Timothy March

COLLINS
COMPACT
FRENCH
DICTIONARY

FRENCH▸ENGLISH ENGLISH▸FRENCH

HarperCollins*Publishers*

First published in this edition 1993

© William Collins Sons & Co. Ltd. 1989

ISBN 0 00 470297 2

A catalogue record for this book
is available from the British Library

Printed in Great Britain by
HarperCollins Manufacturing, Glasgow

INTRODUCTION

This dictionary of French and English is designed to provide the user with wide-ranging and up-to-date coverage of the two languages, and is ideal for both school and reference use.

A special feature of Collins dictionaries is the comprehensive 'signposting' of meanings on both sides of the dictionary, guiding the user to the most appropriate translation for a given context. We hope you will find this dictionary easy and pleasant to consult for all your study and reference needs.

ABRÉVIATIONS

ABBREVIATIONS

adjectif, locution adjective	a	adjective, adjectival phrase
abréviation	ab(b)r	abbreviation
adverbe, locution adverbiale	ad	adverb, adverbial phrase
administration	ADMIN	administration
agriculture	AGR	agriculture
anatomie	ANAT	anatomy
architecture	ARCHIT	architecture
l'automobile	AUT(O)	the motor car and motoring
aviation, voyages aériens	AVIAT	flying, air travel
biologie	BIO(L)	biology
botanique	BOT	botany
anglais de Grande-Bretagne	Brit	British English
conjonction	cj	conjunction
langue familière (! emploi vulgaire)	col (!)	colloquial usage (! particularly offensive)
commerce, finance, banque	COMM	commerce, finance, banking
informatique	COMPUT	computing
construction	CONSTR	building
nom utilisé comme adjectif, ne peut s'employer ni comme attribut, ni après le nom qualifié	cpd	compound element: noun used as an adjective and which cannot follow the noun it qualifies
cuisine, art culinaire	CULIN	cookery
déterminant: article, adjectif démonstratif ou indéfini etc	dét	determiner: article, demonstrative etc.
économie	ECON	economics
électricité, électronique	ELEC	electricity, electronics
exclamation, interjection	excl	exclamation, interjection
féminin	f	feminine
langue familière (! emploi vulgaire)	fam (!)	colloquial usage (! particularly offensive)
emploi figuré	fig	figurative use
(verbe anglais) dont la particule est inséparable du verbe	fus	(phrasal verb) where the particle cannot be separated from main verb
dans la plupart des sens; généralement	gén, gen	in most or all senses; generally
géographie, géologie	GEO	geography, geology
géométrie	GEOM	geometry
informatique	INFORM	computing
invariable	inv	invariable
irrégulier	irg	irregular
domaine juridique	JUR	law
grammaire, linguistique	LING	grammar, linguistics
masculin	m	masculine
mathématiques, algèbre	MATH	mathematics, calculus
médecine	MED	medical term, medicine
masculin ou féminin, suivant le sexe	m/f	either masculine or feminine depending on sex
domaine militaire, armée	MIL	military matters
musique	MUS	music
nom	n	noun

ABRÉVIATIONS

ABBREVIATIONS

navigation, nautisme	**NAVIG, NAUT**	sailing, navigation
adjectif ou nom numérique	**num**	numeral adjective or noun
	o.s.	oneself
péjoratif	**péj, pej**	derogatory, pejorative
photographie	**PHOT(O)**	photography
physiologie	**PHYSIOL**	physiology
pluriel	**pl**	plural
politique	**POL**	politics
participe passé	**pp**	past participle
préposition	**prép, prep**	preposition
psychologie, psychiatrie	**PSYCH**	psychology, psychiatry
temps du passé	**pt**	past tense
nom non comptable: ne peut s'utiliser au pluriel	**q**	collective (uncountable) noun: is not used in the plural
quelque chose	**qch**	
quelqu'un	**qn**	
religions, domaine ecclésiastique	**REL**	religions, church service
	sb	somebody
enseignement, système scolaire et universitaire	**SCOL**	schooling, schools and universities
singulier	**sg**	singular
	sth	something
subjonctif	**sub**	subjunctive
sujet (grammatical)	**su(b)j**	(grammatical) subject
techniques, technologie	**TECH**	technical term, technology
télécommunications	**TEL**	telecommunications
télévision	**TV**	television
typographie	**TYP(O)**	typography, printing
anglais des USA	**US**	American English
verbe	**vb**	verb
verbe ou groupe verbal à fonction intransitive	**vi**	verb or phrasal verb used intransitively
verbe ou groupe verbal à fonction transitive	**vt**	verb or phrasal verb used transitively
zoologie	**ZOOL**	zoology
marque déposée	**®**	registered trademark
indique une équivalence culturelle	**≈**	introduces a cultural equivalent

TRANSCRIPTION PHONÉTIQUE

CONSONNES

CONSONANTS

NB. **p, b, t, d, k, g** sont suivis d'une aspiration en anglais.

NB. **p, b, t, d, k, g** are not aspirated in French.

poupée	p	*puppy*
bombe	b	*baby*
tente thermal	t	*tent*
dinde	d	*daddy*
coq qui képi	k	*cork kiss chord*
gag bague	g	*gag guess*
sale ce nation	s	*so rice kiss*
zéro rose	z	*cousin buzz*
tache chat	ʃ	*sheep sugar*
gilet juge	ʒ	*pleasure beige*
	tʃ	*church*
	dʒ	*judge general*
fer phare	f	*farm raffle*
valve	v	*very rev*
	θ	*thin maths*
	ð	*that other*
lent salle	l	*little ball*
rare rentrer	R	
	r	*rat rare*
maman femme	m	*mummy comb*
non nonne	n	*no ran*
agneau vigne	ɲ	
	ŋ	*singing bank*
hop!	h	*hat reheat*
yeux paille pied	j	*yet*
nouer oui	w	*wall bewail*
huile lui	ɥ	
	x	*loch*

DIVERS

MISCELLANEOUS

pour l'anglais: précède la syllabe accentuée	'	in French wordlist and transcription: no liaison
pour l'anglais: le r final se prononce en liaison devant une voyelle	*	

PHONETIC TRANSCRIPTION

VOYELLES

VOWELS

NB. La mise en équivalence de certains sons n'indique qu'une ressemblance approximative.

NB. The pairing of some vowel sounds only indicates approximate equivalence.

ici v*ie* l*y*re	i i:	*hee*l b*ea*d
	ɪ	*hi*t p*i*ty
jou*er* *été*	e	
l*ai*t jou*et* merc*i*	ɛ	s*e*t t*e*nt
pl*at* *a*mour	a æ	b*a*t *a*pple
b*as* p*â*te	ɑ ɑ:	*a*fter c*a*r c*a*lm
	ʌ	f*u*n c*ou*sin
l*e* prem*ier*	ə	*o*ver *a*bove
b*eu*rre p*eu*r	œ	
p*eu* d*eu*x	ø ə:	*u*rn f*er*n w*or*k
*o*r h*o*mme	ɔ	w*a*sh p*o*t
m*o*t *eau* g*au*che	o ɔ:	b*or*n c*or*k
gen*ou* r*ou*e	u	f*u*ll s*oo*t
	u:	b*oo*n l*ew*d
r*ue* *u*rne	y	

DIPHTONGUES

DIPHTHONGS

ɪə	b*eer* t*ier*
ɛə	t*ear* f*air* th*ere*
eɪ	d*a*te pl*ai*ce d*ay*
aɪ	l*i*fe b*uy* cr*y*
au	*ow*l f*ou*l n*ow*
əu	l*ow* n*o*
ɔɪ	b*oi*l b*oy* *oi*ly
uə	p*oor* t*our*

NASALES

NASAL VOWELS

mat*in* pl*ein*	ɛ̃
br*un*	œ̃
s*an*g *an* d*an*s	ɑ̃
n*on* p*on*t	ɔ̃

FRANÇAIS - ANGLAIS
FRENCH - ENGLISH

A

A *abr de* **autoroute**.

a *vb voir* **avoir**.

à (*à + le =* **au**, *à + les =* **aux**) [a, o] *prép* **1** (*endroit, situation*) at, in; **être à Paris/au Portugal** to be in Paris/Portugal; **être à la maison/à l'école** to be at home/at school; **à la campagne** in the country; **c'est à 10 km/à 20 minutes (d'ici)** it's 10 km/20 minutes away **2** (*direction*) to; **aller à Paris/au Portugal** to go to Paris/Portugal; **aller à la maison/à l'école** to go home/to school; **à la campagne** to the country **3** (*temps*): **à 3 heures/minuit** at 3 o'clock/midnight; **au printemps/mois de juin** in the spring/the month of June **4** (*attribution, appartenance*) to; **le livre est à Paul/à lui/à nous** this book is Paul's/his/ours; **donner qch à qn** to give sth to sb **5** (*moyen*) with; **se chauffer au gaz** to have gas heating; **à bicyclette** on a *ou* by bicycle; **à la main/machine** by hand/machine **6** (*provenance*) from; **boire à la bouteille** to drink from the bottle **7** (*caractérisation, manière*): **l'homme aux yeux bleus** the man with the blue eyes; **à la russe** the Russian way **8** (*but, destination*): **tasse à café** coffee cup; **maison à vendre** house for sale **9** (*rapport, évaluation, distribution*): **100 km/unités à l'heure** 100 km/units per *ou* an hour; **payé à l'heure** paid by the hour; **cinq à six** five to six.

abaisser [abese] *vt* to lower, bring down; (*manette*) to pull down; (*fig*) to debase; to humiliate; **s'~** *vi* to go down; (*fig*) to demean o.s.

abandon [abɑ̃dɔ̃] *nm* abandoning; giving up; withdrawal; **être à l'~** to be in a state of neglect.

abandonner [abɑ̃dɔne] *vt* (*personne*) to abandon; (*projet, activité*) to abandon, give up; (*SPORT*) to retire *ou* withdraw from; (*céder*) to surrender; **s'~** *vi* to let o.s. up to; **s'~ à** (*paresse, plaisirs*) to give o.s. up to.

abasourdir [abazurdir] *vt* to stun, stagger.

abat-jour [abaʒur] *nm inv* lampshade.

abats [aba] *nmpl* (*de bœuf, porc*) offal *sg*; (*de volaille*) giblets.

abattement [abatmɑ̃] *nm* (*déduction*) reduction; **~ fiscal** ≈ tax allowance.

abattis [abati] *nmpl* giblets.

abattoir [abatwar] *nm* slaughterhouse.

abattre [abatr(ə)] *vt* (*arbre*) to cut down, fell; (*mur, maison*) to pull down; (*avion, personne*) to shoot down; (*animal*) to shoot, kill; (*fig*) to wear out, tire out; to demoralize; **s'~** *vi* to crash down; **s'~ sur** to beat down on; to rain down on.

abbaye [abei] *nf* abbey.

abbé [abe] *nm* priest; (*d'une abbaye*) abbot.

abcès [apsɛ] *nm* abscess.

abdiquer [abdike] *vi* to abdicate // *vt* to renounce, give up.

abeille [abɛj] *nf* bee.

aberrant, e [abɛrɑ̃, -ɑ̃t] *a* absurd.

abêtir [abetir] *vt* to make morons of (*ou* a moron of).

abîme [abim] *nm* abyss, gulf.

abîmer [abime] *vt* to spoil, damage; **s'~** *vi* to get spoilt *ou* damaged.

ablation [ablasjɔ̃] *nf* removal.

aboiement [abwamɑ̃] *nm* bark, barking q.

abois [abwa] *nmpl*: **aux ~** at bay.

abolir [abɔlir] *vt* to abolish.

abondance [abɔ̃dɑ̃s] *nf* abundance; (*richesse*) affluence.

abondant, e [abɔ̃dɑ̃, -ɑ̃t] *a* plentiful, abundant, copious.

abonder [abɔ̃de] *vi* to abound, be plentiful; **~ dans le sens de qn** to concur with sb.

abonné, e [abɔne] *nm/f* subscriber; season ticket holder.

abonnement [abɔnmɑ̃] *nm* subscription; (*transports, concerts*) season ticket.

abonner [abɔne] *vt*: **s'~ à** to subscribe to, take out a subscription to.

abord [abɔr] *nm*: **être d'un ~ facile** to be approachable; **~s** *nmpl* surroundings; **au premier ~** at first sight, initially; **d'~** *ad* first.

abordable [abɔrdabl(ə)] *a* approachable; reasonably priced.

aborder [abɔrde] *vi* to land // *vt* (*sujet, difficulté*) to tackle; (*personne*) to approach; (*rivage etc*) to reach; (*NAVIG: attaquer*) to board.

aboutir [abutir] *vi* (*négociations etc*) to succeed; **~ à/dans/sur** to end up at/in/on.

aboyer [abwaje] *vi* to bark.

abrégé [abreʒe] *nm* summary.

abréger [abreʒe] *vt* to shorten.

abreuver [abrœve] *vt* (*fig*): **~ qn de** to

shower *ou* swamp sb with; **s'~** *vi* to drink; **abreuvoir** *nm* watering place.

abréviation [abrevjɑsjɔ̃] *nf* abbreviation.

abri [abri] *nm* shelter; **à l'~** under cover; **à l'~ de** sheltered from; *(fig)* safe from.

abricot [abriko] *nm* apricot; **abricotier** *nm* apricot tree.

abriter [abrite] *vt* to shelter; *(loger)* to accommodate; **s'~** to shelter, take cover.

abroger [abrɔʒe] *vt* to repeal.

abrupt, e [abrypt] *a* sheer, steep; *(ton)* abrupt.

abrutir [abrytir] *vt* to daze; to exhaust; to stupefy.

absence [apsɑ̃s] *nf* absence; *(MÉD)* blackout; mental blank.

absent, e [apsɑ̃, -ɑ̃t] *a* absent; *(distrait: air)* vacant, faraway // *nm/f* absentee; **s'absenter** *vi* to take time off work; *(sortir)* to leave, go out.

absolu, e [apsɔly] *a* absolute; *(caractère)* rigid, uncompromising; **~ment** *ad* absolutely.

absolve *etc vb voir* **absoudre.**

absorber [apsɔrbe] *vt* to absorb; *(gén MÉD: manger, boire)* to take.

absoudre [apsudr(ə)] *vt* to absolve.

abstenir [apstənir]: **s'~** *vi* *(POL)* to abstain; **s'~ de qch/de faire** to refrain from sth/from doing.

abstraction [apstraksjɔ̃] *nf* abstraction; **faire ~ de** to set ou leave aside.

abstrait, e [apstre, -et] *a* abstract.

absurde [apsyrd(ə)] *a* absurd.

abus [aby] *nm* abuse; **~ de confiance** breach of trust.

abuser [abyze] *vi* to go too far, overstep the mark // *vt* to deceive, mislead; **~ de** *vt* to misuse; *(violer, duper)* to take advantage of; **s'~** *vi* to be mistaken; **abusif, ive** *a* exorbitant; excessive; improper.

acabit [akabi] *nm*: **de cet ~** of that type.

académie [akademi] *nf* academy; *(ART: nu)* nude; *(SCOL: circonscription)* ≈ regional education authority.

acajou [akaʒu] *nm* mahogany.

acariâtre [akarjɑtr(ə)] *a* cantankerous.

accablement [akɑbləmɑ̃] *nm* despondency.

accabler [akɑble] *vt* to overwhelm, overcome; *(suj: témoignage)* to condemn, damn; **~ qn d'injures** to heap ou shower abuse on sb.

accalmie [akalmi] *nf* lull.

accaparer [akapare] *vt* to monopolize; *(suj: travail etc)* to take up (all) the time ou attention of.

accéder [aksede]: **~ à** *vt (lieu)* to reach; *(fig)* to accede to, attain; *(accorder: requête)* to grant, accede to.

accélérateur [akseleratœr] *nm* accelerator.

accélération [akselerɑsjɔ̃] *nf* acceleration.

accélérer [akselere] *vt* to speed up // *vi* to accelerate.

accent [aksɑ̃] *nm* accent; *(inflexions expressives)* tone (of voice); *(PHONÉTIQUE, fig)* stress; **mettre l'~ sur** *(fig)* to stress; **~ aigu/grave** acute/grave accent.

accentuer [aksɑ̃tɥe] *vt* *(LING)* to accent; *(fig)* to accentuate, emphasize; **s'~** *vi* to become more marked ou pronounced.

acceptation [akseptɑsjɔ̃] *nf* acceptance.

accepter [aksepte] *vt* to accept; *(tolérer)*: **~ que qn fasse** to agree to sb doing; **~ de faire** to agree to do.

acception [aksepsjɔ̃] *nf* meaning, sense.

accès [akse] *nm* *(à un lieu)* access; *(MÉD)* attack; fit, bout; outbreak // *nmpl* *(routes etc)* means of access, approaches; **d'~ facile** easily accessible; **~ de colère** fit of anger.

accessible [aksesibl(ə)] *a* accessible; *(livre, sujet)*: **~ à qn** within the reach of sb; *(sensible)*: **~ à** open to.

accessoire [akseswar] *a* secondary; incidental // *nm* accessory; *(THÉÂTRE)* prop.

accident [aksidɑ̃] *nm* accident; **par ~** by chance; **~ de la route** road accident; **~ du travail** industrial injury ou accident; **accidenté, e** *a* damaged; injured; *(relief, terrain)* uneven; hilly.

acclamer [aklame] *vt* to cheer, acclaim.

accointances [akwɛ̃tɑ̃s] *nfpl*: **avoir des ~ avec** to have contacts with.

accolade [akɔlad] *nf* *(amicale)* embrace; *(signe)* brace.

accoler [akɔle] *vt* to place side by side.

accommodant, e [akɔmɔdɑ̃, -ɑ̃t] *a* accommodating; easy-going.

accommoder [akɔmɔde] *vt* *(CULIN)* to prepare; *(points de vue)* to reconcile; **s'~ de** to put up with; to make do with.

accompagnateur, trice [akɔ̃paɲatœr, -tris] *nm/f* *(MUS)* accompanist; *(de voyage: guide)* guide; *(: d'enfants)* accompanying adult; *(de voyage organisé)* courier.

accompagner [akɔ̃paɲe] *vt* to accompany, be ou go ou come with; *(MUS)* to accompany.

accompli, e [akɔ̃pli] *a* accomplished.

accomplir [akɔ̃plir] *vt* *(tâche, projet)* to carry out; *(souhait)* to fulfil; **s'~** *vi* to be fulfilled.

accord [akɔr] *nm* agreement; *(entre des styles, tons etc)* harmony; *(MUS)* chord; **d'~!** OK!; **se mettre d'~** to come to an agreement; **être d'~** to agree.

accordéon [akɔrdeɔ̃] *nm* *(MUS)* accordion.

accorder [akɔrde] *vt* *(faveur, délai)* to grant; *(harmoniser)* to match; *(MUS)* to tune; s'~ to get on together; to agree.

accoster [akɔste] (*NAVIG*) *vt* to draw alongside // *vi* to berth.

accotement [akɔtmɑ̃] *nm* verge (*Brit*), shoulder.

accouchement [akuʃmɑ̃] *nm* delivery, (child)birth; labour.

accoucher [akuʃe] *vi* to give birth, have a baby; (*être en travail*) to be in labour // *vt* to deliver; ~ **d'un garçon** to give birth to a boy.

accouder [akude]: s'~ *vi*: s'~ à/contre to rest one's elbows on/against; **accoudoir** *nm* armrest.

accoupler [akuple] *vt* to couple; (*pour la reproduction*) to mate; s'~ to mate.

accourir [akuʀiʀ] *vi* to rush ou run up.

accoutrement [akutʀəmɑ̃] *nm* (*péj: tenue*) outfit.

accoutumance [akutymɑ̃s] *nf* (*gén*) adaptation; (*MÉD*) addiction.

accoutumé, e [akutyme] *a* (*habituel*) customary, usual.

accoutumer [akutyme] *vt*: s'~ à to get accustomed ou used to.

accréditer [akʀedite] *vt* (*nouvelle*) to substantiate.

accroc [akʀo] *nm* (*déchirure*) tear; (*fig*) hitch, snag.

accrochage [akʀɔʃaʒ] *nm* (*AUTO*) collision.

accrocher [akʀɔʃe] *vt* (*suspendre*): ~ qch à to hang sth (up) on; (*attacher: remorque*): ~ qch à to hitch sth (up) to; (*heurter*) to catch; to catch on; to hit; (*déchirer*): ~ qch (à) to catch sth (on); (*MIL*) to engage; (*fig*) to catch, attract; s'~ (*se disputer*) to have a clash ou brush; s'~ à (*rester pris à*) to catch on; (*agripper*, *fig*) to hang on ou cling to.

accroître [akʀwatʀ(ə)] *vt* to increase; s'~ *vi* to increase.

accroupir [akʀupiʀ]: s'~ *vi* to squat, crouch (down).

accru, e [akʀy] *pp de* **accroître**.

accueil [akœj] *nm* welcome; comité d'~ reception committee.

accueillir [akœjiʀ] *vt* to welcome; (*loger*) to accommodate.

acculer [akyle] *vt*: ~ qn à ou contre to drive sb back against.

accumuler [akymyle] *vt* to accumulate, amass; s'~ *vi* to accumulate; to pile up.

accusation [akyzɑsjɔ̃] *nf* (*gén*) accusation; (*JUR*) charge; (*partie*): l'~ the prosecution; **mettre en** ~ to indict.

accusé, e [akyze] *nm/f* accused; defendant; ~ **de réception** acknowledgement of receipt.

accuser [akyze] *vt* to accuse; (*fig*) to emphasize, bring out; to show; ~ qn de to accuse sb of; (*JUR*) to charge sb with; ~ qch (*rendre responsable*) to blame sth for; ~ **réception de** to acknowledge receipt of.

acerbe [asɛʀb(ə)] *a* caustic, acid.

acéré, e [asere] *a* sharp.

achalandé, e [aʃalɑ̃de] *a*: **bien** ~ well-stocked; well-patronized.

acharné, e [aʃaʀne] *a* (*lutte, adversaire*) fierce, bitter; (*travail*) relentless, unremitting.

acharner [aʃaʀne]: s'~ *vi*: s'~ **sur** to go at fiercely; s'~ **contre** to set o.s. against; to dog; s'~ à **faire** to try doggedly to do; to persist in doing.

achat [aʃa] *nm* buying *q*; purchase; **faire des** ~s to do some shopping.

acheminer [aʃmine] *vt* (*courrier*) to forward, dispatch; (*troupes*) to convey, transport; (*train*) to route; s'~ **vers** to head for.

acheter [aʃte] *vt* to buy, purchase; (*soudoyer*) to buy; ~ qch à (*marchand*) to buy ou purchase sth from; (*ami etc: offrir*) to buy sth for; **acheteur, euse** *nm/f* buyer; shopper; (*COMM*) buyer.

achever [aʃve] *vt* to complete, finish; (*blessé*) to finish off; s'~ *vi* to end.

achoppement [aʃɔpmɑ̃] *nm*: **pierre d'**~ stumbling block.

acide [asid] *a* sour, sharp; (*CHIMIE*) acid(ic) // *nm* (*CHIMIE*) acid.

acier [asje] *nm* steel; **aciérie** *nf* steelworks *sg*.

acné [akne] *nf* acne.

acolyte [akɔlit] *nm* (*péj*) associate.

acompte [akɔ̃t] *nm* deposit; (*versement régulier*) instalment; (*sur somme due*) payment on account.

à-côté [akote] *nm* side-issue; (*argent*) extra.

à-coup [aku] *nm* (*du moteur*) (hic)cough; (*fig*) jolt; **par** ~s by fits and starts.

acoustique [akustik] *nf* (*d'une salle*) acoustics *pl*.

acquéreur [akeʀœʀ] *nm* buyer, purchaser.

acquérir [akeʀiʀ] *vt* to acquire.

acquis, e [aki, -iz] *pp de* **acquérir** // *nm* (accumulated) experience; **être** ~ à (*plan, idée*) to fully agree with; **son aide nous est** ~e we can count on her help.

acquit [aki] *vb voir* **acquérir** // *nm* (*quittance*) receipt; **par** ~ **de conscience** to set one's mind at rest.

acquitter [akite] *vt* (*JUR*) to acquit; (*facture*) to pay, settle; s'~ **de** to discharge, fulfil.

âcre [akʀ(ə)] *a* acrid, pungent.

acrobate [akʀɔbat] *nm/f* acrobat.

acte [akt(ə)] *nm* act, action; (*THÉÂTRE*) act; ~s *nmpl* (*compte-rendu*) proceedings; **prendre** ~ **de** to note, take note of; **faire** ~ **de candidature** to apply; **faire** ~ **de présence** to put in an appearance; ~ **de naissance** birth certificate.

acteur [aktœʀ] *nm* actor.

actif, ive [aktif, -iv] *a* active // *nm*

(*COMM*) assets *pl*; (*fig*): **avoir à son ~** to have to one's credit; **population active** working population.

action [aksjɔ̃] *nf* (*gén*) action; (*COMM*) share; **une bonne ~** a good deed; **actionnaire** *nm/f* shareholder; **actionner** *vt* to work; to activate; to operate.

activer [aktive] *vt* to speed up; **s'~** *vi* to bustle about; to hurry up.

activité [aktivite] *nf* activity.

actrice [aktʀis] *nf* actress.

actualiser [aktɥalize] *vt* to actualize; to bring up to date.

actualité [aktɥalite] *nf* (*d'un problème*) topicality; (*événements*): **l'~** current events; **les ~s** (*CINÉMA*, *TV*) the news.

actuel, le [aktɥɛl] *a* (*présent*) present; (*d'actualité*) topical; **~lement** *ad* at present; at the present time.

acuité [akɥite] *nf* acuteness.

adaptateur [adaptatœʀ] *nm* (*ÉLEC*) adapter.

adapter [adapte] *vt* to adapt; **~ qch à** (*approprier*) to adapt sth to (fit); **~ qch sur/dans/à** (*fixer*) to fit sth on/into/to; **s'~** (*à*) (*suj: personne*) to adapt (to).

addition [adisjɔ̃] *nf* addition; (*au café*) bill.

additionner [adisjone] *vt* to add (up).

adepte [adɛpt(ə)] *nm/f* follower.

adéquat, e [adekwa, -at] *a* appropriate, suitable.

adhérent, e [adeʀɑ̃, -ɑ̃t] *nm/f* (*de club*) member.

adhérer [adeʀe]: **~ à** *vi* (*coller*) to adhere *ou* stick to; (*se rallier à*) to join; to support; **adhésif, ive** *a* adhesive, sticky // *nm* adhesive; **adhésion** *nf* joining; membership; support.

adieu, x [adjø] *excl* goodbye // *nm* farewell; **dire ~ à qn** to say goodbye *ou* farewell to sb.

adjectif [adʒɛktif] *nm* adjective.

adjoindre [adʒwɛ̃dʀ(ə)] *vt*: **~ qch à** to attach sth to; to add sth to; **s'~** (*collaborateur etc*) to take on, appoint; **adjoint, e** *nm/f* assistant; **adjoint au maire** deputy mayor; **directeur adjoint** assistant manager.

adjudant [adʒydɑ̃] *nm* (*MIL*) warrant officer.

adjudication [adʒydikasjɔ̃] *nf* sale by auction; (*pour travaux*) invitation to tender (*Brit*) *ou* bid (*US*).

adjuger [adʒyʒe] *vt* (*prix, récompense*) to award; (*lors d'une vente*) to auction (off); **s'~** *vt* to take for o.s.

adjurer [adʒyʀe] *vt*: **~ qn de faire** to implore *ou* beg sb to do.

admettre [admɛtʀ(ə)] *vt* (*laisser entrer*) to admit; (*candidat: SCOL*) to pass; (*tolérer*) to allow, accept; (*reconnaître*) to admit, acknowledge.

administrateur, trice [administʀatœʀ,

-tʀis] *nm/f* (*COMM*) director; (*ADMIN*) administrator; **~ judiciaire** receiver; **~ délégué** managing director.

administration [administʀasjɔ̃] *nf* administration; **l'A~** ≈ the Civil Service.

administrer [administʀe] *vt* (*firme*) to manage, run; (*biens, remède, sacrement etc*) to administer.

admirable [admiʀabl(ə)] *a* admirable, wonderful.

admirateur, trice [admiʀatœʀ, -tʀis] *nm/f* admirer.

admiration [admiʀasjɔ̃] *nf* admiration.

admirer [admiʀe] *vt* to admire.

admis, e *pp de* **admettre**.

admissible [admisibl(ə)] *a* (*candidat*) eligible; (*comportement*) admissible, acceptable.

admission [admisjɔ̃] *nf* admission; acknowledgement; **demande d'~** application for membership.

adolescence [adɔlesɑ̃s] *nf* adolescence.

adolescent, e [adɔlesɑ̃, -ɑ̃t] *nm/f* adolescent, teenager.

adonner [adɔne]: **s'~ à** *vt* (*sport*) to devote o.s. to; (*boisson*) to give o.s. over to.

adopter [adɔpte] *vt* to adopt; (*projet de loi etc*) to pass; **adoptif, ive** *a* (*parents*) adoptive; (*fils, patrie*) adopted.

adorer [adɔʀe] *vt* to adore; (*REL*) to worship.

adosser [adɔse] *vt*: **~ qch à** *ou* **contre** to stand sth against; **s'~ à** *ou* **contre** to lean with one's back against.

adoucir [adusiʀ] *vt* (*goût, température*) to make milder; (*avec du sucre*) to sweeten; (*peau, voix*) to soften; (*caractère*) to mellow.

adresse [adʀɛs] *nf* (*voir adroit*) skill, dexterity; (*domicile*) address; **à l'~ de** (*pour*) for the benefit of.

adresser [adʀese] *vt* (*lettre: expédier*) to send; (*: écrire l'adresse sur*) to address; (*injure, compliments*) to address; **~ la parole à** to speak to, address; **s'~ à** (*parler à*) to speak to, address; (*s'informer auprès de*) to go and see; (*: bureau*) to enquire at; (*suj: livre, conseil*) to be aimed at.

adroit, e [adʀwa, -wat] *a* skilful, skilled.

adulte [adylt(ə)] *nm/f* adult, grown-up // *a* (*chien, arbre*) fully-grown, mature; (*attitude*) adult, grown-up.

adultère [adyltɛʀ] *nm* (*acte*) adultery.

advenir [advəniʀ] *vi* to happen.

adverbe [advɛʀb(ə)] *nm* adverb.

adversaire [advɛʀsɛʀ] *nm/f* (*SPORT*, *gén*) opponent, adversary; (*MIL*) adversary, enemy.

adverse [advɛʀs(ə)] *a* opposing.

aération [aeʀasjɔ̃] *nf* airing; ventilation.

aérer [aeʀe] *vt* to air; (*fig*) to lighten; **s'~** *vi* to get some (fresh) air.

aérien, ne [aeʀjɛ̃ -jɛn] *a* (*AVIAT*) air-

cpd, aerial; (*câble, métro*) overhead; (*fig*) light.

aéro... [aeʀɔ] *préfixe*: **~bic** *nm* aerobics *sg*; **~gare** *nf* airport (buildings); (*en ville*) air terminal; **~glisseur** *nm* hovercraft; **~naval, e** *a* air and sea *cpd*; **~port** *nm* airport; **~porté, e** *a* airborne, airlifted; **~sol** *nm* aerosol.

affaiblir [afeblir] *vt*, **s'~** *vi* to weaken.

affaire [afɛʀ] *nf* (*problème, question*) matter; (*criminelle, judiciaire*) case; (*scandaleuse etc*) affair; (*entreprise*) business; (*marché, transaction*) deal; business *q*; (*occasion intéressante*) bargain; **~s** *nfpl* affairs; (*activité commerciale*) business *sg*; (*effets personnels*) things, belongings; **ce sont mes ~s** (*cela me concerne*) that's my business; **ceci fera l'~** this will do (nicely); **avoir ~ à** to be faced with; to be dealing with; **les A~s étrangères** Foreign Affairs; **s'affairer** *vi* to busy o.s., bustle about.

affaisser [afese]: **s'~** *vi* (*terrain, immeuble*) to subside, sink; (*personne*) to collapse.

affaler [afale]: **s'~** *vi*: **s'~ dans/sur** to collapse *ou* slump into/onto.

affamé, e [afame] *a* starving.

affecter [afɛkte] *vt* to affect; (*telle ou telle forme etc*) to take on; **~ qch à** to allocate *ou* allot sth to; **~ qn à** to appoint sb to; (*diplomate*) to post sb to.

affectif, ive [afɛktif, -iv] *a* emotional.

affection [afɛksjɔ̃] *nf* affection; (*mal*) ailment; **affectionner** *vt* to be fond of.

affectueux, euse [afɛktɥø, -øz] *a* affectionate.

afférent, e [aferɑ̃, -ɑ̃t] *a*: **~ à** pertaining *ou* relating to.

affermir [afɛʀmiʀ] *vt* to consolidate, strengthen.

affichage [afiʃaʒ] *nm* billposting; (*électronique*) display.

affiche [afiʃ] *nf* poster; (*officielle*) notice; (*THÉÂTRE*) bill; **tenir l'~** to run.

afficher [afiʃe] *vt* (*affiche*) to put up; (*réunion*) to put up a notice about; (*électroniquement*) to display; (*fig*) to exhibit, display.

affilée [afile]: **d'~** *ad* at a stretch.

affiler [afile] *vt* to sharpen.

affiner [afine] *vt* to refine.

affirmatif, ive [afiʀmatif, -iv] *a* affirmative.

affirmation [afiʀmasjɔ̃] *nf* assertion.

affirmer [afiʀme] *vt* (*prétendre*) to maintain, assert; (*autorité etc*) to assert.

affligé, e [afliʒe] *a* distressed, grieved; **~ de** (*maladie, tare*) afflicted with.

affliger [afliʒe] *vt* (*peiner*) to distress, grieve.

affluence [aflyɑ̃s] *nf* crowds *pl*; **heures d'~** rush hours; **jours d'~** busiest days.

affluent [aflyɑ̃] *nm* tributary.

affluer [aflye] *vi* (*secours, biens*) to flood in, pour in; (*sang*) to rush, flow.

affolement [afɔlmɑ̃] *nm* panic.

affoler [afɔle] *vt* to throw into a panic; **s'~** *vi* to panic.

affranchir [afʀɑ̃ʃiʀ] *vt* to put a stamp *ou* stamps on; (*à la machine*) to frank (*Brit*), meter (*US*); (*fig*) to free, liberate; **affranchissement** *nm* postage.

affréter [afʀete] *vt* to charter.

affreux, euse [afʀø, -øz] *a* dreadful, awful.

affrontement [afʀɔ̃tmɑ̃] *nm* clash, confrontation.

affronter [afʀɔ̃te] *vt* to confront, face.

affubler [afyble] *vt* (*péj*): **~ qn de** to rig *ou* deck sb out in; (*surnom*) to attach to sb.

affût [afy] *nm*: **à l'~ (de)** (*gibier*) lying in wait (for); (*fig*) on the look-out (for).

affûter [afyte] *vt* to sharpen, grind.

afin [afɛ̃]: **~ que** *cj* so that, in order that; **~ de faire** in order to do, so as to do.

africain, e [afʀikɛ̃, -ɛn] *a*, *nm/f* African.

Afrique [afʀik] *nf*: **l'~** Africa; **l'~ du Sud** South Africa.

agacer [agase] *vt* to pester, tease; (*involontairement*) to irritate.

âge [ɑʒ] *nm* age; **quel ~ as-tu?** how old are you?; **prendre de l'~** to be getting on (in years); **l'~ ingrat** the awkward age; **l'~ mûr** maturity; **âgé, e** *a* old, elderly; **âgé de 10 ans** 10 years old.

agence [aʒɑ̃s] *nf* agency, office; (*succursale*) branch; **~ immobilière** estate (*Brit*) *ou* real estate (*US*) agent's (office); **~ matrimoniale** marriage bureau; **~ de voyages** travel agency.

agencer [aʒɑ̃se] *vt* to put together; to arrange, lay out.

agenda [aʒɛ̃da] *nm* diary.

agenouiller [aʒnuje]: **s'~** *vi* to kneel (down).

agent [aʒɑ̃] *nm* (*aussi*: **~ de police**) policeman; (*ADMIN*) official, officer; (*fig*: *élément, facteur*) agent; **~ d'assurances** insurance broker; **~ de change** stockbroker; **~ (secret)** (secret) agent.

agglomération [aglɔmeʀasjɔ̃] *nf* town; built-up area; **l'~ parisienne** the urban area of Paris.

aggloméré [aglɔmeʀe] *nm* (*bois*) chipboard; (*pierre*) conglomerate.

agglomérer [aglɔmeʀe] *vt* to pile up; (*TECH*: *bois, pierre*) to compress.

aggraver [agʀave] *vt* to worsen, aggravate; (*JUR*: *peine*) to increase; **s'~** *vi* to worsen.

agile [aʒil] *a* agile, nimble.

agir [aʒiʀ] *vi* to act; **il s'agit de** it's a matter *ou* question of; it is about; (*il importe que*): **il s'agit de faire** we (*ou* you *etc*) must do.

agitation [aʒitɑsjɔ̃] *nf* (hustle and) bustle; agitation, excitement; (*politique*) unrest, agitation.

agité, e [aʒite] *a* fidgety, restless; agitated, perturbed; (*mer*) rough.

agiter [aʒite] *vt* (*bouteille, chiffon*) to shake; (*bras, mains*) to wave; (*préoccuper, exciter*) to perturb.

agneau, x [aɲo] *nm* lamb.

agonie [agɔni] *nf* mortal agony, death pangs *pl*; (*fig*) death throes *pl*.

agrafe [agʀaf] *nf* (*de vêtement*) hook, fastener; (*de bureau*) staple; **agrafer** *vt* to fasten; to staple; **agrafeuse** *nf* stapler.

agraire [agʀɛʀ] *a* land *cpd*.

agrandir [agʀɑ̃diʀ] *vt* to enlarge; (*magasin, domaine*) to extend, enlarge; **s'~** *vi* to be extended; to be enlarged; **agrandissement** *nm* (*PHOTO*) enlargement.

agréable [agʀeabl(ə)] *a* pleasant, nice.

agréé, e [agʀee] *a*: concessionnaire ~ registered dealer.

agréer [agʀee] *vt* (*requête*) to accept; ~ à *vt* to please, suit; **veuillez** ~ ... (*formule épistolaire*) yours faithfully.

agrégation [agʀegɑsjɔ̃] *nf* highest teaching diploma in France; **agrégé, e** *nm/f* holder of the *agrégation*.

agrément [agʀemɑ̃] *nm* (*accord*) consent, approval; (*attraits*) charm, attractiveness; (*plaisir*) pleasure.

agrémenter [agʀemɑ̃te] *vt* to embellish, adorn.

agresser [agʀese] *vt* to attack.

agresseur [agʀesœʀ] *nm* aggressor, attacker; (*POL, MIL*) aggressor.

agressif, ive [agʀesif, -iv] *a* aggressive.

agricole [agʀikɔl] *a* agricultural.

agriculteur [agʀikyltœʀ] *nm* farmer.

agriculture [agʀikyltyʀ] *nf* agriculture; farming.

agripper [agʀipe] *vt* to grab, clutch; (*pour arracher*) to snatch, grab; **s'~** à to cling (on) to, to clutch, grip.

agrumes [agʀym] *nmpl* citrus fruit(s).

aguerrir [agɛʀiʀ] *vt* to harden.

aguets [agɛ]: **aux** ~ *ad*: **être aux** ~ to be on the look-out.

aguicher [agiʃe] *vt* to entice.

ahuri, e [ayʀi] *a* (*stupéfait*) flabbergasted; (*idiot*) dim-witted.

ai *vb voir* **avoir**.

aide [ɛd] *nm/f* assistant // *nf* assistance, help; (*secours financier*) aid; **à l'~ de** (*avec*) with the help ou aid of; **appeler (qn) à l'~** to call for help (from sb); ~ **judiciaire** *nf* legal aid; ~ **sociale** *nf* (*assistance*) state aid; ~ **soignant, e** *nm/f* auxiliary nurse; **~-mémoire** *nm inv* memoranda pages *pl*; (*key facts*) handbook.

aider [ɛde] *vt* to help; ~ **à qch** (*faciliter*) to help (towards) sth; **s'~ de** (*se servir de*) to use, make use of.

aie *etc vb voir* **avoir**.

aïe [aj] *excl* ouch.

aïeul, e [ajœl] *nm/f* grandparent, grandfather/grandmother; forebear.

aïeux [ajø] *nmpl* grandparents; forebears, forefathers.

aigle [ɛgl(ə)] *nm* eagle.

aigre [ɛgʀ(ə)] *a* sour, sharp; (*fig*) sharp, cutting; **aigreur** *nf* sourness; sharpness; **aigreurs d'estomac** heartburn *sg*; **aigrir** *vt* (*personne*) to embitter; (*caractère*) to sour.

aigu, ë [egy] *a* (*objet, arête, douleur, intelligence*) sharp; (*son, voix*) high-pitched, shrill; (*note*) high(-pitched).

aiguille [eguij] *nf* needle; (*de montre*) hand; ~ **à tricoter** knitting needle.

aiguiller [eguije] *vt* (*orienter*) to direct.

aiguillon [eguijɔ̃] *nm* (*d'abeille*) sting; **aiguillonner** *vt* to spur ou goad on.

aiguiser [egize] *vt* to sharpen; (*fig*) to stimulate; to excite.

ail [aj] *nm* garlic.

aile [ɛl] *nf* wing; **aileron** *nm* (*de requin*) fin; **ailier** *nm* winger.

aille *etc vb voir* **aller**.

ailleurs [ajœʀ] *ad* elsewhere, somewhere else; **partout/nulle part** ~ everywhere/nowhere else; **d'~** *ad* (*du reste*) moreover, besides; **par** ~ *ad* (*d'autre part*) moreover, furthermore.

ailloli [ajɔli] *nm* garlic mayonnaise.

aimable [ɛmabl(ə)] *a* kind, nice.

aimant [ɛmɑ̃] *nm* magnet.

aimer [eme] *vt* to love; (*d'amitié, affection, par goût*) to like; (*souhait*): **j'aimerais...** I would like...; **bien** ~ **qn/qch** to like sb/sth; **j'aime mieux ou autant vous dire que** I may as well tell you that; **j'aimerais autant y aller maintenant** I'd rather go now; **j'aimerais mieux faire** I'd much rather do.

aine [ɛn] *nf* groin.

aîné, e [ene] *a* elder, older; (*le plus âgé*) eldest, oldest // *nm/f* oldest child ou one, oldest boy ou son/girl ou daughter; **aînesse** *nf*: droit d'aînesse birthright.

ainsi [ɛ̃si] *ad* (*de cette façon*) like this, in this way, thus; (*ce faisant*) thus // *cj* thus, so; ~ **que** (*comme*) (just) as; (*et aussi*) as well as; **pour** ~ **dire** so to speak; **et** ~ **de suite** and so on.

air [ɛʀ] *nm* air; (*mélodie*) tune; (*expression*) look, air; **prendre l'~** to get some (fresh) air; (*avion*) to take off; (*sembler*) to look, appear; **avoir l'~ de** to look like; **avoir l'~ de faire** to look as though one is doing, appear to be doing.

aire [ɛʀ] *nf* (*zone, fig, MATH*) area.

aisance [ɛzɑ̃s] *nf* ease; (*richesse*) affluence.

aise [ɛz] *nf* comfort // *a*: être bien ~ que to be delighted that; être à l'~ ou à son ~ to be comfortable; (*pas embarrassé*) to be at ease; *(financièrement)* to be comfortably off; **se mettre à l'~** to make o.s. comfortable; **être mal à l'~** *ou* **à son ~** to be uncomfortable; to be ill at ease; **en faire à son ~** to do as one likes; **aisé, e** *a* easy; *(assez riche)* well-to-do, well-off.

aisselle [ɛsɛl] *nf* armpit.

ait *vb voir* **avoir**.

ajonc [aʒɔ̃] *nm* gorse q.

ajourner [aʒuRne] *vt (réunion)* to adjourn; *(décision)* to defer, postpone.

ajouter [aʒute] *vt* to add; **~ foi à** to lend *ou* give credence to.

ajusté, e [aʒyste] *a:* **bien ~** *(robe etc)* close-fitting.

ajuster [aʒyste] *vt (régler)* to adjust; *(vêtement)* to alter; *(coup de fusil)* to aim; *(cible)* to aim at; *(TECH, gén: adapter):* **~ qch à** to fit sth to.

alambic [alɑ̃bik] *nm* still.

alarme [alaRm(ə)] *nf* alarm; **donner l'~** to give *ou* raise the alarm; **alarmer** *vt* to alarm; **s'alarmer** *vi* to become alarmed.

album [albɔm] *nm* album.

albumine [albymin] *nf* albumin; **avoir** *ou* **faire de l'~** to suffer from albuminuria.

alcool [alkɔl] *nm:* **l'~** alcohol; **un ~** a spirit, a brandy; **~ à brûler** methylated spirits *(Brit)*, wood alcohol *(US)*; **~ à 90°** surgical spirit; **~ique** *a, nm/f* alcoholic; **~isé, e** *a* alcoholic; **~isme** *nm* alcoholism; **alco(o)test** ® *nm* Breathalyser ®; *(test)* breath-test.

aléas [alea] *nmpl* hazards; **aléatoire** *a* uncertain; *(INFORM)* random.

alentour [alɑ̃tuR] *ad* around (about); **~s** *nmpl* surroundings; **aux ~s de** in the vicinity *ou* neighbourhood of, around about; *(temps)* around about.

alerte [alɛRt(ə)] *a* agile, nimble; brisk, lively // *nf* alert; warning; **alerter** *vt* to alert.

algèbre [alʒɛbR(ə)] *nf* algebra.

Alger [alʒe] *n* Algiers.

Algérie [alʒeRi] *nf:* **l'~** Algeria; **algérien, ne** *a, nm/f* Algerian.

algue [alg(ə)] *nf (gén)* seaweed q; *(BOT)* alga *(pl* algae).

alibi [alibi] *nm* alibi.

aliéné, e [aljene] *nm/f* insane person, lunatic *(péj)*.

aligner [aliɲe] *vt* to align, line up; *(idées, chiffres)* to string together; *(adapter):* **~ qch sur** to bring sth into alignment with; **s'~** *(soldats etc)* to line up; **s'~ sur** *(POL)* to align o.s. on.

aliment [alimɑ̃] *nm* food.

alimentation [alimɑ̃tasjɔ̃] *nf* feeding; supplying; *(commerce)* food trade; *(produits)* groceries *pl; (régime)* diet; *(INFORM)* feed.

alimenter [alimɑ̃te] *vt* to feed; *(TECH):*

~ (en) to supply (with); to feed (with); *(fig)* to sustain, keep going.

alinéa [alinea] *nm* paragraph.

aliter [alite]: **s'~** *vi* to take to one's bed.

allaiter [alete] *vt* to (breast-)feed, nurse; *(suj: animal)* to suckle.

allant [alɑ̃] *nm* drive, go.

allécher [aleʃe] *vt:* **~ qn** to make sb's mouth water; to tempt *ou* entice sb.

allée [ale] *nf (de jardin)* path; *(en ville)* avenue, drive; **~s et venues** *nfpl* comings and goings.

alléger [aleʒe] *vt (voiture)* to make lighter; *(chargement)* to lighten; *(souffrance)* to alleviate, soothe.

allègre [alɛgR(ə)] *a* lively, cheerful.

alléguer [alege] *vt* to put forward (as proof *ou* an excuse).

Allemagne [aləmaɲ] *nf:* **l'~** Germany; **l'~ de l'Est/Ouest** East/West Germany; **allemand, e** *a, nm, nf* German.

aller [ale] *nm (trajet)* outward journey; *(billet: aussi:* **~ simple)** single *(Brit) ou* one-way *(US)* ticket // *vi (gén)* to go; **~ à** *(convenir)* to suit; *(suj: forme, pointure etc)* to fit; **~ avec** *(couleurs, style etc)* to go (well) with; **je vais y aller/me fâcher** I'm going to go/to get angry; **~ voir** to go and see, go to see; **allez! come on!; allons! come now!; comment allez-vous?** how are you?; **comment ça va?** how are you?; *(affaires etc)* how are things?; **il va bien/mal** he's well/not well, he's fine/ill; **ça va bien/mal** *(affaires etc)* it's going well/not going well; **~ mieux** to be better; **cela va sans dire** that goes without saying; **il y va de leur vie** their lives are at stake; **s'en ~** *vi (partir)* to be off, go, leave; *(disparaître)* to go away; **~ (et) retour** *nm (trajet)* return journey *(Brit)*, round trip; *(billet)* return (ticket) *(Brit)*, round trip ticket *(US)*.

allergique [alɛRʒik] *a:* **~ à** allergic to.

alliage [aljaʒ] *nm* alloy.

alliance [aljɑ̃s] *nf (MIL, POL)* alliance; *(mariage)* marriage; *(bague)* wedding ring.

allier [alje] *vt (métaux)* to alloy; *(POL, gén)* to ally; *(fig)* to combine; **s'~** to become allies; to combine.

allô [alo] *excl* hullo, hallo.

allocation [alɔkasjɔ̃] *nf* allowance; **~ (de) chômage** unemployment benefit; **~ (de) logement** rent allowance; **~s familiales** ≈ child benefit.

allocution [alɔkysjɔ̃] *nf* short speech.

allonger [alɔ̃ʒe] *vt* to lengthen, make longer; *(étendre: bras, jambe)* to stretch (out); **s'~** *vi* to get longer; *(se coucher)* to lie down, stretch out; **~ le pas** to hasten one's step(s).

allouer [alwe] *vt* to allocate, allot.

allumage [alymaʒ] *nm (AUTO)* ignition.

allume... [alym] *préfixe:* **~-cigare** *nm*

inv cigar lighter; **~-gaz** *nm inv* gas lighter.

allumer [alyme] *vt* (*lampe, phare, radio*) to put *ou* switch on; (*pièce*) to put *ou* switch the light(s) on in; (*feu*) to light; **s'~** *vi* (*lumière, lampe*) to come *ou* go on.

allumette [alymɛt] *nf* match.

allure [alyʀ] *nf* (*vitesse*) speed, pace; (*démarche*) walk; (*maintien*) bearing; (*aspect, air*) look; **avoir de l'~** to have style; **à toute ~** at top speed.

allusion [alyzjɔ̃] *nf* allusion; (*sous-entendu*) hint; **faire ~ à** to allude *ou* refer to; to hint at.

aloi [alwa] *nm*: **de bon ~** of genuine worth *ou* quality.

alors [alɔʀ] *ad* **1** (*à ce moment-là*) then, at that time; **il habitait ~ à Paris** he lived in Paris at that time
2 (*par conséquent*) then; **tu as fini? ~ je m'en vais** have you finished? I'm going then; **et ~?** so what?
alors que *cj* **1** (*au moment où*) when, as; **il est arrivé ~ que je partais** he arrived as I was leaving
2 (*pendant que*) while, when; **~ qu'il était à Paris, il a visité ...** while *ou* when he was in Paris, he visited ...
3 (*tandis que*) whereas, while; **~ que son frère travaillait dur, lui se reposait** whereas *ou* while his brother was working hard, HE would rest.

alouette [alwɛt] *nf* (sky)lark.

alourdir [aluʀdiʀ] *vt* to weigh down, make heavy.

aloyau [alwajo] *nm* sirloin.

alpage [alpaʒ] *nm* pasture.

Alpes [alp(ə)] *nfpl*: **les ~** the Alps.

alphabet [alfabɛ] *nm* alphabet; (*livre*) ABC (book); **alphabétiser** *vt* to teach to read and write; to eliminate illiteracy in.

alpinisme [alpinism(ə)] *nm* mountaineering, climbing; **alpiniste** *nm/f* mountaineer, climber.

Alsace [alzas] *nf* Alsace; **alsacien, ne** *a*, *nm/f* Alsatian.

altérer [alteʀe] *vt* to falsify; to distort; to debase; to impair.

alternateur [altɛʀnatœʀ] *nm* alternator.

alternatif, ive [altɛʀnatif, -iv] *a* alternating // *nf* (*choix*) alternative; **alternativement** *ad* alternately.

Altesse [altɛs] *nf* Highness.

altitude [altityd] *nf* altitude, height.

alto [alto] *nm* (*instrument*) viola.

altruisme [altʀyism(ə)] *nm* altruism.

aluminium [alyminjɔm] *nm* aluminium (*Brit*), aluminum (*US*).

alunir [alyniʀ] *vi* to land on the moon.

amabilité [amabilite] *nf* kindness, amiability.

amadouer [amadwe] *vt* to coax, cajole; to mollify, soothe.

amaigrir [amegʀiʀ] *vt* to make thin(ner).

amande [amɑ̃d] *nf* (*de l'amandier*) almond; (*de noyau de fruit*) kernel; **amandier** *nm* almond (tree).

amant [amɑ̃] *nm* lover.

amarrer [amaʀe] *vt* (NAVIG) to moor; (*gén*) to make fast.

amas [amɑ] *nm* heap, pile.

amasser [amase] *vt* to amass.

amateur [amatœʀ] *nm* amateur; **en ~** (*péj*) amateurishly; **~ de musique/sport** *etc* music/sport *etc* lover.

amazone [amazon] *nf*: **en ~** sidesaddle.

ambages [ɑ̃baʒ]: **sans ~** *ad* plainly.

ambassade [ɑ̃basad] *nf* embassy; (*mission*): **en ~** on a mission; **ambassadeur, drice** *nm/f* ambassador/ambassadress.

ambiance [ɑ̃bjɑ̃s] *nf* atmosphere.

ambiant, e [ɑ̃bjɑ̃, -ɑ̃t] *a* (*air, milieu*) surrounding; (*température*) ambient.

ambigu, ë [ɑ̃bigy] *a* ambiguous.

ambitieux, euse [ɑ̃bisjø, -øz] *a* ambitious.

ambition [ɑ̃bisjɔ̃] *nf* ambition.

ambulance [ɑ̃bylɑ̃s] *nf* ambulance; **ambulancier, ière** *nm/f* ambulance man/woman (*Brit*), paramedic (*US*).

ambulant, e [ɑ̃bylɑ̃, -ɑ̃t] *a* travelling, itinerant.

âme [ɑm] *nf* soul; **~ sœur** kindred spirit.

améliorer [ameljɔʀe] *vt* to improve; **s'~** *vi* to improve, get better.

aménagements [amenaʒmɑ̃] *nmpl* developments; **~ fiscaux** tax adjustments.

aménager [amenaʒe] *vt* (*agencer, transformer*) to fit out; to lay out; (*: quartier, territoire*) to develop; (*installer*) to fix up, put in; **ferme aménagée** converted farmhouse.

amende [amɑ̃d] *nf* fine; **mettre à l'~** to penalize; **faire ~ honorable** to make amends.

amender [amɑ̃de] *vt* (*loi*) to amend; **s'~** *vi* to mend one's ways.

amène [amɛn] *a* affable; **peu ~** unkind.

amener [amne] *vt* to bring; (*causer*) to bring about; (*baisser: drapeau, voiles*) to strike; **s'~** *vi* (*fam*) to show up, turn up.

amenuiser [amənɥize]: **s'~** *vi* to grow slimmer, lessen; to dwindle.

amer, amère [amɛʀ] *a* bitter.

américain, e [ameʀikɛ̃, -ɛn] *a*, *nm/f* American.

Amérique [ameʀik] *nf* America; **l'~ centrale/latine** Central/Latin America; **l'~ du Nord/du Sud** North/South America.

amerrir [ameʀiʀ] *vi* to land (on the sea).

amertume [amɛʀtym] *nf* bitterness.

ameublement [amœbləmɑ̃] *nm* furnishing; (*meubles*) furniture.

ameuter [amøte] *vt* (*badauds*) to draw a crowd of; (*peuple*) to rouse.

ami, e [ami] *nm/f* friend; *(amant/ maîtresse)* boyfriend/girlfriend // *a: pays/groupe* ~ friendly country/group; **être ~ de l'ordre** to be a lover of order; **un ~ des arts** a patron of the arts.

amiable [amjabl(ə)]: **à l'~** *ad (JUR)* out of court; *(gén)* amicably.

amiante [amjɑ̃t] *nm* asbestos.

amical, e, aux [amikal, -o] *a* friendly // *nf (club)* association; **amicalement** *ad* in a friendly way; *(formule épistolaire)* regards.

amidon [amidɔ̃] *nm* starch.

amincir [amɛ̃siʀ] *vt (objet)* to thin (down); **~ qn** to make sb thinner *ou* slimmer; **s'~** *vi* to get thinner *ou* slimmer.

amiral, aux [amiʀal, -o] *nm* admiral.

amitié [amitje] *nf* friendship; **prendre en ~** to befriend; **faire** *ou* **présenter ses ~s à qn** to send sb one's best wishes.

ammoniac [amɔnjak] *nm:* (gaz) ~ ammonia.

ammoniaque [amɔnjak] *nf* ammonia (water).

amoindrir [amwɛ̃dʀiʀ] *vt* to reduce.

amollir [amɔliʀ] *vt* to soften.

amonceler [amɔ̃sle] *vt*, **s'~** *vi* to pile *ou* heap up; *(fig)* to accumulate.

amont [amɔ̃]: **en ~** *ad* upstream; *(sur une pente)* uphill.

amorce [amɔʀs(ə)] *nf (sur un hameçon)* bait; *(explosif)* cap; primer; priming; *(fig: début)* beginning(s), start.

amorphe [amɔʀf(ə)] *a* passive, lifeless.

amortir [amɔʀtiʀ] *vt (atténuer: choc)* to absorb, cushion; *(bruit, douleur)* to deaden; *(COMM: dette)* to pay off; *(: mise de fonds, matériel)* to write off; ~ **un abonnement** to make a season ticket pay (for itself); **amortisseur** *nm* shock absorber.

amour [amuʀ] *nm* love; *(liaison)* love affair, love; **faire l'~** to make love; **s'~-acher de** *(péj)* to become infatuated with; **~eux, euse** *a (regard, tempérament)* amorous; *(vie, problèmes)* love *cpd*; *(personne):* **~eux (de qn)** in love (with sb) // *nmpl* courting couple(s); **~-propre** *nm* self-esteem, pride.

amovible [amɔvibl(ə)] *a* removable, detachable.

ampère [ɑ̃pɛʀ] *nm* amp(ere).

amphithéâtre [ɑ̃fiteatʀ(ə)] *nm* amphitheatre; *(d'université)* lecture hall *ou* theatre.

ample [ɑ̃pl(ə)] *a (vêtement)* roomy, ample; *(gestes, mouvement)* broad; *(ressources)* ample; **ampleur** *nf (importance)* scale, size; extent.

amplificateur [ɑ̃plifikatœʀ] *nm* amplifier.

amplifier [ɑ̃plifje] *vt (son, oscillation)* to amplify; *(fig)* to expand, increase.

ampoule [ɑ̃pul] *nf (électrique)* bulb; *(de*

médicament) phial; *(aux mains, pieds)* blister.

ampoulé, e [ɑ̃pule] *a (péj)* pompous, bombastic.

amputer [ɑ̃pyte] *vt (MÉD)* to amputate; *(fig)* to cut *ou* reduce drastically.

amusant, e [amyzɑ̃, -ɑ̃t] *a (divertissant, spirituel)* entertaining, amusing; *(comique)* funny, amusing.

amuse-gueule [amyzgœl] *nm inv* appetizer, snack.

amusement [amyzmɑ̃] *nm* amusement; *(jeu etc)* pastime, diversion.

amuser [amyze] *vt (divertir)* to entertain, amuse; *(égayer, faire rire)* to amuse; *(détourner l'attention de)* to distract; **s'~** *vi (jouer)* to amuse o.s., play; *(se divertir)* to enjoy o.s., have fun; *(fig)* to mess around.

amygdale [amidal] *nf* tonsil.

amygdalite [amidalit] *nf* tonsilitis.

an [ɑ̃] *nm* year; **le jour de l'~, le premier de l'~, le nouvel ~** New Year's Day.

analogique [analɔʒik] *a* analogical; *(INFORM, montre)* analog.

analogue [analɔg] *a:* ~ **(à)** analogous (to), similar (to).

analphabète [analfabɛt] *nm/f* illiterate.

analyse [analiz] *nf* analysis; *(MÉD)* test; **analyser** *vt* to analyse; to test.

ananas [anana] *nm* pineapple.

anarchie [anaʀʃi] *nf* anarchy.

anathème [anatɛm] *nm:* **jeter l'~ sur** to curse.

anatomie [anatɔmi] *nf* anatomy.

ancêtre [ɑ̃sɛtʀ(ə)] *nm/f* ancestor.

anchois [ɑ̃ʃwa] *nm* anchovy.

ancien, ne [ɑ̃sjɛ̃, -jɛn] *a* old; *(de jadis, de l'antiquité)* ancient; *(précédent, ex-)* former, old // *nm/f (dans une tribu)* elder; **anciennement** *ad* formerly; **ancienneté** *nf* oldness; antiquity; *(ADMIN)* (length of) service; seniority.

ancre [ɑ̃kʀ(ə)] *nf* anchor; **jeter l'~** to cast/weigh anchor; **à l'~** at anchor.

ancrer [ɑ̃kʀe] *vt (CONSTR: câble etc)* to anchor; *(fig)* to fix firmly; **s'~** *vi (NAVIG)* to (cast) anchor.

Andorre [ɑ̃dɔʀ] *nf* Andorra.

andouille [ɑ̃duj] *nf (CULIN)* sausage made of chitterlings; *(fam)* clot, nit.

âne [ɑn] *nm* donkey, ass; *(péj)* dunce.

anéantir [aneɑ̃tiʀ] *vt* to annihilate, wipe out; *(fig)* to obliterate, destroy; to overwhelm.

anémie [anemi] *nf* anaemia; **anémique** *a* anaemic.

ânerie [ɑnʀi] *nf* stupidity; stupid *ou* idiotic comment *etc*.

anesthésie [anɛstezi] *nf* anaesthesia; **faire une ~ locale/générale à qn** to give sb a local/general anaesthetic.

ange [ɑ̃ʒ] *nm* angel; **être aux ~s** to be over the moon.

angélus [ɑ̃ʒelys] *nm* angelus; evening

bells *pl*.

angine [ãʒin] *nf* throat infection; ~ de poitrine angina.

anglais, e [ãglɛ, -ɛz] *a* English // *nm/f*: A~, e Englishman/woman // *nm* (*LING*) English; les A~ the English; filer à l'~e to take French leave.

angle [ãgl(ə)] *nm* angle; (*coin*) corner; ~ droit right angle.

Angleterre [ãglətɛʀ] *nf*: l'~ England.

anglo... [ãglɔ] *préfixe* Anglo-, anglo(-); ~**phone** *a* English-speaking.

angoissé, e [ãgwase] *a* (*personne*) full of anxieties *ou* hang-ups (*fam*).

angoisser [ãgwase] *vt* to harrow, cause anguish to // *vi* to worry, fret.

anguille [ãgij] *nf* eel.

anicroche [anikʀɔʃ] *nf* hitch, snag.

animal, e, aux [animal, -o] *a, nm* animal.

animateur, trice [animatœʀ, -tʀis] *nm/f* (*de télévision*) host; (*de groupe*) leader, organizer.

animation [animɑsjɔ̃] *nf* (*voir, animé*) busyness; liveliness; (*CINÉMA: technique*) animation.

animé, e [anime] *a* (*lieu*) busy, lively; (*conversation, réunion*) lively, animated; (*opposé à inanimé*) animate.

animer [anime] *vt* (*ville, soirée*) to liven up; (*mettre en mouvement*) to drive.

anis [ani] *nm* (*CULIN*) aniseed; (*BOT*) anise.

ankyloser [ãkiloze]: s'~ *vi* to get stiff.

anneau, x [ano] *nm* (*de rideau, bague*) ring; (*de chaîne*) link.

année [ane] *nf* year.

annexe [anɛks(ə)] *a* (*problème*) related; (*document*) appended; (*salle*) adjoining // *nf* (*bâtiment*) annex(e); (*de document, ouvrage*) annex, appendix; (*jointe à une lettre*) enclosure.

anniversaire [anivɛʀsɛʀ] *nm* birthday; (*d'un événement, bâtiment*) anniversary.

annonce [anɔ̃s] *nf* announcement; (*signe, indice*) sign; (*aussi*: ~ publicitaire) advertisement; les petites ~s the classified advertisements, the small ads.

annoncer [anɔ̃se] *vt* to announce; (*être le signe de*) to herald; s'~ bien/difficile to look promising/difficult; **annonceur, euse** *nm/f* (*TV, RADIO: speaker*) announcer; (*publicitaire*) advertiser.

annuaire [anɥɛʀ] *nm* yearbook, annual; ~ téléphonique (telephone) directory, phone book.

annuel, le [anɥɛl] *a* annual, yearly.

annuité [anɥite] *nf* annual instalment.

annulaire [anɥlɛʀ] *nm* third finger.

annuler [anɥle] *vt* (*rendez-vous, voyage*) to cancel, call off; (*mariage*) to annul; (*jugement*) to quash (*Brit*), repeal (*US*); (*résultats*) to declare void; (*MATH, PHYSIQUE*) to cancel out.

anodin, e [anɔdɛ̃, -in] *a* harmless; in-

significant, trivial.

anonyme [anɔnim] *a* anonymous; (*fig*) impersonal.

anorak [anɔʀak] *nm* anorak.

ANPE *sigle f* (= *Agence nationale pour l'emploi*) national employment agency.

anse [ãs] *nf* (*de panier, tasse*) handle; (*GÉO*) cove.

antan [ãtã]: d'~ *a* of long ago.

antarctique [ãtaʀktik] *a* Antarctic // *nm*: l'A~ the Antarctic.

antécédents [ãtesedã] *nmpl* (*MÉD etc*) past history *sg*.

antenne [ãtɛn] *nf* (*de radio*) aerial; (*d'insecte*) antenna (*pl* ae), feeler; (*poste avancé*) outpost; (*petite succursale*) sub-branch; passer à l'~ to go on the air; prendre l'~ to tune in; 2 heures d'~ 2 hours' broadcasting time.

antérieur, e [ãteʀjœʀ] *a* (*d'avant*) previous, earlier; (*de devant*) front.

anti... [ãti] *préfixe* anti..; ~**aérien, ne** *a* anti-aircraft; abri ~aérien air-raid shelter; ~**alcoolique** *a* anti-alcohol; ~**atomique** *a*: abri ~atomique fallout shelter; ~**biotique** *nm* antibiotic; ~**brouillard** *a*: phare ~brouillard fog lamp.

anticipation [ãtisipɑsjɔ̃] *nf*: livre/film d'~ science fiction book/film.

anticipé, e [ãtisipe] *a*: avec mes remerciements ~s thanking you in advance *ou* anticipation.

anticiper [ãtisipe] *vt* (*événement, coup*) to anticipate, foresee.

anticonceptionnel, le [ãtikɔ̃sɛpsjɔnɛl] *a* contraceptive.

antidote [ãtidɔt] *nm* antidote.

antienne [ãtjɛn] *nf* (*fig*) chant, refrain.

antigel [ãtiʒɛl] *nm* antifreeze.

antihistaminique [ãtiistaminik] *nm* antihistamine.

Antilles [ãtij] *nfpl*: les ~ the West Indies.

antilope [ãtilɔp] *nf* antelope.

antimite(s) [ãtimit] *a, nm*: (produit) mothproofer; moth repellent.

antiparasite [ãtipaʀazit] *a* (*RADIO, TV*): dispositif ~ suppressor.

antipathique [ãtipatik] *a* unpleasant, disagreeable.

antiphrase [ãtifʀaz] *nf*: par ~ ironically.

antipodes [ãtipɔd] *nmpl* (*GÉO*): les ~ the antipodes; (*fig*): être aux ~ de to be the opposite extreme of.

antiquaire [ãtikɛʀ] *nm/f* antique dealer.

antique [ãtik] *a* antique; (*très vieux*) ancient, antiquated.

antiquité [ãtikite] *nf* (*objet*) antique; l'A~ Antiquity; magasin d'~s antique shop.

antirabique [ãtiʀabik] *a* rabies *cpd*.

antirouille [ãtiʀuj] *a inv* anti-rust *cpd*; traitement ~ rustproofing.

antisémite [ɑ̃tisemit] *a* anti-semitic.

antiseptique [ɑ̃tisɛptik] *a, nm* antiseptic.

antivol [ɑ̃tivɔl] *a, nm*: (dispositif) ~ anti-theft device.

antre [ɑ̃tʀ(ə)] *nm* den, lair.

anxieux, euse [ɑ̃ksjø, -øz] *a* anxious, worried.

AOC *sigle f* (= *appellation d'origine contrôlée*) label guaranteeing the quality of wine.

août [u] *nm* August.

apaiser [apeze] *vt* (colère, douleur) to soothe; (faim) to appease; (personne) to calm (down), pacify; s'~ *vi* (tempête, bruit) to die down, subside.

apanage [apanaʒ] *nm*: être l'~ de to be the privilege *ou* prerogative of.

aparté [apaʀte] *nm* (THÉÂTRE) aside; (entretien) private conversation.

apatride [apatʀid] *nm/f* stateless person.

apercevoir [apɛʀsəvwaʀ] *vt* to see; s'~ de *vt* to notice; s'~ que to notice that.

aperçu [apɛʀsy] *nm* (vue d'ensemble) general survey; (intuition) insight.

apéritif [apeʀitif] *nm* (boisson) aperitif; (réunion) drinks *pl*.

à-peu-près [apøpʀɛ] *nm inv* (péj) vague approximation.

apeuré, e [apœʀe] *a* frightened, scared.

aphone [afɔn] *a* voiceless.

aphte [aft(ə)] *nm* mouth ulcer.

aphteuse [aftøz] *af*: fièvre ~ foot-and-mouth disease.

apiculture [apikyltyʀ] *nf* beekeeping, apiculture.

apitoyer [apitwaje] *vt* to move to pity; s'~ (sur) to feel pity (for).

aplanir [aplaniʀ] *vt* to level; (fig) to smooth away, iron out.

aplatir [aplatiʀ] *vt* to flatten; s'~ *vi* to become flatter; to be flattened; (fig) to lie flat on the ground.

aplomb [aplɔ̃] *nm* (équilibre) balance, equilibrium; (fig) self-assurance; nerve; d'~ *ad* steady; (CONSTR) plumb.

apogée [apoʒe] *nm* (fig) peak, apogee.

apologie [apolɔʒi] *nf* vindication, praise.

apostolat [apostola] *nm* (REL) apostolate; (gén) evangelism.

apostrophe [apostʀɔf] *nf* (signe) apostrophe.

apostropher [apostʀɔfe] *vt* (interpeller) to shout at, address sharply.

apothéose [apoteoz] *nf* pinnacle (of achievement); (MUS) grand finale.

apôtre [apotʀ(ə)] *nm* apostle.

apparaître [apaʀɛtʀ(ə)] *vi* to appear // *vb avec attribut* to appear, seem.

apparat [apaʀa] *nm*: tenue/dîner d'~ ceremonial dress/dinner.

appareil [apaʀɛj] *nm* (outil, machine) piece of apparatus, device; appliance; (politique, syndical) machinery; (avion) (aero)plane, aircraft *inv*; (téléphonique)

phone; (dentier) brace (Brit), braces (US); qui est à l'~? who's speaking?; dans le plus simple ~ in one's birthday suit; ~ photographique, ~(-photo) *nm* camera; ~ 24 x 36 *ou* petit format 35mm camera.

appareiller [apaʀeje] *vi* (NAVIG) to cast off, get under way // *vt* (assortir) to match up.

apparemment [apaʀamɑ̃] *ad* apparently.

apparence [apaʀɑ̃s] *nf* appearance.

apparent, e [apaʀɑ̃, -ɑ̃t] *a* visible; obvious; (superficiel) apparent.

apparenté, e [apaʀɑ̃te] *a*: ~ à related to; (fig) similar to.

appariteur [apaʀitœʀ] *nm* attendant, porter (in French universities).

apparition [apaʀisjɔ̃] *nf* appearance; (surnaturelle) apparition.

appartement [apaʀtəmɑ̃] *nm* flat (Brit), apartment (US).

appartenir [apaʀtəniʀ]: ~ à *vt* to belong to; il lui appartient de it is up to him to, it is his duty to.

apparu, e *pp de* apparaître.

appât [apɑ] *nm* (PÊCHE) bait; (fig) lure, bait.

appauvrir [apovʀiʀ] *vt* to impoverish.

appel [apɛl] *nm* call; (nominal) roll call; (: SCOL) register; (MIL: recrutement) call-up; faire ~ à (invoquer) to appeal to; (avoir recours à) to call on; (nécessiter) to call for, require; faire ~ (JUR) to appeal; faire l'~ to call the roll; to call the register; sans ~ (fig) final, irrevocable; ~ d'offres (COMM) invitation to tender; faire un ~ de phares to flash one's headlights; ~ (téléphonique) (tele)phone call.

appelé [aple] *nm* (MIL) conscript.

appeler [aple] *vt* to call; (faire venir: médecin etc) to call, send for; (fig: nécessiter) to call for, demand; être appelé à (fig) to be destined to; ~ qn à comparaître (JUR) to summon sb to appear; en ~ à to appeal to; s'~: elle s'appelle Gabrielle her name is Gabrielle, she's called Gabrielle; comment ça s'appelle? what is it called?

appendice [apɛ̃dis] *nm* appendix; **appendicite** *nf* appendicitis.

appentis [apɑ̃ti] *nm* lean-to.

appesantir [apzɑ̃tiʀ]: s'~ *vi* to grow heavier; s'~ sur (fig) to dwell on.

appétissant, e [apetisɑ̃, -ɑ̃t] *a* appetizing, mouth-watering.

appétit [apeti] *nm* appetite; bon ~! enjoy your meal!

applaudir [aplodiʀ] *vt* to applaud // *vi* to applaud, clap; **applaudissements** *nmpl* applause *sg*, clapping *sg*.

application [aplikasjɔ̃] *nf* application.

applique [aplik] *nf* wall lamp.

appliquer [aplike] *vt* to apply; (loi) to

enforce; **s'~** vi (élève etc) to apply o.s.

appoint [apwɛ̃] nm (extra) contribution ou help; **avoir/faire l'~** (en payant) to have/give the right change ou money; **chauffage d'~** extra heating.

appointements [apwɛ̃tmɑ̃] nmpl salary sg.

appontement [apɔ̃tmɑ̃] nm landing stage, wharf.

apport [apɔʀ] nm supply; contribution.

apporter [apɔʀte] vt to bring.

apposer [apoze] vt to append; to affix.

apprécier [apʀesje] vt to appreciate; (évaluer) to estimate, assess.

appréhender [apʀeɑ̃de] vt (craindre) to dread; (arrêter) to apprehend.

apprendre [apʀɑ̃dʀ(ə)] vt to learn; (événement, résultats) to learn of, hear of; **~ qch à qn** (informer) to tell sb (of) sth; (enseigner) to teach sb sth; **~ à faire qch** to learn to do sth; **~ à qn à faire qch** to teach sb to do sth; **apprenti, e** nm/f apprentice; (fig) novice, beginner; **apprentissage** nm learning; (COMM, SCOL: période) apprenticeship.

apprêté, e [apʀete] a (fig) affected.

apprêter [apʀete] vt to dress, finish.

appris, e pp de **apprendre**.

apprivoiser [apʀivwaze] vt to tame.

approbation [apʀɔbasjɔ̃] nf approval.

approche [apʀɔʃ] nf approaching; approach.

approcher [apʀɔʃe] vi to approach, come near // vt to approach; (rapprocher): **~ qch (de qch)** to bring ou put sth near (to sth); **~ de** vt to draw near to; (quantité, moment) to approach; **s'~ de** vt to approach, go ou come near to.

approfondir [apʀɔfɔ̃diʀ] vt to deepen; (question) to go further into.

approprié, e [apʀɔpʀije] a: **~ (à)** appropriate (to), suited to.

approprier [apʀɔpʀije]: **s'~** vt to appropriate, take over.

approuver [apʀuve] vt to agree with; (autoriser: loi, projet) to approve, pass; (trouver louable) to approve of.

approvisionner [apʀɔvizjɔne] vt to supply; (compte bancaire) to pay funds into; **s'~ en** to stock up with.

approximatif, ive [apʀɔksimatif, -iv] a approximate, rough; vague.

appt abr de **appartement**.

appui [apɥi] nm support; prendre **~ sur** to lean on; to rest on; **l'~ de la fenêtre** the windowsill, the window ledge; **appui-tête, appuie-tête** nm inv headrest.

appuyer [apɥije] vt (poser): **~ qch sur/contre** to lean ou rest sth on/against; (soutenir: personne, demande) to support, back (up) // vi: **~ sur** (bouton, frein) to press, push; (mot, détail) to stress, emphasize; (suj: chose: peser sur) to rest (heavily) on, press against; **s'~ sur** vt to lean on; to rely on; **~ à droite** to bear (to the) right.

âpre [ɑpʀ(ə)] a acrid, pungent; (fig) harsh; bitter; **~ au gain** grasping.

après [apʀe] prép after // ad afterwards; **2 heures ~** 2 hours later; **~ qu'il est** ou **soit parti/avoir fait** after he left/having done; **d'~** prép (selon) according to; **~ coup** ad after the event, afterwards; **~ tout** ad (au fond) after all; **et (puis) ~?** so what?; **~-demain** ad the day after tomorrow; **~-guerre** nm post-war years pl; **~-midi** nm ou nf inv afternoon.

à-propos [apʀopo] nm (d'une remarque) aptness; **faire preuve d'~** to show presence of mind.

apte [apt(ə)] a capable; (MIL) fit.

aquarelle [akwaʀɛl] nf (tableau) watercolour; (genre) watercolours pl.

aquarium [akwaʀjɔm] nm aquarium.

arabe [aʀab] a Arabic; (désert, cheval) Arabian; (nation, peuple) Arab // nm/f: **A~** Arab // nm (LING) Arabic.

Arabie [aʀabi] nf: **l'~ (Saoudite)** Saudi Arabia.

arachide [aʀaʃid] nf (plante) groundnut (plant); (graine) peanut, groundnut.

araignée [aʀeɲe] nf spider.

arbitraire [aʀbitʀɛʀ] a arbitrary.

arbitre [aʀbitʀ(ə)] nm (SPORT) referee; (: TENNIS, CRICKET) umpire; (fig) arbiter, judge; (JUR) arbitrator; **arbitrer** vt to referee; to umpire; to arbitrate.

arborer [aʀbɔʀe] vt to bear, display.

arbre [aʀbʀ(ə)] nm tree; (TECH) shaft; **~ généalogique** family tree; **~ de transmission** (AUTO) driveshaft.

arbuste [aʀbyst(ə)] nm small shrub.

arc [aʀk] nm (arme) bow; (GÉOM) arc; (ARCHIT) arch; **en ~ de cercle** a semicircular.

arcade [aʀkad] nf arch(way); **~s** arcade sg, arches.

arcanes [aʀkan] nmpl mysteries.

arc-boutant [aʀkbutɑ̃] nm flying buttress.

arc-bouter [aʀkbute]: **s'~** vi: **s'~ contre** to lean ou press against.

arceau, x [aʀso] nm (métallique etc) hoop.

arc-en-ciel [aʀkɑ̃sjɛl] nm rainbow.

arche [aʀʃ(ə)] nf arch; **~ de Noé** Noah's Ark.

archéologie [aʀkeɔlɔʒi] nf archeology; **archéologue** nm/f archeologist.

archet [aʀʃɛ] nm bow.

archevêque [aʀʃəvɛk] nm archbishop.

archipel [aʀʃipɛl] nm archipelago.

architecte [aʀʃitɛkt(ə)] nm architect.

architecture [aʀʃitɛktyʀ] nf architecture.

archive [aʀʃiv] *nf* file; ~s *nfpl* archives.

arctique [aʀktik] *a* Arctic // *nm*: l'A~ the Arctic.

ardemment [aʀdamã] *ad* ardently, fervently.

ardent, e [aʀdã, -ãt] *a* (*soleil*) blazing; (*fièvre*) raging; (*amour*) ardent, passionate; (*prière*) fervent.

ardoise [aʀdwaz] *nf* slate.

ardt *abr de* **arrondissement**.

arène [aʀɛn] *nf* arena; ~s *nfpl* bull-ring *sg*.

arête [aʀɛt] *nf* (*de poisson*) bone; (*d'une montagne*) ridge; (*GÉOM etc*) edge.

argent [aʀʒã] *nm* (*métal*) silver; (*monnaie*) money; ~ **liquide** ready money, (ready) cash; ~ **de poche** pocket money; **argenterie** *nf* silverware; silver plate.

argentin, e [aʀʒãtɛ̃, -in] *a* (*son*) silvery; (*d'Argentine*) Argentinian, Argentine.

Argentine [aʀʒãtin] *nf*: l'~ Argentina, the Argentine.

argile [aʀʒil] *nf* clay.

argot [aʀgo] *nm* slang; **argotique** *a* slang *cpd*; slangy.

arguer [aʀgɥe]: ~ **de** *vt* to put forward as a pretext *ou* reason.

argument [aʀgymã] *nm* argument.

argumentaire [aʀgymãtɛʀ] *nm* sales leaflet.

argumenter [aʀgymãte] *vi* to argue.

argus [aʀgys] *nm* guide to second-hand car etc prices.

arguties [aʀgysi] *nfpl* quibbles.

aristocratique [aʀistɔkʀatik] *a* aristocratic.

arithmétique [aʀitmetik] *a* arithmetic(al) // *nf* arithmetic.

armateur [aʀmatœʀ] *nm* shipowner.

armature [aʀmatyʀ] *nf* framework; (*de tente etc*) frame.

arme [aʀm(ə)] *nf* weapon; (*section de l'armée*) arm; ~s *nfpl* weapons, arms; (*blason*) (coat of) arms; ~ **à feu** firearm.

armée [aʀme] *nf* army; ~ **de l'air** Air Force; l'~ **du Salut** the Salvation Army; ~ **de terre** Army.

armement [aʀməmã] *nm* (*matériel*) arms *pl*, weapons *pl*; (: *d'un pays*) arms *pl*, armament.

armer [aʀme] *vt* to arm; (*arme à feu*) to cock; (*appareil-photo*) to wind on; ~ **qch de** to fit sth with; to reinforce sth with.

armistice [aʀmistis] *nm* armistice; l'A~ ≈ Remembrance (*Brit*) *ou* Veterans (*US*) Day.

armoire [aʀmwaʀ] *nf* (tall) cupboard; (*penderie*) wardrobe (*Brit*), closet (*US*).

armoiries [aʀmwaʀi] *nfpl* coat *sg* of arms.

armure [aʀmyʀ] *nf* armour *q*, suit of armour.

armurier [aʀmyʀje] *nm* gunsmith;

armourer.

arnaquer [aʀnake] *vt* to swindle.

aromates [aʀɔmat] *nmpl* seasoning *sg*, herbs (and spices).

aromatisé, e [aʀɔmatize] *a* flavoured.

arôme [aʀom] *nm* aroma; fragrance.

arpenter [aʀpãte] *vt* (*salle, couloir*) to pace up and down.

arpenteur [aʀpãtœʀ] *nm* surveyor.

arqué, e [aʀke] *a* bandy; arched.

arrache-pied [aʀaʃpje]: **d'~** *ad* relentlessly.

arracher [aʀaʃe] *vt* to pull out; (*page etc*) to tear off, tear out; (*légumes, herbe*) to pull up; (*bras etc*) to tear off; ~ **qch à qn** to snatch sth from sb; (*fig*) to wring sth out of sb; **s'~** *vt* (*article recherché*) to fight over.

arraisonner [aʀezɔne] *vt* (*bateau*) to board and search.

arrangeant, e [aʀãʒã, -ãt] *a* accommodating, obliging.

arranger [aʀãʒe] *vt* (*gén*) to arrange; (*réparer*) to fix, put right; (*régler*) to settle, sort out; (*convenir à*) to suit, be convenient for; **s'~** (*se mettre d'accord*) to come to an agreement; **je vais m'~** I'll manage; **ça va s'~** it'll sort itself out.

arrestation [aʀɛstasjɔ̃] *nf* arrest.

arrêt [aʀɛ] *nm* stopping; (*de bus etc*) stop; (*JUR*) judgment, decision; **rester** *ou* **tomber en ~ devant** to stop short in front of; **sans ~** non-stop; continually; ~ **de mort** capital sentence; ~ **de travail** stoppage (of work).

arrêté [aʀete] *nm* order, decree.

arrêter [aʀete] *vt* to stop; (*chauffage etc*) to turn off, switch off; (*fixer: date etc*) to appoint, decide on; (*criminel, suspect*) to arrest; ~ **de faire** to stop doing; **s'~** *vi* to stop.

arrhes [aʀ] *nfpl* deposit *sg*.

arrière [aʀjɛʀ] *nm* back; (*SPORT*) fullback // *a inv*: **siège/roue** ~ back *ou* rear seat/wheel; **à l'~** *ad* behind, at the back; **en ~** *ad* behind; (*regarder*) back, behind; (*tomber, aller*) backwards; **arriéré, e** *a* (*péj*) backward // *nm* (*d'argent*) arrears *pl*; **~-goût** *nm* aftertaste; **~-grand-mère** *nf* great-grandmother; **~-grand-père** *nm* great-grandfather; **~-pays** *nm inv* hinterland; **~-pensée** *nf* ulterior motive; mental reservation; **~-plan** *nm* background; **~-saison** *nf* late autumn; **~-train** *nm* hindquarters *pl*.

arrimer [aʀime] *vt* to stow; to secure.

arrivage [aʀivaʒ] *nm* arrival.

arrivée [aʀive] *nf* arrival; (*ligne d'arrivée*) finish; ~ **d'air/de gaz** air/gas inlet.

arriver [aʀive] *vi* to arrive; (*survenir*) to happen, occur; **il arrive à Paris à 8h** he gets to *ou* arrives in Paris at 8; ~ **à** (*at-*

teindre) to reach; ~ **à faire qch** to succeed in doing sth; **il arrive que** it happens that; **il lui arrive de faire** he sometimes does; **arriviste** *nm/f* go-getter.

arrogant, e [aʀɔɡɑ̃, -ɑ̃t] *a* arrogant.

arroger [aʀɔʒe]: **s'~** *vt* to assume (without right).

arrondir [aʀɔ̃diʀ] *vt* (*forme, objet*) to round; (*somme*) to round off; **s'~** *vi* to become round(ed).

arrondissement [aʀɔ̃dismɑ̃] *nm* (*ADMIN*) ≈ district.

arroser [aʀoze] *vt* to water; (*victoire*) to celebrate (over a drink); (*CULIN*) to baste; **arrosoir** *nm* watering can.

arsenal, aux [aʀsənal, -o] *nm* (*NAVIG*) naval dockyard; (*MIL*) arsenal; (*fig*) gear, paraphernalia.

art [aʀ] *nm* art; **~s ménagers** home economics *sg*.

artère [aʀtɛʀ] *nf* (*ANAT*) artery; (*rue*) main road.

arthrite [aʀtʀit] *nf* arthritis.

artichaut [aʀtiʃo] *nm* artichoke.

article [aʀtikl(ə)] *nm* article; (*COMM*) item, article; **à l'~ de la mort** at the point of death; **~ de fond** (*PRESSE*) feature article.

articulation [aʀtikylɑsjɔ̃] *nf* articulation; (*ANAT*) joint.

articuler [aʀtikyle] *vt* to articulate.

artifice [aʀtifis] *nm* device, trick.

artificiel, le [aʀtifisjɛl] *a* artificial.

artificieux, euse [aʀtifisjø, -øz] *a* guileful, deceitful.

artisan [aʀtizɑ̃] *nm* artisan, (self-employed) craftsman; **artisanal, e, aux** *a* of *ou* made by craftsmen; (*péj*) cottage industry *cpd*, unsophisticated; **artisanat** *nm* arts and crafts *pl*.

artiste [aʀtist(ə)] *nm/f* artist; (*de variétés*) entertainer; performer; **artistique** *a* artistic.

as [a] *vb voir* **avoir** // *nm* [ɑs] ace.

ascendance [asɑ̃dɑ̃s] *nf* (*origine*) ancestry.

ascendant, e [asɑ̃dɑ̃, -ɑ̃t] *a* upward // *nm* influence.

ascenseur [asɑ̃sœʀ] *nm* lift (*Brit*), elevator (*US*).

ascension [asɑ̃sjɔ̃] *nf* ascent; climb; **l'A~** (*REL*) the Ascension.

aseptiser [asɛptize] *vt* to sterilize; to disinfect.

asiatique [azjatik] *a*, *nm/f* Asiatic, Asian.

Asie [azi] *nf*: **l'~** Asia.

asile [azil] *nm* (*refuge*) refuge, sanctuary; (*POL*) **droit d'~** (political) asylum; (*pour malades etc*) home.

aspect [aspɛ] *nm* appearance, look; (*fig*) aspect, side; **à l'~ de** at the sight of.

asperge [aspɛʀʒ(ə)] *nf* asparagus *q*.

asperger [aspɛʀʒe] *vt* to spray, sprinkle.

aspérité [aspeʀite] *nf* excrescence, pro-

truding bit (of rock *etc*).

asphalte [asfalt(ə)] *nm* asphalt.

asphyxier [asfiksje] *vt* to suffocate, asphyxiate; (*fig*) to stifle.

aspirateur [aspiʀatœʀ] *nm* vacuum cleaner.

aspirer [aspiʀe] *vt* (*air*) to inhale; (*liquide*) to suck (up); (*suj: appareil*) to suck up; **~ à** *vt* to aspire to.

aspirine [aspiʀin] *nf* aspirin.

assagir [asaʒiʀ] *vt*, **s'~** *vi* to quieten down, sober down.

assaillir [asajiʀ] *vt* to assail, attack.

assainir [aseniʀ] *vt* to clean up; to purify.

assaisonner [asɛzɔne] *vt* to season.

assassin [asasɛ̃] *nm* murderer; assassin.

assassiner [asasine] *vt* to murder; (*esp POL*) to assassinate.

assaut [aso] *nm* assault, attack; **prendre d'~** to storm, assault; **donner l'~** to attack; **faire ~ de** (*rivaliser*) to vie with each other in.

assécher [aseʃe] *vt* to drain.

assemblée [asɑ̃ble] *nf* (*réunion*) meeting; (*public, assistance*) gathering; assembled people; (*POL*) assembly.

assembler [asɑ̃ble] *vt* (*joindre, monter*) to assemble, put together; (*amasser*) to gather (together), collect (together); **s'~** *vi* to gather.

assener, asséner [asene] *vt*: **~ un coup à qn** to deal sb a blow.

assentiment [asɑ̃timɑ̃] *nm* assent, consent; approval.

asseoir [aswaʀ] *vt* (*malade, bébé*) to sit up; to sit down; (*autorité, réputation*) to establish; **s'~** *vi* to sit (o.s.) down.

assermenté, e [asɛʀmɑ̃te] *a* sworn, on oath.

asservir [asɛʀviʀ] *vt* to subjugate, enslave.

asseye *etc vb voir* **asseoir**.

assez [ase] *ad* (*suffisamment*) enough, sufficiently; (*passablement*) rather, quite, fairly; **~ de pain/livres** enough *ou* sufficient bread/books; **vous en avez ~?** have you got enough?

assidu, e [asidy] *a* assiduous, painstaking; regular; **assiduités** *nfpl* assiduous attentions.

assied *etc vb voir* **asseoir**.

assiéger [asjeʒe] *vt* to besiege.

assiérai *etc vb voir* **asseoir**.

assiette [asjɛt] *nf* plate; (*contenu*) plate(ful); **~ anglaise** assorted cold meats; **~ creuse** (soup) dish, soup plate; **~ à dessert** dessert plate; **~ de l'impôt** basis of (tax) assessment; **~ plate** (dinner) plate.

assigner [asiɲe] *vt*: **~ qch à** (*poste, part, travail*) to assign sth to; (*limites*) to set sth to; (*cause, effet*) to ascribe sth to; **~ qn à** to assign sb to.

assimiler [asimile] *vt* to assimilate, absorb; (*comparer*): ~ **qch/qn à** to liken *ou* compare sth/sb to; s'~ *vi* (*s'intégrer*) to be assimilated *ou* absorbed.

assis, e [asi, -iz] *pp de* **asseoir** // *a* (*sitting* (*down*), seated // *nf* (*fig*) basis (*pl* bases), foundation; ~**es** *nfpl* (*JUR*) assizes; (*congrès*) (annual) conference.

assistance [asistɑ̃s] *nf* (*public*) audience; (*aide*) assistance.

assistant, e [asistɑ̃, -ɑ̃t] *nm/f* assistant; (*d'université*) probationary lecturer; les ~**s** *nmpl* (*auditeurs etc*) those present; ~**e sociale** social worker.

assisté, e [asiste] *a* (*AUTO*) power assisted.

assister [asiste] *vt* to assist; ~ **à** *vt* (*scène, événement*) to witness; (*conférence, séminaire*) to attend, be at; (*spectacle, match*) to be at, see.

association [asɔsjasjɔ̃] *nf* association.

associé, e [asɔsje] *nm/f* associate; partner.

associer [asɔsje] *vt* to associate; ~ **qn à** (*profits*) to give sb a share of; (*affaire*) to make sb a partner in; (*joie, triomphe*) to include sb in; ~ **qch à** (*joindre, allier*) to combine sth with; s'~ (*suj pl*) to join together; (*COMM*) to form a partnership; s'~ *vt* (*collaborateur*) to take on (as a partner); s'~ **à qn pour faire** to join (forces) with sb to do; s'~ **à** to be combined with; (*opinions, joie de qn*) to share in.

assoiffé, e [aswafe] *a* thirsty.

assombrir [asɔ̃bʀiʀ] *vt* to darken; (*fig*) to fill with gloom.

assommer [asɔme] *vt* to batter to death; (*étourdir, abrutir*) to knock out; to stun.

Assomption [asɔ̃psjɔ̃] *nf*: l'~ the Assumption.

assorti, e [asɔʀti] *a* matched, matching; (*varié*) assorted; ~ **à** matching.

assortiment [asɔʀtimɑ̃] *nm* assortment, selection.

assortir [asɔʀtiʀ] *vt* to match; ~ **qch à** to match sth with; ~ **qch de** to accompany sth with; s'~ **de** to be accompanied by.

assoupi, e [asupi] *a* dozing, sleeping; (*fig*) (be)numbed; dulled; stilled.

assouplir [asupliʀ] *vt* to make supple; (*fig*) to relax.

assourdir [asuʀdiʀ] *vt* (*bruit*) to deaden, muffle; (*suj: bruit*) to deafen.

assouvir [asuviʀ] *vt* to satisfy, appease.

assujettir [asyʒetiʀ] *vt* to subject.

assumer [asyme] *vt* (*fonction, emploi*) to assume, take on.

assurance [asyʀɑ̃s] *nf* (*certitude*) assurance; (*confiance en soi*) (self-)confidence; (*contrat*) insurance (policy); (*secteur commercial*) insurance; ~ **maladie** health insurance; ~ **tous risques** (*AUTO*) comprehensive insurance; ~**s**

sociales ≈ National Insurance (*Brit*), ≈ Social Security (*US*); ~**-vie** *nf* life assurance *ou* insurance.

assuré, e [asyʀe] *a* (*certain*): ~ **de** confident of // *nm/f* insured (person); ~**ment** *ad* assuredly, most certainly.

assurer [asyʀe] *vt* to insure; (*stabiliser*) to steady; to stabilize; (*victoire etc*) to ensure; (*frontières, pouvoir*) to make secure; (*service, garde*) to provide; to operate; (*certifier*) to assure; s'~ (*contre*) (*COMM*) to insure o.s. (against); s'~ **de/que** (*vérifier*) to make sure of/that; s'~ (**de**) (*aide de qn*) to secure.

asthme [asm(ə)] *nm* asthma.

asticot [astiko] *nm* maggot.

astiquer [astike] *vt* to polish, shine.

astre [astʀ(ə)] *nm* star.

astreignant, e [astʀɛɲɑ̃, -ɑ̃t] *a* demanding.

astreindre [astʀɛ̃dʀ(ə)] *vt*: ~ **qn à qch** to force sth upon sb; ~ **qn à faire** to compel *ou* force sb to do.

astrologie [astʀɔlɔʒi] *nf* astrology.

astronaute [astʀɔnot] *nm/f* astronaut.

astronomie [astʀɔnɔmi] *nf* astronomy.

astuce [astys] *nf* shrewdness, astuteness; (*truc*) trick, clever way; (*plaisanterie*) wisecrack; **astucieux, euse** *a* clever.

atelier [atəlje] *nm* workshop; (*de peintre*) studio.

athée [ate] *a* atheistic // *nm/f* atheist.

Athènes [atɛn] *n* Athens.

athlète [atlɛt] *nm/f* (*SPORT*) athlete; **athlétisme** *nm* athletics *sg*.

atlantique [atlɑ̃tik] *a* Atlantic // *nm*: l'(océan) A~ the Atlantic (Ocean).

atlas [atlɑs] *nm* atlas.

atmosphère [atmɔsfɛʀ] *nf* atmosphere.

atome [atom] *nm* atom; **atomique** *a* atomic, nuclear; (*nombre, masse*) atomic.

atomiseur [atɔmizœʀ] *nm* atomizer.

atone [atɔn] *a* lifeless.

atours [atuʀ] *nmpl* attire *sg*, finery *sg*.

atout [atu] *nm* trump; (*fig*) asset; trump card.

âtre [ɑtʀ(ə)] *nm* hearth.

atroce [atʀɔs] *a* atrocious.

attabler [atable]: s'~ *vi* to sit down at (the) table.

attachant, e [ataʃɑ̃, -ɑ̃t] *a* engaging, lovable, likeable.

attache [ataʃ] *nf* clip, fastener; (*fig*) tie.

attacher [ataʃe] *vt* to tie up; (*étiquette*) to attach, tie on; (*souliers*) to do up // *vi* (*poêle, riz*) to stick; s'~ **à** (*par affection*) to become attached to; s'~ **à faire** to endeavour to do; ~ **qch à** to tie *ou* attach sth to.

attaque [atak] *nf* attack; (*cérébrale*) stroke; (*d'épilepsie*) fit.

attaquer [atake] *vt* to attack; *(en justice)* to bring an action against, sue; *(travail)* to tackle, set about // *vi* to attack.

attardé, e [ataʀde] *a (passants)* late; *(enfant)* backward; *(conceptions)* old-fashioned.

attarder [ataʀde]: **s'~** *vi* to linger; to stay on.

atteindre [atɛ̃dʀ(ə)] *vt* to reach; *(blesser)* to hit; *(émouvoir)* to affect.

atteint, e [atɛ̃, -ɛ̃t] *a (MÉD)*: être ~ de to be suffering from // *nf* attack; **hors d'~e** out of reach; **porter ~e à** to strike a blow at; to undermine.

atteler [atle] *vt (cheval, bœufs)* to hitch up; *(wagons)* to couple; **s'~ à** *(travail)* to buckle down to.

attelle [atɛl] *nf* splint.

attenant, e [atnɑ̃, -ɑ̃t] *a*: ~ (à) adjoining.

attendre [atɑ̃dʀ(ə)] *vt (gén)* to wait for; *(être destiné ou réservé à)* to await, be in store for // *vi* to wait; **s'~ à (ce que)** to expect (that); ~ **un enfant** to be expecting a baby; ~ **de faire/d'être** to wait until one does/is; ~ **que** to wait until; ~ **qch de** to expect sth of; **en attendant** *ad* meanwhile, in the meantime; be that as it may.

attendrir [atɑ̃dʀiʀ] *vt* to move (to pity); *(viande)* to tenderize.

attendu, e [atɑ̃dy] *a (visiteur)* expected; ~ **que** *cj* considering that, since.

attentat [atɑ̃ta] *nm* assassination attempt; ~ **à la bombe** bomb attack; ~ **à la pudeur** indecent exposure *q*; indecent assault *q*.

attente [atɑ̃t] *nf* wait; *(espérance)* expectation.

attenter [atɑ̃te]: ~ **à** *vt (liberté)* to violate; ~ **à la vie de qn** to make an attempt on sb's life.

attentif, ive [atɑ̃tif, -iv] *a (auditeur)* attentive; *(travail)* scrupulous; careful; ~ **à** mindful of; careful to.

attention [atɑ̃sjɔ̃] *nf* attention; *(prévenance)* attention, thoughtfulness *q*; **à l'~ de** for the attention of; **faire ~ (à)** to be careful (of); **faire ~ (à ce) que** to be ou make sure that; ~! careful!, watch out!; **attentionné, e** *a* thoughtful, considerate.

atténuer [atenɥe] *vt* to alleviate, ease; to lessen.

atterrer [ateʀe] *vt* to dismay, appal.

atterrir [ateʀiʀ] *vi* to land; **atterrissage** *nm* landing.

attestation [atɛstasjɔ̃] *nf* certificate.

attester [atɛste] *vt* to testify to.

attirail [atiʀaj] *nm* gear; *(péj)* paraphernalia.

attirant, e [atiʀɑ̃, -ɑ̃t] *a* attractive, appealing.

attirer [atiʀe] *vt* to attract; *(appâter)* to lure, entice; ~ **qn dans un coin/vers soi** to draw sb into a corner/towards one; ~ **l'attention de qn (sur)** to attract sb's attention (to); to draw sb's attention (to); **s'~ des ennuis** to bring trouble upon o.s., get into trouble.

attiser [atize] *vt (feu)* to poke (up).

attitré, e [atitʀe] *a* qualified; accredited; appointed.

attitude [atityd] *nf* attitude; *(position du corps)* bearing.

attouchements [atuʃmɑ̃] *nmpl* touching *sg*; *(sexuels)* fondling *sg*.

attraction [atʀaksjɔ̃] *nf (gén)* attraction; *(de cabaret, cirque)* number.

attrait [atʀɛ] *nm* appeal, attraction; lure.

attrape-nigaud [atʀapnigo] *nm* con.

attraper [atʀape] *vt (gén)* to catch; *(habitude, amende)* to get, pick up; *(fam: duper)* to con.

attrayant, e [atʀejɑ̃, -ɑ̃t] *a* attractive.

attribuer [atʀibɥe] *vt (prix)* to award; *(rôle, tâche)* to allocate, assign; *(imputer)*: ~ **qch à** to attribute sth to; **s'~** *vt (s'approprier)* to claim for o.s.

attribut [atʀiby] *nm* attribute; *(LING)* complement.

attrister [atʀiste] *vt* to sadden.

attroupement [atʀupmɑ̃] *nm* crowd, mob.

attrouper [atʀupe]: **s'~** *vi* to gather.

au [o] *prép + dét* voir **à**.

aubade [obad] *nf* dawn serenade.

aubaine [obɛn] *nf* godsend; *(financière)* windfall.

aube [ob] *nf* dawn, daybreak; **à l'~** at dawn ou daybreak.

aubépine [obepin] *nf* hawthorn.

auberge [obɛʀʒ(ə)] *nf* inn; ~ **de jeunesse** youth hostel.

aubergine [obɛʀʒin] *nf* aubergine.

aubergiste [obɛʀʒist(ə)] *nm/f* innkeeper, hotel-keeper.

aucun, e [okœ̃, -yn] *dét* no, *tournure négative* + any; *(positif)* any // *pronom* none, *tournure négative* + any; any(one); **sans** ~ **doute** without any doubt; **plus qu'~ autre** more than any other; ~ **des deux** neither of the two; ~ **d'entre eux** none of them; **d'~s** *(certains)* some; **aucunement** *ad* in no way, not in the least.

audace [odas] *nf* daring, boldness; *(péj)* audacity; **audacieux, euse** *a* daring, bold.

au-delà [odla] *ad* beyond // *nm*: **l'~** the hereafter; ~ **de** *prép* beyond.

au-dessous [odsu] *ad* underneath; below; ~ **de** *prép* under(neath); below; *(limite, somme etc)* below, under; *(dignité, condition)* below.

au-dessus [odsy] *ad* above; ~ **de** *prép* above.

au-devant [odvɑ̃]: ~ **de** *prép*: aller ~

de (*personne, danger*) to go (out) and
meet; (*souhaits de qn*) to anticipate.
audience [odjãs] *nf* audience; (*JUR*:
séance) hearing.
audio-visuel, le [odjovizɥɛl] *a* audio-
visual.
auditeur, trice [oditœr, -tris] *nm/f* lis-
tener.
audition [odisjɔ̃] *nf* (*ouïe, écoute*) hearing; (*JUR*: *de témoins*) examination;
(*MUS, THÉÂTRE*: *épreuve*) audition.
auditoire [oditwar] *nm* audience.
auge [oʒ] *nf* trough.
augmentation [ɔgmãtɑsjɔ̃] *nf*: ~ (*de
salaire*) rise (in salary) (*Brit*), (pay)
raise (*US*).
augmenter [ɔgmãte] *vt* (*gén*) to increase; (*salaire, prix*) to increase, raise,
put up; (*employé*) to increase the salary
of // *vi* to increase.
augure [ɔgyr] *nm* soothsayer, oracle; de
bon/mauvais ~ of good/ill omen.
augurer [ɔgyre] *vt*: ~ bien de to augur
well for.
aujourd'hui [oʒurdɥi] *ad* today.
aumône [omon] *nf* alms *sg* (*pl inv*);
faire l'~ (à qn) to give alms (to sb).
aumônier [omonje] *nm* chaplain.
auparavant [oparavã] *ad* before(hand).
auprès [oprɛ]: ~ **de** *prép* next to, close
to; (*recourir, s'adresser*) to; (*en
comparaison de*) compared with.
auquel [okɛl] *prép* + *pronom voir* **lequel**.
aurai *etc vb voir* **avoir**.
auréole [ɔreɔl] *nf* halo; (*tache*) ring.
auriculaire [ɔrikylɛr] *nm* little finger.
aurons *etc vb voir* **avoir**.
aurore [ɔrɔr] *nf* dawn, daybreak.
ausculter [ɔskylte] *vt* to sound.
aussi [osi] *ad* (*également*) also, too; (*de
comparaison*) as // *cj* therefore, consequently; ~ **fort que** as strong as; **moi** ~
me too; ~ **bien que** (*de même que*) as
well as.
aussitôt [osito] *ad* straight away, immediately; ~ **que** as soon as.
austère [ɔstɛr] *a* austere; stern.
austral, e [ɔstral] *a* southern.
Australie [ɔstrali] *nf*: l'~ Australia;
australien, ne *a, nm/f* Australian.
autant [otã] *ad* so much; (*comparatif*):
~ (**que**) as much (as); (*nombre*) as
many (as); ~ (**de**) so much (*ou* many);
as much (*ou* many); ~ **partir** we (*ou*
you *etc*) may as well leave; ~ **dire que**...
one might as well say that...; **pour** ~ for
all that; **pour** ~ **que** *cj* assuming, as long
as; **d'~ plus/mieux** (**que**) all the more/
the better (since).
autel [ɔtɛl] *nm* altar.
auteur [otœr] *nm* author.
authentique [ɔtãtik] *a* authentic,
genuine.
auto [ɔto] *nf* car.

auto... [ɔto] *préfixe* auto..., self-;
~**biographie** *nf* autobiography.
autobus [ɔtɔbys] *nm* bus.
autocar [ɔtɔkar] *nm* coach.
autochtone [ɔtɔktɔn] *nm/f* native.
auto-collant, e [ɔtɔkɔlã, -ãt] *a* self-
adhesive; (*enveloppe*) self-seal // *nm*
sticker.
auto-couchettes [ɔtɔkuʃɛt] *a*: train ~
car sleeper train.
autocuiseur [ɔtɔkɥizœr] *nm* pressure
cooker.
autodéfense [ɔtɔdefãs] *nf* self-defence;
groupe d'~ vigilante committee.
autodidacte [ɔtɔdidakt(ə)] *nm/f* self-
taught person.
auto-école [ɔtɔekɔl] *nf* driving school.
autogestion [ɔtɔʒɛstjɔ̃] *nf* self-
management.
autographe [ɔtɔgraf] *nm* autograph.
auto- mate [ɔtɔmat] *nm* (*machine*)
(automatic) machine.
automatique [ɔtɔmatik] *a* automatic //
nm: l'~ direct dialling; ~**ment** *ad* automatically; **automatiser** *vt* to auto-
mate.
automne [ɔtɔn] *nm* autumn (*Brit*), fall
(*US*).
automobile [ɔtɔmɔbil] *a* motor *cpd* // *nf*
(motor) car; l'~ motoring; the car industry; **automobiliste** *nm/f* motorist.
autonome [ɔtɔnɔm] *a* autonomous;
autonomie *nf* autonomy; (*POL*) self-
government, autonomy.
autopsie [ɔtɔpsi] *nf* post-mortem (examination), autopsy.
autoradio [ɔtɔradjo] *nm* car radio.
autorisation [ɔtɔrizɑsjɔ̃] *nf* permission,
authorization; (*papiers*) permit.
autorisé, e [ɔtɔrize] *a* (*opinion, sour-
ces*) authoritative.
autoriser [ɔtɔrize] *vt* to give permission
for, authorize; (*fig*) to allow (of), sanction.
autoritaire [ɔtɔritɛr] *a* authoritarian.
autorité [ɔtɔrite] *nf* authority; faire ~
to be authoritative.
autoroute [ɔtɔrut] *nf* motorway (*Brit*),
highway (*US*).
auto-stop [ɔtɔstɔp] *nm*: faire de l'~ to
hitch-hike; ~**peur, euse** *nm/f* hitch-
hiker.
autour [otur] *ad* around; ~ **de** *prép*
around; **tout** ~ *ad* all around.
autre [otr(ə)] ♦ *a* **1** (*différent*) other,
different; je préférerais un ~ verre I'd
prefer another *ou* a different glass
2 (*supplémentaire*) other; je voudrais
un ~ verre d'eau I'd like another glass
of water
3: ~ **chose** something else; ~ **part** *ad*
somewhere else; **d'~ part** *ad* on the
other hand
♦ *pronom*: **un** ~ another (one); **nous/
vous** ~**s** us/you; **d'~s** others; l'~ the

other (one); les ~s the others; (*autrui*) others; l'un et l'~ both of them; se détester l'un l'~/les uns les ~s to hate each other *ou* one another; d'une semaine à l'~ from one week to the next; (*incessamment*) any week now; entre ~s among other things.

autrefois [otʀəfwa] *ad* in the past.

autrement [otʀəmã] *ad* differently; in another way; (*sinon*) otherwise; ~ dit in other words.

Autriche [otʀiʃ] *nf*: l'~ Austria; **autrichien, ne** *a*, *nm/f* Austrian.

autruche [otʀyʃ] *nf* ostrich.

autrui [otʀɥi] *pronom* others.

auvent [ovã] *nm* canopy.

aux [o] *prép* + *dét voir* **à**.

auxiliaire [ɔksiljɛʀ] *a*, *nm/f* auxiliary.

auxquels, auxquelles [okɛl] *prép* + *pronom voir* **lequel**.

av. *abr de* **avenue**.

avachi, e [avaʃi] *a* limp, flabby.

aval [aval] *nm* (*accord*) endorsement, backing; (*GÉO*): **en** ~ downstream, downriver; (*sur une pente*) downhill.

avalanche [avalãʃ] *nf* avalanche.

avaler [avale] *vt* to swallow.

avance [avãs] *nf* (*de troupes etc*) advance; progress; (*d'argent*) advance; (*opposé à retard*) lead; being ahead of schedule; ~s *nfpl* overtures; (*amoureuses*) advances; (*être*) **en** ~ (to be) early; (*sur un programme*) (to be) ahead of schedule; **à l'~, d'~ in** advance.

avancé, e [avãse] *a* advanced; well on *ou* under way.

avancement [avãsmã] *nm* (*professionnel*) promotion.

avancer [avãse] *vi* to move forward, advance; (*projet, travail*) to make progress; (*être en saillie*) to overhang; to jut out; (*montre, réveil*) to be fast; to gain // *vt* to move forward, advance; (*argent*) to advance; (*montre, pendule*) to put forward; **s'~** *vi* to move forward, advance; (*fig*) to commit o.s.; to overhang; to jut out.

avant [avã] *prép* before // *ad*: **trop/plus** ~ too far/further forward // *a inv*: **siège/roue** ~ front seat/wheel // *nm* (*d'un véhicule, bâtiment*) front; (*SPORT: joueur*) forward; ~ **qu'il parte/de faire** before he leaves/doing; ~ **tout** (*surtout*) above all; **à l'~** (*dans un véhicule*) in (the) front; **en** ~ *ad* forward(s); **en** ~ **de** *prép* in front of.

avantage [avãtaʒ] *nm* advantage; ~s **sociaux** fringe benefits; **avantager** *vt* (*favoriser*) to favour; (*embellir*) to flatter; **avantageux, euse** *a* attractive; attractively priced.

avant-bras [avãbʀa] *nm inv* forearm.

avant-dernier, ère [avãdɛʀnje, -ɛʀ] *a*, *nm/f* next to last, last but one.

avant-goût [avãgu] *nm* foretaste.

avant-hier [avãtjɛʀ] *ad* the day before yesterday.

avant-première [avãpʀəmjɛʀ] *nf* (*de film*) preview.

avant-projet [avãpʀɔʒɛ] *nm* (preliminary) draft.

avant-propos [avãpʀɔpo] *nm* foreword.

avant-veille [avãvɛj] *nf*: l'~ two days before.

avare [avaʀ] *a* miserly, avaricious // *nm/f* miser; ~ **de** (*compliments etc*) sparing of.

avarié, e [avaʀje] *a* rotting.

avaries [avaʀi] *nfpl* (*NAVIG*) damage *sg*.

avatar [avataʀ] *nm* misadventure.

avec [avɛk] *prép* with; (*à l'égard de*) to(wards), with.

avenant, e [avnã, -ãt] *a* pleasant; **à l'~** *ad* in keeping.

avènement [avɛnmã] *nm* (*d'un roi*) accession, succession; (*d'un changement*) advent, coming.

avenir [avniʀ] *nm* future; **à l'~** in future; **politicien d'~** politician with prospects *ou* a future.

Avent [avã] *nm*: l'~ Advent.

aventure [avãtyʀ] *nf* adventure; (*amoureuse*) affair; **s'aventurer** *vi* to venture; **aventureux, euse** *a* adventurous, venturesome; (*projet*) risky, chancy.

avenue [avny] *nf* avenue.

avérer [aveʀe]: **s'~** *vb avec attribut* to prove to be.

averse [avɛʀs(ə)] *nf* shower.

averti, e [avɛʀti] *a* (well-)informed.

avertir [avɛʀtiʀ] *vt*: ~ **qn** (**de qch/que**) to warn sb (of sth/that); (*renseigner*) to inform sb (of sth/that); **avertissement** *nm* warning; **avertisseur** *nm* horn, siren.

aveu, x [avø] *nm* confession.

aveugle [avœgl(ə)] *a* blind; **aveuglément** *ad* blindly; **aveugler** *vt* to blind.

aviateur, trice [avjatœʀ, -tʀis] *nm/f* aviator, pilot.

aviation [avjasjɔ̃] *nf* aviation; (*sport*) flying; (*MIL*) air force.

avide [avid] *a* eager; (*péj*) greedy, grasping.

avilir [aviliʀ] *vt* to debase.

avion [avjɔ̃] *nm* (aero)plane (*Brit*), (air)plane (*US*); **aller** (**quelque part**) **en** ~ to go (somewhere) by plane, fly (somewhere); **par** ~ by airmail; ~ **à réaction** jet (plane).

aviron [aviʀɔ̃] *nm* oar; (*sport*): l'~ rowing.

avis [avi] *nm* opinion; (*notification*) notice; **changer d'~** to change one's mind; **jusqu'à nouvel** ~ until further notice.

avisé, e [avize] *a* sensible, wise.

aviser [avize] vt (voir) to notice, catch sight of; (informer): ~ qn de/que to advise ou inform sb of/that // vi to think about things, assess the situation; s'~ de qch/que to .become suddenly aware of sth/that; s'~ de faire to take it into one's head to do.

avocat, e [avɔka, -at] nm/f (JUR) barrister (Brit), lawyer // nm (CULIN) avocado (pear); ~ général assistant public prosecutor.

avoine [avwan] nf oats pl.

avoir [avwaʀ] ♦ nm assets pl, resources pl; (COMM) credit
♦ vt 1 (posséder) to have; elle a 2 enfants/une belle maison she has (got) 2 children/a lovely house; il a les yeux bleus he has (got) blue eyes
2 (âge, dimensions) to be; il a 3 ans he is 3 (years old); le mur a 3 mètres de haut the wall is 3 metres high; voir faim, peur etc
3 (fam: duper) to do, have; on vous a eu! you've been done ou had!
4: en ~ contre qn to have a grudge against sb; en ~ assez to be fed up; j'en ai pour une demi-heure it'll take me half an hour
♦ vb auxiliaire 1 to have; ~ mangé/dormi to have eaten/slept
2 (avoir à + inf): ~ à faire qch to have to do sth; vous n'avez qu'à lui demander you only have to ask him
♦ vb impersonnel 1: il y a (+ sing) there is; (+ pl) there are; qu'y-a-t-il?, qu'est-ce qu'il y a? what's the matter?, what is it?; il doit y ~ une explication there must be an explanation; il n'y a qu'à ... we (ou you etc) will just have to ...
2 (temporel): il y a 10 ans 10 years ago; il y a 10 ans/longtemps que je le sais I've known it for 10 years/a long time; il y a 10 ans qu'il est arrivé it's 10 years since he arrived.

avoisiner [avwazine] vt to be near ou close to; (fig) to border ou verge on.

avortement [avɔʀtəmã] nm abortion.

avorter [avɔʀte] vi (MÉD) to have an abortion; (fig) to fail.

avoué, e [avwe] a avowed // nm (JUR) ≈ solicitor.

avouer [avwe] vt (crime, défaut) to confess (to); ~ avoir fait/que to admit ou confess to having done/that.

avril [avʀil] nm April.

axe [aks(ə)] nm axis (pl axes); (de roue etc) axle; (fig) main line; ~ routier trunk road, main road; **axer** vt: axer qch sur to centre sth on.

ayons etc vb voir **avoir**.

azote [azɔt] nm nitrogen.

B

babines [babin] nfpl chops.

babiole [babjɔl] nf (bibelot) trinket; (vétille) trifle.

bâbord [babɔʀ] nm: à ou par ~ to port, on the port side.

baby-foot [babifut] nm table football.

bac [bak] abr m de **baccalauréat** // nm (bateau) ferry; (récipient) tub; tray; tank.

baccalauréat [bakalɔʀea] nm high school diploma.

bachelier, ière [baʃəlje, -jɛʀ] nm/f holder of the baccalauréat.

bâcher [baʃe] vt to cover (with a canvas sheet ou a tarpaulin).

bachot [baʃo] abr m de **baccalauréat**.

bachoter [baʃɔte] vi (fam) to cram (for an exam).

bâcler [bakle] vt to botch (up).

badaud, e [bado, -od] nm/f idle onlooker, stroller.

badigeonner [badiʒɔne] vt to distemper; to colourwash; (barbouiller) to daub.

badin, e [badɛ̃, -in] a playful.

badiner [badine] vi: ~ avec qch to treat sth lightly.

badminton [badmintɔn] nm badminton.

baffe [baf] nf (fam) slap, clout.

bafouer [bafwe] vt to deride, ridicule.

bafouiller [bafuje] vi, vt to stammer.

bagage [bagaʒ] nm: ~s luggage sg; ~s à main hand-luggage.

bagarre [bagaʀ] nf fight, brawl; **se bagarrer** vi to have a fight ou scuffle, fight.

bagatelle [bagatɛl] nf trifle.

bagne [baɲ] nm penal colony.

bagnole [baɲɔl] nf (fam) car.

bagout [bagu] nm: avoir du ~ to have the gift of the gab.

bague [bag] nf ring; ~ de fiançailles engagement ring; ~ de serrage clip.

baguette [bagɛt] nf stick; (cuisine chinoise) chopstick; (de chef d'orchestre) baton; (pain) stick of (French) bread; ~ magique magic wand.

bahut [bay] nm chest.

baie [bɛ] nf (GÉO) bay; (fruit) berry; ~ (vitrée) picture window.

baignade [bɛɲad] nf bathing.

baigner [bɛɲe] vt (bébé) to bath; se ~ vi to have a swim, go swimming ou bathing; **baignoire** nf bath(tub).

bail, baux [baj, bo] nm lease.

bâiller [baje] vi to yawn; (être ouvert) to gape.

bailleur [bajœʀ] nm: ~ de fonds sponsor, backer.

bâillon [bajɔ̃] nm gag; **bâillonner** vt to gag.

bain [bɛ̃] nm bath; prendre un ~ to have a bath; se mettre dans le ~ (fig) to get into it ou things; ~ de foule walkabout; prendre un ~ de soleil to sunbathe; ~s de mer sea bathing sg; faire chauffer au ~-marie (boîte etc) to immerse in boiling water.

baiser [beze] nm kiss // vt (main, front) to kiss; (fam!) to screw (!).

baisse [bɛs] nf fall, drop; '~ sur la viande' 'meat prices down'.

baisser [bese] vt lower; (radio, chauffage) to turn down; (AUTO: phares) to dip (Brit), to lower (US) // vi to fall, drop, go down; se ~ vi to bend down.

bal [bal] nm dance; (grande soirée) ball; ~ costumé fancy-dress ball.

balade [balad] vt (traîner) to trail round; se ~ vi to go for a walk ou stroll; to go for a drive.

balafre [balafʀ(ə)] nf gash, slash; (cicatrice) scar.

balai [balɛ] nm broom, brush; ~-brosse nm (long-handled) scrubbing brush.

balance [balɑ̃s] nf scales pl; (de précision) balance; (signe): la B~ Libra.

balancer [balɑ̃se] vt to swing; (lancer) to fling, chuck; (renvoyer, jeter) to chuck out // vi to swing; se ~ vi to swing; to rock; to sway; se ~ de (fam) not to care about; **balancier** nm (de pendule) pendulum; (perche) (balancing) pole; **balançoire** nf swing; (sur pivot) seesaw.

balayer [baleje] vt (feuilles etc) to sweep up, brush up; (pièce) to sweep; (chasser) to sweep away; to sweep aside; (suj: radar) to scan; **balayeur, euse** nm/f, nf roadsweeper.

balbutier [balbysje] vi, vt to stammer.

balcon [balkɔ̃] nm balcony; (THÉÂTRE) dress circle.

baleine [balɛn] nf whale; (de parapluie, corset) rib; **baleinière** nf whaleboat.

balise [baliz] nf (NAVIG) beacon; (marker) buoy; (AVIAT) runway light, beacon; (AUTO, SKI) sign, marker; **baliser** vt to mark out (with lights etc).

balivernes [balivɛʀn(ə)] nfpl nonsense sg.

ballant, e [balɑ̃, -ɑ̃t] a dangling.

balle [bal] nf (de fusil) bullet; (de sport) ball; (paquet) bale; (fam: franc) franc; ~ perdue stray bullet.

ballerine [balʀin] nf ballet dancer.

ballet [balɛ] nm ballet.

ballon [balɔ̃] nm (de sport) ball; (jouet, AVIAT) balloon; (de vin) glass; ~ de football football.

ballot [balo] nm bundle; (péj) nitwit.

ballottage [balɔtaʒ] nm (POL) second ballot.

ballotter [balɔte] vi to roll around; to toss // vt to shake about; to toss.

balnéaire [balneɛʀ] a seaside cpd.

balourd, e [baluʀ, -uʀd(ə)] a clumsy // nm/f clodhopper.

balustrade [balystʀad] nf railings pl, handrail.

bambin [bɑ̃bɛ̃] nm little child.

ban [bɑ̃] nm round of applause, cheer; ~s nmpl (de mariage) banns; mettre au ~ de to outlaw from.

banal, e [banal] a banal, commonplace; (péj) trite.

banane [banan] nf banana.

banc [bɑ̃] nm seat, bench; (de poissons) shoal; ~ d'essai (fig) testing ground; ~ de sable sandbank.

bancaire [bɑ̃kɛʀ] a banking, bank cpd.

bancal, e [bɑ̃kal] a wobbly; bow-legged.

bandage [bɑ̃daʒ] nm bandage.

bande [bɑ̃d] nf (de tissu etc) strip; (MÉD) bandage; (motif) stripe; (magnétique etc) tape; (groupe) band; (: péj) bunch; par la ~ in a roundabout way; donner de la ~ to list; faire ~ à part to keep to o.s.; ~ dessinée comic strip; ~ sonore sound track.

bandeau, x [bɑ̃do] nm headband; (sur les yeux) blindfold; (MÉD) head bandage.

bander [bɑ̃de] vt (blessure) to bandage; (muscle) to tense; ~ les yeux à qn to blindfold sb.

banderole [bɑ̃dʀɔl] nf banner, streamer.

bandit [bɑ̃di] nm bandit; **banditisme** nm violent crime, armed robberies pl.

bandoulière [bɑ̃duljɛʀ] nf: en ~ (slung ou worn) across the shoulder.

banlieue [bɑ̃ljø] nf suburbs pl; lignes/quartiers de ~ suburban lines/areas; trains de ~ commuter trains.

bannière [banjɛʀ] nf banner.

bannir [baniʀ] vt to banish.

banque [bɑ̃k] nf bank; (activités) banking; ~ d'affaires merchant bank.

banqueroute [bɑ̃kʀut] nf bankruptcy.

banquet [bɑ̃kɛ] nm dinner; (d'apparat) banquet.

banquette [bɑ̃kɛt] nf seat.

banquier [bɑ̃kje] nm banker.

banquise [bɑ̃kiz] nf ice field.

baptême [batɛm] nm christening; baptism; ~ de l'air first flight.

baquet [bakɛ] nm tub, bucket.

bar [baʀ] nm bar.

baraque [baʀak] nf shed; (fam) house; ~ foraine fairground stand.

baraqué, e [baʀake] a well-built, hefty.

baraquements [baʀakmɑ̃] nmpl huts (for refugees, workers etc).

baratin [baʀatɛ̃] nm (fam) smooth talk, patter; **baratiner** vt to chat up.

barbare [baʀbaʀ] a barbaric.

barbe [baʀb(ə)] nf beard; quelle ~! (fam) what a drag ou bore!; à la ~ de qn under sb's nose; ~ à papa candy-floss (Brit), cotton candy (US).

barbelé [baʀbəle] nm barbed wire q.
barboter [baʀbɔte] vi to paddle, dabble.
barboteuse [baʀbɔtøz] nf rompers pl.
barbouiller [baʀbuje] vt to daub; avoir l'estomac barbouillé to feel queasy.
barbu, e [baʀby] a bearded.
barda [baʀda] nm (fam) kit, gear.
barde [baʀd(ə)] nf piece of fat bacon.
barder [baʀde] vi (fam): ça va ~ sparks will fly, things are going to get hot.
barème [baʀɛm] nm scale; table.
baril [baʀil] nm barrel; keg.
baromètre [baʀɔmɛtʀ(ə)] nm barometer.
baron [baʀɔ̃] nm baron; **baronne** nf baroness.
baroque [baʀɔk] a (ART) baroque; (fig) weird.
barque [baʀk(ə)] nf small boat.
barrage [baʀaʒ] nm dam; (sur route) roadblock, barricade.
barre [baʀ] nf bar; (NAVIG) helm; (écrite) line, stroke.
barreau, x [baʀo] nm bar; (JUR): le ~ the Bar.
barrer [baʀe] vt (route etc) to block; (mot) to cross out; (chèque) to cross (Brit); (NAVIG) to steer; se ~ vi (fam) to clear off.
barrette [baʀɛt] nf (pour cheveux) (hair) slide (Brit) ou clip (US).
barricader [baʀikade] vt to barricade.
barrière [baʀjɛʀ] nf fence; (obstacle) barrier; (porte) gate.
barrique [baʀik] nf barrel, cask.
bas, basse [ba, bas] a low // nm bottom, lower part; (vêtement) stocking // nf (MUS) bass // ad low; (parler) softly; avoir la vue basse to be short-sighted; au ~ mot at the lowest estimate; en ~ down below; at (ou to) the bottom; (dans une maison) downstairs; en ~ de at the bottom of; mettre ~ vi to give birth; à ~ ...! 'down with ...!'; ~ morceaux nmpl (viande) cheap cuts.
basané, e [bazane] a tanned, bronzed.
bas-côté [bakote] nm (de route) verge (Brit), shoulder (US).
bascule [baskyl] nf: (jeu de) ~ seesaw; (balance à) ~ scales pl; fauteuil à ~ rocking chair.
basculer [baskyle] vi to fall over, topple (over); (benne) to tip up // vt to topple over; to tip out, tip up.
base [baz] nf base; (POL) rank and file; (fondement, principe) basis (pl bases); de ~ basic; à ~ de café etc coffee etc -based; ~ de données database; **baser** vt to base; se baser sur (preuves) to base one's argument on.
bas-fond [bafɔ̃] nm (NAVIG) shallow; ~s (fig) dregs.
basilic [bazilik] nm (CULIN) basil.
basket [baskɛt] nm trainer (Brit), sneaker (US); (aussi: ~-ball) basket-ball.
basque [bask(ə)] a, nm/f Basque.
basse [bas] a, nf voir bas; ~-cour nf farmyard.
bassin [basɛ̃] nm (cuvette) bowl; (pièce d'eau) pond, pool; (de fontaine, GÉO) basin; (ANAT) pelvis; (portuaire) dock.
basson [basɔ̃] nm bassoon.
bastingage [bastɛ̃gaʒ] nm (ship's) rail.
bas-ventre [bavɑ̃tʀ(ə)] nm (lower part of) the stomach.
bat vb voir battre.
bât [ba] nm packsaddle.
bataille [bataj] nf battle; fight.
bâtard, e [bataʀ, -aʀd(ə)] nm/f illegitimate child, bastard (péj).
bateau, x [bato] nm boat, ship; ~-mouche nm (passenger) pleasure boat (on the Seine).
bateleur, euse [batlœʀ, -øz] nm/f street performer.
batelier, ière [batəlje, -jɛʀ] nm/f (de bac) ferryman/woman.
bâti, e [bati] a: bien ~ well-built.
batifoler [batifole] vi to frolic about.
bâtiment [batimɑ̃] nm building; (NAVIG) ship, vessel; (industrie) building trade.
bâtir [batiʀ] vt to build.
bâtisse [batis] nf building.
bâton [batɔ̃] nm stick; à ~s rompus informally.
bâtonnier [batɔnje] nm ≈ president of the Bar.
bats vb voir battre.
battage [bataʒ] nm (publicité) (hard) plugging.
battant [batɑ̃] nm (de cloche) clapper; (de volets) shutter, flap; (de porte) side; (fig: personne) fighter; porte à double ~ double door.
battement [batmɑ̃] nm (de cœur) beat; (intervalle) interval (between classes, trains etc); ~ de paupières blinking q (of eyelids); 10 minutes de ~ 10 minutes to spare.
batterie [batʀi] nf (MIL, ÉLEC) battery; (MUS) drums pl, drum kit; ~ de cuisine pots and pans pl; kitchen utensils pl.
batteur [batœʀ] nm (MUS) drummer; (appareil) whisk.
battre [batʀ(ə)] vt to beat; (suj: pluie, vagues) to beat ou lash against; (blé) to thresh; (passer au peigne fin) to scour // vi (cœur) to beat; (volets etc) to bang, rattle; se ~ vi to fight; ~ la mesure to beat time; ~ en brèche to demolish; ~ son plein to be at its height, be going full swing; ~ des mains to clap one's hands.
battue [baty] nf (chasse) beat; (policière etc) search, hunt.
baume [bom] nm balm.
bavard, e [bavaʀ, -aʀd(ə)] a (very) talkative; gossipy; **bavarder** vi to chatter; (indiscrètement) to gossip; to blab.

bave [bav] *nf* dribble; (*de chien etc*) slobber; (*d'escargot*) slime; **baver** *vi* to dribble; to slobber; **en baver** (*fam*) to have a hard time (of it); **bavette** *nf* bib; **baveux, euse** *a* (*omelette*) runny.

bavure [bavyʀ] *nf* smudge; (*fig*) hitch; blunder.

bayer [baje] *vi*: ~ **aux corneilles** to stand gaping.

bazar [bazaʀ] *nm* general store; (*fam*) jumble; **bazarder** *vt* (*fam*) to chuck out.

B.C.B.G. *sigle a* (= *bon chic bon genre*) preppy, smart and trendy.

B.C.G. *sigle m* (= *bacille Calmette-Guérin*) BCG.

bd. *abr de* **boulevard**.

B.D. *sigle f de* **bande dessinée**.

béant, e [beɑ̃, -ɑ̃t] *a* gaping.

béat, e [bea, -at] *a* showing open-eyed wonder; blissful; **béatitude** *nf* bliss.

beau(bel), belle, beaux [bo, bɛl] *a* beautiful, lovely; (*homme*) handsome // *nf* (*SPORT*) decider // *ad*: **il fait** ~ **the** weather's fine; **un** ~ **jour** one (fine) day; **de plus belle** more than ever, even more; **on a** ~ **essayer** however hard we try; **bel et bien** well and truly; **faire le** ~ (*chien*) to sit up and beg.

beaucoup [boku] *ad* **1** a lot; **il boit** ~ he drinks a lot; **il ne boit pas** ~ he doesn't drink much *ou* a lot
2 (*suivi de plus, trop etc*) much, a lot, far; **il est** ~ **plus grand** he is much *ou* a lot taller
3: ~ **de** (*nombre*) many, a lot of; (*quantité*) a lot of; ~ **d'étudiants/de touristes** a lot of *ou* many students/tourists; ~ **de courage** a lot of courage; **il n'a pas** ~ **d'argent** he hasn't got much *ou* a lot of money
4: **de** ~ *ad* by far.

beau-fils [bofis] *nm* son-in-law; (*remariage*) stepson.

beau-frère [bofʀɛʀ] *nm* brother-in-law.

beau-père [bopɛʀ] *nm* father-in-law; (*remariage*) stepfather.

beauté [bote] *nf* beauty; **de toute** ~ beautiful; **en** ~ *ad* brilliantly.

beaux-arts [bozaʀ] *nmpl* fine arts.

beaux-parents [bopaʀɑ̃] *nmpl* wife's/husband's family *sg ou pl*, in-laws.

bébé [bebe] *nm* baby.

bec [bɛk] *nm* beak, bill; (*de récipient*) spout; lip; (*fam*) mouth; ~ **de gaz** (street) gaslamp; ~ **verseur** pouring lip.

bécane [bekan] *nf* (*fam*: *vélo*) bike.

bec-de-lièvre [bɛkdəljɛvʀ(ə)] *nm* harelip.

bêche [bɛʃ] *nf* spade; **bêcher** *vt* to dig.

bécoter [bekɔte]: **se** ~ *vi* to smooch.

becqueter [bɛkte] *vt* (*fam*) to eat.

bedaine [bədɛn] *nf* paunch.

bedonnant, e [bədɔnɑ̃, -ɑ̃t] *a* potbellied.

bée [be] *a*: **bouche** ~ gaping.

beffroi [befʀwa] *nm* belfry.

bégayer [begeje] *vt, vi* to stammer.

bègue [bɛg] *nm/f*: **être** ~ to have a stammer.

béguin [begɛ̃] *nm*: **avoir le** ~ **de** *ou* **pour** to have a crush on.

beige [bɛʒ] *a* beige.

beignet [bɛɲe] *nm* fritter.

bel [bɛl] *a voir* **beau**.

bêler [bele] *vi* to bleat.

belette [bəlɛt] *nf* weasel.

belge [bɛlʒ(ə)] *a*, *nm/f* Belgian.

Belgique [bɛlʒik] *nf*: **la** ~ Belgium.

bélier [belje] *nm* ram; (*signe*): **le B**~ Aries.

belle [bɛl] *af, nf voir* **beau**; ~-**fille** *nf* daughter-in-law; (*remariage*) stepdaughter; ~-**mère** *nf* mother-in-law; stepmother; ~-**sœur** *nf* sister-in-law.

belliqueux, euse [belikø, -øz] *a* aggressive, warlike.

belvédère [belvedɛʀ] *nm* panoramic viewpoint (*or small building there*).

bémol [bemɔl] *nm* (*MUS*) flat.

bénédiction [benediksjɔ̃] *nf* blessing.

bénéfice [benefis] *nm* (*COMM*) profit; (*avantage*) benefit; **bénéficier de** *vt* to enjoy; to benefit by *ou* from; to get, be given; **bénéfique** *a* beneficial.

benêt [bənɛ] *nm* simpleton.

bénévole [benevɔl] *a* voluntary, unpaid.

bénin, igne [benɛ̃, -iɲ] *a* minor, mild; (*tumeur*) benign.

bénir [beniʀ] *vt* to bless; **bénit, e** *a* consecrated; **eau bénite** holy water; **bénitier** *nm* font.

benjamin, e [bɛ̃ʒamɛ̃, -in] *nm/f* youngest child.

benne [bɛn] *nf* skip; (*de téléphérique*) (cable) car; ~ **basculante** tipper (*Brit*), dump truck (*US*).

béotien, ne [beɔsjɛ̃, -jɛn] *nm/f* philistine.

B.E.P.C. *sigle m voir* **brevet**.

béquille [bekij] *nf* crutch; (*de bicyclette*) stand.

bercail [bɛʀkaj] *nm* fold.

berceau, x [bɛʀso] *nm* cradle, crib.

bercer [bɛʀse] *vt* to rock, cradle; (*suj: musique etc*) to lull; ~ **qn de** (*promesses etc*) to delude sb with; **berceuse** *nf* lullaby.

béret (basque) [beʀɛ(bask(ə))] *nm* beret.

berge [bɛʀʒ(ə)] *nf* bank.

berger, ère [bɛʀʒe, -ɛʀ] *nm/f* shepherd/shepherdess.

berlingot [bɛʀlɛ̃go] *nm* (*emballage*) carton (*pyramid shaped*).

berlue [bɛʀly] *nf*: **j'ai la** ~ I must be seeing things.

berne [bɛʀn(ə)] *nf*: **en** ~ at half-mast.

berner [bɛʀne] *vt* to fool.

besogne [bəzɔɲ] *nf* work *q*, job; **beso-**

gneux, euse *a* hard-working.

besoin [bəzwɛ̃] *nm* need; (*pauvreté*): le ~ need, want; **faire ses** ~**s** to relieve o.s.; **avoir** ~ **de qch/faire qch** to need sth/to do sth; **au** ~ if need be.

bestiaux [bɛstjo] *nmpl* cattle.

bestiole [bɛstjɔl] *nf* (tiny) creature.

bétail [betaj] *nm* livestock, cattle *pl*.

bête [bɛt] *nf* animal; (*bestiole*) insect, creature // *a* stupid, silly; **il cherche la petite** ~ he's being pernickety *ou* over-fussy; ~ **noire** pet hate.

bêtise [betiz] *nf* stupidity; stupid thing (to say *ou* do).

béton [betɔ̃] *nm* concrete; (**en**) ~ (*alibi*, *argument*) cast iron; ~ **armé** reinforced concrete; **bétonnière** *nf* cement mixer.

betterave [bɛtʀav] *nf* beetroot (*Brit*), beet (*US*); ~ **sucrière** sugar beet.

beugler [bøgle] *vi* to low; (*radio etc*) to blare // *vt* (*chanson*) to bawl out.

beurre [bœʀ] *nm* butter; **beurrer** *vt* to butter; **beurrier** *nm* butter dish.

beuverie [bœvʀi] *nf* drinking session.

bévue [bevy] *nf* blunder.

Beyrouth [beʀut] *n* Beirut.

bi... [bi] *préfixe* bi..., two-.

biais [bjɛ] *nm* (*moyen*) device, expedient; (*aspect*) angle; **en** ~, **de** ~ (*obliquement*) at an angle; (*fig*) indirectly; **biaiser** *vi* (*fig*) to sidestep the issue.

bibelot [biblo] *nm* trinket, curio.

biberon [bibʀɔ̃] *nm* (feeding) bottle; **nourrir au** ~ to bottle-feed.

bible [bibl(ə)] *nf* bible.

biblio... [biblijo] *préfixe*: ~**bus** *nm* mobile library van; ~**phile** *nm/f* booklover; ~**thécaire** *nm/f* librarian; ~**thèque** *nf* library; (*meuble*) bookcase.

bicarbonate [bikaʀbɔnat] *nm*: ~ (**de soude**) bicarbonate of soda.

biceps [bisɛps] *nm* biceps.

biche [biʃ] *nf* doe.

bichonner [biʃɔne] *vt* to groom.

bicolore [bikɔlɔʀ] *a* two-coloured.

bicoque [bikɔk] *nf* (*péj*) shack.

bicyclette [bisiklɛt] *nf* bicycle.

bide [bid] *nm* (*fam*: *ventre*) belly; (*THÉÂTRE*) flop.

bidet [bidɛ] *nm* bidet.

bidon [bidɔ̃] *nm* can // *a inv* (*fam*) phoney.

bidonville [bidɔ̃vil] *nm* shanty town.

bidule [bidyl] *nm* (*fam*) thingumajig.

bielle [bjɛl] *nf* connecting rod.

bien [bjɛ̃] ♦ *nm* **1** (*avantage*, *profit*): **faire du** ~ **à qn** to do sb good; **dire du** ~ **de** to speak well of; **c'est pour son** ~ it's for his own good

2 (*possession*, *patrimoine*) possession, property; **son** ~ **le plus précieux** his most treasured possession; **avoir du** ~ to have property; ~**s** (**de consommation** *etc*) (consumer *etc*) goods

3 (*moral*): **le** ~ good; **distinguer le** ~ **du mal** to tell good from evil

♦ *ad* **1** (*de façon satisfaisante*) well; **elle travaille/mange** ~ she works/eats well; **croyant** ~ **faire, je/il** ... thinking I/he was doing the right thing, I/he ...; **c'est** ~ **fait!** it serves him (*ou* her *etc*) right!

2 (*valeur intensive*) quite; ~ **jeune** quite young; ~ **assez** quite enough; ~ **mieux** (very) much better; **j'espère** ~ **y aller** I do hope to go; **je veux** ~ **le faire** (*concession*) I'm quite willing to do it; **il faut** ~ **le faire** it has to be done

3: ~ **du temps/des gens** quite a time/a number of people

♦ *a inv* **1** (*en bonne forme, à l'aise*): **je me sens** ~ I feel fine; **je ne me sens pas** ~ I don't feel well; **on est** ~ **dans ce fauteuil** this chair is very comfortable

2 (*joli, beau*) good-looking; **tu es** ~ **dans cette robe** you look good in that dress

3 (*satisfaisant*) good; **elle est** ~, **cette maison/secrétaire** it's a good house/she's a good secretary

4 (*moralement*) right; (: *personne*) good, nice; (*respectable*) respectable; **ce n'est pas** ~ **de** ... it's not right to ...; **elle est** ~, **cette femme** she's a nice woman, she's a good sort; **des gens** ~ respectable people

5 (*en bons termes*): **être** ~ **avec qn** to be on good terms with sb

♦ *préfixe*: ~**-aimé, e,** *nm/f* beloved; ~**-être** *nm* well-being; ~**faisance** *nf* charity; ~**faisant, e** *a* (*chose*) beneficial; ~**fait** *nm* act of generosity, benefaction; (*de la science etc*) benefit; ~**faiteur, trice** *nm/f* benefactor/benefactress; ~**fondé** *nm* soundness; ~**fonds** *nm* property; ~**heureux, euse** *a* happy; (*REL*) blessed, blest

bien que *cj* (al)though

bien sûr *ad* certainly.

bienséant, e [bjɛ̃seã, -ãt] *a* seemly.

bientôt [bjɛ̃to] *ad* soon; **à** ~ see you soon.

bienveillant, e [bjɛ̃vejã, -ãt] *a* kindly.

bienvenu, e [bjɛ̃vny] *a* welcome // *nf*: **souhaiter la** ~**e à** to welcome; ~**e à** welcome to.

bière [bjɛʀ] *nf* (*boisson*) beer; (*cercueil*) bier; ~ **blonde** lager; ~ **brune** brown ale; ~ (**à la**) **pression** draught beer.

biffer [bife] *vt* to cross out.

bifteck [biftɛk] *nm* steak.

bifurquer [bifyʀke] *vi* (*route*) to fork; (*véhicule*) to turn off.

bigarré, e [bigaʀe] *a* multicoloured; (*disparate*) motley.

bigarreau, x [bigaʀo] *nm* type of cherry.

bigorneau, x [bigɔʀno] *nm* winkle.

bigot, e [bigo, -ɔt] *a* (*péj*) a bigoted.

bigoudi [bigudi] *nm* curler.

bijou, x [biʒu] *nm* jewel; ~**terie** *nf*

jeweller's (shop); jewellery; **~tier, ière** *nm/f* jeweller.

bikini [bikini] *nm* bikini.

bilan [bilɑ̃] *nm* (*COMM*) balance sheet(s); end of year statement; (*fig*) (net) outcome; (*: de victimes*) toll; faire le ~ de to assess; to review; déposer son ~ to file a bankruptcy statement.

bile [bil] *nf* bile; se faire de la ~ (*fam*) to worry o.s. sick.

bilieux, euse [biljø, -jøz] *a* bilious; (*fig: colérique*) testy.

bilingue [bilɛ̃g] *a* bilingual.

billard [bijaʀ] *nm* billiards *sg*; billiard table; c'est du ~ (*fam*) it's a cinch.

bille [bij] *nf* (*gén*) ball; (*du jeu de billes*) marble; (*de bois*) log.

billet [bijɛ] *nm* (*aussi:* ~ de banque) (bank)note; (*de cinéma, de bus etc*) ticket; (*courte lettre*) note; ~ circulaire round-trip ticket; ~ de faveur complimentary ticket.

billion [biljɔ̃] *nm* billion (*Brit*), trillion (*US*).

billot [bijo] *nm* block.

bimensuel, le [bimɑ̃sɥɛl] *a* bimonthly.

binette [binɛt] *nf* hoe.

binocle [binɔkl(ə)] *nm* pince-nez.

bio... [bjɔ] *préfixe* bio...; **~graphie** *nf* biography; **~logie** *nf* biology; **~logique** *a* biological.

Birmanie [biʀmani] *nf* Burma.

bis, e [bi, biz] *a* (*couleur*) greyish brown // *ad* [bis]: 12 ~ 12a ou A // *excl, nm* [bis] encore // *nf* (*baiser*) kiss; (*vent*) North wind.

bisannuel, le [bizanɥɛl] *a* biennial.

biscornu, e [biskɔʀny] *a* twisted.

biscotte [biskɔt] *nf* (*breakfast*) rusk.

biscuit [biskɥi] *nm* biscuit; sponge cake.

bise [biz] *a, nf voir* **bis**.

bissextile [bisɛkstil] *a*: année ~ leap year.

bistouri [bisturi] *nm* lancet.

bistro(t) [bistʀo] *nm* bistro, café.

bitume [bitym] *nm* asphalt.

bizarre [bizaʀ] *a* strange, odd.

blafard, e [blafaʀ, -aʀd(ə)] *a* wan.

blague [blag] *nf* (*propos*) joke; (*farce*) trick; sans ~! no kidding!; ~ à tabac tobacco pouch.

blaguer [blage] *vi* to joke // *vt* to tease.

blaireau, x [blɛʀo] *nm* (*ZOOL*) badger; (*brosse*) shaving brush.

blairer [blere] *vt* (*fam*): je ne peux pas le ~ I can't bear ou stand him.

blâme [blɑm] *nm* blame; (*sanction*) reprimand.

blâmer [blɑme] *vt* to blame.

blanc, blanche [blɑ̃, blɑ̃ʃ] *a* white; (*non imprimé*) blank; (*innocent*) pure // *nm/f* white, white man/woman // *nm* (*couleur*) white; (*espace non écrit*) blank; (*aussi:* ~ d'œuf) (egg-)white; (*aussi:* ~ de poulet) breast, white meat;

(*aussi:* vin ~) white wine // *nf* (*MUS*) minim (*Brit*), half-note (*US*); ~ cassé off-white; chèque en ~ blank cheque; à ~ *ad* (*chauffer*) white-hot; (*tirer, charger*) with blanks; **~-bec** *nm* greenhorn; **blancheur** *nf* whiteness.

blanchir [blɑ̃ʃiʀ] *vt* (*gén*) to whiten; (*linge*) to launder; (*CULIN*) to blanch; (*fig: disculper*) to clear // *vi* to grow white; (*cheveux*) to go white; **blanchisserie** *nf* laundry.

blaser [blaze] *vt* to make blasé.

blason [blazɔ̃] *nm* coat of arms.

blatte [blat] *nf* cockroach.

blazer [blazɛʀ] *nm* blazer.

blé [ble] *nm* wheat.

bled [blɛd] *nm* (*péj*) hole.

blême [blɛm] *a* pale.

blessé, e [blese] *a* injured // *nm/f* injured person; casualty.

blesser [blese] *vt* to injure; (*délibérément: MIL etc*) to wound; (*suj: souliers etc, offenser*) to hurt; se ~ to injure o.s.; se ~ au pied *etc* to injure one's foot *etc*.

blessure [blesyʀ] *nf* injury; wound.

bleu, e [blø] *a* blue; (*bifteck*) very rare // *nm* (*couleur*) blue; (*novice*) greenhorn; (*contusion*) bruise; (*vêtement: aussi:* ~s) overalls *pl*; ~ marine navy blue.

bleuet [bløɛ] *nm* cornflower.

bleuté, e [bløte] *a* blue-shaded.

blinder [blɛ̃de] *vt* to armour; (*fig*) to harden.

bloc [blɔk] *nm* (*de pierre etc*) block; (*de papier à lettres*) pad; (*ensemble*) group, block; serré à ~ tightened right down; en ~ as a whole; wholesale; ~ opératoire operating ou theatre block; ~ sanitaire toilet block.

blocage [blɔkaʒ] *nm* blocking; jamming; freezing; (*PSYCH*) hang-up.

bloc-notes [blɔknɔt] *nm* note pad.

blocus [blɔkys] *nm* blockade.

blond, e [blɔ̃, -ɔ̃d] *a* fair; blond; (*sable, blés*) golden; ~ cendré ash blond.

bloquer [blɔke] *vt* (*passage*) to block; (*pièce mobile*) to jam; (*crédits, compte*) to freeze.

blottir [blɔtiʀ]: se ~ *vi* to huddle up.

blouse [bluz] *nf* overall.

blouson [bluzɔ̃] *nm* blouson jacket; ~ noir (*fig*) ≈ rocker.

bluffer [blœfe] *vi* to bluff.

bobard [bɔbaʀ] *nm* (*fam*) tall story.

bobine [bɔbin] *nf* reel; (*ÉLEC*) coil.

bocage [bɔkaʒ] *nm* grove.

bocal, aux [bɔkal, -o] *nm* jar.

bock [bɔk] *nm* glass of beer.

bœuf [bœf, *pl* bø] *nm* ox (*pl* oxen), steer; (*CULIN*) beef.

bof! [bɔf] *excl* (*fam*) don't care!; (*: pas terrible*) nothing special.

bohème [bɔɛm] *a* happy-go-lucky, unconventional.

bohémien, ne [bɔemjɛ̃, -jɛn] *nm/f* gipsy.

boire [bwaʀ] *vt* to drink; (*s'imprégner de*) to soak up; ~ **un coup** to have a drink.

bois [bwa] *nm* wood; **de** ~, **en** ~ wooden.

boisé, e [bwaze] *a* woody, wooded.

boisson [bwasɔ̃] *nf* drink; **pris de** ~ drunk, intoxicated.

boîte [bwat] *nf* box; (*entreprise*) place, firm; **aliments en** ~ canned *ou* tinned (*Brit*) foods; ~ **d'allumettes** box of matches; (*vide*) matchbox; ~ (**de conserves**) can *ou* tin (*Brit*) (of food); ~ **à gants** glove compartment; ~ **aux lettres** letter box; ~ **de nuit** night club; ~ **postale** (**B.P.**) PO Box; ~ **de vitesses** gear box.

boiter [bwate] *vi* to limp; (*fig*) to wobble; to be shaky.

boîtier [bwatje] *nm* case.

boive *etc* **voir boire.**

bol [bɔl] *nm* bowl; **un** ~ **d'air** a breath of fresh air.

bolide [bɔlid] *nm* racing car; **comme un** ~ at top speed, like a rocket.

bombance [bɔ̃bɑ̃s] *nf*: **faire** ~ to have a feast, revel.

bombarder [bɔ̃baʀde] *vt* to bomb; ~ **qn de** (*cailloux, lettres*) to bombard sb with; **bombardier** *nm* bomber.

bombe [bɔ̃b] *nf* bomb; (*atomiseur*) (aerosol) spray.

bomber [bɔ̃be] *vi* to bulge; to camber // *vt*: ~ **le torse** to swell out one's chest.

bon, bonne [bɔ̃, bɔn] ♦ *a* **1** (*agréable, satisfaisant*) good; **un** ~ **repas/restaurant** a good meal/restaurant; **être** ~ **en maths** to be good at maths
2 (*charitable*): **être** ~ (**envers**) to be good (to)
3 (*correct*) right; **le** ~ **numéro/moment** the right number/moment
4 (*souhaits*): ~ **anniversaire** happy birthday; ~ **voyage** have a good trip; **bonne chance** good luck; **bonne année** happy New Year; **bonne nuit** good night
5 (*approprié, apte*): ~ **à/pour** fit to/for
6: ~ **enfant** *a inv* accommodating, easygoing; **bonne femme** *nf* (*péj*) woman; **de bonne heure** *ad* early; ~ **marché** *a inv*, *ad* cheap; ~ **mot** *nm* witticism; ~ **sens** *nm* common sense; ~ **vivant** *nm* jovial chap; **bonnes œuvres** *nfpl* charitable works, charities
♦ *nm* **1** (*billet*) voucher; (*aussi*: ~ **cadeau**) gift voucher; ~ **d'essence** petrol coupon; ~ **du Trésor** Treasury bond
2: **avoir du** ~ to have its good points; **pour de** ~ for good
♦ *nf* (*domestique*) maid; **bonne d'enfant** nanny; **bonne à tout faire** general help
♦ *ad*: **il fait** ~ it's *ou* the weather is fine;

sentir ~ to smell good; **tenir** ~ to stand firm
♦ *excl* good!; **ah** ~? really?

bonbon [bɔ̃bɔ̃] *nm* (boiled) sweet.

bonbonne [bɔ̃bɔn] *nf* demijohn.

bond [bɔ̃] *nm* leap; **faire un** ~ to leap in the air.

bonde [bɔ̃d] *nf* (*d'évier etc*) plug; (: *trou*) plughole; (*de tonneau*) bung; bunghole.

bondé, e [bɔ̃de] *a* packed (full).

bondir [bɔ̃diʀ] *vi* to leap.

bonheur [bɔnœʀ] *nm* happiness; **porter** ~ (**à qn**) to bring (sb) luck; **au petit** ~ haphazardly; **par** ~ fortunately.

bonhomie [bɔnɔmi] *nf* goodnaturedness.

bonhomme [bɔnɔm] *nm* (*pl* **bonshommes** [bɔ̃zɔm]) fellow; ~ **de neige** snowman.

bonification [bɔnifikasjɔ̃] *nf* bonus.

bonifier [bɔnifje] *vt* to improve.

boniment [bɔnimɑ̃] *nm* patter *q.*

bonjour [bɔ̃ʒuʀ] *excl*, *nm* hello; good morning (*ou* afternoon).

bonne [bɔn] *a*, *nf* **voir bon**; ~**ment** *ad*: **tout** ~**ment** quite simply.

bonnet [bɔnɛ] *nm* bonnet, hat; (*de soutien-gorge*) cup; ~ **d'âne** dunce's cap; ~ **de bain** bathing cap.

bonneterie [bɔnɛtʀi] *nf* hosiery.

bonsoir [bɔ̃swaʀ] *excl* good evening.

bonté [bɔ̃te] *nf* kindness *q.*

bonus [bɔnys] *nm* no-claims bonus.

bord [bɔʀ] *nm* (*de table, verre, falaise*) edge; (*de rivière, lac*) bank; (*de route*) side; (**monter**) **à** ~ (to go) on board; **jeter par-dessus** ~ to throw overboard; **le commandant/les hommes du** ~ the ship's master/crew; **au** ~ **de la mer** at the seaside; **être au** ~ **des larmes** to be on the verge of tears.

bordeaux [bɔʀdo] *nm* Bordeaux (wine) // *a inv* maroon.

bordel [bɔʀdɛl] *nm* brothel; (*fam!*) bloody mess (!).

border [bɔʀde] *vt* (*être le long de*) to border; to line; (*garnir*): ~ **qch de** to line sth with; to trim sth with; (*qn dans son lit*) to tuck up.

bordereau, x [bɔʀdəʀo] *nm* slip; statement.

bordure [bɔʀdyʀ] *nf* border; **en** ~ **de** on the edge of.

borgne [bɔʀɲ(ə)] *a* one-eyed.

borne [bɔʀn(ə)] *nf* boundary stone; (*aussi*: ~ **kilométrique**) kilometre-marker; ≈ milestone; ~**s** *nfpl* (*fig*) limits; **dépasser les** ~**s** to go too far.

borné, e [bɔʀne] *a* narrow; narrowminded.

borner [bɔʀne] *vt* to limit; to confine; **se** ~ **à faire** to content o.s. with doing; to limit o.s. to doing.

bosquet [bɔskɛ] *nm* grove.

bosse [bɔs] nf (de terrain etc) bump; (enflure) lump; (du bossu, du chameau) hump; **avoir la ~ des maths** etc to have a gift for maths etc; **il a roulé sa ~** he's been around.

bosser [bɔse] vi (fam) to work; to slave (away).

bossu, e [bɔsy] nm/f hunchback.

bot [bo] am: **pied ~** club foot.

botanique [bɔtanik] nf botany // a botanic(al).

botte [bɔt] nf (soulier) (high) boot; (gerbe): **~ de paille** bundle of straw; **~ de radis** bunch of radishes; **~s de caoutchouc** wellington boots.

botter [bɔte] vt to put boots on; to kick; (fam): **ça me botte** I fancy that.

bottin [bɔtɛ̃] nm directory.

bottine [bɔtin] nf ankle boot.

bouc [buk] nm goat; (barbe) goatee; **~ émissaire** scapegoat.

boucan [bukɑ̃] nm din, racket.

bouche [buʃ] nf mouth; **le ~ à ~** the kiss of life; **~ d'égout** manhole; **~ d'incendie** fire hydrant; **~ de métro** métro entrance.

bouché, e [buʃe] a (temps, ciel) overcast; (péj: personne) thick.

bouchée [buʃe] nf mouthful; **~s à la reine** chicken vol-au-vents.

boucher, ère [buʃe, -ɛʀ] nm/f butcher // vt (pour colmater) to stop up; to fill up; (obstruer) to block (up); **se ~ le nez** to hold one's nose; **se ~** vi (tuyau etc) to block up, get blocked up.

boucherie [buʃʀi] nf butcher's (shop); (fig) slaughter.

bouche-trou [buʃtʀu] nm (fig) stopgap.

bouchon [buʃɔ̃] nm stopper; (en liège) cork; (fig: embouteillage) holdup; (PÊCHE) float; **~ doseur** measuring cap.

boucle [bukl(ə)] nf (forme, figure) loop; (objet) buckle; **~ (de cheveux)** curl; **~ d'oreilles** earring.

bouclé, e [bukle] a curly.

boucler [bukle] vt (fermer: ceinture etc) to fasten; (: magasin) to shut; (terminer) to finish off; (: budget) to balance; (enfermer) to shut away; (: quartier) to seal off // vi to curl.

bouclier [buklije] nm shield.

bouddhiste [budist(ə)] nm/f Buddhist.

bouder [bude] vi to sulk // vt to turn one's nose up at; to refuse to have anything to do with.

boudin [budɛ̃] nm (CULIN) black pudding.

boue [bu] nf mud.

bouée [bwe] nf buoy; **~ (de sauvetage)** lifebuoy.

boueux, euse [bwø, -øz] a muddy // nm refuse collector.

bouffe [buf] nf (fam) grub, food.

bouffée [bufe] nf puff; **~ de fièvre/de honte** flush of fever/shame.

bouffer [bufe] vi (fam) to eat.

bouffi, e [bufi] a swollen.

bouge [buʒ] nm (low) dive; hovel.

bougeoir [buʒwaʀ] nm candlestick.

bougeotte [buʒɔt] nf: **avoir la ~** to have the fidgets.

bouger [buʒe] vi to move; (dent etc) to be loose; (changer) to alter; (agir) to stir // vt to move.

bougie [buʒi] nf candle; (AUTO) sparking plug.

bougonner [bugɔne] vi, vt to grumble.

bouillabaisse [bujabɛs] nf type of fish soup.

bouillant, e [bujɑ̃, -ɑ̃t] a (qui bout) boiling; (très chaud) boiling (hot).

bouillie [buji] nf gruel; (de bébé) cereal; **en ~** (fig) crushed.

bouillir [bujiʀ] vi, vt to boil.

bouilloire [bujwaʀ] nf kettle.

bouillon [bujɔ̃] nm (CULIN) stock q.

bouillonner [bujɔne] vi to bubble; (fig) to bubble up; to foam.

bouillotte [bujɔt] nf hot-water bottle.

boulanger, ère [bulɑ̃ʒe, -ɛʀ] nm/f baker.

boulangerie [bulɑ̃ʒʀi] nf bakery.

boule [bul] nf (gén) ball; (pour jouer) bowl; (de machine à écrire) golf-ball; **~ de neige** snowball.

bouleau, x [bulo] nm (silver) birch.

boulet [bulɛ] nm (aussi: **~ de canon**) cannonball.

boulette [bulɛt] nf ball.

boulevard [bulvaʀ] nm boulevard.

bouleversement [bulvɛʀsəmɑ̃] nm upheaval.

bouleverser [bulvɛʀse] vt (émouvoir) to overwhelm; (causer du chagrin) to distress; (pays, vie) to disrupt; (papiers, objets) to turn upside down.

boulier [bulje] nm abacus.

boulon [bulɔ̃] nm bolt.

boulot [bulo] nm (fam: travail) work.

boulot, te [bulo, -ɔt] a plump, tubby.

boum [bum] nm bang // nf party.

bouquet [bukɛ] nm (de fleurs) bunch (of flowers), bouquet; (de persil etc) bunch; (parfum) bouquet.

bouquin [bukɛ̃] nm (fam) book; **bouquiner** vi to read; to browse around (in a bookshop); **bouquiniste** nm/f bookseller.

bourbeux, euse [buʀbø, -øz] a muddy.

bourbier [buʀbje] nm (quag)mire.

bourde [buʀd(ə)] nf (erreur) howler; (gaffe) blunder.

bourdon [buʀdɔ̃] nm bumblebee.

bourdonner [buʀdɔne] vi to buzz.

bourg [buʀ] nm small market town.

bourgeois, e [buʀʒwa, -waz] a (péj) ≈ (upper) middle class; bourgeois.

bourgeoisie [buʀʒwazi] nf ≈ upper

middle classes *pl*; bourgeoisie.
bourgeon [buʀʒ5] *nm* bud.
Bourgogne [buʀgɔɲ] *nf*: la ~ Burgundy // *nm*: b~ burgundy (wine).
bourguignon, ne [buʀgiɲ5, -ɔn] *a* of *ou* from Burgundy, Burgundian.
bourlinguer [buʀlɛ̃ge] *vi* to knock about a lot, get around a lot.
bourrade [buʀad] *nf* shove, thump.
bourrage [buʀaʒ] *nm*: ~ de crâne brainwashing; (SCOL) cramming.
bourrasque [buʀask(ə)] *nf* squall.
bourreau, x [buʀo] *nm* executioner; (*fig*) torturer; ~ de travail workaholic.
bourrelet [buʀlɛ] *nm* draught excluder; (*de peau*) fold *ou* roll (of flesh).
bourrer [buʀe] *vt* (*pipe*) to fill; (*poêle*) to pack; (*valise*) to cram (full); ~ de coups to hammer blows on, pummel.
bourrique [buʀik] *nf* (*âne*) ass.
bourru, e [buʀy] *a* surly, gruff.
bourse [buʀs(ə)] *nf* (*subvention*) grant; (*porte-monnaie*) purse; la B~ the Stock Exchange.
boursoufler [buʀsufle] *vt* to puff up, bloat.
bous *vb voir* bouillir.
bousculade [buskylad] *nf* rush; crush.
bousculer [buskyle] *vt* to knock over; to knock into; (*fig*) to push, rush.
bouse [buz] *nf* dung *q*.
boussole [busɔl] *nf* compass.
bout [bu] *vb voir* bouillir // *nm* bit; (*extrémité: d'un bâton etc*) tip; (: *d'une ficelle, table, rue, période*) end; au ~ de at the end of, after; pousser qn à ~ to push sb to the limit; venir à ~ de to manage to finish; à ~ portant at point-blank range; ~ filtre filter tip.
boutade [butad] *nf* quip, sally.
boute-en-train [butãtʀɛ̃] *nm inv* live wire (*fig*).
bouteille [butɛj] *nf* bottle; (*de gaz butane*) cylinder.
boutique [butik] *nf* shop; **boutiquier, ière** *nm/f* shopkeeper.
bouton [but5] *nm* button; (BOT) bud; (*sur la peau*) spot; (*de porte*) knob; ~ de manchette cuff-link; ~ d'or buttercup; **boutonner** *vt* to button up; **boutonnière** *nf* buttonhole; ~-pression *nm* press stud.
bouture [butyʀ] *nf* cutting.
bovins [bɔvɛ̃] *nmpl* cattle.
bowling [bɔliaj] *nm* (tenpin) bowling; (*salle*) bowling alley.
box [bɔks] *nm* lock-up (garage); (*d'écurie*) loose-box.
boxe [bɔks(ə)] *nf* boxing.
boyau, x [bwajo] *nm* (*galerie*) passage(way); (narrow) gallery // *nmpl* (*viscères*) entrails, guts.
B.P. *abr de* boîte postale.
bracelet [bʀaslɛ] *nm* bracelet; ~-montre *nm* wristwatch.

braconnier [bʀakɔnje] *nm* poacher.
brader [bʀade] *vt* to sell off.
braderie [bʀadʀi] *nf* cut-price shop *ou* stall.
braguette [bʀagɛt] *nf* fly *ou* flies *pl* (*Brit*), zipper (*US*).
brailler [bʀaje] *vi* to bawl, yell.
braire [bʀɛʀ] *vi* to bray.
braise [bʀɛz] *nf* embers *pl*.
brancard [bʀãkaʀ] *nm* (*civière*) stretcher; (*bras, perche*) shaft; **brancardier** *nm* stretcher-bearer.
branchages [bʀãʃaʒ] *nmpl* boughs.
branche [bʀãʃ] *nf* branch.
branché, e [bʀãʃe] *a* (*fam*) trendy.
brancher [bʀãʃe] *vt* to connect (up); (*en mettant la prise*) to plug in.
branle [bʀãl] *nm*: donner le ~ à, mettre en ~ to set in motion.
branle-bas [bʀãlba] *nm inv* commotion.
branler [bʀãle] *vi* to be shaky // *vt*: ~ la tête to shake one's head.
braquer [bʀake] *vi* (AUTO) to turn (the wheel) // *vt* (*revolver etc*): ~ qch sur to aim sth at, point sth at; (*mettre en colère*): ~ qn to put sb's back up.
bras [bʀa] *nm* arm // *nmpl* (*fig: travailleurs*) labour *sg*, hands; saisir qn à ~-le-corps to take hold of sb (a)round the waist; à ~ raccourcis with fists flying; ~ droit (*fig*) right hand man.
brasier [bʀazje] *nm* blaze, inferno.
brassard [bʀasaʀ] *nm* armband.
brasse [bʀas] *nf* (*nage*) breast-stroke; ~ papillon butterfly.
brassée [bʀase] *nf* armful.
brasser [bʀase] *vt* to mix; ~ l'argent/les affaires to handle a lot of money/business.
brasserie [bʀasʀi] *nf* (*restaurant*) café-restaurant; (*usine*) brewery.
bravache [bʀavaʃ] *nm* blusterer, braggart.
brave [bʀav] *a* (*courageux*) brave; (*bon, gentil*) good, kind.
braver [bʀave] *vt* to defy.
bravo [bʀavo] *excl* bravo // *nm* cheer.
bravoure [bʀavuʀ] *nf* bravery.
break [bʀɛk] *nm* (AUTO) estate car.
brebis [bʀəbi] *nf* ewe; ~ galeuse black sheep.
brèche [bʀɛʃ] *nf* breach, gap; être sur la ~ (*fig*) to be on the go.
bredouille [bʀəduj] *a* empty-handed.
bredouiller [bʀəduje] *vi, vt* to mumble, stammer.
bref, brève [bʀɛf, bʀɛv] *a* short, brief // *ad* in short; d'un ton ~ sharply, curtly; en ~ in short, in brief.
Brésil [bʀezil] *nm* Brazil.
Bretagne [bʀətaɲ] *nf* Brittany.
bretelle [bʀətɛl] *nf* (*de fusil etc*) sling; (*de vêtement*) strap; (*d'autoroute*) slip road (*Brit*), entrance/exit ramp (*US*); ~s *nfpl* (*pour pantalon*) braces (*Brit*),

suspenders (US).

breton, ne [brətõ, -ɔn] a, nm/f Breton.

breuvage [brœvaʒ] nm beverage, drink.

brève [brɛv] a, nf voir **bref**.

brevet [brəvɛ] nm diploma, certificate; ~ (d'invention) patent; ~ d'études du premier cycle (B.E.P.C.) school certificate (taken at age 16); **breveté, e** a patented; (diplômé) qualified.

bribes [brib] nfpl bits, scraps; snatches; par ~ piecemeal.

bricolage [brikɔlaʒ] nm: le ~ do-it-yourself.

bricole [brikɔl] nf trifle; small job.

bricoler [brikɔle] vi to do DIY jobs; to potter about // vt to fix up; to tinker with; **bricoleur, euse** nm/f handyman/woman, DIY enthusiast.

bride [brid] nf bridle; (d'un bonnet) string, tie; à ~ abattue flat out, hell for leather; **laisser la ~ sur le cou à** to give free rein to.

bridé, e [bride] a: **yeux ~s** slit eyes.

brider [bride] vt (réprimer) to keep in check; (cheval) to bridle; (CULIN: volaille) to truss.

bridge [bridʒ(ə)] nm bridge.

brièvement [brijɛvmã] ad briefly.

brigade [brigad] nf (POLICE) squad; (MIL) brigade; (gén) team.

brigadier [brigadje] nm sergeant.

brigandage [brigãdaʒ] nm robbery.

briguer [brige] vt to aspire to.

brillamment [brijamã] ad brilliantly.

brillant, e [brijã, -ãt] a brilliant; bright; (luisant) shiny, shining // nm (diamant) brilliant.

briller [brije] vi to shine.

brimer [brime] vt to harass; to bully.

brin [brɛ̃] nm (de laine, ficelle etc) strand; (fig): un ~ de a bit of; ~ d'herbe blade of grass; ~ de muguet sprig of lily of the valley.

brindille [brɛ̃dij] nf twig.

brio [brijo] nm: avec ~ with panache.

brioche [brijɔʃ] nf brioche (bun); (fam: ventre) paunch.

brique [brik] nf brick // a inv brick red.

briquer [brike] vt to polish up.

briquet [brikɛ] nm (cigarette) lighter.

brise [briz] nf breeze.

briser [brize] vt, **se ~** vi to break.

britannique [britanik] a British // nm/f British person, Briton; **les B~s** the British.

broc [bro] nm pitcher.

brocante [brɔkãt] nf junk, second-hand goods pl.

brocanteur, euse [brɔkãtœr, -øz] nm/f junkshop owner; junk dealer.

broche [brɔʃ] nf brooch; (CULIN) spit; (MÉD) pin; à la ~ spit-roasted.

broché, e [brɔʃe] a (livre) paper-backed.

brochet [brɔʃɛ] nm pike inv.

brochette [brɔʃɛt] nf skewer.

brochure [brɔʃyr] nf pamphlet, brochure, booklet.

broder [brɔde] vt to embroider // vi to embroider the facts; **broderie** nf embroidery.

broncher [brɔ̃ʃe] vi: **sans ~** without flinching; without turning a hair.

bronches [brɔ̃ʃ] nfpl bronchial tubes; **bronchite** nf bronchitis.

bronze [brɔ̃z] nm bronze.

bronzer [brɔ̃ze] vt to tan // vi to get a tan; **se ~** to sunbathe.

brosse [brɔs] nf brush; **coiffé en ~** with a crewcut; ~ **à cheveux** hairbrush; ~ **à dents** toothbrush; ~ **à habits** clothesbrush; **brosser** vt (nettoyer) to brush; (fig: tableau etc) to paint; to draw; **se brosser les dents** to brush one's teeth.

brouette [bruɛt] nf wheelbarrow.

brouhaha [bruaa] nm hubbub.

brouillard [brujar] nm fog.

brouille [bruj] nf quarrel.

brouiller [bruje] vt to mix up; to confuse; (rendre trouble) to cloud; (désunir: amis) to set at odds; **se ~** vi (vue) to cloud over; (détails) to become confused; (gens) to fall out.

brouillon, ne [brujõ, -ɔn] a disorganised; unmethodical // nm draft.

broussailles [brusaj] nfpl undergrowth sg; **broussailleux, euse** a bushy.

brousse [brus] nf: la ~ the bush.

brouter [brute] vi to graze.

broutille [brutij] nf trifle.

broyer [brwaje] vt to crush; ~ **du noir** to be down in the dumps.

bru [bry] nf daughter-in-law.

bruiner [brɥine] vb impersonnel: **il bruine** it's drizzling, there's a drizzle.

bruire [brɥir] vi to murmur; to rustle.

bruit [brɥi] nm: **un ~** a noise, a sound; (fig: rumeur) a rumour; **le ~** noise; **sans ~** without a sound, noiselessly; ~ **de fond** background noise.

bruitage [brɥitaʒ] nm sound effects pl.

brûlant, e [brylã, -ãt] a burning; (liquide) boiling (hot); (regard) fiery.

brûlé, e [bryle] a (fig: démasqué) blown // nm: **odeur de ~** smell of burning.

brûle-pourpoint [brylpurpwɛ̃]: **à ~** ad point-blank.

brûler [bryle] vt to burn; (suj: eau bouillante) to scald; (consommer: électricité, essence) to use; (feu rouge, signal) to go through // vi to burn; (jeu) to be warm; **se ~** to burn o.s.; to scald o.s.; **se ~ la cervelle** to blow one's brains out.

brûlure [brylyr] nf (lésion) burn; (sensation) burning (sensation); ~**s d'estomac** heartburn sg.

brume [brym] nf mist.

brun, e [brœ̃, -yn] a brown; (cheveux, personne) dark; **brunir** vi to get a tan.

brusque [bʀysk(ə)] *a* abrupt; **~ment**
ad abruptly; **brusquer** *vt* to rush.
brut, e [bʀyt] *a* raw, crude, rough;
(*COMM*) gross; (*données*) raw // *nf*
brute; (*pétrole*) ~ crude (oil).
brutal, e, aux [bʀytal, -o] *a* brutal;
~iser *vt* to handle roughly, manhandle.
brute [bʀyt] *a, nf voir* **brut.**
Bruxelles [bʀysɛl] *n* Brussels.
bruyamment [bʀɥijamɑ̃] *ad* noisily.
bruyant, e [bʀɥijɑ̃, -ɑ̃t] *a* noisy.
bruyère [bʀɥijɛʀ] *nf* heather.
bu, e *pp de* **boire.**
buccal, e, aux [bykal, -o] *a*: **par voie
~e** orally.
bûche [byʃ] *nf* log; **prendre une ~** (*fig*)
to come a cropper; **~ de Noël** Yule log.
bûcher [byʃe] *nm* pyre; bonfire // *vb*
(*fam*) *vi* to swot (*Brit*), slave (away) //
vt to swot up (*Brit*), slave away at.
bûcheron [byʃʀɔ̃] *nm* woodcutter.
budget [bydʒɛ] *nm* budget.
buée [bɥe] *nf* (*sur une vitre*) mist; (*de
l'haleine*) steam.
buffet [byfɛ] *nm* (*meuble*) sideboard;
(*de réception*) buffet; **~ (de gare)** (station) buffet, snack bar.
buffle [byfl(ə)] *nm* buffalo.
buis [bɥi] *nm* box tree; (*bois*)
box(wood).
buisson [bɥisɔ̃] *nm* bush.
buissonnière [bɥisɔnjɛʀ] *af*: **faire
l'école ~** to skip school.
bulbe [bylb(ə)] *nm* (*BOT, ANAT*) bulb;
(*coupole*) onion-shaped dome.
Bulgarie [bylgaʀi] *nf* Bulgaria.
bulle [byl] *nf* bubble; (*papale*) bull.
bulletin [byltɛ̃] *nm* (*communiqué, journal*) bulletin; (*papier*) form; (*SCOL*) report; **~ d'informations** news bulletin; **~
météorologique** weather report; **~ de
salaire** pay-slip; **~ de santé** medical bulletin; **~ (de vote)** ballot paper.
bureau, x [byʀo] *nm* (*meuble*) desk;
(*pièce, service*) office; **~ de change** (foreign) exchange office *ou* bureau; **~
d'embauche** employment office; **~ de
location** box office; **~ de poste** post
office; **~ de tabac** tobacconist's (shop);
~ de vote polling station; **~cratie**
[-kʀasi] *nf* bureaucracy.
burin [byʀɛ̃] *nm* cold chisel; (*ART*) burin.
burlesque [byʀlɛsk(ə)] *a* ridiculous;
(*LITTÉRATURE*) burlesque.
bus *vb* [by] *voir* **boire** // *nm* [bys] bus.
busqué, e [byske] *a* (*nez*) hook(ed).
buste [byst(ə)] *nm* (*ANAT*) chest; bust.
but [by] *vb voir* **boire** // *nm* (*cible*) target; (*fig*) goal; aim; (*FOOTBALL etc*)
goal; **de ~ en blanc** point-blank; **avoir
pour ~ de faire** to aim to do; **dans le ~
de** with the intention of.
butane [bytan] *nm* butane; Calor gas ®.
buter [byte] *vi*: **~ contre/sur** to bump

into; to stumble against // *vt* to antagonize; **se ~** *vi* to get obstinate; to dig in
one's heels.
butin [bytɛ̃] *nm* booty, spoils *pl*; (*d'un
vol*) loot.
butte [byt] *nf* mound, hillock; **être en ~
à** to be exposed to.
buvais *etc vb voir* **boire.**
buvard [byvaʀ] *nm* blotter.
buvette [byvɛt] *nf* bar.
buveur, euse [byvœʀ, -øz] *nm/f* drinker.

C

c' [s] *dét voir* **ce.**
CA *sigle m de* **chiffre d'affaires.**
ça [sa] *pronom* (*pour désigner*) this; (*:
plus loin*) that; (*comme sujet indéfini*)
it; **~ va?** how are you?; how are
things?; (*d'accord?*) OK?, all right?; **~
alors!** well really!; **~ fait 10 ans que**)
it's 10 years (since); **c'est ~** that's right.
çà [sa] *ad*: **~ et là** here and there.
cabane [kaban] *nf* hut, cabin.
cabaret [kabaʀɛ] *nm* night club.
cabas [kaba] *nm* shopping bag.
cabillaud [kabijo] *nm* cod *inv.*
cabine [kabin] *nf* (*de bateau*) cabin; (*de
plage*) (beach) hut; (*de piscine etc*) cubicle; (*de camion, train*) cab; (*d'avion*)
cockpit; **~ d'essayage** fitting room; **~
spatiale** space capsule; **~ (téléphonique)**
call *ou* (tele)phone box.
cabinet [kabinɛ] *nm* (*petite pièce*)
closet; (*de médecin*) surgery (*Brit*),
office (*US*); (*de notaire etc*) office; (*:
clientèle*) practice; (*POL*) Cabinet; **~s**
nmpl (*w.-c.*) toilet *sg*; **~ d'affaires** business consultants' (bureau), business
partnership; **~ de toilette** toilet; **~ de
travail** study.
câble [kɑbl(ə)] *nm* cable.
cabrer [kabʀe]: **se ~** *vi* (*cheval*) to rear
up; (*avion*) to nose up; (*fig*) to revolt,
rebel.
cabriole [kabʀijɔl] *nf* caper; somersault.
cacahuète [kakaɥɛt] *nf* peanut.
cacao [kakao] *nm* cocoa (powder);
(*boisson*) cocoa.
cache [kaʃ] *nm* mask, card (for masking) // *nf* hiding place.
cache-cache [kaʃkaʃ] *nm*: **jouer à ~** to
play hide-and-seek.
cachemire [kaʃmiʀ] *nm* cashmere.
cache-nez [kaʃne] *nm inv* scarf, muffler.
cacher [kaʃe] *vt* to hide, conceal; **~ qch
à qn** to hide *ou* conceal sth from sb; **se
~** *vi* to hide; to be hidden *ou* concealed;
il ne s'en cache pas he makes no secret
of it.
cachet [kaʃɛ] *nm* (*comprimé*) tablet;
(*sceau: du roi*) seal; (*: de la poste*)

postmark; (*rétribution*) fee; (*fig*) style, character; **cacheter** *vt* to seal.

cachette [kaʃɛt] *nf* hiding place; en ~ on the sly, secretly.

cachot [kaʃo] *nm* dungeon.

cactus [kaktys] *nm* cactus.

cadavre [kadavʀ(ə)] *nm* corpse, (dead) body.

caddie [kadi] *nm* (supermarket) trolley.

cadeau, x [kado] *nm* present, gift; faire un ~ à qn to give sb a present *ou* gift; faire ~ de qch à qn to make a present of sth to sb, give sb sth as a present.

cadenas [kadnɑ] *nm* padlock.

cadence [kadɑ̃s] *nf* (*MUS*) cadence; (: *tempo*) rhythm; (*de travail etc*) rate; en ~ rhythmically; in time.

cadet, te [kade, -ɛt] *a* younger; (*le plus jeune*) youngest // *nm/f* youngest child *ou* one, youngest boy *ou* son/girl *ou* daughter.

cadran [kadʀɑ̃] *nm* dial; ~ solaire sundial.

cadre [kadʀ(ə)] *nm* frame; (*environnement*) surroundings *pl*; (*limites*) scope // *nm/f* (*ADMIN*) managerial employee, executive; rayer qn des ~s to dismiss sb; dans le ~ de (*fig*) within the framework *ou* context of.

cadrer [kadʀe] *vi*: ~ avec to tally *ou* correspond with // *vt* to centre.

caduc, uque [kadyk] *a* obsolete; (*BOT*) deciduous.

cafard [kafaʀ] *nm* cockroach; avoir le ~ to be down in the dumps.

café [kafe] *nm* coffee; (*bistro*) café // *a inv* coffee(-coloured); ~ au lait white coffee; ~ noir black coffee; ~ tabac *tobacconist's or newsagent's also serving coffee and spirits*; **cafetier, ière** *nm/f* café-owner // *nf* (*pot*) coffee-pot.

cafouillage [kafujaʒ] *nm* shambles *sg*.

cage [kaʒ] *nf* cage; ~ (**des buts**) goal; ~ d'escalier (stair)well; ~ thoracique rib cage.

cageot [kaʒo] *nm* crate.

cagibi [kaʒibi] *nm* shed.

cagneux, euse [kaɲø, -øz] *a* knock-kneed.

cagnotte [kaɲɔt] *nf* kitty.

cagoule [kagul] *nf* cowl; hood; (*SKI etc*) cagoule.

cahier [kaje] *nm* notebook; ~ de brouillons roughbook, jotter; ~ d'exercices exercise book.

cahot [kao] *nm* jolt, bump.

caïd [kaid] *nm* big chief, boss.

caille [kaj] *nf* quail.

cailler [kaje] *vi* (*lait*) to curdle; (*sang*) to clot.

caillot [kajo] *nm* (blood) clot.

caillou, x [kaju] *nm* (little) stone; ~**teux, euse** *a* stony; pebbly.

Caire [kɛʀ] *nm*: le ~ Cairo.

caisse [kɛs] *nf* box; (*où l'on met la re-*

cette) cashbox; till; (*où l'on paye*) cash desk (*Brit*), check-out; (*de banque*) cashier's desk; (*TECH*) case, casing; ~ enregistreuse cash register; ~ d'épargne savings bank; ~ de retraite pension fund; **caissier, ière** *nm/f* cashier.

cajoler [kaʒɔle] *vt* to wheedle, coax; to surround with love.

cake [kɛk] *nm* fruit cake.

calandre [kalɑ̃dʀ(ə)] *nf* radiator grill.

calanque [kalɑ̃k] *nf* rocky inlet.

calcaire [kalkɛʀ] *nm* limestone // *a* (*eau*) hard; (*GÉO*) limestone *cpd*.

calciné, e [kalsine] *a* burnt to ashes.

calcul [kalkyl] *nm* calculation; le ~ (*SCOL*) arithmetic; ~ (biliaire) (gall)stone; ~ (rénal) (kidney) stone; ~**ateur** *nm*, ~**atrice** *nf* calculator.

calculer [kalkyle] *vt* to calculate, work out; (*combiner*) to calculate.

calculette [kalkylɛt] *nf* pocket calculator.

cale [kal] *nf* (*de bateau*) hold; (*en bois*) wedge; ~ sèche dry dock.

calé, e [kale] *a* (*fam*) clever, bright.

caleçon [kalsɔ̃] *nm* pair of underpants, trunks *pl*; ~ de bain bathing trunks *pl*.

calembour [kalɑ̃buʀ] *nm* pun.

calendes [kalɑ̃d] *nfpl*: renvoyer aux ~ grecques to postpone indefinitely.

calendrier [kalɑ̃dʀije] *nm* calendar; (*fig*) timetable.

calepin [kalpɛ̃] *nm* notebook.

caler [kale] *vt* to wedge; ~ (son moteur/ véhicule) to stall (one's engine/vehicle).

calfeutrer [kalføtʀe] *vt* to (make) draughtproof; se ~ *vi* to make o.s. snug and comfortable.

calibre [kalibʀ(ə)] *nm* (*d'un fruit*) grade; (*d'une arme*) bore, calibre; (*fig*) calibre.

califourchon [kalifuʀʃɔ̃]: à ~ *ad* astride.

câlin, e [kɑlɛ̃, -in] *a* cuddly, cuddlesome; tender.

câliner [kɑline] *vt* to fondle, cuddle.

calmant [kalmɑ̃] *nm* tranquillizer, sedative; (*pour la douleur*) painkiller.

calme [kalm(ə)] *a* calm, quiet // *nm* calm(ness), quietness.

calmer [kalme] *vt* to calm (down); (*douleur, inquiétude*) to ease, soothe; se ~ *vi* to calm down.

calomnie [kalɔmni] *nf* slander; (*écrite*) libel; **calomnier** *vt* to slander; to libel.

calorie [kalɔʀi] *nf* calorie.

calorifuge [kalɔʀifyʒ] *a* (heat-)insulating, heat-retaining.

calotte [kalɔt] *nf* (*coiffure*) skullcap; (*gifle*) slap.

calquer [kalke] *vt* to trace; (*fig*) to copy exactly.

calvaire [kalvɛʀ] *nm* (*croix*) wayside cross, calvary; (*souffrances*) suffering.

calvitie [kalvisi] *nf* baldness.

camarade [kamaʀad] *nm/f* friend, pal; (*POL*) comrade; **~rie** *nf* friendship.
cambiste [kãbist(ə)] *nm* (*COMM*) foreign exchange dealer, exchange agent.
cambouis [kãbwi] *nm* dirty oil *ou* grease.
cambrer [kãbʀe] *vt* to arch.
cambriolage [kãbʀijɔlaʒ] *nm* burglary.
cambrioler [kãbʀijɔle] *vt* to burgle (*Brit*), burglarize (*US*); **cambrioleur, euse** *nm/f* burglar.
came [kam] *nf*: **arbre à ~s** camshaft.
camelot [kamlo] *nm* street pedlar.
camelote [kamlɔt] *nf* rubbish, trash, junk.
caméra [kameʀa] *nf* (*CINÉMA*, *TV*) camera; (*d'amateur*) cine-camera.
camion [kamjɔ̃] *nm* lorry (*Brit*), truck; (*plus petit, fermé*) van; **~ de dépannage** breakdown (*Brit*) *ou* tow (*US*) truck; **~-citerne** *nm* tanker; **camionnage** *nm* haulage (*Brit*), trucking (*US*); **camionnette** *nf* (small) van; **camionneur** *nm* (*entrepreneur*) haulage contractor (*Brit*), trucker (*US*); (*chauffeur*) lorry (*Brit*) *ou* truck driver; van driver.
camisole [kamizɔl] *nf*: **~ (de force)** straitjacket.
camomille [kamɔmij] *nf* camomile; (*boisson*) camomile tea.
camoufler [kamufle] *vt* to camouflage; (*fig*) to conceal, cover up.
camp [kã] *nm* camp; (*fig*) side.
campagnard, e [kãpaɲaʀ, -aʀd(ə)] *a* country *cpd*.
campagne [kãpaɲ] *nf* country, countryside; (*MIL*, *POL*, *COMM*) campaign; **à la ~** in the country.
camper [kãpe] *vi* to camp // *vt* to sketch; **se ~ devant** to plant o.s. in front of; **campeur, euse** *nm/f* camper.
camphre [kãfʀ(ə)] *nm* camphor.
camping [kãpiŋ] *nm* camping; (*terrain de*) **~** campsite, camping site; **faire du ~** to go camping.
Canada [kanada] *nm*: **le ~** Canada; **canadien, ne** *a*, *nm/f* Canadian // *nf* (*veste*) fur-lined jacket.
canaille [kanaj] *nf* (*péj*) scoundrel.
canal, aux [kanal, -o] *nm* canal; (*naturel*) channel.
canalisation [kanalizɑsjɔ̃] *nf* (*tuyau*) pipe.
canaliser [kanalize] *vt* to canalize; (*fig*) to channel.
canapé [kanape] *nm* settee, sofa.
canard [kanaʀ] *nm* duck.
canari [kanaʀi] *nm* canary.
cancans [kãkã] *nmpl* (malicious) gossip *sg*.
cancer [kãsɛʀ] *nm* cancer; (*signe*): **le C~** Cancer.
cancre [kãkʀ(ə)] *nm* dunce.
candeur [kãdœʀ] *nf* ingenuousness,

guilelessness.
candi [kãdi] *a inv*: **sucre ~** (sugar-)candy.
candidat, e [kãdida, -at] *nm/f* candidate; (*à un poste*) applicant, candidate; **candidature** *nf* candidature; application; **poser sa candidature** to submit an application, apply.
candide [kãdid] *a* ingenuous, guileless.
cane [kan] *nf* (female) duck.
caneton [kantɔ̃] *nm* duckling.
canette [kanɛt] *nf* (*de bière*) (flip-top) bottle.
canevas [kanva] *nm* (*COUTURE*) canvas.
caniche [kaniʃ] *nm* poodle.
canicule [kanikyl] *nf* scorching heat.
canif [kanif] *nm* penknife, pocket knife.
canine [kanin] *nf* canine (tooth).
caniveau, x [kanivo] *nm* gutter.
canne [kan] *nf* (walking) stick; **~ à pêche** fishing rod; **~ à sucre** sugar cane.
cannelle [kanɛl] *nf* cinnamon.
canoë [kanɔe] *nm* canoe; (*sport*) canoeing.
canon [kanɔ̃] *nm* (*arme*) gun; (*HISTOIRE*) cannon; (*d'une arme: tube*) barrel; (*fig*) model; (*MUS*) canon, **~ rayé** rifled barrel.
canot [kano] *nm* ding(h)y; **~ pneumatique** inflatable ding(h)y; **~ de sauvetage** lifeboat; **canotage** *nm* rowing.
canotier [kanɔtje] *nm* boater.
cantatrice [kãtatʀis] *nf* (opera) singer.
cantine [kãtin] *nf* canteen.
cantique [kãtik] *nm* hymn.
canton [kãtɔ̃] *nm* district consisting of several communes; (*en Suisse*) canton.
cantonade [kãtɔnad]: **à la ~** *ad* to everyone in general; from the rooftops.
cantonner [kãtɔne] *vt* (*MIL*) to quarter, station; **se ~ dans** to confine o.s. to.
cantonnier [kãtɔnje] *nm* roadmender.
canular [kanylaʀ] *nm* hoax.
caoutchouc [kautʃu] *nm* rubber; **~ mousse** foam rubber.
cap [kap] *nm* (*GÉO*) cape; headland; (*fig*) hurdle; watershed; (*NAVIG*): **changer de ~** to change course; **mettre le ~ sur** to head *ou* steer for.
C.A.P. *sigle m* (= *Certificat d'aptitude professionnelle*) *vocational training certificate taken at secondary school.*
capable [kapabl(ə)] *a* able, capable; **~ de qch/faire** capable of sth/doing.
capacité [kapasite] *nf* (*compétence*) ability; (*JUR*, *contenance*) capacity; **~ (en droit)** *basic legal qualification.*
cape [kap] *nf* cape, cloak; **rire sous ~** to laugh up one's sleeve.
C.A.P.E.S. [kapɛs] *sigle m* (= *Certificat d'aptitude pédagogique à l'enseignement secondaire*) *teaching diploma.*
capillaire [kapilɛʀ] *a* (*soins, lotion*) hair

cpd; *(vaisseau etc)* capillary.

capitaine [kapitɛn] *nm* captain; ~ **des pompiers** fire chief, firemaster.

capital, e, aux [kapital, -o] *a* major; of paramount importance; fundamental // *nm* capital; *(fig)* stock; asset // *nf (ville)* capital; *(lettre)* capital (letter); // *nmpl (fonds)* capital *sg*; ~ **(social)** authorized capital; **~iser** *vt* to amass, build up; **~isme** *nm* capitalism; **~iste** *a*, *nm/f* capitalist.

capiteux, euse [kapitø, -øz] *a* heady.

capitonné, e [kapitɔne] *a* padded.

caporal, aux [kapɔral, -o] *nm* lance corporal.

capot [kapo] *nm (AUTO)* bonnet *(Brit)*, hood *(US)*.

capote [kapɔt] *nf (de voiture)* hood *(Brit)*, top *(US)*; *(fam)* condom.

capoter [kapɔte] *vi* to overturn.

câpre [kɑpr(ə)] *nf* caper.

caprice [kapʀis] *nm* whim, caprice; passing fancy; **capricieux, euse** *a* capricious; whimsical; temperamental.

Capricorne [kapʀikɔʀn] *nm*: **le ~** Capricorn.

capsule [kapsyl] *nf (de bouteille)* cap; *(BOT etc, spatiale)* capsule.

capter [kapte] *vt (ondes radio)* to pick up; *(eau)* to harness; *(fig)* to win, capture.

captieux, euse [kapsjø, -øz] *a* specious.

captivité [kaptivite] *nf* captivity.

capturer [kaptyʀe] *vt* to capture.

capuche [kapyʃ] *nf* hood.

capuchon [kapyʃɔ̃] *nm* hood; *(de stylo)* cap, top.

capucine [kapysin] *nf (BOT)* nasturtium.

caquet [kakɛ] *nm*: **rabattre le ~ à qn** to bring sb down a peg or two.

caqueter [kakte] *vi* to cackle.

car [kaʀ] *nm* coach // *cj* because, for.

carabine [kaʀabin] *nf* carbine, rifle.

caractère [kaʀaktɛʀ] *nm (gén)* character; **en ~s gras** in bold type; **en petits ~s** in small print; **~s d'imprimerie** (block) capitals; **avoir bon/mauvais ~** to be good-/ill-natured; **caractériel, le** *a* (of) character // *nm/f* emotionally disturbed child.

caractérisé, e [kaʀakteʀize] *a*: **c'est une grippe ~e** it is a clear(-cut) case of flu.

caractéristique [kaʀakteʀistik] *a*, *nf* characteristic.

carafe [kaʀaf] *nf* decanter; carafe.

caraïbe [kaʀaib] *a* Caribbean // *n*: **les C~s** the Caribbean (Islands); **la mer des C~s** the Caribbean Sea.

carambolage [kaʀɑ̃bɔlaʒ] *nm* multiple crash, pileup.

caramel [kaʀamɛl] *nm (bonbon)* caramel, toffee; *(substance)* caramel.

carapace [kaʀapas] *nf* shell.

caravane [kaʀavan] *nf* caravan; **caravaning** *nm* caravanning; *(emplacement)* caravan site.

carbone [kaʀbɔn] *nm* carbon; *(feuille)* carbon, sheet of carbon paper; *(double)* carbon (copy).

carbonique [kaʀbɔnik] *a*: **neige ~** dry ice.

carbonisé, e [kaʀbɔnize] *a* charred.

carboniser [kaʀbɔnize] *vt* to carbonize; to burn down, reduce to ashes.

carburant [kaʀbyʀɑ̃] *nm* (motor) fuel.

carburateur [kaʀbyʀatœʀ] *nm* carburettor.

carcan [kaʀkɑ̃] *nm (fig)* yoke, shackles *pl*.

carcasse [kaʀkas] *nf* carcass; *(de véhicule etc)* shell.

cardiaque [kaʀdjak] *a* cardiac, heart *cpd* // *nm/f* heart patient.

cardigan [kaʀdigɑ̃] *nm* cardigan.

cardiologue [kaʀdjɔlɔg] *nm/f* cardiologist, heart specialist.

carême [kaʀɛm] *nm*: **le C~** Lent.

carence [kaʀɑ̃s] *nf* incompetence, inadequacy; *(manque)* deficiency.

caresse [kaʀɛs] *nf* caress.

caresser [kaʀese] *vt* to caress, fondle; *(fig: projet)* to toy with.

cargaison [kaʀgɛzɔ̃] *nf* cargo, freight.

cargo [kaʀgo] *nm* cargo boat, freighter.

carie [kaʀi] *nf*: **la ~ (dentaire)** tooth decay; **une ~** a bad tooth.

carillon [kaʀijɔ̃] *nm (d'église)* bells *pl*; *(de pendule)* chimes *pl*; *(de porte)* door chime *ou* bell.

carlingue [kaʀlɛ̃g] *nf* cabin.

carnassier, ière [kaʀnasje, -jɛʀ] *a* carnivorous.

carnaval [kaʀnaval] *nm* carnival.

carnet [kaʀnɛ] *nm (calepin)* notebook; *(de tickets, timbres etc)* book; *(d'école)* school report; *(journal intime)* diary; ~ **de chèques** cheque book.

carotte [kaʀɔt] *nf* carrot.

carpette [kaʀpɛt] *nf* rug.

carré, e [kaʀe] *a* square; *(fig: franc)* straightforward // *nm (de terrain, jardin)* patch, plot; *(MATH)* square; **mètre/ kilomètre ~** square metre/kilometre.

carreau, x [kaʀo] *nm (en faïence etc)* (floor) tile; *(wall)* tile; *(de fenêtre)* (window) pane; *(motif)* check, square; *(CARTES: couleur)* diamonds *pl*; *(: carte)* diamond; **tissu à ~x** checked fabric.

carrefour [kaʀfuʀ] *nm* crossroads *sg*.

carrelage [kaʀlaʒ] *nm* tiling; (tiled) floor.

carrelet [kaʀlɛ] *nm (poisson)* plaice.

carrément [kaʀemɑ̃] *ad* straight out, bluntly; completely, altogether.

carrer [kaʀe]: **se ~** *vi*: **se ~ dans** to settle o.s. comfortably in.

carrière [kaʀjɛʀ] *nf (de roches)* quarry;

(*métier*) career; **militaire de ~** professional soldier.

carriole [kaʀjɔl] *nf* (*péj*) old cart.

carrossable [kaʀɔsabl(ə)] *a* suitable for (motor) vehicles.

carrosse [kaʀɔs] *nm* (horse-drawn) coach.

carrosserie [kaʀɔsʀi] *nf* body, coachwork *q*; (*activité, commerce*) coachbuilding.

carrousel [kaʀuzɛl] *nm* (ÉQUITATION) carousel; (*fig*) merry-go-round.

carrure [kaʀyʀ] *nf* build; (*fig*) stature, calibre.

cartable [kaʀtabl(ə)] *nm* (*d'écolier*) satchel, (school)bag.

carte [kaʀt(ə)] *nf* (*de géographie*) map; (*marine, du ciel*) chart; (*de fichier, d'abonnement etc, à jouer*) card; (*au restaurant*) menu; (*aussi: ~ postale*) (post)card; (*aussi: ~ de visite*) (visiting) card; **à la ~** (*au restaurant*) à la carte; **~ bancaire** cash card; **~ de crédit** credit card; **la ~ grise** (AUTO) ≈ the (car) registration book, the logbook; **~ d'identité** identity card; **~ routière** road map; **~ de séjour** residence permit.

carter [kaʀtɛʀ] *nm* sump.

carton [kaʀtɔ̃] *nm* (*matériau*) cardboard; (*boîte*) (cardboard) box; (*d'invitation*) invitation card; **faire un ~** (*au tir*) to have a go at the rifle range; to score a hit; **~** (**à dessin**) portfolio; **cartonné, e** *a* (*livre*) hardback, cased; **~-pâte** *nm* pasteboard.

cartouche [kaʀtuʃ] *nf* cartridge; (*de cigarettes*) carton.

cas [kɑ] *nm* case; **faire peu de ~/grand ~ de** to attach little/great importance to; **en aucun ~** on no account; **au ~ où** in case; **en ~ de** in case of, in the event of; **en ~ de besoin** if need be; **en tout ~** in any case, at any rate; **~ de conscience** matter of conscience.

casanier, ière [kazanje, -jɛʀ] *a* stay-at-home.

casaque [kazak] *nf* (*de jockey*) blouse.

cascade [kaskad] *nf* waterfall, cascade; (*fig*) stream, torrent.

cascadeur, euse [kaskadœʀ, -øz] *nm/f* stuntman/girl.

case [kɑz] *nf* (*hutte*) hut; (*compartiment*) compartment; (*pour le courrier*) pigeonhole; (*sur un formulaire, de mots croisés, d'échiquier*) box.

caser [kaze] *vt* (*trouver de la place pour*) to put in *ou* away; to put up; (*fig*) to find a job for; to marry off.

caserne [kazɛʀn(ə)] *nf* barracks.

cash [kaʃ] *ad*: **payer ~** to pay cash down.

casier [kazje] *nm* (*à journaux etc*) rack; (*de bureau*) filing cabinet; (*: à cases*) set of pigeonholes; (*case*) compartment; pigeonhole; (*: à clef*) locker; **~**

judiciaire police record.

casino [kazino] *nm* casino.

casque [kask(ə)] *nm* helmet; (*chez le coiffeur*) (hair-)drier; (*pour audition*) (head-)phones *pl*, headset.

casquette [kaskɛt] *nf* cap.

cassant, e [kasɑ̃, -ɑ̃t] *a* brittle; (*fig*) brusque, abrupt.

cassation [kasasjɔ̃] *nf*: **cour de ~** final court of appeal.

casse [kas] *nf* (*pour voitures*): **mettre à la ~** to scrap; (*dégâts*): **il y a eu de la ~** there were a lot of breakages.

casse... [kas] *préfixe*: **~-cou** *a inv* daredevil, reckless; **~-croûte** *nm inv* snack; **~-noisette(s)**, **~-noix** *nm inv* nutcrackers *pl*; **~-pieds** (*fam*): **il est ~-pieds** he's a pain (in the neck).

casser [kase] *vt* to break; (ADMIN: *gradé*) to demote; (JUR) to quash; **se ~** *vi* to break.

casserole [kasʀɔl] *nf* saucepan.

casse-tête [kɑstɛt] *nm inv* (*jeu*) brain teaser; (*difficultés*) headache (*fig*).

cassette [kasɛt] *nf* (*bande magnétique*) cassette; (*coffret*) casket.

casseur [kasœʀ] *nm* hooligan.

cassis [kasis] *nm* blackcurrant; (*de la route*) dip, bump.

cassoulet [kasulɛ] *nm* bean and sausage hot-pot.

cassure [kasyʀ] *nf* break, crack.

castor [kastɔʀ] *nm* beaver.

castrer [kastʀe] *vt* (*mâle*) to castrate; (*: cheval*) to geld; (*femelle*) to spay.

catalogue [katalɔg] *nm* catalogue.

cataloguer [katalɔge] *vt* to catalogue, to list; (*péj*) to put a label on.

catalyseur [katalizœʀ] *nm* catalyst.

cataplasme [kataplasm(ə)] *nm* poultice.

cataracte [kataʀakt(ə)] *nf* cataract.

catastrophe [katastʀɔf] *nf* catastrophe, disaster.

catastrophé [katastʀɔfe] *a* (*fam*) deeply saddened.

catch [katʃ] *nm* (all-in) wrestling; **~eur, euse** *nm/f* (all-in) wrestler.

catéchisme [kateʃism(ə)] *nm* catechism.

catégorie [kategɔʀi] *nf* category.

cathédrale [katedʀal] *nf* cathedral.

catholique [katɔlik] *a, nm/f* (Roman) Catholic; **pas très ~** a bit shady *ou* fishy.

catimini [katimini]: **en ~** *ad* on the sly.

cauchemar [koʃmaʀ] *nm* nightmare.

cause [koz] *nf* cause; (JUR) lawsuit, case; **à ~ de** because of, owing to; **pour ~ de** on account of; owing to; **(et) pour ~** and for (a very) good reason; **être en ~** to be at stake; to be involved; to be in question; **mettre en ~** to implicate; to call into question; **remettre en ~** to challenge.

causer [koze] *vt* to cause // *vi* to chat,

talk.

causerie [kozʀi] *nf* talk.

caution [kosjɔ̃] *nf* guarantee, security; deposit; (*JUR*) bail (bond); (*fig*) backing, support; **payer la ~ de qn** to stand bail for sb; **libéré sous ~** released on bail.

cautionner [kosjɔne] *vt* to guarantee; (*soutenir*) to support.

cavalcade [kavalkad] *nf* (*fig*) stampede.

cavalier, ière [kavalje, -jɛʀ] *a* (*désinvolte*) offhand // *nm/f* rider; (*au bal*) partner // *nm* (*ÉCHECS*) knight; **faire ~ seul** to go it alone.

cave [kav] *nf* cellar // *a*: **yeux ~s** sunken eyes.

caveau, x [kavo] *nm* vault.

caverne [kavɛʀn(ə)] *nf* cave.

caviar [kavjaʀ] *nm* caviar(e).

C.C.P. *sigle m voir* **compte.**

CD *sigle m = compact disc.*

ce(c'), **cet, cette, ces** [sə, sɛt, se] ♦ *dét* (*proximité*) this; these *pl*; (*non-proximité*) that; those *pl*; (*maison-ci/-là*) this/that house; **cette nuit** (*qui vient*) tonight; (*passée*) last night ♦ *pronom* **1**: **c'est** it's ou it is; **c'est un peintre** he's ou he is a painter; **ce sont des peintres** they're ou they are painters; **c'est le facteur** *etc* (*à la porte*) it's the postman; **qui est-ce?** who is it?; (*en désignant*) who is he/she?; **qu'est-ce?** what is it? **2**: **~ qui, ~ que** what; (*chose qui*): **il est bête, ~ qui me chagrine** he's stupid, which saddens me; **tout ~ qui bouge** everything that ou which moves; **tout ~ que je sais** all I know; **~ dont j'ai parlé** what I talked about; **~ que c'est grand!** it's so big!; *voir aussi* **-ci, est-ce que, n'est-ce pas, c'est-à-dire.**

ceci [səsi] *pronom* this.

cécité [sesite] *nf* blindness.

céder [sede] *vt* to give up // *vi* (*pont, barrage*) to give way; (*personne*) to give in; **~ à** to yield to, give in to.

CEDEX [sedɛks] *sigle m* (= *courrier d'entreprise à distribution exceptionnelle*) *postal service for bulk users.*

cédille [sedij] *nf* cedilla.

cèdre [sɛdʀ(ə)] *nm* cedar.

C.E.E. *sigle f* (= *Communauté économique européenne*) EEC.

ceinture [sɛ̃tyʀ] *nf* belt; (*taille*) waist; (*fig*) ring; belt; circle; **~ de sécurité** safety *ou* seat belt; **ceinturer** *vt* (*saisir*) to grasp (round the waist).

cela [səla] *pronom* that; (*comme sujet indéfini*) it; **quand/où ~?** when/where (was that)?

célèbre [selɛbʀ(ə)] *a* famous.

célébrer [selebʀe] *vt* to celebrate; (*louer*) to extol.

céleri [sɛlʀi] *nm*: **~(-rave)** celeriac; **~ (en branche)** celery.

célérité [selerite] *nf* speed, swiftness.

célibat [seliba] *nm* celibacy; bachelor/spinsterhood.

célibataire [selibatɛʀ] *a* single, unmarried.

celle, celles [sɛl] *pronom voir* **celui.**

cellier [selje] *nm* storeroom.

cellulaire [selylɛʀ] *a*: **voiture** *ou* **fourgon ~** prison *ou* police van.

cellule [selyl] *nf* (*gén*) cell.

cellulite [selylit] *nf* excess fat, cellulite.

celui, celle, ceux, celles [səlɥi, sɛl, sø] *pronom* **1**: **~-ci/-là, celle-ci/-là** this one/that one; **ceux-ci, celles-ci** these (ones); **ceux-là, celles-là** those (ones); **~ de mon frère** my brother's; **~ du salon/du dessous** the one in (*ou* from) the lounge/below **2**: **~ qui bouge** the one which *ou* that moves; (*personne*) the one who moves; **~ que je vois** the one (which *ou* that) I see; the one (whom) I see; **~ dont je parle** the one I'm talking about **3** (*valeur indéfinie*): **~ qui veut** whoever wants.

cendre [sɑ̃dʀ(ə)] *nf* ash; **~s** (*d'un foyer*) ash(es), cinders; (*volcaniques*) ash *sg*; (*d'un défunt*) ashes; **sous la ~** (*CULIN*) in (the) embers; **cendrier** *nm* ashtray.

cène [sɛn] *nf*: **la ~** (Holy) Communion.

censé, e [sɑ̃se] *a*: **être ~ faire** to be supposed to do.

censeur [sɑ̃sœʀ] *nm* (*SCOL*) deputy-head (*Brit*), vice-principal (*US*); (*CINÉMA, POL*) censor.

censure [sɑ̃syʀ] *nf* censorship.

censurer [sɑ̃syʀe] *vt* (*CINÉMA, PRESSE*) to censor; (*POL*) to censure.

cent [sɑ̃] *num* a hundred, one hundred; **centaine** *nf*: **une centaine (de)** about a hundred, a hundred or so; **plusieurs centaines (de)** several hundred; **des centaines (de)** hundreds (of); **centenaire** *a* hundred-year-old // *nm* (*anniversaire*) centenary; **centième** *num* hundredth; **centigrade** *nm* centigrade; **centilitre** *nm* centilitre; **centime** *nm* centime; **centimètre** *nm* centimetre; (*ruban*) tape measure, measuring tape.

central, e, aux [sɑ̃tʀal, -o] *a* central // *nm*: **~ (téléphonique)** (telephone) exchange // *nf* power station.

centre [sɑ̃tʀ(ə)] *nm* centre; **~ d'apprentissage** training college; **~ commercial** shopping centre; **le ~-ville** the town centre, downtown (area) (*US*).

centuple [sɑ̃typl(ə)] *nm*: **le ~ de qch** a hundred times sth; **au ~** a hundredfold.

cep [sɛp] *nm* (vine) stock.

cèpe [sɛp] *nm* (edible) boletus.

cependant [səpɑ̃dɑ̃] *ad* however.

céramique [seramik] *nf* ceramics *sg*.

cercle [sɛʀkl(ə)] *nm* circle; (*objet*) band, hoop; **~ vicieux** vicious circle.

cercueil [sɛʀkœj] *nm* coffin.

céréale [seʀeal] *nf* cereal.

cérémonie [seʀemɔni] *nf* ceremony; ~s (*péj*) fuss *sg*, to-do *sg*.

cerf [seʀ] *nm* stag.

cerfeuil [seʀfœj] *nm* chervil.

cerf-volant [seʀvɔlɑ̃] *nm* kite.

cerise [s(ə)ʀiz] *nf* cherry; **cerisier** *nm* cherry (tree).

cerné, e [seʀne] *a*: **les yeux ~s** with dark rings *ou* shadows under the eyes.

cerner [seʀne] *vt* (*MIL etc*) to surround; (*fig: problème*) to delimit, define.

certain, e [seʀtɛ̃, -ɛn] *a* certain // *dét* certain; **d'un ~ âge** past one's prime, not so young; **un ~ temps** (quite) some time; ~s *pronom* some; **certainement** *ad* (*probablement*) most probably *ou* likely; (*bien sûr*) certainly, of course.

certes [seʀt(ə)] *ad* admittedly; of course; indeed (yes).

certificat [seʀtifika] *nm* certificate.

certitude [seʀtityd] *nf* certainty.

cerveau, x [seʀvo] *nm* brain.

cervelas [seʀvəla] *nm* saveloy.

cervelle [seʀvɛl] *nf* (*ANAT*) brain.

ces [se] *dét voir* **ce**.

C.E.S. *sigle m* (= *Collège d'Enseignement Secondaire*) ≈ (junior) secondary school (*Brit*), ≈ junior high school (*US*).

cesse [sɛs]: **sans ~** *ad* continually, constantly; continuously; **il n'avait de ~ que** he would not rest until.

cesser [sese] *vt* to stop // *vi* to stop, cease; ~ **de faire** to stop doing.

cessez-le-feu [seselfø] *nm inv* ceasefire.

c'est-à-dire [sɛtadiʀ] *ad* that is (to say).

cet [sɛt] *dét voir* **ce**.

cette [sɛt] *dét voir* **ce**.

ceux [sø] *pronom voir* **celui**.

C.F.D.T. *sigle f* = *Confédération française et démocratique du travail*.

C.G.C. *sigle f* = *Confédération générale des cadres*.

C.G.T. *sigle f* = *Confédération générale du travail*.

chacun, e [ʃakœ̃, -yn] *pronom* each; (*indéfini*) everyone, everybody.

chagrin [ʃagʀɛ̃] *nm* grief, sorrow; **chagriner** *vt* to grieve; to bother.

chahut [ʃay] *nm* uproar; **chahuter** *vt* to rag, bait // *vi* to make an uproar.

chai [ʃe] *nm* wine store.

chaîne [ʃɛn] *nf* chain; (*RADIO, TV: stations*) channel; **travail à la ~** production line work; ~ (**haute-fidélité** *ou* **hi-fi**) hi-fi system; ~ (**de montage** *ou* **de fabrication**) production *ou* assembly line; ~ (**de montagnes**) (mountain) range; ~ (**stéréo**) stereo (system).

chair [ʃeʀ] *nf* flesh // *a*: (**couleur**) ~ flesh-coloured; **avoir la ~ de poule** to have goosepimples *ou* gooseflesh; **bien en ~** plump, well-padded; **en ~ et en os** in the flesh.

chaire [ʃeʀ] *nf* (*d'église*) pulpit; (*d'université*) chair.

chaise [ʃez] *nf* chair; ~ **longue** deckchair.

chaland [ʃalɑ̃] *nm* (*bateau*) barge.

châle [ʃɑl] *nm* shawl.

chaleur [ʃalœʀ] *nf* heat; (*fig*) warmth; fire, fervour; heat.

chaleureux, euse [ʃalœʀø, -øz] *a* warm.

chaloupe [ʃalup] *nf* launch; (*de sauvetage*) lifeboat.

chalumeau, x [ʃalymo] *nm* blowlamp, blowtorch.

chalutier [ʃalytje] *nm* trawler.

chamailler [ʃamaje]: **se ~** *vi* to squabble, bicker.

chambard [ʃɑ̃baʀ] *nm* rumpus.

chambouler [ʃɑ̃bule] *vt* to disrupt, turn upside down.

chambranle [ʃɑ̃bʀɑ̃l] *nm* (door) frame.

chambre [ʃɑ̃bʀ(ə)] *nf* bedroom; (*TECH*) chamber; (*POL*) chamber, house; (*JUR*) court; (*COMM*) chamber; federation; **faire ~ à part** to sleep in separate rooms; ~ **à un lit/deux lits** (*à l'hôtel*) single-/twin-bedded room; ~ **à air** (*de pneu*) (inner) tube; ~ **d'amis** spare *ou* guest room; ~ **à coucher** bedroom; ~ **noire** (*PHOTO*) dark room.

chambrer [ʃɑ̃bʀe] *vt* (*vin*) to bring to room temperature.

chameau, x [ʃamo] *nm* camel.

champ [ʃɑ̃] *nm* field; **prendre du ~** to draw back; ~ **de bataille** battlefield; ~ **de courses** racecourse; ~ **de tir** rifle range.

champagne [ʃɑ̃paɲ] *nm* champagne.

champêtre [ʃɑ̃pɛtʀ(ə)] *a* country *cpd*, rural.

champignon [ʃɑ̃piɲɔ̃] *nm* mushroom; (*terme générique*) fungus (*pl* i); ~ **de Paris** button mushroom.

champion, ne [ʃɑ̃pjɔ̃, -jɔn] *a, nm/f* champion; **championnat** *nm* championship.

chance [ʃɑ̃s] *nf*: **la ~** luck; **une ~** a stroke *ou* piece of luck *ou* good fortune; (*occasion*) a lucky break; ~s *nfpl* (*probabilités*) chances; **avoir de la ~** to be lucky.

chanceler [ʃɑ̃sle] *vi* to totter.

chancelier [ʃɑ̃səlje] *nm* (*allemand*) chancellor.

chanceux, euse [ʃɑ̃sø, -øz] *a* lucky.

chandail [ʃɑ̃daj] *nm* (thick) sweater.

chandelier [ʃɑ̃dəlje] *nm* candlestick.

chandelle [ʃɑ̃dɛl] *nf* (tallow) candle; **dîner aux ~s** candlelight dinner.

change [ʃɑ̃ʒ] *nm* (*COMM*) exchange.

changement [ʃɑ̃ʒmɑ̃] *nm* change; ~ **de vitesses** gears; gear change.

changer [ʃɑ̃ʒe] *vt* (*modifier*) to change, alter; (*remplacer, COMM, rhabiller*) to change // *vi* to change, alter; **se ~** *vi* to change (o.s.); ~ **de** (remplacer: adresse, nom, voiture etc) to change one's; (échanger, alterner: côté, place, train etc) to change + npl; ~ **de couleur/direction** to change colour/direction; ~ **d'idée** to change one's mind; ~ **de vitesse** to change gear.

chanson [ʃɑ̃sɔ̃] nf song.

chant [ʃɑ̃] nm song; (art vocal) singing; (d'église) hymn.

chantage [ʃɑ̃taʒ] nm blackmail; **faire du** ~ to use blackmail.

chanter [ʃɑ̃te] vt, vi to sing; **si cela lui chante** (fam) if he feels like it.

chanteur, euse [ʃɑ̃tœʀ, -øz] nm/f singer.

chantier [ʃɑ̃tje] nm (building) site; (sur une route) roadworks pl; **mettre en** ~ to put in hand; ~ **naval** shipyard.

chantilly [ʃɑ̃tiji] nf voir **crème**.

chantonner [ʃɑ̃tɔne] vi, vt to sing to oneself, hum.

chanvre [ʃɑ̃vʀ(ə)] nm hemp.

chaparder [ʃapaʀde] vt to pinch.

chapeau, x [ʃapo] nm hat; ~ **mou** trilby.

chapelet [ʃaplɛ] nm (REL) rosary.

chapelle [ʃapɛl] nf chapel; ~ **ardente** chapel of rest.

chapelure [ʃaplyʀ] nf (dried) bread-crumbs pl.

chapiteau, x [ʃapito] nm (de cirque) marquee, big top.

chapitre [ʃapitʀ(ə)] nm chapter; (fig) subject, matter.

chapitrer [ʃapitʀe] vt to lecture.

chaque [ʃak] dét each, every; (indéfini) every.

char [ʃaʀ] nm (à foin etc) cart, waggon; (de carnaval) float; ~ **(d'assaut)** tank.

charabia [ʃaʀabja] nm (péj) gibberish.

charade [ʃaʀad] nf riddle; (mimée) charade.

charbon [ʃaʀbɔ̃] nm coal; ~ **de bois** charcoal.

charcuterie [ʃaʀkytʀi] nf (magasin) pork butcher's shop and delicatessen; (produits) cooked pork meats pl; **charcutier, ère** nm/f pork butcher.

chardon [ʃaʀdɔ̃] nm thistle.

charge [ʃaʀʒ(ə)] nf (fardeau) load, burden; (explosif, ÉLEC, MIL, JUR) charge; (rôle, mission) responsibility; ~s nfpl (du loyer) service charges; **à la** ~ **de** (dépendant de) dependent upon;. (aux frais de) chargeable to; **j'accepte, à** ~ **de revanche** I accept, provided I can do the same for you one day; **prendre en** ~ to take charge of; (suj: véhicule) to take on; (dépenses) to take care of; ~s **sociales** social security contributions.

chargement [ʃaʀʒəmɑ̃] nm (objets) load.

charger [ʃaʀʒe] vt (voiture, fusil, caméra) to load; (batterie) to charge // vi (MIL etc) to charge; **se** ~ **de** vt to see to; ~ **qn de (faire) qch** to put sb in charge of (doing) sth.

chariot [ʃaʀjo] nm trolley; (charrette) waggon; (de machine à écrire) carriage.

charité [ʃaʀite] nf charity; **faire la** ~ **à** to give (something) to.

charmant, e [ʃaʀmɑ̃, -ɑ̃t] a charming.

charme [ʃaʀm(ə)] nm charm; **charmer** vt to charm.

charnel, le [ʃaʀnɛl] a carnal.

charnière [ʃaʀnjɛʀ] nf hinge; (fig) turning-point.

charnu, e [ʃaʀny] a fleshy.

charpente [ʃaʀpɑ̃t] nf frame(work); **charpentier** nm carpenter.

charpie [ʃaʀpi] nf: **en** ~ (fig) in shreds ou ribbons.

charrette [ʃaʀɛt] nf cart.

charrier [ʃaʀje] vt to carry (along); to cart, carry.

charrue [ʃaʀy] nf plough (Brit), plow (US).

chasse [ʃas] nf hunting; (au fusil) shooting; (poursuite) chase; (aussi: ~ **d'eau**) flush; **la** ~ **est ouverte** the hunting season is open; ~ **gardée** private hunting grounds pl; **prendre en** ~ to give chase to; **tirer la** ~ **(d'eau)** to flush the toilet, pull the chain; ~ **à courre** hunting.

chassé-croisé [ʃasekwaze] nm (fig) mix-up where people miss each other in turn.

chasse-neige [ʃasnɛʒ] nm inv snow-plough.

chasser [ʃase] vt to hunt; (expulser) to chase away ou out, drive away ou out; **chasseur, euse** nm/f hunter // nm (avion) fighter.

châssis [ʃasi] nm (AUTO) chassis; (cadre) frame; (de jardin) cold frame.

chat [ʃa] nm cat; ~ **sauvage** wildcat.

châtaigne [ʃatɛɲ] nf chestnut; **châtaignier** nm chestnut (tree).

châtain [ʃatɛ̃] a inv chestnut (brown); chestnut-haired.

château, x [ʃato] nm castle; ~ **d'eau** water tower; ~ **fort** stronghold, fortified castle.

châtier [ʃatje] vt to punish; (fig: style) to polish; **châtiment** nm punishment.

chaton [ʃatɔ̃] nm (ZOOL) kitten.

chatouiller [ʃatuje] vt to tickle; (l'odorat, le palais) to titillate; **chatouilleux, euse** a ticklish; (fig) touchy, over-sensitive.

chatoyer [ʃatwaje] vi to shimmer.

châtrer [ʃatʀe] vt (mâle) to castrate; (: cheval) to geld; (femelle) to spay.

chatte [ʃat] nf (she-)cat.

chaud, e [ʃo, -od] a (gén) warm; (très chaud) hot; (fig) hearty; heated; **il fait** ~ it's warm; it's hot; **avoir** ~ to be warm; to be hot; **ça me tient** ~ it keeps me warm; **rester au ~** to stay in the warm.

chaudière [ʃodjɛʀ] *nf* boiler.

chaudron [ʃodʀɔ̃] *nm* cauldron.

chauffage [ʃofaʒ] *nm* heating; **~ central** central heating.

chauffard [ʃofaʀ] *nm* (*péj*) reckless driver; hit-and-run driver.

chauffe-eau [ʃofo] *nm inv* water-heater.

chauffer [ʃofe] *vt* to heat // *vi* to heat up, warm up; (*trop chauffer: moteur*) to overheat; **se ~** *vi* (*se mettre en train*) to warm up; (*au soleil*) to warm o.s.

chauffeur [ʃofœʀ] *nm* driver; (*privé*) chauffeur.

chaume [ʃom] *nm* (*du toit*) thatch.

chaumière [ʃomjɛʀ] *nf* (thatched) cottage.

chaussée [ʃose] *nf* road(way).

chausse-pied [ʃospje] *nm* shoe-horn.

chausser [ʃose] *vt* (*bottes, skis*) to put on; (*enfant*) to put shoes on; **~ du 38/42** to take size 38/42.

chaussette [ʃosɛt] *nf* sock.

chausson [ʃosɔ̃] *nm* slipper; (*de bébé*) bootee; **~ (aux pommes)** (apple) turnover.

chaussure [ʃosyʀ] *nf* shoe; **~s basses** flat shoes; **~s de ski** ski boots.

chauve [ʃov] *a* bald.

chauve-souris [ʃovsuʀi] *nf* bat.

chauvin, e [ʃovɛ̃, -in] *a* chauvinistic.

chaux [ʃo] *nf* lime; **blanchi à la ~** whitewashed.

chavirer [ʃaviʀe] *vi* to capsize.

chef [ʃɛf] *nm* head, leader; (*de cuisine*) chef; **en ~** (*MIL etc*) in chief; **~ d'accusation** charge; **~ d'entreprise** company head; **~ d'état** head of state; **~ de file** (*de parti etc*) leader; **~ de gare** station master; **~ d'orchestre** conductor.

chef-d'œuvre [ʃɛdœvʀ(ə)] *nm* masterpiece.

chef-lieu [ʃɛfljø] *nm* county town.

chemin [ʃmɛ̃] *nm* path; (*itinéraire, direction, trajet*) way; **en ~** on the way; **~ de fer** railway (*Brit*), railroad (*US*); **par ~ de fer** by rail.

cheminée [ʃmine] *nf* chimney; (*à l'intérieur*) chimney piece, fireplace; (*de bateau*) funnel.

cheminement [ʃminmɑ̃] *nm* progress; course.

cheminer [ʃmine] *vi* to walk (along).

cheminot [ʃmino] *nm* railwayman.

chemise [ʃmiz] *nf* shirt; (*dossier*) folder; **~ de nuit** nightdress.

chemisier [ʃmizje] *nm* blouse.

chenal, aux [ʃənal, -o] *nm* channel.

chêne [ʃɛn] *nm* oak (tree); (*bois*) oak.

chenil [ʃənil] *nm* kennels *pl*.

chenille [ʃənij] *nf* (*ZOOL*) caterpillar; (*AUTO*) caterpillar track.

chèque [ʃɛk] *nm* cheque (*Brit*), check

(*US*); **~ sans provision** bad cheque; **~ de voyage** traveller's cheque; **chéquier** *nm* cheque book.

cher, ère [ʃɛʀ] *a* (*aimé*) dear; (*coûteux*) expensive, dear // *ad*: **cela coûte ~** it's expensive // *nf*: **la bonne chère** good food.

chercher [ʃɛʀʃe] *vt* to look for; (*gloire etc*) to seek; **aller ~** to go for, go and fetch; **~ à faire** to try to do.

chercheur, euse [ʃɛʀʃœʀ, -øz] *nm/f* researcher, research worker.

chère [ʃɛʀ] *a, nf voir* **cher**.

chéri, e [ʃeʀi] *a* beloved, dear; (**mon) ~** darling.

chérir [ʃeʀiʀ] *vt* to cherish.

cherté [ʃɛʀte] *nf*: **la ~ de la vie** the high cost of living.

chétif, ive [ʃetif, -iv] *a* puny, stunted.

cheval, aux [ʃval, -o] *nm* horse; (*AUTO*): **~ (vapeur)** (C.V.) horsepower *q*; **faire du ~** to ride; **à ~** on horseback; **à ~ sur** astride; (*fig*) overlapping; **~ de course** race horse.

chevalet [ʃvalɛ] *nm* easel.

chevalier [ʃvalje] *nm* knight.

chevalière [ʃvaljɛʀ] *nf* signet ring.

chevalin, e [ʃvalɛ̃, -in] *a*: **boucherie ~e** horse-meat butcher's.

chevaucher [ʃvoʃe] *vi* (*aussi:* se **~**) to overlap (each other) // *vt* to be astride, straddle.

chevaux [ʃvo] *nmpl voir* **cheval**.

chevelu, e [ʃvly] *a* with a good head of hair, hairy (*péj*).

chevelure [ʃvlyʀ] *nf* hair *q*.

chevet [ʃvɛ] *nm*: **au ~ de qn** at sb's bedside; **lampe de ~** bedside lamp.

cheveu, x [ʃvø] *nm* hair // *nmpl* (*chevelure*) hair *sg*; **avoir les ~x courts** to have short hair.

cheville [ʃvij] *nf* (*ANAT*) ankle; (*de bois*) peg; (*pour une vis*) plug.

chèvre [ʃɛvʀ(ə)] *nf* (she-)goat.

chevreau, x [ʃəvʀo] *nm* kid.

chèvrefeuille [ʃɛvʀəfœj] *nm* honeysuckle.

chevreuil [ʃəvʀœj] *nm* roe deer *inv*; (*CULIN*) venison.

chevronné, e [ʃəvʀone] *a* seasoned.

chevrotant, e [ʃəvʀɔtɑ̃, -ɑ̃t] *a* quavering.

chez [ʃe] *prép* **1** (*à la demeure de*) at; (*: direction*) to; **~ qn** at/to sb's house *ou* place; **~ moi** at home; (*direction*) home **2** (+ *profession*) at; (*: direction*) to; **le boulanger/dentiste** at the baker's/dentist's; to the baker's/dentist's **3** (*dans le caractère, l'œuvre de*) in; **~ les renards/Racine** in foxes/Racine.

chez-soi [ʃeswa] *nm inv* home.

chic [ʃik] *a inv* chic, smart; (*généreux*) nice, decent // *nm* stylishness; **avoir le ~ de** to have the knack of; **~!** great!

chicane [ʃikan] *nf* (*obstacle*) zigzag;

(querelle) squabble.

chiche [ʃiʃ] *a* niggardly, mean // *excl (à un défi)* you're on!

chichi [ʃiʃi] *nm (fam)* fuss.

chicorée [ʃikɔʀe] *nf (café)* chicory; *(salade)* endive.

chien [ʃjɛ̃] *nm* dog; **en ~ de fusil** curled up; **~ de garde** guard dog.

chiendent [ʃjɛ̃dã] *nm* couch grass.

chienne [ʃjɛn] *nf* dog, bitch.

chier [ʃje] *vi (fam!)* to crap (!).

chiffon [ʃifɔ̃] *nm* (piece of) rag.

chiffonner [ʃifɔne] *vt* to crumple; *(tracasser)* to concern.

chiffonnier [ʃifɔnje] *nm* rag-and-bone man.

chiffre [ʃifʀ(ə)] *nm (représentant un nombre)* figure; numeral; *(montant, total)* total, sum; **en ~s ronds** in round figures; **~ d'affaires** turnover; **chiffrer** *vt (dépense)* to put a figure to, assess; *(message)* to (en)code, cipher.

chignon [ʃiɲɔ̃] *nm* chignon, bun.

Chili [ʃili] *nm:* **le ~** Chile.

chimie [ʃimi] *nf* chemistry; **chimique** *a* chemical; **produits chimiques** chemicals.

Chine [ʃin] *nf:* **la ~** China.

chinois, e [ʃinwa, -waz] *a* Chinese // *nm/f* Chinese.

chiot [ʃjo] *nm* pup(py).

chips [ʃips] *nfpl* crisps.

chiquenaude [ʃiknod] *nf* flick, flip.

chiromancien, ne [kiʀɔmãsjɛ̃, -ɛn] *nm/f* palmist.

chirurgical, e, aux [ʃiʀyʀʒikal, -o] *a* surgical.

chirurgie [ʃiʀyʀʒi] *nf* surgery; **~ esthétique** plastic surgery; **chirurgien, ne** *nm/f* surgeon.

choc [ʃɔk] *nm* impact; shock; crash; *(moral)* shock; *(affrontement)* clash.

chocolat [ʃɔkɔla] *nm* chocolate; *(boisson)* (hot) chocolate; **~ au lait** milk chocolate.

chœur [kœʀ] *nm (chorale)* choir; *(OPÉRA, THÉÂTRE)* chorus; **en ~** in chorus.

choisir [ʃwaziʀ] *vt* to choose, select.

choix [ʃwa] *nm* choice, selection; **avoir le ~** to have the choice; **premier ~** *(COMM)* class one; **de ~** choice, selected; **au ~** as you wish.

chômage [ʃomaʒ] *nm* unemployment; **mettre au ~** to make redundant, put out of work; **être au ~** to be unemployed *ou* out of work; **chômeur, euse** *nm/f* unemployed person.

chope [ʃɔp] *nf* tankard.

choquer [ʃɔke] *vt (offenser)* to shock; *(commotionner)* to shake (up).

choriste [kɔʀist(ə)] *nm/f* choir member; *(OPÉRA)* chorus member.

chorus [kɔʀys] *nm:* **faire ~ (avec)** to voice one's agreement (with).

chose [ʃoz] *nf* thing; **c'est peu de ~** it's nothing (really); it's not much.

chou, x [ʃu] *nm* cabbage; **mon petit ~** (my) sweetheart; **~ à la crème** cream bun *(made of choux pastry)*.

chouchou, te [ʃuʃu, -ut] *nm/f (SCOL)* teacher's pet.

choucroute [ʃukʀut] *nf* sauerkraut.

chouette [ʃwɛt] *nf* owl // *a (fam)* great, smashing.

chou-fleur [ʃuflœʀ] *nm* cauliflower.

choyer [ʃwaje] *vt* to cherish; to pamper.

chrétien, ne [kʀetjɛ̃, -ɛn] *a, nm/f* Christian.

Christ [kʀist] *nm:* **le ~** Christ; **christianisme** *nm* Christianity.

chrome [kʀom] *nm* chromium; **chromé, e** *a* chromium-plated.

chronique [kʀɔnik] *a* chronic // *nf (de journal)* column, page; *(historique)* chronicle; *(RADIO, TV):* **la ~ sportive/théâtrale** the sports/theatre review; **la ~ locale** local news and gossip.

chronologique [kʀɔnɔlɔʒik] *a* chronological.

chronomètre [kʀɔnɔmɛtʀ(ə)] *nm* stopwatch; **chronométrer** *vt* to time.

chrysanthème [kʀizãtɛm] *nm* chrysanthemum.

C.H.U. *sigle m (= centre hospitalier universitaire)* ≈ (teaching) hospital.

chuchoter [ʃyʃɔte] *vt, vi* to whisper.

chuinter [ʃɥɛ̃te] *vi* to hiss.

chut [ʃyt] *excl* sh!

chute [ʃyt] *nf* fall; *(de bois, papier: déchet)* scrap; **la ~ des cheveux** hair loss; **faire une ~ (de 10 m)** to fall (10 m); **~s de pluie/neige** rain/snowfalls; **~ (d'eau)** waterfall; **~ libre** free fall.

Chypre [ʃipʀ] Cyprus.

-ci, ci- [si] *ad voir* **par, ci-contre, ci-joint** *etc* // *dét:* **ce garçon-ci/-là** this/that boy; **ces femmes-ci/-là** these/those women.

ci-après [siapʀɛ] *ad* hereafter.

cible [sibl(ə)] *nf* target.

ciboulette [sibulɛt] *nf* (smaller) chive.

cicatrice [sikatʀis] *nf* scar.

cicatriser [sikatʀize] *vt* to heal.

ci-contre [sikɔ̃tʀ(ə)] *ad* opposite.

ci-dessous [sidəsu] *ad* below.

ci-dessus [sidəsy] *ad* above.

cidre [sidʀ(ə)] *nm* cider.

Cie *abr (= compagnie)* Co.

ciel [sjɛl] *nm* sky; *(REL)* heaven; **cieux** *nmpl* sky sg, skies; **à ~ ouvert** open-air; *(mine)* opencast.

cierge [sjɛʀʒ(ə)] *nm* candle.

cieux [sjø] *nmpl voir* **ciel**.

cigale [sigal] *nf* cicada.

cigare [sigaʀ] *nm* cigar.

cigarette [sigaʀɛt] *nf* cigarette.

ci-gît [siʒi] *ad + vb* here lies.

cigogne [sigɔɲ] *nf* stork.

ci-inclus, e [siɛ̃kly, -yz] *a, ad* enclosed.

ci-joint, e [siʒwɛ̃, -ɛ̃t] *a, ad* enclosed.

cil [sil] *nm* (eye)lash.

ciller [sije] *vi* to blink.
cime [sim] *nf* top; (*montagne*) peak.
ciment [simɑ̃] *nm* cement; ~ **armé** reinforced concrete.
cimetière [simtjɛʀ] *nm* cemetery; (*d'église*) churchyard.
cinéaste [sineast(ə)] *nm/f* film-maker.
cinéma [sinema] *nm* cinema; ~**tographique** *a* film *cpd*, cinema *cpd*.
cinéphile [sinefil] *nm/f* cinema-goer.
cinglant, e [sɛ̃glɑ̃, -ɑ̃t] *a* (*échec*) crushing.
cinglé, e [sɛ̃gle] *a* (*fam*) crazy.
cingler [sɛ̃gle] *vt* to lash; (*fig*) to sting.
cinq [sɛ̃k] *num* five.
cinquantaine [sɛ̃kɑ̃tɛn] *nf*: **une ~ (de)** about fifty; **avoir la ~ (**âge) to be around fifty.
cinquante [sɛ̃kɑ̃t] *num* fifty; ~**naire** *a, nm/f* fifty-year-old.
cinquième [sɛ̃kjɛm] *num* fifth.
cintre [sɛ̃tʀ(ə)] *nm* coat-hanger.
cintré, e [sɛ̃tʀe] *a* (*chemise*) fitted.
cirage [siʀaʒ] *nm* (shoe) polish.
circonflexe [siʀkɔ̃flɛks(ə)] *a*: **accent ~** circumflex accent.
circonscription [siʀkɔ̃skʀipsjɔ̃] *nf* district; ~ **électorale** (*d'un député*) constituency.
circonscrire [siʀkɔ̃skʀiʀ] *vt* to define, delimit; (*incendie*) to contain.
circonstance [siʀkɔ̃stɑ̃s] *nf* circumstance; (*occasion*) occasion.
circonstancié, e [siʀkɔ̃stɑ̃sje] *a* detailed.
circonvenir [siʀkɔ̃vniʀ] *vt* to circumvent.
circuit [siʀkɥi] *nm* (*trajet*) tour, (round) trip; (*ÉLEC, TECH*) circuit.
circulaire [siʀkylɛʀ] *a, nf* circular.
circulation [siʀkylasjɔ̃] *nf* circulation; (*AUTO*): **la ~** (the) traffic.
circuler [siʀkyle] *vi* to drive (along); to walk along; (*train etc*) to run; (*sang, devises*) to circulate; **faire ~** (*nouvelle*) to spread (about), circulate; (*badauds*) to move on to.
cire [siʀ] *nf* wax.
ciré [siʀe] *nm* oilskin.
cirer [siʀe] *vt* to wax, polish.
cirque [siʀk(ə)] *nm* circus; (*GÉO*) cirque; (*fig*) chaos, bedlam; carry-on.
cisaille(s) [sizaj] *nf(pl)* (gardening) shears *pl*.
ciseau, x [sizo] *nm*: ~ **(à bois)** chisel // *nmpl* (pair of) scissors.
ciseler [sizle] *vt* to chisel, carve.
citadin, e [sitadɛ̃, -in] *nm/f* city dweller.
citation [sitasjɔ̃] *nf* (*d'auteur*) quotation; (*JUR*) summons *sg*.
cité [site] *nf* town; (*plus grande*) city; ~ **universitaire** students' residences *pl*.
citer [site] *vt* (*un auteur*) to quote (from); (*nommer*) to name; (*JUR*) to summon.

citerne [sitɛʀn(ə)] *nf* tank.
citoyen, ne [sitwajɛ̃, -ɛn] *nm/f* citizen.
citron [sitʀɔ̃] *nm* lemon; ~ **vert** lime; **citronnade** *nf* lemonade; **citronnier** *nm* lemon tree.
citrouille [sitʀuj] *nf* pumpkin.
civet [sive] *nm* stew.
civière [sivjɛʀ] *nf* stretcher.
civil, e [sivil] *a* (*JUR, ADMIN, poli*) civil; (*non militaire*) civilian; **en ~** in civilian clothes; **dans le ~** in civilian life.
civilisation [sivilizasjɔ̃] *nf* civilization.
civisme [sivism(ə)] *nm* public-spiritedness.
clair, e [klɛʀ] *a* light; (*chambre*) light, bright; (*eau, son, fig*) clear // *ad*: **voir ~** to see clearly; **tirer qch au ~** to get sth up, clarify sth; **mettre au ~** (*notes etc*) to tidy up; **le plus ~ de son temps** the better part of his time; ~ **de lune** *nm* moonlight; ~**ement** *ad* clearly.
clairière [klɛʀjɛʀ] *nf* clearing.
clairon [klɛʀɔ̃] *nm* bugle.
clairsemé, e [klɛʀsəme] *a* sparse.
clairvoyant, e [klɛʀvwajɑ̃, -ɑ̃t] *a* perceptive, clear-sighted.
clandestin, e [klɑ̃dɛstɛ̃, -in] *a* clandestine, covert; **passager ~** stowaway.
clapier [klapje] *nm* (rabbit) hutch.
clapoter [klapɔte] *vi* to lap.
claque [klak] *nf* (*gifle*) slap.
claquer [klake] *vi* (*drapeau*) to flap; (*porte*) to bang, slam; (*coup de feu*) to ring out // *vt* (*porte*) to slam, bang; (*doigts*) to snap; **se ~ un muscle** to pull *ou* strain a muscle.
claquettes [klakɛt] *nfpl* tap-dancing *sg*.
clarinette [klaʀinɛt] *nf* clarinet.
clarté [klaʀte] *nf* lightness; brightness; (*d'un son, de l'eau*) clearness; (*d'une explication*) clarity.
classe [klɑs] *nf* class; (*SCOL: local*) class(room); (: *leçon, élèves*) class; **faire la ~** (*SCOL*) to be a *ou* the teacher; to teach.
classement [klɑsmɑ̃] *nm* (*rang: SCOL*) place; (: *SPORT*) placing; (*liste: SCOL*) class list (in order of merit); (: *SPORT*) placings *pl*.
classer [klɑse] *vt* (*idées, livres*) to classify; (*papiers*) to file; (*candidat, concurrent*) to grade; (*JUR: affaire*) to close; **se ~ premier/dernier** to come first/last; (*SPORT*) to finish first/last.
classeur [klɑsœʀ] *nm* (*cahier*) file; (*meuble*) filing cabinet.
classique [klasik] *a* classical; (*sobre: coupe etc*) classic(al); (*habituel*) standard, classic.
claudication [klodikasjɔ̃] *nf* limp.
clause [kloz] *nf* clause.
claustrer [klostʀe] *vt* to confine.
clavecin [klavsɛ̃] *nm* harpsichord.
clavicule [klavikyl] *nf* collarbone.
clavier [klavje] *nm* keyboard.

clé ou **clef** [kle] nf key; (MUS) clef; (de mécanicien) spanner (Brit), wrench (US); **prix ~s en main** (d'une voiture) on-the-road price; **~ anglaise** (monkey) wrench; **~ de contact** ignition key.

clément, e [klemɑ̃, -ɑ̃t] a (temps) mild; (indulgent) lenient.

clerc [klɛʀ] nm: **~ de notaire** solicitor's clerk.

clergé [klɛʀʒe] nm clergy.

cliché [kliʃe] nm (PHOTO) negative; print; (LING) cliché.

client, e [klijɑ̃, -ɑ̃t] nm/f (acheteur) customer, client; (d'hôtel) guest, patron; (du docteur) patient; (de l'avocat) client; **clientèle** nf (du magasin) customers pl, clientèle; (du docteur, de l'avocat) practice.

cligner [kliɲe] vi: **~ des yeux** to blink (one's eyes); **~ de l'œil** to wink.

clignotant [kliɲɔtɑ̃] nm (AUTO) indicator.

clignoter [kliɲɔte] vi (étoiles etc) to twinkle; (lumière) to flash; (: vaciller) to flicker.

climat [klima] nm climate.

climatisation [klimatizasjɔ̃] nf air conditioning; **climatisé, e** a air-conditioned.

clin d'œil [klɛ̃dœj] nm wink; **en un ~** in a flash.

clinique [klinik] nf nursing home.

clinquant, e [klɛ̃kɑ̃, -ɑ̃t] a flashy.

cliqueter [klikte] vi to clash; to jangle, jingle; to chink.

clochard, e [klɔʃaʀ, -aʀd(ə)] nm/f tramp.

cloche [klɔʃ] nf (d'église) bell; (fam) clot; **~ à fromage** cheese-cover.

cloche-pied [klɔʃpje]: **à ~** ad on one leg, hopping (along).

clocher [klɔʃe] nm church tower; (en pointe) steeple // vi (fam) to be ou go wrong; **de ~** (péj) parochial.

cloison [klwazɔ̃] nf partition (wall).

cloître [klwatʀ(ə)] nm cloister.

cloîtrer [klwatʀe] vt: **se ~** to shut o.s. up ou away.

cloque [klɔk] nf blister.

clore [klɔʀ] vt to close; **clos, e** a voir maison, huis // nm (enclosed) field.

clôture [klotyʀ] nf closure; (barrière) enclosure; **clôturer** vt (terrain) to enclose; (débats) to close.

clou [klu] nm nail; (MÉD) boil; **~s** nmpl = passage clouté; **pneus à ~s** studded tyres; **le ~ du spectacle** the highlight of the show; **~ de girofle** clove; **~er** vt to nail down ou up.

clown [klun] nm clown.

club [klœb] nm club.

C.N.R.S. sigle m = centre national de la recherche scientifique.

coasser [kɔase] vi to croak.

cobaye [kɔbaj] nm guinea-pig.

coca [kɔka] nm Coke ®.

cocagne [kɔkaɲ] nf: **pays de ~** land of plenty.

cocaïne [kɔkain] nf cocaine.

cocasse [kɔkas] a comical, funny.

coccinelle [kɔksinɛl] nf ladybird (Brit), ladybug (US).

cocher [kɔʃe] nm coachman // vt to tick off; (entailler) to notch.

cochère [kɔʃɛʀ] af: **porte ~** carriage entrance.

cochon, ne [kɔʃɔ̃, -ɔn] nm pig // a (fam) dirty, smutty; **cochonnerie** nf (fam) filth; rubbish, trash.

cocktail [kɔktɛl] nm cocktail; (réception) cocktail party.

coco [kɔko] nm voir noix; (fam) bloke.

cocorico [kɔkɔʀiko] excl, nm cock-a-doodle-do.

cocotier [kɔkɔtje] nm coconut palm.

cocotte [kɔkɔt] nf (en fonte) casserole; **~ (minute)** pressure cooker; **ma ~** (fam) sweetie (pie).

cocu [kɔky] nm cuckold.

code [kɔd] nm code // a: **phares ~s** dipped lights; **se mettre en ~(s)** to dip one's (head)lights; **~ à barres** bar code; **~ civil** Common Law; **~ pénal** penal code; **~ postal** (numéro) post (Brit) ou zip (US) code; **~ de la route** highway code.

cœur [kœʀ] nm heart; (CARTES: couleur) hearts pl; (: carte) heart; **avoir bon ~** to be kind-hearted; **avoir mal au ~** to feel sick; **en avoir le ~ net** to be clear in one's own mind (about it); **par ~** by heart; **de bon ~** willingly; **cela lui tient à ~** that's (very) close to his heart.

coffre [kɔfʀ(ə)] nm (meuble) chest; (d'auto) boot (Brit), trunk (US); **~(-fort)** nm safe.

coffret [kɔfʀe] nm casket.

cognac [kɔɲak] nm brandy, cognac.

cogner [kɔɲe] vi to knock.

cohérent, e [kɔeʀɑ̃, -ɑ̃t] a coherent, consistent.

cohorte [kɔɔʀt(ə)] nf troop.

cohue [kɔy] nf crowd.

coi, coite [kwa, kwat] a: **rester ~** to remain silent.

coiffe [kwaf] nf headdress.

coiffé, e [kwafe] a: **bien/mal ~** with tidy/untidy hair; **~ en arrière** with one's hair brushed ou combed back.

coiffer [kwafe] vt (fig) to cover, top; **~ qn** to do sb's hair; **se ~** vi to do one's hair; to put on one's hat.

coiffeur, euse [kwafœʀ, -øz] nm/f hairdresser // nf (table) dressing table.

coiffure [kwafyʀ] nf (cheveux) hairstyle, hairdo; (chapeau) hat, headgear q; (art): **la ~** hairdressing.

coin [kwɛ̃] nm corner; (pour coincer) wedge; **l'épicerie du ~** the local grocer; **dans le ~** (aux alentours) in the area, around about; locally; **au ~ du feu** by the fireside; **regard en ~** sideways glance.

coincer [kwēse] *vt* to jam.

coïncidence [kɔēsidɑ̃s] *nf* coincidence.

coïncider [kɔēside] *vi* to coincide.

coite [kwat] *af voir* coi.

col [kɔl] *nm* (*de chemise*) collar; (*encolure, cou*) neck; (*de montagne*) pass; **~ roulé** polo-neck; **~ de l'utérus** cervix.

colère [kɔlɛʀ] *nf* anger; **une ~** a fit of anger; (**se mettre**) **en ~** (to get) angry; **coléreux, euse** *a*, **colérique** *a* quick-tempered, irascible.

colifichet [kɔlifiʃɛ] *nm* trinket.

colimaçon [kɔlimasɔ̃] *nm*: **escalier en ~** spiral staircase.

colin [kɔlē] *nm* hake.

colique [kɔlik] *nf* diarrhoea; colic (pains).

colis [kɔli] *nm* parcel.

collaborateur, trice [kɔlabɔʀatœʀ, -tʀis] *nm/f* (*aussi POL*) collaborator; (*d'une revue*) contributor.

collaborer [kɔlabɔʀe] *vi* to collaborate; **~ à** to collaborate on; (*revue*) to contribute to.

collant, e [kɔlɑ̃, -ɑ̃t] *a* sticky; (*robe etc*) clinging, skintight; (*péj*) clinging // *nm* (*bas*) tights *pl*.

collation [kɔlasjɔ̃] *nf* light meal.

colle [kɔl] *nf* glue; (*à papiers peints*) (wallpaper) paste; (*devinette*) teaser, riddle; (*SCOL fam*) detention.

collecte [kɔlɛkt(ə)] *nf* collection.

collectif, ive [kɔlɛktif, -iv] *a* collective; (*visite, billet*) group *cpd*.

collection [kɔlɛksjɔ̃] *nf* collection; (*ÉDITION*) series; **collectionner** *vt* (*tableaux, timbres*) to collect; **collectionneur, euse** *nm/f* collector.

collectivité [kɔlɛktivite] *nf* group.

collège [kɔlɛʒ] *nm* (*école*) (secondary) school; (*assemblée*) body; **collégien, ne** *nm/f* schoolboy/girl.

collègue [kɔleg] *nm/f* colleague.

coller [kɔle] *vt* (*papier, timbre*) to stick (on); (*affiche*) to stick up; (*enveloppe*) to stick down; (*morceaux*) to stick *ou* glue together; (*fam: mettre, fourrer*) to stick, shove; (*SCOL fam*) to keep in // *vi* (*être collant*) to be sticky; (*adhérer*) to stick; **~ à** to stick to.

collet [kɔlɛ] *nm* (*piège*) snare, noose; (*cou*): **prendre qn au ~** to grab sb by the throat; **~ monté** *a inv* straight-laced.

collier [kɔlje] *nm* (*bijou*) necklace; (*de chien, TECH*) collar; **~ (de barbe)** narrow beard along the line of the jaw.

collimateur [kɔlimatœʀ] *nm*: **avoir qn/qch dans le ~** (*fig*) to have sb/sth in one's sights.

colline [kɔlin] *nf* hill.

collision [kɔlizjɔ̃] *nf* collision, crash; en-

trer en **~ (avec)** to collide (with).

colmater [kɔlmate] *vt* (*fuite*) to seal off; (*brèche*) to plug, fill in.

colombe [kɔlɔ̃b] *nf* dove.

colon [kɔlɔ̃] *nm* settler.

colonel [kɔlɔnɛl] *nm* colonel.

colonie [kɔlɔni] *nf* colony; **~ (de vacances)** holiday camp (*for children*).

colonne [kɔlɔn] *nf* column; **se mettre en ~ par deux** to get into twos; **~ de secours** rescue party; **~ (vertébrale)** spine, spinal column.

colorant [kɔlɔʀɑ̃] *nm* colouring.

colorer [kɔlɔʀe] *vt* to colour.

colorier [kɔlɔʀje] *vt* to colour (in).

coloris [kɔlɔʀi] *nm* colour, shade.

colporter [kɔlpɔʀte] *vt* to hawk, peddle.

colza [kɔlza] *nm* rape.

coma [kɔma] *nm* coma.

combat [kɔ̃ba] *nm* fight; fighting *q*; **~ de boxe** boxing match.

combattant [kɔ̃batɑ̃] *nm*: **ancien ~** war veteran.

combattre [kɔ̃batʀ(ə)] *vt* to fight; (*épidémie, ignorance*) to combat, fight against.

combien [kɔ̃bjē] *ad* (*quantité*) how much; (*nombre*) how many; (*exclamatif*) how; **~ de** how much; how many; **~ de temps** how long; **~ coûte/pèse ceci?** how much does this cost/weigh?

combinaison [kɔ̃binɛzɔ̃] *nf* combination; (*astuce*) device, scheme; (*de femme*) slip; (*d'aviateur*) flying suit; (*d'homme-grenouille*) wetsuit; (*bleu de travail*) boiler suit (*Brit*), coveralls *pl* (*US*).

combine [kɔ̃bin] *nf* trick; (*péj*) scheme, fiddle (*Brit*).

combiné [kɔ̃bine] *nm* (*aussi*: **~ téléphonique**) receiver.

combiner [kɔ̃bine] *vt* to combine; (*plan, horaire*) to work out, devise.

comble [kɔ̃bl(ə)] *a* (*salle*) packed (full) // *nm* (*du bonheur, plaisir*) height; **~s** *nmpl* (*CONSTR*) attic *sg*, loft *sg*; **c'est le ~!** that beats everything!

combler [kɔ̃ble] *vt* (*trou*) to fill in; (*besoin, lacune*) to fill; (*déficit*) to make good; (*satisfaire*) to fulfil.

combustible [kɔ̃bystibl(ə)] *nm* fuel.

comédie [kɔmedi] *nf* comedy; (*fig*) playacting *q*; **~ musicale** musical; **comédien, ne** *nm/f* actor/actress.

comestible [kɔmɛstibl(ə)] *a* edible.

comique [kɔmik] *a* (*drôle*) comical; (*THÉÂTRE*) comic // *nm* (*artiste*) comic, comedian.

comité [kɔmite] *nm* committee; **~ d'entreprise** works council.

commandant [kɔmɑ̃dɑ̃] *nm* (*gén*) commander, commandant; (*NAVIG, AVIAT*) captain.

commande [kɔmɑ̃d] *nf* (*COMM*) order; **~s** *nfpl* (*AVIAT etc*) controls; **sur ~** to order; **~ à distance** remote control.

commandement [kɔmɑ̃dmɑ̃] *nm* command; (*REL*) commandment.

commander [kɔmɑ̃de] *vt* (*COMM*) to order; (*diriger, ordonner*) to command; **~ à qn de faire** to command *ou* order sb to do.

commando [kɔmɑ̃do] *nm* commando (squad).

comme [kɔm] ♦ *prép* **1** (*comparaison*) like; **tout ~ son père** just like his father; **fort ~ un bœuf** as strong as an ox; **joli ~ tout** ever so pretty **2** (*manière*) like; **faites-le ~ ça** do it like this, do it this way; **~ ci, ~ ça** so-so, middling **3** (*en tant que*) as a; **donner ~ prix** to give as a prize; **travailler ~ secrétaire** to work as a secretary ♦ *cj* **1** (*ainsi que*) as; **elle écrit ~ elle parle** she writes as she talks; **~ si** as if **2** (*au moment où, alors que*) as; **il est parti ~ j'arrivais** he left as I arrived **3** (*parce que, puisque*) as; **~ il était en retard, il ...** as he was late, he ... ♦ *ad*: **~ il est fort/c'est bon!** he's so strong/it's so good!

commémorer [kɔmemɔre] *vt* to commemorate.

commencement [kɔmɑ̃smɑ̃] *nm* beginning, start, commencement.

commencer [kɔmɑ̃se] *vt, vi* to begin, start, commence; **~ à** *ou* **de faire** to begin *ou* start doing.

comment [kɔmɑ̃] *ad* how; **~?** (*que dites-vous*) pardon? // *nm*: **le ~ et le pourquoi** the whys and wherefores.

commentaire [kɔmɑ̃tɛʀ] *nm* comment; remark.

commenter [kɔmɑ̃te] *vt* (*jugement, événement*) to comment (up)on; (*RADIO, TV*: *match, manifestation*) to cover.

commérages [kɔmeʀaʒ] *nmpl* gossip *sg*.

commerçant, e [kɔmɛʀsɑ̃, -ɑ̃t] *nm/f* shopkeeper, trader.

commerce [kɔmɛʀs(ə)] *nm* (*activité*) trade, commerce; (*boutique*) business; **vendu dans le ~** sold in the shops; **commercial, e, aux** *a* commercial, trading; (*péj*) commercial; **commercialiser** *vt* to market.

commère [kɔmɛʀ] *nf* gossip.

commettre [kɔmɛtʀ(ə)] *vt* to commit.

commis [kɔmi] *nm* (*de magasin*) (shop) assistant; (*de banque*) clerk; **~ voyageur** commercial traveller.

commissaire [kɔmisɛʀ] *nm* (*de police*) ≈ (police) superintendent; **~-priseur** *nm* auctioneer.

commissariat [kɔmisaʀja] *nm* police station.

commission [kɔmisjɔ̃] *nf* (*comité, pourcentage*) commission; (*message*) message; (*course*) errand; **~s** *nfpl* (*achats*) shopping *sg*.

commissure [kɔmisyʀ] *nf*: **les ~s des lèvres** the corners of the mouth.

commode [kɔmɔd] *a* (*pratique*) convenient, handy; (*facile*) easy; (*air, personne*) easy-going; (*personne*): **pas ~** awkward (to deal with) // *nf* chest of drawers; **commodité** *nf* convenience.

commotion [kɔmosjɔ̃] *nf*: **~ (cérébrale)** concussion; **commotionné, e** *a* shocked, shaken.

commun, e [kɔmœ̃, -yn] *a* common; (*pièce*) communal, shared; (*réunion, effort*) joint // *nf* (*ADMIN*) commune, ≈ district; (: *urbaine*) ≈ borough; **~s** *nmpl* (*bâtiments*) outbuildings; **cela sort du ~** it's out of the ordinary; **le ~ des mortels** the common run of people; **en ~** (*faire*) jointly; **mettre en ~** to pool, share.

communauté [kɔmynote] *nf* community; (*JUR*): **régime de la ~** communal estate settlement.

communication [kɔmynikasjɔ̃] *nf* communication; **~ (téléphonique)** (telephone) call; **~ interurbaine** long distance call.

communier [kɔmynje] *vi* (*REL*) to receive communion; (*fig*) to be united.

communion [kɔmynjɔ̃] *nf* communion.

communiquer [kɔmynike] *vt* (*nouvelle, dossier*) to pass on, convey; (*maladie*) to pass on; (*peur etc*) to communicate; (*chaleur, mouvement*) to transmit // *vi* to communicate; **se ~ à** (*se propager*) to spread to.

communisme [kɔmynism(ə)] *nm* communism; **communiste** *a, nm/f* communist.

commutateur [kɔmytatœʀ] *nm* (*ÉLEC*) (change-over) switch, commutator.

compact, e [kɔpakt] *a* dense; compact.

compagne [kɔpaɲ] *nf* companion.

compagnie [kɔpaɲi] *nf* (*firme, MIL*) company; (*groupe*) gathering; **tenir ~ à qn** to keep sb company; **fausser ~ à qn** to give sb the slip, slip *ou* sneak away from sb; **~ aérienne** airline (company).

compagnon [kɔpaɲɔ̃] *nm* companion.

comparable [kɔparabl(ə)] *a*: **~ (à)** comparable (to).

comparaison [kɔparɛzɔ̃] *nf* comparison.

comparaître [kɔparɛtʀ(ə)] *vi*: **~ (devant)** to appear (before).

comparer [kɔpare] *vt* to compare; **~ qch/qn à** *ou* **et** (*pour choisir*) to compare sth/sb with *ou* and; (*pour établir une similitude*) to compare sth/sb to.

comparse [kɔpars(ə)] *nm/f* (*péj*) associate, stooge.

compartiment [kɔpartimɑ̃] *nm* compartment.

comparution [kɔparysjɔ̃] *nf* appearance.

compas [kɔpa] *nm* (*GÉOM*) (pair of)

compasses pl; (NAVIG) compass.
compassé, e [kɔ̃pɑse] a starchy.
compatible [kɔ̃patibl(ə)] a compatible.
compatir [kɔ̃patiʀ] vi: ~ (à) to sympathize (with).
compatriote [kɔ̃patʀijɔt] nm/f compatriot.
compenser [kɔ̃pɑ̃se] vt to compensate for, make up for.
compère [kɔ̃pɛʀ] nm accomplice.
compétence [kɔ̃petɑ̃s] nf competence.
compétent, e [kɔ̃petɑ̃, -ɑ̃t] a (apte) competent, capable.
compétition [kɔ̃petisjɔ̃] nf (gén) competition; (SPORT: épreuve) event; **la ~** competitive sport; **la ~ automobile** motor racing.
complainte [kɔ̃plɛ̃t] nf lament.
complaire [kɔ̃plɛʀ]: se ~ vi: se ~ dans/parmi to take pleasure in/in being among.
complaisance [kɔ̃plɛzɑ̃s] nf kindness; pavillon de ~ flag of convenience.
complaisant, e [kɔ̃plɛzɑ̃, -ɑ̃t] a (aimable) kind, obliging.
complément [kɔ̃plemɑ̃] nm complement; remainder; **~ d'information** (ADMIN) supplementary ou further information; **complémentaire** a complementary; (additionnel) supplementary.
complet, ète [kɔ̃plɛ, -ɛt] a complete; (plein: hôtel etc) full // nm (aussi: **~veston**) suit; **complètement** ad completely; **compléter** vt (porter à la quantité voulue) to complete; (augmenter) to complement, supplement; to add to.
complexe [kɔ̃plɛks(ə)] a, nm complex; **complexé, e** a mixed-up, hung-up.
complication [kɔ̃plikasjɔ̃] nf complexity, intricacy; (difficulté, ennui) complication.
complice [kɔ̃plis] nm accomplice.
compliment [kɔ̃plimɑ̃] nm (louange) compliment; **~s** nmpl (félicitations) congratulations.
compliqué, e [kɔ̃plike] a complicated, complex; (personne) complicated.
complot [kɔ̃plo] nm plot.
comportement [kɔ̃pɔʀtəmɑ̃] nm behaviour.
comporter [kɔ̃pɔʀte] vt to consist of, comprise; (être équipé de) to have; (impliquer) to entail; se ~ vi to behave.
composante [kɔ̃pozɑ̃t] nf component.
composé [kɔ̃poze] nm compound.
composer [kɔ̃poze] vt (musique, texte) to compose; (mélange, équipe) to make up; (faire partie de) to make up, form // vi (transiger) to come to terms; se ~ de to be composed of, be made up of; **~ un numéro** to dial a number.
compositeur, trice [kɔ̃pozitœʀ, -tʀis] nm/f (MUS) composer.
composition [kɔ̃pozisjɔ̃] nf composi-

tion; (SCOL) test; **de bonne ~** (accommodant) easy to deal with.
composter [kɔ̃pɔste] vt to date stamp; to punch.
compote [kɔ̃pɔt] nf stewed fruit q; **~ de pommes** stewed apples; **compotier** nm fruit dish ou bowl.
compréhensible [kɔ̃pʀeɑ̃sibl(ə)] a comprehensible; (attitude) understandable.
compréhensif, ive [kɔ̃pʀeɑ̃sif, -iv] a understanding.
comprendre [kɔ̃pʀɑ̃dʀ(ə)] vt to understand; (se composer de) to comprise, consist of.
compresse [kɔ̃pʀɛs] nf compress.
compression [kɔ̃pʀɛsjɔ̃] nf compression; reduction.
comprimé [kɔ̃pʀime] nm tablet.
comprimer [kɔ̃pʀime] vt to compress; (fig: crédit etc) to reduce, cut down.
compris, e [kɔ̃pʀi, -iz] pp de comprendre // a (inclus) included; **~ entre** (situé) contained between; **la maison ~e/non ~e, y/non ~ la maison** including/excluding the house; **100 F tout ~** 100 F all inclusive ou all-in.
compromettre [kɔ̃pʀɔmɛtʀ(ə)] vt to compromise.
compromis [kɔ̃pʀɔmi] nm compromise.
comptabilité [kɔ̃tabilite] nf (activité, technique) accounting, accountancy; (d'une société: comptes) accounts pl, books pl; (: service) accounts office.
comptable [kɔ̃tabl(ə)] nm/f accountant.
comptant [kɔ̃tɑ̃] ad: payer ~ to pay cash; acheter ~ to buy for cash.
compte [kɔ̃t] nm count, counting; (total, montant) count, (right) number; (bancaire, facture) account; **~s** nmpl accounts, books; (fig) explanation sg; **en fin de ~** (fig) all things considered; **à bon ~** at a favourable price; (fig) lightly; **avoir son ~** (fig: fam) to have had it; **pour le ~ de** on behalf of; **pour son propre ~** for one's own benefit; **tenir ~ de** to take account of; **travailler à son ~** to work for oneself; **rendre ~ (à qn) de qch** to give (sb) an account of sth; **~ chèques postaux (C.C.P.)** Post Office account; **~ courant** current account; **~ à rebours** countdown; voir aussi rendre.
compte-gouttes [kɔ̃tgut] nm inv dropper.
compter [kɔ̃te] vt to count; (facturer) to charge for; (avoir à son actif, comporter) to have; (prévoir) to allow, reckon; (penser, espérer): **~ réussir** to expect to succeed // vi to count; (être économe) to economize; (figurer): **~ parmi** to be ou rank among; **~ sur** to count (up)on; **~ avec qch/qn** to reckon with ou take account of sth/sb; **sans ~ que** besides which.
compte rendu [kɔ̃tʀɑ̃dy] nm account,

report; (de film, livre) review.
compte-tours [kɔ̃ttuʀ] nm inv rev(olution) counter.
compteur [kɔ̃tœʀ] nm meter; ~ de vitesse speedometer.
comptine [kɔ̃tin] nf nursery rhyme.
comptoir [kɔ̃twaʀ] nm (de magasin) counter.
compulser [kɔ̃pylse] vt to consult.
comte, comtesse [kɔ̃t, kɔ̃tɛs] nm/f count/countess.
con, ne [kɔ̃, kɔn] a (fam!) damned ou bloody (Brit) stupid (!).
concéder [kɔ̃sede] vt to grant; (défaite, point) to concede.
concentrer [kɔ̃sɑ̃tʀe] vt to concentrate; se ~ vi to concentrate.
concept [kɔ̃sɛpt] nm concept.
conception [kɔ̃sɛpsjɔ̃] nf conception; (d'une machine etc) design.
concerner [kɔ̃sɛʀne] vt to concern; en ce qui me concerne as far as I am concerned.
concert [kɔ̃sɛʀ] nm concert; de ~ ad in unison; together.
concerter [kɔ̃sɛʀte] vt to devise; se ~ vi (collaborateurs etc) to put our ou their etc heads together.
concessionnaire [kɔ̃sesjɔnɛʀ] nm/f agent, dealer.
concevoir [kɔ̃svwaʀ] vt (idée, projet) to conceive (of); (méthode, plan d'appartement, décoration etc) to plan, design; (enfant) to conceive; bien/mal conçu well-/badly- designed.
concierge [kɔ̃sjɛʀʒ(ə)] nm/f caretaker; (d'hôtel) head porter.
concile [kɔ̃sil] nm council.
conciliabules [kɔ̃siljabyl] nmpl (private) discussions, confabulations.
concilier [kɔ̃silje] vt to reconcile; se ~ qn to win sb over.
concitoyen, ne [kɔ̃sitwajɛ̃, -jɛn] nm/f fellow citizen.
concluant, e [kɔ̃klyɑ̃, -ɑ̃t] a conclusive.
conclure [kɔ̃klyʀ] vt to conclude.
conclusion [kɔ̃klyzjɔ̃] nf conclusion.
conçois etc vb voir **concevoir**.
concombre [kɔ̃kɔ̃bʀ(ə)] nm cucumber.
concorder [kɔ̃kɔʀde] vi to tally, agree.
concourir [kɔ̃kuʀiʀ] vi (SPORT) to compete; ~ à vt (effet etc) to work towards.
concours [kɔ̃kuʀ] nm competition; (SCOL) competitive examination; (assistance) aid, help; ~ de circonstances combination of circumstances; ~ hippique horse show.
concret, ète [kɔ̃kʀɛ, -ɛt] a concrete.
concrétiser [kɔ̃kʀetize] vt (plan, projet) to put into concrete form; se ~ vi to materialize.
conçu, e [kɔ̃sy] pp de **concevoir**.
concubinage [kɔ̃kybinaʒ] nm (JUR) cohabitation.
concurrence [kɔ̃kyʀɑ̃s] nf competition;

jusqu'à ~ de up to.
concurrent, e [kɔ̃kyʀɑ̃, -ɑ̃t] nm/f (SPORT, ÉCON etc) competitor; (SCOL) candidate.
condamner [kɔ̃dane] vt (blâmer) to condemn; (JUR) to sentence; (porte, ouverture) to fill in, block up; (malade) to give up (hope for); ~ qn à 2 ans de prison to sentence sb to 2 years' imprisonment.
condensation [kɔ̃dɑ̃sasjɔ̃] nf condensation.
condenser [kɔ̃dɑ̃se] vt, se ~ vi to condense.
condisciple [kɔ̃disipl(ə)] nm/f school fellow, fellow student.
condition [kɔ̃disjɔ̃] nf condition; ~s nfpl (tarif, prix) terms; (circonstances) conditions; sans ~ a unconditional // ad unconditionally; à ~ de/que provided that; **conditionnel, le** a conditional // nm conditional (tense); **conditionner** vt (déterminer) to determine; (COMM: produit) to package; (fig: personne) to condition; **air conditionné** air conditioning.
condoléances [kɔ̃dɔleɑ̃s] nfpl condolences.
conducteur, trice [kɔ̃dyktœʀ, -tʀis] nm/f driver // nm (ÉLEC etc) conductor.
conduire [kɔ̃dɥiʀ] vt to drive; (délégation, troupeau) to lead; se ~ vi to behave; ~ vers/à to lead towards/to; ~ qn quelque part to take sb somewhere; to drive sb somewhere.
conduite [kɔ̃dɥit] nf (comportement) behaviour; (d'eau, de gaz) pipe; sous la ~ de led by; ~ à gauche left-hand drive; ~ intérieure saloon (car).
cône [kon] nm cone.
confection [kɔ̃fɛksjɔ̃] nf (fabrication) making; (COUTURE): la ~ the clothing industry; vêtement de ~ ready-to-wear ou off-the-peg garment.
confectionner [kɔ̃fɛksjɔne] vt to make.
conférence [kɔ̃feʀɑ̃s] nf (exposé) lecture; (pourparlers) conference; ~ de presse press conference.
confesser [kɔ̃fese] vt to confess; se ~ vi (REL) to go to confession.
confession [kɔ̃fesjɔ̃] nf confession; (culte: catholique etc) denomination.
confetti [kɔ̃feti] nm confetti q.
confiance [kɔ̃fjɑ̃s] nf confidence, trust; faith; avoir ~ en to have confidence ou faith in, trust; mettre qn en ~ to win sb's trust; ~ en soi self-confidence.
confiant, e [kɔ̃fjɑ̃, -ɑ̃t] a confident; trusting.
confidence [kɔ̃fidɑ̃s] nf confidence.
confidentiel, le [kɔ̃fidɑ̃sjɛl] a confidential.
confier [kɔ̃fje] vt: ~ à qn (objet en dépôt, travail etc) to entrust to sb; (secret, pensée) to confide to sb; se ~ à qn to confide in sb.

confiné, e |kɔ̃fine| *a* enclosed; stale.
confins |kɔ̃fɛ̃| *nmpl*: **aux ~ de** on the borders of.
confirmation |kɔ̃firmasjɔ̃| *nf* confirmation.
confirmer |kɔ̃firme| *vt* to confirm.
confiserie |kɔ̃fizri| *nf* (*magasin*) confectioner's *ou* sweet shop; **~s** *nfpl* (*bonbons*) confectionery *sg*; **confiseur, euse** *nm/f* confectioner.
confisquer |kɔ̃fiske| *vt* to confiscate.
confit, e |kɔ̃fi, -it| *a*: **fruits ~s** crystallized fruits // *nm*: **~ d'oie** conserve of goose.
confiture |kɔ̃fityr| *nf* jam; **~ d'oranges** (orange) marmalade.
conflit |kɔ̃fli| *nm* conflict.
confondre |kɔ̃fɔ̃dr(ə)| *vt* (*jumeaux, faits*) to confuse, mix up; (*témoin, menteur*) to confound; **se ~** *vi* to merge; **se ~ en excuses** to apologize profusely.
confondu, e |kɔ̃fɔ̃dy| *a* (*stupéfait*) speechless, overcome.
conforme |kɔ̃fɔrm(ə)| *a*: **~ à** in accordance with; in keeping with; true to.
conformément |kɔ̃fɔrmemã| *ad*: **~ à** in accordance with.
conformer |kɔ̃fɔrme| *vt*: **se ~ à** to conform to.
conformité |kɔ̃fɔrmite| *nf*: **en ~ avec** in accordance with, in keeping with.
confort |kɔ̃fɔr| *nm* comfort; **tout ~** (*COMM*) with all modern conveniences; **confortable** *a* comfortable.
confrère |kɔ̃frɛr| *nm* colleague; fellow member; **confrérie** *nf* brotherhood.
confronter |kɔ̃frɔ̃te| *vt* to confront; (*textes*) to compare, collate.
confus, e |kɔ̃fy, -yz| *a* (*vague*) confused; (*embarrassé*) embarrassed.
confusion |kɔ̃fyzjɔ̃| *nf* (*voir confus*) confusion; embarrassement; (*voir confondre*) confusion, mixing up.
congé |kɔ̃ʒe| *nm* (*vacances*) holiday; **en ~ on** holiday; (*off work*); **semaine de ~** week off; **prendre ~ de qn** to take one's leave of sb; **donner son ~ à** to give in one's notice to; **~ de maladie** sick leave; **~s payés** paid holiday.
congédier |kɔ̃ʒedje| *vt* to dismiss.
congélateur |kɔ̃ʒelatœr| *nm* freezer, deep freeze.
congeler |kɔ̃ʒle| *vt* to freeze.
congère |kɔ̃ʒɛr| *nf* snowdrift.
congestion |kɔ̃ʒɛstjɔ̃| *nf* congestion; **~ cérébrale** stroke.
congestionner |kɔ̃ʒɛstjɔne| *vt* to congest; (*MÉD*) to flush.
congrès |kɔ̃grɛ| *nm* congress.
congru, e |kɔ̃gry| *a*: **la portion ~e** the smallest *ou* meanest share.
conifère |kɔnifɛr| *nm* conifer.
conjoint, e |kɔ̃ʒwɛ̃, -wɛ̃t| *a* joint // *nm/f* spouse.
conjonction |kɔ̃ʒɔ̃ksjɔ̃| *nf* (*LING*) conjunction.

conjonctivite |kɔ̃ʒɔ̃ktivit| *nf* conjunctivitis.
conjoncture |kɔ̃ʒɔ̃ktyr| *nf* circumstances *pl*; climate.
conjugaison |kɔ̃ʒygɛzɔ̃| *nf* (*LING*) conjugation.
conjuger |kɔ̃ʒyge| *vt* (*LING*) to conjugate; (*efforts etc*) to combine.
conjuration |kɔ̃ʒyrasjɔ̃| *nf* conspiracy.
conjurer |kɔ̃ʒyre| *vt* (*sort, maladie*) to avert; (*implorer*) to beseech, entreat.
connaissance |kɔnɛsɑ̃s| *nf* (*savoir*) knowledge *q*; (*personne connue*) acquaintance; **être sans ~** to be unconscious; **perdre/reprendre ~** to lose/regain consciousness; **à ma/sa ~** to (the best of) my/his knowledge; **avoir ~ de** to be aware of; **prendre ~ de** (*document etc*) to peruse; **en ~ de cause** with full knowledge of the facts.
connaître |kɔnɛtr(ə)| *vt* to know; (*éprouver*) to experience; (*avoir*) to have; to enjoy; **~ de nom/vue** to know by name/sight; **ils se sont connus à Genève** they (first) met in Geneva.
connecté, e |kɔnɛkte| *a* on line.
connecter |kɔnɛkte| *vt* to connect.
connerie |kɔnri| *nf* (*fam!*) stupid thing (to do *ou* say).
connu, e |kɔny| *a* (*célèbre*) well-known.
conquérir |kɔ̃kerir| *vt* to conquer, win; **conquête** *nf* conquest.
consacrer |kɔ̃sakre| *vt* (*REL*) to consecrate; (*fig: usage etc*) to sanction, establish; (*employer*) to devote, dedicate.
conscience |kɔ̃sjɑ̃s| *nf* conscience; **avoir/prendre ~ de** to be/become aware of; **perdre ~** to lose consciousness; **avoir bonne/mauvaise ~** to have a clear/guilty conscience; **consciencieux, euse** *a* conscientious; **conscient, e** *a* conscious.
conscrit |kɔ̃skri| *nm* conscript.
consécutif, ive |kɔ̃sekytif, -iv| *a* consecutive; **~ à** following upon.
conseil |kɔ̃sɛj| *nm* (*avis*) piece of advice, advice *q*; (*assemblée*) council; **prendre ~** (*auprès de qn*) to take advice (from sb); **~ d'administration** board (of directors); **le ~ des ministres** ≈ the Cabinet.
conseiller |kɔ̃seje| *vt* (*personne*) to advise; (*méthode, action*) to recommend, advise; **~ à qn de** to advise sb to.
conseiller, ère |kɔ̃seje, kɔ̃sejɛr| *nm/f* adviser.
consentement |kɔ̃sɑ̃tmɑ̃| *nm* consent.
consentir |kɔ̃sɑ̃tir| *vt* to agree, consent.
conséquence |kɔ̃sekɑ̃s| *nf* consequence; **en ~** (*donc*) consequently; (*de façon appropriée*) accordingly; **ne pas tirer à ~** to be unlikely to have any repercussions.
conséquent, e |kɔ̃sekɑ̃, -ɑ̃t| *a* logical, rational; (*fam: important*) substantial;

par ~ consequently.

conservateur, trice [kɔ̃sɛʀvatœʀ, -tʀis] nm/f (POL) conservative; (de musée) curator.

conservatoire [kɔ̃sɛʀvatwaʀ] nm academy; (ÉCOLOGIE) conservation area.

conserve [kɔ̃sɛʀv(ə)] nf (gén pl) canned ou tinned (Brit) food; **en ~** canned, tinned (Brit).

conserver [kɔ̃sɛʀve] vt (faculté) to retain, keep; (amis, livres) to keep; (préserver, aussi CULIN) to preserve.

considérable [kɔ̃sideʀabl(ə)] a considerable, significant, extensive.

considération [kɔ̃sideʀasjɔ̃] nf consideration; (estime) esteem.

considérer [kɔ̃sideʀe] vt to consider; ~ qch comme to regard sth as.

consigne [kɔ̃siɲ] nf (de gare) left luggage (office) (Brit), checkroom (US); (ordre, instruction) instructions pl; ~ (automatique) left-luggage locker.

consigner [kɔ̃siɲe] vt (note, pensée) to record; (punir) to confine to barracks; to put in detention; (COMM) to put a deposit on.

consistant, e [kɔ̃sistɑ̃, -ɑ̃t] a thick; solid.

consister [kɔ̃siste] vi: ~ en/dans/à faire to consist of/in/in doing.

consœur [kɔ̃sœʀ] nf (lady) colleague; fellow member.

consoler [kɔ̃sɔle] vt to console.

consolider [kɔ̃sɔlide] vt to strengthen; (fig) to consolidate.

consommateur, trice [kɔ̃sɔmatœʀ, -tʀis] nm/f (ÉCON) consumer; (dans un café) customer.

consommation [kɔ̃sɔmasjɔ̃] nf (boisson) drink; ~ **aux 100 km** (AUTO) (fuel) consumption per 100 km.

consommer [kɔ̃sɔme] vt (suj: personne) to eat ou drink, consume; (suj: voiture, usine, poêle) to use, consume // vi (dans un café) to have (a) drink.

consonne [kɔ̃sɔn] nf consonant.

conspirer [kɔ̃spiʀe] vi to conspire.

conspuer [kɔ̃spɥe] vt to boo, shout down.

constamment [kɔ̃stamɑ̃] ad constantly.

constant, e [kɔ̃stɑ̃, -ɑ̃t] a constant; (personne) steadfast.

constat [kɔ̃sta] nm (d'huissier) certified report; (de police) report; (affirmation) statement.

constatation [kɔ̃statasjɔ̃] nf (observation) (observed) fact, observation; (affirmation) statement.

constater [kɔ̃state] vt (remarquer) to note; (ADMIN, JUR: attester) to certify; (dire) to state.

consterner [kɔ̃stɛʀne] vt to dismay.

constipé, e [kɔ̃stipe] a constipated.

constitué, e [kɔ̃stitɥe] a: ~ de made up ou composed of.

constituer [kɔ̃stitɥe] vt (comité, équipe) to set up; (dossier, collection) to put together; (suj: éléments: composer) to make up, constitute; (représenter, être) to constitute; **se ~ prisonnier** to give o.s. up.

constitution [kɔ̃stitysjɔ̃] nf (composition) composition, make-up; (santé, POL) constitution.

constructeur [kɔ̃stʀyktœʀ] nm manufacturer, builder.

construction [kɔ̃stʀyksjɔ̃] nf construction, building.

construire [kɔ̃stʀɥiʀ] vt to build, construct.

consul [kɔ̃syl] nm consul; **~at** nm consulate.

consultation [kɔ̃syltasjɔ̃] nf consultation; **~s** nfpl (POL) talks; **heures de ~** (MÉD) surgery (Brit) ou office (US) hours.

consulter [kɔ̃sylte] vt to consult // vi (médecin) to hold surgery (Brit), be in (the office) (US).

consumer [kɔ̃syme] vt to consume; se ~ vi to burn.

contact [kɔ̃takt] nm contact; **au ~ de** (air, peau) on contact with; (gens) through contact with; **mettre/couper le ~** (AUTO) to switch on/off the ignition; **entrer en ou prendre ~ avec** to get in touch ou contact with; **~er** vt to contact, get in touch with.

contagieux, euse [kɔ̃taʒjø, -øz] a contagious; infectious.

contaminer [kɔ̃tamine] vt to contaminate.

conte [kɔ̃t] nm tale; ~ **de fées** fairy tale.

contempler [kɔ̃tɑ̃ple] vt to contemplate, gaze at.

contemporain, e [kɔ̃tɑ̃pɔʀɛ̃, -ɛn] a, nm/f contemporary.

contenance [kɔ̃tnɑ̃s] nf (d'un récipient) capacity; (attitude) bearing, attitude; **perdre ~** to lose one's composure.

conteneur [kɔ̃tnœʀ] nm container.

contenir [kɔ̃tniʀ] vt to contain; (avoir une capacité de) to hold.

content, e [kɔ̃tɑ̃, -ɑ̃t] a pleased, glad; ~ **de** pleased with; **contenter** vt to satisfy, please; **se contenter de** to content o.s. with.

contentieux [kɔ̃tɑ̃sjø] nm (COMM) litigation; litigation department.

contenu [kɔ̃tny] nm (d'un bol) contents pl; (d'un texte) content.

conter [kɔ̃te] vt to recount, relate.

contestable [kɔ̃tɛstabl(ə)] a questionable.

contestation [kɔ̃tɛstasjɔ̃] nf (POL) protest.

conteste [kɔ̃tɛst(ə)]: **sans ~** ad unquestionably, indisputably.

contester [kɔ̃tɛste] vt to question, contest // vi (POL, gén) to protest, rebel (against established authority).

contexte [kɔ̃tɛkst(ə)] *nm* context.

contigu, ë [kɔ̃tigy] *a*: ~ (à) adjacent (to).

continent [kɔ̃tinɑ̃] *nm* continent.

continu, e [kɔ̃tiny] *a* continuous; (*courant*) ~ direct current, DC.

continuel, le [kɔ̃tinɥɛl] *a* (*qui se répète*) constant, continual; (*continu*) continuous.

continuer [kɔ̃tinɥe] *vt* (*travail, voyage etc*) to continue (with), carry on (with), go on (with); (*prolonger: alignement, rue*) to continue // *vi* (*pluie, vie, bruit*) to continue, go on; (*voyageur*) to go on; ~ à *ou* de faire to go on ou continue doing.

contorsionner [kɔ̃tɔʀsjɔne]: se ~ *vi* to contort o.s., writhe about.

contour [kɔ̃tuʀ] *nm* outline, contour.

contourner [kɔ̃tuʀne] *vt* to go round.

contraceptif, ive [kɔ̃tʀasɛptif, -iv] *a*, *nm* contraceptive.

contraception [kɔ̃tʀasɛpsjɔ̃] *nf* contraception.

contracté, e [kɔ̃tʀakte] *a* tense.

contracter [kɔ̃tʀakte] *vt* (*muscle etc*) to tense, contract; (*maladie, dette, obligation*) to contract; (*assurance*) to take out; se ~ *vi* (*métal, muscles*) to contract.

contractuel, le [kɔ̃tʀaktɥɛl] *nm/f* (*agent*) traffic warden.

contradiction [kɔ̃tʀadiksjɔ̃] *nf* contradiction; **contradictoire** *a* contradictory, conflicting.

contraindre [kɔ̃tʀɛ̃dʀ(ə)] *vt*: ~ qn à faire to compel sb to do.

contraint, e [kɔ̃tʀɛ̃, -ɛ̃t] *a* (*mine, air*) constrained, forced // *nf* constraint.

contraire [kɔ̃tʀɛʀ] *a, nm* opposite; ~ à contrary to; au ~ on the contrary.

contrarier [kɔ̃tʀaʀje] *vt* (*personne*) to annoy, bother; (*fig*) to impede; to thwart, frustrate.

contraste [kɔ̃tʀast(ə)] *nm* contrast.

contrat [kɔ̃tʀa] *nm* contract; ~ de travail employment contract.

contravention [kɔ̃tʀavɑ̃sjɔ̃] *nf* (*amende*) fine; (*P.V. pour stationnement interdit*) parking ticket.

contre [kɔ̃tʀ(ə)] *prép* against; (*en échange*) (in exchange) for; par ~ on the other hand.

contrebande [kɔ̃tʀəbɑ̃d] *nf* (*trafic*) contraband, smuggling; (*marchandise*) contraband, smuggled goods *pl*; faire la ~ de to smuggle.

contrebas [kɔ̃tʀəba]: en ~ *ad* (down) below.

contrebasse [kɔ̃tʀəbas] *nf* (double) bass.

contrecarrer [kɔ̃tʀəkaʀe] *vt* to thwart.

contrecœur [kɔ̃tʀəkœʀ]: à ~ *ad* (be)grudgingly, reluctantly.

contrecoup [kɔ̃tʀəku] *nm* repercussions

pl; par ~ as an indirect consequence.

contredire [kɔ̃tʀədiʀ] *vt* (*personne*) to contradict; (*témoignage, assertion, faits*) to refute.

contrée [kɔ̃tʀe] *nf* region; land.

contrefaçon [kɔ̃tʀəfasɔ̃] *nf* forgery.

contrefaire [kɔ̃tʀəfɛʀ] *vt* (*document, signature*) to forge, counterfeit; (*personne, démarche*) to mimic; (*dénaturer: sa voix etc*) to disguise.

contre-jour [kɔ̃tʀəʒuʀ]: à ~ *ad* against the sunlight.

contremaître [kɔ̃tʀəmɛtʀ(ə)] *nm* foreman.

contrepartie [kɔ̃tʀəpaʀti] *nf* compensation; en ~ in return.

contre-performance [kɔ̃tʀəpɛʀfɔʀmɑ̃s] *nf* below-average performance.

contre-pied [kɔ̃tʀəpje] *nm*: prendre le ~ de to take the opposing view of; to take the opposite course to.

contre-plaqué [kɔ̃tʀəplake] *nm* plywood.

contrepoids [kɔ̃tʀəpwa] *nm* counterweight, counterbalance.

contrer [kɔ̃tʀe] *vt* to counter.

contresens [kɔ̃tʀəsɑ̃s] *nm* misinterpretation; mistranslation; nonsense *q*; à ~ *ad* the wrong way.

contretemps [kɔ̃tʀətɑ̃] *nm* hitch; à ~ *ad* (*MUS*) out of time; (*fig*) at an inopportune moment.

contrevenir [kɔ̃tʀəvniʀ]: ~ à *vt* to contravene.

contribuable [kɔ̃tʀibɥabl(ə)] *nm/f* taxpayer.

contribuer [kɔ̃tʀibɥe]: ~ à *vt* to contribute towards; **contribution** *nf* contribution; contributions directes/indirectes direct/indirect taxation; mettre à contribution to call upon.

contrôle [kɔ̃tʀol] *nm* checking *q*, check; supervision; monitoring; (*test*) test, examination; perdre le ~ de (*véhicule*) to lose control of; ~ continu (*SCOL*) continuous assessment; ~ d'identité identity check; ~ des naissances birth control.

contrôler [kɔ̃tʀole] *vt* (*vérifier*) to check; (*surveiller*) to supervise; to monitor, control; (*maîtriser, COMM: firme*) to control; **contrôleur, euse** *nm/f* (*de train*) (ticket) inspector; (*de bus*) (bus) conductor/tress.

contrordre [kɔ̃tʀɔʀdʀ(ə)] *nm*: sauf ~ unless otherwise directed.

controversé, e [kɔ̃tʀɔvɛʀse] *a* (*personnage, question*) controversial.

contusion [kɔ̃tyzjɔ̃] *nf* bruise, contusion.

convaincre [kɔ̃vɛ̃kʀ(ə)] *vt*: ~ qn (de qch) to convince sb (of sth); ~ qn (de faire) to persuade sb (to do); ~ qn de (*JUR: délit*) to convict sb of.

convalescence [kɔ̃valesɑ̃s] *nf* convalescence.

convenable [kɔ̃vnabl(ə)] a suitable; (assez bon, respectable) decent.

convenance [kɔ̃vnɑ̃s] nf: à ma/votre ~ to my/your liking; ~s nfpl proprieties.

convenir [kɔ̃vniʀ] vi to be suitable; ~ à to suit; **il convient de** it is advisable to; (bienséant) it is right ou proper to; ~ de (bien-fondé de qch) to admit (to), acknowledge; (date, somme etc) to agree upon; ~ **que** (admettre) to admit that; ~ **de faire** to agree to do.

convention [kɔ̃vɑ̃sjɔ̃] nf convention; ~s nfpl (convenances) convention sg; ~ **collective** (ÉCON) collective agreement; **conventionné, e** a (ADMIN) applying charges laid down by the state.

convenu, e [kɔ̃vny] pp de **convenir** // a agreed.

conversation [kɔ̃vɛʀsasjɔ̃] nf conversation.

convertir [kɔ̃vɛʀtiʀ] vt: ~ **qn** (à) to convert sb (to); ~ **qch en** to convert sth into; **se** ~ (à) to be converted (to).

conviction [kɔ̃viksjɔ̃] nf conviction.

convienne etc vb voir **convenir**.

convier [kɔ̃vje] vt: ~ **qn à** (dîner etc) to (cordially) invite sb to.

convive [kɔ̃viv] nm/f guest (at table).

convivial, e [kɔ̃vivjal] a (INFORM) user-friendly.

convocation [kɔ̃vɔkasjɔ̃] nf (document) notification to attend; summons sg.

convoi [kɔ̃vwa] nm (de voitures, prisonniers) convoy; (train) train; ~ (**funèbre**) funeral procession.

convoiter [kɔ̃vwate] vt to covet.

convoquer [kɔ̃vɔke] vt (assemblée) to convene; (subordonné) to summon; (candidat) to ask to attend; ~ **qn** (à) (réunion) to invite sb (to attend).

convoyeur [kɔ̃vwajœʀ] nm (NAVIG) escort ship; ~ **de fonds** security guard.

coopération [kɔɔpeʀasjɔ̃] nf cooperation; (ADMIN): **la** C~ ≈ Voluntary Service Overseas (Brit), ≈ Peace Corps (US alternative to military service).

coopérer [kɔɔpeʀe] vi: ~ (à) to cooperate (in).

coordonner [kɔɔʀdɔne] vt to coordinate.

copain, copine [kɔpɛ̃, kɔpin] nm/f mate, pal.

copeau, x [kɔpo] nm shaving.

copie [kɔpi] nf copy; (SCOL) script, paper; exercise.

copier [kɔpje] vt, vi to copy; ~ **sur** to copy from.

copieur [kɔpjœʀ] nm (photo)copier.

copieux, euse [kɔpjø, -øz] a copious.

copine [kɔpin] nf voir **copain**.

copropriété [kɔpʀɔpʀijete] nf coownership, joint ownership.

coq [kɔk] nm cock, rooster.

coq-à-l'âne [kɔkalɑn] nm inv abrupt change of subject.

coque [kɔk] nf (de noix, mollusque) shell; (de bateau) hull; **à la** ~ (CULIN) (soft-)boiled.

coquelicot [kɔkliko] nm poppy.

coqueluche [kɔklyʃ] nf whooping-cough.

coquet, te [kɔkɛ, -ɛt] a flirtatious; appearance-conscious; pretty.

coquetier [kɔktje] nm egg-cup.

coquillage [kɔkijaʒ] nm (mollusque) shellfish inv; (coquille) shell.

coquille [kɔkij] nf shell; (TYPO) misprint; ~ **St Jacques** scallop.

coquin, e [kɔkɛ̃, -in] a mischievous, roguish; (polisson) naughty.

cor [kɔʀ] nm (MUS) horn; (MÉD): ~ (**au pied**) corn; **réclamer à** ~ **et à cri** to clamour for.

corail, aux [kɔʀaj, -o] nm coral q.

Coran [kɔʀɑ̃] nm: **le** ~ the Koran.

corbeau, x [kɔʀbo] nm crow.

corbeille [kɔʀbɛj] nf basket; ~ **à papier** waste paper basket ou bin.

corbillard [kɔʀbijaʀ] nm hearse.

corde [kɔʀd(ə)] nf rope; (de violon, raquette, d'arc) string; (ATHLÉTISME, AUTO): **la** ~ the rails pl; ~ **à linge** washing ou clothes line; ~ **raide** tight-rope; ~ **à sauter** skipping rope; ~s **vocales** vocal cords; **usé jusqu'à la** ~ threadbare.

cordée [kɔʀde] nf (d'alpinistes) rope, roped party.

cordialement [kɔʀdjalmɑ̃] ad (formule épistolaire) (kind) regards.

cordon [kɔʀdɔ̃] nm cord, string; ~ **sanitaire/de police** sanitary/police cordon; ~ **ombilical** umbilical cord.

cordonnerie [kɔʀdɔnʀi] nf shoe repairer's (shop).

cordonnier [kɔʀdɔnje] nm shoe repairer.

coriace [kɔʀjas] a tough.

corne [kɔʀn(ə)] nf horn; (de cerf) antler.

corneille [kɔʀnɛj] nf crow.

cornemuse [kɔʀnəmyz] nf bagpipes pl.

corner [kɔʀnɛʀ] nm (FOOTBALL) corner (kick).

cornet [kɔʀnɛ] nm (paper) cone; (de glace) cornet, cone; ~ **à piston** cornet.

corniaud [kɔʀnjo] nm (chien) mongrel; (péj) twit, clot.

corniche [kɔʀniʃ] nf (de meuble, neigeuse) cornice; (route) coast road.

cornichon [kɔʀniʃɔ̃] nm gherkin.

Cornouailles [kɔʀnwaj] nf Cornwall.

corporation [kɔʀpɔʀasjɔ̃] nf corporate body.

corporel, le [kɔʀpɔʀɛl] a bodily; (punition) corporal.

corps [kɔʀ] nm body; **à son** ~ **défendant** against one's will; **à** ~ **perdu** headlong; **perdu** ~ **et biens** lost with all hands; **prendre** ~ to take shape; **à** ~ **à** ~ ad hand-to-hand // nm clinch; **le** ~ **électoral** the electorate; **le** ~ **enseignant** the teach-

ing profession; ~ **de garde** guardroom.
corpulent, e [kɔʀpylɑ̃, -ɑ̃t] *a* stout.
correct, e [kɔʀɛkt] *a* correct; (*passable*) adequate.
correction [kɔʀɛksjɔ̃] *nf* (*voir corriger*) correction; (*voir correct*) correctness; (*rature, surcharge*) correction, emendation; (*coups*) thrashing.
correctionnel, le [kɔʀɛksjɔnɛl] *a* (*JUR*): **tribunal ~** ≈ criminal court.
correspondance [kɔʀɛspɔ̃dɑ̃s] *nf* correspondence; (*de train, d'avion*) connection; **cours par ~** correspondence course; **vente par ~** mail-order business.
correspondant, e [kɔʀɛspɔ̃dɑ̃, -ɑ̃t] *nm/f* correspondent; (*TÉL*) person phoning (*ou* being phoned).
correspondre [kɔʀɛspɔ̃dʀ(ə)] *vi* to correspond, tally; ~ **à** to correspond to; ~ **avec qn** to correspond with sb.
corrida [kɔʀida] *nf* bullfight.
corridor [kɔʀidɔʀ] *nm* corridor.
corriger [kɔʀiʒe] *vt* (*devoir*) to correct; (*punir*) to thrash; ~ **qn de** (*défaut*) to cure sb of.
corrompre [kɔʀɔ̃pʀ(ə)] *vt* to corrupt; (*acheter: témoin etc*) to bribe.
corruption [kɔʀypsjɔ̃] *nf* corruption; bribery.
corsage [kɔʀsaʒ] *nm* bodice; blouse.
corse [kɔʀs(ə)] *a, nm/f* Corsican // *nf*: la C~ Corsica.
corsé, e [kɔʀse] *a* vigorous; (*vin, goût*) full-flavoured; (*fig*) spicy; tricky.
corset [kɔʀsɛ] *nm* corset; bodice.
cortège [kɔʀtɛʒ] *nm* procession.
corvée [kɔʀve] *nf* chore, drudgery *q*.
cosmétique [kɔsmetik] *nm* beauty care product.
cossu, e [kɔsy] *a* well-to-do.
costaud, e [kɔsto, -od] *a* strong, sturdy.
costume [kɔstym] *nm* (*d'homme*) suit; (*de théâtre*) costume; **costumé, e** *a* dressed up.
cote [kɔt] *nf* (*en Bourse etc*) quotation; quoted value; (*d'un cheval*): **la ~ de** the odds *pl* on; (*d'un candidat etc*) rating; (*sur un croquis*) dimension; ~ **d'alerte** danger *ou* flood level.
côte [kot] *nf* (*rivage*) coast(line); (*pente*) slope; (: *sur une route*) hill; (*ANAT*) rib; (*d'un tricot, tissu*) rib, ribbing *q*; ~ **à** ~ *ad* side by side; **la C~** (**d'Azur**) the (French) Riviera.
côté [kote] *nm* (*gén*) side; (*direction*) way, direction; **de chaque ~** (**de**) on each side (of); **de tous les ~s** from all directions; **de quel ~ est-il parti?** which way did he go?; **de ce/de l'autre ~** this/the other way; **du ~ de** (*provenance*) from; (*direction*) towards; (*proximité*) near; **de ~** *ad* sideways; on one side; to one side; aside; **laisser/mettre de ~** to leave/put to one side; **à ~** *ad* (*right*)

nearby; beside; next door; (*d'autre part*) besides; **à ~ de** beside; next to; **être aux ~s de** to be by the side of.
coteau, x [kɔto] *nm* hill.
côtelette [kotlɛt] *nf* chop.
coter [kɔte] *vt* (*en Bourse*) to quote.
côtier, ière [kotje, -jɛʀ] *a* coastal.
cotisation [kɔtizasjɔ̃] *nf* subscription, dues *pl*; (*pour une pension*) contributions *pl*.
cotiser [kɔtize] *vi*: ~ (**à**) to pay contributions (to); **se ~** *vi* to club together.
coton [kɔtɔ̃] *nm* cotton; ~ **hydrophile** cotton wool (*Brit*), absorbent cotton (*US*).
côtoyer [kotwaje] *vt* to be close to; to rub shoulders with; to run alongside.
cou [ku] *nm* neck.
couchant [kuʃɑ̃] *a*: **soleil ~** setting sun.
couche [kuʃ] *nf* (*strate: gén, GÉO*) layer; (*de peinture, vernis*) coat; (*de bébé*) nappy (*Brit*), diaper (*US*); (*MÉD*) confinement *sg*; ~s **sociales** social levels *ou* strata; ~-**culotte** *nf* disposable nappy (*Brit*) *ou* diaper (*US*) and waterproof pants in one.
couché, e [kuʃe] *a* lying down; (*au lit*) in bed.
coucher [kuʃe] *nm* (*du soleil*) setting // *vt* (*personne*) to put to bed; (: *loger*) to put up; (*objet*) to lay on its side // *vi* to sleep; **se ~** *vi* (*pour dormir*) to go to bed; (*pour se reposer*) to lie down; (*soleil*) to set; ~ **de soleil** sunset.
couchette [kuʃɛt] *nf* couchette; (*de marin*) bunk.
coucou [kuku] *nm* cuckoo.
coude [kud] *nm* (*ANAT*) elbow; (*de tuyau, de la route*) bend; ~ **à** ~ *ad* shoulder to shoulder, side by side.
coudre [kudʀ(ə)] *vt* (*bouton*) to sew on; (*robe*) to sew (up) // *vi* to sew.
couenne [kwan] *nf* (*de lard*) rind.
couette [kwɛt] *nf/pl* duvet, quilt.
couffin [kufɛ̃] *nm* Moses basket.
couiner [kwine] *vi* to squeal.
couler [kule] *vi* to flow, run; (*fuir: stylo, récipient*) to leak; (*sombrer: bateau*) to sink // *vt* (*cloche, sculpture*) to cast; (*bateau*) to sink; (*fig*) to ruin, bring down.
couleur [kulœʀ] *nf* colour; (*CARTES*) suit; **film/télévision en ~s** colour film/television.
couleuvre [kulœvʀ(ə)] *nf* grass snake.
coulisse [kulis] *nf*: ~s *nfpl* (*THÉÂTRE*) wings; (*fig*): **dans les ~s** behind the scenes; **coulisser** *vi* to slide, run.
couloir [kulwaʀ] *nm* corridor, passage; (*de bus*) gangway; (*sur la route*) bus lane; (*SPORT: de piste*) lane; (*GÉO*) gully; ~ **aérien/de navigation** air/shipping lane.
coup [ku] *nm* (*heurt, choc*) knock; (*affectif*) blow, shock; (*agressif*) blow;

(avec arme à feu) shot; (de l'horloge) chime; stroke; (SPORT) stroke; shot; blow; (fam: fois) time; ~ **de coude** nudge (with the elbow); ~ **de tonnerre** clap of thunder; ~ **de sonnette** ring of the bell; ~ **de crayon** stroke of the pencil; **donner un** ~ **de balai** to give the floor a sweep; **avoir le** ~ (fig) to have the knack; **boire un** ~ to have a drink; **être dans le** ~ to be in on it; **du** ~... so (you see)...; **d'un seul** ~ (subitement) suddenly; (à la fois) at one go; in one blow; **du premier** ~ first time; **du même** ~ at the same time; **à** ~ **sûr** definitely, without fail; ~ **sur** ~ in quick succession; **sur le** ~ outright; **sous le** ~ **de** (surprise etc) under the influence of; ~ **de chance** stroke of luck; ~ **de couteau** stab (of a knife); ~ **d'envoi** kick-off; ~ **d'essai** first attempt; ~ **de feu** shot; ~ **de filet** (POLICE) haul; ~ **franc** free kick; ~ **de frein** (sharp) braking q; ~ **de main:** **donner un** ~ **de main à qn** to give sb a (helping) hand; ~ **d'œil** glance; ~ **de pied** kick; ~ **de poing** punch; ~ **de soleil** sunburn q; ~ **de téléphone** phone call; ~ **de tête** (fig) (sudden) impulse; ~ **de théâtre** (fig) dramatic turn of events; ~ **de vent** gust of wind; **en** ~ **de vent** in a tearing hurry.

coupable [kupabl(ə)] a guilty // nm/f (gén) culprit; (JUR) guilty party.

coupe [kup] nf (verre) goblet; (à fruits) dish; (SPORT) cup; (de cheveux, de vêtement) cut; (graphique, plan) (cross) section; **être sous la** ~ **de** to be under the control of.

coupe-papier [kuppapje] nm inv paper knife.

couper [kupe] vt to cut; (retrancher) to cut (out); (route, courant) to cut off; (appétit) to take away; (vin, cidre) to blend; (: à table) to dilute // vi to cut; (prendre un raccourci) to take a short-cut; **se** ~ vi (se blesser) to cut o.s.; ~ **la parole à qn** to cut sb short.

couperosé, e [kupʀoze] a blotchy.

couple [kupl(ə)] nm couple.

couplet [kuplɛ] nm verse.

coupole [kupɔl] nf dome; cupola.

coupon [kupɔ̃] nm (ticket) coupon; (de tissu) remnant; roll; ~-**réponse** nm reply coupon.

coupure [kupyʀ] nf cut; (billet de banque) note; (de journal) cutting; ~ **de courant** power cut.

cour [kuʀ] nf (de ferme, jardin) (court)yard; (d'immeuble) back yard; (JUR, royale) court; **faire la** ~ **à qn** to court sb; ~ **d'assises** court of assizes; ~ **martiale** court-martial.

courage [kuʀaʒ] nm courage, bravery; **courageux, euse** a brave, courageous.

couramment [kuʀamɑ̃] ad commonly; (parler) fluently.

courant, e [kuʀɑ̃, -ɑ̃t] a (fréquent) common; (COMM, gén: normal) standard; (en cours) current // nm current; (fig) movement; trend; **être au** ~ (de) (fait, nouvelle) to know (about); **mettre qn au** ~ (de) (fait, nouvelle) to tell sb (about); (nouveau travail etc) to teach sb the basics (of); **se tenir au** ~ (de) (techniques etc) to keep o.s. up-to-date (on); **dans le** ~ **de** (pendant) in the course of; **le 10** ~ (COMM) the 10th inst; ~ **d'air** draught; ~ **électrique** (electric) current, power.

courbature [kuʀbatyʀ] nf ache.

courbe [kuʀb(ə)] a curved // nf curve.

courber [kuʀbe] vt to bend.

coureur, euse [kuʀœʀ, -øz] nm/f (SPORT) runner (ou driver); (péj) womanizer/manhunter; ~ **automobile** racing driver.

courge [kuʀʒ(ə)] nf (CULIN) marrow.

courgette [kuʀʒɛt] nf courgette (Brit), zucchini (US).

courir [kuʀiʀ] vi to run // vt (SPORT: épreuve) to compete in; (risque) to run; (danger) to face; ~ **les magasins** to go round the shops; **le bruit court que** the rumour is going round that.

couronne [kuʀɔn] nf crown; (de fleurs) wreath, circlet.

courons etc vb voir **courir**.

courrier [kuʀje] nm mail, post; (lettres à écrire) letters pl; **long/moyen** ~ a (AVIAT) long-/medium-haul.

courroie [kuʀwa] nf strap; (TECH) belt.

courrons etc vb voir **courir**.

cours [kuʀ] nm (leçon) lesson; class; (série de leçons) course; (cheminement) course; (écoulement) flow; (COMM) rate; price; **donner libre** ~ **à** to give free expression to; **avoir** ~ (monnaie) to be legal tender; (fig) to be current; (SCOL) to have a class ou lecture; **en** ~ (année) current; (travaux) in progress; **en** ~ **de route** on the way; **au** ~ **de** in the course of, during; ~ **d'eau** waterway; ~ **du soir** night school.

course [kuʀs(ə)] nf running; (SPORT: épreuve) race; (d'un taxi, autocar) journey, trip; (petite mission) errand; ~s nfpl (achats) shopping sg; **faire des** ~s to do some shopping.

court, e [kuʀ, kuʀt(ə)] a short // ad short // nm: ~ **(de tennis)** (tennis) court; **tourner** ~ to come to a sudden end; **ça fait** ~ that's not very long; **à** ~ **de short** of; **prendre qn de** ~ to catch sb unawares; **tirer à la** ~**e paille** to draw lots; ~-**circuit** nm short-circuit.

courtier, ère [kuʀtje, -jɛʀ] nm/f broker.

courtiser [kuʀtize] vt to court, woo.

courtois, e [kuʀtwa, -waz] a courteous.

couru, e [kuʀy] pp de **courir** // a: **c'est** ~ it's a safe bet.

cousais etc vb voir **coudre**.

couscous [kuskus] *nm* couscous.
cousin, e [kuzɛ̃, -in] *nm/f* cousin.
coussin [kusɛ̃] *nm* cushion.
cousu, e [kuzy] *pp de* coudre.
coût [ku] *nm* cost; **le ~ de la vie** the cost of living.
coûtant [kutɑ̃] *am*: **au prix ~** at cost price.
couteau, x [kuto] *nm* knife; **~ à cran d'arrêt** flick-knife.
coûter [kute] *vt, vi* to cost; **combien ça coûte?** how much is it?, what does it cost?; **coûte que coûte** at all costs; **coûteux, euse** *a* costly, expensive.
coutume [kutym] *nf* custom.
couture [kutyʀ] *nf* sewing; dressmaking; (*points*) seam.
couturier [kutyʀje] *nm* fashion designer.
couturière [kutyʀjɛʀ] *nf* dressmaker.
couvée [kuve] *nf* brood, clutch.
couvent [kuvɑ̃] *nm* (*de sœurs*) convent; (*de frères*) monastery.
couver [kuve] *vt* to hatch; (*maladie*) to be sickening for // *vi* (*feu*) to smoulder; (*révolte*) to be brewing.
couvercle [kuvɛʀkl(ə)] *nm* lid; (*de bombe aérosol etc, qui se visse*) cap, top.
couvert, e [kuvɛʀ, -ɛʀt(ə)] *pp de* couvrir // *a* (*ciel*) overcast // *nm* place setting; (*place à table*) place; (*au restaurant*) cover charge; **~s** *nmpl* cutlery *sg*; **~ de** covered with *ou* in; **mettre le ~** to lay the table.
couverture [kuvɛʀtyʀ] *nf* blanket; (*de bâtiment*) roofing; (*de livre, assurance, fig*) cover; (*presse*) coverage; **~ chauffante** electric blanket.
couveuse [kuvøz] *nf* (*de maternité*) incubator.
couvre... [kuvʀ(ə)] *préfixe*: **~-chef** *nm* hat; **~-feu** *nm* curfew; **~-lit** *nm* bedspread.
couvrir [kuvʀiʀ] *vt* to cover; **se ~** *vi* (*ciel*) to cloud over; (*s'habiller*) to cover up; (*se coiffer*) to put on one's hat.
crabe [kʀab] *nm* crab.
cracher [kʀaʃe] *vi, vt* to spit.
crachin [kʀaʃɛ̃] *nm* drizzle.
craie [kʀɛ] *nf* chalk.
craindre [kʀɛ̃dʀ(ə)] *vt* to fear, be afraid of; (*être sensible à: chaleur, froid*) to be easily damaged by.
crainte [kʀɛ̃t] *nf* fear; **de ~ de/que** for fear of/that; **craintif, ive** *a* timid.
cramoisi, e [kʀamwazi] *a* crimson.
crampe [kʀɑ̃p] *nf* cramp.
cramponner [kʀɑ̃pɔne]: **se ~** *vi*: **se ~ (à)** to hang *ou* cling on (to).
cran [kʀɑ̃] *nm* (*entaille*) notch; (*de courroie*) hole; (*courage*) guts *pl*; **~ d'arrêt** safety catch.
crâne [kʀɑn] *nm* skull.
crâner [kʀane] *vi* (*fam*) to show off.
crapaud [kʀapo] *nm* toad.

crapule [kʀapyl] *nf* villain.
craquement [kʀakmɑ̃] *nm* crack, snap; (*du plancher*) creak, creaking *q*.
craquer [kʀake] *vi* (*bois, plancher*) to creak; (*fil, branche*) to snap; (*couture*) to come apart; (*fig*) to break down // *vt* (*allumette*) to strike.
crasse [kʀas] *nf* grime, filth.
cravache [kʀavaʃ] *nf* (*riding*) crop.
cravate [kʀavat] *nf* tie.
crawl [kʀol] *nm* crawl; **dos crawlé** backstroke.
crayeux, euse [kʀɛjø, -øz] *a* chalky.
crayon [kʀɛjɔ̃] *nm* pencil; **~ à bille** ballpoint pen; **~ de couleur** crayon, colouring pencil; **~ optique** light pen.
créancier, ière [kʀeɑ̃sje, -jɛʀ] *nm/f* creditor.
création [kʀeɑsjɔ̃] *nf* creation.
créature [kʀeatyʀ] *nf* creature.
crécelle [kʀesɛl] *nf* rattle.
crèche [kʀɛʃ] *nf* (*de Noël*) crib; (*garderie*) crèche, day nursery.
crédit [kʀedi] *nm* (*gén*) credit; **~s** *nmpl* funds; **payer/acheter à ~** to pay/buy on credit *ou* on easy terms; **faire ~ à qn** to give sb credit; **créditer** *vt*: **créditer un compte (de)** to credit an account (with).
crédule [kʀedyl] *a* credulous, gullible.
créer [kʀee] *vt* to create; (*THÉÂTRE*) to produce (for the first time).
crémaillère [kʀemajɛʀ] *nf* (*RAIL*) rack; **pendre la ~** to have a house-warming party.
crématoire [kʀematwaʀ] *a*: **four ~** crematorium.
crème [kʀɛm] *nf* cream; (*entremets*) cream dessert // *a inv* cream(-coloured); **un (café) ~** ≈ a white coffee; **~ chantilly, ~ fouettée** whipped cream; **~ à raser** shaving cream; **crémerie** *nf* dairy; **crémeux, euse** *a* creamy.
créneau, x [kʀeno] *nm* (*de fortification*) crenel(le); (*fig*) gap, slot; (*AUTO*): **faire un ~** to reverse into a parking space (*between cars alongside the kerb*).
crêpe [kʀɛp] *nf* (*galette*) pancake // *nm* (*tissu*) crepe; **crêpé, e** *a* (*cheveux*) backcombed; **~rie** *nf* pancake shop *ou* restaurant.
crépir [kʀepiʀ] *vt* to roughcast.
crépiter [kʀepite] *vi* to sputter, splutter; to crackle.
crépon [kʀepɔ̃] *nm* seersucker.
crépu, e [kʀepy] *a* frizzy, fuzzy.
crépuscule [kʀepyskyl] *nm* twilight, dusk.
cresson [kʀesɔ̃] *nm* watercress.
crête [kʀɛt] *nf* (*de coq*) comb; (*de vague, montagne*) crest.
creuser [kʀøze] *vt* (*trou, tunnel*) to dig; (*sol*) to dig a hole in; (*bois*) to hollow out; (*fig*) to go (deeply) into; **ça creuse** that gives you a real appetite; **se ~** (*la cervelle*) to rack one's brains.

creux, euse [krø, -øz] *a* a hollow // *nm* hollow; (*fig: sur graphique etc*) trough; **heures creuses** slack periods; off-peak periods.

crevaison [krəvɛzɔ̃] *nf* puncture.

crevasse [krəvas] *nf* (*dans le sol*) crack, fissure; (*de glacier*) crevasse.

crevé, e [krəve] *a* (*fatigué*) all in, exhausted.

crever [krəve] *vt* (*papier*) to tear, break; (*tambour, ballon*) to burst // *vi* (*pneu*) to burst; (*automobiliste*) to have a puncture (*Brit*) *ou* a flat (tire) (*US*); (*fam*) to die; **cela lui a crevé un œil** it blinded him in one eye.

crevette [krəvɛt] *nf:* ~ **(rose)** prawn; ~ **grise** shrimp.

cri [kri] *nm* cry, shout; (*d'animal: spécifique*) cry, call; **c'est le dernier** ~ (*fig*) it's the latest fashion.

criant, e [krijɑ̃, -ɑ̃t] *a* (*injustice*) glaring.

criard, e [krijar, -ard(ə)] *a* (*couleur*) garish, loud; yelling.

crible [kribl(ə)] *nm* riddle; **passer qch au** ~ (*fig*) to go over sth with a fine-tooth comb.

cric [krik] *nm* (*AUTO*) jack.

crier [krije] *vi* (*pour appeler*) to shout, cry (out); (*de peur, de douleur etc*) to scream, yell // *vt* (*ordre, injure*) to shout (out), yell (out).

crime [krim] *nm* crime; (*meurtre*) murder; **criminel, le** *nm/f* criminal; murderer.

crin [krɛ̃] *nm* hair *q*; (*fibre*) horsehair.

crinière [krinjɛr] *nf* mane.

crique [krik] *nf* creek, inlet.

criquet [krikɛ] *nm* locust; grasshopper.

crise [kriz] *nf* crisis (*pl* crises); (*MÉD*) attack; fit; ~ **cardiaque** heart attack; ~ **de foie** bilious attack; ~ **de nerfs** attack of nerves.

crisper [krispe] *vt* to tense; (*poings*) to clench; **se** ~ *vi* to tense; to clench; (*personne*) to get tense.

crisser [krise] *vi* (*neige*) to crunch; (*pneu*) to screech.

cristal, aux [kristal, -o] *nm* crystal.

cristallin, e [kristalɛ̃, -in] *a* crystal-clear.

critère [kritɛr] *nm* criterion (*pl* ia).

critiquable [kritikabl(ə)] *a* open to criticism.

critique [kritik] *a* a critical // *nm/f* (*de théâtre, musique*) critic // *nf* criticism; (*THÉÂTRE etc: article*) review.

critiquer [kritike] *vt* (*dénigrer*) to criticize; (*évaluer, juger*) to assess, examine (critically).

croasser [krɔase] *vi* to caw.

croc [kro] *nm* (*dent*) fang; (*de boucher*) hook.

croc-en-jambe [krɔkɑ̃ʒɑ̃b] *nm:* **faire un** ~ **à qn** to trip sb up.

croche [krɔʃ] *nf* (*MUS*) quaver (*Brit*), eighth note (*US*).

croche-pied [krɔʃpje] *nm* = **croc-en-jambe**.

crochet [krɔʃɛ] *nm* hook; (*détour*) detour; (*TRICOT: aiguille*) crochet hook; (: *technique*) crochet; ~**s** *nmpl* (*TYPO*) square brackets; **vivre aux** ~**s de qn** to live *ou* sponge off sb; **crocheter** *vt* (*serrure*) to pick.

crochu, e [krɔʃy] *a* hooked; claw-like.

crocodile [krɔkɔdil] *nm* crocodile.

crocus [krɔkys] *nm* crocus.

croire [krwar] *vt* to believe; **se** ~ **fort** to think one is strong; ~ **que** to believe *ou* think that; ~ **à**, ~ **en** to believe in.

crois *vb voir* **croître**.

croisade [krwazad] *nf* crusade.

croisé, e [krwaze] *a* (*veston*) double-breasted.

croisement [krwazmɑ̃] *nm* (*carrefour*) crossroads *sg*; (*BIO*) crossing; cross-breed.

croiser [krwaze] *vt* (*personne, voiture*) to pass; (*route*) to cross, cut across; (*BIO*) to cross // *vi* (*NAVIG*) to cruise; ~ **les jambes/bras** to cross one's legs/fold one's arms; **se** ~ *vi* (*personnes, véhicules*) to pass each other; (*routes, lettres*) to cross; (*regards*) to meet.

croiseur [krwazœr] *nm* cruiser (*warship*).

croisière [krwazjɛr] *nf* cruise; **vitesse de** ~ (*AUTO etc*) cruising speed.

croisillon [krwazijɔ̃] *nm* lattice.

croissance [krwasɑ̃s] *nf* growth.

croissant [krwasɑ̃] *nm* (*à manger*) croissant; (*motif*) crescent.

croître [krwatr(ə)] *vi* to grow.

croix [krwa] *nf* cross; **en** ~ *a, ad* in the form of a cross; **la C~ Rouge** the Red Cross.

croque... [krɔk] *préfixe:* ~**-monsieur** *nm inv* toasted ham and cheese sandwich.

croquer [krɔke] *vt* (*manger*) to crunch; to munch; (*dessiner*) to sketch // *vi* to be crisp *ou* crunchy; **chocolat à** ~ plain dessert chocolate.

croquis [krɔki] *nm* sketch.

crosse [krɔs] *nf* (*de fusil*) butt; (*de revolver*) grip.

crotte [krɔt] *nf* droppings *pl*.

crotté, e [krɔte] *a* muddy, mucky.

crottin [krɔtɛ̃] *nm* dung, manure.

crouler [krule] *vi* (*s'effondrer*) to collapse; (*être délabré*) to be crumbling.

croupe [krup] *nf* rump; **en** ~ pillion.

croupir [krupir] *vi* to stagnate.

croustillant, e [krustijɑ̃, -ɑ̃t] *a* crisp; (*fig*) spicy.

croûte [krut] *nf* crust; (*du fromage*) rind; (*MÉD*) scab; **en** ~ (*CULIN*) in pastry.

croûton [krutɔ̃] *nm* (*CULIN*) crouton;

(*bout du pain*) crust, heel.
croyable [krwajabl(ə)] *a* credible.
croyant, e [krwajã, -ãt] *nm/f* believer.
C.R.S. *sigle fpl* (= *Compagnies républicaines de sécurité*) *a* state security police force // *sigle m* member of the C.R.S.
cru, e [kry] *pp de* croire // *a* (*non cuit*) raw; (*lumière, couleur*) harsh; (*paroles, description*) crude // *nm* (*vignoble*) vineyard; (*vin*) wine.
crû *pp de* **croître.**
cruauté [kryote] *nf* cruelty.
cruche [kryʃ] *nf* pitcher, jug.
crucifix [krysifi] *nm* crucifix.
crucifixion [krysifiksjɔ̃] *nf* crucifixion.
crudités [krydite] *nfpl* (*CULIN*) salads.
crue [kry] *nf voir* **cru.**
cruel, le [kryɛl] *a* cruel.
crus *etc* **crûs** *etc, vb voir* **croire, croître.**
crustacés [krystase] *nmpl* shellfish.
Cuba [kyba] *nf* Cuba.
cube [kyb] *nm* cube; (*jouet*) brick; mètre ~ cubic metre; 2 au ~ 2 cubed.
cueillir [kœjir] *vt* (*fruits, fleurs*) to pick, gather; (*fig*) to catch.
cuiller *ou* **cuillère** [kɥijɛr] *nf* spoon; ~ à café coffee spoon; (*CULIN*) ≈ teaspoonful; ~ à soupe soup-spoon; (*CULIN*) ≈ tablespoonful; **cuillerée** *nf* spoonful.
cuir [kɥir] *nm* leather; ~ chevelu scalp.
cuirassé [kɥirase] *nm* (*NAVIG*) battleship.
cuire [kɥir] *vt* (*aliments*) to cook; (*au four*) to bake; (*poterie*) to fire // *vi* to cook; **bien cuit** (*viande*) well done; **trop cuit** overdone.
cuisant, e [kɥizã, -ãt] *a* (*douleur*) stinging; (*fig: souvenir, échec*) bitter.
cuisine [kɥizin] *nf* (*pièce*) kitchen; (*art culinaire*) cookery, cooking; (*nourriture*) cooking, food; **faire la** ~ to cook; **cuisiner** *vt* to cook; (*fam*) to grill // *vi* to cook; **cuisinier, ière** *nm/f* cook // *nf* (*poêle*) cooker.
cuisse [kɥis] *nf* thigh; (*CULIN*) leg.
cuisson [kɥisɔ̃] *nf* cooking; firing.
cuit, e *pp de* **cuire.**
cuivre [kɥivr(ə)] *nm* copper; les ~s (*MUS*) the brass.
cul [ky] *nm* (*fam!*) arse (!).
culasse [kylas] *nf* (*AUTO*) cylinder-head; (*de fusil*) breech.
culbute [kylbyt] *nf* somersault; (*accidentelle*) tumble, fall.
culminant, e [kylminã, -ãt] *a*: **point** ~ highest point.
culminer [kylmine] *vi* to reach its highest point; to tower.
culot [kylo] *nm* (*effronterie*) cheek.
culotte [kylɔt] *nf* (*pantalon*) trousers *pl* (*Brit*), pants *pl* (*US*); (*de femme*) knickers *pl* (*Brit*), panties *pl*; ~ de cheval riding breeches *pl*.

culpabilité [kylpabilite] *nf* guilt.
culte [kylt(ə)] *nm* (*religion*) religion; (*hommage, vénération*) worship; (*protestant*) service.
cultivateur, trice [kyltivatœr, -tris] *nm/f* farmer.
cultivé, e [kyltive] *a* (*personne*) cultured, cultivated.
cultiver [kyltive] *vt* to cultivate; (*légumes*) to grow, cultivate.
culture [kyltyr] *nf* cultivation; growing; (*connaissances etc*) culture; ~ **physique** physical training; **culturisme** *nm* bodybuilding.
cumin [kymɛ̃] *nm* (*CULIN*) caraway seeds *pl*; cumin.
cumuler [kymyle] *vt* (*emplois, honneurs*) to hold concurrently; (*salaires*) to draw concurrently; (*JUR: droits*) to accumulate.
cupide [kypid] *a* greedy, grasping.
cure [kyr] *nf* (*MÉD*) course of treatment; **n'avoir** ~ **de** to pay no attention to.
curé [kyre] *nm* parish priest.
cure-dent [kyrdã] *nm* toothpick.
cure-pipe [kyrpip] *nm* pipe cleaner.
curer [kyre] *vt* to clean out.
curieux, euse [kyrjø, -øz] *a* (*étrange*) strange, curious; (*indiscret*) curious, inquisitive // *nmpl* (*badauds*) onlookers; **curiosité** *nf* curiosity; (*site*) unusual feature.
curriculum vitae [kyrikylɔmvite] *nm inv* (*abr* C.V.) curriculum vitae (C.V.).
curseur [kyrsœr] *nm* (*INFORM*) cursor.
cuti-réaction [kytireaksjɔ̃] *nf* (*MÉD*) skin-test.
cuve [kyv] *nf* vat; (*à mazout etc*) tank.
cuvée [kyve] *nf* vintage.
cuvette [kyvɛt] *nf* (*récipient*) bowl, basin; (*GÉO*) basin.
C.V. *sigle m* (*AUTO*) *voir* **cheval**; (*COMM*) = curriculum vitae.
cyanure [sjanyr] *nm* cyanide.
cyclable [siklabl(ə)] *a*: **piste** ~ cycle track.
cycle [sikl(ə)] *nm* cycle.
cyclisme [siklism(ə)] *nm* cycling.
cycliste [siklist(ə)] *nm/f* cyclist // *a* cycle *cpd*; **coureur** ~ racing cyclist.
cyclomoteur [siklomotœr] *nm* moped.
cyclone [siklon] *nm* hurricane.
cygne [siɲ] *nm* swan.
cylindre [silɛ̃dr(ə)] *nm* cylinder; **cylindrée** *nf* (*AUTO*) (cubic) capacity.
cymbale [sɛ̃bal] *nf* cymbal.
cynique [sinik] *a* cynical.
cystite [sistit] *nf* cystitis.

D

d' *prép de* **de.**
dactylo [daktilo] *nf* (*aussi:* ~graphe) typist; (*aussi:* ~graphie) typing;

~**graphier** vt to type (out).

dada [dada] nm hobby-horse.

daigner [deɲe] vt to deign.

daim [dɛ̃] nm (fallow) deer inv; (peau) buckskin; (imitation) suede.

dalle [dal] nf paving stone; slab.

daltonien, ne [daltɔnjɛ̃, -jɛn] a colour-blind.

dam [dam] nm: au grand ~ de much to the detriment (ou annoyance) of.

dame [dam] nf lady; (CARTES, ÉCHECS) queen; ~s nfpl (jeu) draughts sg (Brit), checkers (US).

damner [dɑne] vt to damn.

dancing [dɑ̃siŋ] nm dance hall.

Danemark [danmaʀk] nm Denmark.

danger [dɑ̃ʒe] nm danger; **dangereux, euse** a dangerous.

danois, e [danwa, -waz] a Danish // nm/f: D~, e Dane // nm (LING) Danish.

dans [dɑ̃] prép
1 (position) in; (à l'intérieur de) inside; c'est ~ le tiroir/le salon it's in the drawer/lounge; ~ la boîte in ou inside the box; marcher ~ la ville to walk about the town
2 (direction) into; elle a couru ~ le salon she ran into the lounge
3 (provenance) out of, from; je l'ai pris ~ le tiroir/salon I took it out of ou from the drawer/lounge; boire ~ un verre to drink out of ou from a glass
4 (temps) in; ~ 2 mois in 2 months, in 2 months' time
5 (approximation) about; ~ les 20 F about 20 F.

danse [dɑ̃s] nf: la ~ dancing; une ~ a dance; **danser** vi, vt to dance; **danseur, euse** nm/f ballet dancer/ballerina; (au bal etc) dancer; partner.

dard [daʀ] nm sting (organ).

date [dat] nf date; de longue ~ a long-standing; ~ de naissance date of birth; **dater** vt, vi to date; dater de to date from; à dater de (as) from.

datte [dat] nf date; **dattier** nm date palm.

dauphin [dofɛ̃] nm (ZOOL) dolphin.

davantage [davɑ̃taʒ] ad more; (plus longtemps) longer; ~ de more.

de (de + le = du, de + les = des) [də, dy, de] ♦ prép **1** (appartenance) of; le toit de la maison the roof of the house; la voiture d'Élisabeth/de mes parents Elizabeth's/my parents' car
2 (provenance) from; il vient de Londres he comes from London; elle est sortie du cinéma she came out of the cinema
3 (caractérisation, mesure): un mur de brique/bureau d'acajou a brick wall/mahogany desk; un billet de 50 F a 50 franc note; une pièce de 2m de large ou large de 2m a room 2m wide, a 2m-wide room; un bébé de 10 mois a 10-month-old

baby; 12 mois de crédit/travail 12 months' credit/work; augmenter de 10 F to increase by 10 F; de 14 à 18 from 14 to 18
♦ dét **1** (phrases affirmatives) some (souvent omis); du vin, de l'eau, des pommes (some) wine, (some) water, (some) apples; des enfants sont venus some children came; pendant des mois for months
2 (phrases interrogatives et négatives) any; a-t-il du vin? has he got any wine?; il n'a pas de pommes/d'enfants he hasn't (got) any apples/children, he has no apples/children.

dé [de] nm (à jouer) die ou dice (pl dice); (aussi: ~ à coudre) thimble.

déambuler [deɑ̃byle] vi to stroll about.

débâcle [debɑkl(ə)] nf rout.

déballer [debale] vt to unpack.

débandade [debɑ̃dad] nf rout; scattering.

débarbouiller [debaʀbuje] vt to wash; se ~ vi to wash (one's face).

débarcadère [debaʀkadɛʀ] nm wharf.

débardeur [debaʀdœʀ] nm docker, stevedore; (maillot) tank top.

débarquer [debaʀke] vt to unload, land // vi to disembark; (fig) to turn up.

débarras [debaʀa] nm lumber room; junk cupboard; bon ~! good riddance!

débarrasser [debaʀase] vt to clear; ~ qn de (vêtements, paquets) to relieve sb of; se ~ de vt to get rid of.

débat [deba] nm discussion, debate.

débattre [debatʀ(ə)] vt to discuss, debate; se ~ vi to struggle.

débaucher [debofe] vt (licencier) to lay off, dismiss; (entraîner) to lead astray, debauch.

débile [debil] a weak, feeble; (fam: idiot) dim-witted; ~ mental, e nm/f mental defective.

débit [debi] nm (d'un liquide, fleuve) flow; (d'un magasin) turnover (of goods); (élocution) delivery; (bancaire) debit; ~ de boissons drinking establishment; ~ de tabac tobacconist's; **débiter** vt (compte) to debit; (liquide, gaz) to give out; (couper: bois, viande) to cut up; (péj: paroles etc) to churn out; **débiteur, trice** nm/f debtor // a in debit; (compte) debit cpd.

déblayer [debleje] vt to clear.

débloquer [debloke] vt (frein) to release; (prix, crédits) to free.

déboires [debwaʀ] nmpl setbacks.

déboiser [debwaze] vt to deforest.

déboîter [debwate] vt (AUTO) to pull out; se ~ le genou etc to dislocate one's knee etc.

débonnaire [debɔnɛʀ] a easy-going, good-natured.

débordé, e [debɔʀde] a: être ~ (de) (travail, demandes) to be snowed under (with).

déborder [debɔʀde] vi to overflow; *(lait etc)* to boil over; ~ **(de)** qch *(dépasser)* to extend beyond sth.

débouché [debuʃe] nm *(pour vendre)* outlet; *(perspective d'emploi)* opening.

déboucher [debuʃe] vt *(évier, tuyau etc)* to unblock; *(bouteille)* to uncork // vi: ~ **de** to emerge from; ~ **sur** to come out onto; to open out onto.

débourser [debuʀse] vt to pay out.

debout [dəbu] ad: être ~ *(personne)* to be standing, stand; *(: levé, éveillé)* to be up; *(chose)* to be upright; être encore ~ *(fig: en état)* to be still going; se mettre ~ to stand up; se tenir ~ to stand; ~! stand up!; *(du lit)* get up!; cette histoire ne tient pas ~ this story doesn't hold water.

déboutonner [debutɔne] vt to undo, unbutton.

débraillé, e [debʀaje] a slovenly, untidy.

débrancher [debʀɑ̃ʃe] vt to disconnect; *(appareil électrique)* to unplug.

débrayage [debʀɛjaʒ] nm *(AUTO)* clutch.

débrayer [debʀeje] vi *(AUTO)* to declutch; *(cesser le travail)* to stop work.

débris [debʀi] nm *(fragment)* fragment // nmpl rubbish sg; debris sg.

débrouillard, e [debʀujaʀ, -aʀd(ə)] a smart, resourceful.

débrouiller [debʀuje] vt to disentangle, untangle; se ~ vi to manage.

débusquer [debyske] vt to drive out (from cover).

début [deby] nm beginning, start; ~s beginnings; début sg.

débutant, e [debytɑ̃, -ɑ̃t] nm/f beginner, novice.

débuter [debyte] vi to begin, start; *(faire ses débuts)* to start out.

deçà [dəsa]: en ~ de prép this side of.

décacheter [dekaʃte] vt to unseal.

décadence [dekadɑ̃s] nf decadence; decline.

décaféiné, e [dekafeine] a decaffeinated.

décalage [dekalaʒ] nm gap; discrepancy; ~ **horaire** time difference (between time zones); time-lag.

décaler [dekale] vt *(dans le temps: avancer)* to bring forward; *(: retarder)* to put back; *(changer de position)* to shift forward ou back.

décalquer [dekalke] vt to trace; *(par pression)* to transfer.

décamper [dekɑ̃pe] vi to clear out ou off.

décanter [dekɑ̃te] vt to allow to settle (and decant).

décaper [dekape] vt to strip; *(avec abrasif)* to scour; *(avec papier de verre)* to sand.

décapiter [dekapite] vt to behead; *(par accident)* to decapitate.

décapotable [dekapɔtabl(ə)] a convertible.

décapsuler [dekapsyle] vt to take the cap ou top off; **décapsuleur** nm bottle-opener.

décédé, e [desede] a deceased.

décéder [desede] vi to die.

déceler [desle] vt to discover, detect; to indicate, reveal.

décembre [desɑ̃bʀ(ə)] nm December.

décemment [desamɑ̃] ad decently.

décennie [deseni] nf decade.

décent, e [desɑ̃, -ɑ̃t] a decent.

déception [desɛpsjɔ̃] nf disappointment.

décerner [desɛʀne] vt to award.

décès [desɛ] nm death, decease.

décevoir [desvwaʀ] vt to disappoint.

déchaîner [deʃene] vt to unleash, arouse; se ~ to be unleashed.

déchanter [deʃɑ̃te] vi to become disillusioned.

décharge [deʃaʀʒ(ə)] nf *(dépôt d'ordures)* rubbish tip ou dump; *(électrique)* electrical discharge; à la ~ de in defence of.

décharger [deʃaʀʒe] vt *(marchandise, véhicule)* to unload; *(ÉLEC, faire feu)* to discharge; ~ qn de *(responsabilité)* to release sb from.

décharné, e [deʃaʀne] a emaciated.

déchausser [deʃose] vt *(skis)* to take off; se ~ vi to take off one's shoes; *(dent)* to come ou work loose.

déchéance [deʃeɑ̃s] nf degeneration; decay, decline; fall.

déchet [deʃɛ] nm *(de bois, tissu etc)* scrap; *(perte: gén COMM)* wastage, waste; ~s nmpl *(ordures)* refuse sg, rubbish sg.

déchiffrer [deʃifʀe] vt to decipher.

déchiqueter [deʃikte] vt to tear ou pull to pieces.

déchirement [deʃiʀmɑ̃] nm *(chagrin)* wrench, heartbreak; *(gén pl: conflit)* rift, split.

déchirer [deʃiʀe] vt to tear; *(en morceaux)* to tear up; *(pour ouvrir)* to tear off; *(arracher)* to tear out; *(fig)* to rack; to tear (apart); se ~ vi to tear, rip; se ~ un muscle to tear a muscle.

déchirure [deʃiʀyʀ] nf *(accroc)* tear, rip; ~ **musculaire** torn muscle.

déchoir [deʃwaʀ] vi *(personne)* to lower o.s., demean o.s.

déchu, e [deʃy] a fallen; deposed.

décidé, e [deside] a *(personne, air)* determined; **c'est ~** it's decided.

décidément [desidemɑ̃] ad undoubtedly; really.

décider [deside] vt: ~ qch to decide on sth; ~ de faire/que to decide to do/that; ~ qn (à faire qch) to persuade sb (to do sth); ~ de qch to decide upon sth; *(suj:*

chose) to determine sth; **se ~ (à faire)** to decide (to do), make up one's mind (to do); **se ~ pour** to decide on *ou* in favour of.

décilitre [desilitʀ(ə)] *nm* decilitre.

décimal, e, aux [desimal, -o] *a, nf* decimal.

décimètre [desimɛtʀ(ə)] *nm* decimetre; **double ~** (20 cm) ruler.

décisif, ive [desizif, -iv] *a* decisive.

décision [desizjɔ̃] *nf* decision; (*fermeté*) decisiveness, decision.

déclaration [deklaʀasjɔ̃] *nf* declaration; registration; (*discours*: POL *etc*) statement; **~ (d'impôts)** ≈ tax return; **~ (de sinistre)** (insurance) claim.

déclarer [deklaʀe] *vt* to declare; (*décès, naissance*) to register; **se ~** *vi* (*feu, maladie*) to break out.

déclasser [deklɑse] *vt* to relegate; to downgrade; to lower in status.

déclencher [deklɑ̃ʃe] *vt* (*mécanisme etc*) to release; (*sonnerie*) to set off, activate; (*attaque, grève*) to launch; (*provoquer*) to trigger off; **se ~** *vi* to release itself; to go off.

déclic [deklik] *nm* trigger mechanism; (*bruit*) click.

décliner [dekline] *vi* to decline // *vt* (*invitation*) to decline; (*responsabilité*) to refuse to accept; (*nom, adresse*) to state.

déclivité [deklivite] *nf* slope, incline.

décocher [dekɔʃe] *vt* to throw; to shoot.

décoiffer [dekwafe] *vt*: **~ qn** to mess up sb's hair; to take sb's hat off; **se ~** *vi* to take off one's hat.

déçois *etc vb voir* **décevoir**.

décollage [dekɔlaʒ] *nm* (AVIAT) takeoff.

décoller [dekɔle] *vt* to unstick // *vi* (*avion*) to take off; **se ~** *vi* to come unstuck.

décolleté, e [dekɔlte] *a* low-cut; wearing a low-cut dress // *nm* low neck(line); (*bare*) neck and shoulders; (*plongeant*) cleavage.

décolorer [dekɔlɔʀe] *vt* (*tissu*) to fade; (*cheveux*) to bleach, lighten; **se ~** *vi* to fade.

décombres [dekɔ̃bʀ(ə)] *nmpl* rubble *sg*, debris *sg*.

décommander [dekɔmɑ̃de] *vt* to cancel; (*invités*) to put off; **se ~** *vi* to cancel one's appointment *etc*, cry off.

décomposé, e [dekɔ̃poze] *a* (*pourri*) decomposed; (*visage*) haggard, distorted.

décompte [dekɔ̃t] *nm* deduction; (*facture*) detailed account.

déconcerter [dekɔ̃sɛʀte] *vt* to disconcert, confound.

déconfit, e [dekɔ̃fi, -it] *a* crestfallen.

déconfiture [dekɔ̃fityʀ] *nf* failure, defeat; collapse, ruin.

décongeler [dekɔ̃ʒle] *vt* to thaw.

déconner [dekɔne] *vi* (*fam*) to talk rubbish.

déconseiller [dekɔ̃seje] *vt*: **~ qch (à qn)** to advise (sb) against sth.

déconsidérer [dekɔ̃sideʀe] *vt* to discredit.

décontracter [dekɔ̃tʀakte] *vt, se ~ vi* to relax.

déconvenue [dekɔ̃vny] *nf* disappointment.

décor [dekɔʀ] *nm* décor; (*paysage*) scenery; **~s** *nmpl* (THÉÂTRE) scenery *sg*, décor *sg*; (CINÉMA) set *sg*.

décorateur [dekɔʀatœʀ] *nm* (interior) decorator; (CINÉMA) set designer.

décoration [dekɔʀasjɔ̃] *nf* decoration.

décorer [dekɔʀe] *vt* to decorate.

décortiquer [dekɔʀtike] *vt* to shell; (*riz*) to hull; (*fig*) to dissect.

découcher [dekuʃe] *vi* to spend the night away from home.

découdre [dekudʀ(ə)] *vt* to unpick; **se ~** *vi* to come unstitched; **en ~** (*fig*) to fight, do battle.

découler [dekule] *vi*: **~ de** to ensue *ou* follow from.

découper [dekupe] *vt* (*papier, tissu etc*) to cut up; (*volaille, viande*) to carve; (*détacher: manche, article*) to cut out; **se ~ sur** (*ciel, fond*) to stand out against.

décourager [dekuʀaʒe] *vt* to discourage; **se ~** *vi* to lose heart, become discouraged.

décousu, e [dekuzy] *a* unstitched; (*fig*) disjointed, disconnected.

découvert, e [dekuvɛʀ, -ɛʀt(ə)] *a* (*tête*) bare, uncovered; (*lieu*) open, exposed // *nm* (*bancaire*) overdraft // *nf* discovery.

découvrir [dekuvʀiʀ] *vt* to discover; (*apercevoir*) to see; (*enlever ce qui couvre ou protège*) to uncover; (*montrer, dévoiler*) to reveal; **se ~** *vi* to take off one's hat; to take something off; (*au lit*) to uncover o.s.; (*ciel*) to clear.

décret [dekʀɛ] *nm* decree; **décréter** *vt* to decree; to order; to declare.

décrié, e [dekʀije] *a* disparaged.

décrire [dekʀiʀ] *vt* to describe.

décrocher [dekʀɔʃe] *vt* (*dépendre*) to take down; (*téléphone*) to take off the hook; (: *pour répondre*): **~ (le téléphone)** to lift the receiver; (*fig: contrat etc*) to get, land // *vi* to drop out; to switch off.

décroître [dekʀwatʀ(ə)] *vi* to decrease, decline.

décrypter [dekʀipte] *vt* to decipher.

déçu, e [desy] *pp de* **décevoir**.

décupler [dekyple] *vt, vi* to increase tenfold.

dédaigner [dedeɲe] *vt* to despise, scorn; (*négliger*) to disregard, spurn.

dédain [dedɛ̃] *nm* scorn, disdain.

dédale [dedal] *nm* maze.

dedans [dədɑ̃] *ad* inside; (*pas en plein air*) indoors, inside // *nm* inside; **au ~** on the inside; inside; **en ~** (*vers l'intérieur*) inwards; *voir aussi* **là**.

dédicacer [dedikase] *vt:* **~ (à qn)** to sign (for sb), autograph (for sb).

dédier [dedje] *vt* to dedicate.

dédire [dediʀ]: **se ~** *vi* to go back on one's word; to retract, recant.

dédommager [dedɔmaʒe] *vt:* **~ qn (de)** to compensate sb (for); (*fig*) to repay sb (for).

dédouaner [dedwane] *vt* to clear through customs.

dédoubler [deduble] *vt* (*classe, effectifs*) to split (into two); **~ les trains** to run additional trains.

déduire [dedɥiʀ] *vt:* **~ qch (de)** (*ôter*) to deduct sth (from); (*conclure*) to deduce *ou* infer sth (from).

déesse [deɛs] *nf* goddess.

défaillance [defajɑ̃s] *nf* (*syncope*) blackout; (*fatigue*) (sudden) weakness *q*; (*technique*) fault, failure; (*morale etc*) weakness; **~ cardiaque** heart failure.

défaillir [defajiʀ] *vi* to faint; to feel faint; (*mémoire etc*) to fail.

défaire [defɛʀ] *vt* (*installation*) to take down, dismantle; (*paquet etc, nœud, vêtement*) to undo; **se ~** *vi* to come undone; **se ~ de** *vt* (*se débarrasser de*) to get rid of; (*se séparer de*) to part with.

défait, e [defɛ, -ɛt] *a* (*visage*) haggard, ravaged // *nf* defeat.

défalquer [defalke] *vt* to deduct.

défaut [defo] *nm* (*moral*) fault, failing, defect; (*d'étoffe, métal*) fault, flaw, defect; (*manque, carence*): **~ de** lack of; shortage of; **en ~** at fault; in the wrong; **faire ~** (*manquer*) to be lacking; **à ~** *ad* failing that; **à ~ de** for lack *ou* want of; **par ~** (*JUR*) in his (*ou* her *etc*) absence.

défavoriser [defavɔʀize] *vt* to put at a disadvantage.

défection [defɛksjɔ̃] *nf* defection, failure to give support *ou* assistance; failure to appear; **faire ~** (*d'un parti etc*) to withdraw one's support, leave.

défectueux, euse [defɛktɥø, -øz] *a* faulty, defective.

défendre [defɑ̃dʀ(ə)] *vt* to defend; (*interdire*) to forbid; **~ à qn qch/de faire** to forbid sb sth/to do; **se ~** *vi* to defend o.s.; **il se défend** (*fig*) he can hold his own; **se ~ de/contre** (*se protéger*) to protect o.s. from/against; **se ~ de** (*se garder de*) to refrain from; (*nier*): **se ~ de vouloir** to deny wanting.

défense [defɑ̃s] *nf* defence; (*d'éléphant etc*) tusk; **'~ de fumer/cracher'** 'no smoking/spitting'.

déférer [defeʀe] *vt* (*JUR*) to refer; **~ à** *vt* (*requête, décision*) to defer to.

déferler [defɛʀle] *vi* (*vagues*) to break;

(*fig*) to surge.

défi [defi] *nm* (*provocation*) challenge; (*bravade*) defiance.

défiance [defjɑ̃s] *nf* mistrust, distrust.

déficit [defisit] *nm* (*COMM*) deficit.

défier [defje] *vt* (*provoquer*) to challenge; (*fig*) to defy, brave; **se ~ de** *vi* (*se méfier de*) to distrust.

défigurer [defigyʀe] *vt* to disfigure.

défilé [defile] *nm* (*GÉO*) (narrow) gorge *ou* pass; (*soldats*) parade; (*manifestants*) procession, march.

défiler [defile] *vi* (*troupes*) to march past; (*sportifs*) to parade; (*manifestants*) to march; (*visiteurs*) to pour, stream; **se ~** *vi* (*se dérober*) to slip away, sneak off.

définir [definiʀ] *vt* to define.

définitif, ive [definitif, -iv] *a* (*final*) final, definitive; (*pour longtemps*) permanent, definitive; (*sans appel*) final, definite // *nf:* **en définitive** eventually; (*somme toute*) when all is said and done.

définitivement [definitivmɑ̃] *ad* definitively; permanently; definitely.

déflagration [deflagʀasjɔ̃] *nf* explosion.

défoncer [defɔ̃se] *vt* (*caisse*) to stave in; (*porte*) to smash in *ou* down; (*lit, fauteuil*) to burst (the springs of); (*terrain, route*) to rip *ou* plough up.

déformation [defɔʀmasjɔ̃] *nf:* **~ professionnelle** conditioning by one's job.

déformer [defɔʀme] *vt* to put out of shape; (*corps*) to deform; (*pensée, fait*) to distort; **se ~** *vi* to lose its shape.

défouler [defule]: **se ~** *vi* to unwind, let off steam.

défraîchir [defʀeʃiʀ]: **se ~** *vi* to fade; to become worn.

défrayer [defʀeje] *vt:* **~ qn** to pay sb's expenses; **~ la chronique** to be in the news.

défricher [defʀiʃe] *vt* to clear (for cultivation).

défroquer [defʀɔke] *vi* (*aussi:* **se ~**) to give up the cloth.

défunt, e [defœ̃, -œ̃t] *a:* **son ~ père** his late father // *nm/f* deceased.

dégagé, e [degaʒe] *a* clear; (*ton, air*) casual, jaunty.

dégagement [degaʒmɑ̃] *nm:* **voie de ~** slip road; **itinéraire de ~** alternative route (*to relieve traffic congestion*).

dégager [degaʒe] *vt* (*exhaler*) to give off; (*délivrer*) to free, extricate; (*désencombrer*) to clear; (*isoler: idée, aspect*) to bring out; **se ~** *vi* (*odeur*) to be given off; (*passage, ciel*) to clear.

dégainer [degene] *vt* to draw.

dégarnir [degaʀniʀ] *vt* (*vider*) to empty, clear; **se ~** *vi* (*tempes, crâne*) to go bald.

dégâts [dega] *nmpl* damage *sg*.

dégel [deʒɛl] *nm* thaw.

dégeler [deʒle] *vt* to thaw (out); *(fig)* to unfreeze // *vi* to thaw (out).

dégénérer [deʒenere] *vi* to degenerate; *(empirer)* to go from bad to worse.

dégingandé, e [deʒɛ̃gɑ̃de] *a* gangling.

dégivrer [deʒivre] *vt* (*frigo*) to defrost; *(vitres)* to de-ice.

déglutir [deglytiʀ] *vt*, *vi* to swallow.

dégonflé, e [degɔ̃fle] *a* (*pneu*) flat.

dégonfler [degɔ̃fle] *vt* (*pneu, ballon*) to let down, deflate; se ~ *vi* (*fam*) to chicken out.

dégouliner [deguline] *vi* to trickle, drip.

dégourdi, e [degurdi] *a* smart, resourceful.

dégourdir [degurdiʀ] *vt*: se ~ (les jambes) to stretch one's legs *(fig)*.

dégoût [degu] *nm* disgust, distaste.

dégoûtant, e [degutɑ̃, -ɑ̃t] *a* disgusting.

dégoûté, e [degute] *a* disgusted; ~ de sick of.

dégoûter [degute] *vt* to disgust; ~ qn de qch to put sb off sth.

dégoutter [degute] *vi* to drip.

dégradé [degrade] *nm* (*PEINTURE*) gradation.

dégrader [degrade] *vt* (*MIL: officier*) to degrade; *(abîmer)* to damage, deface; se ~ *vi* (*relations, situation*) to deteriorate.

dégrafer [degrafe] *vt* to unclip, unhook.

degré [dəgre] *nm* degree; *(d'escalier)* step; alcool à 90 ~s surgical spirit.

dégressif, ive [degresif, -iv] *a* on a decreasing scale.

dégrèvement [degrɛvmɑ̃] *nm* tax relief.

dégringoler [degrɛ̃gɔle] *vi* to tumble (down).

dégrossir [degrosiʀ] *vt* (*fig*) to work out roughly; to knock the rough edges off.

déguenillé, e [dɛgnije] *a* ragged, tattered.

déguerpir [degɛrpiʀ] *vi* to clear off.

dégueulasse [degølas] *a* (*fam*) disgusting.

déguisement [degizmɑ̃] *nm* disguise.

déguiser [degize] *vt* to disguise; se ~ *vi* (*se costumer*) to dress up; *(pour tromper)* to disguise o.s.

déguster [degyste] *vt* (*vins*) to taste; *(fromages etc)* to sample; *(savourer)* to enjoy, savour.

dehors [dəɔʀ] *ad* outside; *(en plein air)* outdoors // *nm* outside // *nmpl* (*apparences*) appearances; mettre *ou* jeter ~ *(expulser)* to throw out; au ~ outside; outwardly; au ~ de outside; en ~ (*vers l'extérieur*) outside; outwards; en ~ de (*hormis*) apart from.

déjà [deʒa] *ad* already; *(auparavant)* before, already.

déjeuner [deʒœne] *vi* to (have) lunch; *(le matin)* to have breakfast // *nm* lunch; breakfast.

déjouer [deʒwe] *vt* to elude; to foil.

delà [dəla] *ad*: par ~, en ~ (de), au ~ (de) beyond.

délabrer [delabre]: se ~ *vi* to fall into decay, become dilapidated.

délacer [delase] *vt* to unlace.

délai [dele] *nm* (*attente*) waiting period; *(sursis)* extension (of time); *(temps accordé)* time limit; à bref ~ shortly, very soon; at short notice; dans les ~s within the time limit.

délaisser [delese] *vt* to abandon, desert.

délasser [delase] *vt* (*reposer*) to relax; *(divertir)* to divert, entertain; se ~ *vi* to relax.

délateur, trice [delatœʀ, -tʀis] *nm/f* informer.

délavé, e [delave] *a* faded.

délayer [deleje] *vt* (*CULIN*) to mix (with water *etc*); *(peinture)* to thin down.

delco [dɛlko] *nm* (*AUTO*) distributor.

délecter [delɛkte]: se ~ *vi*: se ~ de to revel *ou* delight in.

délégué, e [delege] *nm/f* delegate; representative.

déléguer [delege] *vt* to delegate.

délibéré, e [delibere] *a* (*conscient*) deliberate; *(déterminé)* determined.

délibérer [delibere] *vi* to deliberate.

délicat, e [delika, -at] *a* delicate; *(plein de tact)* tactful; *(attentionné)* thoughtful; *(exigeant)* fussy, particular; procédés peu ~s unscrupulous methods; **délicatement** *ad* delicately; *(avec douceur)* gently.

délice [delis] *nm* delight.

délicieux, euse [delisjø, -jøz] *a* (*au goût*) delicious; *(sensation, impression)* delightful.

délier [delje] *vt* to untie; ~ qn de *(serment etc)* to release sb from.

délimiter [delimite] *vt* to delimit, demarcate; to determine; to define.

délinquance [delɛ̃kɑ̃s] *nf* criminality.

délinquant, e [delɛ̃kɑ̃, -ɑ̃t] *a*, *nm/f* delinquent.

délirer [delire] *vi* to be delirious; *(fig)* to be raving, be going wild.

délit [deli] *nm* (criminal) offence.

délivrer [delivre] *vt* (*prisonnier*) to (set) free, release; *(passeport, certificat)* to issue; ~ qn de (*ennemis*) to deliver *ou* free sb from; *(fig)* to relieve sb of; to rid sb of.

déloger [delɔʒe] *vt* (*locataire*) to turn out; *(objet coincé, ennemi)* to dislodge.

deltaplane [dɛltaplan] *nm* hang-glider.

déluge [delyʒ] *nm* (*biblique*) Flood.

déluré, e [delyre] *a* smart, resourceful; *(péj)* forward, pert.

demain [dəmɛ̃] *ad* tomorrow.

demande [dəmɑ̃d] *nf* (*requête*) request; *(revendication)* demand; (*ADMIN, formulaire*) application; (*ÉCON*): la ~ de-

mand; '~s d'emploi' 'situations wanted';
~ **en mariage** (marriage) proposal; ~ **de**
poste job application.
demandé, e [dəmɑ̃de] a (article etc):
très ~ (very) much in demand.
demander [dəmɑ̃de] vt to ask for;
(date, heure etc) to ask; (nécessiter) to
require, demand; ~ **qch à qn** to ask sb
for sth; to ask sb sth; ~ **à qn de faire** to
ask sb to do; **se ~ si/pourquoi** etc to wonder if/why etc; (sens purement réfléchi)
to ask o.s. if/why etc; **on vous demande**
au téléphone you're wanted on the
phone.
demandeur, euse [dəmɑ̃dœʀ, -øz]
nm/f: ~ **d'emploi** job-seeker; (job) applicant.
démangeaison [demɑ̃ʒɛzɔ̃] nf itching.
démanger [demɑ̃ʒe] vi to itch.
démanteler [demɑ̃tle] vt to break up;
to demolish.
démaquillant [demakijɑ̃] nm make-up
remover.
démaquiller [demakije] vt: se ~ to remove one's make-up.
démarche [demaʀʃ(ə)] nf (allure) gait,
walk; (intervention) step; approach;
(fig: intellectuelle) thought processes pl;
approach; **faire des ~s auprès de qn** to
approach sb.
démarcheur, euse [demaʀʃœʀ, -øz]
nm/f (COMM) door-to-door salesman/
woman.
démarquer [demaʀke] vt (prix) to
mark down; (joueur) to stop marking.
démarrage [demaʀaʒ] nm start.
démarrer [demaʀe] vi (conducteur) to
start (up); (véhicule) to move off; (travaux) to get moving; **démarreur** nm
(AUTO) starter.
démêler [demele] vt to untangle.
démêlés [demele] nmpl problems.
déménagement [demenaʒmɑ̃] nm
move, removal; **camion de ~** removal
van.
déménager [demenaʒe] vt (meubles) to
(re)move // vi to move (house);
déménageur nm removal man; (entrepreneur) furniture remover.
démener [demne]: se ~ vi to thrash
about; (fig) to exert o.s.
dément, e [demɑ̃, -ɑ̃t] a (fou) mad,
crazy; (fam) brilliant, fantastic.
démentiel, le [demɑ̃sjɛl] a insane.
démentir [demɑ̃tiʀ] vt to refute; ~ **que**
to deny that.
démerder [demɛʀde] (fam): se ~ vi to
sort things out for o.s.
démesuré, e [demzyʀe] a immoder-
ate.
démettre [demɛtʀ(ə)] vt: ~ **qn de**
(fonction, poste) to dismiss sb from; **se**
~ **(de ses fonctions)** to resign (from)
one's duties; **se ~ l'épaule** etc to dislocate one's shoulder etc.

demeurant [dəmœʀɑ̃]: au ~ ad for all
that.
demeure [dəmœʀ] nf residence; **mettre**
qn en ~ de faire to enjoin ou order sb to
do; à ~ ad permanently.
demeurer [dəmœʀe] vi (habiter) to
live; (séjourner) to stay; (rester) to remain.
demi, e [dəmi] a: et ~: **trois heures/**
bouteilles et ~es three and a half hours/
bottles, three hours/bottles and a half; **il**
est 2 heures/midi et ~e it's half past 2/12
// nm (bière) ≈ half-pint (.25 litre); à ~
ad half-; **à la ~e** (heure) on the half-
hour.
demi... [dəmi] préfixe half-, semi...,
demi-; **~-cercle** nm semicircle; **en ~-**
cercle a semicircular // ad in a half circle; **~-douzaine** nf half-dozen, half a
dozen; **~-finale** nf semifinal; **~-frère**
nm half-brother; **~-heure** nf half-hour,
half an hour; **~-jour** nm half-light; **~-**
journée nf half-day, half a day; **~-litre**
nm half-litre, half a litre; **~-livre** nf
half-pound, half a pound; **~-mot**: à ~-
mot ad without having to spell things
out; **~-pension** nf (à l'hôtel) half-
board; **~-place** nf half-fare.
démis, e [demi, -iz] a (épaule etc) dislocated.
demi-saison [dəmisɛzɔ̃] nf: **vêtements**
de ~ spring ou autumn clothing.
demi-sel [dəmisɛl] a inv (beurre, fromage) slightly salted.
demi-sœur [dəmisœʀ] nf half-sister.
démission [demisjɔ̃] nf resignation;
donner sa ~ to give ou hand in one's notice; **démissionner** vi (de son poste) to
resign.
demi-tarif [dəmitaʀif] nm half-price;
(TRANSPORTS) half-fare.
demi-tour [dəmituʀ] nm about-turn;
faire ~ to turn (and go) back; (AUTO) to
do a U-turn.
démocratie [demɔkʀasi] nf democracy.
démocratique [demɔkʀatik] a democratic.
démodé, e [demɔde] a old-fashioned.
démographique [demɔgʀafik] a demo-
graphic, population cpd.
demoiselle [dəmwazɛl] nf (jeune fille)
young lady; (célibataire) single lady,
maiden lady; ~ **d'honneur** bridesmaid.
démolir [demɔliʀ] vt to demolish.
démon [demɔ̃] nm (enfant turbulent)
devil, demon; **le D~** the Devil.
démonstration [demɔ̃stʀasjɔ̃] nf demonstration; (aérienne, navale) display.
démonté, e [demɔ̃te] a (fig) raging,
wild.
démonter [demɔ̃te] vt (machine etc) to
take down, dismantle; **se ~** vi (personne) to lose countenance.
démontrer [demɔ̃tʀe] vt to demon-

strate.

démordre [demɔʀdʀ(ə)] *vi*: ne pas ~ de to refuse to give up, stick to.

démouler [demule] *vt* (*gâteau*) to turn out.

démuni, e [demyni] *a* (*sans argent*) impoverished.

démunir [demyniʀ] *vt*: ~ qn de to deprive sb of; se ~ de to part with, give up.

dénatalité [denatalite] *nf* fall in the birth rate.

dénaturer [denatyʀe] *vt* (*goût*) to alter; (*pensée, fait*) to distort.

dénégations [denegɑsjɔ̃] *nfpl* denials.

déniaiser [denjeze] *vt*: ~ qn to teach sb about life.

dénicher [denife] *vt* to unearth; to track *ou* hunt down.

dénier [denje] *vt* to deny.

dénigrer [denigʀe] *vt* to denigrate, run down.

dénivellation [denivɛlɑsjɔ̃] *nf*, **dénivellement** [denivɛlmɑ̃] *nm* ramp; dip; difference in level.

dénombrer [denɔ̃bʀe] *vt* (*compter*) to count; (*énumérer*) to enumerate, list.

dénomination [denɔminɑsjɔ̃] *nf* designation, appellation.

dénommer [denɔme] *vt* to name.

dénoncer [denɔ̃se] *vt* to denounce; se ~ *vi* to give o.s. up, come forward.

dénouement [denumɑ̃] *nm* outcome.

dénouer [denwe] *vt* to unknot, undo.

dénoyauter [denwajote] *vt* to stone.

denrée [dɑ̃ʀe] *nf*: ~s (alimentaires) foodstuffs.

dense [dɑ̃s] *a* dense.

densité [dɑ̃site] *nf* density.

dent [dɑ̃] *nf* tooth (*pl* teeth); en ~s de scie serrated; jagged; ~ de lait/sagesse milk/wisdom tooth; **dentaire** *a* dental.

dentelé, e [dɑ̃tle] *a* jagged, indented.

dentelle [dɑ̃tɛl] *nf* lace *q*.

dentier [dɑ̃tje] *nm* denture.

dentifrice [dɑ̃tifʀis] *nm* toothpaste.

dentiste [dɑ̃tist(ə)] *nm/f* dentist.

dénuder [denyde] *vt* to bare.

dénué, e [denɥe] *a*: ~ de devoid of; lacking in.

dénuement [denymɑ̃] *nm* destitution.

déodorant [deɔdɔʀɑ̃] *nm* deodorant.

dépannage [depanaʒ] *nm*: service de ~ (*AUTO*) breakdown service.

dépanner [depane] *vt* (*voiture, télévision*) to fix, repair; (*fig*) to bail out, help out; **dépanneuse** *nf* breakdown lorry (*Brit*), tow truck (*US*).

dépareillé, e [depaʀeje] *a* (*collection, service*) incomplete; (*objet*) odd.

déparer [depaʀe] *vt* to spoil, mar.

départ [depaʀ] *nm* leaving *q*, departure; (*SPORT*) start; (*sur un horaire*) departure; au ~ at the start; à son ~ when he left.

départager [depaʀtaʒe] *vt* to decide between.

département [depaʀtəmɑ̃] *nm* department.

départir [depaʀtiʀ]: se ~ de *vt* to abandon, depart from.

dépassé, e [depase] *a* superseded, outmoded; (*affolé*) panic-stricken.

dépasser [depase] *vt* (*véhicule, concurrent*) to overtake; (*endroit*) to pass, go past; (*somme, limite*) to exceed; (*fig: en beauté etc*) to surpass, outshine; (*être en saillie sur*) to jut out above (*ou* in front of) // *vi* (*jupon*) to show.

dépaysé, e [depeize] *a* disoriented.

dépecer [depəse] *vt* to joint, cut up.

dépêche [depɛʃ] *nf* dispatch.

dépêcher [depeʃe] *vt* to dispatch; se ~ *vi* to hurry.

dépeindre [depɛ̃dʀ(ə)] *vt* to depict.

dépendre [depɑ̃dʀ(ə)]: ~ de *vt* to depend on; (*financièrement etc*) to be dependent on.

dépens [depɑ̃] *nmpl*: aux ~ de at the expense of.

dépense [depɑ̃s] *nf* spending *q*, expense, expenditure *q*; (*fig*) consumption; expenditure.

dépenser [depɑ̃se] *vt* to spend; (*gaz, eau*) to use; (*fig*) to expend, use up; se ~ *vi* (*se fatiguer*) to exert o.s.

dépensier, ière [depɑ̃sje, -jɛʀ] *a*: il est ~ he's a spendthrift.

déperdition [depɛʀdisjɔ̃] *nf* loss.

dépérir [depeʀiʀ] *vi* to waste away; to wither.

dépêtrer [depetʀe] *vt*: se ~ de to extricate o.s. from.

dépeupler [depœple] *vt* to depopulate; se ~ *vi* to be depopulated.

déphasé, e [defaze] *a* (*fig*) out of touch.

dépilatoire [depilatwaʀ] *a* depilatory, hair removing.

dépister [depiste] *vt* to detect; (*voleur*) to track down; (*poursuivants*) to throw off the scent.

dépit [depi] *nm* vexation, frustration; en ~ de *prép* in spite of; en ~ du bon sens contrary to all good sense; **dépité, e** *a* vexed, frustrated.

déplacé, e [deplase] *a* (*propos*) out of place, uncalled-for.

déplacement [deplasmɑ̃] *nm* (*voyage*) trip, travelling *q*.

déplacer [deplase] *vt* (*table, voiture*) to move, shift; (*employé*) to transfer, move; se ~ *vi* to move; (*voyager*) to travel // *vt* (*vertèbre etc*) to displace.

déplaire [deplɛʀ] *vi*: ceci me déplaît I don't like this, I dislike this; **déplaisant, e** *a* disagreeable.

dépliant [deplijɑ̃] *nm* leaflet.

déplier [deplije] *vt* to unfold.

déployer [deplwaje] *vt* to open out, spread; to deploy; to display, exhibit.

dépoli, e [depɔli] *a*: **verre ~** frosted glass.

déporter [depɔrte] *vt* (*POL*) to deport; (*dévier*) to carry off course.

déposer [depoze] *vt* (*gén: mettre, poser*) to lay *ou* put down; (*à la banque, à la consigne*) to deposit; (*passager*) to drop (off), set down; (*roi*) to depose; (*ADMIN: faire enregistrer*) to file; to register; (*JUR*): ~ **(contre)** to testify *ou* give evidence (against); **se ~** *vi* to settle; **dépositaire** *nm/f* (*COMM*) agent.

dépôt [depo] *nm* (*à la banque, sédiment*) deposit; (*entrepôt, réserve*) warehouse, store; (*gare*) depot; (*prison*) cells *pl*.

dépotoir [depɔtwar] *nm* dumping ground, rubbish dump.

dépouille [depuj] *nf* (*d'animal*) skin, hide; (*humaine*): ~ **(mortelle)** mortal remains *pl*.

dépouillé, e [depuje] *a* (*fig*) bare, bald.

dépouiller [depuje] *vt* (*animal*) to skin; (*spolier*) to deprive of one's possessions; (*documents*) to go through, peruse; ~ **qn/qch de** to strip sb/sth of; ~ **le scrutin** to count the votes.

dépourvu, e [depurvy] *a*: ~ **de** lacking in, without; **au ~** *ad* unprepared.

déprécier [depresje] *vt*, **se ~** *vi* to depreciate.

déprédations [depredasjɔ̃] *nfpl* damage *sg*.

dépression [depresjɔ̃] *nf* depression; ~ **(nerveuse)** (nervous) breakdown.

déprimer [deprime] *vt* to depress.

depuis [dəpɥi] ♦ *prép* **1** (*point de départ dans le temps*) since; **il habite Paris ~ 1983/l'an dernier** he has been living in Paris since 1983/last year; ~ **quand le connaissez-vous?** how long have you known him?
2 (*temps écoulé*) for; **il habite Paris ~ 5 ans** he has been living in Paris for 5 years; **je le connais ~ 3 ans** I've known him for 3 years
3 (*lieu*): **il a plu ~ Metz** it's been raining since Metz; **elle a téléphoné ~ Valence** she rang from Valence
4 (*quantité, rang*) from; ~ **les plus petits jusqu'aux plus grands** from the youngest to the oldest
♦ *ad* (*temps*) since (then); **je ne lui ai pas parlé ~** I haven't spoken to him since (then)

depuis que *cj* (ever) since; ~ **qu'il m'a dit ça** (ever) since he said that to me.

député, e [depyte] *nm/f* (*POL*) ≈ Member of Parliament (*Brit*), ≈ Member of Congress (*US*).

députer [depyte] *vt* to delegate.

déraciner [derasine] *vt* to uproot.

dérailler [deraje] *vi* (*train*) to be derailed; **faire ~** to derail.

déraisonner [derɛzɔne] *vi* to talk non-sense, rave.

dérangement [derɑ̃ʒmɑ̃] *nm* (*gêne*) trouble; (*gastrique etc*) disorder; (*mécanique*) breakdown; **en ~** (*téléphone*) out of order.

déranger [derɑ̃ʒe] *vt* (*personne*) to trouble, bother; to disturb; (*projets*) to disrupt, upset; (*objets, vêtements*) to disarrange; **se ~** *vi* to put o.s. out; to (take the trouble to) come *ou* go out; **est-ce que cela vous dérange si...?** do you mind if...?

déraper [derape] *vi* (*voiture*) to skid; (*personne, semelles, couteau*) to slip.

déréglé, e [deregle] *a* (*mœurs*) dissolute.

dérégler [deregle] *vt* (*mécanisme*) to put out of order; (*estomac*) to upset.

dérider [deride] *vt*, **se ~** *vi* to brighten up.

dérision [derizjɔ̃] *nf*: **tourner en ~** to deride.

dérivatif [derivatif] *nm* distraction.

dérive [deriv] *nf* (*de dériveur*) centreboard; **aller à la ~** (*NAVIG, fig*) to drift.

dérivé, e [derive] *nm* (*TECH*) by-product // *nf* (*MATH*) derivative.

dériver [derive] *vt* (*MATH*) to derive; (*cours d'eau etc*) to divert // *vi* (*bateau*) to drift; ~ **de** to derive from.

dermatologue [dermatɔlɔg] *nm/f* dermatologist.

dernier, ière [dernje, -jɛr] *a* last; (*le plus récent*) latest, last; **lundi/le mois ~** last Monday/month; **du ~ chic** extremely smart; **les ~s honneurs** the last tribute; **en ~** *ad* last; **ce ~** the latter; **dernièrement** *ad* recently.

dérobé, e [derɔbe] *a* (*porte*) secret, hidden; **à la ~e** surreptitiously.

dérober [derɔbe] *vt* to steal; ~ **qch à (la vue de)** qn to conceal *ou* hide sth from sb('s view); **se ~** *vi* (*s'esquiver*) to slip away; to shy away; **se ~ sous** (*s'effondrer*) to give way beneath; **se ~ à** (*justice, regards*) to hide from; (*obligation*) to shirk.

dérogation [derɔgasjɔ̃] *nf* (special) dispensation.

déroger [derɔʒe]: ~ **à** *vt* to go against, depart from.

dérouiller [deruje] *vt*: **se ~ les jambes** to stretch one's legs (*fig*).

déroulement [derulmɑ̃] *nm* (*d'une opération etc*) progress.

dérouler [derule] *vt* (*ficelle*) to unwind; (*papier*) to unroll; **se ~** *vi* (*avoir lieu*) to take place; (*se passer*) to go on; to go (off); to unfold.

déroute [derut] *nf* rout; total collapse.

dérouter [derute] *vt* (*avion, train*) to reroute, divert; (*étonner*) to disconcert, throw (out).

derrière [derjɛr] *ad, prép* behind // *nm* (*d'une maison*) back; (*postérieur*) be-

hind, bottom; **les pattes de ~** the back
ou hind legs; **par ~** from behind; *(fig)*
behind one's back.

des [de] *dét, prép* + *dét voir* **de**.

dès [dɛ] *prép* from; **~ que** *cj* as soon as;
~ son retour as soon as he was *(ou* is)
back; **~ lors** *ad* from then on; **~ lors
que** *cj* from the moment (that).

désabusé, e [dezabyze] *a* disillusioned.

désaccord [dezakɔʀ] *nm* disagreement.

désaccordé, e [dezakɔʀde] *a* *(MUS)* out
of tune.

désaffecté, e [dezafɛkte] *a* disused.

désaffection [dezafɛksjɔ̃] *nf*: **~ pour**
estrangement from.

désagréable [dezagʀeable(ə)] *a* unpleasant.

désagréger [dezagʀeʒe]: **se ~** *vi* to disintegrate, break up.

désagrément [dezagʀemɑ̃] *nm* annoyance, trouble *q*.

désaltérer [dezalteʀe] *vt*: **se ~** to
quench one's thirst.

désamorcer [dezamɔʀse] *vt* to defuse;
to forestall.

désapprouver [dezapʀuve] *vt* to disapprove of.

désarçonner [dezaʀsɔne] *vt* to unseat,
throw; *(fig)* to throw, puzzle.

désarroi [dezaʀwa] *nm* disarray.

désarticulé, e [dezaʀtikyle] *a* *(pantin,
corps)* dislocated.

désastre [dezastʀ(ə)] *nm* disaster.

désavantage [dezavɑ̃taʒ] *nm* disadvantage; *(inconvénient)* drawback, disadvantage; **désavantager** *vt* to put at a
disadvantage.

désavouer [dezavwe] *vt* to disown.

désaxé, e [dezakse] *a* *(fig)* unbalanced.

descendre [desɑ̃dʀ(ə)] *vt* *(escalier,
montagne)* to go *(ou* come) down;
(valise, paquet) to take *ou* get down;
(étagère etc) to lower; *(fam: abattre)* to
shoot down // *vi* to go *(ou* come) down;
(passager: s'arrêter) to get out, alight;
~ à pied/en voiture to walk/drive down;
~ de *(famille)* to be descended from; **~
du train** to get out of *ou* get off the train;
~ d'un arbre to climb down from a tree;
~ de cheval to dismount; **~ à l'hôtel** to
stay at a hotel.

descente [desɑ̃t] *nf* descent, going
down; *(chemin)* way down; *(SKI)* downhill (race); **au milieu de la ~** halfway
down; **~ de lit** bedside rug; **~ (de
police)** (police) raid.

description [dɛskʀipsjɔ̃] *nf* description.

désemparé, e [dezɑ̃paʀe] *a* bewildered,
distraught.

désemparer [dezɑ̃paʀe] *vi*: **sans ~**
without stopping.

désemplir [dezɑ̃pliʀ] *vi*: **ne pas ~** to be
always full.

déséquilibre [dezekilibʀ(ə)] *nm* *(position)*: **en ~** unsteady; *(fig: des forces,*

du budget) imbalance.

déséquilibré, e [dezekilibʀe] *nm/f*
(PSYCH) unbalanced person.

déséquilibrer [dezekilibʀe] *vt* to throw
off balance.

désert, e [dezɛʀ, -ɛʀt(ə)] *a* deserted //
nm desert.

déserter [dezɛʀte] *vi, vt* to desert.

désertique [dezɛʀtik] *a* desert *cpd*; barren, empty.

désespéré, e [dezɛspeʀe] *a* desperate.

désespérer [dezɛspeʀe] *vt* to drive to
despair // *vi*: **~ de** to despair of.

désespoir [dezɛspwaʀ] *nm* despair; **en
~ de cause** in desperation.

déshabillé [dezabije] *nm* négligée.

déshabiller [dezabije] *vt* to undress; **se
~** *vi* to undress (o.s.).

désherbant [dezɛʀbɑ̃] *nm* weed-killer.

déshériter [dezeʀite] *vt* to disinherit.

déshérités [dezeʀite] *nmpl*: **les ~** the
underprivileged.

déshonneur [dezɔnœʀ] *nm* dishonour.

déshydraté, e [dezidʀate] *a* dehydrated.

desiderata [dezideʀata] *nmpl* requirements.

désigner [deziɲe] *vt* *(montrer)* to point
out, indicate; *(dénommer)* to denote;
(candidat etc) to name.

désinfectant, e [dezɛ̃fɛktɑ̃, -ɑ̃t] *a, nm*
disinfectant.

désinfecter [dezɛ̃fɛkte] *vt* to disinfect.

désintégrer [dezɛ̃tegʀe] *vt*, **se ~** *vi* to
disintegrate.

désintéressé, e [dezɛ̃teʀese] *a* disinterested, unselfish.

désintéresser [dezɛ̃teʀese] *vt*: **se ~
(de)** to lose interest (in).

désintoxication [dezɛ̃tɔksikasjɔ̃] *nf*:
faire une cure de ~ to undergo treatment
for alcoholism *(ou* drug addiction).

désinvolte [dezɛ̃vɔlt(ə)] *a* casual, offhand; **désinvolture** *nf* casualness.

désir [deziʀ] *nm* wish; *(fort, sensuel)* desire.

désirer [deziʀe] *vt* to want, wish for;
(sexuellement) to desire; **je désire ...**
(formule de politesse) I would like ...

désister [deziste]: **se ~** *vi* to stand
down, withdraw.

désobéir [dezɔbeiʀ] *vi*: **~ (à qn/qch)** to
disobey (sb/sth); **désobéissant, e** *a* disobedient.

désobligeant, e [dezɔbliʒɑ̃, -ɑ̃t] *a* disagreeable.

désodorisant [dezɔdɔʀizɑ̃] *nm* air
freshener, deodorizer.

désœuvré, e [dezœvʀe] *a* idle.

désolé, e [dezɔle] *a* *(paysage)* desolate;
je suis ~ I'm sorry.

désoler [dezɔle] *vt* to distress, grieve.

désolidariser [desɔlidaʀize] *vt*: **se ~ de
ou d'avec** to dissociate o.s. from.

désopilant, e [dezɔpilɑ̃, -ɑ̃t] *a* hilarious.

désordonné, e [dezɔʀdɔne] a untidy.

désordre [dezɔʀdʀ(ə)] nm disorder(liness), untidiness; (anarchie) disorder; ~s nmpl (POL) disturbances, disorder sg; **en** ~ in a mess, untidy.

désorienté, e [dezɔʀjɑ̃te] a disorientated.

désormais [dezɔʀmɛ] ad from now on.

désosser [dezose] vt to bone.

desquels, desquelles [dekɛl] prép + pronom voir **lequel**.

dessaisir [deseziʀ]: **se** ~ **de** vt to give up, part with.

dessaler [desale] vt (eau de mer) to desalinate; (CULIN) to soak.

desséché, e [deseʃe] a dried up.

dessécher [deseʃe] vt to dry out, parch; **se** ~ vi to dry out.

dessein [desɛ̃] nm design; **à** ~ intentionally, deliberately.

desserrer [deseʀe] vt to loosen; (frein) to release.

dessert [desɛʀ] nm dessert, pudding.

desserte [desɛʀt(ə)] nf (table) side table; (transport): **la** ~ **du village est assurée par autocar** there is a coach service to the village.

desservir [desɛʀviʀ] vt (ville, quartier) to serve; (nuire à) to go against, put at a disadvantage; (débarrasser): ~ (**la table**) to clear the table.

dessin [desɛ̃] nm (œuvre, art) drawing; (motif) pattern, design; (contour) (out)line; ~ **animé** cartoon (film); ~ **humoristique** cartoon.

dessinateur, trice [desinatœʀ, -tʀis] nm/f drawer; (de bandes dessinées) cartoonist; (industriel) draughtsman (Brit), draftsman (US).

dessiner [desine] vt to draw; (concevoir) to design.

dessoûler [desule] vt, vi to sober up.

dessous [dəsu] ad underneath, beneath // nm underside // nmpl (sousvêtements) underwear sg; **en** ~, **par** ~ underneath; **below**; **au-**~ (**de**) below; (peu digne de) beneath; **avoir le** ~ to get the worst of it; ~**-de-plat** nm inv tablemat.

dessus [dəsy] ad on top; (collé, écrit) on it // nm top; **en** ~ above; **par** ~ ad over it // prép over; **au-**~ (**de**) above; **avoir le** ~ to get the upper hand; ~**-de-lit** nm inv bedspread.

destin [destɛ̃] nm fate; (avenir) destiny.

destinataire [dɛstinatɛʀ] nm/f (POSTES) addressee; (d'un colis) consignee.

destination [dɛstinasjɔ̃] nf (lieu) destination; (usage) purpose; **à** ~ **de** bound for, travelling to.

destinée [dɛstine] nf fate; (existence, avenir) destiny.

destiner [dɛstine] vt: ~ **qn à** (poste, sort) to destine sb for; ~ **qn/qch à** (pré-

destiner) to destine sb/sth to + verbe; ~ **qch à qn** (envisager de donner) to intend sb to have sth; (adresser) to intend sth for sb; to aim sth at sb; **être destiné à** (sort) to be destined to + verbe; (usage) to be meant for; (suj: sort) to be in store for.

destituer [dɛstitɥe] vt to depose.

désuet, ète [desɥɛ, -ɛt] a outdated, outmoded; **désuétude** nf: **tomber en désuétude** to fall into disuse.

détachant [detaʃɑ̃] nm stain remover.

détacher [detaʃe] vt (enlever) to detach, remove; (délier) to untie; (ADMIN): ~ **qn (auprès de/à)** to post sb (to); **se** ~ vi (tomber) to come off; to come out; (se défaire) to come undone; **se** ~ **sur** to stand out against; **se** ~ **de** (se désintéresser) to grow away from.

détail [detaj] nm detail; (COMM): **le** ~ retail; **au** ~ ad (COMM) retail; separately; **en** ~ in detail.

détaillant [detajɑ̃] nm retailer.

détailler [detaje] vt (expliquer) to explain in detail; to detail; (examiner) to look over, examine.

détartrant [detaʀtʀɑ̃] nm scale remover.

détecter [detɛkte] vt to detect.

détective [detɛktiv] nm (Brit: policier) detective; ~ (**privé**) private detective.

déteindre [detɛ̃dʀ(ə)] vi (tissu) to fade; (fig): ~ **sur** to rub off on.

dételer [detle] vt to unharness.

détendre [detɑ̃dʀ(ə)] vt: **se** ~ to lose its tension; to relax.

détenir [detniʀ] vt (fortune, objet, secret) to be in possession of; (prisonnier) to detain, hold; (record, pouvoir) to hold.

détente [detɑ̃t] nf relaxation; (d'une arme) trigger.

détention [detɑ̃sjɔ̃] nf possession; detention; holding; ~ **préventive** (pre-trial) custody.

détenu, e [detny] nm/f prisoner.

détergent [detɛʀʒɑ̃] nm detergent.

détériorer [deteʀjɔʀe] vt to damage; **se** ~ vi to deteriorate.

déterminé, e [detɛʀmine] a (résolu) determined; (précis) specific, definite.

déterminer [detɛʀmine] vt (fixer) to determine; (décider): ~ **qn à faire** to decide sb to do.

déterrer [detɛʀe] vt to dig up.

détersif [detɛʀsif] nm detergent.

détestable [detɛstabl(ə)] a foul, ghastly; detestable, odious.

détester [detɛste] vt to hate, detest.

détonation [detɔnasjɔ̃] nf detonation, bang, report (of a gun).

détonner [detɔne] vi (MUS) to go out of tune; (fig) to clash.

détour [detuʀ] nm detour; (tournant) bend, curve; **sans** ~ (fig) plainly.

détourné, e [detuʀne] a (moyen)

roundabout.

détournement [deturnəmɑ̃] nm: ~ d'avion hijacking; ~ de mineur corruption of a minor.

détourner [deturne] vt to divert; (par la force) to hijack; (yeux, tête) to turn away; (de l'argent) to embezzle; se ~ vi to turn away.

détracteur, trice [detraktœr, -tris] nm/f disparager, critic.

détraquer [detrake] vt to put out of order; (estomac) to upset; se ~ vi to go wrong.

détrempé, e [detrɑ̃pe] a (sol) sodden, waterlogged.

détresse [detrɛs] nf distress.

détriment [detrimɑ̃] nm: au ~ de to the detriment of.

détritus [detritys] nmpl rubbish sg, refuse sg.

détroit [detrwa] nm strait.

détromper [detrɔ̃pe] vt to disabuse.

détrôner [detrone] vt to dethrone.

détrousser [detruse] vt to rob.

détruire [detruir] vt to destroy.

dette [dɛt] nf debt.

D.E.U.G. [dœg] sigle m = diplôme d'études universitaires générales.

deuil [dœj] nm (perte) bereavement; (période) mourning; (chagrin) grief; être en ~ to be in mourning.

deux [dø] num two; les ~ both; ses ~ mains both his hands, his two hands; ~ points colon sg; **deuxième** num second; **deuxièmement** ad secondly, in the second place; ~**-pièces** nm inv (tailleur) two-piece suit; (de bain) two-piece (swimsuit); (appartement) two-roomed flat (Brit) ou apartment (US); ~**-roues** nm inv two-wheeled vehicle.

devais etc vb voir **devoir**.

dévaler [devale] vt to hurtle down.

dévaliser [devalize] vt to rob, burgle.

dévaloriser [devalɔrize] vt, se ~ vi to depreciate.

dévaluation [devalɥasjɔ̃] nf depreciation; (ÉCON: mesure) devaluation.

devancer [dəvɑ̃se] vt to be ahead of; to get ahead of; to arrive before; (prévenir) to anticipate.

devant [dəvɑ̃] ad in front; (à distance: en avant) ahead // prép in front; ahead of; (avec mouvement: passer) past; (fig) before, in front of; faced with; in view of // nm front; **prendre les** ~**s** to make the first move; **les pattes de** ~ the front legs, the forelegs; **par** ~ (boutonner) at the front; (entrer) the front way; **aller au** ~ **de qn** to go out to meet sb; **aller au** ~ **de** (désirs de qn) to anticipate.

devanture [dəvɑ̃tyr] nf (façade) (shop) front; (étalage) display; (shop) window.

déveine [devɛn] nf rotten luck q.

développement [devlɔpmɑ̃] nm development.

développer [devlɔpe] vt to develop; ~ vi to develop.

devenir [dəvnir] vb avec attribut to become; ~ **instituteur** to become a teacher; **que sont-ils devenus?** what has become of them?

dévergondé, e [devɛrgɔ̃de] a wild, shameless.

déverser [devɛrse] vt (liquide) to pour (out); (ordures) to tip (out); se ~ **dans** (fleuve, mer) to flow into.

dévêtir [devetir] vt, se ~ to undress.

devez etc vb voir **devoir**.

déviation [devjasjɔ̃] nf deviation; (AUTO) diversion (Brit), detour (US).

dévider [devide] vt to unwind.

devienne etc vb voir **devenir**.

dévier [devje] vt (fleuve, circulation) to divert; (coup) to deflect // vi to veer (off course).

devin [dəvɛ̃] nm soothsayer, seer.

deviner [dəvine] vt to guess; (prévoir) to foresee; (apercevoir) to distinguish.

devinette [dəvinɛt] nf riddle.

devins etc vb voir **devenir**.

devis [dəvi] nm estimate, quotation.

dévisager [devizaʒe] vt to stare at.

devise [dəviz] nf (formule) motto, watchword; (ÉCON: monnaie) currency; ~**s** nfpl (argent) currency sg.

deviser [dəvize] vi to converse.

dévisser [devise] vt to unscrew, undo; se ~ vi to come unscrewed.

dévoiler [devwale] vt to unveil.

devoir [dəvwar] nm duty; (SCOL) homework q; (: en classe) exercise // vt (argent, respect): ~ **qch** (à qn) to owe (sb) sth; (suivi de l'infinitif: obligation): **il doit le faire** he has to do it, he must do it; (: intention): **il doit partir demain** he is (due) to leave tomorrow; (: probabilité): **il doit être tard** it must be late.

dévolu, e [devɔly] a: ~ **à** allotted to // nm: **jeter son** ~ **sur** to fix one's choice on.

dévorer [devɔre] vt to devour; (suj: feu, soucis) to consume.

dévot, e [devo, -ɔt] a devout, pious.

dévotion [devɔsjɔ̃] nf devoutness; **être à la** ~ **de qn** to be totally devoted to sb.

dévoué, e [devwe] a devoted.

dévouer [devwe]: se ~ vi (se sacrifier): se ~ (**pour**) to sacrifice o.s. (for); (se consacrer): se ~ **à** to devote ou dedicate o.s. to.

dévoyé, e [devwaje] a delinquent.

devrai etc vb voir **devoir**.

diabète [djabɛt] nm diabetes sg; **diabétique** nm/f diabetic.

diable [djɑbl(ə)] nm devil.

diacre [djakr(ə)] nm deacon.

diagnostic [djagnɔstik] nm diagnosis sg.

diagonal, e, aux [djagɔnal, -o] a, nf diagonal; **en** ~**e** diagonally; **lire en** ~**e** to skim through.

diagramme [djagʀam] *nm* chart, graph.

dialecte [djalɛkt(ə)] *nm* dialect.

dialogue [djalɔg] *nm* dialogue.

diamant [djamɑ̃] *nm* diamond; **diamantaire** *nm* diamond dealer.

diamètre [djamɛtʀ(ə)] *nm* diameter.

diapason [djapazɔ̃] *nm* tuning fork.

diaphragme [djafʀagm] *nm* diaphragm.

diaporama [djapɔʀama] *nm* slide show.

diapositive [djapozitiv] *nf* transparency, slide.

diarrhée [djaʀe] *nf* diarrhoea.

dictateur [diktatœʀ] *nm* dictator; **dictature** *nf* dictatorship.

dictée [dikte] *nf* dictation.

dicter [dikte] *vt* to dictate.

dictionnaire [diksjɔnɛʀ] *nm* dictionary.

dicton [diktɔ̃] *nm* saying, dictum.

dièse [djɛz] *nm* sharp.

diesel [djezɛl] *nm, a inv* diesel.

diète [djɛt] *nf* (*jeûne*) starvation diet; (*régime*) diet.

diététique [djetetik] *a*: **magasin ~** health food shop.

dieu, x [djø] *nm* god; **D~** God; **mon D~!** good heavens!

diffamation [difamɑsjɔ̃] *nf* slander; (*écrite*) libel.

différé [difeʀe] *nm* (*TV*): **en ~** (pre-)recorded.

différence [difeʀɑ̃s] *nf* difference; **à la ~ de** unlike.

différencier [difeʀɑ̃sje] *vt* to differentiate.

différend [difeʀɑ̃] *nm* difference (of opinion), disagreement.

différent, e [difeʀɑ̃, -ɑ̃t] *a*: **~ (de)** different (from); **~s objets** different *ou* various objects.

différer [difeʀe] *vt* to postpone, put off // *vi*: **~ (de)** to differ (from).

difficile [difisil] *a* difficult; (*exigeant*) hard to please; **~ment** *ad* with difficulty.

difficulté [difikylte] *nf* difficulty; **en ~** (*bateau, alpiniste*) in difficulties.

difforme [difɔʀm(ə)] *a* deformed, misshapen.

diffuser [difyze] *vt* (*chaleur, bruit*) to diffuse; (*émission, musique*) to broadcast; (*nouvelle, idée*) to circulate; (*COMM*) to distribute.

digérer [diʒeʀe] *vt* to digest; (*fig: accepter*) to stomach, put up with; **digestif** *nm* (after-dinner) liqueur.

digne [diɲ] *a* dignified; **~ de** worthy of; **~ de foi** trustworthy.

dignité [diɲite] *nf* dignity.

digression [digʀesjɔ̃] *nf* digression.

digue [dig] *nf* dike, dyke.

dilapider [dilapide] *vt* to squander.

dilemme [dilɛm] *nm* dilemma.

diligence [diliʒɑ̃s] *nf* stagecoach; (*empressement*) despatch.

diluer [dilɥe] *vt* to dilute.

diluvien, ne [dilyvjɛ̃, -jɛn] *a*: **pluie ~ne** torrential rain.

dimanche [dimɑ̃ʃ] *nm* Sunday.

dimension [dimɑ̃sjɔ̃] *nf* (*grandeur*) size; (*cote, de l'espace*) dimension.

diminuer [diminɥe] *vt* to reduce, decrease; (*ardeur etc*) to lessen; (*personne: physiquement*) to undermine; (*dénigrer*) to belittle // *vi* to decrease, diminish; **diminutif** *nm* (*surnom*) pet name; **diminution** *nf* decreasing, diminishing.

dinde [dɛ̃d] *nf* turkey.

dindon [dɛ̃dɔ̃] *nm* turkey.

dîner [dine] *nm* dinner // *vi* to have dinner.

dingue [dɛ̃g] *a* (*fam*) crazy.

diplomate [diplɔmat] *a* diplomatic // *nm* diplomat; (*fig*) diplomatist.

diplomatie [diplɔmasi] *nf* diplomacy.

diplôme [diplom] *nm* diploma; **diplômé, e** *a* qualified.

dire [diʀ] *nm*: **au ~ de** according to; **leur ~s** what they say // *vt* to say; (*secret, mensonge*) to tell; **~ l'heure/la vérité** to tell the time/the truth; **~ qch à qn** to tell sb sth; **~ à qn qu'il fasse** *ou* **de faire** to tell sb to do; **on dit que** they say that; **ceci dit** that being said; (*à ces mots*) whereupon; **si cela lui dit** (*plaire*) if he fancies it; **que dites-vous de** (*penser*) what do you think of; **on dirait que** it looks (*ou* sounds *etc*) as if; **dis/dites (donc)** I say; (*à propos*) by the way.

direct, e [diʀɛkt] *a* direct // *nm* (*TV*): **en ~** live; **~ement** *ad* directly.

directeur, trice [diʀɛktœʀ, -tʀis] *nm/f* (*d'entreprise*) director; (*de service*) manager/eress; (*d'école*) head(teacher) (*Brit*), principal (*US*).

direction [diʀɛksjɔ̃] *nf* management; conducting; supervision; (*AUTO*) steering; (*sens*) direction; **'toutes ~s'** 'all routes'.

dirent *vb voir* dire.

dirigeant, e [diʀiʒɑ̃, -ɑ̃t] *a* managerial; ruling // *nm/f* (*d'un parti etc*) leader; (*d'entreprise*) manager.

diriger [diʀiʒe] *vt* (*entreprise*) to manage, run; (*véhicule*) to steer; (*orchestre*) to conduct; (*recherches, travaux*) to supervise; (*braquer: regard, arme*): **~ sur** to point *ou* level at; **se ~** (*s'orienter*) to find one's way; **se ~ vers** *ou* **sur** to make *ou* head for.

dirigisme [diʀiʒism(ə)] *nm* (*ÉCON*) state intervention, interventionism.

dis *etc vb voir* dire.

discerner [disɛʀne] *vt* to discern, make out.

discipline [disiplin] *nf* discipline; **discipliner** *vt* to discipline; to control.

discontinu, e [diskɔ̃tiny] *a* intermittent.

discontinuer [diskɔ̃tinɥe] *vi*: **sans ~**

without stopping, without a break.

disconvenir [diskɔ̃vniʀ] *vi*: ne pas ~ de qch/que not to deny sth/that.

discordant, e [diskɔʀdɑ̃, -ɑ̃t] *a* discordant; conflicting.

discothèque [diskɔtɛk] *nf* (*disques*) record collection; (: *dans une bibliothèque*) record library; (*boîte de nuit*) disco(thèque).

discourir [diskuʀiʀ] *vi* to discourse, hold forth.

discours [diskuʀ] *nm* speech.

discret, ète [diskʀɛ, -ɛt] *a* discreet; (*fig*) unobtrusive; quiet.

discrétion [diskʀesjɔ̃] *nf* discretion; être à la ~ de qn to be in sb's hands; à ~ unlimited; as much as one wants.

discrimination [diskʀiminasjɔ̃] *nf* discrimination; sans ~ indiscriminately.

disculper [diskylpe] *vt* to exonerate.

discussion [diskysjɔ̃] *nf* discussion.

discutable [diskytabl(ə)] *a* debatable.

discuté, e [diskyte] *a* controversial.

discuter [diskyte] *vt* (*contester*) to question, dispute; (*débattre: prix*) to discuss // *vi* to talk; (*ergoter*) to argue; ~ de to discuss.

dise *etc vb voir* **dire.**

disette [dizɛt] *nf* food shortage.

diseuse [dizøz] *nf*: ~ de bonne aventure fortuneteller.

disgracieux, euse [disgʀasjø, -jøz] *a* ungainly, awkward.

disjoindre [disʒwɛ̃dʀ(ə)] *vt* to take apart; se ~ *vi* to come apart.

disjoncteur [disʒɔ̃ktœʀ] *nm* (ÉLEC) circuit breaker.

disloquer [dislɔke] *vt* (*chaise*) to dismantle; (*parti, empire*) to break up; se ~ l'épaule to dislocate one's shoulder.

disons *vb voir* **dire.**

disparaître [dispaʀɛtʀ(ə)] *vi* to disappear; (*à la vue*) to vanish, disappear; to be hidden *ou* concealed; (*se perdre: traditions etc*) to die out; faire ~ to remove; to get rid of.

disparition [dispaʀisjɔ̃] *nf* disappearance.

disparu, e [dispaʀy] *nm/f* missing person; (*défunt*) departed.

dispensaire [dispɑ̃sɛʀ] *nm* community clinic.

dispenser [dispɑ̃se] *vt* (*donner*) to lavish, bestow; (*exempter*): ~ qn de to exempt sb from; se ~ de *vt* to avoid; to get out of.

disperser [dispɛʀse] *vt* to scatter; (*fig: son attention*) to dissipate.

disponibilité [dispɔnibilite] *nf* (ADMIN): être en ~ to be on leave of absence.

disponible [dispɔnibl(ə)] *a* available.

dispos [dispo] *am*: (frais et) ~ fresh (as a daisy).

disposé, e [dispoze] *a*: bien/mal ~ (*humeur*) in a good/bad mood; ~ à (*prêt à*) willing *ou* prepared to.

disposer [dispoze] *vt* (*arranger, placer*) to arrange // *vi*: vous pouvez ~ you may leave; ~ de *vt* to have (at one's disposal); to use; se ~ à faire to prepare to do, be about to do.

dispositif [dispozitif] *nm* device; (*fig*) system, plan of action; set-up.

disposition [dispozisjɔ̃] *nf* (*arrangement*) arrangement, layout; (*humeur*) mood; (*tendance*) tendency; ~s *nfpl* (*mesures*) steps, measures; (*préparatifs*) arrangements; (*loi, testament*) provisions; (*aptitudes*) bent *sg*, aptitude *sg*; à la ~ de qn at sb's disposal.

disproportionné, e [dispʀɔpɔʀsjɔne] *a* disproportionate, out of all proportion.

dispute [dispyt] *nf* quarrel, argument.

disputer [dispyte] *vt* (*match*) to play; (*combat*) to fight; (*course*) to run, fight; se ~ *vi* to quarrel; ~ qch à qn to fight with sb over sth.

disquaire [diskɛʀ] *nm/f* record dealer.

disqualifier [diskalifje] *vt* to disqualify.

disque [disk(ə)] *nm* (MUS) record; (*forme, pièce*) disc; (SPORT) discus; ~ compact compact disc; ~ d'embrayage (AUTO) clutch plate.

disquette [diskɛt] *nf* floppy disk, diskette.

disséminer [disemine] *vt* to scatter.

disséquer [diseke] *vt* to dissect.

dissertation [disɛʀtasjɔ̃] *nf* (SCOL) essay.

disserter [disɛʀte] *vi*: ~ sur to discourse upon.

dissimuler [disimyle] *vt* to conceal.

dissiper [disipe] *vt* to dissipate; (*fortune*) to squander; se ~ *vi* (*brouillard*) to clear, disperse; (*doutes*) to melt away; (*élève*) to become unruly.

dissolu, e [disɔly] *a* dissolute.

dissolvant, e [disɔlvɑ̃, -ɑ̃t] *nm* solvent; ~ (gras) nail polish remover.

dissonant, e [disɔnɑ̃, -ɑ̃t] *a* discordant.

dissoudre [disudʀ(ə)] *vt* to dissolve; se ~ *vi* to dissolve.

dissuader [disɥade] *vt*: ~ qn de faire/de qch to dissuade sb from doing/from sth.

dissuasion [disɥazjɔ̃] *nf*: force de ~ deterrent power.

distance [distɑ̃s] *nf* distance; (*fig: écart*) gap; à ~ at *ou* from a distance; **distancer** *vt* to outdistance.

distant, e [distɑ̃, -ɑ̃t] *a* (*réservé*) distant; ~ de (*lieu*) far away from.

distendre [distɑ̃dʀ(ə)] *vt*, se ~ *vi* to distend.

distiller [distile] *vt* to distil; **distillerie** *nf* distillery.

distinct, e [distɛ̃(kt), distɛ̃kt(ə)] *a* distinct; **distinctif, ive** *a* distinctive.

distingué, e [distɛ̃ge] *a* distinguished.

distinguer [distɛ̃ge] *vt* to distinguish.
distraction [distraksjɔ̃] *nf* (*manque d'attention*) absent-mindedness; (*oubli*) lapse (in concentration); (*détente*) diversion, recreation; (*passe-temps*) distraction, entertainment.
distraire [distrɛr] *vt* (*déranger*) to distract; (*divertir*) to entertain, divert; se ~ *vi* to amuse *ou* enjoy o.s.
distrait, e [distrɛ, -ɛt] *a* absent-minded.
distribuer [distribɥe] *vt* to distribute; to hand out; (*CARTES*) to deal (out); (*courrier*) to deliver; **distributeur** *nm* (*COMM*) distributor; (*automatique*) (*vending*) machine; (: *de billets*) (cash) dispenser; **distribution** *nf* distribution; (*postale*) delivery; (*choix d'acteurs*) casting, cast.
dit, e [di, dit] *pp de* **dire** // *a* (*fixé*): **le jour** ~ the arranged day; (*surnommé*): **X, ~ Pierrot** X, known as Pierrot.
dites *vb voir* **dire**.
divaguer [divage] *vi* to ramble; to rave.
divan [divɑ̃] *nm* divan.
divers, e [divɛr, -ɛrs(ə)] *a* (*varié*) diverse, varied; (*différent*) different, various // *dét* (*plusieurs*) various, several; (**frais**) ~ sundries, miscellaneous (expenses).
divertir [divɛrtir] *vt* to amuse, entertain; se ~ *vi* to amuse *ou* enjoy o.s.
divin, e [divɛ̃, -in] *a* divine.
diviser [divize] *vt* (*gén*, *MATH*) to divide; (*morceler*, *subdiviser*) to divide (up), split (up); **division** *nf* division.
divorce [divɔrs(ə)] *nm* divorce; **divorcé, e** *nm/f* divorcee; **divorcer** *vi* to get a divorce, get divorced; **divorcer de** *ou* **d'avec qn** to divorce sb.
divulguer [divylge] *vt* to divulge, disclose.
dix [dis] *num* ten; **dixième** *num* tenth.
dizaine [dizɛn] *nf* (*10*) ten; (*environ 10*): **une** ~ (**de**) about ten, ten or so.
do [do] *nm* (*note*) C; (*en chantant la gamme*) doh.
dock [dɔk] *nm* dock.
docker [dɔkɛr] *nm* docker.
docte [dɔkt(ə)] *a* learned.
docteur [dɔktœr] *nm* doctor.
doctorat [dɔktɔra] *nm*: ~ (**d'Université**) doctorate; ~ **d'état** ≈ Ph.D.
doctrine [dɔktrin] *nf* doctrine.
document [dɔkymɑ̃] *nm* document.
documentaire [dɔkymãtɛr] *a*, *nm* documentary.
documentaliste [dɔkymãtalist(ə)] *nm/f* archivist; researcher.
documentation [dɔkymãtasjɔ̃] *nf* documentation, literature; (*PRESSE*, *TV*: *service*) research.
documenter [dɔkymãte] *vt*: se ~ (**sur**) to gather information (on).
dodeliner [dɔdline] *vi*: ~ **de la tête** to

nod one's head gently.
dodo [dodo] *nm*: **aller faire** ~ to go to beddy-byes.
dodu, e [dɔdy] *a* plump.
dogue [dɔg] *nm* mastiff.
doigt [dwa] *nm* finger; **à deux ~s de** within an inch of; **un** ~ **de lait** a drop of milk; ~ **de pied** toe.
doigté [dwate] *nm* (*MUS*) fingering; (*fig*: *habileté*) diplomacy, tact.
doit *etc vb voir* **devoir**.
doléances [dɔleɑ̃s] *nfpl* complaints; grievances.
dolent, e [dɔlɑ̃, -ɑ̃t] *a* doleful.
dollar [dɔlar] *nm* dollar.
D.O.M. [deɔm, dɔm] *sigle m ou mpl* = **département(s) d'outre-mer**.
domaine [dɔmɛn] *nm* estate, property; (*fig*) domain, field.
domanial, e, aux [dɔmanjal, -o] *a* (*forêt*, *biens*) national, state *cpd*.
domestique [dɔmɛstik] *a* domestic // *nm/f* servant, domestic.
domicile [dɔmisil] *nm* home, place of residence; **à** ~ at home; **domicilié, e** *a*: **être domicilié à** to have one's home in *ou* at.
dominant, e [dɔminɑ̃, -ɑ̃t] *a* dominant; predominant.
dominateur, trice [dɔminatœr, -tris] *a* dominating; domineering.
dominer [dɔmine] *vt* to dominate; (*passions etc*) to control, master; (*surpasser*) to outclass, surpass // *vi* to be in the dominant position; se ~ *vi* to control o.s.
domino [dɔmino] *nm* domino.
dommage [dɔmaʒ] *nm* (*préjudice*) harm, injury; (*dégâts*, *pertes*) damage *q*; **c'est** ~ **de faire/que** it's a shame *ou* pity to do/that; ~**s-intérêts** *nmpl* damages.
dompter [dɔ̃te] *vt* to tame; **dompteur, euse** *nm/f* trainer; liontamer.
don [dɔ̃] *nm* (*cadeau*) gift; (*charité*) donation; (*aptitude*) gift, talent; **avoir des** ~**s pour** to have a gift *ou* talent for.
donc [dɔ̃k] *cj* therefore, so; (*après une digression*) so, then.
donjon [dɔ̃ʒɔ̃] *nm* keep.
donné, e [dɔne] *a* (*convenu*) given; (*pas cher*): **c'est** ~ it's a gift // *nf* (*MATH*, *gén*) datum (*pl* data); **étant** ~ ... given ....
donner [dɔne] *vt* to give; (*vieux habits etc*) to give away; (*spectacle*) to put on; (*film*) to show; ~ **qch à qn** to give sb sth, give sth to sb; ~ **sur** (*suj*: *fenêtre*, *chambre*) to look (out) onto; ~ **dans** (*piège etc*) to fall into; se ~ **à fond** to give one's all; **s'en** ~ **à cœur joie** (*fam*) to have a great time.
dont [dɔ̃] *pronom relatif* **1** (*appartenance*: *objets*) whose, of which; (: *êtres animés*) whose; **la maison** ~ **le toit est**

rouge the house the roof of which is red, the house whose roof is red; **l'homme ~ je connais la sœur** the man whose sister I know

2 (*parmi lesquel(le)s*): **2 livres, ~ l'un est ... 2** books, one of which is ...; **il y avait plusieurs personnes, ~ Gabrielle** there were several people, among them Gabrielle; **10 blessés, ~ 2 grièvement** 10 injured, 2 of them seriously

3 (*complément d'adjectif, de verbe*): **le fils ~ il est si fier** the son he's so proud of; **ce ~ je parle** what I'm talking about; *voir adjectifs et verbes à complément prépositionnel:* **responsable de, souffrir de** etc.

doré, e [dɔʀe] *a* golden; (*avec dorure*) gilt, gilded.

dorénavant [dɔʀenavɑ̃] *ad* henceforth.

dorer [dɔʀe] *vt* (*cadre*) to gild; (*faire*) ~ (*CULIN*) to brown.

dorloter [dɔʀlɔte] *vt* to pamper.

dormir [dɔʀmiʀ] *vi* to sleep; (*être endormi*) to be asleep.

dortoir [dɔʀtwaʀ] *nm* dormitory.

dorure [dɔʀyʀ] *nf* gilding.

dos [do] *nm* back; (*de livre*) spine; **'voir au ~'** 'see over'; **de ~** from the back.

dosage [dozaʒ] *nm* mixture.

dose [doz] *nf* dose.

doser [doze] *vt* to measure out; to mix in the correct proportions; (*fig*) to expend in the right amounts; to strike a balance between.

dossard [dosaʀ] *nm* number (*worn by competitor*).

dossier [dosje] *nm* (*renseignements, fichier*) file; (*de chaise*) back; (*PRESSE*) feature.

dot [dɔt] *nf* dowry.

doter [dɔte] *vt* to equip.

douane [dwan] *nf* (*poste, bureau*) customs *pl*; (*taxes*) (customs) duty; **douanier, ière** *a* customs *cpd* // *nm* customs officer.

double [dubl(ə)] *a, ad* double // *nm* (*2 fois plus*): **le ~ (de)** twice as much (*ou* many) (as); (*autre exemplaire*) duplicate, copy; (*sosie*) double; (*TENNIS*) doubles *sg*; **en ~** (*exemplaire*) in duplicate; **faire ~ emploi** to be redundant.

doubler [duble] *vt* (*multiplier par 2*) to double; (*vêtement*) to line; (*dépasser*) to overtake, pass; (*film*) to dub; (*acteur*) to stand in for // *vi* to double.

doublure [dublyʀ] *nf* lining; (*CINÉMA*) stand-in.

douce [dus] *a voir* **doux**; **~âtre** *a* sickly sweet; **~ment** *ad* gently; slowly; **~reux, euse** *a* (*péj*) sugary; **douceur** *nf* softness; sweetness; mildness; gentleness; **douceurs** *nfpl* (*friandises*) sweets.

douche [duʃ] *nf* shower; **~s** *nfpl* (*salle*) shower room *sg*; **se doucher** *vi* to have

ou take a shower.

doué, e [dwe] *a* gifted, talented; **~ de** endowed with.

douille [duj] *nf* (*ÉLEC*) socket; (*de projectile*) case.

douillet, te [dujɛ, -ɛt] *a* cosy; (*péj*) soft.

douleur [dulœʀ] *nf* pain; (*chagrin*) grief, distress; **douloureux, euse** *a* painful.

doute [dut] *nm* doubt; **sans ~** *ad* no doubt; (*probablement*) probably.

douter [dute] *vt* to doubt; **~ de** *vt* (*allié*) to doubt, have (one's) doubts about; (*résultat*) to be doubtful of; **se ~ de qch/que** to suspect sth/that; **je m'en doutais** I suspected as much.

douteux, euse [dutø, -øz] *a* (*incertain*) doubtful; (*discutable*) dubious, questionable; (*péj*) dubious-looking.

Douvres [duvʀ(ə)] *n* Dover.

doux, douce [du, dus] *a* (*gén*) soft; (*sucré, agréable*) sweet; (*peu fort: moutarde, clément: climat*) mild; (*pas brusque*) gentle.

douzaine [duzɛn] *nf* (*12*) dozen; (*environ 12*): **une ~ (de)** a dozen or so, twelve or so.

douze [duz] *num* twelve; **douzième** *num* twelfth.

doyen, ne [dwajɛ̃, -ɛn] *nm/f* (*en âge, ancienneté*) most senior member; (*de faculté*) dean.

dragée [dʀaʒe] *nf* sugared almond; (*MÉD*) (sugar-coated) pill.

dragon [dʀagɔ̃] *nm* dragon.

draguer [dʀage] *vt* (*rivière*) to dredge; to drag; (*fam*) to try to pick up.

dramatique [dʀamatik] *a* dramatic; (*tragique*) tragic // *nf* (*TV*) (television) drama.

dramaturge [dʀamatyʀʒ(ə)] *nm* dramatist, playwright.

drame [dʀam] *nm* (*THÉÂTRE*) drama.

drap [dʀa] *nm* (*de lit*) sheet; (*tissu*) woollen fabric.

drapeau, x [dʀapo] *nm* flag; **sous les ~x** with the colours, in the army.

dresser [dʀese] *vt* (*mettre vertical, monter*) to put up, erect; (*fig: liste, bilan, contrat*) to draw up; (*animal*) to train; **se ~** *vi* (*falaise, obstacle*) to stand; to tower (up); (*personne*) to draw o.s. up; **~ qn contre qn** to set sb against sb; **~ l'oreille** to prick up one's ears.

drogue [dʀɔg] *nf* drug; **la ~** drugs *pl*.

drogué, e [dʀɔge] *nm/f* drug addict.

droguer [dʀɔge] *vt* (*victime*) to drug; (*malade*) to give drugs to; **se ~** *vi* (*aux stupéfiants*) to take drugs; (*péj: de médicaments*) to dose o.s. up.

droguerie [dʀɔgʀi] *nf* hardware shop.

droguiste [dʀɔgist(ə)] *nm* keeper (*ou* owner) of a hardware shop.

droit, e [dʀwa, dʀwat] *a* (*non courbe*)

straight; (*vertical*) upright, straight; (*fig: loyal*) upright, straight(forward); (*opposé à gauche*) right, right-hand // *ad* straight // *nm* (*prérogative*) right; (*taxe*) duty, tax; (*: d'inscription*) fee; (JUR): le ~ law // *nf* (POL): la ~e the right (wing); avoir le ~ de to be allowed to; avoir ~ à to be entitled to; être en ~ de to have a *ou* the right to; être dans son ~ to be within one's rights; à ~e on the right; (*direction*) (to the) right; ~s d'auteur royalties.

droitier, ière [dʀwatje, -jɛʀ] *nm/f* right-handed person.

droiture [dʀwatyʀ] *nf* uprightness, straightness.

drôle [dʀol] *a* funny; ~**ment** *ad* (*très*) terribly, awfully; une ~ d'idée a funny idea.

dromadaire [dʀɔmadɛʀ] *nm* dromedary.

dru, e [dʀy] *a* (*cheveux*) thick, bushy; (*pluie*) heavy.

du [dy] *prép* + *dét*, *dét voir* **de**.

dû, due [dy] *vb voir* devoir // *a* (*somme*) owing, owed; (*: venant à échéance*) due; (*causé par*): ~ à due to // *nm* due; (*somme*) dues *pl*.

dubitatif, ive [dybitatif, -iv] *a* doubtful, dubious.

duc [dyk] *ĸm* duke; **duchesse** *nf* duchess.

dûment [dymɑ̃] *ad* duly.

Dunkerque [dœ̃kɛʀk] *n* Dunkirk.

duo [dyo] *nm* (MUS) duet.

dupe [dyp] *nf* dupe // *a*: (ne pas) être ~ de (not) to be taken in by.

duplex [dyplɛks] *nm* (*appartement*) split-level apartment, duplex.

duplicata [dyplikata] *nm* duplicate.

duquel [dykɛl] *prép* + *pronom voir* **lequel**.

dur, e [dyʀ] *a* (*pierre, siège, travail, problème*) hard; (*lumière, voix, climat*) harsh; (*sévère*) hard, harsh; (*cruel*) hard(-hearted); (*porte, col*) stiff; (*viande*) tough // *ad* hard; ~ d'oreille hard of hearing.

durant [dyʀɑ̃] *prép* (*au cours de*) during; (*pendant*) for; des mois ~ for months.

durcir [dyʀsiʀ] *vt, vi, se* ~ *vi* to harden.

durée [dyʀe] *nf* length; (*d'une pile etc*) life; (*déroulement: des opérations etc*) duration.

durement [dyʀmɑ̃] *ad* harshly.

durer [dyʀe] *vi* to last.

dureté [dyʀte] *nf* hardness; harshness; stiffness; toughness.

durit [dyʀit] *nf* ® (car radiator) hose.

dus *etc vb voir* devoir.

duvet [dyvɛ] *nm* down; (*sac de couchage*) down-filled sleeping bag.

dynamique [dinamik] *a* dynamic.

dynamite [dinamit] *nf* dynamite.

dynamiter [dinamite] *vt* to (blow up with) dynamite.

dynamo [dinamo] *nf* dynamo.

dysenterie [disɑ̃tʀi] *nf* dysentery.

dyslexie [dislɛksi] *nf* dyslexia, word-blindness.

E

eau, x [o] *nf* water // *nfpl* waters; prendre l'~ to leak, let in water; tomber à l'~ (*fig*) to fall through; ~ de Cologne Eau de Cologne; ~ courante running water; ~ douce fresh water; ~ de Javel bleach; ~ minérale mineral water; ~ plate still water; ~ salée salt water; ~ de toilette toilet water; ~-de-vie *nf* brandy; ~-forte *nf* etching.

ébahi, e [ebai] *a* dumbfounded.

ébattre [ebatʀ(ə)]: s'~ *vi* to frolic.

ébaucher [eboʃe] *vt* to sketch out, outline; s'~ *vi* to take shape.

ébène [ebɛn] *nf* ebony.

ébéniste [ebenist(ə)] *nm* cabinetmaker.

éberlué, e [ebɛʀlɥe] *a* astounded.

éblouir [ebluiʀ] *vt* to dazzle.

éblouissement [ebluismɑ̃] *nm* (*faiblesse*) dizzy turn.

éborgner [ebɔʀɲe] *vt*: ~ qn to blind sb in one eye.

éboueur [ebwœʀ] *nm* dustman (*Brit*), garbageman (*US*).

ébouillanter [ebujɑ̃te] *vt* to scald; (*CULIN*) to blanch.

éboulement [ebulmɑ̃] *nm* rock fall.

ébouler [ebule]: s'~ *vi* to crumble, collapse.

éboulis [ebuli] *nmpl* fallen rocks.

ébouriffé, e [eburife] *a* tousled.

ébranler [ebʀɑ̃le] *vt* to shake; (*rendre instable: mur*) to weaken; s'~ *vi* (*partir*) to move off.

ébrécher [ebʀeʃe] *vt* to chip.

ébriété [ebʀijete] *nf*: en état d'~ in a state of intoxication.

ébrouer [ebʀue]: s'~ *vi* to shake o.s.; (*souffler*) to snort.

ébruiter [ebʀɥite] *vt* to spread, disclose.

ébullition [ebylisjɔ̃] *nf* boiling point; en ~ boiling; (*fig*) in an uproar.

écaille [ekaj] *nf* (*de poisson*) scale; (*de coquillage*) shell; (*matière*) tortoiseshell.

écailler [ekaje] *vt* (*poisson*) to scale; (*huître*) to open; s'~ *vi* to flake *ou* peel (off).

écarlate [ekaʀlat] *a* scarlet.

écarquiller [ekaʀkije] *vt*: ~ les yeux to stare wide-eyed.

écart [ekaʀ] *nm* gap; (*embardée*) swerve; sideways leap; (*fig*) departure, deviation; à l'~ *ad* out of the way; à l'~ de *prép* away from.

écarté, e [ekaʀte] *a* (*lieu*) out-of-the-way, remote; (*ouvert*): les jambes ~es legs apart; les bras ~s arms outstretched.

écarteler [ekartəle] *vt* to quarter; (*fig*) to tear.

écarter [ekarte] *vt* (*séparer*) to move apart, separate; (*éloigner*) to push back, move away; (*ouvrir: bras, jambes*) to spread, open; (: *rideau*) to draw (back); (*éliminer: candidat, possibilité*) to dismiss; s'~ *vi* to part; to move away; s'~ de to wander from.

écervelé, e [esɛrvəle] *a* scatterbrained, featherbrained.

échafaud [eʃafo] *nm* scaffold.

échafaudage [eʃafodaʒ] *nm* scaffolding.

échafauder [eʃafode] *vt* (*plan*) to construct.

échalote [eʃalɔt] *nf* shallot.

échancrure [eʃɑ̃kryr] *nf* (*de robe*) scoop neckline; (*de côte, arête rocheuse*) indentation.

échange [eʃɑ̃ʒ] *nm* exchange; en ~ de in exchange *ou* return for.

échanger [eʃɑ̃ʒe] *vt*: ~ qch (contre) to exchange sth (for); **échangeur** *nm* (*AUTO*) interchange.

échantillon [eʃɑ̃tijɔ̃] *nm* sample.

échappée [eʃape] *nf* (*vue*) vista.

échappement [eʃapmɑ̃] *nm* (*AUTO*) exhaust.

échapper [eʃape]: ~ à *vt* (*gardien*) escape (from); (*punition, péril*) to escape; ~ à qn (*détail, sens*) to escape sb; (*objet qu'on tient*) to slip out of sb's hands; s'~ *vi* to escape; laisser ~ (*cri etc*) to let out; l'~ belle to have a narrow escape.

écharde [eʃard(ə)] *nf* splinter (of wood).

écharpe [eʃarp(ə)] *nf* scarf (*pl* scarves); (*de maire*) sash; (*MÉD*) sling.

échasse [eʃas] *nf* stilt.

échauffer [eʃofe] *vt* (*métal, moteur*) to overheat; (*fig: exciter*) to fire, excite; s'~ *vi* (*SPORT*) to warm up; (*dans la discussion*) to become heated.

échauffourée [eʃofure] *nf* clash, brawl.

échéance [eʃeɑ̃s] *nf* (*d'un paiement: date*) settlement date; (: *somme due*) financial commitment(s); (*fig*) deadline; à brève/longue ~ *a* short-/long-term // *ad* in the short/long run.

échéant [eʃeɑ̃]: le cas ~ *ad* if the case arises.

échec [eʃɛk] *nm* failure; (*ÉCHECS*): ~ et mat/au roi checkmate/check; ~s *nmpl* (*jeu*) chess *sg*; tenir en ~ to hold in check; faire ~ à to foil ou thwart.

échelle [eʃɛl] *nf* ladder; (*fig, d'une carte*) scale.

échelon [eʃlɔ̃] *nm* (*d'échelle*) rung; (*ADMIN*) grade.

échelonner [eʃlɔne] *vt* to space out.

échevelé, e [eʃəvle] *a* tousled, dishevelled; wild, frenzied.

échine [eʃin] *nf* backbone, spine.

échiquier [eʃikje] *nm* chessboard.

écho [eko] *nm* echo; ~s *nmpl* (*potins*) gossip *sg*, rumours.

échoir [eʃwar] *vi* (*dette*) to fall due; (*délais*) to expire; ~ à *vt* to fall to.

échoppe [eʃɔp] *nf* stall, booth.

échouer [eʃwe] *vi* to fail; s'~ *vi* to run aground.

échu, e [eʃy] *pp* de **échoir**.

éclabousser [eklabuse] *vt* to splash.

éclair [eklɛr] *nm* (*d'orage*) flash of lightning, lightning *q*; (*gâteau*) éclair.

éclairage [eklɛraʒ] *nm* lighting.

éclaircie [eklɛrsi] *nf* bright interval.

éclaircir [eklɛrsir] *vt* to lighten; (*fig*) to clear up; to clarify; (*CULIN*) to thin (down); s'~ (*ciel*) to clear; s'~ la voix to clear one's throat; **éclaircissement** *nm* clearing up; clarification.

éclairer [eklere] *vt* (*lieu*) to light (up); (*personne: avec une lampe etc*) to light the way for; (*fig*) to enlighten; to shed light on // *vi*: ~ mal/bien to give a poor/ good light; s'~ à l'électricité to have electric lighting.

éclaireur, euse [eklɛrœr, -øz] *nm/f* (*scout*) (boy) scout/(girl) guide // *nm* (*MIL*) scout.

éclat [ekla] *nm* (*de bombe, de verre*) fragment; (*du soleil, d'une couleur etc*) brightness, brilliance; (*d'une cérémonie*) splendour; (*scandale*): faire un ~ to cause a commotion; ~s de voix shouts.

éclatant, e [eklatɑ̃, -ɑ̃t] *a* brilliant.

éclater [eklate] *vi* (*pneu*) to burst; (*bombe*) to explode; (*guerre, épidémie*) to break out; (*groupe, parti*) to break up; ~ en sanglots/de rire to burst out sobbing/laughing.

éclipse [eklips(ə)] *nf* eclipse.

éclipser [eklipse]: s'~ *vi* to slip away.

éclopé, e [eklɔpe] *a* lame.

éclore [eklɔr] *vi* (*œuf*) to hatch; (*fleur*) to open (out).

écluse [eklyz] *nf* lock.

écœurant, e [ekœrɑ̃, -ɑ̃t] *a* (*gâteau etc*) sickly.

écœurer [ekœre] *vt*: ~ qn to make sb feel sick.

école [ekɔl] *nf* school; aller à l'~ to go to school; ~ normale teachers' training college; **écolier, ière** *nm/f* schoolboy/ girl.

écologie [ekɔlɔʒi] *nf* ecology; environmental studies *pl*.

éconduire [ekɔ̃dɥir] *vt* to dismiss.

économe [ekɔnɔm] *a* thrifty // *nm/f* (*de lycée etc*) bursar (*Brit*), treasurer (*US*).

économie [ekɔnɔmi] *nf* economy; (*gain: d'argent, de temps etc*) saving; (*science*) economics *sg*; ~s *nfpl* (*pécule*) savings; **économique** *a* (*avantageux*) economical; (*ÉCON*) economic.

économiser [ekɔnɔmize] *vt, vi* to save.
écoper [ekɔpe] *vi* to bale out; *(fig)* to cop it; ~ **(de)** *vt* to get.
écorce [ekɔrs(ə)] *nf* bark; *(de fruit)* peel.
écorcher [ekɔrʃe] *vt (animal)* to skin; *(égratigner)* to graze; **écorchure** *nf* graze.
écossais, e [ekɔsɛ, -ɛz] *a* Scottish // *nm/f*: É~, e Scot.
Écosse [ekɔs] *nf*: l'~ Scotland.
écosser [ekɔse] *vt* to shell.
écouler [ekule] *vt* to sell; to dispose of; s'~ *vi (eau)* to flow (out); *(jours, temps)* to pass (by).
écourter [ekurte] *vt* to curtail, cut short.
écoute [ekut] *nf (RADIO, TV):* **temps/ heure d'~** (listening *ou* viewing) time/ hour; **prendre l'~** to tune in; **rester à l'~ (de)** to stay tuned in; ~s **télé-phoniques** phone tapping *sg*.
écouter [ekute] *vt* to listen to; **écouteur** *nm (TÉL)* receiver; *(RADIO)* headphones *pl*, headset.
écoutille [ekutij] *nf* hatch.
écran [ekrã] *nm* screen.
écrasant, e [ekrazã, -ãt] *a* overwhelming.
écraser [ekraze] *vt* to crush; *(piéton)* to run over; s'~ *vi (fam)* to pipe down; s'~ **(au sol)** to crash; s'~ **contre** to crash into.
écrémer [ekreme] *vt* to skim.
écrevisse [ekrəvis] *nf* crayfish *inv*.
écrier [ekrije]: s'~ *vi* to exclaim.
écrin [ekrɛ̃] *nm* case, box.
écrire [ekrir] *vt* to write; s'~ to write to each other; **ça s'écrit comment?** how is it spelt?; **écrit** *nm* document; *(examen)* written paper; **par écrit** in writing.
écriteau, x [ekrito] *nm* notice, sign.
écriture [ekrityr] *nf* writing; *(COMM)* entry; ~s *nfpl (COMM)* accounts, books; **l'É~, les É~s** the Scriptures.
écrivain [ekrivɛ̃] *nm* writer.
écrou [ekru] *nm* nut.
écrouer [ekrue] *vt* to imprison; to remand in custody.
écrouler [ekrule]: s'~ *vi* to collapse.
écru, e [ekry] *a (toile)* raw, unbleached; *(couleur)* off-white, écru.
écueil [ekœj] *nm* reef; *(fig)* pitfall; stumbling block.
écuelle [ekɥɛl] *nf* bowl.
éculé, e [ekyle] *a (chaussure)* down-at-heel; *(fig: péj)* hackneyed.
écume [ekym] *nf* foam; *(CULIN)* scum; **écumer** *vt (CULIN)* to skim; *(fig)* to plunder.
écureuil [ekyrœj] *nm* squirrel.
écurie [ekyri] *nf* stable.
écusson [ekysɔ̃] *nm* badge.
écuyer, ère [ekɥije, -ɛr] *nm/f* rider.
eczéma [ɛgzema] *nm* eczema.

édenté, e [edãte] *a* toothless.
E.D.F. *sigle f* (= *Électricité de France*) national electricity company.
édifier [edifje] *vt* to build, erect; *(fig)* to edify.
édiles [edil] *nmpl* city fathers.
édit [edi] *nm* edict.
éditer [edite] *vt (publier)* to publish; *(: disque)* to produce; **éditeur, trice** *nm/f* editor; publisher; **édition** *nf* editing *q*; edition; *(industrie du livre)* publishing.
édredon [edrədɔ̃] *nm* eiderdown.
éducatif, ive [edykatif, -iv] *a* educational.
éducation [edykasjɔ̃] *nf* education; *(familiale)* upbringing; *(manières)* (good) manners *pl*; ~ **physique** physical education.
édulcorer [edylkɔre] *vt* to sweeten; *(fig)* to tone down.
éduquer [edyke] *vt* to educate; *(élever)* to bring up; *(faculté)* to train.
effacé, e [efase] *a* unassuming.
effacer [efase] *vt* to erase, rub out; s'~ *vi (inscription etc)* to wear off; *(pour laisser passer)* to step aside.
effarer [efare] *vt* to alarm.
effaroucher [efaruʃe] *vt* to frighten *ou* scare away; to alarm.
effectif, ive [efɛktif, -iv] *a* real; effective // *nm (MIL)* strength; *(SCOL)* (pupil) numbers *pl*; **effectivement** *ad* effectively; *(réellement)* actually, really; *(en effet)* indeed.
effectuer [efɛktɥe] *vt (opération)* to carry out; *(déplacement, trajet)* to make; *(mouvement)* to execute.
efféminé, e [efemine] *a* effeminate.
effervescent, e [efɛrvesã, -ãt] *a* effervescent; *(fig)* agitated.
effet [efɛ] *nm (résultat, artifice)* effect; *(impression)* impression; ~s *nmpl (vêtements etc)* things; **faire de l'~** *(médicament, menace)* to have an effect; **en ~** *ad* indeed.
efficace [efikas] *a (personne)* efficient; *(action, médicament)* effective.
effilé, e [efile] *a* slender; sharp; streamlined.
effiler [efile] *vt (tissu)* to fray.
effilocher [efiloʃe]: s'~ *vi* to fray.
efflanqué, e [eflãke] *a* emaciated.
effleurer [eflœre] *vt* to brush (against); *(sujet)* to touch upon; *(suj: idée, pensée)*: ~ **qn** to cross sb's mind.
effluves [eflyv] *nmpl* exhalation(s).
effondrer [efɔ̃dre]: s'~ *vi* to collapse.
efforcer [efɔrse]: s'~ **de** *vt*: s'~ **de faire** to try hard to do, try hard to.
effort [efɔr] *nm* effort.
effraction [efraksjɔ̃] *nf*: **s'introduire par ~ dans** to break into.
effrayant, e [efrɛjã, -ãt] *a* frightening.
effrayer [efrɛje] *vt* to frighten, scare.
effréné, e [efrene] *a* wild.

effriter [efʀite]: s'~ *vi* to crumble.
effroi [efʀwa] *nm* terror, dread *q*.
effronté, e [efʀɔ̃te] *a* insolent, brazen.
effroyable [efʀwajabl(ə)] *a* horrifying, appalling.
effusion [efyzjɔ̃] *nf* effusion; **sans ~ de sang** without bloodshed.
égal, e, aux [egal, -o] *a* equal; (*plan: surface*) even, level; (*constant: vitesse*) steady; (*équitable*) even // *nm/f* equal; **être ~ à** (*prix, nombre*) to be equal to; **ça lui est ~** it's all the same to him; he doesn't mind; **sans ~** matchless, unequalled; **à l'~ de** (*comme*) just like; **d'~ à ~** as equals; **~ement** *ad* equally; evenly; steadily; (*aussi*) too, as well; **~er** *vt* to equal; **~iser** *vt* (*sol, salaires*) to level (out); (*chances*) to equalize // *vi* (*SPORT*) to equalize; **~ité** *nf* equality; evenness; steadiness; (*MATH*) identity; **être à ~ité (de points)** to be level.
égard [egaʀ] *nm*: **~s** *nmpl* consideration *sg*; **à cet ~** in this respect; **eu ~ à** in view of; **par ~ pour** out of consideration for; **sans ~ pour** without regard for; **à l'~ de** *prép* towards; concerning.
égarement [egaʀmɑ̃] *nm* distraction; aberration.
égarer [egaʀe] *vt* to mislay; (*moralement*) to lead astray; **s'~** *vi* to get lost, lose one's way; (*objet*) to go astray; (*dans une discussion*) to wander.
égayer [egeje] *vt* (*personne*) to amuse; to cheer up; (*récit, endroit*) to brighten up, liven up.
églantine [eglɑ̃tin] *nf* wild *ou* dog rose.
églefin [egləfɛ̃] *nm* haddock.
église [egliz] *nf* church; **aller à l'~** to go to church.
égoïsme [egɔism(ə)] *nm* selfishness; **égoïste** *a* selfish.
égorger [egɔʀʒe] *vt* to cut the throat of.
égosiller [egozije]: **s'~** *vi* to shout o.s. hoarse.
égout [egu] *nm* sewer.
égoutter [egute] *vt* (*linge*) to wring out; (*vaisselle*) to drain // *vi*, **s'~** *vi* to drip; **égouttoir** *nm* draining board; (*mobile*) draining rack.
égratigner [egʀatiɲe] *vt* to scratch; **égratignure** *nf* scratch.
égrillard, e [egʀijaʀ, -aʀd(ə)] *a* ribald.
Égypte [eʒipt(ə)] *nf*: **l'~** Egypt; **égyptien, ne** *a*, *nm/f* Egyptian.
eh [e] *excl* hey!; **~ bien** well.
éhonté, e [eɔ̃te] *a* shameless, brazen.
éjecter [eʒɛkte] *vt* (*TECH*) to eject; (*fam*) to kick *ou* chuck out.
élaborer [elabɔʀe] *vt* to elaborate; (*projet, stratégie*) to work out; (*rapport*) to draft.
élaguer [elage] *vt* to prune.
élan [elɑ̃] *nm* (*ZOOL*) elk, moose; (*SPORT: avant le saut*) run up; (*d'objet en mouvement*) momentum; (*fig: de ten-*

dresse etc) surge; **prendre de l'~** to gather speed.
élancé, e [elɑ̃se] *a* slender.
élancement [elɑ̃smɑ̃] *nm* shooting pain.
élancer [elɑ̃se]: **s'~** *vi* to dash, hurl o.s.; (*fig: arbre, clocher*) to soar (upwards).
élargir [elaʀʒiʀ] *vt* to widen; (*vêtement*) to let out; (*JUR*) to release; **s'~** *vi* to widen; (*vêtement*) to stretch.
élastique [elastik] *a* elastic // *nm* (*de bureau*) rubber band; (*pour la couture*) elastic *q*.
électeur, trice [elɛktœʀ, -tʀis] *nm/f* elector, voter.
élection [elɛksjɔ̃] *nf* election.
électorat [elɛktɔʀa] *nm* electorate.
électricien, ne [elɛktʀisjɛ̃, -jɛn] *nm/f* electrician.
électricité [elɛktʀisite] *nf* electricity; **allumer/éteindre l'~** to put on/off the light.
électrique [elɛktʀik] *a* electric(al).
électro... [elɛktʀo] *préfixe*: **~choc** *nm* electric shock treatment; **~ménager** *a*, *nm*: **appareils ~ménagers, l'~ménager** domestic (electrical) appliances.
électronique [elɛktʀɔnik] *a* electronic // *nf* electronics *sg*.
électrophone [elɛktʀɔfɔn] *nm* record player.
élégant, e [elegɑ̃, -ɑ̃t] *a* elegant; (*solution*) neat, elegant; (*attitude, procédé*) courteous, civilized.
élément [elemɑ̃] *nm* element; (*pièce*) component, part; **élémentaire** *a* elementary.
éléphant [elefɑ̃] *nm* elephant.
élevage [elvaʒ] *nm* breeding; (*de bovins*) cattle rearing.
élévation [elevasjɔ̃] *nf* (*gén*) elevation; (*voir élever*) raising; (*voir s'élever*) rise.
élevé, e [elve] *a* (*prix, sommet*) high; (*fig: noble*) elevated; **bien/mal ~** well-/ill-mannered.
élève [elɛv] *nm/f* pupil.
élever [elve] *vt* (*enfant*) to bring up, raise; (*bétail, volaille*) to breed; (*abeilles*) to keep; (*hausser: taux, niveau*) to raise; (*fig: âme, esprit*) to elevate; (*édifier: monument*) to put up, erect; **s'~** *vi* (*avion, alpiniste*) to go up; (*niveau, température, aussi: cri etc*) to rise; (*survenir: difficultés*) to arise; **s'~ à** (*suj: frais, dégâts*) to amount to, add up to; **s'~ contre qch** to rise up against sth; **~ la voix** to raise one's voice; **éleveur, euse** *nm/f* breeder.
élimé, e [elime] *a* threadbare.
éliminatoire [eliminatwaʀ] *nf* (*SPORT*) heat.
éliminer [elimine] *vt* to eliminate.
élire [eliʀ] *vt* to elect.
elle [ɛl] *pronom* (*sujet*) she; (: *chose*) it; (*complément*) her; it; **~s** they; them;

~-**même** herself; itself; ~**s-mêmes** themselves; *voir* il.

élocution [elɔkysjɔ̃] *nf* delivery; **défaut d'~** speech impediment.

éloge [elɔʒ] *nm* praise (*gén q*); **élogieux, euse** *a* laudatory, full of praise.

éloigné, e [elwaɲe] *a* distant, far-off.

éloignement [elwaɲmɑ̃] *nm* removal; putting off; estrangement; (*fig*) distance.

éloigner [elwaɲe] *vt* (*objet*): ~ **qch (de)** to move ou take sth away (from); (*personne*): ~ **qn (de)** to take sb away ou remove sb (from); (*échéance*) to put off, postpone; (*soupçons, danger*) to ward off; **s'~ (de)** (*personne*) to go away (from); (*véhicule*) to move away (from); (*affectivement*) to become estranged (from).

élongation [elɔ̃gasjɔ̃] *nf* strained muscle.

éloquent, e [elɔkɑ̃, -ɑ̃t] *a* eloquent.

élu, e [ely] *pp de* **élire** // *nm/f* (*POL*) elected representative.

élucubrations [elykybʀasjɔ̃] *nfpl* wild imaginings.

éluder [elyde] *vt* to evade.

émacié, e [emasje] *a* emaciated.

émail, aux [emaj, -o] *nm* enamel.

émaillé, e [emaje] *a* (*fig*): ~ **de** dotted with.

émanciper [emɑ̃sipe] *vt* to emancipate; **s'~** *vi* (*fig*) to become emancipated ou liberated.

émaner [emane]: ~ **de** *vt* to come from; (*ADMIN*) to proceed from.

emballage [ɑ̃balaʒ] *nm* wrapping; packaging.

emballer [ɑ̃bale] *vt* to wrap (up); (*dans un carton*) to pack (up); (*fig: fam*) to thrill (to bits); **s'~** *vi* (*moteur*) to race; (*cheval*) to bolt; (*fig: personne*) to get carried away.

embarcadère [ɑ̃baʀkadɛʀ] *nm* wharf, pier.

embarcation [ɑ̃baʀkasjɔ̃] *nf* (small) boat, (small) craft *inv*.

embardée [ɑ̃baʀde] *nf*: **faire une ~** to swerve.

embarquement [ɑ̃baʀkəmɑ̃] *nm* embarkation; loading; boarding.

embarquer [ɑ̃baʀke] *vt* (*personne*) to embark; (*marchandise*) to load; (*fam*) to cart off; to nick // *vi* (*passager*) to board; **s'~** *vi* to board; **s'~ dans** (*affaire, aventure*) to embark upon.

embarras [ɑ̃baʀa] *nm* (*obstacle*) hindrance; (*confusion*) embarrassment.

embarrassant, e [ɑ̃baʀasɑ̃, -ɑ̃t] *a* embarrassing.

embarrasser [ɑ̃baʀase] *vt* (*encombrer*) to clutter (up); (*gêner*) to hinder, hamper; (*fig*) to cause embarrassment to; to put in an awkward position.

embauche [ɑ̃boʃ] *nf* hiring; **bureau d'~** labour office.

embaucher [ɑ̃boʃe] *vt* to take on, hire.

embaumer [ɑ̃bome] *vt* to embalm; to fill with its fragrance; ~ **la lavande** to be fragrant with (the scent of) lavender.

embellie [ɑ̃beli] *nf* brighter period.

embellir [ɑ̃beliʀ] *vt* to make more attractive; (*une histoire*) to embellish // *vi* to grow lovelier ou more attractive.

embêtements [ɑ̃bɛtmɑ̃] *nmpl* trouble *sg*.

embêter [ɑ̃bɛte] *vt* to bother; **s'~** *vi* (*s'ennuyer*) to be bored.

emblée [ɑ̃ble]: **d'~** *ad* straightaway.

emboîter [ɑ̃bwate] *vt* to fit together; **s'~ (dans)** to fit (into); ~ **le pas à qn** to follow in sb's footsteps.

embonpoint [ɑ̃bɔ̃pwɛ̃] *nm* stoutness.

embouchure [ɑ̃buʃyʀ] *nf* (*GÉO*) mouth.

embourber [ɑ̃buʀbe]: **s'~** *vi* to get stuck in the mud.

embourgeoiser [ɑ̃buʀʒwaze]: **s'~** *vi* to adopt a middle-class outlook.

embouteillage [ɑ̃buteja3] *nm* traffic jam.

emboutir [ɑ̃butiʀ] *vt* (*heurter*) to crash into, ram.

embranchement [ɑ̃bʀɑ̃ʃmɑ̃] *nm* (*routier*) junction; (*classification*) branch.

embraser [ɑ̃bʀaze]: **s'~** *vi* to flare up.

embrasser [ɑ̃bʀase] *vt* to kiss; (*sujet, période*) to embrace, encompass; (*carrière, métier*) to enter upon.

embrasure [ɑ̃bʀazyʀ] *nf*: **dans l'~ de la porte** in the door(way).

embrayage [ɑ̃bʀeja3] *nm* clutch.

embrayer [ɑ̃bʀeje] *vi* (*AUTO*) to let in the clutch.

embrigader [ɑ̃bʀigade] *vt* to recruit.

embrocher [ɑ̃bʀɔʃe] *vt* to put on a spit.

embrouiller [ɑ̃bʀuje] *vt* (*fils*) to tangle (up); (*fiches, idées, personne*) to muddle up; **s'~** *vi* (*personne*) to get in a muddle.

embruns [ɑ̃bʀœ̃] *nmpl* sea spray *sg*.

embûches [ɑ̃byʃ] *nfpl* pitfalls, traps.

embué, e [ɑ̃bɥe] *a* misted up.

embuscade [ɑ̃byskad] *nf* ambush.

éméché, e [emeʃe] *a* tipsy, merry.

émeraude [emʀod] *nf* emerald.

émerger [emɛʀʒe] *vi* to emerge; (*faire saillie, aussi fig*) to stand out.

émeri [emʀi] *nm*: **toile** ou **papier ~** emery paper.

émérite [emeʀit] *a* highly skilled.

émerveiller [emɛʀveje] *vt* to fill with wonder; **s'~ de** to marvel at.

émetteur, trice [emetœʀ, -tʀis] *a* transmitting; (*poste*) ~ transmitter.

émettre [emɛtʀ(ə)] *vt* (*son, lumière*) to give out, emit; (*message etc: RADIO*) to transmit; (*billet, timbre, emprunt*) to issue; (*hypothèse, avis*) to voice, put forward // *vi* to broadcast.

émeus *etc vb voir* **émouvoir**.

émeute [emøt] *nf* riot.

émietter [emjete] *vt* to crumble.

émigrer [emigʀe] *vi* to emigrate.

éminence [eminɑ̃s] *nf* distinction; *(colline)* knoll, hill; **Son É~** his *(ou* her) Eminence.

éminent, e [eminɑ̃, -ɑ̃t] *a* distinguished.

émission [emisjɔ̃] *nf* emission; transmission; issue; *(RADIO, TV)* programme, broadcast.

emmagasiner [ɑ̃magazine] *vt* to (put into) store; *(fig)* to store up.

emmailloter [ɑ̃majɔte] *vt* to wrap up.

emmanchure [ɑ̃mɑ̃ʃyʀ] *nf* armhole.

emmêler [ɑ̃mele] *vt* to tangle (up); *(fig)* to muddle up; **s'~** *vi* to get into a tangle.

emménager [ɑ̃menaʒe] *vi* to move in; **~ dans** to move into.

emmener [ɑ̃mne] *vt* to take (with one); *(comme otage, capture)* to take away; **~ qn au cinéma** to take sb to the cinema.

emmerder [ɑ̃mɛʀde] *(fam!)* *vt* to bug, bother; **s'~** *vi* to be bored stiff.

emmitoufler [ɑ̃mitufle] *vt* to wrap up (warmly).

émoi [emwa] *nm* commotion; *(trouble)* agitation.

émoluments [emɔlymɑ̃] *nmpl* remuneration *sg*, fee *sg*.

émonder [emɔ̃de] *vt* to prune.

émotif, ive [emɔtif, -iv] *a* emotional.

émotion [emɔsjɔ̃] *nf* emotion.

émousser [emuse] *vt* to blunt; *(fig)* to dull.

émouvoir [emuvwaʀ] *vt* *(troubler)* to stir, affect; *(toucher, attendrir)* to move; *(indigner)* to rouse; **s'~** *vi* to be affected; to be moved; to be roused.

empailler [ɑ̃paje] *vt* to stuff.

empaler [ɑ̃pale] *vt* to impale.

emparer [ɑ̃paʀe]: **s'~ de** *vt (objet)* to seize, grab; *(comme otage, MIL)* to seize; *(suj: peur etc)* to take hold of.

empâter [ɑ̃pɑte]: **s'~** *vi* to thicken out.

empêchement [ɑ̃pɛʃmɑ̃] *nm* (unexpected) obstacle, hitch.

empêcher [ɑ̃peʃe] *vt* to prevent; **~ qn de faire** to prevent *ou* stop sb (from) doing; **il n'empêche que** nevertheless; **il n'a pas pu s'~ de rire** he couldn't help laughing.

empereur [ɑ̃pʀœʀ] *nm* emperor.

empeser [ɑ̃pɔze] *vt* to starch.

empester [ɑ̃peste] *vi* to stink, reek.

empêtrer [ɑ̃petʀe] *vt*: **s'~ dans** *(fils etc)* to get tangled up in.

emphase [ɑ̃faz] *nf* pomposity, bombast.

empiéter [ɑ̃pjete] *vi*: **~ sur** to encroach upon.

empiffrer [ɑ̃pifʀe]: **s'~** *vi (péj)* to stuff o.s.

empiler [ɑ̃pile] *vt* to pile (up).

empire [ɑ̃piʀ] *nm* empire; *(fig)* influence.

empirer [ɑ̃piʀe] *vi* to worsen, deteriorate.

emplacement [ɑ̃plasmɑ̃] *nm* site.

emplettes [ɑ̃plɛt] *nfpl* shopping *sg*.

emplir [ɑ̃pliʀ] *vt* to fill; **s'~ (de)** to fill (with).

emploi [ɑ̃plwa] *nm* use; *(COMM, ÉCON)* employment; *(poste)* job, situation; **~ du temps** timetable, schedule.

employé, e [ɑ̃plwaje] *nm/f* employee; **~ de bureau** office employee *ou* clerk.

employer [ɑ̃plwaje] *vt (outil, moyen, méthode, mot)* to use; *(ouvrier, main-d'œuvre)* to employ; **s'~ à faire** to apply *ou* devote o.s. to doing; **employeur, euse** *nm/f* employer.

empocher [ɑ̃pɔʃe] *vt* to pocket.

empoignade [ɑ̃pwaɲad] *nf* row, set-to.

empoigner [ɑ̃pwaɲe] *vt* to grab.

empoisonner [ɑ̃pwazɔne] *vt* to poison; *(empester: air, pièce)* to stink out; *(fam)*: **~ qn** to drive sb mad.

emporter [ɑ̃pɔʀte] *vt* to take (with one); *(en dérobant ou enlevant, emmener: blessés, voyageurs)* to take away; *(entraîner)* to carry away; *(arracher)* to tear off; *(avantage, approbation)* to win; **s'~** *vi (de colère)* to lose one's temper; **l'~ (sur)** to get the upper hand (of); *(méthode etc)* to prevail (over); **boissons à ~** take-away drinks.

empreint, e [ɑ̃pʀɛ̃, -ɛ̃t] *a*: **~ de** marked with; tinged with // *nf (de pied, main)* print; *(fig)* stamp, mark; **~e (digitale)** fingerprint.

empressé, e [ɑ̃pʀese] *a* attentive.

empressement [ɑ̃pʀɛsmɑ̃] *nm (hâte)* eagerness.

empresser [ɑ̃pʀese]: **s'~** *vi*: **s'~ auprès de qn** to surround sb with attentions; **s'~ de faire** *(se hâter)* to hasten to do.

emprise [ɑ̃pʀiz] *nf* hold, ascendancy.

emprisonner [ɑ̃pʀizɔne] *vt* to imprison.

emprunt [ɑ̃pʀœ̃] *nm* borrowing *q*, loan.

emprunté, e [ɑ̃pʀœ̃te] *a (fig)* ill-at-ease, awkward.

emprunter [ɑ̃pʀœ̃te] *vt* to borrow; *(itinéraire)* to take, follow; *(style, manière)* to adopt, assume.

ému, e [emy] *pp de* **émouvoir** // *a* excited; touched; moved.

émulsion [emylsjɔ̃] *nf (cosmetic)* (water-based) lotion.

en [ɑ̃] ♦ *prép* **1** *(endroit, pays)* in; *(direction)* to; **habiter ~ France/ville** to live in France/town; **aller ~ France/ville** to go to France/town
2 *(moment, temps)* in; **~ été/juin** in summer/June
3 *(moyen)* by; **~ avion/taxi** by plane/taxi
4 *(composition)* made of; **c'est ~ verre** it's (made of) glass; **un collier ~ argent** a silver necklace
5 *(description, état)*: **une femme (habillée) ~ rouge** a woman (dressed) in red; **peindre qch ~ rouge** to paint sth red; **~ T/étoile** T-/star-shaped; **~**

chemise/chaussettes in one's shirt-sleeves/socks; **~ soldat** as a soldier; **cassé ~** plusieurs morceaux broken into several pieces; **~ réparation** being repaired, under repair; **~ vacances** on holiday; **~ deuil** in mourning; le **même ~ plus grand** the same but *ou* only bigger

6 (*avec gérondif*) while; on; by; **~ dormant** while sleeping, as one sleeps; **~ sortant** on going out, as he *etc* went out; **sortir ~ courant** to run out

♦ *pronom* **1** (*indéfini*): **j'~ ai/veux** I have/want some; **~ as-tu?** have you got any?; **je n'~ veux pas** I don't want any; **j'~ ai 2** I've got 2; **combien y ~ a-t-il?** how many (of them) are there?; **j'~ ai assez** I've got enough (of it *ou* them); (*j'en ai marre*) I've had enough **2** (*provenance*) from there; **j'~ viens** I've come from there **3** (*cause*): **il ~ est malade/perd le sommeil** he is ill/can't sleep because of it **4** (*complément de nom, d'adjectif, de verbe*): **j'~ connais les dangers** I know its *ou* the dangers; **j'~ suis fier/ai besoin** I am proud of it/need it; *voir le verbe ou l'adjectif lorsque 'en' correspond à 'de' introduisant un complément prépositionnel.*

E.N.A. [ena] *sigle f* (= *École Nationale d'Administration*) one of the *Grandes Écoles.*

encadrer [ãkɑdʀe] *vt* (*tableau, image*) to frame; (*fig: entourer*) to surround; (*personnel, soldats etc*) to train.

encaisse [ãkɛs] *nf* cash in hand; **~ or/ métallique** gold/gold and silver reserves.

encaissé, e [ãkese] *a* steep-sided; with steep banks.

encaisser [ãkese] *vt* (*chèque*) to cash; (*argent*) to collect; (*fig: coup, défaite*) to take.

encan [ãkã]: **à l'~** *ad* by auction.

encart [ãkaʀ] *nm* insert.

encastrer [ãkastʀe] *vt*: **~ qch dans** (*mur*) to embed sth in(to); (*boîtier*) to fit sth into.

encaustique [ãkɔstik] *nf* polish, wax.

enceinte [ãsɛ̃t] *af*: **~ (de 6 mois)** (6 months) pregnant // *nf* (*mur*) wall; (*espace*) enclosure.

encens [ãsã] *nm* incense.

encercler [ãsɛʀkle] *vt* to surround.

enchaîner [ãʃene] *vt* to chain up; (*mouvements, séquences*) to link (together) // *vi* to carry on.

enchanté, e [ãʃãte] *a* delighted; enchanted; **~ (de faire votre connaissance)** pleased to meet you.

enchantement [ãʃãtmã] *nm* delight; (*magie*) enchantment.

enchâsser [ãʃase] *vt* to set.

enchère [ãʃɛʀ] *nf* bid; **mettre/vendre aux ~s** to put up for (sale by)/sell by

auction.

enchevêtrer [ãʃvetʀe] *vt* to tangle (up).

enclencher [ãklãʃe] *vt* (*mécanisme*) to engage; **s'~** *vi* to engage.

enclin, e [ãklɛ̃, -in] *a*: **~ à** inclined *ou* prone to.

enclos [ãklo] *nm* enclosure.

enclume [ãklym] *nf* anvil.

encoche [ãkɔʃ] *nf* notch.

encoignure [ãkɔɲyʀ] *nf* corner.

encolure [ãkɔlyʀ] *nf* (*tour de cou*) collar size; (*col, cou*) neck.

encombrant, e [ãkɔ̃bʀã, -ãt] *a* cumbersome, bulky.

encombre [ãkɔ̃bʀ(ə)]: **sans ~** *ad* without mishap *ou* incident.

encombrer [ãkɔ̃bʀe] *vt* to clutter (up); (*gêner*) to hamper; **s'~ de** (*bagages etc*) to load *ou* burden o.s. with.

encontre [ãkɔ̃tʀ(ə)]: **à l'~ de** *prép* against, counter to.

encore [ãkɔʀ] *ad* **1** (*continuation*) still; **il y travaille ~** he's still working on it; **pas ~** not yet **2** (*de nouveau*) again; **j'irai ~ demain** I'll go again tomorrow; **~ une fois** (once) again; **~ deux jours** two more days **3** (*intensif*) even, still; **~ plus fort/ mieux** even louder/better, louder/better still **4** (*restriction*) even so *ou* then, only; **~ pourrais-je le faire si ...** even so, I might be able to do it if ...; **si ~** if only **encore que** *cj* although.

encourager [ãkuʀaʒe] *vt* to encourage.

encourir [ãkuʀiʀ] *vt* to incur.

encre [ãkʀ(ə)] *nf* ink; **~ de Chine** Indian ink; **encrier** *nm* inkwell.

encroûter [ãkʀute]: **s'~** *vi* (*fig*) to get into a rut, get set in one's ways.

encyclopédie [ãsiklɔpedi] *nf* encyclopaedia.

endetter [ãdete] *vt*, **s'~** *vi* to get into debt.

endiablé, e [ãdjable] *a* furious; boisterous.

endiguer [ãdige] *vt* to dyke (up); (*fig*) to check, hold back.

endimancher [ãdimãʃe] *vt*: **s'~** to put on one's Sunday best.

endive [ãdiv] *nf* chicory *q.*

endoctriner [ãdɔktʀine] *vt* to indoctrinate.

endommager [ãdɔmaʒe] *vt* to damage.

endormi, e [ãdɔʀmi] *a* asleep.

endormir [ãdɔʀmiʀ] *vt* to put to sleep; (*suj: chaleur etc*) to send to sleep; (*MÉD: dent, nerf*) to anaesthetize; (*fig: soupçons*) to allay; **s'~** *vi* to fall asleep, go to sleep.

endosser [ãdose] *vt* (*responsabilité*) to take, shoulder; (*chèque*) to endorse; (*uniforme, tenue*) to put on, don.

endroit [ãdʀwa] *nm* place; (*opposé à*

l'envers) right side; **à l'~** the right way out; the right way up; **à l'~ de** *prép* regarding.

enduire [ãduiʀ] *vt* to coat.

endurant, e [ãdyʀã, -ãt] *a* tough, hardy.

endurcir [ãdyʀsiʀ] *vt* (*physiquement*) to toughen; (*moralement*) to harden; **s'~** *vi* to become tougher; to become hardened.

endurer [ãdyʀe] *vt* to endure, bear.

énergie [enɛʀʒi] *nf* (*PHYSIQUE*) energy; (*TECH*) power; (*morale*) vigour, spirit; **énergique** *a* energetic; vigorous; (*mesures*) drastic, stringent.

énergumène [enɛʀgymɛn] *nm* rowdy character *ou* customer.

énerver [enɛʀve] *vt* to irritate, annoy; **s'~** *vi* to get excited, get worked up.

enfance [ãfãs] *nf* (*âge*) childhood; (*fig*) infancy; (*enfants*) children *pl*.

enfant [ãfã] *nm/f* child (*pl* children); **~ de chœur** *nm* (*REL*) altar boy; **enfanter** *vi* to give birth to // *vt* to give birth to; **enfantillage** *nm* (*péj*) childish behaviour *q*; **enfantin, e** *a* childlike; child *cpd*.

enfer [ãfɛʀ] *nm* hell.

enfermer [ãfɛʀme] *vt* to shut up; (*à clef, interner*) to lock up.

enfiévré, e [ãfjevʀe] *a* (*fig*) feverish.

enfiler [ãfile] *vt* (*vêtement*) to slip on, slip into; (*insérer*): **~ qch dans** to stick sth into; (*rue, couloir*) to take; (*perles*) to string; (*aiguille*) to thread.

enfin [ãfɛ̃] *ad* at last; (*en énumérant*) lastly; (*de restriction, résignation*) still; well; (*pour conclure*) in a word.

enflammer [ãflame] *vt* to set fire to; (*MÉD*) to inflame; **s'~** *vi* to catch fire; to become inflamed.

enflé, e [ãfle] *a* swollen.

enfler [ãfle] *vi* to swell (up).

enfoncer [ãfɔ̃se] *vt* (*clou*) to drive in; (*faire pénétrer*): **~ qch dans** to push (*ou* drive) sth into; (*forcer: porte*) to break open; (: *plancher*) to cause to cave in // *vi* (*dans la vase etc*) to sink in; (*sol, surface*) to give way; **s'~** *vi* to sink; **s'~ dans** to sink into; (*forêt, ville*) to disappear into.

enfouir [ãfwiʀ] *vt* (*dans le sol*) to bury; (*dans un tiroir etc*) to tuck away.

enfourcher [ãfuʀʃe] *vt* to mount.

enfourner [ãfuʀne] *vt* to put in the oven.

enfreindre [ãfʀɛ̃dʀ(ə)] *vt* to infringe, break.

enfuir [ãfɥiʀ]: **s'~** *vi* to run away *ou* off.

enfumer [ãfyme] *vt* to smoke out.

engageant, e [ãgaʒã, -ãt] *a* attractive, appealing.

engagement [ãgaʒmã] *nm* (*promesse, contrat, POL*) commitment; (*MIL: combat*) engagement.

engager [ãgaʒe] *vt* (*embaucher*) to take on, engage; (*commencer*) to start; (*lier*) to bind, commit; (*impliquer, entraîner*) to involve; (*investir*) to invest, lay out; (*faire intervenir*) to engage; (*inciter*) to urge; (*faire pénétrer*) to insert; **s'~** *vi* to hire o.s., engage; (*MIL*) to enlist; (*promettre, politiquement*) to commit o.s.; (*débuter*) to start (up); **s'~ à faire** to undertake to do; **s'~ dans** (*rue, passage*) to turn into; (*s'emboîter*) to engage into; (*fig: affaire, discussion*) to enter into, embark on.

engelures [ãʒlyʀ] *nfpl* chilblains.

engendrer [ãʒãdʀe] *vt* to father.

engin [ãʒɛ̃] *nm* machine; instrument; vehicle; (*AVIAT*) aircraft *inv*; missile.

englober [ãglɔbe] *vt* to include.

engloutir [ãglutiʀ] *vt* to swallow up.

engoncé, e [ãgɔ̃se] *a*: **~ dans** cramped in.

engorger [ãgɔʀʒe] *vt* to obstruct, block.

engouement [ãgumã] *nm* (sudden) passion.

engouffrer [ãgufʀe] *vt* to swallow up, devour; **s'~ dans** to rush into.

engourdir [ãguʀdiʀ] *vt* to numb; (*fig*) to dull, blunt; **s'~** *vi* to go numb.

engrais [ãgʀɛ] *nm* manure; **~ (chimique)** (chemical) fertilizer.

engraisser [ãgʀese] *vt* to fatten (up).

engrenage [ãgʀənaʒ] *nm* gears *pl*, gearing; (*fig*) chain.

engueuler [ãgœle] *vt* (*fam*) to bawl at.

enhardir [ãaʀdiʀ]: **s'~** *vi* to grow bolder.

énigme [enigm(ə)] *nf* riddle.

enivrer [ãnivʀe] *vt*: **s'~** to get drunk; **s'~ de** (*fig*) to become intoxicated with.

enjambée [ãʒãbe] *nf* stride.

enjamber [ãʒãbe] *vt* to stride over; (*suj: pont etc*) to span, straddle.

enjeu, x [ãʒø] *nm* stakes *pl*.

enjoindre [ãʒwɛ̃dʀ(ə)] *vt* to enjoin, order.

enjôler [ãʒole] *vt* to coax, wheedle.

enjoliver [ãʒɔlive] *vt* to embellish; **enjoliveur** *nm* (*AUTO*) hub cap.

enjoué, e [ãʒwe] *a* playful.

enlacer [ãlase] *vt* (*étreindre*) to embrace, hug.

enlaidir [ãlediʀ] *vt* to make ugly // *vi* to become ugly.

enlèvement [ãlɛvmã] *nm* (*rapt*) abduction, kidnapping.

enlever [ãlve] *vt* (*ôter: gén*) to remove; (: *vêtement, lunettes*) to take off; (*emporter: ordures etc*) to take away; (*prendre*): **~ qch à qn** to take sth (away) from sb; (*kidnapper*) to abduct, kidnap; (*obtenir: prix, contrat*) to win.

enliser [ãlize]: **s'~** *vi* to sink, get stuck.

enluminure [ãlyminyʀ] *nf* illumination.

enneigé, e [ãneʒe] *a* snowy; snowed-up.

ennemi, e [ɛnmi] *a* hostile; (*MIL*) enemy *cpd* // *nm/f* enemy.

ennui [ãnɥi] *nm* (*lassitude*) boredom; (*difficulté*) trouble *q*; **avoir des ~s** to have problems; **ennuyer** *vt* to bother; (*lasser*) to bore; **s'ennuyer** *vi* to be bored; **s'ennuyer de** (*regretter*) to miss; **ennuyeux, euse** *a* boring, tedious; annoying.

énoncé [enɔse] *nm* terms *pl*; wording.

énoncer [enɔse] *vt* to say, express; (*conditions*) to set out, state.

enorgueillir [ãnɔrgœjir]: **s'~ de** *vt* to pride o.s. on; to boast.

énorme [enɔrm(ə)] *a* enormous, huge; **énormément** *ad* enormously; **enormément de neige/gens** an enormous amount of snow/number of people.

enquérir [ãkerir]: **s'~ de** *vt* to inquire about.

enquête [ãkɛt] *nf* (*de journaliste, de police*) investigation; (*judiciaire, administrative*) inquiry; (*sondage d'opinion*) survey; **enquêter** *vi* to investigate; to hold an inquiry; to conduct a survey.

enquiers *etc vb voir* **enquérir**.

enraciné, e [ãrasine] *a* deep-rooted.

enragé, e [ãraʒe] *a* (*MÉD*) rabid, with rabies; (*fig*) fanatical.

enrageant, e [ãraʒã, -ãt] *a* infuriating.

enrager [ãraʒe] *vi* to be in a rage.

enrayer [ãreje] *vt* to check, stop; **s'~** *vi* (*arme à feu*) to jam.

enregistrement [ãrʒistrəmã] *nm* recording; (*ADMIN*) registration; **~ des bagages** (*à l'aéroport*) baggage check-in.

enregistrer [ãrʒistre] *vt* (*MUS etc, remarquer, noter*) to record; (*fig: mémoriser*) to make a mental note of; (*ADMIN*) to register; (*bagages: par train*) to register; (: *à l'aéroport*) to check in.

enrhumer [ãryme]: **s'~** *vi* to catch a cold.

enrichir [ãriʃir] *vt* to make rich(er); (*fig*) to enrich; **s'~** *vi* to get rich(er).

enrober [ãrɔbe] *vt*: **~ qch de** to coat sth with; (*fig*) to wrap sth up in.

enrôler [ãrole] *vt* to enlist; **s'~** (*dans*) to enlist (in).

enrouer [ãrwe]: **s'~** *vi* to go hoarse.

enrouler [ãrule] *vt* (*fil, corde*) to wind (up); **~ qch autour de** to wind sth (a)round; **s'~** *vi* to coil up; to wind.

ensanglanté, e [ãsãglãte] *a* covered with blood.

enseignant, e [ãsɛɲã, -ãt] *nm/f* teacher.

enseigne [ãsɛɲ] *nf* sign; **à telle ~ que** so much so that; **~ lumineuse** neon sign.

enseignement [ãsɛɲmã] *nm* teaching; (*ADMIN*) education.

enseigner [ãsɛɲe] *vt, vi* to teach; **~ qch à qn/à qn que** to teach sb sth/sb that.

ensemble [ãsãbl(ə)] *ad* together // *nm* (*assemblage, MATH*) set; (*totalité*): **l'~ du/de la** the whole *ou* entire; (*unité, harmonie*) unity; **impression/idée d'~** over-

all *ou* general impression/idea; **dans l'~** (*en gros*) on the whole.

ensemencer [ãsmãse] *vt* to sow.

ensevelir [ãsəvlir] *vt* to bury.

ensoleillé, e [ãsɔleje] *a* sunny.

ensommeillé, e [ãsɔmeje] *a* drowsy.

ensorceler [ãsɔrsəle] *vt* to enchant, bewitch.

ensuite [ãsɥit] *ad* then, next; (*plus tard*) afterwards, later; **~ de quoi** after which.

ensuivre [ãsɥivr(ə)]: **s'~** *vi* to follow, ensue.

entailler [ãtaje] *vt* to notch; to cut.

entamer [ãtame] *vt* (*pain, bouteille*) to start; (*hostilités, pourparlers*) to open; (*fig: altérer*) to make a dent in; to shake; to damage.

entasser [ãtase] *vt* (*empiler*) to pile up, heap up; (*tenir à l'étroit*) to cram together; **s'~** *vi* to pile up; to cram.

entendre [ãtãdr(ə)] *vt* to hear; (*comprendre*) to understand; (*vouloir dire*) to mean; (*vouloir*): **~ être obéi/que** to mean to be obeyed/that; **j'ai entendu dire que** I've heard (it said) that; **s'~** *vi* (*sympathiser*) to get on; (*se mettre d'accord*) to agree; **s'~ à qch/à faire** (*être compétent*) to be good at sth/doing.

entendu, e [ãtãdy] *a* (*réglé*) agreed; (*au courant: air*) knowing; (**c'est**) **~** all right, agreed; **c'est ~** (*concession*) all right, granted; **bien ~** of course.

entente [ãtãt] *nf* understanding; (*accord, traité*) agreement; **à double ~** (*sens*) with a double meaning.

entériner [ãterine] *vt* to ratify, confirm.

enterrement [ãtɛrmã] *nm* (*cérémonie*) funeral, burial.

enterrer [ãtɛre] *vt* to bury.

entêtant, e [ãtɛtã, -ãt] *a* heady.

entêté, e [ãtete] *a* stubborn.

en-tête [ãtɛt] *nm* heading; **papier à ~** headed notepaper.

entêter [ãtete]: **s'~** *vi*: **s'~ (à faire)** to persist in doing).

enthousiasme [ãtuzjasm(ə)] *nm* enthusiasm; **enthousiasmer** *vt* to fill with enthusiasm; **s'enthousiasmer (pour qch)** to get enthusiastic (about sth).

enticher [ãtiʃe]: **s'~ de** *vt* to become infatuated with.

entier, ère [ãtje, -jɛr] *a* (*non entamé, en totalité*) whole; (*total, complet*) complete; (*fig: caractère*) unbending // *nm* (*MATH*) whole; **en ~** totally; **in its entirety**; **lait ~** full-cream milk; **entièrement** *ad* entirely, wholly.

entonner [ãtɔne] *vt* (*chanson*) to strike up.

entonnoir [ãtɔnwar] *nm* funnel.

entorse [ãtɔrs(ə)] *nf* (*MÉD*) sprain; (*fig*): **~ au reglement** infringement of the rule.

entortiller [ãtɔrtije] *vt* (*envelopper*) to wrap; (*enrouler*) to twist, wind; (*duper*) to deceive.

entourage [ãturaʒ] *nm* circle; family (circle); entourage; (*ce qui enclôt*) surround.

entourer [ãture] *vt* to surround; (*apporter son soutien à*) to rally round; ~ **de** to surround with; (*trait*) to encircle with.

entourloupettes [ãturlupet] *nfpl* mean tricks.

entracte [ãtrakt(ə)] *nm* interval.

entraide [ãtrɛd] *nf* mutual aid; **s'entraider** *vi* to help each other.

entrain [ãtrɛ̃] *nm* spirit; **avec/sans** ~ spiritedly/half-heartedly.

entraînement [ãtrɛnmã] *nm* training; (*TECH*) drive.

entraîner [ãtrene] *vt* (*tirer: wagons*) to pull; (*charrier*) to carry *ou* drag along; (*TECH*) to drive; (*emmener: personne*) to take (off); (*mener à l'assaut, influencer*) to lead; (*SPORT*) to train; (*impliquer*) to entail; (*causer*) to lead to, bring about; ~ **qn à faire** (*inciter*) to lead sb to do; **s'**~ *vi* (*SPORT*) to train; **s'**~ **à qch/à faire** to train o.s. for sth/to do; **entraîneur, euse** *nm/f* (*SPORT*) coach, trainer // *nm* (*HIPPISME*) trainer // *nf* (*de bar*) hostess.

entraver [ãtrave] *vt* (*circulation*) to hold up; (*action, progrès*) to hinder.

entre [ãtr(ə)] *prép* between; (*parmi*) among(st); **l'un d'**~ **eux/nous** one of them/us; ~ **eux** among(st) themselves.

entrebâillé, e [ãtrəbaje] *a* half-open, ajar.

entrechoquer [ãtrəʃɔke]: **s'**~ *vi* to knock *ou* bang together.

entrecôte [ãtrəkot] *nf* entrecôte *ou* rib steak.

entrecouper [ãtrəkupe] *vt*: ~ **qch de** to intersperse sth with.

entrecroiser [ãtrəkrwaze]: **s'**~ *vi* intertwine.

entrée [ãtre] *nf* entrance; (*accès: au cinéma etc*) admission; (*billet*) (admission) ticket; (*CULIN*) first course; **d'**~ *ad* from the outset; ~ **en matière** introduction.

entrefaites [ãtrəfɛt]: **sur ces** ~ *ad* at this juncture.

entrefilet [ãtrəfile] *nm* paragraph (*short article*).

entrejambes [ãtrəʒãb] *nm* crotch.

entrelacer [ãtrəlase] *vt* to intertwine.

entrelarder [ãtrəlarde] *vt* to lard.

entremêler [ãtrəmele] *vt*: ~ **qch de** to (inter)mingle sth with.

entremets [ãtrəmɛ] *nm* (cream) dessert.

entremetteur, euse [ãtrəmɛtœr, -øz] *nm/f* go-between.

entremise [ãtrəmiz] *nf* intervention; **par l'**~ **de** through.

entreposer [ãtrəpoze] *vt* to store, put into storage.

entrepôt [ãtrəpo] *nm* warehouse.

entreprenant, e [ãtrəprənã, -ãt] *a* (*actif*) enterprising; (*trop galant*) forward.

entreprendre [ãtrəprãdr(ə)] *vt* (*se lancer dans*) to undertake; (*commencer*) to begin *ou* start (upon); (*personne*) to buttonhole; to tackle.

entrepreneur [ãtrəprənœr] *nm*: ~ **(en bâtiment**) (building) contractor.

entreprise [ãtrəpriz] *nf* (*société*) firm, concern; (*action*) undertaking, venture.

entrer [ãtre] *vi* to go (*ou* come) in, enter // *vt* (*INFORM*) to enter, input; (*faire*) ~ **qch dans** to get sth into; ~ **dans** (*gén*) to enter; (*pièce*) to go (*ou* come) into, enter; (*club*) to join; (*heurter*) to run into; (*être une composante de*) to go into; to form part of; ~ **à l'hôpital** to go into hospital; **faire** ~ (*visiteur*) to show in.

entresol [ãtrəsɔl] *nm* mezzanine.

entre-temps [ãtrətã] *ad* meanwhile.

entretenir [ãtrətnir] *vt* to maintain; (*famille, maîtresse*) to support, keep; ~ **qn (de)** to speak to sb (about); **s'**~ **(de)** to converse (about).

entretien [ãtrətjɛ̃] *nm* maintenance; (*discussion*) discussion, talk; (*audience*) interview.

entrevoir [ãtrəvwar] *vt* (*à peine*) to make out; (*brièvement*) to catch a glimpse of.

entrevue [ãtrəvy] *nf* meeting; (*audience*) interview.

entrouvert, e [ãtruver, -ɛrt(ə)] *a* half-open.

énumérer [enymere] *vt* to list, enumerate.

envahir [ãvair] *vt* to invade; (*suj: inquiétude, peur*) to come over; **envahissant, e** *a* (*péj: personne*) interfering, intrusive.

enveloppe [ãvlɔp] *nf* (*de lettre*) envelope; (*TECH*) casing; outer layer.

envelopper [ãvlɔpe] *vt* to wrap; (*fig*) to envelop, shroud.

envenimer [ãvnime] *vt* to aggravate.

envergure [ãvergyr] *nf* (*fig*) scope; calibre.

enverrai *etc vb voir* **envoyer**.

envers [ãver] *prép* towards, to // *nm* other side; (*d'une étoffe*) wrong side; **à l'**~ upside down; back to front; (*vêtement*) inside out.

envie [ãvi] *nf* (*sentiment*) envy; (*souhait*) desire, wish; **avoir** ~ **de (faire)** to feel like (doing); (*plus fort*) to want (to do); **avoir** ~ **que** to wish that; **ça lui fait** ~ he would like that; **envier** *vt* to envy; **envieux, euse** *a* envious.

environ [ãvirɔ̃] *ad*: ~ **3 h/2 km** (around) about 3 o'clock/2 km; ~**s** *nmpl* surroundings.

environnement [ãvirɔnmã] *nm* environment.

environner [ãvirɔne] vt to surround.

envisager [ãvizaʒe] vt (examiner, considérer) to view, contemplate; (avoir en vue) to envisage.

envoi [ãvwa] nm (paquet) parcel, consignment.

envoler [ãvɔle]: s'~ vi (oiseau) to fly away ou off; (avion) to take off; (papier, feuille) to blow away; (fig) to vanish (into thin air).

envoûter [ãvute] vt to bewitch.

envoyé, e [ãvwaje] nm/f (POL) envoy; (PRESSE) correspondent.

envoyer [ãvwaje] vt to send; (lancer) to hurl, throw; ~ chercher to send for.

épagneul, e [epaɲœl] nm/f spaniel.

épais, se [epɛ, -ɛs] a thick; **épaisseur** nf thickness.

épancher [epãʃe]: s'~ vi to open one's heart.

épanouir [epanwir]: s'~ vi (fleur) to bloom, open out; (visage) to light up; (fig) to blossom; to open up.

épargne [eparɲ(ə)] nf saving.

épargner [eparɲe] vt to save; (ne pas tuer ou endommager) to spare // vi to save; ~ qch à qn to spare sb sth.

éparpiller [eparpije] vt to scatter; (pour répartir) to disperse; s'~ vi to scatter; (fig) to dissipate one's efforts.

épars, e [epar, -ars(ə)] a scattered.

épatant, e [epatã, -ãt] a (fam) super.

épater [epate] vt to amaze; to impress.

épaule [epol] nf shoulder.

épauler [epole] vt (aider) to back up, support; (arme) to raise (to one's shoulder) // vi to (take) aim.

épave [epav] nf wreck.

épée [epe] nf sword.

épeler [eple] vt to spell.

éperdu, e [eperdy] a distraught, overcome; passionate; frantic.

éperon [eprõ] nm spur.

épi [epi] nm (de blé, d'orge) ear.

épice [epis] nf spice.

épicer [epise] vt to spice.

épicerie [episri] nf grocer's shop; (denrées) groceries pl; ~ fine delicatessen; **épicier, ière** nm/f grocer.

épidémie [epidemi] nf epidemic.

épier [epje] vt to spy on, watch closely; (occasion) to look out for.

épilepsie [epilepsi] nf epilepsy.

épiler [epile] vt (jambes) to remove the hair from; (sourcils) to pluck.

épilogue [epilɔg] nm (fig) conclusion, dénouement.

épiloguer [epilɔge] vi: ~ sur to hold forth on.

épinards [epinar] nmpl spinach sg.

épine [epin] nf thorn, prickle; (d'oursin etc) spine; ~ dorsale backbone.

épingle [epɛ̃gl(ə)] nf pin; ~ de nourrice ou de sûreté ou double safety pin.

épingler [epɛ̃gle] vt (badge, décoration): ~ qch sur to pin sth on(to); (fam) to catch, nick.

épique [epik] a epic.

épisode [epizɔd] nm episode; **film/roman à ~s** serial; **épisodique** a occasional.

épître [epitr(ə)] nf epistle.

éploré, e [eplɔre] a tearful.

épluche-légumes [eplyʃlegym] nm inv (potato) peeler.

éplucher [eplyʃe] vt (fruit, légumes) to peel; (fig) to go over with a fine-tooth comb; **épluchures** nfpl peelings.

épointer [epwɛ̃te] vt to blunt.

éponge [epɔ̃ʒ] nf sponge; **éponger** vt (liquide) to mop up; (surface) to sponge; (fig: déficit) to soak up; s'~ le front to mop one's brow.

épopée [epɔpe] nf epic.

époque [epɔk] nf (de l'histoire) age, era; (de l'année, la vie) time; d'~ a (meuble) period cpd.

époumoner [epumɔne]: s'~ vi to shout o.s. hoarse.

épouse [epuz] nf wife (pl wives).

épouser [epuze] vt to marry; (fig: idées) to espouse; (: forme) to fit.

épousseter [epuste] vt to dust.

époustouflant, e [epustuflã, -ãt] a staggering, mind-boggling.

épouvantable [epuvãtabl(ə)] a appalling, dreadful.

épouvantail [epuvãtaj] nm (à moineaux) scarecrow.

épouvante [epuvãt] nf terror; **film d'~** horror film; **épouvanter** vt to terrify.

époux [epu] nm husband // nmpl (married) couple.

éprendre [eprãdr(ə)]: s'~ de vt to fall in love with.

épreuve [eprœv] nf (d'examen) test; (malheur, difficulté) trial, ordeal; (PHOTO) print; (TYPO) proof; (SPORT) event; à l'~ des balles bulletproof; à toute ~ unfailing; mettre à l'~ to put to the test.

épris, e [epri, -iz] vb voir **éprendre**.

éprouver [epruve] vt (tester) to test; (marquer, faire souffrir) to afflict, distress; (ressentir) to experience.

éprouvette [epruvεt] nf test tube.

épuisé, e [epɥize] a exhausted; (livre) out of print.

épuisement [epɥizmã] nm exhaustion.

épuiser [epɥize] vt (fatiguer) to exhaust, wear ou tire out; (stock, sujet) to exhaust; s'~ vi to wear ou tire o.s. out, exhaust o.s.; (stock) to run out.

épurer [epyre] vt (liquide) to purify; (parti etc) to purge; (langue, texte) to refine.

équateur [ekwatœr] nm equator; (la république de) l'É~ Ecuador.

équation [ekwasjõ] nf equation.

équerre [ekɛʀ] nf (à dessin) (set) square; (pour fixer) brace; **en ~** at right angles; **à l'~, d'~** straight.

équilibre [ekilibʀ(ə)] nm balance; (d'une balance) equilibrium; **garder/perdre l'~** to keep/lose one's balance; **être en ~** to be balanced; **équilibré, e** a (fig) well-balanced, stable; **équilibrer** vt to balance; **s'équilibrer** vi (poids) to balance; (fig: défauts etc) to balance each other out.

équipage [ekipaʒ] nm crew.

équipe [ekip] nf team; (bande: parfois péj) bunch.

équipé, e [ekipe] a: **bien/mal ~** well-/poorly-equipped.

équipée [ekipe] nf escapade.

équipement [ekipmã] nm equipment; **~s** nmpl amenities, facilities; installations.

équiper [ekipe] vt to equip; (voiture, cuisine) to equip, fit out; **~ qn/qch de** to equip sb/sth with.

équitable [ekitabl(ə)] a fair.

équitation [ekitasjɔ̃] nf (horse-)riding.

équivalent, e [ekivalã, -ãt] a, nm equivalent.

équivaloir [ekivalwaʀ]: **~ à** vt to be equivalent to.

équivoque [ekivɔk] a equivocal, ambiguous; (louche) dubious.

érable [eʀabl(ə)] nm maple.

érafler [eʀafle] vt to scratch; **éraflure** nf scratch.

éraillé, e [eʀaje] a (voix) rasping.

ère [ɛʀ] nf era; **en l'an 1050 de notre ~** in the year 1050 A.D.

érection [eʀɛksjɔ̃] nf erection.

éreinter [eʀɛ̃te] vt to exhaust, wear out.

ériger [eʀiʒe] vt (monument) to erect.

ermite [ɛʀmit] nm hermit.

éroder [eʀɔde] vt to erode.

érotique [eʀɔtik] a erotic.

errer [eʀe] vi to wander.

erreur [eʀœʀ] nf mistake, error; (morale) error; **faire ~** to be mistaken; **par ~** by mistake; **~ judiciaire** miscarriage of justice.

érudit, e [eʀyde, -it] nm/f scholar.

éruption [eʀypsjɔ̃] nf eruption; (MÉD) rash.

es vb voir **être**.

ès [ɛs] prép: **licencié ~ lettres/sciences** ≈ Bachelor of Arts/Science.

escabeau, x [ɛskabo] nm (tabouret) stool; (échelle) stepladder.

escadre [ɛskadʀ(ə)] nf (NAVIG) squadron; (AVIAT) wing.

escadrille [ɛskadʀij] nf (AVIAT) flight.

escadron [ɛskadʀɔ̃] nm squadron.

escalade [ɛskalad] nf climbing q; (POL etc) escalation.

escalader [ɛskalade] vt to climb.

escale [ɛskal] nf (NAVIG) call; port of call; (AVIAT) stop(over); **faire ~ à** to

put in at; to stop over at.

escalier [ɛskalje] nm stairs pl; **dans l'~ ou les ~s** on the stairs; **~ roulant** escalator.

escamoter [ɛskamɔte] vt (esquiver) to get round, evade; (faire disparaître) to conjure away.

escapade [ɛskapad] nf: **faire une ~** to go on a jaunt; to run away ou off.

escargot [ɛskaʀgo] nm snail.

escarmouche [ɛskaʀmuʃ] nf skirmish.

escarpé, e [ɛskaʀpe] a steep.

escient [ɛsjã] nm: **à bon ~** advisedly.

esclaffer [ɛsklafe]: **s'~** vi to guffaw.

esclandre [ɛsklãdʀ(ə)] nm scene, fracas.

esclavage [ɛsklavaʒ] nm slavery.

esclave [ɛsklav] nm/f slave.

escompter [ɛskɔ̃te] vt (COMM) to discount; (espérer) to expect, reckon upon.

escorte [ɛskɔʀt(ə)] nf escort.

escouade [ɛskwad] nf squad.

escrime [ɛskʀim] nf fencing.

escrimer [ɛskʀime]: **s'~** vi: **s'~ à faire** to wear o.s. out doing.

escroc [ɛskʀo] nm swindler, conman.

escroquer [ɛskʀɔke] vt: **~ qn (de qch)/qch (à qn)** to swindle sb (out of sth)/sth (out of sb); **escroquerie** nf swindle.

espace [ɛspas] nm space.

espacer [ɛspase] vt to space out; **s'~** vi (visites etc) to become less frequent.

espadon [ɛspadɔ̃] nm swordfish inv.

espadrille [ɛspadʀij] nf rope-soled sandal.

Espagne [ɛspaɲ(ə)] nf: **l'~** Spain; **espagnol, e** a Spanish // nm/f: Espagnol, e Spaniard // nm (LING) Spanish.

espagnolette [ɛspaɲɔlɛt] nf (window) catch; **fermé à l'~** resting on the catch.

espèce [ɛspɛs] nf (BIO, BOT, ZOOL) species inv; (gén: sorte) sort, kind, type; (péj): **~ de maladroit!** you clumsy oaf!; **en ~** in cash; **~s** nfpl (COMM) cash sg; **en l'~** ad in the case in point.

espérance [ɛspeʀãs] nf hope; **~ de vie** life expectancy.

espérer [ɛspeʀe] vt to hope for; **j'espère (bien)** I hope so; **~ que/faire** to hope that/to do; **~ en** to trust in.

espiègle [ɛspjɛgl(ə)] a mischievous.

espion, ne [ɛspjɔ̃, -ɔn] nm/f spy.

espionnage [ɛspjɔnaʒ] nm espionage, spying.

espionner [ɛspjɔne] vt to spy (up)on.

esplanade [ɛsplanad] nf esplanade.

espoir [ɛspwaʀ] nm hope.

esprit [ɛspʀi] nm (pensée, intellect) mind; (humour, ironie) wit; (mentalité, d'une loi etc, fantôme etc) spirit; **faire de l'~** to try to be witty; **reprendre ses ~s** to come to; **perdre l'~** to lose one's mind.

esquimau, de, x [ɛskimo, -od] a, nm/f Eskimo // nm ice lolly (Brit), popsicle

(US).
esquinter [ɛskɛ̃te] vt (fam) to mess up.
esquisse [ɛskis] nf sketch.
esquisser [ɛskise] vt to sketch; **s'~** vi (amélioration) to begin to be detectable; **~ un sourire** to give a vague smile.
esquiver [ɛskive] vt to dodge; **s'~** vi to slip away.
essai [ɛsɛ] nm trying; testing; (tentative) attempt, try; (RUGBY) try; (LITTÉRATURE) essay; **~s** (AUTO) trials; **~ gratuit** (COMM) free trial; **à l'~** on a trial basis.
essaim [ɛsɛ̃] nm swarm.
essayer [eseje] vt (gén) to try; (vêtement, chaussures) to try (on); (restaurant, méthode, voiture) to try (out) // vi to try; **~ de faire** to try ou attempt to do.
essence [esɑ̃s] nf (de voiture) petrol (Brit), gas(oline) (US); (extrait de plante, PHILOSOPHIE) essence; (espèce: d'arbre) species inv.
essentiel, le [esɑ̃sjɛl] a essential; **c'est l'~** (ce qui importe) that's the main thing; **l'~ de** the main part of.
essieu, x [esjø] nm axle.
essor [esɔʀ] nm (de l'économie etc) rapid expansion.
essorer [esɔʀe] vt (en tordant) to wring (out); (par la force centrifuge) to spin-dry; **essoreuse** nf mangle, wringer; spin-dryer.
essouffler [esufle] vt to make breathless; **s'~** vi to get out of breath; (fig) to run out of steam.
essuie-glace [esɥiglas] nm inv windscreen (Brit) ou windshield (US) wiper.
essuie-main [esɥimɛ̃] nm hand towel.
essuyer [esɥije] vt to wipe; (fig: subir) to suffer; **s'~** vi (après le bain) to dry o.s.; **~ la vaisselle** to dry up.
est [ɛst] vb [ɛ] voir être // nm east // a inv east; (région) east(ern); **à l'~** in the east; (direction) to the east, east(wards); **à l'~ de** (to the) east of.
estafette [ɛstafɛt] nf (MIL) dispatch rider.
estaminet [ɛstaminɛ] nm tavern.
estampe [ɛstɑ̃p] nf print, engraving.
estampille [ɛstɑ̃pij] nf stamp.
est-ce que [ɛskə] ad: **~ c'est cher/ c'était bon?** is it expensive/was it good?; **quand est-ce qu'il part?** when does he leave?, when is he leaving?; voir aussi que.
esthéticienne [ɛstetisjɛn] nf beautician.
esthétique [ɛstetik] a attractive; aesthetically pleasing.
estimation [ɛstimasjɔ̃] nf valuation; assessment.
estime [ɛstim] nf esteem, regard.
estimer [ɛstime] vt (respecter) to es-

teem; (expertiser) to value; (évaluer) to assess, estimate; (penser): **~ que/être** to consider that/o.s. to be.
estival, e, aux [ɛstival, -o] a summer cpd.
estivant, e [ɛstivɑ̃, -ɑ̃t] nm/f (summer) holiday-maker.
estomac [ɛstɔma] nm stomach.
estomaqué, e [ɛstɔmake] a flabbergasted.
estomper [ɛstɔ̃pe] vt (fig) to blur, dim; **s'~** vi to soften; to become blurred.
estrade [ɛstʀad] nf platform, rostrum.
estragon [ɛstʀagɔ̃] nm tarragon.
estropier [ɛstʀɔpje] vt to cripple, maim; (fig) to twist, distort.
et [e] cj and; **~ lui?** what about him?; **~ alors!** so what!
étable [etabl(ə)] nf cowshed.
établi [etabli] nm (work)bench.
établir [etabliʀ] vt (papiers d'identité, facture) to make out; (liste, programme) to draw up; (entreprise, camp, gouvernement, artisan) to set up; (réputation, usage, fait, culpabilité) to establish; **s'~** vi (se faire: entente etc) to be established; **s'~** (à son compte) to set up in business; **s'~** à/près de to settle in/near.
établissement [etablismɑ̃] nm making out; drawing up; setting up, establishing; (entreprise, institution) establishment; **~ scolaire** school, educational establishment.
étage [etaʒ] nm (d'immeuble) storey, floor; (de fusée) stage; (GÉO: de culture, végétation) level; **à l'~** upstairs; **au 2ème ~** on the 2nd (Brit) ou 3rd (US) floor; **de bas ~** a low.
étagère [etaʒɛʀ] nf (rayon) shelf; (meuble) shelves pl.
étai [etɛ] nm stay, prop.
étain [etɛ̃] nm (ORFÈVRERIE) pewter q.
étais etc vb voir être.
étal [etal] nm stall.
étalage [etalaʒ] nm display; display window; **faire ~ de** to show off, parade.
étaler [etale] vt (carte, nappe) to spread (out); (peinture, liquide) to spread; (échelonner: paiements, vacances) to spread, stagger; (marchandises) to display; (richesses, connaissances) to parade; **s'~** vi (liquide) to spread out; (fam) to fall flat on one's face; **s'~ sur** (suj: paiements etc) to be spread out over.
étalon [etalɔ̃] nm (mesure) standard; (cheval) stallion.
étamer [etame] vt (casserole) to tin(plate); (glace) to silver.
étanche [etɑ̃ʃ] a (récipient) watertight; (montre, vêtement) waterproof.
étancher [etɑ̃ʃe] vt: **~ sa soif** to quench

one's thirst.

étang [etɑ̃] *nm* pond.

étant [etɑ̃] *vb voir* **être, donné**.

étape [etap] *nf* stage; (*lieu d'arrivée*) stopping place; (: CYCLISME) staging point; **faire ~ à** to stop off at.

état [eta] *nm* (POL, *condition*) state; (*liste*) inventory, statement; **en mauvais ~** in poor condition; **en ~ (de marche)** in (working) order; **remettre en ~** to repair; **hors d'~** out of order; **être en ~/ hors d'~ de faire** to be in a/in no fit state to do; **en tout ~ de cause** in any event; **être dans tous ses ~s** to be in a state; **faire ~ de** (*alléguer*) to put forward; **en ~ d'arrestation** under arrest; **~ civil** civil status; **~ des lieux** inventory of fixtures; **~s d'âme** moods; **étatiser** *vt* to bring under state control.

état-major [etamaʒɔʀ] *nm* (MIL) staff.

Etats-Unis [etazyni] *nmpl*: **les ~** the United States.

étau, x [eto] *nm* vice (*Brit*), vise (*US*).

étayer [eteje] *vt* to prop *ou* shore up.

et c(a)etera [ɛtsetera], **etc.** *ad* et cetera, and so on, etc.

été [ete] *pp de* être // *nm* summer.

éteignoir [etɛɲwaʀ] *nm* (candle) extinguisher; (*péj*) killjoy, wet blanket.

éteindre [etɛ̃dʀ(ə)] *vt* (*lampe, lumière, radio*) to turn *ou* switch off; (*cigarette, incendie, bougie*) to put out, extinguish; (JUR: *dette*) to extinguish; **s'~** *vi* to go out; to go off; (*mourir*) to pass away; **éteint, e** *a* (*fig*) lacklustre, dull; (*volcan*) extinct.

étendard [etɑ̃daʀ] *nm* standard.

étendre [etɑ̃dʀ(ə)] *vt* (*pâte, liquide*) to spread; (*carte etc*) to spread out; (*linge*) to hang up; (*bras, jambes, par terre: blessé*) to stretch out; (*diluer*) to dilute, thin; (*fig: agrandir*) to extend; **s'~** *vi* (*augmenter, se propager*) to spread; (*terrain, forêt etc*) to stretch; (*s'allonger*) to stretch out; (*se coucher*) to lie down; (*fig: expliquer*) to elaborate. **étendu, e** [etɑ̃dy] *a* extensive // *nf* (*d'eau, de sable*) stretch, expanse; (*importance*) extent.

éternel, le [etɛʀnɛl] *a* eternal.

éterniser [etɛʀnize]: **s'~** *vi* to last for ages; to stay for ages.

éternité [etɛʀnite] *nf* eternity.

éternuer [etɛʀnɥe] *vi* to sneeze.

êtes *vb voir* **être**.

éthique [etik] *a* ethical.

ethnie [ɛtni] *nf* ethnic group.

éthylisme [etilism(ə)] *nm* alcoholism.

étiez *vb voir* **être**.

étinceler [etɛ̃sle] *vi* to sparkle.

étincelle [etɛ̃sɛl] *nf* spark.

étioler [etjɔle]: **s'~** *vi* to wilt.

étiqueter [etikte] *vt* to label.

étiquette [etiket] *nf* label; (*protocole*): **l'~** etiquette.

étirer [etiʀe] *vt* to stretch; **s'~** *vi* (*personne*) to stretch; (*convoi, route*): **s'~ sur** to stretch out over.

étoffe [etɔf] *nf* material, fabric.

étoffer [etɔfe] *vt*, **s'~** *vi* to fill out.

étoile [etwal] *nf* star; **à la belle ~** in the open; **~ filante** shooting star; **~ de mer** starfish; **étoilé, e** *a* starry.

étole [etɔl] *nf* stole.

étonnant, e [etɔnɑ̃, -ɑ̃t] *a* amazing.

étonner [etɔne] *vt* to surprise, amaze; **s'~ que/de** to be amazed that/at; **cela m'étonnerait (que)** (*j'en doute*) I'd be very surprised (if).

étouffée [etufe]: **à l'~** *ad* (CULIN) steamed; braised.

étouffer [etufe] *vt* to suffocate; (*bruit*) to muffle; (*scandale*) to hush up // *vi* to suffocate; **s'~** *vi* (*en mangeant etc*) to choke.

étourderie [etuʀdəʀi] *nf* heedlessness *q*; thoughtless blunder.

étourdi, e [etuʀdi] *a* (*distrait*) scatterbrained, heedless.

étourdir [etuʀdiʀ] *vt* (*assommer*) to stun, daze; (*griser*) to make dizzy *ou* giddy; **étourdissement** *nm* dizzy spell.

étourneau, x [etuʀno] *nm* starling.

étrange [etʀɑ̃ʒ] *a* strange.

étranger, ère [etʀɑ̃ʒe, -ɛʀ] *a* foreign; (*pas de la famille, non familier*) strange // *nm/f* foreigner; stranger // *nm*: **à l'~** abroad; **de l'~** from abroad; **~ à** (*fig*) unfamiliar to; irrelevant to.

étranglement [etʀɑ̃gləmɑ̃] *nm* (*d'une vallée etc*) constriction.

étrangler [etʀɑ̃gle] *vt* to strangle; **s'~** *vi* (*en mangeant etc*) to choke.

étrave [etʀav] *nf* stem.

être [etʀ(ə)] ♦ *nm* being; **~ humain** human being

♦ *vb avec attribut* **1** (*état, description*) to be; **il est instituteur** he is *ou* he's a teacher; **vous êtes grand/intelligent/ fatigué** you are *ou* you're tall/clever/tired **2** (+ à: *appartenir*) to be; **le livre est à Paul** the book is Paul's *ou* belongs to Paul; **c'est à moi/eux** it is *ou* it's mine/ theirs

3 (+ de: *provenance*) to be; **il est de Paris** he is from Paris; (: *appartenance*): **il est des nôtres** he is one of us

4 (*date*): **nous sommes le 10 janvier** it's the 10th of January (today)

♦ *vi* to be; **je ne serai pas ici demain** I won't be here tomorrow

♦ *vb auxiliaire* **1** to have; to be; **être arrivé/allé** to have arrived/gone; **il est parti** he has left, he is gone

2 (*forme passive*) to be; **être fait par** to be made by; **il a été promu** he has been promoted

3 (+ à: *obligation*): **c'est à réparer** it needs repairing; **c'est à essayer** it should be tried

♦ *vb impersonnel* **1**: il est + *adjectif* it is + *adjective*; **il est impossible de le faire** it's impossible to do it **2** (*heure, date*): **il est 10 heures, c'est 10 heures** it is *ou* it's 10 o'clock **3** (*emphatique*): **c'est moi** it's me; **c'est à lui de le faire** it's up to him to do it.

étreindre [etʀɛ̃dʀ(ə)] *vt* to clutch, grip; (*amoureusement, amicalement*) to embrace; **s'~** *vi* to embrace.

étrenner [etʀene] *vt* to use (*ou* wear) for the first time.

étrennes [etʀɛn] *nfpl* Christmas box *sg*.

étrier [etʀije] *nm* stirrup.

étriller [etʀije] *vt* (*cheval*) to curry; (*fam: battre*) to slaughter (*fig*).

étriqué, e [etʀike] *a* skimpy.

étroit, e [etʀwa, -wat] *a* narrow; (*vêtement*) tight; (*fig: serré*) close, tight; **à l'~** cramped; **~ d'esprit** narrow-minded.

étude [etyd] *nf* studying; (*ouvrage, rapport*) study; (*de notaire: bureau*) office; (: *charge*) practice; (*SCOL: salle de travail*) study room; **~s** (*SCOL*) studies; **être à l'~** (*projet etc*) to be under consideration; **faire des ~s** (**de droit/médecine**) to study (law/medicine).

étudiant, e [etydjɑ̃, -ɑ̃t] *nm/f* student.

étudié, e [etydje] *a* (*démarche*) studied; (*système*) carefully designed; (*prix*) keen.

étudier [etydje] *vt, vi* to study.

étui [etɥi] *nm* case.

étuve [etyv] *nf* steamroom.

étuvée, e [etyve] : **à l'~** *ad* braised.

eu, eue [y] *pp de* **avoir**.

euh [ø] *excl* er.

Europe [øʀɔp] *nf*: **l'~** Europe; **européen, ne** *a, nm/f* European.

eus *etc vb voir* **avoir**.

eux [ø] *pronom* (*sujet*) they; (*objet*) them.

évacuer [evakɥe] *vt* to evacuate.

évader [evade] : **s'~** *vi* to escape.

évangile [evɑ̃ʒil] *nm* gospel.

évanouir [evanwiʀ] : **s'~** *vi* to faint; (*disparaître*) to vanish, disappear.

évanouissement [evanwismɑ̃] *nm* (*syncope*) fainting fit; (*dans un accident*) loss of consciousness.

évaporer [evapɔʀe] : **s'~** *vi* to evaporate.

évaser [evaze] *vt* (*tuyau*) to widen, open out; (*jupe, pantalon*) to flare.

évasif, ive [evazif, -iv] *a* evasive.

évasion [evazjɔ̃] *nf* escape.

évêché [eveʃe] *nm* bishopric; bishop's palace.

éveil [evɛj] *nm* awakening; **être en ~** to be alert.

éveillé, e [eveje] *a* awake; (*vif*) alert, sharp.

éveiller [eveje] *vt* to (a)waken; **s'~** *vi* to (a)waken; (*fig*) to be aroused.

événement [evɛnmɑ̃] *nm* event.

éventail [evɑ̃taj] *nm* fan; (*choix*) range.

éventaire [evɑ̃tɛʀ] *nm* stall, stand.

éventer [evɑ̃te] *vt* (*secret*) to uncover; **s'~** *vi* (*parfum*) to go stale.

éventrer [evɑ̃tʀe] *vt* to disembowel; (*fig*) to tear *ou* rip open.

éventualité [evɑ̃tɥalite] *nf* eventuality; possibility; **dans l'~ de** in the event of.

éventuel, le [evɑ̃tɥel] *a* possible; **~lement** *ad* possibly.

évêque [evɛk] *nm* bishop.

évertuer [evɛʀtɥe] : **s'~** *vi*: **s'~ à faire** to try very hard to do.

éviction [eviksjɔ̃] *nf* ousting; (*de locataire*) eviction.

évidemment [evidamɑ̃] *ad* obviously.

évidence [evidɑ̃s] *nf* obviousness; obvious fact; **de toute ~** quite obviously *ou* evidently; **en ~** conspicuous; **mettre en ~** to highlight; to bring to the fore.

évident, e [evidɑ̃, -ɑ̃t] *a* obvious, evident.

évider [evide] *vt* to scoop out.

évier [evje] *nm* (kitchen) sink.

évincer [evɛ̃se] *vt* to oust.

éviter [evite] *vt* to avoid; **~ de faire/que qch ne se passe** to avoid doing/sth happening; **~ qch à qn** to spare sb sth.

évolué, e [evolɥe] *a* advanced.

évoluer [evolɥe] *vi* (*enfant, maladie*) to develop; (*situation, moralement*) to evolve, develop; (*aller et venir: danseur etc*) to move about, circle; **évolution** *nf* development; evolution; **évolutions** *nfpl* movements.

évoquer [evɔke] *vt* to call to mind, evoke; (*mentionner*) to mention.

ex... [ɛks] *préfixe* ex-.

exact, e [ɛgzakt] *a* (*précis*) exact, accurate, precise; (*correct*) correct; (*ponctuel*) punctual; **l'heure ~e** the right *ou* exact time; **~ement** *ad* exactly, accurately, precisely; correctly; (*c'est cela même*) exactly.

ex aequo [ɛgzeko] *a* equally placed.

exagéré, e [ɛgzaʒeʀe] *a* (*prix etc*) excessive.

exagérer [ɛgzaʒeʀe] *vt* to exaggerate // *vi* (*abuser*) to go too far; to overstep the mark; (*déformer les faits*) to exaggerate.

exalter [ɛgzalte] *vt* (*enthousiasmer*) to excite, elate; (*glorifier*) to exalt.

examen [ɛgzamɛ̃] *nm* examination; (*SCOL*) exam, examination; **à l'~** under consideration; (*COMM*) on approval.

examiner [ɛgzamine] *vt* to examine.

exaspérant, e [ɛgzaspeʀɑ̃, -ɑ̃t] *a* exasperating.

exaspérer [ɛgzaspeʀe] *vt* to exasperate; to exacerbate.

exaucer [ɛgzose] *vt* (*vœu*) to grant.

excédent [ɛksedɑ̃] *nm* surplus; **en ~** surplus; **~ de bagages** excess luggage.

excéder [ɛksede] *vt* (*dépasser*) to exceed; *(agacer)* to exasperate.

excellence [ɛksɛlɑ̃s] *nf (titre)* Excellency.

excellent, e [ɛksɛlɑ̃, -ɑ̃t] *a* excellent.

excentrique [ɛksɑ̃tʀik] *a* eccentric; *(quartier)* outlying.

excepté, e [ɛksɛpte] *a*, *prép*: les élèves ~s, ~ les élèves except for the pupils; ~ si except if.

exception [ɛksɛpsjɔ̃] *nf* exception; à l'~ de except for, with the exception of; d'~ *(mesure, loi)* special, exceptional; **exceptionnel, le** *a* exceptional.

excès [ɛksɛ] *nm* surplus // *nmpl* excesses; à l'~ to excess; ~ de vitesse speeding *q*; **excessif, ive** *a* excessive.

excitant, e [ɛksitɑ̃, -ɑ̃t] *a* exciting // *nm* stimulant.

excitation [ɛksitasjɔ̃] *nf (état)* excitement.

exciter [ɛksite] *vt* to excite; *(suj: café etc)* to stimulate; **s'~** *vi* to get excited.

exclamation [ɛksklamasjɔ̃] *nf* exclamation.

exclamer [ɛksklame]: **s'~** *vi* to exclaim.

exclure [ɛksklyʀ] *vt (faire sortir)* to expel; *(ne pas compter)* to exclude, leave out; *(rendre impossible)* to exclude, rule out; **ce n'est pas exclu** it's not impossible, I don't rule that out; **exclusif, ive** *a* exclusive; **exclusion** *nf* expulsion; à l'exclusion de with the exclusion *ou* exception of; **exclusivité** *nf (COMM)* exclusive rights *pl*; **film passant en exclusivité à** film showing only at.

excursion [ɛkskyʀsjɔ̃] *nf (en autocar)* excursion, trip; *(à pied)* walk, hike.

excuse [ɛkskyz] *nf* excuse; **~s** *nfpl* apology *sg*, apologies.

excuser [ɛkskyze] *vt* to excuse; **s'~ (de)** to apologize (for); **'excusez-moi'** 'I'm sorry'; *(pour attirer l'attention)* 'excuse me'.

exécrable [ɛgzekʀabl(ə)] *a* atrocious.

exécrer [ɛgzekʀe] *vt* to loathe, abhor.

exécuter [ɛgzekyte] *vt (prisonnier)* to execute; *(tâche etc)* to execute, carry out; *(MUS: jouer)* to perform, execute; *(INFORM)* to run; **s'~** *vi* to comply; **exécutif, ive** *a*, *nm (POL)* executive; **exécution** *nf* execution; carrying out; **mettre à exécution** to carry out.

exemplaire [ɛgzɑ̃plɛʀ] *nm* copy.

exemple [ɛgzɑ̃pl(ə)] *nm* example; **par ~** for instance, for example; **donner l'~** to set an example; **prendre ~ sur** to take as a model; **à l'~ de** just like.

exempt, e [ɛgzɑ̃, -ɑ̃t] *a*: ~ **de** *(dispensé de)* exempt from; *(sans)* free from.

exercer [ɛgzɛʀse] *vt (pratiquer)* to exercise, practise; *(prérogative)* to exercise; *(influence, contrôle)* to exert; *(former)* to exercise, train; **s'~** *vi (sportif, musicien)* to practise; *(se faire sentir: pression etc)* to be exerted.

exercice [ɛgzɛʀsis] *nm (tâche, travail)* exercise; **l'~** exercise; *(MIL)* drill; **en ~** *(juge)* in office; *(médecin)* practising.

exhaustif, ive [ɛgzostif, -iv] *a* exhaustive.

exhiber [ɛgzibe] *vt (montrer: papiers, certificat)* to present, produce; *(péj)* to display, flaunt; **s'~** *vi* to parade; *(suj: exhibitionniste)* to expose o.s.

exhorter [ɛgzɔʀte] *vt* to urge.

exigeant, e [ɛgziʒɑ̃, -ɑ̃t] *a* demanding; *(péj)* hard to please.

exigence [ɛgziʒɑ̃s] *nf* demand, requirement.

exiger [ɛgziʒe] *vt* to demand, require.

exigu, ë [ɛgzigy] *a (lieu)* cramped, tiny.

exil [ɛgzil] *nm* exile; **~er** *vt* to exile; **s'~er** *vi* to go into exile.

existence [ɛgzistɑ̃s] *nf* existence.

exister [ɛgziste] *vi* to exist; **il existe un/ des** there is a/are (some).

exonérer [ɛgzɔneʀe] *vt*: ~ **de** to exempt from.

exorbité, e [ɛgzɔʀbite] *a*: yeux ~s bulging eyes.

exotique [ɛgzɔtik] *a* exotic.

expatrier [ɛkspatʀije] *vt*: **s'~** to leave one's country.

expectative [ɛkspɛktativ] *nf*: être dans l'~ to be still waiting.

expédient [ɛkspedjɑ̃] *nm (péj)* expedient; **vivre d'~s** to live by one's wits.

expédier [ɛkspedje] *vt (lettre, paquet)* to send; *(troupes)* to dispatch; *(péj: travail etc)* to dispose of, dispatch; **expéditeur, trice** *nm/f* sender.

expédition [ɛkspedisjɔ̃] *nf* sending; *(scientifique, sportive, MIL)* expedition.

expérience [ɛkspeʀjɑ̃s] *nf (de la vie)* experience; *(scientifique)* experiment.

expérimenté, e [ɛkspeʀimɑ̃te] *a* experienced.

expérimenter [ɛkspeʀimɑ̃te] *vt* to test out, experiment with.

expert, e [ɛkspɛʀ, -ɛʀt(ə)] *a*, *nm* expert; ~ **en assurances** insurance valuer; **~-comptable** *nm* ≈ chartered accountant *(Brit)*, ≈ certified public accountant *(US)*.

expertise [ɛkspɛʀtiz] *nf* valuation; assessment; valuer's *(ou* assessor's) report; *(JUR)* (forensic) examination.

expertiser [ɛkspɛʀtize] *vt (objet de valeur)* to value; *(voiture accidentée etc)* to assess damage to.

expier [ɛkspje] *vt* to expiate, atone for.

expirer [ɛkspiʀe] *vi (prendre fin, mourir)* to expire; *(respirer)* to breathe out.

explicatif, ive [ɛksplikatif, -iv] *a* explanatory.

explication [ɛksplikasjɔ̃] *nf* explanation; *(discussion)* discussion; argument; ~ **de texte** *(SCOL)* critical analysis.

explicite [ɛksplisit] *a* explicit.

expliquer [ɛksplike] *vt* to explain; s'~ to explain (o.s.); (*discuter*) to discuss things; to have it out; **son erreur s'explique** one can understand his mistake.

exploit [ɛksplwa] *nm* exploit, feat.

exploitation [ɛksplwatasjɔ̃] *nf* exploitation; running; ~ **agricole** farming concern.

exploiter [ɛksplwate] *vt* (*mine*) to exploit, work; (*entreprise, ferme*) to run, operate; (*clients, ouvriers, erreur, don*) to exploit.

explorer [ɛksplɔRe] *vt* to explore.

exploser [ɛksploze] *vi* to explode, blow up; (*engin explosif*) to go off; (*fig: joie, colère*) to burst out, explode; **explosif, ive** *a, nm* explosive; **explosion** *nf* explosion.

exportateur, trice [ɛkspɔRtatœR, -tRis] *a* export *cpd*, exporting // *nm* exporter.

exportation [ɛkspɔRtasjɔ̃] *nf* exportation; export.

exporter [ɛkspɔRte] *vt* to export.

exposant [ɛkspozɑ̃] *nm* exhibitor.

exposé, e [ɛkspoze] *nm* talk // *a*: ~ **au sud** facing south; **bien** ~ well situated.

exposer [ɛkspoze] *vt* (*marchandise*) to display; (*peinture*) to exhibit, show; (*parler de*) to explain, set out; (*mettre en danger, orienter, PHOTO*) to expose; **exposition** *nf* (*manifestation*) exhibition; (*PHOTO*) exposure.

exprès [ɛkspRɛ] *ad* (*délibérément*) on purpose; (*spécialement*) specially.

exprès, esse [ɛkspRɛs] *a* (*ordre, défense*) express, formal // *a inv, ad* (*PTT*) express.

express [ɛkspRɛs] *a, nm*: (**café**) ~ espresso (coffee); (**train**) ~ fast train.

expressément [ɛkspRɛsemɑ̃] *ad* expressly; specifically.

expression [ɛkspRɛsjɔ̃] *nf* expression.

exprimer [ɛkspRime] *vt* (*sentiment, idée*) to express; (*jus, liquide*) to press out; s'~ *vi* (*personne*) to express o.s.

exproprier [ɛkspRopRije] *vt* to buy up by compulsory purchase, expropriate.

expulser [ɛkspylse] *vt* to expel; (*locataire*) to evict; (*SPORT*) to send off.

exquis, e [ɛkski, -iz] *a* exquisite; delightful.

exsangue [ɛksɑ̃g] *a* bloodless, drained of blood.

extase [ɛkstɑz] *nf* ecstasy; **s'extasier sur** to go into raptures over.

extension [ɛkstɑ̃sjɔ̃] *nf* (*d'un muscle, ressort*) stretching; (*fig*) extension; expansion.

exténuer [ɛkstenɥe] *vt* to exhaust.

extérieur, e [ɛksteRjœR] *a* (*porte, mur etc*) outer, outside; (*au dehors: escalier, w.-c.*) outside; (*commerce*) foreign; (*influences*) external; (*apparent: calme, gaieté etc*) surface *cpd* // *nm* (*d'une*

maison, *d'un récipient etc*) outside, exterior; (*apparence*) exterior; (*d'un groupe social*): **l'~** the outside world; **à l'~** outside; (*à l'étranger*) abroad; **~ement** *ad* on the outside; (*en apparence*) on the surface.

exterminer [ɛkstɛRmine] *vt* to exterminate, wipe out.

externat [ɛkstɛRna] *nm* day school.

externe [ɛkstɛRn(ə)] *a* external, outer // *nm/f* (*MÉD*) non-resident medical student (*Brit*), extern (*US*); (*SCOL*) day pupil.

extincteur [ɛkstɛ̃ktœR] *nm* (fire) extinguisher.

extinction [ɛkstɛ̃ksjɔ̃] *nf*: ~ **de voix** loss of voice.

extorquer [ɛkstɔRke] *vt* to extort.

extra [ɛkstRa] *a inv* first-rate; top-quality // *nm inv* extra help.

extrader [ɛkstRade] *vt* to extradite.

extraire [ɛkstRɛR] *vt* to extract; **extrait** *nm* extract.

extraordinaire [ɛkstRaɔRdinɛR] *a* extraordinary; (*POL: mesures etc*) special.

extravagant, e [ɛkstRavagɑ̃, -ɑ̃t] *a* extravagant; wild.

extraverti, e [ɛkstRavɛRti] *a* extrovert.

extrême [ɛkstRɛm] *a, nm* extreme; **~ment** *ad* extremely; **~-onction** *nf* last rites *pl*; **E~-Orient** *nm* Far East.

extrémité [ɛkstRemite] *nf* end; (*situation*) straits *pl*, plight; (*geste désespéré*) extreme action; ~**s** *nfpl* (*pieds et mains*) extremities; **à la dernière** ~ on the point of death.

exutoire [ɛgzytwaR] *nm* outlet, release.

F

F *abr de* **franc**.

fa [fa] *nm inv* (*MUS*) F; (*en chantant la gamme*) fa.

fable [fɑbl(ə)] *nf* fable.

fabricant [fabRikɑ̃] *nm* manufacturer.

fabrication [fabRikasjɔ̃] *nf* manufacture.

fabrique [fabRik] *nf* factory.

fabriquer [fabRike] *vt* to make; (*industriellement*) to manufacture; (*fig*): **qu'est-ce qu'il fabrique?** what is he doing?

fabulation [fabylasjɔ̃] *nf* fantasizing.

fac [fak] *abr f* (*fam: SCOL*) *de* **faculté**.

façade [fasad] *nf* front, façade.

face [fas] *nf* face; (*fig: aspect*) side // *a*: **le côté** ~ heads; **perdre la** ~ to lose face; **en** ~ **de** *prép* opposite; (*fig*) in front of; **de** ~ *ad* from the front; face on; ~ **à** *prép* facing; (*fig*) faced with, in the face of; **faire** ~ **à** to face; ~ **à** ~ *ad* facing each other // *nm inv* encounter.

facétieux, euse [fasesjø, -øz] *a* mischievous.

fâché, e [fɑʃe] *a* angry; (*désolé*) sorry.

fâcher [fɑʃe] vt to anger; **se ~** vi to get angry; **se ~ avec** (se brouiller) to fall out with.

fâcheux, euse [fɑʃø, -øz] a unfortunate, regrettable.

facile [fasil] a easy; (accommodant) easy-going; **~ment** ad easily; **facilité** nf easiness; (disposition, don) aptitude; **facilités** nfpl facilities; **facilités de paiement** easy terms; **faciliter** vt to make easier.

façon [fasɔ̃] nf (manière) way; (d'une robe etc) making-up; cut; **~s** nfpl (péj) fuss sg; **de quelle ~?** (in) what way?; **de ~ à/à ce que** so as to/that; **de toute ~** anyway, in any case.

façonner [fasɔne] vt (fabriquer) to manufacture; (travailler: matière) to shape, fashion; (fig) to mould, shape.

facteur, trice [faktœʀ, -tʀis] nm/f postman/woman (Brit), mailman/woman (US) // nm (MATH, fig: élément) factor; **~ d'orgues** organ builder; **~ de pianos** piano maker.

factice [faktis] a artificial.

faction [faksjɔ̃] nf faction; (MIL) guard ou sentry (duty); watch.

facture [faktyʀ] nf (à payer: gén) bill; (: COMM) invoice; (d'un artisan, artiste) technique, workmanship; **facturer** vt to invoice.

facultatif, ive [fakyltatif, -iv] a optional; (arrêt de bus) request cpd.

faculté [fakylte] nf (intellectuelle, d'université) faculty; (pouvoir, possibilité) power.

fade [fad] a insipid.

fagot [fago] nm bundle of sticks.

faible [fɛbl(ə)] a weak; (voix, lumière, vent) faint; (rendement, intensité, revenu etc) low // nm weak point; (pour quelqu'un) weakness, soft spot; **~ d'esprit** feeble-minded; **faiblesse** nf weakness; **faiblir** vi to weaken; (lumière) to dim; (vent) to drop.

faïence [fajɑ̃s] nf earthenware q; piece of earthenware.

faignant, e [fɛɲɑ̃, -ɑ̃t] nm/f = **fainéant, e.**

faille [faj] vb voir **falloir** // nf (GÉO) fault; (fig) flaw, weakness.

faillir [fajiʀ] vi: **j'ai failli tomber** I almost ou very nearly fell.

faillite [fajit] nf bankruptcy.

faim [fɛ̃] nf hunger; **avoir ~** to be hungry; **rester sur sa ~** (aussi fig) to be left wanting more.

fainéant, e [fɛneɑ̃, -ɑ̃t] nm/f idler, loafer.

faire [fɛʀ] ♦ vt 1 (fabriquer, être l'auteur de) to make; (~ du vin/une offre/un film to make wine/an offer/a film; **~ du bruit** to make a noise
2 (effectuer: travail, opération) to do; **que faites-vous?** (quel métier etc) what

do you do?; (quelle activité: au moment de la question) what are you doing?; **~ la lessive** to do the washing
3 (études) to do; (sport, musique) to play; **~ du droit/du français** to do law/French; **~ du rugby/piano** to play rugby/the piano
4 (simuler): **~ le malade/l'ignorant** to act the invalid/the fool
5 (transformer, avoir un effet sur): **~ de qn un frustré/avocat** to make sb frustrated/a lawyer; **ça ne me fait rien** (m'est égal) I don't care ou mind; (me laisse froid) it has no effect on me; **ça ne fait rien** it doesn't matter; **~ que** (impliquer) to mean that
6 (calculs, prix, mesures): **2 et 2 font 4** 2 and 2 are ou make 4; **ça fait 10 m/15 F** it's 10 m/15 F; **je vous le fais 10 F** I'll let you have it for 10 F
7: **qu'a-t-il fait de sa valise?** what has he done with his case?
8: **ne ~ que**: **il ne fait que critiquer** (sans cesse) all he (ever) does is criticize; (seulement) he's only criticizing
9 (dire) to say; **'vraiment?' fit-il** 'really?' he said
10 (maladie) to have; **~ du diabète** to have diabetes sg
♦ vi 1 (agir, s'y prendre) to act, do; **il faut ~ vite** we (ou you etc) must act quickly; **comment a-t-il fait pour?** how did he manage to?; **faites comme chez vous** make yourself at home
2 (paraître) to look; **~ vieux/démodé** to look old/old-fashioned; **ça fait bien** it looks good
♦ vb substitut to do; **ne le casse pas comme je l'ai fait** don't break it as I did; **je peux le voir? - faites!** can I see it? - please do!
♦ vb impersonnel 1: **il fait beau** etc the weather is fine etc; voir **jour, froid** etc
2 (temps écoulé, durée): **ça fait 2 ans qu'il est parti** it's 2 years since he left; **ça fait 2 ans qu'il y est** he's been there for 2 years
♦ vb semi-auxiliaire: **~ + infinitif** 1 (action directe) to make; **~ tomber/bouger qch** to make sth fall/move; **~ démarrer un moteur/chauffer de l'eau** to start up an engine/heat some water; **cela fait dormir** it makes you sleep; **~ travailler les enfants** to make the children work ou get the children to work
2 (indirectement, par un intermédiaire): **~ réparer qch** to get ou have sth repaired; **~ punir les enfants** to have the children punished
se faire vi 1 (vin, fromage) to mature
2: **cela se fait beaucoup/ne se fait pas** it's done a lot/not done
3: **se ~ + nom ou pronom**: **se ~ une jupe** to make o.s. a skirt; **se ~ des amis** to make friends; **se ~ du souci** to worry;

il ne s'en fait pas he doesn't worry

4: se ~ + *adjectif* (*devenir*): se ~ **vieux** to be getting old; (*délibérément*): se ~ **beau** to do o.s. up

5: se ~ à (*s'habituer*) to get used to; je n'arrive pas à me ~ à la nourriture/au climat I can't get used to the food/climate

6: se ~ + *infinitif*: se ~ **examiner la vue/opérer** to have one's eyes tested/have an operation; se ~ **couper les cheveux** to get one's hair cut; il va se ~ **tuer/punir** he's going to get himself killed/get (himself) punished; il s'est fait aider he got somebody to help him; il s'est fait aider par Simon he got Simon to help him; se ~ **faire un vêtement** to get a garment made for o.s.

7 (*impersonnel*): **comment se fait-il/faisait-il que?** how is it/was it that?

faire-part [fɛʀpaʀ] *nm inv* announcement (*of birth, marriage etc*).

faisable [fəzabl(ə)] *a* feasible.

faisan, e [fəzɑ̃, -an] *nm/f* pheasant.

faisandé, e [fəzɑ̃de] *a* high (*bad*).

faisceau, x [fɛso] *nm* (*de lumière etc*) beam; (*de branches etc*) bundle.

faisons *vb voir* **faire.**

fait [fɛ] *nm* (*événement*) event, occurrence; (*réalité, donnée*) fact; **être le ~ de** (*causé par*) to be the work of; **être au ~ (de)** to be informed (of); **au ~** (*à propos*) by the way; **en venir au ~** to get to the point; **de ~** *a* (*opposé à: de droit*) de facto // *ad* in fact; **du ~ de ceci/qu'il a menti** because of *ou* on account of this/his having lied; **de ce ~** for this reason; **en ~** in fact; **en ~ de repas** by way of a meal; **prendre ~ et cause pour qn** to support sb, side with sb; **prendre qn sur le ~** to catch sb in the act; **~ divers** news item; **les ~s et gestes de qn** sb's actions *ou* doings.

fait, e [fɛ, fɛt] *a* (*mûr: fromage, melon*) ripe; **c'en est ~ de** that's the end of.

faîte [fɛt] *nm* top; (*fig*) pinnacle, height.

faites *vb voir* **faire.**

fait-tout *nm inv*, **faitout** *nm* [fɛtu] stewpot.

falaise [falɛz] *nf* cliff.

fallacieux, euse [falasjø, -øz] *a* fallacious; deceptive; illusory.

falloir [falwaʀ] *vb impersonnel*: il va ~ 100 F we'll (*ou* I'll) need 100 F; il doit ~ du temps that must take time; il me faudrait 100 F I would need 100 F; il vous faut tourner à gauche après l'église you have to turn left past the church; **nous avons ce qu'il (nous) faut** we have what we need; **il faut qu'il parte/a fallu qu'il parte** (*obligation*) he has to *ou* must leave/had to leave; **il a fallu le faire** it had to be done // **s'en ~**: il s'en est fallu de 100 F/5 minutes we (*ou* they) were 100 F short/5 minutes late (*ou* ear-

ly); il s'en faut de beaucoup qu'il soit he is far from being; il s'en est fallu de peu que cela n'arrive it very nearly happened; ou peu s'en faut or as good as.

falot, e [falo, -ɔt] *a* dreary, colourless.

falsifier [falsifje] *vt* to falsify; to doctor.

famé, e [fame] *a*: **mal ~** disreputable, of ill repute.

famélique [famelik] *a* half-starved.

fameux, euse [famø, -øz] *a* (*illustre*) famous; (*bon: repas, plat etc*) first-rate, first-class; (*valeur intensive*) real, downright.

familial, e, aux [familjal, -o] *a* family *cpd* // *nf* (*AUTO*) estate car (*Brit*), station wagon (*US*).

familiarité [familjaʀite] *nf* informality; familiarity; ~s *nfpl* familiarities.

familier, ère [familje, -ɛʀ] *a* (*connu, impertinent*) familiar; (*dénotant une certaine intimité*) informal, friendly; (*LING*) informal, colloquial // *nm* regular (visitor).

famille [famij] *nf* family; **il a de la ~ à Paris** he has relatives in Paris.

famine [famin] *nf* famine.

fanal, aux [fanal, -o] *nm* beacon; lantern.

fanatique [fanatik] *a* fanatical // *nm/f* fanatic; **fanatisme** *nm* fanaticism.

faner [fane]: se ~ *vi* to fade.

fanfare [fɑ̃faʀ] *nf* (*orchestre*) brass band; (*musique*) fanfare.

fanfaron, ne [fɑ̃faʀɔ̃, -ɔn] *nm/f* braggart.

fange [fɑ̃ʒ] *nf* mire.

fanion [fanjɔ̃] *nm* pennant.

fantaisie [fɑ̃tezi] *nf* (*spontanéité*) fancy, imagination; (*caprice*) whim; extravagance // *a*: **bijou/pain (de) ~** costume jewellery/fancy bread; **fantaisiste** *a* (*péj*) unorthodox, eccentric // *nm/f* (*de music-hall*) variety artist *ou* entertainer.

fantasme [fɑ̃tasm(ə)] *nm* fantasy.

fantasque [fɑ̃task(ə)] *a* whimsical, capricious; fantastic.

fantastique [fɑ̃tastik] *a* fantastic.

fantôme [fɑ̃tom] *nm* ghost, phantom.

faon [fɑ̃] *nm* fawn.

farce [faʀs(ə)] *nf* (*viande*) stuffing; (*blague*) (practical) joke; (*THÉÂTRE*) farce; **farcir** *vt* (*viande*) to stuff.

fard [faʀ] *nm* make-up.

fardeau, x [faʀdo] *nm* burden.

farder [faʀde] *vt* to make up.

farfelu, e [faʀfəly] *a* hare-brained.

farine [faʀin] *nf* flour; **farineux, euse** *a* (*sauce, pomme*) floury // *nmpl* (*aliments*) starchy foods.

farouche [faʀuʃ] *a* shy, timid; savage, wild; fierce.

fart [faʀ(t)] *nm* (ski) wax.

fascicule [fasikyl] *nm* volume.

fasciner [fasine] *vt* to fascinate.

fascisme [faʃism(ə)] *nm* fascism.

fasse *etc vb voir* **faire**.

faste [fast(ə)] *nm* splendour // *a:* c'est un jour ~ this is our (*ou* our) lucky day.

fastidieux, euse [fastidjø, -øz] *a* tedious, tiresome.

fastueux, euse [fastɥø, -øz] *a* sumptuous, luxurious.

fat [fa] *am* conceited, smug.

fatal, e [fatal] *a* fatal; (*inévitable*) inevitable; **~ité** *nf* fate; fateful coincidence; inevitability.

fatidique [fatidik] *a* fateful.

fatigant, e [fatigɑ̃, -ɑ̃t] *a* tiring; (*agaçant*) tiresome.

fatigue [fatig] *nf* tiredness, fatigue.

fatigué, e [fatige] *a* tired.

fatiguer [fatige] *vt* to tire, make tired; (*TECH*) to put a strain on, strain; (*fig: importuner*) to wear out // *vi* (*moteur*) to labour, strain; **se ~** to get tired; to tire o.s. (out).

fatras [fatʀɑ] *nm* jumble, hotchpotch.

fatuité [fatɥite] *nf* conceitedness, smugness.

faubourg [fobuʀ] *nm* suburb.

fauché, e [foʃe] *a* (*fam*) broke.

faucher [foʃe] *vt* (*herbe*) to cut; (*champs, blés*) to reap; (*fig*) to cut down; to mow down.

faucille [fosij] *nf* sickle.

faucon [fokɔ̃] *nm* falcon, hawk.

faudra *vb voir* **falloir**.

faufiler [fofile] *vt* to tack, baste; **se ~** *vi:* se ~ dans to edge one's way into; se ~ parmi/entre to thread one's way among/between.

faune [fon] *nf* (*ZOOL*) wildlife, fauna.

faussaire [fosɛʀ] *nm* forger.

fausse [fos] *a voir* **faux**.

faussement [fosmɑ̃] *ad* (*accuser*) wrongly, wrongfully; (*croire*) falsely.

fausser [fose] *vt* (*objet*) to bend, buckle; (*fig*) to distort.

fausseté [foste] *nf* wrongness; falseness.

faut *vb voir* **falloir**.

faute [fot] *nf* (*erreur*) mistake, error; (*péché, manquement*) misdemeanour; (*FOOTBALL etc*) offence; (*TENNIS*) fault; c'est de sa/ma ~ it's his/my fault; être en ~ to be in the wrong; ~ de (*temps, argent*) for *ou* through lack of; sans ~ *ad* without fail; ~ de frappe typing error; ~ professionnelle professional misconduct *q*.

fauteuil [fotœj] *nm* armchair; ~ d'orchestre seat in the front stalls; ~ roulant wheelchair.

fauteur [fotœʀ] *nm:* ~ de troubles trouble-maker.

fautif, ive [fotif, -iv] *a* (*incorrect*) incorrect, inaccurate; (*responsable*) at fault, in the wrong; guilty.

fauve [fov] *nm* wildcat // *a* (*couleur*) fawn.

faux [fo] *nf* scythe.

faux, fausse [fo, fos] *a* (*inexact*) wrong; (*piano, voix*) out of tune; (*falsifié*) fake; forged; (*sournois, postiche*) false // *ad* (*MUS*) out of tune // *nm* (*copie*) fake, forgery; (*opposé au vrai*): le ~ falsehood; faire ~ bond à qn to stand sb up; ~ frais *nmpl* extras, incidental expenses; ~ pas tripping *q*; (*fig*) faux pas; ~ témoignage (*délit*) perjury; **fausse alerte** false alarm; **fausse couche** miscarriage; **~-filet** *nm* sirloin; **~-fuyant** *nm* equivocation; **~-monnayeur** *nm* counterfeiter, forger.

faveur [favœʀ] *nf* favour; traitement de ~ preferential treatment; à la ~ de under cover of; thanks to; en ~ de in favour of.

favorable [favɔʀabl(ə)] *a* favourable.

favori, te [favɔʀi, -it] *a, nm/f* favourite; **~s** *nmpl* (*barbe*) sideboards (*Brit*), sideburns.

favoriser [favɔʀize] *vt* to favour.

fébrile [febʀil] *a* feverish, febrile.

fécond, e [fekɔ̃, -ɔ̃d] *a* fertile; **féconder** *vt* to fertilize; **fécondité** *nf* fertility.

fécule [fekyl] *nf* potato flour.

fédéral, e, aux [fedeʀal, -o] *a* federal.

fée [fe] *nf* fairy; **~rie** *nf* enchantment; **~rique** *a* magical, fairytale *cpd*.

feignant, e [fɛɲɑ̃, -ɑ̃t] *nm/f* = **fainéant, e**.

feindre [fɛ̃dʀ(ə)] *vt* to feign // *vi* to dissemble; ~ de faire to pretend to do.

feinte [fɛ̃t] *nf* (*SPORT*) dummy.

fêler [fele] *vt* to crack.

félicitations [felisitasjɔ̃] *nfpl* congratulations.

féliciter [felisite] *vt:* ~ qn (de) to congratulate sb (on); se ~ (de) to congratulate o.s. (on).

félin, e [felɛ̃, -in] *a* feline // *nm* (big) cat.

fêlure [felyʀ] *nf* crack.

femelle [fəmɛl] *a, nf* female.

féminin, e [feminɛ̃, -in] *a* feminine; (*sexe*) female; (*équipe, vêtements etc*) women's // *nm* feminine; **féministe** *a* feminist.

femme [fam] *nf* woman; (*épouse*) wife (*pl* wives); ~ de chambre, ~ de ménage cleaning lady.

fémur [femyʀ] *nm* femur, thighbone.

fendre [fɑ̃dʀ(ə)] *vt* (*couper en deux*) to split; (*fissurer*) to crack; (*fig: traverser*) to cut through; to cleave through; **se ~** *vi* to crack.

fenêtre [fənɛtʀ(ə)] *nf* window.

fenouil [fənuj] *nm* fennel.

fente [fɑ̃t] *nf* (*fissure*) crack; (*de boîte à lettres etc*) slit.

féodal, e, aux [feɔdal, -o] *a* feudal.

fer [fɛʀ] *nm* iron; (*de cheval*) shoe; ~ à cheval horseshoe; ~ forgé wrought iron; ~ (à repasser) iron.

ferai *etc vb voir* **faire.**

fer-blanc [fɛʀblɑ̃] *nm* tin(plate).

férié, e [feʀje] *a:* **jour ~** public holiday.

ferions *etc vb voir* **faire.**

férir [feʀiʀ]: **sans coup ~** *ad* without meeting any opposition.

ferme [fɛʀm(ə)] *a* firm // *ad (travailler etc)* hard // *nf (exploitation)* farm; *(maison)* farmhouse.

fermé, e [fɛʀme] *a* closed, shut; *(gaz, eau etc)* off; *(fig: personne)* uncommunicative; *(: milieu)* exclusive.

fermenter [fɛʀmɑ̃te] *vi* to ferment.

fermer [fɛʀme] *vt* to close, shut; *(cesser l'exploitation de)* to close down, shut down; *(eau, lumière, électricité, robinet)* to put off, turn off; *(aéroport, route)* to close // *vi* to close, shut; to close down, shut down; **se ~** *vi (yeux)* to close, shut; *(fleur, blessure)* to close up.

fermeté [fɛʀməte] *nf* firmness.

fermeture [fɛʀmətyʀ] *nf* closing; shutting; closing *ou* shutting down; putting *ou* turning off; *(dispositif)* catch; fastening, fastener; **~ éclair** ® *ou* **à glissière** zip (fastener) (*Brit*), zipper (*US*).

fermier, ière [fɛʀmje, -jɛʀ] *nm* farmer // *nf* woman farmer; farmer's wife.

fermoir [fɛʀmwaʀ] *nm* clasp.

féroce [feʀɔs] *a* ferocious, fierce.

ferons *vb voir* **faire.**

ferraille [feʀaj] *nf* scrap iron; **mettre à la ~** to scrap.

ferré, e [feʀe] *a* hobnailed; steel-tipped; *(fam):* **~ en** well up on, hot at.

ferrer [feʀe] *vt (cheval)* to shoe.

ferronnerie [feʀɔnʀi] *nf* ironwork.

ferroviaire [feʀɔvjɛʀ] *a* rail(way) *cpd* (*Brit*), rail(road) *cpd* (*US*).

ferry(-boat) [feʀe(bot)] *nm* ferry.

fertile [fɛʀtil] *a* fertile; **~ en incidents** eventful, packed with incidents.

féru, e [feʀy] *a:* **~ de** with a keen interest in.

férule [feʀyl] *nf:* **être sous la ~ de** qn to be under sb's (iron) rule.

fervent, e [fɛʀvɑ̃, -ɑ̃t] *a* fervent.

fesse [fɛs] *nf* buttock; **fessée** *nf* spanking.

festin [fɛstɛ̃] *nm* feast.

festival [fɛstival] *nm* festival.

festoyer [fɛstwaje] *vi* to feast.

fêtard [fɛtaʀ] *nm (péj)* high liver, merry-maker.

fête [fɛt] *nf (religieuse)* feast; *(publique)* holiday; *(en famille etc)* celebration; *(kermesse)* fête, fair, festival; *(du nom)* feast day, name day; **faire la ~** to live it up; **faire ~ à** qn to give sb a warm welcome; **les ~s (de fin d'année)** the festive season; **la salle/le comité des ~s** the village hall/festival committee; **~ foraine** (fun) fair; **la F~ Nationale** the national holiday; **fêter** *vt* to celebrate; *(personne)* to have a celebration for.

fétu [fety] *nm:* **~ de paille** wisp of straw.

feu [fø] *a inv:* **~ son père** his late father.

feu, x [fø] *nm (gén)* fire; *(signal lumineux)* light; *(de cuisinière)* ring; *(sensation de brûlure)* burning (sensation); **~x** *nmpl (éclat, lumière)* fire *sg*; *(AUTO)* (traffic) lights; **au ~!** *(incendie)* fire!; **à ~ doux/vif** over a slow/brisk heat; **à petit ~** *(CULIN)* over a gentle heat; *(fig)* slowly; **faire ~** to fire; **prendre ~** to catch fire; **mettre le ~ à** to set fire to; **faire du ~** to make a fire; **avez-vous du ~?** *(pour cigarette)* have you (got) a light?; **~ rouge/vert/orange** red/green/amber (*Brit*) *ou* yellow (*US*) light; **~ arrière** rear light; **~ d'artifice** firework; *(spectacle)* fireworks *pl*; **~ de joie** bonfire; **~x de brouillard** fog-lamps; **~x de croisement** dipped (*Brit*) *ou* dimmed (*US*) headlights; **~x de position** sidelights; **~x de route** headlights.

feuillage [fœjaʒ] *nm* foliage, leaves *pl*.

feuille [fœj] *nf (d'arbre)* leaf *(pl* leaves); *(de papier)* sheet; **~ d'impôts** tax form; **~ de maladie** medical expenses claim form; **~ de paie** pay slip; **~ de vigne** *(BOT)* vine leaf; *(sur statue)* fig leaf; **~ volante** loose sheet.

feuillet [fœje] *nm* leaf *(pl* leaves).

feuilleté, e [fœjte] *a (CULIN)* flaky; *(verre)* laminated.

feuilleter [fœjte] *vt (livre)* to leaf through.

feuilleton [fœjtɔ̃] *nm* serial.

feuillu, e [fœjy] *a* leafy // *nm* broadleaved tree.

feutre [føtʀ(ə)] *nm* felt; *(chapeau)* felt hat; *(aussi: stylo-~)* felt-tip pen; **feutré, e** *a* feltlike; *(pas, voix)* muffled.

fève [fɛv] *nf* broad bean.

février [fevʀije] *nm* February.

fi [fi] *excl:* **faire ~ de** to snap one's fingers at.

fiable [fjabl(ə)] *a* reliable.

fiacre [fjakʀ(ə)] *nm* (hackney) cab *ou* carriage.

fiançailles [fjɑ̃saj] *nfpl* engagement *sg*.

fiancé, e [fjɑ̃se] *nm/f* fiancé/fiancée // *a:* **être ~ (à)** to be engaged (to).

fiancer [fjɑ̃se]: **se ~** *vi* to become engaged.

fibre [fibʀ(ə)] *nf* fibre; **~ de verre** fibreglass, glass fibre.

ficeler [fisle] *vt* to tie up.

ficelle [fisɛl] *nf* string *q*; piece *ou* length of string.

fiche [fiʃ] *nf (pour fichier)* (index) card; *(formulaire)* form; *(ÉLEC)* plug.

ficher [fiʃe] *vt (dans un fichier)* to file; *(POLICE)* to put on file; *(planter)* to stick, drive; *(fam)* to do; to give; to stick *ou* shove; **fiche(-moi) le camp** *(fam)* clear off; **fiche-moi la paix** *(fam)* leave me alone; **se ~ de** *(fam)* to make fun of; not to care about.

fichier [fiʃje] nm file; card index.
fichu, e [fiʃy] pp de **ficher** (fam) // a (fam: fini, inutilisable) bust, done for; (: intensif) wretched, darned // nm (foulard) (head)scarf (pl scarves); **mal ~** (fam) feeling lousy; useless.
fictif, ive [fiktif, -iv] a fictitious.
fiction [fiksjɔ̃] nf fiction; (fait imaginé) invention.
fidèle [fidɛl] a faithful // nm/f (REL): les **~s** the faithful; (à l'église) the congregation.
fief [fjɛf] nm fief; (fig) preserve; stronghold.
fier [fje]: se **~ à** vt to trust.
fier, fière [fjɛʀ] a proud; **~té** nf pride.
fièvre [fjɛvʀ(ə)] nf fever; **avoir de la ~/39 de ~** to have a high temperature/a temperature of 39°C; **fiévreux, euse** a feverish.
fifre [fifʀ(ə)] nm fife; fife-player.
figer [fiʒe] vt to congeal; (fig: personne) to freeze, root to the spot; se **~** vi to congeal; to freeze; (institutions etc) to become set, stop evolving.
figue [fig] nf fig; **figuier** nm fig tree.
figurant, e [figyʀɑ̃, -ɑ̃t] nm/f (THÉÂTRE) walk-on; (CINÉMA) extra.
figure [figyʀ] nf (visage) face; (image, tracé, forme, personnage) figure; (illustration) picture, diagram; **faire ~ de** to look like.
figuré, e [figyʀe] a (sens) figurative.
figurer [figyʀe] vi to appear // vt to represent; se **~ que** to imagine that.
fil [fil] nm (brin, fig: d'une histoire) thread; (du téléphone) cable, wire; (textile de lin) linen; (d'un couteau) edge; **au ~ des années** with the passing of the years; **au ~ de l'eau** with the stream ou current; **coup de ~** phone call; **~ à coudre** (sewing) thread; **~ électrique** electric wire; **~ de fer** wire; **~ de fer barbelé** barbed wire; **~ à pêche** fishing line; **~ à plomb** plumbline.
filament [filamɑ̃] nm (ÉLEC) filament; (de liquide) trickle, thread.
filandreux, euse [filɑ̃dʀø, -øz] a stringy.
filasse [filas] a inv white blond.
filature [filatyʀ] nf (fabrique) mill; (policière) shadowing q, tailing q.
file [fil] nf line; (AUTO) lane; **~ (d'attente)** queue (Brit), line (US); **en ~ indienne** in single file; **à la ~** ad (d'affilée) in succession.
filer [file] vt (tissu, toile) to spin; (prendre en filature) to shadow, tail; (fam: donner): **~ qch à qn** to slip sb sth // vi (bas, liquide, pâte) to run; (aller vite) to fly past; (fam: partir) to make off; **~ doux** to toe the line.
filet [filɛ] nm net; (CULIN) fillet; (d'eau, de sang) trickle; **~ (à provisions)** string bag.

filiale [filjal] nf (COMM) subsidiary.
filière [filjɛʀ] nf: **passer par la ~** to go through the (administrative) channels; **suivre la ~** (dans sa carrière) to work one's way up (through the hierarchy).
filiforme [filifɔʀm(ə)] a spindly; threadlike.
filigrane [filigʀan] nm (d'un billet, timbre) watermark; **en ~** (fig) showing just beneath the surface.
fille [fij] nf girl; (opposé à fils) daughter; **vieille ~** old maid; **~-mère** nf (péj) unmarried mother; **fillette** nf (little) girl.
filleul, e [fijœl] nm/f godchild, godson/daughter.
film [film] nm (pour photo) (roll of) film; (œuvre) film, picture, movie; (couche) film; **~ muet/parlant** silent/talking picture ou movie; **~ d'animation** animated film; **~ policier** thriller.
filon [filɔ̃] nm vein, lode; (fig) lucrative line, money spinner.
fils [fis] nm son; **~ de famille** moneyed young man; **~ à papa** daddy's boy.
filtre [filtʀ(ə)] nm filter; **~ à air** (AUTO) air filter; **filtrer** vt to filter; (fig: candidats, visiteurs) to screen // vi to filter (through).
fin [fɛ̃] nf end; **~s** nfpl (but) ends; **prendre ~** to come to an end; **mettre ~ à** to put an end to; **à la ~** ad in the end, eventually; **sans ~** a endless // ad endlessly.
fin, e [fɛ̃, fin] a (papier, couche, fil) thin; (cheveux, poudre, pointe, visage) fine; (taille) neat, slim; (esprit, remarque) subtle; shrewd // ad (moudre, couper) finely // nf (alcool) liqueur brandy; **~ prêt** quite ready; **un ~ tireur** a crack shot; **avoir la vue/l'ouïe ~e** to have sharp ou keen eyes/ears; **vin ~** fine wine; **~ gourmet** gourmet; **une ~e mouche** (fig) a sharp customer; **~es herbes** mixed herbs.
final, e [final] a, nf final // nm (MUS) finale; **quarts de ~e** quarter finals; **8èmes/16èmes de ~e** 2nd/1st round (in 5 round knock-out competition); **~ement** ad finally, in the end; (après tout) after all.
finance [finɑ̃s] nf finance; **~s** nfpl (situation) finances; (activités) finance sg; **moyennant ~** for a fee; **financer** vt to finance; **financier, ière** a financial.
finaud, e [fino, -od] a wily.
finesse [finɛs] nf thinness; fineness; neatness, slimness; subtlety; shrewdness.
fini, e [fini] a finished; (MATH) finite; (intensif): **un menteur ~** a liar through and through // nm (d'un objet manufacturé) finish.
finir [finiʀ] vt to finish // vi to finish, end; **~ quelque part/par faire** to end ou finish

up somewhere/doing; ~ de faire to finish doing; (*cesser*) to stop doing; il finit par m'agacer he's beginning to get on my nerves; ~ en pointe/tragédie to end in a point/in tragedy; en ~ avec to be *ou* have done with; il va mal ~ he will come to a bad end.

finition [finisjɔ̃] *nf* finishing; finish.

finlandais, e [fɛ̃lɑ̃dɛ, -ɛz] *a* Finnish // *nm/f*: F~, e Finn.

Finlande [fɛ̃lɑ̃d] *nf*: la ~ Finland.

fiole [fjɔl] *nf* phial.

fioriture [fjɔrityr] *nf* embellishment, flourish.

firme [firm(ə)] *nf* firm.

fis *vb voir* faire.

fisc [fisk] *nm* tax authorities *pl*; ~al, e, aux *a* tax *cpd*, fiscal; ~alité *nf* tax system; (*charges*) taxation.

fissure [fisyr] *nf* crack.

fissurer [fisyre] *vt*, se ~ *vi* to crack.

fiston [fistɔ̃] *nm* (*fam*) son, lad.

fit *vb voir* faire.

fixation [fiksasjɔ̃] *nf* fixing; fastening; setting; (*de ski*) binding; (*PSYCH*) fixation.

fixe [fiks(ə)] *a* fixed; (*emploi*) steady, regular // *nm* (*salaire*) basic salary; à heure ~ at a set time; menu à prix ~ set menu.

fixé, e [fikse] *a*: être ~ (sur) (*savoir à quoi s'en tenir*) to have made up one's mind (about); to know for certain (about).

fixer [fikse] *vt* (*attacher*): ~ qch (à/sur) to fix *ou* fasten sth (to/onto); (*déterminer*) to fix, set; (*CHIMIE, PHOTO*) to fix; (*regarder*) to stare at; se ~ *vi* (*s'établir*) to settle down; se ~ sur (*suj: attention*) to focus on.

flacon [flakɔ̃] *nm* bottle.

flageller [flaʒele] *vt* to flog, scourge.

flageoler [flaʒɔle] *vi* (*jambes*) to sag.

flageolet [flaʒɔle] *nm* (*MUS*) flageolet; (*CULIN*) dwarf kidney bean.

flagrant, e [flagrɑ̃, -ɑ̃t] *a* flagrant, blatant; en ~ délit in the act.

flair [flɛr] *nm* sense of smell; (*fig*) intuition; **flairer** *vt* (*humer*) to sniff (at); (*détecter*) to scent.

flamand, e [flamɑ̃, -ɑ̃d] *a*, *nm* (*LING*) Flemish // *nm/f*: F~, e Fleming; les F~s the Flemish.

flamant [flamɑ̃] *nm* flamingo.

flambant [flɑ̃bɑ̃] *ad*: ~ neuf brand new.

flambé, e [flɑ̃be] *a* (*CULIN*) flambé // *nf* blaze; (*fig*) flaring-up, explosion.

flambeau, x [flɑ̃bo] *nm* (flaming) torch.

flamber [flɑ̃be] *vi* to blaze (up).

flamboyer [flɑ̃bwaje] *vi* to blaze (up); to flame.

flamme [flam] *nf* flame; (*fig*) fire, fervour; en ~s on fire, ablaze.

flan [flɑ̃] *nm* (*CULIN*) custard tart *ou* pie.

flanc [flɑ̃] *nm* side; (*MIL*) flank; prêter le ~ à (*fig*) to lay o.s. open to.

flancher [flɑ̃ʃe] *vi* to fail, pack up; to quit.

flanelle [flanɛl] *nf* flannel.

flâner [flɑne] *vi* to stroll; **flânerie** *nf* stroll.

flanquer [flɑ̃ke] *vt* to flank; (*fam: mettre*) to chuck, shove; (: *jeter*): ~ par terre/à la porte to fling to the ground/ chuck out.

flaque [flak] *nf* (*d'eau*) puddle; (*d'huile, de sang etc*) pool.

flash, pl flashes [flaʃ] *nm* (*PHOTO*) flash; ~ (d'information) newsflash.

flasque [flask(ə)] *a* flabby.

flatter [flate] *vt* to flatter; se ~ de qch to pride o.s. on sth; **flatterie** *nf* flattery *q*; **flatteur, euse** *a* flattering // *nm/f* flatter-er.

fléau, x [fleo] *nm* scourge.

flèche [flɛʃ] *nf* arrow; (*de clocher*) spire; (*de grue*) jib; monter en ~ (*fig*) to soar, rocket; partir en ~ to be off like a shot; **fléchette** *nf* dart; **fléchettes** *nfpl* (*jeu*) darts *sg*.

fléchir [fleʃir] *vt* (*corps, genou*) to bend; (*fig*) to sway, weaken // *vi* (*poutre*) to sag, bend; (*fig*) to weaken, flag; to yield.

flemmard, e [flemar, -ard(ə)] *nm/f* lazybones *sg*, loafer.

flétrir [fletrir] *vt*, se ~ *vi* to wither.

fleur [flœr] *nf* flower; (*d'un arbre*) blossom; en ~ (*arbre*) in blossom; à ~ de terre just above the ground.

fleurer [flœre] *vt*: ~ la lavande to have the scent of lavender.

fleuri, e [flœri] *a* in flower *ou* bloom; surrounded by flowers; (*fig*) flowery; florid.

fleurir [flœrir] *vi* (*rose*) to flower; (*arbre*) to blossom; (*fig*) to flourish // *vt* (*tombe*) to put flowers on; (*chambre*) to decorate with flowers.

fleuriste [flœrist(ə)] *nm/f* florist.

fleuron [flœrɔ̃] *nm* jewel (*fig*).

fleuve [flœv] *nm* river.

flexible [fleksibl(ə)] *a* flexible.

flexion [fleksjɔ̃] *nf* flexing, bending.

flic [flik] *nm* (*fam: péj*) cop.

flipper [flipœr] *nm* pinball (machine).

flirter [flœrte] *vi* to flirt.

flocon [flɔkɔ̃] *nm* flake.

floraison [flɔrezɔ̃] *nf* flowering; blossoming; flourishing.

flore [flɔr] *nf* flora.

florissant, e [flɔrisɑ̃, -ɑ̃t] *vb voir* fleurir.

flot [flo] *nm* flood, stream; ~s *nmpl* (*de la mer*) waves; être à ~ (*NAVIG*) to be afloat; (*fig*) to be on an even keel; entrer à ~s to stream *ou* pour in.

flotte [flɔt] *nf* (*NAVIG*) fleet; (*fam*) water; rain.

flottement [flɔtmɑ̃] *nm* (*fig*) wavering, hesitation.

flotter [flɔte] *vi* to float; (*nuage, odeur*) to drift; (*drapeau*) to fly; (*vêtements*) to hang loose; (*monnaie*) to float // *vt* to float; **faire ~** to float; **flotteur** *nm* float.

flou, e [flu] *a* fuzzy, blurred; (*fig*) woolly, vague.

flouer [flue] *vt* to swindle.

fluctuation [flyktɥɑsjɔ̃] *nf* fluctuation.

fluet, te [flɥɛ, -ɛt] *a* thin, slight.

fluide [flɥid] *a* fluid; (*circulation etc*) flowing freely // *nm* fluid; (*force*) (mysterious) power.

fluor [flyɔʀ] *nm* fluorine.

fluorescent, e [flyɔʀesã, -ãt] *a* fluorescent.

flûte [flyt] *nf* flute; (*verre*) flute glass; (*pain*) long loaf (*pl* loaves); **~!** drat it!; **~ à bec** recorder.

flux [fly] *nm* incoming tide; (*écoulement*) flow; **le ~ et le reflux** the ebb and flow.

FM *sigle f* (= *fréquence modulée*) FM.

foc [fɔk] *nm* jib.

foi [fwa] *nf* faith; **sous la ~ du serment** under *ou* on oath; **ajouter ~ à** to lend credence to; **digne de ~** reliable; **sur la ~ de** on the word *ou* strength of; **être de bonne/mauvaise ~** to be sincere/insincere; **ma ~...** well....

foie [fwa] *nm* liver.

foin [fwɛ̃] *nm* hay; **faire du ~** (*fig: fam*) to kick up a row.

foire [fwaʀ] *nf* fair; (*fête foraine*) (fun) fair; **faire la ~** (*fig: fam*) to whoop it up; **~** (*exposition*) trade fair.

fois [fwa] *nf* time; **une/deux ~** once/ twice; **2 ~ 2** 2 times 2; **quatre ~ plus grand (que)** four times as big (as); **une ~** (*passé*) once; (*futur*) sometime; **une ~ pour toutes** once and for all; **une ~ que** once; **des ~** (*parfois*) sometimes; **à la ~** (*ensemble*) at once.

foison [fwazɔ̃] *nf*: **une ~ de** an abundance of; **à ~** *ad* in plenty.

foisonner [fwazɔne] *vi* to abound.

fol [fɔl] *a voir* **fou**.

folâtrer [fɔlɑtʀe] *vi* to frolic (about).

folie [fɔli] *nf* (*d'une décision, d'un acte*) madness, folly; (*état*) madness, insanity; (*acte*) folly; **la ~ des grandeurs** delusions of grandeur; **faire des ~s** (*en dépenses*) to be extravagant.

folklorique [fɔlklɔʀik] *a* folk *cpd*; (*fam*) weird.

folle [fɔl] *a, nf voir* **fou**; **~ment** *ad* (*très*) madly, wildly.

foncé, e [fɔ̃se] *a* dark.

foncer [fɔ̃se] *vi* to go darker; (*fam: aller vite*) to tear *ou* belt along; **~ sur** to charge at.

foncier, ère [fɔ̃sje, -ɛʀ] *a* (*honnêteté etc*) basic, fundamental; (*malhonnêteté*) deep-rooted; (*COMM*) real estate *cpd*.

fonction [fɔ̃ksjɔ̃] *nf* (*rôle*, MATH, LING) function; (*emploi, poste*) post, position; **~s** (*professionnelles*) duties; **entrer en ~s** to take up one's post *ou* duties; to take up office; **voiture de ~** company car; **être ~ de** (*dépendre de*) to depend on; **en ~ de** (*par rapport à*) according to; **faire ~ de** to serve as; **la ~ publique** the state *ou* civil (*Brit*) service.

fonctionnaire [fɔ̃ksjɔnɛʀ] *nm/f* state employee, local authority employee; (*dans l'administration*) ≈ civil servant.

fonctionner [fɔ̃ksjɔne] *vi* to work, function; (*entreprise*) to operate, function.

fond [fɔ̃] *nm voir aussi* **fonds**; (*d'un récipient, trou*) bottom; (*d'une salle, scène*) back; (*d'un tableau, décor*) background; (*opposé à la forme*) content; (SPORT): **le ~** long distance (running); **sans ~** bottomless; **au ~ de** at the bottom of; at the back of; **à ~** *ad* (*connaître, soutenir*) thoroughly; (*appuyer, visser*) right down *ou* home; **à ~** (*de train*) *ad* (*fam*) full tilt; **dans le ~, au ~** *ad* (*en somme*) basically, really; **de ~ en comble** *ad* from top to bottom; **~ sonore** background noise; background music; **~ de teint** (make-up) foundation.

fondamental, e, aux [fɔ̃damãtal, -o] *a* fundamental.

fondant, e [fɔ̃dã, -ãt] *a* (*neige*) melting; (*poire*) that melts in the mouth.

fondateur, trice [fɔ̃datœʀ, -tʀis] *nm/f* founder.

fondation [fɔ̃dasjɔ̃] *nf* founding; (*établissement*) foundation; **~s** *nfpl* (*d'une maison*) foundations.

fondé, e [fɔ̃de] *a* (*accusation etc*) well-founded; **être ~ à** to have grounds for *ou* good reason to // *nm*: **~ de pouvoir** authorized representative.

fondement [fɔ̃dmɑ̃] *nm* (*derrière*) behind; **~s** *nmpl* foundations; **sans ~** *a* (*rumeur etc*) groundless, unfounded.

fonder [fɔ̃de] *vt* to found; (*fig*) to base; **se ~ sur** (*suj: personne*) to base o.s. on.

fonderie [fɔ̃dʀi] *nf* smelting works *sg*.

fondre [fɔ̃dʀ(ə)] *vt* (*aussi*: **faire ~**) to melt; (*dans l'eau*) to dissolve; (*fig: mélanger*) to merge, blend // *vi* to melt; to dissolve; (*fig*) to melt away; (*se précipiter*): **~ sur** to swoop down on; **~ en larmes** to burst into tears.

fonds [fɔ̃] *nm* (*de bibliothèque*) collection; (*COMM*): **~ (de commerce)** business // *nmpl* (*argent*) funds; **à ~ perdus** *ad* with little or no hope of getting the money back.

fondu, e [fɔ̃dy] *a* (*beurre, neige*) melted; (*métal*) molten // *nf* (CULIN) fondue.

font *vb voir* **faire**.

fontaine [fɔ̃tɛn] *nf* fountain; (*source*) spring.

fonte [fɔ̃t] *nf* melting; (*métal*) cast iron; **la ~ des neiges** the (spring) thaw.

fonts baptismaux [fɔ̃batismo] *nmpl* (baptismal) font *sg*.

foot [fut] *nm* (*fam*) football.

football [futbol] *nm* football, soccer; **~eur** *nm* footballer.

footing [futiaj] *nm* jogging; **faire du ~** to go jogging.

for [fɔR] *nm*: **dans son ~ intérieur** in one's heart of hearts.

forain, e [fɔRɛ̃, -ɛn] *a* fairground *cpd* // *nm* stallholder; fairground entertainer.

forçat [fɔRsa] *nm* convict.

force [fɔRs(ə)] *nf* strength; (*puissance: surnaturelle etc*) power; (*PHYSIQUE, MÉCANIQUE*) force; **~s** *nfpl* (*physiques*) strength *sg*; (*MIL*) forces; **à ~ d'insister** by dint of insisting; as he (*ou* I *etc*) kept on insisting; **de ~** *ad* forcibly, by force; **être de ~ à faire** to be up to doing; **de première ~** first class; **~ d'âme** fortitude; **les ~s de l'ordre** the police.

forcé, e [fɔRse] *a* forced; unintended; inevitable.

forcément [fɔRsemã] *ad* necessarily; inevitably; (*bien sûr*) of course.

forcené, e [fɔRsəne] *nm/f* maniac.

forcer [fɔRse] *vt* (*porte, serrure, plante*) to force; (*moteur, voix*) to strain // *vi* (*SPORT*) to overtax o.s.; **~ la dose/ l'allure** to overdo it/increase the pace; **se ~ (pour faire)** to force o.s. (to do).

forcir [fɔRsiR] *vi* (*grossir*) to broaden out; (*vent*) to freshen.

forer [fɔRe] *vt* to drill, bore.

forestier, ère [fɔRɛstje, -ɛR] *a* forest *cpd*.

forêt [fɔRɛ] *nf* forest.

foreuse [fɔRøz] *nf* (electric) drill.

forfait [fɔRfɛ] *nm* (*COMM*) fixed *ou* set price; all-in deal *ou* price; (*crime*) infamy; **déclarer ~** to withdraw; **travailler à ~** to work for a lump sum; **forfaitaire** *a* inclusive; set.

forfanterie [fɔRfãtRi] *nf* boastfulness *q*.

forge [fɔRʒ(ə)] *nf* forge, smithy.

forger [fɔRʒe] *vt* to forge; (*fig: personnalité*) to form; (*: prétexte*) to contrive, make up.

forgeron [fɔRʒərɔ̃] *nm* (black)smith.

formaliser [fɔRmalize]: **se ~** *vi*: **se ~ (de)** to take offence (at).

format [fɔRma] *nm* size.

formater [fɔRmate] *vt* (*disque*) to format.

formation [fɔRmasjɔ̃] *nf* forming; training; (*MUS*) group; (*MIL, AVIAT, GÉO*) formation; **~ permanente** continuing education; **~ professionnelle** vocational training.

forme [fɔRm(ə)] *nf* (*gén*) form; (*d'un objet*) shape, form; **~s** *nfpl* (*bonnes manières*) proprieties; (*d'une femme*) figure *sg*; **en ~ de poire** pear-shaped; **être en ~** (*SPORT etc*) to be on form; en

bonne et due **~** in due form.

formel, le [fɔRmɛl] *a* (*preuve, décision*) definite, positive; (*logique*) formal; **~lement** *ad* (*absolument*) positively.

former [fɔRme] *vt* to form; (*éduquer*) to train; **se ~** *vi* to form.

formidable [fɔRmidabl(ə)] *a* tremendous.

formulaire [fɔRmylɛR] *nm* form.

formule [fɔRmyl] *nf* (*gén*) formula; (*formulaire*) form; **~ de politesse** polite phrase; letter ending.

formuler [fɔRmyle] *vt* (*émettre: réponse, vœux*) to formulate; (*expliciter: sa pensée*) to express.

fort, e [fɔR, fɔRt(ə)] *a* strong; (*intensité, rendement*) high, great; (*corpulent*) stout; (*doué*) good, able // *ad* (*serrer, frapper*) hard; (*sonner*) loud(ly); (*beaucoup*) greatly, very much; (*très*) very // *nm* (*édifice*) fort; (*point fort*) strong point, forte; **se faire ~ de ...** to claim one can ...; **au plus ~ de** (*au milieu de*) in the thick of; at the height of; **~e tête** rebel.

fortifiant [fɔRtifjã] *nm* tonic.

fortifier [fɔRtifje] *vt* to strengthen, fortify; (*MIL*) to fortify.

fortiori [fɔRtjɔRi]: **à ~** *ad* all the more so.

fortuit, e [fɔRtɥi, -it] *a* fortuitous, chance *cpd*.

fortune [fɔRtyn] *nf* fortune; **faire ~** to make one's fortune; **de ~** *a* makeshift; chance *cpd*.

fortuné, e [fɔRtyne] *a* wealthy.

fosse [fos] *nf* (*grand trou*) pit; (*tombe*) grave; **~ (d'orchestre)** (orchestra) pit *pl*; **~ septique** septic tank.

fossé [fose] *nm* ditch; (*fig*) gulf, gap.

fossette [fosɛt] *nf* dimple.

fossile [fosil] *nm* fossil.

fossoyeur [foswajœR] *nm* gravedigger.

fou(fol), folle [fu, fɔl] *a* mad; (*déréglé etc*) wild, erratic; (*fam: extrême, très grand*) terrific, tremendous // *nm/f* madman/woman // *nm* (*du roi*) jester; **être ~ de** to be mad *ou* crazy about; **faire le ~** to act the fool; **avoir le ~ rire** to have the giggles.

foudre [fudR(ə)] *nf*: **la ~** lightning; **~s** *nfpl* (*colère*) wrath *sg*.

foudroyant, e [fudRwajã, -ãt] *a* lightning *cpd*, stunning; (*maladie, poison*) violent.

foudroyer [fudRwaje] *vt* to strike down; **être foudroyé(e)** to be struck by lightning; **~ qn du regard** to glare at sb.

fouet [fwɛ] *nm* whip; (*CULIN*) whisk; **de plein ~** *ad* (*se heurter*) head on; **~ter** *vt* to whip; to whisk.

fougère [fuʒɛR] *nf* fern.

fougue [fug] *nf* ardour, spirit.

fouille [fuj] *nf* search; **~s** *nfpl* (*archéologiques*) excavations.

fouiller [fuje] vt to search; (creuser) to dig // vi to rummage.

fouillis [fuji] nm jumble, muddle.

fouiner [fwine] vi (péj): ~ **dans** to nose around ou about in.

foulard [fulaʀ] nm scarf (pl scarves).

foule [ful] nf crowd; **la ~** crowds pl; **les ~s** the masses; **une ~ de** masses of.

foulée [fule] nf stride.

fouler [fule] vt to press; (sol) to tread upon; **se ~** vi (fam) to overexert o.s.; **se ~ la cheville** to sprain one's ankle; **~ aux pieds** to trample underfoot.

foulure [fulyʀ] nf sprain.

four [fuʀ] nm oven; (de potier) kiln; (THÉÂTRE: échec) flop.

fourbe [fuʀb(ə)] a deceitful.

fourbu, e [fuʀby] a exhausted.

fourche [fuʀʃ(ə)] nf pitchfork; (de bicyclette) fork.

fourchette [fuʀʃɛt] nf fork; (STATISTIQUE) bracket, margin.

fourgon [fuʀgɔ̃] nm van; (RAIL) wag(g)on.

fourmi [fuʀmi] nf ant; **~s** nfpl (fig) pins and needles; **~lière** nf ant-hill.

fourmiller [fuʀmije] vi to swarm.

fournaise [fuʀnɛz] nf blaze; (fig) furnace, oven.

fourneau, x [fuʀno] nm stove.

fournée [fuʀne] nf batch.

fourni, e [fuʀni] a (barbe, cheveux) thick; (magasin): **bien ~ (en)** well stocked (with).

fournir [fuʀniʀ] vt to supply; (preuve, exemple) to provide, supply; (effort) to put in; **fournisseur, euse** nm/f supplier; **fourniture** [fuʀnityʀ] nf supply(ing); **~s** nfpl supplies.

fourrage [fuʀaʒ] nm fodder.

fourrager, ère [fuʀaʒe, -ɛʀ] a fodder cpd.

fourré, e [fuʀe] a (bonbon etc) filled; (manteau etc) fur-lined // nm thicket.

fourreau, x [fuʀo] nm sheath.

fourrer [fuʀe] vt (fam) to stick, shove; **se ~ dans/sous** to get into/under.

fourre-tout [fuʀtu] nm inv (sac) holdall; (péj) junk room (ou cupboard); (fig) rag-bag.

fourrière [fuʀjɛʀ] nf pound.

fourrure [fuʀyʀ] nf fur; (sur l'animal) coat.

fourvoyer [fuʀvwaje]: **se ~** vi to go astray, stray.

foutre [futʀ(ə)] vt (fam!) = **ficher** (fam); **foutu, e** a (fam!) = **fichu, e** a.

foyer [fwaje] nm (de cheminée) hearth; (famille) family; (maison) home; (de jeunes etc) (social) club; hostel; (salon) foyer; (OPTIQUE, PHOTO) focus sg; **lunettes à double ~** bi-focal glasses.

fracas [fʀaka] nm din; crash; roar.

fracasser [fʀakase] vt to smash.

fraction [fʀaksjɔ̃] nf fraction;

fractionner vt to divide (up), split (up).

fracture [fʀaktyʀ] nf fracture; **~ du crâne** fractured skull; **~ de la jambe** broken leg.

fracturer [fʀaktyʀe] vt (coffre, serrure) to break open; (os, membre) to fracture.

fragile [fʀaʒil] a fragile, delicate; (fig) frail; **fragilité** nf fragility.

fragment [fʀagmɑ̃] nm (d'un objet) fragment, piece; (d'un texte) passage, extract.

fraîche [fʀɛʃ] a voir **frais**; **fraîcheur** nf coolness; freshness; **fraîchir** vi to get cooler; (vent) to freshen.

frais, fraîche [fʀɛ, fʀɛʃ] a fresh; (froid) cool // ad (récemment) newly, fresh(ly); **il fait ~** it's cool; **servir ~** serve chilled // nm: **mettre au ~** to put in a cool place; **prendre le ~** to take a breath of cool air // nmpl (débours) expenses; (COMM) costs; charges; **faire des ~** to spend; to go to a lot of expense; **faire les ~ de** to bear the brunt of; **~ généraux** overheads; **~ de scolarité** school fees (Brit), tuition (US).

fraise [fʀɛz] nf strawberry; (TECH) countersink (bit); (de dentiste) drill; **~ des bois** wild strawberry.

framboise [fʀɑ̃bwaz] nf raspberry.

franc, franche [fʀɑ̃, fʀɑ̃ʃ] a (personne) frank, straightforward; (visage) open; (net: refus, couleur) clear; (: coupure) clean; (intensif) downright; (exempt): **~ de port** postage paid // ad: **parler ~** to be frank ou candid // nm franc.

français, e [fʀɑ̃sɛ, -ɛz] a French // nm/f: **F~, e** Frenchman/woman // nm (LING) French; **les F~** the French.

France [fʀɑ̃s] nf: **la ~** France.

franche [fʀɑ̃ʃ] a voir **franc**; **~ment** ad frankly; clearly; (tout à fait) downright.

franchir [fʀɑ̃ʃiʀ] vt (obstacle) to clear, get over; (seuil, ligne, rivière) to cross; (distance) to cover.

franchise [fʀɑ̃ʃiz] nf frankness; (douanière, d'impôt) exemption; (ASSURANCES) excess.

franciser [fʀɑ̃size] vt to gallicize, Frenchify.

franc-maçon [fʀɑ̃masɔ̃] nm freemason.

franco [fʀɑ̃ko] ad (COMM): **~ (de port)** postage paid.

francophone [fʀɑ̃kɔfɔn] a French-speaking; **~phonie** nf French-speaking communities.

franc-parler [fʀɑ̃paʀle] nm inv outspokenness.

franc-tireur [fʀɑ̃tiʀœʀ] nm (MIL) irregular; (fig) freelance.

frange [fʀɑ̃ʒ] nf fringe.

frangipane [fʀɑ̃ʒipan] nf almond paste.

franquette [fʀɑ̃kɛt]: **à la bonne ~** ad without any fuss.

frappe [fʀap] nf (d'une dactylo, pianiste, machine à écrire) touch; (BOXE) punch.

frappé, e [fʀape] a iced.
frapper [fʀape] vt to hit, strike; (étonner) to strike; (monnaie) to strike, stamp; **se ~** vi (s'inquiéter) to get worked up; **~ dans ses mains** to clap one's hands; **~ du poing sur** to bang one's fist on; **frappé de stupeur** dumbfounded.
frasques [fʀask(ə)] nfpl escapades.
fraternel, le [fʀatɛʀnɛl] a brotherly, fraternal.
fraternité [fʀatɛʀnite] nf brotherhood.
fraude [fʀod] nf fraud; (SCOL) cheating; **passer qch en ~** to smuggle sth in (ou out); **~ fiscale** tax evasion; **frauder** vi, vt to cheat; **frauduleux, euse** a fraudulent.
frayer [fʀeje] vt to open up, clear // vi to spawn; (fréquenter): **~ avec** to mix with.
frayeur [fʀejœʀ] nf fright.
fredonner [fʀədɔne] vt to hum.
freezer [fʀizœʀ] nm freezing compartment.
frein [fʀɛ̃] nm brake; **~ à main** handbrake; **~s à disques/tambour** disc/drum brakes.
freiner [fʀene] vi to brake // vt (progrès etc) to check.
frelaté, e [fʀəlate] a adulterated; (fig) tainted.
frêle [fʀɛl] a frail, fragile.
frelon [fʀəlɔ̃] nm hornet.
frémir [fʀemiʀ] vi to tremble, shudder; to shiver; to quiver.
frêne [fʀɛn] nm ash.
frénétique [fʀenetik] a frenzied, frenetic.
fréquemment [fʀekamɑ̃] ad frequently.
fréquent, e [fʀekɑ̃, -ɑ̃t] a frequent.
fréquentation [fʀekɑ̃tasjɔ̃] nf frequenting; seeing; **~s** nfpl company sg.
fréquenté, e [fʀekɑ̃te] a: **très ~** (very) busy; **mal ~** patronized by disreputable elements.
fréquenter [fʀekɑ̃te] vt (lieu) to frequent; (personne) to see; **se ~** to see each other.
frère [fʀɛʀ] nm brother.
fresque [fʀɛsk(ə)] nf (ART) fresco.
fret [fʀɛ] nm freight.
fréter [fʀete] vt to charter.
frétiller [fʀetije] vi to wriggle; to quiver; (chien): **~ de la queue** to wag its tail.
fretin [fʀətɛ̃] nm: **menu ~** small fry.
friable [fʀijabl(ə)] a crumbly.
friand, e [fʀijɑ̃, -ɑ̃d] a: **~ de** very fond of.
friandise [fʀijɑ̃diz] nf sweet.
fric [fʀik] nm (fam) cash, bread.
friche [fʀiʃ]: **en ~** a, ad (lying) fallow.
friction [fʀiksjɔ̃] nf (massage) rub, rubdown; (TECH, fig) friction; **frictionner** vt to rub (down); to massage.
frigidaire [fʀiʒidɛʀ] nm ® refrigerator.

frigide [fʀiʒid] a frigid.
frigo [fʀigo] nm fridge.
frigorifier [fʀigɔʀifje] vt to refrigerate; **frigorifique** a refrigerating.
frileux, euse [fʀilø, -øz] a sensitive to (the) cold.
frimer [fʀime] vi to put on an act.
frimousse [fʀimus] nf (sweet) little face.
fringale [fʀɛ̃gal] nf: **avoir la ~** to be ravenous.
fringant, e [fʀɛ̃gɑ̃, -ɑ̃t] a dashing.
fripé, e [fʀipe] a crumpled.
fripon, ne [fʀipɔ̃, -ɔn] a roguish, mischievous // nm/f rascal, rogue.
fripouille [fʀipuj] nf scoundrel.
frire [fʀiʀ] vt, vi: **faire ~** to fry.
frisé, e [fʀize] a curly; curly-haired.
frisson [fʀisɔ̃] nm shudder, shiver; quiver; **frissonner** vi to shudder; to shiver; to quiver.
frit, e [fʀi, fʀit] pp de **frire** // nf: (pommes) **~es** chips (Brit), French fries; **friteuse** nf chip pan; **friture** nf (huile) (deep) fat; (plat): **friture (de poissons)** fried fish; (RADIO) crackle.
frivole [fʀivɔl] a frivolous.
froid, e [fʀwa, fʀwad] a, nm cold; **il fait ~** it's cold; **avoir/prendre ~** to be/catch cold; **être en ~ avec** to be on bad terms with; **froidement** ad (accueillir) coldly; (décider) coolly.
froisser [fʀwase] vt to crumple (up), crease; (fig) to hurt, offend; **se ~** vi to crumple, crease; to take offence; **se ~ un muscle** to strain a muscle.
frôler [fʀole] vt to brush against; (suj: projectile) to skim past; (fig) to come very close to.
fromage [fʀɔmaʒ] nm cheese; **~ blanc** soft white cheese; **fromager, ère** nm/f cheese merchant.
froment [fʀɔmɑ̃] nm wheat.
froncer [fʀɔ̃se] vt to gather; **~ les sourcils** to frown.
frondaisons [fʀɔ̃dɛzɔ̃] nfpl foliage sg.
fronde [fʀɔ̃d] nf sling; (fig) rebellion, rebelliousness.
front [fʀɔ̃] nm forehead, brow; (MIL) front; **de ~** ad (se heurter) head-on; (rouler) together (i.e. 2 or 3 abreast); (simultanément) at once; **faire ~ à** to face up to; **~ de mer** (sea) front.
frontalier, ère [fʀɔ̃talje, -ɛʀ] a border cpd, frontier cpd // nm/f: (travailleurs) **~s** commuters from across the border.
frontière [fʀɔ̃tjɛʀ] nf frontier, border; (fig) frontier, boundary.
fronton [fʀɔ̃tɔ̃] nm pediment.
frotter [fʀɔte] vi to rub, scrape // vt to rub; (pour nettoyer) to rub (up); to scrub; **~ une allumette** to strike a match.
fructifier [fʀyktifje] vi to yield a profit; **faire ~** to turn to good account.

fructueux, euse [fʀyktyø, -øz] a fruit-ful; profitable.

fruit [fʀɥi] nm fruit gén q; ~s de mer seafood(s); ~s secs dried fruit sg; **fruité, e** a fruity; **fruitier, ère** a: arbre **fruitier** fruit tree // nm/f fruiterer (Brit), fruit merchant (US).

fruste [fʀyst(ə)] a unpolished, unculti-vated.

frustrer [fʀystʀe] vt to frustrate.

fuel(-oil) [fjul(ɔjl)] nm fuel oil; heating oil.

fugace [fygas] a fleeting.

fugitif, ive [fyʒitif, -iv] a (lueur, amour) fleeting; (prisonnier etc) fugitive, run-away // nm/f fugitive.

fugue [fyg] nf: faire une ~ to run away, abscond.

fuir [fɥir] vt to flee from; (éviter) to shun // vi to run away; (gaz, robinet) to leak.

fuite [fɥit] nf flight; (écoulement, divul-gation) leak; être en ~ to be on the run; mettre en ~ to put to flight.

fulgurant, e [fylgyʀɑ̃, -ɑ̃t] a lightning cpd, dazzling.

fulminer [fylmine] vi to thunder forth.

fumé, e [fyme] a (CULIN) smoked; (verre) tinted // nf smoke.

fume-cigarette [fymsigaʀɛt] nm inv cigarette holder.

fumer [fyme] vi to smoke; (soupe) to steam // vt to smoke; (terre, champ) to manure.

fûmes etc vb voir **être**.

fumet [fyme] nm aroma.

fumeur, euse [fymœʀ, -øz] nm/f smoker.

fumeux, euse [fymø, -øz] a (péj) woolly, hazy.

fumier [fymje] nm manure.

fumiste [fymist(ə)] nm/f (péj) shirker; phoney.

fumisterie [fymistəʀi] nf (péj) fraud, con. .

funambule [fynɑ̃byl] nm tightrope walk-er.

funèbre [fynɛbʀ(ə)] a funeral cpd; (fig) doleful; funereal.

funérailles [fyneʀɑj] nfpl funeral sg.

funeste [fynɛst(ə)] a disastrous; death-ly.

fur [fyʀ]: au ~ et à mesure ad as one goes along; au ~ et à mesure que as.

furet [fyʀɛ] nm ferret.

fureter [fyʀte] vi (péj) to nose about.

fureur [fyʀœʀ] nf fury; (passion): ~ de passion for; faire ~ to be all the rage.

furibond, e [fyʀibɔ̃, -ɔ̃d] a furious.

furie [fyʀi] nf fury; (femme) shrew, vix-en; en ~ (mer) raging; **furieux, euse** a furious.

furoncle [fyʀɔ̃kl(ə)] nm boil.

furtif, ive [fyʀtif, -iv] a furtive.

fus vb voir **être**.

fusain [fyzɛ̃] nm (ART) charcoal.

fuseau, x [fyzo] nm (pour filer) spindle; (pantalon) (ski) pants; ~ horaire time zone.

fusée [fyze] nf rocket; ~ éclairante flare.

fuselé, e [fyzle] a slender; tapering.

fuser [fyze] vi (rires etc) to burst forth.

fusible [fyzibl(ə)] nm (ÉLEC: fil) fuse wire; (: fiche) fuse.

fusil [fyzi] nm (de guerre, à canon rayé) rifle, gun; (de chasse, à canon lisse) shotgun, gun; **fusillade** [-jad] nf gunfire q, shooting q; shooting battle; **fusiller** vt to shoot; ~-mitrailleur nm machine gun.

fusionner [fyzjɔne] vi to merge.

fustiger [fystiʒe] vt to denounce.

fut vb voir **être**.

fût [fy] vb voir **être** // nm (tonneau) bar-rel, cask.

futaie [fytɛ] nf forest, plantation.

futile [fytil] a futile; frivolous.

futur, e [fytyʀ] a, nm future.

fuyant, e [fɥijɑ̃, -ɑ̃t] vb voir **fuir** // a (regard etc) evasive; (lignes etc) reced-ing; (perspective) vanishing.

fuyard, e [fɥijaʀ, -aʀd(ə)] nm/f run-away.

G

gabarit [gabaʀi] nm (fig) size; calibre.

gâcher [gɑʃe] vt (gâter) to spoil, ruin; (gaspiller) to waste.

gâchette [gɑʃɛt] nf trigger.

gâchis [gɑʃi] nm waste q.

gadoue [gadu] nf sludge.

gaffe [gaf] nf (instrument) boat hook; (erreur) blunder; faire ~ (fam) to be careful.

gage [gaʒ] nm (dans un jeu) forfeit; (fig: de fidélité) token; ~s nmpl (sa-laire) wages; (garantie) guarantee sg; mettre en ~ to pawn.

gager [gaʒe] vt to bet, wager.

gageure [gaʒyʀ] nf: c'est une ~ it's at-tempting the impossible.

gagnant, e [gaɲɑ̃, -ɑ̃t] nm/f winner.

gagne-pain [gaɲpɛ̃] nm inv job.

gagner [gaɲe] vt to win; (somme d'argent, revenu) to earn; (aller vers, atteindre) to reach; (envahir) to over-come; to spread to // vi to win; (fig) to gain; ~ du temps/de la place to gain time/save space; ~ sa vie to earn one's living.

gai, e [ge] a gay, cheerful; (un peu ivre) merry.

gaieté [gete] nf cheerfulness; ~s nfpl (souvent ironique) delights; de ~ de cœur with a light heart.

gaillard, e [gajaʀ, -aʀd(ə)] a (grivois) bawdy, ribald // nm (strapping) fellow.

gain [gɛ̃] nm (revenu) earnings pl;

(*bénéfice: gén pl*) profits *pl*; (*au jeu: gén pl*) winnings *pl*; (*fig: de temps, place*) saving; **avoir ~ de cause** to win the case; (*fig*) to be proved right.

gaine [gɛn] *nf* (*corset*) girdle; (*fourreau*) sheath.

galant, e [galã, -ãt] *a* (*courtois*) courteous, gentlemanly; (*entreprenant*) flirtatious, gallant; (*aventure, poésie*) amorous.

galbe [galb(ə)] *nm* curve(s); shapeliness.

galère [galɛʀ] *nf* galley.

galérer [galeʀe] *vi* (*fam*) to slog away, work hard.

galerie [galʀi] *nf* gallery; (*THÉÂTRE*) circle; (*de voiture*) roof rack; (*fig: spectateurs*) audience; **~ marchande** shopping arcade; **~ de peinture** (private) art gallery.

galet [galɛ] *nm* pebble; (*TECH*) wheel.

galette [galɛt] *nf* flat cake.

Galles [gal]: **le pays de ~** Wales.

gallois, e [galwa, -waz] *a, nm* (*langue*) Welsh // *nm/f*: **G~, e** Welshman/woman.

galon [galɔ̃] *nm* (*MIL*) stripe; (*décoratif*) piece of braid.

galop [galo] *nm* gallop.

galoper [galɔpe] *vi* to gallop.

galopin [galɔpɛ̃] *nm* urchin, ragamuffin.

galvauder [galvode] *vt* to debase.

gambader [gãbade] *vi* (*animal, enfant*) to leap about.

gamelle [gamɛl] *nf* mess tin; billy can.

gamin, e [gamɛ̃, -in] *nm/f* kid // *a* mischievous, playful.

gamme [gam] *nf* (*MUS*) scale; (*fig*) range.

gammé, e [game] *a*: **croix ~e** swastika.

gant [gã] *nm* glove; **~ de toilette** (face) flannel (*Brit*), face cloth.

garage [gaʀaʒ] *nm* garage; **garagiste** *nm/f* garage owner; garage mechanic.

garant, e [gaʀã, -ãt] *nm/f* guarantor // *nm* guarantee; **se porter ~ de** to vouch for; to be answerable for.

garantie [gaʀãti] *nf* guarantee; (*gage*) security, surety; **(bon de) ~** guarantee *ou* warranty slip.

garantir [gaʀãtiʀ] *vt* to guarantee; (*protéger*): **~ de** to protect from.

garçon [gaʀsɔ̃] *nm* boy; (*célibataire*) bachelor; (*serveur*): **~ (de café)** waiter; **~ de courses** messenger; **garçonnet** *nm* small boy; **garçonnière** *nf* bachelor flat.

garde [gaʀd(ə)] *nm* (*de prisonnier*) guard; (*de domaine etc*) warden; (*soldat, sentinelle*) guardsman // *nf* guarding; looking after; (*soldats, BOXE, ESCRIME*) guard; (*faction*) watch; (*TYPO*): **(page de) ~** endpaper; flyleaf; **de ~** *a, ad* on duty; **monter la ~** to stand guard; **mettre en ~** to warn; **prendre ~ (à)** to be careful (of); **~ champêtre** *nm* rural policeman; **~ du corps** *nm* body-

guard; **~ des enfants** *nf* (*après divorce*) custody of the children; **~ des Sceaux** *nm* ≈ Lord Chancellor (*Brit*), ≈ Attorney General (*US*); **à vue** *nf* (*JUR*) ≈ police custody; **être/se mettre au ~-à-vous** to be at/stand to attention.

garde... [gaʀd(ə)] *préfixe*: **~-barrière** *nm/f* level-crossing keeper; **~-boue** *nm inv* mudguard; **~-chasse** *nm* gamekeeper; **~-fou** *nm* railing, parapet; **~-malade** *nf* home nurse; **~-manger** *nm inv* meat safe; pantry, larder.

garder [gaʀde] *vt* (*conserver*) to keep; (*surveiller: enfants*) to look after; (*: immeuble, lieu, prisonnier*) to guard; **le lit/la chambre** to stay in bed/indoors; **se ~** *vi* (*aliment: se conserver*) to keep; **se ~ de faire** to be careful not to do; **pêche/chasse gardée** private fishing/hunting (ground).

garderie [gaʀdəʀi] *nf* day nursery, crèche.

garde-robe [gaʀdəʀɔb] *nf* wardrobe.

gardien, ne [gaʀdjɛ̃, -jɛn] *nm/f* (*garde*) guard; (*de prison*) warder; (*de domaine, réserve*) warden; (*de musée etc*) attendant; (*de phare, cimetière*) keeper; (*d'immeuble*) caretaker; (*fig*) guardian; **~ de but** goalkeeper; **~ de nuit** night watchman; **~ de la paix** policeman.

gare [gaʀ] *nf* (*railway*) station, train station (*US*) // *excl* watch out!; **~ routière** bus station.

garer [gaʀe] *vt* to park; **se ~** *vi* to park; (*pour laisser passer*) to draw into the side.

gargariser [gaʀgaʀize]: **se ~** *vi* to gargle; **gargarisme** *nm* gargling *q*; gargle.

gargote [gaʀgɔt] *nf* cheap restaurant.

gargouille [gaʀguj] *nf* gargoyle.

gargouiller [gaʀguje] *vi* to gurgle.

garnement [gaʀnəmã] *nm* rascal, scallywag.

garni, e [gaʀni] *a* (*plat*) served with vegetables (*and chips ou pasta ou rice*) // *nm* furnished accommodation *q*.

garnir [gaʀniʀ] *vt* (*orner*) to decorate; to trim; (*approvisionner*) to fill, stock; (*protéger*) to fit.

garnison [gaʀnizɔ̃] *nf* garrison.

garniture [gaʀnityʀ] *nf* (*CULIN*) vegetables *pl*; filling; (*décoration*) trimming; (*protection*) fittings *pl*; **~ de frein** brake lining.

garrot [gaʀo] *nm* (*MÉD*) tourniquet.

gars [gɑ] *nm* lad; guy.

Gascogne [gaskɔɲ] *nf* Gascony; **le golfe de ~** the Bay of Biscay.

gas-oil [gazɔjl] *nm* diesel oil.

gaspiller [gaspije] *vt* to waste.

gastronomique [gastʀɔnɔmik] *a* gastronomic.

gâteau, x [gɑto] *nm* cake; **~ sec** biscuit.

gâter [gɑte] *vt* to spoil; **se ~** *vi* (*dent, fruit*) to go bad; (*temps, situation*) to change for the worse.

gâterie [gɑtʀi] nf little treat.

gâteux, euse [gɑtø, -øz] a senile.

gauche [goʃ] a left, left-hand; (maladroit) awkward, clumsy // nf (POL) left (wing); à ~ on the left; (direction) (to the) left; **gaucher, ère** a left-handed; **gauchiste** nm/f leftist.

gaufre [gofʀ(ə)] nf waffle.

gaufrette [gofʀɛt] nf wafer.

gaulois, e [golwa, -waz] a Gallic; (grivois) bawdy // nm/f: G~, e Gaul.

gausser [gose] : se ~ de vt to deride.

gaver [gave] vt to force-feed; (fig): ~ de to cram with, fill up with.

gaz [gaz] nm inv gas.

gaze [gaz] nf gauze.

gazéifié, e [gazeifje] a aerated.

gazette [gazɛt] nf news sheet.

gazeux, euse [gazø, -øz] a gaseous; (boisson) fizzy; (eau) sparkling.

gazoduc [gazɔdyk] nm gas pipeline.

gazon [gazɔ̃] nm (herbe) turf; grass; (pelouse) lawn.

gazouiller [gazuje] vi to chirp; (enfant) to babble.

geai [ʒɛ] nm jay.

géant, e [ʒeɑ̃, -ɑ̃t] a gigantic, giant; (COMM) giant-size // nm/f giant.

geindre [ʒɛ̃dʀ(ə)] vi to groan, moan.

gel [ʒɛl] nm frost; freezing.

gélatine [ʒelatin] nf gelatine.

gelée [ʒəle] nf jelly; (gel) frost.

geler [ʒəle] vt, vi to freeze; **il gèle** it's freezing; **gelures** nfpl frostbite sg.

gélule [ʒelyl] nf (MÉD) capsule.

Gémeaux [ʒemo] nmpl: les ~ Gemini.

gémir [ʒemiʀ] vi to groan, moan.

gemme [ʒɛm] nf gem(stone).

gênant, e [ʒɛnɑ̃, -ɑ̃t] a annoying; embarrassing.

gencive [ʒɑ̃siv] nf gum.

gendarme [ʒɑ̃daʀm(ə)] nm gendarme; ~**rie** nf military police force in countryside and small towns; their police station or barracks.

gendre [ʒɑ̃dʀ(ə)] nm son-in-law.

gêne [ʒɛn] nf (à respirer, bouger) discomfort, difficulty; (dérangement) bother, trouble; (manque d'argent) financial difficulties pl ou straits pl; (confusion) embarrassment.

gêné, e [ʒene] a embarrassed.

gêner [ʒene] vt (incommoder) to bother; (encombrer) to hamper; to be in the way; (embarrasser): ~ **qn** to make sb feel ill-at-ease; se ~ vi to put o.s. out.

général, e, aux [ʒeneʀal, -o] a, nm general // nf: (répétition) ~e final dress rehearsal; en ~ usually, in general; ~**ement** ad generally.

généraliser [ʒeneʀalize] vt, vi to generalize; se ~ vi to become widespread.

généraliste [ʒeneʀalist(ə)] nm/f general practitioner, G.P.

générateur, trice [ʒeneʀatœʀ, -tʀis] a: ~ **de** which causes // nf generator.

génération [ʒeneʀasjɔ̃] nf generation.

généreux, euse [ʒeneʀø, -øz] a generous.

générique [ʒeneʀik] nm (CINÉMA) credits pl, credit titles pl.

générosité [ʒeneʀozite] nf generosity.

genêt [ʒənɛ] nm broom q (shrub).

génétique [ʒenetik] a genetic.

Genève [ʒənɛv] n Geneva.

génial, e, aux [ʒenjal, -o] a of genius; (fam: formidable) fantastic, brilliant.

génie [ʒeni] nm genius; (MIL): le ~ the Engineers pl; ~ **civil** civil engineering.

genièvre [ʒənjɛvʀ(ə)] nm juniper.

génisse [ʒenis] nf heifer.

genou, x [ʒnu] nm knee; à ~x on one's knees; se mettre à ~x to kneel down.

genre [ʒɑ̃ʀ] nm kind, type, sort; (allure) manner; (LING) gender.

gens [ʒɑ̃] nmpl (f in some phrases) people pl.

gentil, le [ʒɑ̃ti, -ij] a kind; (enfant: sage) good; (endroit etc) nice; **gentillesse** nf kindness; **gentiment** ad kindly.

géographie [ʒeɔgʀafi] nf geography.

geôlier [ʒolje] nm jailer.

géologie [ʒeɔlɔʒi] nf geology.

géomètre [ʒeɔmɛtʀ(ə)] nm/f: (arpenteur-)~ (land) surveyor.

géométrie [ʒeɔmetʀi] nf geometry; **géométrique** a geometric.

gérance [ʒeʀɑ̃s] nf management; **mettre en ~** to appoint a manager for.

géranium [ʒeʀanjɔm] nm geranium.

gérant, e [ʒeʀɑ̃, -ɑ̃t] nm/f manager/manageress.

gerbe [ʒɛʀb(ə)] nf (de fleurs) spray; (de blé) sheaf (pl sheaves); (fig) shower, burst.

gercé, e [ʒeʀse] a chapped.

gerçure [ʒeʀsyʀ] nf crack.

gérer [ʒeʀe] vt to manage.

germain, e [ʒeʀmɛ̃, -ɛn] a: cousin ~ first cousin.

germe [ʒeʀm(ə)] nm germ.

germer [ʒeʀme] vi to sprout; to germinate.

gésir [ʒeziʀ] vi to be lying (down); voir aussi ci-gît.

geste [ʒɛst(ə)] nm gesture; move; motion.

gestion [ʒɛstjɔ̃] nf management.

gibecière [ʒibsjɛʀ] nf gamebag.

gibet [ʒibɛ] nm gallows sg.

gibier [ʒibje] nm (animaux) game; (fig) prey.

giboulée [ʒibule] nf sudden shower.

gicler [ʒikle] vi to spurt, squirt.

gifle [ʒifl(ə)] nf slap (in the face); **gifler** vt to slap (in the face).

gigantesque [ʒigɑ̃tɛsk(ə)] a gigantic.

gigogne [ʒigɔɲ] a: lits ~s truckle (Brit)

ou trundle beds.

gigot [ʒigo] *nm* leg (of mutton *ou* lamb).

gigoter [ʒigɔte] *vi* to wriggle (about).

gilet [ʒilɛ] *nm* waistcoat; (*pull*) cardigan; (*de corps*) vest; ~ **pare-balles** bulletproof jacket; ~ **de sauvetage** life jacket.

gingembre [ʒɛ̃ʒɑ̃bʀ(ə)] *nm* ginger.

girafe [ʒiʀaf] *nf* giraffe.

giratoire [ʒiʀatwaʀ] *a*: **sens** ~ roundabout.

girouette [ʒiʀwɛt] *nf* weather vane *ou* cock.

gisait *etc vb voir* **gésir**.

gisement [ʒizmɑ̃] *nm* deposit.

gît *vb voir* **gésir**.

gitan, e [ʒitɑ̃, -an] *nm/f* gipsy.

gîte [ʒit] *nm* home; shelter; ~ (**rural**) holiday cottage *ou* apartment.

givre [ʒivʀ(ə)] *nm* (hoar) frost.

glabre [glabʀ(ə)] *a* hairless; clean-shaven.

glace [glas] *nf* ice; (*crème glacée*) ice cream; (*verre*) sheet of glass; (*miroir*) mirror; (*de voiture*) window.

glacé, e [glase] *a* icy; (*boisson*) iced.

glacer [glase] *vt* to freeze; (*boisson*) to chill, ice; (*gâteau*) to ice; (*papier, tissu*) to glaze; (*fig*): ~ **qn** to chill sb; to make sb's blood run cold.

glacial, e [glasjal] *a* icy.

glacier [glasje] *nm* (*GÉO*) glacier; (*marchand*) ice-cream maker.

glacière [glasjɛʀ] *nf* icebox.

glaçon [glasɔ̃] *nm* icicle; (*pour boisson*) ice cube.

glaise [glɛz] *nf* clay.

gland [glɑ̃] *nm* acorn; (*décoration*) tassel.

glande [glɑ̃d] *nf* gland.

glaner [glane] *vt, vi* to glean.

glapir [glapiʀ] *vi* to yelp.

glas [glɑ] *nm* knell, toll.

glauque [glok] *a* a dull blue-green.

glissant, e [glisɑ̃, -ɑ̃t] *a* slippery.

glissement [glismɑ̃] *nm*: ~ **de terrain** landslide.

glisser [glise] *vi* (*avancer*) to glide *ou* slide along; (*coulisser, tomber*) to slide; (*déraper*) to slip; (*être glissant*) to be slippery // *vt* to slip; se ~ **dans** to slip into.

global, e, aux [glɔbal, -o] *a* overall.

globe [glɔb] *nm* globe.

globule [glɔbyl] *nm* (*du sang*) corpuscle.

globuleux, euse [glɔbylø, -øz] *a*: **yeux** ~ protruding eyes.

gloire [glwaʀ] *nf* glory; (*mérite*) distinction, credit; (*personne*) celebrity; **glorieux, euse** *a* glorious.

glousser [gluse] *vi* to cluck; (*rire*) to chuckle.

glouton, ne [glutɔ̃, -ɔn] *a* gluttonous.

gluant, e [glyɑ̃, -ɑ̃t] *a* sticky, gummy.

glycine [glisin] *nf* wisteria.

go [go]: **tout de** ~ *ad* straight out.

G.O. *sigle* = **grandes ondes**.

gobelet [gɔblɛ] *nm* tumbler; beaker; (*à dés*) cup.

gober [gɔbe] *vt* to swallow.

godasse [gɔdas] *nf* (*fam*) shoe.

godet [gɔdɛ] *nm* pot.

goéland [gɔelɑ̃] *nm* (sea)gull.

goélette [gɔelɛt] *nf* schooner.

goémon [gɔemɔ̃] *nm* wrack.

gogo [gɔgo]: **à** ~ *ad* galore.

goguenard, e [gɔgnaʀ, -aʀd(ə)] *a* mocking.

goinfre [gwɛ̃fʀ(ə)] *nm* glutton.

golf [gɔlf] *nm* golf; golf course.

golfe [gɔlf(ə)] *nm* gulf; bay.

gomme [gɔm] *nf* (à *effacer*) rubber (*Brit*), eraser; **gommer** *vt* to rub out (*Brit*), erase.

gond [gɔ̃] *nm* hinge; **sortir de ses** ~s (*fig*) to fly off the handle.

gondoler [gɔ̃dɔle]: se ~ *vi* to warp; to buckle.

gonflé, e [gɔ̃fle] *a* swollen; bloated.

gonfler [gɔ̃fle] *vt* (*pneu, ballon*) to inflate, blow up; (*nombre, importance*) to inflate // *vi* to swell (up); (*CULIN: pâte*) to rise.

gonzesse [gɔ̃zɛs] *nf* (*fam*) chick, bird (*Brit*).

goret [gɔʀɛ] *nm* piglet.

gorge [gɔʀʒ(ə)] *nf* (*ANAT*) throat; (*poitrine*) breast.

gorgé, e [gɔʀʒe] *a*: ~ **de** filled with; (*eau*) saturated with // *nf* mouthful; sip; gulp.

gorille [gɔʀij] *nm* gorilla; (*fam*) bodyguard.

gosier [gozje] *nm* throat.

gosse [gɔs] *nm/f* kid.

goudron [gudʀɔ̃] *nm* tar; **goudronner** *vt* to tar(mac) (*Brit*), asphalt (*US*).

gouffre [gufʀ(ə)] *nm* abyss, gulf.

goujat [guʒa] *nm* boor.

goulot [gulo] *nm* neck; **boire au** ~ to drink from the bottle.

goulu, e [guly] *a* greedy.

gourd, e [guʀ, guʀd(ə)] *a* numb (with cold).

gourde [guʀd(ə)] *nf* (*récipient*) flask; (*fam*) (clumsy) clot *ou* oaf // *a* oafish.

gourdin [guʀdɛ̃] *nm* club, bludgeon.

gourmand, e [guʀmɑ̃, -ɑ̃d] *a* greedy; **gourmandise** *nf* greed; (*bonbon*) sweet.

gousse [gus] *nf*: ~ **d'ail** clove of garlic.

goût [gu] *nm* taste; **de bon** ~ tasteful; **de mauvais** ~ tasteless; **prendre** ~ **à** to develop a taste *ou* a liking for.

goûter [gute] *vt* (*essayer*) to taste; (*apprécier*) to enjoy // *vi* to have (afternoon) tea // *nm* (afternoon) tea.

goutte [gut] *nf* drop; (*MÉD*) gout; (*alcool*) brandy.

goutte-à-goutte [gutagut] *nm* (*MÉD*) drip; **tomber** ~ to drip.

gouttière [gutjɛʀ] nf gutter.
gouvernail [guvɛʀnaj] nm rudder; (barre) helm, tiller.
gouvernante [guvɛʀnɑ̃t] nf governess.
gouverne [guvɛʀn(ə)] nf: pour sa ~ for his guidance.
gouvernement [guvɛʀnəmɑ̃] nm government; **gouvernemental, e, aux** a government cpd; pro-government.
gouverner [guvɛʀne] vt to govern.
grâce [gʀɑs] nf grace; favour; (JUR) pardon; ~s nfpl (REL) grace sg; faire ~ à qn de qch to spare sb sth; rendre ~(s) à to give thanks to; demander ~ to beg for mercy; ~ à prép thanks to; **gracier** vt to pardon; **gracieux, euse** a graceful.
grade [gʀad] nm rank; monter en ~ to be promoted.
gradé [gʀade] nm officer.
gradin [gʀadɛ̃] nm tier; step; ~s nmpl (de stade) terracing sg.
graduel, le [gʀadɥɛl] a gradual; progressive.
graduer [gʀadɥe] vt (effort etc) to increase gradually; (règle, verre) to graduate.
grain [gʀɛ̃] nm (gén) grain; (NAVIG) squall; ~ de beauté beauty spot; ~ de café coffee bean; ~ de poivre peppercorn; ~ de poussière speck of dust; ~ de raisin grape.
graine [gʀɛn] nf seed.
graissage [gʀɛsaʒ] nm lubrication, greasing.
graisse [gʀɛs] nf fat; (lubrifiant) grease; **graisser** vt to lubricate, grease; (tacher) to make greasy.
grammaire [gʀamɛʀ] nf grammar; **grammatical, e, aux** a grammatical.
gramme [gʀam] nm gramme.
grand, e [gʀɑ̃, gʀɑ̃d] a (haut) tall; (gros, vaste, large) big, large; (long) long; (sens abstraits) great // ad: ~ ouvert wide open; au ~ air in the open (air); les ~s blessés the severely injured; ~ ensemble housing scheme; ~ magasin department store; ~e personne grown-up; ~e surface hypermarket; ~es écoles prestige schools of university level; ~es lignes (RAIL) main lines; ~es vacances summer holidays; **grand-chose** nm/f inv: pas grand-chose not much; **Grande-Bretagne** nf (Great) Britain; **grandeur** nf (dimension) size; magnitude; (fig) greatness; **grandeur nature** life-size; **grandir** vi to grow // vt: grandir qn (suj: vêtement, chaussure) to make sb look taller; ~-mère nf grandmother; ~-messe nf high mass; ~-peine: à ~-peine ad with difficulty; ~-père nm grandfather; ~-route nf main road; ~-rue nf high street; ~s-parents nmpl grandparents.
grange [gʀɑ̃ʒ] nf barn.

granit(e) [gʀanit] nm granite.
graphique [gʀafik] a graphic // nm graph.
grappe [gʀap] nf cluster; ~ de raisin bunch of grapes.
grappiller [gʀapije] vt to glean.
grappin [gʀapɛ̃] nm grapnel; mettre le ~ sur (fig) to get one's claws on.
gras, se [gʀɑ, gʀɑs] a (viande, soupe) fatty; (personne) fat; (surface, main) greasy; (plaisanterie) coarse; (TYPO) bold // nm (CULIN) fat; faire la ~se matinée to have a lie-in (Brit), sleep late (US); ~sement ad: ~sement payé handsomely paid; ~souillet, te a podgy, plump.
gratifier [gʀatifje] vt: ~ qn de to favour sb with; to reward sb with.
gratiné, e [gʀatine] a (CULIN) au gratin.
gratis [gʀatis] ad free.
gratitude [gʀatityd] nf gratitude.
gratte-ciel [gʀatsjɛl] nm inv skyscraper.
gratte-papier [gʀatpapje] nm inv (péj) penpusher.
gratter [gʀate] vt (frotter) to scrape; (enlever) to scrape off; (bras, bouton) to scratch.
gratuit, e [gʀatɥi, -ɥit] a (entrée, billet) free; (fig) gratuitous.
gravats [gʀava] nmpl rubble sg.
grave [gʀav] a (maladie, accident) serious, bad; (sujet, problème) serious, grave; (air) grave, solemn; (voix, son) deep, low-pitched; ~ment ad seriously, gravely.
graver [gʀave] vt to engrave.
gravier [gʀavje] nm gravel q; **gravillons** nmpl loose gravel sg.
gravir [gʀaviʀ] vt to climb (up).
gravité [gʀavite] nf seriousness; gravity.
graviter [gʀavite] vi to revolve.
gravure [gʀavyʀ] nf engraving; (reproduction) print; plate.
gré [gʀe] nm: à son ~ to his liking; as he pleases; au ~ de according to, following; contre le ~ de qn against sb's will; de son (plein) ~ of one's own free will; bon ~ mal ~ like it or not; de ~ ou de force whether one likes it or not; savoir ~ à qn de qch to be grateful to sb for sth.
grec, grecque [gʀɛk] a Greek; (classique: vase etc) Grecian // nm/f Greek.
Grèce [gʀɛs] nf: la ~ Greece.
gréement [gʀemɑ̃] nm rigging.
greffer [gʀefe] vt (BOT, MÉD: tissu) to graft; (MÉD: organe) to transplant.
greffier [gʀefje] nm clerk of the court.
grêle [gʀɛl] a (very) thin // nf hail.
grêlé, e [gʀele] a pockmarked.
grêler [gʀele] vb impersonnel: il grêle it's hailing.
grêlon [gʀelɔ̃] nm hailstone.

grelot [grəlo] nm little bell.
grelotter [grəlɔte] vi to shiver.
grenade [grənad] nf (explosive) grenade; (BOT) pomegranate.
grenat [grəna] a inv dark red.
grenier [grənje] nm attic; (de ferme) loft.
grenouille [grənuj] nf frog.
grès [grɛ] nm sandstone; (poterie) stoneware.
grésiller [grezije] vi to sizzle; (RADIO) to crackle.
grève [grɛv] nf (d'ouvriers) strike; (plage) shore; se mettre en/faire ~ to go on/be on strike; ~ de la faim hunger strike; ~ du zèle work-to-rule (Brit), slowdown (US).
grever [grəve] vt to put a strain on.
gréviste [grevist(ə)] nm/f striker.
gribouiller [gribuje] vt to scribble, scrawl.
grief [grijɛf] nm grievance; faire ~ à qn de to reproach sb for.
grièvement [grijɛvmã] ad seriously.
griffe [grif] nf claw; (fig) signature.
griffer [grife] vt to scratch.
griffonner [grifɔne] vt to scribble.
grignoter [griɲɔte] vt to nibble ou gnaw at.
gril [gril] nm steak ou grill pan.
grillade [grijad] nf grill.
grillage [grijaʒ] nm (treillis) wire netting; wire fencing.
grille [grij] nf (clôture) railings; (portail) (metal) gate; (d'égout) (metal) grate; (fig) grid.
grille-pain [grijpɛ̃] nm inv toaster.
griller [grije] vt (aussi: faire ~: pain) to toast; (: viande) to grill; (fig: ampoule etc) to burn out, blow.
grillon [grijɔ̃] nm cricket.
grimace [grimas] nf grimace; (pour faire rire): faire des ~s to pull ou make faces.
grimer [grime] vt to make up.
grimper [grɛ̃pe] vi, vt to climb.
grincer [grɛ̃se] vi (porte, roue) to grate; (plancher) to creak; ~ des dents to grind one's teeth.
grincheux, euse [grɛ̃ʃø, -øz] a grumpy.
grippe [grip] nf flu, influenza; **grippé, e** a: être grippé to have flu.
gris, e [gri, griz] a grey; (ivre) tipsy; faire ~e mine to pull a miserable ou wry face.
grisaille [grizaj] nf greyness, dullness.
griser [grize] vt to intoxicate.
grisonner [grizɔne] vi to be going grey.
grisou [grizu] nm firedamp.
grive [griv] nf thrush.
grivois, e [grivwa, -waz] a saucy.
Groenland [grɔɛnlãd] nm Greenland.
grogner [grɔɲe] vi to growl; (fig) to grumble.

groin [grwɛ̃] nm snout.
grommeler [grɔmle] vi to mutter to o.s.
gronder [grɔ̃de] vi to rumble; (fig: révolte) to be brewing // vt to scold.
gros, se [gro, gros] a big, large; (obèse) fat; (travaux, dégâts) extensive; (large: trait, fil) thick, heavy // ad: risquer/ gagner ~ to risk/win a lot // nm (COMM): le ~ the wholesale business; prix de ~ wholesale price; par ~ temps/ ~se mer in rough weather/heavy seas; le ~ de the main body of; the bulk of; en ~ roughly; (COMM) wholesale; ~ lot jackpot; ~ mot coarse word; ~ plan (PHOTO) close-up; ~ sel cooking salt; ~se caisse big drum.
groseille [grozɛj] nf: ~ (rouge)/ (blanche) red/white currant; ~ à maquereau gooseberry.
grosse [gros] a voir gros.
grossesse [grosɛs] nf pregnancy.
grosseur [grosœr] nf size; fatness; (tumeur) lump.
grossier, ière [grosje, -jɛr] a coarse; (travail) rough; crude; (évident: erreur) gross.
grossir [grosir] vi (personne) to put on weight; (fig) to grow, get bigger; (rivière) to swell // vt to increase; to exaggerate; (au microscope) to magnify; (suj: vêtement): ~ qn to make sb look fatter.
grossiste [grosist(ə)] nm/f wholesaler.
grosso modo [grosomodo] ad roughly.
grotte [grɔt] nf cave.
grouiller [gruje] vi to mill about; to swarm about; ~ de to be swarming with.
groupe [grup] nm group.
groupement [grupmã] nm grouping; group.
grouper [grupe] vt to group; se ~ vi to get together.
grue [gry] nf crane.
grumeaux [grymo] nmpl lumps.
gué [ge] nm ford; passer à ~ to ford.
guenilles [gənij] nfpl rags.
guenon [gənɔ̃] nf female monkey.
guépard [gepar] nm cheetah.
guêpe [gɛp] nf wasp.
guêpier [gepje] nm (fig) trap.
guère [gɛr] ad (avec adjectif, adverbe): ne ... ~ hardly; (avec verbe): ne ... ~ tournure négative + much; hardly ever; tournure négative + (very) long; il n'y a ~ que/de there's hardly anybody (ou anything) but/hardly any.
guéridon [geridɔ̃] nm pedestal table.
guérilla [gerija] nf guerrilla warfare.
guérir [gerir] vt (personne, maladie) to cure; (membre, plaie) to heal // vi to recover, be cured; to heal; **guérison** nf curing; healing; recovery.
guérite [gerit] nf sentry box.
guerre [gɛr] nf war; (méthode): ~ atomique atomic warfare q; en ~ at

war; **faire la ~ à** to wage war against; **de ~ lasse** finally; **~ d'usure** war of attrition; **guerrier, ière** *a* warlike // *nm/f* warrior.

guet [gɛ] *nm*: **faire le ~** to be on the watch *ou* look-out.

guet-apens [gɛtapɑ̃] *nm* ambush.

guetter [gete] *vt* (*épier*) to watch (intently); (*attendre*) to watch (out) for; to be lying in wait for.

gueule [gœl] *nf* mouth; (*fam*) face; mouth; **ta ~!** (*fam*) shut up!; **~ de bois** (*fam*) hangover.

gueuler [gœle] *vi* (*fam*) to bawl.

gui [gi] *nm* mistletoe.

guichet [giʃɛ] *nm* (*de bureau, banque*) counter, window; (*d'une porte*) wicket, hatch; **les ~s** (*à la gare, au théâtre*) the ticket office.

guide [gid] *nm* guide.

guider [gide] *vt* to guide.

guidon [gidɔ̃] *nm* handlebars *pl*.

guignol [giɲɔl] *nm* ≈ Punch and Judy show; (*fig*) clown.

guillemets [gijmɛ] *nmpl*: **entre ~** in inverted commas.

guillotiner [gijɔtine] *vt* to guillotine.

guindé, e [gɛ̃de] *a* stiff, starchy.

guirlande [giʀlɑ̃d] *nf* garland; (*de papier*) paper chain.

guise [giz] *nf*: **à votre ~** as you wish *ou* please; **en ~ de** by way of.

guitare [gitaʀ] *nf* guitar.

gymnase [ʒimnɑz] *nm* gym(nasium).

gymnastique [ʒimnastik] *nf* gymnastics *sg*; (*au réveil etc*) keep-fit exercises *pl*.

gynécologie [ʒinekɔlɔʒi] *nf* gynaecology; **gynécologue** *nm/f* gynaecologist.

H

habile [abil] *a* skilful; (*malin*) clever; **~té** *nf* skill, skilfulness; cleverness.

habilité, e [abilite] *a*: **~ à faire** entitled to do, empowered to do.

habillé, e [abije] *a* dressed; (*chic*) dressy; (*TECH*): **~ de** covered with; encased in.

habillement [abijmɑ̃] *nm* clothes *pl*.

habiller [abije] *vt* to dress; (*fournir en vêtements*) to clothe; **s'~** *vi* to dress (o.s.); (*se déguiser, mettre des vêtements chic*) to dress up.

habit [abi] *nm* outfit; **~s** *nmpl* (*vêtements*) clothes; **~** (**de soirée**) tails *pl*; evening dress.

habitant, e [abitɑ̃, -ɑ̃t] *nm/f* inhabitant; (*d'une maison*) occupant.

habitation [abitasjɔ̃] *nf* living; residence, home; house; **~s à loyer modéré** (**HLM**) low-rent housing *sg*.

habiter [abite] *vt* to live in; (*suj: sentiment*) to dwell in // *vi*: **~ à/dans** to live in *ou* at/in.

habitude [abityd] *nf* habit; **avoir l'~ de faire** to be in the habit of doing; (*expé-´rience*) to be used to doing; **d'~** usually; **comme d'~** as usual.

habitué, e [abitye] *nm/f* regular visitor; regular (customer).

habituel, le [abitɥɛl] *a* usual.

habituer [abitɥe] *vt*: **~ qn à** to get sb used to; **s'~ à** to get used to.

'hache [ˈaʃ] *nf* axe.

'hacher [ˈaʃe] *vt* (*viande*) to mince; (*persil*) to chop.

'hachis [ˈaʃi] *nm* mince *q*.

'hachoir [ˈaʃwaʀ] *nm* chopper; (*meat*) mincer; chopping board.

'hagard, e [ˈagaʀ, -aʀd(ə)] *a* wild, distraught.

'haie [ˈɛ] *nf* hedge; (*SPORT*) hurdle; (*fig: rang*) line, row.

'haillons [ˈajɔ̃] *nmpl* rags.

'haine [ˈɛn] *nf* hatred.

'haïr [ˈaiʀ] *vt* to detest, hate.

'hâlé, e [ˈɑle] *a* (sun)tanned, sunburnt.

haleine [alɛn] *nf* breath; **hors d'~** out of breath; **tenir en ~** to hold spellbound; to keep in suspense; **de longue ~** *a* long-term.

'haler [ˈale] *vt* to haul in; to tow.

'haleter [ˈalte] *vt* to pant.

'hall [ˈol] *nm* hall.

'halle [ˈal] *nf* (covered) market; **~s** *nfpl* central food market *sg*.

hallucinant, e [alysinɑ̃, -ɑ̃t] *a* staggering.

hallucination [alysinasjɔ̃] *nf* hallucination.

'halte [ˈalt(ə)] *nf* stop, break; stopping place; (*RAIL*) halt // *excl* stop!; **faire ~** to stop.

haltère [altɛʀ] *nm* dumbbell, barbell; (**poids et**) **~s** *nmpl* (*activité*) weight lifting *sg*.

'hamac [ˈamak] *nm* hammock.

'hameau, x [ˈamo] *nm* hamlet.

hameçon [amsɔ̃] *nm* (fish) hook.

'hanche [ˈɑ̃ʃ] *nf* hip.

'handicapé, e [ˈɑ̃dikape] *nm/f* physically (*ou* mentally) handicapped person; **~ moteur** spastic.

'hangar [ˈɑ̃gaʀ] *nm* shed; (*AVIAT*) hangar.

'hanneton [ˈantɔ̃] *nm* cockchafer.

'hanter [ˈɑ̃te] *vt* to haunt.

'hantise [ˈɑ̃tiz] *nf* obsessive fear.

'happer [ˈape] *vt* to snatch; (*suj: train etc*) to hit.

'haras [ˈaʀɑ] *nm* stud farm.

'harassant, e [ˈaʀasɑ̃, -ɑ̃t] *a* exhausting.

'harceler [ˈaʀsəle] *vt* (*MIL, CHASSE*) to harass, harry; (*importuner*) to plague.

'hardi, e [ˈaʀdi] *a* bold, daring.

'hareng [ˈaʀɑ̃] *nm* herring.

'hargne [ˈaʀɲ(ə)] *nf* aggressiveness.

'haricot [ˈaʀiko] *nm* bean; **~ blanc** hari-

cot bean; ~ **vert** green bean.
harmonica [aʀmɔnika] *nm* mouth organ.
harmonie [aʀmɔni] *nf* harmony.
'harnacher ['aʀnaʃe] *vt* to harness.
'harnais ['aʀnɛ] *nm* harness.
'harpe ['aʀp(ə)] *nf* harp.
'harponner ['aʀpɔne] *vt* to harpoon; (*fam*) to collar.
'hasard ['azaʀ] *nm*: **le ~** chance, fate; **un ~** a coincidence; a stroke of luck; **au ~** aimlessly; at random; haphazardly; **par ~** by chance; **à tout ~** just in case; on the off chance (*Brit*).
'hasarder ['azaʀde] *vt* (*mot*) to venture; (*fortune*) to risk.
'hâte ['ɑt] *nf* haste; **à la ~** hurriedly, hastily; **en ~** posthaste, with all possible speed; **avoir ~ de** to be eager *ou* anxious to; **'hâter** *vt* to hasten; **se hâter** *vi* to hurry.
'hâtif, ive ['ɑtif, -iv] *a* hurried; hasty; (*légume*) early.
'hausse ['os] *nf* rise, increase.
'hausser ['ose] *vt* to raise; **~ les épaules** to shrug (one's shoulders).
'haut, e ['o, 'ot] *a* high; (*grand*) tall; (*son, voix*) high(-pitched) // *ad* high // *nm* top (part); **de 3 m de ~** 3 m high, 3 m in height; **des ~s et des bas** ups and downs; **en ~ lieu** in high places; **à ~e voix, (tout) ~** aloud, out loud; **du ~ de** from the top of; **de ~ en bas** from top to bottom; downwards; **plus ~** higher up, further up; (*dans un texte*) above; (*parler*) louder; **en ~** up above; at (*ou* to) the top; (*dans une maison*) upstairs; **en ~ de** at the top of.
'hautain, e ['otɛ̃, -ɛn] *a* haughty.
'hautbois ['obwa] *nm* oboe.
'haut-de-forme ['odfɔʀm(ə)] *nm* top hat.
'hauteur ['otœʀ] *nf* height; (*fig*) loftiness; haughtiness; **à la ~ de** (*sur la même ligne*) level with; by; (*fig*) equal to; **à la ~** (*fig*) up to it.
'haut-fond ['ofɔ̃] *nm* shallow, shoal.
'haut-fourneau ['ofuʀno] *nm* blast *ou* smelting furnace.
'haut-le-cœur ['olkœʀ] *nm inv* retch, heave.
'haut-parleur ['opaʀlœʀ] *nm* (loud)speaker.
'havre ['ɑvʀ(ə)] *nm* haven.
'Haye ['ɛ] *n*: **la ~** the Hague.
'hayon ['ɛjɔ̃] *nm* tailgate.
hebdo [ɛbdo] *nm* (*fam*) weekly.
hebdomadaire [ɛbdɔmadɛʀ] *a*, *nm* weekly.
héberger [ebɛʀʒe] *vt* to accommodate, lodge; (*réfugiés*) to take in.
hébété, e [ebete] *a* dazed.
hébreu, x [ebʀø] *am, nm* Hebrew.
hécatombe [ekatɔ̃b] *nf* slaughter.
hectare [ɛktaʀ] *nm* hectare.

'hein ['ɛ̃] *excl* eh?
'hélas ['elɑs] *excl* alas! // *ad* unfortunately.
'héler ['ele] *vt* to hail.
hélice [elis] *nf* propeller.
hélicoptère [elikɔptɛʀ] *nm* helicopter.
helvétique [elvetik] *a* Swiss.
hémicycle [emisikl(ə)] *nm* semicircle; (*POL*): **l'~** ≈ the benches (of the Commons) (*Brit*), ≈ the floor (of the House of Representatives) (*US*).
hémorragie [emɔʀaʒi] *nf* bleeding *q*, haemorrhage.
hémorroïdes [emɔʀɔid] *nfpl* piles, haemorrhoids.
'hennir ['eniʀ] *vi* to neigh, whinny.
herbe [ɛʀb(ə)] *nf* grass; (*CULIN, MÉD*) herb; **en ~** unripe; (*fig*) budding; **herbicide** *nm* weed-killer; **herboriste** *nm/f* herbalist.
'hère ['ɛʀ] *nm*: **pauvre ~** poor wretch.
héréditaire [eʀeditɛʀ] *a* hereditary.
'hérisser ['eʀise] *vt*: **~ qn** (*fig*) to ruffle sb; **se ~** *vi* to bristle, bristle up.
'hérisson ['eʀisɔ̃] *nm* hedgehog.
héritage [eʀitaʒ] *nm* inheritance; (*fig*) heritage; legacy.
hériter [eʀite] *vi*: **~ de qch (de qn)** to inherit sth (from sb); **héritier, ière** *nm/f* heir/heiress.
hermétique [eʀmetik] *a* airtight; watertight; (*fig*) abstruse; impenetrable.
hermine [eʀmin] *nf* ermine.
'hernie ['eʀni] *nf* hernia.
héroïne [eʀɔin] *nf* heroine; (*drogue*) heroin.
'héron ['eʀɔ̃] *nm* heron.
'héros ['eʀo] *nm* hero.
hésitation [ezitasjɔ̃] *nf* hesitation.
hésiter [ezite] *vi*: **~ (à faire)** to hesitate (to do).
hétéroclite [eteʀɔklit] *a* heterogeneous; (*objets*) sundry.
'hêtre ['ɛtʀ(ə)] *nm* beech.
heure [œʀ] *nf* hour; (*SCOL*) period; (*moment*) time; **c'est l'~** it's time; **quelle ~ est-il?** what time is it?; **2 ~s (du matin)** 2 o'clock (in the morning); **être à l'~** to be on time; (*montre*) to be right; **mettre à l'~** to set right; **à toute ~** at any time; **24 ~s sur 24** round the clock, 24 hours a day; **à l'~ qu'il est** at this time (of day); **by now**; **sur l'~** at once; **~s supplémentaires** overtime *sg*.
heureusement [œʀøzmɑ̃] *ad* (*par bonheur*) fortunately, luckily.
heureux, euse [œʀø, -øz] *a* happy; (*chanceux*) lucky, fortunate; (*judicieux*) felicitous, fortunate.
'heurt ['œʀ] *nm* (*choc*) collision; **~s** (*fig*) clashes.
'heurter ['œʀte] *vt* (*mur*) to strike, hit; (*personne*) to collide with; (*fig*) to go against, upset; **se ~ à** *vt* (*fig*) to come up against; **'heurtoir** *nm* door knocker.

hexagone [ɛgzagɔn] *nm* hexagon; *(la France)* France *(because of its roughly hexagonal shape)*.

hiberner [ibɛʀne] *vi* to hibernate.

'hibou, x ['ibu] *nm* owl.

'hideux, euse ['idø, -øz] *a* hideous.

hier [jɛʀ] *ad* yesterday; **toute la journée d'~** all day yesterday; **toute la matinée d'~** all yesterday morning.

'hiérarchie ['jeʀaʀʃi] *nf* hierarchy.

hilare [ilaʀ] *a* mirthful.

hippique [ipik] *a* equestrian, horse *cpd*.

hippodrome [ipɔdʀom] *nm* racecourse.

hippopotame [ipɔpɔtam] *nm* hippopotamus.

hirondelle [iʀɔdɛl] *nf* swallow.

hirsute [iʀsyt] *a* hairy; shaggy; tousled.

'hisser ['ise] *vt* to hoist, haul up.

histoire [istwaʀ] *nf (science, événements)* history; *(anecdote, récit, mensonge)* story; *(affaire)* business *q*; **~s** *nfpl (chichis)* fuss *q*; *(ennuis)* trouble *sg*; **historique** *a* historical; *(important)* historic.

hiver [ivɛʀ] *nm* winter; **~nal, e, aux** *a* winter *cpd*; wintry; **~ner** *vi* to winter.

HLM *sigle m ou f voir* **habitation**.

'hobby ['ɔbi] *nm* hobby.

'hocher ['ɔʃe] *vt*: **~ la tête** to nod; *(signe négatif ou dubitatif)* to shake one's head.

'hochet ['ɔʃe] *nm* rattle.

'hockey ['ɔke] *nm*: **~ (sur glace/gazon)** (ice/field) hockey.

'hold-up ['ɔldœp] *nm inv* hold-up.

'hollandais, e ['ɔlɑ̃dɛ, -ɛz] *a, nm (LING)* Dutch // *nm/f*: **H~, e** Dutchman/woman; **les H~** the Dutch.

'Hollande ['ɔlɑ̃d] *nf*: **la ~** Holland.

'homard ['ɔmaʀ] *nm* lobster.

homéopathique [ɔmeopatik] *a* homoeopathic.

homicide [ɔmisid] *nm* murder; **~ involontaire** manslaughter.

hommage [ɔmaʒ] *nm* tribute; **~s** *nmpl*: **présenter ses ~s** to pay one's respects; **rendre ~ à** to pay tribute *ou* homage to.

homme [ɔm] *nm* man; **~ d'affaires** businessman; **~ d'État** statesman; **~ de main** hired man; **~ de paille** stooge; **~-grenouille** *nm* frogman.

homogène [ɔmɔʒɛn] *a* homogeneous.

homologue [ɔmɔlɔg] *nm/f* counterpart, opposite number.

homologué, e [ɔmɔlɔge] *a (SPORT)* officially recognized, ratified; *(tarif)* authorized.

homonyme [ɔmɔnim] *nm (LING)* homonym; *(d'une personne)* namesake.

homosexuel, le [ɔmɔsɛksɥɛl] *a* homosexual.

'Hongrie ['ɔ̃gʀi] *nf*: **la ~** Hungary.

'hongrois, e *a, nm/f* Hungarian.

honnête [ɔnɛt] *a (intègre)* honest; *(juste, satisfaisant)* fair; **~ment** *ad*

honestly; **~té** *nf* honesty.

honneur [ɔnœʀ] *nm* honour; *(mérite)* credit; **en l'~ de** in honour of; *(événement)* on the occasion of; **faire ~ à** *(engagements)* to honour; *(famille)* to be a credit to; *(fig: repas etc)* to do justice to.

honorable [ɔnɔʀabl(ə)] *a* worthy, honourable; *(suffisant)* decent.

honoraire [ɔnɔʀɛʀ] *a* honorary; **~s** *nmpl* fees *pl*; **professeur ~** professor emeritus.

honorer [ɔnɔʀe] *vt* to honour; *(estimer)* to hold in high regard; *(faire honneur à)* to do credit to; **s'~ de** to pride o.s. upon; **honorifique** *a* honorary.

'honte ['ɔ̃t] *nf* shame; **avoir ~ de** to be ashamed of; **faire ~ à qn** to make sb (feel) ashamed; **'honteux, euse** *a* ashamed; *(conduite, acte)* shameful, disgraceful.

'hôpital, aux [ɔpital, -o] *nm* hospital.

'hoquet ['ɔke] *nm*: **avoir le ~** to have (the) hiccoughs; **'hoqueter** ['ɔkte] *vi* to hiccough.

horaire [ɔʀɛʀ] *a* hourly // *nm* timetable, schedule; **~ souple** flexitime; **~s** *nmpl (d'employé)* hours.

horizon [ɔʀizɔ̃] *nm* horizon; *(paysage)* landscape, view.

horizontal, e, aux [ɔʀizɔ̃tal, -o] *a* horizontal.

horloge [ɔʀlɔʒ] *nf* clock; **horloger, ère** *nm/f* watchmaker; clockmaker; **~rie** *nf* watch-making; watchmaker's (shop); clockmaker's (shop).

'hormis ['ɔʀmi] *prép* save.

horoscope [ɔʀɔskɔp] *nm* horoscope.

horreur [ɔʀœʀ] *nf* horror; **avoir ~ de** to loathe *ou* detest; **horrible** *a* horrible.

horripiler [ɔʀipile] *vt* to exasperate.

'hors ['ɔʀ] *prép* except (for); **~ de** out of; **~ pair** outstanding; **~ de propos** inopportune; **être ~ de soi** to be beside o.s.; **~-bord** *nm inv* speedboat (with outboard motor); **~-concours** *a* ineligible to compete; **~-d'œuvre** *nm inv* hors d'œuvre; **~-jeu** *nm inv* offside; **~-la-loi** *nm inv* outlaw; **~-taxe** *a (boutique, articles)* duty-free.

hospice [ɔspis] *nm (de vieillards)* home.

hospitalier, ière [ɔspitalje, -jɛʀ] *a (accueillant)* hospitable; *(MÉD: service, centre)* hospital *cpd*.

hospitalité [ɔspitalite] *nf* hospitality.

hostie [ɔsti] *nf* host *(REL)*.

hostile [ɔstil] *a* hostile; **hostilité** *nf* hostility.

hôte [ot] *nm (maître de maison)* host; *(invité)* guest.

hôtel [otɛl] *nm* hotel; **aller à l'~** to stay in a hotel; **~ (particulier)** (private) mansion; **~ de ville** town hall; **hôtelier, ière** *a* hotel *cpd* // *nm/f* hotelier; **~lerie** *nf* hotel business; *(auberge)* inn.

hôtesse [otɛs] nf hostess; ~ **de l'air** air stewardess.

'hotte ['ɔt] nf (panier) basket (carried on the back); (de cheminée) hood; ~ **aspirante** cooker hood.

'houblon ['ubl5] nm (BOT) hop; (pour la bière) hops pl.

'houille ['uj] nf coal; ~ **blanche** hydroelectric power.

'houle ['ul] nf swell.

'houlette ['ulɛt] nf: **sous la** ~ **de** under the guidance of.

'houleux, euse ['ulø, -øz] a heavy, swelling; (fig) stormy, turbulent.

'houspiller ['uspije] vt to scold.

'housse ['us] nf cover; dust cover; loose ou stretch cover.

'houx ['u] nm holly.

'hublot ['yblo] nm porthole.

'huche ['yʃ] nf: ~ **à pain** bread bin.

'huer ['ɥe] vt to boo.

huile [ɥil] nf oil; ~ **de foie de morue** cod-liver oil; **huiler** vt to oil; **huileux, euse** a oily.

huis [ɥi] nm: **à** ~ **clos** in camera.

huissier [ɥisje] nm usher; (JUR) ≈ bailiff.

'huit ['ɥit] num eight; **samedi en** ~ **a** week on Saturday; **une huitaine de jours** a week or so; **'huitième** num eighth.

huître [ɥitʀ(ə)] nf oyster.

humain, e [ymɛ̃, -ɛn] a human; (compatissant) humane // nm human (being); **humanité** nf humanity.

humble [œ̃bl(ə)] a humble.

humecter [ymɛkte] vt to dampen.

'humer ['yme] vt to smell; to inhale.

humeur [ymœʀ] nf mood; (tempérament) temper; (irritation) bad temper; **de bonne/mauvaise** ~ in a good/bad mood.

humide [ymid] a damp; (main, yeux) moist; (climat, chaleur) humid; (saison, route) wet.

humilier [ymilje] vt to humiliate.

humilité [ymilite] nf humility, humbleness.

humoristique [ymɔʀistik] a humorous; humoristic.

humour [ymuʀ] nm humour; **avoir de l'**~ to have a sense of humour; ~ **noir** sick humour.

'hurlement ['yʀləmɑ̃] nm howling q, howl, yelling q, yell.

'hurler ['yʀle] vi to howl, yell.

hurluberlu [yʀlybɛʀly] nm (péj) crank.

'hutte ['yt] nf hut.

hydratant, e [idʀatɑ̃, -ɑ̃t] a (crème) moisturizing.

hydrate [idʀat] nm: ~s **de carbone** carbohydrates.

hydraulique [idʀolik] a hydraulic.

hydravion [idʀavj5] nm seaplane.

hydrogène [idʀɔʒɛn] nm hydrogen.

hydroglisseur [idʀɔglisœʀ] nm hydro-

plane.

hygiénique [iʒjenik] a hygienic.

hymne [imn(ə)] nm hymn; ~ **national** national anthem.

hypermarché [ipɛʀmaʀʃe] nm hypermarket.

hypermétrope [ipɛʀmetʀɔp] a longsighted.

hypnotiser [ipnɔtize] vt to hypnotize.

hypocrite [ipɔkʀit] a hypocritical.

hypothèque [ipɔtɛk] nf mortgage.

hypothèse [ipɔtɛz] nf hypothesis.

hystérique [isteʀik] a hysterical.

I

iceberg [isbɛʀg] nm iceberg.

ici [isi] ad here; **jusqu'**~ as far as this; until now; **d'**~ **là** by then; in the meantime; **d'**~ **peu** before long.

idéal, e, aux [ideal, -o] a ideal // nm ideal; ideals pl.

idée [ide] nf idea; **avoir dans l'**~ **que** to have an idea that; ~s **noires** black ou dark thoughts.

identifier [idɑ̃tifje] vt to identify; **s'**~ **à** (héros etc) to identify with.

identique [idɑ̃tik] a: ~ **(à)** identical (to).

identité [idɑ̃tite] nf identity.

idiot, e [idjo, idjɔt] a idiotic // nm/f idiot.

idole [idɔl] nf idol.

if [if] nm yew.

ignare [iɲaʀ] a ignorant.

ignifugé, e [iɲifyʒe] a fireproof(ed).

ignoble [iɲɔbl(ə)] a vile.

ignorant, e [iɲɔʀɑ̃, -ɑ̃t] a ignorant.

ignorer [iɲɔʀe] vt (ne pas connaître) not to know, be unaware ou ignorant of; (être sans expérience de: plaisir, guerre etc) not to know about, have no experience of; (bouder: personne) to ignore.

il [il] pronom he; (animal, chose, en tournure impersonnelle) it; ~s they; voir aussi **avoir**.

île [il] nf island; **les** ~s **anglo-normandes** the Channel Islands; **les** ~s **Britanniques** the British Isles.

illégal, e, aux [ilegal, -o] a illegal.

illégitime [ileʒitim] a illegitimate.

illettré, e [iletʀe] a, nm/f illiterate.

illimité, e [ilimite] a unlimited.

illisible [ilizibl(ə)] a illegible; (roman) unreadable.

illumination [ilyminɑsj5] nf illumination, floodlighting; (idée) flash of inspiration.

illuminer [ilymine] vt to light up; (monument, rue: pour une fête) to illuminate, floodlight.

illusion [ilyzj5] nf illusion; **se faire des** ~s to delude o.s.; **faire** ~ to delude ou fool people; **illusionniste** nm/f conjuror.

illustration 106 important

illustration [ilystʀɑsjɔ̃] nf illustration.
illustre [ilystʀ(ə)] a illustrious.
illustré, e [ilystʀe] a illustrated // nm illustrated magazine; comic.
illustrer [ilystʀe] vt to illustrate; s'~ to become famous, win fame.
îlot [ilo] nm small island, islet; (de maisons) block.
ils [il] pronom voir il.
image [imaʒ] nf (gén) picture; (comparaison, ressemblance, OPTIQUE) image; ~ de marque brand image; (fig) public image.
imagination [imaʒinɑsjɔ̃] nf imagination; (chimère) fancy; avoir de l'~ to be imaginative.
imaginer [imaʒine] vt to imagine; (inventer: expédient) to devise, think up; s'~ vt (se figurer: scène etc) to imagine, picture; s'~ que to imagine that.
imbécile [ɛ̃besil] a idiotic // nm/f idiot.
imberbe [ɛ̃bɛʀb(ə)] a beardless.
imbiber [ɛ̃bibe] vt to moisten, wet; s'~ de to become saturated with.
imbu, e [ɛ̃by] a: ~ de full of.
imitateur, trice [imitatœʀ, -tʀis] nm/f (gén) imitator; (MUSIC-HALL) impersonator.
imitation [imitɑsjɔ̃] nf imitation; (sketch) imitation, impression; impersonation.
imiter [imite] vt to imitate; (contrefaire) to forge; (ressembler à) to look like.
immaculé, e [imakyle] a spotless; immaculate.
immatriculation [imatʀikylɑsjɔ̃] nf registration.
immatriculer [imatʀikyle] vt to register; faire/se faire ~ to register.
immédiat, e [imedja, -at] a immediate // nm: dans l'~ for the time being; **immédiatement** ad immediately.
immense [imɑ̃s] a immense.
immerger [imɛʀʒe] vt to immerse, submerge.
immeuble [imœbl(ə)] nm building; ~ locatif block of rented flats (Brit), rental building (US).
immigration [imigʀɑsjɔ̃] nf immigration.
immigré, e [imigʀe] nm/f immigrant.
imminent, e [iminɑ̃, -ɑ̃t] a imminent.
immiscer [imise]: s'~ vi: s'~ dans to interfere in ou with.
immobile [imɔbil] a still, motionless; (fig) unchanging.
immobilier, ière [imɔbilje, -jɛʀ] a property cpd // nm: l'~ the property business.
immobiliser [imɔbilize] vt (gén) to immobilize; (circulation, véhicule, affaires) to bring to a standstill; s'~ (personne) to stand still; (machine, véhicule) to come to a halt.
immonde [imɔ̃d] a foul.

immondices [imɔ̃dis] nmpl refuse sg; filth sg.
immoral, e, aux [imɔʀal, -o] a immoral.
immuable [imyabl(ə)] a immutable; unchanging.
immunisé, e [imynize] a: ~ contre immune to.
immunité [imynite] nf immunity.
impact [ɛ̃pakt] nm impact.
impair, e [ɛ̃pɛʀ] a odd // nm faux pas, blunder.
impardonnable [ɛ̃paʀdɔnabl(ə)] a unpardonable, unforgivable.
imparfait, e [ɛ̃paʀfɛ, -ɛt] a imperfect.
impartial, e, aux [ɛ̃paʀsjal, -o] a impartial, unbiased.
impartir [ɛ̃paʀtiʀ] vt to assign; to bestow.
impasse [ɛ̃pɑs] nf dead-end, cul-de-sac; (fig) deadlock.
impassible [ɛ̃pasibl(ə)] a impassive.
impatience [ɛ̃pasjɑ̃s] nf impatience.
impatient, e [ɛ̃pasjɑ̃, -ɑ̃t] a impatient; **impatienter** vt to irritate, annoy; s'impatienter to get impatient.
impayable [ɛ̃pɛjabl(ə)] a (drôle) priceless.
impeccable [ɛ̃pekabl(ə)] a faultless, impeccable; spotlessly clean; impeccably dressed; (fam) smashing.
impensable [ɛ̃pɑ̃sabl(ə)] a unthinkable; unbelievable.
impératif, ive [ɛ̃peʀatif, -iv] a imperative // nm (LING) imperative; ~s nmpl requirements; demands.
impératrice [ɛ̃peʀatʀis] nf empress.
impérial, e, aux [ɛ̃peʀjal, -o] a imperial // nf top deck.
impérieux, euse [ɛ̃peʀjø, -øz] a (caractère, ton) imperious; (obligation, besoin) pressing, urgent.
impérissable [ɛ̃peʀisabl(ə)] a undying; imperishable.
imperméable [ɛ̃pɛʀmeabl(ə)] a waterproof; (GÉO) impermeable; (fig): ~ à impervious to // nm raincoat.
impertinent, e [ɛ̃pɛʀtinɑ̃, -ɑ̃t] a impertinent.
impétueux, euse [ɛ̃petɥø, -øz] a fiery.
impie [ɛ̃pi] a impious, ungodly.
impitoyable [ɛ̃pitwajabl(ə)] a pitiless, merciless.
implanter [ɛ̃plɑ̃te] vt (usine, industrie, usage) to establish; (colons etc) to settle; (idée, préjugé) to implant.
impliquer [ɛ̃plike] vt to imply; ~ qn (dans) to implicate sb (in).
impoli, e [ɛ̃pɔli] a impolite, rude.
importance [ɛ̃pɔʀtɑ̃s] nf importance; sans ~ unimportant.
important, e [ɛ̃pɔʀtɑ̃, -ɑ̃t] a important; (en quantité) considerable, sizeable; extensive; (péj: airs, ton) self-important // nm: l'~ the important thing.

importateur, trice [ɛ̃pɔʀtatœʀ, -tʀis] *nm/f* importer.

importation [ɛ̃pɔʀtasjɔ̃] *nf* importation; introduction; (*produit*) import.

importer [ɛ̃pɔʀte] *vt* (*COMM*) to import; (*maladies, plantes*) to introduce // *vi* (*être important*) to matter; **il importe qu'il fasse** it is important that he should do; **peu m'importe** I don't mind; I don't care; **peu importe (que)** it doesn't matter (if); *voir aussi* **n'importe**.

importun, e [ɛ̃pɔʀtœ̃, -yn] *a* irksome, importunate; (*arrivée, visite*) inopportune, ill-timed // *nm* intruder; **importuner** *vt* to bother.

imposant, e [ɛ̃pozɑ̃, -ɑ̃t] *a* imposing.

imposer [ɛ̃poze] *vt* (*taxer*) to tax; ~ **qch à qn** to impose sth on sb; **s'~** (*être nécessaire*) to be imperative; (*montrer sa prominence*) to stand out, emerge; (*artiste: se faire connaître*) to win recognition; **en ~ à** to impress.

imposition [ɛ̃pozisjɔ̃] *nf* (*ADMIN*) taxation.

impossible [ɛ̃pɔsibl(ə)] *a* impossible; **il m'est ~ de le faire** it is impossible for me to do it, I can't possibly do it; **faire l'~** to do one's utmost.

impôt [ɛ̃po] *nm* tax; (*taxes*) taxation; **taxes** *pl*; **~s** *nmpl* (*contributions*) (income) tax *sg*; **payer 1000 F d'~s** to pay 1,000 F in tax; **~ sur le chiffre d'affaires** corporation (*Brit*) *ou* corporate (*US*) tax; **~ foncier** land tax; **~ sur le revenu** income tax.

impotent, e [ɛ̃potɑ̃, -ɑ̃t] *a* disabled.

impraticable [ɛ̃pʀatikabl(ə)] *a* (*projet*) impracticable, unworkable; (*piste*) impassable.

imprécis, e [ɛ̃pʀesi, -iz] *a* imprecise.

imprégner [ɛ̃pʀeɲe] *vt* (*tissu, tampon*) to soak, impregnate; (*lieu, air*) to fill; **s'~ de** (*fig*) to absorb.

imprenable [ɛ̃pʀənabl(ə)] *a* (*forteresse*) impregnable; **vue ~** unimpeded outlook.

impression [ɛ̃pʀesjɔ̃] *nf* impression; (*d'un ouvrage, tissu*) printing; **faire bonne ~** to make a good impression.

impressionnant, e [ɛ̃pʀesjɔnɑ̃, -ɑ̃t] *a* impressive; upsetting.

impressionner [ɛ̃pʀesjɔne] *vt* (*frapper*) to impress; (*troubler*) to upset.

imprévisible [ɛ̃pʀevizibl(ə)] *a* unforeseeable.

imprévoyant, e [ɛ̃pʀevwajɑ̃, -ɑ̃t] *a* lacking in foresight; (*en matière d'argent*) improvident.

imprévu, e [ɛ̃pʀevy] *a* unforeseen, unexpected // *nm* unexpected incident; **en cas d'~** if anything unexpected happens.

imprimante [ɛ̃pʀimɑ̃t] *nf* printer; ~ **matricielle** dot-matrix printer.

imprimé [ɛ̃pʀime] *nm* (*formulaire*) printed form; (*POSTES*) printed matter *q*.

imprimer [ɛ̃pʀime] *vt* to print; (*empreinte etc*) to imprint; (*publier*) to publish; (*communiquer: mouvement, impulsion*) to impart, transmit; **imprimerie** *nf* printing; (*établissement*) printing works *sg*; **imprimeur** *nm* printer.

impromptu, e [ɛ̃pʀɔ̃pty] *a* impromptu; sudden.

impropre [ɛ̃pʀɔpʀ(ə)] *a* inappropriate; ~ **à** unsuitable for.

improviser [ɛ̃pʀɔvize] *vt*, *vi* to improvise.

improviste [ɛ̃pʀɔvist(ə)]: **à l'~** *ad* unexpectedly, without warning.

imprudence [ɛ̃pʀydɑ̃s] *nf* carelessness *q*; imprudence *q*.

imprudent, e [ɛ̃pʀydɑ̃, -ɑ̃t] *a* (*conducteur, geste, action*) careless; (*remarque*) unwise, imprudent; (*projet*) foolhardy.

impudent, e [ɛ̃pydɑ̃, -ɑ̃t] *a* impudent; brazen.

impudique [ɛ̃pydik] *a* shameless.

impuissant, e [ɛ̃pɥisɑ̃, -ɑ̃t] *a* helpless; (*sans effet*) ineffectual; (*sexuellement*) impotent; ~ **à faire** powerless to do.

impulsif, ive [ɛ̃pylsif, -iv] *a* impulsive.

impulsion [ɛ̃pylsjɔ̃] *nf* (*ÉLEC, instinct*) impulse; (*élan, influence*) impetus.

impunément [ɛ̃pynemɑ̃] *ad* with impunity.

imputer [ɛ̃pyte] *vt* (*attribuer*) to ascribe, impute; (*COMM*): ~ **à** *ou* **sur** to charge to.

inabordable [inabɔʀdabl(ə)] *a* (*cher*) prohibitive.

inaccessible [inaksesibl(ə)] *a* inaccessible; unattainable; (*insensible*): ~ **à** impervious to.

inachevé, e [inaʃve] *a* unfinished.

inadapté, e [inadapte] *a* (*gén*): ~ **à** not adapted to, unsuited to; (*PSYCH*) maladjusted.

inadmissible [inadmisibl(ə)] *a* inadmissible.

inadvertance [inadvɛʀtɑ̃s]: **par ~** *ad* inadvertently.

inaltérable [inalteʀabl(ə)] *a* (*matière*) stable; (*fig*) unchanging; ~ **à** unaffected by.

inamovible [inamɔvibl(ə)] *a* fixed; (*JUR*) irremovable.

inanimé, e [inanime] *a* (*matière*) inanimate; (*évanoui*) unconscious; (*sans vie*) lifeless.

inanition [inanisjɔ̃] *nf*: **tomber d'~** to faint with hunger (and exhaustion).

inaperçu, e [inapɛʀsy] *a*: **passer ~** to go unnoticed.

inappréciable [inapʀesjabl(ə)] *a* (*service*) invaluable.

inapte [inapt(ə)] *a*: ~ **à** incapable of; (*MIL*) unfit for.

inattaquable [inatakabl(ə)] *a* (*texte, preuve*) irrefutable.

inattendu, e [inatɑ̃dy] *a* unexpected.
inattentif, ive [inatɑ̃tif, -iv] *a* inattentive; ~ à (*dangers, détails*) heedless of; **inattention** *nf*: **faute d'inattention** careless mistake.
inaugurer [inɔgyʀe] *vt* (*monument*) to unveil; (*exposition, usine*) to open; (*fig*) to inaugurate.
inavouable [inavwabl(ə)] *a* shameful; undisclosable.
inavoué, e [inavwe] *a* unavowed.
incandescence [ɛ̃kɑ̃desɑ̃s] *nf*: **porter à ~** to heat white-hot.
incapable [ɛ̃kapabl(ə)] *a* incapable; ~ **de faire** incapable of doing; (*empêché*) unable to do.
incapacité [ɛ̃kapasite] *nf* incapability; (*JUR*) incapacity.
incarner [ɛ̃kaʀne] *vt* to embody, personify; (*THÉÂTRE*) to play.
incartade [ɛ̃kaʀtad] *nf* prank.
incassable [ɛ̃kasabl(ə)] *a* unbreakable.
incendiaire [ɛ̃sɑ̃djɛʀ] *a* incendiary; (*fig: discours*) inflammatory // *nm/f* fire-raiser, arsonist.
incendie [ɛ̃sɑ̃di] *nm* fire; ~ **criminel** arson *q*; ~ **de forêt** forest fire.
incendier [ɛ̃sɑ̃dje] *vt* (*mettre le feu à*) to set fire to, set alight; (*brûler complètement*) to burn down.
incertain, e [ɛ̃sɛʀtɛ̃, -ɛn] *a* uncertain; (*temps*) uncertain, unsettled; (*imprécis: contours*) indistinct, blurred; **incertitude** *nf* uncertainty.
incessamment [ɛ̃sɛsamɑ̃] *ad* very shortly.
incidemment [ɛ̃sidamɑ̃] *ad* in passing.
incident [ɛ̃sidɑ̃] *nm* incident; ~ **de parcours** minor hitch *ou* setback; ~ **technique** technical difficulties *pl*.
incinérer [ɛ̃sineʀe] *vt* (*ordures*) to incinerate; (*mort*) to cremate.
incisive [ɛ̃siziv] *nf* incisor.
inclinaison [ɛ̃klinɛzɔ̃] *nf* (*déclivité: d'une route etc*) incline; (: *d'un toit*) slope; (*état penché*) tilt.
inclination [ɛ̃klinasjɔ̃] *nf*: ~ **de (la) tête** nod (of the head); ~ **(de buste)** bow.
incliner [ɛ̃kline] *vt* (*tête, bouteille*) to tilt // *vi*: ~ **à qch/à faire** to incline towards sth/doing; **s'~ (devant)** to bow (before); (*céder*) to give in *ou* yield (to); ~ **la tête** *ou* **le front** to give a slight bow.
inclure [ɛ̃klyʀ] *vt* to include; (*joindre à un envoi*) to enclose; **jusqu'au 10 mars inclus** until 10th March inclusive.
incoercible [ɛ̃kɔɛʀsibl(ə)] *a* uncontrollable.
incohérent, e [ɛ̃kɔeʀɑ̃, -ɑ̃t] *a* inconsistent; incoherent.
incollable [ɛ̃kɔlabl(ə)] *a*: **il est ~** he's got all the answers.
incolore [ɛ̃kɔlɔʀ] *a* colourless.
incomber [ɛ̃kɔ̃be]: ~ **à** *vt* (*suj: devoirs, responsabilité*) to rest upon; (: *frais, travail*) to be the responsibility of.
incommensurable [ɛ̃kɔmɑ̃syʀabl(ə)] *a* immeasurable.
incommode [ɛ̃kɔmɔd] *a* inconvenient; (*posture, siège*) uncomfortable.
incommoder [ɛ̃kɔmɔde] *vt*: ~ **qn** to inconvenience sb; (*embarrasser*) to make sb feel uncomfortable.
incompétent, e [ɛ̃kɔ̃petɑ̃, -ɑ̃t] *a* incompetent.
incompris, e [ɛ̃kɔ̃pʀi, -iz] *a* misunderstood.
inconcevable [ɛ̃kɔ̃svabl(ə)] *a* incredible.
inconciliable [ɛ̃kɔ̃siljabl(ə)] *a* irreconcilable.
inconditionnel, le [ɛ̃kɔ̃disjɔnɛl] *a* unconditional; (*partisan*) unquestioning.
inconduite [ɛ̃kɔ̃dɥit] *nf* wild behaviour *q*.
incongru, e [ɛ̃kɔ̃gʀy] *a* unseemly.
inconnu, e [ɛ̃kɔny] *a* unknown; new, strange // *nm/f* stranger; unknown person (*ou* artist etc) // *nm*: **l'~** the unknown // *nf* unknown.
inconsciemment [ɛ̃kɔ̃sjamɑ̃] *ad* unconsciously.
inconscient, e [ɛ̃kɔ̃sjɑ̃, -ɑ̃t] *a* unconscious; (*irréfléchi*) thoughtless, reckless // *nm* (*PSYCH*): **l'~** the unconscious; ~ **de** unaware of.
inconsidéré, e [ɛ̃kɔ̃sidere] *a* ill-considered.
inconsistant, e [ɛ̃kɔ̃sistɑ̃, -ɑ̃t] *a* flimsy, weak; runny.
incontestable [ɛ̃kɔ̃tɛstabl(ə)] *a* indisputable.
inconvenant, e [ɛ̃kɔ̃vnɑ̃, -ɑ̃t] *a* unseemly, improper.
inconvénient [ɛ̃kɔ̃venjɑ̃] *nm* (*d'une situation, d'un projet*) disadvantage, drawback; (*d'un remède, changement etc*) inconvenience; **si vous n'y voyez pas d'~** if you have no objections.
incorporer [ɛ̃kɔʀpɔʀe] *vt*: ~ **(à)** to mix in (with); (*paragraphe etc*): ~ **(dans)** to incorporate (in); (*MIL: appeler*) to recruit, call up.
incorrect, e [ɛ̃kɔʀɛkt] *a* (*impropre, inconvenant*) improper; (*défectueux*) faulty; (*inexact*) incorrect; (*impoli*) impolite; (*déloyal*) underhand.
incrédule [ɛ̃kʀedyl] *a* incredulous; (*REL*) unbelieving.
increvable [ɛ̃kʀəvabl(ə)] *a* (*fam*) tireless.
incriminer [ɛ̃kʀimine] *vt* (*personne*) to incriminate; (*action, attitude*) to bring under attack; (*bonne foi, honnêteté*) to call into question.
incroyable [ɛ̃kʀwajabl(ə)] *a* incredible; unbelievable.
incruster [ɛ̃kʀyste] *vt* (*ART*) to inlay; **s'~** *vi* (*invité*) to take root; (*radiateur etc*) to become coated with fur *ou* scale.

incubateur [ɛ̃kybatœʀ] nm incubator.
inculpé, e [ɛ̃kylpe] nm/f accused.
inculper [ɛ̃kylpe] vt: ~ (de) to charge (with).
inculquer [ɛ̃kylke] vt: ~ qch à to inculcate sth into ou instil sth into.
inculte [ɛ̃kylt(ə)] a uncultivated; (esprit, peuple) uncultured; (barbe) unkempt.
Inde [ɛ̃d] nf: l'~ India.
indécis, e [ɛ̃desi, -iz] a indecisive; (perplexe) undecided.
indéfendable [ɛ̃defɑ̃dabl(ə)] a indefensible.
indéfini, e [ɛ̃defini] a (imprécis, incertain) undefined; (illimité, LING) indefinite; ~ment ad indefinitely; ~ssable a indefinable.
indélicat, e [ɛ̃delika, -at] a tactless; dishonest.
indemne [ɛ̃dɛmn(ə)] a unharmed.
indemniser [ɛ̃dɛmnize] vt: ~ qn (de) to compensate sb (for).
indemnité [ɛ̃dɛmnite] nf (dédommagement) compensation q; (allocation) allowance; ~ de licenciement redundancy payment.
indépendamment [ɛ̃depɑ̃damɑ̃] ad independently; ~ de (abstraction faite de) irrespective of; (en plus de) over and above.
indépendance [ɛ̃depɑ̃dɑ̃s] nf independence.
indépendant, e [ɛ̃depɑ̃dɑ̃, -ɑ̃t] a independent; ~ de independent of.
indescriptible [ɛ̃dɛskʀiptibl(ə)] a indescribable.
indétermination [ɛ̃detɛʀminɑsjɔ̃] nf indecision; indecisiveness.
indéterminé, e [ɛ̃detɛʀmine] a unspecified; indeterminate.
index [ɛ̃dɛks] nm (doigt) index finger; (d'un livre etc) index; **mettre à l'~** to blacklist.
indexé, e [ɛ̃dɛkse] a (ÉCON): ~ (sur) index-linked (to).
indicateur [ɛ̃dikatœʀ] nm (POLICE) informer; (livre) guide; directory; (TECH) gauge; indicator; ~ des chemins de fer railway timetable.
indicatif, ive [ɛ̃dikatif, -iv] a: à titre ~ for (your) information // nm (LING) indicative; (RADIO) theme ou signature tune; (TÉL) dialling code.
indication [ɛ̃dikɑsjɔ̃] nf indication; (renseignement) information q; ~s nfpl (directives) instructions.
indice [ɛ̃dis] nm (marque, signe) indication, sign; (POLICE: lors d'une enquête) clue; (JUR: présomption) piece of evidence; (SCIENCE, ÉCON, TECH) index.
indicible [ɛ̃disibl(ə)] a inexpressible.
indien, ne [ɛ̃djɛ̃, -jɛn] a, nm/f Indian.
indifféremment [ɛ̃difeʀamɑ̃] ad (sans distinction) equally (well); indiscriminately.

indifférence [ɛ̃difeʀɑ̃s] nf indifference.
indifférent, e [ɛ̃difeʀɑ̃, -ɑ̃t] a (peu intéressé) indifferent.
indigence [ɛ̃diʒɑ̃s] nf poverty.
indigène [ɛ̃diʒɛn] a native, indigenous; local // nm/f native.
indigeste [ɛ̃diʒɛst(ə)] a indigestible.
indigestion [ɛ̃diʒɛstjɔ̃] nf indigestion q.
indigne [ɛ̃diɲ] a unworthy.
indigner [ɛ̃diɲe] vt: s'~ (de/contre) to be indignant (at).
indiqué, e [ɛ̃dike] a (date, lieu) given; (adéquat, conseillé) suitable.
indiquer [ɛ̃dike] vt (désigner): ~ qch/qn à qn to point sth/sb out to sb; (suj: pendule, aiguille) to show; (suj: étiquette, plan) to show, indicate; (faire connaître: médecin, restaurant): ~ qch/qn à qn to tell sb of sth/sb; (renseigner sur) to point out, tell; (déterminer: date, lieu) to give, state; (dénoter) to indicate, point to.
indirect, e [ɛ̃diʀɛkt] a indirect.
indiscipline [ɛ̃disiplin] nf lack of discipline; **indiscipliné, e** a undisciplined; (fig) unmanageable.
indiscret, ète [ɛ̃diskʀɛ, -ɛt] a indiscreet.
indiscutable [ɛ̃diskytabl(ə)] a indisputable.
indispensable [ɛ̃dispɑ̃sabl(ə)] a indispensable; essential.
indisposer [ɛ̃dispoze] vt (incommoder) to upset; (déplaire à) to antagonize.
indistinct, e [ɛ̃distɛ̃, -ɛkt(ə)] a indistinct; **indistinctement** ad (voir, prononcer) indistinctly; (sans distinction) indiscriminately.
individu [ɛ̃dividy] nm individual.
individuel, le [ɛ̃dividɥɛl] a (gén) individual; (opinion, livret, contrôle, avantages) personal; **chambre ~le** single room; **maison ~le** detached house.
indolore [ɛ̃dɔlɔʀ] a painless.
indomptable [ɛ̃dɔ̃tabl(ə)] a untameable; (fig) invincible, indomitable.
Indonésie [ɛ̃donezi] nf Indonesia.
indu, e [ɛ̃dy] a: à des heures ~es at some ungodly hour.
induire [ɛ̃dɥiʀ] vt: ~ qn en erreur to lead sb astray, mislead sb.
indulgent, e [ɛ̃dylʒɑ̃, -ɑ̃t] a (parent, regard) indulgent; (juge, examinateur) lenient.
indûment [ɛ̃dymɑ̃] ad wrongfully; without due cause.
industrie [ɛ̃dystʀi] nf industry; **industriel, le** a industrial // nm industrialist; manufacturer.
inébranlable [inebʀɑ̃labl(ə)] a (masse, colonne) solid; (personne, certitude, foi) steadfast, unwavering.
inédit, e [inedi, -it] a (correspondance etc) hitherto unpublished; (spectacle, moyen) novel, original.

ineffaçable |incfasabl(ə)| a indelible.
inefficace |incfikas| a (remède, moyen) ineffective; (machine, employé) inefficient.
inégal, e, aux |incgal, -o| a unequal; uneven.
inégalable |incgalabl(c)| a matchless.
inégalé, e |incgalc| a unmatched, unequalled.
inerte |incʀt(ə)| a lifeless; inert.
inestimable |incstimabl(c)| a priceless; (fig: bienfait) invaluable.
inévitable |incvitabl(ə)| a unavoidable; (fatal, habituel) inevitable.
inexact, e |incgzakt| a inaccurate, inexact; unpunctual.
in extenso |incks(tēso| ad in full.
in extremis |inckstʀcmis| ad at the last minute // a last-minute.
infaillible |ēfajibl(ə)| a infallible.
infâme |ēfɑm| a vile.
infanticide |ēfūtisid| nm/f child-murderer/eress // nm (meurtre) infanticide.
infarctus |ēfaʀktys| nm: ~ (du myocarde) coronary (thrombosis).
infatigable |ēfatigabl(ə)| a tireless.
infect, e |ēfɛkt| a vile; foul; (repas, vin) revolting.
infecter |ēfɛkte| vt (atmosphère, eau) to contaminate; (MÉD) to infect; s'~ to become infected ou septic; **infection** |-sjɔ̃| nf infection.
inférieur, e |ēfcʀjœʀ| a lower; (en qualité, intelligence) inferior; ~ à (somme, quantité) less ou smaller than; (moins bon que) inferior to.
infernal, e, aux |ēfɛʀnal, -o| a (chaleur, rythme) infernal; (méchanceté, complot) diabolical.
infidèle |ēfidɛl| a unfaithful.
infiltrer |ēfiltʀe| s'~ vi: s'~ dans to penetrate into; (liquide) to seep into; (fig: noyauter) to infiltrate.
infime |ēfim| a minute, tiny; (inférieur) lowly.
infini, e |ēfini| a infinite // nm infinity; à l'~ (MATH) to infinity; (agrandir, varier) infinitely; (interminablement) endlessly; **infinité** nf: une infinité de an infinite number of.
infinitif |ēfinitif| nm infinitive.
infirme |ēfiʀm(ə)| a disabled // nm/f disabled person; ~ de guerre war cripple.
infirmer |ēfiʀme| vt to invalidate.
infirmerie |ēfiʀməʀi| nf sick bay.
infirmier, ière |ēfiʀmje, -jɛʀ| nm/f nurse; **infirmière chef** sister; **infirmière visiteuse** ≈ district nurse.
infirmité |ēfiʀmite| nf disability.
inflammable |ēflamabl(ə)| a (in)flammable.
inflation |ēflɑsjɔ̃| nf inflation.
inflexion |ēflɛksjɔ̃| nf inflexion; ~ de la tête slight nod (of the head).

infliger |ēfliʒe| vt: ~ qch (à qn) to inflict sth (on sb); (amende, sanction) to impose sth (on sb).
influence |ēflyɑ̃s| nf influence; (d'un médicament) effect; **influencer** vt to influence; **influent, e** a influential.
influer |ēflye|: ~ sur vt to have an influence upon.
informaticien, ne |ēfɔʀmatisjē, -jɛn| nm/f computer scientist.
information |ēfɔʀmasjɔ̃| nf (renseignement) piece of information; (PRESSE, TV: nouvelle) item of news; ~s (TV) news sg; (diffusion de renseignements, INFORM) information; (JUR) inquiry, investigation; **voyage d'~** fact-finding trip.
informatique |ēfɔʀmatik| nf (technique) data processing; (science) computer science // a computer cpd; **informatiser** vt to computerize.
informe |ēfɔʀm(ə)| a shapeless.
informer |ēfɔʀme| vt: ~ qn (de) to inform sb (of); s'~ (de/si) to inquire ou find out (about/whether ou if).
infortune |ēfɔʀtyn| nf misfortune.
infraction |ēfʀaksjɔ̃| nf offence; ~ à violation ou breach of; **être en ~** to be in breach of the law.
infranchissable |ēfʀɑ̃ʃisabl(ə)| a impassable; (fig) insuperable.
infrastructure |ēfʀastʀyktyʀ| nf (AVIAT, MIL) ground installations pl; (ÉCON: touristique etc) infrastructure.
infuser |ēfyze| vt, vi (thé) to brew; (tisane) to infuse; **infusion** nf (tisane) herb tea.
ingénier |ēʒenje|: s'~ vi: s'~ à faire to strive to do.
ingénierie |ēʒenjəʀi| nf engineering.
ingénieur |ēʒenjœʀ| nm engineer; ~ du son sound engineer.
ingénieux, euse |ēʒenjø, -øz| a ingenious, clever.
ingénu, e |ēʒeny| a ingenuous, artless.
ingérer |ēʒeʀe|: s'~ vi: s'~ dans to interfere in.
ingrat, e |ēgʀa, -at| a (personne) ungrateful; (sol) poor; (travail, sujet) thankless; (visage) unprepossessing.
ingrédient |ēgʀedjɑ̃| nm ingredient.
ingurgiter |ēgyʀʒite| vt to swallow.
inhabitable |inabitabl(ə)| a uninhabitable.
inhérent, e |ineʀɑ̃, -ɑ̃t| a: ~ à inherent in.
inhibition |inibisjɔ̃| nf inhibition.
inhumain, e |inymē, -ɛn| a inhuman.
inhumer |inyme| vt to inter, bury.
inimitié |inimitje| nf enmity.
initial, e, aux |inisjal, -o| a, nf initial.
initiateur, trice |inisjatœʀ, -tʀis| nm/f initiator; (d'une mode, technique) innovator, pioneer.
initiative |inisjativ| nf initiative.
initier |inisje| vt: ~ qn à to initiate sb

into; (*faire découvrir: art, jeu*) to introduce sb to.

injecté, e [ɛ̃ʒɛkte] a: yeux ~s de sang
bloodshot eyes.

injecter [ɛ̃ʒɛkte] vt to inject; **injection**
[-sjɔ̃] nf injection; **à injection** a (AUTO)
fuel injection cpd.

injure [ɛ̃ʒyʀ] nf insult, abuse q.

injurier [ɛ̃ʒyʀje] vt to insult, abuse; **in-
jurieux, euse** a abusive, insulting.

injuste [ɛ̃ʒyst(ə)] a unjust, unfair;
injustice nf injustice.

inlassable [ɛ̃lasabl(ə)] a tireless.

inné, e [ine] a innate, inborn.

innocent, e [inɔsɑ̃, -ɑ̃t] a innocent;
innocenter vt to clear, prove innocent.

innombrable [inɔ̃bʀabl(ə)] a innumerable.

innommable [inɔmabl(ə)] a unspeakable.

innover [inɔve] vi to break new ground.

inoccupé, e [inɔkype] a unoccupied.

inoculer [inɔkyle] vt (*volontairement*) to
inoculate; (*accidentellement*) to infect.

inodore [inɔdɔʀ] a (*gaz*) odourless;
(*fleur*) scentless.

inoffensif, ive [inɔfɑ̃sif, -iv] a harmless, innocuous.

inondation [inɔ̃dasjɔ̃] nf flooding q;
flood.

inonder [inɔ̃de] vt to flood; (*fig*) to inundate, overrun.

inopérant, e [inɔpeʀɑ̃, -ɑ̃t] a inopera-
tive, ineffective.

inopiné, e [inɔpine] a unexpected, sudden.

inopportun, e [inɔpɔʀtœ̃, -yn] a ill-
timed, untimely; inappropriate.

inoubliable [inublijabl(ə)] a unforgettable.

inouï, e [inwi] a unheard-of, extraordinary.

inox(ydable) [inɔks(idabl(ə))] a stain-
less.

inqualifiable [ɛ̃kalifjabl(ə)] a unspeakable.

inquiet, ète [ɛ̃kjɛ, -ɛt] a anxious.

inquiétant, e [ɛ̃kjetɑ̃, -ɑ̃t] a worrying,
disturbing.

inquiéter [ɛ̃kjete] vt to worry; (*harceler*) to harass; s'~ to worry; s'~ de to
worry about; (*s'enquérir de*) to inquire
about.

inquiétude [ɛ̃kjetyd] nf anxiety.

insaisissable [ɛ̃sezisabl(ə)] a elusive.

insatisfait, e [ɛ̃satisfɛ, -ɛt] a (*non com-
blé*) unsatisfied; unfulfilled; (*mécontent*)
dissatisfied.

inscription [ɛ̃skʀipsjɔ̃] nf inscription;
(*voir s'inscrire*) enrolment; registration.

inscrire [ɛ̃skʀiʀ] vt (*marquer: sur son
calepin etc*) to note ou write down; (:
sur un mur, une affiche etc) to write; (:
dans la pierre, le métal) to inscribe;

(*mettre: sur une liste, un budget etc*) to
put down; ~ qn à (*club, école etc*) to enrol sb at; s'~ (*pour une excursion etc*) to
put one's name down; s'~ (à) (*club, parti*) to join; (*université*) to register ou enrol (at); (*examen, concours etc*) to register
(for); s'~ **en faux contre** to challenge.

insecte [ɛ̃sɛkt(ə)] nm insect;
insecticide nm insecticide.

insensé, e [ɛ̃sɑ̃se] a mad.

insensibiliser [ɛ̃sɑ̃sibilize] vt to
anaesthetize.

insensible [ɛ̃sɑ̃sibl(ə)] a (*nerf, membre*)
numb; (*dur, indifférent*) insensitive;
(*imperceptible*) imperceptible.

insérer [ɛ̃seʀe] vt to insert; s'~ **dans** to
fit into; to come within.

insigne [ɛ̃siɲ] nm (*d'un parti, club*)
badge // a distinguished; ~s nmpl
(*d'une fonction*) insignia pl.

insignifiant, e [ɛ̃siɲifjɑ̃, -ɑ̃t] a insigni-
cant; trivial.

insinuer [ɛ̃sinɥe] vt to insinuate, imply;
s'~ **dans** (*fig*) to creep into.

insister [ɛ̃siste] vi to insist; (*s'obstiner*)
to keep on; ~ **sur** (*détail, note*) to stress.

insolation [ɛ̃sɔlasjɔ̃] nf (MÉD) sunstroke
q.

insolent, e [ɛ̃sɔlɑ̃, -ɑ̃t] a insolent.

insolite [ɛ̃sɔlit] a strange, unusual.

insomnie [ɛ̃sɔmni] nf insomnia q, sleep-
lessness q.

insondable [ɛ̃sɔ̃dabl(ə)] a unfathom-
able.

insonoriser [ɛ̃sɔnɔʀize] vt to sound-
proof.

insouciant, e [ɛ̃susjɑ̃, -ɑ̃t] a carefree;
(*imprévoyant*) heedless.

insoumis, e [ɛ̃sumi, -iz] a (*caractère,
enfant*) rebellious, refractory; (*contrée,
tribu*) unsubdued.

insoupçonnable [ɛ̃supsɔnabl(ə)] a un-
suspected; (*personne*) above suspicion.

insoutenable [ɛ̃sutnabl(ə)] a (*argument*) untenable; (*chaleur*) unbearable.

inspecter [ɛ̃spɛkte] vt to inspect.

inspecteur, trice [ɛ̃spɛktœʀ, -tʀis] nm/
f inspector; ~ **d'Académie** (regional) director of education; ~ **des finances** ≈ tax
inspector (*Brit*), ≈ Internal Revenue Service agent (US).

inspection [ɛ̃spɛksjɔ̃] nf inspection.

inspirer [ɛ̃spiʀe] vt (*gén*) to inspire // vi
(*aspirer*) to breathe in; s'~ de (*suj: artiste*) to draw one's inspiration from.

instable [ɛ̃stabl(ə)] a (*meuble, équilibre*) unsteady; (*population, temps*) unsettled; (*régime, caractère*) unstable.

installation [ɛ̃stalasjɔ̃] nf putting in ou
up; fitting out; settling in; (*appareils
etc*) fittings pl, installations pl; ~s nfpl
equipment; facilities.

installer [ɛ̃stale] vt (*loger*): ~ qn to get
sb settled; (*placer*) to put, place; (*meuble, gaz, électricité*) to put in; (*rideau,*

étagère, tente) to put up; (*appartement*) to fit out; s'~ (*s'établir: artisan, dentiste etc*) to set o.s. up; (*se loger*) to settle (o.s.); (*emménager*) to settle in; (*sur un siège, à un emplacement*) to settle (down); (*fig: maladie, grève*) to take a firm hold.

instamment [ɛ̃stamɑ̃] *ad* urgently.

instance [ɛ̃stɑ̃s] *nf* (ADMIN: *autorité*) authority; ~s *nfpl* (*prières*) entreaties; **affaire en** ~ matter pending; **être en** ~ **de divorce** to be awaiting a divorce.

instant [ɛ̃stɑ̃] *nm* moment, instant; **dans un** ~ in a moment; **à l'**~ this instant; **à tout** *ou* **chaque** ~ at any moment; constantly; **pour l'**~ for the moment, for the time being; **par** ~s at times; **de tous les** ~s perpetual.

instantané, e [ɛ̃stɑ̃tane] *a* (*lait, café*) instant; (*explosion, mort*) instantaneous // *nm* snapshot.

instar [ɛ̃staʀ]: **à l'**~ **de** *prép* following the example of, like.

instaurer [ɛ̃stɔʀe] *vt* to institute.

instinct [ɛ̃stɛ̃] *nm* instinct.

instituer [ɛ̃stitɥe] *vt* to set up.

institut [ɛ̃stity] *nm* institute; ~ **de beauté** beauty salon; **I~ Universitaire de Technologie (IUT)** ≈ polytechnic.

instituteur, trice [ɛ̃stitytœʀ, -tʀis] *nm/f* (primary school) teacher.

institution [ɛ̃stitysjɔ̃] *nf* institution; (*collège*) private school.

instruction [ɛ̃stʀyksjɔ̃] *nf* (*enseignement, savoir*) education; (JUR) (preliminary) investigation and hearing; ~s *nfpl* directions, instructions; ~ **civique** civics *sg*.

instruire [ɛ̃stʀɥiʀ] *vt* (*élèves*) to teach; (*recrues*) to train; (JUR: *affaire*) to conduct the investigation for; s'~ to educate o.s.; **instruit, e** *a* educated.

instrument [ɛ̃stʀymɑ̃] *nm* instrument; ~ **à cordes/vent** stringed/wind instrument; ~ **de mesure** measuring instrument; ~ **de musique** musical instrument; ~ **de travail** (working) tool.

insu [ɛ̃sy] *nm*: **à l'**~ **de qn** without sb knowing (it).

insubmersible [ɛ̃sybmɛʀsibl(ə)] *a* unsinkable.

insubordination [ɛ̃sybɔʀdinasjɔ̃] *nf* rebelliousness; (MIL) insubordination.

insuccès [ɛ̃syksɛ] *nm* failure.

insuffisant, e [ɛ̃syfizɑ̃, -ɑ̃t] *a* insufficient; (*élève, travail*) inadequate.

insuffler [ɛ̃syfle] *vt* to blow; to inspire.

insulaire [ɛ̃sylɛʀ] *a* island *cpd*; (*attitude*) insular.

insuline [ɛ̃sylin] *nf* insulin.

insulte [ɛ̃sylt(ə)] *nf* insult; **insulter** *vt* to insult.

insupportable [ɛ̃sypɔʀtabl(ə)] *a* unbearable.

insurger [ɛ̃syʀ ʒe]: s'~ *vi*: s'~ (**contre**)

to rise up *ou* rebel (against).

insurmontable [ɛ̃syʀmɔ̃tabl(ə)] *a* (*difficulté*) insuperable; (*aversion*) unconquerable.

intact, e [ɛ̃takt] *a* intact.

intangible [ɛ̃tɑ̃ʒibl(ə)] *a* intangible; (*principe*) inviolable.

intarissable [ɛ̃taʀisabl(ə)] *a* inexhaustible.

intégral, e, aux [ɛ̃tegʀal, -o] *a* complete.

intégrant, e [ɛ̃tegʀɑ̃, -ɑ̃t] *a*: **faire partie** ~**e de** to be an integral part of.

intègre [ɛ̃tegʀ(ə)] *a* upright.

intégrer [ɛ̃tegʀe] *vt* to integrate; s'~ **à/dans** to become integrated into.

intellectuel, le [ɛ̃telɛktɥɛl] *a* intellectual // *nm/f* intellectual; (*péj*) highbrow.

intelligence [ɛ̃teliʒɑ̃s] *nf* intelligence; (*compréhension*): **l'**~ **de** the understanding of; (*complicité*): **regard d'**~ glance of complicity; (*accord*): **vivre en bonne** ~ **avec qn** to be on good terms with sb.

intelligent, e [ɛ̃teliʒɑ̃, -ɑ̃t] *a* intelligent.

intempéries [ɛ̃tɑ̃peʀi] *nfpl* bad weather *sg*.

intempestif, ive [ɛ̃tɑ̃pestif, -iv] *a* untimely.

intenable [ɛ̃tnabl(ə)] *a* (*chaleur*) unbearable.

intendant, e [ɛ̃tɑ̃dɑ̃, -ɑ̃t] *nm/f* (MIL) quartermaster; (SCOL) bursar; (*d'une propriété*) steward.

intense [ɛ̃tɑ̃s] *a* intense; **intensif, ive** *a* intensive.

intenter [ɛ̃tɑ̃te] *vt*: ~ **un procès contre** *ou* **à** to start proceedings against.

intention [ɛ̃tɑ̃sjɔ̃] *nf* intention; (JUR) intent; **avoir l'**~ **de faire** to intend to do; **à l'**~ **de** *prép* for; (*renseignement*) for the benefit of; (*film, ouvrage*) aimed at; **à cette** ~ with this aim in view; **intentionné, e** *a*: **bien intentionné** wellmeaning *ou* -intentioned; **mal intentionné** ill-intentioned.

intercaler [ɛ̃tɛʀkale] *vt* to insert.

intercepter [ɛ̃tɛʀsɛpte] *vt* to intercept; (*lumière, chaleur*) to cut off.

interchangeable [ɛ̃tɛʀʃɑ̃ʒabl(ə)] *a* interchangeable.

interclasse [ɛ̃tɛʀklɑs] *nm* (SCOL) break (between classes).

interdiction [ɛ̃tɛʀdiksjɔ̃] *nf* ban.

interdire [ɛ̃tɛʀdiʀ] *vt* to forbid; (ADMIN) to ban, prohibit; (: *journal, livre*) to ban; ~ **à qn de faire** to forbid sb to do, prohibit sb from doing; (*suj: empêchement*) to prevent sb from doing.

interdit, e [ɛ̃tɛʀdi, -it] *a* (*stupéfait*) taken aback // *nm* prohibition.

intéressant, e [ɛ̃teʀesɑ̃, -ɑ̃t] *a* interesting.

intéressé, e [ɛ̃teʀese] *a* (*parties*) involved, concerned; (*amitié, motifs*) self-interested.

intéresser [ɛ̃terese] *vt* (*captiver*) to interest; (*toucher*) to be of interest to; (*ADMIN: concerner*) to affect, concern; s'~ à to be interested in.

intérêt [ɛ̃terɛ] *nm* (*aussi COMM*) interest; (*égoïsme*) self-interest; avoir ~ à faire to do well to do.

intérieur, e [ɛ̃terjœr] *a* (*mur, escalier, poche*) inside; (*commerce, politique*) domestic; (*cour, calme, vie*) inner; (*navigation*) inland // *nm* (*d'une maison, d'un récipient etc*) inside; (*d'un pays, aussi: décor, mobilier*) interior; (*POL*): l'I~ the Interior; à l'~ (de) inside; (*fig*) within.

intérim [ɛ̃terim] *nm* interim period; assurer l'~ (de) to deputize (for); par ~ *a* interim.

intérioriser [ɛ̃terjɔrize] *vt* to internalize.

interlocuteur, trice [ɛ̃terlɔkytœr, -tris] *nm/f* speaker; son ~ the person he was speaking to.

interloquer [ɛ̃terlɔke] *vt* to take aback.

intermède [ɛ̃termɛd] *nm* interlude.

intermédiaire [ɛ̃termedjɛr] *a* intermediate; middle; half-way // *nm/f* intermediary; (*COMM*) middleman; sans ~ directly; par l'~ de through.

intermittence [ɛ̃termitɑ̃s] *nf*: par ~ sporadically, intermittently.

internat [ɛ̃terna] *nm* (*SCOL*) boarding school.

international, e, aux [ɛ̃ternasjɔnal, -o] *a, nm/f* international.

interne [ɛ̃tern(ə)] *a* internal // *nm/f* (*SCOL*) boarder; (*MÉD*) houseman.

interner [ɛ̃terne] *vt* (*POL*) to intern; (*MÉD*) to confine to a mental institution.

interpeller [ɛ̃terpele] *vt* (*appeler*) to call out to; (*apostropher*) to shout at; (*POLICE*) to take in for questioning; (*POL*) to question.

interphone [ɛ̃terfɔn] *nm* intercom.

interposer [ɛ̃terpoze] *vt* to interpose; s'~ *vi* to intervene; par personnes interposées through a third party.

interprète [ɛ̃terprɛt] *nm/f* interpreter; (*porte-parole*) spokesman.

interpréter [ɛ̃terprete] *vt* to interpret.

interrogateur, trice [ɛ̃terɔgatœr, -tris] *a* questioning, inquiring.

interrogatif, ive [ɛ̃terɔgatif, -iv] *a* (*LING*) interrogative.

interrogation [ɛ̃terɔgasjɔ̃] *nf* question; (*SCOL*) (written *ou* oral) test.

interrogatoire [ɛ̃terɔgatwar] *nm* (*POLICE*) questioning *q*; (*JUR*) cross-examination.

interroger [ɛ̃terɔʒe] *vt* to question; (*INFORM*) to consult; (*SCOL*) to test.

interrompre [ɛ̃terɔ̃pr(ə)] *vt* (*gén*) to interrupt; (*travail, voyage*) to break off, interrupt; s'~ to break off.

interrupteur [ɛ̃teryptœr] *nm* switch.

interruption [ɛ̃terypsjɔ̃] *nf* interruption;

(*pause*) break.

interstice [ɛ̃terstis] *nm* crack; slit.

interurbain [ɛ̃teryrbɛ̃] *nm* (*TÉL*) long-distance call service // *a* (*TÉL*) long-distance.

intervalle [ɛ̃terval] *nm* (*espace*) space; (*de temps*) interval; dans l'~ in the meantime.

intervenir [ɛ̃tervənir] *vi* (*gén*) to intervene; (*survenir*) to take place; ~ auprès de qn to intervene with sb.

intervention [ɛ̃tervɑ̃sjɔ̃] *nf* intervention; (*discours*) paper; ~ chirurgicale (surgical) operation.

intervertir [ɛ̃tervertir] *vt* to invert (the order of), reverse.

interview [ɛ̃tervju] *nf* interview.

intestin, e [ɛ̃testɛ̃, -in] *a* internal // *nm* intestine.

intime [ɛ̃tim] *a* intimate; (*vie, journal*) private; (*conviction*) inmost; (*dîner, cérémonie*) quiet // *nm/f* close friend.

intimer [ɛ̃time] *vt* (*JUR*) to notify; ~ à qn l'ordre de faire to order sb to do.

intimité [ɛ̃timite] *nf*: dans l'~ in private; (*sans formalités*) with only a few friends, quietly.

intitulé, e [ɛ̃tityle] *a* entitled.

intolérable [ɛ̃tɔlerabl(ə)] *a* intolerable.

intoxication [ɛ̃tɔksikasjɔ̃] *nf*: ~ alimentaire food poisoning.

intoxiquer [ɛ̃tɔksike] *vt* to poison; (*fig*) to brainwash.

intraduisible [ɛ̃traduizibl(ə)] *a* untranslatable; (*fig*) inexpressible.

intraitable [ɛ̃tretabl(ə)] *a* inflexible, uncompromising.

intransigeant, e [ɛ̃trɑ̃ziʒɑ̃, -ɑ̃t] *a* intransigent; (*morale*) uncompromising.

intransitif, ive [ɛ̃trɑ̃zitif, -iv] *a* (*LING*) intransitive.

intrépide [ɛ̃trepid] *a* dauntless.

intrigue [ɛ̃trig] *nf* (*scénario*) plot.

intriguer [ɛ̃trige] *vi* to scheme // *vt* to puzzle, intrigue.

intrinsèque [ɛ̃trɛ̃sek] *a* intrinsic.

introduction [ɛ̃trɔdyksjɔ̃] *nf* introduction.

introduire [ɛ̃trɔduir] *vt* to introduce; (*visiteur*) to show in; (*aiguille, clef*): ~ qch dans to insert *ou* introduce sth into; s'~ dans to gain entry into; to get o.s. accepted into; (*eau, fumée*) to get into.

introuvable [ɛ̃truvabl(ə)] *a* which cannot be found; (*COMM*) unobtainable.

introverti, e [ɛ̃trɔverti] *nm/f* introvert.

intrus, e [ɛ̃try, -yz] *nm/f* intruder.

intrusion [ɛ̃tryzjɔ̃] *nf* intrusion; interference.

intuition [ɛ̃tɥisjɔ̃] *nf* intuition.

inusable [inyzabl(ə)] *a* hard-wearing.

inusité, e [inyzite] *a* rarely used.

inutile [inytil] *a* useless; (*superflu*) unnecessary; **inutilisable** *a* unusable.

invalide [ɛ̃valid] *a* disabled // *nm*: ~ de

guerre disabled ex-serviceman.
invasion [ɛ̃vɑzjɔ̃] nf invasion.
invectiver [ɛ̃vɛktive] vt to hurl abuse at.
invendable [ɛ̃vɑ̃dabl(ə)] a unsaleable; unmarketable; **invendus** nmpl unsold goods.
inventaire [ɛ̃vɑ̃tɛR] nm inventory; (COMM: liste) stocklist; (: opération) stocktaking q; (fig) survey.
inventer [ɛ̃vɑ̃te] vt to invent; (subterfuge) to devise, invent; (histoire, excuse) to make up, invent; **inventeur** nm inventor; **inventif, ive** a inventive; **invention** [-sjɔ̃] nf invention.
inverse [ɛ̃vɛRs(ə)] a reverse; opposite; inverse // nm inverse, reverse; dans l'ordre ~ in the reverse order; en sens ~ in (ou from) the opposite direction; **~ment** ad conversely; **inverser** vt to invert, reverse; (ÉLEC) to reverse.
investir [ɛ̃vɛstiR] vt to invest; **investissement** nm investment; **investiture** nf investiture; (à une élection) nomination.
invétéré, e [ɛ̃vetere] a (habitude) ingrained; (bavard, buveur) inveterate.
invisible [ɛ̃vizibl(ə)] a invisible.
invitation [ɛ̃vitɑsjɔ̃] nf invitation.
invité, e [ɛ̃vite] nm/f guest.
inviter [ɛ̃vite] vt to invite; ~ qn à faire (suj: chose) to induce ou tempt sb to do.
involontaire [ɛ̃vɔlɔ̃tɛR] a (mouvement) involuntary; (insulte) unintentional; (complice) unwitting.
invoquer [ɛ̃vɔke] vt (Dieu, muse) to call upon, invoke; (prétexte) to put forward (as an excuse); (loi, texte) to refer to.
invraisemblable [ɛ̃vRɛsɑ̃blabl(ə)] a unlikely, improbable; incredible.
iode [jɔd] nm iodine.
irai etc vb voir **aller**.
Irak [iRak] nm Iraq.
Iran [iRɑ̃] nm Iran.
irions etc vb voir **aller**.
irlandais, e [iRlɑ̃dɛ, -ɛz] a Irish // nm/f: I~, e Irishman/woman; les I~ the Irish.
Irlande [iRlɑ̃d] nf Ireland; ~ du Nord Northern Ireland.
ironie [iRɔni] nf irony; **ironique** a ironical; **ironiser** vi to be ironical.
irons etc vb voir **aller**.
irradier [iRadje] vi to radiate // vt (aliment) to irradiate.
irraisonné, e [iRezɔne] a irrational, unreasoned.
irrationnel, le [iRasjɔnɛl] a irrational.
irréalisable [iRealizabl(ə)] a unrealizable; impracticable.
irrécupérable [iRekypeRabl(ə)] a unreclaimable, beyond repair; (personne) beyond redemption.
irrécusable [iRekyzabl(ə)] a unimpeachable; incontestable.
irréductible [iRedyktibl(ə)] a indomitable, implacable.

irréel, le [iRɛɛl] a unreal.
irréfléchi, e [iReflefi] a thoughtless.
irrégularité [iRegylaRite] nf irregularity; unevenness q.
irrégulier, ière [iRegylje, -jɛR] a irregular; uneven; (élève, athlète) erratic.
irrémédiable [iRemedjabl(ə)] a irreparable.
irréprochable [iRepRɔfabl(ə)] a irreproachable, beyond reproach; (tenue) impeccable.
irrésistible [iRezistibl(ə)] a irresistible; (preuve, logique) compelling.
irrespectueux, euse [iRɛspɛktɥø, -øz] a disrespectful.
irriguer [iRige] vt to irrigate.
irritable [iRitabl(ə)] a irritable.
irriter [iRite] vt to irritate.
irruption [iRypsjɔ̃] nf irruption q; faire ~ dans to burst into.
islamic [islamik] a Islamic.
Islande [islɑ̃d] nf Iceland.
isolant, e [izɔlɑ̃, -ɑ̃t] a insulating; (insonorisant) soundproofing.
isolation [izɔlɑsjɔ̃] nf insulation.
isolé, e [izɔle] a isolated; insulated.
isoler [izɔle] vt to isolate; (prisonnier) to put in solitary confinement; (ville) to cut off, isolate; (ÉLEC) to insulate; **isoloir** nm polling booth.
Israël [isRaɛl] nm Israel; **israélien, ne** a, nm/f Israeli; **israélite** a Jewish // nm/f Jew/Jewess.
issu, e [isy] a: ~ de descended from; (fig) stemming from // nf (ouverture, sortie) exit; (solution) way out, solution; (dénouement) outcome; à l'~e de at the conclusion ou close of; rue sans ~e dead end.
Italie [itali] nf Italy; **italien, ne** a, nm, nf Italian.
italique [italik] nm: en ~ in italics.
itinéraire [itineRɛR] nm itinerary, route.
IUT sigle m voir **institut**.
ivoire [ivwaR] nm ivory.
ivre [ivR(ə)] a drunk; ~ de (colère, bonheur) wild with; **ivresse** nf drunkenness; **ivrogne** nm/f drunkard.

J

jachère [zafɛR] nf: (être) en ~ (to lie) fallow.
jacinthe [zasɛ̃t] nf hyacinth.
jack [zak] nm jack plug.
jadis [zadis] ad in times past, formerly.
jaillir [zajiR] vi (liquide) to spurt out; (fig); to burst out; to flood out.
jais [zɛ] nm jet; (d'un noir) de ~ jet-black.
jalon [zalɔ̃] nm range pole; (fig) milestone; **jalonner** vt to mark out; (fig) to mark, punctuate.
jalousie [zaluzi] nf jealousy; (store) (ve-

netian) blind.
jaloux, se [ʒalu, -uz] *a* jealous.
jamais [ʒamɛ] *ad* never; (*sans négation*) ever; ne ... ~ never; à ~ for ever.
jambe [ʒɑ̃b] *nf* leg.
jambon [ʒɑ̃bɔ̃] *nm* ham.
jante [ʒɑ̃t] *nf* (*wheel*) rim.
janvier [ʒɑ̃vje] *nm* January.
Japon [ʒapɔ̃] *nm* Japan; **japonais, e** *a, nm, nf* Japanese.
japper [ʒape] *vi* to yap, yelp.
jaquette [ʒakɛt] *nf* (*de cérémonie*) morning coat; (*de dame*) jacket.
jardin [ʒaʀdɛ̃] *nm* garden; ~ **d'enfants** nursery school; **jardinage** *nm* gardening; **jardinier, ière** *nm/f* gardener // *nf* (*de fenêtre*) window box.
jarre [ʒaʀ] *nf* (*earthenware*) jar.
jarret [ʒaʀɛ] *nm* back of knee, ham; (*CULIN*) knuckle, shin.
jarretelle [ʒaʀtɛl] *nf* suspender (*Brit*), garter (*US*).
jarretière [ʒaʀtjɛʀ] *nf* garter.
jaser [ʒaze] *vi* to chatter, prattle; (*indiscrètement*) to gossip.
jatte [ʒat] *nf* basin, bowl.
jauge [ʒoʒ] *nf* (*instrument*) gauge; **jauger** *vt* (*fig*) to size up.
jaune [ʒon] *a, nm* yellow // *ad* (*fam*): rire ~ to laugh on the other side of one's face; ~ **d'œuf** (*egg*) yolk; **jaunir** *vi, vt* to turn yellow.
jaunisse [ʒonis] *nf* jaundice.
Javel [ʒavɛl] *nf voir* eau.
javelot [ʒavlo] *nm* javelin.
jazz [dʒɑz] *nm* jazz.
J.-C. *sigle voir* Jésus-Christ.
je, j' [ʒ(ə)] *pronom* I.
jean [dʒin] *nm* jeans *pl.*
Jésus-Christ [ʒezykʀi(st)] *n* Jesus Christ; **600 avant/après ~ ou J.-C.** 600 B.C./A.D.
jet [ʒɛ] *nm* (*lancer*) throwing *q*, throw; (*jaillissement*) jet; spurt; (*de tuyau*) nozzle; (*avion*) [dʒɛt] jet; **du premier ~** at the first attempt or shot; ~ **d'eau** fountain; spray.
jetable [ʒətabl(ə)] *a* disposable.
jetée [ʒəte] *nf* jetty; pier.
jeter [ʒəte] *vt* (*gén*) to throw; (*se défaire de*) to throw away *ou* out; (*son, lueur etc*) to give out; ~ **qch à qn** to throw sth to sb; (*de façon agressive*) to throw sth at sb; ~ **un coup d'œil (à)** to take a look (at); ~ **un sort à qn** to cast a spell on sb; se ~ **dans** (*fleuve*) to flow into.
jeton [ʒətɔ̃] *nm* (*au jeu*) counter; (*de téléphone*) token.
jette *etc vb voir* **jeter.**
jeu, x [ʒø] *nm* (*divertissement, TECH: d'une pièce*) play; (*TENNIS: partie, FOOTBALL etc: façon de jouer*) game; (*THÉÂTRE etc*) acting; (*au casino*): le ~ gambling; (*fonctionnement*) working, interplay; (*série d'objets, jouet*) set;

(*CARTES*) hand; en ~ at stake; at work; remettre en ~ to throw in; entrer/mettre en ~ to come/bring into play; ~ **de cartes** pack of cards; ~ **d'échecs** chess set; ~ **de hasard** game of chance; ~ **de mots** pun.
jeudi [ʒødi] *nm* Thursday.
jeun [ʒœ̃]: à ~ *ad* on an empty stomach.
jeune [ʒœn] *a* young; ~ **fille** *nf* girl; ~ **homme** *nm* young man.
jeûne [ʒøn] *nm* fast.
jeunesse [ʒœnɛs] *nf* youth; (*aspect*) youthfulness; youngness.
joaillerie [ʒɔajʀi] *nf* jewel trade; jewellery; **joaillier, ière** *nm/f* jeweller.
joie [ʒwa] *nf* joy.
joindre [ʒwɛ̃dʀ(ə)] *vt* to join; (*à une lettre*): ~ **qch à** to enclose sth with; (*contacter*) to contact, get in touch with; ~ **les mains** to put one's hands together; se ~ **à** to join.
joint, e [ʒwɛ̃, ʒwɛ̃t] *a*: pièce ~e enclosure // *nm* joint; (*ligne*) join; ~ **de culasse** cylinder head gasket; ~ **de robinet** washer.
joli, e [ʒɔli] *a* pretty, attractive; c'est du ~! (*ironique*) that's very nice!; c'est bien ~, mais... that's all very well but...
jonc [ʒɔ̃] *nm* (bul)rush.
joncher [ʒɔ̃ʃe] *vt* (*suj: choses*) to be strewed on.
jonction [ʒɔ̃ksjɔ̃] *nf* joining; (**point de**) ~ junction.
jongleur, euse [ʒɔ̃glœʀ, -øz] *nm/f* juggler.
jonquille [ʒɔ̃kij] *nf* daffodil.
Jordanie [ʒɔʀdani] *nf*: la ~ Jordan.
joue [ʒu] *nf* cheek; mettre en ~ to take aim at.
jouer [ʒwe] *vt* to play; (*somme d'argent, réputation*) to stake, wager; (*pièce, rôle*) to perform; (*film*) to show; (*simuler: sentiment*) to affect, feign // *vi* to play; (*THÉÂTRE, CINÉMA*) to act, perform; (*bois, porte: se voiler*) to warp; (*clef, pièce: avoir du jeu*) to be loose; ~ **sur** (*miser*) to gamble on; ~ **de** (*MUS*) to play; ~ **des coudes** to use one's elbows; ~ **à** (*jeu, sport, roulette*) to play; ~ **avec** (*risquer*) to gamble with; se ~ **de** (*difficultés*) to make light of; to deceive; ~ **un tour à qn** to play a trick on sb; ~ **serré** to play a close game; ~ **de malchance** to be dogged with ill-luck.
jouet [ʒwɛ] *nm* toy; **être le ~ de** (*illusion etc*) to be the victim of.
joueur, euse [ʒwœʀ, -øz] *nm/f* player; **être beau ~** to be a good loser.
joufflu, e [ʒufly] *a* chubby-cheeked.
joug [ʒu] *nm* yoke.
jouir [ʒwiʀ]: ~ **de** *vt* to enjoy; **jouissance** *nf* pleasure; (*JUR*) use.
joujou [ʒuʒu] *nm* (*fam*) toy.
jour [ʒuʀ] *nm* day; (*opposé à la nuit*)

day, daytime; (*clarté*) daylight; (*fig: aspect*) light; (*ouverture*) opening; **au ~ le ~** from day to day; **de nos ~s** these days; **il fait ~** it's daylight; **au grand ~** (*fig*) in the open; **mettre au ~** to disclose; **mettre à ~** to update; **donner le ~ à** to give birth to; **voir le ~** to be born.

journal, aux [ʒuʀnal, -o] *nm* (news)paper; (*personnel*) journal, diary; **~ parlé/télévisé** radio/television news *sg*; **~ de bord** log.

journalier, ière [ʒuʀnalje, -jɛʀ] *a* daily; (*banal*) everyday.

journalisme [ʒuʀnalism(ə)] *nm* journalism; **journaliste** *nm/f* journalist.

journée [ʒuʀne] *nf* day; **la ~ continue** the 9 to 5 working day.

journellement [ʒuʀnɛlmɑ̃] *ad* daily.

joyau, x [ʒwajo] *nm* gem, jewel.

joyeux, euse [ʒwajø, -øz] *a* joyful, merry; **~ Noël!** merry Christmas!; **~ anniversaire!** happy birthday!

jubiler [ʒybile] *vi* to be jubilant, exult.

jucher [ʒyʃe] *vt, vi* to perch.

judas [ʒyda] *nm* (*trou*) spy-hole.

judiciaire [ʒydisjɛʀ] *a* judicial.

judicieux, euse [ʒydisjø, -øz] *a* judicious.

judo [ʒydo] *nm* judo.

juge [ʒyʒ] *nm* judge; **~ d'instruction** examining (*Brit*) *ou* committing (*US*) magistrate; **~ de paix** justice of the peace.

jugé [ʒyʒe] : **au ~** *ad* by guesswork.

jugement [ʒyʒmɑ̃] *nm* judgment; (*JUR: au pénal*) sentence; (: *au civil*) decision.

juger [ʒyʒe] *vt* to judge; **~ qn/qch satisfaisant** to consider sb/sth (to be) satisfactory; **~ bon de faire** to see fit to do; **~ de** *vt* to appreciate.

juif, ive [ʒɥif, -iv] *a* Jewish // *nm/f* Jew/ Jewess.

juillet [ʒɥijɛ] *nm* July.

juin [ʒɥɛ̃] *nm* June.

jumeau, elle, x [ʒymo, -ɛl] *a, nm/f* twin; **jumelles** *nfpl* binoculars.

jumeler [ʒymle] *vt* to twin.

jumelle [ʒymɛl] *a, nf voir* **jumeau**.

jument [ʒymɑ̃] *nf* mare.

jungle [ʒɔ̃gl(ə)] *nf* jungle.

jupe [ʒyp] *nf* skirt.

jupon [ʒypɔ̃] *nm* waist slip.

juré, e [ʒyʀe] *nm/f* juror.

jurer [ʒyʀe] *vt* (*obéissance etc*) to swear, vow // *vi* (*dire des jurons*) to swear, curse; (*dissoner*): **~ (avec)** to clash (with); (*s'engager*): **~ de faire/que** to swear *ou* vow to do/that; (*affirmer*): **~ que** to swear *ou* vouch that; **~ de qch** (*s'en porter garant*) to swear to sth.

juridique [ʒyʀidik] *a* legal.

juron [ʒyʀɔ̃] *nm* curse, swearword.

jury [ʒyʀi] *nm* jury; board.

jus [ʒy] *nm* juice; (*de viande*) gravy, (meat) juice; **~ de fruit** fruit juice.

jusque [ʒysk(ə)]: **jusqu'à** *prép* (*endroit*) as far as, (up) to; (*moment*) until, till; (*limite*) up to; **~ sur/dans** up to; (*y compris*) even on/in; **jusqu'à ce que** until; **jusqu'à présent** until now.

juste [ʒyst(ə)] *a* (*équitable*) just, fair; (*légitime*) just, justified; (*exact, vrai*) right; (*étroit, insuffisant*) tight // *ad* right; tight; (*chanter*) in tune; (*seulement*) just; **~ assez/au-dessus** just enough/above; **au ~** exactly; **le ~ milieu** the happy medium; **~ment** *ad* rightly, justly; (*précisément*) just, precisely; **justesse** *nf* (*précision*) accuracy; (*d'une remarque*) aptness; (*d'une opinion*) soundness; **de justesse** just.

justice [ʒystis] *nf* (*équité*) fairness, justice; (*ADMIN*) justice; **rendre la ~** to dispense justice; **rendre ~ à qn** to do sb justice.

justicier, ière [ʒystisje, -jɛʀ] *nm/f* judge, righter of wrongs.

justifier [ʒystifje] *vt* to justify; **~ de** *vt* to prove.

juteux, euse [ʒytø, -øz] *a* juicy.

juvénile [ʒyvenil] *a* young, youthful.

K

K [ka] *nm* (*INFORM*) K.

kaki [kaki] *a inv* khaki.

kangourou [kɑ̃guʀu] *nm* kangaroo.

karaté [kaʀate] *nm* karate.

karting [kaʀtiŋ] *nm* go-carting, karting.

kermesse [kɛʀmɛs] *nf* bazaar, (charity) fête; village fair.

kidnapper [kidnape] *vt* to kidnap.

kilogramme [kilɔgʀam] *nm*, **kilo** *nm* kilogramme.

kilométrage [kilɔmetʀaʒ] *nm* number of kilometres travelled, ≈ mileage.

kilomètre [kilɔmɛtʀ(ə)] *nm* kilometre.

kilométrique [kilɔmetʀik] *a* (*distance*) in kilometres.

kinésithérapeute [kineziteʀapøt] *nm/f* physiotherapist.

kiosque [kjɔsk(ə)] *nm* kiosk, stall.

klaxon [klaksɔn] *nm* horn; **klaxonner** *vi, vt* to hoot (*Brit*), honk (*US*).

km. *abr de* **kilomètre**; **~/h** (= *kilomètres/heure*) ≈ m.p.h. (= *miles per hour*).

Ko [kao] *nm* (*INFORM:* = *kilo-octet*) K.

K.-O. [kao] *a inv* (knocked) out.

kyste [kist(ə)] *nm* cyst.

L

l' [l] *dét voir* **le**.

la [la] *dét voir* **le** // *nm* (*MUS*) A; (*en chantant la gamme*) la.

là [la] *ad* (*voir aussi* -ci, celui) there; (*ici*) here; (*dans le temps*) then; **elle n'est pas ~** she isn't here; **c'est ~ que**

this is where; **~ où** where; **de ~** (*fig*) hence; **par ~** (*fig*) by that; **tout est ~** (*fig*) that's what it's all about; **~-bas** *ad* there.

label [label] *nm* stamp, seal.

labeur [labœʀ] *nm* toil *q*, toiling *q*.

labo [labo] *abr m* (= *laboratoire*) lab.

laboratoire [labɔʀatwaʀ] *nm* laboratory; **~ de langues** language laboratory.

laborieux, euse [labɔʀjø, -øz] *a* (*tâche*) laborious; **classes ~euses** working classes.

labour [labuʀ] *nm* ploughing *q*; **~s** *nmpl* ploughed fields; **cheval de ~** plough- *ou* cart-horse; **bœuf de ~** ox (*pl* oxen).

labourer [labuʀe] *vt* to plough; (*fig*) to make deep gashes *ou* furrows in.

labyrinthe [labiʀɛ̃t] *nm* labyrinth, maze.

lac [lak] *nm* lake.

lacer [lase] *vt* to lace *ou* do up.

lacérer [laseʀe] *vt* to tear to shreds.

lacet [lasɛ] *nm* (*de chaussure*) lace; (*de route*) sharp bend; (*piège*) snare.

lâche [lɑʃ] *a* (*poltron*) cowardly; (*desserré*) loose, slack // *nm/f* coward.

lâcher [lɑʃe] *nm* (*de ballons, oiseaux*) release // *vt* to let go of; (*ce qui tombe, abandonner*) to drop; (*oiseau, animal: libérer*) to release, set free; (*fig: mot, remarque*) to let slip, come out with; (*SPORT: distancer*) to leave behind // *vi* (*fil, amarres*) to break, give way; (*freins*) to fail; **~ les amarres** (*NAVIG*) to cast off (the moorings); **~ les chiens** to unleash the dogs; **~ prise** to let go.

lâcheté [lɑʃte] *nf* cowardice; lowness.

lacrymogène [lakʀimɔʒɛn] *a*: **gaz ~** teargas.

lacté, e [lakte] *a* (*produit, régime*) milk *cpd*.

lacune [lakyn] *nf* gap.

là-dedans [ladədɑ̃] *ad* inside (there), in it; (*fig*) in that; **là-dessous** *ad* underneath, under there; (*fig*) behind that; **là-dessus** *ad* on there; (*fig*) at that point; about that.

ladite [ladit] *dét voir* **ledit**.

lagune [lagyn] *nf* lagoon.

là-haut [laˈo] *ad* up there.

laïc [laik] *a, nm/f* = **laïque**.

laid, e [lɛ, lɛd] *a* ugly; **laideur** *nf* ugliness *q*.

lainage [lɛnaʒ] *nm* woollen garment; woollen material.

laine [lɛn] *nf* wool.

laïque [laik] *a* a lay, civil; (*SCOL*) state *cpd* // *nm/f* layman/woman.

laisse [lɛs] *nf* (*de chien*) lead, leash; **tenir en ~** to keep on a lead *ou* leash.

laisser [lese] *vt* to leave // *vb auxiliaire*: **~ qn faire** to let sb do; **se ~ aller** to let o.s. go; **laisse-toi faire** let me (*ou* him) do it; **~-aller** *nm* carelessness, slovenliness; **laissez-passer** *nm inv* pass.

lait [lɛ] *nm* milk; **frère/sœur de ~** foster brother/sister; **~ condensé/concentré** evaporated/condensed milk; **laiterie** *nf* dairy; **laitier, ière** *a* dairy *cpd* // *nm/f* milkman/dairywoman.

laiton [lɛtɔ̃] *nm* brass.

laitue [lety] *nf* lettuce.

laïus [lajys] *nm* (*péj*) spiel.

lambeau, x [lɑ̃bo] *nm* scrap; **en ~x** in tatters, tattered.

lambris [lɑ̃bʀi] *nm* panelling *q*.

lame [lam] *nf* blade; (*vague*) wave; (*lamelle*) strip; **~ de fond** ground swell *q*; **~ de rasoir** razor blade.

lamelle [lamɛl] *nf* thin strip *ou* blade.

lamentable [lamɑ̃tabl(ə)] *a* appalling; pitiful.

lamenter [lamɑ̃te]: **se ~** *vi*: **se ~ (sur)** to moan (over).

lampadaire [lɑ̃padɛʀ] *nm* (*de salon*) standard lamp; (*dans la rue*) street lamp.

lampe [lɑ̃p(ə)] *nf* lamp; (*TECH*) valve; **~ de poche** torch (*Brit*), flashlight (*US*); **~ à souder** blowlamp.

lampion [lɑ̃pjɔ̃] *nm* Chinese lantern.

lance [lɑ̃s] *nf* spear; **~ d'incendie** fire hose.

lancée [lɑ̃se] *nf*: **être/continuer sur sa ~** to be under way/keep going.

lancement [lɑ̃smɑ̃] *nm* launching.

lance-pierres [lɑ̃spjɛʀ] *nm inv* catapult.

lancer [lɑ̃se] *nm* (*SPORT*) throwing *q*, throw // *vt* to throw; (*émettre, projeter*) to throw out, send out; (*produit, fusée, bateau, artiste*) to launch; (*injure*) to hurl, fling; (*proclamation, mandat d'arrêt*) to issue; **~ qch à qn** to throw sth to sb; (*de façon agressive*) to throw sth at sb; **se ~** *vi* (*prendre de l'élan*) to build up speed; (*se précipiter*): **se ~ sur** *ou* **contre** to rush at; **se ~ dans** (*discussion*) to launch into; (*aventure*) to embark on; **~ du poids** *nm* putting the shot.

lancinant, e [lɑ̃sinɑ̃, -ɑ̃t] *a* (*regrets etc*) haunting; (*douleur*) shooting.

landau [lɑ̃do] *nm* pram (*Brit*), baby carriage (*US*).

lande [lɑ̃d] *nf* moor.

langage [lɑ̃gaʒ] *nm* language.

langer [lɑ̃ʒe] *vt* to change (the nappy (*Brit*) *ou* diaper (*US*) of).

langouste [lɑ̃gust(ə)] *nf* crayfish *inv*; **langoustine** *nf* Dublin Bay prawn.

langue [lɑ̃g] *nf* (*ANAT, CULIN*) tongue; (*LING*) language; **tirer la ~ (à)** to stick out one's tongue (at); **de ~ française** French-speaking; **~ maternelle** native language, mother tongue; **~ verte** slang; **~ vivante** modern language.

langueur [lɑ̃gœʀ] *nf* languidness.

languir [lɑ̃giʀ] *vi* to languish; (*conversation*) to flag; **faire ~ qn** to keep sb waiting.

lanière [lanjɛʀ] *nf* (*de fouet*) lash; (*de valise, bretelle*) strap.

lanterne [lɑ̃tɛʀn(ə)] nf (portable) lantern; (électrique) light, lamp; (de voiture) (side)light.

laper [lape] vt to lap up.

lapidaire [lapidɛʀ] a stone cpd; (fig) terse.

lapin [lapɛ̃] nm rabbit; (peau) rabbitskin; (fourrure) coney.

Laponie [lapɔni] nf Lapland.

laps [laps] nm: ~ de temps space of time, time q.

laque [lak] nf lacquer; (brute) shellac; (pour cheveux) hair spray.

laquelle [lakɛl] pronom voir **lequel**.

larcin [laʀsɛ̃] nm theft.

lard [laʀ] nm (graisse) fat; (bacon) (streaky) bacon.

lardon [laʀdɔ̃] nm: ~s chopped bacon.

large [laʀʒ(ə)] a wide; broad; (fig) generous // ad: calculer/voir ~ to allow extra/think big // nm (largeur): 5 m de ~ 5 m wide ou in width; (mer): le ~ the open sea; au ~ de off; ~ d'esprit broad-minded; ~ment ad widely; greatly; easily; generously; **largesse** nf generosity; **largeur** nf (qu'on mesure) width; (impression visuelle) wideness, width; breadth; broadness.

larguer [laʀge] vt to drop: ~ les amarres to cast off (the moorings).

larme [laʀm(ə)] nf tear; (fig) drop; en ~s in tears; **larmoyer** vi (yeux) to water; (se plaindre) to whimper.

larvé, e [laʀve] a (fig) latent.

laryngite [laʀɛ̃ʒit] nf laryngitis.

las, lasse [lɑ, lɑs] a weary.

laser [lazɛʀ] nm: (rayon) ~ laser (beam); chaîne ~ compact disc (player); disque ~ compact disc.

lasse [lɑs] af voir **las**.

lasser [lɑse] vt to weary, tire; se ~ de to grow weary ou tired of.

latéral, e, aux [lateʀal, -o] a side cpd, lateral.

latin, e [latɛ̃, -in] a, nm, nf Latin.

latitude [latityd] nf latitude.

latte [lat] nf lath, slat; (de plancher) board.

lauréat, e [lɔʀea, -at] nm/f winner.

laurier [lɔʀje] nm (BOT) laurel; (CULIN) bay leaves pl; ~s nmpl (fig) laurels.

lavable [lavabl(ə)] a washable.

lavabo [lavabo] nm washbasin; ~s nmpl toilet sg.

lavage [lavaʒ] nm washing q, wash; ~ de cerveau brainwashing q.

lavande [lavɑ̃d] nf lavender.

lave [lav] nf lava q.

lave-glace [lavglas] nm windscreen (Brit) ou windshield (US) washer.

laver [lave] vt to wash; (tache) to wash off; se ~ vi to have a wash, wash; se ~ les mains/dents to wash one's hands/clean one's teeth; ~ qn de (accusation) to clear sb of; **laverie** nf: laverie (automatique) launderette.

lavette [lavɛt] nf dish cloth; (fam) drip.

laveur, euse [lavœʀ, -øz] nm/f cleaner.

lave-vaisselle [lavvɛsɛl] nm inv dishwasher.

lavoir [lavwaʀ] nm wash house.

laxatif, ive [laksatif, -iv] a, nm laxative.

le(l'), la, les [l(ə), la, le] ♦ article défini
1 the; le livre/la pomme/l'arbre the book/the apple/the tree; les étudiants the students

2 (noms abstraits): le courage/l'amour/la jeunesse courage/love/youth

3 (indiquant la possession): se casser la jambe etc to break one's leg etc; levez la main put your hand up; avoir les yeux gris/le nez rouge to have grey eyes/a red nose

4 (temps): le matin/soir in the morning/evening; mornings/evenings; le jeudi etc (d'habitude) on Thursdays etc; (ce jeudi-là etc) on (the) Thursday

5 (distribution, évaluation) a, an; 10 F le mètre/kilo 10 F a ou per metre/kilo; le tiers/quart a third/quarter of

♦ pronom **1** (personne: mâle) him; (: femelle) her; (: pluriel) them; je le/la/les vois I can see him/her/them

2 (animal, chose: sing) it; (: pl) them; je le (ou la) vois I can see it; je les vois I can see them

3 (remplaçant une phrase): je ne le savais pas I didn't know (about it); il était riche et ne l'est plus he was once rich but no longer is.

lécher [leʃe] vt to lick; (laper: lait, eau) to lick ou lap up; ~ les vitrines to go window-shopping.

leçon [ləsɔ̃] nf lesson; faire la ~ à (fig) to give a lecture to; ~s de conduite driving lessons.

lecteur, trice [lɛktœʀ, -tʀis] nm/f reader; (d'université) foreign language assistant // nm (TECH): ~ de cassettes cassette player; ~ de disquette disk drive.

lecture [lɛktyʀ] nf reading.

ledit [lədi], **ladite** [ladit], mpl **lesdits** [ledi], fpl **lesdites** [ledit] dét the aforesaid.

légal, e, aux [legal, -o] a legal.

légende [leʒɑ̃d] nf (mythe) legend; (de carte, plan) key; (de dessin) caption.

léger, ère [leʒe, -ɛʀ] a light; (bruit, retard) slight; (superficiel) thoughtless; (volage) free and easy; flighty; à la légère ad (parler, agir) rashly, thoughtlessly; **légèrement** ad lightly; thoughtlessly; slightly.

législatif, ive [leʒislatif, -iv] a legislative; **législatives** nfpl general election sg.

législature [leʒislatyʀ] nf legislature; term (of office).

légitime [leʒitim] a (JUR) lawful, legitimate; (*fig*) rightful, legitimate; **en état de ~ défense** in self-defence.

legs [lɛg] *nm* legacy.

léguer [lege] *vt*: ~ **qch à qn** (*JUR*) to bequeath sth to sb; (*fig*) to hand sth down *ou* pass sth on to sb.

légume [legym] *nm* vegetable.

lendemain [lɑ̃dmɛ̃] *nm*: **le ~** the next *ou* following day; **le ~ matin/soir** the next *ou* following morning/evening; **le ~ de** the day after; **sans ~** short-lived.

lent, e [lɑ̃, lɑ̃t] *a* slow; **lentement** *ad* slowly; **lenteur** *nf* slowness *q*.

lentille [lɑ̃tij] *nf* (*OPTIQUE*) lens *sg*; (*CULIN*) lentil.

léopard [leɔpaʀ] *nm* leopard.

lèpre [lɛpʀ(ə)] *nf* leprosy.

lequel [ləkɛl], **laquelle** [lakɛl], *mpl* **lesquels**, *fpl* **lesquelles** [lekɛl] (*avec à, de*: **auquel, duquel** etc) *pronom* (*interrogatif*) which, which one; (*relatif: personne: sujet*) who; (*: objet, après préposition*) whom; (*: chose*) which // *a*: **auquel cas** in which case.

les [le] *dét voir* **le**.

lesbienne [lɛsbjɛn] *nf* lesbian.

lesdits [ledi], **lesdites** [ledit] *dét voir* **ledit**.

léser [leze] *vt* to wrong.

lésiner [lezine] *vi*: ~ (**sur**) to skimp (on).

lésion [lezjɔ̃] *nf* lesion, damage *q*.

lesquels, lesquelles [lekɛl] *pronom voir* **lequel**.

lessive [lesiv] *nf* (*poudre*) washing powder; (*linge*) washing *q*, wash.

lessiver [lesive] *vt* to wash.

lest [lɛst] *nm* ballast.

leste [lɛst(ə)] *a* sprightly, nimble.

lettre [lɛtʀ(ə)] *nf* letter; ~**s** *nfpl* literature *sg*; (*SCOL*) arts (subjects); **à la ~** literally; **en toutes ~s** in full.

lettré, e [letʀe] *a* well-read.

leucémie [løsemi] *nf* leukaemia.

leur [lœʀ] ♦ *a possessif* their; ~ **maison** their house; ~**s amis** their friends ♦ *pronom* **1** (*objet indirect*) (to) them; **je ~ ai dit la vérité** I told them the truth; **je le ~ ai donné** I gave it to them, I gave them it **2** (*possessif*): **le(la) ~, les ~s** theirs.

leurre [lœʀ] *nm* (*appât*) lure; (*fig*) delusion; snare.

leurrer [lœʀe] *vt* to delude, deceive.

levain [ləvɛ̃] *nm* leaven.

levé, e [ləve] *a*: **être ~** to be up.

levée [ləve] *nf* (*POSTES*) collection; (*CARTES*) trick; ~ **de boucliers** general outcry.

lever [ləve] *vt* (*vitre, bras etc*) to raise; (*soulever de terre, supprimer: interdiction, siège*) to lift; (*séance*) to close; (*impôts, armée*) to levy // *vi* to rise // *nm*: **au ~** on getting up; **se ~** *vi* to get up; (*soleil*) to rise; (*jour*) to

break; (*brouillard*) to lift; ~ **du jour** daybreak; ~ **de rideau** curtain raiser; ~ **de soleil** sunrise.

levier [ləvje] *nm* lever.

lèvre [lɛvʀ(ə)] *nf* lip.

lévrier [levʀije] *nm* greyhound.

levure [ləvyʀ] *nf* yeast; ~ **chimique** baking powder.

lexique [lɛksik] *nm* vocabulary; lexicon.

lézard [lezaʀ] *nm* lizard.

lézarde [lezaʀd(ə)] *nf* crack.

liaison [ljezɔ̃] *nf* link; (*amoureuse*) affair; (*PHONÉTIQUE*) liaison; **entrer/être en ~ avec** to get/be in contact with.

liane [ljan] *nf* creeper.

liant, e [ljɑ̃, -ɑ̃t] *a* sociable.

liasse [ljas] *nf* wad, bundle.

Liban [libɑ̃] *nm*: **le ~** (the) Lebanon; **libanais, e** *a, nm/f* Lebanese.

libeller [libele] *vt* (*chèque, mandat*): ~ (**au nom de**) to make out (to); (*lettre*) to word.

libellule [libelyl] *nf* dragonfly.

libéral, e, aux [liberal, -o] *a, nm/f* liberal.

libérer [libere] *vt* (*délivrer*) to free, liberate; (*: moralement, PSYCH*) to liberate; (*relâcher, dégager: gaz*) to release; to discharge; **se ~** *vi* (*de rendez-vous*) to get out of previous engagements.

liberté [libɛʀte] *nf* freedom; (*loisir*) free time; ~**s** *nfpl* (*privautés*) liberties; **mettre/être en ~** to set/be free; **en ~ provisoire/surveillée/conditionnelle** on bail/probation/parole; ~**s individuelles** personal freedom *sg*.

libraire [libʀɛʀ] *nm/f* bookseller.

librairie [libʀɛʀi] *nf* bookshop.

libre [libʀ(ə)] *a* free; (*route*) clear; (*place etc*) vacant; empty; not engaged; not taken; (*SCOL*) non-state; **de ~ de qch/de faire** free from sth/to do; ~ **arbitre** free will; ~**-échange** *nm* free trade; ~**-service** *nm* self-service store.

Libye [libi] *nf*: **la ~** Libya.

licence [lisɑ̃s] *nf* (*permis*) permit; (*diplôme*) degree; (*liberté*) liberty; licence (*Brit*), license (*US*); licentiousness; **licencié, e** *nm/f* (*SCOL*): **licencié ès lettres/en droit**; ≈ Bachelor of Arts/Law; (*SPORT*) member of a sports federation.

licencier [lisɑ̃sje] *vt* (*renvoyer*) to dismiss; (*débaucher*) to make redundant; to lay off.

licite [lisit] *a* lawful.

lie [li] *nf* dregs *pl*, sediment.

lié, e [lje] *a*: **très ~ avec** very friendly with *ou* close to; ~ **par** (*serment*) bound by.

liège [ljɛʒ] *nm* cork.

lien [ljɛ̃] *nm* (*corde, fig: affectif*) bond; (*rapport*) link, connection; ~ **de parenté** family tie.

lier [lje] *vt* (*attacher*) to tie up; (*joindre*)

to link up; (*fig: unir, engager*) to bind; (*CULIN*) to thicken; ~ **qch à** to tie *ou* link sth to; ~ **conversation avec** to strike up a conversation with; **se ~ avec** to make friends with.

lierre [ljɛʀ] *nm* ivy.

liesse [ljɛs] *nf*: **être en ~** to be celebrating *ou* jubilant.

lieu, x [ljø] *nm* place // *nmpl* (*habitation*) premises; (*endroit: d'un accident etc*) scene *sg*; **en ~ sûr** in a safe place; **en premier/dernier ~** in the first place/ lastly; **avoir ~** to take place; **avoir ~ de faire** to have grounds for doing; **tenir ~ de** to take the place of; to serve as; **donner ~ à** to give rise to; **au ~ de** instead of.

lieu-dit *nm* (*pl* **lieux-dits**) [ljødi] locality.

lieutenant [ljøtnā] *nm* lieutenant.

lièvre [ljɛvʀ(ə)] *nm* hare.

ligament [ligamā] *nm* ligament.

ligne [liɲ] *nf* (*gén*) line; (*TRANSPORTS: liaison*) service; (*: trajet*) route; (*silhouette*) figure; **entrer en ~ de compte** to come into it.

lignée [liɲe] *nf* line; lineage; descendants *pl*.

ligoter [ligɔte] *vt* to tie up.

ligue [lig] *nf* league; **liguer** *vt*: **se liguer contre** (*fig*) to combine against.

lilas [lila] *nm* lilac.

limace [limas] *nf* slug.

limaille [limaj] *nf*: ~ **de fer** iron filings *pl*.

limande [limãd] *nf* dab.

lime [lim] *nf* file; ~ **à ongles** nail file; **limer** *vt* to file.

limier [limje] *nm* bloodhound; (*détective*) sleuth.

limitation [limitasjɔ̃] *nf*: ~ **de vitesse** speed limit.

limite [limit] *nf* (*de terrain*) boundary; (*partie ou point extrême*) limit; **vitesse/ charge ~** maximum speed/load; **cas ~** borderline case; **date ~** deadline.

limiter [limite] *vt* (*restreindre*) to limit, restrict; (*délimiter*) to border.

limitrophe [limitʀɔf] *a* border *cpd*.

limoger [limɔʒe] *vt* to dismiss.

limon [limɔ̃] *nm* silt.

limonade [limɔnad] *nf* lemonade.

lin [lɛ̃] *nm* flax.

linceul [lɛ̃sœl] *nm* shroud.

linge [lɛ̃ʒ] *nm* (*serviettes etc*) linen; (*pièce de tissu*) cloth; (*aussi*: ~ **de corps**) underwear; (*aussi*: ~ **de toilette**) towel; (*lessive*) washing.

lingerie [lɛ̃ʒʀi] *nf* lingerie, underwear.

lingot [lɛ̃go] *nm* ingot.

linguistique [lɛ̃gɥistik] *a* linguistic // *nf* linguistics *sg*.

lion, ne [ljɔ̃, ljɔn] *nm/f* lion/lioness; (*signe*): **le L~** Leo; **lionceau, x** *nm* lion cub.

liqueur [likœʀ] *nf* liqueur.

liquide [likid] *a* liquid // *nm* liquid; (*COMM*): **en ~** in ready money *ou* cash.

liquider [likide] *vt* (*société, biens, témoin gênant*) to liquidate; (*compte, problème*) to settle; (*COMM: articles*) to clear, sell off.

liquidités [likidite] *nfpl* (*COMM*) liquid assets.

lire [liʀ] *nf* (*monnaie*) lira // *vt, vi* to read.

lis [lis] *nm* = **lys**.

lisible [lizibl(ə)] *a* legible.

lisière [lizjɛʀ] *nf* (*de forêt*) edge; (*de tissu*) selvage.

lisons *vb voir* **lire**.

lisse [lis] *a* smooth.

liste [list(ə)] *nf* list; **faire la ~ de** to list; ~ **électorale** electoral roll.

listing [listiŋ] *nm* (*INFORM*) printout.

lit [li] *nm* (*gén*) bed; **faire son ~** to make one's bed; **aller/se mettre au ~** to go to/ get into bed; ~ **de camp** campbed; ~ **d'enfant** cot (*Brit*), crib (*US*).

literie [litʀi] *nf* bedding, bedclothes *pl*.

litière [litjɛʀ] *nf* litter.

litige [litiʒ] *nm* dispute.

litre [litʀ(ə)] *nm* litre; (*récipient*) litre measure.

littéraire [literɛʀ] *a* literary.

littéral, e, aux [literal, -o] *a* literal.

littérature [literatyʀ] *nf* literature.

littoral, aux [litɔral, -o] *nm* coast.

liturgie [lityʀʒi] *nf* liturgy.

livide [livid] *a* livid, pallid.

livraison [livʀɛzɔ̃] *nf* delivery.

livre [livʀ(ə)] *nm* book // *nf* (*poids, monnaie*) pound; ~ **de bord** logbook; ~ **de poche** paperback (*pocket size*).

livré, e [livʀe] *a*: ~ **à soi-même** left to o.s. *ou* one's own devices // *nf* livery.

livrer [livʀe] *vt* (*COMM*) to deliver; (*otage, coupable*) to hand over; (*secret, information*) to give away; **se ~ à** (*se confier*) to confide in; (*se rendre, s'abandonner*) to give o.s. up to; (*faire: pratiques, actes*) to indulge in; (*travail*) to engage in; (*: sport*) to practise; (*: enquête*) to carry out.

livret [livʀɛ] *nm* booklet; (*d'opéra*) libretto (*pl* s); ~ **de caisse d'épargne** (savings) bank-book; ~ **de famille** (official) family record book; ~ **scolaire** (school) report book.

livreur, euse [livʀœʀ, -øz] *nm/f* delivery boy *ou* man/girl *ou* woman.

local, e, aux [lɔkal, -o] *a* local // *nm* (*salle*) premises *pl* // *nmpl* premises.

localiser [lɔkalize] *vt* (*repérer*) to locate, place; (*limiter*) to confine.

localité [lɔkalite] *nf* locality.

locataire [lɔkatɛʀ] *nm/f* tenant; (*de chambre*) lodger.

location [lɔkasjɔ̃] *nf* (*par le locataire, le loueur*) renting; (*par le propriétaire*) renting out, letting; (*THÉÂTRE*) booking office; '~ de voitures' 'car rental'.

locomotive [lɔkɔmɔtiv] *nf* locomotive, engine; *(fig)* pacesetter, pacemaker.

locution [lɔkysjɔ̃] *nf* phrase.

loge [lɔʒ] *nf* (THÉÂTRE: *d'artiste*) dressing room; (: *de spectateurs*) box; *(de concierge, franc-maçon*) lodge.

logement [lɔʒmɑ̃] *nm* accommodation *q*; flat *(Brit)*, apartment *(US)*; housing *q*.

loger [lɔʒe] *vt* to accommodate // *vi* to live; **trouver à se ~** to find accommodation; **se ~ dans** *(suj: balle, flèche)* to lodge itself in; **logeur, euse** *nm/f* landlord/landlady.

logiciel [lɔʒisjɛl] *nm* software.

logique [lɔʒik] *a* logical // *nf* logic.

logis [lɔʒi] *nm* home; abode, dwelling.

loi [lwa] *nf* law; **faire la ~** to lay down the law.

loin [lwɛ̃] *ad* far; *(dans le temps)* a long way off; *a long time ago*; **plus ~** further; **~ de** far from; **au ~** far off; **de ~** *ad* from a distance; *(fig: de beaucoup)* by far; **il vient de ~** *(fig)* he's come a long way.

lointain, e [lwɛ̃tɛ̃, -ɛn] *a* faraway, distant; *(dans le futur, passé)* distant, far-off; *(cause, parent)* remote, distant // *nm*: **dans le ~** in the distance.

loir [lwaʀ] *nm* dormouse *(pl* -mice).

loisir [lwaziʀ] *nm*: **heures de ~** spare time; **~s** *nmpl* leisure *sg*; leisure activities; **avoir le ~ de faire** to have the time *ou* opportunity to do; **à ~** at leisure; at one's pleasure.

londonien, ne [lɔ̃dɔnjɛ̃, -jɛn] *a* London *cpd*, of London // *nm/f*: **L~, ne** Londoner.

Londres [lɔ̃dʀ(ə)] *n* London.

long, longue [lɔ̃, lɔ̃g] *a* long // *ad*: **en savoir ~** to know a great deal // *nm*: **de 3 m de ~** 3 m long, 3 m in length // *nf*: **à la longue** in the end; **ne pas faire ~ feu** not to last long; **(tout) le ~ de** (all) along; **tout au ~ de** *(année, vie)* throughout; **de ~ en large** *(marcher)* to and fro, up and down.

longer [lɔ̃ʒe] *vt* to go *(ou* walk *ou* drive) along(side); *(suj: mur, route)* to border.

longiligne [lɔ̃ʒiliɲ] *a* long-limbed.

longitude [lɔ̃ʒityd] *nf* longitude.

longitudinal, e, aux [lɔ̃ʒitydinal, -o] *a* (running) lengthways.

longtemps [lɔ̃tɑ̃] *ad* (for) a long time, (for) long; **avant ~** before long; **pour/ pendant ~** for a long time; **mettre ~ à faire** to take a long time to do.

longue [lɔ̃g] *af voir* long; **~ment** *ad* for a long time.

longueur [lɔ̃gœʀ] *nf* length; **~s** *nfpl* *(fig: d'un film etc)* tedious parts; **en ~** *ad* lengthwise; **tirer en ~** to drag on; **à ~ de journée** all day long; **~ d'onde** wavelength.

longue-vue [lɔ̃gvy] *nf* telescope.

lopin [lɔpɛ̃] *nm*: **~ de terre** patch of land.

loque [lɔk] *nf* *(personne)* wreck; **~s** *nfpl* *(habits)* rags.

loquet [lɔkɛ] *nm* latch.

lorgner [lɔʀɲe] *vt* to eye; *(fig)* to have one's eye on.

lors [lɔʀ]: **~ de** *prép* at the time of; during; **~ même que** even though.

lorsque [lɔʀsk(ə)] *cj* when, as.

losange [lozɑ̃ʒ] *nm* diamond; (GÉOM) lozenge.

lot [lo] *nm* *(part)* share; *(de loterie)* prize; *(fig: destin)* fate, lot; *(COMM, IN-FORM)* batch.

loterie [lɔtʀi] *nf* lottery; raffle.

loti, e [lɔti] *a*: **bien/mal ~** well-/badly off.

lotion [losjɔ̃] *nf* lotion.

lotir [lɔtiʀ] *vt* *(terrain)* to divide into plots; to sell by lots; **lotissement** *nm* housing development; plot, lot.

loto [lɔto] *nm* lotto; numerical lottery.

louable [lwabl(ə)] *a* commendable.

louanges [lwɑ̃ʒ] *nfpl* praise *sg*.

loubard [lubaʀ] *nm* *(fam)* lout.

louche [luʃ] *a* shady, fishy, dubious // *nf* ladle.

loucher [luʃe] *vi* to squint.

louer [lwe] *vt* *(maison: suj: propriétaire)* to let, rent (out); (: *locataire)* to rent; *(voiture etc)* to hire out *(Brit)*, rent (out); to hire, rent; *(réserver)* to book; *(faire l'éloge de)* to praise; **'à louer'** 'to let' *(Brit)*, 'for rent' *(US)*.

loup [lu] *nm* wolf *(pl* wolves).

loupe [lup] *nf* magnifying glass.

louper [lupe] *vt* *(manquer)* to miss.

lourd, e [luʀ, luʀd(ə)] *a, ad* heavy; **~ de** *(conséquences, menaces)* charged with; **lourdaud, e** *a* *(péj)* clumsy.

loutre [lutʀ(ə)] *nf* otter.

louve [luv] *nf* she-wolf.

louveteau, x [luvto] *nm* wolf-cub; *(scout)* cub (scout).

louvoyer [luvwaje] *vi* (NAVIG) to tack; *(fig)* to hedge, evade the issue.

lover [lɔve]: **se ~** *vi* to coil up.

loyal, e, aux [lwajal, -o] *a* *(fidèle)* loyal, faithful; *(fair-play)* fair; **loyauté** *nf* loyalty, faithfulness; fairness.

loyer [lwaje] *nm* rent.

lu, e [ly] *pp de* lire.

lubie [lybi] *nf* whim, craze.

lubrifiant [lybʀifjɑ̃] *nm* lubricant.

lubrifier [lybʀifje] *vt* to lubricate.

lubrique [lybʀik] *a* lecherous.

lucarne [lykaʀn(ə)] *nf* skylight.

lucratif, ive [lykʀatif, -iv] *a* lucrative; profitable; **à but non ~** non profit-making.

lueur [lɥœʀ] *nf* *(chatoyante)* glimmer *q*; *(métallique, mouillée)* gleam *q*; *(rougeoyante, chaude)* glow *q*; *(pâle)* (faint) light; *(fig)* glimmer; gleam.

luge [lyʒ] *nf* sledge *(Brit)*, sled *(US)*.

lugubre [lygybʀ(ə)] *a* gloomy; dismal.
lui [lɥi] *pronom* **1** (*objet indirect: mâle*) (to) him; (*: femelle*) (to) her; (*: chose, animal*) (to) it; **je ~ ai parlé** I have spoken to him (*ou* to her); **il ~ a offert un cadeau** he gave him (*ou* her) a present **2** (*après préposition, comparatif: personne*) him; (*: chose, animal*) it; **elle est contente de ~** she is pleased with him; **je la connais mieux que ~** I know her better than he does; I know her better than him **3** (*sujet, forme emphatique*) he; **~, il est à Paris** HE is in Paris **4**: **~-même** himself; itself.
luire [lɥiʀ] *vi* to shine; to glow.
lumière [lymjɛʀ] *nf* light; **~s** *nfpl* (*d'une personne*) wisdom *sg*; **mettre en ~** (*fig*) to highlight; **~ du jour/soleil** day/sunlight.
luminaire [lyminɛʀ] *nm* lamp, light.
lumineux, euse [lyminø, -øz] *a* (*émettant de la lumière*) luminous; (*éclairé*) illuminated; (*ciel, couleur*) bright; (*relatif à la lumière: rayon etc*) of light, light *cpd*; (*fig: regard*) radiant.
lunaire [lynɛʀ] *a* lunar, moon *cpd*.
lunatique [lynatik] *a* whimsical, temperamental.
lundi [lœdi] *nm* Monday; **~ de Pâques** Easter Monday.
lune [lyn] *nf* moon; **~ de miel** honeymoon.
lunette [lynɛt] *nf*: **~s** *nfpl* glasses, spectacles; (*protectrices*) goggles; **~ arrière** (AUTO) rear window; **~s noires** dark glasses; **~s de soleil** sunglasses.
lus *etc vb voir* **lire.**
lustre [lystʀ(ə)] *nm* (*de plafond*) chandelier; (*fig: éclat*) lustre.
lustrer [lystʀe] *vt* to shine.
lut *vb voir* **lire.**
luth [lyt] *nm* lute.
lutin [lytɛ̃] *nm* imp, goblin.
lutte [lyt] *nf* (*conflit*) struggle; (*sport*) wrestling; **lutter** *vi* to fight, struggle.
luxe [lyks(ə)] *nm* luxury; **de ~** a luxury *cpd*.
Luxembourg [lyksãbuʀ] *nm*: **le ~** Luxembourg.
luxer [lykse] *vt*: **se ~ l'épaule** to dislocate one's shoulder.
luxueux, euse [lyksɥø, -øz] *a* luxurious.
luxure [lyksyʀ] *nf* lust.
lycée [lise] *nm* secondary school; **lycéen, ne** *nm/f* secondary school pupil.
lyrique [liʀik] *a* lyrical; (OPÉRA) lyric; **artiste ~** opera singer.
lys [lis] *nm* lily.

M

M *abr de* **Monsieur.**
m' [m] *pronom voir* **me.**
ma [ma] *dét voir* **mon.**
macaron [makaʀɔ̃] *nm* (*gâteau*) macaroon; (*insigne*) (round) badge.
macaronis [makaʀɔni] *nmpl* macaroni *sg*.
macédoine [masedwan] *nf*: **~ de fruits** fruit salad.
macérer [maseʀe] *vi*, *vt* to macerate; (*dans du vinaigre*) to pickle.
mâcher [maʃe] *vt* to chew; **ne pas ~ ses mots** not to mince one's words.
machin [maʃɛ̃] *nm* (*fam*) thing(umajig).
machinal, e, aux [maʃinal, -o] *a* mechanical, automatic.
machination [maʃinasjɔ̃] *nf* scheming, frame-up.
machine [maʃin] *nf* machine; (*locomotive*) engine; (*fig: rouages*) machinery; **~ à laver/coudre** washing/sewing machine; **~ à écrire** typewriter; **~ à sous** fruit machine; **~ à vapeur** steam engine; **~rie** *nf* machinery, plant; (*d'un navire*) engine room; **machinisme** *nm* mechanization; **machiniste** *nm* (*de bus, métro*) driver.
mâchoire [maʃwaʀ] *nf* jaw; **~ de frein** brake shoe.
mâchonner [maʃɔne] *vt* to chew (at).
maçon [masɔ̃] *nm* bricklayer; builder.
maçonnerie [masɔnʀi] *nf* (*murs*) brickwork; masonry, stonework; (*activité*) bricklaying; building.
maculer [makyle] *vt* to stain.
Madame [madam], *pl* **Mesdames** [medam] *nf*: **~ X** Mrs X ['mɪsɪz]; **occupez-vous de ~/Monsieur/Mademoiselle** please serve this lady/gentleman/(young) lady; **bonjour ~/Monsieur/Mademoiselle** good morning; (*ton déférent*) good morning Madam/Sir/Madam; (*le nom est connu*) good morning Mrs/Mr/Miss X; **~/Monsieur/Mademoiselle!** (*pour appeler*) Madam/Sir/Miss!; **~/Monsieur/Mademoiselle** (*sur lettre*) Dear Madam/Sir/Madam; **chère ~/cher Monsieur/chère Mademoiselle** Dear Mrs/Mr/Miss X; **Mesdames** Ladies.
Mademoiselle [madmwazɛl], *pl* **Mesdemoiselles** [medmwazɛl] *nf* Miss; *voir aussi* **Madame.**
madère [madɛʀ] *nm* Madeira (wine).
magasin [magazɛ̃] *nm* (*boutique*) shop; (*entrepôt*) warehouse; (*d'une arme*) magazine; **en ~** (COMM) in stock.
magazine [magazin] *nm* magazine.
magicien, ne [maʒisjɛ̃, -jɛn] *nm/f* magician.
magie [maʒi] *nf* magic; **magique** *a* magic; (*enchanteur*) magical.

magistral, e, aux [maʒistʀal, -o] a (œuvre, adresse) masterly; (ton) authoritative; (ex cathedra): **enseignement ~** lecturing, lectures pl.

magistrat [maʒistʀa] nm magistrate.

magnétique [maɲetik] a magnetic.

magnétiser [maɲetize] vt to magnetize; (fig) to mesmerize, hypnotize.

magnétophone [maɲetɔfɔn] nm tape recorder; **~ à cassettes** cassette recorder.

magnétoscope [maɲetɔskɔp] nm video-tape recorder.

magnifique [maɲifik] a magnificent.

magot [mago] nm (argent) pile (of money); nest egg.

magouille [maguj] nf scheming.

mai [mɛ] nm May.

maigre [mɛgʀ(ə)] a (very) thin, skinny; (viande) lean; (fromage) low-fat; (végétation) thin, sparse; (fig) poor, meagre, skimpy // ad: **faire ~** not to eat meat; **jours ~s** days of abstinence, fish days; **maigreur** nf thinness; **maigrir** vi to get thinner, lose weight.

maille [maj] nf stitch; **~ à l'endroit/à l'envers** plain/purl stitch; **avoir ~ à partir avec qn** to have a brush with sb.

maillet [maje] nm mallet.

maillon [majɔ̃] nm link.

maillot [majo] nm (aussi: **~ de corps**) vest; (de danseur) leotard; (de sportif) jersey; **~ de bain** swimsuit; (d'homme) bathing trunks pl.

main [mɛ̃] nf hand; **à la ~** in one's hand; **se donner la ~** to hold hands; **donner ou tendre la ~ à qn** to hold out one's hand to sb; **se serrer la ~** to shake hands; **serrer la ~ à qn** to shake hands with sb; **sous la ~** to ou at hand; **attaque à ~ armée** armed attack; **à ~ droite/gauche** to the right/left; **à remettre en ~s propres** to be delivered personally; **de première ~** (COMM: voiture etc) second-hand with only one previous owner; **mettre la dernière ~ à** to put the finishing touches to; **se faire/perdre la ~** to get one's hand in/lose one's touch; **avoir qch bien en ~** to have a (got) the hang of sth.

main-d'œuvre [mɛ̃dœvʀ(ə)] nf manpower, labour.

main-forte [mɛ̃fɔʀt(ə)] nf: **prêter ~ à qn** to come to sb's assistance.

mainmise [mɛ̃miz] nf seizure; (fig): **~ sur** complete hold on.

maint, e [mɛ̃, mɛ̃t] a many a; **~s** many; **à ~es reprises** time and (time) again.

maintenant [mɛ̃tnɑ̃] ad now; (actuellement) nowadays.

maintenir [mɛ̃tniʀ] vt (retenir, soutenir) to support; (contenir: foule etc) to hold back; (conserver, affirmer) to maintain; **se ~** vi to hold; to keep steady; to per-

sist.

maintien [mɛ̃tjɛ̃] nm maintaining; (attitude) bearing.

maire [mɛʀ] nm mayor.

mairie [meʀi] nf (bâtiment) town hall; (administration) town council.

mais [mɛ] cj but; **~ non!** of course not!; **~ enfin** but after all; (indignation) look here!; **~ encore?** is that all?

maïs [mais] nm maize (Brit), corn (US).

maison [mɛzɔ̃] nf house; (chez-soi) home; (COMM) firm // a inv (CULIN) home-made; made by the chef; (fig) in-house, own; **à la ~** at home; (direction) home; **~ close ou de passe** brothel; **~ de correction** reformatory; **~ des jeunes** ≈ youth club; **~ mère** parent company; **~ de repos** convalescent home; **~ de santé** mental home; **maisonnée** nf household, family; **maisonnette** nf small house, cottage.

maître, esse [mɛtʀ(ə), mɛtʀɛs] nm/f master/mistress; (SCOL) teacher, schoolmaster/mistress // nm (peintre etc) master; (titre): **M~ (Me) Maître,** term of address gen for a barrister // nf (amante) mistress // a (principal, essentiel) main; **être ~ de** (soi-même, situation) to be in control of; **une maîtresse femme** a managing woman; **~ chanteur** blackmailer; **~/maîtresse d'école** schoolmaster/mistress; **~ d'hôtel** (domestique) butler; (d'hôtel) head waiter; **~ de maison** host; **~ nageur** lifeguard; **maîtresse de maison** hostess; housewife (pl wives).

maîtrise [mɛtʀiz] nf (aussi: **~ de soi**) self-control, self-possession; (habileté) skill, mastery; (suprématie) mastery, command; (diplôme) ≈ master's degree.

maîtriser [mɛtʀize] vt (cheval, incendie) to (bring under) control; (sujet) to master; (émotion) to control, master; **se ~** to control o.s.

majestueux, euse [maʒɛstɥø, -øz] a majestic.

majeur, e [maʒœʀ] a (important) major; (JUR) of age; (fig) adult // nm (doigt) middle finger; **en ~e partie** for the most part.

majorer [maʒɔʀe] vt to increase.

majoritaire [maʒɔʀitɛʀ] a majority cpd.

majorité [maʒɔʀite] nf (gén) majority; (parti) party in power; **en ~** mainly.

majuscule [maʒyskyl] a, nf: (lettre) **~** capital (letter).

mal, maux [mal, mo] nm (opposé au bien) evil; (tort, dommage) harm; (douleur physique) pain, ache; (maladie) illness, sickness q // ad badly // a bad, wrong; **être ~** to be uncomfortable; **être ~ avec qn** to be on bad terms with sb; **être au plus ~** (malade) to be at death's door; (*brouillé*) to be at daggers drawn; **il a ~ compris** he misunderstood; **dire/penser du ~ de** to speak/think ill of; **ne voir aucun ~ à** to see no harm in, see nothing wrong in; **craignant ~ faire** fearing he was doing the wrong thing; **faire du ~ à qn** to hurt sb; to harm sb; **se faire ~ to** hurt o.s.; **se donner du ~ pour faire qch** to go to a lot of trouble to do sth; **ça fait ~** it hurts; **j'ai ~ au dos** my back hurts; **avoir ~ à la tête/à la gorge/aux dents** to have a headache/a sore throat/toothache; **avoir le ~ du pays** to be homesick; **prendre ~** to be taken ill, feel unwell; **~ de mer** seasickness; **~ en point** *a inv* in a bad state; **maux de ventre** stomach ache *sg*; *voir* **coeur.**

malade [malad] *a* ill, sick; (*poitrine, jambe*) bad; (*plante*) diseased // *nm/f* invalid, sick person; (*à l'hôpital etc*) patient; **tomber ~** to fall ill; **être ~ du coeur** to have heart trouble *ou* a bad heart; **~ mental** mentally sick *ou* ill person.

maladie [maladi] *nf* (*spécifique*) disease, illness; (*mauvaise santé*) illness, sickness; **maladif, ive** *a* sickly; (*curiosité, besoin*) pathological.

maladresse [maladRɛs] *nf* clumsiness *q*; (*gaffe*) blunder.

maladroit, e [maladRwa, -wat] *a* clumsy.

malaise [malɛz] *nm* (*MÉD*) feeling of faintness; feeling of discomfort; (*fig*) uneasiness, malaise.

malaisé, e [maleze] *a* difficult.

malappris, e [malapRi, -iz] *nm/f* ill-mannered *ou* boorish person.

malaria [malaRja] *nf* malaria.

malaxer [malakse] *vt* to knead; to mix.

malchance [malʃɑ̃s] *nf* misfortune, ill luck *q*; **par ~** unfortunately.

mâle [mal] *a* (*aussi ÉLEC, TECH*) male; (*viril: voix, traits*) manly // *nm* male.

malédiction [malediksjɔ̃] *nf* curse.

malencontreux, euse [malɑ̃kɔ̃tRø, -øz] *a* unfortunate, untoward.

malentendu [malɑ̃tɑ̃dy] *nm* misunderstanding.

malfaçon [malfasɔ̃] *nf* fault.

malfaisant, e [malfəzɑ̃, -ɑ̃t] *a* evil, harmful.

malfaiteur [malfɛtœR] *nm* lawbreaker, criminal; burglar, thief (*pl* thieves).

malgache [malgaʃ] *a*, *nm/f* Madagascan, Malagasy // *nm* (*langue*) Malagasy.

malgré [malgRe] *prép* in spite of, despite; **~ tout** *ad* all the same.

malheur [malœR] *nm* (*situation*) adversity, misfortune; (*événement*) misfortune; disaster, tragedy; **faire un ~** to be a smash hit; **malheureusement** *ad* unfortunately; **malheureux, euse** *a* (*triste*) unhappy, miserable; (*infortuné,*

regrettable) unfortunate; (*malchanceux*) unlucky; (*insignifiant*) wretched // *nm/f* poor soul; unfortunate creature; **les malheureux** the destitute.

malhonnête [malɔnɛt] *a* dishonest.

malice [malis] *nf* mischievousness; (*méchanceté*): **par ~** out of malice *ou* spite; **sans ~** guileless; **malicieux, euse** *a* mischievous.

malin, igne [malɛ̃, -iɲ] *a* (*futé: f gén: maline*) smart, shrewd; (*MÉD*) malignant.

malingre [malɛ̃gR(ə)] *a* puny.

malle [mal] *nf* trunk.

mallette [malɛt] *nf* (small) suitcase; overnight case; attaché case.

malmener [malmane] *vt* to manhandle; (*fig*) to give a rough handling to.

malodorant, e [malɔdɔRɑ̃, -ɑ̃t] *a* foul-*ou* ill-smelling.

malotru [malɔtRy] *nm* lout, boor.

malpropre [malpRɔpR(ə)] *a* dirty.

malsain, e [malsɛ̃, -ɛn] *a* unhealthy.

malt [malt] *nm* malt.

Malte [malt(ə)] *nf* Malta.

maltraiter [maltRɛte] *vt* (*brutaliser*) to manhandle, ill-treat.

malveillance [malvejɑ̃s] *nf* (*animosité*) ill will; (*intention de nuire*) malevolence; (*JUR*) malicious intent *q*.

malversation [malvɛRsasjɔ̃] *nf* embezzlement.

maman [mamɑ̃] *nf* mum(my), mother.

mamelle [mamɛl] *nf* teat.

mamelon [mamlɔ̃] *nm* (*ANAT*) nipple; (*colline*) knoll, hillock.

mamie [mami] *nf* (*fam*) granny.

mammifère [mamifɛR] *nm* mammal.

manche [mɑ̃ʃ] *nf* (*de vêtement*) sleeve; (*d'un jeu, tournoi*) round; (*GÉO*): **la M~** the Channel // *nm* (*d'outil, casserole*) handle; (*de pelle, pioche etc*) shaft; **~ à balai** *nm* broomstick; (*AVIAT, INFORM*) joystick.

manchette [mɑ̃ʃɛt] *nf* (*de chemise*) cuff; (*coup*) forearm blow; (*titre*) headline.

manchon [mɑ̃ʃɔ̃] *nm* (*de fourrure*) muff.

manchot [mɑ̃ʃo] *nm* one-armed man; armless man; (*ZOOL*) penguin.

mandarine [mɑ̃daRin] *nf* mandarin (orange), tangerine.

mandat [mɑ̃da] *nm* (*postal*) postal *ou* money order; (*d'un député etc*) mandate; (*procuration*) power of attorney, proxy; (*POLICE*) warrant; **~ d'amener** summons *sg*; **~ d'arrêt** warrant for arrest; **mandataire** *nm/f* representative, proxy.

mander [mɑ̃de] *vt* to summon.

manège [manɛʒ] *nm* riding school; (*à la foire*) roundabout, merry-go-round; (*fig*) game, ploy.

manette [manɛt] *nf* lever, tap; **~ de jeu**

joystick.

mangeable [mɑ̃ʒabl(ə)] a edible, eatable.

mangeoire [mɑ̃ʒwaʀ] nf trough, manger.

manger [mɑ̃ʒe] vt to eat; (ronger: suj: rouille etc) to eat into ou away // vi to eat.

mangue [mɑ̃g] nf mango.

maniable [manjabl(ə)] a (outil) handy; (voiture, voilier) easy to handle.

maniaque [manjak] a finicky, fussy; suffering from a mania // nm/f maniac.

manie [mani] nf mania; (tic) odd habit.

manier [manje] vt to handle.

manière [manjɛʀ] nf (façon) way, manner; ~s nfpl (attitude) manners; (chichis) fuss sg; de ~ à so as to; de telle ~ que in such a way that; de cette ~ in this way ou manner; d'une certaine ~ in a way; d'une ~ générale generally speaking, as a general rule; de toute ~ in any case.

maniéré, e [manjeʀe] a affected.

manifestant, e [manifɛstɑ̃, -ɑ̃t] nm/f demonstrator.

manifestation [manifɛstasjɔ̃] nf (de joie, mécontentement) expression, demonstration; (symptôme) outward sign; (fête etc) event; (POL) demonstration.

manifeste [manifɛst(ə)] a obvious, evident // nm manifesto (pl s).

manifester [manifɛste] vt (volonté, intentions) to show, indicate; (joie, peur) to express, show // vi to demonstrate; se ~ vi (émotion) to show ou express itself; (difficultés) to arise; (symptômes) to appear; (témoin etc) to come forward.

manigance [manigɑ̃s] nf scheme.

manipuler [manipyle] vt to handle; (fig) to manipulate.

manivelle [manivɛl] nf crank.

mannequin [mankɛ̃] nm (COUTURE) dummy; (MODE) model.

manœuvre [manœvʀ(ə)] nf (gén) manœuvre (Brit), maneuver (US) // nm labourer.

manœuvrer [manœvʀe] vt to manœuvre (Brit), maneuver (US); (levier, machine) to operate // vi to manœuvre.

manoir [manwaʀ] nm manor ou country house.

manque [mɑ̃k] nm (insuffisance): ~ de lack of; (vide) emptiness, gap; (MÉD) withdrawal; ~s nmpl (lacunes) faults, defects.

manqué, e [mɑ̃ke] a failed; garçon ~ tomboy.

manquer [mɑ̃ke] vi (faire défaut) to be lacking; (être absent) to be missing; (échouer) to fail // vt to miss // vb impersonnel: il (nous) manque encore 100 F we are still 100 F short; il manque des pages (au livre) there are some pages missing ou some pages missing

(from the book); il/cela me manque I miss him/this; ~ à vt (règles etc) to be in breach of, fail to observe; ~ de vt to lack; il a manqué (de) se tuer he very nearly got killed.

mansarde [mɑ̃saʀd(ə)] nf attic.

mansuétude [mɑ̃sɥetyd] nf leniency.

manteau, x [mɑ̃to] nm coat; ~ de cheminée mantelpiece.

manucure [manykyʀ] nf manicurist.

manuel, le [manɥɛl] a manual // nm (ouvrage) manual, handbook.

manufacture [manyfaktyʀ] nf factory.

manufacturé, e [manyfaktyʀe] a manufactured.

manuscrit, e [manyskʀi, -it] a handwritten // nm manuscript.

manutention [manytɑ̃sjɔ̃] nf (COMM) handling; (local) storehouse.

mappemonde [mapmɔ̃d] nf (plane) map of the world; (sphère) globe.

maquereau, x [makʀo] nm (ZOOL) mackerel inv; (fam) pimp.

maquette [makɛt] nf (d'un décor, bâtiment, véhicule) (scale) model; (d'une page illustrée) paste-up.

maquillage [makijaʒ] nm making up; faking; (crème etc) make-up.

maquiller [makije] vt (personne, visage) to make up; (truquer: passeport, statistique) to fake; (: voiture volée) to do over (respray etc); se ~ vi to make up (one's face).

maquis [maki] nm (GÉO) scrub; (MIL) maquis, underground fighting q.

maraîcher, ère [maʀɛʃe, maʀɛʃɛʀ] a: cultures maraîchères market gardening sg // nm/f market gardener.

marais [maʀɛ] nm marsh, swamp.

marasme [maʀasm(ə)] nm stagnation, slump.

marathon [maʀatɔ̃] nm marathon.

marâtre [maʀɑtʀ(ə)] nf cruel mother.

maraudeur [maʀodœʀ] nm prowler.

marbre [maʀbʀ(ə)] nm (pierre, statue) marble; (d'une table, commode) marble top; **marbrer** vt to mottle, blotch.

marc [maʀ] nm (de raisin, pommes) marc; ~ de café coffee grounds pl ou dregs pl.

marchand, e [maʀʃɑ̃, -ɑ̃d] nm/f shopkeeper, tradesman/woman; (au marché) stallholder // a: prix/valeur ~(e) market price/value; ~ de charbon/vins coal/wine merchant; ~/e de couleurs ironmonger (Brit), hardware dealer (US); ~/e de fruits fruiterer (Brit), fruit seller (US); ~/e de journaux newsagent; ~/e de légumes greengrocer (Brit), produce dealer (US); ~/e de quatre saisons costermonger (Brit), street vendor (selling fresh fruit and vegetables); ~/e de tableaux art dealer.

marchander [maʀʃɑ̃de] vi to bargain, haggle.

marchandise [maʀʃɑ̃diz] nf goods pl, merchandise q.

marche [maʀʃ(ə)] nf (d'escalier) step; (activité) walking; (promenade, trajet, allure) walk; (démarche) walk, gait; (MIL etc, MUS) march; (fonctionnement) running; (progression) progress; course; ouvrir/fermer la ~ to lead the way/bring up the rear; dans le sens de la ~ (RAIL) facing the engine; en ~ (monter etc) while the vehicle is moving ou in motion; mettre en ~ to start; se mettre en ~ (personne) to get moving; (machine) to start; ~ arrière reverse (gear); faire ~ arrière to reverse; (fig) to backtrack, back-pedal; ~ à suivre (correct) procedure; (sur notice) (step by step) instructions pl.

marché [maʀʃe] nm (lieu, COMM, ÉCON) market; (ville) trading centre; (transaction) bargain, deal; M~ commun Common Market; faire du ~ noir to buy and sell on the black market; ~ aux puces flea market.

marchepied [maʀʃəpje] nm (RAIL) step; (fig) stepping stone.

marcher [maʀʃe] vi to walk; (MIL) to march; (aller: voiture, train, affaires) to go; (prospérer) to go well; (fonctionner) to work, run; (fam) to go along, agree; to be taken in; ~ sur to walk on; (mettre le pied sur) to step on ou in; (MIL) to march upon; ~ dans (herbe etc) to walk in ou on; (flaque) to step in; faire ~ qn to pull sb's leg; to lead sb up the garden path; **marcheur, euse** nm/f walker.

mardi [maʀdi] nm Tuesday; M~ gras Shrove Tuesday.

mare [maʀ] nf pond; ~ de sang pool of blood.

marécage [maʀekaʒ] nm marsh, swamp.

maréchal, aux [maʀeʃal, -o] nm marshal.

marée [maʀe] nf tide; (poissons) fresh (sea) fish; ~ haute/basse high/low tide; ~ montante/descendante rising/ebb tide.

marémotrice [maʀemɔtʀis] af tidal.

margarine [maʀgaʀin] nf margarine.

marge [maʀʒ(ə)] nf margin; en ~ de (fig) on the fringe of; cut off from; ~ bénéficiaire profit margin.

marguerite [maʀgəʀit] nf marguerite, (oxeye) daisy; (d'imprimante) daisy-wheel.

mari [maʀi] nm husband.

mariage [maʀjaʒ] nm (union, état, fig) marriage; (noce) wedding; ~ civil/religieux registry office (Brit) ou civil/church wedding.

marié, e [maʀje] a married // nm/f (bride)groom/bride; les ~s the bride and groom; les (jeunes) ~s the newly-weds.

marier [maʀje] vt to marry; (fig) to blend; se ~ (avec) to marry.

marin, e [maʀɛ̃, -in] a sea cpd, marine // nm sailor // nf navy; ~e de guerre navy; ~e marchande merchant navy.

marine [maʀin] af, nf voir marin // a inv navy (blue) // nm (MIL) marine.

marionnette [maʀjɔnɛt] nf puppet.

maritime [maʀitim] a sea cpd, maritime.

mark [maʀk] nm mark.

marmelade [maʀməlad] nf stewed fruit, compote; ~ d'oranges marmalade.

marmite [maʀmit] nf (cooking-)pot.

marmonner [maʀmɔne] vt, vi to mumble, mutter.

marmotter [maʀmɔte] vt to mumble.

Maroc [maʀɔk] nm: le ~ Morocco; **marocain, e** a, nm/f Moroccan.

maroquinerie [maʀɔkinʀi] nf leather craft; fine leather goods pl.

marquant, e [maʀkɑ̃, -ɑ̃t] a outstanding.

marque [maʀk(ə)] nf mark; (SPORT, JEU: décompte des points) score; (COMM: de produits) brand; make; (: de disques) label; de ~ a (COMM) brand-name cpd; proprietary; (fig) high-class; distinguished; ~ déposée registered trademark; ~ de fabrique trademark.

marquer [maʀke] vt to mark; (inscrire) to write down; (bétail) to brand; (SPORT: but etc) to score; (: joueur) to mark; (accentuer: taille etc) to emphasize; (manifester: refus, intérêt) to show // vi (événement, personnalité) to stand out, be outstanding; (SPORT) to score; ~ les points (tenir la marque) to keep the score.

marqueterie [maʀkətʀi] nf inlaid work, marquetry.

marquis, e [maʀki, -iz] nm/f marquis ou marquess/marchioness // nf (auvent) glass canopy ou awning.

marraine [maʀɛn] nf godmother.

marrant, e [maʀɑ̃, -ɑ̃t] a (fam) funny.

marre [maʀ] ad (fam): en avoir ~ de to be fed up with.

marrer [maʀe]: se ~ vi (fam) to have a (good) laugh.

marron [maʀɔ̃] nm (fruit) chestnut // a inv brown; **marronnier** nm chestnut (tree).

mars [maʀs] nm March.

marsouin [maʀswɛ̃] nm porpoise.

marteau, x [maʀto] nm hammer; (de porte) knocker; ~-piqueur nm pneumatic drill.

marteler [maʀtəle] vt to hammer.

martien, ne [maʀsjɛ̃, -jɛn] a Martian, of ou from Mars.

martinet [maʀtinɛ] nm (fouet) small whip; (ZOOL) swift.

martyr, e [maʀtiʀ] nm/f martyr.

martyre [maʀtiʀ] nm martyrdom; (fig: sens affaibli) agony, torture.

martyriser [maʀtiʀize] *vt* (*REL*) to martyr; (*fig*) to bully; (*enfant*) to batter, beat.

marxiste [maʀksist(ə)] *a, nm/f* Marxist.

masculin, e [maskylɛ̃, -in] *a* masculine; (*sexe, population*) male; (*équipe, vêtements*) men's; (*viril*) manly // *nm* masculine.

masque [mask(ə)] *nm* mask.

masquer [maske] *vt* (*cacher: paysage, porte*) to hide, conceal; (*dissimuler: vérité, projet*) to mask, obscure.

massacre [masakʀ(ə)] *nm* massacre, slaughter.

massacrer [masakʀe] *vt* to massacre, slaughter; (*fig: texte etc*) to murder.

massage [masaʒ] *nm* massage.

masse [mas] *nf* mass; (*péj*): **la ~ the** masses *pl*; (*ÉLEC*) earth; (*maillet*) sledgehammer; **une ~ de** (*fam*) masses *ou* loads of; **en ~** *ad* (*en bloc*) in bulk; (*en foule*) mass cpd. // *a* (*exécutions, production*) mass cpd.

masser [mase] *vt* (*assembler*) to gather; (*pétrir*) to massage; **se ~** *vi* to gather; **masseur, euse** *nm/f* masseur/masseuse.

massif, ive [masif, -iv] *a* (*porte*) solid, massive; (*visage*) heavy, large; (*bois, or*) solid; (*dose*) massive; (*déportations etc*) mass cpd // *nm* (*montagneux*) massif; (*de fleurs*) clump, bank.

massue [masy] *nf* club, bludgeon.

mastic [mastik] *nm* (*pour vitres*) putty; (*pour fentes*) filler.

mastiquer [mastike] *vt* (*aliment*) to chew, masticate; (*fente*) to fill; (*vitre*) to putty.

mat, e [mat] *a* (*couleur, métal*) mat(t); (*bruit, son*) dull // *a inv* (*ÉCHECS*): **être ~ to be** checkmate.

mât [mɑ] *nm* (*NAVIG*) mast; (*poteau*) pole, post.

match [matʃ] *nm* match; **faire ~ nul** to draw; **~ aller** first leg; **~ retour** second leg, return match.

matelas [matlɑ] *nm* mattress; **~ pneumatique** air bed *ou* mattress.

matelassé, e [matlase] *a* padded; quilted.

matelot [matlo] *nm* sailor, seaman.

mater [mate] *vt* (*personne*) to bring to heel, subdue; (*révolte*) to put down.

matérialiste [mateʀjalist(ə)] *a* materialistic.

matériaux [mateʀjo] *nmpl* material(s).

matériel, le [mateʀjɛl] *a* material // *nm* equipment *q*; (*de camping etc*) gear *q*; **~ d'exploitation** (*COMM*) plant.

maternel, le [mateʀnɛl] *a* (*amour, geste*) motherly, maternal; (*grand-père, oncle*) maternal // *nf* (*aussi:* **école ~le**) (state) nursery school.

maternité [mateʀnite] *nf* (*établissement*) maternity hospital; (*état de mère*) motherhood, maternity; (*gros-*

sesse) pregnancy.

mathématique [matematik] *a* mathematical; **~s** *nfpl* (*science*) mathematics *sg*.

matière [matjɛʀ] *nf* (*PHYSIQUE*) matter; (*COMM, TECH*) material, matter *q*; (*fig: d'un livre etc*) subject matter, material; (*SCOL*) subject; **en ~ de** as regards; **~s grasses** fat content *sg*; **~s premières** raw materials.

matin [matɛ̃] *nm, ad* morning; **du ~ au soir** from morning till night; **de bon *ou* grand ~** early in the morning; **matinal, e, aux** *a* (*toilette, gymnastique*) morning cpd; (*de bonne heure*) early; **être matinal** (*personne*) to be up early; to be an early riser.

matinée [matine] *nf* morning; (*spectacle*) matinée.

matou [matu] *nm* tom(cat).

matraque [matʀak] *nf* club; (*de policier*) truncheon (*Brit*), billy (*US*).

matricule [matʀikyl] *nf* (*aussi: registre* **~**) roll, register // *nm* (*aussi:* **numéro ~**: *MIL*) regimental number; (*: ADMIN*) reference number.

matrimonial, e, aux [matʀimɔnjal, -o] *a* marital, marriage cpd.

maudire [modiʀ] *vt* to curse.

maudit, e [modi, -it] *a* (*fam: satané*) blasted, confounded.

maugréer [mogʀee] *vi* to grumble.

maussade [mosad] *a* sullen.

mauvais, e [mɔvɛ, -ɛz] *a* bad; (*faux*): **le ~ numéro/moment** the wrong number/ moment; (*méchant, malveillant*) malicious, spiteful // *ad*: **il fait ~** the weather is bad; **la mer est ~e** the sea is rough; **~ plaisant** hoaxer; **~e herbe** weed; **~e langue** gossip, scandalmonger (*Brit*); **~e passe** difficult situation; bad patch; **~e tête** rebellious *ou* headstrong customer.

maux [mo] *nmpl voir* **mal**.

maximum [maksimɔm] *a, nm* maximum; **au ~** *ad* (*le plus possible*) to the full; as much as one can; (*tout au plus*) at the (very) most *ou* maximum.

mayonnaise [majɔnɛz] *nf* mayonnaise.

mazout [mazut] *nm* (fuel) oil.

Me *abr de* **Maître**.

me, m' [m(ə)] *pronom* me; (*réfléchi*) myself.

mec [mɛk] *nm* (*fam*) bloke, guy.

mécanicien, ne [mekanisjɛ̃, -jɛn] *nm/f* mechanic; (*RAIL*) (train *ou* engine) driver.

mécanique [mekanik] *a* mechanical // *nf* (*science*) mechanics *sg*; (*technologie*) mechanical engineering; (*mécanisme*) mechanism; engineering; works *pl*; **ennui ~** engine trouble *q*.

mécanisme [mekanism(ə)] *nm* mechanism.

méchamment [meʃamɑ̃] *ad* nastily,

maliciously, spitefully.

méchanceté [meʃɑ̃ste] *nf* nastiness, maliciousness; nasty *ou* spiteful *ou* malicious remark (*ou* action).

méchant, e [meʃɑ̃, -ɑ̃t] *a* nasty, malicious, spiteful; (*enfant: pas sage*) naughty; (*animal*) vicious; (*avant le nom: valeur péjorative*) nasty; miserable; (: *intensive*) terrific.

mèche [mɛʃ] *nf* (*de lampe, bougie*) wick; (*d'un explosif*) fuse; (*de vilebrequin, perceuse*) bit; (*de cheveux*) lock; de ~ avec in league with.

mécompte [mekɔ̃t] *nm* miscalculation; (*déception*) disappointment.

méconnaissable [mekɔnɛsabl(ə)] *a* unrecognizable.

méconnaître [mekɔnɛtʀ(ə)] *vt* (*ignorer*) to be unaware of; (*mésestimer*) to misjudge.

mécontent, e [mekɔ̃tɑ̃, -ɑ̃t] *a*: ~ (de) discontented *ou* dissatisfied *ou* displeased (with); (*contrarié*) annoyed (at); **mécontentement** *nm* dissatisfaction, discontent, displeasure; annoyance.

médaille [medaj] *nf* medal.

médaillon [medajɔ̃] *nm* (*portrait*) medallion; (*bijou*) locket.

médecin [medsɛ̃] *nm* doctor; ~ légiste forensic surgeon.

médecine [medsin] *nf* medicine; ~ légale forensic medicine.

média [medja] *nmpl*: les ~ the media.

médiatique [medjatik] *a* media *cpd*.

médical, e, aux [medikal, -o] *a* medical.

médicament [medikamɑ̃] *nm* medicine, drug.

médiéval, e, aux [medjeval, -o] *a* medieval.

médiocre [medjɔkʀ(ə)] *a* mediocre, poor.

médire [mediʀ] *vi*: ~ de to speak ill of; **médisance** *nf* scandalmongering (*Brit*); piece of scandal *ou* of malicious gossip.

méditer [medite] *vt* (*approfondir*) to meditate on, ponder (over); (*combiner*) to meditate // *vi* to meditate.

Méditerranée [mediteʀane] *nf*: la (mer) ~ the Mediterranean (Sea); **méditerranéen, ne** *a, nm/f* Mediterranean.

méduse [medyz] *nf* jellyfish.

meeting [mitiŋ] *nm* (*POL, SPORT*) rally.

méfait [mefɛ] *nm* (*faute*) misdemeanour, wrongdoing; ~s *nmpl* (*ravages*) ravages, damage *sg*.

méfiance [mefjɑ̃s] *nf* mistrust, distrust.

méfiant, e [mefjɑ̃, -ɑ̃t] *a* mistrustful, distrustful.

méfier [mefje]: se ~ *vi* to be wary; to be careful; se ~ de to mistrust, distrust, be wary of; (*faire attention*) to be careful about.

mégarde [megaʀd(ə)] *nf*: par ~ accidentally; by mistake.

mégère [meʒɛʀ] *nf* shrew.

mégot [mego] *nm* cigarette end.

meilleur, e [mɛjœʀ] *a, ad* better; (*valeur superlative*) best // *nm*: le ~ (celui qui ...) the best (one); (ce qui ...) the best // *nf*: la ~e the best (one); le ~ des deux the better of the two; de ~e heure earlier; ~ marché cheaper.

mélancolie [melɑ̃kɔli] *nf* melancholy, gloom; **mélancolique** *a* melancholic, melancholy.

mélange [melɑ̃ʒ] *nm* mixture.

mélanger [melɑ̃ʒe] *vt* (*substances*) to mix; (*vins, couleurs*) to blend; (*mettre en désordre*) to mix up, muddle (up).

mélasse [melas] *nf* treacle, molasses *sg*.

mêlée [mele] *nf* mêlée, scramble; (*RUGBY*) scrum(mage).

mêler [mele] *vt* (*substances, odeurs, races*) to mix; (*embrouiller*) to muddle (up), mix up; se ~ *vi* to mix; to mingle; se ~ à (*suj: personne*) to join; to mix with; (: *odeurs etc*) to mingle with; se ~ de (*suj: personne*) to meddle with, interfere in; ~ qn à (*affaire*) to get sb mixed up *ou* involved in.

mélodie [melɔdi] *nf* melody.

melon [məlɔ̃] *nm* (*BOT*) (honeydew) melon; (*aussi*: **chapeau ~**) bowler (hat).

membre [mɑ̃bʀ(ə)] *nm* (*ANAT*) limb; (*personne, pays, élément*) member // *a* member.

mémé [meme] *nf* (*fam*) granny.

même [mɛm] ♦ *a* **1** (*avant le nom*) same; en ~ temps at the same time

2 (*après le nom: renforcement*): il est la loyauté ~ he is loyalty itself; ce sont ses paroles/celles-là ~s they are his very words/the very ones

♦ *pronom*: le(la) ~ the same one

♦ *ad* **1** (*renforcement*): il n'a ~ pas pleuré he didn't even cry; ~ lui l'a dit even HE said it; ici ~ at this very place

2: à ~: à ~ la bouteille straight from the bottle; à ~ la peau next to the skin; être à ~ de faire to be in a position to do, be able to do

3: de ~: faire de ~ to do likewise; lui de ~ so does (*ou* did *ou* is) he; de ~ que just as; il en va de ~ pour the same goes for.

mémento [memɛ̃to] *nm* (*agenda*) appointments diary; (*ouvrage*) summary.

mémoire [memwaʀ] *nf* memory // *nm* (*ADMIN, JUR*) memorandum (pl à) s); (*SCOL*) dissertation, paper; ~s *nmpl* memoirs; à la ~ de to the *ou* in memory of; pour ~ *ad* for the record; de ~ *ad* from memory; ~ morte/vive (*INFORM*) ROM/RAM.

menace [mənas] *nf* threat.

menacer [mənase] *vt* to threaten.

ménage [menaʒ] *nm* (*travail*) housekeeping, housework; (*couple*) (married) couple; (*famille*, ADMIN) household; faire le ~ to do the housework.

ménagement [menaʒmɑ̃] nm care and attention; ~s nmpl (*égards*) consideration sg, attention sg.

ménager [menaʒe] vt (*traiter*) to handle with tact; to treat considerately; (*utiliser*) to use sparingly; to use with care; (*prendre soin de*) to take (great) care of, look after; (*organiser*) to arrange; (*installer*) to put in; to make; ~ qch à qn (*réserver*) to have sth in store for sb.

ménager, ère [menaʒe, -ɛʀ] a household cpd, domestic // nf housewife (pl wives).

mendiant, e [mɑ̃djɑ̃, -ɑ̃t] nm/f beggar.

mendier [mɑ̃dje] vi to beg // vt to beg (for).

menées [məne] nfpl intrigues.

mener [məne] vt to lead; (*enquête*) to conduct; (*affaires*) to manage // vi: ~ (à la marque) to lead, be in the lead; ~ à/ dans (*emmener*) to take to/into; ~ qch à terme ou à bien to see sth through (to a successful conclusion), complete sth successfully.

meneur, euse [mənœʀ, -øz] nm/f leader; (*péj*) agitator; ~ de jeu host, quizmaster.

méningite [menɛ̃ʒit] nf meningitis q.

ménopause [menɔpoz] nf menopause.

menottes [mənɔt] nfpl handcuffs.

mensonge [mɑ̃sɔ̃ʒ] nm lie; lying q; **mensonger, ère** a false.

mensualité [mɑ̃sɥalite] nf monthly payment; monthly salary.

mensuel, le [mɑ̃sɥɛl] a monthly.

mensurations [mɑ̃syʀasjɔ̃] nfpl measurements.

mentalité [mɑ̃talite] nf mentality.

menteur, euse [mɑ̃tœʀ, -øz] nm/f liar.

menthe [mɑ̃t] nf mint.

mention [mɑ̃sjɔ̃] nf (*note*) note, comment; (SCOL): ~ bien etc ≈ grade B etc (*ou* upper 2nd class etc) pass (*Brit*), ≈ pass with (high) honors (US); **mentionner** vt to mention.

mentir [mɑ̃tiʀ] vi to lie; to be lying.

menton [mɑ̃tɔ̃] nm chin.

menu, e [məny] a slim, slight; tiny; (*frais, difficulté*) minor // ad (*couper, hacher*) very fine // nm menu; **par le ~** (*raconter*) in minute detail; **~e monnaie** small change.

menuiserie [mənɥizʀi] nf (*travail*) joinery, carpentry; woodwork; (*local*) joiner's workshop; (*ouvrage*) woodwork q.

menuisier [mənɥizje] nm joiner, carpenter.

méprendre [mepʀɑ̃dʀ(ə)]: se ~ vi: se ~ sur to be mistaken (about).

mépris [mepʀi] nm (*dédain*) contempt, scorn; (*indifférence*): le ~ de contempt *ou* disregard for; au ~ de regardless of, in defiance of.

méprisable [mepʀizabl(ə)] a contemptible, despicable.

méprise [mepʀiz] nf mistake, error; misunderstanding.

mépriser [mepʀize] vt to scorn, despise; (*gloire, danger*) to scorn, spurn.

mer [mɛʀ] nf sea; (*marée*) tide; **en ~** at sea; **prendre la ~** to put out to sea; **en haute** *ou* **pleine ~** off shore, on the open sea; **la ~ du Nord/Rouge** the North/Red Sea.

mercantile [mɛʀkɑ̃til] a (*péj*) mercenary.

mercenaire [mɛʀsənɛʀ] nm mercenary, hired soldier.

mercerie [mɛʀsəʀi] nf haberdashery (*Brit*); notions (US); haberdasher's shop (*Brit*), notions store (US).

merci [mɛʀsi] excl thank you // nf: à la ~ de qn/qch at sb's mercy/the mercy of sth; ~ de thank you for; **sans ~** merciless(ly).

mercredi [mɛʀkʀədi] nm Wednesday.

mercure [mɛʀkyʀ] nm mercury.

merde [mɛʀd(ə)] (*fam!*) nf shit (!) // excl (*bloody*) hell (!).

mère [mɛʀ] nf mother; ~ **célibataire** unmarried mother.

méridional, e, aux [meʀidjɔnal, -o] a southern // nm/f Southerner.

meringue [məʀɛ̃g] nf meringue.

mérite [meʀit] nm merit; **le ~ (de ceci) lui revient** the credit (for this) is his.

mériter [meʀite] vt to deserve.

merlan [mɛʀlɑ̃] nm whiting.

merle [mɛʀl(ə)] nm blackbird.

merveille [mɛʀvɛj] nf marvel, wonder; **faire ~** to work wonders; **à ~** perfectly, wonderfully.

merveilleux, euse [mɛʀvɛjø, -øz] a marvellous, wonderful.

mes [me] dét voir **mon**.

mésange [mezɑ̃ʒ] nf tit(mouse) (pl mice).

mésaventure [mezavɑ̃tyʀ] nf misadventure, misfortune.

Mesdames voir **Madame**.

Mesdemoiselles voir **Mademoiselle**.

mésentente [mezɑ̃tɑ̃t] nf dissension, disagreement.

mesquin, e [mɛskɛ̃, -in] a mean, petty.

message [mesaʒ] nm message; **messager, ère** nm/f messenger.

messe [mes] nf mass; **aller à la ~** to go to mass; **~ de minuit** midnight mass.

Messieurs [mesjø] nmpl voir **Monsieur**.

mesure [məzyʀ] nf (*évaluation, dimension*) measurement; (*étalon, récipient, contenu*) measure; (MUS: *cadence*) time, tempo; (: *division*) bar; (*retenue*) moderation; (*disposition*) measure, step; **sur ~** (*costume*) made-to-measure; **à la ~ de** (*fig*) worthy of; on the same scale as; **dans la ~ où** insofar as, inasmuch as; **à**

~ que as; être en ~ de to be in a position to.

mesurer [məzyʀe] *vt* to measure; *(juger)* to weigh up, assess; *(limiter)* to limit, ration; *(modérer)* to moderate; se ~ avec to have a confrontation with; to tackle; il mesure 1 m 80 he's 1 m 80 tall.

met *vb voir* **mettre**.

métal, aux [metal, -o] *nm* metal; ~**lique** *a* metallic.

météo [meteo] *nf* weather report; ≈ Met Office *(Brit)*, ≈ National Weather Service *(US)*.

météorologie [meteɔrɔlɔʒi] *nf* meteorology.

méthode [metɔd] *nf* method; *(livre, ouvrage)* manual, tutor.

métier [metje] *nm (profession: gén)* job; *(: manuel)* trade; *(artisanal)* craft; *(technique, expérience)* (acquired) skill *ou* technique; *(aussi: ~ à tisser)* (weaving) loom.

métis, se [metis] *a, nm/f* half-caste, half-breed.

métisser [metise] *vt* to cross.

métrage [metraʒ] *nm (de tissu)* length; ≈ yardage; *(CINÉMA)* footage, length; **long/moyen/court** ~ full-length/medium-length/short film.

mètre [metr(ə)] *nm* metre; *(règle)* (metre) rule; *(ruban)* tape measure; **métrique** *a* metric.

métro [metro] *nm* underground *(Brit)*, subway.

métropole [metrɔpɔl] *nf (capitale)* metropolis; *(pays)* home country.

mets [mɛ] *nm* dish.

metteur [metœr] *nm:* ~ **en scène** *(THÉÂTRE)* producer; *(CINÉMA)* director; ~ **en ondes** producer.

mettre [metr(ə)] *vt* **1** *(placer)* to put; ~ **en bouteille/en sac** to bottle/put in bags *ou* sacks

2 *(vêtements: revêtir)* to put on; *(: porter)* to wear; **mets ton gilet** put your cardigan on; **je ne mets plus mon manteau** I no longer wear my coat

3 *(faire fonctionner: chauffage, électricité)* to put on; *(: réveil, minuteur)* to set; *(installer: gaz, eau)* to put in, lay on; ~ **en marche** to start up

4 *(consacrer):* ~ **du temps à faire qch** to take time to do sth *ou* over sth

5 *(noter, écrire)* to say, put (down); **qu'est-ce qu'il a mis sur la carte?** what did he say *ou* write on the card?; **mettez au pluriel** ... put ... into the plural

6 *(supposer):* **mettons que** ... let's suppose *ou* say that ...

7: **y** ~ **du sien** to pull one's weight

se mettre *vi* **1** *(se placer):* **vous pouvez vous** ~ **là** you can sit *(ou* stand) there; **où ça se met?** where does it go?; **se** ~ **au lit** to get into bed; **se** ~ **au piano** to sit down at the piano; **se** ~ **de l'encre**

sur les doigts to get ink on one's fingers

2 *(s'habiller):* **se** ~ **en maillot de bain** to get into *ou* put on a swimsuit; **n'avoir rien à se** ~ to have nothing to wear

3: **se** ~ **à** to begin, start; **se** ~ **à faire** to begin *ou* start doing *ou* to do; **se** ~ **au piano** to start learning the piano; **se** ~ **au travail/à l'étude** to get down to work/ one's studies.

meuble [mœbl(ə)] *nm* piece of furniture; furniture *q // a (terre)* loose, friable; **meublé** *nm* furnished flatlet *(Brit) ou* room; **meubler** *vt* to furnish; *(fig)*: **meubler qch (de)** to fill sth (with).

meugler [møgle] *vi* to low, moo.

meule [møl] *nf (à broyer)* millstone; *(à aiguiser)* grindstone; *(de foin, blé)* stack; *(de fromage)* round.

meunier, ière [mønje, -jɛr] *nm* miller *// nf* miller's wife.

meure *etc vb voir* **mourir**.

meurtre [mœrtr(ə)] *nm* murder; **meurtrier, ière** *a (arme etc)* deadly; *(fureur, instincts)* murderous *// nm/f* murderer/ eress *// nf (ouverture)* loophole.

meurtrir [mœrtrir] *vt* to bruise; *(fig)* to wound; **meurtrissure** *nf* bruise; *(fig)* scar.

meus *etc vb voir* **mouvoir**.

meute [møt] *nf* pack.

Mexico [mɛksiko] *n* Mexico City.

Mexique [mɛksik] *nm:* **le** ~ Mexico.

MF *sigle f voir* **modulation**.

Mgr *abr de* **Monseigneur**.

mi [mi] *nm (MUS)* E; *(en chantant la gamme)* mi.

mi... [mi] *préfixe* half(-); mid-; **à la** ~-**janvier** in mid-January; **à** ~-**jambes/ -corps** up to the knees/waist; **à** ~-**hauteur/-pente** halfway up *ou* down/ up *ou* down the hill.

miauler [mjole] *vi* to mew.

miche [miʃ] *nf* round *ou* cob loaf.

mi-chemin [miʃmɛ̃]: **à** ~ *ad* halfway, midway.

mi-clos, e [miklo, -kloz] *a* half-closed.

micro [mikro] *nm* mike, microphone; *(INFORM)* micro.

microbe [mikrɔb] *nm* germ, microbe.

micro-onde [mikrɔ̃d] *nf:* **four à** ~s microwave oven.

micro-ordinateur [mikrɔɔrdinatœr] *nm* microcomputer.

microscope [mikrɔskɔp] *nm* microscope.

midi [midi] *nm* midday, noon; *(moment du déjeuner)* lunchtime; **à** ~ at 12 (o'clock) *ou* midday *ou* noon; *(sud)* south; **en plein** ~ (right) in the middle of the day; facing south; **le M~** the South (of France), the Midi.

mie [mi] *nf* crumb (of the loaf).

miel [mjɛl] *nm* honey.

mien, ne [mjɛ̃, mjɛn] *pronom:* **le(la)** ~(ne), **les** ~s mine; **les** ~s my family.

miette [mjɛt] *nf* (*de pain, gâteau*) crumb; (*fig: de la conversation etc*) scrap; **en ~s** (*fig*) in pieces *ou* bits.

mieux [mjø] ♦ *ad* **1** (*d'une meilleure fa-çon*): **~ (que)** better (than); **elle travaille/mange ~** she works/eats better; **elle va ~** she is better

2 (*de la meilleure façon*) best; **ce que je sais le ~** what I know best; **les livres les ~ faits** the best made books

3: **de ~ en ~** better and better

♦ *a* **1** (*plus à l'aise, en meilleure forme*) better; **se sentir ~** to feel better

2 (*plus satisfaisant*) better; **c'est ~ ainsi** it's better like this; **c'est le ~ des deux** it's the better of the two; **le(la) ~, les ~** the best; **demandez-lui, c'est le ~** ask him, it's the best thing

3 (*plus joli*) better-looking

4: **au ~** at best; **au ~ avec** on the best of terms with; **pour le ~** for the best

♦ *nm* **1** (*progrès*) improvement

2: **de mon/ton ~** as best I/you can (*ou* could); **faire de son ~** to do one's best.

mièvre [mjɛvʀ(ə)] *a* mawkish (*Brit*), sickly sentimental.

mignon, ne [miɲɔ̃, -ɔn] *a* sweet, cute.

migraine [migʀɛn] *nf* headache; mi-graine.

mijoter [miʒɔte] *vt* to simmer; (*préparer avec soin*) to cook lovingly; (*affaire, projet*) to plot, cook up // *vi* to simmer.

mil [mil] *num* = **mille**.

milieu, x [miljø] *nm* (*centre*) middle; (*fig*) middle course *ou* way; happy me-dium; (*BIO, GÉO*) environment; (*entourage social*) milieu; background; circle; (*pègre*): **le ~** the underworld; **au ~ de** in the middle of; **au beau *ou* en plein ~ (de)** right in the middle (of).

militaire [militɛʀ] *a* military, army *cpd* // *nm* serviceman.

militant, e [militɑ̃, -ɑ̃t] *a, nm/f* militant.

militer [milite] *vi* to be a militant; **~ pour/contre** (*suj: faits, raisons etc*) to militate in favour of/against.

mille [mil] *num a ou* one thousand // *nm* (*mesure*): **~ (marin)** nautical mile; **met-tre dans le ~** to hit the bull's-eye; to be bang on target; **~feuille** *nm* cream *ou* vanilla slice; **millénaire** *nm* millennium // *a* thousand-year-old; (*fig*) ancient; **~-pattes** *nm inv* centipede.

millésime [milezim] *nm* year; **mil-lésimé, e** *a* vintage *cpd*.

millet [mijɛ] *nm* millet.

milliard [miljaʀ] *nm* milliard, thousand million (*Brit*), billion (*US*); **milliardaire** *nm/f* multimillionaire (*Brit*), billionaire (*US*).

millier [milje] *nm* thousand; **un ~ (de)** a thousand or so, about a thousand; **par ~s** in (their) thousands, by the thousand.

milligramme [miligʀam] *nm* milli-gramme.

millimètre [milimɛtʀ(ə)] *nm* millimetre.

million [miljɔ̃] *nm* million; **deux ~s de** two million; **millionnaire** *nm/f* million-aire.

mime [mim] *nm/f* (*acteur*) mime(r) // *nm* (*art*) mime, miming.

mimer [mime] *vt* to mime; (*singer*) to mimic, take off.

mimique [mimik] *nf* (*funny*) face; (*signes*) gesticulations *pl*, sign language *q*.

minable [minabl(ə)] *a* shabby(-looking); pathetic.

mince [mɛ̃s] *a* thin; (*personne, taille*) slim, slender; (*fig: profit, connaissances*) slight, small, weak // *excl*: **~ alors!** drat it!, darn it! (*US*); **minceur** *nf* thinness; slimness, slenderness.

mine [min] *nf* (*physionomie*) expression, look; (*extérieur*) exterior, appearance; (*de crayon*) lead; (*gisement, ex-ploitation, explosif, fig*) mine; **avoir bonne ~** (*personne*) to look well; (*ironi-que*) to look an utter idiot; **avoir mauvaise ~** to look unwell *ou* poorly; **faire ~ de faire** to make a pretence of doing; to make as if to do; **~ de rien** *ad* with a casual air; although you wouldn't think so.

miner [mine] *vt* (*saper*) to undermine, erode; (*MIL*) to mine.

minerai [minʀɛ] *nm* ore.

minéral, e, aux [mineʀal, -o] *a, nm* mineral.

minéralogique [mineʀalɔʒik] *a*: **numéro ~** registration number.

minet, te [minɛ, -ɛt] *nm/f* (*chat*) pussy-cat; (*péj*) young trendy.

mineur, e [minœʀ] *a* minor // *nm/f* (*JUR*) minor, person under age // *nm* (*travailleur*) miner.

miniature [minjatyʀ] *a, nf* miniature.

minibus [minibys] *nm* minibus.

mini-cassette [minikasɛt] *nf* cassette (recorder).

minier, ière [minje, -jɛʀ] *a* mining.

mini-jupe [miniʒyp] *nf* mini-skirt.

minime [minim] *a* minor, minimal.

minimiser [minimize] *vt* to minimize; (*fig*) to play down.

minimum [minimɔm] *a, nm* minimum; **au ~** (*au moins*) at the very least.

ministère [ministɛʀ] *nm* (*aussi REL*) ministry; (*cabinet*) government; **~ pu-blic** (*JUR*) Prosecution, State Prosecutor; **ministériel, le** *a* cabinet *cpd*; minis-terial.

ministre [ministʀ(ə)] *nm* (*aussi REL*) minister; **~ d'État** senior minister.

Minitel [minitɛl] *nm* ® videotext terminal and service.

minorité [minɔʀite] *nf* minority; **être en ~** to be in the *ou* a minority; **mettre en ~** (*POL*) to defeat.

minoterie [minɔtʀi] *nf* flour-mill.

minuit [minɥi] *nm* midnight.

minuscule [minyskyl] *a* minute, tiny // *nf*: (lettre) ~ small letter.

minute [minyt] *nf* minute; (JUR: original) minute, draft; **à la** ~ (just) this instant; there and then; **minuter** *vt* to time; **minuterie** *nf* time switch.

minutieux, euse [minysjø, -øz] *a* meticulous; minutely detailed.

mirabelle [miʀabɛl] *nf* (cherry) plum.

miracle [miʀakl(ə)] *nm* miracle.

mirage [miʀaʒ] *nm* mirage.

mire [miʀ] *nf*: **point de** ~ target; (fig) focal point; **ligne de** ~ line of sight.

miroir [miʀwaʀ] *nm* mirror.

miroiter [miʀwate] *vi* to sparkle, shimmer; **faire** ~ **qch à qn** to paint sth in glowing colours for sb, dangle sth in front of sb's eyes.

mis, e [mi, miz] *pp de* **mettre** // *a*: **bien** ~ well dressed // (argent: au jeu) stake; (tenue) clothing; attire; **être de** ~e to be acceptable *ou* in season; ~e à **feu** blast-off; ~e **de fonds** capital outlay; ~e **en plis** set; ~e **au point** (fig) clarification (voir aussi **point**); ~e **en scène** production.

miser [mize] *vt* (enjeu) to stake, bet; ~ **sur** *vt* (cheval, numéro) to bet on; (fig) to bank *ou* count on.

misérable [mizeʀabl(ə)] *a* (lamentable, malheureux) pitiful, wretched; (pauvre) poverty-stricken; (insignifiant, mesquin) miserable // *nm/f* wretch; (miséreux) poor wretch.

misère [mizɛʀ] *nf* (extreme) poverty, destitution; ~s *nfpl* woes, miseries; little troubles; **salaire de** ~ starvation wage.

miséricorde [mizeʀikɔʀd(ə)] *nf* mercy, forgiveness.

missile [misil] *nm* missile.

mission [misjɔ̃] *nf* mission; **partir en** ~ (ADMIN, POL) to go on an assignment; **missionnaire** *nm/f* missionary.

mit *vb voir* **mettre**.

mité, e [mite] *a* moth-eaten.

mi-temps [mitɑ̃] *nf inv* (SPORT: période) half (pl halves); (: pause) half-time; **à** ~ *a*, *ad* part-time.

mitigé, e [mitiʒe] *a* lukewarm; mixed.

mitonner [mitɔne] *vt* to cook with loving care; (fig) to cook up quietly.

mitoyen, ne [mitwajɛ̃, -ɛn] *a* common, party *cpd*.

mitrailler [mitʀaje] *vt* to machine-gun; (fig: photographier) to take shot after shot of; to pelt, bombard; **mitraillette** *nf* submachine gun; **mitrailleuse** *nf* machine gun.

mi-voix [mivwa]: **à** ~ *ad* in a low *ou* hushed voice.

mixage [miksaʒ] *nm* (CINÉMA) (sound) mixing.

mixer [miksœʀ] *nm* (food) mixer.

mixte [mikst(ə)] *a* (gén) mixed; (SCOL) mixed, coeducational; **à usage** ~ dual-purpose.

mixture [mikstyʀ] *nf* mixture; (fig) concoction.

MLF *sigle m* = *Mouvement de libération de la femme*.

Mlle, *pl* **Mlles** *abr de* **Mademoiselle**.

MM *abr de* **Messieurs**.

Mme, *pl* **Mmes** *abr de* **Madame**.

Mo *abr de* **métro**.

mobile [mɔbil] *a* mobile; (pièce de machine) moving; (élément de meuble etc) movable // *nm* (motif) motive; (œuvre d'art) mobile.

mobilier, ière [mɔbilje, -jɛʀ] *a* (JUR) personal // *nm* furniture.

mobiliser [mɔbilize] *vt* (MIL, gén) to mobilize.

moche [mɔʃ] *a* (fam) ugly; rotten.

modalité [mɔdalite] *nf* form, mode; ~s *nfpl* (d'un accord etc) clauses, terms.

mode [mɔd] *nf* fashion // *nm* (manière) form, mode; **à la** ~ fashionable, in fashion; ~ **d'emploi** directions *pl* (for use).

modèle [mɔdɛl] *a*, *nm* model; (qui pose: de peintre) sitter; ~ **déposé** registered design; ~ **réduit** small-scale model.

modeler [mɔdle] *vt* (ART) to model, mould; (suj: vêtement, érosion) to mould, shape.

modem [mɔdɛm] *nm* modem.

modéré, e [mɔdeʀe] *a*, *nm/f* moderate.

modérer [mɔdeʀe] *vt* to moderate; **se** ~ *vi* to restrain o.s.

moderne [mɔdɛʀn(ə)] *a* modern // *nm* modern style; modern furniture; **moderniser** *vt* to modernize.

modeste [mɔdɛst(ə)] *a* modest; **modestie** *nf* modesty.

modifier [mɔdifje] *vt* to modify, alter; **se** ~ *vi* to alter.

modique [mɔdik] *a* modest.

modiste [mɔdist(ə)] *nf* milliner.

modulation [mɔdylasjɔ̃] *nf*: ~ **de fréquence** (**FM** *ou* **MF**) frequency modulation.

module [mɔdyl] *nm* module.

moelle [mwal] *nf* marrow.

moelleux, euse [mwalø, -øz] *a* soft; (au goût, à l'ouie) mellow.

moellon [mwalɔ̃] *nm* rubble stone.

mœurs [mœʀ] *nfpl* (conduite) morals; (manières) manners; (pratiques sociales, mode de vie) habits.

mohair [mɔɛʀ] *nm* mohair.

moi [mwa] *pronom* me; (emphatique): ~, **je ...** for my part, I ..., I myself ....

moignon [mwaɲɔ̃] *nm* stump.

moi-même [mwamɛm] *pronom* myself; (emphatique) I myself.

moindre [mwɛ̃dʀ(ə)] *a* lesser; lower; **le(la)** ~, **les** ~s the least, the slightest.

moine [mwan] *nm* monk, friar.

moineau, x [mwano] *nm* sparrow.

moins [mwɛ̃] ♦ ad **1** (comparatif): ~ (que) less (than); ~ **grand que** less tall than, not as tall as; ~ **je travaille, mieux je me porte** the less I work, the better I feel

2 (superlatif): **le ~** (the) least; **c'est ce que j'aime le ~** it's what I like (the) least; **le(la) ~ doué(e)** the least gifted; **au ~, du ~** at least; **pour le ~** at the very least

3: ~ **de** (quantité) less (than); (nombre) fewer (than); ~ **de sable/d'eau** less sand/water; ~ **de livres/gens** fewer books/people; ~ **de 2 ans** less than 2 years; ~ **de midi** not yet midday

4: **de ~, en ~**: 100 F/3 jours de ~ 100 F/3 days less; **3 livres en ~** 3 books fewer; **3 books too few; de l'argent en ~** less money; **le soleil en ~** but for the sun, minus the sun; **de ~ en ~** less and less

5: **à ~ de, à ~ que** unless; **à ~ de faire** unless we do (ou he does etc); **à ~ que tu ne fasses** unless you do; **à ~ d'un accident** barring any accident

♦ prép: 4 ~ 2 4 minus 2; **il est ~ 5** it's 5 to; **il fait ~ 5** it's 5 (degrees) below (freezing), it's minus 5.

mois [mwa] nm month; ~ **double** (COMM) extra month's salary.

moisi [mwazi] nm mould, mildew; **odeur de ~** musty smell.

moisir [mwaziʀ] vi to go mouldy; (fig) to rot; to hang about.

moisissure [mwazisyʀ] nf mould q.

moisson [mwasɔ̃] nf harvest; **moissonner** vt to harvest, reap; **moissonneuse** nf (machine) harvester.

moite [mwat] a sweaty, sticky.

moitié [mwatje] nf half (pl halves); **la ~** half; **la ~ de** half (of); **la ~ du temps/ des gens** half the time/the people; **à la ~ de** halfway through; **à ~** half (avant le verbe); half- (avant l'adjectif); **de ~** by half; ~ ~ half-and-half.

mol [mɔl] a voir **mou**.

molaire [mɔlɛʀ] nf molar.

molester [mɔleste] vt to manhandle, maul (about).

molette [mɔlɛt] nf toothed ou cutting wheel.

molle [mɔl] af voir **mou**; ~**ment** ad softly; (péj) sluggishly; (protester) feebly.

mollet [mɔlɛ] nm calf (pl calves) // am: **œuf ~** soft-boiled egg.

molletonné, e [mɔltɔne] a fleece-lined.

mollir [mɔliʀ] vi to give way; to relent; to go soft.

môme [mom] nm/f (fam: enfant) brat; (: fille) chick.

moment [mɔmɑ̃] nm moment; **ce n'est pas le ~** this is not the (right) time; **à un certain ~** at some point; **à un ~ donné** at a certain point; **pour un bon ~** for a good while; **pour le ~** for the moment, for the time being; **au ~ de** at the time of; **au ~ où** as; at a time when; **à tout ~** at any time ou moment; constantly, continually; **en ce ~** at the moment; at present; **sur le ~** at the time; **par ~s** now and then, at times; **du ~ où** ou **que** seeing that, since; **momentané, e** a temporary, momentary.

momie [mɔmi] nf mummy.

mon [mɔ̃], **ma** [ma], pl **mes** [me] dét my.

Monaco [mɔnako] nm: **le ~** Monaco.

monarchie [mɔnaʀʃi] nf monarchy.

monastère [mɔnastɛʀ] nm monastery.

monceau, x [mɔ̃so] nm heap.

mondain, e [mɔ̃dɛ̃, -ɛn] a society cpd; social; fashionable // nf: **la M~e, la police ~e** ≈ the vice squad.

monde [mɔ̃d] nm world; (haute société): **le ~** (high) society; (milieu): **être du même ~** to move in the same circles; (gens): **il y a du ~** (beaucoup de gens) there are a lot of people; (quelques personnes) there are some people; **beaucoup/peu de ~** many/few people; **le meilleur** etc **du ~** the best etc in the world ou on earth; **mettre au ~** to bring into the world; **pas le moins du ~** not in the least; **se faire un ~ de qch** to make a great deal of fuss about sth; **mondial, e, aux** a (population) world cpd; (influence) world-wide; **mondiale-ment** ad throughout the world.

monégasque [mɔnegask(ə)] a Monegasque, of ou from Monaco.

monétaire [mɔnetɛʀ] a monetary.

moniteur, trice [mɔnitœʀ, -tʀis] nm/f (SPORT) instructor/instructress; (de colonie de vacances) supervisor // nm (écran) monitor.

monnaie [mɔnɛ] nf (pièce) coin; (ÉCON, gén: moyen d'échange) currency; (petites pièces): **avoir de la ~** to have (some) change; **faire de la ~** to get (some) change; **avoir/faire la ~ de 20 F** to have change of/get change for 20 F; **rendre à qn la ~** (sur 20 F) to give sb the change (out of ou from 20 F); **monnayer** vt to convert into cash; (talent) to capitalize on.

monologue [mɔnɔlɔg] nm monologue, soliloquy; **monologuer** vi to soliloquize.

monopole [mɔnɔpɔl] nm monopoly.

monotone [mɔnɔtɔn] a monotonous.

monseigneur [mɔ̃sɛɲœʀ] nm (archevêque, évêque) Your (ou His) Grace; (cardinal) Your (ou His) Eminence.

Monsieur [məsjø], pl **Messieurs** [mesjø] titre Mr ['mistə*] // nm (homme quelconque): **un/le m~** a/the gentleman; voir aussi **Madame**.

monstre [mɔ̃stʀ(ə)] nm monster // a: **un travail ~** a fantastic amount of work; an enormous job.

mont [mɔ̃] *nm*: par ~s et par vaux up hill and down dale; **le M~ Blanc** Mont Blanc.

montage [mɔ̃taʒ] *nm* putting up; mounting, setting; assembly; (*PHOTO*) photomontage; (*CINÉMA*) editing.

montagnard, e [mɔ̃taɲaʀ, -aʀd(ə)] *a* mountain *cpd* // *nm/f* mountain-dweller.

montagne [mɔ̃taɲ] *nf* (*cime*) mountain; (*région*): **la ~** the mountains *pl*; **~s russes** big dipper *sg*, switchback *sg*.

montagneux, euse [mɔ̃taɲø, -øz] *a* mountainous; hilly.

montant, e [mɔ̃tɑ̃, -ɑ̃t] *a* rising; (*robe, corsage*) high-necked // *nm* (*somme, total*) (sum) total, (total) amount; (*de fenêtre*) upright; (*de lit*) post.

mont-de-piété [mɔ̃dpjete] *nm* pawnshop.

monte-charge [mɔ̃tʃaʀʒ(ə)] *nm inv* goods lift, hoist.

montée [mɔ̃te] *nf* rising, rise; ascent, climb; (*chemin*) way up; (*côte*) hill; **au milieu de la ~** halfway up.

monter [mɔ̃te] *vt* (*escalier, côte*) to go (*ou* come) up; (*valise, paquet*) to take (*ou* bring) up; (*cheval*) to mount; (*étagère*) to raise; (*tente, échafaudage*) to put up; (*machine*) to assemble; (*bijou*) to mount, set; (*COUTURE*) to set in; to sew on; (*CINÉMA*) to edit; (*THÉÂTRE*) to put on, stage; (*société etc*) to set up // *vi* to go (*ou* come) up; (*avion etc*) to climb, go up; (*chemin, niveau, température*) to go up, rise; (*passager*) to get on; (*à cheval*): **~ bien/mal** to ride well/badly; **~ à pied** to walk up, go up on foot; **~ à bicyclette/en voiture** to cycle/drive up, go up by bicycle/by car; **~ dans le train/l'avion** to get into the train/plane, board the train/plane; **~ sur** to climb up onto; **~ à cheval** to get on *ou* mount a horse; **se ~ à** (*frais etc*) to add up to, come to.

monticule [mɔ̃tikyl] *nm* mound.

montre [mɔ̃tʀ(ə)] *nf* watch; **faire ~ de** to show, display; **contre la ~** (*SPORT*) against the clock; **~-bracelet** *nf* wrist watch.

montrer [mɔ̃tʀe] *vt* to show; **~ qch à qn** to show sb sth.

monture [mɔ̃tyʀ] *nf* (*bête*) mount; (*d'une bague*) setting; (*de lunettes*) frame.

monument [mɔnymɑ̃] *nm* monument; **~ aux morts** war memorial.

moquer [mɔke]: **se ~ de** *vt* to make fun of, laugh at; (*fam: se désintéresser de*) not to care about; (*tromper*): **se ~ de qn** to take sb for a ride.

moquette [mɔkɛt] *nf* fitted carpet.

moqueur, euse [mɔkœʀ, -øz] *a* mocking.

moral, e, aux [mɔʀal, -o] *a* moral // *nm* morale // *nf* (*conduite*) morals *pl*; (*règles*) moral code, ethic; (*valeurs*) moral standards *pl*, morality; (*science*) ethics *sg*, moral philosophy; (*conclusion: d'une fable etc*) moral; **avoir le ~ à zéro** to be really down; **faire la ~e à** to lecture, preach at; **~ité** *nf* morality; (*conduite*) morals *pl*; (*conclusion, enseignement*) moral.

morceau, x [mɔʀso] *nm* piece, bit; (*d'une œuvre*) passage, extract; (*MUS*) piece; (*CULIN: de viande*) cut; **mettre en ~x** to pull to pieces *ou* bits.

morceler [mɔʀsəle] *vt* to break up, divide up.

mordant, e [mɔʀdɑ̃, -ɑ̃t] *a* scathing, cutting; biting.

mordiller [mɔʀdije] *vt* to nibble at, chew at.

mordre [mɔʀdʀ(ə)] *vt* to bite; (*suj: lime, vis*) to bite into // *vi* (*poisson*) to bite; **~ sur** (*fig*) to go over into, overlap into; **~ à l'hameçon** to bite, rise to the bait.

mordu, e [mɔʀdy] *nm/f*: **un ~ du jazz** a jazz fanatic.

morfondre [mɔʀfɔ̃dʀ(ə)]: **se ~** *vi* to mope.

morgue [mɔʀg(ə)] *nf* (*arrogance*) haughtiness; (*lieu: de la police*) morgue; (*: à l'hôpital*) mortuary.

morne [mɔʀn(ə)] *a* dismal, dreary.

mors [mɔʀ] *nm* bit.

morse [mɔʀs(ə)] *nm* (*ZOOL*) walrus; (*TÉL*) Morse (code).

morsure [mɔʀsyʀ] *nf* bite.

mort [mɔʀ] *nf* death.

mort, e [mɔʀ, mɔʀt(ə)] *pp de* **mourir** // *a* dead // *nm/f* (*défunt*) dead man/ woman; (*victime*): **il y a eu plusieurs ~s** several people were killed, there were several killed // *nm* (*CARTES*) dummy; **~ ou vif** dead or alive; **~ de peur/fatigue** frightened to death/dead tired.

mortalité [mɔʀtalite] *nf* mortality, death rate.

mortel, le [mɔʀtɛl] *a* (*poison etc*) deadly, lethal; (*accident, blessure*) fatal; (*REL*) mortal; (*fig*) deathly; deadly boring.

mortier [mɔʀtje] *nm* (*gén*) mortar.

mort-né, e [mɔʀne] *a* (*enfant*) stillborn.

mortuaire [mɔʀtɥɛʀ] *a* funeral *cpd*.

morue [mɔʀy] *nf* (*ZOOL*) cod *inv*.

mosaïque [mɔzaik] *nf* (*ART*) mosaic; (*fig*) patchwork.

Moscou [mɔsku] *n* Moscow.

mosquée [mɔske] *nf* mosque.

mot [mo] *nm* word; (*message*) line, note; (*bon mot etc*) saying; sally; **~ à a, ad** word for word; **~s croisés** crossword (puzzle) *sg*; **~ d'ordre** watchword; **~ de passe** password.

motard [mɔtaʀ] *nm* biker; (*policier*) motorcycle cop.

motel [mɔtɛl] *nm* motel.

moteur, trice [mɔtœʀ, -tʀis] *a* (*ANAT*,

PHYSIOL) motor; (*TECH*) driving; (*AUTO*): **à 4 roues motrices** 4-wheel drive // *nm* engine, motor; **à ~** power-driven, motor *cpd*.

motif [mɔtif] *nm* (*cause*) motive; (*décoratif*) design, pattern, motif; (*d'un tableau*) subject, motif; **~s** *nmpl* (*JUR*) grounds *pl*; **sans ~** a groundless.

motiver [mɔtive] *vt* (*justifier*) to justify, account for; (*ADMIN, JUR, PSYCH*) to motivate.

moto [mɔto] *nf* (motor)bike; **~cyclisme** *nm* motorcycle racing; **~cycliste** *nm/f* motorcyclist.

motorisé, e [mɔtɔrize] *a* (*troupe*) motorized; (*personne*) having transport *ou* a car.

motrice [mɔtris] *a voir* **moteur**.

motte [mɔt] *nf*: **~ de terre** lump of earth, clod (of earth); **~ de gazon** turf, sod; **~ de beurre** lump of butter.

mou(mol), molle [mu, mɔl] *a* soft; (*péj*) flabby; sluggish // *nm* (*abats*) lights *pl*, lungs *pl*; (*de la corde*): **avoir du ~** to be slack.

mouche [muʃ] *nf* fly.

moucher [muʃe] *vt* (*enfant*) to blow the nose of; (*chandelle*) to snuff (out); **se ~** *vi* to blow one's nose.

moucheron [muʃrɔ̃] *nm* midge.

moucheté, e [muʃte] *a* dappled; flecked.

mouchoir [muʃwar] *nm* handkerchief, hanky; **~ en papier** tissue, paper hanky.

moudre [mudr(ə)] *vt* to grind.

moue [mu] *nf* pout; **faire la ~** to pout; (*fig*) to pull a face.

mouette [mwɛt] *nf* (sea)gull.

moufle [mufl(ə)] *nf* (*gant*) mitt(en).

mouillé, e [muje] *a* wet.

mouiller [muje] *vt* (*humecter*) to wet, moisten; (*tremper*): **~ qn/qch** to make sb/sth wet; (*couper, diluer*) to water down; (*mine etc*) to lay // *vi* (*NAVIG*) to lie *ou* to be at anchor; **se ~** to get wet; (*fam*) to commit o.s.; to get o.s. involved.

moule [mul] *nf* mussel // *nm* (*creux, CULIN*) mould; (*modèle plein*) cast; **~ à gâteaux** *nm* cake tin (*Brit*) *ou* pan (*US*).

moulent *vb voir* **moudre, mouler**.

mouler [mule] *vt* (*suj: vêtement*) to hug, fit closely round; **~ qch sur** (*fig*) to model sth on.

moulin [mulɛ̃] *nm* mill; **~ à café** *ou* **poivre** coffee/pepper mill; **~ à légumes** (vegetable) shredder; **~ à paroles** (*fig*) chatterbox; **~ à vent** windmill.

moulinet [mulinɛ] *nm* (*de treuil*) winch; (*de canne à pêche*) reel; (*mouvement*): **faire des ~s avec qch** to whirl sth around.

moulinette [mulinɛt] *nf* (vegetable) shredder.

moulu, e [muly] *pp de* **moudre**.

moulure [mulyr] *nf* (*ornement*) moulding.

mourant, e [murɑ̃, -ɑ̃t] *a* dying.

mourir [murir] *vi* to die; (*civilisation*) to die out; **~ de froid/faim** to die of exposure/hunger; **~ de faim/d'ennui** (*fig*) to be starving/be bored to death; **~ d'envie de faire** to be dying to do.

mousse [mus] *nf* (*BOT*) moss; (*écume: sur eau, bière*) froth, foam; (: *shampooing*) lather; (*CULIN*) mousse // *nm* (*NAVIG*) ship's boy; **bas ~** stretch stockings; **~ carbonique** (fire-fighting) foam; **~ à raser** shaving foam.

mousseline [muslin] *nf* muslin; chiffon.

mousser [muse] *vi* to foam; to lather.

mousseux, euse [musø, -øz] *a* frothy // *nm*: (*vin*) ~ sparkling wine.

mousson [musɔ̃] *nf* monsoon.

moustache [mustaʃ] *nf* moustache; **~s** (*du chat*) whiskers *pl*.

moustiquaire [mustiker] *nf* mosquito net (*ou* screen).

moustique [mustik] *nm* mosquito.

moutarde [mutard(ə)] *nf* mustard.

mouton [mutɔ̃] *nm* (*ZOOL, péj*) sheep *inv*; (*peau*) sheepskin; (*CULIN*) mutton.

mouvant, e [muvɑ̃, -ɑ̃t] *a* unsettled; changing; shifting.

mouvement [muvmɑ̃] *nm* (*gén, aussi: mécanisme*) movement; (*fig*) activity; impulse; gesture; (*MUS: rythme*) tempo (*pl* s); **en ~** in motion; on the move; **mouvementé, e** *a* (*vie, poursuite*) eventful; (*réunion*) turbulent.

mouvoir [muvwar] *vt* (*levier, membre*) to move; **se ~** *vi* to move.

moyen, ne [mwajɛ̃, -ɛn] *a* average; (*tailles, prix*) medium; (*de grandeur moyenne*) medium-sized // *nm* (*façon*) means *sg*, way // *nf* average; (*MATH*) mean; (*SCOL: à l'examen*) pass mark; (*AUTO*) average speed; **~s** (*capacités*) means; **au ~ de** by means of; **par tous les ~s** by every possible means, every possible way; **par ses propres ~s** all by oneself; **en ~ne** on (an) average; **~ de transport** means of transport; **~ âge** Middle Ages; **~ne d'âge** average age.

moyennant [mwajɛnɑ̃] *prép* (*somme*) for; (*service, conditions*) in return for; (*travail, effort*) with.

Moyen-Orient [mwajɛnɔrjɑ̃] *nm*: **le ~** the Middle East.

moyeu, x [mwajø] *nm* hub.

MST *sigle f* (= *maladie sexuellement transmissible*) sexually transmitted disease.

mû, mue [my] *pp de* **mouvoir**.

muer [mɥe] *vi* (*oiseau, mammifère*) to moult; (*serpent*) to slough; (*jeune garçon*): **il mue** his voice is breaking; **se ~ en** to transform into.

muet, te [mɥɛ, -ɛt] *a* dumb; (*fig*): **~**

d'admiration *etc* speechless with admiration *etc*; *(joie, douleur, CINÉMA)* silent; *(carte)* blank // *nm/f* mute.

mufle [myfl(ə)] *nm* muzzle; *(goujat)* boor.

mugir [myʒiʀ] *vi (taureau)* to bellow; *(vache)* to low; *(fig)* to howl.

muguet [mygɛ] *nm* lily of the valley.

mule [myl] *nf (ZOOL)* (she-)mule.

mulet [mylɛ] *nm (ZOOL)* (he-)mule.

multiple [myltipl(ə)] *a* multiple, numerous; *(varié)* many, manifold // *nm (MATH)* multiple.

multiplication [myltiplikɑsjɔ̃] *nf* multiplication.

multiplier [myltiplije] *vt* to multiply; se ~ *vi* to multiply; to increase in number.

municipal, e, aux [mynisipal, -o] *a* municipal; town *cpd*, ≈ borough *cpd*.

municipalité [mynisipalite] *nf (corps municipal)* town council, corporation.

munir [myniʀ] *vt:* ~ **qn/qch de** to equip sb/sth with.

munitions [mynisjɔ̃] *nfpl* ammunition *sg.*

mur [myʀ] *nm* wall; ~ **du son** sound barrier.

mûr, e [myʀ] *a* ripe; *(personne)* mature // *nf* blackberry; mulberry.

muraille [myʀɑj] *nf* (high) wall.

mural, e, aux [myʀal, -o] *a* wall *cpd*; mural.

murer [myʀe] *vt (enclos)* to wall (in); *(porte, issue)* to wall up; *(personne)* to wall up *ou* in.

muret [myʀɛ] *nm* low wall.

mûrir [myʀiʀ] *vi (fruit, blé)* to ripen; *(abcès, furoncle)* to come to a head; *(fig: idée, personne)* to mature // *vt* to ripen; to (make) mature.

murmure [myʀmyʀ] *nm* murmur; ~**s** *(plaintes)* murmurings, mutterings; **murmurer** *vi* to murmur; *(se plaindre)* to mutter, grumble.

muscade [myskad] *nf (aussi:* **noix** ~*)* nutmeg.

muscat [myska] *nm* muscat grape; muscatel (wine).

muscle [myskl(ə)] *nm* muscle; **musclé, e** *a* muscular; *(fig)* strong-arm.

museau, x [myzo] *nm* muzzle.

musée [myze] *nm* museum; art gallery.

museler [myzle] *vt* to muzzle; **muselière** *nf* muzzle.

musette [myzɛt] *nf (sac)* lunchbag // *a inv (orchestre etc)* accordion *cpd*.

musical, e, aux [myzikal, -o] *a* musical.

music-hall [myzikol] *nm* variety theatre; *(genre)* variety.

musicien, ne [myzisjɛ̃, -jɛn] *a* musical // *nm/f* musician.

musique [myzik] *nf* music; *(fanfare)* band; ~ **de chambre** chamber music.

musulman, e [myzylmɑ̃, -an] *a, nm/f* Moslem, Muslim.

mutation [mytɑsjɔ̃] *nf (ADMIN)* transfer.

mutilé, e [mytile] *nm/f* disabled person *(through loss of limbs)*.

mutiler [mytile] *vt* to mutilate, maim.

mutin, e [mytɛ̃, -in] *a (air, ton)* mischievous, impish // *nm/f (MIL, NAVIG)* mutineer.

mutinerie [mytinʀi] *nf* mutiny.

mutisme [mytism(ə)] *nm* silence.

mutuel, le [mytɥɛl] *a* mutual // *nf* mutual benefit society.

myope [mjɔp] *a* short-sighted.

myosotis [mjozɔtis] *nm* forget-me-not.

myrtille [miʀtij] *nf* bilberry.

mystère [mistɛʀ] *nm* mystery; **mystérieux, euse** *a* mysterious.

mystifier [mistifje] *vt* to fool; to mystify.

mythe [mit] *nm* myth.

mythologie [mitɔlɔʒi] *nf* mythology.

N

n' [n] *ad voir* **ne.**

nacelle [nasɛl] *nf (de ballon)* basket.

nacre [nakʀ(ə)] *nf* mother of pearl; **nacré, e** *a* pearly.

nage [naʒ] *nf* swimming; style of swimming, stroke; **traverser/s'éloigner à la** ~ to swim across/away; **en** ~ bathed in perspiration.

nageoire [naʒwaʀ] *nf* fin.

nager [naʒe] *vi* to swim; **nageur, euse** *nm/f* swimmer.

naguère [nagɛʀ] *ad* formerly.

naïf, ïve [naif, naiv] *a* naïve.

nain, e [nɛ̃, nɛn] *nm/f* dwarf.

naissance [nɛsɑ̃s] *nf* birth; **donner** ~ **à** to give birth to; *(fig)* to give rise to.

naître [nɛtʀ(ə)] *vi* to be born; *(fig):* ~ **de** to arise from, be born out of; **il est né en 1960** he was born in 1960; **faire** ~ *(fig)* to give rise to, arouse.

nana [nana] *nf (fam: fille)* chick, bird *(Brit).*

nantir [nɑ̃tiʀ] *vt:* ~ **qn de** to provide sb with; **les nantis** *(péj)* the well-to-do.

nappe [nap] *nf* tablecloth; *(fig)* sheet; layer; ~**ron** *nm* table-mat.

naquit *etc vb voir* **naître.**

narguer [naʀge] *vt* to taunt.

narine [naʀin] *nf* nostril.

narquois, e [naʀkwa, -waz] *a* derisive, mocking.

narrer [naʀe] *vt* to tell the story of, recount.

naseau, x [nazo] *nm* nostril.

natal, e [natal] *a* native.

natalité [natalite] *nf* birth rate.

natation [natɑsjɔ̃] *nf* swimming.

natif, ive [natif, -iv] *a* native.

nation [nɑsjɔ̃] *nf* nation.

national, e, aux [nasjɔnal, -o] *a* national // *nf:* **(route)** ~**e** ≈ A road *(Brit),*

≈ state highway (*US*); **~iser** *vt* to nationalize; **~ité** *nf* nationality.

natte [nat] *nf* (*tapis*) mat; (*cheveux*) plait.

naturaliser [natyʀalize] *vt* to naturalize.

nature [natyʀ] *nf* nature // *a, ad* (*CULIN*) plain, without seasoning or sweetening; (*café, thé*) black, without sugar; **payer en ~** to pay in kind; **~ morte** still-life; **naturel, le** *a* (*gén, aussi: enfant*) natural // *nm* naturalness; disposition, nature; (*autochtone*) native; **naturellement** *ad* naturally; (*bien sûr*) of course.

naufrage [nofʀaʒ] *nm* (ship)wreck; (*fig*) wreck; **faire ~** to be shipwrecked.

nauséabond, e [nozeabɔ̃, -ɔ̃d] *a* foul, nauseous.

nausée [noze] *nf* nausea.

nautique [notik] *a* nautical, water *cpd*.

nautisme [notism] *nm* water sports.

navet [navɛ] *nm* turnip.

navette [navɛt] *nf* shuttle; **faire la ~** (**entre**) to go to and fro *ou* shuttle (between).

navigable [navigabl(ə)] *a* navigable.

navigateur [navigatœʀ] *nm* (*NAVIG*) seafarer, sailor; (*AVIAT*) navigator.

navigation [navigasjɔ̃] *nf* navigation, sailing; shipping.

naviguer [navige] *vi* to navigate, sail.

navire [naviʀ] *nm* ship.

navrer [navʀe] *vt* to upset, distress; **je suis navré** I'm so sorry.

ne, n' [n(ə)] *ad voir* pas, plus, jamais *etc*; (*explétif*) *non traduit*.

né, e [ne] *pp* (*voir* **naître**): **~ en 1960** born in 1960; **~e Scott** née Scott.

néanmoins [neɑ̃mwɛ̃] *ad* nevertheless.

néant [neɑ̃] *nm* nothingness; **réduire à ~** to bring to nought; (*espoir*) to dash.

nécessaire [nesesɛʀ] *a* necessary // *nm* necessary; (*sac*) kit; **~ de couture** sewing kit; **~ de toilette** toilet bag; **nécessité** *nf* necessity; **nécessiter** *vt* to require; **nécessiteux, euse** *a* needy.

nécrologique [nekʀɔlɔʒik] *a*: **article ~** obituary; **rubrique ~** obituary column.

néerlandais, e [neɛʀlɑ̃dɛ, -ɛz] *a* Dutch.

nef [nɛf] *nf* (*d'église*) nave.

néfaste [nefast(ə)] *a* baneful; ill-fated.

négatif, ive [negatif, iv] *a* negative // *nm* (*PHOTO*) negative.

négligé, e [negliʒe] *a* (*en désordre*) slovenly // *nm* (*tenue*) negligee.

négligent, e [negliʒɑ̃, -ɑ̃t] *a* careless; negligent.

négliger [negliʒe] *vt* (*épouse, jardin*) to neglect; (*tenue*) to be careless about; (*avis, précautions*) to disregard; **~ de faire** to fail to do, not bother to do.

négoce [negɔs] *nm* trade.

négociant [negɔsjɑ̃] *nm* merchant.

négociation [negɔsjasjɔ̃] *nf* negotiation.

négocier [negɔsje] *vi, vt* to negotiate.

nègre [nɛgʀ(ə)] *nm* Negro; ghost (writer).

négresse [negʀɛs] *nf* Negro woman.

neige [nɛʒ] *nf* snow; **neiger** *vi* to snow; **neigeux, euse** *a* snowy, snow-covered.

nénuphar [nenyfaʀ] *nm* water-lily.

néon [neɔ̃] *nm* neon.

néophyte [neɔfit] *nm/f* novice.

néo-zélandais, e [neozelɑ̃dɛ, -ɛz] *a* New Zealand *cpd* //; **N~, e** *nm/f* New Zealander.

nerf [nɛʀ] *nm* nerve; (*fig*) spirit; stamina; **nerveux, euse** *a* nervous; (*voiture*) nippy, responsive; (*tendineux*) sinewy; **nervosité** *nf* excitability; state of agitation; nervousness.

nervure [nɛʀvyʀ] *nf* vein.

n'est-ce pas [nɛspa] *ad* isn't it?, won't you? *etc*, *selon le verbe qui précède*.

net, nette [nɛt] *a* (*sans équivoque, distinct*) clear; (*évident*) definite; (*propre*) neat, clean; (*COMM: prix, salaire*) net // *ad* (*refuser*) flatly; **s'arrêter ~** to stop dead // *nm*: **mettre au ~** to copy out; **nettement** *ad* clearly, distinctly; **~teté** *nf* clearness.

nettoyage [nɛtwajaʒ] *nm* cleaning; **~ à sec** dry cleaning.

nettoyer [nɛtwaje] *vt* to clean; (*fig*) to clean out.

neuf [nœf] *num* nine.

neuf, neuve [nœf, nœv] *a* new // *nm*: **repeindre à ~** to redecorate; **remettre à ~** to do up (as good as new), refurbish.

neutre [nøtʀ(ə)] *a* neutral; (*LING*) neuter // *nm* (*LING*) neuter.

neuve [nœv] *a voir* **neuf**.

neuvième [nœvjɛm] *num* ninth.

neveu, x [nəvø] *nm* nephew.

névrosé, e [nevʀoze] *a, nm/f* neurotic.

nez [ne] *nm* nose; **~ à ~ avec** face to face with; **avoir du ~** to have flair.

ni [ni] *cj*: **~ l'un ~ l'autre ne sont** neither one nor the other are; **il n'a rien dit ~ fait** he hasn't said or done anything.

niais, e [njɛ, -ɛz] *a* silly, thick.

niche [niʃ] *nf* (*du chien*) kennel; (*de mur*) recess, niche.

nicher [niʃe] *vi* to nest.

nid [ni] *nm* nest; **~ de poule** pothole.

nièce [njɛs] *nf* niece.

nier [nje] *vt* to deny.

nigaud, e [nigo, -od] *nm/f* booby, fool.

Nil [nil] *nm*: **le ~** the Nile.

n'importe [nɛ̃pɔʀt(ə)] *ad*: **~ qui/quoi/où** anybody/anything/anywhere; **~ quand** any time; **~ quel/quelle** any; **~ lequel/laquelle** any (one); **~ comment** (*sans soin*) carelessly.

niveau, x [nivo] *nm* level; (*des élèves, études*) standard; **de ~** (*avec*) level (with); **~ (à bulle)** spirit level; **le ~ de la mer** sea level; **~ de vie** standard of living.

niveler [nivle] *vt* to level.

NN *abr* (= *nouvelle norme*) *revised standard of hotel classification*.

noble [nɔbl(ə)] *a* a noble; **noblesse** *nf* nobility; (*d'une action etc*) nobleness.

noce [nɔs] *nf* wedding; (*gens*) wedding party (*ou* guests *pl*); **faire la ~** (*fam*) to go on a binge; **~s d'or/d'argent** golden/silver wedding.

nocif, ive [nɔsif, -iv] *a* harmful, noxious.

noctambule [nɔktãbyl] *nm* night-bird.

nocturne [nɔktyrn(ə)] *a* nocturnal // *nf* late-night opening.

Noël [nɔɛl] *nm* Christmas.

nœud [nø] *nm* (*de corde, du bois*, NAVIG) knot; (*ruban*) bow; (*fig: liens*) bond, tie; **~ papillon** bow tie.

noir, e [nwar] *a* (*obscur, sombre*) dark // *nm/f* black man/woman, Negro/Negro woman // *nm*: **dans le ~** in the dark; **travail au ~** moonlighting // *nf* (*MUS*) crotchet (*Brit*), quarter note (*US*); **~ceur** *nf* blackness; darkness; **~cir** *vt, vi* to blacken.

noisette [nwazɛt] *nf* hazelnut.

noix [nwa] *nf* walnut; (*CULIN*): **une ~ de beurre** a knob of butter; **~ de cajou** cashew nut; **~ de coco** coconut.

nom [nɔ̃] *nm* name; (*LING*) noun; **~ d'emprunt** assumed name; **~ de famille** surname; **~ de jeune fille** maiden name.

nombre [nɔ̃br(ə)] *nm* number; **venir en ~** to come in large numbers; **depuis ~ d'années** for many years; **ils sont au ~ de 3** there are 3 of them; **au ~ de mes amis** among my friends.

nombreux, euse [nɔ̃brø, -øz] *a* many, numerous; (*avec nom sg: foule etc*) large; **peu ~** few; small.

nombril [nɔ̃bri] *nm* navel.

nommer [nɔme] *vt* (*baptiser, mentionner*) to name; (*qualifier*) to call; (*élire*) to appoint, nominate; **se ~**: **il se nomme Pascal** his name's Pascal, he's called Pascal.

non [nɔ̃] *ad* (*réponse*) no; (*avec loin, sans, seulement*) not; **~ que, ~ pas que** not that; **moi ~ plus** neither do I, I don't either.

non-alcoolisé, e [nɔnalkɔlize] *a* non-alcoholic.

non-fumeur [nɔ̃fymœr] *nm* non-smoker.

non-lieu [nɔ̃ljø] *nm*: **il y a eu ~** the case was dismissed.

non-sens [nɔ̃sãs] *nm* absurdity.

nord [nɔr] *nm* North // *a* northern; north; **au ~** (*situation*) in the north; (*direction*) to the north; **au ~ de** (to the) north of; **~-est** *nm* North-East; **~-ouest** *nm* North-West.

normal, e, aux [nɔrmal, -o] *a* normal // *nf*: **la ~e** the norm, the average; **~ement** *ad* (*en général*) normally; **~iser** *vt* (*COMM, TECH*) to standardize.

normand, e [nɔrmã, -ãd] *a* of Normandy.

Normandie [nɔrmãdi] *nf* Normandy.

norme [nɔrm(ə)] *nf* norm; (*TECH*) standard.

Norvège [nɔrvɛʒ] *nf* Norway; **norvégien, ne** *a, nm, nf* Norwegian.

nos [no] *dét voir* **notre**.

nostalgie [nɔstalʒi] *nf* nostalgia.

notable [nɔtabl(ə)] *a* notable, noteworthy; (*marqué*) noticeable, marked // *nm* prominent citizen.

notaire [nɔtɛr] *nm* notary; solicitor.

notamment [nɔtamã] *ad* in particular, among others.

note [nɔt] *nf* (*écrite*, MUS) note; (*SCOL*) mark (*Brit*), grade; (*facture*) bill; **~ de service** memorandum.

noté, e [nɔte] *a*: **être bien/mal ~** (*employé etc*) to have a good/bad record.

noter [nɔte] *vt* (*écrire*) to write down; (*remarquer*) to note, notice.

notice [nɔtis] *nf* summary, short article; (*brochure*) leaflet, instruction book.

notifier [nɔtifje] *vt*: **~ qch à qn** to notify sb of sth, notify sth to sb.

notion [nosjɔ̃] *nf* notion, idea.

notoire [nɔtwar] *a* widely known; (*en mal*) notorious.

notre, nos [nɔtr(ə), no] *dét* our.

nôtre [notr(ə)] *pronom*: **le/la ~** ours; **les ~s** ours; (*alliés etc*) our own people; **soyez des ~s** join us // *a* ours.

nouer [nwe] *vt* to tie, knot; (*fig: alliance etc*) to strike up.

noueux, euse [nwø, -øz] *a* gnarled.

nouilles [nuj] *nfpl* noodles; pasta *sg*.

nourrice [nuris] *nf* wet-nurse.

nourrir [nurir] *vt* to feed; (*fig: espoir*) to harbour, nurse; **logé nourri** with board and lodging; **nourrissant, e** *a* nourishing, nutritious.

nourrisson [nurisɔ̃] *nm* (unweaned) infant.

nourriture [nurityr] *nf* food.

nous [nu] *pronom* (*sujet*) we; (*objet*) us; **~-mêmes** *pronom* ourselves.

nouveau(nouvel), elle, x [nuvo, -ɛl] *a* new // *nm/f* new pupil (*ou* employee) // *nf* (piece of) news *sg*; (*LITTÉRATURE*) short story; **de ~, à ~** again; **je suis sans nouvelles de lui** I haven't heard from him; **~ venu, nouvelle venue** *nm/f* newcomer; **Nouvel An** New Year; **~-né, e** *nm/f* newborn baby; **Nouvelle-Calédonie** *nf* New Caledonia; **Nouvelle-Zélande** *nf* New Zealand; **~té** *nf* novelty; (*COMM*) new film (*ou* book *ou* creation *etc*).

novembre [nɔvãbr(ə)] *nm* November.

novice [nɔvis] *a* inexperienced.

noyade [nwajad] *nf* drowning *q*.

noyau, x [nwajo] *nm* (*de fruit*) stone; (*BIO, PHYSIQUE*) nucleus; (*ÉLEC, GÉO, fig: centre*) core; **~ter** *vt* (*POL*) to infiltrate.

noyer [nwaje] *nm* walnut (tree); (*bois*)

walnut // vt to drown; (fig) to flood; to submerge; **se ~** vi to be drowned, drown; (suicide) to drown o.s.

nu, e [ny] a naked; (membres) naked, bare; (chambre, fil, plaine) bare // nm (ART) nude; **~-pieds** a inv barefoot; **~-tête** a inv bareheaded; **se mettre à ~** to strip; **mettre à ~** to bare.

nuage [nɥaʒ] nm cloud; **nuageux, euse** a cloudy.

nuance [nɥɑ̃s] nf (de couleur, sens) shade; **il y a une ~** (entre) there's a slight difference (between); **nuancer** vt (opinion) to bring some reservations ou qualifications to.

nucléaire [nykleɛʀ] a nuclear.

nudiste [nydist(ə)] nm/f nudist.

nuée [nɥe] nf: **une ~ de** a cloud ou host ou swarm of.

nues [ny] nfpl: **tomber des ~** to be taken aback; **porter qn aux ~** to praise sb to the skies.

nuire [nɥiʀ] vi to be harmful; **~ à** to harm, do damage to; **nuisible** a harmful; **animal nuisible** pest.

nuit [nɥi] nf night; **il fait ~** it's dark; **cette ~** last night; tonight; **~ blanche** sleepless night; **~ de noces** wedding night.

nul, nulle [nyl] a (aucun) no; (minime) nil, non-existent; (non valable) null; (péj) useless, hopeless // pronom none, no one; **résultat ~, match ~** draw; **~le part** ad nowhere; **~lement** ad by no means.

numérique [nymeʀik] a numerical.

numéro [nymeʀo] nm number; (spectacle) act, turn; **~ de téléphone** (tele)phone number; **~ter** vt to number.

nuque [nyk] nf nape of the neck.

nutritif, ive [nytʀitif, -iv] a nutritional; (aliment) nutritious.

nylon [nilɔ̃] nm nylon.

O

oasis [ɔazis] nf oasis (pl oases).

obéir [ɔbeiʀ] vi to obey; **~ à** to obey; (suj: moteur, véhicule) to respond to; **obéissant, e** a obedient.

objecter [ɔbʒɛkte] vt (prétexter) to plead, put forward as an excuse; **~ (à qn) que** to object (to sb) that.

objecteur [ɔbʒɛktœʀ] nm: **~ de conscience** conscientious objector.

objectif, ive [ɔbʒɛktif, -iv] a objective // nm (OPTIQUE, PHOTO) lens sg, objective; (MIL, fig) objective; **~ à focale variable** zoom lens.

objection [ɔbʒɛksjɔ̃] nf objection.

objet [ɔbʒɛ] nm object; (d'une discussion, recherche) subject; **être ou faire l'~ de** (discussion) to be the subject of; (soins) to be given ou shown;

sans **~** a purposeless; groundless; **~ d'art** objet d'art; **~s personnels** personal items; **~s trouvés** lost property sg (Brit), lost-and-found sg (US).

obligation [ɔbligasjɔ̃] nf obligation; (COMM) bond, debenture; **obligatoire** a compulsory, obligatory.

obligé, e [ɔbliʒe] a (redevable): **être très ~ à qn** to be most obliged to sb; **obligeant, e** a obliging; kind.

obliger [ɔbliʒe] vt (contraindre): **~ qn à faire** to force ou oblige sb to do; (JUR: engager) to bind; (rendre service à) to oblige; **je suis bien obligé** I have to.

oblique [ɔblik] a oblique; **regard ~** sidelong glance; **en ~** ad diagonally; **obliquer** vi: **obliquer vers** to turn off towards.

oblitérer [ɔbliteʀe] vt (timbre-poste) to cancel.

obscène [ɔpsɛn] a obscene.

obscur, e [ɔpskyʀ] a dark; (fig) obscure; lowly; **~cir** vt to darken; (fig) to obscure; **s'~cir** vi to grow dark; **~ité** nf darkness; **dans l'~ité** in the dark, in darkness.

obséder [ɔpsede] vt to obsess, haunt.

obsèques [ɔpsɛk] nfpl funeral sg.

observateur, trice [ɔpsɛʀvatœʀ, -tʀis] a observant, perceptive // nm/f observer.

observation [ɔpsɛʀvasjɔ̃] nf observation; (d'un règlement etc) observance; (reproche) reproof.

observatoire [ɔpsɛʀvatwaʀ] nm observatory; (lieu élevé) observation post, vantage point.

observer [ɔpsɛʀve] vt (regarder) to observe, watch; (examiner) to examine; (scientifiquement, aussi: règlement, jeûne etc) to observe; (surveiller) to watch; (remarquer) to observe, notice; **faire ~ qch à qn** (dire) to point out sth to sb.

obstacle [ɔpstakl(ə)] nm obstacle; (ÉQUITATION) jump, hurdle; **faire ~ à** (lumière) to block out; (projet) to hinder, put obstacles in the path of.

obstiné, e [ɔpstine] a obstinate.

obstiner [ɔpstine]: **s'~** vi to insist, dig one's heels in; **s'~ à faire** to persist (obstinately) in doing; **s'~ sur qch** to keep working at sth, labour away at sth.

obstruer [ɔpstʀye] vt to block, obstruct.

obtempérer [ɔptɑ̃peʀe] vi to obey.

obtenir [ɔptəniʀ] vt to obtain, get; (total, résultat) to achieve, at reach; **~ de pouvoir faire** to obtain permission to do; **~ de qn qu'il fasse** to get sb to agree to do; **obtention** nf obtaining.

obturateur [ɔptyʀatœʀ] nm (PHOTO) shutter.

obturer [ɔptyʀe] vt to close (up); (dent) to fill.

obus [ɔby] nm shell.

occasion [ɔkazjɔ̃] *nf* (*aubaine, possibilité*) opportunity; (*circonstance*) occasion; (*COMM: article non neuf*) second-hand buy; (: *acquisition avantageuse*) bargain; **à plusieurs ~s** on several occasions; **être l'~ de** to occasion, give rise to; **à l'~** *ad* sometimes, on occasions; some time; **d'~** *a, ad* secondhand; **occasionnel, le** *a* (*fortuit*) chance *cpd*; (*non régulier*) occasional; casual.

occasionner [ɔkazjɔne] *vt* to cause, bring about; **~ qch à qn** to cause sb sth.

occident [ɔksidã] *nm*: **l'O~** the West; **occidental, e, aux** western; (*POL*) Western.

occupation [ɔkypasjɔ̃] *nf* occupation.

occupé, e [ɔkype] *a* (*MIL, POL*) occupied; (*personne: affairé, pris*) busy; (*place, sièges*) taken; (*toilettes, ligne*) engaged.

occuper [ɔkype] *vt* to occupy; (*main-d'œuvre*) to employ; **s'~ (à qch)** to occupy o.s. ou keep o.s. busy (with sth); **s'~ de** (*être responsable de*) to be in charge of; (*se charger de: affaire*) to take charge of, deal with; (: *clients etc*) to attend to; (*s'intéresser à, pratiquer*) to be involved in; **ça occupe trop de place** it takes up too much room.

occurrence [ɔkyʀãs] *nf*: **en l'~** in this case.

océan [ɔseã] *nm* ocean; **l'~ Indien** the Indian Ocean.

octet [ɔktɛt] *nm* byte.

octobre [ɔktɔbʀ(ə)] *nm* October.

octroyer [ɔktʀwaje] *vt*: **~ qch à qn** to grant sth to sb, grant sb sth.

oculiste [ɔkylist(ə)] *nm/f* eye specialist.

odeur [ɔdœʀ] *nf* smell.

odieux, euse [ɔdjø, -øz] *a* hateful.

odorant, e [ɔdɔʀɑ̃, -ɑ̃t] *a* sweet-smelling, fragrant.

odorat [ɔdɔʀa] *nm* (sense of) smell.

œil [œj], *pl* **yeux** [jø] *nm* eye; **à l'~** (*fam*) for free; **à l'~ nu** with the naked eye; **tenir qn à l'~** to keep an eye ou a watch on sb; **avoir l'~ à** to keep an eye on; **fermer les yeux (sur)** (*fig*) to turn a blind eye (to).

œillade [œjad] *nf*: **lancer une ~ à qn** to wink at sb, give sb a wink; **faire des ~s à** to make eyes at.

œillères [œjɛʀ] *nfpl* blinkers (*Brit*), blinders (*US*).

œillet [œjɛ] *nm* (*BOT*) carnation.

œuf [œf, *pl* ø] *nm* egg; **~ dur** hard-boiled egg; **~ au plat** fried egg; **~s brouillés** scrambled eggs; **~ de Pâques** Easter egg.

œuvre [œvʀ(ə)] *nf* (*tâche*) task, undertaking; (*ouvrage achevé, livre, tableau etc*) work; (*ensemble de la production artistique*) works *pl*; (*organisation charitable*) charity // *nm* (*d'un artiste*) works *pl*; (*CONSTR*): **le gros ~** the shell; **être à**

l'~ to be at work; **mettre en ~** (*moyens*) to make use of; **~ d'art** work of art.

offense [ɔfɑ̃s] *nf* insult.

offenser [ɔfɑ̃se] *vt* to offend, hurt; (*principes, Dieu*) to offend against; **s'~ de** to take offence at.

offert, e [ɔfɛʀ, -ɛʀt(ə)] *pp de* **offrir**.

office [ɔfis] *nm* (*charge*) office; (*agence*) bureau, agency; (*REL*) service // *nm ou nf* (*pièce*) pantry; **faire ~ de** to act as; to do duty as; **d'~** *ad* automatically; **~ du tourisme** tourist bureau.

officiel, le [ɔfisjɛl] *a, nm/f* official.

officier [ɔfisje] *nm* officer // *vi* to officiate; **~ de l'état-civil** registrar.

officieux, euse [ɔfisjø, -øz] *a* unofficial.

officinal, e, aux [ɔfisinal, -o] *a*: **plantes ~es** medicinal plants.

officine [ɔfisin] *nf* (*de pharmacie*) dispensary; (*bureau*) agency, office.

offrande [ɔfʀɑ̃d] *nf* offering.

offre [ɔfʀ(ə)] *nf* offer; (*aux enchères*) bid; (*ADMIN: soumission*) tender; (*ÉCON*): **l'~** supply; **~ d'emploi** job advertised; **'~s d'emploi'** 'situations vacant'; **~ publique d'achat** (O.P.A.) takeover bid.

offrir [ɔfʀiʀ] *vt*: **~ (à qn)** to offer (to sb); (*faire cadeau de*) to give (to sb); **s'~** *vi* (*occasion, paysage*) to present itself // *vt* (*vacances, voiture*) to treat o.s. to; **~ (à qn) de faire qch** to offer to do sth (for sb); **~ à boire à qn** to offer sb a drink; **s'~ comme guide/en otage** to offer one's services as (a) guide/offer o.s. as hostage.

offusquer [ɔfyske] *vt* to offend.

ogive [ɔʒiv] *nf*: **~ nucléaire** nuclear warhead.

oie [wa] *nf* (*ZOOL*) goose (*pl* geese).

oignon [ɔɲɔ̃] *nm* (*BOT, CULIN*) onion; (*de tulipe etc: bulbe*) bulb; (*MÉD*) bunion.

oiseau, x [wazo] *nm* bird; **~ de proie** bird of prey.

oiseux, euse [wazø, -øz] *a* pointless; trivial.

oisif, ive [wazif, -iv] *a* idle // *nm/f* (*péj*) man/woman of leisure.

oléoduc [ɔleɔdyk] *nm* (oil) pipeline.

olive [ɔliv] *nf* (*BOT*) olive; **olivier** *nm* olive.

olympique [ɔlɛ̃pik] *a* Olympic.

ombrage [ɔ̃bʀaʒ] *nm* (*ombre*) (leafy) shade; **ombragé, e** *a* shaded, shady; **ombrageux, euse** *a* (*cheval*) skittish, nervous; (*personne*) touchy, easily offended.

ombre [ɔ̃bʀ(ə)] *nf* (*espace non ensoleillé*) shade; (*ombre portée, tache*) shadow; **à l'~** in the shade; **tu me fais de l'~** you're in my light; **ça nous donne de l'~** it gives us (some) shade; **dans l'~** (*fig*) in obscurity; in the dark; **~ à paupières** eyeshadow.

ombrelle [ɔ̃bʀɛl] nf parasol, sunshade.

omelette [ɔmlɛt] nf omelette.

omettre [ɔmɛtʀ(ə)] vt to omit, leave out.

omnibus [ɔmnibys] nm slow ou stopping train.

omoplate [ɔmɔplat] nf shoulder blade.

on [ɔ̃] pronom
1 (indéterminé) you, one; ~ peut le faire ainsi you ou one can do it like this, it can be done like this
2 (quelqu'un): ~ les a attaqués they were attacked; ~ vous demande au téléphone there's a phone call for you, you're wanted on the phone
3 (nous) we; ~ va y aller demain we're going tomorrow
4 (les gens) they; autrefois, ~ croyait ... they used to believe ...
5: ~ ne peut plus ad: ~ ne peut plus stupide as stupid as can be.

oncle [ɔ̃kl(ə)] nm uncle.

onctueux, euse [ɔ̃ktɥø, -øz] a creamy, smooth; (fig) smooth, unctuous.

onde [ɔ̃d] nf (PHYSIQUE) wave; sur les ~s on the radio; mettre en ~s to produce for the radio; sur ~s courtes (o.c.) on short wave sg; moyennes/longues ~s medium/long wave sg.

ondée [ɔ̃de] nf shower.

on-dit [ɔ̃di] nm inv rumour.

ondoyer [ɔ̃dwaje] vi to ripple, wave.

onduler [ɔ̃dyle] vi to undulate; (cheveux) to wave.

onéreux, euse [ɔneʀø, -øz] a costly; à titre ~ in return for payment.

ongle [ɔ̃gl(ə)] nm (ANAT) nail; se faire les ~ to do one's nails.

onguent [ɔ̃gɑ̃] nm ointment.

ont vb voir avoir.

O.N.U. [ɔny] sigle f voir organisation.

onze [ɔ̃z] num eleven; **onzième** num eleventh.

O.P.A. sigle f voir offre.

opale [ɔpal] nf opal.

opaque [ɔpak] a opaque.

opéra [ɔpeʀa] nm opera; (édifice) opera house; **~-comique** nm light opera.

opérateur, trice [ɔpeʀatœʀ, -tʀis] nm/f operator; ~ (de prise de vues) cameraman.

opération [ɔpeʀasjɔ̃] nf operation; (COMM) dealing.

opératoire [ɔpeʀatwaʀ] a operating; (choc etc) post-operative.

opérer [ɔpeʀe] vt (MÉD) to operate on; (faire, exécuter) to carry out, make // vi (remède: faire effet) to act, work; (procéder) to proceed; (MÉD) to operate; s'~ vi (avoir lieu) to occur, take place; se faire ~ to have an operation.

opiner [ɔpine] vi: ~ de la tête to nod assent.

opinion [ɔpinjɔ̃] nf opinion; l'~ (publique) public opinion.

opportun, e [ɔpɔʀtœ̃, -yn] a timely, opportune; en temps ~ at the appropriate time.

opposant, e [ɔpozɑ̃, -ɑ̃t] a opposing; ~s nmpl opponents.

opposé, e [ɔpoze] a (direction, rive) opposite; (faction) opposing; (couleurs) contrasting; (opinions, intérêts) conflicting; (contre): ~ à opposed to, against // nm: l'~ the other ou opposite side (ou direction); (contraire) the opposite; à l'~ (fig) on the other hand; à l'~ de on the other ou opposite side from; (fig) contrary to, unlike.

opposer [ɔpoze] vt (personnes, armées, équipes) to oppose; (couleurs, termes, tons) to contrast; ~ qch à (comme obstacle, défense) to set sth against; (comme objection) to put sth forward against; s'~ (sens réciproque) to conflict; to clash; to contrast; s'~ à (interdire, empêcher) to oppose; (tenir tête à) to rebel against.

opposition [ɔpozisjɔ̃] nf opposition; par ~ à as opposed to, in contrast with; entrer en ~ avec to come into conflict with; être en ~ avec (idées, conduite) to be at variance with; faire ~ à un chèque to stop a cheque.

oppresser [ɔpʀese] vt to oppress; **oppression** nf oppression; (malaise) feeling of suffocation.

opprimer [ɔpʀime] vt to oppress; (liberté, opinion) to suppress, stifle; (suj: chaleur etc) to suffocate, oppress.

opter [ɔpte] vi: ~ pour to opt for; ~ entre to choose between.

opticien, ne [ɔptisjɛ̃, -ɛn] nm/f optician.

optimiste [ɔptimist(ə)] nm/f optimist // a optimistic.

option [ɔpsjɔ̃] nf option; matière à ~ (SCOL) optional subject.

optique [ɔptik] a (nerf) optic; (verres) optical // nf (PHOTO: lentilles etc) optics pl; (science, industrie) optics sg; (fig: manière de voir) perspective.

opulent, e [ɔpylɑ̃, -ɑ̃t] a wealthy, opulent; (formes, poitrine) ample, generous.

or [ɔʀ] nm gold // cj now, but; en ~ gold cpd; (fig) golden, marvellous.

orage [ɔʀaʒ] nm (thunder)storm; **orageux, euse** a stormy.

oraison [ɔʀezɔ̃] nf orison, prayer; ~ funèbre funeral oration.

oral, e, aux [ɔʀal, -o] a, nm oral.

orange [ɔʀɑ̃ʒ] nf, a inv orange; **oranger** nm orange tree.

orateur [ɔʀatœʀ] nm speaker; orator.

orbite [ɔʀbit] nf (ANAT) (eye-)socket; (PHYSIQUE) orbit.

orchestre [ɔʀkɛstʀ(ə)] nm orchestra; (de jazz, danse) band; (places) stalls pl (Brit), orchestra (US); **orchestrer** vt (MUS) to orchestrate; (fig) to mount, stage-manage.

orchidée [ɔʀkide] *nf* orchid.
ordinaire [ɔʀdinɛʀ] *a* ordinary; everyday; standard // *nm* ordinary; (*menus*)
everyday fare // *nf* (*essence*) ≈ two-star
(petrol) (*Brit*), ≈ regular (gas) (*US*);
d'~ usually, normally; à l'~ usually, or-
dinarily.
ordinateur [ɔʀdinatœʀ] *nm* computer;
~ domestique home computer; ~
individuel personal computer.
ordonnance [ɔʀdɔnɑ̃s] *nf* organization;
layout; (*MÉD*) prescription; (*JUR*) order;
(*MIL*) orderly, batman (*Brit*).
ordonné, e [ɔʀdɔne] *a* tidy, orderly;
(*MATH*) ordered.
ordonner [ɔʀdɔne] *vt* (*agencer*) to organize, arrange; (*donner un ordre*): ~ à
qn de faire to order sb to do; (*REL*) to
ordain; (*MÉD*) to prescribe.
ordre [ɔʀdʀ(ə)] *nm* (*gén*) order; (*propreté et soin*) orderliness, tidiness; (*nature*): d'~ pratique of a practical nature; ~s *nmpl* (*REL*) holy orders; mettre
en ~ to tidy (up), put in order; à l'~ de
qn payable to sb; être aux ~s de qn/sous
les ~s de qn to be at sb's disposal/under
sb's command; jusqu'à nouvel ~ until
further notice; dans le même ~ d'idées
in this connection; donnez-nous un ~ de
grandeur give us some idea as regards
size (ou the amount); de premier ~
first-rate; ~ du jour (*d'une réunion*)
agenda; (*MIL*) order of the day; à l'~ du
jour (*fig*) topical.
ordure [ɔʀdyʀ] *nf* filth *q*; ~s (*balayures,
déchets*) rubbish *sg*, refuse *sg*; ~s
ménagères household refuse.
oreille [ɔʀɛj] *nf* (*ANAT*) ear; (*de
marmite, tasse*) handle; avoir de l'~ to
have a good ear (for music).
oreiller [ɔʀeje] *nm* pillow.
oreillons [ɔʀɛjɔ̃] *nmpl* mumps *sg*.
ores [ɔʀ]: d'~ et déjà *ad* already.
orfèvrerie [ɔʀfɛvʀəʀi] *nf* goldsmith's (*ou
silversmith's*) trade; (*ouvrage*) gold (*ou
silver*) plate.
organe [ɔʀgan] *nm* organ; (*porte-
parole*) representative, mouthpiece.
organigramme [ɔʀganigʀam] *nm* organization chart; flow chart.
organique [ɔʀganik] *a* organic.
organisateur, trice [ɔʀganizatœʀ,
-tʀis] *nm/f* organizer.
organisation [ɔʀganizasjɔ̃] *nf* organization; O~ des Nations Unies
(O.N.U.) United Nations (Organization)
(UN, UNO); O~ du traité de l'Atlantique
Nord (O.T.A.N.) North Atlantic Treaty
Organization (NATO).
organiser [ɔʀganize] *vt* to organize;
(*mettre sur pied: service etc*) to set up;
s'~ to get organized.
organisme [ɔʀganism(ə)] *nm* (*BIO*) or-
ganism; (*corps, ADMIN*) body.
organiste [ɔʀganist(ə)] *nm/f* organist.

orgasme [ɔʀgasm(ə)] *nm* orgasm, climax.
orge [ɔʀʒ(ə)] *nf* barley.
orgie [ɔʀʒi] *nf* orgy.
orgue [ɔʀg(ə)] *nm* organ; ~s *nfpl* organ
sg.
orgueil [ɔʀgœj] *nm* pride; **orgueilleux,
euse** *a* proud.
Orient [ɔʀjɑ̃] *nm*: l'~ the East, the
Orient.
oriental, e, aux [ɔʀjɑ̃tal, -o] *a* oriental,
eastern; (*frontière*) eastern.
orientation [ɔʀjɑ̃tasjɔ̃] *nf* positioning;
orientation; (*d'une maison etc*) aspect;
(*d'un journal*) leanings *pl*; avoir le sens
de l'~ to have a (good) sense of direction; ~ professionnelle careers advising;
careers advisory service.
orienté, e [ɔʀjɑ̃te] *a* (*fig: article, journal*) slanted; bien/mal ~ (*appartement*)
well/badly positioned; ~ au sud facing
south *ou* with a southern aspect.
orienter [ɔʀjɑ̃te] *vt* (*placer, disposer:
pièce mobile*) to adjust, position; (*tourner*) to direct, turn; (*voyageur, touriste,
recherches*) to direct; (*fig: élève*) to
orientate; s'~ (*se repérer*) to find
one's bearings; s'~ vers (*fig*) to turn
towards.
originaire [ɔʀiʒinɛʀ] *a*: être ~ de to be
a native of.
original, e, aux [ɔʀiʒinal, -o] *a* original; (*bizarre*) eccentric // *nm/f* eccentric
// *nm* (*document etc, ART*) original;
(*dactylographie*) top copy.
origine [ɔʀiʒin] *nf* origin; dès l'~ at *ou*
from the outset; à l'~ originally; **origi-
nel, le** *a* original.
O.R.L. *sigle nm/f de* oto-rhino-
laryngologiste.
orme [ɔʀm(ə)] *nm* elm.
ornement [ɔʀnəmɑ̃] *nm* ornament; (*fig*)
embellishment, adornment.
orner [ɔʀne] *vt* to decorate, adorn.
ornière [ɔʀnjɛʀ] *nf* rut.
orphelin, e [ɔʀfəlɛ̃, -in] *a* orphan(ed) //
nm/f orphan; ~ de père/mère fatherless/
motherless; **orphelinat** *nm* orphanage.
orteil [ɔʀtɛj] *nm* toe; gros ~ big toe.
orthographe [ɔʀtɔgʀaf] *nf* spelling; **orthographier** *vt* to spell.
orthopédiste [ɔʀtɔpedist(ə)] *nm/f*
orthopaedic specialist.
ortie [ɔʀti] *nf* (stinging) nettle.
os [ɔs, *pl o*] *nm* bone.
osciller [ɔsile] *vi* (*pendule*) to swing; (*au
vent etc*) to rock; (*TECH*) to oscillate;
(*fig*): ~ entre to waver *ou* fluctuate between.
osé, e [oze] *a* daring, bold.
oseille [ozɛj] *nf* sorrel.
oser [oze] *vi, vt* to dare; ~ faire to dare
(to) do.
osier [ozje] *nm* willow; d'~, en ~
wicker(work).

ossature [osatyʀ] *nf* (ANAT) frame, skeletal structure; *(fig)* framework.

osseux, euse [ɔsø, -øz] *a* bony; *(tissu, maladie, greffe)* bone *cpd*.

ostensible [ɔstɑ̃sibl(ə)] *a* conspicuous.

otage [ɔtaʒ] *nm* hostage; **prendre qn comme ~** to take sb hostage.

O.T.A.N. [ɔtɑ̃] *sigle f voir* **organisation**.

otarie [ɔtaʀi] *nf* sea-lion.

ôter [ote] *vt* to remove; *(soustraire)* to take away; **~ qch à qn** to take sth (away) from sb; **~ qch de** to remove sth from.

otite [ɔtit] *nf* ear infection.

oto-rhino-(laryngologiste) [ɔtɔʀino(laʀɛ̃gɔlɔʒist(ə)] *nm/f* ear nose and throat specialist.

ou [u] *cj* or; **~ ... ~** either ... or; **~ bien** or (else).

où [u] ♦ *pronom relatif* **1** *(position, situation)* where, that *(souvent omis)*; **la chambre ~ il était** the room (that) he was in, the room where he was; **la ville ~ je l'ai rencontré** the town where I met him; **la pièce d'~ il est sorti** the room he came out of; **le village d'~ je viens** the village I come from; **les villes par ~ il est passé** the towns he went through **2** *(temps, état) (souvent omis)*; **le jour ~ il est parti** the day (that) he left; **au prix ~ c'est** at the price it is ♦ *ad* **1** *(interrogation)* where; **~ est-il/va-t-il?** where is he/is he going?; **par ~?** which way?; **d'~ vient que ...?** how come ...? **2** *(position)* where; **je sais ~ il est** I know where he is; **~ que l'on aille** wherever you go.

ouate [wat] *nf* cotton wool *(Brit)*, cotton *(US)*; *(bourre)* padding, wadding.

oubli [ubli] *nm (acte)*: **l'~ de** forgetting; *(étourderie)* forgetfulness *q*; *(négligence)* omission, oversight; *(absence de souvenirs)* oblivion.

oublier [ublije] *vt (gén)* to forget; *(ne pas voir: erreurs etc)* to miss; *(ne pas mettre: virgule, nom)* to leave out; *(laisser quelque part: chapeau etc)* to leave behind; **s'~** to forget o.s.

oubliettes [ublijɛt] *nfpl* dungeon *sg*.

oublieux, euse [ublijø, -øz] *a* forgetful.

ouest [wɛst] *nm* west // *a inv* west; *(région)* western; **à l'~** in the west; **(to the) west, westwards; **à l'~ de** (to the) west of.

ouf [uf] *excl* phew!

oui [wi] *ad* yes.

ouï-dire [widiʀ]: **par ~** *ad* by hearsay.

ouïe [wi] *nf* hearing; **~s** *nfpl (de poisson)* gills.

ouïr [wiʀ] *vt* to hear; **avoir ouï dire que** to have heard it said that.

ouragan [uʀagɑ̃] *nm* hurricane.

ourlet [uʀlɛ] *nm* hem.

ours [uʀs] *nm* bear; **~ brun/blanc** brown/polar bear; **~ (en peluche)** teddy (bear).

oursin [uʀsɛ̃] *nm* sea urchin.

ourson [uʀsɔ̃] *nm* (bear-)cub.

ouste [ust(ə)] *excl* hop it!

outil [uti] *nm* tool.

outiller [utije] *vt (ouvrier, usine)* to equip.

outrage [utʀaʒ] *nm* insult; **faire subir les derniers ~s à** *(femme)* to ravish; **~ à la pudeur** indecent conduct *q*.

outrager [utʀaʒe] *vt* to offend gravely.

outrance [utʀɑ̃s]: **à ~** *ad* excessively, to excess.

outre [utʀ(ə)] *nf* goatskin, water skin // *prép* besides // *ad*: **passer ~ à** to disregard, take no notice of; **en ~** besides, moreover; **~ que** apart from the fact that; **~ mesure** immoderately; unduly.

outre-Atlantique [utʀatlɑ̃tik] *ad* across the Atlantic.

outre-Manche [utʀəmɑ̃ʃ] *ad* across the Channel.

outremer [utʀəmɛʀ] *a inv* ultramarine.

outre-mer [utʀəmɛʀ] *ad* overseas.

outrepasser [utʀəpɑse] *vt* to go beyond, exceed.

outrer [utʀe] *vt* to exaggerate; *(choquer)* to outrage.

ouvert, e [uvɛʀ, -ɛʀt(ə)] *pp de* **ouvrir** // *a* open; *(robinet, gaz etc)* on; **ouvertement** *ad* openly.

ouverture [uvɛʀtyʀ] *nf* opening; *(MUS)* overture; *(PHOTO)*: **~ (du diaphragme)** aperture; **~s** *nfpl (propositions)* overtures; **~ d'esprit** open-mindedness.

ouvrable [uvʀabl(ə)] *a*: **jour ~** working day, weekday.

ouvrage [uvʀaʒ] *nm (tâche, de tricot etc, MIL)* work *q*; *(texte, livre)* work.

ouvragé, e [uvʀaʒe] *a* finely embroidered *(ou worked ou carved)*.

ouvre-boîte(s) [uvʀəbwat] *nm inv* tin *(Brit)* ou can opener.

ouvre-bouteille(s) [uvʀəbutɛj] *nm inv* bottle-opener.

ouvreuse [uvʀøz] *nf* usherette.

ouvrier, ière [uvʀije, -jɛʀ] *nm/f* worker // *a* working-class; industrial, labour *cpd*; **classe ouvrière** working class.

ouvrir [uvʀiʀ] *vt (gén)* to open; *(brèche, passage, MÉD: abcès)* to open up; *(commencer l'exploitation de, créer)* to open (up); *(eau, électricité, chauffage, robinet)* to turn on // *vi* to open; to open up; **s'~** *vi* to open; **s'~ à qn** to open one's heart to sb; **~ l'appétit à qn** to whet sb's appetite.

ovaire [ɔvɛʀ] *nm* ovary.

ovale [ɔval] *a* oval.

ovni [ɔvni] *sigle m* (= *objet volant non identifié*) UFO.

oxyder [ɔkside]: **s'~** *vi* to become oxidized.

oxygène [ɔksiʒɛn] *nm* oxygen; *(fig)*:

cure d'~ fresh air cure.

oxygéné, e [ɔksiʒene] a: eau ~e hydrogen peroxide.

P

pacifique [pasifik] a peaceful // nm: le P~, l'océan P~ the Pacific (Ocean).

pacte [pakt(ə)] nm pact, treaty.

pactiser [paktize] vi: ~ avec to come to terms with.

pagaie [pagɛ] nf paddle.

pagaille [pagaj] nf mess, shambles sg.

page [paʒ] nf page // nm page; à la ~ (fig) up-to-date.

paie [pɛ] nf = paye.

paiement [pɛmɑ̃] nm = payement.

païen, ne [pajɛ̃, -jɛn] a, nm/f pagan, heathen.

paillard, e [pajaʀ, -aʀd(ə)] a bawdy.

paillasson [pajasɔ̃] nm doormat.

paille [paj] nf straw; (défaut) flaw.

paillettes [pajɛt] nfpl (décoratives) sequins, spangles; lessive en ~ soapflakes pl.

pain [pɛ̃] nm (substance) bread; (unité) loaf (pl loaves) (of bread); (morceau): ~ de cire etc bar of wax etc; ~ bis/complet brown/wholemeal (Brit) ou wholewheat (US) bread; ~ d'épice gingerbread; ~ grillé toast; ~ de mie sandwich loaf; ~ de sucre sugar loaf.

pair, e [pɛʀ] a (nombre) even // nm peer; aller de ~ to go hand in hand ou together; jeune fille au ~ au pair.

paire [pɛʀ] nf pair.

paisible [pezibl(ə)] a peaceful, quiet.

paître [pɛtʀ(ə)] vi to graze.

paix [pɛ] nf peace; (fig) peacefulness, peace; faire/avoir la ~ to make/have peace.

Pakistan [pakistɑ̃] nm: le ~ Pakistan.

palace [palas] nm luxury hotel.

palais [palɛ] nm palace; (ANAT) palate.

pale [pal] nf (d'hélice, de rame) blade.

pâle [pɑl] a pale; bleu ~ pale blue.

Palestine [palɛstin] nf: la ~ Palestine; **palestinien, ne** a, nm/f Palestinian.

palet [palɛ] nm disc; (HOCKEY) puck.

palette [palɛt] nf (de peintre) palette; (produits) range.

pâleur [palœʀ] nf paleness.

palier [palje] nm (d'escalier) landing; (fig) level, plateau; (TECH) bearing; par ~s in stages.

pâlir [paliʀ] vi to turn ou go pale; (couleur) to fade.

palissade [palisad] nf fence.

palliatif [paljatif] nm palliative; (expédient) stopgap measure.

pallier [palje] vt: ~ à; vt to offset, make up for.

palmarès [palmaʀɛs] nm record (of achievements); (SCOL) prize list; (SPORT) list of winners.

palme [palm(ə)] nf (symbole) palm; (de plongeur) flipper; **palmé, e** a (pattes) webbed.

palmier [palmje] nm palm tree.

palombe [palɔ̃b] nf woodpigeon.

pâlot, te [palo, -ɔt] a pale, peaky.

palourde [paluʀd(ə)] nf clam.

palper [palpe] vt to feel, finger.

palpitant, e [palpitɑ̃, -ɑ̃t] a thrilling.

palpiter [palpite] vi (cœur, pouls) to beat; (: plus fort) to pound, throb.

paludisme [palydism(ə)] nm malaria.

pamphlet [pɑ̃flɛ] nm lampoon, satirical tract.

pamplemousse [pɑ̃pləmus] nm grapefruit.

pan [pɑ̃] nm section, piece // excl bang!; ~ de chemise shirt tail.

panachage [panaʃaʒ] nm blend, mix.

panache [panaʃ] nm plume; (fig) spirit, panache.

panaché, e [panaʃe] a: glace ~e mixed-flavour ice cream; bière ~e shandy.

pancarte [pɑ̃kaʀt(ə)] nf sign, notice; (dans un défilé) placard.

pancréas [pɑ̃kʀeas] nm pancreas.

pané, e [pane] a fried in breadcrumbs.

panier [panje] nm basket; mettre au ~ to chuck away; ~ à provisions shopping basket.

panique [panik] nf, a panic; **paniquer** vi to panic.

panne [pan] nf (d'un mécanisme, moteur) breakdown; être/tomber en ~ to have broken down/break down; être en ~ d'essence ou sèche to have run out of petrol (Brit) ou gas (US); ~ d'électricité ou de courant power ou electrical failure.

panneau, x [pano] nm (écriteau) sign, notice; (de boiserie, de tapisserie etc) panel; ~ d'affichage notice board; ~ de signalisation roadsign.

panonceau, x [panɔ̃so] nm sign.

panoplie [panɔpli] nf (jouet) outfit; (d'armes) display; (fig) array.

panorama [panɔʀama] nm panorama.

panse [pɑ̃s] nf paunch.

pansement [pɑ̃smɑ̃] nm dressing, bandage; ~ adhésif sticking plaster.

panser [pɑ̃se] vt (plaie) to dress, bandage; (bras) to put a dressing on, bandage; (cheval) to groom.

pantalon [pɑ̃talɔ̃] nm (aussi: ~s, paire de ~s) trousers pl, pair of trousers; ~ de ski ski pants pl.

pantelant, e [pɑ̃tlɑ̃, -ɑ̃t] a gasping for breath, panting.

panthère [pɑ̃tɛʀ] nf panther.

pantin [pɑ̃tɛ̃] nm jumping jack; (péj) puppet.

pantois [pɑ̃twa] am: rester ~ to be flabbergasted.

pantomime [pɑ̃tɔmim] nf mime;

(pièce) mime show.

pantoufle [pɑ̃tufl(ə)] *nf* slipper.

paon [pɑ̃] *nm* peacock.

papa [papa] *nm* dad(dy).

pape [pap] *nm* pope.

paperasse [papRas] *nf* (péj) bumf *q*, papers *pl*; **~s** *nf* (péj) red tape *q*; paperwork *q*.

papeterie [papetRi] *nf* (usine) paper mill; *(magasin)* stationer's (shop).

papier [papje] *nm* paper; *(article)* article; **~s** *(aussi:* **~s d'identité)** (identity) papers; **~ (d')aluminium** aluminium (Brit) *ou* aluminum (US) foil, tinfoil; **~ buvard** blotting paper; **~ carbone** carbon paper; **~ hygiénique** toilet paper; **~ journal** newsprint; *(pour emballer)* newspaper; **~ à lettres** writing paper, notepaper; **~ peint** wallpaper; **~ de verre** sandpaper.

papillon [papijɔ̃] *nm* butterfly; *(fam: contravention)* (parking) ticket; *(TECH: écrou)* wing nut; **~ de nuit** moth.

papilloter [papijɔte] *vi* to blink, flicker.

paquebot [pakbo] *nm* liner.

pâquerette [pakRɛt] *nf* daisy.

Pâques [pak] *nm, nfpl* Easter.

paquet [pakɛ] *nm* packet; *(colis)* parcel; *(fig: tas):* **~ de** pile *ou* heap of; **~-cadeau** *nm* gift-wrapped parcel.

par [paR] *prép* by; **finir** *etc* **~** to end *etc* with; **~ amour** out of love; **passer ~ Lyon/la côte** to go via *ou* through Lyons/along by the coast; **~ la fenêtre** *(jeter, regarder)* out of the window; **3 ~ jour/personne** 3 a *ou* per day/head; **2 ~ 2** two at a time; in twos; **~ ici** this way; *(dans le coin)* round here; **~-ci, ~-là** here and there.

parabole [paRabɔl] *nf* (REL) parable.

parachever [paRaʃve] *vt* to perfect.

parachute [paRaʃyt] *nm* parachute.

parachutiste [paRaʃytist(ə)] *nm/f* parachutist; *(MIL)* paratrooper.

parade [paRad] *nf* (spectacle, défilé) parade; *(ESCRIME, BOXE)* parry.

paradis [paRadi] *nm* heaven, paradise.

paradoxe [paRadɔks(ə)] *nm* paradox.

paraffine [paRafin] *nf* paraffin.

parages [paRaʒ] *nmpl:* **dans les ~ (de)** in the area *ou* vicinity (of).

paragraphe [paRagRaf] *nm* paragraph.

paraître [paRɛtR(ə)] *vb avec attribut* to seem, look, appear // *vi* to appear; *(être visible)* to show; *(PRESSE, ÉDITION)* to be published, come out, appear; *(briller)* to show off // *vb impersonnel:* **il paraît que** it seems *ou* appears that; they say that; **il me paraît que** it seems to me that.

parallèle [paRalɛl] *a* parallel; *(police, marché)* unofficial // *nm (comparaison):* **faire un ~ entre** to draw a parallel between; *(GÉO)* parallel // *nf* parallel (line).

paralyser [paRalize] *vt* to paralyze.

parapet [paRapɛ] *nm* parapet.

parapher [paRafe] *vt* to initial; to sign.

paraphrase [paRafRɑz] *nf* paraphrase.

parapluie [paRaplɥi] *nm* umbrella.

parasite [paRazit] *nm* parasite; **~s** *(TÉL)* interference *sg*.

parasol [paRasɔl] *nm* parasol, sunshade.

paratonnerre [paRatɔnɛR] *nm* lightning conductor.

paravent [paRavɑ̃] *nm* folding screen.

parc [paRk] *nm* (public) park, gardens *pl*; *(de château etc)* grounds *pl*; *(pour le bétail)* pen, enclosure; *(d'enfant)* playpen; *(MIL: entrepôt)* depot; *(ensemble d'unités)* stock; *(de voitures etc)* fleet; **~ automobile** *(d'un pays)* number of cars on the roads; **~ de stationnement** car park.

parcelle [paRsɛl] *nf* fragment, scrap; *(de terrain)* plot, parcel.

parce que [paRsk(ə)] *cj* because.

parchemin [paRʃəmɛ̃] *nm* parchment.

parc(o)mètre [paRk(ɔ)mɛtR(ə)] *nm* parking meter.

parcourir [paRkuRiR] *vt* (trajet, distance) to cover; *(article, livre)* to skim *ou* glance through; *(lieu)* to go all over, travel up and down; *(suj: frisson, vibration)* to run through.

parcours [paRkuR] *nm* (trajet) journey; *(itinéraire)* route; *(SPORT: terrain)* course; *(: tour)* round; run; lap.

par-dessous [paRdəsu] *prép, ad* under(neath).

pardessus [paRdəsy] *nm* overcoat.

par-dessus [paRdəsy] *prép* over (the top of) // *ad* over (the top); **~ le marché** on top of all that.

par-devant [paRdəvɑ̃] *prép* in the presence of, before // *ad* at the front; round the front.

pardon [paRdɔ̃] *nm* forgiveness *q* // *excl* sorry!; *(pour interpeller etc)* excuse me!; **demander ~ à qn (de)** to apologize to sb (for); **je vous demande ~** I'm sorry; excuse me.

pardonner [paRdɔne] *vt* to forgive; **~ qch à qn** to forgive sb for sth.

pare-balles [paRbal] *a inv* bulletproof.

pare-boue [paRbu] *nm inv* mudguard.

pare-brise [paRbRiz] *nm inv* windscreen (Brit), windshield (US).

pare-chocs [paRʃɔk] *nm inv* bumper.

pareil, le [paRɛj] *a (identique)* the same, alike; *(similaire)* similar; *(tel):* **un courage/livre ~** such courage/a book, courage/a book like this; **de ~s livres** such books; **ses ~s** one's fellow men; one's peers; **ne pas avoir son(sa) ~(le)** to be second to none; **~ à** the same as; similar to; **sans ~** unparalleled, unequalled.

parent, e [paRɑ̃, -ɑ̃t] *nm/f:* **un/une ~/e** a relative *ou* relation // *a:* **être ~ de** to be related to; **~š** *nmpl* (*père et mère*) parents; **parenté** *nf* (*lien*) relationship.

parenthèse [paʀɑ̃tɛz] *nf* (*ponctuation*) bracket, parenthesis; (*MATH*) bracket; (*digression*) parenthesis, digression; **ouvrir/fermer la ~** to open/close the brackets; **entre ~s** in brackets; (*fig*) incidentally.

parer [paʀe] *vt* to adorn; (*CULIN*) to dress, trim; (*éviter*) to ward off.

pare-soleil [paʀsɔlej] *nm inv* sun visor.

paresse [paʀɛs] *nf* laziness; **paresseux, euse** *a* lazy; (*fig*) slow, sluggish.

parfaire [paʀfɛʀ] *vt* to perfect.

parfait, e [paʀfɛ, -ɛt] *a* perfect // *nm* (*LING*) perfect (tense); **parfaitement** *ad* perfectly // *excl* (*most*) certainly.

parfois [paʀfwa] *ad* sometimes.

parfum [paʀfœ̃] *nm* (*produit*) perfume, scent; (*odeur: de fleur*) scent, fragrance; (: *de tabac, vin*) aroma; (*goût*) flavour; **parfumé, e** *a* (*fleur, fruit*) fragrant; (*femme*) perfumed; **parfumé au café** coffee-flavoured; **parfumer** *vt* (*suj: odeur, bouquet*) to perfume; (*mouchoir*) to put scent on; **se parfumer** to perfume; (*crème, gâteau*) to flavour; **parfumerie** *nf* (*commerce*) perfumery; (*produits*) perfumes *pl*; (*boutique*) perfume shop.

pari [paʀi] *nm* bet, wager; (*SPORT*) bet.

paria [paʀja] *nm* outcast.

parier [paʀje] *vt* to bet.

Paris [paʀi] *n* Paris; **parisien, ne** *a* Parisian; (*GÉO, ADMIN*) Paris *cpd* // *nm/f*: **Parisien, ne** Parisian.

paritaire [paʀitɛʀ] *a* joint.

parjure [paʀʒyʀ] *nm* perjury; **se parjurer** *vi* to forswear *ou* perjure o.s.

parking [paʀkiŋ] *nm* (*lieu*) car park.

parlant, e [paʀlɑ̃, -ɑ̃t] *a* (*fig*) graphic, vivid; eloquent; (*CINÉMA*) talking.

parlement [paʀləmɑ̃] *nm* parliament; **parlementaire** *a* parliamentary // *nm/f* member of parliament.

parlementer [paʀləmɑ̃te] *vi* to negotiate, parley.

parler [paʀle] *vi* to speak, talk; (*avouer*) to talk; **~ à qn** de to talk *ou* speak (to sb) about; **~ le/en français** to speak French/in French; **~ affaires** to talk business; **~ en dormant** to talk in one's sleep; **sans ~ de** (*fig*) not to mention, to say nothing of; **tu parles!** you must be joking!

parloir [paʀlwaʀ] *nm* (*de prison, d'hôpital*) visiting room; (*REL*) parlour.

parmi [paʀmi] *prép* among(st).

paroi [paʀwa] *nf* wall; (*cloison*) partition; **~ rocheuse** rock face.

paroisse [paʀwas] *nf* parish.

parole [paʀɔl] *nf* (*faculté*): **la ~** speech; (*mot, promesse*) word; **~s** (*MUS*) words, lyrics; **tenir ~** to keep one's word; **prendre la ~** to speak; **demander la ~** to ask for permission to speak; **je le crois sur ~**

I'll take his word for it.

parquer [paʀke] *vt* (*voiture, matériel*) to park; (*bestiaux*) to pen in *ou* up).

parquet [paʀkɛ] *nm* (*parquet*) floor; (*JUR*): **le ~** the Public Prosecutor's department.

parrain [paʀɛ̃] *nm* godfather; (*d'un nouvel adhérent*) sponsor, proposer.

pars *vb voir* **partir**.

parsemer [paʀsəme] *vt* (*suj: feuilles, papiers*) to be scattered over; **~ qch de** to scatter sth with.

part [paʀ] *nf* (*qui revient à qn*) share; (*fraction, partie*) part; (*FINANCE*) (non-voting) share; **prendre ~ à** (*débat etc*) to take part in; (*soucis, douleur de qn*) to share in; **faire ~ de qch à qn** to announce sth to sb, inform sb of sth; **pour ma ~** as for me, as far as I'm concerned; **à ~ entière** *a* full; **de la ~ de** (*au nom de*) on behalf of; (*donné par*) from; **de toute(s) ~(s)** from all sides *ou* quarters; **de ~ et d'autre** on both sides, on either side; **de ~ en ~** right through; **d'une ~ ... d'autre ~** on the one hand ... on the other hand; **à ~** *ad* separately; (*de côté*) aside // *prép* apart from, except for // *a* exceptional, special; **faire la ~ des choses** to make allowances.

partage [paʀtaʒ] *nm* dividing up; sharing (out) *q*, share-out; sharing; **recevoir qch en ~** to receive sth as one's share (*ou* lot).

partager [paʀtaʒe] *vt* to share; (*distribuer, répartir*) to share (out); (*morceler, diviser*) to divide (up); **se ~** *vt* (*héritage etc*) to share between themselves (*ou* ourselves).

partance [paʀtɑ̃s]: **en ~** *ad* outbound, due to leave; **en ~ pour** (bound) for.

partant, e [paʀtɑ̃] *vb voir* **partir** // *nm* (*SPORT*) starter; (*HIPPISME*) runner.

partenaire [paʀtənɛʀ] *nm/f* partner.

parterre [paʀtɛʀ] *nm* (*de fleurs*) (flower) bed; (*THÉÂTRE*) stalls *pl*.

parti [paʀti] *nm* (*POL*) party; (*décision*) course of action; (*personne à marier*) match; **tirer ~ de** to take advantage of, turn to good account; **prendre le ~ de qn** to stand up for sb, side with sb; **prendre ~ (pour/contre)** to take sides *ou* a stand (for/against); **prendre son ~ de** to come to terms with; **~ pris** bias.

partial, e, aux [paʀsjal, -o] *a* biased, partial.

participant, e [paʀtisipɑ̃, -ɑ̃t] *nm/f* participant; (*à un concours*) entrant.

participation [paʀtisipasjɔ̃] *nf* participation; sharing; (*COMM*) interest; **la ~ aux bénéfices** profit-sharing.

participe [paʀtisip] *nm* participle.

participer [paʀtisipe]: **~ à** *vt* (*course, réunion*) to take part in; (*profits etc*) to share in; (*frais etc*) to contribute to; (*chagrin, succès de qn*) to share (in).

particularité [partikylarite] *nf* particularity; (*distinctive*) characteristic.

particule [partikyl] *nf* particle.

particulier, ière [partikylje, -jɛʀ] *a* (*personnel, privé*) private; (*spécial*) special, particular; (*caractéristique*) characteristic, distinctive; (*spécifique*) particular // *nm* (*individu: ADMIN*) private individual; ~ **à** peculiar to; **en** ~ *ad* (*surtout*) in particular, particularly; (*en privé*) in private; **particulièrement** *ad* particularly.

partie [parti] *nf* (*gén*) part; (*profession, spécialité*) field, subject; (*JUR etc: protagonistes*) party; (*de cartes, tennis etc*) game; **une** ~ **de campagne/de pêche** an outing in the country/a fishing party *ou* trip; **en** ~ *ad* partly, in part; **faire** ~ **de** to belong to; (*suj: chose*) to be part of; **prendre qn à** ~ to take sb to task; (*malmener*) to set on sb; **en grande** ~ largely, in the main; ~ **civile** (*JUR*) party claiming damages in a criminal case.

partiel, le [parsjɛl] *a* partial // *nm* (*SCOL*) class exam.

partir [partir] *vi* (*gén*) to go; (*quitter*) to go, leave; (*s'éloigner*) to go (*ou* drive etc) away *ou* off; (*moteur*) to start; ~ **de** (*lieu: quitter*) to leave; (: *commencer à*) to start from; (*date*) to run *ou* start from; **à** ~ **de** from.

partisan, e [partizɑ̃, -an] *nm/f* partisan // *a*: **être** ~ **de qch/faire** to be in favour of sth/doing.

partition [partisjɔ̃] *nf* (*MUS*) score.

partout [partu] *ad* everywhere; ~ **où il allait** everywhere *ou* wherever he went; **trente** ~ (*TENNIS*) thirty all.

paru *pp de* **paraître**.

parure [paryr] *nf* (*bijoux etc*) finery *q*; jewellery *q*; (*assortiment*) set.

parution [parysjɔ̃] *nf* publication, appearance.

parvenir [parvənir]: ~ **à** *vt* (*atteindre*) to reach; (*réussir*): ~ **à faire** to manage to do, succeed in doing; **faire** ~ **qch à qn** to have sth sent to sb.

parvis [parvi] *nm* square (*in front of a church*).

pas [pɑ] *ad voir le mot suivant* // *nm* (*allure, mesure*) pace; (*démarche*) tread; (*enjambée, DANSE*) step; (*bruit*) (foot)step; (*trace*) footprint; (*TECH: de vis, d'écrou*) thread; ~ **à** ~ step by step; **au** ~ at walking pace; **à** ~ **de loup** stealthily; **faire les cent** ~ to pace up and down; **faire les premiers** ~ to make the first move; **sur le** ~ **de la porte** on the doorstep.

pas [pɑ] ♦ *nm voir le mot précédent* ♦ *ad* **1** (*en corrélation avec ne, non etc*) not; **il ne pleure** ~ he does not *ou* doesn't cry; he's not *ou* isn't crying; **il n'a** ~ **pleuré/ne pleurera** ~ he did not *ou*

didn't/will not *ou* won't cry; **ils n'ont** ~ **de voiture/d'enfants** they haven't got a car/any children, they have no car/ children; **il m'a dit de ne** ~ **le faire** he told me not to do it; **non** ~ **que ...** not that ...

2 (*employé sans ne etc*): ~ **moi** not me; not I, I don't (*ou* can't etc); **une pomme** ~ **mûre** an apple which isn't ripe; ~ **plus tard qu'hier** only yesterday; ~ **du tout** not at all

3: ~ **mal** not bad; not badly; ~ **mal de** quite a lot of.

passage [pasaʒ] *nm* (*fait de passer*) *voir* **passer**; (*lieu, prix de la traversée, extrait de livre etc*) passage; (*chemin*) way; **de** ~ (*touristes*) passing through; (*amants etc*) casual; ~ **clouté** pedestrian crossing; **'**~ **interdit'** 'no entry'; ~ **à niveau** level crossing; **'**~ **protégé'** *right of way over secondary road(s) on your right*; ~ **souterrain** subway (*Brit*), underpass.

passager, ère [pasaʒe, -ɛʀ] *a* passing // *nm/f* passenger; ~ **clandestin** stowaway.

passant, e [pasɑ̃, -ɑ̃t] *a* (*rue, endroit*) busy // *nm/f* passer-by; **en** ~ in passing.

passe [pas] *nf* (*SPORT, magnétique, NAVIG*) pass // *nm* (*passe-partout*) master *ou* skeleton key; **être en** ~ **de faire** to be on the way to doing.

passé, e [pase] *a* (*événement, temps*) past; (*couleur, tapisserie*) faded // *prép* after // *nm* past; (*LING*) past (tense); ~ **de mode** out of fashion; ~ **composé** perfect (tense); ~ **simple** past historic.

passe-droit [pasdrwa] *nm* special privilege.

passementerie [pasmɑ̃tri] *nf* trimmings *pl*.

passe-montagne [pasmɔ̃taɲ] *nm* balaclava.

passe-partout [paspartu] *nm inv* master *ou* skeleton key // *a inv* all-purpose.

passe-passe [paspas] *nm*: **tour de** ~ trick, sleight of hand *q*.

passeport [paspɔʀ] *nm* passport.

passer [pase] *vi* (*se rendre, aller*) to go; (*voiture, piétons: défiler*) to pass (by), go by; (*faire une halte rapide: facteur, laitier etc*) to call *ou* drop in; (: *pour rendre visite*) to call *ou* drop in; (*courant, air, lumière, franchir un obstacle etc*) to get through; (*accusé, projet de loi*): ~ **devant** to come before; (*film, émission*) to be on; (*temps, jours*) to pass, go by; (*couleur, papier*) to fade; (*mode*) to die out; (*douleur*) to pass, go away; (*CARTES*) to pass; (*SCOL*) to go up (to the next class) // *vt* (*frontière, rivière etc*) to cross; (*douane*) to go through; (*examen*) to sit, take; (*visite médicale etc*) to have; (*journée, temps*) to spend; (*donner*): ~ **qch à qn** to pass sth to sb; to give sb sth; (*transmettre*): ~ **qch à**

qn to pass sth on to sb; *(enfiler: vête-ment)* to slip on; *(faire entrer, mettre)*: **(faire)** ~ qch dans/par to get sth into/ through; *(café)* to pour the water on; *(thé, soupe)* to strain; *(film, pièce)* to show, put on; *(disque)* to play, put on; *(marché, accord)* to agree on; *(tolérer)*: ~ qch à qn to let sb get away with sth; **se** ~ *vi (avoir lieu: scène, action)* to take place; *(se dérouler: entretien etc)* to go; *(arriver)*: **que s'est-il passé?** what happened?; *(s'écouler: semaine etc)* to pass, go by; **se** ~ **de** *vt* to go *ou* do without; **se** ~ **les mains sous l'eau/de l'eau sur le visage** to put one's hands under the tap/run water over one's face; ~ **par** to go through; ~ **sur** *vt (faute, détail inutile)* to pass over; ~ **avant** qch/qn *(fig)* to come before sth/sb; **laisser** ~ *(air, lumière, personne)* to let through; *(occasion)* to let slip, miss; *(erreur)* to overlook; ~ **à la radio/télévision** to be on the radio/on television; ~ **pour riche** to be taken for a rich man; ~ **en seconde**, ~ **la seconde** *(AUTO)* to change into second; ~ **le balai/l'aspirateur** to sweep up/ hoover; **je vous passe M. X** *(je vous mets en communication avec lui)* I'm putting you through to Mr X; *(je lui passe l'appareil)* here is Mr X, I'll pass you over to Mr X.

passerelle [pasʀɛl] *nf* footbridge; *(de navire, avion)* gangway.

passe-temps [pɑstɑ̃] *nm inv* pastime.

passette [pasɛt] *nf* (tea-)strainer.

passeur, euse [pasœʀ, -øz] *nm/f* smuggler.

passible [pasibl(ə)] *a*: ~ **de** liable to.

passif, ive [pasif, -iv] *a* passive // *nm (LING)* passive; *(COMM)* liabilities *pl*.

passion [pasjɔ̃] *nf* passion; **passion-nant, e** *a* fascinating; **passionné, e** *a* passionate; impassioned; **passionner** *vt (personne)* to fascinate, grip; **se passionner pour** to take an avid interest in; to have a passion for.

passoire [paswaʀ] *nf* sieve; *(à légumes)* colander; *(à thé)* strainer.

pastèque [pastɛk] *nf* watermelon.

pasteur [pastœʀ] *nm (protestant)* minister, pastor.

pastille [pastij] *nf (à sucer)* lozenge, pastille; *(de papier etc)* (small) disc.

patate [patat] *nf*: ~ **douce** sweet potato.

patauger [patoʒe] *vi (pour s'amuser)* to splash about; *(avec effort)* to wade about.

pâte [pɑt] *nf (à tarte)* pastry; *(à pain)* dough; *(à frire)* batter; *(substance molle)* paste; cream; ~**s** *nfpl (macaroni etc)* pasta *sg*; ~ **d'amandes** almond paste; ~ **brisée** shortcrust pastry; ~ **de fruits** crystallized fruit *q*; ~ **à modeler** modelling clay, Plasticine ® *(Brit)*.

pâté [pɑte] *nm (charcuterie)* pâté; *(tache)* ink blot; *(de sable)* sandpie; ~ **en croûte** ≈ pork pie; ~ **de maisons** block (of houses).

pâtée [pɑte] *nf* mash, feed.

patente [patɑ̃t] *nf (COMM)* trading licence.

patère [pateʀ] *nf* (coat-)peg.

paternel, le [patɛʀnɛl] *a (amour, soins)* fatherly; *(ligne, autorité)* paternal.

pâteux, euse [pɑtø, -øz] *a* thick; pasty.

pathétique [patetik] *a* moving.

patience [pasjɑ̃s] *nf* patience.

patient, e [pasjɑ̃, -ɑ̃t] *a, nm/f* patient.

patienter [pasjɑ̃te] *vi* to wait.

patin [patɛ̃] *nm* skate; *(sport)* skating; ~**s (à glace)** (ice) skates; ~**s à roulettes** roller skates.

patinage [patinaʒ] *nm* skating.

patiner [patine] *vi* to skate; *(em-brayage)* to slip; *(roue, voiture)* to spin; **se** ~ *vi (meuble, cuir)* to acquire a sheen; **patineur, euse** *nm/f* skater; **patinoire** *nf* skating rink, (ice) rink.

pâtir [pɑtiʀ]: ~ **de** *vt* to suffer because of.

pâtisserie [pɑtisʀi] *nf (boutique)* cake shop; *(métier)* confectionery; *(à la maison)* pastry- *ou* cake-making, baking; ~**s** *nfpl (gâteaux)* pastries, cakes; **pâtis-sier, ière** *nm/f* pastrycook; confectioner.

patois [patwa] *nm* dialect, patois.

patrie [patʀi] *nf* homeland.

patrimoine [patʀimwan] *nm* inheritance, patrimony; *(culture)* heritage.

patriotique [patʀijɔtik] *a* patriotic.

patron, ne [patʀɔ̃, -ɔn] *nm/f* boss; *(REL)* patron saint // *nm (COUTURE)* pattern.

patronat [patʀɔna] *nm* employers *pl*.

patronner [patʀɔne] *vt* to sponsor, support.

patrouille [patʀuj] *nf* patrol.

patte [pat] *nf (jambe)* leg; *(pied: de chien, chat)* paw; *(: d'oiseau)* foot; *(lan-guette)* strap.

pâturage [pɑtyʀaʒ] *nm* pasture.

pâture [pɑtyʀ] *nf* food.

paume [pom] *nf* palm.

paumé, e [pome] *nm/f (fam)* drop-out.

paumer [pome] *vt (fam)* to lose.

paupière [popjɛʀ] *nf* eyelid.

pause [poz] *nf (arrêt)* break; *(en parlant, MUS)* pause.

pauvre [povʀ(ə)] *a* poor; ~**té** *nf (état)* poverty.

pavaner [pavane]: **se** ~ *vi* to strut about.

pavé, e [pave] *a* paved; cobbled // *nm (bloc)* paving stone; cobblestone; *(pavage)* paving.

pavillon [pavijɔ̃] *nm (de banlieue)* small (detached) house; *(kiosque)* lodge; pavilion; *(drapeau)* flag.

pavoiser [pavwaze] *vi* to put out flags; *(fig)* to rejoice, exult.

pavot [pavo] nm poppy.

payant, e [pɛjɑ̃, -ɑ̃t] a (spectateurs etc) paying; (fig: entreprise) profitable; **c'est ~** you have to pay, there is a charge.

paye [pɛj] nf pay, wages pl.

payement [pɛjmɑ̃] nm payment.

payer [peje] vt (créancier, employé, loyer) to pay; (achat, réparations, fig: faute) to pay for // vi to pay; (métier) to be well-paid; (tactique etc) to pay off; **il me l'a fait ~ 10 F** he charged me 10 F for it; **~ qch à qn** to buy sth for sb, buy sb sth; **cela ne le paie pas de mine** it doesn't look much.

pays [pei] nm country; land; region; village; **du ~** a local.

paysage [peizaʒ] nm landscape.

paysan, ne [peizɑ̃, -an] nm/f countryman/woman; farmer; (péj) peasant // a country cpd, farming; farmers'.

Pays-Bas [peiba] nmpl: **les ~** the Netherlands.

PC nm (INFORM) PC.

PDG sigle m voir **président**.

péage [peaʒ] nm toll; (endroit) tollgate; **pont à ~** toll bridge.

peau, x [po] nf skin; **gants de ~** fine leather gloves; **~ de chamois** (chiffon) chamois leather, shammy; **P~-Rouge** nm/f Red Indian, redskin.

péché [peʃe] nm sin.

pêche [pɛʃ] nf (sport, activité) fishing; (poissons pêchés) catch; (fruit) peach; **~ à la ligne** (en rivière) angling.

pécher [peʃe] vi (REL) to sin; (fig: personne) to err; (: chose) to be flawed.

pêcher [peʃe] nm peach tree // vi to go fishing // vt to catch; to fish for.

pêcheur, eresse [peʃœʀ, peʃʀɛs] nm/f sinner.

pêcheur [peʃœʀ] nm fisherman; angler.

pécule [pekyl] nm savings pl, nest egg.

pécuniaire [pekynjɛʀ] a financial.

pédagogie [pedagoʒi] nf educational methods pl, pedagogy; **pédagogique** a educational.

pédale [pedal] nf pedal.

pédalo [pedalo] nm pedal-boat.

pédant, e [pedɑ̃, -ɑ̃t] a (péj) pedantic.

pédestre [pedɛstʀ(ə)] a: **tourisme ~** hiking.

pédiatre [pedjatʀ(ə)] nm/f paediatrician, child specialist.

pédicure [pedikyʀ] nm/f chiropodist.

pègre [pɛgʀ(ə)] nf underworld.

peignais etc vb voir **peindre, peigner**.

peigne [pɛɲ] nm comb.

peigner [pɛɲe] vt to comb (the hair of); **se ~** vi to comb one's hair.

peignoir [pɛɲwaʀ] nm dressing gown; **~ de bain** bathrobe.

peindre [pɛ̃dʀ(ə)] vt to paint; (fig) to portray, depict.

peine [pɛn] nf (affliction) sorrow, sad-

ness q; (mal, effort) trouble q, effort; (difficulté) difficulty; (punition, châtiment) punishment; (JUR) sentence; **faire de la ~ à qn** to distress ou upset sb; **prendre la ~ de faire** to go to the trouble of doing; **se donner de la ~** to make an effort; **ce n'est pas la ~ de faire** there's no point in doing, it's not worth doing; **à ~** scarcely, hardly, barely; **à ~ ...** **que** hardly ... than; **défense d'afficher sous ~ d'amende** billposters will be fined; **~ capitale** ou **de mort** capital punishment, death sentence; **peiner** vi to work hard; to struggle; (moteur, voiture) to labour // vt to grieve, sadden.

peintre [pɛ̃tʀ(ə)] nm painter; **~ en bâtiment** house painter.

peinture [pɛ̃tyʀ] nf painting; (couche de couleur, couleur) paint; (surfaces peintes: aussi: ~s) paintwork; **~ mate/brillante** matt/gloss paint; **'~ fraîche'** 'wet paint'.

péjoratif, ive [peʒoʀatif, -iv] a pejorative, derogatory.

pelage [pəlaʒ] nm coat, fur.

pêle-mêle [pɛlmɛl] ad higgledy-piggledy.

peler [pəle] vt, vi to peel.

pèlerin [pɛlʀɛ̃] nm pilgrim.

pelle [pɛl] nf shovel; (d'enfant, de terrassier) spade; **~ mécanique** mechanical digger.

pellicule [pelikyl] nf film; **~s** nfpl (MÉD) dandruff sg.

pelote [pəlɔt] nf (de fil, laine) ball; (d'épingles) pin cushion; **~ basque** pelota.

peloton [pəlɔtɔ̃] nm group, squad; (CYCLISME) pack; **~ d'exécution** firing squad.

pelotonner [pəlɔtɔne]: **se ~** vi to curl (o.s.) up.

pelouse [pəluz] nf lawn.

peluche [pəlyʃ] nf: **animal en ~** fluffy animal, soft toy.

pelure [pəlyʀ] nf peeling, peel q.

pénal, e, aux [penal, -o] a penal.

pénalité [penalite] nf penalty.

penaud, e [pəno, -od] a sheepish, contrite.

penchant [pɑ̃ʃɑ̃] nm tendency, propensity; liking, fondness.

pencher [pɑ̃ʃe] vi to tilt, lean over // vt to tilt; **se ~** vi to lean over; (se baisser) to bend down; **se ~ sur** to bend over; (fig: problème) to look into; **se ~ au dehors** to lean out; **~ pour** to be inclined to favour.

pendaison [pɑ̃dɛzɔ̃] nf hanging.

pendant [pɑ̃dɑ̃] nm: **faire ~ à** to match; to be the counterpart of // prép during; **~ que** while.

pendentif [pɑ̃dɑ̃tif] nm pendant.

penderie [pɑ̃dʀi] nf wardrobe.

pendre [pɑ̃dʀ(ə)] vt, vi to hang; **se ~**

(à) (se suicider) to hang o.s. (on); ~ à to hang (down) from; ~ qch à to hang sth (up) on.

pendule [pãdyl] nf clock // nm pendulum.

pêne [pɛn] nm bolt.

pénétrer [penetre] vi, vt to penetrate; ~ **dans** to enter; (suj: projectile) to penetrate; (: air, eau) to come into, get into.

pénible [penibl(ə)] a (astreignant) hard; (affligeant) painful; (personne, caractère) tiresome; ~**ment** ad with difficulty.

péniche [peniʃ] nf barge.

pénicilline [penisilin] nf penicillin.

péninsule [penɛ̃syl] nf peninsula.

pénis [penis] nm penis.

pénitence [penitãs] nf (repentir) penitence; (peine) penance.

pénitencier [penitãsje] nm penitentiary.

pénombre [penɔ̃br(ə)] nf half-light; darkness.

pensée [pãse] nf thought; (démarche, doctrine) thinking q; (BOT) pansy; en ~ in one's mind.

penser [pãse] vi to think // vt to think; (concevoir: problème, machine) to think out; ~ à to think of; (songer à: ami, vacances) to think of ou about; (réfléchir à: problème, offre): ~ à qch to think about sth ou think sth over; faire ~ à to remind one of; ~ **faire qch** to be thinking of doing sth, intend to do sth.

pension [pãsjɔ̃] nf (allocation) pension; (prix du logement) board and lodgings, bed and board; (maison particulière) boarding house; (hôtel) guesthouse, hotel; (école) boarding school; **prendre qn en** ~ to take sb (in) as a lodger; **mettre en** ~ to send to boarding school; ~ **alimentaire** (d'étudiant) living allowance; (de divorcée) maintenance allowance; alimony; ~ **complète** full board; ~ **de famille** boarding house, guesthouse; **pensionnaire** nm/f boarder; guest; **pensionnat** nm boarding school.

pente [pãt] nf slope; en ~ a sloping.

Pentecôte [pãtkot] nf: la ~ Whitsun (Brit), Pentecost.

pénurie [penyri] nf shortage.

pépé [pepe] nm (fam) grandad.

pépin [pepɛ̃] nm (BOT: graine) pip; (ennui) snag, hitch.

pépinière [pepinjɛr] nf nursery.

perçant, e [pɛrsã, -ãt] a sharp, keen; piercing, shrill.

percée [pɛrse] nf (trouée) opening; (MIL, technologique) breakthrough; (SPORT) break.

perce-neige [pɛrsənɛʒ] nf inv snowdrop.

percepteur [pɛrsɛptœr] nm tax collector.

perception [pɛrsɛpsjɔ̃] nf perception;

(d'impôts etc) collection; (bureau) tax office.

percer [pɛrse] vt to pierce; (ouverture etc) to make; (mystère, énigme) to penetrate // vi to come through; to break through; ~ **une dent** to cut a tooth.

perceuse [pɛrsøz] nf drill.

percevoir [pɛrsəvwar] vt (distinguer) to perceive, detect; (taxe, impôt) to collect; (revenu, indemnité) to receive.

perche [pɛrʃ(ə)] nf (bâton) pole.

percher [pɛrʃe] vt: ~ **qch sur** to perch sth on // vi, se ~ vi (oiseau) to perch; **perchoir** nm perch.

perçois etc vb voir **percevoir**.

percolateur [pɛrkɔlatœr] nm percolator.

perçu, e pp de **percevoir**.

percussion [pɛrkysjɔ̃] nf percussion.

percuter [pɛrkyte] vt to strike; (suj: véhicule) to crash into.

perdant, e [pɛrdã, -ãt] nm/f loser.

perdition [pɛrdisjɔ̃] nf: en ~ (NAVIG) in distress; lieu de ~ den of vice.

perdre [pɛrdr(ə)] vt to lose; (gaspiller: temps, argent) to waste; (personne: moralement etc) to ruin // vi to lose; (sur une vente etc) to lose out; se ~ vi (s'égarer) to get lost, lose one's way; (fig) to go to waste; to disappear, vanish.

perdrix [pɛrdri] nf partridge.

perdu, e [pɛrdy] pp de **perdre** // a (isolé) out-of-the-way; (COMM: emballage) non-returnable; (malade): **il est** ~ there's no hope left for him; à vos moments ~s in your spare time.

père [pɛr] nm father; ~s (ancêtres) forefathers; ~ **de famille** father; family man; **le** ~ **Noël** Father Christmas.

perfectionné, e [pɛrfɛksjɔne] a sophisticated.

perfectionner [pɛrfɛksjɔne] vt to improve, perfect.

perforatrice [pɛrfɔratris] nf (pour cartes) card-punch; (de bureau) punch.

perforer [pɛrfɔre] vt to perforate; to punch a hole (ou holes) in; (ticket, bande, carte) to punch.

performant, e [pɛrfɔrmã, -ãt] a: très ~ high-performance cpd.

perfusion [pɛrfyzjɔ̃] nf: **faire une** ~ à qn to put sb on a drip.

péril [peril] nm peril.

périmé, e [perime] a (out)dated; (ADMIN) out-of-date, expired.

périmètre [perimɛtr(ə)] nm perimeter.

période [perjɔd] nf period; **périodique** a (phases) periodic; (publication) periodical // nm periodical.

péripéties [peripesi] nfpl events, episodes.

périphérique [periferik] a (quartiers) outlying; (ANAT, TECH) peripheral; (station de radio) operating from outside

France // nm (AUTO) ring road; (IN-FORM) peripheral.

périple [peripl(ə)] nm journey.

périr [peʀiʀ] vi to die, perish.

périssable [peʀisabl(ə)] a perishable.

perle [peʀl(ə)] nf pearl; (de plastique, métal, sueur) bead.

perlé, e [peʀle] a: **grève ~e** go-slow.

perler [peʀle] vi to form in droplets.

permanence [peʀmanãs] nf permanence; (local) (duty) office; emergency service; **assurer une ~** (service public, bureaux) to operate ou maintain a basic service; **être de ~** to be on call ou duty; **en ~** ad permanently; continuously.

permanent, e [peʀmanã, -ãt] a permanent; (spectacle) continuous // nf perm.

perméable [peʀmeabl(ə)] a (terrain) permeable; **~ à** (fig) receptive ou open to.

permettre [peʀmetʀ(ə)] vt to allow, permit; **~ à qn de faire/qch** to allow sb to do/sth; **se ~ de faire** to take the liberty of doing; **permettez!** excuse me!

permis [peʀmi] nm permit, licence; **~ de chasse** hunting permit; **~ (de conduire)** (driving) licence (Brit), (driver's) license (US); **~ de construire** planning permission (Brit), building permit (US); **~ d'inhumer** burial certificate; **~ de séjour** residence permit; **~ de travail** work permit.

permission [peʀmisjõ] nf permission; (MIL) leave; **en ~** on leave; **avoir la ~ de faire** to have permission to do.

permuter [peʀmyte] vt to change around, permutate // vi to change, swap.

Pérou [peʀu] nm Peru.

perpétuel, le [peʀpetɥɛl] a perpetual; (ADMIN etc) permanent; for life.

perpétuité [peʀpetɥite] nf: **à ~** a, ad for life; **être condamné à ~** to receive a life sentence.

perplexe [peʀpleks(ə)] a perplexed, puzzled.

perquisitionner [peʀkizisjone] vi to carry out a search.

perron [peʀõ] nm steps pl (in front of mansion etc).

perroquet [peʀɔke] nm parrot.

perruche [peʀyʃ] nf budgerigar (Brit), budgie (Brit), parakeet (US).

perruque [peʀyk] nf wig.

persan, e [peʀsã, -an] a Persian.

persécuter [peʀsekyte] vt to persecute.

persévérer [peʀseveʀe] vi to persevere.

persiennes [peʀsjɛn] nfpl (metal) shutters.

persiflage [peʀsiflaʒ] nm mockery q.

persil [peʀsi] nm parsley.

Persique [peʀsik] a: **le golfe ~** the (Persian) Gulf.

persistant, e [peʀsistã, -ãt] a persistent; (feuilles) evergreen.

persister [peʀsiste] vi to persist; **~ à faire qch** to persist in doing sth.

personnage [peʀsɔnaʒ] nm (notable) personality; figure; (individu) character, individual; (THÉÂTRE) character; (PEINTURE) figure.

personnalité [peʀsɔnalite] nf personality; (personnage) prominent figure.

personne [peʀsɔn] nf person // pronom nobody, no one; (quelqu'un) anybody, anyone; **~s** people pl; **il n'y a ~** there's nobody there, there isn't anybody there; **~ âgée** elderly person; **personnel, le** a personal // nm staff, personnel; **personnellement** ad personally.

perspective [peʀspɛktiv] nf (ART) perspective; (vue, coup d'œil) view; (point de vue) viewpoint, angle; (chose escomptée, envisagée) prospect; **en ~** in prospect.

perspicace [peʀspikas] a clear-sighted, gifted with (ou showing) insight.

persuader [peʀsɥade] vt: **~ qn (de/de faire)** to persuade sb (of/to do).

perte [peʀt(ə)] nf loss; (de temps) waste; (fig: morale) ruin; **à ~** (COMM) at a loss; **à ~ de vue** as far as the eye can (ou could) see; **~ sèche** dead loss; **~s blanches** (vaginal) discharge sg.

pertinemment [peʀtinamã] ad to the point; full well.

pertinent, e [peʀtinã, -ãt] a apt, relevant.

perturbation [peʀtyʀbasjõ] nf disruption; perturbation; **~ (atmosphérique)** atmospheric disturbance.

perturber [peʀtyʀbe] vt to disrupt; (PSYCH) to perturb, disturb.

pervers, e [peʀvɛʀ, -ɛʀs(ə)] a perverted, depraved; perverse.

pervertir [peʀvɛʀtiʀ] vt to pervert.

pesant, e [pəzã, -ãt] a heavy; (fig) burdensome.

pesanteur [pəzãtœʀ] nf gravity.

pèse-personne [pɛzpɛʀsɔn] nm (bathroom) scales pl.

peser [pəze] vt, vb avec attribut to weigh // vi to be heavy; (fig) to carry weight; **~ sur** (fig) to lie heavy on; to influence.

pessimiste [pesimist(ə)] a pessimistic // nm/f pessimist.

peste [pɛst(ə)] nf plague.

pester [pɛste] vi: **~ contre** to curse.

pétale [petal] nm petal.

pétanque [petãk] nf type of bowls.

pétarader [petaʀade] vi to backfire.

pétard [petaʀ] nm banger (Brit), firecracker.

péter [pete] vi (fam: casser, sauter) to burst; to bust; (fam!) to fart (!).

pétiller [petije] vi (flamme, bois) to crackle; (mousse, champagne) to bubble; (yeux) to sparkle.

petit, e [pəti, -it] a (gén) small; (main,

objet, colline, en âge: enfant) small, little; (*voyage*) short, little; (*bruit etc*) faint, slight; (*mesquin*) mean // *nmpl* (*d'un animal*) young *pl*; **faire des ~s** to have kittens (*ou* puppies *etc*); **les tout-petits** the little ones, the tiny tots; **~ à ~** bit by bit, gradually; **~(e) ami/e** boyfriend/girlfriend; **les ~es annonces** the small ads; **~ déjeuner** breakfast; **~ pain** (bread) roll; **~s pois** garden peas; **~-bourgeois, ~e-bourgeoise** *a* (*péj*) middle-class; **~e-fille** *nf* granddaughter; **~-fils** *nm* grandson; **~s-enfants** *nmpl* grandchildren.

pétition [petisjɔ̃] *nf* petition.

pétrin [petrɛ̃] *nm* kneading-trough; (*fig*): **dans le ~** in a jam *ou* fix.

pétrir [petrir] *vt* to knead.

pétrole [petrɔl] *nm* oil; (*pour lampe, réchaud etc*) paraffin (oil); **pétrolier, ière** *a* oil *cpd* // *nm* oil tanker.

peu [pø] ♦ *ad* 1 (*modifiant verbe, adjectif, adverbe*): **il boit ~** he doesn't drink (very) much; **il est ~ bavard** he's not very talkative; **~ avant/après** shortly before/afterwards
2 (*modifiant nom*): **~ de**: **~ de gens/ d'arbres** few *ou* not (very) many people/ trees; **il a ~ d'espoir** he hasn't (got) much hope, he has little hope; **pour ~ de temps** for (only) a short while
3: **~ à ~** little by little; **à ~ près** just about, more or less; **à ~ près 10 kg/10 F** approximately 10 kg/10 F
♦ *nm* 1: **le ~ de gens qui** the few people who; **le ~ de sable qui** what little sand, the little sand which
2: **un ~** a little; **un petit ~** a little bit; **un ~ d'espoir** a little hope
♦ *pronom*: **~ le savent** few know (it); **avant** *ou* **sous ~** shortly, before long; **de ~** (only) just.

peuple [pœpl(ə)] *nm* people.

peupler [pœple] *vt* (*pays, région*) to populate; (*étang*) to stock; (*suj: hommes, poissons*) to inhabit; (*fig: imagination, rêves*) to fill.

peuplier [pøplije] *nm* poplar (tree).

peur [pœr] *nf* fear; **avoir ~ (de/de faire/ que)** to be frightened *ou* afraid (of/of doing/that); **faire ~ à** to frighten; **de ~ de/que** for fear of/that; **~eux, euse** *a* fearful, timorous.

peut *vb voir* **pouvoir.**

peut-être [pøtɛtr(ə)] *ad* perhaps, maybe; **~ que** perhaps, maybe; **~ bien qu'il fera/est** he may well do/be.

peux *etc vb voir* **pouvoir.**

phare [far] *nm* (*en mer*) lighthouse; (*de véhicule*) headlight; **mettre ses ~s** to put on one's headlights; **~s de recul** reversing lights.

pharmacie [farmasi] *nf* (*magasin*) chemist's (*Brit*), pharmacy; (*officine*) dispensary; (*de salle de bain*) medicine

cabinet; **pharmacien, ne** *nm/f* pharmacist, chemist (*Brit*).

phase [faz] *nf* phase.

phénomène [fenɔmɛn] *nm* phenomenon (*pl* a); (*monstre*) freak.

philanthrope [filɑ̃trɔp] *nm/f* philanthropist.

philosophe [filɔzɔf] *nm/f* philosopher // *a* philosophical.

philosophie [filɔzɔfi] *nf* philosophy; **philosophique** *a* philosophical.

phobie [fɔbi] *nf* phobia.

phonétique [fɔnetik] *nf* phonetics *sg*.

phoque [fɔk] *nm* seal; (*fourrure*) sealskin.

phosphorescent, e [fɔsfɔresɑ̃, -ɑ̃t] *a* luminous.

photo [fɔto] *nf* photo(graph); **en ~** in *ou* on a photograph; **prendre en ~** to take a photo of; **aimer la/faire de la ~** to like taking/take photos; **~ d'identité** passport photograph.

photo... [fɔto] *préfixe*: **~copie** *nf* photo-copying; photocopy; **~copier** *vt* to photocopy; **~graphe** *nm/f* photographer; **~graphie** *nf* (*procédé, technique*) photography; (*cliché*) photograph; **~graphier** *vt* to photograph.

phrase [fraz] *nf* (*LING*) sentence; (*propos, MUS*) phrase.

physicien, ne [fizisjɛ̃, -ɛn] *nm/f* physicist.

physionomie [fizjɔnɔmi] *nf* face.

physique [fizik] *a* physical // *nm* physique // *nf* physics *sg*; **au ~** physically, **~ment** *ad* physically.

piaffer [pjafe] *vi* to stamp.

piailler [pjaje] *vi* to squawk.

pianiste [pjanist(ə)] *nm/f* pianist.

piano [pjano] *nm* piano.

pianoter [pjanɔte] *vi* to tinkle away (at the piano); (*tapoter*): **~ sur** to drum one's fingers on.

pic [pik] *nm* (*instrument*) pick(axe); (*montagne*) peak; (*ZOOL*) woodpecker; **à ~** *ad* vertically; (*fig*) just at the right time.

pichet [piʃɛ] *nm* jug.

picorer [pikɔre] *vt* to peck.

picoter [pikɔte] *vt* (*suj: oiseau*) to peck // *vi* (*irriter*) to smart, prickle.

pie [pi] *nf* magpie; (*fig*) chatterbox.

pièce [pjɛs] *nf* (*d'un logement*) room; (*THÉÂTRE*) play; (*de mécanisme, machine*) part; (*de monnaie*) coin; (*COUTURE*) patch; (*document*) document; (*de drap, fragment, de collection*) piece; **dix francs ~** ten francs each; **vendre à la ~** to sell separately; **travailler/ payer à la ~** to do piecework/pay piece rate; **un maillot une ~** a one-piece swimsuit; **un deux-~s cuisine** a two-room(ed) flat (*Brit*) *ou* apartment (*US*) with kitchen; **~ à conviction** exhibit; **~ d'eau** ornamental lake *ou* pond; **~ d'identité:**

avez-vous une ~ d'identité? have you got any (means of) identification?; ~ montée tiered cake; ~s détachées spares, (spare) parts; ~s justificatives supporting documents.

pied [pje] nm foot (pl feet); (de verre) stem; (de table) leg; (de lampe) base; (plante) plant; à ~ on foot; à ~ sec without getting one's feet wet; au ~ de la lettre literally; de ~ en cap from head to foot; en ~ (portrait) full-length; avoir ~ to be able to touch the bottom, not to be out of one's depth; avoir le ~ marin to be a good sailor; sur ~ (debout, rétabli) up and about; mettre sur ~ (entreprise) to set up; mettre à ~ to dismiss; to lay off; ~ de vigne vine.

piédestal, aux [pjedɛstal, -o] nm pedestal.

pied-noir [pjenwaʀ] nm Algerian-born Frenchman.

piège [pjɛʒ] nm trap; **prendre au** ~ to trap; **piéger** vt (avec une bombe) to booby-trap; **lettre/voiture piégée** letter-/car-bomb.

pierraille [pjɛʀaj] nf loose stones pl.

pierre [pjɛʀ] nf stone; ~ à briquet flint; ~ fine semiprecious stone; ~ de taille freestone q; ~ tombale tombstone.

pierreries [pjɛʀʀi] nfpl gems, precious stones.

piétiner [pjetine] vi (trépigner) to stamp (one's foot); (marquer le pas) to stand about; (fig) to be at a standstill // vt to trample on.

piéton, ne [pjetɔ̃, -ɔn] nm/f pedestrian; **piétonnier, ière** a: **rue/zone piétonnière** pedestrian precinct.

pieu, x [pjø] nm post; (pointu) stake.

pieuvre [pjœvʀ(ə)] nf octopus.

pieux, euse [pjø, -øz] a pious.

piffer [pife] vt (fam): **je ne peux pas le** ~ I can't stand him.

pigeon [piʒɔ̃] nm pigeon.

piger [piʒe] vi, vt (fam) to understand.

pigiste [piʒist(ə)] nm/f freelance(r).

pignon [piɲɔ̃] nm (de mur) gable; (d'engrenage) cog(wheel), gearwheel.

pile [pil] nf (tas) pile; (ÉLEC) battery // ad (s'arrêter etc) dead; à deux heures ~ at two on the dot; **jouer à** ~ **ou face** to toss up (for it); ~ **ou face?** heads or tails?

piler [pile] vt to crush, pound.

pileux, euse [pilø, -øz] a: **système** ~ (body) hair.

pilier [pilje] nm pillar.

piller [pije] vt to pillage, plunder, loot.

pilon [pilɔ̃] nm pestle.

pilote [pilɔt] nm pilot; (de char, voiture) driver // a pilot cpd; ~ **de ligne/d'essai/ de chasse** airline/test/fighter pilot; ~ **de course** racing driver.

piloter [pilɔte] vt to pilot, fly; to drive.

pilule [pilyl] nf pill; **prendre la** ~ to be

on the pill.

piment [pimɑ̃] nm (BOT) pepper, capsicum; (fig) spice, piquancy.

pimpant, e [pɛ̃pɑ̃, -ɑ̃t] a spruce.

pin [pɛ̃] nm pine (tree); (bois) pine(wood).

pinard [pinaʀ] nm (fam) (cheap) wine, plonk (Brit).

pince [pɛ̃s] nf (outil) pliers pl; (de homard, crabe) pincer, claw; (COUTURE: pli) dart; ~ à sucre/glace sugar/ ice tongs pl; ~ à épiler tweezers pl; ~ à linge clothes peg (Brit) ou pin (US).

pincé, e [pɛ̃se] a (air) stiff // nf: **une** ~**e** de a pinch of.

pinceau, x [pɛ̃so] nm (paint)brush.

pincer [pɛ̃se] vt to pinch; (MUS: cordes) to pluck; (fam) to nab.

pincettes [pɛ̃sɛt] nfpl (pour le feu) (fire) tongs.

pinède [pinɛd] nf pinewood, pine forest.

pingouin [pɛ̃gwɛ̃] nm penguin.

ping-pong [piɑjpɔ̃g] nm table tennis.

pingre [pɛ̃gʀ(ə)] a niggardly.

pinson [pɛ̃sɔ̃] nm chaffinch.

pintade [pɛ̃tad] nf guinea-fowl.

pioche [pjɔʃ] nf pickaxe; **piocher** vt to dig up (with a pickaxe).

piolet [pjɔlɛ] nm ice axe.

pion [pjɔ̃] nm (ÉCHECS) pawn; (DAMES) piece.

pionnier [pjɔnje] nm pioneer.

pipe [pip] nf pipe.

pipeau, x [pipo] nm (reed-)pipe.

piquant, e [pikɑ̃, -ɑ̃t] a (barbe, rosier etc) prickly; (saveur, sauce) hot, pungent; (fig) racy; biting // nm (épine) thorn, prickle; (fig) spiciness, spice.

pique [pik] nf pike; (fig) cutting remark // nm (CARTES: couleur) spades pl; (: carte) spade.

pique-nique [piknik] nm picnic.

piquer [pike] vt (percer) to prick; (planter) to give a jab to; (MÉD) ~ **qch dans** to stick sth into; (: animal blessé etc) to put to sleep; (suj: insecte, fumée, ortie) to sting; (suj: poivre) to burn; (: froid) to bite; (COUTURE) to machine (stitch); (intérêt etc) to arouse; (fam) to pick up; (: voler) to pinch; (: arrêter) to nab // vi (avion) to go into a dive; **se** ~ **de faire** to pride o.s. on doing; ~ **un galop/un cent mètres** to break into a gallop/put on a sprint.

piquet [pikɛ] nm (pieu) post, stake; (de tente) peg; ~ **de grève** (strike-)picket; ~ **d'incendie** fire-fighting squad.

piqûre [pikyʀ] nf (d'épingle) prick; (d'ortie) sting; (de moustique) bite; (MÉD) injection, shot (US); (COUTURE) (straight) stitch; straight stitching; **faire une** ~ **à qn** to give sb an injection.

pirate [piʀat] nm, a pirate; ~ **de l'air** hijacker.

pire [piʀ] *a* worse; (*superlatif*): le(la) ~
... the worst ... // *nm*: le ~ (de) the worst
(of).

pis [pi] *nm* (*de vache*) udder; (*pire*): le
~ the worst // *a, ad* worse; **pis-aller** *nm
inv* stopgap.

piscine [pisin] *nf* (swimming) pool; ~
couverte indoor (swimming) pool.

pissenlit [pisãli] *nm* dandelion.

pistache [pistaʃ] *nf* pistachio (nut).

piste [pist(ə)] *nf* (*d'un animal, sentier*)
track, trail; (*indice*) lead; (*de stade, de
magnétophone*) track; (*de cirque*) ring;
(*de danse*) floor; (*de patinage*) rink; (*de
ski*) run; (AVIAT) runway; ~ cyclable
cycle track.

pistolet [pistɔlɛ] *nm* (*arme*) pistol, gun;
(*à peinture*) spray gun; ~ à air
comprimé airgun; ~-mitrailleur *nm*
submachine gun.

piston [pistɔ̃] *nm* (TECH) piston;
pistonner *vt* (*candidat*) to pull strings
for.

piteux, euse [pitø, -øz] *a* pitiful, sorry
(*avant le nom*).

pitié [pitje] *nf* pity; **faire** ~ to inspire
pity; **avoir** ~ **de** (*compassion*) to pity,
feel sorry for; (*merci*) to have pity *ou*
mercy on.

piton [pitɔ̃] *nm* (*clou*) peg; ~ rocheux
rocky outcrop.

pitoyable [pitwajabl(ə)] *a* pitiful.

pitre [pitʀ(ə)] *nm* clown; **pitrerie** *nf*
tomfoolery *q*.

pittoresque [pitɔʀɛsk(ə)] *a* picturesque.

pivot [pivo] *nm* pivot; **pivoter** *vi* to
swivel; to revolve.

P.J. *sigle f voir* **police**.

placard [plakaʀ] *nm* (*armoire*) cupboard; (*affiche*) poster, notice;
placarder *vt* (*affiche*) to put up.

place [plas] *nf* (*emplacement, situation,
classement*) place; (*de ville, village*)
square; (*espace libre*) room, space; (*de
parking*) space; (*siège: de train,
cinéma, voiture*) seat; (*emploi*) job; **en**
~ (*mettre*) in its place; **sur** ~ on the
spot; **faire** ~ **à** to give way to; **faire de
la** ~ **à** to make room for; **ça prend de la
~** it takes up a lot of room *ou* space; **à
la** ~ **de** in place of, instead of; **il y a 20
~s assises/debout** there are 20 seats/there
is standing room for 20.

placement [plasmã] *nm* placing; (FI-
NANCE) investment; **bureau de** ~ employment agency.

placer [plase] *vt* to place; (*convive,
spectateur*) to seat; (*capital, argent*) to
place, invest; (*dans la conversation*) to
put *ou* get in; **se** ~ **au premier rang** to
go and stand (*ou* sit) in the first row.

plafond [plafɔ̃] *nm* ceiling.

plafonner [plafɔne] *vi* to reach one's (*ou*
a) ceiling.

plage [plaʒ] *nf* beach; (*fig*) band, brack-

et; (*de disque*) track, band; ~ arrière
(AUTO) parcel *ou* back shelf.

plagiat [plaʒja] *nm* plagiarism.

plaider [plede] *vi* (*avocat*) to plead;
(*plaignant*) to go to court, litigate // *vt*
to plead; ~ **pour** (*fig*) to speak for;
plaidoyer *nm* (JUR) speech for the defence; (*fig*) plea.

plaie [plɛ] *nf* wound.

plaignant, e [plɛɲã, -ãt] *nm/f* plaintiff.

plaindre [plɛ̃dʀ(ə)] *vt* to pity, feel sorry
for; **se** ~ *vi* (*gémir*) to moan; (*protester,
rouspéter*): **se** ~ (**à qn**) (**de**) to complain
(to sb) (about); (*souffrir*): **se** ~ **de** to
complain of.

plaine [plɛn] *nf* plain.

plain-pied [plɛ̃pje]: **de** ~ (**avec**) on the
same level (as).

plainte [plɛ̃t] *nf* (*gémissement*) moan,
groan; (*doléance*) complaint; **porter** ~ to
lodge a complaint.

plaire [plɛʀ] *vi* to be a success, be successful; to please; ~ **à**: **cela me plaît** I
like it; **se** ~ **quelque part** to like being
somewhere *ou* like it somewhere; **s'il
vous plaît** please.

plaisance [plɛzãs] *nf* (*aussi*: navigation
de ~) (pleasure) sailing, yachting.

plaisant, e [plɛzã, -ãt] *a* pleasant;
(*histoire, anecdote*) amusing.

plaisanter [plɛzãte] *vi* to joke;
plaisanterie *nf* joke; joking *q*.

plaise *etc vb voir* **plaire**.

plaisir [plɛziʀ] *nm* pleasure; **faire** ~ **à
qn** (*délibérément*) to be nice to sb,
please sb; (*suj*: *cadeau, nouvelle etc*):
ceci me fait ~ I'm delighted *ou* very
pleased with this; **pour le** *ou* **par** ~ for
pleasure.

plaît *vb voir* **plaire**.

plan, e [plã, -an] *a* flat // *nm* plan;
(GÉOM) plane; (*fig*) level, plane; (CINÉ-
MA) shot; **au premier/second** ~ **in** the
foreground/middle distance; **à l'arrière**
~ in the background; ~ **d'eau** lake;
pond.

planche [plãʃ] *nf* (*pièce de bois*) plank,
(wooden) board; (*illustration*) plate; **les
~s** (THÉÂTRE) the stage *sg*, the boards;
~ **à repasser** ironing board; ~ **à
roulettes** skateboard; ~ **de salut** (*fig*)
sheet anchor.

plancher [plãʃe] *nm* floor; floorboards
pl; (*fig*) minimum level // *vi* to work
hard.

planer [plane] *vi* to glide; ~ **sur** (*fig*) to
hang over; to hover above.

planète [planɛt] *nf* planet.

planeur [planœʀ] *nm* glider.

planification [planifikasjɔ̃] *nf* (economic) planning.

planifier [planifje] *vt* to plan.

planning [planiŋ] *nm* programme,
schedule; ~ **familial** family planning.

plant [plã] *nm* seedling, young plant.

plante [plɑ̃t] *nf* plant; ~ **d'appartement** house *ou* pot plant; ~ **du pied** sole (of the foot).

planter [plɑ̃te] *vt* (*plante*) to plant; (*enfoncer*) to hammer *ou* drive in; (*tente*) to put up, pitch; (*fam*) to dump; to ditch; **se** ~ (*fam: se tromper*) to get it wrong.

plantureux, euse [plɑ̃tyʀø, -øz] *a* copious, lavish; (*femme*) buxom.

plaque [plak] *nf* plate; (*de verglas, d'eczéma*) patch; (*avec inscription*) plaque; ~ (**minéralogique** *ou* **d'immatriculation**) number (*Brit*) *ou* license (*US*) plate; ~ **chauffante** hotplate; ~ **de chocolat** bar of chocolate; ~ **d'identité** identity disc; ~ **tournante** (*fig*) centre.

plaqué, e [plake] *a*: ~ **or/argent** gold-/silver-plated; ~ **acajou** veneered in mahogany.

plaquer [plake] *vt* (*aplatir*): ~ **qch sur/contre** to make sth stick *ou* cling to; (*RUGBY*) to bring down; (*fam: laisser tomber*) to drop.

plastic [plastik] *nm* plastic explosive.

plastique [plastik] *a, nm* plastic.

plastiquer [plastike] *vt* to blow up (*with a plastic bomb*).

plat, e [pla, -at] *a* flat; (*cheveux*) straight; (*personne, livre*) dull // *nm* (*récipient, CULIN*) dish; (*d'un repas*): **premier** ~ the first course; **à** ~ **ventre** *ad* face down; **à** ~ *ad, a* (*pneu, batterie*) flat; (*personne*) dead beat; ~ **cuisiné** pre-cooked meal; ~ **du jour** day's special (*menu*); ~ **de résistance** main course.

platane [platan] *nm* plane tree.

plateau, x [plato] *nm* (*support*) tray; (*GÉO*) plateau; (*de tourne-disques*) turntable; (*CINÉMA*) set; ~ **à fromages** cheeseboard.

plate-bande [platbɑ̃d] *nf* flower bed.

plate-forme [platfɔrm(ə)] *nf* platform; ~ **de forage/pétrolière** drilling/oil rig.

platine [platin] *nm* platinum // *nf* (*d'un tourne-disque*) turntable.

plâtras [plɑtʀa] *nm* rubble *q*.

plâtre [plɑtʀ(ə)] *nm* (*matériau*) plaster; (*statue*) plaster statue; (*MÉD*) (plaster) cast; **avoir un bras dans le** ~ to have an arm in plaster.

plein, e [plɛ̃, -ɛn] *a* full; (*porte, roue*) solid; (*chienne, jument*) big (with young) // *nm*: **faire le** ~ (**d'essence**) to fill up (with petrol); **à** ~**es mains** (*ramasser*) in handfuls; (*empoigner*) firmly; **à** ~ **régime** at maximum revs; (*fig*) full steam; **à** ~ **temps** full-time; **en** ~ **air** in the open air; **en** ~ **soleil** in direct sunlight; **en** ~**e nuit/rue** in the middle of the night/street; **en** ~ **jour** in broad daylight; **en** ~ **sur** right on; ~**-emploi** *nm* full employment.

plénitude [plenityd] *nf* fullness.

pleurer [plœʀe] *vi* to cry; (*yeux*) to wa-

ter // *vt* to mourn (for); to lament (over), to bemoan.

pleurnicher [plœʀniʃe] *vi* to snivel, whine.

pleurs [plœʀ] *nmpl*: **en** ~ in tears.

pleut *vb voir* **pleuvoir**.

pleuvoir [pløvwaʀ] *vb impersonnel* to rain // *vi* (*fig*): ~ (**sur**) to shower down (upon); to be showered upon; **il pleut** it's raining.

pli [pli] *nm* fold; (*de jupe*) pleat; (*de pantalon*) crease; (*aussi*: **faux** ~) crease; (*enveloppe*) envelope; (*lettre*) letter; (*CARTES*) trick.

pliant, e [plijɑ̃, -ɑ̃t] *a* folding // *nm* folding stool, campstool.

plier [plije] *vt* to fold; (*pour ranger*) to fold up; (*table pliante*) to fold down; (*genou, bras*) to bend // *vi* to bend; (*fig*) to yield; **se** ~ **à** to submit to.

plinthe [plɛ̃t] *nf* skirting board.

plisser [plise] *vt* (*rider, chiffonner*) to crease; (*jupe*) to put pleats in.

plomb [plɔ̃] *nm* (*métal*) lead; (*d'une cartouche*) (lead) shot; (*PÊCHE*) sinker; (*sceau*) (lead) seal; (*ÉLEC*) fuse.

plombage [plɔ̃baʒ] *nm* (*de dent*) filling.

plomber [plɔ̃be] *vt* (*canne, ligne*) to weight (with lead); (*dent*) to fill.

plomberie [plɔ̃bʀi] *nf* plumbing.

plombier [plɔ̃bje] *nm* plumber.

plongeant, e [plɔ̃ʒɑ̃, -ɑ̃t] *a* (*vue*) from above; (*tir, décolleté*) plunging.

plongée [plɔ̃ʒe] *nf* (*SPORT*) diving *q*; (: *sans scaphandre*) skin diving.

plongeoir [plɔ̃ʒwaʀ] *nm* diving board.

plongeon [plɔ̃ʒɔ̃] *nm* dive.

plonger [plɔ̃ʒe] *vi* to dive // *vt*: ~ **qch dans** to plunge sth into.

ployer [plwaje] *vt* to bend // *vi* to sag; to bend.

plu *pp de* **plaire**, **pleuvoir**.

pluie [plɥi] *nf* rain; (*fig*): ~ **de** shower of.

plume [plym] *nf* feather; (*pour écrire*) (pen) nib; (*fig*) pen.

plumer [plyme] *vt* to pluck.

plumier [plymje] *nm* pencil box.

plupart [plypaʀ]: **la** ~ *pronom* the majority, most (of them); **la** ~ **des** most, the majority of; **la** ~ **du temps/d'entre nous** most of the time/of us; **pour la** ~ *ad* for the most part, mostly.

pluriel [plyʀjɛl] *nm* plural.

plus ♦ *vb voir* **plaire**
♦ *ad* **1** [ply] (*forme négative*): **ne ...** ~ no more, no longer; **je n'ai** ~ **d'argent** I've got no more money *ou* no money left; **il ne travaille** ~ he's no longer working, he doesn't work any more
2 [ply, plyz + *voyelle*] (*comparatif*) more, ...+er; (*superlatif*): **le** ~ the most, the ...+est; ~ **grand/intelligent (que)** bigger/more intelligent (than); **le** ~

grand/intelligent the biggest/most intelligent; **tout au ~** at the very most
3 [plys] (*davantage*) more; **il travaille ~ (que)** he works more (than); **~ il travaille**, **~ il est heureux** the more he works, the happier he is; **~ de pain** more bread; **~ de 10 personnes** more than 10 people, over 10 people; **3 heures de ~ que** 3 hours more than; **de ~** what's more, moreover; **3 kilos en ~** 3 kilos more; **en ~** de in addition to; **de ~ en ~** more and more; **~ ou moins** more or less; **ni ~ ni moins** no more, no less
♦ *prép* [plys]: **4 ~ 2** 4 plus 2.
plusieurs [plyzjœʀ] *dét, pronom* several; **ils sont ~** there are several of them.
plus-que-parfait [plyskəpaʀfɛ] *nm* pluperfect, past perfect.
plus-value [plyvaly] *nf* appreciation; capital gain; surplus.
plut *vb voir* **plaire**.
plutôt [plyto] *ad* rather; **je ferais ~ ceci** I'd rather *ou* sooner do this; **fais ~ comme ça** try this way instead, you'd better try this way; **~ que (de) faire** rather than *ou* instead of doing.
pluvieux, euse [plyvjø, -øz] *a* rainy, wet.
PMU *sigle m* (= *pari mutuel urbain*) system of betting on horses; (*café*) betting agency.
pneu [pnø] *nm* tyre (*Brit*), tire (*US*).
pneumatique [pnømatik] *nm* tyre (*Brit*), tire (*US*).
pneumonie [pnømɔni] *nf* pneumonia.
poche [pɔʃ] *nf* pocket; (*déformation*): **faire une/des ~(s)** to bag; (*sous les yeux*) bag, pouch; **de ~** pocket *cpd*.
pocher [pɔʃe] *vt* (*CULIN*) to poach.
pochette [pɔʃɛt] *nf* (*de timbres*) wallet, envelope; (*d'aiguilles etc*) case; (*mouchoir*) breast pocket handkerchief; **~ de disque** record sleeve.
pochoir [pɔʃwaʀ] *nm* (*ART*) stencil.
poêle [pwal] *nm* stove // *nf*: **~ (à frire)** frying pan.
poêlon [pwalɔ̃] *nm* casserole.
poème [pɔɛm] *nm* poem.
poésie [pɔezi] *nf* (*poème*) poem; (*art*): **la ~** poetry.
poète [pɔɛt] *nm* poet.
poids [pwa] *nm* weight; (*SPORT*) shot; **vendre au ~** to sell by weight; **prendre du ~** to put on weight; **~ lourd** (*camion*) lorry (*Brit*), truck (*US*).
poignard [pwaɲaʀ] *nm* dagger; **poignarder** *vt* to stab, knife.
poigne [pwaɲ] *nf* grip; (*fig*): **à ~** firm-handed.
poignée [pwaɲe] *nf* (*de sel etc, fig*) handful; (*de couvercle, porte*) handle; **~ de main** handshake.
poignet [pwaɲɛ] *nm* (*ANAT*) wrist; (*de chemise*) cuff.

poil [pwal] *nm* (*ANAT*) hair; (*de pinceau, brosse*) bristle; (*de tapis*) strand; (*pelage*) coat; **à ~** (*fam*) starkers; **au ~** *a* (*fam*) hunky-dory; **poilu, e** *a* hairy.
poinçon [pwɛ̃sɔ̃] *nm* awl; bodkin; (*marque*) hallmark; **poinçonner** *vt* to stamp; to hallmark; (*billet*) to punch.
poing [pwɛ̃] *nm* fist.
point [pwɛ̃] *nm* (*marque, signe*) dot; (*: de ponctuation*) full stop, period (*US*); (*moment, de score etc, fig: question*) point; (*endroit*) spot; (*COUTURE, TRICOT*) stitch // *ad* = **pas**; **faire le ~** (*NAVIG*) to take a bearing; (*fig*) to take stock (of the situation); **en tout ~** in every respect; **sur le ~ de faire** (just) about to do; **à tel ~ que** so much so that; **mettre au ~** (*mécanisme, procédé*) to develop; (*appareil-photo*) to focus; (*affaire*) to settle; **à ~** (*CULIN*) medium; just right; **à ~ (nommé)** just at the right time; **~ (de côté)** stitch (*pain*); **~ d'eau** spring; water point; **~ d'exclamation** exclamation mark; **~ faible** weak point; **~ final** full stop, period; **~ d'interrogation** question mark; **~ mort** (*AUTO*): **au ~ mort** in neutral; **~ de repère** landmark; (*dans le temps*) point of reference; **~ de vente** retail outlet; **~ de vue** viewpoint; (*fig: opinion*) point of view; **~s de suspension** suspension points.
pointe [pwɛ̃t] *nf* point; (*fig*): **une ~ de** a hint of; **être à la ~ de** (*fig*) to be in the forefront of; **sur la ~ des pieds** on tiptoe; **en ~** *ad* (*tailler*) into a point // *a* pointed, tapered; **de ~** *a* (*technique etc*) leading; **heures/jours de ~** peak hours/days; **~ de vitesse** burst of speed.
pointer [pwɛ̃te] *vt* (*cocher*) to tick off; (*employés etc*) to check in; (*diriger: canon, doigt*): **~ vers qch** to point at sth // *vi* (*employé*) to clock in.
pointillé [pwɛ̃tije] *nm* (*trait*) dotted line.
pointilleux, euse [pwɛ̃tijø, -øz] *a* particular, pernickety.
pointu, e [pwɛ̃ty] *a* pointed; (*clou*) sharp; (*voix*) shrill; (*analyse*) precise.
pointure [pwɛ̃tyʀ] *nf* size.
point-virgule [pwɛ̃viʀgyl] *nm* semicolon.
poire [pwaʀ] *nf* pear; (*fam: péj*) mug.
poireau, x [pwaʀo] *nm* leek.
poirier [pwaʀje] *nm* pear tree.
pois [pwa] *nm* (*BOT*) pea; (*sur une étoffe*) dot, spot; **à ~** (*cravate etc*) spotted, polka-dot *cpd*.
poison [pwazɔ̃] *nm* poison.
poisse [pwas] *nf* rotten luck.
poisseux, euse [pwasø, -øz] *a* sticky.
poisson [pwasɔ̃] *nm* fish *gén inv*; **les P~s** (*signe*) Pisces; **~ d'avril!** April fool!; **~ rouge** goldfish; **poissonnerie** *nf* fish-shop; **poissonnier, ière** *nm/f* fishmonger (*Brit*), fish merchant (*US*).

poitrine [pwatʀin] nf chest; (seins) bust, bosom; (CULIN) breast; ~ **de bœuf** brisket.

poivre [pwavʀ(ə)] nm pepper; **poivrier** nm (ustensile) pepperpot.

poivron [pwavʀɔ̃] nm pepper, capsicum.

pôle [pol] nm (GÉO, ÉLEC) pole.

poli, e [pɔli] a polite; (lisse) smooth; polished.

police [pɔlis] nf police; **peine de simple ~** sentence given by magistrates' or police court; **~ judiciaire (P.J.)** ≈ Criminal Investigation Department (Brit), ≈ Federal Bureau of Investigation (US); **des mœurs** ≈ vice squad; **~ secours** ≈ emergency services pl (Brit), ≈ paramedics pl (US).

policier, ière [pɔlisje, -jɛʀ] a police cpd // nm policeman; (aussi: roman ~) detective novel.

polio [pɔljo] nf polio.

polir [pɔliʀ] vt to polish.

polisson, ne [pɔlisɔ̃, -ɔn] a naughty.

politesse [pɔlitɛs] nf politeness.

politicien, ne [pɔlitisjɛ̃, -ɛn] nm/f politician.

politique [pɔlitik] a political // nf (science, pratique, activité) politics sg; (mesures, méthode) policies pl; **politiser** vt to politicize.

pollen [pɔlɛn] nm pollen.

pollution [pɔlysjɔ̃] nf pollution.

Pologne [pɔlɔɲ] nf: **la ~** Poland; **polonais, e** a, nm (LING) Polish; **Polonais, e** nm/f Pole.

poltron, ne [pɔltʀɔ̃, -ɔn] a cowardly.

poly... [pɔli] préfixe: **~copier** vt to duplicate.

Polynésie [pɔlinezi] nf: **la ~** Polynesia.

polyvalent, e [pɔlivalɑ̃, -ɑ̃t] a versatile; multi-purpose.

pommade [pɔmad] nf ointment, cream.

pomme [pɔm] nf (BOT) apple; **tomber dans les ~s** (fam) to pass out; **~ d'Adam** Adam's apple; **~ d'arrosoir** (sprinkler) rose; **~ de pin** pine ou fir cone; **~ de terre** potato.

pommeau, x [pɔmo] nm (boule) knob; (de selle) pommel.

pommette [pɔmɛt] nf cheekbone.

pommier [pɔmje] nm apple tree.

pompe [pɔ̃p] nf pump; (faste) pomp (and ceremony); **~ à essence** petrol pump; **~s funèbres** funeral parlour sg, undertaker's sg.

pomper [pɔ̃pe] vt to pump; (évacuer) to pump out; (aspirer) to pump up; (absorber) to soak up.

pompeux, euse [pɔ̃pø, -øz] a pompous.

pompier [pɔ̃pje] nm fireman.

pompiste [pɔ̃pist(ə)] nm/f petrol (Brit) ou gas (US) pump attendant.

poncer [pɔ̃se] vt to sand (down).

ponctuation [pɔ̃ktɥasjɔ̃] nf punctuation.

ponctuel, le [pɔ̃ktɥɛl] a (à l'heure, aussi TECH) punctual; (fig: opération etc) one-off, single; (scrupuleux) punctilious, meticulous.

ponctuer [pɔ̃ktɥe] vt to punctuate.

pondéré, e [pɔ̃deʀe] a level-headed, composed.

pondre [pɔ̃dʀ(ə)] vt to lay; (fig) to produce.

poney [pɔnɛ] nm pony.

pont [pɔ̃] nm bridge; (AUTO) axle; (NAVIG) deck; **faire le ~** to take the extra day off; **~ de graissage** ramp (in garage); **~ suspendu** suspension bridge; **P~s et Chaussées** highways department.

pont-levis [pɔ̃lvi] nm drawbridge.

pop [pɔp] a inv pop.

populace [pɔpylas] nf (péj) rabble.

populaire [pɔpylɛʀ] a popular; (manifestation) mass cpd; (milieux, clientèle) working-class.

population [pɔpylasjɔ̃] nf population.

populeux, euse [pɔpylø, -øz] a densely populated.

porc [pɔʀ] nm (ZOOL) pig; (CULIN) pork; (peau) pigskin.

porcelaine [pɔʀsəlɛn] nf porcelain, china; piece of china(ware).

porcelet [pɔʀsəlɛ] nm piglet.

porc-épic [pɔʀkepik] nm porcupine.

porche [pɔʀʃ(ə)] nm porch.

porcherie [pɔʀʃəʀi] nf pigsty.

pore [pɔʀ] nm pore.

pornographique [pɔʀnɔgʀafik] a (abr **porno**) pornographic.

port [pɔʀ] nm (NAVIG) harbour, port; (ville) port; (de l'uniforme etc) wearing; (pour lettre) postage; (pour colis, aussi: posture) carriage; **~ d'arme** (JUR) carrying of a firearm.

portail [pɔʀtaj] nm gate; (de cathédrale) portal.

portant, e [pɔʀtɑ̃, -ɑ̃t] a: **bien/mal ~** in good/poor health.

portatif, ive [pɔʀtatif, -iv] a portable.

porte [pɔʀt(ə)] nf door; (de ville, forteresse, SKI) gate; **mettre à la ~** to throw out; **~ d'entrée** front door; **~ à ~** nm door-to-door selling.

porte- [pɔʀt(ə)] préfixe: **~-à-faux** nm: **en ~-à-faux** cantilevered; (fig) in an awkward position; **~-avions** nm inv aircraft carrier; **~-bagages** nm inv luggage rack; **~-clefs** nm inv key ring; **~-documents** nm inv attaché ou document case.

portée [pɔʀte] nf (d'une arme) range; (fig) impact, import; scope, capability; (de chatte etc) litter; (MUS) stave, staff (pl staves); **à/hors de ~** (de) within/out of reach (of); **à ~ de (la) main** within (arm's) reach; **à ~ de voix** within earshot; **à la ~ de qn** (fig) at sb's level, within sb's capabilities.

porte-fenêtre [pɔʀtfənɛtʀ(ə)] nf French window.

portefeuille [pɔʀtəfœj] nm wallet; (POL, BOURSE) portfolio.

porte-jarretelles [pɔʀtʒaʀtɛl] nm inv suspender belt.

portemanteau, x [pɔʀtmɑ̃to] nm coat hanger; coat rack.

porte-mine [pɔʀtəmin] nm propelling (Brit) ou mechanical (US) pencil.

porte-monnaie [pɔʀtmɔnɛ] nm inv purse.

porte-parole [pɔʀtpaʀɔl] nm inv spokesman.

porter [pɔʀte] vt to carry; (sur soi: vêtement, barbe, bague) to wear; (fig: responsabilité etc) to bear, carry; (inscription, marque, titre, patronyme, suj: arbre: fruits, fleurs) to bear; (apporter): ~ **qch quelque part/à qn** to take sth somewhere/to sb // vi (voix, regard, canon) to carry; (coup, argument) to hit home; ~ **sur** (peser) to rest on; (accent) to fall on; (conférence etc) to concern; (heurter) to strike; **se** ~ vi (se sentir): **se** ~ **bien/mal** to be well/unwell; **être porté à faire** to be apt ou inclined to do; **se faire** ~ **malade** to report sick; ~ **la main à son chapeau** to raise one's hand to one's hat; ~ **son effort sur** to direct one's efforts towards; ~ **à croire** to lead one to believe.

porte-serviettes [pɔʀtsɛʀvjɛt] nm inv towel rail.

porteur [pɔʀtœʀ] nm (de bagages) porter; (de chèque) bearer.

porte-voix [pɔʀtəvwa] nm inv megaphone.

portier [pɔʀtje] nm doorman.

portière [pɔʀtjɛʀ] nf door.

portillon [pɔʀtijɔ̃] nm gate.

portion [pɔʀsjɔ̃] nf (part) portion, share; (partie) portion, section.

portique [pɔʀtik] nm (RAIL) gantry.

porto [pɔʀto] nm port (wine).

portrait [pɔʀtʀɛ] nm portrait; photograph; ~-**robot** nm Identikit ® ou photo-fit ® picture.

portuaire [pɔʀtɥɛʀ] a port cpd, harbour cpd.

portugais, e [pɔʀtygɛ, -ɛz] a, nm/f Portuguese.

Portugal [pɔʀtygal] nm: **le** ~ Portugal.

pose [poz] nf laying; hanging; (attitude, d'un modèle) pose; (PHOTO) exposure.

posé, e [poze] a serious.

poser [poze] vt (déposer): ~ **qch (sur)/ qn à** to put sth down (on)/drop sb at; (placer): ~ **qch sur/quelque part** to put sth on/somewhere; (installer: moquette, carrelage) to lay; (rideaux, papier peint) to hang; (question) to ask; (principe, conditions) to lay ou set down; (problème) to formulate; (difficulté) to pose // vi (modèle) to pose; **se** ~ vi

(oiseau, avion) to land; (question) to arise.

positif, ive [pozitif, -iv] a positive.

position [pozisjɔ̃] nf position; **prendre** ~ (fig) to take a stand.

posséder [posede] vt to own, possess; (qualité, talent) to have, possess; (bien connaître: métier, langue) to have mastered, have a thorough knowledge of; (sexuellement, aussi: suj: colère etc) to possess; **possession** nf ownership q; possession.

possibilité [posibilite] nf possibility; ~**s** nfpl (moyens) means; (potentiel) potential sg.

possible [posibl(ə)] a possible; (projet, entreprise) feasible // nm: **faire son** ~ to do all one can, do one's utmost; **le plus/ moins de livres** ~ as many/few books as possible; **le plus/moins d'eau** ~ as much/little water as possible; **dès que** ~ as soon as possible.

postal, e, aux [pɔstal, -o] a postal.

poste [pɔst(ə)] nf (service) post, postal service; (administration, bureau) post office // nm (fonction, MIL) post; (TÉL) extension; (de radio etc) set; **mettre à la** ~ to post; **P~s, Télécommunications et Télédiffusion (P.T.T.)** postal and telecommunications service; ~ **d'essence** nm petrol ou filling station; ~ **d'incendie** nm fire point; ~ **de pilotage** nm cockpit; ~ **(de police)** nm police station; ~ **restante** nf poste restante (Brit), general delivery (US); ~ **de secours** nm first-aid post; ~ **de travail** nm work station.

poster vt [pɔste] to post // nm [pɔstɛʀ] poster.

postérieur, e [pɔsteʀjœʀ] a (date) later; (partie) back // nm (fam) behind.

posthume [pɔstym] a posthumous.

postiche [pɔstiʃ] nm hairpiece.

postuler [pɔstyle] vt (emploi) to apply for, put in for.

posture [pɔstyʀ] nf posture; position.

pot [po] nm jar, pot; (en plastique, carton) carton; (en métal) tin; **boire** ou **prendre un** ~ (fam) to have a drink; ~ **(de chambre)** (chamber)pot; ~ **d'échappement** exhaust pipe; ~ **de fleurs** plant pot, flowerpot; (plante) potted plant.

potable [pɔtabl(ə)] a: **eau (non)** ~ (not) drinking water.

potage [pɔtaʒ] nm soup; soup course.

potager, ère [pɔtaʒe, -ɛʀ] a (plante) edible, vegetable cpd; (jardin) ~ kitchen ou vegetable garden.

pot-au-feu [pɔtofø] nm inv (beef) stew.

pot-de-vin [pɔdvɛ̃] nm bribe.

pote [pɔt] nm (fam) pal.

poteau, x [pɔto] nm post; ~ **indicateur** signpost.

potelé, e [pɔtle] a plump, chubby.

potence [pɔtɑ̃s] nf gallows sg.

potentiel, le [pɔtɑ̃sjɛl] a, nm potential.

poterie [pɔtʀi] nf pottery; piece of pottery.

potier [pɔtje] nm potter.

potins [pɔtɛ̃] nmpl gossip sg.

potiron [pɔtiʀɔ̃] nm pumpkin.

pou, x [pu] nm louse (pl lice).

poubelle [pubɛl] nf (dust)bin.

pouce [pus] nm thumb.

poudre [pudʀ(ə)] nf powder; (fard) (face) powder; (explosif) gunpowder; en ~: café en ~ instant coffee; lait en ~ dried ou powdered milk; **poudrier** nm (powder) compact.

pouffer [pufe] vi: ~ (de rire) to snigger; to giggle.

pouilleux, euse [pujø, -øz] a flea-ridden; (fig) grubby; seedy.

poulailler [pulaje] nm henhouse.

poulain [pulɛ̃] nm foal; (fig) protégé.

poule [pul] nf (ZOOL) hen; (CULIN) (boiling) fowl.

poulet [pulɛ] nm chicken; (fam) cop.

poulie [puli] nf pulley; block.

pouls [pu] nm pulse; prendre le ~ de qn to feel sb's pulse.

poumon [pumɔ̃] nm lung.

poupe [pup] nf stern; en ~ astern.

poupée [pupe] nf doll.

poupon [pupɔ̃] nm babe-in-arms; **pouponnière** nf crèche, day nursery.

pour [puʀ] prép for // nm: le ~ et le contre the pros and cons; ~ faire (so as) to do, in order to do; ~ avoir fait for having done; ~ que so that, in order that; ~ 100 francs d'essence 100 francs' worth of petrol; ~ cent per cent; ~ ce qui est de as for.

pourboire [puʀbwaʀ] nm tip.

pourcentage [puʀsɑ̃taʒ] nm percentage.

pourchasser [puʀʃase] vt to pursue.

pourparlers [puʀpaʀle] nmpl talks, negotiations.

pourpre [puʀpʀ(ə)] a crimson.

pourquoi [puʀkwa] ad, cj why // nm inv: le ~ (de) the reason (for).

pourrai etc vb voir **pouvoir**.

pourri, e [puʀi] a rotten.

pourrir [puʀiʀ] vi to rot; (fruit) to go rotten ou bad // vt to rot; (fig) to spoil thoroughly; **pourriture** nf rot.

pourrons etc vb voir **pouvoir**.

poursuite [puʀsɥit] nf pursuit, chase; ~s (JUR) legal proceedings.

poursuivre [puʀsɥivʀ(ə)] vt to pursue, chase (after); (relancer) to hound, harry; (obséder) to haunt; (JUR) to bring proceedings against, prosecute; (: au civil); (but) to strive towards; (voyage, études) to carry on with, continue // vi to carry on, go on; se ~ vi to go on, continue.

pourtant [puʀtɑ̃] ad yet; c'est ~ facile (and) yet it's easy.

pourtour [puʀtuʀ] nm perimeter.

pourvoir [puʀvwaʀ] vt: ~ qch/qn de to equip sth/sb with // vi: ~ à to provide for; (emploi) to fill; se ~ (JUR): se ~ en cassation to take one's case to the Court of Appeal.

pourvoyeur [puʀvwajœʀ] nm supplier.

pourvu, e [puʀvy] a: ~ de equipped with; ~ que cj (si) provided that, so long as; (espérons que) let's hope (that).

pousse [pus] nf growth; (bourgeon) shoot.

poussé, e [puse] a exhaustive.

poussée [puse] nf thrust; (coup) push; (MÉD) eruption; (fig) upsurge.

pousser [puse] vt to push; (inciter): ~ qn à to urge ou press sb to + infinitif; (acculer): ~ qn à to drive sb to; (émettre: cri etc) to give; (stimuler) to urge on; to drive hard; (poursuivre) to carry on (further) // vi to push; (croître) to grow; se ~ vi to move over; faire ~ (plante) to grow.

poussette [pusɛt] nf (voiture d'enfant) push chair (Brit), stroller (US).

poussière [pusjɛʀ] nf dust; (grain) speck of dust; **poussiéreux, euse** a dusty.

poussin [pusɛ̃] nm chick.

poutre [putʀ(ə)] nf beam; (en fer, ciment armé) girder.

pouvoir [puvwaʀ] ♦ nm power; (POL: dirigeants): le ~ those in power; les ~s publics the authorities; ~ d'achat purchasing power

♦ vb semi-auxiliaire 1 (être en état de) can, be able to; je ne peux pas le réparer I can't ou I am not able to repair it; déçu de ne pas ~ le faire disappointed not to be able to do it

2 (avoir la permission) can, may, be allowed to; vous pouvez aller au cinéma you can ou may go to the pictures

3 (probabilité, hypothèse) may, might, could; il a pu avoir un accident he may ou might ou could have had an accident; il aurait pu le dire! he might ou could have said (so)!

♦ vb impersonnel may, might, could; il peut arriver que it may ou might ou could happen that

♦ vt can, be able to; j'ai fait tout ce que j'ai pu I did all I could; je n'en peux plus (épuisé) I'm exhausted; (à bout) I can't take any more

se pouvoir vi: il se peut que it may ou might be that; cela se pourrait that's quite possible.

prairie [pʀeʀi] nf meadow.

praline [pʀalin] nf sugared almond.

praticable [pʀatikabl(ə)] a passable, practicable.

praticien, ne [pʀatisjɛ̃, -jɛn] nm/f practitioner.

pratique [pʀatik] nf practice // a practical.

pratiquement [pratikmã] *ad (pour ainsi dire)* practically, virtually.

pratiquer [pratike] *vt* to practise; *(SPORT etc)* to go (in for); to play; *(intervention, opération)* to carry out; *(ouverture, abri)* to make.

pré [pre] *nm* meadow.

préalable [prealabl(ə)] *a* preliminary; **condition ~ (de)** precondition (for), prerequisite (for); **au ~** beforehand.

préambule [preãbyl] *nm* preamble; *(fig)* prelude; **sans ~** straight away.

préavis [preavi] *nm* notice; **communication avec ~** *(TÉL)* personal *ou* person to person call.

précaution [prekosjõ] *nf* precaution; **avec ~** cautiously; **par ~** as a precaution.

précédemment [presedamã] *ad* before, previously.

précédent, e [presedã, -ãt] *a* previous // *nm* precedent; **sans ~** unprecedented; **le jour ~** the day before, the previous day.

précéder [presede] *vt* to precede; *(marcher ou rouler devant)* to be in front of.

précepteur, trice [preseptœr, -tris] *nm/f* (private) tutor.

prêcher [preʃe] *vt* to preach.

précieux, euse [presjø, -øz] *a* precious; invaluable; *(style, écrivain)* précieux, precious.

précipice [presipis] *nm* drop, chasm; *(fig)* abyss.

précipitamment [presipitamã] *ad* hurriedly, hastily.

précipitation [presipitasjõ] *nf (hâte)* haste; **~s** *(pluie)* rain.

précipité, e [presipite] *a* hurried, hasty.

précipiter [presipite] *vt (faire tomber)*: **~ qn/qch du haut de** to throw sb/sth off *ou* from; *(hâter: marche)* to quicken; *(: départ)* to hasten; **se ~** *vi* to speed up; **se ~ sur/vers** to rush at/towards.

précis, e [presi, -iz] *a* precise; *(tir, mesures)* accurate, precise // *nm* handbook; **précisément** *ad* precisely; **préciser** *vt (expliquer)* to be more specific about, clarify; *(spécifier)* to state, specify; **se préciser** *vi* to become clear(er); **précision** *nf* precision; accuracy; **point ou detail** *(made clear or to be clarified)*.

précoce [prekos] *a* early; *(enfant)* precocious; *(calvitie)* premature.

préconiser [prekɔnize] *vt* to advocate.

prédécesseur [predesesœr] *nm* predecessor.

prédilection [predileksjõ] *nf*: **avoir une ~ pour** to be partial to; **de ~** favourite.

prédire [predir] *vt* to predict.

prédominer [predɔmine] *vi* to predominate; *(avis)* to prevail.

préface [prefas] *nf* preface.

préfecture [prefɛktyr] *nf* prefecture; **~ de police** police headquarters.

préférable [preferabl(ə)] *a* preferable.

préféré, e [prefere] *a, nm/f* favourite.

préférence [preferãs] *nf* preference; **de ~** preferably.

préférer [prefere] *vt*: **~ qn/qch (à)** to prefer sb/sth (to), like sb/sth better (than); **~ faire** to prefer to do; **je préférerais du thé** I would rather have tea, I'd prefer tea.

préfet [prefɛ] *nm* prefect.

préfixe [prefiks(ə)] *nm* prefix.

préhistorique [preistɔrik] *a* prehistoric.

préjudice [preʒydis] *nm (matériel)* loss; *(moral)* harm *q*; **porter ~ à** to harm, be detrimental to; **au ~ de** at the expense of.

préjugé [preʒyʒe] *nm* prejudice; **avoir un ~ contre** to be prejudiced *ou* biased against.

préjuger [preʒyʒe]: **~ de** *vt* to prejudge.

prélasser [prelase]: **se ~** *vi* to lounge.

prélèvement [prelɛvmã] *nm*: **faire un ~ de sang** to take a blood sample.

prélever [prelve] *vt (échantillon)* to take; *(argent)*: **~ (sur)** to deduct (from); *(: sur son compte)*: **~ (sur)** to withdraw (from).

prématuré, e [prematyre] *a* premature; *(retraite)* early // *nm* premature baby.

premier, ière [prəmje, -jɛr] *a* first; *(branche, marche)* bottom; *(fig)* basic; prime; initial // *nf (THÉÂTRE)* first night; *(AUTO)* first (gear); *(AVIAT, RAIL etc)* first class; *(CINÉMA)* première; *(exploit)* first; **le ~ venu** the first person to come along; **P~ Ministre** Prime Minister; **premièrement** *ad* firstly.

prémonition [premɔnisjõ] *nf* premonition.

prémunir [premynir]: **se ~** *vi*: **se ~ contre** to guard against.

prénatal, e [prenatal] *a (MÉD)* antenatal.

prendre [prãdr(ə)] *vt* to take; *(ôter)*: **~ qch à** to take sth from; *(aller chercher)* to get, fetch; *(se procurer)* to get; *(malfaiteur, poisson)* to catch; *(passager)* to pick up; *(personnel, aussi: couleur, goût)* to take on; *(locataire)* to take in; *(élève etc: traiter)* to handle; *(voix, ton)* to put on; *(coincer)*: **se ~ les doigts dans** to get one's fingers caught in // *vi (liquide, ciment)* to set; *(greffe, vaccin)* to take; *(feu: foyer)* to go; *(: incendie)* to start; *(allumette)* to light; *(se diriger)*: **~ à gauche** to turn (to the) left; **à tout ~** on the whole, all in all; **~ pour** to think one is; **s'en ~ à** to attack; **se ~ d'amitié/d'affection pour** to befriend/become fond of; s'y ~ (*procéder*) to set about it.

preneur [prənœr] *nm*: être/trouver ~ to be willing to buy/find a buyer.

preniez, prenne *etc vb voir* **prendre**.

prénom [prenɔ̃] *nm* first *ou* Christian name.

prénuptial, e, aux [prenypsjal, -o] *a* premarital.

préoccupation [preɔkypasjɔ̃] *nf* (*souci*) concern; (*idée fixe*) preoccupation.

préoccuper [preɔkype] *vt* to concern; to preoccupy.

préparatifs [preparatif] *nmpl* preparations.

préparation [preparasjɔ̃] *nf* preparation; (*SCOL*) piece of homework.

préparer [prepare] *vt* to prepare; (*café*) to make; (*examen*) to prepare for; (*voyage, entreprise*) to plan; se ~ *vi* (*orage, tragédie*) to brew, be in the air; se ~ (à qch/faire) to prepare (o.s.) *ou* get ready (for sth/to do); ~ qch à qn (*surprise etc*) to have sth in store for sb.

prépondérant, e [prepɔ̃derɑ̃, -ɑ̃t] *a* major, dominating.

préposé, e [prepoze] *a*: ~ à in charge of *// nm/f* employee; official; attendant.

préposition [prepozisjɔ̃] *nf* preposition.

près [prɛ] *ad* near, close; ~ de *prép* near (to), close to; (*environ*) nearly, almost; de ~ *ad* closely; à 5 kg ~ to within about 5 kg; à cela ~ que apart from the fact that.

présage [prezaʒ] *nm* omen.

présager [prezaʒe] *vt* to foresee.

presbyte [presbit] *a* long-sighted.

presbytère [presbitɛr] *nm* presbytery.

prescription [preskripsjɔ̃] *nf* (*instruction*) order, instruction; (*MÉD, JUR*) prescription.

prescrire [preskrir] *vt* to prescribe.

préséance [preseɑ̃s] *nf* precedence *q*.

présence [prezɑ̃s] *nf* presence; (*au bureau etc*) attendance; ~ d'esprit presence of mind.

présent, e [prezɑ̃, -ɑ̃t] *a, nm* present; à ~ (que) now (that).

présentation [prezɑ̃tasjɔ̃] *nf* introduction; presentation; (*allure*) appearance.

présenter [prezɑ̃te] *vt* to present; (*sympathie, condoléances*) to offer; (*soumettre*) to submit; (*invité, conférencier*): ~ qn (à) to introduce sb (to) *// vi*: ~ mal/bien to have an unattractive/a pleasing appearance; se ~ *vi* (*sur convocation*) to report, come; (*à une élection*) to stand; (*occasion*) to arise; se ~ bien/mal to look good/not too good; se ~ à (*examen*) to sit.

préservatif [prezɛrvatif] *nm* sheath, condom.

préserver [prezɛrve] *vt*: ~ de to protect from; to save from.

président [prezidɑ̃] *nm* (*POL*) president; (*d'une assemblée, COMM*) chairman; ~ directeur général (PDG) chairman and managing director.

présider [prezide] *vt* to preside over; (*dîner*) to be the guest of honour at; ~ à *vt* to direct; to govern.

présomptueux, euse [prezɔ̃ptɥø, -øz] *a* presumptuous.

presque [prɛsk(ə)] *ad* almost, nearly; ~ rien hardly anything; ~ pas hardly (at all); ~ pas de hardly any.

presqu'île [prɛskil] *nf* peninsula.

pressant, e [presɑ̃, -ɑ̃t] *a* urgent; se faire ~ to become insistent.

presse [prɛs] *nf* press; (*affluence*): heures de ~ busy times.

pressé, e [prese] *a* in a hurry; (*air*) hurried; (*besogne*) urgent; orange ~e fresh orange juice.

pressentiment [presɑ̃timɑ̃] *nm* foreboding, premonition.

pressentir [presɑ̃tir] *vt* to sense; (*prendre contact avec*) to approach.

presse-papiers [prespapje] *nm inv* paperweight.

presser [prese] *vt* (*fruit, éponge*) to squeeze; (*bouton*) to press; (*allure, affaire*) to speed up; (*inciter*): ~ qn de faire to urge *ou* press sb to do *// vi* to be urgent; rien ne presse there's no hurry; se ~ *vi* (*se hâter*) to hurry (up); se ~ contre qn to squeeze up against sb.

pressing [presiaʒ] *nm* steam-pressing; (*magasin*) dry-cleaner's.

pression [presjɔ̃] *nf* pressure; faire ~ sur to put pressure on; ~ artérielle blood pressure.

pressoir [preswar] *nm* (*wine ou oil etc*) press.

pressurer [presyre] *vt* (*fig*) to squeeze.

prestance [prestɑ̃s] *nf* presence, imposing bearing.

prestataire [prestatɛr] *nm/f* supplier.

prestation [prestasjɔ̃] *nf* (*allocation*) benefit; (*d'une entreprise*) service provided; (*d'un artiste*) performance.

prestidigitateur, trice [prestidiʒitatœr, -tris] *nm/f* conjurer.

prestigieux, euse [prestiʒjø, -øz] *a* prestigious.

présumer [prezyme] *vt*: ~ que to presume *ou* assume that; ~ de to overrate.

présupposer [presypoze] *vt* to presuppose.

prêt, e [prɛ, prɛt] *a* ready *// nm* lending *q*; loan; **prêt-à-porter** *nm* ready-to-wear *ou* off-the-peg (*Brit*) clothes *pl*.

prétendant [pretɑ̃dɑ̃] *nm* pretender; (*d'une femme*) suitor.

prétendre [pretɑ̃dr(ə)] *vt* (*affirmer*): ~ que to claim that; (*avoir l'intention de*): ~ faire qch to mean *ou* intend to do sth; ~ à *vt* (*droit, titre*) to lay claim to; **prétendu, e** *a* (*supposé*) so-called.

prête-nom [prɛtnɔ̃] *nm* (*péj*) figurehead.

prétentieux, euse |prɛtɑ̃sjø, -øz| *a* pretentious.

prétention |prɛtɑ̃sjɔ̃| *nf* claim; pretentiousness.

prêter |prɛte| *vt* (*livres, argent*): ~ qch (à) to lend sth (to); (*supposer*): ~ à qn (*caractère, propos*) to attribute to sb // *vi* (*aussi*: se ~: *tissu, cuir*) to give; ~ à (*commentaires etc*) to be open to, give rise to; se ~ à to lend o.s. (*ou* itself) to; (*manigances etc*) to go along with; ~ assistance à to give help to; ~ attention à to pay attention to; ~ serment to take the oath; ~ l'oreille to listen.

prétexte |prɛtɛkst(ə)| *nm* pretext, excuse; **sous aucun** ~ on no account; **prétexter** *vt* to give as a pretext *ou* an excuse.

prêtre |prɛtr(ə)| *nm* priest.

preuve |prœv| *nf* proof; (*indice*) proof, evidence *q*; **faire** ~ **de** to show; **faire ses** ~s to prove o.s. (*ou* itself).

prévaloir |prevalwar| *vi* to prevail; se ~ **de** *vt* to take advantage of; to pride o.s. on.

prévenant, e |prevnɑ̃, -ɑ̃t| *a* thoughtful, kind.

prévenir |prevnir| *vt* (*avertir*): ~ qn (**de**) to warn sb (about); (*informer*): ~ qn (**de**) to tell *ou* inform sb (about); (*éviter*): to avoid, prevent; (*anticiper*) to forestall; to anticipate.

prévention |prevɑ̃sjɔ̃| *nf* prevention; ~ **routière** road safety.

prévenu, e |prevny| *nm/f* (*JUR*) defendant, accused.

prévision |previzjɔ̃| *nf*: ~s predictions; forecast *sg*; **en** ~ **de** in anticipation of; ~s **météorologiques** weather forecast *sg*.

prévoir |prevwar| *vt* (*deviner*) to foresee; (*s'attendre à*) to expect, reckon on; (*prévenir*) to anticipate; (*organiser*) to plan; (*préparer, réserver*) to allow; **prévu pour 10h** scheduled for 10 o'clock.

prévoyance |prevwajɑ̃s| *nf*: **caisse de** ~ contingency fund.

prévoyant, e |prevwajɑ̃, -ɑ̃t| *a* gifted with (*ou* showing) foresight.

prévu, e |prevy| *pp de* **prévoir**.

prier |prije| *vi* to pray // *vt* (*Dieu*) to pray to; (*implorer*) to beg; (*demander*): ~ qn **de faire** to ask sb to do; se **faire** ~ to need coaxing *ou* persuading; **je vous en prie** (*allez-y*) please do; (*de rien*) don't mention it.

prière |prijɛr| *nf* prayer; '~ **de faire ...**' 'please do ...'.

primaire |primɛr| *a* primary; (*péj*) simple-minded; simplistic // *nm* (*SCOL*) primary education.

prime |prim| *nf* (*bonification*) bonus; (*subside*) premium; allowance; (*COMM*: *cadeau*) free gift; (*ASSURANCES,*

BOURSE) premium // *a*: **de** ~ **abord** at first glance.

primer |prime| *vt* (*l'emporter sur*) to prevail over; (*récompenser*) to award a prize to // *vi* to dominate; to prevail.

primeurs |primœr| *nfpl* early fruits and vegetables.

primevère |primvɛr| *nf* primrose.

primitif, ive |primitif, -iv| *a* primitive; (*originel*) original.

prince, esse |prɛ̃s, prɛ̃sɛs| *nm/f* prince/princess.

principal, e, aux |prɛ̃sipal, -o| *a* principal, main // *nm* (*SCOL*) principal, head(master); (*essentiel*) main thing.

principe |prɛ̃sip| *nm* principle; **pour le** ~ on principle; **de** ~ *a* (*accord, hostilité*) automatic; **par** ~ on principle; **en** ~ (*habituellement*) as a rule; (*théoriquement*) in principle.

printemps |prɛ̃tɑ̃| *nm* spring.

priorité |prijɔrite| *nf* (*AUTO*): **avoir la** ~ (**sur**) to have right of way (over); ~ **à droite** right of way to vehicles coming from the right.

pris, e |pri, priz| *pp de* **prendre** // *a* (*place*) taken; (*journée, mains*) full; (*billets*) sold; (*personne*) busy; **avoir le nez/la gorge** ~ (**e**) to have a stuffy nose/ a hoarse throat; **être** ~ **de panique** to be panic-stricken.

prise |priz| *nf* (*d'une ville*) capture; (*PÊCHE, CHASSE*) catch; (*de judo ou catch, point d'appui ou pour empoigner*) hold; (*ÉLEC: fiche*) plug; (: *femelle*) socket; **être aux** ~s **avec** to be grappling with; ~ **de courant** power point; ~ **multiple** adaptor; ~ **de sang** blood test; ~ **de terre** earth; ~ **de vue** (*photo*) shot.

priser |prize| *vt* (*tabac, héroïne*) to take; (*estimer*) to prize, value // *vi* to take snuff.

prison |prizɔ̃| *nf* prison; **aller/être en** ~ to go to/be in prison *ou* jail; **faire de la** ~ to serve time; **prisonnier, ière** *nm/f* prisoner // *a* captive.

prit *vb voir* **prendre**.

privé, e |prive| *a* private; **en** ~ in private.

priver |prive| *vt*: ~ qn **de** to deprive sb of; se ~ **de** to do without.

privilège |privilɛʒ| *nm* privilege.

prix |pri| *nm* (*valeur*) price; (*récompense, SCOL*) prize; **hors de** ~ exorbitantly priced; **à aucun** ~ not at any price; **à tout** ~ at all costs; ~ **d'achat/de vente/de revient** purchasing/selling/cost price.

probable |prɔbabl(ə)| *a* likely, probable; ~**ment** *ad* probably.

probant, e |prɔbɑ̃, -ɑ̃t| *a* convincing.

problème |prɔblɛm| *nm* problem.

procédé |prɔsede| *nm* (*méthode*) process; (*comportement*) behaviour *q*.

procéder |prɔsede| *vi* to proceed; to behave; ~ à vt to carry out.

procès |pRɔsɛ| nm trial; (poursuites) proceedings pl; être en ~ avec to be involved in a lawsuit with.

processus |pRɔsɛsys| nm process.

procès-verbal, aux |pRɔsɛvɛRbal, -o| nm (constat) statement; (aussi: P.V.): avoir un ~ to get a parking ticket; to be booked; (de réunion) minutes pl.

prochain, e |pRɔʃɛ̃, -ɛn| a next; (proche) impending; near // nm fellow man; la ~e fois/semaine ~e next time/ week; **prochainement** ad soon, shortly.

proche |pRɔʃ| a nearby; (dans le temps) imminent; (parent, ami) close; ~s nmpl close relatives; être ~ (de) to be near, be close (to); de ~ en ~ gradually; le P~ Orient the Middle East.

proclamer |pRɔklame| vt to proclaim.

procuration |pRɔkyRɑsjɔ̃| nf proxy; power of attorney.

procurer |pRɔkyRe| vt: ~ qch à qn (fournir) to obtain sth for sb; (causer: plaisir etc) to bring sb sth; se ~ vt to get.

procureur |pRɔkyRœR| nm public prosecutor.

prodige |pRɔdiʒ| nm marvel, wonder; (personne) prodigy.

prodigue |pRɔdig| a generous; extravagant; fils ~ prodigal son.

prodiguer |pRɔdige| vt (argent, biens) to be lavish with; (soins, attentions): ~ qch à qn to give sb sth.

producteur, trice |pRɔdyktœR, -tRis| nm/f producer.

production |pRɔdyksjɔ̃| nf (gén) production; (rendement) output.

produire |pRɔdɥiR| vt to produce; se ~ vi (acteur) to perform, appear; (événement) to happen, occur.

produit |pRɔdɥi| nm (gén) product; ~s agricoles farm produce sg; ~ d'entretien cleaning product.

prof |pRɔf| nm (fam) teacher.

profane |pRɔfan| a (REL) secular // nm/f layman.

proférer |pRɔfeRe| vt to utter.

professer |pRɔfese| vi to teach.

professeur |pRɔfesœR| nm teacher; (titulaire d'une chaire) professor; ~ (de faculté) (university) lecturer.

profession |pRɔfesjɔ̃| nf profession; sans ~ unemployed; **professionnel, le** a, nm/f professional.

profil |pRɔfil| nm profile; (d'une voiture) line, contour; de ~ in profile; ~er vt to streamline.

profit |pRɔfi| nm (avantage) benefit, advantage; (COMM, FINANCE) profit; au ~ de in aid of; tirer ~ de to profit from.

profitable |pRɔfitabl(ə)| a beneficial; profitable.

profiter |pRɔfite| vi: ~ de to take advantage of; to make the most of; ~ à to

benefit; to be profitable to.

profond, e |pRɔfɔ̃, -ɔ̃d| a deep; (méditation, mépris) profound; **profondeur** nf depth.

progéniture |pRɔʒenityR| nf offspring inv.

programme |pRɔgRam| nm programme; (TV, RADIO) programmes pl; (SCOL) syllabus, curriculum; (INFORM) program; **programmer** vt (TV, RADIO) to put on, show; (INFORM) to program; **programmeur, euse** nm/f programmer.

progrès |pRɔgRɛ| nm progress q; faire des ~ to make progress.

progresser |pRɔgRese| vi to progress; (troupes etc) to make headway ou progress; **progressif, ive** a progressive.

prohiber |pRɔibe| vt to prohibit, ban.

proie |pRwa| nf prey q.

projecteur |pRɔʒɛktœR| nm projector; (de théâtre, cirque) spotlight.

projectile |pRɔʒɛktil| nm missile.

projection |pRɔʒɛksjɔ̃| nf projection; showing; conférence avec ~s lecture with slides (ou a film).

projet |pRɔʒɛ| nm plan; (ébauche) draft; ~ de loi bill.

projeter |pRɔʒte| vt (envisager) to plan; (film, photos) to project; (passer) to show; (ombre, lueur) to throw, cast; (jeter) to throw up (ou off ou out).

prolixe |pRɔliks(ə)| a verbose.

prolongations |pRɔlɔ̃gɑsjɔ̃| nfpl (FOOTBALL) extra time sg.

prolongement |pRɔlɔ̃ʒmɑ̃| nm extension; ~s (fig) repercussions, effects; dans le ~ de to be running on from.

prolonger |pRɔlɔ̃ʒe| vt (débat, séjour) to prolong; (délai, billet, rue) to extend; (suj: chose) to be a continuation ou an extension of; se ~ vi to go on.

promenade |pRɔmnad| nf walk (ou drive ou ride); faire une ~ to go for a walk; une ~ en voiture/à vélo a drive/ (bicycle) ride.

promener |pRɔmne| vt (chien) to take out for a walk; (doigts, regard): ~ qch sur to run sth over; se ~ vi to go for (ou be out for) a walk.

promesse |pRɔmɛs| nf promise.

promettre |pRɔmɛtR(ə)| vt to promise // vi to be ou look promising; ~ à qn de faire to promise sb that one will do.

promiscuité |pRɔmiskɥite| nf crowding; lack of privacy.

promontoire |pRɔmɔ̃twaR| nm headland.

promoteur, trice |pRɔmɔtœR, -tRis| nm/f (instigateur) instigator, promoter; ~ (immobilier) property developer (Brit), real estate promoter (US).

promotion |pRɔmɔsjɔ̃| nf promotion.

promouvoir |pRɔmuvwaR| vt to promote.

prompt, e |pRɔ̃, pRɔ̃t| a swift, rapid.

prôner [prone] vt to advocate.

pronom [prɔnɔ̃] nm pronoun.

prononcer [prɔnɔ̃se] vt (son, mot, jugement) to pronounce; (dire) to utter; (allocution) to deliver; se ~ vi to reach a decision, give a verdict; se ~ sur to give an opinion on; se ~ contre to come down against; **prononciation** nf pronunciation.

pronostic [prɔnɔstik] nm (MÉD) prognosis (pl oses); (fig: aussi: ~s) forecast.

propagande [prɔpagɑ̃d] nf propaganda.

propager [prɔpaʒe] vt, se ~ vi to spread.

prophète [prɔfɛt] nm prophet.

prophétie [prɔfesi] nf prophecy.

propice [prɔpis] a favourable.

proportion [prɔpɔrsjɔ̃] nf proportion; **toute(s) ~(s) gardée(s)** making due allowance(s).

propos [prɔpo] nm (paroles) talk q, remark; (intention) intention, aim; (sujet): à quel ~? what about?; à ~ de about, regarding; à tout ~ for no reason at all; à ~ ad by the way; (opportunément) at the right moment.

proposer [prɔpoze] vt (suggérer): ~ qch (à qn)/de faire to suggest sth (to sb)/doing, propose sth (to sb)/to do; (offrir): ~ qch à qn/de faire to offer sb sth/to do; (candidat) to put forward; (loi, motion) to propose; se ~ to offer one's services; se ~ de faire to intend ou propose to do; **proposition** nf suggestion; proposal; offer; (LING) clause.

propre [prɔpr(ə)] a clean; (net) neat, tidy; (possessif) own; (sens) literal; (particulier): ~ à peculiar to; (approprié): ~ à suitable for; (de nature à): ~ à faire likely to do // nm: recopier au ~ to make a fair copy of; **~ment** ad cleanly; neatly, tidily; le village ~ment dit the village itself; à ~ment parler strictly speaking; **~té** nf cleanliness; neatness; tidiness.

propriétaire [prɔprijetɛr] nm/f owner; (pour le locataire) landlord/lady.

propriété [prɔprijete] nf (gén) property; (droit) ownership; (objet, immeuble, terres) property gén q.

propulser [prɔpylse] vt (missile) to propel; (projeter) to hurl, fling.

proroger [prɔrɔʒe] vt to put back, defer; (prolonger) to extend.

proscrire [prɔskrir] vt (bannir) to banish; (interdire) to ban, prohibit.

prose [proz] nf prose (style).

prospecter [prɔspɛkte] vt to prospect; (COMM) to canvass.

prospectus [prɔspɛktys] nm leaflet.

prospère [prɔspɛr] a prosperous.

prosterner [prɔstɛrne]: se ~ vi to bow low, prostrate o.s.

prostituée [prɔstitɥe] nf prostitute.

protecteur, trice [prɔtɛktœr, -tris] a protective; (air, ton: péj) patronizing // nm/f protector.

protection [prɔtɛksjɔ̃] nf protection; (d'un personnage influent: aide) patronage.

protéger [prɔteʒe] vt to protect; se ~ de/contre to protect o.s. from.

protéine [prɔtein] nf protein.

protestant, e [prɔtɛstɑ̃, -ɑ̃t] a, nm/f Protestant.

protestation [prɔtɛstasjɔ̃] nf (plainte) protest.

protester [prɔtɛste] vi: ~ (contre) to protest (against ou about); ~ de (son innocence, sa loyauté) to protest.

prothèse [prɔtɛz] nf artificial limb, prosthesis; ~ dentaire denture.

protocole [prɔtɔkɔl] nm (fig) etiquette.

proue [pru] nf bow(s pl), prow.

prouesse [prues] nf feat.

prouver [pruve] vt to prove.

provenance [prɔvnɑ̃s] nf origin; (de mot, coutume) source; **avion en ~ de** plane (arriving) from.

provenir [prɔvnir]: ~ de vt to come from; (résulter de) to be the result of.

proverbe [prɔvɛrb(ə)] nm proverb.

province [prɔvɛ̃s] nf province.

proviseur [prɔvizœr] nm ≈ head-(teacher) (Brit), ≈ principal (US).

provision [prɔvizjɔ̃] nf (réserve) stock, supply; (avance: à un avocat, avoué) retainer, retaining fee; (COMM) funds pl (in account); reserve; ~s (vivres) provisions, food q.

provisoire [prɔvizwar] a temporary; (JUR) provisional.

provoquer [prɔvɔke] vt (inciter): ~ qn à to incite sb to; (défier) to provoke; (causer) to cause, bring about.

proxénète [prɔksenɛt] nm procurer.

proximité [prɔksimite] nf nearness, closeness; (dans le temps) imminence, closeness; à ~ near ou close by; à ~ de near (to), close to.

prude [pryd] a prudish.

prudemment [prydamɑ̃] ad carefully, cautiously; wisely, sensibly.

prudence [prydɑ̃s] nf carefulness; caution; **avec ~** carefully; cautiously; **par (mesure de) ~** as a precaution.

prudent, e [prydɑ̃, -ɑ̃t] a (pas téméraire) careful, cautious; (: en général) safety-conscious; (sage, conseillé) wise, sensible; (réservé) cautious.

prune [pryn] nf plum.

pruneau, x [pryno] nm prune.

prunelle [prynɛl] nf pupil; eye.

prunier [prynje] nm plum tree.

psaume [psom] nm psalm.

pseudonyme [psødɔnim] nm (gén) fictitious name; (d'écrivain) pseudonym, pen name; (de comédien) stage name.

psychanalyste [psikanalist(ə)] nm/f

psychoanalyst.

psychiatre [psikjatʀ(ə)] nm/f psychiatrist.

psychiatrique [psikjatʀik] a psychiatric.

psychique [psiʃik] a psychological.

psychologie [psikɔlɔʒi] nf psychology; **psychologique** a psychological; **psychologue** nm/f psychologist.

P.T.T. sigle fpl voir **poste**.

pu pp de **pouvoir**.

puanteur [pɥɑ̃tœʀ] nf stink, stench.

pub [pyb] abr f (fam: = publicité): la ~ advertising.

public, ique [pyblik] a public; (école, instruction) state cpd // nm public; (assistance) audience; **en** ~ in public.

publicitaire [pyblisitɛʀ] a advertising cpd; (film, voiture) publicity cpd.

publicité [pyblisite] nf (méthode, profession) advertising; (annonce) advertisement; (révélations) publicity.

publier [pyblije] vt to publish.

publique [pyblik] af voir **public**.

puce [pys] nf flea; (INFORM) chip; **~s** nfpl (marché) flea market sg.

pucelle [pysɛl] af: **être** ~ to be a virgin.

pudeur [pydœʀ] nf modesty.

pudique [pydik] a (chaste) modest; (discret) discreet.

puer [pɥe] (péj) vi to stink.

puéricultrice [pɥeʀikyltʀis] nf p(a)ediatric nurse.

puériculture [pɥeʀikyltyʀ] nf p(a)ediatric nursing; infant care.

puéril, e [pɥeʀil] a childish.

pugilat [pyʒila] nm (fist) fight.

puis [pɥi] vb voir **pouvoir** // ad then.

puiser [pɥize] vt: ~ (**dans**) to draw (from).

puisque [pɥisk(ə)] cj since.

puissance [pɥisɑ̃s] nf power; **en** ~ a potential.

puissant, e [pɥisɑ̃, -ɑ̃t] a powerful.

puisse etc vb voir **pouvoir**.

puits [pɥi] nm well; ~ **de mine** mine shaft.

pull(-over) [pul(ɔvœʀ)] nm sweater.

pulluler [pylyle] vi to swarm.

pulpe [pylp(ə)] nf pulp.

pulvérisateur [pylveʀizatœʀ] nm spray.

pulvériser [pylveʀize] vt to pulverize; (liquide) to spray.

punaise [pynɛz] nf (ZOOL) bug; (clou) drawing pin (Brit), thumbtack (US).

punch [pɔ̃ʃ] nm (boisson) punch; [pœnʃ] (BOXE, fig) punch.

punir [pyniʀ] vt to punish; **punition** nf punishment.

pupille [pypij] nf (ANAT) pupil // nm/f (enfant) ward; ~ **de l'État** child in care.

pupitre [pypitʀ(ə)] nm (SCOL) desk; (REL) lectern; (de chef d'orchestre) rostrum.

pur, e [pyʀ] a pure; (vin) undiluted;

(whisky) neat; **en** ~**e perte** to no avail.

purée [pyʀe] nf: ~ (**de pommes de terre**) mashed potatoes pl; ~ **de marrons** chestnut purée.

purger [pyʀʒe] vt (radiateur) to drain; (circuit hydraulique) to bleed; (MÉD, POL) to purge; (JUR: peine) to serve.

purin [pyʀɛ̃] nm liquid manure.

pur-sang [pyʀsɑ̃] nm inv thoroughbred.

pusillanime [pyzilanim] a fainthearted.

putain [pytɛ̃] nf (fam!) whore (!).

puzzle [pœzl(ə)] nm jigsaw (puzzle).

P.V. sigle m = **procès-verbal**.

pyjama [piʒama] nm pyjamas pl.

pyramide [piʀamid] nf pyramid.

Pyrénées [piʀene] nfpl: **les** ~ the Pyrenees.

Q

QG [kyʒe] voir **quartier**.

QI [kyi] sigle m (= quotient intellectuel) IQ.

quadragénaire [kadʀaʒenɛʀ] nm/f man/woman in his/her forties.

quadriller [kadʀije] vt (papier) to mark out in squares; (POLICE) to keep under tight control.

quadruple [k(w)adʀypl(ə)] nm: **le** ~ **de** four times as much as; **quadruplés, ées** nm/fpl quadruplets, quads.

quai [ke] nm (de port) quay; (de gare) platform; **être à** ~ (navire) to be alongside; (train) to be in the station.

qualifier [kalifje] vt, **se** ~ vi (SPORT) to qualify; ~ **qch/qn de** to describe sth/sb as.

qualité [kalite] nf quality; (titre, fonction) position.

quand [kɑ̃] cj, ad when; ~ **je serai riche** when I'm rich; ~ **même** all the same; really; ~ **bien même** even though.

quant [kɑ̃]: ~ **à** prép as for, as to; regarding.

quant-à-soi [kɑ̃taswa] nm: **rester sur son** ~ to remain aloof.

quantité [kɑ̃tite] nf quantity, amount; (SCIENCE) quantity; (grand nombre): **une** ou **des** ~**(s) de** a great deal of.

quarantaine [kaʀɑ̃tɛn] nf (MÉD) quarantine; **avoir la** ~ (âge) to be around forty; **une** ~ (**de**) forty or so, about forty.

quarante [kaʀɑ̃t] num forty.

quart [kaʀ] nm (fraction, partie) quarter; (surveillance) watch; **un** ~ **de beurre** a quarter kilo of butter; **un** ~ **de vin** a quarter litre of wine; **une livre un** ~ ou **et** ~ one and a quarter pounds; **le** ~ **de** a quarter of; ~ **d'heure** quarter of an hour.

quartier [kaʀtje] nm (de ville) district, area; (de bœuf) quarter; (de fruit, fromage) piece; ~**s** nmpl (MIL, BLASON) quarters; **cinéma de** ~ local cinema; **avoir** ~ **libre** *(fig)* to be free; ~ **général (QG)** headquarters (HQ).

quartz [kwaʀts] *nm* quartz.

quasi [kazi] *ad* almost, nearly; ~**ment** *ad* almost, nearly.

quatorze [katɔʀz(ə)] *num* fourteen.

quatre [katʀ(ə)] *num* four; **à** ~ **pattes** on all fours; **tiré à** ~ **épingles** dressed up to the nines; **faire les** ~ **cent coups** to get a bit wild; **se mettre en** ~ **pour qn** to go out of one's way for sb; ~ **à** ~ *(monter, descendre)* four at a time; ~-**vingt-dix** *num* ninety; ~-**vingts** *num* eighty; **quatrième** *num* fourth.

quatuor [kwatyɔʀ] *nm* quartet(te).

que [kə] ♦ *cj* **1** *(introduisant complétive)* that; **il sait** ~ **tu es là** he knows (that) you're here; **je veux** ~ **tu acceptes** I want you to accept; **il a dit** ~ **oui** he said he would *(ou it was etc)*
2 *(reprise d'autres conjonctions)*: **quand il rentrera et qu'il aura mangé** when he gets back and (when) he has eaten; **si vous y allez ou** ~ **vous** ... if you go there or if you ...
3 *(en tête de phrase: hypothèse, souhait etc)*: **qu'il le veuille ou non** whether he likes it or not; **qu'il fasse ce qu'il voudra!** let him do as he pleases!
4 *(après comparatif)* than; as; *voir* **plus, aussi, autant** *etc*
5 *(seulement)*: **ne** ... ~ only; **il ne boit** ~ **de l'eau** he only drinks water
♦ *ad (exclamation)*: **qu'il** *ou* **qu'est-ce qu'il est bête/court vite!** he's so silly!/he runs so fast!; ~ **de livres!** what a lot of books!
♦ *pronom* **1** *(relatif: personne)* whom; *(: chose)* that, which; **l'homme** ~ **je vois** the man (whom) I see; **le livre** ~ **tu vois** the book (that *ou* which) you see; **un jour** ~ **j'étais** ... a day when I was ...
2 *(interrogatif)* what; ~ **fais-tu?, qu'est-ce que tu fais?** what are you doing?; **qu'est-ce que c'est?** what is it?, what's that?; ~ **faire?** what can one do?

quel, quelle [kɛl] *a* **1** *(interrogatif: personne)* who; *(: chose)* what; which; ~ **est cet homme?** who is this man?; ~ **est ce livre?** what is this book?; ~ **livre/ homme?** what book/man?; *(parmi un certain choix)* which book/man?; ~**s acteurs préférez-vous?** which actors do you prefer?; **dans** ~**s pays êtes-vous allé?** which *ou* what countries did you go to?
2 *(exclamatif)*: ~**le surprise!** what a surprise!
3: ~**(le) que soit**: ~ **que soit le coupable** whoever is guilty; ~ **que soit votre avis** whatever your opinion.

quelconque [kɛlkɔ̃k] *a (médiocre)* indifferent, poor; *(sans attrait)* ordinary, plain; *(indéfini)*: **un ami/pretexte** ~ some friend/pretext or other.

quelque [kɛlkə] ♦ *a* **1** some; a few; *(tournure interrogative)* any; ~ **espoir** some hope; **il a** ~**s amis** he has a few *ou* some friends; **a-t-il** ~**s amis?** has he any friends?; **les** ~**s livres qui** the few books which; **20 kg et** ~**(s)** a bit over 20 kg
2: ~ ... **que**: ~ **livre qu'il choisisse** whatever *(ou* whichever) book he chooses
3: ~ **chose** something; *(tournure interrogative)* anything; ~ **chose d'autre** something else; anything else; ~ **part** somewhere; anywhere; **en** ~ **sorte** as it were
♦ *ad* **1** *(environ)*: ~ **100 mètres** some 100 metres
2: ~ **peu** rather, somewhat.

quelquefois [kɛlkəfwa] *ad* sometimes.

quelques-uns, -unes [kɛlkəzœ̃, -yn] *pronom* a few, some.

quelqu'un [kɛlkœ̃] *pronom* someone, somebody, *tournure interrogative* + anyone *ou* anybody; ~ **d'autre** someone *ou* somebody else; anybody else.

quémander [kemɑ̃de] *vt* to beg for.

qu'en dira-t-on [kɑ̃diʀatɔ̃] *nm inv*: **le** ~ gossip, what people say.

querelle [kəʀɛl] *nf* quarrel.

quereller [kəʀele]: **se** ~ *vi* to quarrel.

qu'est-ce que *(ou* **qui)** [kɛskə(ki)] *voir* **que, qui.**

question [kɛstjɔ̃] *nf (gén)* question; *(fig)* matter; issue; **il a été** ~ **de we** *(ou* they) spoke about; **de quoi est-il** ~? what is it about?; **il n'en est pas** ~ there's no question of it; **hors de** ~ out of the question; **remettre en** ~ to question.

questionnaire [kɛstjɔnɛʀ] *nm* questionnaire; **questionner** *vt* to question.

quête [kɛt] *nf* collection; *(recherche)* quest, search; **faire la** ~ *(à l'église)* to take the collection; *(artiste)* to pass the hat round; **quêter** *vi (à l'église)* to take the collection.

quetsche [kwɛtʃ(ə)] *nf* damson.

queue [kø] *nf* tail; *(fig: du classement)* bottom; *(: de poêle)* handle; *(: de fruit, feuille)* stalk; *(: de train, colonne, file)* rear; **faire la** ~ to queue (up); ~ **de cheval** ponytail; ~-**de-pie** *nf (habit)* tails *pl*, tail coat.

qui [ki] *pronom (personne)* who, *prép* + whom; *(chose, animal)* which, that; **qu'est-ce** ~ **est sur la table?** what is on the table?; ~ **est-ce qui?** who?; ~ **est-ce que?** who?; whom?; **à** ~ **est ce sac?** whose bag is this?; **à** ~ **parlais-tu?** who were you talking to?, to whom were you talking?; **amenez** ~ **vous voulez** bring who you like; ~ **que ce soit** whoever it may be.

quiconque [kikɔ̃k] *pronom (celui qui)* whoever, anyone who; *(personne)* anyone, anybody.

quiétude [kjetyd] *nf (d'un lieu)* quiet, tranquillity; **en toute** ~ in complete peace.

quille [kij] *nf*: (jeu de) ~s skittles *sg* (*Brit*), bowling (*US*).
quincaillerie [kɛ̃kajʀi] *nf* (*ustensiles*) hardware; (*magasin*) hardware shop; **quincaillier, ière** *nm/f* hardware dealer.
quinine [kinin] *nf* quinine.
quinquagénaire [kɛ̃kaʒenɛʀ] *nm/f* man/woman in his/her fifties.
quintal, aux [kɛ̃tal, -o] *nm* quintal (*100 kg*).
quinte [kɛ̃t] *nf*: ~ (de toux) coughing fit.
quintuple [kɛ̃typl(ə)] *nm*: le ~ de five times as much as; **quintuplés, ées** *nm/fpl* quintuplets, quins.
quinzaine [kɛ̃zɛn] *nf*: une ~ (de) about fifteen, fifteen or so; une ~ (de jours) a fortnight, two weeks.
quinze [kɛ̃z] *num* fifteen; demain en ~ a fortnight *ou* two weeks tomorrow; dans ~ jours in a fortnight('s time), in two weeks(' time).
quiproquo [kipʀɔko] *nm* misunderstanding.
quittance [kitɑ̃s] *nf* (*reçu*) receipt; (*facture*) bill.
quitte [kit] *a*: être ~ envers qn to be no longer in sb's debt; (*fig*) to be quits with sb; être ~ de (*obligation*) to be clear of; en être ~ à bon compte to have got off lightly; ~ à faire even if it means doing.
quitter [kite] *vt* to leave; (*espoir, illusion*) to give up; (*vêtement*) to take off; se ~ *vi* (*couples, interlocuteurs*) to part; ne quittez pas (*au téléphone*) hold the line.
qui-vive [kiviv] *nm*: être sur le ~ to be on the alert.
quoi [kwa] *pronom* (*interrogatif*) what; ~ de neuf? what's the news?; as-tu de ~ écrire? have you anything to write with?; il n'a pas de ~ se l'acheter he can't afford it; ~ qu'il arrive whatever happens; ~ qu'il en soit be that as it may; ~ que ce soit anything at all; 'il n'y a pas de ~' (please) don't mention it'; à ~ bon? what's the use?; en ~ puis-je vous aider? how can I help you?
quoique [kwak(ə)] *cj* (al)though.
quolibet [kɔlibɛ] *nm* gibe, jeer.
quote-part [kɔtpaʀ] *nf* share.
quotidien, ne [kɔtidjɛ̃, -ɛn] *a* daily; (*banal*) everyday // *nm* (*journal*) daily (paper).

R

r. *abr de* **route, rue.**
rab [ʀab] *abr m* (*fam*) *de* **rabiot.**
rabâcher [ʀabaʃe] *vt* to keep on repeating.
rabais [ʀabɛ] *nm* reduction, discount.
rabaisser [ʀabese] *vt* (*rabattre*) to reduce; (*dénigrer*) to belittle.
rabattre [ʀabatʀ(ə)] *vt* (*couvercle,*

siège) to pull down; (*gibier*) to drive; se ~ *vi* (*bords, couvercle*) to fall shut; (*véhicule, coureur*) to cut in; **se ~ sur** *vt* to fall back on.
rabbin [ʀabɛ̃] *nm* rabbi.
rabiot [ʀabjo] *nm* (*fam*) extra, more.
râblé, e [ʀable] *a* stocky.
rabot [ʀabo] *nm* plane.
rabougri, e [ʀabugʀi] *a* stunted.
rabrouer [ʀabʀue] *vt* to snub.
racaille [ʀakaj] *nf* (*péj*) rabble, riffraff.
raccommoder [ʀakɔmɔde] *vt* to mend, repair; (*chaussette etc*) to darn.
raccompagner [ʀakɔ̃paɲe] *vt* to take *ou* see back.
raccord [ʀakɔʀ] *nm* link.
raccorder [ʀakɔʀde] *vt* to join (up), link up; (*suj: pont etc*) to connect, link.
raccourci [ʀakuʀsi] *nm* short cut.
raccourcir [ʀakuʀsiʀ] *vt* to shorten.
raccrocher [ʀakʀɔʃe] *vt* (*tableau*) to hang back up; (*récepteur*) to put down // *vi* (*TÉL*) to hang up, ring off; se ~ à *vt* to cling to, hang on to.
race [ʀas] *nf* race; (*d'animaux, fig*) breed; (*ascendance*) stock, race; de ~ *a* purebred, pedigree.
rachat [ʀaʃa] *nm* buying; buying back.
racheter [ʀaʃte] *vt* (*article perdu*) to buy another; (*davantage*): ~ du lait/3 œufs to buy more milk/another 3 eggs *ou* 3 more eggs; (*après avoir vendu*) to buy back; (*d'occasion*) to buy up; (*: COMM: part, firme*) to buy up; (*: pension, rente*) to redeem; se ~ *vi* (*fig*) to make amends.
racial, e, aux [ʀasjal, -o] *a* racial.
racine [ʀasin] *nf* root; ~ carrée/cubique square/cube root.
raciste [ʀasist(ə)] *a, nm/f* raci(al)ist.
racket [ʀakɛt] *nm* racketeering *q*.
racler [ʀakle] *vt* (*surface*) to scrape; (*tache, boue*) to scrape off.
racoler [ʀakɔle] *vt* (*attirer: suj: prostituée*) to solicit; (*: parti, marchand*) to tout for.
racontars [ʀakɔ̃taʀ] *nmpl* gossip *sg*.
raconter [ʀakɔ̃te] *vt*: ~ (à qn) (*décrire*) to relate (to sb), tell (sb) about; (*dire*) to tell (sb).
racorni, e [ʀakɔʀni] *a* hard(ened).
radar [ʀadaʀ] *nm* radar.
rade [ʀad] *nf* (natural) harbour; rester en ~ (*fig*) to be left stranded.
radeau, x [ʀado] *nm* raft.
radiateur [ʀadjatœʀ] *nm* radiator, heater; (*AUTO*) radiator; ~ électrique/à gaz electric/gas heater *ou* fire.
radiation [ʀadjasjɔ̃] *nf* (*voir radier*) striking off *q*; (*PHYSIQUE*) radiation.
radical, e, aux [ʀadikal, -o] *a* radical.
radier [ʀadje] *vt* to strike off.
radieux, euse [ʀadjø, -øz] *a* radiant; brilliant, glorious.
radin, e [ʀadɛ̃, -in] *a* (*fam*) stingy.
radio [ʀadjo] *nf* radio; (*MÉD*) X-ray //

nm radio operator; **à la ~** on the radio.
radio... [Radjo] *préfixe:* **~actif, ive** *a*
radioactive; **radiodiffuser** *vt* to broadcast; **~graphie** *nf* radiography; *(photo)*
X-ray photograph; **~phonique** *a* radio
cpd; **~télévisé, e** *a* broadcast on radio
and television.
radis [Radi] *nm* radish.
radoter [Radote] *vi* to ramble on.
radoucir [Radusir]: **se ~** *vi (se réchauffer)* to become milder; *(se calmer)* to
calm down; to soften.
rafale [Rafal] *nf (vent)* gust (of wind);
(tir) burst of gunfire.
raffermir [RafɛRmiR] *vt,* **se ~** *vi (tissus,
muscle)* to firm up; *(fig)* to strengthen.
raffiner [Rafine] *vt* to refine; **raffinerie**
nf refinery.
raffoler [Rafɔle]: **~ de** *vt* to be very
keen on.
rafle [Rafl(ə)] *nf (de police)* raid.
rafler [Rafle] *vt (fam)* to swipe, nick.
rafraîchir [RafRɛʃiR] *vt (atmosphère,
température)* to cool (down); *(aussi:
mettre à ~)* to chill; *(fig: rénover)* to
brighten up; **se ~** *vi* to grow cooler; to
freshen up; to refresh o.s.; **rafraîchis-
sant, e** *a* refreshing; **rafraîchissement**
nm cooling; *(boisson)* cool drink; **rafraîchissements** *(boissons, fruits etc)* re-
freshments.
rage [Raʒ] *nf (MÉD):* **la ~** rabies; *(fureur)* rage, fury; **faire ~** to rage; **~ de
dents** (raging) toothache.
ragot [Rago] *nm (fam)* malicious gossip
q.
ragoût [Ragu] *nm (plat)* stew.
raide [Rɛd] *a (tendu)* taut, tight; *(escarpé)* steep; *(droit: cheveux)* straight;
(ankylosé, dur, guindé) stiff; *(fam)*
steep, stiff; flat broke // *ad (en pente)*
steeply; **~ mort** stone dead; **raidir** *vt
(muscles)* to stiffen; *(câble)* to pull taut;
se raidir *vi* to stiffen; to become taut;
(personne) to tense up; to brace o.s.
raie [Rɛ] *nf (ZOOL)* skate, ray; *(rayure)*
stripe; *(des cheveux)* parting.
raifort [RɛfɔR] *nm* horseradish.
rail [Rɑj] *nm* rail; *(chemins de fer)* railways *pl;* **par ~** by rail.
railler [Rɑje] *vt* to scoff at, jeer at.
rainure [RenyR] *nf* groove; slot.
raisin [Rɛzɛ̃] *nm (aussi: ~s)* grapes *pl;*
~s secs raisins.
raison [Rɛzɔ̃] *nf* reason; **avoir ~** to be
right; **donner ~ à qn** to agree with sb; to
prove sb right; **se faire une ~** to learn to
live with it; **perdre la ~** to become insane; to take leave of one's senses; **de
plus** all the more reason; **à plus forte ~**
all the more so; **en ~ de** because of; **à
cause de**; **à ~ de** at
the rate of; **~ sociale** corporate name;
raisonnable *a* reasonable, sensible.
raisonnement [Rɛzɔnmɑ̃] *nm* reasoning; arguing; argument.
raisonner [Rɛzɔne] *vi (penser)* to reason; *(argumenter, discuter)* to argue //
vt (personne) to reason with.
rajeunir [RaʒœniR] *vt (suj: coiffure,
robe):* **~ qn** to make sb look younger;
(suj: cure etc) to rejuvenate; *(fig)* to
give a new look to; to inject new blood
into // *vi* to become *(ou* look*)* younger.
rajouter [Raʒute] *vt:* **~ du sel/un œuf** to
add some more salt/another egg.
rajuster [Raʒyste] *vt (vêtement)* to
straighten, tidy; *(salaires)* to adjust;
(machine) to readjust.
ralenti [Ralɑ̃ti] *nm:* **au ~** *(AUTO):*
tourner au ~ to tick over, idle; *(CINÉ-
MA)* in slow motion; *(fig)* at a slower
pace.
ralentir [Ralɑ̃tiR] *vt, vi,* **se ~** *vi* to slow
down.
râler [Rɑle] *vi* to groan; *(fam)* to grouse,
moan (and groan).
rallier [Ralje] *vt (rassembler)* to rally;
(rejoindre) to rejoin; *(gagner à sa
cause)* to win over; **se ~ à** *(avis)* to
come over *ou* round to.
rallonge [Ralɔ̃ʒ] *nf (de table)* (extra)
leaf *(pl* leaves*); (argent etc)* extra *q.*
rallonger [Ralɔ̃ʒe] *vt* to lengthen.
rallye [Rali] *nm* rally; *(POL)* march.
ramassage [Ramasaʒ] *nm:* **~ scolaire**
school bus service.
ramassé, e *a (trapu)* squat.
ramasser [Ramase] *vt (objet tombé ou
par terre, fam)* to pick up; *(recueillir)* to
collect; *(récolter)* to gather; **se ~** *vi (sur
soi-même)* to huddle up; to crouch;
ramassis *nm (péj)* bunch; jumble.
rambarde [Rɑ̃baRd(ə)] *nf* guardrail.
rame [Ram] *nf (aviron)* oar; *(de métro)*
train; *(de papier)* ream.
rameau, x [Ramo] *nm (small)* branch;
les R~x *(REL)* Palm Sunday *sg.*
ramener [Ramne] *vt* to bring back; *(reconduire)* to take back; *(rabattre:
couverture, visière):* **~ qch sur** to pull
sth back over; **~ qch à** *(réduire à, aussi
MATH)* to reduce sth to.
ramer [Rame] *vi* to row.
ramollir [RamɔliR] *vt* to soften; **se ~** *vi*
to go soft.
ramoner [Ramɔne] *vt* to sweep.
rampe [Rɑ̃p] *nf (d'escalier)* banister(s
pl); (dans un garage, d'un terrain)
ramp; *(THÉÂTRE):* **la ~** the footlights
pl; **~ de lancement** launching pad.
ramper [Rɑ̃pe] *vi* to crawl.
rancard [Rɑ̃kaR] *nm (fam)* date; tip.
rancart [Rɑ̃kaR] *nm:* **mettre au ~** to
scrap.
rance [Rɑ̃s] *a* rancid.
rancœur [Rɑ̃kœR] *nf* rancour.
rançon [Rɑ̃sɔ̃] *nf* ransom; *(fig)* price.
rancune [Rɑ̃kyn] *nf* grudge, rancour;
garder ~ à qn (de qch) to bear sb a

randonnée 169 rattacher

grudge (for sth); **sans ~!** no hard feelings!; **rancunier, ière** *a* vindictive, spiteful.
randonnée [ʀɑ̃dɔne] *nf* ride; (à pied) walk, ramble; hike, hiking *q*.
rang [ʀɑ̃] *nm* (rangée) row; (grade, classement) rank; **~s** (MIL) ranks; **se mettre en ~s/sur un ~** to get into *ou* form rows/a line; **au premier ~** in the first row; (fig) ranking first.
rangé, e [ʀɑ̃ʒe] *a* (sérieux) orderly, steady.
rangée [ʀɑ̃ʒe] *nf* row.
ranger [ʀɑ̃ʒe] *vt* (classer, grouper) to order, arrange; (mettre à sa place) to put away; (voiture dans la rue) to park; (mettre de l'ordre dans) to tidy up; (arranger) to arrange; (fig: classer): **~ qn/qch parmi** to rank sb/sth among; **se ~** *vi* (véhicule, conducteur) to pull over *ou* in; (piéton) to step aside; (s'assagir) to settle down; **se ~ à** (avis) to come round to.
ranimer [ʀanime] *vt* (personne) to bring round; (forces, courage) to restore; (troupes etc) to kindle new life in; (douleur, souvenir) to revive; (feu) to rekindle.
rapace [ʀapas] *nm* bird of prey.
râpe [ʀɑp] *nf* (CULIN) grater.
râpé, e [ʀɑpe] *a* (tissu) threadbare.
râper [ʀɑpe] *vt* (CULIN) to grate.
rapetisser [ʀaptise] *vt* to shorten.
rapide [ʀapid] *a* fast; (prompt) quick // *nm* express (train); (de cours d'eau) rapid; **~ment** *ad* fast; quickly.
rapiécer [ʀapjese] *vt* to patch.
rappel [ʀapɛl] *nm* (THÉÂTRE) curtain call; (MÉD: vaccination) booster; (ADMIN: de salaire) back pay *q*; (d'une aventure, d'un nom) reminder.
rappeler [ʀaple] *vt* to call back; (ambassadeur, MIL) to recall; (faire se souvenir): **~ qch à qn** to remind sb of sth; **se ~** *vt* (se souvenir de) to remember, recall.
rapport [ʀapɔʀ] *nm* (compte rendu) report; (profit) yield, return; revenue; (lien, analogie) relationship; (MATH, TECH) ratio (pl s); **~s** (entre personnes, pays) relations; **avoir ~ à** to have something to do with; **être en ~ avec** (idée de corrélation) to be related to; **être/se mettre en ~ avec qn** to be/get in touch with sb; **par ~ à** in relation to; **~s** (sexuels) (sexual) intercourse *q*.
rapporter [ʀapɔʀte] *vt* (rendre, ramener) to bring back; (apporter davantage) to bring more; (suj: investissement) to yield; (: activité) to bring in; (relater) to report // *vi* (investissement) to give a good return *ou* yield; (: activité) to be very profitable; **~ qch à** (fig: rattacher) to relate sth to; **se ~ à** (correspondre à) to relate to; **s'en ~ à** to

rely on; **rapporteur, euse** *nm/f* (de procès, commission) reporter; (péj) telltale // *nm* (GÉOM) protractor.
rapprochement [ʀapʀɔʃmɑ̃] *nm* (de nations, familles) reconciliation; (analogie, rapport) parallel.
rapprocher [ʀapʀɔʃe] *vt* (chaise d'une table): **~ qch (de)** to bring sth closer (to); (deux objets) to bring closer together; (réunir) to bring together; (comparer) to establish a parallel between; **se ~** *vi* to draw closer *ou* nearer; **se ~ de** to come closer to; (présenter une analogie avec) to be close to.
rapt [ʀapt] *nm* abduction.
raquette [ʀakɛt] *nf* (de tennis) racket; (de ping-pong) bat; (à neige) snowshoe.
rare [ʀɑʀ] *a* rare; (main-d'œuvre, denrées) scarce; (cheveux, herbe) sparse.
rarement [ʀaʀmɑ̃] *ad* rarely, seldom.
ras, e [ʀɑ, ʀɑz] *a* (tête, cheveux) close-cropped; (poil, herbe) short // *ad* short; **en ~e campagne** in open country; **à ~ bords** to the brim; **au ~ de** level with; **en avoir ~ le bol** (fam) to be fed up; **~ du cou** (pull, robe) crew-neck.
rasade [ʀazad] *nf* glassful.
raser [ʀaze] *vt* (barbe, cheveux) to shave off; (menton, personne) to shave; (fam: ennuyer) to bore; (démolir) to raze (to the ground); (frôler) to graze, skim; **se ~** *vi* to shave; (fam) to be bored (to tears); **rasoir** *nm* razor.
rassasier [ʀasazje] *vt* to satisfy.
rassemblement [ʀasɑ̃bləmɑ̃] *nm* (groupe) gathering; (POL) union.
rassembler [ʀasɑ̃ble] *vt* (réunir) to assemble, gather; (regrouper, amasser) to gather together, collect; **se ~** *vi* to gather.
rassis, e [ʀasi, -iz] *a* (pain) stale.
rassurer [ʀasyʀe] *vt* to reassure; **se ~** *vi* to be reassured; **rassure-toi** don't worry.
rat [ʀa] *nm* rat.
rate [ʀat] *nf* spleen.
raté, e [ʀate] *a* (tentative) unsuccessful, failed // *nm/f* failure // *nm* misfiring *q*.
râteau, x [ʀɑto] *nm* rake.
râtelier [ʀɑtəlje] *nm* rack; (fam) false teeth *pl*.
rater [ʀate] *vi* (affaire, projet etc) to go wrong, fail // *vt* (cible, train, occasion) to miss; (démonstration, plat) to spoil; (examen) to fail.
ration [ʀasjɔ̃] *nf* ration; (fig) share.
ratisser [ʀatise] *vt* (allée) to rake; (feuilles) to rake up; (suj: armée, police) to comb.
R.A.T.P. sigle *f* (= Régie autonome des transports parisiens) Paris transport authority.
rattacher [ʀataʃe] *vt* (animal, cheveux) to tie up again; (incorporer: ADMIN etc): **~ qch à** to join sth to; (fig: relier): **~ qch à** to link sth with; (: lier): **~ qn à**

to bind *ou* tie sb to.

rattraper [ʀatʀape] *vt* (*fugitif*) to recapture; (*empêcher de tomber*) to catch (hold of); (*atteindre, rejoindre*) to catch up with; (*réparer: imprudence, erreur*) to make up for; **se ~** *vi* to make good one's losses; to make up for it; **se ~** (**à**) (*se raccrocher*) to stop o.s. falling (by catching hold of).

rature [ʀatyʀ] *nf* deletion, erasure.

rauque [ʀok] *a* raucous; hoarse.

ravages [ʀavaʒ] *nmpl:* **faire des ~** to wreak havoc.

ravaler [ʀavale] *vt* (*mur, façade*) to restore; (*déprécier*) to lower.

ravi, e [ʀavi] *a:* **être ~ de/que** to be delighted with/that.

ravin [ʀavɛ̃] *nm* gully, ravine.

ravir [ʀaviʀ] *vt* (*enchanter*) to delight; (*enlever*): **~ qch à qn** to rob sb of sth; **à ~** *ad* beautifully.

raviser [ʀavize]: **se ~** *vi* to change one's mind.

ravissant, e [ʀavisɑ̃, -ɑ̃t] *a* delightful.

ravisseur, euse [ʀavisœʀ, -øz] *nm/f* abductor, kidnapper.

ravitailler [ʀavitaje] *vt* to resupply; (*véhicule*) to refuel; **se ~** *vi* to get fresh supplies.

raviver [ʀavive] *vt* (*feu, douleur*) to revive; (*couleurs*) to brighten up.

rayé, e [ʀeje] *a* (*à rayures*) striped.

rayer [ʀeje] *vt* (*érafler*) to scratch; (*barrer*) to cross out; (*d'une liste*) to cross off.

rayon [ʀejɔ̃] *nm* (*de soleil etc*) ray; (*GÉOM*) radius; (*de roue*) spoke; (*étagère*) shelf (*pl* shelves); (*de grand magasin*) department; **dans un ~ de** within a radius of; **~ d'action** range; **~ de soleil** sunbeam; **~s X** X-rays.

rayonnement [ʀejɔnmɑ̃] *nm* radiation; (*fig*) radiance; influence.

rayonner [ʀejɔne] *vi* (*chaleur, énergie*) to radiate; (*fig*) to shine forth; to be radiant; (*touriste*) to go touring (*from one base*).

rayure [ʀejyʀ] *nf* (*motif*) stripe; (*éraflure*) scratch; (*rainure, d'un fusil*) groove.

raz-de-marée [ʀɑdmaʀe] *nm inv* tidal wave.

ré [ʀe] *nm* (*MUS*) D; (*en chantant la gamme*) re.

réacteur [ʀeaktœʀ] *nm* jet engine.

réaction [ʀeaksjɔ̃] *nf* reaction; **moteur à ~** jet engine.

réadapter [ʀeadapte] *vt* to readjust; (*MÉD*) to rehabilitate; **se ~** (**à**) to readjust (to).

réagir [ʀeaʒiʀ] *vi* to react.

réalisateur, trice [ʀealizatœʀ, -tʀis] *nm/f* (*TV, CINÉMA*) director.

réalisation [ʀealizasjɔ̃] *nf* carrying out; realization; fulfilment; achievement; production; (*œuvre*) production; creation; work.

réaliser [ʀealize] *vt* (*projet, opération*) to carry out, realize; (*rêve, souhait*) to realize, fulfil; (*exploit*) to achieve; (*achat, vente*) to make; (*film*) to produce; (*se rendre compte de, COMM: bien, capital*) to realize; **se ~** *vi* to be realized.

réaliste [ʀealist(ə)] *a* realistic.

réalité [ʀealite] *nf* reality; **en ~** in (actual) fact; **dans la ~** in reality.

réanimation [ʀeanimasjɔ̃] *nf* resuscitation; **service de ~** intensive care unit.

réarmer [ʀeaʀme] *vt* (*arme*) to reload // *vi* (*état*) to rearm.

rébarbatif, ive [ʀebaʀbatif, -iv] *a* forbidding.

rebattu, e [ʀəbaty] *a* hackneyed.

rebelle [ʀəbɛl] *nm/f* rebel // *a* (*troupes*) rebel; (*enfant*) rebellious; (*mèche etc*) unruly; **~ à** unamenable to.

rebeller [ʀəbele]: **se ~** *vi* to rebel.

rebondi, e [ʀəbɔ̃di] *a* rounded; chubby.

rebondir [ʀəbɔ̃diʀ] *vi* (*ballon: au sol*) to bounce; (*: contre un mur*) to rebound; (*fig*) to get moving again; **rebondissement** *nm* new development.

rebord [ʀəbɔʀ] *nm* edge.

rebours [ʀəbuʀ]: **à ~** *ad* the wrong way.

rebrousse-poil [ʀəbʀuspwal]: **à ~** *ad* the wrong way.

rebrousser [ʀəbʀuse] *vt:* **~ chemin** to turn back.

rebut [ʀəby] *nm:* **mettre au ~** to scrap.

rebuter [ʀəbyte] *vt* to put off.

récalcitrant, e [ʀekalsitʀɑ̃, -ɑ̃t] *a* refractory.

recaler [ʀəkale] *vt* (*SCOL*) to fail.

récapituler [ʀekapityle] *vt* to recapitulate; to sum up.

receler [ʀəsəle] *vt* (*produit d'un vol*) to receive; (*malfaiteur*) to harbour; (*fig*) to conceal; **receleur, euse** *nm/f* receiver.

récemment [ʀesamɑ̃] *ad* recently.

recenser [ʀəsɑ̃se] *vt* (*population*) to take a census of; (*inventorier*) to list.

récent, e [ʀesɑ̃, -ɑ̃t] *a* recent.

récépissé [ʀesepise] *nm* receipt.

récepteur [ʀeseptœʀ] *nm* receiver; **~ (de radio)** radio set *ou* receiver.

réception [ʀesɛpsjɔ̃] *nf* receiving *q*; (*accueil*) reception, welcome; (*bureau*) reception desk; (*réunion mondaine*) reception, party; **réceptionniste** *nm/f* receptionist.

recette [ʀəsɛt] *nf* (*CULIN*) recipe; (*fig*) formula, recipe; (*COMM*) takings *pl*; **~s** *nfpl* (*COMM: rentrées*) receipts.

receveur, euse [ʀəsəvœʀ, -øz] *nm/f* (*des contributions*) tax collector; (*des postes*) postmaster/mistress; (*d'autobus*) conductor/conductress.

recevoir [ʀəsəvwaʀ] *vt* to receive;

(*client, patient*) to see // *vi* to receive visitors; to give parties; to see patients *etc*; se ~ *vi* (*athlète*) to land; être reçu (à un examen) to pass.

rechange [ʀəʃɑ̃ʒ]: de ~ a (*pièces, roue*) spare; (*fig: solution*) alternative; des vêtements de ~ a change of clothes.

rechaper [ʀəʃape] *vt* to remould, re-tread.

réchapper [ʀeʃape]: ~ de ou à *vt* (*accident, maladie*) to come through.

recharge [ʀəʃaʀʒ(ə)] *nf* refill.

recharger [ʀəʃaʀʒe] *vt* (*camion, fusil, appareil-photo*) to reload; (*briquet, sty-lo*) to refill; (*batterie*) to recharge.

réchaud [ʀeʃo] *nm* (portable) stove; plate-warmer.

réchauffer [ʀeʃofe] *vt* (*plat*) to reheat; (*mains, personne*) to warm; se ~ *vi* (*température*) to get warmer.

rêche [ʀɛʃ] a rough.

recherche [ʀəʃɛʀʃ(ə)] *nf* (*action*): la ~ de the search for; (*raffinement*) af-fectedness, studied elegance; (*scien-tifique etc*): la ~ research; ~s *nfpl* (*de la police*) investigations; (*scientifiques*) research *sg*; se mettre à la ~ de to go in search of.

recherché, e [ʀəʃɛʀʃe] a (*rare, de-mandé*) much sought-after; (*raffiné*) studied, affected.

rechercher [ʀəʃɛʀʃe] *vt* (*objet égaré, personne*) to look for; (*causes, nouveau procédé*) to try to find; (*bonheur, amitié*) to seek.

rechute [ʀəʃyt] *nf* (MÉD) relapse.

récidiver [ʀesidive] *vi* to commit a sub-sequent offence; (*fig*) to do it again.

récif [ʀesif] *nm* reef.

récipient [ʀesipjɑ̃] *nm* container.

réciproque [ʀesipʀɔk] a reciprocal.

récit [ʀesi] *nm* story.

récital [ʀesital] *nm* recital.

réciter [ʀesite] *vt* to recite.

réclamation [ʀeklamasjɔ̃] *nf* complaint; ~s (*bureau*) complaints department *sg*.

réclame [ʀeklam] *nf* ad, ad-vert(isement); article en ~ special offer.

réclamer [ʀeklame] *vt* (*aide, nourriture etc*) to ask for; (*revendiquer*) to claim, demand; (*nécessiter*) to demand, require // *vi* to complain.

réclusion [ʀeklyzjɔ̃] *nf* imprisonment.

recoin [ʀəkwɛ̃] *nm* nook, corner; (*fig*) hidden recess.

reçois *etc* **vb** *voir* **recevoir**.

récolte [ʀekɔlt(ə)] *nf* harvesting; gather-ing; (*produits*) harvest, crop; (*fig*) crop, collection.

récolter [ʀekɔlte] *vt* to harvest, gather (in); (*fig*) to collect; to get.

recommandé [ʀəkɔmɑ̃de] *nm* (POSTES): en ~ by registered mail.

recommander [ʀəkɔmɑ̃de] *vt* to recom-mend; (*suj: qualités etc*) to commend;

(POSTES) to register; se ~ de qn to give sb's name as a reference.

recommencer [ʀəkɔmɑ̃se] *vt* (*repren-dre: lutte, séance*) to resume, start again; (*refaire: travail, explications*) to start afresh, start (over) again; (*récidiver: erreur*) to make again // *vi* to start again; (*récidiver*) to do it again.

récompense [ʀekɔ̃pɑ̃s] *nf* reward; (*prix*) award; **récompenser** *vt*: récompenser qn (de ou pour) to reward sb (for).

réconcilier [ʀekɔ̃silje] *vt* to reconcile; se ~ (avec) to be reconciled (with).

reconduire [ʀəkɔ̃dɥiʀ] *vt* (*raccompa-gner*) to take ou see back; (JUR, POL: *renouveler*) to renew.

réconfort [ʀekɔ̃fɔʀ] *nm* comfort.

réconforter [ʀekɔ̃fɔʀte] *vt* (*consoler*) to comfort; (*revigorer*) to fortify.

reconnaissance [ʀəkɔnɛsɑ̃s] *nf* recogni-tion; acknowledgement; (*gratitude*) gratitude, gratefulness; (MIL) reconnais-sance, recce.

reconnaissant, e [ʀəkɔnɛsɑ̃, -ɑ̃t] a grateful.

reconnaître [ʀəkɔnɛtʀ(ə)] *vt* to recog-nize; (MIL: *lieu*) to reconnoitre; (JUR: *enfant, dette, droit*) to acknowledge; ~ que to admit ou acknowledge that; ~ qn/qch à to recognize sb/sth by.

reconstituer [ʀəkɔ̃stitɥe] *vt* (*monument ancien*) to recreate; (*fresque, vase brisé*) to piece together, reconstitute; (*événement, accident*) to reconstruct; (*fortune, patrimoine*) to rebuild.

reconstruire [ʀəkɔ̃stʀɥiʀ] *vt* to rebuild.

record [ʀəkɔʀ] *nm*, a record.

recoupement [ʀəkupmɑ̃] *nm*: par ~ by cross-checking.

recouper [ʀəkupe]: se ~ *vi* (*témoi-gnages*) to tie ou match up.

recourbé, e [ʀəkuʀbe] a curved; hooked; bent.

recourir [ʀəkuʀiʀ]: ~ à *vt* (*ami, agence*) to turn ou appeal to; (*force, ruse, emprunt*) to resort to.

recours [ʀəkuʀ] *nm* (JUR) appeal; avoir ~ à = recourir à; en dernier ~ as a last resort; ~ en grâce plea for clemency.

recouvrer [ʀəkuvʀe] *vt* (*vue, santé etc*) to recover, regain; (*impôts*) to collect; (*créance*) to recover.

recouvrir [ʀəkuvʀiʀ] *vt* (*couvrir à nou-veau*) to re-cover; (*couvrir entièrement, aussi fig*) to cover; (*cacher, masquer*) to conceal, hide; se ~ (*se superposer*) to overlap.

récréation [ʀekʀeasjɔ̃] *nf* recreation, en-tertainment; (SCOL) break.

récrier [ʀekʀije]: se ~ *vi* to exclaim.

récriminations [ʀekʀiminasjɔ̃] *nfpl* re-monstrations, complaints.

recroqueviller [ʀəkʀɔkvije]: se ~ *vi* (*feuilles*) to curl ou shrivel up; (*per-*

sonne) to huddle up.

recrudescence [ʀəkʀydesɑ̃s] *nf* fresh outbreak.

recrue [ʀəkʀy] *nf* recruit.

recruter [ʀəkʀyte] *vt* to recruit.

rectangle [ʀɛktɑ̃gl(ə)] *nm* rectangle; **rectangulaire** *a* rectangular.

recteur [ʀɛktœʀ] *nm* ≈ (regional) director of education (*Brit*), ≈ state superintendent of education (*US*).

rectifier [ʀɛktifje] *vt* (*tracé, virage*) to straighten; (*calcul, adresse*) to correct; (*erreur, faute*) to rectify.

rectiligne [ʀɛktiliɲ] *a* straight; (*GÉOM*) rectilinear.

reçu, e [ʀəsy] *pp de* **recevoir** // *a* (*admis, consacré*) accepted // *nm* (*COMM*) receipt.

recueil [ʀəkœj] *nm* collection.

recueillir [ʀəkœjiʀ] *vt* to collect; (*voix, suffrages*) to win; (*accueillir: réfugiés, chat*) to take in; se ~ *vi* to gather one's thoughts; to meditate.

recul [ʀəkyl] *nm* retreat; recession; decline; (*d'arme à feu*) recoil, kick; **avoir un mouvement de ~** to recoil; **prendre du ~** to stand back.

reculé, e [ʀəkyle] *a* remote.

reculer [ʀəkyle] *vi* to move back, back away; (*AUTO*) to reverse, back (up); (*fig*) to be (on the) decline; to be loosing ground; (*: se dérober*) to shrink back // *vt* to move back; to reverse, back (up); (*fig: possibilités, limites*) to extend; (*: date, décision*) to postpone.

reculons [ʀəkylɔ̃]: **à ~** *ad* backwards.

récupérer [ʀekypeʀe] *vt* to recover, get back; (*heures de travail*) to make up; (*déchets*) to salvage; (*délinquant etc*) to rehabilitate // *vi* to recover.

récurer [ʀekyʀe] *vt* to scour.

récuser [ʀekyze] *vt* to challenge; se ~ *vi* to decline to give an opinion.

reçut *vb voir* **recevoir**.

recycler [ʀəsikle] *vt* (*SCOL*) to reorientate; (*employés*) to retrain; (*TECH*) to recycle.

rédacteur, trice [ʀedaktœʀ, -tʀis] *nm/f* (*journaliste*) writer; subeditor; (*d'ouvrage de référence*) editor, compiler; ~ **en chef** chief editor; ~ **publicitaire** copywriter.

rédaction [ʀedaksjɔ̃] *nf* writing; (*rédacteurs*) editorial staff; (*bureau*) editorial office(s); (*SCOL: devoir*) essay, composition.

reddition [ʀedisjɔ̃] *nf* surrender.

redemander [ʀədmɑ̃de] *vt* to ask again for; to ask for more of.

redescendre [ʀədesɑ̃dʀ(ə)] *vi* to go back down // *vt* (*pente etc*) to go down.

redevable [ʀədvabl(ə)] *a*: **être ~ de qch à qn** (*somme*) to owe sb sth; (*fig*) to be indebted to sb for sth.

redevance [ʀədvɑ̃s] *nf* (*TÉL*) rental

charge; (*TV*) licence fee.

rédiger [ʀediʒe] *vt* to write; (*contrat*) to draw up.

redire [ʀədiʀ] *vt* to repeat; **trouver à ~ à** to find fault with.

redoublé, e [ʀəduble] *a*: **à coups ~s** even harder, twice as hard.

redoubler [ʀəduble] *vi* (*tempête, violence*) to intensify; (*SCOL*) to repeat a year; ~ **de** *vt* to be twice as + *adjectif*.

redoutable [ʀədutabl(ə)] *a* formidable, fearsome.

redouter [ʀədute] *vt* to fear; (*appréhender*) to dread.

redresser [ʀədʀese] *vt* (*arbre, mât*) to set upright; (*pièce tordue*) to straighten out; (*situation, économie*) to put right; se ~ *vi* (*objet penché*) to right itself; (*personne*) to sit (*ou* stand) up (straight).

réduction [ʀedyksjɔ̃] *nf* reduction.

réduire [ʀeduiʀ] *vt* to reduce; (*prix, dépenses*) to cut, reduce; (*MÉD: fracture*) to set; se ~ **à** (*revenir à*) to boil down to; se ~ **en** (*se transformer en*) to be reduced to.

réduit [ʀedui] *nm* tiny room; recess.

rééducation [ʀeedykasjɔ̃] *nf* (*d'un membre*) re-education; (*de délinquants, d'un blessé*) rehabilitation; ~ **de la parole** speech therapy.

réel, le [ʀeɛl] *a* real.

réellement [ʀeɛlmɑ̃] *ad* really.

réévaluer [ʀeevalɥe] *vt* to revalue.

réexpédier [ʀeɛkspedje] *vt* (*à l'envoyeur*) to return, send back; (*au destinataire*) to send on, forward.

refaire [ʀəfɛʀ] *vt* (*faire de nouveau, recommencer*) to do again; (*réparer, restaurer*) to do up.

réfection [ʀefɛksjɔ̃] *nf* repair.

réfectoire [ʀefɛktwaʀ] *nm* refectory.

référence [ʀefeʀɑ̃s] *nf* reference; ~**s** (*recommandations*) reference *sg*.

référer [ʀefeʀe]: se ~ **à** *vt* to refer to; **en ~ à qn** to refer the matter to sb.

réfléchi, e [ʀefleʃi] *a* (*caractère*) thoughtful; (*action*) well-thought-out; (*LING*) reflexive.

réfléchir [ʀefleʃiʀ] *vt* to reflect // *vi* to think; ~ **à** *ou* **sur** to think about.

reflet [ʀəflɛ] *nm* reflection; (*sur l'eau etc*) sheen *q*, glint.

refléter [ʀəflete] *vt* to reflect; se ~ *vi* to be reflected.

réflexe [ʀeflɛks(ə)] *nm, a* reflex.

réflexion [ʀeflɛksjɔ̃] *nf* (*de la lumière etc, pensée*) reflection; (*fait de penser*) thought; (*remarque*) remark; ~ **faite, à la** ~ on reflection.

refluer [ʀəflɥe] *vi* to flow back; (*foule*) to surge back.

reflux [ʀəfly] *nm* (*de la mer*) ebb.

réforme [ʀefɔʀm(ə)] *nf* reform; (*REL*): **la R~** the Reformation.

réformer [Refɔrme] *vt* to reform; (*MIL*) to declare unfit for service.

refouler [Rəfule] *vt* (*envahisseurs*) to drive back; (*liquide*) to force back; (*fig*) to suppress; (*PSYCH*) to repress.

réfractaire [Refraktɛr] *a*: être ~ à to resist.

refrain [Rəfrɛ̃] *nm* (*MUS*) refrain, chorus; (*air, fig*) tune.

refréner, réfréner [Rəfrene, Refrene] *vt* to curb, check.

réfrigérateur [Refriʒeratœr] *nm* refrigerator, fridge.

refroidir [Rəfrwadir] *vt* to cool // *vi* to cool (down); **se** ~ *vi* (*prendre froid*) to catch a chill; (*temps*) to get cooler *ou* colder; (*fig*) to cool (off); **refroidissement** *nm* (*grippe etc*) chill.

refuge [Rəfyʒ] *nm* refuge; (*pour piétons*) (traffic) island.

réfugié, e [Refyʒje] *a, nm/f* refugee.

réfugier [Refyʒje]: **se** ~ *vi* to take refuge.

refus [Rəfy] *nm* refusal; ce n'est pas de ~ I won't say no, it's welcome.

refuser [Rəfyze] *vt* to refuse; (*SCOL*: *candidat*) to fail; ~ qch à qn to refuse sb sth; ~ du monde to have to turn people away; **se** ~ à faire to refuse to do.

regagner [Rəgaɲe] *vt* (*argent, faveur*) to win back; (*lieu*) to get back to; ~ **le temps perdu** to make up (for) lost time.

regain [Rəgɛ̃] *nm* (*renouveau*): **un** ~ **de** renewed + *nom*.

régal [Regal] *nm* treat.

régaler [Regale]: **se** ~ *vi* to have a delicious meal; (*fig*) to enjoy o.s.

regard [Rəgar] *nm* (*coup d'œil*) look, glance; (*expression*) look (in one's eye); **au** ~ **de** (*loi, morale*) from the point of view of; **en** ~ (*vis à vis*) opposite; **en** ~ **de** in comparison with.

regardant, e [Rəgardɑ̃, -ɑ̃t] *a*: **très/peu** ~ (**sur**) quite fussy/very free (about); (*économe*) very tight-fisted/quite generous (with).

regarder [Rəgarde] *vt* (*examiner, observer, lire*) to look at; (*film, télévision, match*) to watch; (*envisager: situation, avenir*) to view; (*considérer: son intérêt etc*) to be concerned with; (*être orienté vers*): ~ (**vers**) to face; (*concerner*) to concern // *vi* to look; ~ à *vt* (*dépense*) to be fussy with *ou* over; ~ **qn/qch comme** to regard sb/sth as.

régie [Reʒi] *nf* (*COMM, INDUSTRIE*) state-owned company; (*THÉÂTRE, CINÉMA*) production; (*RADIO, TV*) control room.

regimber [Rəʒɛ̃be] *vi* to balk, jib.

régime [Reʒim] *nm* (*POL*) régime; (*ADMIN: carcéral, fiscal etc*) system; (*MÉD*) diet; (*TECH*) (engine) speed; (*fig*) rate, pace; (*de bananes, dattes*) bunch; **se mettre au/suivre un** ~ to go on/be on a

diet.

régiment [Reʒimɑ̃] *nm* regiment; (*fig: fam*): **un** ~ **de** an army of.

région [Reʒjɔ̃] *nf* region; **régional, e, aux** *a* regional.

régir [Reʒir] *vt* to govern.

régisseur [Reʒisœr] *nm* (*d'un domaine*) steward; (*CINÉMA, TV*) assistant director; (*THÉÂTRE*) stage manager.

registre [Rəʒistr(ə)] *nm* (*livre*) register; logbook; ledger; (*MUS, LING*) register.

réglage [Reglaʒ] *nm* adjustment; tuning.

règle [Regl(ə)] *nf* (*instrument*) ruler; (*loi, prescription*) rule; ~**s** *nfpl* (*PHYSIOL*) period *sg*; **en** ~ (*papiers d'identité*) in order; **en** ~ **générale** as a (general) rule; ~ à calcul slide rule.

réglé, e [Regle] *a* well-ordered; steady; (*papier*) ruled; (*arrangé*) settled.

règlement [Rəglmɑ̃] *nm* (*paiement*) settlement; (*arrêté*) regulation; (*règles, statuts*) regulations *pl*, rules *pl*; **réglementaire** *a* conforming to the regulations; (*tenue*) regulation *cpd*.

réglementer [Rəglmɑ̃te] *vt* to regulate.

régler [Regle] *vt* (*mécanisme, machine*) to regulate, adjust; (*moteur*) to tune; (*thermostat etc*) to set, adjust; (*conflit, facture*) to settle; (*fournisseur*) to settle up with.

réglisse [Reglis] *nf* liquorice.

règne [Rɛɲ] *nm* (*d'un roi etc, fig*) reign; (*BIO*): **le** ~ **végétal/animal** the vegetable/animal kingdom.

régner [Reɲe] *vi* (*roi*) to rule, reign; (*fig*) to reign.

regorger [Rəgɔrʒe] *vi*: ~ **de** to overflow with, be bursting with.

regret [Rəgrɛ] *nm* regret; **à** ~ with regret; **avec** ~ regretfully; **être au** ~ **de devoir faire** to regret having to do.

regrettable [Rəgrɛtabl(ə)] *a* regrettable.

regretter [Rəgrɛte] *vt* to regret; (*personne*) to miss; **je regrette** I'm sorry.

regrouper [Rəgrupe] *vt* (*grouper*) to group together; (*contenir*) to include, comprise; **se** ~ *vi* to gather (together).

régulier, ière [Regylje, -jɛr] *a* (*gén*) regular; (*vitesse, qualité*) steady; (*répartition, pression, paysage*) even; (*TRANSPORTS: ligne, service*) scheduled, regular; (*légal, réglementaire*) lawful, in order; (*fam: correct*) straight, on the level; **régulièrement** *ad* regularly; steadily; evenly; normally.

rehausser [Rəose] *vt* to heighten, raise.

rein [Rɛ̃] *nm* kidney; ~**s** *nmpl* (*dos*) back *sg*.

reine [Rɛn] *nf* queen.

reine-claude [Rɛnklod] *nf* greengage.

réintégrer [Reɛ̃tegre] *vt* (*lieu*) to return to; (*fonctionnaire*) to reinstate.

rejaillir [Rəʒajir] *vi* to splash up; ~ **sur** to splash up onto; (*fig*) to rebound on; to fall upon.

rejet [Rəʒɛ] nm (action, aussi MÉD) rejection.

rejeter [Rəʒte] vt (relancer) to throw back; (vomir) to bring ou throw up; (écarter) to reject; (déverser) to throw out, discharge; ~ **la responsabilité de qch sur qn** to lay the responsibility for sth at sb's door.

rejoindre [Rəʒwɛ̃dR(ə)] vt (famille, régiment) to rejoin, return to; (lieu) to get (back) to; (suj: route etc) to meet, join; (rattraper) to catch up (with); **se ~ vi** to meet; **je te rejoins au café** I'll see ou meet you at the café.

réjouir [ReʒwiR] vt to delight; **se ~ vi** to be delighted; **se réjouir; réjouissances** nfpl (joie) rejoicing sg; (fête) festivities.

relâche [Rəlaʃ]: **faire ~ vi** (CINÉMA) to be closed; **sans ~ ad** without respite ou a break.

relâché, e [Rəlaʃe] a loose, lax.

relâcher [Rəlaʃe] vt to release; (étreinte) to loosen; **se ~ vi** to loosen; (discipline) to become slack ou lax; (élève etc) to slacken off.

relais [Rələ] nm (SPORT): (course de) ~ relay (race); **équipe de ~** shift team; (SPORT) relay team; **prendre le ~ (de)** to take over (from); ~ **routier** ≈ transport café (Brit), ≈ truck stop (US).

relancer [Rələ̃se] vt (balle) to throw back; (moteur) to restart; (fig) to boost, revive; (personne): ~ **qn** to pester sb.

relater [Rəlate] vt to relate, recount.

relatif, ive [Rəlatif, -iv] a relative.

relation [Rəlasjɔ̃] nf (récit) account, report; (rapport) relation(ship); ~**s** nfpl (rapports) relations; relationship sg; (connaissances) connections; **être/entrer en ~(s) avec** to be/get in contact with.

relaxer [Rəlakse] vt to relax; (JUR) to discharge; **se ~ vi** to relax.

relayer [Rəleje] vt (collaborateur, coureur etc) to relieve; **se ~ vi** (dans une activité) to take it in turns.

reléguer [Rəlege] vt to relegate.

relent(s) [Rəlɑ̃] nm(pl) (foul) smell.

relevé, e [Rəlve] a (manches) rolled-up; (sauce) highly-seasoned // nm (lecture) reading; (liste) statement; list; (facture) account; ~ **de compte** bank statement.

relève [Rəlɛv] nf relief; relief team (ou troops pl); **prendre la ~** to take over.

relever [Rəlve] vt (statue, meuble) to stand up again; (personne tombée) to help up; (vitre, niveau de vie) to raise; (col) to turn up; (style, conversation) to elevate; (plat, sauce) to season; (sentinelle, équipe) to relieve; (fautes, points) to pick out; (constater: traces etc) to find, pick up; (répliquer à: remarque) to react to, reply to; (: défi) to accept, take up; (noter: adresse etc) to

take down, note; (: plan) to sketch; (: cotes etc) to plot; (compteur) to read; (ramasser: cahiers) to collect, take in; ~ **de** vt (maladie) to be recovering from; (être du ressort de) to be a matter for; (ADMIN: dépendre de) to come under; (fig) to pertain to; **se ~ vi** (se remettre debout) to get up; ~ **qn de** (fonctions) to relieve sb of; ~ **la tête** to look up; to hold one's head up.

relief [Rəljɛf] nm relief; ~**s** nmpl (restes) remains; **mettre en ~** (fig) to bring out, highlight.

relier [Rəlje] vt to link up; (livre) to bind; ~ **qch à** to link sth to.

religieux, euse [Rəliʒjø, -øz] a religious // nm monk // nf nun; (gâteau) cream bun.

religion [Rəliʒjɔ̃] nf religion; (piété, dévotion) faith.

relire [RəliR] vt (à nouveau) to reread, read again; (vérifier) to read over.

reliure [RəljyR] nf binding.

reluire [RəlɥiR] vi to gleam.

remanier [Rəmanje] vt to reshape, recast; (POL) to reshuffle.

remarquable [Rəmarkabl(ə)] a remarkable.

remarque [Rəmark(ə)] nf remark; (écrite) note.

remarquer [Rəmarke] vt (voir) to notice; **se ~ vi** to be noticeable; **faire ~ (à qn) que** to point out (to sb) that; **faire ~ qch (à qn)** to point sth out (to sb); **remarquez, ...** mind you ....

remblai [Rɑ̃blɛ] nm embankment.

rembourrer [Rɑ̃bure] vt to stuff; (dossier, vêtement, souliers) to pad.

remboursement [Rɑ̃bursəmɑ̃] nm repayment; **envoi contre ~** cash on delivery.

rembourser [Rɑ̃burse] vt to pay back, repay.

remède [Rəmɛd] nm (médicament) medicine; (traitement, fig) remedy, cure.

remémorer [Rəmemɔre]: **se ~ vt** to recall, recollect.

remerciements [Rəmɛrsimɑ̃] nmpl thanks.

remercier [Rəmɛrsje] vt to thank; (congédier) to dismiss; ~ **qn de/d'avoir fait** to thank sb for/for having done.

remettre [Rəmɛtr(ə)] vt (vêtement): ~ **qch** to put sth back on; (replacer): ~ **qch quelque part** to put sth back somewhere; (ajouter): ~ **du sel/un sucre** to add more salt/another lump of sugar; (ajourner): ~ **qch (à)** to postpone sth (until); ~ **qch à qn** (rendre, restituer) to give sth back to sb; (donner, confier: paquet, argent) to hand over sth to sb, deliver sth to sb; (: prix, décoration) to present sb with sth; **se ~ vi** to get better, recover; **se ~ de** to recover from,

get over; s'en ~ à to leave it (up) to.
remise [Rəmiz] nf delivery; presentation; (rabais) discount; (local) shed; ~ en jeu (FOOTBALL) throw-in; ~ de peine reduction of sentence.
remontant [Rəmɔ̃tɑ̃] nm tonic, pick-me-up.
remonte-pente [Rəmɔ̃tpɑ̃t] nm skilift.
remonter [Rəmɔ̃te] vi to go back up; (jupe) to ride up // vt (pente) to go up; (fleuve) to sail (ou swim etc) up; (manches, pantalon) to roll up; (col) to turn up; (niveau, limite) to raise; (fig: personne) to buck up; (moteur, meuble) to put back together, reassemble; (montre, mécanisme) to wind up; ~ le moral à qn to raise sb's spirits; ~ à (dater de) to date ou go back to.
remontrance [Rəmɔ̃trɑ̃s] nf reproof, reprimand.
remontrer [Rəmɔ̃tre] vt (fig): en ~ à to prove one's superiority over.
remords [Rəmɔr] nm remorse q; avoir des ~ to feel remorse.
remorque [Rəmɔrk(ə)] nf trailer; être en ~ to be on tow; **remorquer** vt to tow; **remorqueur** nm tug(boat).
remous [Rəmu] nm (d'un navire) (back)wash q; (de rivière) swirl, eddy // nmpl (fig) stir sg.
remparts [Rɑ̃par] nmpl walls, ramparts.
remplaçant, e [Rɑ̃plasɑ̃, -ɑ̃t] nm/f replacement, stand-in; (THÉÂTRE) understudy; (SCOL) supply teacher.
remplacement [Rɑ̃plasmɑ̃] nm replacement; (job) replacement work q.
remplacer [Rɑ̃plase] vt to replace; (tenir lieu de) to take the place of; ~ qch/qn par to replace sth/sb with.
rempli, e [Rɑ̃pli] a (emploi du temps) full, busy; ~ de full of, filled with.
remplir [Rɑ̃plir] vt to fill (up); (questionnaire) to fill out ou up; (obligations, fonction, condition) to fulfil; se ~ vi to fill up.
remporter [Rɑ̃pɔrte] vt (marchandise) to take away; (fig) to win, achieve.
remuant, e [Rəmɥɑ̃, -ɑ̃t] a restless.
remue-ménage [Rəmymenaʒ] nm inv commotion.
remuer [Rəmɥe] vt to move; (café, sauce) to stir // vi, se ~ vi to move.
rémunérer [Remynere] vt to remunerate.
renard [Rənar] nm fox.
renchérir [Rɑ̃ʃerir] vi (fig): ~ (sur) to add something (to).
rencontre [Rɑ̃kɔ̃tr(ə)] nf meeting; (imprévue) encounter; aller à la ~ de qn to go and meet sb.
rencontrer [Rɑ̃kɔ̃tre] vt to meet; (mot, expression) to come across; (difficultés) to meet with; se ~ vi to meet; (véhicules) to collide.
rendement [Rɑ̃dmɑ̃] nm (d'un

travailleur, d'une machine) output; (d'une culture) yield; (d'un investissement) return; à plein ~ at full capacity.
rendez-vous [Rɑ̃devu] nm (rencontre) appointment; (: d'amoureux) date; (lieu) meeting place; donner ~ à qn to arrange to meet sb; avoir/prendre ~ (avec) to have/make an appointment (with).
rendre [Rɑ̃dr(ə)] vt (livre, argent etc) to give back, return; (otages, visite etc) to return; (sang, aliments) to bring up; (exprimer, traduire) to render; (faire devenir): ~ qn célèbre/qch possible to make sb famous/sth possible; se ~ vi (capituler) to surrender, give o.s. up; (aller): se ~ quelque part to go somewhere; se ~ compte de qch to realize sth.
rênes [Rɛn] nfpl reins.
renfermé, e [Rɑ̃fɛrme] a (fig) withdrawn // nm: sentir le ~ to smell stuffy.
renfermer [Rɑ̃fɛrme] vt to contain.
renflement [Rɑ̃fləmɑ̃] nm bulge.
renflouer [Rɑ̃flue] vt to refloat; (fig) to set back on its (ou his/her etc) feet.
renfoncement [Rɑ̃fɔ̃smɑ̃] nm recess.
renforcer [Rɑ̃fɔrse] vt to reinforce.
renfort [Rɑ̃fɔr]: ~s nmpl reinforcements; à grand ~ de with a great deal of.
renfrogné, e [Rɑ̃frɔɲe] a sullen.
rengaine [Rɑ̃gɛn] nf (péj) old tune.
renier [Rənje] vt (parents) to disown, repudiate; (foi) to renounce.
renifler [Rənifle] vi, vt to sniff.
renne [Rɛn] nm reindeer inv.
renom [Rənɔ̃] nm reputation; (célébrité) renown; **renommé, e** a celebrated, renowned // nf fame.
renoncer [Rənɔ̃se] vi: ~ à vt to give up; ~ à faire to give up the idea of doing.
renouer [Rənwe] vt: ~ avec (tradition) to revive; (habitude) to take up again; ~ avec qn to take up with sb again.
renouveler [Rənuvle] vt to renew; (exploit, méfait) to repeat; se ~ vi (incident) to recur, happen again; **renouvellement** nm renewal; recurrence.
rénover [Renɔve] vt (immeuble) to renovate, do up; (enseignement) to reform; (quartier) to redevelop.
renseignement [Rɑ̃sɛɲmɑ̃] nm information q, piece of information; (guichet des) ~s information desk.
renseigner [Rɑ̃sɛɲe] vt: ~ qn (sur) to give information to sb (about); se ~ vi to ask for information, make inquiries.
rentable [Rɑ̃tabl(ə)] a profitable.
rente [Rɑ̃t] nf income; pension; government stock ou bond; **rentier, ière** nm/f person of private means.
rentrée [Rɑ̃tre] nf: ~ (d'argent) cash q coming in; la ~ (des classes) the start of

the new school year.

rentrer [rɑ̃tre] *vi* (*entrer de nouveau*) to go (*ou* come) back in; (*entrer*) to go (*ou* come) in; (*revenir chez soi*) to go (*ou* come) (back) home; (*air, clou: pénétrer*) to go in; (*revenu, argent*) to come in // *vt* (*foins*) to bring in; (*véhicule*) to put away; (*chemise dans pantalon etc*) to tuck in; (*griffes*) to draw in; (*fig: larmes, colère etc*) to hold back; **~ le ventre** to pull in one's stomach; **~ dans** (*heurter*) to crash into; **~ dans l'ordre** to be back to normal; **~ dans ses frais** to recover one's expenses.

renversant, e [rɑ̃vɛrsɑ̃, -ɑ̃t] *a* astounding.

renverse [rɑ̃vɛrs(ə)]: **à la ~** *ad* backwards.

renverser [rɑ̃vɛrse] *vt* (*faire tomber: chaise, verre*) to knock over, overturn; (*piéton*) to knock down; (*liquide, contenu*) to spill, upset; (*retourner*) to turn upside down; (: *ordre des mots etc*) to reverse; (*fig: gouvernement etc*) to overthrow; (*stupéfier*) to bowl over; **se ~** *vi* to fall over; to overturn; to spill.

renvoi [rɑ̃vwa] *nm* (*référence*) cross-reference; (*éructation*) belch.

renvoyer [rɑ̃vwaje] *vt* to send back; (*congédier*) to dismiss; (*lumière*) to reflect; (*son*) to echo; (*ajourner*): **~ qch (à)** to put sth off *ou* postpone sth (until); **~ qn à** (*fig*) to refer sb to.

repaire [rəpɛr] *nm* den.

répandre [repɑ̃dr(ə)] *vt* (*renverser*) to spill; (*étaler, diffuser*) to spread; (*lumière*) to shed; (*chaleur, odeur*) to give off; **se ~** *vi* to spill; to spread; **répandu, e** *a* (*opinion, usage*) widespread.

réparation [reparasjɔ̃] *nf* repair.

réparer [repare] *vt* to repair; (*fig: offense*) to make up for, atone for; (: *oubli, erreur*) to put right.

repartie [rəparti] *nf* retort; **avoir de la ~** to be quick at repartee.

repartir [rəpartir] *vi* to set off again; to leave again; (*fig*) to get going again; **~ à zéro** to start from scratch (again).

répartir [repartir] *vt* (*pour attribuer*) to share out; (*pour disperser, disposer*) to divide up; (*poids, chaleur*) to distribute; **se ~** *vt* (*travail, rôles*) to share out between themselves; **répartition** *nf* sharing out; dividing up; distribution.

repas [rəpa] *nm* meal.

repasser [rəpase] *vi* to come (*ou* go) back // *vt* (*vêtement, tissu*) to iron; (*examen*) to retake, resit; (*film*) to show again; (*leçon, rôle: revoir*) to go over (again).

repêcher [rəpeʃe] *vt* (*noyé*) to recover the body of; (*candidat*) to pass (*by inflating marks*).

repentir [rəpɑ̃tir] *nm* repentance; **se ~** *vi* to repent; **se ~ de** to repent of.

répercuter [repɛrkyte] *vt* (*information, hausse des prix*) to pass on; **se ~** *vi* (*bruit*) to reverberate; (*fig*): **se ~ sur** to have repercussions on.

repère [rəpɛr] *nm* mark; (*monument etc*) landmark.

repérer [rəpere] *vt* (*erreur, connaissance*) to spot; (*abri, ennemi*) to locate; **se ~** *vi* to find one's way about.

répertoire [repɛrtwar] *nm* (*liste*) (alphabetical) list; (*carnet*) index notebook; (*d'un artiste*) repertoire.

répéter [repete] *vt* to repeat; (*préparer: leçon: aussi vi*) to learn, go over; (*THÉÂTRE*) to rehearse; **se ~** *vi* (*redire*) to repeat o.s.; (*se reproduire*) to be repeated, recur.

répétition [repetisjɔ̃] *nf* repetition; (*THÉÂTRE*) rehearsal; **~ générale** final dress rehearsal.

répit [repi] *nm* respite.

replet, ète [rəplɛ, -ɛt] *a* chubby.

replier [rəplije] *vt* (*rabattre*) to fold down *ou* over; **se ~** *vi* (*troupes, armée*) to withdraw, fall back.

réplique [replik] *nf* (*repartie, fig*) reply; (*THÉÂTRE*) line; (*copie*) replica.

répliquer [replike] *vi* to reply; (*riposter*) to retaliate.

répondre [repɔ̃dr(ə)] *vi* to answer, reply; (*freins, mécanisme*) to respond; **~ à** *vt* to reply to, answer; (*avec impertinence*): **~ à qn** to answer sb back; (*affection, salut*) to return; (*provocation, suj: mécanisme etc*) to respond to; (*correspondre à: besoin*) to answer; (: *conditions*) to meet; (: *description*) to match; **~ de** to answer for.

réponse [repɔ̃s] *nf* answer, reply; **en ~ à** in reply to.

reportage [rəpɔrtaʒ] *nm* (*bref*) report; (*écrit: documentaire*) story; article; (*en direct*) commentary; (*genre, activité*): **le ~** reporting.

reporter *nm* [rəpɔrtɛr] reporter // *vt* [rəpɔrte] (*total*): **~ qch sur** to carry sth forward *ou* over to; (*ajourner*): **~ qch (à)** to postpone sth (until); (*transférer*): **~ qch sur** to transfer sth to; **se ~ à** (*époque*) to think back to; (*document*) to refer to.

repos [rəpo] *nm* rest; (*fig*) peace (and quiet); peace of mind; (*MIL*): **~!** stand at ease!; **en ~** at rest; **de tout ~** safe.

reposant, e [rəpozɑ̃, -ɑ̃t] *a* restful.

reposer [rəpoze] *vt* (*verre, livre*) to put down; (*délasser*) to rest; (*problème*) to reformulate // *vi* (*liquide, pâte*) to settle, rest; **~ sur** to be built on; (*fig*) to rest on; **se ~** *vi* to rest; **se ~ sur qn** to rely on sb.

repoussant, e [rəpusɑ̃, -ɑ̃t] *a* repulsive.

repousser [rəpuse] *vi* to grow again // *vt* to repel, repulse; (*offre*) to turn down, reject; (*tiroir, personne*) to push back; (*différer*) to put back.

reprendre [ʀǝpʀɑ̃dʀ(ǝ)] *vt* (*prisonnier, ville*) to recapture; (*objet prêté, donné*) to take back; (*chercher*): **je viendrai te ~ à 4h** I'll come and fetch you at 4; (*se resservir de*): **~ du pain/un œuf** to take (*ou eat*) more bread/another egg; (*firme, entreprise*) to take over; (*travail, promenade*) to resume; (*emprunter: argument, idée*) to take up, use; (*refaire: article etc*) to go over again; (*jupe etc*) to alter; (*émission, pièce*) to put on again; (*réprimander*) to tell off; (*corriger*) to correct // *vi* (*classes, pluie*) to start (up) again; (*activités, travaux, combats*) to resume, start up again; (*affaires, industrie*) to pick up; (*dire*): **reprit-il** he went on; **se ~** *vi* (*se ressaisir*) to recover; **s'y ~** to make another attempt; **~ des forces** to recover one's strength; **~ courage** to take new heart; **~ la route** to set off again; **~ haleine** *ou* **son souffle** to get one's breath back.

représailles [ʀǝpʀezɑj] *nfpl* reprisals.

représentant, e [ʀǝpʀezɑ̃tɑ̃, -ɑ̃t] *nm/f* representative.

représentation [ʀǝpʀezɑ̃tɑsjɔ̃] *nf* (*symbole, image*) representation; (*spectacle*) performance.

représenter [ʀǝpʀezɑ̃te] *vt* to represent; (*donner: pièce, opéra*) to perform; **se ~** *vt* (*se figurer*) to imagine; to visualize.

répression [ʀepʀesjɔ̃] *nf* (*voir réprimer*) suppression; repression.

réprimer [ʀepʀime] *vt* (*émotions*) to suppress; (*peuple etc*) to repress.

repris [ʀǝpʀi] *nm*: **~ de justice** ex-prisoner, ex-convict.

reprise [ʀǝpʀiz] *nf* (*recommencement*) resumption; recovery; (*TV*) repeat; (*CINÉMA*) rerun; (*AUTO*) acceleration *q*; (*COMM*) trade-in, part exchange; **à plusieurs ~s** on several occasions.

repriser [ʀǝpʀize] *vt* to darn; to mend.

reproche [ʀǝpʀɔʃ] *nm* (*remontrance*) reproach; **faire des ~s à qn** to reproach sb; **sans ~(s)** beyond reproach.

reprocher [ʀǝpʀɔʃe] *vt*: **~ qch à qn** to reproach *ou* blame sb for sth; **~ qch à** (*machine, théorie*) to have sth against.

reproduction [ʀǝpʀɔdyksjɔ̃] *nf* reproduction.

reproduire [ʀǝpʀɔdɥiʀ] *vt* to reproduce; **se ~** *vi* (*BIO*) to reproduce; (*recommencer*) to recur, re-occur.

reptile [ʀɛptil] *nm* reptile.

repu, e [ʀǝpy] *a* satisfied, sated.

républicain, e [ʀepyblikɛ̃, -ɛn] *a, nm/f* republican.

république [ʀepyblik] *nf* republic.

répugnant, e [ʀepyɲɑ̃, -ɑ̃t] *a* repulsive; loathsome.

répugner [ʀepyɲe]: **~ à** *vt*: **~ à qn** to

repel *ou* disgust sb; **~ à faire** to be loath *ou* reluctant to do.

réputation [ʀepytasjɔ̃] *nf* reputation; **réputé, e** *a* renowned.

requérir [ʀǝkeʀiʀ] *vt* (*nécessiter*) to require, call for; (*JUR: peine*) to call for, demand.

requête [ʀǝkɛt] *nf* request; (*JUR*) petition.

requin [ʀǝkɛ̃] *nm* shark.

requis, e [ʀǝki, -iz] *a* required.

R.E.R. *sigle m* (= réseau express régional) Greater Paris high speed train service.

rescapé, e [ʀɛskape] *nm/f* survivor.

rescousse [ʀɛskus] *nf*: **aller à la ~ de qn** to go to sb's aid *ou* rescue.

réseau, x [ʀezo] *nm* network.

réservation [ʀezɛʀvasjɔ̃] *nf* booking, reservation.

réserve [ʀezɛʀv(ǝ)] *nf* (*retenue*) reserve; (*entrepôt*) storeroom; (*restriction, d'Indiens*) reservation; (*de pêche, chasse*) preserve; **sous ~ de** subject to; **sans ~** *ad* unreservedly; **de ~** (*provisions etc*) in reserve.

réservé, e [ʀezɛʀve] *a* (*discret*) reserved; (*chasse, pêche*) private.

réserver [ʀezɛʀve] *vt* (*gén*) to reserve; (*chambre, billet etc*) to book, reserve; (*garder*): **~ qch pour/à** to keep *ou* save sth for; **~ qch à qn** to reserve (*ou* book) sth for sb.

réservoir [ʀezɛʀvwaʀ] *nm* tank.

résidence [ʀezidɑ̃s] *nf* residence; **~ secondaire** second home; **(en) ~ surveillée** (under) house arrest; **résidentiel, le** *a* residential.

résider [ʀezide] *vi*: **~ à/dans/en** to reside in; **~ dans** (*fig*) to lie in.

résidu [ʀezidy] *nm* residue *q*.

résigner [ʀezine]: **se ~** *vi*: **se ~ (à qch/à faire)** to resign o.s. (to sth/to doing).

résilier [ʀezilje] *vt* to terminate.

résistance [ʀezistɑ̃s] *nf* resistance; (*de réchaud, bouilloire: fil*) element.

résistant, e [ʀezistɑ̃, -ɑ̃t] *a* (*personne*) robust, tough; (*matériau*) strong, hard-wearing.

résister [ʀeziste] *vi* to resist; **~ à** *vt* (*assaut, tentation*) to resist; (*effort, souffrance*) to withstand; (*désobéir à*) to stand up to, resist.

résolu, e [ʀezɔly] *pp de* **résoudre** // *a*: **être ~ à qch/faire** to be set upon sth/doing.

résolution [ʀezɔlysjɔ̃] *nf* solving; (*fermeté, décision*) resolution.

résolve *etc vb voir* **résoudre**.

résonner [ʀezɔne] *vi* (*cloche, pas*) to reverberate, resound; (*salle*) to be resonant; **~ de** to resound with.

résorber [ʀezɔʀbe]: **se ~** *vi* (*fig*) to be reduced; to be absorbed.

résoudre [ʀezudʀ(ǝ)] *vt* to solve; **se ~ à**

faire to bring o.s. to do.

respect [ʀɛspɛ] *nm* respect; **tenir en ~** to keep at bay.

respecter [ʀɛspɛkte] *vt* to respect.

respectueux, euse [ʀɛspɛktyø, -øz] *a* respectful; **~ de** respectful of.

respiration [ʀɛspiʀasjɔ̃] *nf* breathing *q*; **~ artificielle** artificial respiration.

respirer [ʀɛspiʀe] *vi* to breathe; *(fig)* to get one's breath; to breathe again // *vt* to breathe (in), inhale; *(manifester: santé, calme etc)* to exude.

resplendir [ʀɛsplɑ̃diʀ] *vi* to shine; *(fig)*: **~ (de)** to be radiant (with).

responsabilité [ʀɛspɔ̃sabilite] *nf* responsibility; *(légale)* liability.

responsable [ʀɛspɔ̃sabl(ə)] *a* responsible // *nm/f (du ravitaillement etc)* person in charge; *(de parti, syndicat)* official; **~ de** responsible for; *(chargé de)* in charge of, responsible for.

ressaisir [ʀəseziʀ]: **se ~** *vi* to regain one's self-control.

ressasser [ʀəsase] *vt* to keep going over.

ressemblance [ʀəsɑ̃blɑ̃s] *nf* resemblance, similarity, likeness.

ressemblant, e [ʀəsɑ̃blɑ̃, -ɑ̃t] *a (portrait)* lifelike, true to life.

ressembler [ʀəsɑ̃ble]: **~ à** *vt* to be like; to resemble; *(visuellement)* to look like; **se ~** *vi* to be *(ou* look) alike.

ressemeler [ʀəsəmle] *vt* to (re)sole.

ressentiment [ʀəsɑ̃timɑ̃] *nm* resentment.

ressentir [ʀəsɑ̃tiʀ] *vt* to feel; **se ~ de** to feel *(ou* show) the effects of.

resserrer [ʀəseʀe] *vt (nœud, boulon)* to tighten (up); *(fig: liens)* to strengthen; **se ~** *vi (vallée)* to narrow.

resservir [ʀəseʀviʀ] *vi* to do *ou* serve again // *vt*: **~ qn (d'un plat)** to give sb a second helping of a dish).

ressort [ʀəsɔʀ] *nm (pièce)* spring; *(force morale)* spirit; *(recours)*: **en dernier ~** as a last resort; *(compétence)*: **être du ~ de** to fall within the competence of.

ressortir [ʀəsɔʀtiʀ] *vi* to go *(ou* come) out (again); *(contraster)* to stand out; **~ de** to emerge from; **faire ~** *(fig: souligner)* to bring out.

ressortissant, e [ʀəsɔʀtisɑ̃, -ɑ̃t] *nm/f* national.

ressource [ʀəsuʀs(ə)] *nf*: **avoir la ~ de** to have the possibility of; **leur seule ~ était de** the only course open to them was to; **~s** *nfpl* resources.

ressusciter [ʀesysite] *vt (fig)* to revive, bring back // *vi* to rise (from the dead).

restant, e [ʀɛstɑ̃, -ɑ̃t] *a* remaining // *nm*: **le ~ (de)** the remainder (of); **un ~ de** *(de trop)* some left-over.

restaurant [ʀɛstoʀɑ̃] *nm* restaurant.

restauration [ʀɛstoʀasjɔ̃] *nf* restoration; *(hôtellerie)* catering; **~ rapide** fast food.

restaurer [ʀɛstoʀe] *vt* to restore; **se ~** *vi* to have something to eat.

reste [ʀɛst(ə)] *nm (restant)*: **le ~ (de)** the rest (of); *(de trop)*: **un ~ (de)** some left over; *(vestige)*: **un ~ de** a remnant *ou* last trace of; *(MATH)* remainder; **~s** *nmpl* left-overs; *(d'une cité etc, dépouille mortelle)* remains; **du ~, au ~** *ad* besides, moreover.

rester [ʀɛste] *vi* to stay, remain; *(subsister)* to remain, be left; *(durer)* to last, live on // *vb impersonnel*: **il reste du pain/2 œufs** there's some bread/there are 2 eggs left (over); **il me reste assez de temps** I have enough time left; **ce qui reste à faire** what remains to be done; **restons-en là** let's leave it at that.

restituer [ʀɛstitɥe] *vt (objet, somme)*: **~ qch (à qn)** to return sth (to sb); *(TECH)* to release; *(: son)* to reproduce.

restoroute [ʀɛstoʀut] *nm* motorway *(Brit)* ou highway *(US)* restaurant.

restreindre [ʀɛstʀɛ̃dʀ(ə)] *vt* to restrict, limit.

restriction [ʀɛstʀiksjɔ̃] *nf* restriction; **~s** *(mentales)* reservations.

résultat [ʀezylta] *nm* result; *(d'élection etc)* results *pl*.

résulter [ʀezylte]: **~ de** *vt* to result from, be the result of.

résumé [ʀezyme] *nm* summary, résumé.

résumer [ʀezyme] *vt (texte)* to summarize; *(récapituler)* to sum up; **se ~ à** to come down to.

résurrection [ʀezyʀɛksjɔ̃] *nf* resurrection; *(fig)* revival.

rétablir [ʀetabliʀ] *vt* to restore, re-establish; **se ~** *vi (guérir)* to recover; *(silence, calme)* to return, be restored; **rétablissement** *nm* restoring; recovery; *(SPORT)* pull-up.

retaper [ʀətape] *vt (maison, voiture etc)* to do up; *(fam: revigorer)* to buck up; *(redactylographier)* to retype.

retard [ʀətaʀ] *nm (d'une personne attendue)* lateness *q*; *(sur l'horaire, un programme)* delay; *(fig: scolaire, mental etc)* backwardness; **en ~ (de 2 heures)** (2 hours) late; **avoir du ~** to be late; *(sur un programme)* to be behind (schedule); **prendre du ~** *(train, avion)* to be delayed; *(montre)* to lose (time); **sans ~** *ad* without delay.

retardement [ʀətaʀdəmɑ̃]: **à ~** *a* delayed action *cpd*; **bombe à ~** time bomb.

retarder [ʀətaʀde] *vt (sur un horaire)*: **~ qn (d'une heure)** to delay sb (an hour); *(départ, date)*: **~ qch (de 2 jours)** to put sth back (2 days), delay sth (for *ou* by 2 days); *(horloge)* to put back // *vi (montre)* to be slow; to lose (time).

retenir [ʀətniʀ] *vt (garder, retarder)* to keep, detain; *(maintenir: objet qui glisse, fig: colère, larmes)* to hold back;

(*: objet suspendu*) to hold; (*fig: empêcher d'agir*): ~ **qn (de faire)** to hold sb back (from doing); (*se rappeler*) to retain; (*réserver*) to reserve; (*accepter*) to accept; (*prélever*): ~ **qch (sur)** to deduct sth (from); **se** ~ **vi** (*se raccrocher*): **se** ~ **à** to hold onto; (*se contenir*): **se** ~ **de faire** to restrain o.s. from doing; ~ **son souffle** to hold one's breath.

retentir [Rətɑ̃tir] *vi* to ring out; (*salle*): ~ **de** to ring *ou* resound with.

retentissant, e [Rətɑ̃tisɑ̃, -ɑ̃t] *a* resounding; (*fig*) impact-making.

retentissement [Rətɑ̃tismɑ̃] *nm* repercussion; effect, impact; stir.

retenue [Rətny] *nf* (*prélèvement*) deduction; (*SCOL*) detention; (*modération*) (self-)restraint; (*réserve*) reserve, reticence.

réticence [Retisɑ̃s] *nf* hesitation, reluctance *q*.

rétine [Retin] *nf* retina.

retiré, e [Rətire] *a* secluded; remote.

retirer [Rətire] *vt* to withdraw; (*vêtement, lunettes*) to take off, remove; (*extraire*): ~ **qch de** to take sth out of, remove sth from; (*reprendre: bagages, billets*) to collect, pick up.

retombées [Rətɔ̃be] *nfpl* (*radioactives*) fallout *sg*; (*fig*) fallout; spin-offs.

retomber [Rətɔ̃be] *vi* (*à nouveau*) to fall again; (*atterrir: après un saut etc*) to land; (*tomber, redescendre*) to fall back; (*pendre*) to fall, hang (down); (*échoir*): ~ **sur qn** to fall on sb.

rétorquer [Retɔrke] *vt*: ~ **(à qn) que** to retort (to sb) that.

retors, e [Rətɔr, -ɔrs(ə)] *a* wily.

rétorsion [Retɔrsjɔ̃] *nf*: **mesures de** ~ reprisals.

retoucher [Rətuʃe] *vt* (*photographie*) to touch up; (*texte, vêtement*) to alter.

retour [Rətur] *nm* return; **au** ~ when we (*ou* they *etc*) get (*ou* got) back; (*en route*) on the way back; **être de** ~ **(de)** to be back (from); **par** ~ **du courrier** by return of post.

retourner [Rəturne] *vt* (*dans l'autre sens: matelas, crêpe, foin, terre*) to turn (over); (*: caisse*) to turn upside down; (*: sac, vêtement*) to turn inside out; (*émouvoir: personne*) to shake; (*renvoyer, restituer*): ~ **qch à qn** to return sth to sb // *vi* (*aller, revenir*): ~ **quelque part/à** to go back *ou* return somewhere/to; ~ **à** (*état, activité*) to return to, go back to; **se** ~ *vi* to turn over; (*tourner la tête*) to turn round; **se** ~ **contre** (*fig*) to turn against; **savoir de quoi il retourne** to know what it is all about.

retracer [Rətrase] *vt* to relate, recount.

retrait [Rətrɛ] *nm* (*voir retirer*) withdrawal; collection; **en** ~ set back; ~ **du permis (de conduire)** disqualification

from driving (*Brit*), revocation of driver's license (*US*).

retraite [Rətrɛt] *nf* (*d'une armée, REL, refuge*) retreat; (*d'un employé*) retirement; (*revenu*) pension; **prendre sa** ~ to retire; ~ **anticipée** early retirement; **retraité, e** *a* retired // *nm/f* pensioner.

retrancher [Rətrɑ̃ʃe] *vt* (*passage, détails*) to take out, remove; (*nombre, somme*): ~ **qch de** to take *ou* deduct sth from; (*couper*) to cut off; **se** ~ **derrière/dans** to take refuge behind/in.

retransmettre [Rətrɑ̃smɛtr(ə)] *vt* (*RADIO*) to broadcast; (*TV*) to show.

rétrécir [Retresir] *vt* (*vêtement*) to take in // *vi* to shrink; **se** ~ *vi* to narrow.

rétribution [Retribysjɔ̃] *nf* payment.

rétro [Retro] *a inv*: **la mode** ~ the nostalgia vogue.

rétrograde [Retrograd] *a* reactionary, backward-looking.

rétrograder [Retrograde] *vi* (*économie*) to regress; (*AUTO*) to change down.

rétroprojecteur [Retroprɔʒɛktœr] *nm* overhead projector.

rétrospective [Retrospɛktiv] *nf*; retrospective exhibition/season; ~**ment** *ad* in retrospect.

retrousser [Rətruse] *vt* to roll up.

retrouvailles [Rətruvɑj] *nfpl* reunion *sg*.

retrouver [Rətruve] *vt* (*fugitif, objet perdu*) to find; (*occasion*) to find again; (*calme, santé*) to regain; (*revoir*) to see again; (*rejoindre*) to meet (again), join; **se** ~ *vi* to meet; (*s'orienter*) to find one's way; **se** ~ **quelque part** to find o.s. somewhere; **s'y** ~ (*rentrer dans ses frais*) to break even.

rétroviseur [Retrovizœr] *nm* (rearview) mirror.

réunion [Reynjɔ̃] *nf* bringing together; joining; (*séance*) meeting.

réunir [Reynir] *vt* (*convoquer*) to call together; (*rassembler*) to gather together; (*cumuler*) to combine; (*rapprocher*) to bring together (again), reunite; (*rattacher*) to join (together); **se** ~ *vi* (*se rencontrer*) to meet.

réussi, e [Reysi] *a* successful.

réussir [Reysir] *vi* to succeed, be successful; (*à un examen*) to pass; (*plante, culture*) to thrive, do well // *vt* to make a success of; ~ **à faire** to succeed in doing; ~ **à qn** to go right for sb; (*aliment*) to agree with sb.

réussite [Reysit] *nf* success; (*CARTES*) patience.

revaloir [Rəvalwar] *vt*: **je vous revaudrai cela** I'll repay you some day; (*en mal*) I'll pay you back for this.

revaloriser [Rəvalɔrize] *vt* (*monnaie*) to revalue; (*salaires*) to raise the level of.

revanche [Rəvɑ̃ʃ] *nf* revenge; **en** ~ on the other hand.

rêve [REV] nm dream; (activité psychique): le ~ dreaming.

revêche [RəvƐʃ] a surly, sour-tempered.

réveil [Revɛj] nm (d'un dormeur) waking up q; (fig) awakening; (pendule) alarm (clock); (MIL) reveille; **au ~** on waking (up).

réveille-matin [Revɛjmatɛ̃] nm inv alarm clock.

réveiller [Revɛje] vt (personne) to wake up; (fig) to awaken, revive; **se ~** vi to wake up; (fig) to reawaken.

réveillon [Revɛjɔ̃] nm Christmas Eve; (de la Saint-Sylvestre) New Year's Eve; **réveillonner** vi to celebrate Christmas Eve (ou New Year's Eve).

révélateur, trice [RevelatœR, -tRis] a: ~ **(de qch)** revealing (sth) // nm (PHOTO) developer.

révéler [Revele] vt (gén) to reveal; (faire connaître au public): ~ **qn/qch** to make sb/sth widely known, bring sb/sth to the public's notice; **se ~** vi to be revealed, reveal itself // vb avec attribut to prove (to be).

revenant, e [Rəvnɑ̃, -ɑ̃t] nm/f ghost.

revendeur, euse [Rəvɑ̃dœR, -øz] nm/f (détaillant) retailer; (d'occasions) secondhand dealer.

revendication [Rəvɑ̃dikasjɔ̃] nf claim, demand; **journée de ~** day of action.

revendiquer [Rəvɑ̃dike] vt to claim, demand; (responsabilité) to claim.

revendre [Rəvɑ̃dR(ə)] vt (d'occasion) to resell; (détailler) to sell; **à ~** ad (en abondance) to spare.

revenir [RəvniR] vi to come back; (CULIN): **faire ~** to brown; (coûter): ~ **cher/à 100 F (à qn)** to cost (sb) a lot/100 F; ~ **à** (études, projet) to return to, go back to; (équivaloir à) to amount to; ~ **à qn** (part, honneur) to go to sb, be sb's; (souvenir, nom) to come back to sb; ~ **de** (fig: maladie, étonnement) to recover from; ~ **sur** (question, sujet) to go back over; (engagement) to go back on; ~ **à la charge** to return to the attack; ~ **à soi** to come round; **n'en pas ~: je n'en reviens pas** I can't get over it; ~ **sur ses pas** to retrace one's steps; **cela revient à dire que/au même** it amounts to saying that/the same thing.

revenu [Rəvny] nm income; (de l'État) revenue; (d'un capital) yield; ~**s** nmpl income sg.

rêver [Reve] vi, vt to dream; ~ **de/à** to dream of.

réverbère [RevƐRbƐR] nm street lamp ou light.

réverbérer [RevƐRbeRe] vt to reflect.

révérence [RevƐRɑ̃s] nf (salut) bow; (: de femme) curtsey.

rêverie [RevRi] nf daydreaming q, daydream.

revers [RəvƐR] nm (de feuille, main)

back; (d'étoffe) wrong side; (de pièce, médaille) back, reverse; (TENNIS, PING-PONG) backhand; (de veston) lapel; (de pantalon) turn-up; (fig: échec) setback.

revêtement [RəvƐtmɑ̃] nm (de paroi) facing; (des sols) flooring; (de chaussée) surface; (de tuyau etc: enduit) coating.

revêtir [RəvetiR] vt (habit) to don, put on; (fig) to take on; ~ **qn de** (fig) to endow ou invest sb with; ~ **qch de** to cover sth with; (fig) to cloak sth in.

rêveur, euse [RevœR, -øz] a dreamy // nm/f dreamer.

revient [Rəvjɛ̃] vb voir **revenir**.

revigorer [RəvigoRe] vt to invigorate, brace up; to revive, buck up.

revirement [RəviRmɑ̃] nm change of mind; (d'une situation) reversal.

réviser [Revize] vt (texte, SCOL: matière) to revise; (machine, installation, moteur) to overhaul, service; (JUR: procès) to review.

révision [Revizjɔ̃] nf revision; auditing q; overhaul; servicing q; review; **la ~ des 10000 km** (AUTO) the 10,000 km service.

revivre [RəvivR(ə)] vi (reprendre des forces) to come alive again; (traditions) to be revived // vt (épreuve, moment) to relive.

revoir [RəvwaR] vt to see again; (réviser) to revise // nm: **au ~** goodbye.

révoltant, e [Revɔltɑ̃, -ɑ̃t] a revolting; appalling.

révolte [Revɔlt(ə)] nf rebellion, revolt.

révolter [Revɔlte] vt to revolt; to outrage, appal; **se ~ (contre)** to rebel (against).

révolu, e [Revɔly] a past; (ADMIN): **âgé de 18 ans ~s** over 18 years of age; **après 3 ans ~s** when 3 full years have passed.

révolution [Revɔlysjɔ̃] nf revolution; **révolutionnaire** a, nm/f revolutionary.

revolver [RevɔlvƐR] nm gun; (à barillet) revolver.

révoquer [Revɔke] vt (fonctionnaire) to dismiss; (arrêt, contrat) to revoke.

revue [Rəvy] nf (inventaire, examen, MIL) review; (périodique) review, magazine; (de music-hall) variety show; **passer en ~** to review; to go through.

rez-de-chaussée [Redʃose] nm inv ground floor.

RF sigle = République Française.

RFA sigle f = République fédérale d'Allemagne.

Rhin [Rɛ̃] nm: **le ~** the Rhine.

rhinocéros [RinoseRɔs] nm rhinoceros.

Rhône [Ron] nm: **le ~** the Rhone.

rhubarbe [RybaRb(ə)] nf rhubarb.

rhum [Rɔm] nm rum.

rhumatisme [Rymatism(ə)] nm rheumatism q.

rhume [Rym] nm cold; ~ **de cerveau** head cold; **le ~ des foins** hay fever.

ri [ʀi] *pp de* **rire**.
riant, e [ʀjɑ̃, -ɑ̃t] *a* smiling, cheerful.
ricaner [ʀikane] *vi (avec méchanceté)* to snigger; *(bêtement)* to giggle.
riche [ʀiʃ] *a (gén)* rich; *(personne, pays)* rich, wealthy; ~ **en** rich in; ~ **de** full of; rich in; **richesse** *nf* wealth; *(fig)* richness; **richesses** *nfpl* wealth *sg*; treasures.
ricin [ʀisɛ̃] *nm*: **huile de** ~ castor oil.
ricocher [ʀikɔʃe] *vi*: ~ **(sur)** to rebound (off); *(sur l'eau)* to bounce (on *ou* off).
ricochet [ʀikɔʃe] *nm*: **faire des** ~s to skip stones; **par** ~ *ad* on the rebound; *(fig)* as an indirect result.
rictus [ʀiktys] *nm* grin; *(snarling)* grimace.
ride [ʀid] *nf* wrinkle; *(fig)* ripple.
rideau, x [ʀido] *nm* curtain; *(POL)*: **le** ~ **de fer** the Iron Curtain.
rider [ʀide] *vt* to wrinkle; *(eau)* to ripple; **se** ~ *vi* to become wrinkled.
ridicule [ʀidikyl] *a* ridiculous // *nm*: **le** ~ ridicule; **se ridiculiser** *vi* to make a fool of o.s.
rien [ʀjɛ̃] ♦ *pronom*
1: (ne) ... ~ nothing, *tournure négative* + anything; **qu'est-ce que vous avez?** - ~ what have you got? - nothing; **il n'a** ~ **dit/fait** he said/did nothing; **he hasn't** said/done anything; **il n'a** ~ *(n'est pas blessé)* he's all right; **de** ~! not at all!
2 *(quelque chose)*: **a-t-il jamais** ~ **fait pour nous?** has he ever done anything for us?
3: ~ **de**: ~ **d'intéressant** nothing interesting; ~ **d'autre** nothing else; ~ **du tout** nothing at all
4: ~ **que** just, only; nothing but; ~ **que pour lui faire plaisir** only *ou* just to please him; ~ **que la vérité** nothing but the truth; ~ **que cela** that alone
♦ *nm*: **un petit** ~ *(cadeau)* a little something; **des** ~s trivia *pl*; **un** ~ **de** a hint of; **en un** ~ **de temps** in no time at all.
rieur, euse [ʀjœʀ, -øz] *a* cheerful.
rigide [ʀiʒid] *a* stiff; *(fig)* rigid; strict.
rigole [ʀigɔl] *nf (conduit)* channel; *(filet d'eau)* rivulet.
rigoler [ʀigɔle] *vi (rire)* to laugh; *(s'amuser)* to have (some) fun; *(plaisanter)* to be joking *ou* kidding.
rigolo, ote [ʀigɔlo, -ɔt] *a (fam)* funny // *nm/f* comic; *(péj)* fraud, phoney.
rigoureux, euse [ʀiguʀø, -øz] *a (morale)* rigorous, strict; *(personne)* stern, strict; *(climat, châtiment)* rigorous, harsh; *(interdiction, neutralité)* strict.
rigueur [ʀigœʀ] *nf* rigour; strictness; harshness; **être de** ~ to be the rule; **à la** ~ at a pinch; possibly; **tenir** ~ **à qn de qch** to hold sth against sb.
rime [ʀim] *nf* rhyme.
rinçage [ʀɛ̃saʒ] *nm* rinsing (out); *(opération)* rinse.

rincer [ʀɛ̃se] *vt* to rinse; *(récipient)* to rinse out.
ring [ʀiŋ] *nm* (boxing) ring.
ringard, e [ʀɛ̃gaʀ, -aʀd(ə)] *a* old-fashioned.
rions *vb voir* **rire**.
riposter [ʀipɔste] *vi* to retaliate // *vt*: ~ **que** to retort that; ~ **à** *vt* to counter; to reply to.
rire [ʀiʀ] *vi* to laugh; *(se divertir)* to have fun // *nm* laugh; **le** ~ laughter; ~ **de** *vt* to laugh at; **pour** ~ *(pas sérieusement)* for a joke *ou* a laugh.
risée [ʀize] *nf*: **être la** ~ **de** to be the laughing stock of.
risible [ʀizibl(ə)] *a* laughable.
risque [ʀisk(ə)] *nm* risk; **le** ~ danger; **à ses** ~s **et périls** at his own risk.
risqué, e [ʀiske] *a* risky; *(plaisanterie)* risqué, daring.
risquer [ʀiske] *vt* to risk; *(allusion, question)* to venture, hazard; **ça ne risque rien** it's quite safe; ~ **de**: **il risque de se tuer** he could get himself killed; **ce qui risque de se produire** what might *ou* could well happen; **il ne risque pas de recommencer** there's no chance of him doing that again; **se** ~ **à faire** *(tenter)* to venture *ou* dare to do.
rissoler [ʀisɔle] *vi, vt*: **(faire)** ~ to brown.
ristourne [ʀistuʀn(ə)] *nf* rebate.
rite [ʀit] *nm* rite; *(fig)* ritual.
rivage [ʀivaʒ] *nm* shore.
rival, e, aux [ʀival, -o] *a, nm/f* rival.
rivaliser [ʀivalize] *vi*: ~ **avec** to rival, vie with; *(être comparable)* to hold its own against, compare with.
rivalité [ʀivalite] *nf* rivalry.
rive [ʀiv] *nf* shore; *(de fleuve)* bank.
river [ʀive] *vt (clou, pointe)* to clinch; *(plaques)* to rivet together.
riverain, e [ʀivʀɛ̃, -ɛn] *nm/f* riverside *(ou* lakeside) resident; local resident.
rivet [ʀive] *nm* rivet.
rivière [ʀivjɛʀ] *nf* river.
rixe [ʀiks(ə)] *nf* brawl, scuffle.
riz [ʀi] *nm* rice.
R.N. *sigle f de* **route nationale**.
robe [ʀɔb] *nf* dress; *(de juge, d'ecclésiastique)* robe; *(de professeur)* gown; *(pelage)* coat; ~ **de soirée/de mariée** evening/wedding dress; ~ **de chambre** dressing gown; ~ **de grossesse** maternity dress.
robinet [ʀɔbinɛ] *nm* tap.
robot [ʀɔbo] *nm* robot.
robuste [ʀɔbyst(ə)] *a* robust, sturdy.
roc [ʀɔk] *nm* rock.
rocaille [ʀɔkaj] *nf* loose stones *pl*; rocky *ou* stony ground; *(jardin)* rockery, rock garden.
roche [ʀɔʃ] *nf* rock.
rocher [ʀɔʃe] *nm* rock.
rocheux, euse [ʀɔʃø, -øz] *a* rocky.

rodage [ʀɔdaʒ] *nm*: en ~ running in.
roder [ʀɔde] *vt* (*AUTO*) to run in.
rôder [ʀode] *vi* to roam about; (*de façon suspecte*) to lurk (about *ou* around); **rôdeur, euse** *nm/f* prowler.
rogne [ʀɔɲ] *nf*: être en ~ to be in a temper.
rogner [ʀɔɲe] *vt* to clip; ~ **sur** (*fig*) to cut down on back on.
rognons [ʀɔɲɔ̃] *nmpl* kidneys.
roi [ʀwa] *nm* king; le jour *ou* la fête des R~s, les R~s Twelfth Night.
roitelet [ʀwatlɛ] *nm* wren.
rôle [ʀol] *nm* role; (*contribution*) part.
romain, e [ʀɔmɛ̃, -ɛn] *a*, *nm/f* Roman.
roman, e [ʀɔmɑ̃, -an] *a* (*ARCHIT*) Romanesque // *nm* novel; ~ **d'espionnage** spy novel *ou* story; ~ **photo** romantic picture story.
romance [ʀɔmɑ̃s] *nf* ballad.
romancer [ʀɔmɑ̃se] *vt* to make into a novel; to romanticize.
romancier, ière [ʀɔmɑ̃sje, -jɛʀ] *nm/f* novelist.
romanesque [ʀɔmanɛsk(ə)] *a* (*fantastique*) fantastic; storybook *cpd*; (*sentimental*) romantic.
roman-feuilleton [ʀɔmɑ̃fœjtɔ̃] *nm* serialized novel.
romanichel, le [ʀɔmaniʃɛl] *nm/f* gipsy.
romantique [ʀɔmɑ̃tik] *a* romantic.
romarin [ʀɔmaʀɛ̃] *nm* rosemary.
rompre [ʀɔ̃pʀ(ə)] *vt* to break; (*entretien, fiançailles*) to break off // *vi* (*fiancés*) to break it off; se ~ *vi* to break; (*MÉD*) to burst, rupture.
rompu, e [ʀɔ̃py] *a*: ~ **à** with wide experience of; inured to.
ronces [ʀɔ̃s] *nfpl* brambles.
ronchonner [ʀɔ̃ʃɔne] *vi* (*fam*) to grouse, grouch.
rond, e [ʀɔ̃, ʀɔ̃d] *a* a round; (*joues, mollets*) well-rounded; (*fam: ivre*) tight // *nm* (*cercle*) ring; (*fam: sou*): je n'ai plus un ~ I haven't a penny left // *nf* (*gén: de surveillance*) rounds *pl*, patrol; (*danse*) round (dance); (*MUS*) semibreve (*Brit*), whole note (*US*); en ~ (*s'asseoir, danser*) in a ring; à la ~e (*alentour*): à 10 km à la ~e for 10 km round; **rondelet, te** *a* plump.
rondelle [ʀɔ̃dɛl] *nf* (*TECH*) washer; (*tranche*) slice, round.
rondement [ʀɔ̃dmɑ̃] *ad* briskly; frankly.
rondin [ʀɔ̃dɛ̃] *nm* log.
rond-point [ʀɔ̃pwɛ̃] *nm* roundabout.
ronéotyper [ʀɔneɔtipe] *vt* to duplicate.
ronfler [ʀɔ̃fle] *vi* to snore; (*moteur, poêle*) to hum; to roar.
ronger [ʀɔ̃ʒe] *vt* to gnaw (at); (*suj: vers, rouille*) to eat into; se ~ **les sangs** to worry o.s. sick; se ~ **les ongles** to bite one's nails; **rongeur** *nm* rodent.

ronronner [ʀɔ̃ʀɔne] *vi* to purr.
roquet [ʀɔkɛ] *nm* nasty little lap-dog.
roquette [ʀɔkɛt] *nf* rocket.
rosace [ʀɔzas] *nf* (*vitrail*) rose window.
rosbif [ʀɔsbif] *nm*: du ~ roasting beef; (*cuit*) roast beef; un ~ a joint of beef.
rose [ʀoz] *nf* rose // a pink.
rosé, e [ʀoze] *a* pinkish; (*vin*) ~ rosé.
roseau, x [ʀozo] *nm* reed.
rosée [ʀoze] *nf* dew.
roseraie [ʀozʀɛ] *nf* rose garden.
rosier [ʀozje] *nm* rosebush, rose tree.
rosse [ʀɔs] *nf* (*péj: cheval*) nag // *a* nasty, vicious.
rossignol [ʀɔsiɲɔl] *nm* (*ZOOL*) nightingale.
rot [ʀo] *nm* belch; (*de bébé*) burp.
rotatif, ive [ʀɔtatif, -iv] *a* rotary.
rotation [ʀɔtasjɔ̃] *nf* rotation; (*fig*) rotation, swap-around; turnover.
roter [ʀɔte] *vi* (*fam*) to burp, belch.
rôti [ʀoti] *nm*: du ~ roasting meat; (*cuit*) roast meat; un ~ **de bœuf/porc** a joint of beef/pork.
rotin [ʀɔtɛ̃] *nm* rattan (cane); **fauteuil en** ~ cane (arm)chair.
rôtir [ʀotiʀ] *vt*, *vi* (*aussi: faire* ~) to roast; **rôtisserie** *nf* steakhouse; roast meat counter (*ou* shop); **rôtissoire** *nf* (roasting) spit.
rotule [ʀɔtyl] *nf* kneecap, patella.
roturier, ière [ʀɔtyʀje, -jɛʀ] *nm/f* commoner.
rouage [ʀwaʒ] *nm* cog(wheel), gearwheel; (*de montre*) part; (*fig*) cog.
roucouler [ʀukule] *vi* to coo.
roue [ʀu] *nf* wheel; ~ **dentée** cogwheel; ~ **de secours** spare wheel.
roué, e [ʀwe] *a* wily.
rouer [ʀwe] *vt*: ~ **qn de coups** to give sb a thrashing.
rouet [ʀwɛ] *nm* spinning wheel.
rouge [ʀuʒ] *a*, *nm/f* red // *nm* red; (*fard*) rouge; (*vin*) ~ red wine; **sur la liste** ~ ex-directory (*Brit*), unlisted (*US*); **passer au** ~ (*signal*) to go red; (*automobiliste*) to go through a red light; ~ (**à lèvres**) lipstick; ~**-gorge** *nm* robin (redbreast).
rougeole [ʀuʒɔl] *nf* measles *sg*.
rougeoyer [ʀuʒwaje] *vi* to glow red.
rouget [ʀuʒɛ] *nm* mullet.
rougeur [ʀuʒœʀ] *nf* redness.
rougir [ʀuʒiʀ] *vi* (*de honte, timidité*) to blush, flush; (*de plaisir, colère*) to flush; (*fraise, tomate*) to go ou turn red; (*ciel*) to redden.
rouille [ʀuj] *nf* rust.
rouillé, e [ʀuje] *a* rusty.
rouiller [ʀuje] *vt* to rust // *vi* to rust, go rusty; se ~ *vi* to rust.
roulant, e [ʀulɑ̃, -ɑ̃t] *a* (*meuble*) on wheels; (*surface, trottoir*) moving.
rouleau, x [ʀulo] *nm* (*de papier, tissu,*

SPORT) roll; (*de machine à écrire*) roller, platen; (*à mise en plis, à peinture, vague*) roller; ~ **compresseur** steamroller; ~ **à pâtisserie** rolling pin.

roulement [Rulmɑ̃] *nm* (*bruit*) rumbling *q*, rumble; (*rotation*) rotation; turnover; **par ~** on a rota (*Brit*) *ou* rotation (*US*) basis; ~ (**à billes**) ball bearings *pl*; ~ **de tambour** drum roll.

rouler [Rule] *vt* to roll; (*papier, tapis*) to roll up; (*CULIN: pâte*) to roll out; (*fam*) to do, con // *vi* (*bille, boule*) to roll; (*voiture, train*) to go, run; (*automobiliste*) to drive; (*cycliste*) to ride; (*bateau*) to roll; (*tonnerre*) to rumble, roll; **se ~ dans** (*boue*) to roll in; (*couverture*) to roll o.s. (up) in.

roulette [Rulɛt] *nf* (*de table, fauteuil*) castor; (*de pâtissier*) pastry wheel; (*jeu*): **la ~** roulette; **à ~s** on castors.

roulis [Ruli] *nm* roll(ing).

roulotte [Rulɔt] *nf* caravan.

Roumanie [Rumani] *nf* Rumania.

rouquin, e [Rukɛ̃, -in] *nm/f* (*péj*) redhead.

rouspéter [Ruspete] *vi* (*fam*) to moan.

rousse [Rus] *a voir* **roux**.

roussi [Rusi] *nm*: **ça sent le ~** there's a smell of burning; (*fig*) I can smell trouble.

roussir [Rusir] *vt* to scorch // *vi* (*feuilles*) to go *ou* turn brown; (*CULIN*): **faire ~** to brown.

route [Rut] *nf* road; (*fig: chemin*) way; (*itinéraire, parcours*) route; (*fig: voie*) road, path; **par (la) ~** by road; **il y a 3h de ~** it's a 3-hour ride *ou* journey; **en ~** *ad* on the way; **mettre en ~** to start up; **se mettre en ~** to set off; **faire ~ vers** to head towards; ~ **nationale** ≈ A road (*Brit*), ≈ state highway (*US*); **routier, ière** *a* road *cpd* // *nm* (*camionneur*) (long-distance) lorry (*Brit*) *ou* truck (*US*) driver; (*restaurant*) ≈ transport café (*Brit*), ≈ truck stop (*US*) // *nf* (*voiture*) touring car.

routine [Rutin] *nf* routine; **routinier, ière** *a* (*péj*) humdrum; addicted to routine.

rouvrir [Ruvrir] *vt, vi,* **se ~** *vi* to reopen, open again.

roux, rousse [Ru, Rus] *a* red; (*personne*) red-haired // *nm/f* redhead.

royal, e, aux [Rwajal, -o] *a* royal; (*fig*) princely.

royaume [Rwajom] *nm* kingdom; (*fig*) realm; **le R~-Uni** the United Kingdom.

royauté [Rwajote] *nf* (*dignité*) kingship; (*régime*) monarchy.

ruban [Rybɑ̃] *nm* (*gén*) ribbon; (*d'acier*) strip; ~ **adhésif** adhesive tape.

rubéole [Rybeɔl] *nf* German measles *sg*, rubella.

rubis [Rybi] *nm* ruby.

rubrique [Rybrik] *nf* (*titre, catégorie*) heading; (*PRESSE: article*) column.

ruche [Ryʃ] *nf* hive.

rude [Ryd] *a* (*barbe, toile*) rough; (*métier, tâche*) hard, tough; (*climat*) severe, harsh; (*bourru*) harsh, rough; (*fruste*) rugged, tough; (*fam*) jolly good; ~**ment** *ad*; (*fam: très*) terribly; (*: beaucoup*) terribly hard.

rudimentaire [Rydimɑ̃tɛR] *a* rudimentary, basic.

rudoyer [Rydwaje] *vt* to treat harshly.

rue [Ry] *nf* street.

ruée [Rɥe] *nf* rush.

ruelle [Rɥɛl] *nf* alley(-way).

ruer [Rɥe] *vi* (*cheval*) to kick out; **se ~** *vi*: **se ~ sur** to pounce on; **se ~ vers/dans/hors de** to rush *ou* dash towards/into/out of.

rugby [Rygbi] *nm* Rugby (football).

rugir [Ryʒir] *vi* to roar.

rugueux, euse [Rygø, -øz] *a* rough.

ruine [Rɥin] *nf* ruin; ~**s** *nfpl* ruins.

ruiner [Rɥine] *vt* to ruin.

ruisseau, x [Rɥiso] *nm* stream, brook.

ruisseler [Rɥisle] *vi* to stream.

rumeur [RymœR] *nf* (*bruit confus*) rumbling; hubbub *q*; murmur(ing); (*nouvelle*) rumour.

ruminer [Rymine] *vt* (*herbe*) to ruminate; (*fig*) to ruminate on *ou* over, chew over.

rupture [RyptyR] *nf* (*de câble, digue*) breaking; (*de tendon*) rupture, tearing; (*de négociations etc*) breakdown; (*de contrat*) breach; (*séparation, désunion*) break-up, split.

rural, e, aux [RyRal, -o] *a* rural, country *cpd*.

ruse [Ryz] *nf*: **la ~** cunning, craftiness; **trickery**; **une ~** a trick, a ruse; **rusé, e** *a* cunning, crafty.

russe [Rys] *a, nm, nf* Russian.

Russie [Rysi] *nf*: **la ~** Russia.

rustique [Rystik] *a* rustic.

rustre [RystR(ə)] *nm* boor.

rutilant, e [Rytilɑ̃, -ɑ̃t] *a* gleaming.

rythme [Ritm(ə)] *nm* rhythm; (*vitesse*) rate; (*: de la vie*) pace, tempo.

S

s' [s] *pronom voir* **se**.

sa [sa] *dét voir* **son**.

S.A. *sigle voir* **société**.

sable [sabl(ə)] *nm* sand; ~**s mouvants** quicksand(s).

sablé [sable] *nm* shortbread biscuit.

sabler [sable] *vt* to sand; (*contre le verglas*) to grit; ~ **le champagne** to drink champagne.

sablier [sablije] *nm* hourglass; (*de cuisine*) egg timer.

sablonneux, euse [sablɔnø, -øz] *a* sandy.

saborder [sabɔʀde] *vt* (*navire*) to scuttle; (*fig*) to wind up, shut down.

sabot [sabo] *nm* clog; (*de cheval, bœuf*) hoof; ~ **de frein** brake shoe.

saboter [sabɔte] *vt* to sabotage.

sac [sak] *nm* bag; (*à charbon etc*) sack; **mettre à ~** to sack; ~ **à provisions/de voyage** shopping/travelling bag; ~ **de couchage** sleeping bag; ~ **à dos** rucksack; ~ **à main** handbag.

saccade [sakad] *nf* jerk.

saccager [sakaʒe] *vt* (*piller*) to sack; (*dévaster*) to create havoc in.

saccharine [sakaʀin] *nf* saccharin(e).

sacerdoce [saseʀdɔs] *nm* priesthood; (*fig*) calling, vocation.

sache *etc vb voir* **savoir**.

sachet [saʃɛ] *nm* (small) bag; (*de lavande, poudre, shampooing*) sachet; ~ **de thé** tea bag.

sacoche [sakɔʃ] *nf* (*gén*) bag; (*de bicyclette*) saddlebag.

sacre [sakʀ(ə)] *nm* coronation; consecration.

sacré, e [sakʀe] *a* sacred; (*fam: satané*) blasted; (*: fameux*): **un ~ ...** a heck of a ...

sacrement [sakʀəmã] *nm* sacrament.

sacrifice [sakʀifis] *nm* sacrifice.

sacrifier [sakʀifje] *vt* to sacrifice; ~ **à** *vt* to conform to.

sacristie [sakʀisti] *nf* sacristy; (*culte protestant*) vestry.

sadique [sadik] *a* sadistic.

sage [saʒ] *a* wise; (*enfant*) good // *nm* wise man; sage.

sage-femme [saʒfam] *nf* midwife (*pl* wives).

sagesse [saʒɛs] *nf* wisdom.

Sagittaire [saʒitɛʀ] *nm*: **le ~** Sagittarius.

Sahara [saaʀa] *nm*: **le ~** the Sahara (desert).

saignant, e [sɛɲã, -ãt] *a* (*viande*) rare.

saignée [seɲe] *nf* (*fig*) heavy losses *pl*.

saigner [seɲe] *vi* to bleed // *vt* to bleed; (*animal*) to kill (by bleeding); ~ **du nez** to have a nosebleed.

saillie [saji] *nf* (*sur un mur etc*) projection; (*trait d'esprit*) witticism.

saillir [sajiʀ] *vi* to project, stick out; (*veine, muscle*) to bulge.

sain, e [sɛ̃, sɛn] *a* healthy; (*lectures*) wholesome; ~ **et sauf** safe and sound, unharmed; ~ **d'esprit** sound in mind, sane.

saindoux [sɛ̃du] *nm* lard.

saint, e [sɛ̃, sɛ̃t] *a* holy; (*fig*) saintly // *nm/f* saint; **le S~ Esprit** the Holy Spirit *ou* Ghost; **la S~e Vierge** the Blessed Virgin; **la S~-Sylvestre** New Year's Eve; **sainteté** *nf* holiness.

sais *etc vb voir* **savoir**.

saisie [sezi] *nf* seizure; ~ **(de données)** (data) capture.

saisir [seziʀ] *vt* to take hold of, grab; (*fig: occasion*) to seize; (*comprendre*) to grasp; (*entendre*) to get, catch; (*données*) to capture; (*suj: émotions*) to take hold of, come over; (*CULIN*) to fry quickly; (*JUR: biens, publication*) to seize; (*: juridiction*): ~ **un tribunal d'une affaire** to submit *ou* refer a case to a court; **se ~ de** *vt* to seize; **saisissant, e** *a* startling, striking.

saison [sɛzɔ̃] *nf* season; **morte ~** slack season; **saisonnier, ière** *a* seasonal.

sait *vb voir* **savoir**.

salade [salad] *nf* (*BOT*) lettuce *etc*; (*CULIN*) (green) salad; (*fam*) tangle, muddle; ~ **de fruits** fruit salad; **saladier** *nm* (salad) bowl.

salaire [salɛʀ] *nm* (*annuel, mensuel*) salary; (*hebdomadaire, journalier*) pay, wages *pl*; (*fig*) reward; ~ **de base** basic salary (*ou* wage); ~ **minimum interprofessionnel de croissance** (SMIC) *index-linked guaranteed minimum wage*.

salarié, e [salaʀje] *nm/f* salaried employee; wage-earner.

salaud [salo] *nm* (*fam!*) sod (!), bastard (!).

sale [sal] *a* dirty, filthy.

salé, e [sale] *a* (*liquide, saveur*) salty; (*CULIN*) salted; (*fig*) spicy; steep.

saler [sale] *vt* to salt.

saleté [salte] *nf* (*état*) dirtiness; (*crasse*) dirt, filth; (*tache etc*) dirt *q*; (*fig*) dirty trick; rubbish *q*; filth *q*.

salière [saljɛʀ] *nf* saltcellar.

salin, e [salɛ̃, -in] *a* saline // *nf* saltworks *sg*; salt marsh.

salir [saliʀ] *vt* to (make) dirty; (*fig*) to soil the reputation of; **se ~** *vi* to get dirty; **salissant, e** *a* (*tissu*) which shows the dirt; (*métier*) dirty, messy.

salle [sal] *nf* room; (*d'hôpital*) ward; (*de restaurant*) dining room; (*d'un cinéma*) auditorium; (*: public*) audience; **faire ~ comble** to have a full house; ~ **d'attente** waiting room; ~ **de bain(s)** bathroom; ~ **de classe** classroom; ~ **commune** (*d'hôpital*) ward; ~ **de concert** concert hall; ~ **de consultation** consulting room; ~ **d'eau** shower-room; ~ **d'embarquement** (*à l'aéroport*) departure lounge; ~ **de jeux** games room; playroom; ~ **à manger** dining room; ~ **d'opération** (*d'hôpital*) operating theatre; ~ **de séjour** living room; ~ **de spectacle** theatre; cinema; ~ **des ventes** saleroom.

salon [salɔ̃] *nm* lounge, sitting room; (*mobilier*) lounge suite; (*exposition*) exhibition, show; ~ **de thé** tearoom.

salopard [salɔpaʀ] *nm* (*fam!*) bastard (!).

salope [salɔp] *nf* (*fam!*) bitch (!).

saloperie [salɔpʀi] *nf* (*fam!*) filth *q*; dirty trick; rubbish *q*.

salopette [salɔpɛt] *nf* dungarees *pl*;

(d'ouvrier) overall(s).

salsifis [salsifi] nm salsify.

salubre [salybʀ(ə)] a healthy, salubrious.

saluer [salɥe] vt (pour dire bonjour, fig) to greet; (pour dire au revoir) to take one's leave; (MIL) to salute.

salut [saly] nm (sauvegarde) safety; (REL) salvation; (geste) wave; (parole) greeting; (MIL) salute // excl (fam) hi (there).

salutations [salytɑsjɔ̃] nfpl greetings; **recevez mes ~ distinguées ou respectueuses** yours faithfully.

samedi [samdi] nm Saturday.

SAMU [samy] sigle f (= service d'assistance médicale d'urgence) ≈ ambulance (service) (Brit), ≈ paramedics pl (US).

sanction [sɑ̃ksjɔ̃] nf sanction; (fig) penalty; **sanctionner** vt (loi, usage) to sanction; (punir) to punish.

sandale [sɑ̃dal] nf sandal.

sandwich [sɑ̃dwitʃ] nm sandwich.

sang [sɑ̃] nm blood; **en ~** covered in blood; **se faire du mauvais ~** to fret, get in a state.

sang-froid [sɑ̃fʀwa] nm calm, sang-froid; **de ~** in cold blood.

sanglant, e [sɑ̃glɑ̃, -ɑ̃t] a bloody, covered in blood; (combat) bloody.

sangle [sɑ̃gl(ə)] nf strap.

sanglier [sɑ̃glije] nm (wild) boar.

sanglot [sɑ̃glo] nm sob.

sangsue [sɑ̃sy] nf leech.

sanguin, e [sɑ̃gɛ̃, -in] a blood cpd; (fig) fiery.

sanguinaire [sɑ̃ginɛʀ] a bloodthirsty; bloody.

sanisette [sanizɛt] nf (automatic) public toilet.

sanitaire [sanitɛʀ] a health cpd; **~s** nmpl bathroom sg.

sans [sɑ̃] prép without; **~ qu'il s'en aperçoive** without him ou his noticing; **~-abri** nmpl homeless; **~-façon** a inv fuss-free; free and easy; **~-gêne** a inv inconsiderate; **~-logis** nmpl homeless.

santé [sɑ̃te] nf health; **en bonne ~** in good health; **boire à la ~ de qn** to drink (to) sb's health; **'à la ~ de'** 'here's to'; **à ta/votre ~!** cheers!

saoudien, ne [saudjɛ̃, -jɛn] a Saudi Arabian // nm/f: **S~(ne)** Saudi Arabian.

saoul, e [su, sul] a = **soûl, e**.

saper [sape] vt to undermine, sap.

sapeur [sapœʀ] nm sapper; **~-pompier** nm fireman.

saphir [safiʀ] nm sapphire.

sapin [sapɛ̃] nm fir (tree); (bois) fir; **~ de Noël** Christmas tree.

sarcastique [saʀkastik] a sarcastic.

sarcler [saʀkle] vt to weed.

Sardaigne [saʀdɛɲ] nf: **la ~** Sardinia.

sardine [saʀdin] nf sardine.

S.A.R.L. sigle voir **société**.

sas [sas] nm (de sous-marin, d'engin spatial) airlock; (d'écluse) lock.

satané, e [satane] a confounded.

satellite [satelit] nm satellite.

satin [satɛ̃] nm satin.

satire [satiʀ] nf satire; **satirique** a satirical.

satisfaction [satisfaksjɔ̃] nf satisfaction.

satisfaire [satisfɛʀ] vt to satisfy; **~ à** vt (engagement) to fulfil; (revendications, conditions) to satisfy, meet; to comply with; **satisfaisant, e** a satisfactory; (qui fait plaisir) satisfying; **satisfait, e** a satisfied; **satisfait de** happy ou satisfied with.

saturer [satyʀe] vt to saturate.

sauce [sos] nf sauce; (avec un rôti) gravy; **saucière** nf sauceboat.

saucisse [sosis] nf sausage.

saucisson [sosisɔ̃] nm (slicing) sausage.

sauf [sof] prép except; **~ si** (à moins que) unless; **~ erreur** if I'm not mistaken; **~ avis contraire** unless you hear to the contrary.

sauf, sauve [sof, sov] a unharmed, unhurt; (fig: honneur) intact, saved; **laisser la vie sauve à qn** to spare sb's life.

sauge [soʒ] nf sage.

saugrenu, e [sogʀəny] a preposterous.

saule [sol] nm willow (tree).

saumon [somɔ̃] nm salmon inv.

saumure [somyʀ] nf brine.

sauna [sona] nm sauna.

saupoudrer [supudʀe] vt: **~ qch de** to sprinkle sth with.

saur [sɔʀ] am: **hareng ~** smoked ou red herring, kipper.

saurai etc vb voir **savoir**.

saut [so] nm jump; (discipline sportive) jumping; **faire un ~ chez qn** to pop over to sb's (place); **au ~ du lit** on getting out of bed; **~ en hauteur/longueur** high/long jump; **~ à la corde** skipping; **~ à la perche** pole vaulting; **~ périlleux** somersault.

saute [sot] nf sudden change.

saute-mouton [sotmutɔ̃] nm: **jouer à ~** to play leapfrog.

sauter [sote] vi to jump, leap; (exploser) to blow up, explode; (: fusibles) to blow; (se rompre) to snap, burst; (se détacher) to pop out (ou off) // vt to jump (over), leap (over); (fig: omettre) to skip, miss (out); **faire ~** to blow up; to burst open; (CULIN) to sauté; **~ au cou de qn** to fly into sb's arms.

sauterelle [sotʀɛl] nf grasshopper.

sautiller [sotije] vi to hop; to skip.

sautoir [sotwaʀ] nm: **~ (de perles)** string of pearls.

sauvage [sovaʒ] a (gén) wild; (peuplade) savage; (farouche) unsociable;

(*barbare*) wild, savage; (*non officiel*) unauthorized, unofficial // *nm/f* savage; (*timide*) unsociable type.

sauve [sov] *af voir* **sauf**.

sauvegarde [sovgaʀd(ə)] *nf* safeguard; **sauvegarder** *vt* to safeguard; (*INFORM: enregistrer*) to save; (*: copier*) to back up.

sauve-qui-peut [sovkipø] *excl* run for your life!

sauver [sove] *vt* to save; (*porter secours à*) to rescue; (*récupérer*) to salvage, rescue; **se ~** *vi* (*s'enfuir*) to run away; (*fam: partir*) to be off; **sauvetage** *nm* rescue; **sauveteur** *nm* rescuer; **sauvette: à la sauvette** *ad* (*vendre*) without authorization; (*se marier etc*) hastily, hurriedly; **sauveur** *nm* saviour (*Brit*), savior (*US*).

savais *etc vb voir* **savoir**.

savamment [savamɑ̃] *ad* (*avec érudition*) learnedly; (*habilement*) skilfully, cleverly.

savant, e [savɑ̃, -ɑ̃t] *a* scholarly, learned; (*calé*) clever // *nm* scientist.

saveur [savœʀ] *nf* flavour; (*fig*) savour.

savoir [savwaʀ] *vt* to know; (*être capable de*): **il sait nager** he can swim // *nm* knowledge; **se ~** *vi* (*être connu*) to be known; **à ~** *ad* that is, namely; **faire ~ qch à qn** to let sb know sth; **pas que je sache** not as far as I know.

savon [savɔ̃] *nm* (*produit*) soap; (*morceau*) bar of soap; (*fam*): **passer un ~ à qn** to give sb a good dressing-down; **savonnette** *nf* bar of soap; **savonneux, euse** *a* soapy.

savons *vb voir* **savoir**.

savourer [savuʀe] *vt* to savour.

savoureux, euse [savuʀø, -øz] *a* tasty; (*fig*) spicy, juicy.

saxo(phone) [saksɔ(fɔn)] *nm* sax(o-phone).

scabreux, euse [skabʀø, -øz] *a* risky; (*indécent*) improper, shocking.

scandale [skɑ̃dal] *nm* scandal; (*tapage*): **faire du ~** to make a scene, create a disturbance; **faire ~** to scandalize people; **scandaleux, euse** *a* scandalous, outrageous.

scandinave [skɑ̃dinav] *a*, *nm/f* Scandinavian.

Scandinavie [skɑ̃dinavi] *nf* Scandinavia.

scaphandre [skafɑ̃dʀ(ə)] *nm* (*de plongeur*) diving suit; (*de cosmonaute*) space-suit.

scarabée [skaʀabe] *nm* beetle.

sceau, x [so] *nm* seal; (*fig*) stamp, mark.

scélérat, e [seleʀa, -at] *nm/f* villain.

sceller [sele] *vt* to seal.

scénario [senaʀjo] *nm* (*CINÉMA*) scenario; script; (*fig*) scenario.

scène [sɛn] *nf* (*gén*) scene; (*estrade, fig: théâtre*) stage; **entrer en ~** to come on

stage; **mettre en ~** (*THÉÂTRE*) to stage; (*CINÉMA*) to direct; (*fig*) to present, introduce.

sceptique [sɛptik] *a* sceptical.

schéma [ʃema] *nm* (*diagramme*) diagram, sketch; (*fig*) outline; pattern; **schématique** *a* diagrammatic(al), schematic; (*fig*) oversimplified.

sciatique [sjatik] *nf* sciatica.

scie [si] *nf* saw; **~ à découper** fretsaw; **~ à métaux** hacksaw.

sciemment [sjamɑ̃] *ad* knowingly.

science [sjɑ̃s] *nf* science; (*savoir*) knowledge; (*savoir-faire*) art, skill; **~s naturelles** (*SCOL*) natural science *sg*, biology *sg*; **scientifique** *a* scientific // *nm/f* scientist; science student.

scier [sje] *vt* to saw; (*retrancher*) to saw off; **scierie** *nf* sawmill.

scinder [sɛ̃de] *vt*, **se ~** *vi* to split (up).

scintiller [sɛ̃tije] *vi* to sparkle.

scission [sisjɔ̃] *nf* split.

sciure [sjyʀ] *nf*: **~ (de bois)** sawdust.

sclérose [skleʀoz] *nf*: **~ en plaques** multiple sclerosis.

scolaire [skɔlɛʀ] *a* school *cpd*; (*péj*) schoolish; **scolariser** *vt* to provide with schooling (*ou* schools); **scolarité** *nf* schooling.

scooter [skutœʀ] *nm* (motor) scooter.

score [skɔʀ] *nm* score.

scorpion [skɔʀpjɔ̃] *nm* (*signe*): **le S~** Scorpio.

Scotch [skɔtʃ] *nm* ® adhesive tape.

scout, e [skut] *a*, *nm* scout.

script [skʀipt] *nm* printing; (*CINÉMA*) (shooting) script; **~-girl** [-gœʀl] *nf* continuity girl.

scrupule [skʀypyl] *nm* scruple.

scruter [skʀyte] *vt* to scrutinize; (*l'obscurité*) to peer into.

scrutin [skʀytɛ̃] *nm* (*vote*) ballot; (*ensemble des opérations*) poll.

sculpter [skylte] *vt* to sculpt; (*suj: érosion*) to carve; **sculpteur** *nm* sculptor.

sculpture [skyltyʀ] *nf* sculpture; **~ sur bois** wood carving.

se, s' [s(ə)] *pronom* **1** (*emploi réfléchi*) oneself, *m* himself, *f* herself, *sujet non humain* itself; *pl* themselves; **~ voir comme l'on est** to see o.s. as one is

2 (*réciproque*) one another, each other; **ils s'aiment** they love one another *ou* each other

3 (*passif*): **cela ~ répare facilement** it is easily repaired

4 (*possessif*): **~ casser la jambe/laver les mains** to break one's leg/wash one's hands; *autres emplois pronominaux: voir le verbe en question.*

séance [seɑ̃s] *nf* (*d'assemblée, récréative*) meeting, session; (*de tribunal*) sitting, session; (*musicale, CINÉMA, THÉÂTRE*) performance; **~ tenante** forthwith.

seau, x [so] *nm* bucket, pail.

sec, sèche [sɛk, sɛʃ] *a* dry; (*raisins, figues*) dried; (*cœur, personne: insensible*) hard, cold // *nm*: **tenir au ~** to keep in a dry place // *ad* hard; **je le bois ~** I drink it straight *ou* neat; **à ~** *a* dried up.

sécateur [sekatœr] *nm* secateurs *pl* (*Brit*), shears *pl*.

sèche [sɛʃ] *af voir* **sec.**

sèche-cheveux [sɛʃʃəvø] *nm inv* hairdrier.

sécher [seʃe] *vt* to dry; (*dessécher: peau, blé*) to dry (out); (: *étang*) to dry up // *vi* to dry; to dry out; to dry up; (*fam: candidat*) to be stumped; **se ~** (*après le bain*) to dry o.s.

sécheresse [sɛʃrɛs] *nf* dryness; (*absence de pluie*) drought.

séchoir [seʃwar] *nm* drier.

second, e [səgɔ̃, -ɔ̃d] *a* second // *nm* (*assistant*) second in command; (*NAVIG*) first mate // *nf* second; **voyager en ~e** to travel second-class; **de ~e main** secondhand; **secondaire** *a* secondary; **seconder** *vt* to assist.

secouer [səkwe] *vt* to shake; (*passagers*) to rock; (*traumatiser*) to shake (up).

secourir [səkurir] *vt* (*aller sauver*) to (go and) rescue; (*prodiguer des soins à*) to help, assist; (*venir en aide à*) to assist, aid; **secourisme** *nm* first aid; life saving.

secours [səkur] *nm* help, aid, assistance // *nmpl* aid *sg*; **au ~!** help!; **appeler au ~** to shout *ou* call for help; **porter ~ à qn** to give sb assistance, help sb; **les premiers ~** first aid *sg*.

secousse [səkus] *nf* jolt, bump; (*électrique*) shock; (*fig: psychologique*) jolt, shock; **~ sismique** *ou* **tellurique** earth tremor.

secret, ète [səkrɛ, -ɛt] *a* secret; (*fig: renfermé*) reticent, reserved // *nm* secret; (*discrétion absolue*): **le ~** secrecy; **au ~** in solitary confinement.

secrétaire [səkretɛr] *nm/f* secretary // *nm* (*meuble*) writing desk; **~ de direction** private *ou* personal secretary; **~ d'État** junior minister; **secrétariat** *nm* (*profession*) secretarial work; (*bureau*) office; (: *d'organisation internationale*) secretariat.

secteur [sɛktœr] *nm* sector; (*ADMIN*) district; (*ÉLEC*): **branché sur le ~** plugged into the mains (supply).

section [sɛksjɔ̃] *nf* section; (*de parcours d'autobus*) fare stage; (*MIL: unité*) platoon; **sectionner** *vt* to sever.

Sécu [seky] *abr f de* **sécurité sociale.**

séculaire [sekylɛr] *a* secular; (*très vieux*) age-old.

sécuriser [sekyrize] *vt* to give (a feeling of) security to.

sécurité [sekyrite] *nf* safety; security; **système de ~** safety system; **être en ~** to be safe; **la ~ routière** road safety; **la ~ sociale** ≈ (the) Social Security (*Brit*), ≈ Welfare (*US*).

sédition [sedisjɔ̃] *nf* insurrection; sedition.

séduction [sedyksjɔ̃] *nf* seduction; (*charme, attrait*) appeal, charm.

séduire [seduir] *vt* to charm; (*femme: abuser de*) to seduce; **séduisant, e** *a* (*femme*) seductive; (*homme, offre*) very attractive.

ségrégation [segregasjɔ̃] *nf* segregation.

seigle [sɛgl(ə)] *nm* rye.

seigneur [sɛɲœr] *nm* lord.

sein [sɛ̃] *nm* breast; (*entrailles*) womb; **au ~ de** *prép* (*équipe, institution*) within; (*flots, bonheur*) in the midst of.

séisme [seism(ə)] *nm* earthquake.

seize [sɛz] *num* sixteen; **seizième** *num* sixteenth.

séjour [seʒur] *nm* stay; (*pièce*) living room; **~ner** *vi* to stay.

sel [sɛl] *nm* salt; (*fig*) wit; spice; **~ de cuisine/de table** cooking/table salt.

sélection [selɛksjɔ̃] *nf* selection; **sélectionner** *vt* to select.

self-service [sɛlfsɛrvis] *a, nm* self-service.

selle [sɛl] *nf* saddle; **~s** *nfpl* (*MÉD*) stools; **seller** *vt* to saddle.

sellette [sɛlɛt] *nf*: **être sur la ~** to be on the carpet.

selon [səlɔ̃] *prép* according to; (*en se conformant à*) in accordance with; **~ que** according to whether; **~ moi** as I see it.

semaine [səmɛn] *nf* week; **en ~** during the week, on weekdays.

semblable [sɑ̃blabl(ə)] *a* similar; (*de ce genre*): **de ~s mésaventures** such mishaps // *nm* fellow creature *ou* man; **~ à** similar to, like.

semblant [sɑ̃blɑ̃] *nm*: **un ~ de vérité** a semblance of truth; **faire ~ (de faire)** to pretend (to do).

sembler [sɑ̃ble] *vb avec attribut* to seem // *vb impersonnel*: **il semble (bien) que/ inutile de** it (really) seems *ou* appears that/useless to; **il me semble que** it seems to me that; I think (that); **comme bon lui semble** as he sees fit.

semelle [səmɛl] *nf* sole; (*intérieure*) insole, inner sole.

semence [səmɑ̃s] *nf* (*graine*) seed.

semer [səme] *vt* to sow; (*fig: éparpiller*) to scatter; (: *confusion*) to spread; (: *poursuivants*) to lose, shake off; **semé de** (*difficultés*) riddled with.

semestre [səmɛstr(ə)] *nm* half-year; (*SCOL*) semester.

séminaire [seminɛr] *nm* seminar.

semi-remorque [səmirəmɔrk(ə)] *nm*

semonce [səmɔ̃s] *nf*: un coup de ~ a shot across the bows.

semoule [səmul] *nf* semolina.

sempiternel, le [sɛ̃pitɛʀnɛl] *a* eternal, never-ending.

sénat [sena] *nm* Senate; **sénateur** *nm* Senator.

sens [sɑ̃s] *nm* (PHYSIOL, *instinct*) sense; (*signification*) meaning, sense; (*direction*) direction; **à mon ~** to my mind; **reprendre ses ~** to regain consciousness; **dans le ~ des aiguilles d'une montre** clockwise; **~ commun** common sense; **~ dessus dessous** upside down; **~ interdit, ~ unique** one-way street.

sensass [sɑ̃sas] *a* (*fam*) fantastic.

sensation [sɑ̃sɑsjɔ̃] *nf* sensation; **à ~** (*péj*) sensational.

sensé, e [sɑ̃se] *a* sensible.

sensibiliser [sɑ̃sibilize] *vt*: **~ qn à** to make sb sensitive to.

sensibilité [sɑ̃sibilite] *nf* sensitivity.

sensible [sɑ̃sibl(ə)] *a* sensitive; (*aux sens*) perceptible; (*appréciable: différence, progrès*) appreciable, noticeable; **~ment** *ad* (*notablement*) appreciably, noticeably; (*à peu près*): **ils ont ~ment le même poids** they weigh approximately the same; **~rie** *nf* sentimentality; squeamishness.

sensuel, le [sɑ̃sɥel] *a* sensual; sensuous.

sentence [sɑ̃tɑ̃s] *nf* (*jugement*) sentence; (*adage*) maxim.

sentier [sɑ̃tje] *nm* path.

sentiment [sɑ̃timɑ̃] *nm* feeling; **recevez mes ~s respectueux** yours faithfully; **sentimental, e, aux** *a* sentimental; (*vie, aventure*) love *cpd*.

sentinelle [sɑ̃tinɛl] *nf* sentry.

sentir [sɑ̃tiʀ] *vt* (*par l'odorat*) to smell; (*par le goût*) to taste; (*au toucher, fig*) to feel; (*répandre une odeur de*) to smell of; (: *ressemblance*) to smell like; (*avoir la saveur de*) to taste of; to taste like // *vi* to smell; **~ mauvais** to smell bad; **se ~ bien** to feel good; **se ~ mal** (*être indisposé*) to feel unwell *ou* ill; **se ~ le courage/la force de faire** to feel brave/strong enough to do; **il ne peut pas le ~** (*fam*) he can't stand him.

séparation [sepaʀɑsjɔ̃] *nf* separation; (*cloison*) division, partition; **~ de corps** legal separation.

séparé, e [separe] *a* (*appartements, pouvoirs*) separate; (*époux*) separated; **~ment** *ad* separately.

séparer [separe] *vt* (*gén*) to separate; (*suj: divergences etc*) to divide; to drive apart; (: *différences, obstacles*) to stand between; (*détacher*): **~ qch de** to pull sth (off) from; (*diviser*): **~ qch par** to divide sth (up) with; **~ une pièce en deux** to divide a room into two; **se ~** *vi*

(*époux, amis, adversaires*) to separate, part; (*se diviser: route, tige etc*) to divide; (*se détacher*): **se ~ (de)** to split off (from); to come off; **se ~ de** (*époux*) to separate *ou* part from; (*employé, objet personnel*) to part with.

sept [sɛt] *num* seven.

septembre [sɛptɑ̃bʀ(ə)] *nm* September.

septentrional, e, aux [sɛptɑ̃tʀijɔnal, -o] *a* northern.

septicémie [sɛptisemi] *nf* blood poisoning, septicaemia.

septième [sɛtjɛm] *num* seventh.

septique [sɛptik] *a*: **fosse ~** septic tank.

sépulture [sepyltyʀ] *nf* burial; burial place, grave.

séquelles [sekɛl] *nfpl* after-effects; (*fig*) aftermath *sg*; consequences.

séquestrer [sekɛstʀe] *vt* (*personne*) to confine illegally; (*biens*) to impound.

serai *etc vb voir* **être**.

serein, e [səʀɛ̃, -ɛn] *a* serene; (*jugement*) dispassionate.

serez *vb voir* **être**.

sergent [sɛʀʒɑ̃] *nm* sergeant.

série [seʀi] *nf* (*de questions, d'accidents*) series *inv*; (*de clés, casseroles, outils*) set; (*catégorie: SPORT*) rank; class; **en ~** in quick succession; (COMM) mass *cpd*; **de ~** *a* standard; **hors ~** (COMM) custom-built; (*fig*) outstanding.

sérieusement [seʀjøzmɑ̃] *ad* seriously; reliably; responsibly.

sérieux, euse [seʀjø, -øz] *a* serious; (*élève, employé*) reliable, responsible; (*client, maison*) reliable, dependable // *nm* seriousness; reliability; **garder son ~** to keep a straight face; **prendre qch/qn au ~** to take sth/sb seriously.

serin [səʀɛ̃] *nm* canary.

seringue [səʀɛ̃g] *nf* syringe.

serions *vb voir* **être**.

serment [sɛʀmɑ̃] *nm* (*juré*) oath; (*promesse*) pledge, vow.

sermon [sɛʀmɔ̃] *nm* sermon.

serpent [sɛʀpɑ̃] *nm* snake; **~ à sonnettes** rattlesnake.

serpenter [sɛʀpɑ̃te] *vi* to wind.

serpentin [sɛʀpɑ̃tɛ̃] *nm* (*tube*) coil; (*ruban*) streamer.

serpillière [sɛʀpijɛʀ] *nf* floorcloth.

serre [sɛʀ] *nf* (AGR) greenhouse; **~s** *nfpl* (*griffes*) claws, talons.

serré, e [seʀe] *a* (*réseau*) dense; (*écriture*) close; (*habits*) tight; (*fig: lutte, match*) tight, close-fought; (*passagers etc*) (tightly) packed.

serrer [seʀe] *vt* (*tenir*) to grip *ou* hold tight; (*comprimer, coincer*) to squeeze; (*poings, mâchoires*) to clench; (*suj: vêtement*) to be too tight for; to fit tightly; (*rapprocher*) to close up, move closer together; (*ceinture, nœud, frein, vis*) to tighten // *vi*: **~ à droite** to keep *ou* get over to the right; **se ~** *vi* (*se rap-*

procher) to squeeze up; se ~ **contre qn**
to huddle up to sb; ~ **la main à qn** to
shake sb's hand; ~ **qn dans ses bras** to
hug sb, clasp sb in one's arms.
serrure [seryr] *nf* lock.
serrurier [seryrje] *nm* locksmith.
sert *etc vb voir* **servir**.
sertir [sertir] *vt (pierre)* to set.
servante [servãt] *nf* (maid)servant.
serveur, euse [servœr, -øz] *nm/f*
waiter/waitress.
serviable [servjabl(ə)] *a* obliging, willing to help.
service [servis] *nm (gén)* service; *(série
de repas)*: **premier ~** first sitting;
(assortiment de vaisselle) set, service;
(bureau: de la vente etc) department,
section; *(travail)*: **pendant le ~** on duty;
~**s** *nmpl (travail, ÉCON)* services; **faire
le ~** to serve; **rendre ~ à** to help; **rendre
un ~ à qn** to do sb a favour; **mettre en
~** to put into service *ou* operation; **hors
~** out of order; ~ **après vente** after-sales
service; ~ **militaire** military service; ~
d'ordre police *(ou* stewards) in charge of
maintaining order; ~**s secrets** secret service *sg*.
serviette [servjet] *nf (de table)* (table)
napkin, serviette; *(de toilette)* towel;
(porte-documents) briefcase; ~ **hygiénique** sanitary towel.
servir [servir] *vt (gén)* to serve; *(au
restaurant)* to wait on; *(au magasin)* to
serve, attend to; *(fig: aider)*: ~ **qn** to
aid sb; to serve sb's interests; *(COMM:
rente)* to pay // *vi (TENNIS)* to serve;
(CARTES) to deal; **vous êtes servi?** are
you being served?; **se** ~ *vi (prendre
d'un plat)* to help o.s.; **se** ~ **de** *(plat)* to
help o.s. to; *(voiture, outil, relations)* to
use; ~ **à qn** *(diplôme, livre)* to be of use
to sb; ~ **à qch/faire** *(outil etc)* to be used
for sth/doing; **à quoi cela sert-il** *(de
faire)?* what's the use (of doing)?; **cela
ne sert à rien** it's no use; ~ **(à qn) de** to
serve as (for sb); ~ **à dîner (à qn)** to
serve dinner (to sb).
serviteur [servitœr] *nm* servant.
servitude [servityd] *nf* servitude; *(fig)*
constraint.
ses [se] *dét voir* **son**.
seuil [sœj] *nm* doorstep; *(fig)* threshold.
seul, e [sœl] *a (sans compagnie)* alone;
(avec nuance affective: isolé) lonely;
(unique): **un ~ livre** only one book, a
single book; **le ~ livre** the only book; ~
ce livre, ce livre ~ this book alone, only
this book // *ad (vivre)* alone, on one's
own; **parler tout ~** to talk to oneself;
faire qch (tout) ~ to do sth (all) on one's
own *ou* (all) by oneself // *nm, nf*: **il en
reste un(e)** ~**(e)** there's only one left; **à
lui (tout)** ~ single-handed, on his own.
seulement [sœlmã] *ad* only; **non** ~ ...
mais aussi *ou* **encore** not only ... but

also.
sève [sev] *nf* sap.
sévère [sever] *a* severe.
sévices [sevis] *nmpl* (physical) cruelty
sg, ill treatment *sg*.
sévir [sevir] *vi (punir)* to use harsh
measures, crack down; *(suj: fléau)* to
rage, be rampant.
sevrer [səvre] *vt (enfant etc)* to wean.
sexe [seks(ə)] *nm* sex; *(organe mâle)*
member.
sexuel, le [seksɥel] *a* sexual.
seyant, e [sejã, -ãt] *a* becoming.
shampooing [ʃãpwɛ̃] *nm* shampoo; **se
faire un** ~ to shampoo one's hair.
short [ʃɔrt] *nm* (pair of) shorts *pl*.
si [si] ♦ *nm (MUS)* B; *(en chantant la
gamme)* ti
♦ *ad* **1** *(oui)* yes
2 *(tellement)* so; ~ **gentil/rapidement** so
kind/fast; *(tant et)* ~ **bien que** so much
so that; ~ **rapide qu'il soit** however fast
he may be
♦ *cj* if; ~ **tu veux** if you want; **je me
demande** ~ I wonder if *ou* whether; ~
seulement if only.
Sicile [sisil] *nf*: **la** ~ Sicily.
SIDA [sida] *sigle m* (= *syndrome
immuno-déficitaire acquis)* AIDS *sg*.
sidéré, e [sidere] *a* staggered.
sidérurgie [sideryrʒi] *nf* steel industry.
siècle [sjɛkl(ə)] *nm* century; *(époque)*
age.
siège [sjɛʒ] *nm* seat; *(d'entreprise)* head
office; *(d'organisation)* headquarters *pl*;
(MIL) siege; ~ **social** registered office.
siéger [sjeʒe] *vi* to sit.
sien, ne [sjɛ̃, sjɛn] *pronom*: **le(la)
~(ne), les** ~**s(~nes)** his; hers; its; **faire
des** ~**nes** *(fam)* to be up to one's (usual)
tricks; **les** ~**s** *(sa famille)* one's family.
sieste [sjɛst(ə)] *nf* (afternoon) snooze *ou*
nap, siesta; **faire la** ~ to have a snooze
ou nap.
sieur [sjœr] *nm*: **le** ~ **Thomas** Master
Thomas.
sifflement [sifləmã] *nm* whistle, whis-
tling *q*; wheezing *q*; hissing *q*.
siffler [sifle] *vi (gén)* to whistle; *(en
respirant)* to wheeze; *(serpent, vapeur)*
to hiss // *vt (chanson)* to whistle; *(chien
etc)* to whistle for; *(fille)* to whistle at;
(pièce, orateur) to hiss, boo; *(faute)* to
blow one's whistle at; *(fin du match, départ)* to blow one's whistle for; *(fam:
verre)* to guzzle.
sifflet [sifle] *nm* whistle; **coup de** ~ whistle.
siffloter [siflote] *vi, vt* to whistle.
sigle [sigl(ə)] *nm* acronym.
signal, aux [sinal, -o] *nm (signe
convenu, appareil)* signal; *(indice, écriteau)* sign; **donner le** ~ **de** to give the
signal for; ~ **d'alarme** alarm signal; **signaux (lumineux)** *(AUTO)* traffic signals.

signalement [siɲalmɑ̃] *nm* description, particulars *pl*.

signaler [siɲale] *vt* to indicate; to announce; to report; (*faire remarquer*): ~ qch à qn/(à qn) que to point out sth to sb/(to sb) that; se ~ (par) to distinguish o.s. (by).

signaliser [siɲalize] *vt* to put up roadsigns on; to put signals on.

signature [siɲatyʀ] *nf* signature (*action*), signing.

signe [siɲ] *nm* sign; (*TYPO*) mark; faire un ~ de la main to give a sign with one's hand; faire ~ à qn (*fig*) to get in touch with sb; faire ~ à qn d'entrer to motion (to) sb to come in.

signer [siɲe] *vt* to sign; se ~ *vi* to cross o.s.

signet [siɲɛ] *nm* bookmark.

significatif, ive [siɲifikatif, -iv] *a* significant.

signification [siɲifikasjɔ̃] *nf* meaning.

signifier [siɲifje] *vt* (*vouloir dire*) to mean; (*faire connaître*): ~ qch à qn to make sth known (to sb); (*JUR*): ~ qch à qn to serve notice of sth on sb.

silence [silɑ̃s] *nm* silence; (*MUS*) rest; garder le ~ to keep silent, say nothing; passer sous ~ to pass over (in silence); **silencieux, euse** *a* quiet, silent // *nm* silencer.

silex [silɛks] *nm* flint.

silhouette [silwɛt] *nf* outline, silhouette; (*lignes, contour*) outline; (*figure*) figure.

silicium [silisjɔm] *nm* silicon; plaquette de ~ silicon chip.

sillage [sijaʒ] *nm* wake; (*fig*) trail.

sillon [sijɔ̃] *nm* furrow; (*de disque*) groove; **sillonner** *vt* to criss-cross.

simagrées [simagʀe] *nfpl* fuss *sg*; airs and graces.

similaire [similɛʀ] *a* similar; **similicuir** *nm* imitation leather; **similitude** *nf* similarity.

simple [sɛ̃pl(ə)] *a* (*gén*) simple; (*non multiple*) single; ~s *nmpl* (*MÉD*) medicinal plants; ~ messieurs *nm* (*TENNIS*) men's singles *sg*; un ~ particulier an ordinary citizen; ~ d'esprit *nm/f* simpleton; ~ soldat private.

simulacre [simylakʀ(ə)] *nm* (*péj*): un ~ de a pretence of.

simuler [simyle] *vt* to sham, simulate.

simultané, e [simyltane] *a* simultaneous.

sincère [sɛ̃sɛʀ] *a* sincere; genuine; **sincérité** *nf* sincerity.

sine qua non [sinekwanɔn] *a*: condition ~ indispensable condition.

singe [sɛ̃ʒ] *nm* monkey; (*de grande taille*) ape.

singer [sɛ̃ʒe] *vt* to ape, mimic.

singeries [sɛ̃ʒʀi] *nfpl* antics; (*simagrées*) airs and graces.

singulariser [sɛ̃gylaʀize] *vt* to mark

out; se ~ *vi* to call attention to o.s.

singularité [sɛ̃gylaʀite] *nf* peculiarity.

singulier, ière [sɛ̃gylje, -jɛʀ] *a* remarkable, singular // *nm* singular.

sinistre [sinistʀ(ə)] *a* sinister // *nm* (*incendie*) blaze; (*catastrophe*) disaster; (*ASSURANCES*) damage (*giving rise to a claim*); **sinistré, e** *a* disaster-stricken // *nm/f* disaster victim.

sinon [sinɔ̃] *cj* (*autrement, sans quoi*) otherwise, or else; (*sauf*) except, other than; (*si ce n'est*) if not.

sinueux, euse [sinɥø, -øz] *a* winding; (*fig*) tortuous.

sinus [sinys] *nm* (*ANAT*) sinus; (*GÉOM*) sine; **sinusite** *nf* sinusitis.

siphon [sifɔ̃] *nm* (*tube, d'eau gazeuse*) siphon; (*d'évier etc*) U-bend.

sirène [siʀɛn] *nf* siren; ~ d'alarme air-raid siren; fire alarm.

sirop [siʀo] *nm* (à *diluer: de fruit etc*) syrup; (*boisson*) fruit drink; (*pharmaceutique*) syrup, mixture.

siroter [siʀɔte] *vt* to sip.

sis, e [si, siz] *a* located.

sismique [sismik] *a* seismic.

site [sit] *nm* (*paysage, environnement*) setting; (*d'une ville etc: emplacement*) site; ~ (*pittoresque*) beauty spot; ~s touristiques places of interest.

sitôt [sito] *ad*: ~ parti as soon as he *etc* had left; ~ après straight after; pas de ~ not for a long time.

situation [sitɥasjɔ̃] *nf* (*gén*) situation; (*d'un édifice, d'une ville*) situation, position; location.

situé, e [sitɥe] *a*: bien ~ well situated; ~ à situated at.

situer [sitɥe] *vt* to site, situate; (*en pensée*) to set, place; se ~ *vi*: se ~ à/près de to be situated at/near.

six [sis] *num* six; **sixième** *num* sixth.

ski [ski] *nm* (*objet*) ski; (*sport*) skiing; faire du ~ to ski; ~ de fond cross-country skiing; ~ nautique water-skiing; ~ de piste downhill skiing; ~ de randonnée cross-country skiing; **skier** *vi* to ski; **skieur, euse** *nm/f* skier.

slip [slip] *nm* (*sous-vêtement*) pants *pl*, briefs *pl*; (*de bain: d'homme*) trunks *pl*; (: *du bikini*) (bikini) briefs *pl*.

slogan [slɔgɑ̃] *nm* slogan.

S.M.I.C. [smik] *sigle m voir* **salaire**.

smoking [smɔkiaj] *nm* dinner *ou* evening suit.

S.N.C.F. *sigle f* (= *société nationale des chemins de fer français*) French railways.

snob [snɔb] *a* snobbish // *nm/f* snob.

sobre [sɔbʀ(ə)] *a* temperate, abstemious; (*élégance, style*) sober; ~ de (*gestes, compliments*) sparing of.

sobriquet [sɔbʀikɛ] *nm* nickname.

social, e, aux [sɔsjal, -o] *a* social.

socialisme [sɔsjalism(ə)] *nm* socialism;

socialiste *nm/f* socialist.
société [sɔsjete] *nf* society; (*sportive*) club; (*COMM*) company; **la ~ d'abondance/de consommation** the affluent/consumer society; **~ anonyme (S.A.)** ≈ limited (*Brit*) *ou* incorporated (*US*) company; **~ à responsabilité limitée (S.A.R.L.)** *type of limited liability company (with non-negotiable shares)*.
sociologie [sɔsjɔlɔʒi] *nf* sociology.
socle [sɔkl(ə)] *nm* (*de colonne, statue*) plinth, pedestal; (*de lampe*) base.
socquette [sɔkɛt] *nf* ankle sock.
sœur [sœʀ] *nf* sister; (*religieuse*) nun, sister.
soi [swa] *pronom* oneself; **cela va de ~** that *ou* it goes without saying; **~-disant** *a inv* so-called // *ad* supposedly.
soie [swa] *nf* silk; (*de porc, sanglier: poil*) bristle; **~rie** *nf* (*tissu*) silk.
soif [swaf] *nf* thirst; **avoir ~** to be thirsty; **donner ~ à qn** to make sb thirsty.
soigné, e [swaɲe] *a* (*tenue*) well-groomed, neat; (*travail*) careful, meticulous; (*fam*) whopping; stiff.
soigner [swaɲe] *vt* (*malade, maladie: suj: docteur*) to treat; (*suj: infirmière, mère*) to nurse, look after; (*blessé*) to tend; (*travail, détails*) to take care over; (*jardin, chevelure, invités*) to look after.
soigneux, euse [swaɲø, -øz] *a* (*propre*) tidy, neat; (*méticuleux*) painstaking, careful; **~ de** careful with.
soi-même [swamɛm] *pronom* oneself.
soin [swɛ̃] *nm* (*application*) care; (*propreté, ordre*) tidiness, neatness; **~s** *nmpl* (*à un malade, blessé*) treatment *sg*, medical attention *sg*; (*attentions, prévenance*) care and attention *sg*; (*hygiène*) care *sg*; **prendre ~ de** to take care of, look after; **prendre ~ de faire** to take care to do; **les premiers ~s** first aid *sg*; **aux bons ~s de** c/o, care of.
soir [swaʀ] *nm* evening; **ce ~** this evening, tonight; **demain ~** tomorrow evening, tomorrow night.
soirée [swaʀe] *nf* evening; (*réception*) party.
soit [swa] *vb voir* être // *cj* (*à savoir*) namely; (*ou*): **~ ... ~** either ... or // *ad* so be it, very well; **~ que ... ~ que ou que** whether ... or whether.
soixantaine [swasɑ̃tɛn] *nf*: **une ~ (de)** sixty or so, about sixty; **avoir la ~ (âge)** to be around sixty.
soixante [swasɑ̃t] *num* sixty; **~-dix** seventy.
soja [sɔʒa] *nm* soya; (*graines*) soya beans *pl*.
sol [sɔl] *nm* ground; (*de logement*) floor; (*revêtement*) flooring *q*; (*territoire, AGR, GÉO*) soil; (*MUS*) G; (: *en chantant la gamme*) so(h).

solaire [sɔlɛʀ] *a* solar, sun *cpd*.
soldat [sɔlda] *nm* soldier.
solde [sɔld(ə)] *nf* pay // *nm* (*COMM*) balance; **~s** *nmpl ou nfpl* (*COMM*) sale goods; sales; **en ~** at sale price.
solder [sɔlde] *vt* (*compte*) to settle; (*marchandise*) to sell at sale price, sell off; **se ~ par** (*fig*) to end in; **article soldé (à) 10 F** item reduced to 10 F.
sole [sɔl] *nf* sole *inv* (*fish*).
soleil [sɔlɛj] *nm* sun; (*lumière*) sun(light); (*temps ensoleillé*) sun(shine); (*BOT*) sunflower; **il fait du ~** it's sunny; **au ~** in the sun.
solennel, le [sɔlanɛl] *a* solemn; ceremonial; **solennité** *nf* (*d'une fête*) solemnity.
solfège [sɔlfɛʒ] *nm* rudiments *pl* of music; (*exercices*) ear training *q*.
solidaire [sɔlidɛʀ] *a* (*personnes*) who stand together, who show solidarity; (*pièces mécaniques*) interdependent; **être ~ de** (*collègues*) to stand by; **solidarité** *nf* solidarity; interdependence; **par solidarité (avec)** in sympathy (with).
solide [sɔlid] *a* solid; (*mur, maison, meuble*) solid, sturdy; (*connaissances, argument*) sound; (*personne, estomac*) robust, sturdy // *nm* solid.
soliste [sɔlist(ə)] *nm/f* soloist.
solitaire [sɔlitɛʀ] *a* (*sans compagnie*) solitary, lonely; (*lieu*) lonely // *nm/f* recluse; loner.
solitude [sɔlityd] *nf* loneliness; (*paix*) solitude.
solive [sɔliv] *nf* joist.
sollicitations [sɔlisitasjɔ̃] *nfpl* entreaties, appeals; enticements; (*TECH*) stress *sg*.
solliciter [sɔlisite] *vt* (*personne*) to appeal to; (*emploi, faveur*) to seek; (*suj: occupations, attractions etc*): **~ qn** to appeal to sb's curiosity *etc*; to entice sb; to make demands on sb's time.
sollicitude [sɔlisityd] *nf* concern.
soluble [sɔlybl(ə)] *a* soluble.
solution [sɔlysjɔ̃] *nf* solution; **~ de facilité** easy way out.
solvable [sɔlvabl(ə)] *a* solvent.
sombre [sɔ̃bʀ(ə)] *a* dark; (*fig*) gloomy.
sombrer [sɔ̃bʀe] *vi* (*bateau*) to sink; **~ dans** (*misère, désespoir*) to sink into.
sommaire [sɔmɛʀ] *a* (*simple*) basic; (*expéditif*) summary // *nm* summary.
sommation [sɔmasjɔ̃] *nf* (*JUR*) summons *sg*; (*avant de faire feu*) warning.
somme [sɔm] *nf* (*MATH*) sum; (*fig*) amount; (*argent*) sum, amount // *nm*: **faire un ~** to have a (short) nap; **en ~** *ad* all in all; **~ toute** *ad* all in all.
sommeil [sɔmɛj] *nm* sleep; **avoir ~** to be sleepy; **sommeiller** *vi* to doze; (*fig*) to lie dormant.
sommelier [sɔməlje] *nm* wine waiter.

sommer [sɔme] vt: ~ qn de faire to command ou order sb to do; (JUR) to summon sb to do.

sommes vb voir **être**.

sommet [sɔmɛ] nm top; (d'une montagne) summit, top; (fig: de la perfection, gloire) height.

sommier [sɔmje] nm (bed) base.

sommité [sɔmite] nf prominent person, leading light.

somnambule [sɔmnãbyl] nm/f sleepwalker.

somnifère [sɔmnifɛr] nm sleeping drug q (ou pill).

somnoler [sɔmnɔle] vi to doze.

somptueux, euse [sɔptɥø, -øz] a sumptuous; lavish.

son [sɔ̃], **sa** [sa], pl **ses** [se] dét (antécédent humain mâle) his; (: femelle) her; (: valeur indéfinie) one's, his/her; (: non humain) its.

son [sɔ̃] nm sound; (de blé) bran.

sondage [sɔ̃daʒ] nm: ~ (d'opinion) (opinion) poll.

sonde [sɔ̃d] nf (NAVIG) lead ou sounding line; (MÉD) probe; catheter; feeding tube; (TECH) borer, driller; (pour fouiller etc) probe.

sonder [sɔ̃de] vt (NAVIG) to sound; (atmosphère, plaie, bagages etc) to probe; (TECH) to bore, drill; (fig) to sound out; to probe.

songe [sɔ̃ʒ] nm dream.

songer [sɔ̃ʒe] vi: ~ à (penser à) to think of; ~ que to consider that; to think that; **songeur, euse** a pensive.

sonnant, e [sɔnã, -ãt] a: à 8 heures ~es on the stroke of 8.

sonné, e [sɔne] a (fam) cracked; il est midi ~ it's gone twelve.

sonner [sɔne] vi to ring // vt (cloche) to ring; (glas, tocsin) to sound; (portier, infirmière) to ring for; (messe) to ring the bell for; ~ faux (instrument) to sound out of tune; (rire) to ring false; ~ les heures to strike the hours.

sonnerie [sɔnri] nf (son) ringing; (sonnette) bell; (mécanisme d'horloge) striking mechanism; ~ d'alarme alarm bell.

sonnette [sɔnɛt] nf bell; ~ d'alarme alarm bell; ~ de nuit night-bell.

sono [sɔno] abr f de **sonorisation**.

sonore [sɔnɔr] a (voix) sonorous, ringing; (salle, métal) resonant; (ondes, film, signal) sound cpd.

sonorisation [sɔnɔrizasjɔ̃] nf (installations) public address system, P.A. system.

sonorité [sɔnɔrite] nf (de piano, violon) tone; (de voix, mot) sonority; (d'une salle) resonance; acoustics pl.

sont vb voir **être**.

sophistiqué, e [sɔfistike] a sophisticated.

sorbet [sɔrbɛ] nm water ice, sorbet.

sorcellerie [sɔrsɛlri] nf witchcraft q.

sorcier, ière [sɔrsje, -jɛr] nm/f sorcerer/witch ou sorceress.

sordide [sɔrdid] a sordid; squalid.

sornettes [sɔrnɛt] nfpl twaddle sg.

sort [sɔr] nm (fortune, destinée) fate; (condition, situation) lot; (magique) curse, spell; tirer au ~ to draw lots.

sorte [sɔrt(ə)] nf sort, kind; de la ~ ad in that way; de (telle) ~ que, en ~ que so that; so much so that; faire en ~ que to see to it that.

sortie [sɔrti] nf (issue) way out, exit; (MIL) sortie; (fig: verbale) outburst; sally; (promenade) outing; (le soir: au restaurant etc) night out; (COMM: somme): ~s items of expenditure; outgoings sans sg; ~ de bain (vêtement) bathrobe; ~ de secours emergency exit.

sortilège [sɔrtilɛʒ] nm (magic) spell.

sortir [sɔrtir] vi (gén) to come out; (partir, se promener, aller au spectacle etc) to go out; (numéro gagnant) to come up // vt (gén) to take out; (produit, ouvrage, modèle) to bring out; (INFORM) to output; (: sur papier) to print out; (fam: expulser) to throw out; ~ de (gén) to leave; (endroit) to go (ou come) out of, leave; (rainure etc) to come out of; (cadre, compétence) to be outside; se ~ de (affaire, situation) to get out of; s'en ~ (malade) to pull through; (d'une difficulté etc) to get through.

sosie [sozi] nm double.

sot, sotte [so, sɔt] a silly, foolish // nm/f fool; **sottise** nf silliness, foolishness; silly ou foolish thing.

sou [su] nm: près de ses ~s tight-fisted; sans le ~ penniless.

soubresaut [subrəso] nm start; jolt.

souche [suʃ] nf (d'arbre) stump; (de carnet) counterfoil (Brit), stub; de vieille ~ of old stock.

souci [susi] nm (inquiétude) worry; (préoccupation) concern; (BOT) marigold; se faire du ~ to worry.

soucier [susje]: se ~ de vt to care about.

soucieux, euse [susjø, -øz] a concerned, worried.

soucoupe [sukup] nf saucer; ~ volante flying saucer.

soudain, e [sudɛ̃, -ɛn] a (douleur, mort) sudden // ad suddenly, all of a sudden.

soude [sud] nf soda.

souder [sude] vt (avec fil à souder) to solder; (par soudure autogène) to weld; (fig) to bind together.

soudoyer [sudwaje] vt (péj) to bribe.

soudure [sudyr] nf soldering; welding; (joint) soldered joint; weld.

souffert, e [sufɛr, -ɛrt(ə)] pp de **souffrir**.

souffle [sufl(ə)] nm (en expirant) breath; (en soufflant) puff, blow;

(respiration) breathing; (d'explosion, de ventilateur) blast; (du vent) blowing; **être à bout de ~** to be out of breath; **un ~ d'air** ou **de vent** a breath of air, a puff of wind.

soufflé, e [sufle] a (fam: stupéfié) staggered // nm (CULIN) soufflé.

souffler [sufle] vi (gén) to blow; (haleter) to puff (and blow) // vt (feu, bougie) to blow out; (chasser: poussière etc) to blow away; (TECH: verre) to blow; (suj: explosion) to destroy (with its blast); (dire): **~ qch à qn** to whisper sth to sb; (fam: voler): **~ qch à qn** to pinch sth from sb.

soufflet [sufle] nm (instrument) bellows pl; (gifle) slap (in the face).

souffleur [suflœʀ] nm (THÉÂTRE) prompter.

souffrance [sufʀɑ̃s] nf suffering; **en ~** (marchandise) awaiting delivery; (affaire) pending.

souffrant, e [sufʀɑ̃, -ɑ̃t] a unwell.

souffre-douleur [sufʀədulœʀ] nm inv butt, underdog.

souffrir [sufʀiʀ] vi to suffer; to be in pain // vt to suffer, endure; (supporter) to bear, stand; (admettre: exception etc) to allow ou admit of; **~ de** (maladie, froid) to suffer from.

soufre [sufʀ(ə)] nm sulphur.

souhait [swe] nm wish; **tous nos ~s de** good wishes ou our best wishes for; **riche etc à ~** as rich etc as one could wish; **à vos ~s!** bless you!

souhaitable [swetabl(ə)] a desirable.

souhaiter [swete] vt to wish for; **~ la bonne année à qn** to wish sb a happy New Year.

souiller [suje] vt to dirty, soil; (fig) to sully, tarnish.

soûl, e [su, sul] a drunk // nm: **tout son ~** to one's heart's content.

soulagement [sulaʒmɑ̃] nm relief.

soulager [sulaʒe] vt to relieve.

soûler [sule] vt: **~ qn** to get sb drunk; (suj: boisson) to make sb drunk; (fig) to make sb's head spin ou reel; **se ~** vi to get drunk.

soulever [sulve] vt to lift; (vagues, poussière) to send up; (peuple) to stir up (to revolt); (enthousiasme) to arouse; (question, débat) to raise; **se ~** vi (peuple) to rise up; (personne couchée) to lift o.s. up; **cela me soulève le cœur** it makes me feel sick.

soulier [sulje] nm shoe.

souligner [suliɲe] vt to underline; (fig) to emphasize; to stress.

soumettre [sumɛtʀ] vt (pays) to subject, subjugate; (rebelle) to put down, subdue; **~ qn/qch à** to subject sb/sth to; **~ qch à qn** (projet etc) to submit sth to sb; **se ~ (à)** to submit (to).

soumis, e [sumi, -iz] a submissive;

revenus ~ à l'impôt taxable income.

soumission [sumisjɔ̃] nf submission; (docilité) submissiveness; (COMM) tender.

soupape [supap] nf valve.

soupçon [supsɔ̃] nm suspicion; (petite quantité): **un ~ de** a hint ou touch of; **soupçonner** vt to suspect; **soupçonneux, euse** a suspicious.

soupe [sup] nf soup; **~ au lait** a inv quick-tempered.

souper [supe] vi to have supper // nm supper.

soupeser [supəze] vt to weigh in one's hand(s); (fig) to weigh up.

soupière [supjɛʀ] nf (soup) tureen.

soupir [supiʀ] nm sigh; (MUS) crotchet rest.

soupirail, aux [supiʀaj, -o] nm (small) basement window.

soupirer [supiʀe] vi to sigh; **~ après qch** to yearn for sth.

souple [supl(ə)] a supple; (fig: règlement, caractère) flexible; (: démarche, taille) lithe, supple.

source [suʀs(ə)] nf (point d'eau) spring; (d'un cours d'eau, fig) source; **de bonne ~** on good authority.

sourcil [suʀsij] nm (eye)brow.

sourciller [suʀsije] vi: **sans ~** without turning a hair ou batting an eyelid.

sourcilleux, euse [suʀsijø, -øz] a pernickety.

sourd, e [suʀ, suʀd(ə)] a deaf; (bruit, voix) muffled; (douleur) dull; (lutte) silent, hidden // nm/f deaf person.

sourdine [suʀdin] nf (MUS) mute; **en ~** ad softly, quietly.

sourd-muet, sourde-muette [suʀmɥɛ, suʀdmɥɛt] a deaf-and-dumb // nm/f deaf-mute.

souriant, e [suʀjɑ̃, -ɑ̃t] a cheerful.

souricière [suʀisjɛʀ] nf mousetrap; (fig) trap.

sourire [suʀiʀ] nm smile // vi to smile; **~ à qn** to smile at sb; (fig) to appeal to sb; to smile on sb; **garder le ~** to keep smiling.

souris [suʀi] nf mouse (pl mice).

sournois, e [suʀnwa, -waz] a deceitful, underhand.

sous [su] prép (gén) under; **~ la pluie/le soleil** in the rain/sunshine; **~ terre** a, ad underground; **~ peu** ad shortly, before long.

sous-alimenté, e [suzalimɑ̃te] a undernourished.

sous-bois [subwa] nm inv undergrowth.

souscrire [suskʀiʀ] vt: **~ à** vt to subscribe to.

sous-directeur, trice [sudiʀɛktœʀ, -tʀis] nm/f assistant manager/manageress.

sous-entendre [suzɑ̃tɑ̃dʀ(ə)] vt to imply, infer; **sous-entendu, e** a implied;

(LING) understood // *nm* innuendo, insinuation.

sous-estimer [suzɛstime] *vt* to underestimate.

sous-jacent, e [suʒasɑ̃, -ɑ̃t] *a* underlying.

sous-louer [sulwe] *vt* to sublet.

sous-main [sumɛ̃] *nm inv* desk blotter; en ~ *ad* secretly.

sous-marin, e [sumaRɛ̃, -in] *a (flore, volcan)* submarine; *(navigation, pêche, explosif)* underwater // *nm* submarine.

sous-officier [suzɔfisje] *nm* ≈ non-commissioned officer (N.C.O.).

sous-produit [supRɔdɥi] *nm* by-product; *(fig: péj)* pale imitation.

soussigné, e [susiɲe] *a*: je ~ I the undersigned.

sous-sol [susɔl] *nm* basement.

sous-titre [sutitR(ə)] *nm* subtitle.

soustraction [sustRaksjɔ̃] *nf* subtraction.

soustraire [sustRɛR] *vt* to subtract, take away; *(dérober)*: ~ **qch à qn** to remove sth from sb; se ~ **à** *(danger)* to shield sb from; se ~ **à** *(autorité etc)* to elude, escape from.

sous-traitant [sutRɛtɑ̃] *nm* subcontractor.

sous-vêtements [suvɛtmɑ̃] *nmpl* underwear *sg*.

soutane [sutan] *nf* cassock, soutane.

soute [sut] *nf* hold.

soutènement [sutɛnmɑ̃] *nm*: mur de ~ retaining wall.

souteneur [sutnœR] *nm* procurer.

soutenir [sutniR] *vt* to support; *(assaut, choc)* to stand up to, withstand; *(intérêt, effort)* to keep up; *(assurer)*: ~ **que** to maintain that; ~ **la comparaison avec** to bear *ou* stand comparison with; **soutenu, e** *a (efforts)* sustained, unflagging; *(style)* elevated.

souterrain, e [sutɛRɛ̃, -ɛn] *a* underground // *nm* underground passage.

soutien [sutjɛ̃] *nm* support; ~ **de famille** breadwinner.

soutien-gorge [sutjɛ̃gɔRʒ(ə)] *nm* bra.

soutirer [sutiRe] *vt*: ~ **qch à qn** to squeeze *ou* get sth out of sb.

souvenir [suvniR] *nm (réminiscence)* memory; *(objet)* souvenir // *vb*: se ~ **de** *vt* to remember; se ~ **que** to remember that; en ~ **de** in memory *ou* remembrance of.

souvent [suvɑ̃] *ad* often; peu ~ seldom, infrequently.

souverain, e [suvRɛ̃, -ɛn] *a* sovereign; *(fig: mépris)* supreme // *nm/f* sovereign, monarch.

soviétique [sɔvjetik] *a* Soviet // *nm/f*: S~ Soviet citizen.

soyeux, euse [swajø, øz] *a* silky.

soyons etc *vb voir* **être**.

spacieux, euse [spasjø, -øz] *a* spa-cious; roomy.

spaghettis [spageti] *nmpl* spaghetti *sg*.

sparadrap [spaRadRa] *nm* sticking plaster *(Brit)*, bandaid ® *(US)*.

spatial, e, aux [spasjal, -o] *a (AVIAT)* space *cpd*.

speaker, ine [spikœR, -kRin] *nm/f* announcer.

spécial, e, aux [spesjal, -o] *a* special; *(bizarre)* peculiar; ~**ement** *ad* especially, particularly; *(tout exprès)* specially.

spécialiser [spesjalize]: se ~ *vi* to specialize.

spécialiste [spesjalist(ə)] *nm/f* specialist.

spécialité [spesjalite] *nf* speciality; *(SCOL)* special field.

spécifier [spesifje] *vt* to specify, state.

spécimen [spesimɛn] *nm* specimen; *(revue etc)* specimen *ou* sample copy.

spectacle [spɛktakl(ə)] *nm (tableau, scène)* sight; *(représentation)* show; *(industrie)* show business; **spectaculaire** *a* spectacular.

spectateur, trice [spɛktatœR, -tRis] *nm/f (CINÉMA etc)* member of the audience; *(SPORT)* spectator; *(d'un événement)* onlooker, witness.

spéculer [spekyle] *vi* to speculate; ~ **sur** *(COMM)* to speculate in; *(réfléchir)* to speculate on.

spéléologie [speleɔlɔʒi] *nf* potholing.

sperme [spɛRm(ə)] *nm* semen, sperm.

sphère [sfɛR] *nf* sphere.

spirale [spiRal] *nf* spiral.

spirituel, le [spiRitɥɛl] *a* spiritual; *(fin, piquant)* witty.

spiritueux [spiRitɥø] *nm* spirit.

splendide [splɑ̃did] *a* splendid; magnificent.

spontané, e [spɔ̃tane] *a* spontaneous.

sport [spɔR] *nm* sport // *a inv (vêtement)* casual; **faire du** ~ to do sport; ~**s d'hiver** winter sports; **sportif, ive** *a (journal, association, épreuve)* sports *cpd*; *(allure, démarche)* athletic; *(attitude, esprit)* sporting.

spot [spɔt] *nm (lampe)* spot(light); *(annonce)*: ~ **(publicitaire)** commercial (break).

square [skwaR] *nm* public garden(s).

squelette [skəlɛt] *nm* skeleton; **squelettique** *a* scrawny; *(fig)* skimpy.

stabiliser [stabilize] *vt* to stabilize; *(terrain)* to consolidate.

stable [stabl(ə)] *a* stable, steady.

stade [stad] *nm (SPORT)* stadium; *(phase, niveau)* stage.

stage [staʒ] *nm* training period; training course; **stagiaire** *nm/f, a* trainee.

stalle [stal] *nf* stall, box.

stand [stɑ̃d] *nm (d'exposition)* stand; *(de foire)* stall; ~ **de tir** *(à la foire, SPORT)* shooting range.

standard [stɑ̃daʀ] *a inv* standard // *nm* switchboard; **standardiste** *nm/f* switchboard operator.

standing [stɑ̃diaj] *nm* standing; **immeuble de grand ~** block of luxury flats (*Brit*), condo(minium) (*US*).

starter [staʀtɛʀ] *nm* (*AUTO*) choke.

station [stɑsjɔ̃] *nf* station; (*de bus*) stop; (*de villégiature*) resort; (*posture*): **la ~ debout** standing, an upright posture; **~ de ski** ski resort; **~ de taxis** taxi rank (*Brit*) *ou* stand (*US*).

stationnement [stɑsjɔnmɑ̃] *nm* parking.

stationner [stɑsjɔne] *vi* to park.

station-service [stɑsjɔ̃sɛʀvis] *nf* service station.

statistique [statistik] *nf* (*science*) statistics *sg*; (*rapport, étude*) statistic // *a* statistical.

statue [staty] *nf* statue.

statuer [statɥe] *vi*: **~ sur** to rule on, give a ruling on.

statut [staty] *nm* status; **~s** *nmpl* (*JUR, ADMIN*) statutes; **statutaire** *a* statutory.

Sté *abr de* **société**.

steak [stɛk] *nm* steak.

sténo... [stenɔ] *préfixe*: **~(dactylo)** *nf* shorthand typist (*Brit*), stenographer (*US*); **~(graphie)** *nf* shorthand.

stéréo(phonique) [steʀeɔ(fɔnik)] *a* stereo(phonic).

stérile [steʀil] *a* sterile; (*terre*) barren; (*fig*) fruitless, futile.

stérilet [steʀilɛ] *nm* coil, loop.

stériliser [steʀilize] *vt* to sterilize.

stigmates [stigmat] *nmpl* scars, marks.

stimulant [stimylɑ̃] *nm* (*fig*) stimulus (*pl* i), incentive.

stimuler [stimyle] *vt* to stimulate.

stipuler [stipyle] *vt* to stipulate.

stock [stɔk] *nm* stock; **~ d'or** (*FINANCE*) gold reserves *pl*; **~er** *vt* to stock.

stop [stɔp] *nm* (*AUTO*: *écriteau*) stop sign; (: *signal*) brake-light.

stopper [stɔpe] *vt* to stop, halt; (*COUTURE*) to mend // *vi* to stop, halt.

store [stɔʀ] *nm* blind; (*de magasin*) shade, awning.

strabisme [stʀabism(ə)] *nm* squinting.

strapontin [stʀapɔ̃tɛ̃] *nm* jump *ou* foldaway seat.

stratégie [stʀateʒi] *nf* strategy; **stratégique** *a* strategic.

stressant, e [stʀesɑ̃, -ɑ̃t] *a* stressful.

strict, e [stʀikt(ə)] *a* strict; (*tenue, décor*) severe, plain; **son droit le plus ~** his most basic right; **le ~ nécessaire/minimum** the bare essentials/minimum.

strie [stʀi] *nf* streak.

strophe [stʀɔf] *nf* verse, stanza.

structure [stʀyktyʀ] *nf* structure; **~s d'accueil** reception facilities.

studieux, euse [stydjø, -øz] *a* studious; devoted to study.

studio [stydjo] *nm* (*logement*) (one-roomed) flatlet (*Brit*) *ou* apartment (*US*); (*d'artiste, TV etc*) studio (*pl* s).

stupéfait, e [stypefɛ, -ɛt] *a* astonished.

stupéfiant [stypefjɑ̃] *nm* (*MÉD*) drug, narcotic.

stupéfier [stypefje] *vt* to stupefy; (*étonner*) to stun, astonish.

stupeur [stypœʀ] *nf* astonishment.

stupide [stypid] *a* stupid; **stupidité** *nf* stupidity; stupid thing (to do *ou* say).

style [stil] *nm* style; **meuble de ~** piece of period furniture.

stylé, e [stile] *a* well-trained.

stylo [stilo] *nm*: **~ (à encre)** (fountain) pen; **~ (à) bille** ball-point pen.

su, e [sy] *pp de* **savoir** // *nm*: **au ~ de** with the knowledge of.

suave [sɥav] *a* sweet; (*goût*) mellow.

subalterne [sybaltɛʀn(ə)] *a* (*employé, officier*) junior; (*rôle*) subordinate, subsidiary // *nm/f* subordinate.

subconscient [sypkɔ̃sjɑ̃] *nm* subconscious.

subir [sybiʀ] *vt* (*affront, dégâts*) to suffer; (*influence, charme*) to be under; (*opération, châtiment*) to undergo.

subit, e [sybi, -it] *a* sudden; **subitement** *ad* suddenly, all of a sudden.

subjectif, ive [sybʒɛktif, -iv] *a* subjective.

subjonctif [sybʒɔ̃ktif] *nm* subjunctive.

submerger [sybmɛʀʒe] *vt* to submerge; (*fig*) to overwhelm.

subordonné, e [sybɔʀdɔne] *a, nm/f* subordinate; **~ à** subordinate to; subject to, depending on.

subornation [sybɔʀnɑsjɔ̃] *nf* bribing.

subrepticement [sybʀɛptismɑ̃] *ad* surreptitiously.

subside [sypsid] *nm* grant.

subsidiaire [sypsidjɛʀ] *a*: **question ~** deciding question.

subsister [sybziste] *vi* (*rester*) to remain, subsist; (*vivre*) to live; (*survivre*) to live on.

substance [sypstɑ̃s] *nf* substance.

substituer [sypstitɥe] *vt*: **~ qn/qch à** to substitute sb/sth for; **se ~ à qn** (*évincer*) to substitute o.s. for sb.

substitut [sypstity] *nm* (*JUR*) deputy public prosecutor; (*succédané*) substitute.

subtil, e [syptil] *a* subtle.

subtiliser [syptilize] *vt*: **~ qch (à qn)** to spirit sth away (from sb).

subvenir [sybvəniʀ] **~ à** *vt* to meet.

subvention [sybvɑ̃sjɔ̃] *nf* subsidy, grant; **subventionner** *vt* to subsidize.

suc [syk] *nm* (*BOT*) sap; (*de viande, fruit*) juice.

succédané [syksedane] *nm* substitute.

succéder [syksede]: **~ à** *vt* (*directeur, roi etc*) to succeed; (*venir après: dans* *une série*) to follow, succeed; **se ~** *vi* (*accidents, années*) to follow one another.

succès [syksɛ] *nm* success; **avoir du ~** to be a success, be successful; **~ de librairie** bestseller; **~** (*féminins*) conquests; **à ~** successful.

succession [syksesjɔ̃] *nf* (*série, POL*) succession; (*JUR: patrimoine*) estate, inheritance.

succomber [sykɔ̃be] *vi* to die, succumb; (*fig*): **~ à** to give way to, succumb to.

succursale [sykyrsal] *nf* branch.

sucer [syse] *vt* to suck.

sucette [sysɛt] *nf* (*bonbon*) lollipop; (*de bébé*) dummy (*Brit*), pacifier (*US*).

sucre [sykr(ə)] *nm* (*substance*) sugar; (*morceau*) lump of sugar, sugar lump *ou* cube; **~ en morceaux/cristallisé/en poudre** lump/granulated/caster sugar; **~ d'orge** barley sugar; **sucré, e** *a* (*produit alimentaire*) sweetened; (*au goût*) sweet; (*péj*) sugary, honeyed; **sucrer** *vt* (*thé, café*) to sweeten, put sugar in; **sucreries** *nfpl* (*bonbons*) sweets, sweet things; **sucrier** *nm* (*récipient*) sugar bowl.

sud [syd] *nm*: **le ~** the south // *a inv* south; (*côte*) south, southern; **au ~** (*situation*) in the south; (*direction*) to the south; **au ~ de** (to the) south of; **~africain, e** *a, nm/f* South African; **~américain, e** *a, nm/f* South American.

sud-est [sydɛst] *nm, a inv* south-east.

sud-ouest [sydwɛst] *nm, a inv* south-west.

Suède [sɥɛd] *nf*: **la ~** Sweden; **suédois, e** *a* Swedish // *nm/f*: **Suédois, e** Swede // *nm* (*LING*) Swedish.

suer [sɥe] *vi* to sweat; (*suinter*) to ooze.

sueur [sɥœr] *nf* sweat; **en ~** sweating, in a sweat.

suffire [syfir] *vi* (*être assez*): **~** (**à qn/pour qch/pour faire**) to be enough *ou* sufficient (for sb/for sth/to do); **cela suffit pour les irriter/qu'ils se fâchent** it's enough to annoy them/for them to get angry; **il suffit d'une négligence/qu'on oublie pour que ...** it only takes one act of carelessness/one only needs to forget for ....

suffisamment [syfizamɑ̃] *ad* sufficiently, enough; **~ de** sufficient, enough.

suffisant, e [syfizɑ̃, -ɑ̃t] *a* (*temps, ressources*) sufficient; (*résultats*) satisfactory; (*vaniteux*) self-important, bumptious.

suffixe [syfiks(ə)] *nm* suffix.

suffoquer [syfɔke] *vt* to choke, suffocate; (*stupéfier*) to stagger, astound // *vi* to choke, suffocate.

suffrage [syfraʒ] *nm* (*POL: voix*) vote; (*du public etc*) approval *q*.

suggérer [syʒere] *vt* to suggest; **suggestion** *nf* suggestion.

suicide [sɥisid] *nm* suicide.

suicider [sɥiside]: **se ~** *vi* to commit suicide.

suie [sɥi] *nf* soot.

suinter [sɥɛ̃te] *vi* to ooze.

suis *vb voir* **être; suivre**.

suisse [sɥis] *a* Swiss // *nm*: **S~** Swiss *pl inv*; (*bedeau*) ≈ verger // *nf*: **la S~** Switzerland; **la S~ romande/allemande** French-speaking/German-speaking Switzerland; **Suissesse** *nf* Swiss (woman *ou* girl).

suite [sɥit] *nf* (*continuation: d'énumération etc*) rest, remainder; (: *de feuilleton*) continuation; (: *second film etc sur le même thème*) sequel; (*série: de maisons, succès*): **une ~ de** a series *ou* succession of; (*MATH*) series *sg*; (*conséquence*) result; (*ordre, liaison logique*) coherence; (*appartement, MUS*) suite; (*escorte*) retinue, suite; **~s** *nfpl* (*d'une maladie etc*) effects; **prendre la ~ de** (*directeur etc*) to succeed, take over from; **donner ~ à** (*requête, projet*) to follow up; **faire ~ à** to follow; (*faisant*) **~ à votre lettre du** further to your letter of the; **à la ~** in succession; (*immédiatement*) at once; **par la ~** afterwards, subsequently; **à la ~ ad** one after the other; **à la ~ de** (*derrière*) behind; (*en conséquence de*) following; **par ~ de** owing to, as a result of.

suivant, e [sɥivɑ̃, -ɑ̃t] *a* next, following; (*ci-après*): **l'exercice ~** the following exercise // *prép* (*selon*) according to; **au ~!** next!

suivi, e [sɥivi] *a* (*régulier*) regular; (*cohérent*) consistent; coherent; **très/peu ~** (*cours*) well-/poorly-attended.

suivre [sɥivr(ə)] *vt* (*gén*) to follow; (*SCOL: cours*) to attend; (: *programme*) to keep up with; (*COMM: article*) to continue to stock // *vi* to follow; (*élève*) to attend; to keep up; **se ~** *vi* (*accidents etc*) to follow one after the other; (*raisonnement*) to be coherent; **faire ~** (*lettre*) to forward; **~ son cours** (*suj: enquête etc*) to run *ou* take its course; **'à ~'** 'to be continued'.

sujet, te [syʒɛ, -ɛt] *a*: **être ~ à** (*vertige etc*) to be liable *ou* subject to // *nm/f* (*d'un souverain*) subject // *nm* subject; **au ~ de** *prép* about; **~ à caution** *a* questionable; **~ de conversation** topic *ou* subject of conversation; **~ d'examen** (*SCOL*) examination question; examination paper.

summum [sɔmɔm] *nm*: **le ~ de** the height of.

superbe [sypɛrb(ə)] *a* magnificent, superb.

super(carburant) [sypɛr(karbyrɑ̃)] *nm* ≈ 4-star petrol (*Brit*), ≈ high-octane gasoline (*US*).

supercherie [sypɛrʃəri] *nf* trick.

superficie [sypɛrfisi] nf (surface) area; (fig) surface.

superficiel, le [sypɛrfisjɛl] a superficial.

superflu, e [sypɛrfly] a superfluous.

supérieur, e [sypɛrjœr] a (lèvre, étages, classes) upper; (plus élevé: température, niveau): ~ (à) higher (than); (meilleur: qualité, produit): ~ (à) superior (to); (excellent, hautain) superior // nm, nf superior; à l'étage ~ on the next floor up; **supériorité** nf superiority.

superlatif [sypɛrlatif] nm superlative.

supermarché [sypɛrmarʃe] nm supermarket.

superposer [sypɛrpoze] vt (faire chevaucher) to superimpose; lits superposés bunk beds.

superproduction [sypɛrprɔdyksjɔ̃] nf (film) spectacular.

superpuissance [sypɛrpɥisɑ̃s] nf super-power.

superstitieux, euse [sypɛrstisjø, -øz] a superstitious.

superviser [sypɛrvize] vt to supervise.

suppléant, e [sypleɑ̃, -ɑ̃t] a (juge, fonctionnaire) deputy cpd; (professeur) supply cpd // nm/f deputy; supply teacher.

suppléer [syplee] vt (ajouter: mot manquant etc) to supply, provide; (compenser: lacune) to fill in; (: défaut) to make up for; (remplacer) to stand in for; ~ à vt to make up for; to substitute for.

supplément [syplemɑ̃] nm supplement; (de frites etc) extra portion; un ~ de travail extra ou additional work; ceci est en ~ (au menu etc) this is extra, there is an extra charge for this; **supplémentaire** a additional, further; (train, bus) relief cpd, extra.

supplications [syplikasjɔ̃] nfpl pleas, entreaties.

supplice [syplis] nm (peine corporelle) torture q; form of torture; (douleur physique, morale) torture, agony.

supplier [syplije] vt to implore, beseech.

supplique [syplik] nf petition.

support [sypɔr] nm support; (pour livre, outils) stand.

supportable [sypɔrtabl(ə)] a (douleur) bearable.

supporter nm [sypɔrtɛr] supporter, fan // vt [sypɔrte] (poids, poussée) to support; (conséquences, épreuve) to bear, endure; (défauts, personne) to put up with; (suj: chose: chaleur etc) to withstand; (suj: personne: chaleur, vin) to be able to take.

supposé, e [sypoze] a (nombre) estimated; (auteur) supposed.

supposer [sypoze] vt to suppose; (impliquer) to presuppose; à ~ que supposing (that).

suppositoire [sypozitwar] nm suppository.

suppression [sypresjɔ̃] nf removal; deletion; cancellation; suppression.

supprimer [syprime] vt (cloison, cause, anxiété) to remove; (clause, mot) to delete; (congés, service d'autobus etc) to cancel; (emplois, privilèges, témoin gênant) to do away with.

supputer [sypyte] vt to calculate.

suprême [syprɛm] a supreme.

sur, e [syr] a sour.

sur [syr] prép **1** (position) on; (par-dessus) over; (au-dessus) above; pose-le ~ la table put it on the table; je n'ai pas d'argent ~ moi I haven't any money on me

2 (direction) towards; en allant ~ Paris going towards Paris; ~ votre droite on ou to your right

3 (à propos de) on, about; un livre/une conférence ~ Balzac a book/lecture on ou about Balzac

4 (proportion, mesures) out of; by; un ~ 10 one in 10; (SCOL) one out of 10; 4 m ~ 2 4 m by 2

sur ce ad hereupon.

sûr, e [syr] a sure, certain; (digne de confiance) reliable; (sans danger) safe; ~ de soi self-confident; le plus ~ est de the safest thing is to; ~ et certain absolutely certain.

suranné, e [syrane] a outdated, outmoded.

surbaissé, e [syrbese] a lowered, low.

surcharge [syrʃarʒ(ə)] nf (de passagers, marchandises) excess load; (correction) alteration.

surcharger [syrʃarʒe] vt to overload.

surchoix [syrʃwa] a inv top-quality.

surclasser [syrklase] vt to outclass.

surcroît [syrkrwa] nm: un ~ de additional + nom; par ou de ~ moreover; en ~ in addition.

surdité [syrdite] nf deafness.

surélever [syrelve] vt to raise, heighten.

sûrement [syrmɑ̃] ad reliably; safely, securely; (certainement) certainly.

surenchère [syrɑ̃ʃɛr] nf (aux enchères) higher bid; (sur prix fixe) overbid; (fig) overstatement; outbidding tactics pl; **surenchérir** vi to bid higher; (fig) to try and outbid each other.

surent vb voir **savoir**.

surestimer [syrɛstime] vt to overestimate.

sûreté [syrte] nf (voir sûr) reliability; safety; (JUR) guaranty; surety; mettre en ~ to put in a safe place; pour plus de ~ as an extra precaution; to be on the safe side.

surf [syrf] nm surfing.

surface [syrfas] nf surface; (superficie) surface area; faire ~ to surface; en ~ ad near the surface; (fig) superficially.

surfait, e [syrfɛ, -ɛt] a overrated.

surfin, e [syrfɛ̃, -in] *a* superfine.

surgelé, e [syrʒəle] *a* (deep-)frozen.

surgir [syrʒir] *vi* to appear suddenly; *(jaillir)* to shoot up; *(fig: problème, conflit)* to arise.

surhumain, e [syrymɛ̃, -ɛn] *a* superhuman.

surimpression [syrɛ̃presjɔ̃] *nf* (PHOTO) double exposure; **en ~** superimposed.

sur-le-champ [syrləʃɑ̃] *ad* immediately.

surlendemain [syrlɑ̃dmɛ̃] *nm*: **le ~ (soir)** two days later (in the evening); **le ~ de** two days after.

surligneur [syrliɲœr] *nm* highlighter (pen).

surmener [syrmǝne] *vt*, **se ~** *vi* to overwork.

surmonter [syrmɔ̃te] *vt* *(suj: coupole etc)* to top; *(vaincre)* to overcome.

surnager [syrnaʒe] *vi* to float.

surnaturel, le [syrnatyrɛl] *a*, *nm* supernatural.

surnom [syrnɔ̃] *nm* nickname.

surnombre [syrnɔ̃br(ǝ)] *nm*: **être en ~** to be too many (*ou* one too many).

surpeuplé, e [syrpœple] *a* overpopulated.

sur-place [syrplas] *nm*: **faire du ~** to mark time.

surplomber [syrplɔ̃be] *vi* to be overhanging // *vt* to overhang; to tower above.

surplus [syrply] *nm* (COMM) surplus; *(reste)*: **~ de bois** wood left over.

surprenant, e [syrprǝnɑ̃, -ɑ̃t] *a* amazing.

surprendre [syrprɑ̃dr(ǝ)] *vt* *(étonner, prendre à l'improviste)* to surprise; *(tomber sur: intrus etc)* to catch; *(fig)* to detect; to chance upon; to overhear.

surpris, e [syrpri, -iz] *a*: **~ (de/que)** surprised (at/that).

surprise [syrpriz] *nf* surprise; **faire une ~ à qn** to give sb a surprise.

surprise-partie [syrprizparti] *nf* party.

sursaut [syrso] *nm* start, jump; **~ de** *(énergie, indignation)* sudden fit *ou* burst of; **en ~** *ad* with a start; **sursauter** *vi* to (give a) start, jump.

surseoir [syrswar]: **~ à** *vt* to defer.

sursis [syrsi] *nm* (JUR) *gén*: suspended sentence; *(à l'exécution capitale, aussi fig)* reprieve; *(MIL)* deferment.

surtaxe [syrtaks(ǝ)] *nf* surcharge.

surtout [syrtu] *ad* *(avant tout, d'abord)* above all; *(spécialement, particulièrement)* especially; **~, ne dites rien!** whatever you do don't say anything!; **~ pas!** certainly *ou* definitely not!; **~ que ...** especially as ...

surveillance [syrvɛjɑ̃s] *nf* watch; *(POLICE, MIL)* surveillance; **sous ~ médicale** under medical supervision.

surveillant, e [syrvɛjɑ̃, -ɑ̃t] *nm/f* *(de prison)* warder; *(SCOL)* monitor; *(de travaux)* supervisor, overseer.

surveiller [syrveje] *vt* *(enfant, élèves, bagages)* to watch, keep an eye on; *(malade)* to watch over; *(prisonnier, suspect)* to keep (a) watch on; *(territoire, bâtiment)* to (keep) watch over; *(travaux, cuisson)* to supervise; *(SCOL: examen)* to invigilate; **se ~** *vi* to keep a check *ou* watch on o.s.; **~ son langage/sa ligne** to watch one's language/figure.

survenir [syrvǝnir] *vi* *(incident, retards)* to occur, arise; *(événement)* to take place; *(personne)* to appear, arrive.

survêt(ement) [syrvɛt(mɑ̃)] *nm* tracksuit.

survie [syrvi] *nf* survival; *(REL)* afterlife.

survivant, e [syrvivɑ̃, -ɑ̃t] *nm/f* survivor.

survivre [syrvivr(ǝ)] *vi* to survive; **~ à** *vt* *(accident etc)* to survive; *(personne)* to outlive.

survoler [syrvɔle] *vt* to fly over; *(fig: livre)* to skim through.

survolté, e [syrvɔlte] *a* *(fig)* worked up.

sus [sy(s)]: **en ~ de** *prép* in addition to, over and above; **en ~** *ad* in addition; **~ à** *excl*: **~ au tyran!** at the tyrant!

susceptible [syseptibl(ǝ)] *a* touchy, sensitive; **~ d'amélioration** that can be improved, open to improvement; **~ de faire** able to do; liable to do.

susciter [sysite] *vt* *(admiration)* to arouse; *(obstacles, ennuis)*: **~ (à qn)** to create (for sb).

suspect, e [syspɛ(kt), -ɛkt(ǝ)] *a* suspicious; *(témoignage, opinions)* suspect // *nm/f* suspect.

suspecter [syspɛkte] *vt* to suspect; *(honnêteté de qn)* to question, have one's suspicions about.

suspendre [syspɑ̃dr(ǝ)] *vt* *(accrocher: vêtement)*: **~ qch (à)** to hang sth up (on); *(fixer: lustre etc)*: **~ qch à** to hang sth from; *(interrompre, démettre)* to suspend; *(remettre)* to defer; **se ~ à** to hang from.

suspendu, e [syspɑ̃dy] *a* *(accroché)*: **~ à** hanging on (*ou* from); *(perché)*: **~ au-dessus de** suspended over.

suspens [syspɑ̃]: **en ~** *ad* *(affaire)* in abeyance; **tenir en ~** to keep in suspense.

suspense [syspɑ̃s] *nm* suspense.

suspension [syspɑ̃sjɔ̃] *nf* suspension; **~ d'audience** adjournment.

sut *vb voir* **savoir.**

suture [sytyr] *nf*: **point de ~** stitch.

svelte [svɛlt(ǝ)] *a* slender, svelte.

S.V.P. *sigle* (= *s'il vous plaît*) please.

syllabe [silab] *nf* syllable.

sylviculture [silvikyltyr] *nf* forestry.

symbole [sɛ̃bɔl] *nm* symbol; **symbolique** *a* symbolic(al); *(geste, of-*

frande) token _cpd_; (_salaire, dommage-intérêts_) nominal; **symboliser** _vt_ to symbolize.

symétrique [simetʀik] _a_ symmetrical.

sympa [sɛpa] _a abr de_ **sympathique**.

sympathie [sɛpati] _nf_ (_inclination_) liking; (_affinité_) fellow feeling; (_condoléances_) sympathy; **accueillir avec ~** (_projet_) to receive favourably; **croyez à toute ma ~** you have my deepest sympathy.

sympathique [sɛpatik] _a_ nice, friendly; likeable; pleasant.

sympathisant, e [sɛpatizɑ̃, -ɑ̃t] _nm/f_ sympathizer.

sympathiser [sɛpatize] _vi_ (_voisins etc_: _s'entendre_) to get on (_Brit_) _ou_ along (_US_) (well).

symphonie [sɛ̃fɔni] _nf_ symphony.

symptôme [sɛ̃ptom] _nm_ symptom.

synagogue [sinagɔg] _nf_ synagogue.

syncope [sɛ̃kɔp] _nf_ (_MÉD_) blackout; **tomber en ~** to faint, pass out.

syndic [sɛ̃dik] _nm_ managing agent.

syndical, e, aux [sɛ̃dikal, -o] _a_ (trade-)union _cpd_; **~iste** _nm/f_ trade unionist.

syndicat [sɛ̃dika] _nm_ (_d'ouvriers, employés_) (trade) union; (_autre association d'intérêts_) union, association; **~ d'initiative** tourist office.

syndiqué, e [sɛ̃dike] _a_ belonging to a (trade) union; **non ~** non-union.

syndiquer [sɛ̃dike]: **se ~** _vi_ to form a trade union; (_adhérer_) to join a trade union.

synonyme [sinɔnim] _a_ synonymous // _nm_ synonym; **~ de** synonymous with.

syntaxe [sɛ̃taks(ə)] _nf_ syntax.

synthèse [sɛ̃tɛz] _nf_ synthesis (_pl_ es).

synthétique [sɛ̃tetik] _a_ synthetic.

Syrie [siʀi] _nf_: **la ~** Syria.

systématique [sistematik] _a_ systematic.

système [sistɛm] _nm_ system; **le ~ D** resourcefulness.

T

t' [t(ə)] _pronom voir_ **te**.

ta [ta] _dét voir_ **ton**.

tabac [taba] _nm_ tobacco; tobacconist's (shop); **~ blond/brun** light/dark tobacco; **~ à priser** snuff.

table [tabl(ə)] _nf_ table; **à ~!** dinner _etc_ is ready!; **se mettre à ~** to sit down to eat; (_fig: fam_) to come clean; **mettre la ~** to lay the table; **faire ~ rase de** to make a clean sweep of; **~ des matières** (table of) contents _pl_; **~ de nuit** _ou_ **de chevet** bedside table.

tableau, x [tablo] _nm_ painting; (_reproduction, fig_) picture; (_panneau_) board; (_schéma_) table, chart; **~ d'affichage** notice board; **~ de bord** dashboard; (_AVIAT_) instrument panel; **~ noir** blackboard.

tabler [table] _vi_: **~ sur** to bank on.

tablette [tablɛt] _nf_ (_planche_) shelf (_pl_ shelves); **~ de chocolat** bar of chocolate.

tableur [tablœʀ] _nm_ spreadsheet.

tablier [tablije] _nm_ apron.

tabouret [tabuʀɛ] _nm_ stool.

tac [tak] _nm_: **du ~ au ~** tit for tat.

tache [taʃ] _nf_ (_saleté_) stain, mark; (_ART, de couleur, lumière_) spot; splash, patch.

tâche [tɑʃ] _nf_ task; **travailler à la ~** to do piecework.

tacher [taʃe] _vt_ to stain, mark; (_fig_) to sully, stain.

tâcher [tɑʃe] _vi_: **~ de faire** to try _ou_ endeavour to do.

tacot [tako] _nm_ (_péj_) banger (_Brit_), (old) heap.

tact [takt] _nm_ tact; **avoir du ~** to be tactful.

tactique [taktik] _a_ tactical // _nf_ (_technique_) tactics _sg_; (_plan_) tactic.

taie [tɛ] _nf_: **~ (d'oreiller)** pillowslip, pillowcase.

taille [taj] _nf_ cutting; pruning; (_milieu du corps_) waist; (_hauteur_) height; (_grandeur_) size; **de ~ à faire** capable of doing; **de ~** _a_ sizeable.

taille-crayon(s) [tajkʀɛjɔ̃] _nm_ pencil sharpener.

tailler [taje] _vt_ (_pierre, diamant_) to cut; (_arbre, plante_) to prune; (_vêtement_) to cut out; (_crayon_) to sharpen.

tailleur [tajœʀ] _nm_ (_couturier_) tailor; (_vêtement_) suit; **en ~** (_assis_) cross-legged.

taillis [taji] _nm_ copse.

taire [tɛʀ] _vt_ to keep to o.s., conceal // _vi_: **faire ~ qn** to make sb be quiet; (_fig_) to silence sb; **se ~** _vi_ to be silent _ou_ quiet.

talc [talk] _nm_ talc, talcum powder.

talent [talɑ̃] _nm_ talent.

talon [talɔ̃] _nm_ heel; (_de chèque, billet_) stub, counterfoil (_Brit_); **~s plats/aiguilles** flat/stiletto heels.

talonner [talɔne] _vt_ to follow hard behind; (_fig_) to hound.

talus [taly] _nm_ embankment.

tambour [tɑ̃buʀ] _nm_ (_MUS, aussi TECH_) drum; (_musicien_) drummer; (_porte_) revolving door(s _pl_).

tamis [tami] _nm_ sieve.

Tamise [tamiz] _nf_: **la ~** the Thames.

tamisé, e [tamize] _a_ (_fig_) subdued, soft.

tamiser [tamize] _vt_ to sieve, sift.

tampon [tɑ̃pɔ̃] _nm_ (_de coton, d'ouate_) wad, pad; (_amortisseur_) buffer; (_bouchon_) plug, stopper; (_cachet, timbre_) stamp; (_mémoire_) **~** (_INFORM_) buffer; **~** (_hygiénique_) tampon; **tamponner** _vt_ (_timbres_) to stamp; (_heurter_) to crash _ou_ ram into;

tamponneuse *a*: autos tamponneuses dodgems.

tandis [tɑ̃di]: ~ que *cj* while.

tanguer [tɑ̃ge] *vi* to pitch (and toss).

tanière [tanjɛʀ] *nf* lair, den.

tanné, e [tane] *a* weather-beaten.

tanner [tane] *vt* to tan.

tant [tɑ̃] *ad* so much; ~ de (*sable, eau*) so much; (*gens, livres*) so many; ~ que *cj* as long as; ~ que (*comparatif*) as much as; ~ **mieux** that's great; so much the better; ~ **pis** never mind; too bad.

tante [tɑ̃t] *nf* aunt.

tantôt [tɑ̃to] *ad* (*parfois*): ~ ... ~ now ... now; (*cet après-midi*) this afternoon.

tapage [tapaʒ] *nm* uproar, din.

tapageur, euse [tapaʒœʀ, -øz] *a* loud, flashy; noisy.

tape [tap] *nf* slap.

tape-à-l'œil [tapalœj] *a inv* flashy, showy.

taper [tape] *vt* (*porte*) to bang; slam; (*dactylographier*) to type (out); (*fam: emprunter*): ~ **qn de 10 F** to touch sb for 10 F // *vi* (*soleil*) to beat down; ~ **sur qn** to thump sb; (*fig*) to run sb down; ~ **sur qch** to hit sth; to bang on sth; ~ **à** (*porte etc*) to knock on; ~ **dans** *vt* (*se servir*) to dig into; ~ **des mains/pieds** to clap one's hands/stamp one's feet; ~ (**à la machine**) to type; **se ~ un travail** to land o.s. with a job.

tapi, e [tapi] *a* crouching, cowering; hidden away.

tapis [tapi] *nm* carpet; (*de table*) cloth; **mettre sur le ~** (*fig*) to bring up for discussion; ~ **roulant** conveyor belt; ~ **de sol** (*de tente*) groundsheet.

tapisser [tapise] *vt* (*avec du papier peint*) to paper; (*recouvrir*): ~ **qch (de)** to cover sth (with).

tapisserie [tapisʀi] *nf* (*tenture, broderie*) tapestry; (*papier peint*) wallpaper.

tapissier, ière [tapisje, -jɛʀ] *nm/f*: ~(**-décorateur**) upholsterer (and decorator).

tapoter [tapote] *vt* to pat, tap.

taquiner [takine] *vt* to tease.

tarabiscoté, e [taʀabiskote] *a* overornate, fussy.

tard [taʀ] *ad* late; **plus ~** later (on); **au plus ~** at the latest; **sur le ~** late in life.

tarder [taʀde] *vi* (*chose*) to be a long time coming; (*personne*): ~ **à faire** to delay doing; **il me tarde d'être** I am longing to be; **sans (plus) ~** without (further) delay.

tardif, ive [taʀdif, -iv] *a* late.

targuer [taʀge]: **se ~ de** *vt* to boast about.

tarif [taʀif] *nm* (*liste*) price list; tariff; (*barème*) rates *pl*; fares *pl*; tariff; (*prix*) rate; fare.

tarir [taʀiʀ] *vi* to dry up, run dry.

tarte [taʀt(ə)] *nf* tart.

tartine [taʀtin] *nf* slice of bread; ~ **de miel** slice of bread and honey; **tartiner** *vt* to spread; **fromage à tartiner** cheese spread.

tartre [taʀtʀ(ə)] *nm* (*des dents*) tartar; (*de chaudière*) fur, scale.

tas [tɑ] *nm* heap, pile; (*fig*): **un ~ de** heaps of, lots of; **en ~** in a heap *ou* pile; **formé sur le ~** trained on the job.

tasse [tɑs] *nf* cup; ~ **à café** coffee cup.

tassé, e [tɑse] *a*: **bien ~** (*café etc*) strong.

tasser [tɑse] *vt* (*terre, neige*) to pack down; (*entasser*): ~ **qch dans** to cram sth into; **se ~** *vi* (*terrain*) to settle; (*fig*) to sort itself out, settle down.

tâter [tɑte] *vt* to feel; (*fig*) to try out; ~ **de** (*prison etc*) to have a taste of; **se ~** (*hésiter*) to be in two minds.

tatillon, ne [tatijɔ̃, -ɔn] *a* pernickety.

tâtonnement [tɑtɔnmɑ̃] *nm*: **par ~s** (*fig*) by trial and error.

tâtonner [tɑtɔne] *vi* to grope one's way along.

tâtons [tɑtɔ̃]: **à ~** *ad*: **chercher/avancer à ~** to grope around for/grope one's way forward.

tatouer [tatwe] *vt* to tattoo.

taudis [todi] *nm* hovel, slum.

taule [tol] *nf* (*fam*) nick (*fam*), prison.

taupe [top] *nf* mole.

taureau, x [tɔʀo] *nm* bull; (*signe*): **le T~** Taurus.

tauromachie [tɔʀɔmaʃi] *nf* bullfighting.

taux [to] *nm* rate; (*d'alcool*) level; ~ **d'intérêt** interest rate.

taxe [taks] *nf* tax; (*douanière*) duty; ~ **de séjour** tourist tax; ~ **à la valeur ajoutée (T.V.A.)** value added tax (V.A.T.).

taxer [takse] *vt* (*personne*) to tax; (*produit*) to put a tax on, tax; (*fig*): ~ **qn de** to call sb + *attribut*; to accuse sb of, tax sb with.

taxi [taksi] *nm* taxi.

tchao [tʃao] *excl* (*fam*) bye(-bye)!

Tchécoslovaquie [tʃekɔslɔvaki] *nf* Czechoslovakia; **tchèque** *a, nm, nf* Czech.

te, t' [t(ə)] *pronom* you; (*réfléchi*) yourself.

technicien, ne [tɛknisjɛ̃, -jɛn] *nm/f* technician.

technique [tɛknik] *a* technical // *nf* technique; ~**ment** *ad* technically.

technologie [tɛknɔlɔʒi] *nf* technology; **technologique** *a* technological.

teck [tɛk] *nm* teak.

teignais *etc vb voir* **teindre**.

teindre [tɛ̃dʀ(ə)] *vt* to dye.

teint, e [tɛ̃, tɛ̃t] *a* dyed // *nm* (*du visage*) complexion; colour // *nf* shade; **grand ~** *a inv* colourfast.

teinté, e [tɛ̃te] *a*: ~ **de** (*fig*) tinged with.

teinter [tɛ̃te] *vt* to tint; (*bois*) to stain;

teinture nf dyeing; (*substance*) dye; (*MÉD*) tincture.

teinturerie [tɛ̃tyʀʀi] nf dry cleaner's.

teinturier [tɛ̃tyʀje] nm dry cleaner.

tel, telle [tɛl] a (*pareil*) such; (*comme*): ~ un/des ... like a/like ...; (*indéfini*) such-and-such a, a given; (*intensif*): un ~/de ~s ... such (a)/such ...; rien de ~ nothing like it, no such thing; ~ que cj like, such as; ~ quel as it is ou stands (ou was etc).

télé [tele] abr f (= télévision) TV, telly (*Brit*); (*poste*) TV (set), telly à la ~ on TV, on telly.

télé... [tele] préfixe: ~**benne**, ~**cabine** nf (benne) cable car; ~**commande** nf remote control; ~**copie** nf fax; ~**distribution** nf cable TV; ~**férique** nm = ~phérique; ~**gramme** nm telegram.

télégraphe [telegraf] nm telegraph; **télégraphier** vt to telegraph, cable.

téléguider [telegide] vt to operate by remote control, radio-control.

téléjournal [teleʒuʀnal] nm TV news magazine programme.

télématique [telematik] nf telematics sg.

téléobjectif [teleɔbʒɛktif] nm telephoto lens sg.

téléphérique [teleferik] nm cable-car.

téléphone [telefɔn] nm telephone; avoir le ~ to be on the (tele)phone; au ~ on the phone; **téléphoner** vi to telephone, ring; to make a phone call; **téléphoner à** to phone, call up; **téléphonique** a (tele)phone cpd.

télescope [telɛskɔp] nm telescope.

télescoper [telɛskɔpe] vt to smash up; se ~ (véhicules) to concertina.

téléscripteur [teleskriptœʀ] nm teleprinter.

télésiège [telesjɛʒ] nm chairlift.

téléski [teleski] nm ski-tow.

téléspectateur, trice [telespɛktatœʀ, -tʀis] nm/f (television) viewer.

téléviseur [televizœʀ] nm television set.

télévision [televizjɔ̃] nf television; à la ~ on television.

télex [telɛks] nm telex.

telle [tɛl] a voir tel.

tellement [tɛlmɑ̃] ad (tant) so much; (si) so; ~ de (sable, eau) so much; (gens, livres) so many; il s'est endormi ~ il était fatigué he was so tired (that) he fell asleep; pas ~ not (all) that much; not (all) that + adjectif.

téméraire [temeʀɛʀ] a reckless, rash; **témérité** nf recklessness, rashness.

témoignage [temwaɲaʒ] nm (JUR: déclaration) testimony q, evidence q; (: faits) evidence q; (rapport, récit) account; (fig: d'affection etc) token, mark; expression.

témoigner [temwaɲe] vt (intérêt, grati-

tude) to show // vi (JUR) to testify, give evidence; ~ de vt to bear witness to, testify to.

témoin [temwɛ̃] nm witness; (fig) testimony // a control cpd, test cpd; **appartement** ~ show flat (Brit); **être** ~ **de** to witness; ~ **oculaire** eyewitness.

tempe [tɑ̃p] nf temple.

tempérament [tɑ̃peʀamɑ̃] nm temperament, disposition; à ~ (vente) on deferred (payment) terms; (achat) by instalments, hire purchase cpd.

température [tɑ̃peʀatyʀ] nf temperature; avoir ou faire de la ~ to be running ou have a temperature.

tempéré, e [tɑ̃peʀe] a temperate.

tempête [tɑ̃pɛt] nf storm; ~ de sable/neige sand/snowstorm.

temple [tɑ̃pl(ə)] nm temple; (protestant) church.

temporaire [tɑ̃pɔʀɛʀ] a temporary.

temps [tɑ̃] nm (atmosphérique) weather; (durée) time; (époque) time, times pl; (LING) tense; (MUS) beat; (TECH) stroke; il fait beau/mauvais ~ the weather is fine/bad; avoir le ~/tout le ~ to have time/plenty of time; en ~ de paix/guerre in peacetime/wartime; en ~ utile ou voulu in due time ou course; de ~ en ~, de ~ à autre from time to time; à ~ (partir, arriver) in time; à ~ partiel ad, a part-time; dans le ~ at one time; de tout ~ always; ~ d'arrêt pause, halt; ~ mort (COMM) slack period.

tenable [tənabl(ə)] a bearable.

tenace [tənas] a tenacious, persistent.

tenailler [tənaje] vt (fig) to torment.

tenailles [tənaj] nfpl pincers.

tenais etc vb voir tenir.

tenancier, ière [tənɑ̃sje, -jɛʀ] nm/f manager/manageress.

tenant, e [tənɑ̃, -ɑ̃t] nm/f (SPORT): ~ du titre title-holder.

tendance [tɑ̃dɑ̃s] nf (opinions) leanings pl, sympathies pl; (inclination) tendency; (évolution) trend; avoir ~ à to have a tendency to, tend to.

tendeur [tɑ̃dœʀ] nm (attache) elastic strap.

tendre [tɑ̃dʀ(ə)] a tender; (bois, roche, couleur) soft // vt (élastique, peau) to stretch, draw tight; (muscle) to tense; (donner): ~ qch à qn to hold sth out to sb; to offer sb sth; (fig: piège) to set, lay; se ~ vi (corde) to tighten; (relations) to become strained; ~ à qch/à faire to tend towards sth/to do; ~ l'oreille to prick up one's ears; ~ la main/le bras to hold out one's hand/stretch out one's arm; ~**ment** ad tenderly; **tendresse** nf tenderness.

tendu, e [tɑ̃dy] pp de tendre // a tight; tensed; strained.

ténèbres [tenɛbʀ(ə)] nfpl darkness sg.

teneur [tənœʀ] nf content; (d'une lettre)

terms pl, content.

tenir [tənir] vt to hold; (magasin, hôtel) to run; (promesse) to keep // vi to hold; (neige, gel) to last; se ~ vi (avoir lieu) to be held, take place; (être: personne) to stand; se ~ droit to stand up (ou sit up) straight; bien se ~ to behave well; se ~ à qch to hold on to sth; s'en ~ à qch to confine o.s. to sth; to stick to sth; ~ à vt to be attached to; to care about; to depend on; to stem from; ~ à faire to want to do; ~ de vt to partake of; to take after; ça ne tient qu'à lui it is entirely up to him; ~ qn pour to take sb for; ~ qch de qn (histoire) to have heard ou learnt sth from sb; (qualité, défaut) to have inherited ou got sth from sb; ~ les comptes to keep the books; ~ le coup to hold out; ~ au chaud to keep hot; tiens/tenez, voilà le stylo there's the pen!; tiens, Alain! look, here's Alain!; tiens? (surprise) really?

tennis [tenis] nm tennis; (court) tennis court // nmpl ou fpl (aussi: chaussures de ~) tennis ou gym shoes; ~ de table table tennis; **~man** nm tennis player.

tension [tɑ̃sjɔ̃] nf tension; (fig) tension; strain; (MÉD) blood pressure; faire ou avoir de la ~ to have high blood pressure.

tentation [tɑ̃tɑsjɔ̃] nf temptation.

tentative [tɑ̃tativ] nf attempt, bid.

tente [tɑ̃t] nf tent.

tenter [tɑ̃te] vt (éprouver, attirer) to tempt; (essayer): ~ qch/de faire to attempt ou try sth/to do; ~ sa chance to try one's luck.

tenture [tɑ̃tyr] nf hanging.

tenu, e [təny] pp de tenir // a (maison, comptes): bien ~ well-kept; (obligé): ~ de faire under an obligation to do // nf (action de tenir) running; keeping; holding; (vêtements) clothes pl, gear; (allure) dress q, appearance; (comportement) manners pl, behaviour; en petite ~e scantily dressed ou clad; ~e de route (AUTO) road-holding; ~e de soirée evening dress.

ter [ter] a: 16 ~ 16b ou B.

térébenthine [terebɑ̃tin] nf: (essence de) ~ (oil of) turpentine.

terme [term(ə)] nm term; (fin) end; à court/long ~ a short-/long-term ou -range // ad in the short/long term; avant ~ (MÉD) prematurely; mettre un ~ à to put an end ou a stop to.

terminaison [terminezɔ̃] nf (LING) ending.

terminal, e, aux [terminal, -o] a final // nm terminal // nf (SCOL) ≈ sixth form ou year (Brit), ≈ twelfth grade (US).

terminer [termine] vt to end; (travail, repas) to finish; se ~ vi to end.

terne [tern(ə)] a dull.

ternir [ternir] vt to dull; (fig) to sully,

tarnish; se ~ vi to become dull.

terrain [terɛ̃] nm (sol, fig) ground; (COMM) land q, plot (of land); site; sur le ~ (fig) on the field; ~ de football/rugby football/rugby pitch (Brit) ou field (US); ~ d'aviation airfield; ~ de camping campsite; ~ de golf golf course; ~ de jeu games field; playground; ~ de sport sports ground; ~ vague waste ground q.

terrasse [teras] nf terrace; à la ~ (café) outside.

terrassement [terasmɑ̃] nm earthmoving, earthworks pl; embankment.

terrasser [terase] vt (adversaire) to floor; (suj: maladie etc) to lay low.

terre [ter] nf (gén, aussi ÉLEC) earth; (substance) soil, earth; (opposé à mer) land q; (contrée) land; ~s nfpl (terrains) lands, land sg; en ~ (pipe, poterie) clay cpd; à ~ ou par ~ (mettre, être) on the ground (ou floor); (jeter, tomber) to the ground, down; ~ cuite earthenware; terracotta; la ~ ferme dry land; ~ glaise clay; ~ à ~ a inv down-to-earth.

terreau [tero] nm compost.

terre-plein [terplɛ̃] nm platform.

terrer [tere]: se ~ vi to hide away; to go to ground.

terrestre [terɛstr(ə)] a (surface) earth's, of the earth; (BOT, ZOOL, MIL) land cpd; (REL) earthly, worldly.

terreur [terœr] nf terror q.

terrible [teribl(ə)] a terrible, dreadful; (fam) terrific.

terrien, ne [terjɛ̃, -jɛn] a: propriétaire ~ landowner // nm/f (non martien etc) earthling.

terrier [terje] nm burrow, hole; (chien) terrier.

terril [teril] nm slag heap.

terrine [terin] nf (récipient) terrine; (CULIN) pâté.

territoire [teritwar] nm territory.

terroir [terwar] nm (AGR) soil; region.

terrorisme [terorism(ə)] nm terrorism; **terroriste** nm/f terrorist.

tertiaire [tersjer] a tertiary // nm (ÉCON) service industries pl.

tertre [tertr(ə)] nm hillock, mound.

tes [te] dét voir ton.

tesson [tesɔ̃] nm: ~ de bouteille piece of broken bottle.

test [test] nm test.

testament [testamɑ̃] nm (JUR) will; (REL) Testament; (fig) legacy.

tester [teste] vt to test.

testicule [testikyl] nm testicle.

tétanos [tetanos] nm tetanus.

têtard [tetar] nm tadpole.

tête [tet] nf head; (cheveux) hair q; (visage) face; de ~ a (wagon etc) front cpd // ad (calculer) in one's head, mentally; tenir ~ à qn to stand up to sb; la

~ **en bas** with one's head down; **la ~ la première** (*tomber*) headfirst; **faire une ~** (*FOOTBALL*) to head the ball; **faire la ~** (*fig*) to sulk; **en ~** (*SPORT*) in the lead; at the front; **en ~ à ~** in private, alone together; **de la ~ aux pieds** from head to toe; ~ **de lecture** (playback) head; ~ **de liste** (*POL*) chief candidate; ~ **de série** (*TENNIS*) seeded player, seed; ~-**à-queue** *nm inv*: **faire un ~-à-queue** to spin round.

téter [tete] *vt*: ~ (**sa mère**) to suck at one's mother's breast, feed.

tétine [tetin] *nf* teat; (*sucette*) dummy (*Brit*), pacifier (*US*).

têtu, e [tety] *a* stubborn, pigheaded.

texte [tɛkst(ə)] *nm* text.

textile [tɛkstil] *a* textile *cpd* // *nm* textile; textile industry.

texture [tɛkstyʀ] *nf* texture.

TGV *sigle m* (= *train à grande vitesse*) high-speed train.

thé [te] *nm* tea; **prendre le ~** to have tea; **faire le ~** to make the tea.

théâtral, e, aux [teatʀal, -o] *a* theatrical.

théâtre [teatʀ(ə)] *nm* theatre; (*œuvres*) plays *pl*, dramatic works *pl*; (*fig: lieu*): **le ~ de** the scene of; (*péj*) histrionics *pl*, playacting; **faire du ~** to be on the stage; to do some acting.

théière [tejɛʀ] *nf* teapot.

thème [tɛm] *nm* theme; (*SCOL: traduction*) prose (composition).

théologie [teɔlɔʒi] *nf* theology.

théorie [teɔʀi] *nf* theory; **théorique** *a* theoretical.

thérapie [teʀapi] *nf* therapy.

thermal, e, aux [tɛʀmal, -o] *a*: **station ~e** spa; **cure ~e** water cure.

thermes [tɛʀm(ə)] *nmpl* thermal baths.

thermomètre [tɛʀmɔmɛtʀ(ə)] *nm* thermometer.

thermos ® [tɛʀmos] *nm ou nf*: (**bouteille**) ~ vacuum *ou* Thermos ® flask.

thermostat [tɛʀmɔsta] *nm* thermostat.

thèse [tɛz] *nf* thesis (*pl* theses).

thon [tɔ̃] *nm* tuna (fish).

thym [tɛ̃] *nm* thyme.

tibia [tibja] *nm* shinbone, tibia; shin.

tic [tik] *nm* tic, (nervous) twitch; (*de langage etc*) mannerism.

ticket [tikɛ] *nm* ticket; ~ **de quai** platform ticket.

tiède [tjɛd] *a* lukewarm; tepid; (*vent, air*) mild, warm; **tiédir** *vi* to cool; to grow warmer.

tien, tienne [tjɛ̃, tjɛn] *pronom*: **le ~** (**la tienne**), **les ~s** (**tiennes**) yours; **à la tienne!** cheers!

tiens [tjɛ̃] *vb, excl voir* **tenir**.

tiercé [tjɛʀse] *nm* system of forecast betting giving first 3 horses.

tiers, tierce [tjɛʀ, tjɛʀs(ə)] *a* third //

nm (*JUR*) third party; (*fraction*) third; **le ~ monde** the third world.

tige [tiʒ] *nf* stem; (*baguette*) rod.

tignasse [tiɲas] *nf* (*péj*) mop of hair.

tigre [tigʀ(ə)] *nm* tiger.

tigré, e [tigʀe] *a* striped; spotted.

tilleul [tijœl] *nm* lime (tree), linden (tree); (*boisson*) lime(-blossom) tea.

timbale [tɛ̃bal] *nf* (metal) tumbler; ~**s** *nfpl* (*MUS*) timpani, kettledrums.

timbre [tɛ̃bʀ(ə)] *nm* (*tampon*) stamp; (*aussi*: ~-**poste**) (postage) stamp; (*MUS: de voix, instrument*) timbre, tone.

timbré, e [tɛ̃bʀe] *a* (*fam*) daft.

timbrer [tɛ̃bʀe] *vt* to stamp.

timide [timid] *a* shy; timid; (*timoré*) timid, timorous; ~**ment** *ad* shyly; timidly; **timidité** *nf* shyness; timidity.

tins *etc vb voir* **tenir**.

tintamarre [tɛ̃tamaʀ] *nm* din, uproar.

tinter [tɛ̃te] *vi* to ring, chime; (*argent, clefs*) to jingle.

tir [tiʀ] *nm* (*sport*) shooting; (*fait ou manière de tirer*) firing *q*; (*stand*) shooting gallery; ~ **à l'arc** archery; ~ **au pigeon** clay pigeon shooting.

tirage [tiʀaʒ] *nm* (*action*) printing; (*PHOTO*) print; (*de journal*) circulation; (*de livre*) (print-)run; edition; (*de cheminée*) draught; (*de loterie*) draw; (*désaccord*) friction; ~ **au sort** drawing lots.

tirailler [tiʀaje] *vt* to pull at, tug at // *vi* to fire at random.

tirant [tiʀɑ̃] *nm*: ~ **d'eau** draught.

tire [tiʀ] *nf*: **vol à la ~** pickpocketing.

tiré, e [tiʀe] *a* (*traits*) drawn // *nm* (*COMM*) drawee; ~ **par les cheveux** far-fetched.

tire-au-flanc [tiʀoflɑ̃] *nm inv* (*péj*) skiver.

tire-bouchon [tiʀbuʃɔ̃] *nm* corkscrew.

tirelire [tiʀliʀ] *nf* moneybox.

tirer [tiʀe] *vt* (*gén*) to pull; (*extraire*): ~ **qch de** to take *ou* pull sth out of; to get sth out of; to extract sth from; (*tracer: ligne, trait*) to draw, trace; (*fermer: rideau*) to draw, close; (*choisir: carte, conclusion, aussi COMM: chèque*) to draw; (*en faisant feu: balle, coup*) to fire; (: *animal*) to shoot; (*journal, livre, photo*) to print; (*FOOTBALL: corner etc*) to take // *vi* (*faire feu*) to fire; (*faire du tir, FOOTBALL*) to shoot; (*cheminée*) to draw; **se ~** *vi* (*fam*) to push off; **s'en ~** to pull through, get off; ~ **sur** to pull on *ou* at; to shoot *ou* fire at; (*pipe*) to draw on; (*fig: avoisiner*) to verge *ou* border on; ~ **qn de** (*embarras etc*) to help *ou* get sb out of; ~ **à l'arc/la carabine** to shoot with a bow and arrow/with a rifle.

tiret [tiʀɛ] *nm* dash.

tireur, euse [tiʀœʀ, -øz] *nm/f* gunman; (*COMM*) drawer; ~ **d'élite** marksman.

tiroir [tiʀwaʀ] *nm* drawer; ~-**caisse** *nm*

till.
tisane [tizan] *nf* herb tea.
tisonnier [tizɔnje] *nm* poker.
tisser [tise] *vt* to weave; **tisserand** *nm* weaver.
tissu [tisy] *nm* fabric, material, cloth *q*; (*ANAT, BIO*) tissue.
tissu-éponge [tisyepɔ̃ʒ] *nm* (terry) towelling *q*.
titre [titʀ(ə)] *nm* (*gén*) title; (*de journal*) headline; (*diplôme*) qualification; (*COMM*) security; **en ~** (*champion*) official; **à juste ~** with just cause, rightly; **à quel ~?** on what grounds?; **à aucun ~** on no account; **au même ~ (que)** in the same way (as); **à ~ d'information for** (your) information; **à ~ gracieux** free of charge; **à ~ d'essai** on a trial basis; **à ~ privé** in a private capacity; **~ de propriété** title deed; **~ de transport** ticket.
tituber [titybe] *vi* to stagger (along).
titulaire [tityleʀ] (*ADMIN*) *a* appointed, with tenure // *nm* incumbent; **être ~ de** (*poste*) to hold; (*permis*) to be the holder of.
toast [tost] *nm* slice *ou* piece of toast; (*de bienvenue*) (welcoming) toast; **porter un ~ à qn** to propose *ou* drink a toast to sb.
toboggan [tɔbɔgã] *nm* toboggan; (*jeu*) slide.
tocsin [tɔksɛ̃] *nm* alarm (bell).
toge [tɔʒ] *nf* toga; (*de juge*) gown.
toi [twa] *pronom* you.
toile [twal] *nf* (*matériau*) cloth *q*; (*bâche*) piece of canvas; (*tableau*) canvas; **~ d'araignée** cobweb; **~ cirée** oilcloth; **~ de fond** (*fig*) backdrop.
toilette [twalɛt] *nf* wash; (*habits*) outfit; dress *q*; **~s** *nfpl* (*w.-c.*) toilet *sg*; **faire sa ~** to have a wash, get washed; **articles de ~** toiletries.
toi-même [twamɛm] *pronom* yourself.
toiser [twaze] *vt* to eye up and down.
toison [twazɔ̃] *nf* (*de mouton*) fleece; (*cheveux*) mane.
toit [twa] *nm* roof; **~ ouvrant** sunroof.
toiture [twatyʀ] *nf* roof.
tôle [tol] *nf* (*plaque*) steel *ou* iron sheet; **~ ondulée** corrugated iron.
tolérable [tɔleʀabl(ə)] *a* tolerable, bearable.
tolérant, e [tɔleʀã, -ãt] *a* tolerant.
tolérer [tɔleʀe] *vt* to tolerate; (*ADMIN*: hors taxe etc) to allow.
tollé [tɔle] *nm* outcry.
tomate [tɔmat] *nf* tomato.
tombe [tɔ̃b] *nf* (*sépulture*) grave; (*avec monument*) tomb.
tombeau, x [tɔ̃bo] *nm* tomb.
tombée [tɔ̃be] *nf*: **à la ~ de la nuit** at the close of day, at nightfall.
tomber [tɔ̃be] *vi* to fall; **laisser ~** to drop; **~ sur** *vt* (*rencontrer*) to come across; (*attaquer*) to set about; **~ de**

fatigue/sommeil to drop from exhaustion/be falling asleep on one's feet; **ça tombe bien** that's come at the right time; **il est bien tombé** he's been lucky.
tome [tɔm] *nm* volume.
ton, ta, *pl* **tes** [tɔ̃, ta, te] *dét* your.
ton [tɔ̃] *nm* (*gén*) tone; (*MUS*) key; (*couleur*) shade, tone; **de bon ~** in good taste.
tonalité [tɔnalite] *nf* (*au téléphone*) dialling tone; (*MUS*) key; (*fig*) tone.
tondeuse [tɔ̃døz] *nf* (*à gazon*) (lawn)mower; (*du coiffeur*) clippers *pl*; (*pour la tonte*) shears *pl*.
tondre [tɔ̃dʀ(ə)] *vt* (*pelouse, herbe*) to mow; (*haie*) to cut, clip; (*mouton, toison*) to shear; (*cheveux*) to crop.
tonifier [tɔnifje] *vt* (*peau, organisme*) to tone up.
tonique [tɔnik] *a* fortifying // *nm* tonic.
tonne [tɔn] *nf* metric ton, tonne.
tonneau, x [tɔno] *nm* (*à vin, cidre*) barrel; (*NAVIG*) ton; **faire des ~x** (*voiture, avion*) to roll over.
tonnelle [tɔnɛl] *nf* bower, arbour.
tonner [tɔne] *vi* to thunder; **il tonne** it is thundering, there's some thunder.
tonnerre [tɔnɛʀ] *nm* thunder.
tonus [tɔnys] *nm* dynamism.
top [tɔp] *nm*: **au 3ème ~** at the 3rd stroke.
topinambour [tɔpinãbuʀ] *nm* Jerusalem artichoke.
toque [tɔk] *nf* (*de fourrure*) fur hat; **~ de jockey/juge** jockey's/judge's cap; **~ de cuisinier** chef's hat.
toqué, e [tɔke] *a* (*fam*) cracked.
torche [tɔʀʃ(ə)] *nf* torch.
torchon [tɔʀʃɔ̃] *nm* cloth, duster; (*à vaisselle*) tea towel *ou* cloth.
tordre [tɔʀdʀ(ə)] *vt* (*chiffon*) to wring; (*barre, fig: visage*) to twist; **se ~** *vi* (*barre*) to bend; (*roue*) to twist, buckle; (*ver, serpent*) to writhe; **se ~ le pied/bras** to twist one's foot/arm.
tordu, e [tɔʀdy] *a* (*fig*) warped, twisted.
tornade [tɔʀnad] *nf* tornado.
torpille [tɔʀpij] *nf* torpedo; **torpiller** *vt* to torpedo.
torréfier [tɔʀefje] *vt* to roast.
torrent [tɔʀã] *nm* torrent.
torse [tɔʀs(ə)] *nm* (*ANAT*) torso; chest.
torsion [tɔʀsjɔ̃] *nf* twisting; torsion.
tort [tɔʀ] *nm* (*défaut*) fault; (*préjudice*) wrong *q*; **~s** *nmpl* (*JUR*) fault *sg*; **avoir ~** to be wrong; **être dans son ~** to be in the wrong; **donner ~ à qn** to lay the blame on sb; (*fig*) to prove sb wrong; **causer du ~ à** to harm; to be harmful *ou* detrimental to; **à ~** wrongly; **à ~ et à travers** wildly.
torticolis [tɔʀtikɔli] *nm* stiff neck.
tortiller [tɔʀtije] *vt* to twist; to twiddle; **se ~** *vi* to wriggle, squirm.

tortionnaire [tɔʀsjɔnɛʀ] *nm* torturer.
tortue [tɔʀty] *nf* tortoise.
tortueux, euse [tɔʀtɥø, -øz] *a* (*rue*) twisting; (*fig*) tortuous.
torture [tɔʀtyʀ] *nf* torture; **torturer** *vt* to torture; (*fig*) to torment.
tôt [to] *ad* early; **~ ou tard** sooner or later; **si ~** so early; (*déjà*) so soon; **au plus ~** at the earliest; **il eut ~ fait de** faire he soon did.
total, e, aux [tɔtal, -o] *a, nm* total; **au ~** in total *ou* all; **faire le ~** to work out the total, add up; **~ement** *ad* totally, completely; **~iser** *vt* total (up).
totalité [tɔtalite] *nf*: **la ~ de** all of, the total amount (*ou* number) of; the whole + *sg*; **en ~** entirely.
toubib [tubib] *nm* (*fam*) doctor.
touchant, e [tuʃɑ̃, -ɑ̃t] *a* touching.
touche [tuʃ] *nf* (*de piano, de machine à écrire*) key; (*PEINTURE etc*) stroke, touch; (*fig: de nostalgie*) touch, hint; (*FOOTBALL: aussi: remise en ~*) throw-in; (*aussi: ligne de ~*) touch-line.
toucher [tuʃe] *nm* touch // *vt* to touch; (*palper*) to feel; (*atteindre: d'un coup de feu etc*) to hit; (*concerner*) to concern, affect; (*contacter*) to reach, contact; (*recevoir: récompense*) to receive, get; (*: salaire*) to draw, get; (*: chèque*) to cash; **au ~** to the touch; **se ~** (*être en contact*) to touch; **~ à** to touch; (*concerner*) to have to do with, concern; **je vais lui en ~ un mot** I'll have a word with him about it; **~ à sa fin** to be drawing to a close.
touffe [tuf] *nf* tuft.
touffu, e [tufy] *a* thick, dense.
toujours [tuʒuʀ] *ad* always; (*encore*) still; (*constamment*) forever; **~ plus** more and more; **pour ~** forever; **~ est-il que** the fact remains that; **essaie ~** (you can) try anyway.
toupet [tupɛ] *nm* (*fam*) cheek.
toupie [tupi] *nf* (spinning) top.
tour [tuʀ] *nf* tower; (*immeuble*) high-rise block (*Brit*) *ou* building (*US*); (*ÉCHECS*) castle, rook // *nm* (*excursion*) stroll, walk; run, ride; trip; (*SPORT: aussi:* **~ de piste**) lap; (*d'être servi ou de jouer etc, tournure, de vis ou clef*) turn; (*de roue etc*) revolution; (*circonférence*): **de 3 m de ~** 3 m round, with a circumference *ou* girth of 3 m; (*POL: aussi:* **~ de scrutin**) ballot; (*ruse, de prestidigitation*) trick; (*de potier*) wheel; (*à bois, métaux*) lathe; **faire le ~ de** to go round; (*à pied*) to walk round; **c'est au ~ de Renée** it's Renée's turn; **à ~ de rôle**, **~ à ~** in turn; **~ de taille/tête** waist/head measurement; **~ de chant** song recital; **~ de contrôle** *nf* control tower; **~ de garde** spell of duty; **~ d'horizon** (*fig*) general survey.
tourbe [tuʀb(ə)] *nf* peat.

tourbillon [tuʀbijɔ̃] *nm* whirlwind; (*d'eau*) whirlpool; (*fig*) whirl, swirl; **tourbillonner** *vi* to whirl (round).
tourelle [tuʀɛl] *nf* turret.
tourisme [tuʀism(ə)] *nm* tourism; **agence de ~** tourist agency; **faire du ~** to go sightseeing; to go touring; **touriste** *nm/f* tourist; **touristique** *a* tourist *cpd*; (*région*) touristic.
tourment [tuʀmɑ̃] *nm* torment.
tourmenter [tuʀmɑ̃te] *vt* to torment; **se ~** *vi* to fret, worry o.s.
tournant [tuʀnɑ̃] *nm* (*de route*) bend; (*fig*) turning point.
tournebroche [tuʀnəbʀɔʃ] *nm* roasting spit.
tourne-disque [tuʀnədisk(ə)] *nm* record player.
tournée [tuʀne] *nf* (*du facteur etc*) round; (*d'artiste, politicien*) tour; (*au café*) round of drinks).
tourner [tuʀne] *vt* to turn; (*sauce, mélange*) to stir; (*contourner*) to get round; (*CINÉMA*) to shoot; to make // *vi* to turn; (*moteur*) to run; (*compteur*) to tick away; (*lait etc*) to turn (sour); **se ~** *vi* to turn round; **se ~ vers** to turn to; to turn towards; **bien ~** to turn out well; **~ autour de** to go round; (*péj*) to hang round; **~ à/en** to turn into; **~ le dos à** to turn one's back on; to have one's back to; **~ de l'œil** to pass out.
tournesol [tuʀnəsɔl] *nm* sunflower.
tournevis [tuʀnəvis] *nm* screwdriver.
tourniquet [tuʀnikɛ] *nm* (*pour arroser*) sprinkler; (*portillon*) turnstile; (*présentoir*) revolving stand, spinner.
tournoi [tuʀnwa] *nm* tournament.
tournoyer [tuʀnwaje] *vi* to whirl round; to swirl round.
tournure [tuʀnyʀ] *nf* (*LING*) turn of phrase; form; phrasing; (*évolution*): **la ~ de qch** the way sth is developing; (*aspect*): **la ~ de** the look of; **~ d'esprit** turn *ou* cast of mind; **la ~ des événements** the turn of events.
tourte [tuʀt(ə)] *nf* pie.
tous *dét* [tu] , *pronom* [tus] *voir* **tout**.
Toussaint [tusɛ̃] *nf*: **la ~** All Saints' Day.
tousser [tuse] *vi* to cough.
tout, e, *pl* tous, toutes [tu, tut, tus] ♦ *a* **1** (*avec article sing*) all; **~ le lait** all the milk; **~e la nuit** all night, the whole night; **~ le livre** the whole book; **~ un pain** a whole loaf; **~ le temps** all the time; the whole time; **c'est ~ le contraire** it's quite the opposite **2** (*avec article pl*) every; all; **tous les livres** all the books; **toutes les nuits** every night; **toutes les fois** every time; **toutes les trois/deux semaines** every third/other *ou* second week, every three/two weeks; **tous les deux** both *ou* each of us (*ou* them *ou* you); **toutes les 3** all 3 of us (*ou*

them *ou* you)
3 (*sans article*): à ~ âge at any age; **pour** ~e **nourriture, il avait** ... his only food was ...

♦ *pronom* everything, all; **il a ~ fait** he's done everything; **je les vois tous** I can see them all *ou* all of them; **nous y sommes tous allés** all of us went, we all went; **en** ~ in all; ~ **ce qu'il sait** all he knows

♦ *nm* whole; **le** ~ all of it (*ou* them); **le** ~ **est de** ... the main thing is to ...; **pas du** ~ not at all

♦ *ad* **1** (*très, complètement*) very; ~ **près** very near; **le** ~ **premier** the very first; ~ **seul** all alone; **le livre** ~ **entier** the whole book; ~ **en haut** right at the top; ~ **droit** straight ahead

2: ~ **en while**; ~ **en travaillant** while working, as he *etc* works

3: ~ **d'abord** first of all; ~ **à coup** suddenly; ~ **à fait** absolutely; ~ **à l'heure** a short while ago; (*futur*) in a short while, shortly; **à** ~ **à l'heure!** see you later!; ~ **de même** all the same; ~ **le monde** *pronom* everybody; ~ **de suite** immediately, straight away; ~ **terrain, tous terrains** *a inv* all-terrain.

toutefois [tutfwa] *ad* however.

toux [tu] *nf* cough.

toxicomane [tɔksikɔman] *nm/f* drug addict.

trac [trak] *nm* nerves *pl.*

tracasser [trakase] *vt* to worry, bother; **to harass.**

trace [tras] *nf* (*empreintes*) tracks *pl*; (*marques, aussi fig*) mark; (*restes, vestige*) trace; (*indice*) sign; ~**s de pas** footprints.

tracé [trase] *nm* line; layout.

tracer [trase] *vt* to draw; (*mot*) to trace; (*piste*) to open up.

tract [trakt] *nm* tract, pamphlet.

tractations [traktɑsjɔ̃] *nfpl* dealings, bargaining *sg.*

tracteur [traktœr] *nm* tractor.

traction [traksjɔ̃] *nf*: ~ **avant/arrière** front-wheel/rear-wheel drive.

tradition [tradisjɔ̃] *nf* tradition; **traditionnel, le** *a* traditional.

traducteur, trice [tradyktœr, -tris] *nm/f* translator.

traduction [tradyksjɔ̃] *nf* translation.

traduire [traduir] *vt* to translate; (*exprimer*) to render, convey.

trafic [trafik] *nm* traffic; ~ **d'armes** arms dealing; **trafiquant, e** *nm/f* trafficker; dealer; **trafiquer** *vt* (*péj*) to doctor, tamper with.

tragédie [traʒedi] *nf* tragedy.

tragique [traʒik] *a* tragic.

trahir [trair] *vt* to betray; (*fig*) to give away, reveal; **trahison** *nf* betrayal; (*JUR*) treason.

train [trɛ̃] *nm* (*RAIL*) train; (*allure*) pace; (*fig: ensemble*) set; **mettre qch en** ~ to get sth under way; **mettre qn en** ~ to put sb in good spirits; **se mettre en** ~ to get started; to warm up; **se sentir en** ~ to feel in good form; ~ **d'atterrissage** undercarriage; ~**autos-couchettes** car-sleeper train; ~ **électrique** (*jouet*) (electric) train set; ~ **de vie** style of living.

traîne [trɛn] *nf* (*de robe*) train; **être à la** ~ to be in tow; to lag behind.

traîneau, x [trɛno] *nm* sleigh, sledge.

traînée [trɛne] *nf* streak, trail; (*péj*) slut.

traîner [trɛne] *vt* (*remorque*) to pull; (*enfant, chien*) to drag *ou* trail along // *vi* (*être en désordre*) to lie around; (*marcher*) to dawdle (along); (*vagabonder*) to hang about; (*agir lentement*) to idle about; (*durer*) to drag on; **se** ~ *vi* to drag o.s. along; ~ **les pieds** to drag one's feet.

train-train [trɛ̃trɛ̃] *nm* humdrum routine.

traire [trɛr] *vt* to milk.

trait [trɛ] *nm* (*ligne*) line; (*de dessin*) stroke; (*caractéristique*) feature, trait; ~**s** *nmpl* (*du visage*) features; **d'un** ~ (*boire*) in one gulp; **de** ~ *a* (*animal*) draught; **avoir** ~ **à** to concern; ~ **d'union** hyphen; (*fig*) link.

traitant, e [trɛtɑ̃, -ɑ̃t] *a*: **votre médecin** ~ your usual *ou* family doctor; **crème** ~**e** conditioning cream.

traite [trɛt] *nf* (*COMM*) draft; (*AGR*) milking; **d'une** ~ without stopping; **la** ~ **des noirs** the slave trade.

traité [trɛte] *nm* treaty.

traitement [trɛtmɑ̃] *nm* treatment; processing; (*salaire*) salary; ~ **de données/texte** data/word processing.

traiter [trɛte] *vt* (*gén*) to treat; (*TECH, INFORM*) to process; (*affaire*) to deal with, handle; (*qualifier*): ~ **qn d'idiot** to call sb a fool // *vi* to deal; ~ **de** *vt* to deal with.

traiteur [trɛtœr] *nm* caterer.

traître, esse [trɛtr(ə), -trɛs] *a* (*dangereux*) treacherous // *nm* traitor.

trajectoire [traʒɛktwar] *nf* path.

trajet [traʒɛ] *nm* journey; (*itinéraire*) route; (*fig*) path, course.

trame [tram] *nf* (*de tissu*) weft; (*fig*) framework; texture.

tramer [trame] *vt* to plot, hatch.

trampolino [trɑ̃pɔlino] *nm* trampoline.

tramway [tramwɛ] *nm* tram(way); tram(car) (*Brit*), streetcar (*US*).

tranchant, e [trɑ̃ʃɑ̃, -ɑ̃t] *a* sharp; (*fig*) peremptory // *nm* (*d'un couteau*) cutting edge; (*de la main*) edge.

tranche [trɑ̃ʃ] *nf* (*morceau*) slice; (*arête*) edge; (*partie*) section; (*série*) block; issue; bracket.

tranché, e [trɑ̃ʃe] *a* (*couleurs*) distinct, sharply contrasted; (*opinions*) clear-cut, definite // nf trench.

trancher [tʀɑ̃ʃe] vt to cut, sever; (fig: résoudre) to settle // vi to take a decision; ~ **avec** to contrast sharply with.

tranquille [tʀɑ̃kil] a calm, quiet; (enfant, élève) quiet; (rassuré) easy in one's mind, with one's mind at rest; **se tenir** ~ (enfant) to be quiet; **laisse-moi/ laisse-ça** ~ leave me/it alone; **tranquillité** nf quietness; peace (and quiet).

transat [tʀɑ̃zat] nm deckchair.

transborder [tʀɑ̃sbɔʀde] vt to tran(s)ship.

transférer [tʀɑ̃sfeʀe] vt to transfer; **transfert** nm transfer.

transfigurer [tʀɑ̃sfiɡyʀe] vt to transform.

transformation [tʀɑ̃sfɔʀmasjɔ̃] nf transformation; (RUGBY) conversion.

transformer [tʀɑ̃sfɔʀme] vt to transform, alter; (matière première, appartement, RUGBY) to convert; ~ **en** to transform into; to turn into; to convert into.

transfusion [tʀɑ̃sfyzjɔ̃] nf: ~ **sanguine** blood transfusion.

transgresser [tʀɑ̃sɡʀese] vt to contravene, disobey.

transi, e [tʀɑ̃zi] a numb (with cold), chilled to the bone.

transiger [tʀɑ̃ziʒe] vi to compromise.

transistor [tʀɑ̃zistɔʀ] nm transistor.

transit [tʀɑ̃zit] nm transit; ~**er** vi to pass in transit.

transitif, ive [tʀɑ̃zitif, -iv] a transitive.

transition [tʀɑ̃zisjɔ̃] nf transition; **transitoire** a transitional; transient.

translucide [tʀɑ̃slysid] a translucent.

transmetteur [tʀɑ̃smetœʀ] nm transmitter.

transmettre [tʀɑ̃smetʀ(ə)] vt (passer): ~ **qch à qn** to pass sth on to sb; (TECH, TÉL, MÉD) to transmit; (TV, RADIO: retransmettre) to broadcast.

transmission [tʀɑ̃smisjɔ̃] nf transmission.

transparaître [tʀɑ̃spaʀetʀ(ə)] vi to show (through).

transparence [tʀɑ̃spaʀɑ̃s] nf transparence; **par** ~ (regarder) against the light; (voir) showing through.

transparent, e [tʀɑ̃spaʀɑ̃, -ɑ̃t] a transparent.

transpercer [tʀɑ̃speʀse] vt to go through, pierce.

transpiration [tʀɑ̃spiʀasjɔ̃] nf perspiration.

transpirer [tʀɑ̃spiʀe] vi to perspire.

transplanter [tʀɑ̃splɑ̃te] vt (MÉD, BOT) to transplant; (personne) to uproot.

transport [tʀɑ̃spɔʀ] nm transport; ~**s en commun** public transport sg.

transporter [tʀɑ̃spɔʀte] vt to carry, move; (COMM) to transport, convey; **transporteur** nm haulage contractor

(Brit), trucker (US).

transversal, e, aux [tʀɑ̃sveʀsal, -o] a transverse, cross(-); cross-country; running at right angles.

trapèze [tʀapez] nm (au cirque) trapeze.

trappe [tʀap] nf trap door.

trapu, e [tʀapy] a squat, stocky.

traquenard [tʀaknaʀ] nm trap.

traquer [tʀake] vt to track down; (harceler) to hound.

traumatiser [tʀomatize] vt to traumatize.

travail, aux [tʀavaj, -o] nm (gén) work; (tâche, métier) work q, job; (ÉCON, MÉD) labour // nmpl (de réparation, agricoles etc) work sg; (sur route) roadworks pl; (de construction) building (work); **être sans** ~ (employé) to be out of work ou unemployed; ~ **(au) noir** moonlighting; **travaux des champs** farmwork sg; **travaux dirigés** (SCOL) supervised practical work sg; **travaux forcés** hard labour sg; **travaux manuels** (SCOL) handicrafts; **travaux ménagers** housework sg.

travailler [tʀavaje] vi to work; (bois) to warp // vt (bois, métal) to work; (objet d'art, discipline, fig: influencer) to work on; **cela le travaille** it is on his mind; ~ **à** to work on; (fig: contribuer à) to work towards; **travailleur, euse** a hardworking // nm/f worker; **travailliste** a ≈ Labour cpd.

travée [tʀave] nf row; (ARCHIT) bay; span.

travers [tʀaveʀ] nm fault, failing; **en** ~ (de) across; **au** ~ (de) through; **de** ~ a askew ou sideways; (fig) the wrong way; **à** ~ through; **regarder de** ~ (fig) to look askance at.

traverse [tʀaveʀs(ə)] nf (de voie ferrée) sleeper; **chemin de** ~ shortcut.

traversée [tʀaveʀse] nf crossing.

traverser [tʀaveʀse] vt (gén) to cross; (ville, tunnel, aussi: percer, fig) to go through; (suj: ligne, trait) to run across.

traversin [tʀaveʀsɛ̃] nm bolster.

travestir [tʀavestiʀ] vt (vérité) to misrepresent; **se** ~ vi to dress up; to dress as a woman.

trébucher [tʀebyʃe] vi: ~ **(sur)** to stumble (over), trip (against).

trèfle [tʀefl(ə)] nm (BOT) clover; (CARTES: couleur) clubs pl; (: carte) club.

treille [tʀej] nf vine arbour; climbing vine.

treillis [tʀeji] nm (métallique) wiremesh.

treize [tʀez] num thirteen; **treizième** num thirteenth.

tréma [tʀema] nm diaeresis.

tremblement [tʀɑ̃bləmɑ̃] nm: ~ **de terre** earthquake.

trembler [tʀɑ̃ble] vi to tremble, shake; ~ de (froid, fièvre) to shiver ou tremble with; (peur) to shake ou tremble with; ~ pour qn to fear for sb.

trémousser [tʀemuse]: se ~ vi to jig about, wriggle about.

trempe [tʀɑ̃p] nf (fig): de cette/sa ~ of this/his calibre.

trempé, e [tʀɑ̃pe] a soaking (wet), drenched; (TECH) tempered.

tremper [tʀɑ̃pe] vt to soak, drench; (aussi: faire ~, mettre à ~) to soak (plonger): ~ qch dans to dip sth in(to) // vi to soak; (fig): ~ dans to be involved ou have a hand in; se ~ vi to have a quick dip; **trempette** nf: faire trempette to go paddling.

tremplin [tʀɑ̃plɛ̃] nm springboard; (SKI) ski-jump.

trentaine [tʀɑ̃tɛn] nf: une ~ (de) thirty or so, about thirty; avoir la ~ (âge) to be around thirty.

trente [tʀɑ̃t] num thirty; **trentième** num thirtieth.

trépied [tʀepje] nm tripod.

trépigner [tʀepiɲe] vi to stamp (one's feet).

très [tʀɛ] ad very; much + pp, highly + pp.

trésor [tʀezɔʀ] nm treasure; (ADMIN) finances pl; funds pl; T~ (public) public revenue.

trésorerie [tʀezɔʀʀi] nf (gestion) accounts pl; (bureaux) accounts department; difficultés de ~ cash problems, shortage of cash ou funds.

trésorier, ière [tʀezɔʀje, -jɛʀ] nm/f treasurer.

tressaillir [tʀesajiʀ] vi to shiver, shudder; to quiver.

tressauter [tʀesote] vi to start, jump.

tresse [tʀɛs] nf braid, plait.

tresser [tʀese] vt (cheveux) to braid, plait; (fil, jonc) to plait; (corbeille) to weave; (corde) to twist.

tréteau, x [tʀeto] nm trestle.

treuil [tʀœj] nm winch.

trêve [tʀɛv] nf (MIL, POL) truce; (fig) respite; ~ de ... enough of this ....

tri [tʀi] nm sorting out q; selection; (POSTES) sorting; sorting office.

triangle [tʀijɑ̃gl(ə)] nm triangle.

tribord [tʀibɔʀ] nm: à ~ to starboard, on the starboard side.

tribu [tʀiby] nf tribe.

tribunal, aux [tʀibynal, -o] nm (JUR) court; (MIL) tribunal.

tribune [tʀibyn] nf (estrade) platform, rostrum; (débat) forum; (d'église, de tribunal) gallery; (de stade) stand.

tribut [tʀiby] nm tribute.

tributaire [tʀibytɛʀ] a: être ~ de to be dependent on.

tricher [tʀiʃe] vi to cheat.

tricolore [tʀikɔlɔʀ] a three-coloured; (français) red, white and blue.

tricot [tʀiko] nm (technique, ouvrage) knitting q; (tissu) knitted fabric; (vêtement) jersey, sweater.

tricoter [tʀikɔte] vt to knit.

trictrac [tʀiktʀak] nm backgammon.

tricycle [tʀisikl(ə)] nm tricycle.

triennal, e, aux [tʀiɛnal, -o] a three-yearly; three-year.

trier [tʀije] vt to sort out; (POSTES, fruits) to sort.

trimestre [tʀimɛstʀ(ə)] nm (SCOL) term; (COMM) quarter; **trimestriel, le** a quarterly; (SCOL) end-of-term.

tringle [tʀɛ̃gl(ə)] nf rod.

trinquer [tʀɛ̃ke] vi to clink glasses.

triomphe [tʀijɔ̃f] nm triumph.

triompher [tʀijɔ̃fe] vi to triumph, win; ~ de to triumph over, overcome.

tripes [tʀip] nfpl (CULIN) tripe sg.

triple [tʀipl(ə)] a triple; treble // nm: le ~ (de) (comparaison) three times as much (as); en ~ exemplaire in triplicate; **triplés, ées** nm/fpl triplets; **tripler** vi, vt to triple, treble.

tripoter [tʀipɔte] vt to fiddle with.

trique [tʀik] nf cudgel.

triste [tʀist(ə)] a sad; (péj): ~ personnage/affaire sorry individual/ affair; **tristesse** nf sadness.

trivial, e, aux [tʀivjal, -o] a coarse, crude; (commun) mundane.

troc [tʀɔk] nm barter.

trognon [tʀɔɲɔ̃] nm (de fruit) core; (de légume) stalk.

trois [tʀwa] num three; **troisième** num third; ~-quarts nmpl: les ~-quarts de three-quarters of.

trombe [tʀɔ̃b] nf: des ~s d'eau a downpour; en ~ like a whirlwind.

trombone [tʀɔ̃bɔn] nm (MUS) trombone; (de bureau) paper clip.

trompe [tʀɔ̃p] nf (d'éléphant) trunk; (MUS) trumpet, horn.

tromper [tʀɔ̃pe] vt to deceive; (vigilance, poursuivants) to elude; se ~ vi to make a mistake, be mistaken; se ~ de voiture/jour to take the wrong car/get the day wrong; se ~ de 3 cm/20 F to be out by 3 cm/20 F; **tromperie** nf deception, trickery q.

trompette [tʀɔ̃pɛt] nf trumpet; en ~ (nez) turned-up.

tronc [tʀɔ̃] nm (BOT, ANAT) trunk; (d'église) collection box.

tronçon [tʀɔ̃sɔ̃] nm section.

tronçonner [tʀɔ̃sɔne] vt to saw up.

trône [tʀon] nm throne.

trop [tʀo] ad vb +, too much, too + adjectif, adverbe; ~ (nombreux) too many; ~ peu (nombreux) too few; ~ (souvent) too often; ~ (longtemps) (for) too long; ~ de (nombre) too many; (quantité) too much; de ~, en ~: des livres en ~ a few books too many; du lait

en ~ too much milk; **3 livres/3 F de ~** 3 books too many/3 F too much.
tropical, e, aux [tʀɔpikal, -o] *a* tropical.
tropique [tʀɔpik] *nm* tropic.
trop-plein [tʀɔplɛ̃] *nm (tuyau)* overflow *ou* outlet (pipe); *(liquide)* overflow.
troquer [tʀɔke]: **~ qch contre** to barter *ou* trade sth for; *(fig)* to swap sth for.
trot [tʀo] *nm* trot.
trotter [tʀɔte] *vi* to trot; *(fig)* to scamper along *(ou* about).
trottiner [tʀɔtine] *vi (fig)* to scamper along *(ou* about).
trottinette [tʀɔtinɛt] *nf* (child's) scooter.
trottoir [tʀɔtwaʀ] *nm* pavement; **faire le ~** *(péj)* to walk the streets; **~ roulant** moving walkway, travellator.
trou [tʀu] *nm* hole; *(fig)* gap; *(COMM)* deficit; **~ d'air** air pocket; **~ de mémoire** blank, lapse of memory; **le ~ de la serrure** the keyhole.
trouble [tʀubl(ə)] *a (liquide)* cloudy; *(image, mémoire)* indistinct, hazy; *(affaire)* shady, murky // *nm (désarroi)* agitation; *(embarras)* confusion; *(zizanie)* unrest, discord; **~s** *nmpl (POL)* disturbances, troubles, unrest *sg*; *(MÉD)* trouble *sg*, disorders.
troubler [tʀuble] *vt (embarrasser)* to confuse, disconcert; *(émouvoir)* to agitate; to disturb; *(perturber: ordre etc)* to disrupt; *(liquide)* to make cloudy; **se ~** *vi (personne)* to become flustered *ou* confused.
trouée [tʀue] *nf* gap; *(MIL)* breach.
trouer [tʀue] *vt* to make a hole *(ou* holes) in; *(fig)* to pierce.
trouille [tʀuj] *nf (fam)*: **avoir la ~** to be scared to death.
troupe [tʀup] *nf* troop; **~ (de théâtre)** (theatrical) company.
troupeau, x [tʀupo] *nm (de moutons)* flock; *(de vaches)* herd.
trousse [tʀus] *nf* case, kit; *(d'écolier)* pencil case; *(de docteur)* instrument case; **aux ~s de** *(fig)* on the heels *ou* tail of; **~ à outils** toolkit; **~ de toilette** toilet bag.
trousseau, x [tʀuso] *nm (de mariée)* trousseau; **~ de clefs** bunch of keys.
trouvaille [tʀuvaj] *nf* find.
trouver [tʀuve] *vt* to find; *(rendre visite)*: **aller/venir ~ qn** to go/come and see sb; **je trouve que** I find *ou* think that; **~ à boire/critiquer** to find something to drink/criticize; **se ~** *vi (être)* to be; *(être soudain)* to find o.s.; **il se trouve que** it happens that, it turns out that; **se ~ bien** to feel well; **se ~ mal** to pass out.
truand [tʀyɑ̃] *nm* villain, crook.
truander [tʀyɑ̃de] *vt* to cheat.
truc [tʀyk] *nm (astuce)* way, device; *(de cinéma, prestidigitateur)* trick effect; *(chose)* thing, thingumajig; **avoir le ~ to** have the knack.
truchement [tʀyʃmɑ̃] *nm*: **par le ~ de qn** through the intervention of) sb.
truelle [tʀyɛl] *nf* trowel.
truffe [tʀyf] *nf* truffle; *(nez)* nose.
truffé [tʀyfe] *a*: **~ de** *(fig)* peppered with; bristling with.
truie [tʀɥi] *nf* sow.
truite [tʀɥit] *nf* trout *inv*.
truquer [tʀyke] *vt (élections, serrure, dés)* to fix; *(CINÉMA)* to use special effects in.
T.S.V.P. *sigle* (= *tournez s.v.p.*) P.T.O.
T.T.C. *sigle* = *toutes taxes comprises*.
tu [ty] *pronom* you.
tu, e [ty] *pp de* **taire**.
tuba [tyba] *nm (MUS)* tuba; *(SPORT)* snorkel.
tube [tyb] *nm* tube; pipe; *(chanson, disque)* hit song *ou* record.
tuer [tɥe] *vt* to kill; **se ~** *vi* to be killed; *(suicide)* to kill o.s.; **tuerie** *nf* slaughter *q*.
tue-tête [tytɛt]: **à ~** *ad* at the top of one's voice.
tueur [tɥœʀ] *nm* killer; **~ à gages** hired killer.
tuile [tɥil] *nf* tile; *(fam)* spot of bad luck, blow.
tulipe [tylip] *nf* tulip.
tuméfié, e [tymefje] *a* puffy, swollen.
tumeur [tymœʀ] *nf* growth, tumour.
tumulte [tymylt(ə)] *nm* commotion.
tumultueux, euse [tymyltɥø, -øz] *a* stormy, turbulent.
tunique [tynik] *nf* tunic.
Tunisie [tynizi] *nf*: **la ~** Tunisia; **tunisien, ne** *a*, *nm/f* Tunisian.
tunnel [tynɛl] *nm* tunnel.
turbulences [tyʀbylɑ̃s] *nfpl (AVIAT)* turbulence *sg*.
turbulent, e [tyʀbylɑ̃, -ɑ̃t] *a* boisterous, unruly.
turc, turque [tyʀk(ə)] *a* Turkish // *nm/f*: **T~, Turque** Turk/Turkish woman // *nm (LING)* Turkish.
turf [tyʀf] *nm* racing; **~iste** *nm/f* racegoer.
Turquie [tyʀki] *nf*: **la ~** Turkey.
turquoise [tyʀkwaz] *nf*, *a inv* turquoise.
tus *etc vb voir* **taire**.
tutelle [tytɛl] *nf (JUR)* guardianship; *(POL)* trusteeship; **sous la ~ de** *(fig)* under the supervision of.
tuteur [tytœʀ] *nm (JUR)* guardian; *(de plante)* stake, support.
tutoyer [tytwaje] *vt*: **~ qn** to address sb as 'tu'.
tuyau, x [tɥijo] *nm* pipe; *(flexible)* tube; *(fam)* tip; gen *q*; **~ d'arrosage** hosepipe; **~ d'échappement** exhaust pipe; **~terie** *nf* piping *q*.
T.V.A. *sigle f voir* **taxe**.

tympan [tɛ̃pɑ̃] nm (ANAT) eardrum.
type [tip] nm type; (fam) chap, guy // a typical, standard.
typé, e [tipe] a ethnic (euph).
typhoïde [tifɔid] nf typhoid.
typique [tipik] a typical.
tyran [tiʀɑ̃] nm tyrant.
tzigane [dzigan] a gipsy, tzigane.

U

ulcère [ylsɛʀ] nm ulcer.
ulcérer [ylseʀe] vt (fig) to sicken, appal.
ultérieur, e [ylteʀjœʀ] a later, subsequent; **remis à une date** ~e postponed to a later date.
ultime [yltim] a final.
ultra... [yltʀa] préfixe: ~**moderne/-rapide** ultra-modern/-fast.
un, une [œ̃, yn] ♦ article indéfini a; (devant voyelle) an; ~ **garçon/vieillard** a boy/an old man; **une fille** a girl
♦ pronom one; **l'~ des meilleurs** one of the best; **l'~ ..., l'autre** (the) one ..., the other; **les** ~**s ..., les autres** some ..., others; **l'~ et l'autre** both (of them); **l'~ ou l'autre** either (of them); **l'~ l'autre, les** ~**s les autres** each other, one another; **pas** ~ **seul** not a single one; ~ **par** ~ one by one
♦ num one; **une pomme seulement** one apple only.
unanime [ynanim] a unanimous; **unanimité** nf: **à l'unanimité** unanimously.
uni, e [yni] a (ton, tissu) plain; (surface) smooth, even; (famille) close(-knit); (pays) united.
unifier [ynifje] vt to unite, unify.
uniforme [ynifɔʀm(ə)] a (mouvement) regular, uniform; (surface, ton) even; (objets, maisons) uniform // nm uniform; **uniformiser** vt to make uniform; (systèmes) to standardize.
union [ynjɔ̃] nf union; ~ **de consommateurs** consumers' association; **l'U~ soviétique** the Soviet Union.
unique [ynik] a (seul) only; (le même): **un prix/système** ~ a single price/system; (exceptionnel) unique; **fils/fille** ~ son/daughter, only child; ~**ment** ad only, solely; (juste) only, merely.
unir [yniʀ] vt (nations) to unite; (éléments, couleurs) to combine; (en mariage) to unite, join together; ~ **qch à** to unite sth with; to combine sth with; **s'~** to unite; (en mariage) to be joined together.
unité [ynite] nf (harmonie, cohésion) unity; (COMM, MIL, de mesure, MATH) unit.
univers [ynivɛʀ] nm universe.
universel, le [ynivɛʀsɛl] a universal; (esprit) all-embracing.

universitaire [ynivɛʀsitɛʀ] a university cpd; (diplôme, études) academic, university cpd // nm/f academic.
université [ynivɛʀsite] nf university.
urbain, e [yʀbɛ̃, -ɛn] a urban, city cpd, town cpd; (poli) urbane; **urbanisme** nm town planning.
urgence [yʀʒɑ̃s] nf urgency; (MÉD etc) emergency; **d'~** a emergency cpd // ad as a matter of urgency.
urgent, e [yʀʒɑ̃, -ɑ̃t] a urgent.
urine [yʀin] nf urine; **urinoir** nm (public) urinal.
urne [yʀn(ə)] nf (électorale) ballot box; (vase) urn.
URSS [fareois: yʀs] sigle f: **l'~** the USSR.
urticaire [yʀtikɛʀ] nf nettle rash.
us [ys] nmpl: ~ **et coutumes** (habits and) customs.
USA sigle mpl: **les** ~ the USA.
usage [yzaʒ] nm (emploi, utilisation) use; (coutume) custom; (LING): **l'~** usage; **à l'~ de** (pour) for (use of); **en** ~ in use; **hors d'~** out of service; wrecked; **à** ~ **interne** to be taken; **à** ~ **externe** for external use only.
usagé, e [yzaʒe] a (usé) worn; (d'occasion) used.
usager, ère [yzaʒe, -ɛʀ] nm/f user.
usé, e [yze] a worn; (banal) hackneyed.
user [yze] vt (outil) to wear down; (vêtement) to wear out; (matière) to wear away; (consommer: charbon etc) to use; **s'~** vi to wear; to wear out; (fig) to decline; ~ **de** (moyen, procédé) to use, employ; (droit) to exercise.
usine [yzin] nf factory; ~ **marémotrice** tidal power station.
usiner [yzine] vt (TECH) to machine.
usité, e [yzite] a common.
ustensile [ystɑ̃sil] nm implement; ~ **de cuisine** kitchen utensil.
usuel, le [yzɥɛl] a everyday, common.
usure [yzyʀ] nf wear; worn state.
utérus [yteʀys] nm uterus, womb.
utile [ytil] a useful.
utilisation [ytilizasjɔ̃] nf use.
utiliser [ytilize] vt to use.
utilitaire [ytilitɛʀ] a utilitarian; (objets) practical.
utilité [ytilite] nf usefulness q; use; **reconnu d'~ publique** state-approved.

V

va vb voir **aller**.
vacance [vakɑ̃s] nf (ADMIN) vacancy; ~**s** nfpl holiday(s pl), vacation sg; **prendre des/ses** ~**s** to take a holiday/one's holiday(s); **aller en** ~**s** to go on holiday; **vacancier, ière** nm/f holiday-maker.
vacant, e [vakɑ̃, -ɑ̃t] a vacant.

vacarme [vakaʀm(ə)] *nm* row, din.
vaccin [vaksɛ̃] *nm* vaccine; (*opération*) vaccination; **vaccination** *nf* vaccination; **vacciner** *vt* to vaccinate; (*fig*) to make immune.
vache [vaʃ] *nf* (*ZOOL*) cow; (*cuir*) cowhide // *a* (*fam*) rotten, mean; **vachement** *ad* (*fam*) damned, hellish.
vaciller [vasije] *vi* to sway, wobble; (*bougie, lumière*) to flicker; (*fig*) to be failing, falter.
va-et-vient [vaevjɛ̃] *nm inv* (*de personnes, véhicules*) comings and goings *pl*, to-ings and fro-ings *pl*.
vagabond [vagabɔ̃] *nm* (*rôdeur*) tramp, vagrant; (*voyageur*) wanderer.
vagabonder [vagabɔ̃de] *vi* to roam, wander.
vagin [vaʒɛ̃] *nm* vagina.
vague [vag] *nf* wave // *a* vague; (*regard*) faraway; (*manteau, robe*) loose(-fitting); (*quelconque*): **un ~ bureau/cousin** some office/cousin or other; **~ de fond** *nf* ground swell.
vaillant, e [vajɑ̃, -ɑ̃t] *a* (*courageux*) gallant; (*robuste*) hale and hearty.
vaille *vb voir* **valoir**.
vain, e [vɛ̃, vɛn] *a* vain; **en ~** *ad* in vain.
vaincre [vɛ̃kʀ(ə)] *vt* to defeat; (*fig*) to conquer, overcome; **vaincu, e** *nm/f* defeated party; **vainqueur** *nm* victor; (*SPORT*) winner.
vais *vb voir* **aller**.
vaisseau, x [veso] *nm* (*ANAT*) vessel; (*NAVIG*) ship, vessel; **~ spatial** spaceship.
vaisselier [vesəlje] *nm* dresser.
vaisselle [vesɛl] *nf* (*service*) crockery; (*plats etc à laver*) (dirty) dishes *pl*; (*lavage*) washing-up (*Brit*), dishes *pl*.
val, vaux *ou* **vals** [val, vo] *nm* valley.
valable [valabl(ə)] *a* valid; (*acceptable*) decent, worthwhile.
valent *etc vb voir* **valoir**.
valet [valɛ] *nm* valet; (*CARTES*) jack.
valeur [valœʀ] *nf* (*gén*) value; (*mérite*) worth, merit; (*COMM: titre*) security; **mettre en ~** (*terrain, région*) to develop; (*fig*) to highlight; to show off to advantage; **avoir de la ~** to be valuable; **sans ~** worthless; **prendre de la ~** to go up *ou* gain in value.
valide [valid] *a* (*en bonne santé*) fit; (*valable*) valid; **valider** *vt* to validate.
valions *vb voir* **valoir**.
valise [valiz] *nf* (suit)case.
vallée [vale] *nf* valley.
vallon [valɔ̃] *nm* small valley.
valoir [valwaʀ] *vi* (*être valable*) to hold, apply // *vt* (*prix, valeur, effort*) to be worth; (*causer*): **~ qch à qn** to earn sb sth; **se ~** *vi* to be of equal merit; (*péj*) to be two of a kind; **faire ~** (*droits, prérogatives*) to assert; **faire ~ que** to point

out that; **à ~ sur** to be deducted from; **vaille que vaille** somehow or other; **cela ne me dit rien qui vaille** I don't like the look of it at all; **ce climat ne me vaut rien** this climate doesn't suit me; **~ la peine** to be worth the trouble *ou* worth it; **~ mieux: il vaut mieux se taire** it's better to say nothing; **ça ne vaut rien** it's worthless; **que vaut ce candidat?** how good is this applicant?
valoriser [valɔʀize] *vt* (*ÉCON*) to develop (the economy of); (*PSYCH*) to increase the standing of.
valse [vals(ə)] *nf* waltz.
valu, e [valy] *pp de* **valoir**.
vandale [vɑ̃dal] *nm/f* vandal; **vandalisme** *nm* vandalism.
vanille [vanij] *nf* vanilla.
vanité [vanite] *nf* vanity; **vaniteux, euse** *a* vain, conceited.
vanne [van] *nf* gate; (*fig*) joke.
vannerie [vanʀi] *nf* basketwork.
vantail, aux [vɑ̃taj, -o] *nm* door, leaf (*pl* leaves).
vantard, e [vɑ̃taʀ, -aʀd(ə)] *a* boastful.
vanter [vɑ̃te] *vt* to speak highly of, vaunt; **se ~** *vi* to boast, brag; **se ~ de** to pride o.s. on; (*péj*) to boast of.
vapeur [vapœʀ] *nf* steam; (*émanation*) vapour, fumes *pl*; **~s** *nfpl* (*bouffées*) vapours; **à ~** steam-powered, steam *cpd*; **cuit à la ~** steamed.
vapocuiseur [vapokɥizœʀ] *nm* pressure cooker.
vaporeux, euse [vapoʀø, -øz] *a* (*flou*) hazy, misty; (*léger*) filmy.
vaporisateur [vapoʀizatœʀ] *nm* spray.
vaporiser [vapoʀize] *vt* (*parfum etc*) to spray.
varappe [vaʀap] *nf* rock climbing.
vareuse [vaʀøz] *nf* (*blouson*) pea jacket; (*d'uniforme*) tunic.
variable [vaʀjabl(ə)] *a* variable; (*temps, humeur*) changeable; (*divers: résultats*) varied, various.
varice [vaʀis] *nf* varicose vein.
varicelle [vaʀisɛl] *nf* chickenpox.
varié, e [vaʀje] *a* varied; (*divers*) various.
varier [vaʀje] *vi* to vary; (*temps, humeur*) to change // *vt* to vary.
variété [vaʀjete] *nf* variety.
variole [vaʀjɔl] *nf* smallpox.
vas *vb voir* **aller**.
vase [vaz] *nm* vase // *nf* silt, mud.
vaseux, euse [vazø, -øz] *a* silty, muddy; (*fig: confus*) woolly, hazy; (*: fatigué*) peaky; woozy.
vasistas [vazistas] *nm* fanlight.
vaste [vast(ə)] *a* vast, immense.
vaudrai *etc vb voir* **valoir**.
vaurien, ne [voʀjɛ̃, -ɛn] *nm/f* good-for-nothing, guttersnipe.
vaut *vb voir* **valoir**.
vautour [votuʀ] *nm* vulture.

vautrer [votre]: se ~ vi: se ~ dans/sur to wallow in/sprawl on.

vaux [vo] pl de **val** // vb voir **valoir**.

veau, x [vo] nm (ZOOL) calf (pl calves); (CULIN) veal; (peau) calfskin.

vécu, e [veky] pp de **vivre**.

vedette [vədɛt] nf (artiste etc) star; (canot) patrol boat; launch.

végétal, e, aux [veʒetal, -o] a vegetable // nm vegetable, plant.

végétarien, ne [veʒetarjɛ̃, -ɛn] a, nm/f vegetarian.

végétation [veʒetasjɔ̃] nf vegetation; ~s nfpl (MÉD) adenoids.

véhicule [veikyl] nm vehicle; ~ utilitaire commercial vehicle.

veille [vɛj] nf (garde) watch; (PSYCH) wakefulness; (jour): la ~ (de) the day before; la ~ au soir the previous evening; à la ~ de on the eve of.

veillée [veje] nf (soirée) evening; (réunion) evening gathering; ~ (mortuaire) watch.

veiller [veje] vi to stay up; to be awake; to be on watch // vt (malade, mort) to watch over, sit up with; ~ à vt to attend to, see to; ~ à ce que to make sure that; ~ sur vt to keep a watch on; **veilleur de nuit** nm night watchman.

veilleuse [vejøz] nf (lampe) night light; (AUTO) sidelight; (flamme) pilot light; en ~ a, ad (lampe) dimmed.

veine [vɛn] nf (ANAT, du bois etc) vein; (filon) vein, seam; (fam: chance): avoir de la ~ to be lucky.

velléités [veleite] nfpl vague impulses.

vélo [velo] nm bike, cycle; faire du ~ to go cycling.

vélomoteur [velomotœr] nm moped.

velours [vəluʀ] nm velvet; ~ côtelé corduroy.

velouté, e [vəlute] a (au toucher) velvety; (à la vue) soft, mellow; (au goût) smooth, mellow.

velu, e [vəly] a hairy.

venais etc vb voir **venir**.

venaison [vənɛzɔ̃] nf venison.

vendange [vɑ̃dɑ̃ʒ] nf (opération, période: aussi: ~s) grape harvest; (raisins) grape crop, grapes pl.

vendanger [vɑ̃dɑ̃ʒe] vi to harvest the grapes.

vendeur, euse [vɑ̃dœʀ, -øz] nm/f (de magasin) shop assistant; (COMM) salesman/woman // nm (JUR) vendor, seller; ~ de journaux newspaper seller.

vendre [vɑ̃dʀ(ə)] vt to sell; ~ qch à qn to sell sb sth; 'à ~' 'for sale'.

vendredi [vɑ̃dʀədi] nm Friday; V~ saint Good Friday.

vénéneux, euse [venenø, -øz] a poisonous.

vénérien, ne [venerjɛ̃, -ɛn] a venereal.

vengeance [vɑ̃ʒɑ̃s] nf vengeance q, revenge q.

venger [vɑ̃ʒe] vt to avenge; se ~ vi to avenge o.s.; se ~ de qch to avenge o.s. for sth; to take one's revenge for sth; se ~ de qn to take revenge on sb; se ~ sur to take revenge on; to take it out on.

venimeux, euse [vənimø, -øz] a poisonous, venomous; (fig: haineux) venomous, vicious.

venin [vənɛ̃] nm venom, poison.

venir [vəniʀ] vi to come; ~ de to come from; ~ de faire: je viens d'y aller/de le voir I've just been there/seen him; s'il vient à pleuvoir if it should rain; j'en viens à croire que I have come to believe that; faire ~ (docteur, plombier) to call (out).

vent [vɑ̃] nm wind; il y a du ~ it's windy; c'est du ~ it's all hot air; au ~ to windward; sous le ~ to leeward; avoir le ~ debout/arrière to head into the wind/have the wind astern; dans le ~ (fam) trendy.

vente [vɑ̃t] nf sale; la ~ (activité) selling; (secteur) sales pl; mettre en ~ to put on sale; (objets personnels) to put up for sale; ~ de charité jumble sale; ~ aux enchères auction sale.

venteux, euse [vɑ̃tø, -øz] a windy.

ventilateur [vɑ̃tilatœʀ] nm fan.

ventiler [vɑ̃tile] vt to ventilate; (total, statistiques) to break down.

ventouse [vɑ̃tuz] nf (de caoutchouc) suction pad; (ZOOL) sucker.

ventre [vɑ̃tʀ(ə)] nm (ANAT) stomach; (fig) belly; avoir mal au ~ to have stomach ache (Brit) ou a stomach ache (US).

ventriloque [vɑ̃tʀilɔk] nm/f ventriloquist.

venu, e [vəny] pp de **venir** // a: être mal ~ à ou de faire to have no grounds for doing, be in no position to do // nf coming.

ver [vɛʀ] nm voir aussi **vers**; worm; (des fruits etc) maggot; (du bois) woodworm q; ~ luisant glow-worm; ~ à soie silkworm; ~ solitaire tapeworm; ~ de terre earthworm.

verbaliser [vɛʀbalize] vi (POLICE) to book ou report an offender.

verbe [vɛʀb(ə)] nm verb.

verdeur [vɛʀdœʀ] nf (vigueur) vigour, vitality; (crudité) forthrightness.

verdict [vɛʀdik(t)] nm verdict.

verdir [vɛʀdiʀ] vi, vt to turn green.

verdure [vɛʀdyʀ] nf greenery.

véreux, euse [veʀø, -øz] a worm-eaten; (malhonnête) shady, corrupt.

verge [vɛʀʒ(ə)] nf (ANAT) penis; (baguette) stick, cane.

verger [vɛʀʒe] nm orchard.

verglacé, e [vɛʀglase] a icy, iced-over.

verglas [vɛʀgla] nm (black) ice.

vergogne [vɛʀgɔɲ]: sans ~ ad shamelessly.

véridique [veʀidik] a truthful.
vérification [veʀifikasjɔ̃] nf checking q, check.
vérifier [veʀifje] vt to check; (corroborer) to confirm, bear out.
véritable [veʀitabl(ə)] a real; (ami, amour) true.
vérité [veʀite] nf truth; (d'un portrait romanesque) lifelikeness; (sincérité) truthfulness, sincerity.
vermeil, le [veʀmej] a ruby red.
vermine [veʀmin] nf vermin pl.
vermoulu, e [veʀmuly] a worm-eaten, with woodworm.
verni, e [veʀni] a (fam) lucky; cuir ~ patent leather.
vernir [veʀniʀ] vt (bois, tableau, ongles) to varnish; (poterie) to glaze.
vernis [veʀni] nm (enduit) varnish; glaze; (fig) veneer; ~ à ongles nail polish ou varnish.
vernissage [veʀnisaʒ] nm varnishing; glazing; (d'une exposition) preview.
vérole [veʀɔl] nf (variole) smallpox.
verrai etc vb voir **voir**.
verre [veʀ] nm glass; (de lunettes) lens sg; boire ou prendre un ~ to have a drink; ~s de contact contact lenses.
verrerie [veʀʀi] nf (fabrique) glassworks sg; (activité) glass-making; (objets) glassware.
verrière [veʀjɛʀ] nf (grand vitrage) window; (toit vitré) glass roof.
verrons etc vb voir **voir**.
verrou [veʀu] nm (targette) bolt; (fig) constriction; mettre qn sous les ~s to put sb behind bars; **verrouillage** nm locking; **verrouiller** vt to bolt; to lock.
verrue [veʀy] nf wart.
vers [veʀ] nm line // nmpl (poésie) verse sg // prép (en direction de) toward(s); (près de) around (about); (temporel) about, around.
versant [veʀsɑ̃] nm slopes pl, side.
versatile [veʀsatil] a fickle, changeable.
verse [veʀs(ə)]: à ~ ad: il pleut à ~ it's pouring (with rain).
Verseau [veʀso] nm: le ~ Aquarius.
versement [veʀsəmɑ̃] nm payment; en 3 ~s in 3 instalments.
verser [veʀse] vt (liquide, grains) to pour; (larmes, sang) to shed; (argent) to pay // vi (véhicule) to overturn; (fig): ~ dans to lapse into.
verset [veʀse] nm verse.
version [veʀsjɔ̃] nf version; (SCOL) translation (into the mother tongue).
verso [veʀso] nm back; voir au ~ see over(leaf).
vert, e [veʀ, veʀt(ə)] a green; (vin) young; (vigoureux) sprightly; (cru) forthright // nm green.
vertèbre [veʀtɛbʀ(ə)] nf vertebra (pl ae).
vertement [veʀtəmɑ̃] ad (réprimander)
sharply.
vertical, e, aux [veʀtikal, -o] a, nf vertical; à la ~e ad vertically; ~ement ad vertically.
vertige [veʀtiʒ] nm (peur du vide) vertigo; (étourdissement) dizzy spell; (fig) fever; **vertigineux, euse** a breathtaking.
vertu [veʀty] nf virtue; en ~ de prép in accordance with; ~eux, euse a virtuous.
verve [veʀv(ə)] nf witty eloquence; être en ~ to be in brilliant form.
verveine [veʀven] nf (BOT) verbena, vervain; (infusion) verbena tea.
vésicule [vezikyl] nf vesicle; ~ biliaire gall-bladder.
vessie [vesi] nf bladder.
veste [vest(ə)] nf jacket; ~ droite/croisée single-/double-breasted jacket.
vestiaire [vestjɛʀ] nm (au théâtre etc) cloakroom; (de stade etc) changing-room (Brit), locker-room (US).
vestibule [vestibyl] nm hall.
vestige [vestiʒ] nm relic; (fig) vestige; ~s nmpl remains.
veston [vestɔ̃] nm jacket.
vêtement [vɛtmɑ̃] nm garment, item of clothing; ~s nmpl clothes.
vétérinaire [veteʀinɛʀ] nm/f vet, veterinary surgeon.
vêtir [vetiʀ] vt to clothe, dress.
veto [veto] nm veto; opposer un ~ à to veto.
vêtu, e [vety] pp de **vêtir**.
vétuste [vetyst(ə)] a ancient, timeworn.
veuf, veuve [vœf, vœv] a widowed // nm widower // nf widow.
veuille, veuillez etc vb voir **vouloir**.
veule [vøl] a spineless.
veux vb voir **vouloir**.
vexations [veksasjɔ̃] nfpl humiliations.
vexer [vekse] vt to hurt, upset; se ~ vi to be hurt, get upset.
viabiliser [vjabilize] vt to provide with services (water etc).
viable [vjabl(ə)] a viable.
viager, ère [vjaʒe, -ɛʀ] a: rente viagère life annuity.
viande [vjɑ̃d] nf meat.
vibrer [vibʀe] vi to vibrate; (son, voix) to be vibrant; (fig) to be stirred; faire ~ to (cause to) vibrate; to stir, thrill.
vice [vis] nm vice; (défaut) fault; ~ de forme legal flaw ou irregularity.
vice... [vis] préfixe vice-.
vichy [viʃi] nm (toile) gingham.
vicié, e [visje] a (air) polluted, tainted; (JUR) invalidated.
vicieux, euse [visjø, -øz] a (pervers) dirty(-minded); nasty; (fautif) incorrect, wrong.
vicinal, e, aux [visinal, -o] a: chemin ~ by-road, byway.
victime [viktim] nf victim; (d'accident)

casualty.

victoire [viktwaʀ] *nf* victory.

vidange [vidɑ̃ʒ] *nf* (*d'un fossé, réservoir*) emptying; (*AUTO*) oil change; (*de lavabo: bonde*) waste outlet; **~s** *nfpl* (*matières*) sewage *sg*; **vidanger** *vt* to empty.

vide [vid] *a* empty // *nm* (*PHYSIQUE*) vacuum; (*espace*) (empty) space, gap; (*futilité, néant*) void; **avoir peur du ~** to be afraid of heights; **emballé sous ~** vacuum packed; **à ~** *ad* (*sans occupants*) empty; (*sans charge*) unladen.

vidéo [video] *nf* video // *a*: **cassette ~** video cassette.

vide-ordures [vidɔʀdyʀ] *nm inv* (rubbish) chute.

vide-poches [vidpɔʃ] *nm inv* tidy; (*AUTO*) glove compartment.

vider [vide] *vt* to empty; (*CULIN: volaille, poisson*) to gut, clean out; **se ~** *vi* to empty; **~ les lieux** to quit *ou* vacate the premises; **videur** *nm* (*de boîte de nuit*) bouncer.

vie [vi] *nf* life (*pl* lives); **être en ~** to be alive; **sans ~** lifeless; **à ~** for life.

vieil [vjɛj] *am voir* **vieux**.

vieillard [vjɛjaʀ] *nm* old man; **les ~s** old people, the elderly.

vieille [vjɛj] *a, nf voir* **vieux**.

vieilleries [vjɛjʀi] *nfpl* old things.

vieillesse [vjɛjɛs] *nf* old age.

vieillir [vjɛjiʀ] *vi* (*prendre de l'âge*) to grow old; (*population, vin*) to age; (*doctrine, auteur*) to become dated // *vt* to age; **vieillissement** *nm* growing old; ageing.

Vienne [vjɛn] *nf* Vienna.

vienne, viens *etc vb voir* **venir**.

vierge [vjɛʀʒ] *a* virgin; (*page*) clean, blank // *nf* virgin; (*signe*): **la V~** Virgo; **~ de** (*sans*) free from, unsullied by.

Viet-Nam, Vietnam [vjɛtnam] *nm* Vietnam.

vietnamien, ne [vjɛtnamjɛ̃, -jɛn] *a, nm/f* Vietnamese.

vieux(vieil), vieille [vjø, vjɛj] *a* old // *nm/f* old man/woman // *nmpl* old people; **mon ~/ma vieille** (*fam*) old man/girl; **prendre un coup de ~** to put years on; **~ garçon** *nm* bachelor; **~ jeu** *a inv* old-fashioned.

vif, vive [vif, viv] *a* (*animé*) lively; (*alerte, brusque, aigu*) sharp; (*lumière, couleur*) brilliant; (*air*) crisp; (*vent, émotion*) keen; (*fort: regret, déception*) great, deep; (*vivant*): **brûlé ~** burnt alive; **de vive voix** personally; **piquer qn au ~** to cut sb to the quick; **à ~** (*plaie*) open; **avoir les nerfs à ~** to be on edge.

vigie [viʒi] *nf* look-out, look-out post.

vigne [viɲ] *nf* (*plante*) vine; (*plantation*) vineyard.

vigneron [viɲʀɔ̃] *nm* wine grower.

vignette [viɲɛt] *nf* (*motif*) vignette; (*de marque*) manufacturer's label *ou* seal; (*ADMIN*) ≈ (road) tax disc (*Brit*), ≈ license plate sticker (*US*); price label (*on medicines for reimbursement by Social Security*).

vignoble [viɲɔbl(ə)] *nm* (*plantation*) vineyard; (*vignes d'une région*) vineyards *pl*.

vigoureux, euse [viguʀø, -øz] *a* vigorous, robust.

vigueur [vigœʀ] *nf* vigour; **entrer en ~** to come into force; **en ~** current.

vil, e [vil] *a* vile, base; **à ~ prix** at a very low price.

vilain, e [vilɛ̃, -ɛn] *a* (*laid*) ugly; (*affaire, blessure*) nasty; (*pas sage: enfant*) naughty.

vilebrequin [vilbʀəkɛ̃] *nm* (*outil*) (bit-)brace.

villa [vila] *nf* (detached) house.

village [vilaʒ] *nm* village; **villageois, e** *a* village *cpd* // *nm/f* villager.

ville [vil] *nf* town; (*importante*) city; (*administration*): **la ~** ≈ the Corporation; ≈ the (town) council.

villégiature [vileʒiatyʀ] *nf* holiday; (holiday) resort.

vin [vɛ̃] *nm* wine; **avoir le ~ gai** to get happy after a few drinks; **~ d'honneur** reception (*with wine and snacks*); **~ ordinaire** table wine; **~ de pays** local wine.

vinaigre [vinɛgʀ(ə)] *nm* vinegar; **vinaigrette** *nf* vinaigrette, French dressing.

vindicatif, ive [vɛ̃dikatif, -iv] *a* vindictive.

vineux, euse [vinø, -øz] *a* win(e)y.

vingt [vɛ̃, vɛ̃t] *num* twenty; **vingtaine** *nf*: **une vingtaine (de)** about twenty, twenty or so; **vingtième** *num* twentieth.

vinicole [vinikɔl] *a* wine *cpd*, wine-growing.

vins *etc vb voir* **venir**.

vinyle [vinil] *nm* vinyl.

viol [vjɔl] *nm* (*d'une femme*) rape; (*d'un lieu sacré*) violation.

violacé, e [vjɔlase] *a* purplish, mauvish.

violemment [vjɔlamɑ̃] *ad* violently.

violence [vjɔlɑ̃s] *nf* violence.

violent, e [vjɔlɑ̃, -ɑ̃t] *a* violent; (*remède*) drastic.

violer [vjɔle] *vt* (*femme*) to rape; (*sépulture, loi, traité*) to violate.

violet, te [vjɔle, -ɛt] *a, nm* purple, mauve // *nf* (*fleur*) violet.

violon [vjɔlɔ̃] *nm* violin; (*fam: prison*) lock-up.

violoncelle [vjɔlɔ̃sɛl] *nm* cello.

violoniste [vjɔlɔnist(ə)] *nm/f* violinist.

vipère [vipɛʀ] *nf* viper, adder.

virage [viʀaʒ] *nm* (*d'un véhicule*) turn; (*d'une route, piste*) bend; (*fig: POL*) about-turn.

virée [viʀe] *nf* (*courte*) run; (*: à pied*) walk; (*longue*) trip; hike, walking tour.

virement [viʀmɑ̃] nm (COMM) transfer.

virent vb voir aussi vire.

virer [viʀe] vt (COMM): ~ qch (sur) to transfer sth (into) // vi to turn; (CHIMIE) to change colour; ~ de bord to tack.

virevolter [viʀvɔlte] vi to twirl around.

virgule [viʀgyl] nf comma; (MATH) point.

viril, e [viʀil] a (propre à l'homme) masculine; (énergique, courageux) manly, virile.

virtuel, le [viʀtɥɛl] a potential; (théorique) virtual.

virtuose [viʀtɥoz] nm/f (MUS) virtuoso; (gén) master.

virus [viʀys] nm virus.

vis vb [vi] voir voir, vivre // nf [vis] screw.

visa [viza] nm (sceau) stamp; (validation de passeport) visa.

visage [vizaʒ] nm face.

vis-à-vis [vizavi] ad face to face // nm person opposite; house etc opposite; ~ de prép opposite; (fig) vis-à-vis; en ~ facing each other.

viscéral, e, aux [viseʀal, -o] a (fig) deep-seated, deep-rooted.

visée [vize]: ~s nfpl (intentions) designs.

viser [vize] vi to aim // vt to aim at; (concerner) to be aimed ou directed at; (apposer un visa sur) to stamp, visa; ~ à qch/faire to aim at sth/at doing ou to do.

viseur [vizœʀ] nm (d'arme) sights pl; (PHOTO) viewfinder.

visibilité [vizibilite] nf visibility.

visible [vizibl(ə)] a visible; (disponible): est-il ~? can he see me?, will he see visitors?

visière [vizjɛʀ] nf (de casquette) peak; (qui s'attache) eyeshade.

vision [vizjɔ̃] nf vision; (sens) (eye)sight, vision; (fait de voir): la ~ de the sight of.

visite [vizit] nf visit; (visiteur) visitor; (médicale, à domicile) visit, call; la ~ (MÉD) medical examination; faire une ~ à qn to call on sb, pay sb a visit; rendre ~ à qn to visit sb, pay sb a visit; être en ~ (chez qn) to be visiting (sb); heures de ~ (hôpital, prison) visiting hours.

visiter [vizite] vt to visit; (musée, ville) to visit, go round; **visiteur, euse** nm/f visitor.

vison [vizɔ̃] nm mink.

visser [vise] vt: ~ qch (fixer, serrer) to screw sth on.

visuel, le [vizɥɛl] a visual.

vit vb voir voir; vivre.

vital, e, aux [vital, -o] a vital.

vitamine [vitamin] nf vitamin.

vite [vit] ad (rapidement) quickly, fast; (sans délai) quickly; soon; **faire** ~ to act quickly; to be quick.

vitesse [vites] nf speed; (AUTO: disposi-

tif) gear; **prendre qn de** ~ to outstrip sb; get ahead of sb; **prendre de la** ~ to pick up ou gather speed; **à toute** ~ at full ou top speed.

viticole [vitikɔl] a wine cpd, wine-growing.

viticulteur [vitikyltœʀ] nm wine grower.

vitrage [vitraʒ] nm glass q; (rideau) net curtain.

vitrail, aux [vitraj, -o] nm stained-glass window.

vitre [vitr(ə)] nf (window) pane; (de portière, voiture) window.

vitré, e [vitre] a glass cpd.

vitrer [vitre] vt to glaze.

vitreux, euse [vitrø, -øz] a (terne) glassy.

vitrine [vitrin] nf (devanture) (shop) window; (étalage) display; (petite armoire) display cabinet; ~ publicitaire display case, showcase.

vitupérer [vitypere] vi to rant and rave.

vivace a [vivas] (arbre, plante) hardy; (fig) indestructible, inveterate.

vivacité [vivasite] nf liveliness, vivacity; sharpness; brilliance.

vivant, e [vivɑ̃, -ɑ̃t] a (qui vit) living, alive; (animé) lively; (preuve, exemple) living // nm: du ~ de qn in sb's lifetime.

vivats [viva] nmpl cheers.

vive [viv] af voir vif // vb voir vivre // excl: ~ le roi! long live the king!; ~ment ad vivaciously; sharply // excl: ~ment les vacances! roll on the holidays!

viveur [vivœʀ] nm (péj) high liver, pleasure-seeker.

vivier [vivje] nm fish tank; fishpond.

vivifiant, e [vivifjɑ̃, -ɑ̃t] a invigorating.

vivions vb voir vivre.

vivre [vivr(ə)] vi, vt to live; ~s nmpl provisions, food supplies; il vit encore he is still alive; se laisser ~ to take life as it comes; ne plus ~ (être anxieux) to live on one's nerves; il a vécu (eu une vie aventureuse) he has seen life; être facile à ~ to be easy to get on with; faire ~ qn (pourvoir à sa subsistance) to provide (a living) for sb.

vlan [vlɑ̃] excl wham!, bang!

vocable [vɔkabl(ə)] nm term.

vocabulaire [vɔkabylɛʀ] nm vocabulary.

vocation [vɔkasjɔ̃] nf vocation, calling.

vociférer [vɔsifeʀe] vi, vt to scream.

vodka [vɔdka] nf vodka.

vœu, x [vø] nm wish; (à Dieu) vow; **faire** ~ **de** to take a vow of; ~x de bonne année best wishes for the New Year.

vogue [vɔg] nf fashion, vogue.

voguer [vɔge] vi to sail.

voici [vwasi] prép (pour introduire, désigner) here is + sg, here are + pl; et ~ que ... and now it (ou he) ...; voir aussi voilà.

voie [vwa] *nf* way; (*RAIL*) track, line; (*AUTO*) lane; **être en bonne ~** to be going well; **mettre qn sur la ~** to put sb on the right track; **être en ~ d'achèvement/de rénovation** to be nearing completion/in the process of renovation; **par ~ buccale** *ou* **orale** orally; **à ~ étroite** narrow-gauge; **~ d'eau** (*NAVIG*) leak; **~ ferrée** track; railway line; **~ de garage** (*RAIL*) siding.

voilà [vwala] *prép* (*en désignant*) there is + *sg*, there are + *pl*; **les ~** *ou* **voici** here *ou* there they are; **en ~ un** here's one, there's one; **~** *ou* **voici deux ans** two years ago; **~** *ou* **voici deux ans que** it's two years since; **et ~!** there we are!; **~ tout** that's all; **'~** *ou* **voici'** (*en offrant etc*) 'there *ou* here you are'.

voile [vwal] *nm* veil; (*tissu léger*) net // *nf* sail; (*sport*) sailing.

voiler [vwale] *vt* to veil; (*fausser: roue*) to buckle; (*: bois*) to warp; **se ~** *vi* (*lune, regard*) to mist over; (*voix*) to become husky; (*roue, disque*) to buckle; (*planche*) to warp.

voilier [vwalje] *nm* sailing ship; (*de plaisance*) sailing boat.

voilure [vwalyʀ] *nf* (*de voilier*) sails *pl*.

voir [vwaʀ] *vi, vt* to see; **se ~** *vt*: **se ~ critiquer/transformer** to be criticized/transformed; **cela se voit** (*cela arrive*) it happens; (*c'est visible*) that's obvious, it shows; **~ venir** (*fig*) to wait and see; **faire ~ qch à qn** to show sb sth; **en faire ~ à qn** (*fig*) to give sb a hard time; **ne pas pouvoir ~ qn** (*fig*) not to be able to stand sb; **voyons!** let's see now; (*indignation etc*) come (along) now!; **avoir quelque chose à ~ avec** to have something to do with.

voire [vwaʀ] *ad* indeed; nay; or even.

voisin, e [vwazɛ̃, -in] *a* (*proche*) neighbouring; (*contigu*) next; (*ressemblant*) connected // *nm/f* neighbour; **voisinage** *nm* (*proximité*) proximity; (*environs*) vicinity; (*quartier, voisins*) neighbourhood.

voiture [vwatyʀ] *nf* car; (*wagon*) coach, carriage; **~ d'enfant** pram (*Brit*), baby carriage (*US*); **~ de sport** sports car; **~-lit** *nf* sleeper.

voix [vwa] *nf* voice; (*POL*) vote; **à haute ~** aloud; **à ~ basse** in a low voice; **à 2/4 ~** (*MUS*) in 2/4 parts; **avoir ~ au chapitre** to have a say in the matter.

vol [vɔl] *nm* (*mode de locomotion*) flying; (*trajet, voyage, groupe d'oiseaux*) flight; (*larcin*) theft; **à ~ d'oiseau** as the crow flies; **au ~: attraper qch au ~** to catch sth as it flies past; **en ~** in flight; **~ libre** hang-gliding; **~ à main armée** armed robbery; **~ à voile** gliding.

volage [vɔlaʒ] *a* fickle.

volaille [vɔlaj] *nf* (*oiseaux*) poultry *pl*; (*viande*) poultry *q*; (*oiseau*) fowl.

volant, e [vɔlɑ̃, -ɑ̃t] *a voir* **feuille** etc //

nm (*d'automobile*) (steering) wheel; (*de commande*) wheel; (*objet lancé*) shuttlecock; (*bande de tissu*) flounce.

volcan [vɔlkɑ̃] *nm* volcano.

volée [vɔle] *nf* (*TENNIS*) volley; **~ de coups/de flèches** volley of blows/arrows; **à la ~: rattraper à la ~** to catch in mid air; **à toute ~** (*sonner les cloches*) vigorously; (*lancer un projectile*) with full force.

voler [vɔle] *vi* (*avion, oiseau, fig*) to fly; (*voleur*) to steal // *vt* (*objet*) to steal; (*personne*) to rob; **~ qch à qn** to steal sth from sb.

volet [vɔlɛ] *nm* (*de fenêtre*) shutter; (*de feuillet, document*) section.

voleter [vɔlte] *vi* to flutter (about).

voleur, euse [vɔlœʀ, -øz] *nm/f* thief (*pl* thieves) // *a* thieving.

volontaire [vɔlɔ̃tɛʀ] *a* voluntary; (*caractère, personne: décidé*) self-willed // *nm/f* volunteer.

volonté [vɔlɔ̃te] *nf* (*faculté de vouloir*) will; (*énergie, fermeté*) will(power); (*souhait, désir*) wish; **à ~** as much as one likes; **bonne ~** goodwill, willingness; **mauvaise ~** lack of goodwill, unwillingness.

volontiers [vɔlɔ̃tje] *ad* (*de bonne grâce*) willingly; (*avec plaisir*) willingly, gladly; (*habituellement, souvent*) readily, willingly.

volt [vɔlt] *nm* volt.

volte-face [vɔltəfas] *nf inv* about-turn.

voltige [vɔltiʒ] *nf* (*ÉQUITATION*) trick riding; (*au cirque*) acrobatics *sg*.

voltiger [vɔltiʒe] *vi* to flutter (about).

volume [vɔlym] *nm* volume; (*GÉOM: solide*) solid; **volumineux, euse** *a* voluminous, bulky.

volupté [vɔlypte] *nf* sensual delight *ou* pleasure.

vomir [vɔmiʀ] *vi* to vomit, be sick // *vt* to vomit, bring up; (*fig*) to belch out, spew out; (*exécrer*) to loathe, abhor.

vont [vɔ̃] *vb voir* **aller**.

vos [vo] *dét voir* **votre**.

vote [vɔt] *nm* vote; **~ par correspondance/procuration** postal/proxy vote.

voter [vɔte] *vi* to vote // *vt* (*loi, décision*) to vote for.

votre [vɔtʀ(ə)], *pl* **vos** [vo] *dét* your.

vôtre [votʀ(ə)] *pronom*: **le ~, la ~, les ~s** yours; **les ~s** (*fig*) your family *ou* folks; **à la ~** (*toast*) your (good) health!

voudrai etc *vb voir* **vouloir**.

voué, e [vwe] *a*: **~ à** doomed to.

vouer [vwe] *vt*: **~ qch à** (*Dieu/un saint*) to dedicate sth to; **~ sa vie à** (*étude, cause etc*) to devote one's life to; **~ une amitié éternelle à qn** to vow undying friendship to sb.

vouloir [vulwaʀ] ♦ *nm*: **le bon ~ de qn** sb's goodwill; sb's pleasure

♦ *vt* **1** (*exiger, désirer*) to want; **~**

faire/que qn fasse to want to do/sb to do; **voulez-vous du thé?** would you like ou do you want some tea?; **que me veut-il?** what does he want with me?; **sans le ~** (*involontairement*) without meaning to, unintentionally; **je voudrais ceci/faire** I would ou I'd like this/to do
2 (*consentir*): **je veux bien** (*bonne volonté*) I'll be happy to; (*concession*) fair enough, that's fine; **oui, si on veut** (*en quelque sorte*) yes, if you like; **veuillez attendre** please wait; **veuillez agréer ...** (*formule épistolaire*) yours faithfully
3: **en ~ à**: **en ~ à qn** to bear sb a grudge; **s'en ~ (de)** to be annoyed with o.s. (for); **il en veut à mon argent** he's after my money
4: **~ de**: **l'entreprise ne veut plus de lui** the firm doesn't want him any more; **elle ne veut pas de son aide** she doesn't want his help
5: **~ dire** to mean.
voulu, e [vuly] *a* (*requis*) required, requisite; (*délibéré*) deliberate, intentional.
vous [vu] *pronom* you; (*objet indirect*) (to) you; (*réfléchi*) yourself (*pl* yourselves); (*réciproque*) each other; **~-même** yourself; **~-mêmes** yourselves.
voûte [vut] *nf* vault.
voûter [vute] *vt*: **se ~** *vi* (*dos, personne*) to become stooped.
vouvoyer [vuvwaje] *vt*: **~ qn** to address sb as 'vous'.
voyage [vwajaʒ] *nm* journey, trip; (*fait de voyager*): **le ~** travel(ling); **partir/être en ~** to go off/be away on a journey ou trip; **faire bon ~** to have a good journey; **~ d'agrément/d'affaires** pleasure/business trip; **~ de noces** honeymoon; **~ organisé** package tour.
voyager [vwajaʒe] *vi* to travel; **voyageur, euse** *nm/f* traveller; (*passager*) passenger.
voyant, e [vwajã, -ãt] *a* (*couleur*) loud, gaudy // *nm* (*signal*) (warning) light // *nf* clairvoyant.
voyelle [vwajɛl] *nf* vowel.
voyons *etc vb voir* **voir**.
voyou [vwaju] *nm* lout, hoodlum; (*enfant*) guttersnipe.
vrac [vʀak]: **en ~** *ad* higgledy-piggledy; (*COMM*) in bulk.
vrai, e [vʀɛ] *a* (*véridique: récit, faits*) true; (*non factice, authentique*) real; **à ~ dire** to tell the truth.
vraiment [vʀɛmã] *ad* really.
vraisemblable [vʀɛsãblabl(ə)] *a* likely, probable.
vraisemblance [vʀɛsãblãs] *nf* likelihood; (*romanesque*) verisimilitude.
vrille [vʀij] *nf* (*de plante*) tendril; (*outil*) gimlet; (*spirale*) spiral; (*AVIAT*) spin.
vrombir [vʀɔ̃biʀ] *vi* to hum.
vu [vy] *prép* (*en raison de*) in view of; **~**

que in view of the fact that.
vu, e [vy] *pp de* **voir** // *a*: **bien/mal ~** (*fig*) well/poorly thought of; good/bad form.
vue [vy] *nf* (*fait de voir*): **la ~ de** the sight of; (*sens, faculté*) (eye)sight; (*panorama, image, photo*) view; **~s** *nfpl* (*idées*) views; (*dessein*) designs; **hors de ~** out of sight; **tirer à ~** to shoot on sight; **à ~ d'œil** *ad* visibly; at a quick glance; **en ~** (*visible*) in sight; (*COMM*) in the public eye; **en ~ de faire** with a view to doing.
vulgaire [vylgɛʀ] *a* (*grossier*) vulgar, coarse; (*trivial*) commonplace, mundane; (*péj: quelconque*): **de ~s touristes** common tourists; (*BOT, ZOOL: non latin*) common; **vulgariser** *vt* to popularize.
vulnérable [vylneʀabl(ə)] *a* vulnerable.

W X Y Z

wagon [vagɔ̃] *nm* (*de voyageurs*) carriage; (*de marchandises*) truck, wagon; **~-citerne** *nm* tanker; **~-lit** *nm* sleeper, sleeping car; **~-restaurant** *nm* restaurant ou dining car.
wallon, ne [walɔ̃, -ɔn] *a* Walloon.
waters [watɛʀ] *nmpl* toilet *sg*.
watt [wat] *nm* watt.
w.-c. [vese] *nmpl* toilet *sg*, lavatory *sg*.
week-end [wikɛnd] *nm* weekend.
western [wɛstɛʀn] *nm* western.
whisky, *pl* whiskies [wiski] *nm* whisky.
xérès [gzeʀɛs] *nm* sherry.
xylophone [ksilɔfɔn] *nm* xylophone.
y [i] *ad* (*à cet endroit*) there; (*dessus*) on it (*ou* them); (*dedans*) in it (*ou* them) // *pronom* (about ou on ou of) it : *vérifier la syntaxe du verbe employé*; **j'~ pense** I'm thinking about it; *voir aussi* **aller**, **avoir**.
yacht [jɔt] *nm* yacht.
yaourt [jauʀt] *nm* yoghourt.
yeux [jø] *pl de* **œil**.
yoga [jɔga] *nm* yoga.
yoghourt [jɔguʀt] *nm* = **yaourt**.
yougoslave [jugɔslav] *a*, *nm/f* Yugoslav(ian).
Yougoslavie [jugɔslavi] *nf* Yugoslavia.
zèbre [zɛbʀ(ə)] *nm* (*ZOOL*) zebra.
zébré, e [zebʀe] *a* striped, streaked.
zèle [zɛl] *nm* zeal; **faire du ~** (*péj*) to be over-zealous.
zéro [zeʀo] *nm* zero, nought (*Brit*); **au-dessous de ~** below zero (Centigrade) ou freezing; **partir de ~** to start from scratch; **trois (buts) à ~** 3 (goals) to nil.
zeste [zɛst(ə)] *nm* peel, zest.
zézayer [zezeje] *vi* to have a lisp.
zigzag [zigzag] *nm* zigzag.
zinc [zɛ̃g] *nm* (*CHIMIE*) zinc; (*comptoir*) bar, counter.

zizanie [zizani] *nf*: semer la ~ to stir up ill-feeling.
zodiaque [zɔdjak] *nm* zodiac.
zona [zona] *nm* shingles *sg*.
zone [zon] *nf* zone, area; *(quartiers)*: la ~ the slum belt; ~ **bleue** ≈ restricted parking area.
zoo [zoo] *nm* zoo.
zoologie [zɔɔlɔʒi] *nf* zoology; **zoologique** *a* zoological.
zut [zyt] *excl* dash (it)! *(Brit)*, nuts! *(US)*.

ENGLISH - FRENCH
ANGLAIS - FRANÇAIS

A

A [eɪ] n (MUS) la m; (AUT): ~ **road** route nationale.

a (before vowel or silent h: **an**) [æ, æn] indefinite article **1** un(e); ~ **book** un livre; **an apple** une pomme; **she's** ~ **doctor** elle est médecin
2 (instead of the number 'one') un(e); ~ **year ago** il y a un an; ~ **hundred/ thousand** etc **pounds** cent/mille etc livres
3 (in expressing ratios, prices etc): 3 ~ **day/week** 3 par jour/semaine; **10 km an hour** 10 km à l'heure; **30p** ~ **kilo** 30p le kilo.

A.A. n abbr =Alcoholics Anonymous; (Brit: =Automobile Association) ≈TCF m.

A.A.A. n abbr (US: =American Automobile Association) ≈TCF m.

aback [ə'bæk] ad: **to be taken** ~ être stupéfait(e).

abandon [ə'bændən] vt abandonner // n abandon m; **with** ~ avec désinvolture.

abashed [ə'bæʃt] a confus(e), embarrassé(e).

abate [ə'beɪt] vi s'apaiser, se calmer.

abbey ['æbɪ] n abbaye f.

abbot ['æbət] n père supérieur.

abbreviation [əbriːˈvɪ'eɪʃən] n abréviation f.

abdicate ['æbdɪkeɪt] vt, vi abdiquer.

abdomen ['æbdəmɛn] n abdomen m.

abduct [æb'dʌkt] vt enlever.

aberration [æbə'reɪʃən] n anomalie f.

abet [ə'bɛt] vt see **aid**.

abeyance [ə'beɪəns] n: **in** ~ (law) en désuétude; (matter) en suspens.

abide [ə'baɪd] vt: **I can't** ~ **it/him** je ne peux pas le souffrir or supporter; **to** ~ **by** vt fus observer, respecter.

ability [ə'bɪlɪtɪ] n compétence f; capacité f; (skill) talent m.

abject ['æbdʒɛkt] a (poverty) sordide; (apology) plat(e).

ablaze [ə'bleɪz] a en feu, en flammes.

able ['eɪbl] a compétent(e); **to be** ~ **to do sth** pouvoir faire qch, être capable de faire qch; **ably** ad avec compétence or talent, habilement.

abnormal [æb'nɔːməl] a anormal(e).

aboard [ə'bɔːd] ad à bord // prep à bord de.

abode [ə'bəʊd] n: **of no fixed** ~ sans domicile fixe.

abolish [ə'bɒlɪʃ] vt abolir.

aborigine [æbə'rɪdʒɪnɪ] n aborigène m/f.

abort [ə'bɔːt] vt faire avorter; ~**ion**

[ə'bɔːʃən] n avortement m; **to have an** ~**ion** se faire avorter; ~**ive** a manqué(e).

abound [ə'baʊnd] vi abonder; **to** ~ **in** abonder en, regorger de.

about [ə'baʊt] ♦ ad **1** (approximately) environ, à peu près; ~ **a hundred/ thousand** etc environ cent/mille etc, une centaine/un millier etc; **it takes** ~ **10 hours** ça prend environ or à peu près 10 heures; **at** ~ **2 o'clock** vers 2 heures; **I've just** ~ **finished** j'ai presque fini
2 (referring to place) çà et là, de côté et d'autre; **to run** ~ courir çà et là; **to walk** ~ se promener, aller et venir
3: **to be** ~ **to do sth** être sur le point de faire qch
♦ prep **1** (relating to) au sujet de, à propos de; **a book** ~ **London** un livre sur Londres; **what is it** ~? de quoi s'agit-il?; **we talked** ~ **it** nous en avons parlé; **what or how** ~ **doing this?** et si nous faisions ceci?
2 (referring to place) dans; **to walk** ~ **the town** se promener dans la ville.

about turn n demi-tour m.

above [ə'bʌv] ad au-dessus // prep au-dessus de; **mentioned** ~ mentionné ci-dessus; ~ **all** par-dessus tout, surtout; ~**board** a franc(franche), loyal(e); honnête.

abrasive [ə'breɪzɪv] a abrasif(ive); (fig) caustique, agressif(ive).

abreast [ə'brɛst] ad de front; **to keep** ~ **of** se tenir au courant de.

abridge [ə'brɪdʒ] vt abréger.

abroad [ə'brɔːd] ad à l'étranger.

abrupt [ə'brʌpt] a (steep, blunt) abrupt(e); (sudden, gruff) brusque.

abscess ['æbsɪs] n abcès m.

abscond [əb'skɒnd] vi disparaître, s'enfuir.

absence ['æbsəns] n absence f.

absent ['æbsənt] a absent(e); ~**ee** [-'tiː] n absent/e; ~**-minded** a distrait(e).

absolute ['æbsəluːt] a absolu(e); ~**ly** [-'luːtlɪ] ad absolument.

absolve [əb'zɒlv] vt: **to** ~ **sb (from)** (sin etc) absoudre qn (de); **to** ~ **sb from** (oath) délier qn de.

absorb [əb'zɔːb] vt absorber; **to be** ~**ed in a book** être plongé dans un livre; ~**ent cotton** n (US) coton m hydrophile.

absorption [əb'zɔːpʃən] n absorption f; amortissement m; intégration f; (fig) concentration *f*.

abstain [əb'steɪn] *vi*: to ~ **(from)** s'abstenir (de).

abstemious [əb'sti:mɪəs] *a* sobre, frugal(e).

abstract ['æbstrækt] *a* abstrait(e).

absurd [əb'sə:d] *a* absurde.

abuse *n* [ə'bju:s] abus *m*, insultes *fpl*, injures *fpl* // *vt* [ə'bju:z] abuser de; **abusive** *a* grossier(ère), injurieux(euse).

abysmal [ə'bɪzməl] *a* exécrable; (*ignorance etc*) sans bornes.

abyss [ə'bɪs] *n* abîme *m*, gouffre *m*.

AC *abbr* (=*alternating current*) courant alternatif.

academic [ækə'dɛmɪk] *a* universitaire; (*pej: issue*) oiseux(euse), purement théorique // *n* universitaire *m/f*.

academy [ə'kædəmɪ] *n* (*learned body*) académie *f*; (*school*) collège *m*; ~ of music conservatoire *m*.

accelerate [æk'sɛləreɪt] *vt*, *vi* accélérer; **accelerator** *n* accélérateur *m*.

accent ['æksənt] *n* accent *m*.

accept [ək'sɛpt] *vt* accepter; ~**able** *a* acceptable; ~**ance** *n* acceptation *f*.

access ['æksɛs] *n* accès *m*; ~**ible** [æk'sɛsəbl] *a* accessible.

accessory [æk'sɛsərɪ] *n* accessoire *m*; toilet accessories *npl* articles *mpl* de toilette.

accident ['æksɪdənt] *n* accident *m*; (*chance*) hasard *m*; by ~ par hasard; accidentellement; ~**al** [-'dɛntl] *a* accidentel(le); ~**ally** [-'dɛntlɪ] *ad* accidentellement; ~-**prone** *a* sujet(te) aux accidents.

acclaim [ə'kleɪm] *n* acclamation *f*.

accommodate [ə'kɔmədeɪt] *vt* loger, recevoir; (*oblige, help*) obliger.

accommodating [ə'kɔmədeɪtɪŋ] *a* obligeant(e), arrangeant(e).

accommodation [əkɔmə'deɪʃən] *n* (*US*: ~s) logement *m*.

accompany [ə'kʌmpənɪ] *vt* accompagner.

accomplice [ə'kʌmplɪs] *n* complice *m/f*.

accomplish [ə'kʌmplɪʃ] *vt* accomplir; ~**ment** *n* accomplissement *m*; réussite *f*, résultat *m*; ~**ments** *npl* talents *mpl*.

accord [ə'kɔ:d] *n* accord *m* // *vt* accorder; **of his own** ~ de son plein gré; ~**ance** *n*: **in** ~**ance with** conformément à; ~**ing to** *prep* selon; ~**ingly** *ad* en conséquence.

accordion [ə'kɔ:dɪən] *n* accordéon *m*.

accost [ə'kɔst] *vt* aborder.

account [ə'kaunt] *n* (*COMM*) compte *m*; (*report*) compte rendu; récit *m*; ~**s** *npl* comptabilité *f*, comptes; **of little** ~ de peu d'importance; **on** ~ en acompte; **on no** ~ en aucun cas; **on** ~ **of** à cause de; **to take into** ~, **take** ~ **of** tenir compte de; **to** ~ **for** *vt fus* expliquer, rendre compte de; ~**able** *a* responsable.

accountancy [ə'kauntənsɪ] *n* comptabilité *f*.

accountant [ə'kauntənt] *n* comptable *m/f*.

account number *n* (*at bank etc*) numéro *m* de compte.

accumulate [ə'kju:mjuleɪt] *vt* accumuler, amasser // *vi* s'accumuler, s'amasser.

accuracy ['ækjurəsɪ] *n* exactitude *f*, précision *f*.

accurate ['ækjurɪt] *a* exact(e), précis(e); ~**ly** *ad* avec précision.

accusation [ækju'zeɪʃən] *n* accusation *f*.

accuse [ə'kju:z] *vt* accuser; ~**d** *n* accusé/e.

accustom [ə'kʌstəm] *vt* accoutumer, habituer; ~**ed** *a* (*usual*) habituel(le); ~**ed to** habitué(e) *or* accoutumé(e) à.

ace [eɪs] *n* as *m*.

ache [eɪk] *n* mal *m*, douleur *f* // *vi* (*be sore*) faire mal, être douloureux(euse); **my head** ~s j'ai mal à la tête.

achieve [ə'tʃi:v] *vt* (*aim*) atteindre; (*victory, success*) remporter, obtenir; (*task*) accomplir; ~**ment** *n* exploit *m*, réussite *f*.

acid ['æsɪd] *a*, *n* acide (*m*); ~ **rain** *n* pluies *fpl* acides.

acknowledge [ək'nɔlɪdʒ] *vt* (*letter: also*: ~ **receipt of**) accuser réception de; (*fact*) reconnaître; ~**ment** *n* accusé *m* de réception.

acne ['æknɪ] *n* acné *m*.

acorn ['eɪkɔ:n] *n* gland *m*.

acoustic [ə'ku:stɪk] *a* acoustique; ~**s** *n*, *npl* acoustique *f*.

acquaint [ə'kweɪnt] *vt*: to ~ **sb with sth** mettre qn au courant de qch; **to be** ~**ed with** (*person*) connaître; ~**ance** *n* connaissance *f*.

acquire [ə'kwaɪə*] *vt* acquérir.

acquit [ə'kwɪt] *vt* acquitter; **to** ~ **o.s. well** bien se comporter, s'en tirer très honorablement; ~**tal** *n* acquittement *m*.

acre ['eɪkə*] *n* acre *f* (= 4047 m²).

acrid ['ækrɪd] *a* âcre.

acrobat ['ækrəbæt] *n* acrobate *m/f*.

across [ə'krɔs] *prep* (*on the other side*) de l'autre côté de; (*crosswise*) en travers de // *ad* de l'autre côté; en travers; **to run/swim** ~ traverser en courant/à la nage; ~ **from** en face de.

acrylic [ə'krɪlɪk] *a*, *n* acrylique (*m*).

act [ækt] *n* acte *m*, action *f*; (*THEATRE*) acte; (*in music-hall etc*) numéro *m*; (*LAW*) loi *f* // *vi* agir; (*THEATRE*) jouer; (*pretend*) jouer la comédie // *vt* (*part*) jouer, tenir; **to** ~ **as** servir de; ~**ing** *a* suppléant(e), par intérim // *n* (*of actor*) jeu *m*; (*activity*): **to do some** ~**ing** faire du théâtre (*or* du cinéma).

action ['ækʃən] *n* action *f*; (*MIL*) combat(s) *m(pl)*; (*LAW*) procès *m*, action en justice; **out of** ~ hors de combat; hors d'usage; **to take ~** agir, prendre des mesures; **~ replay** n (TV) répétition f d'une séquence.

activate ['æktɪveɪt] vt (mechanism) actionner, faire fonctionner; (CHEM, PHYSICS) activer.

active ['æktɪv] a actif(ive); (volcano) en activité; **~ly** ad activement.

activity [æk'tɪvɪtɪ] n activité f.

actor ['æktə*] n acteur m.

actress ['æktrɪs] n actrice f.

actual ['æktjuəl] a réel(le), véritable; **~ly** ad réellement, véritablement; en fait.

acumen ['ækjumən] n perspicacité f.

acute [ə'kju:t] a aigu(ë); (mind, observer) pénétrant(e).

ad [æd] n abbr of **advertisement**.

A.D. ad abbr (= Anno Domini) ap. J.-C.

adamant ['ædəmənt] a inflexible.

adapt [ə'dæpt] vt adapter // vi: **to ~ (to)** s'adapter (à); **~able** a (device) adaptable; (person) qui s'adapte facilement; **~er** or **~or** n (ELEC) adapteur m.

add [æd] vt ajouter; (figures: also: **to ~ up)** additionner // vi: **to ~ to** (increase) ajouter à, accroître; **it doesn't ~ up** (fig) cela ne rime à rien.

adder ['ædə*] n vipère f.

addict ['ædɪkt] n intoxiqué/e; (fig) fanatique m/f; **~ed** [ə'dɪktɪd] a: **to be ~ed to** (drink etc) être adonné(e) à; (fig: football etc) être un(e) fanatique de; **~ion** [ə'dɪkʃən] n (MED) dépendance f; **~ive** a qui crée une dépendance.

addition [ə'dɪʃən] n addition f; **in ~** de plus; de surcroît; **in ~ to** en plus de; **~al** a supplémentaire.

additive ['ædɪtɪv] n additif m.

address [ə'drɛs] n adresse f; (talk) discours m, allocution f // vt adresser; (speak to) s'adresser à.

adept ['ædɛpt] a: **~ at** expert(e) à or en.

adequate ['ædɪkwɪt] a adéquat(e); suffisant(e); compétent(e).

adhere [əd'hɪə*] vi: **to ~ to** adhérer à; (fig: rule, decision) se tenir à.

adhesive [əd'hi:zɪv] a adhésif(ive) // n adhésif m; **~ tape** n (Brit) ruban adhésif; (US: MED) sparadrap m.

adjective ['ædʒɛktɪv] n adjectif m.

adjoining [ə'dʒɔɪnɪŋ] a voisin(e), adjacent(e), attenant(e).

adjourn [ə'dʒə:n] vt ajourner // vi suspendre la séance; lever la séance; clore la session; (go) se retirer.

adjudicate [ə'dʒu:dɪkeɪt] vi se prononcer.

adjust [ə'dʒʌst] vt ajuster, régler; rajuster // vi: **to ~ (to)** s'adapter (à); **~able** a réglable.

ad-lib [æd'lɪb] vt, vi improviser // ad: **ad lib** à volonté, à discrétion.

administer [əd'mɪnɪstə*] vt adminis-

trer; (justice) rendre.

administration [ədmɪnɪs'treɪʃən] n administration f.

administrative [əd'mɪnɪstrətɪv] a administratif(ive).

admiral ['ædmərəl] n amiral m; **A~ty** n (Brit: also: **A~ty Board**) ministère m de la Marine.

admiration [ædmə'reɪʃən] n admiration f.

admire [əd'maɪə*] vt admirer.

admission [əd'mɪʃən] n admission f; (to exhibition, night club etc) entrée f; (confession) aveu m.

admit [əd'mɪt] vt laisser entrer; admettre; (agree) reconnaître, admettre; **to ~ to** vt fus reconnaître, avouer; **~tance** n admission f, (droit m d')entrée f; **~tedly** ad il faut en convenir.

admonish [əd'mɒnɪʃ] vt donner un avertissement à; réprimander.

ad nauseam [æd'nɔ:zɪəm] ad (repeat, talk) à satiété.

ado [ə'du:] n: **without (any) more ~** sans plus de cérémonies.

adolescence [ædəu'lɛsns] n adolescence f.

adolescent [ædəu'lɛsnt] a, n adolescent(e).

adopt [ə'dɒpt] vt adopter; **~ed** a adoptif(ive), adopté(e); **~ion** [ə'dɒpʃən] n adoption f.

adore [ə'dɔ:*] vt adorer.

adorn [ə'dɔ:n] vt orner.

Adriatic (Sea) [eɪdrɪ'ætɪk('si:)] n Adriatique f.

adrift [ə'drɪft] ad à la dérive.

adult ['ædʌlt] n adulte m/f.

adultery [ə'dʌltərɪ] n adultère m.

advance [əd'vɑ:ns] n avance f // vt avancer // vi s'avancer; **in ~** en avance, d'avance; **~d** a avancé(e); (SCOL: studies) supérieur(e).

advantage [əd'vɑ:ntɪdʒ] n (also TENNIS) avantage m; **to take ~ of** profiter de.

advent ['ædvənt] n avènement m, venue f; **A~** Avent m.

adventure [əd'vɛntʃə*] n aventure f.

adverb ['ædvə:b] n adverbe m.

adverse ['ædvə:s] a contraire, adverse; **~ to** hostile à.

advert ['ædvə:t] n abbr (Brit) of **advertisement**.

advertise ['ædvətaɪz] vi (vt) faire de la publicité or de la réclame (pour); mettre une annonce (pour vendre); **to ~ for** (staff) faire paraître une annonce pour trouver.

advertisement [əd'və:tɪsmənt] n (COMM) réclame f, publicité f; (in classified ads) annonce f.

advertiser ['ædvətaɪzə*] n (in newspaper etc) annonceur m.

advertising ['ædvətaɪzɪŋ] n publicité f,

réclame f.

advice [əd'vaɪs] n conseils mpl; (notification) avis m; **piece of ~** conseil; **to take legal ~** consulter un avocat.

advisable [əd'vaɪzəbl] a recommandable, indiqué(e).

advise [əd'vaɪz] vt conseiller; **to ~ sb of sth** aviser or informer qn de qch; **to ~ against sth/doing sth** déconseiller qch/conseiller de ne pas faire qch; **~dly** [-'vaɪzədlɪ] ad (deliberately) délibérément; **~r** n conseiller/ère; **advisory** [-ərɪ] a consultatif(ive).

advocate n ['ædvəkɪt] (upholder) défenseur m, avocat/e ♦ vt ['ædvəkeɪt] recommander, prôner; **to be an ~ of** être partisan(e) de.

aerial ['ɛərɪəl] n antenne f // a aérien(ne).

aerobics [ɛə'rəʊbɪks] n aérobic m.

aeroplane ['ɛərəpleɪn] n (Brit) avion m.

aerosol ['ɛərəsɒl] n aérosol m.

aesthetic [ɪs'θɛtɪk] a esthétique.

afar [ə'fɑ:*] ad: **from ~** de loin.

affair [ə'fɛə*] n affaire f; (also: **love ~**) liaison f; aventure f.

affect [ə'fɛkt] vt affecter.

affection [ə'fɛkʃən] n affection f; **~ate** a affectueux(euse).

affirmation [æfə'meɪʃən] n affirmation f, assertion f.

affix [ə'fɪks] vt apposer, ajouter.

afflict [ə'flɪkt] vt affliger.

affluence ['æfluəns] n abondance f, opulence f.

affluent ['æfluənt] a abondant(e); opulent(e); (person) dans l'aisance, riche.

afford [ə'fɔ:d] vt se permettre; avoir les moyens d'acheter or d'entretenir; (provide) fournir, procurer.

afield [ə'fi:ld] ad: **far ~** loin.

afloat [ə'fləʊt] a, ad à flot; **to stay ~** surnager.

afoot [ə'fʊt] ad: **there is something ~** il se prépare quelque chose.

afraid [ə'freɪd] a effrayé(e); **to be ~ of** or **to** avoir peur de; **I am ~ that** je crains que + sub.

afresh [ə'frɛʃ] ad de nouveau.

Africa ['æfrɪkə] n Afrique f; **~n** a africain(e) // n Africain/e.

aft [ɑ:ft] ad à l'arrière, vers l'arrière.

after ['ɑ:ftə*] prep, ad après // cj après que, après avoir or être + pp; **what/who are you ~?** que/qui cherchez-vous?; **~ he left/having done** après qu'il fut parti/après avoir fait; **ask ~ him** demandez de ses nouvelles; **~ all** après tout; **~ you!** après vous, Monsieur (or Madame etc); **~-effects** npl répercussions fpl; (of illness) séquelles fpl, suites fpl; **~life** n vie future; **~math** n conséquences fpl; **in the ~math of** dans les mois or années etc qui suivirent, au lendemain de;

~noon n après-midi m or f; **~s** n (col: dessert) dessert m; **~-sales service** n (Brit: for car, washing machine etc) service m après-vente (S.A.V.); **~-shave (lotion)** n after-shave m; **~-thought** n: **I had an ~thought** il m'est venu une idée après coup; **~wards** ad après.

again [ə'gɛn] ad de nouveau; **to do sth ~** refaire qch; **not ~** ne — plus; **~ and ~** à plusieurs reprises.

against [ə'gɛnst] prep contre.

age [eɪdʒ] n âge m // vt, vi vieillir; **it's been ~s since** ça fait une éternité que — ne; **he is 20 years of ~** il a 20 ans; **to come of ~** atteindre sa majorité; **~d 10** âgé de 10 ans; **the ~d** ['eɪdʒɪd] les personnes âgées; **~ group** n tranche f d'âge; **~ limit** n limite f d'âge.

agency ['eɪdʒənsɪ] n agence f; **through or by the ~ of** par l'entremise or l'action de.

agenda [ə'dʒɛndə] n ordre m du jour.

agent ['eɪdʒənt] n agent m.

aggregate ['ægrɪgeɪt] n ensemble m, total m.

aggressive [ə'grɛsɪv] a agressif(ive).

aggrieved [ə'gri:vd] a chagriné(e), affligé(e).

aghast [ə'gɑ:st] a consterné(e), atterré(e).

agitate ['ædʒɪteɪt] vt rendre inquiet(ète) or agité(e); agiter; **to ~ for** faire campagne pour.

ago [ə'gəʊ] ad: **2 days ~** il y a deux jours; **not long ~** il n'y a pas longtemps; **how long ~?** il y a combien de temps (de cela)?

agog [ə'gɒg] a en émoi.

agonizing ['ægənaɪzɪŋ] a angoissant(e); déchirant(e).

agony ['ægənɪ] n grande souffrance or angoisse.

agree [ə'gri:] vt (price) convenir de // vi: **to ~ (with)** (person) être d'accord (avec); (statements etc) concorder (avec); (LING) s'accorder (avec); **to ~ to do** accepter or consentir à faire; **to ~ to sth** consentir à qch; **to ~ that** (admit) convenir or reconnaître que; **garlic doesn't ~ with me** je ne supporte pas l'ail; **~able** a agréable; (willing) consentant(e), d'accord; **~d** a (time, place) convenu(e); **~ment** n accord m; **in ~ment** d'accord.

agricultural [ægrɪ'kʌltʃərəl] a agricole.

agriculture ['ægrɪkʌltʃə*] n agriculture f.

aground [ə'graʊnd] ad: **to run ~** s'échouer.

ahead [ə'hɛd] ad en avant; devant; **~ of** devant; (fig: schedule etc) en avance sur; **~ of time** en avance; **go right or straight ~** allez tout droit; **they were (right) ~ of us** ils nous précédaient (de peu), ils étaient (juste) devant nous.

aid [eɪd] n aide f // vt aider; **in ~ of** en faveur de; **to ~ and abet** (LAW) se faire le complice de.

aide [eɪd] n (person) collaborateur/trice, assistant/e.

AIDS [eɪdz] n abbr (=acquired immune deficiency syndrome) SIDA m.

ailing ['eɪlɪŋ] a malade.

ailment ['eɪlmənt] n petite maladie, affection f.

aim [eɪm] vt: **to ~ sth at** (such as gun, camera) braquer or pointer qch sur, diriger qch contre; (missile) lancer qch à or contre or en direction de; (remark, blow) destiner or adresser qch à // vi (also: **to take ~**) viser // n but m; **to ~ at** viser; (fig) viser (à); avoir pour but or ambition; **to ~ to do** avoir l'intention de faire; **~less** a sans but.

ain't [eɪnt] (col) =am not, aren't, isn't.

air [eə*] n air m // vt aérer; (grievances, ideas) exposer (librement) // cpd (currents, attack etc) aérien(ne); **to throw sth into the ~** jeter qch en l'air; **to be on the ~** (RADIO, TV: programme) être diffusé(e); (: station) diffuser; **~bed** n matelas m pneumatique; **~borne** a en vol; aéroporté(e); **~ conditioning** n climatisation f; **~craft** n, pl inv avion m; **~craft carrier** n porte-avions m inv; **~field** n terrain m d'aviation; **A~ Force** n Armée f de l'air; **~ freshener** n désodorisant m; **~gun** n fusil m à air comprimé; **~ hostess** n (Brit) hôtesse f de l'air; **~letter** n (Brit) aérogramme m; **~lift** n pont aérien; **~line** n ligne aérienne, compagnie f d'aviation; **~liner** n avion m de ligne; **~lock** n sas m; **~mail** n: **by ~mail** par avion; **~ mattress** n matelas m pneumatique; **~plane** n (US) avion m; **~port** n aéroport m; **~ raid** n attaque aérienne; **~sick** a: **to be ~sick** avoir le mal de l'air; **~strip** n terrain m d'atterrissage; **~ terminal** n aérogare f; **~tight** a hermétique; **~ traffic controller** n aiguilleur m du ciel; **~y** a bien aéré(e); (manners) dégagé(e).

aisle [aɪl] n (of church) allée centrale; nef latérale.

ajar [ə'dʒɑ:*] a entrouvert(e).

akin [ə'kɪn] a: **~ to** (similar) qui tient de or ressemble à.

alacrity [ə'lækrɪtɪ] n empressement m.

alarm [ə'lɑ:m] n alarme f // vt alarmer; **~ clock** n réveille-matin m, réveil m.

alas [ə'læs] excl hélas!

albeit [ɔ:l'bi:ɪt] cj (although) bien que + sub, encore que + sub.

album ['ælbəm] n album m; (L.P.) 33 tours m inv.

alcohol ['ælkəhɔl] n alcool m; **~ic** [-'hɔlɪk] a, n alcoolique (m/f).

alderman ['ɔ:ldəmən] n conseiller

municipal (en Angleterre).

ale [eɪl] n bière f.

alert [ə'lə:t] a alerte, vif(vive); vigilant(e) // n alerte f // vt alerter; (fig) éveiller l'attention de; **on the ~** sur le qui-vive; (MIL) en état d'alerte.

algebra ['ældʒɪbrə] n algèbre m.

Algeria [æl'dʒɪərɪə] n Algérie f.

alias ['eɪlɪəs] ad alias // n faux nom, nom d'emprunt.

alibi ['ælɪbaɪ] n alibi m.

alien ['eɪlɪən] n étranger/ère // a: **~ (to)** étranger(ère) (à); **~ate** vt aliéner; s'aliéner.

alight [ə'laɪt] a, ad en feu // vi mettre pied à terre; (passenger) descendre; (bird) se poser.

alike [ə'laɪk] a semblable, pareil(le) // ad de même; **to look ~** se ressembler.

alimony ['ælɪmənɪ] n (payment) pension f alimentaire.

alive [ə'laɪv] a vivant(e); (active) plein(e) de vie.

all [ɔ:l] ♦ a (singular) tout(e); (plural) tous(toutes); **~ day** tout le jour; **~ night** toute la nuit; **~ men** tous les hommes; **~ five** tous les cinq; **~ the food** toute la nourriture; **~ the books** tous les livres; **~ the time** tout le temps; **~ his life** toute sa vie

♦ pronoun **1** tout; I ate it ~, I ate ~ of it j'ai tout mangé; **~ of us went** nous y sommes tous allés; **~ of the boys went** tous les garçons y sont allés

2 (in phrases): **above ~** surtout, pardessus tout; **after ~** après tout; **at ~: not at ~** (in answer to question) pas du tout; (in answer to thanks) je vous en prie!; **I'm not at ~ tired** je ne suis pas du tout fatigué(e); **anything at ~ will do** n'importe quoi fera l'affaire; **~ in ~** tout bien considéré, en fin de compte

♦ ad: **~ alone** tout(e) seul(e); **it's not as hard as ~ that** ce n'est pas si difficile que ça; **~ the more/the better** d'autant plus/mieux; **~ but** presque, pratiquement; **the score is 2 ~** le score est 2 partout.

allay [ə'leɪ] vt (fears) apaiser, calmer.

all clear n (after attack etc, also fig) fin f d'alerte.

allege [ə'ledʒ] vt alléguer, prétendre; **~dly** [ə'ledʒɪdlɪ] ad à ce que l'on prétend, paraît-il.

allegiance [ə'li:dʒəns] n fidélité f, obéissance f.

allergic [ə'lə:dʒɪk] a: **~ to** allergique à.

allergy ['ælədʒɪ] n allergie f.

alleviate [ə'li:vɪeɪt] vt soulager, adoucir.

alley ['ælɪ] n ruelle f; (in garden) allée f.

alliance [ə'laɪəns] n alliance f.

allied ['ælaɪd] a allié(e).

all-in ['ɔ:lɪn] a (Brit: also ad: charge) tout compris; **~ wrestling** n catch m.

all-night ['ɔ:l'naɪt] a ouvert(e) or qui

dure toute la nuit.

allocate ['æləkeɪt] vt (share out) répartir, distribuer; (duties): **to ~ sth to** assigner or attribuer qch à; (sum, time): **to ~ sth to** allouer qch à; **to ~ sth for** affecter qch à.

allot [ə'lɔt] vt (share out) répartir, distribuer; (time): **to ~ sth to** allouer qch à; (duties): **to ~ sth to** assigner qch à; **~ment** n (share) part f; (garden) lopin m de terre (loué à la municipalité).

all-out ['ɔːlaut] a (effort etc) total(e) // ad: **all out** à fond.

allow [ə'lau] vt (practice, behaviour) permettre, autoriser; (sum to spend etc) accorder; allouer; (sum, time estimated) compter, prévoir; (concede): **to ~ that** convenir que; **to ~ sb to do** permettre à qn de faire, autoriser qn à faire; he is ~ed to — on lui permet de —; **to ~ for** vt fus tenir compte de; **~ance** n (money received) allocation f; subside m; indemnité f; (TAX) somme f déductible du revenu imposable, abattement m; **to make ~ances for** tenir compte de.

alloy ['ælɔɪ] n alliage m.

all right ['ɔːl'raɪt] ad (feel, work) bien; (as answer) d'accord.

all-round ['ɔːl'raund] a compétent(e) dans tous les domaines; (athlete etc) complet(ète).

all-time ['ɔːl'taɪm] a (record) sans précédent, absolu(e).

allude [ə'luːd] vi: **to ~ to** faire allusion à.

alluring [ə'ljuərɪŋ] a séduisant(e), alléchant(e).

ally ['ælaɪ] n allié m.

almighty [ɔːl'maɪtɪ] a tout-puissant.

almond ['ɑːmənd] n amande f.

almost ['ɔːlməust] ad presque.

alms [ɑːmz] npl aumône(s) f(pl).

aloft [ə'lɔft] ad en haut, en l'air; (NAUT) dans la mâture.

alone [ə'ləun] a, ad seul(e); **to leave sb ~** laisser qn tranquille; **to leave sth ~** ne pas toucher à qch; **let ~** — sans parler de —; encore moins —.

along [ə'lɔŋ] prep le long de // ad: **is he coming ~?** vient-il avec nous?; **he was hopping/limping ~** il venait or avançait en sautillant/boitant; **~ with** en compagnie de; avec, en plus de; **all ~** (all the time) depuis le début; **~side** prep le long de; au côté de // ad bord à bord; côte à côte.

aloof [ə'luːf] a, ad à distance, à l'écart.

aloud [ə'laud] ad à haute voix.

alphabet ['ælfəbɛt] n alphabet m; **~ical** [-'bɛtɪkəl] a alphabétique.

alpine ['ælpaɪn] a alpin(e), alpestre.

Alps [ælps] npl: **the ~** les Alpes fpl.

already [ɔːl'rɛdɪ] ad déjà.

alright ['ɔːl'raɪt] ad (Brit) = **all right**.

Alsatian [æl'seɪʃən] n (dog) berger allemand.

also ['ɔːlsəu] ad aussi.

altar ['ɔltə*] n autel m.

alter ['ɔltə*] vt, vi changer, modifier.

alternate a [ɔl'təːnɪt] alterné(e), alternant(e), alternatif(ive) // vi ['ɔltəːneɪt] alterner; **on ~ days** un jour sur deux, tous les deux jours; **alternating** a (current) alternatif(ive).

alternative [ɔl'təːnətɪv] a (solutions) interchangeable, possible; (solution) autre, de remplacement // n (choice) alternative f; (other possibility) solution f de remplacement or de rechange, autre possibilité f; **~ly** ad: **~ly one could** une autre or l'autre solution serait de.

alternator ['ɔltəːneɪtə*] n (AUT) alternateur m.

although [ɔːl'ðəu] cj bien que + sub.

altitude ['æltɪtjuːd] n altitude f.

alto ['æltəu] n (female) contralto m; (male) haute-contre f.

altogether [ɔːltə'gɛðə*] ad entièrement, tout à fait; (on the whole) tout compte fait; (in all) en tout.

aluminium [ælju'mɪnɪəm] , (US) **aluminum** [ə'luːmɪnəm] n aluminium m.

always ['ɔːlweɪz] ad toujours.

am [æm] vb see **be**.

a.m. ad abbr (=ante meridiem) du matin.

amalgamate [ə'mælgəmeɪt] vt, vi fusionner.

amateur ['æmətə*] n amateur m // a (SPORT) amateur inv; **~ish** a (pej) d'amateur.

amaze [ə'meɪz] vt stupéfier; **to be ~d (at)** être surpris(e) or étonné(e) (de); **~ment** n stupéfaction f, stupeur f; **amazing** a étonnant(e); exceptionnel(le).

ambassador [æm'bæsədə*] n ambassadeur m.

amber ['æmbə*] n ambre m; **at ~** (Brit AUT) à l'orange.

ambiguous [æm'bɪgjuəs] a ambigu(ë).

ambition [æm'bɪʃən] n ambition f.

ambitious [æm'bɪʃəs] a ambitieux(euse).

amble ['æmbl] vi (also: **to ~ along**) aller d'un pas tranquille.

ambulance ['æmbjuləns] n ambulance f.

ambush ['æmbuʃ] n embuscade f // vt tendre une embuscade à.

amenable [ə'miːnəbl] a: **~ to** (advice etc) disposé(e) à écouter or suivre.

amend [ə'mɛnd] vt (law) amender; (text) corriger; **to make ~s** réparer ses torts, faire amende honorable.

amenities [ə'miːnɪtɪz] npl aménagements mpl (prévus pour le loisir des habitants).

America [ə'mɛrɪkə] n Amérique f; **~n** a américain(e) // n Américain/e.

amiable ['eɪmɪəbl] a aimable, affable.

amicable ['æmɪkəbl] *a* amical(e).

amid(st) [ə'mɪd(st)] *prep* parmi, au milieu de.

amiss [ə'mɪs] *a, ad*: there's something ~ il y a quelque chose qui ne va pas *or* qui cloche; to take sth ~ prendre qch mal *or* de travers.

ammonia [ə'məʊnɪə] *n* (*gas*) ammoniac *m*; (*liquid*) ammoniaque *f*.

ammunition [æmju'nɪʃən] *n* munitions *fpl*.

amok [ə'mɔk] *ad*: to run ~ être pris(e) d'un accès de folie furieuse.

among(st) [ə'mʌŋ(st)] *prep* parmi, entre.

amorous ['æmərəs] *a* amoureux(euse).

amount [ə'maʊnt] *n* (*sum*) somme *f*, montant *m*; (*quantity*) quantité *f* // *vi*: to ~ to (*total*) s'élever à; (*be same as*) équivaloir à, revenir à.

amp(ère) ['æmp(εə*)] *n* ampère *m*.

ample ['æmpl] *a* ample; spacieux(euse); (*enough*): this is ~ c'est largement suffisant; to have ~ time/room avoir bien assez de temps/place.

amplifier ['æmplɪfaɪə*] *n* amplificateur *m*.

amuck [ə'mʌk] *ad* = amok.

amuse [ə'mju:z] *vt* amuser; ~ment *n* amusement *m*; ~ment arcade *n* salle *f* de jeu.

an [æn] *indefinite article see* **a**.

anaemic [ə'ni:mɪk] *a* anémique.

anaesthetic [ænɪs'θεtɪk] *a, n* anesthésique (*m*).

analog(ue) ['ænəlɔg] *a* (*watch, computer*) analogique.

analyse ['ænəlaɪz] *vt* (*Brit*) analyser.

analysis, pl analyses [ə'næləsɪs, -sɪːz] *n* analyse *f*.

analyst ['ænəlɪst] *n* (*POL etc*) spécialiste *m/f*; (*US*) psychanalyste *m/f*.

analyze ['ænəlaɪz] *vt* (*US*) = analyse.

anarchist ['ænəkɪst] *a, n* anarchiste (*m/f*).

anarchy ['ænəkɪ] *n* anarchie *f*.

anathema [ə'næθɪmə] *n*: it is ~ to him il a cela en abomination.

anatomy [ə'nætəmɪ] *n* anatomie *f*.

ancestor ['ænsɪstə*] *n* ancêtre *m*, aïeul *m*.

anchor ['æŋkə*] *n* ancre *f* // *vi* (*also*: to drop ~) jeter l'ancre, mouiller // *vt* mettre à l'ancre; to weigh ~ lever l'ancre.

anchovy ['æntʃəvɪ] *n* anchois *m*.

ancient ['eɪnʃənt] *a* ancien(ne), antique; (*fig*) d'un âge vénérable, antique.

ancillary [æn'sɪlərɪ] *a* auxiliaire.

and [ænd] *cj* et; ~ so on et ainsi de suite; try ~ come tâchez de venir; he talked ~ talked il n'a pas arrêté de parler; better ~ better de mieux en mieux.

anew [ə'nju:] *ad* à nouveau.

angel ['eɪndʒəl] *n* ange *m*.

anger ['æŋgə*] *n* colère *f* // *vt* mettre en colère, irriter.

angina [æn'dʒaɪnə] *n* angine *f* de poitrine.

angle ['æŋgl] *n* angle *m*; from their ~ de leur point de vue; ~r *n* pêcheur/euse à la ligne.

Anglican ['æŋglɪkən] *a, n* anglican(e).

angling ['æŋglɪŋ] *n* pêche *f* à la ligne.

Anglo- ['æŋgləʊ] *prefix* anglo(-).

angry ['æŋgrɪ] *a* en colère, furieux(euse); to be ~ with sb/at sth être furieux contre qn/de qch; to get ~ se fâcher, se mettre en colère; to make sb ~ mettre qn en colère.

anguish ['æŋgwɪʃ] *n* angoisse *f*.

angular ['æŋgjulə*] *a* anguleux(euse).

animal ['ænɪməl] *n* animal *m* // *a* animal(e).

animate *vt* ['ænɪmeɪt] animer // *a* ['ænɪmɪt] animé(e), vivant(e); ~d *a* animé(e).

aniseed ['ænɪsi:d] *n* anis *m*.

ankle ['æŋkl] *n* cheville *f*; ~ sock *n* socquette *f*.

annex ['ænɛks] (*also*: *Brit*: **annexe**) *n* annexe *f* // *vt* [ə'nɛks] annexer.

anniversary [ænɪ'vɜ:sərɪ] *n* anniversaire *m*.

announce [ə'naʊns] *vt* annoncer; (*birth, death*) faire part de; ~ment *n* annonce *f*; (*for births etc: in newspaper*) avis *m* de faire-part; (*: letter, card*) faire-part *m*; ~r *n* (*RADIO, TV: between programmes*) speaker/ine; (*: in a programme*) présentateur/trice.

annoy [ə'nɔɪ] *vt* agacer, ennuyer, contrarier; don't get ~ed! ne vous fâchez pas!; ~ance *n* mécontentement *m*, contrariété *f*; ~ing *a* ennuyeux(euse), agaçant(e), contrariant(e).

annual ['ænjuəl] *a* annuel(le) // *n* (*BOT*) plante annuelle; (*book*) album *m*.

annul [ə'nʌl] *vt* annuler; (*law*) abroger.

annum ['ænəm] *n see* **per**.

anonymous [ə'nɔnɪməs] *a* anonyme.

anorak ['ænəræk] *n* anorak *m*.

another [ə'nʌðə*] *a*: ~ book (*one more*) un autre livre, encore un livre, un livre de plus; (*a different one*) un autre livre // *pronoun* un(e) autre, encore un(e), un(e) de plus; see **one**.

answer ['ɑ:nsə*] *n* réponse *f*; solution *f* // *vi* répondre // *vt* (*reply to*) répondre à; (*problem*) résoudre; (*prayer*) exaucer; to ~ the phone répondre (au téléphone); in ~ to your letter suite à *or* en réponse à votre lettre; to ~ the bell *or* the door aller *or* venir ouvrir (la porte); to ~ back *vi* répondre, répliquer; to ~ for *vt fus* répondre de, se porter garant de; être responsable de; to ~ to *vt fus* (*description*) répondre *or* correspondre à; ~able *a*: ~able (to sb/for sth) responsable (devant qn/de qch); ~ing

machine n répondeur m automatique.
ant [ænt] n fourmi f.
antagonism [æn'tægənɪzəm] n antagonisme m.
antagonize [æn'tægənaɪz] vt éveiller l'hostilité de, contrarier.
Antarctic [ænt'ɑːktɪk] n: the ~ l'Antarctique m.
antenatal ['æntɪ'neɪtl] a prénatal(e); ~ **clinic** n service m de consultation prénatale.
anthem ['ænθəm] n motet m; **national** ~ hymne national.
anthology [æn'θɔlədʒɪ] n anthologie f.
antibiotic ['æntɪbaɪ'ɔtɪk] a, n antibiotique (m).
antibody ['æntɪbɔdɪ] n anticorps m.
anticipate [æn'tɪsɪpeɪt] vt s'attendre à; prévoir; (wishes, request) aller au devant de, devancer.
anticipation [æntɪsɪ'peɪʃən] n attente f.
anticlimax ['æntɪ'klaɪmæks] n réalisation décevante d'un événement que l'on escomptait important, intéressant etc.
anticlockwise ['æntɪ'klɔkwaɪz] a, ad dans le sens inverse des aiguilles d'une montre.
antics ['æntɪks] npl singeries fpl.
antifreeze ['æntɪfriːz] n antigel m.
antihistamine [æntɪ'hɪstəmiːn] n antihistaminique m.
antiquated ['æntɪkweɪtɪd] a vieilli(e), suranné(e), vieillot(te).
antique [æn'tiːk] n objet m d'art ancien, meuble ancien or d'époque, antiquité f // a ancien(ne); (pre-mediaeval) antique; ~ **shop** n magasin m d'antiquités.
anti-Semitism [æntɪ'sɛmɪtɪzəm] n antisémitisme m.
antiseptic [æntɪ'sɛptɪk] a, n antiseptique (m).
antisocial ['æntɪ'səʊʃəl] a peu liant(e), sauvage, insociable; (against society) anti-social(e).
antlers ['æntləz] npl bois mpl, ramure f.
anvil ['ænvɪl] n enclume f.
anxiety [æŋ'zaɪətɪ] n anxiété f; (keenness): ~ **to do** grand désir or impatience f de faire.
anxious ['æŋkʃəs] a anxieux(euse), (très) inquiet(ète); (keen): ~ **to do/that** qui tient beaucoup à faire/à ce que; impatient(e) de faire/que.
any ['ɛnɪ] ♦ a 1 (in questions etc: singular) du, de l', de la; (: plural) des; **have you** ~ **butter/children/ink?** avez-vous du beurre/des enfants/de l'encre?
2 (with negative) de, d'; **I haven't** ~ **money/books** je n'ai pas d'argent/de livres
3 (no matter which) n'importe quel(le); **choose** ~ **book you like** vous pouvez choisir n'importe quel livre
4 (in phrases): **in** ~ **case** de toute façon; ~ **day now** d'un jour à l'autre; **at**

~ **moment** à tout moment, d'un instant à l'autre; **at** ~ **rate** en tout cas
♦ pronoun 1 (in questions etc) en; **have you got** ~? est-ce que vous en avez?; **can** ~ **of you sing?** est-ce que parmi vous il y en a qui chantent?
2 (with negative): en; **I haven't** ~ (of them) je n'en ai pas, je n'en ai aucun
3 (no matter which one(s)) n'importe lequel (or laquelle); **take** ~ **of those books (you like)** vous pouvez prendre n'importe lequel de ces livres
♦ ad 1 (in questions etc): **do you want** ~ **more soup/sandwiches?** voulez-vous encore de la soupe/des sandwichs?; **are you feeling** ~ **better?** est-ce que vous vous sentez mieux?
2 (with negative): **I can't hear him** ~ **more** je ne l'entends plus; **don't wait** ~ **longer** n'attendez pas plus longtemps.
anybody ['ɛnɪbɔdɪ] pronoun n'importe qui; (in interrogative sentences) quelqu'un; (in negative sentences): **I don't see** ~ je ne vois personne.
anyhow ['ɛnɪhaʊ] ad (at any rate) de toute façon, quand même; (haphazard) n'importe comment.
anyone ['ɛnɪwʌn] pronoun = **anybody**.
anything ['ɛnɪθɪŋ] pronoun (see anybody) n'importe quoi; quelque chose; ne — rien.
anyway ['ɛnɪweɪ] ad de toute façon.
anywhere ['ɛnɪwɛə*] ad (see anybody) n'importe où; quelque part; **I don't see him** ~ je ne le vois nulle part.
apart [ə'pɑːt] ad (to one side) à part; de côté; à l'écart; (separately) séparément; **with one's legs** ~ les jambes écartées; **10 miles** ~ à 10 milles l'un de l'autre; **to take** ~ démonter; ~ **from** prep à part, excepté.
apartheid [ə'pɑːteɪt] n apartheid m.
apartment [ə'pɑːtmənt] n (US) appartement m, logement m; ~ **building** n (US) immeuble m; maison divisée en appartements.
ape [eɪp] n (grand) singe // vt singer.
aperture ['æpətʃjʊə*] n orifice m, ouverture f; (PHOT) ouverture (du diaphragme).
apex ['eɪpɛks] n sommet m.
apiece [ə'piːs] ad (for each person) chacun(e).
apologetic [əpɔlə'dʒɛtɪk] a (tone, letter) d'excuse.
apologize [ə'pɔlədʒaɪz] vi: **to** ~ (for sth to sb) s'excuser (de qch auprès de qn), présenter ses excuses (à qn pour qch).
apology [ə'pɔlədʒɪ] n excuses fpl.
apostle [ə'pɔsl] n apôtre m.
apostrophe [ə'pɔstrəfɪ] n apostrophe f.
appalling [ə'pɔːlɪŋ] a épouvantable; (stupidity) consternant(e).
apparatus [æpə'reɪtəs] n appareil m, dispositif m; (in gymnasium) agrès mpl.

apparel [əˈpærl] n (US) habillement m.

apparent [əˈpærənt] a apparent(e); **~ly** ad apparemment.

appeal [əˈpiːl] vi (LAW) faire or interjeter appel // n (LAW) appel m; (request) prière f; appel m; (charm) attrait m, charme m; **to ~ for** demander (instamment); implorer; **to ~ to** (subj: person) faire appel à; (subj: thing) plaire à; **it doesn't ~ to me** cela ne m'attire pas; **~ing** a (nice) attrayant(e); (touching) attendrissant(e).

appear [əˈpɪə*] vi apparaître, se montrer; (LAW) comparaître; (publication) paraître, sortir, être publié(e); (seem) paraître, sembler; **it would ~ that il** semble que; **to ~ in Hamlet** jouer dans Hamlet; **to ~ on TV** passer à la télé; **~ance** n apparition f; parution f; (look, aspect) apparence f, aspect m.

appease [əˈpiːz] vt apaiser, calmer.

appendicitis [əpɛndɪˈsaɪtɪs] n appendicite f.

appendix, pl **appendices** [əˈpɛndɪks, -siːz] n appendice m.

appetite [ˈæpɪtaɪt] n appétit m.

appetizer [ˈæpɪtaɪzə*] n amuse-gueule mpl.

applaud [əˈplɔːd] vt, vi applaudir.

applause [əˈplɔːz] n applaudissements mpl.

apple [ˈæpl] n pomme f; **~ tree** n pommier m.

appliance [əˈplaɪəns] n appareil m.

applicant [ˈæplɪkənt] n: **~ (for)** (post) candidat/e (à).

application [æplɪˈkeɪʃən] n application f; (for a job, a grant etc) demande f; candidature f; **~ form** n formulaire m de demande.

applied [əˈplaɪd] a appliqué(e).

apply [əˈplaɪ] vt (paint, ointment): **to ~ (to)** appliquer (sur); (theory, technique): **to ~ (to)** appliquer (à) // vi: **to ~ to** (ask) s'adresser à; (be suitable for, relevant to) s'appliquer à; se rapporter à; être valable pour; **to ~ (for)** (permit, grant) faire une demande (en vue d'obtenir); (job) poser sa candidature (pour), faire une demande d'emploi (concernant); **to ~ the brakes** actionner les freins, freiner; **to ~ o.s. to** s'appliquer à.

appoint [əˈpɔɪnt] vt nommer, engager; (date, place) fixer, désigner; **~ment** n nomination f; rendez-vous m; **to make an ~ment (with)** prendre rendez-vous (avec).

appraisal [əˈpreɪzl] n évaluation f.

appreciate [əˈpriːʃɪeɪt] vt (like) apprécier, faire cas de; être reconnaissant(e) de; (assess) évaluer; (be aware of) comprendre; se rendre compte de // vi (FINANCE) prendre de la valeur.

appreciation [əpriːʃɪˈeɪʃən] n ap-

préciation f; reconnaissance f; (COMM) hausse f, valorisation f.

appreciative [əˈpriːʃɪətɪv] a (person) sensible; (comment) élogieux(euse).

apprehensive [æprɪˈhɛnsɪv] a inquiet(ète), appréhensif(ive).

apprentice [əˈprɛntɪs] n apprenti m; **~ship** n apprentissage m.

approach [əˈprəʊtʃ] vi approcher // vt (come near) approcher de; (ask, apply to) s'adresser à; (subject, passer-by) aborder // n approche f; accès m, abord m; démarche f (auprès de qn); démarche (intellectuelle) f; **~able** a accessible.

appropriate [əˈprəʊprɪɪt] a opportun(e); qui convient, approprié(e) // vt [əˈprəʊprɪeɪt] (take) s'approprier.

approval [əˈpruːvəl] n approbation f; **on ~** (COMM) à l'examen.

approve [əˈpruːv] vt approuver; **to ~ of** vt fus approuver; **~d school** n (Brit) centre m d'éducation surveillée.

approximate a [əˈprɒksɪmɪt] approximatif(ive); **~ly** ad approximativement.

apricot [ˈeɪprɪkɒt] n abricot m.

April [ˈeɪprəl] n avril m; **~ Fool's Day** le premier avril.

apron [ˈeɪprən] n tablier m.

apt [æpt] a (suitable) approprié(e); (likely): **~ to do** susceptible de faire; ayant tendance à faire.

aqualung [ˈækwəlʌŋ] n scaphandre m autonome.

aquarium [əˈkwɛərɪəm] n aquarium m.

Aquarius [əˈkwɛərɪəs] n le Verseau.

Arab [ˈærəb] n Arabe m/f.

Arabian [əˈreɪbɪən] a arabe.

Arabic [ˈærəbɪk] a arabe // n arabe m; **~ numerals** chiffres mpl arabes.

arbitrary [ˈɑːbɪtrərɪ] a arbitraire.

arbitration [ɑːbɪˈtreɪʃən] n arbitrage m.

arcade [ɑːˈkeɪd] n arcade f; (passage with shops) passage m, galerie f.

arch [ɑːtʃ] n arche f; (of foot) cambrure f, voûte f plantaire // vt arquer, cambrer // a malicieux(euse).

archaeologist [ɑːkɪˈɒlədʒɪst] n archéologue m/f.

archaeology [ɑːkɪˈɒlədʒɪ] n archéologie f.

archbishop [ɑːtʃˈbɪʃəp] n archevêque m.

arch-enemy [ˈɑːtʃˈɛnəmɪ] n ennemi m de toujours or par excellence.

archeology etc [ɑːkɪˈɒlədʒɪ] (US) **=archaeology** etc.

archer [ˈɑːtʃə*] n archer m; **~y** n tir m à l'arc.

architect [ˈɑːkɪtɛkt] n architecte m; **~ure** [ˈɑːkɪtɛktʃə*] n architecture f.

archives [ˈɑːkaɪvz] npl archives fpl.

archway [ˈɑːtʃweɪ] n voûte f, porche voûté or cintré.

Arctic ['ɑ:ktɪk] *a* arctique // *n*: the ~ l'Arctique *m*.

ardent ['ɑ:dənt] *a* fervent(e).

are [ɑ:*] *vb see* **be**.

area ['ɛərɪə] *n* (*GEOM*) superficie *f*; (*zone*) région *f*; (: *smaller*) secteur *m*.

aren't [ɑ:nt] =**are not**.

Argentina [ɑ:dʒən'ti:nə] *n* Argentine *f*; **Argentinian** [-'tɪnɪən] *a* argentin(e) // *n* Argentin/e.

arguably ['ɑ:gjuəblɪ] *ad*: it is ~ — on peut soutenir que c'est —.

argue ['ɑ:gju:] *vi* (*quarrel*) se disputer; (*reason*) argumenter; to ~ that objecter *or* alléguer que, donner comme argument que.

argument ['ɑ:gjumənt] *n* (*reasons*) argument *m*; (*quarrel*) dispute *f*, discussion *f*; (*debate*) discussion *f*, controverse *f*; ~**ative** [-'mentətɪv] *a* ergoteur(euse), raisonneur(euse).

Aries ['ɛərɪz] *n* le Bélier.

arise, *pt* **arose**, *pp* **arisen** [ə'raɪz, ə'rəuz, ə'rɪzn] *vi* survenir, se présenter; to ~ from survenir de.

aristocrat ['ærɪstəkræt] *n* aristocrate *m/f*.

arithmetic [ə'rɪθmətɪk] *n* arithmétique *f*.

ark [ɑ:k] *n*: Noah's A~ l'Arche *f* de Noé.

arm [ɑ:m] *n* bras *m* // *vt* armer; ~s *npl* (*weapons*, *HERALDRY*) armes *fpl*; ~ in ~ bras dessus bras dessous.

armaments ['ɑ:məmənts] *npl* armements *mpl*.

arm: ~**chair** *n* fauteuil *m*; ~**ed** *a* armé(e); ~**ed robbery** *n* vol *m* à main armée.

armour, (*US*) **armor** ['ɑ:mə*] *n* armure *f*; (*also*: ~-**plating**) blindage *m*; (*MIL*: *tanks*) blindés *mpl*; ~**ed car** *n* véhicule blindé; ~**y** *n* arsenal *m*.

armpit ['ɑ:mpɪt] *n* aisselle *f*.

armrest ['ɑ:mrest] *n* accoudoir *m*.

army ['ɑ:mɪ] *n* armée *f*.

aroma [ə'rəumə] *n* arôme *m*.

arose [ə'rəuz] *pt of* **arise**.

around [ə'raund] *ad* (tout) autour; dans les parages // *prep* autour de; (*fig*: *about*) environ; vers.

arouse [ə'rauz] *vt* (*sleeper*) éveiller; (*curiosity*, *passions*) éveiller, susciter; exciter.

arrange [ə'reɪndʒ] *vt* arranger; (*programme*) arrêter, convenir de; to ~ to do sth prévoir de faire qch; ~**ment** *n* arrangement *m*; (*plans etc*): ~**ments** dispositions *fpl*.

array [ə'reɪ] *n*: ~ of déploiement *m or* étalage *m* de.

arrears [ə'rɪəz] *npl* arriéré *m*; to be in ~ with one's rent devoir un arriéré de loyer.

arrest [ə'rest] *vt* arrêter; (*sb's attention*) retenir, attirer // *n* arrestation *f*; under ~

en état d'arrestation.

arrival [ə'raɪvəl] *n* arrivée *f*; (*COMM*) arrivage *m*; (*person*) arrivant/e; new ~ nouveau venu, nouvelle venue.

arrive [ə'raɪv] *vi* arriver.

arrogant ['ærəgənt] *a* arrogant(e).

arrow ['ærəu] *n* flèche *f*.

arse [ɑ:s] *n* (*col!*) cul *m* (!).

arson ['ɑ:sn] *n* incendie criminel.

art [ɑ:t] *n* art *m*; (*craft*) métier *m*; A~s *npl* (*SCOL*) les lettres *fpl*.

artefact ['ɑ:tɪfækt] *n* objet fabriqué.

artery ['ɑ:tərɪ] *n* artère *f*.

art gallery *n* musée *m* d'art; (*small and private*) galerie *f* de peinture.

arthritis [ɑ:'θraɪtɪs] *n* arthrite *f*.

artichoke ['ɑ:tɪtʃəuk] *n* artichaut *m*; Jerusalem ~ topinambour *m*.

article ['ɑ:tɪkl] *n* article *m*; (*Brit LAW*: *training*): ~s *npl* ≈stage *m*; ~ of clothing vêtement *m*.

articulate *a* [ɑ:'tɪkjulɪt] (*person*) qui s'exprime clairement et aisément; (*speech*) bien articulé(e), prononcé(e) clairement // *vi* [ɑ:'tɪkjuleɪt] articuler, parler distinctement; ~**d lorry** *n* (*Brit*) (camion *m*) semi-remorque *m*.

artificial [ɑ:tɪ'fɪʃəl] *a* artificiel(le).

artist ['ɑ:tɪst] *n* artiste *m/f*; ~**ic** [ɑ:'tɪstɪk] *a* artistique; ~**ry** *n* art *m*, talent *m*.

artless ['ɑ:tlɪs] *a* naïf(naïve), simple, ingénu(e).

art school *n* ≈école *f* des beaux-arts.

as [æz] ♦ *cj* **1** (*referring to time*) comme, alors que; à mesure que; he came in ~ I was leaving il est arrivé comme je partais; ~ the years went by à mesure que les années passaient; ~ from tomorrow à partir de demain

2 (*in comparisons*): ~ big ~ aussi grand que; twice ~ big ~ deux fois plus grand que; ~ much *or* many ~ autant que; ~ much money/many books ~ autant d'argent/de livres que; ~ soon ~ dès que

3 (*since*, *because*) comme, puisque; he left early, ~ he had to be home by 10 comme il *or* puisqu'il devait être de retour avant 10h il est parti tôt

4 (*referring to manner*, *way*) comme; do ~ you wish faites comme vous voudrez

5 (*concerning*): ~ for *or* to that quant à cela, pour ce qui est de cela

6: ~ if *or* though comme si; he looked ~ if he was ill il avait l'air d'être malade; *see also* long, such, well

♦ *prep*: he works ~ a driver il travaille comme chauffeur; ~ chairman of the company, he — en tant que président de la compagnie, il —; dressed up ~ a cowboy déguisé en cowboy; he gave me it ~ a present il me l'a offert, il m'en a fait cadeau.

a.s.a.p. *abbr* (=*as soon as possible*) dès

que possible.

ascend [ə'sɛnd] *vt* gravir.

ascent [ə'sɛnt] *n* ascension *f*.

ascertain [æsə'teɪn] *vt* s'assurer de, vérifier; établir.

ash [æʃ] *n* (*dust*) cendre *f*; (*also*: ~ tree) frêne *m*.

ashamed [ə'ʃeɪmd] *a* honteux(euse), confus(e); **to be ~ of** avoir honte de.

ashen ['æʃn] *a* (*pale*) cendreux(euse), blême.

ashore [ə'ʃɔ:*] *ad* à terre.

ashtray ['æʃtreɪ] *n* cendrier *m*.

Ash Wednesday *n* mercredi *m* des cendres.

Asia ['eɪʃə] *n* Asie *f*; ~**n** *n* Asiatique *m/f* // *a* asiatique.

aside [ə'saɪd] *ad* de côté; à l'écart // *n* aparté *m*.

ask [ɑ:sk] *vt* demander; (*invite*) inviter; **to ~ sb sth/to do sth** demander à qn qch/ de faire qch; **to ~ sb about sth** questionner qn au sujet de qch; se renseigner auprès de qn au sujet de qch; **to ~ (sb) a question** poser une question (à qn); **to ~ sb out to dinner** inviter qn au restaurant; **to ~ after** *vt fus* demander des nouvelles de; **to ~ for** *vt fus* demander.

askance [ə'skɑːns] *ad*: **to look ~ at sb** regarder qn de travers *or* d'un œil désapprobateur.

askew [ə'skjuː] *ad* de travers, de guinguois.

asleep [ə'sliːp] *a* endormi(e); **to be ~** dormir, être endormi; **to fall ~** s'endormir.

asparagus [əs'pærəgəs] *n* asperges *fpl*.

aspect ['æspɛkt] *n* aspect *m*; (*direction in which a building etc faces*) orientation *f*, exposition *f*.

aspersions [əs'pəːʃənz] *npl*: **to cast ~ on** dénigrer.

aspire [əs'paɪə*] *vi*: **to ~ to** aspirer à.

aspirin ['æsprɪn] *n* aspirine *f*.

ass [æs] *n* âne *m*; (*col*) imbécile *m/f*; (*US col!*) cul *m* (!).

assailant [ə'seɪlənt] *n* agresseur *m*; assaillant *m*.

assassinate [ə'sæsɪneɪt] *vt* assassiner; **assassination** [əsæsɪ'neɪʃən] *n* assassinat *m*.

assault [ə'sɔːlt] *n* (*MIL*) assaut *m*; (*gen: attack*) agression *f* // *vt* attaquer; (*sexually*) violenter.

assemble [ə'sɛmbl] *vt* assembler // *vi* s'assembler, se rassembler.

assembly [ə'sɛmblɪ] *n* (*meeting*) rassemblement *m*; (*construction*) assemblage *m*; ~ **line** *n* chaîne *f* de montage.

assent [ə'sɛnt] *n* assentiment *m*, consentement *m*.

assert [ə'səːt] *vt* affirmer, déclarer; établir.

assess [ə'sɛs] *vt* évaluer, estimer; (*tax,*

damages, établir *or* fixer le montant de; (*property etc: for tax*) calculer la valeur imposable de; ~**ment** *n* évaluation *f*, estimation *f*; ~**or** *n* expert *m* (*en matière d'impôt et d'assurance*).

asset ['æsɛt] *n* avantage *m*, atout *m*; ~**s** *npl* capital *m*; avoir(s) *m(pl)*; actif *m*.

assign [ə'saɪn] *vt* (*date*) fixer, arrêter; (*task*): **to ~ sth to** assigner qch à; (*resources*): **to ~ sth to** affecter qch à; (*cause, meaning*): **to ~ sth to** attribuer qch à; ~**ment** *n* tâche *f*, mission *f*.

assist [ə'sɪst] *vt* aider, assister; secourir; ~**ance** *n* aide *f*, assistance *f*; secours *mpl*; ~**ant** *n* assistant/e, adjoint/e; (*Brit: also*: **shop ~ant**) vendeur/euse.

associate *a, n* [ə'səʊʃɪɪt] associé(e) // *vb* [ə'səʊʃɪeɪt] *vt* associer // *vi*: **to ~ with sb** fréquenter qn.

association [əsəʊsɪ'eɪʃən] *n* association *f*.

assorted [ə'sɔːtɪd] *a* assorti(e).

assortment [ə'sɔːtmənt] *n* assortiment *m*.

assume [ə'sjuːm] *vt* supposer; (*responsibilities etc*) assumer; (*attitude, name*) prendre, adopter; ~**d name** *n* nom *m* d'emprunt.

assumption [ə'sʌmpʃən] *n* supposition *f*, hypothèse *f*.

assurance [ə'ʃʊərəns] *n* assurance *f*.

assure [ə'ʃʊə*] *vt* assurer.

astern [ə'stəːn] *ad* à l'arrière.

asthma ['æsmə] *n* asthme *m*.

astonish [ə'stɒnɪʃ] *vt* étonner, stupéfier; ~**ment** *n* étonnement *m*.

astound [ə'staʊnd] *vt* stupéfier, sidérer.

astray [ə'streɪ] *ad*: **to go ~** s'égarer; (*fig*) quitter le droit chemin.

astride [ə'straɪd] *ad* à cheval // *prep* à cheval sur.

astrology [əs'trɒlədʒɪ] *n* astrologie *f*.

astronaut ['æstrənɔːt] *n* astronaute *m/f*.

astronomy [əs'trɒnəmɪ] *n* astronomie *f*.

astute [əs'tjuːt] *a* astucieux(euse).

asylum [ə'saɪləm] *n* asile *m*.

at [æt] *prep*
1 (*referring to position, direction*) à; ~ **the top** au sommet; ~ **home/school** à la maison *or* chez soi/à l'école; ~ **the baker's** à la boulangerie, chez le boulanger; **to look ~ sth** regarder qch
2 (*referring to time*) à; ~ **4 o'clock** à 4 heures; ~ **Christmas** à Noël; ~ **night** la nuit; ~ **times** par moments, parfois
3 (*referring to rates, speed etc*) à; ~ **£1 a kilo** une livre le kilo; **two ~ a time** deux à la fois; ~ **50 km/h** à 50 km/h
4 (*referring to manner*): ~ **a stroke** d'un seul coup; ~ **peace** en paix
5 (*referring to activity*): **to be ~ work** être à l'œuvre, travailler; **to play ~ cowboys** jouer aux cowboys; **to be good ~ sth** être bon en qch

6 (referring to cause): shocked/surprised/annoyed ~ sth choqué par/étonné de/agacé par qch; I went ~ his suggestion j'y suis allé sur son conseil.

ate [eɪt] pt of **eat**.

atheist ['eɪθɪɪst] n athée m/f.

Athens ['æθɪnz] n Athènes.

athlete ['æθli:t] n athlète m/f.

athletic [æθ'letɪk] a athlétique; **~s** n athlétisme m.

Atlantic [ət'læntɪk] a atlantique // n: the ~ (**Ocean**) l'Atlantique m, l'océan m Atlantique.

atlas ['ætləs] n atlas m.

atmosphere ['ætməsfɪə*] n atmosphère f.

atom ['ætəm] n atome m; **~ic** [ə'tɔmɪk] a atomique; **~(ic) bomb** n bombe f atomique; **~izer** ['ætəmaɪzə*] n atomiseur m.

atone [ə'təun] vi: to ~ for expier, racheter.

atrocious [ə'trəuʃəs] a (very bad) atroce, exécrable.

attach [ə'tætʃ] vt (gen) attacher; (document, letter) joindre; (employee, troops) affecter; to be ~ed to sb/sth (to like) être attaché à qn/qch.

attaché case [ə'tæʃeɪ-] n mallette f, attaché-case m.

attachment [ə'tætʃmənt] n (tool) accessoire m; (love): ~ (to) affection f (pour), attachement m (à).

attack [ə'tæk] vt attaquer; (task etc) s'attaquer à // n attaque f; (also: **heart** ~) crise f cardiaque.

attain [ə'teɪn] vt (also: to ~ to) parvenir à, atteindre; acquérir; **~ments** npl connaissances fpl, résultats mpl.

attempt [ə'tempt] n tentative f // vt essayer, tenter; to make an ~ on sb's life attenter à la vie de qn.

attend [ə'tend] vt (course) suivre; (meeting, talk) assister à; (school, church) aller à, fréquenter; (patient) soigner, s'occuper de; to ~ to vt fus (needs, affairs etc) s'occuper de; (customer) s'occuper de, servir; **~ance** n (being present) présence f; (people present) assistance f; **~ant** n employé/e; gardien/ne // a concomitant(e), qui accompagne or s'ensuit.

attention [ə'tenʃən] n attention f; **~!** (MIL) garde-à-vous!; for the ~ of (ADMIN) à l'attention de.

attentive [ə'tentɪv] a attentif(ive); (kind) prévenant(e).

attic ['ætɪk] n grenier m, combles mpl.

attitude ['ætɪtjuːd] n attitude f, manière f; pose f, maintien m.

attorney [ə'tə:nɪ] n (lawyer) avoué m; (having proxy) mandataire m; **A~ General** n (Brit) ≈procureur général; (US) ≈garde m des Sceaux, ministre m de la Justice.

attract [ə'trækt] vt attirer; **~ion** [ə'trækʃən] n (gen pl: pleasant things) attraction f, attrait m; (PHYSICS) attraction f; (fig: towards sth) attirance f; **~ive** a séduisant(e), attrayant(e).

attribute n ['ætrɪbjuːt] attribut m // vt [ə'trɪbjuːt]: to ~ sth to attribuer qch à.

attrition [ə'trɪʃən] n: war of ~ guerre f d'usure.

aubergine ['əubəʒiːn] n aubergine f.

auction ['ɔːkʃən] n (also: **sale by** ~) vente f aux enchères // vt (also: **to sell by** ~) vendre aux enchères; (also: **to put up for** ~) mettre aux enchères; **~eer** [-'nɪə*] n commissaire-priseur m.

audience ['ɔːdɪəns] n (people) assistance f, auditoire m; auditeurs mpl; spectateurs mpl; (interview) audience f.

audio-visual [ɔːdɪəu'vɪzjuəl] a audiovisuel(le); ~ **aids** npl supports or moyens audiovisuels.

audit ['ɔːdɪt] vt vérifier, apurer.

audition [ɔː'dɪʃən] n audition f.

auditor ['ɔːdɪtə*] n vérificateur m des comptes.

augur ['ɔːgə*] vi: it ~s well c'est bon signe or de bon augure.

August ['ɔːgəst] n août m.

aunt [ɑːnt] n tante f; **~ie**, **~y** n diminutive of **aunt**.

au pair ['əu'pɛə*] n (also: ~ **girl**) jeune fille f au pair.

aura ['ɔːrə] n atmosphère f.

auspicious [ɔːs'pɪʃəs] a de bon augure, propice.

austerity [ɔs'terɪtɪ] n austérité f.

Australia [ɔs'treɪlɪə] n Australie f; **~n** a australien(ne) // n Australien/ne.

Austria ['ɔstrɪə] n Autriche f; **~n** a autrichien(ne) // n Autrichien/ne.

authentic [ɔː'θentɪk] a authentique.

author ['ɔːθə*] n auteur m.

authoritarian [ɔːθɔrɪ'tɛərɪən] a autoritaire.

authoritative [ɔː'θɔrɪtətɪv] a (account) digne de foi; (study, treatise) qui fait autorité; (manner) autoritaire.

authority [ɔː'θɔrɪtɪ] n autorité f; (permission) autorisation (formelle); **the authorities** npl les autorités fpl, l'administration f.

authorize ['ɔːθəraɪz] vt autoriser.

auto ['ɔːtəu] n (US) auto f, voiture f.

autobiography [ɔːtəbaɪ'ɔgrəfɪ] n autobiographie f.

autograph ['ɔːtəgrɑːf] n autographe m // vt signer, dédicacer.

automatic [ɔːtə'mætɪk] a automatique // n (gun) automatique m; (Brit AUT) voiture f à transmission automatique; **~ally** ad automatiquement.

automation [ɔːtə'meɪʃən] n automatisation f.

automobile ['ɔːtəməbiːl] n (US) automobile f.

autonomy [ɔː'tɒnəmɪ] *n* autonomie *f*.

autumn ['ɔːtəm] *n* automne *m*.

auxiliary [ɔːg'zɪlɪərɪ] *a, n* auxiliaire (*m/f*).

Av. *abbr of* avenue.

avail [ə'veɪl] *vt*: to ~ o.s. of user de; profiter de // *n*: to no ~ sans résultat, en vain, en pure perte.

available [ə'veɪləbl] *a* disponible.

avalanche ['ævəlɑːnʃ] *n* avalanche *f*.

Ave. *abbr of* avenue.

avenge [ə'vendʒ] *vt* venger.

avenue ['ævənjuː] *n* avenue *f*.

average ['ævərɪdʒ] *n* moyenne *f* // *a* moyen(ne) // *vt* (*a certain figure*) atteindre *or* faire *etc* en moyenne; **on** ~ en moyenne; **to** ~ **out** *vi*: to ~ out at représenter en moyenne, donner une moyenne de.

averse [ə'vɜːs] *a*: to be ~ to sth/doing éprouver une forte répugnance envers qch/à faire.

avert [ə'vɜːt] *vt* prévenir, écarter; (*one's eyes*) détourner.

aviary ['eɪvɪərɪ] *n* volière *f*.

avocado [ævə'kɑːdəu] *n* (*also: Brit* ~ pear) avocat *m*.

avoid [ə'vɔɪd] *vt* éviter.

await [ə'weɪt] *vt* attendre.

awake [ə'weɪk] *a* éveillé(e); (*fig*) en éveil // *vb* (*pt* awoke, *pp* awoken, awaked) *vt* éveiller // *vi* s'éveiller; to be ~ être réveillé(e); ne pas dormir; ~ning [ə'weɪknɪŋ] *n* réveil *m*.

award [ə'wɔːd] *n* récompense *f*, prix *m* // *vt* (*prize*) décerner; (*LAW: damages*) accorder.

aware [ə'wɛə*] *a*: ~ of (*conscious*) conscient(e) de; (*informed*) au courant de; to become ~ of avoir conscience de, prendre conscience de; se rendre compte de; ~ness *n* le fait d'être conscient, au courant *etc*.

awash [ə'wɒʃ] *a* recouvert(e) (d'eau); ~ with inondé(e) de.

away [ə'weɪ] *a, ad* (au) loin; absent(e); two kilometres ~ à (une distance de) deux kilomètres, à deux kilomètres de distance; **two hours** ~ **by car** à deux heures de voiture *or* par route; **the holiday was two weeks** ~ il restait deux semaines jusqu'aux vacances; ~ **from** loin de; **he's** ~ **for a week** il est parti (pour) une semaine; **to take** ~ *vt* emporter; **to pedal/work/laugh** *etc* ~ la particule indique la constance et l'énergie de l'action: il pédalait *etc* tant qu'il pouvait; **to fade** *etc* ~ la particule renforce l'idée de la disparition, l'éloignement; ~ **game** *n* (*SPORT*) match *m* à l'extérieur.

awe [ɔː] *n* respect mêlé de crainte, effroi mêlé d'admiration; ~**-inspiring**, ~**some** *a* impressionnant(e).

awful ['ɔːfəl] *a* affreux(euse); ~**ly** *ad*

(*very*) terriblement, vraiment.

awhile [ə'waɪl] *ad* un moment, quelque temps.

awkward ['ɔːkwəd] *a* (*clumsy*) gauche, maladroit(e); (*inconvenient*) malaisé(e), d'emploi malaisé, peu pratique; (*embarrassing*) gênant(e), délicat(e).

awning ['ɔːnɪŋ] *n* (*of tent*) auvent *m*; (*of shop*) store *m*; (*of hotel etc*) marquise *f* (de toile).

awoke, awoken [ə'wəuk, -kən] *pt, pp of* awake.

awry [ə'raɪ] *ad, a* de travers; **to go** ~ mal tourner.

axe, (*US*) **ax** [æks] *n* hache *f* // *vt* (*employee*) renvoyer; (*project etc*) abandonner; (*jobs*) supprimer.

axis, *pl* **axes** ['æksɪs, -siːz] *n* axe *m*.

axle ['æksl] *n* (*also: ~*-tree) essieu *m*.

ay(e) [aɪ] *excl* (*yes*) oui.

B

B [biː] *n* (*MUS*) si *m*.

B.A. *abbr see* bachelor.

baby ['beɪbɪ] *n* bébé *m*; ~ **carriage** *n* (*US*) voiture *f* d'enfant; ~**-sit** *vi* garder les enfants; ~**-sitter** *n* baby-sitter *m/f*.

bachelor ['bætʃələ*] *n* célibataire *m*; B~ **of Arts/Science** (**B.A./B.Sc.**) ≈ licencié/e ès *or* en lettres/sciences.

back [bæk] *n* (*of person, horse*) dos *m*; (*of hand*) dos, revers *m*; (*of house*) derrière *m*; (*of car, train*) arrière *m*; (*of chair*) dossier *m*; (*of page*) verso *m*; (*FOOTBALL*) arrière *m* // *vt* (*candidate: also:* ~ **up**) soutenir, appuyer; (*horse: at races*) parier *or* miser sur; (*car*) (faire) reculer // *vi* reculer; (*car etc*) faire marche arrière // *a* (*in compounds*) de derrière, à l'arrière; ~ **seats/wheels** (*AUT*) sièges *mpl*/roues *fpl* arrière; ~ **payments/rent** arriéré *m* de paiements/loyer // *ad* (*not forward*) en arrière; (*returned*): **he's** ~ il est rentré, il est de retour; **he ran** ~ il est revenu en courant; (*restitution*): **throw the ball** ~ renvoie la balle; **can I have it** ~? puis-je le ravoir?; (*again*): **he called** ~ il a rappelé; **to** ~ **down** *vi* rabattre de ses prétentions; **to** ~ **out** *vi* (*of promise*) se dédire; **to** ~ **up** *vt* (*candidate etc*) soutenir, appuyer; (*COMPUT*) sauvegarder; ~**bencher** *n* (*Brit*) membre du parlement sans portefeuille; ~**bone** *n* colonne vertébrale, épine dorsale; ~**-cloth** *n* toile *f* de fond; ~**date** *vt* (*letter*) antidater; ~**dated pay rise** augmentation *f* avec effet rétroactif; ~**drop** *n* = ~**-cloth**; ~**fire** *vi* (*AUT*) pétarader; (*plans*) mal tourner; ~**ground** *n* arrière-plan *m*; (*of events*) situation *f*, conjoncture *f*; (*basic knowledge*) éléments *mpl* de base;

(*experience*) formation *f*; **family ~ground** milieu familial; **~hand** *n* (*TENNIS: also:* **~hand stroke**) revers *m*; **~handed** *a* (*fig*) déloyal(e), équivoque; **~hander** *n* (*Brit: bribe*) pot-de-vin *m*; **~ing** *n* (*fig*) soutien *m*, appui *m*; **~lash** *n* contre-coup *m*, répercussion *f*; **~log** *n*: **~log of work** travail *m* en retard; **~ number** *n* (*of magazine etc*) vieux numéro; **~pack** *n* sac *m* à dos; **~ pay** *n* rappel *m* de salaire; **~side** *n* (*col*) derrière *m*, postérieur *m*; **~stage** *ad* derrière la scène, dans la coulisse; **~stroke** *n* dos crawlé; **~up** *a* (*train, plane*) supplémentaire, de réserve; (*COMPUT*) de sauvegarde // *n* (*support*) appui *m*, soutien *m*; (*also:* **~up file**) sauvegarde *f*; **~ward** *a* (*movement*) en arrière; (*person, country*) arriéré(e); attardé(e); **~wards** *ad* (*move, go*) en arrière; (*read a list*) à l'envers, à rebours; (*fall*) à la renverse; (*walk*) à reculons; **~water** *n* (*fig*) coin reculé; bled perdu; **~yard** *n* arrière-cour *f*.

bacon ['beɪkən] *n* bacon *m*, lard *m*.

bad [bæd] *a* mauvais(e); (*child*) vilain(e); (*meat, food*) gâté(e), avarié(e); **his ~ leg** sa jambe malade; **to go ~** (*meat, food*) se gâter; (*milk*) tourner.

bade [bæd] *pt of* **bid**.

badge [bædʒ] *n* insigne *m*; (*of policeman*) plaque *f*.

badger ['bædʒə*] *n* blaireau *m*.

badly ['bædlɪ] *ad* (*work, dress etc*) mal; **~ wounded** grièvement blessé; **he needs it ~** il en a absolument besoin; **~ off**, *ad* dans la gêne.

badminton ['bædmɪntən] *n* badminton *m*.

bad-tempered ['bæd'tɛmpəd] *a* ayant mauvais caractère; de mauvaise humeur.

baffle ['bæfl] *vt* (*puzzle*) déconcerter.

bag [bæg] *n* sac *m*; (*of hunter*) gibecière *f*; chasse *f* // *vt* (*col: take*) empocher; s'approprier; **~s of** (*col: lots of*) des masses de; **~gage** *n* bagages *mpl*; **~gy** *a* avachi(e), qui fait des poches; **~pipes** *npl* cornemuse *f*.

bail [beɪl] *n* caution *f* // *vt* (*prisoner: also: grant ~ to*) mettre en liberté sous caution; (*boat: also: ~ out*) écoper; **on ~** (*prisoner*) sous caution; **to ~ out** *vt* (*prisoner*) payer la caution de; *see also* **bale**.

bailiff ['beɪlɪf] *n* huissier *m*.

bait [beɪt] *n* appât *m* // *vt* appâter; (*fig*) tourmenter.

bake [beɪk] *vt* (faire) cuire au four // *vi* cuire (au four); faire de la pâtisserie; **~d beans** *npl* haricots blancs à la sauce tomate; **~r** *n* boulanger *m*; **~ry** *n* boulangerie *f*; boulangerie industrielle; **baking** *n* cuisson *f*.

balance ['bæləns] *n* équilibre *m*; (*COMM: sum*) solde *m*; (*scales*) balance *f* // *vt* mettre or faire tenir en équilibre; (*pros and cons*) peser; (*budget*) équilibrer; (*account*) balancer; (*compensate*) compenser, contrebalancer; **~ of trade/ payments** balance commerciale/des comptes or paiements; **~d** *a* (*personality, diet*) équilibré(e); **~ sheet** *n* bilan *m*.

balcony ['bælkənɪ] *n* balcon *m*.

bald [bɔːld] *a* chauve; (*tyre*) lisse.

bale [beɪl] *n* balle *f*, ballot *m*; **to ~ out** *vi* (*of a plane*) sauter en parachute.

baleful ['beɪlful] *a* funeste, maléfique.

ball [bɔːl] *n* boule *f*; (*football*) ballon *m*; (*for tennis, golf*) balle *f*; (*dance*) bal *m*.

ballast ['bæləst] *n* lest *m*.

ball bearings *npl* roulement *m* à billes.

ballerina [bælə'riːnə] *n* ballerine *f*.

ballet ['bæleɪ] *n* ballet *m*; (*art*) danse *f* (classique).

balloon [bə'luːn] *n* ballon *m*; (*in comic strip*) bulle *f*.

ballot ['bælət] *n* scrutin *m*.

ball-point pen ['bɔːlpɔɪnt-] *n* stylo *m* à bille.

ballroom ['bɔːlrum] *n* salle *f* de bal.

balm [bɑːm] *n* baume *m*.

ban [bæn] *n* interdiction *f* // *vt* interdire.

banana [bə'nɑːnə] *n* banane *f*.

band [bænd] *n* bande *f*; (*at a dance*) orchestre *m*; (*MIL*) musique *f*, fanfare *f*; **to ~ together** *vi* se liguer.

bandage ['bændɪdʒ] *n* bandage *m*, pansement *m*.

bandaid ['bændeɪd] *n* (*US*) pansement adhésif.

bandwagon ['bændwægən] *n*: **to jump on the ~** (*fig*) monter dans or prendre le train en marche.

bandy ['bændɪ] *vt* (*jokes, insults*) échanger.

bandy-legged ['bændɪ'lɛgɪd] *a* aux jambes arquées.

bang [bæŋ] *n* détonation *f*; (*of door*) claquement *m*; (*blow*) coup (violent) // *vt* frapper (violemment); (*door*) claquer // *vi* détoner, claquer.

bangle ['bæŋgl] *n* bracelet *m*.

bangs [bæŋz] *npl* (*US: fringe*) frange *f*.

banish ['bænɪʃ] *vt* bannir.

banister(s) ['bænɪstə(z)] *n(pl)* rampe *f* (d'escalier).

bank [bæŋk] *n* banque *f*; (*of river, lake*) bord *m*, rive *f*; (*of earth*) talus *m*, remblai *m* // *vi* (*AVIAT*) virer sur l'aile; **to ~ on** *vt fus* miser or tabler sur; **~ ac- count** *n* compte *m* en banque; **~ card** *n* carte *f* d'identité bancaire; **~er** *n* banquier *m*; **~er's card** *n* (*Brit*) = **~ card**; **B~ holiday** *n* (*Brit*) jour férié (*où les banques sont fermées*); **~ing** *n* opérations *fpl* bancaires; profession *f* de banquier; **~note** *n* billet *m* de banque;

~ **rate** n taux m de l'escompte.
bankrupt ['bæŋkrʌpt] a en faillite; **to go** ~ faire faillite; ~**cy** n faillite f.
bank statement n relevé m de compte.
banner ['bænə*] n bannière f.
baptism ['bæptɪzəm] n baptême m.
bar [ba:*] n barre f; (of window etc) barreau m; (of chocolate) tablette f, plaque f; (fig) obstacle m; mesure f d'exclusion; (pub) bar m; (counter: in pub) comptoir m, bar; (MUS) mesure f // vt (road) barrer; (window) munir de barreaux; (person) exclure; (activity) interdire; ~ **of soap** savonnette f; **the B**~ (LAW) le barreau; **behind** ~**s** (prisoner) sous les verrous; ~ **none** sans exception.
barbaric [ba:'bærɪk] a barbare.
barbecue ['ba:bɪkju:] n barbecue m.
barbed wire ['ba:bd-] n fil m de fer barbelé.
barber ['ba:bə*] n coiffeur m (pour hommes).
bar code n (on goods) code m à barres.
bare [bɛə*] a nu(e) // vt mettre à nu, dénuder; (teeth) montrer; ~**back** ad à cru, sans selle; ~**faced** a impudent(e), effronté(e); ~**foot** a, ad nu-pieds, (les) pieds nus; ~**ly** ad à peine.
bargain ['ba:gɪn] n (transaction) marché m; (good buy) affaire f, occasion f // vi (haggle) marchander; (trade) négocier, traiter; **into the** ~ par-dessus le marché; **to** ~ **for** vt fus: **he got more than he** ~**ed for** il ne s'attendait pas à un coup pareil.
barge [ba:dʒ] n péniche f; **to** ~ **in** vi (walk in) faire irruption; (interrupt talk) intervenir mal à propos; **to** ~ **into** vt fus rentrer dans.
bark [ba:k] n (of tree) écorce f; (of dog) aboiement m // vi aboyer.
barley ['ba:lɪ] n orge f.
barmaid ['ba:meɪd] n serveuse f (de bar), barmaid f.
barman ['ba:mən] n serveur m (de bar), barman m.
barn [ba:n] n grange f.
barometer [bə'rɔmɪtə*] n baromètre m.
baron ['bærən] n baron m; ~**ess** n baronne f.
barracks ['bærəks] npl caserne f.
barrage ['bæra:ʒ] n (MIL) tir m de barrage; (dam) barrage m; (fig) pluie f.
barrel ['bærəl] n tonneau m; (of gun) canon m.
barren ['bærən] a stérile; (hills) aride.
barricade [bærɪ'keɪd] n barricade f.
barrier ['bærɪə*] n barrière f.
barring ['ba:rɪŋ] prep sauf.
barrister ['bærɪstə*] n (Brit) avocat (plaidant).
barrow ['bærəu] n (cart) charrette f à bras.
bartender ['ba:tɛndə*] n (US) serveur

m (de bar), barman m.
barter ['ba:tə*] vt: **to** ~ **sth for** échanger qch contre.
base [beɪs] n base f // vt: **to** ~ **sth on** baser or fonder qch sur // a vil(e), bas(se).
baseball ['beɪsbɔ:l] n base-ball m.
basement ['beɪsmənt] n sous-sol m.
bases ['beɪsi:z] npl of **base**; ['beɪsɪz] npl of **base**.
bash [bæʃ] vt (col) frapper, cogner.
bashful ['bæʃful] a timide; modeste.
basic ['beɪsɪk] a fondamental(e), de base; réduit(e) au minimum, rudimentaire; ~**ally** [-lɪ] ad fondamentalement, à la base; en fait, au fond.
basil ['bæzl] n basilic m.
basin ['beɪsn] n (vessel, also GEO) cuvette f, bassin m; (also: **wash**~) lavabo m.
basis, pl bases ['beɪsɪs, -si:z] n base f.
bask [ba:sk] vi: **to** ~ **in the sun** se chauffer au soleil.
basket ['ba:skɪt] n corbeille f; (with handle) panier m; ~**ball** n basket-ball m.
bass [beɪs] n (MUS) basse f.
bassoon [bə'su:n] n basson m.
bastard ['ba:stəd] n enfant naturel(le), bâtard/e; (col!) salaud m (!).
bat [bæt] n chauve-souris f; (for baseball etc) batte f; (Brit: for table tennis) raquette f // vt: **he didn't** ~ **an eyelid** il n'a pas sourcillé or bronché.
batch [bætʃ] n (of bread) fournée f; (of papers) liasse f.
bated ['beɪtɪd] a: **with** ~ **breath** en retenant son souffle.
bath [ba:θ, pl ba:ðz] n see also **baths**; bain m; (bathtub) baignoire f // vt baigner, donner un bain à; **to have a** ~ prendre un bain.
bathe [beɪð] vi se baigner // vt baigner.
bathing ['beɪðɪŋ] n baignade f; ~ **cap** n bonnet m de bain; ~ **costume**, (US) ~ **suit** n maillot m (de bain).
bath: ~**robe** n peignoir m de bain; ~**room** n salle f de bains.
baths [ba:ðz] npl établissement m de bains(-douches).
bath towel n serviette f de bain.
baton ['bætən] n bâton m; (MUS) baguette f; (club) matraque f.
batter ['bætə*] vt battre // n pâte f à frire; ~**ed** a (hat, pan) cabossé(e).
battery ['bætərɪ] n batterie f; (of torch) pile f.
battle ['bætl] n bataille f, combat m // vi se battre, lutter; ~**field** n champ m de bataille; ~**ship** n cuirassé m.
bawdy ['bɔ:dɪ] a paillard(e).
bawl [bɔ:l] vi hurler, brailler.
bay [beɪ] n (of sea) baie f; **to hold sb at** ~ tenir qn à distance or en échec.
bay window n baie vitrée.

bazaar [bə'zɑ:*] n bazar m; vente f de charité.

b. & b. B. & B. abbr see **bed**.

BBC n abbr (= British Broadcasting Corporation) office de la radiodiffusion et télévision britannique.

B.C. ad abbr (= before Christ) av. J.-C.

be [bi:], pt **was, were**, pp **been** ♦ auxiliary vb **1** (with present participle: forming continuous tenses): **what are you doing?** que faites-vous?; **they're coming tomorrow** ils viennent demain; **I've been waiting for you for 2 hours** je t'attends depuis 2 heures

2 (with pp: forming passives) être; **to ~ killed** être tué(e); **he was nowhere to ~ seen** on ne le voyait nulle part

3 (in tag questions): **it was fun, wasn't it?** c'était drôle, n'est-ce pas?; **she's back, is she?** elle est rentrée, n'est-ce pas or alors?

4 (+ to + infinitive): **the house is to ~ sold** la maison doit être vendue; **he's not to open it** il ne doit pas l'ouvrir

♦ vb + complement **1** (gen) être; **I'm English** je suis anglais(e); **I'm tired** je suis fatigué(e); **I'm hot/cold** j'ai chaud/froid; **he's a doctor** il est médecin; **2 and 2 are 4** 2 et 2 font 4

2 (of health) aller; **how are you?** comment allez-vous?; **I'm better now** je vais mieux maintenant; **he's very ill** il est très malade

3 (of age) avoir; **how old are you?** quel âge avez-vous?; **I'm sixteen (years old)** j'ai seize ans

4 (cost) coûter; **how much was the meal?** combien a coûté le repas?; **that'll ~ £5, please** ça fera 5 livres, s'il vous plaît

♦ vi **1** (exist, occur etc) être, exister; **the best singer that ever was** le meilleur chanteur qui ait jamais existé; **~ that as it may** quoi qu'il en soit; **so ~ it** soit

2 (referring to place) être, se trouver; **I won't ~ here tomorrow** je ne serai pas là demain; **Edinburgh is in Scotland** Édimbourg est or se trouve en Écosse

3 (referring to movement) aller; **where have you been?** où êtes-vous allé(s)?

♦ impersonal vb **1** (referring to time, distance) être; **it's 5 o'clock** il est 5 heures; **it's the 28th of April** c'est le 28 avril; **it's 10 km to the village** le village est à 10 km

2 (referring to the weather) faire; **it's too hot/cold** il fait trop chaud/froid; **it's windy** il y a du vent

3 (emphatic): **it's me/the postman** c'est moi/le facteur.

beach [bi:tʃ] n plage f // vt échouer.

beacon ['bi:kən] n (lighthouse) fanal m; (marker) balise f.

bead [bi:d] n perle f.

beak [bi:k] n bec m.

beaker ['bi:kə*] n gobelet m.

beam [bi:m] n poutre f; (of light) rayon m // vi rayonner.

bean [bi:n] n haricot m; (of coffee) grain m; **runner ~** haricot m (à rames); **broad ~** fève f; **~sprouts** npl germes mpl de soja.

bear [bɛə*] n ours m // vb (pt **bore**, pp **borne**) vt porter; (endure) supporter // vi: **to ~ right/left** obliquer à droite/gauche, se diriger vers la droite/gauche; **to ~ out** vt corroborer, confirmer; **to ~ up** vi (person) tenir le coup.

beard [bɪəd] n barbe f.

bearer ['bɛərə*] n porteur m.

bearing ['bɛərɪŋ] n maintien m, allure f; (connection) rapport m; **~s** npl (also: **ball ~s**) roulement m (à billes); **to take a ~** faire le point; **to find one's ~s** s'orienter.

beast [bi:st] n bête f; **~ly** a infect(e).

beat [bi:t] n battement m; (MUS) temps m, mesure f; (of policeman) ronde f // vt (pt **beat**, pp **beaten**) battre; **off the ~en track** hors des chemins or sentiers battus; **to ~ time** battre la mesure; **~ it!** (col) fiche(-moi) le camp!; **to ~ off** vt repousser; **to ~ up** vt (col: person) tabasser; (eggs) battre; **~ing** n raclée f.

beautiful ['bju:tɪful] a beau(belle); **~ly** ad admirablement.

beauty ['bju:tɪ] n beauté f; **~ salon** n institut m de beauté; **~ spot** n grain m de beauté; (Brit TOURISM) site naturel (d'une grande beauté).

beaver ['bi:və*] n castor m.

became [bɪ'keɪm] pt of **become**.

because [bɪ'kɒz] cj parce que; **~ of** prep à cause de.

beck [bɛk] n: **to be at sb's ~ and call** être à l'entière disposition de qn.

beckon ['bɛkən] vt (also: **~ to**) faire signe (de venir) à.

become [bɪ'kʌm] vt (irg: like **come**) devenir; **to ~ thin** maigrir.

becoming [bɪ'kʌmɪŋ] a (behaviour) convenable, bienséant(e); (clothes) seyant(e).

bed [bɛd] n lit m; (of flowers) parterre m; (of coal, clay) couche f; **to go to ~** aller se coucher; **single ~** lit à une place; **double ~** grand lit; **~ and breakfast (b. & b.)** n (terms) chambre et petit déjeuner; **~clothes** npl couvertures fpl et draps mpl; **~ding** n literie f.

bedlam ['bɛdləm] n chahut m, cirque m.

bedraggled [bɪ'dræɡld] a dépenaillé(e), les vêtements en désordre.

bed: ~ridden a cloué(e) au lit; **~room** n chambre f (à coucher); **~side** n: at sb's **~side** au chevet de qn; **~sit(ter)** n (Brit) chambre meublée, studio m;

~**spread** n couvre-lit m, dessus-de-lit m; ~**time** n heure f du coucher.

bee [bi:] n abeille f.

beech [bi:tʃ] n hêtre m.

beef [bi:f] n bœuf m; roast ~ rosbif m; ~**burger** n hamburger m; ~**eater** n hallebardier de la Tour de Londres.

beehive ['bi:haɪv] n ruche f.

beeline ['bi:laɪn] n: to make a ~ for se diriger tout droit vers.

been [bi:n] pp of be.

beer [bɪə*] n bière f.

beetle ['bi:tl] n scarabée m.

beetroot ['bi:tru:t] n (Brit) betterave f.

before [bɪ'fɔ:*] prep (in time) avant; (in space) devant // cj avant que + sub; avant de // ad avant; ~ going avant de partir; ~ she goes avant qu'elle (ne) parte; the week ~ la semaine précédente or d'avant; I've seen it ~ je l'ai déjà vu; ~**hand** ad au préalable, à l'avance.

beg [bɛg] vi mendier // vt mendier; (favour) quémander, solliciter; (entreat) supplier.

began [bɪ'gæn] pt of begin.

beggar ['bɛgə*] n mendiant/e.

begin [bɪ'gɪn], pt began, pp begun vt, vi commencer; to ~ doing or to do sth commencer à or de faire qch; ~**ner** n débutant/e; ~**ning** n commencement m, début m.

begun [bɪ'gʌn] pp of begin.

behalf [bɪ'hɑ:f] n: on ~ of de la part de; au nom de; pour le compte de.

behave [bɪ'heɪv] vi se conduire, se comporter; (well: also: ~ o.s.) se conduire bien or comme il faut.

behaviour, (US) **behavior** [bɪ'heɪvjə*] n comportement m, conduite f.

behead [bɪ'hɛd] vt décapiter.

beheld [bɪ'hɛld] pt, pp of behold.

behind [bɪ'haɪnd] prep derrière; (time) en retard sur // ad derrière; en retard // n derrière m; to be ~ (schedule) être en retard; ~ the scenes dans les coulisses.

behold [bɪ'həʊld] vt (irg: like hold) apercevoir, voir.

beige [beɪʒ] a beige.

being ['bi:ɪŋ] n être m; to come into ~ prendre naissance.

Beirut [beɪ'ru:t] n Beyrouth.

belated [bɪ'leɪtɪd] a tardif(ive).

belch [bɛltʃ] vi avoir un renvoi, roter // vt (also: ~ out: smoke etc) vomir, cracher.

belfry ['bɛlfrɪ] n beffroi m.

Belgian ['bɛldʒən] a belge, de Belgique // n Belge m/f.

Belgium ['bɛldʒəm] n Belgique f.

belie [bɪ'laɪ] vt démentir.

belief [bɪ'li:f] n (opinion) conviction f; (trust, faith) foi f; (acceptance as true) croyance f.

believe [bɪ'li:v] vt, vi croire; to ~ in (God) croire en; (method, ghosts) croire

à; ~**r** n (in idea, activity): ~**r** in partisan/e de; (REL) croyant/e.

belittle [bɪ'lɪtl] vt déprécier, rabaisser.

bell [bɛl] n cloche f; (small) clochette f, grelot m; (on door) sonnette f; (electric) sonnerie f.

bellow ['bɛləʊ] vi mugir.

bellows ['bɛləʊz] npl soufflet m.

belly ['bɛlɪ] n ventre m.

belong [bɪ'lɒŋ] vi: to ~ to appartenir à; (club etc) faire partie de; this book ~s here ce livre va ici; ~**ings** npl affaires fpl, possessions fpl.

beloved [bɪ'lʌvɪd] a (bien-)aimé(e).

below [bɪ'ləʊ] prep sous, au-dessous de // ad en dessous; en contre-bas; see ~ voir plus bas or plus loin or ci-dessous.

belt [bɛlt] n ceinture f; (TECH) courroie f // vt (thrash) donner une raclée à; ~**way** n (US AUT) route f de ceinture; (: motorway) périphérique m.

bemused [bɪ'mju:zd] a stupéfié(e).

bench [bɛntʃ] n banc m; (in workshop) établi m; the B~ (LAW) la magistrature, la Cour.

bend [bɛnd] vb (pt, pp bent) vt courber; (leg, arm) plier // vi se courber // n (Brit: in road) virage m, tournant m; (in pipe, river) coude m; to ~ down vi se baisser; to ~ over vi se pencher.

beneath [bɪ'ni:θ] prep sous, au-dessous de; (unworthy of) indigne de // ad dessous, au-dessous, en bas.

benefactor ['bɛnɪfæktə*] n bienfaiteur m.

beneficial [bɛnɪ'fɪʃəl] a salutaire; avantageux(euse).

benefit ['bɛnɪfɪt] n avantage m, profit m; (allowance of money) allocation f // vt faire du bien à, profiter à // vi: he'll ~ from it cela lui fera du bien, il y gagnera or s'en trouvera bien.

benevolent [bɪ'nɛvələnt] a bienveillant(e).

benign [bɪ'naɪn] a (person, smile) bienveillant(e), affable; (MED) bénin(igne).

bent [bɛnt] pt, pp of bend // n inclination f, penchant m // a (col: dishonest) véreux(euse); to be ~ on être résolu(e) à.

bequest [bɪ'kwɛst] n legs m.

bereaved [bɪ'ri:vd] n: the ~ la famille du disparu.

beret ['bɛreɪ] n béret m.

berm [bə:m] n (US AUT) accotement m.

berry ['bɛrɪ] n baie f.

berserk [bə'sə:k] a: to go ~ être pris(e) d'une rage incontrôlable; se déchaîner.

berth [bə:θ] n (bed) couchette f; (for ship) poste m d'amarrage, mouillage m // vi (in harbour) venir à quai; (at anchor) mouiller.

beseech [bɪ'si:tʃ], pt, pp **besought** vt implorer, supplier.

beset, *pt, pp* **beset** [bɪ'sɛt] *vt* assaillir.

beside [bɪ'saɪd] *prep* à côté de; **to be ~ o.s. (with anger)** être hors de soi; **that's ~ the point** cela n'a rien à voir.

besides [bɪ'saɪdz] *ad* en outre, de plus // *prep* en plus de; excepté.

besiege [bɪ'siːdʒ] *vt (town)* assiéger; *(fig)* assaillir.

besought [bɪ'sɔːt] *pt, pp of* **beseech**.

best [bɛst] *a* meilleur(e) // *ad* le mieux; **the ~ part of** *(quantity)* le plus clair de, la plus grande partie de; **at ~** au mieux; **to make the ~ of sth** s'accommoder de qch (du mieux que l'on peut); **to do one's ~** faire de son mieux; **to the ~ of my knowledge** pour autant que je sache; **to the ~ of my ability** du mieux que je pourrai; **~ man** *n* garçon *m* d'honneur.

bestow [bɪ'stəu] *vt* accorder; *(title)* conférer.

bet [bɛt] *n* pari *m* // *vt, vi (pt, pp* **bet** *or* **betted)** parier.

betray [bɪ'treɪ] *vt* trahir; **~al** *n* trahison *f*.

better ['bɛtə*] *a* meilleur(e) // *ad* mieux // *vt* améliorer // *n*: **to get the ~ of** triompher de, l'emporter sur; **you had ~ do it** vous feriez mieux de le faire; **he thought ~ of it** il s'est ravisé; **to get ~** aller mieux; s'améliorer; **~ off** *a* plus à l'aise financièrement; *(fig)*: **you'd be ~ off this way** vous vous en trouveriez mieux ainsi.

betting ['bɛtɪŋ] *n* paris *mpl*; **~ shop** *n (Brit)* bureau *m* de paris.

between [bɪ'twiːn] *prep* entre // *ad* au milieu; dans l'intervalle.

beverage ['bɛvərɪdʒ] *n* boisson *f (gén sans alcool).*

bevy ['bɛvɪ] *n*: **a ~ of** un essaim *or* une volée de.

beware [bɪ'wɛə*] *vi*: **to ~ (of)** prendre garde (à).

bewildered [bɪ'wɪldəd] *a* dérouté(e), ahuri(e).

bewitching [bɪ'wɪtʃɪŋ] *a* enchanteur(teresse).

beyond [bɪ'jɒnd] *prep (in space)* au-delà de; *(exceeding)* au-dessus de // *ad* au-delà; **~ doubt** hors de doute.

bias ['baɪəs] *n (prejudice)* préjugé *m*, parti pris; *(preference)* prévention *f*; **~(s)ed** *a* partial(e), montrant un parti pris.

bib [bɪb] *n* bavoir *m*, bavette *f*.

Bible ['baɪbl] *n* Bible *f*.

bicarbonate of soda [baɪ'kɑːbənɪt-] *n* bicarbonate *m* de soude.

bicker ['bɪkə*] *vi* se chamailler.

bicycle ['baɪsɪkl] *n* bicyclette *f*.

bid [bɪd] *n* offre *f*; *(at auction)* enchère *f*; *(attempt)* tentative *f* // *vb (pt* **bid** *or* **bade,** *pp* **bid** *or* **bidden)** *vi* faire une enchère *or* offre // *vt* faire une enchère *or* offre de; **to ~ sb good day** souhaiter le

bonjour à qn; **~der** *n*: **the highest ~der** le plus offrant; **~ding** *n* enchères *fpl*.

bide [baɪd] *vt*: **to ~ one's time** attendre son heure.

bifocals [baɪ'fəuklz] *npl* verres *mpl* à double foyer, lunettes bifocales.

big [bɪg] *a* grand(e); gros(se).

big dipper [-'dɪpə*] *n* montagnes *fpl* russes.

bigheaded ['bɪg'hɛdɪd] *a* prétentieux(euse).

bigot ['bɪgət] *n* fanatique *m/f*, sectaire *m/f*; **~ed** *a* fanatique, sectaire; **~ry** *n* fanatisme *m*, sectarisme *m*.

big top *n* grand chapiteau.

bike [baɪk] *n* vélo *m*, bécane *f*.

bikini [bɪ'kiːnɪ] *n* bikini *m*.

bilingual [baɪ'lɪŋwəl] *a* bilingue.

bill [bɪl] *n* note *f*, facture *f*; *(POL)* projet *m* de loi; *(US: banknote)* billet *m* (de banque); *(of bird)* bec *m*; **'post no ~s'** 'défense d'afficher'; **to fit** *or* **fill the ~** *(fig)* faire l'affaire; **~board** *n* panneau *m* d'affichage.

billet ['bɪlɪt] *n* cantonnement *m* (chez l'habitant).

billfold ['bɪlfəuld] *n (US)* portefeuille *m*.

billiards ['bɪljədz] *n* (jeu de) billard *m*.

billion ['bɪljən] *n (Brit)* billion *m (million de millions);* *(US)* milliard *m*.

bin [bɪn] *n* boîte *f*; *(also: dust~)* poubelle *f*; *(for coal)* coffre *m*.

bind [baɪnd], *pt, pp* **bound** *vt* attacher; *(book)* relier; *(oblige)* obliger, contraindre; **~ing** *n (of book)* reliure *f* // *a (contract)* constituant une obligation.

binge [bɪndʒ] *n (col):* **to go on a ~** aller faire la bringue.

bingo ['bɪŋgəu] *n* sorte de jeu de loto pratiqué dans des établissements publics.

binoculars [bɪ'nɒkjuləz] *npl* jumelles *fpl*.

bio... [baɪə'...] *prefix:* **~chemistry** *n* biochimie *f*; **~graphy** [baɪ'ɒgrəfɪ] *n* biographie *f*; **~logical** *a* biologique; **~logy** [baɪ'ɒlədʒɪ] *n* biologie *f*.

birch [bəːtʃ] *n* bouleau *m*.

bird [bəːd] *n* oiseau *m*; *(Brit col: girl)* nana *f*; **~'s-eye view** *n* vue *f* à vol d'oiseau; *(fig)* vue d'ensemble *or* générale; **~ watcher** *n* ornithologue *m/f* amateur.

Biro ['baɪərəu] *n* ® stylo *m* à bille.

birth [bəːθ] *n* naissance *f*; **~ certificate** *n* acte *m* de naissance; **~ control** *n* limitation *f* des naissances; méthode(s) contraceptive(s); **~day** *n* anniversaire *m*; **~ rate** *n* (taux *m* de) natalité *f*.

biscuit ['bɪskɪt] *n (Brit)* biscuit *m*.

bisect [baɪ'sɛkt] *vt* couper *or* diviser en deux.

bishop ['bɪʃəp] *n* évêque *m*.

bit [bɪt] *pt of* **bite** // *n* morceau *m*; *(of*

tool) mèche f; (of horse) mors m;
(COMPUT) élément m binaire; **a ~ of** un
peu de; **a ~ mad** un peu fou; **~ by ~**
petit à petit.
bitch [bɪtʃ] n (dog) chienne f; (col!)
salope f (!), garce f.
bite [baɪt] vt, vi (pt **bit**, pp **bitten**) mordre // n morsure f; (insect ~) piqûre f;
(mouthful) bouchée f; let's have a ~ (to
eat) mangeons un morceau; to ~ one's
nails se ronger les ongles.
bitter ['bɪtə*] a amer(ère); (wind,
criticism) cinglant(e) // n (Brit: beer)
bière f (à forte teneur en houblon);
~ness n amertume f; goût amer.
blab [blæb] vi jaser, trop parler.
black [blæk] a noir(e) // n (colour) noir
m; (person): B~ noir/e // vt (shoes)
cirer; (Brit INDUSTRY) boycotter; to give
sb a ~ eye pocher l'œil à qn, faire un œil
au beurre noir à qn; ~ and blue a
couvert(e) de bleus; to be in the ~ (in
credit) être créditeur(trice); **~berry** n
mûre f; **~bird** n merle m; **~board** n
tableau noir; **~currant** n cassis m;
~en vt noircir; **~ ice** n verglas m;
~leg n (Brit) briseur m de grève, jaune
m; **~list** n liste noire; **~mail** n
chantage m // vt faire chanter, soumettre
au chantage; **~ market** n marché noir;
~out n panne f d'électricité; (fainting)
syncope f; **the B~ Sea** n la mer Noire;
~ sheep n brebis galeuse; **~smith** n
forgeron m; **~ spot** n (AUT) point noir.
bladder ['blædə*] n vessie f.
blade [bleɪd] n lame f; (of oar) plat m;
~ of grass brin m d'herbe.
blame [bleɪm] n faute f, blâme m // vt:
to ~ sb/sth for sth attribuer à qn/qch la
responsabilité de qch; reprocher qch à
qn/qch; who's to ~? qui est le fautif or
coupable or responsable?
bland [blænd] a affable; (taste)
doux(douce), fade.
blank [blæŋk] a blanc(blanche); (look)
sans expression, dénué(e) d'expression //
n espace m vide, blanc m; (cartridge)
cartouche f à blanc; ~ cheque n
chèque m en blanc.
blanket ['blæŋkɪt] n couverture f.
blare [blɛə*] vi beugler.
blast [blɑːst] n souffle m; explosion f // vt
faire sauter or exploser; **~-off** n
(SPACE) lancement m.
blatant ['bleɪtənt] a flagrant(e),
criant(e).
blaze [bleɪz] n (fire) incendie m; (fig)
flamboiement m // vi (fire) flamber; (fig)
flamboyer, resplendir // vt: to ~ a trail
(fig) montrer la voie.
blazer ['bleɪzə*] n blazer m.
bleach [bliːtʃ] n (also: household ~) eau
f de Javel // vt (linen) blanchir; **~ed** a
(hair) oxygéné(e), décoloré(e); **~ers**
npl (US SPORT) gradins mpl (en plein

soleil).
bleak [bliːk] a morne, désolé(e).
bleary-eyed ['blɪərɪ'aɪd] a aux yeux
pleins de sommeil.
bleat [bliːt] vi bêler.
bleed [bliːd], pt, pp **bled** [bliːd, blɛd] vt, vi
saigner; my nose is ~ing je saigne du
nez.
bleeper ['bliːpə*] n (device) bip m.
blemish ['blɛmɪʃ] n défaut m.
blend [blɛnd] n mélange m // vt
mélanger // vi (colours etc) se mélanger,
se fondre, s'allier.
bless [blɛs], pt, pp **blessed** or **blest** [blɛs,
blɛst] vt bénir; **~ing** n bénédiction f;
bienfait m.
blew [bluː] pt of **blow**.
blight [blaɪt] vt (hopes etc) anéantir,
briser.
blimey ['blaɪmɪ] excl (Brit col) mince
alors!
blind [blaɪnd] a aveugle // n (for
window) store m // vt aveugler; ~ alley
n impasse f; ~ corner n (Brit) virage
m sans visibilité; **~fold** n bandeau m //
a, ad les yeux bandés // vt bander les
yeux à; **~ly** ad aveuglément; **~ness** n
cécité f; (fig) aveuglement m; ~ spot n
(AUT etc) angle mort.
blink [blɪŋk] vi cligner des yeux; (light)
clignoter; **~ers** npl œillères fpl.
bliss [blɪs] n félicité f, bonheur m sans
mélange.
blister ['blɪstə*] n (on skin) ampoule f,
cloque f; (on paintwork) boursouflure f //
vi (paint) se boursoufler, se cloquer.
blithely ['blaɪðlɪ] ad joyeusement.
blitz [blɪts] n bombardement (aérien).
blizzard ['blɪzəd] n blizzard m, tempête
f de neige.
bloated ['bləʊtɪd] a (face) bouffi(e);
(stomach) gonflé(e).
blob [blɒb] n (drop) goutte f; (stain,
spot) tache f.
block [blɒk] n bloc m; (in pipes) obstruction f; (toy) cube m; (of buildings)
pâté m (de maisons) // vt bloquer; **~ade**
[-'keɪd] n blocus m // vt faire le blocus
de; **~age** n obstruction f; **~buster** n
(film, book) grand succès; ~ of flats n
(Brit) immeuble (locatif); ~ letters npl
majuscules fpl.
bloke [bləʊk] n (Brit col) type m.
blonde [blɒnd] a, n blond(e).
blood [blʌd] n sang m; ~ donor n
donneur/euse de sang; ~ group n
groupe sanguin; **~hound** n limier m; ~
poisoning n empoisonnement m du
sang; ~ pressure n tension f
(artérielle); **~shed** n effusion f de sang,
carnage m; **~shot** a: ~shot eyes yeux
injectés de sang; **~stream** n sang m,
système sanguin; ~ test n prise f de
sang; **~thirsty** a sanguinaire; **~y** a
sanglant(e); (Brit col!): this ~y ... ce

foutu ..., ce putain de ... (!); ~y strong/ good vachement or sacrément fort/bon; ~y-minded a (Brit col) contrariant(e), obstiné(e).

bloom [blu:m] n fleur f; (fig) épanouissement m // vi être en fleur; (fig) s'épanouir; être florissant(e).

blossom ['blɔsəm] n fleur(s) f(pl) // vi être en fleurs; (fig) s'épanouir.

blot [blɔt] n tache f // vt tacher; to ~out vt (memories) effacer; (view) cacher, masquer; (nation, city) annihiler.

blotchy ['blɔtʃɪ] a (complexion) couvert(e) de marbrures.

blotting paper ['blɔtɪŋ-] n buvard m.

blouse [blauz] n (feminine garment) chemisier m, corsage m.

blow [bləu] n coup m // vb (pt blew, pp blown [blu:, bləun]) vi souffler // vt (fuse) faire sauter; to ~ one's nose se moucher; to ~ a whistle siffler; to ~away vt chasser, faire s'envoler; to ~down vt faire tomber, renverser; to ~off vt emporter; to ~ out vi éclater, sauter; to ~ over vi s'apaiser; to ~up vi exploser, sauter // vt faire sauter; (tyre) gonfler; (PHOT) agrandir; ~-dry n brushing m; ~lamp n (Brit) chalumeau m; ~out n (of tyre) éclatement m; ~-torch n = ~lamp.

blue [blu:] a bleu(e); ~ film/joke film m/ histoire f pornographique; to come out of the ~ (fig) être complètement inattendu; to have the ~s avoir le cafard; ~bottle n mouche f à viande; ~ jeans npl bluejeans mpl; ~print n (fig) projet m, plan directeur.

bluff [blʌf] vi bluffer // n bluff m; to call sb's ~ mettre qn au défi d'exécuter ses menaces.

blunder ['blʌndə*] n gaffe f, bévue f // vi faire une gaffe or une bévue.

blunt [blʌnt] a émoussé(e), peu tranchant(e); (person) brusque, ne mâchant pas ses mots // vt émousser.

blur [blə:*] n tache or masse floue or confuse // vt brouiller, rendre flou(e).

blurb [blə:b] n notice f publicitaire; (for book) texte m de présentation.

blurt [blə:t] : to ~ out vt (reveal) lâcher; (say) balbutier, dire d'une voix entrecoupée.

blush [blʌʃ] vi rougir // n rougeur f.

blustery ['blʌstərɪ] a (weather) à bourrasques.

boar [bɔ:*] n sanglier m.

board [bɔ:d] n planche f; (on wall) panneau m; (committee) conseil m, comité m; (in firm) conseil d'administration // vt (ship) monter à bord de; (train) monter dans; (NAUT, AVIAT): on ~ à bord; full ~ (Brit) pension complète; half ~ (Brit) demi-pension f; ~ and lodging n chambre f avec pension; which goes by the ~ (fig) qu'on

laisse tomber, qu'on abandonne; to ~up vt (door) condamner (au moyen de planches, de tôle); ~er n pensionnaire m/f; (SCOL) interne m/f, pensionnaire ~ing card n (AVIAT, NAUT) carte f d'embarquement; ~ing house n pension f; ~ing school n internat m, pensionnat m; ~ room n salle f du conseil d'administration.

boast [bəust] vi: to ~ (about or of) se vanter (de) // vt s'enorgueillir de // n vantardise f; sujet m d'orgueil or de fierté.

boat [bəut] n bateau m; (small) canot m; barque f; ~er n (hat) canotier m; ~swain ['bəusn] n maître m d'équipage.

bob [bɔb] vi (boat, cork on water: also: ~ up and down) danser, se balancer // n (Brit col) = shilling; to ~ up vi surgir or apparaître brusquement.

bobby ['bɔbɪ] n (Brit col) ≈ agent m (de police).

bobsleigh ['bɔbsleɪ] n bob m.

bode [bəud] vi: to ~ well/ill (for) être de bon/mauvais augure (pour).

bodily ['bɔdɪlɪ] a corporel(le) // ad physiquement; dans son entier or ensemble; en personne.

body [bɔdɪ] n corps m; (of car) carrosserie f; (of plane) fuselage m; (fig: society) organe m, organisme m; (fig: quantity) ensemble m, masse f; (of wine) corps m; ~-building n culturisme m; ~guard n garde m du corps; ~work n carrosserie f.

bog [bɔg] n tourbière f // vt: to get ~ged down (fig) s'enliser.

boggle ['bɔgl] vi: the mind ~s c'est incroyable, on en reste sidéré.

bogus ['bəugəs] a bidon inv; fantôme.

boil [bɔɪl] vt (faire) bouillir // vi bouillir // n (MED) furoncle m; to come to the (Brit) or a (US) ~ bouillir; to ~ down vi (fig): to ~ down to se réduire or ramener à; to ~ over vi déborder; ~ed egg n œuf m à la coque; ~ed potatoes npl pommes fpl à l'anglaise or à l'eau; ~er n chaudière f; ~er suit n (Brit) bleu m de travail, combinaison f; ~ing point n point m d'ébullition.

boisterous ['bɔɪstərəs] a bruyant(e), tapageur(euse).

bold [bəuld] a hardi(e), audacieux(euse); (pej) effronté(e); (outline, colour) franc(franche), tranché(e), marqué(e).

bollard ['bɔləd] n (Brit AUT) borne lumineuse or de signalisation.

bolster ['bəulstə*] n traversin m; to ~up vt soutenir.

bolt [bəult] n verrou m; (with nut) boulon m // ad: ~ upright droit(e) comme un piquet // vt verrouiller; (food) engloutir // vi se sauver, filer (comme une flèche).

bomb [bɔm] *n* bombe *f* // *vt* bombarder; ~ **disposal unit** *n* section *f* de déminage; ~**er** *n* (*AVIAT*) bombardier *m*; ~**shell** *n* (*fig*) bombe *f*.

bona fide ['bəunə'faidi] *a* de bonne foi; (*offer*) sérieux(euse);

bond [bɔnd] *n* lien *m*; (*binding promise*) engagement *m*, obligation *f*; (*COMM*) obligation *f*; **in** ~ (*of goods*) en douane.

bondage ['bɔndidʒ] *n* esclavage *m*.

bone [bəun] *n* os *m*; (*of fish*) arête *f* // *vt* désosser; ôter les arêtes de; ~ **idle** *a*, ~ **lazy** *a* fainéant(e).

bonfire ['bɔnfaiə*] *n* feu *m* (de joie); (*for rubbish*) feu.

bonnet ['bɔnit] *n* bonnet *m*; (*Brit: of car*) capot *m*.

bonus ['bəunəs] *n* prime *f*, gratification *f*.

bony ['bəuni] *a* (*arm, face, MED: tissue*) osseux(euse); (*meat*) plein(e) d'os; (*fish*) plein d'arêtes.

boo [bu:] *excl* hou!, peuh! // *vt* huer.

booby trap ['bu:bi-] *n* engin piégé.

book [buk] *n* livre *m*; (*of stamps etc*) carnet *m*; (*COMM*): ~**s** comptes *mpl*, comptabilité *f* // *vt* (*ticket*) prendre; (*seat, room*) réserver; (*driver*) dresser un procès-verbal à; (*football player*) prendre le nom de; ~**case** *n* bibliothèque *f* (*meuble*); ~**ing office** *n* (*Brit*) bureau *m* de location; ~**keeping** *n* comptabilité *f*; ~**let** *n* brochure *f*; ~**maker** *n* bookmaker *m*; ~**seller** *n* libraire *m/f*; ~**shop** *n*, ~**store** *n* librairie *f*.

boom [bu:m] *n* (*noise*) grondement *m*; (*busy period*) boom *m*, vague *f* de prospérité // *vi* gronder; prospérer.

boon [bu:n] *n* bénédiction *f*, grand avantage.

boost [bu:st] *n* stimulant *m*, remontant *m* // *vt* stimuler; ~**er** *n* (*MED*) rappel *m*.

boot [bu:t] *n* botte *f*; (*for hiking*) chaussure *f* (de marche); (*for football etc*) soulier *m*; (*Brit: of car*) coffre *m* // *vt* (*COMPUT*) remettre à zéro; **to** ~ (*in addition*) par-dessus le marché, en plus.

booth [bu:ð] *n* (*at fair*) baraque (foraine); (*of cinema, telephone etc*) cabine *f*; (*also*: **voting** ~) isoloir *m*.

booty ['bu:ti] *n* butin *m*.

booze [bu:z] *n* (*col*) boissons *fpl* alcooliques, alcool *m*.

border ['bɔ:də*] *n* bordure *f*; bord *m*; (*of a country*) frontière *f*; **the B~s** la région frontière entre l'Écosse et l'Angleterre; **to** ~ **on** *vt fus* être voisin(e) de, toucher à; ~**line** *n* (*fig*) ligne *f* de démarcation; ~**line case** *n* cas *m* limite.

bore [bɔ:*] *pt* of **bear** // *vt* (*hole*) percer; (*person*) ennuyer, raser // *n* (*person*) raseur/euse; (*of gun*) calibre

m; **to be** ~**d** s'ennuyer; ~**dom** *n* ennui *m*; **boring** *a* ennuyeux(euse).

born [bɔ:n] *a*: **to be** ~ naître; **I was** ~ **in 1960** je suis né en 1960.

borne [bɔ:n] *pp* of **bear**.

borough ['bʌrə] *n* municipalité *f*.

borrow ['bɔrəu] *vt*: **to** ~ **sth (from sb)** emprunter qch (à qn).

bosom ['buzəm] *n* poitrine *f*; (*fig*) sein *m*.

boss [bɔs] *n* patron/ne // *vt* commander; ~**y** *a* autoritaire.

bosun ['bəusn] *n* maître *m* d'équipage.

botany ['bɔtəni] *n* botanique *f*.

botch [bɔtʃ] *vt* (*also*: ~ **up**) saboter, bâcler.

both [bəuθ] *a* les deux, l'un(e) et l'autre // *pronoun*: ~ (**of them**) les deux, tous(toutes) les deux, l'un(e) et l'autre; ~ **of us went, we** ~ **went** nous y sommes allés (tous) les deux // *ad*: **they sell** ~ **the fabric and the finished curtains** ils vendent (et) le tissu et les rideaux (finis), ils vendent à la fois le tissu et les rideaux (finis).

bother ['bɔðə*] *vt* (*worry*) tracasser; (*needle, bait*) importuner, ennuyer; (*disturb*) déranger // *vi* (*also*: ~ **o.s.**) se tracasser, se faire du souci // *n*: **it is a** ~ **to have to do** c'est vraiment ennuyeux d'avoir à faire; **it's no** ~ aucun problème; **to** ~ **doing** prendre la peine de faire.

bottle ['bɔtl] *n* bouteille *f*; (*baby's*) biberon *m* // *vt* mettre en bouteille(s); **to** ~ **up** *vt* refouler, contenir; ~**neck** *n* étranglement *m*; ~**-opener** *n* ouvre-bouteille *m*.

bottom ['bɔtəm] *n* (*of container, sea etc*) fond *m*; (*buttocks*) derrière *m*; (*of page, list*) bas *m*; (*of chair*) siège *m* // *a* du fond; du bas.

bough [bau] *n* branche *f*, rameau *m*.

bought [bɔ:t] *pt, pp* of **buy**.

boulder ['bəuldə*] *n* gros rocher.

bounce [bauns] *vi* (*ball*) rebondir; (*cheque*) être refusé (*étant sans provision*) // *vt* faire rebondir // *n* (*rebound*) rebond *m*; ~**r** *n* (*col*) videur *m*.

bound [baund] *pt, pp* of **bind** // *n* (*gen pl*) limite *f*; (*leap*) bond *m* // *vt* (*leap*) bondir; (*limit*) borner // *a*: **to be** ~ **to do sth** (*obliged*) être obligé(e) or avoir obligation de faire qch; **he's** ~ **to fail** (*likely*) il est sûr d'échouer, son échec est inévitable or assuré; ~ **for** à destination de; **out of** ~**s** dont l'accès est interdit.

boundary ['baundri] *n* frontière *f*.

bout [baut] *n* période *f*; (*of malaria etc*) accès *m*, crise *f*, attaque *f*; (*BOXING etc*) combat *m*, match *m*.

bow *n* [bəu] nœud *m*; (*weapon*) arc *m*; (*MUS*) archet *m*; [bau] (*with body*) révérence f, inclination f (du buste or corps); (NAUT: also: ~s) proue f // vi [bau] faire une révérence, s'incliner; (yield): to ~ to or before s'incliner devant, se soumettre à.

bowels [bauəlz] npl intestins mpl; (fig) entrailles fpl.

bowl [bəul] n (for eating) bol m; (for washing) cuvette f; (ball) boule f; (of pipe) fourneau m // vi (CRICKET) lancer (la balle); ~s n (jeu m de) boules fpl.

bow-legged ['bəu'lɛgɪd] a aux jambes arquées.

bowler ['bəulə*] n (CRICKET) lanceur m (de la balle); (Brit: also: ~ hat) (chapeau m) melon m.

bowling ['bəulɪŋ] n (game) jeu m de boules; jeu m de quilles; ~ alley n bowling m; ~ green n terrain m de boules (gazonné et carré).

bow tie n nœud m papillon.

box [bɔks] n boîte f; (also: cardboard ~) carton m; (THEATRE) loge f // vt mettre en boîte; (SPORT) boxer // vi boxer, faire de la boxe; ~er n (person) boxeur m; ~ing n (SPORT) boxe f; B~ing Day n (Brit) le lendemain de Noël; ~ing gloves npl gants mpl de boxe; ~ing ring n ring m; ~ office n bureau m de location; ~ room n débarras m; chambrette f.

boy [bɔɪ] n garçon m.

boycott ['bɔɪkɔt] n boycottage m // vt boycotter.

boyfriend ['bɔɪfrɛnd] n (petit) ami.

B.R. abbr of **British Rail**.

bra [brɑ:] n soutien-gorge m.

brace [breɪs] n attache f, agrafe f; (on teeth) appareil m (dentaire); (tool) vilbrequin m // vt consolider, soutenir; ~s npl (Brit) bretelles fpl; to ~ o.s. (fig) se préparer mentalement.

bracelet ['breɪslɪt] n bracelet m.

bracing ['breɪsɪŋ] a tonifiant(e), tonique.

bracken ['brækən] n fougère f.

bracket ['brækɪt] n (TECH) tasseau m, support m; (group) classe f, tranche f; (also: brace ~) accolade f; (also: round ~) parenthèse f; (also: square ~) crochet m // vt mettre entre parenthèse(s).

brag [bræg] vi se vanter.

braid [breɪd] n (trimming) galon m; (of hair) tresse f, natte f.

brain [breɪn] n cerveau m; ~s npl cervelle f; he's got ~s il est intelligent; ~child n invention personnelle; ~wash vt faire subir un lavage de cerveau à; ~wave n idée géniale; ~y a intelligent(e), doué(e).

brake [breɪk] n (on vehicle) frein m // vt, vi freiner; ~ fluid n liquide m de freins; ~ light n feu m de stop.

bramble ['bræmbl] n (bush) ronce f; (berry) mûre f sauvage.

bran [bræn] n son m.

branch [brɑ:ntʃ] n branche f; (COMM) succursale f // vi bifurquer.

brand [brænd] n marque (commerciale) // vt (cattle) marquer (au fer rouge).

brand-new ['brænd'nju:] a tout(e) neuf(neuve), flambant neuf(neuve).

brandy ['brændɪ] n cognac m, fine f.

brash [bræʃ] a effronté(e).

brass [brɑ:s] n cuivre m (jaune), laiton m; the ~ (MUS) les cuivres; ~ band n fanfare f.

brassière ['bræsɪə*] n soutien-gorge m.

brat [bræt] n (pej) mioche m/f, môme m/f.

brave [breɪv] a courageux(euse), brave // n guerrier indien // vt braver, affronter; ~ry n bravoure f, courage m.

brawl [brɔ:l] n rixe f, bagarre f.

brawn [brɔ:n] n muscle m; (meat) fromage m de tête.

bray [breɪ] vi braire.

brazen ['breɪzn] a impudent(e), effronté(e) // vt: to ~ it out payer d'effronterie, crâner.

brazier ['breɪzɪə*] n brasero m.

Brazil [brə'zɪl] n Brésil m.

breach [bri:tʃ] vt ouvrir une brèche dans // n (gap) brèche f; (breaking): ~ of contract rupture f de contract; ~ of the peace attentat m à l'ordre public.

bread [brɛd] n pain m; ~ and butter n tartines (beurrées); (fig) subsistance f; ~bin, (US) ~box n boîte f à pain; (bigger) huche f à pain; ~crumbs npl miettes fpl de pain; (CULIN) chapelure f, panure f; ~line n: to be on the ~line être sans le sou or dans l'indigence.

breadth [brɛtθ] n largeur f.

breadwinner ['brɛdwɪnə*] n soutien m de famille.

break [breɪk] vb (pt broke, pp broken) vt casser, briser; (promise) rompre; (law) violer // vi (se) casser, se briser; (weather) tourner // n (gap) brèche f; (fracture) cassure f; (rest) interruption f, arrêt m; (: short) pause f; (: at school) récréation f; (chance) chance f, occasion f favorable; to ~ one's leg etc se casser la jambe etc; to ~ a record battre un record; to ~ the news to sb annoncer la nouvelle à qn; to ~ down vt (figures, data) décomposer, analyser // vi s'effondrer; (MED) faire une dépression (nerveuse); (AUT) tomber en panne; to ~ even vi rentrer dans ses frais; to ~ free or loose vi se dégager, s'échapper; to ~ in vt (horse etc) dresser // vi (burglar) entrer par effraction; to ~ into vt fus (house) s'introduire or pénétrer par effraction dans; to ~ off vi (speaker) s'interrompre; (branch) se rompre; to ~ open vt (door etc) forcer, fracturer; to ~ out vi éclater, se déclarer; to ~ out in spots se couvrir de boutons; to ~ up vi (*partnership*) cesser, prendre fin; (*friends*) se séparer // *vt* fracasser, casser; (*fight etc*) interrompre, faire cesser; **~age** *n* casse *f*; **~down** *n* (*AUT*) panne *f*; (*in communications*) rupture *f*; (*MED: also:* **nervous ~down**) dépression (nerveuse); **~down van** *n* (*Brit*) dépanneuse *f*; **~er** *n* brisant *m*.

breakfast ['brɛkfəst] *n* petit déjeuner *m*.

break: **~-in** *n* cambriolage *m*; **~ing and entering** *n* (*LAW*) effraction *f*; **~through** *n* percée *f*; **~water** *n* brise-lames *m inv*, digue *f*.

breast [brɛst] *n* (*of woman*) sein *m*; (*chest*) poitrine *f*; **~-feed** *vt, vi* (*irg: like* feed) allaiter; **~-stroke** *n* brasse *f*.

breath [brɛθ] *n* haleine *f*, souffle *m*; out of **~** à bout de souffle, essoufflé(e).

Breathalyser ['brɛθəlaɪzə*] *n* ® alcootest *m*.

breathe [bri:ð] *vt, vi* respirer; **to ~ in** *vt, vi* aspirer, inspirer; **to ~ out** *vt, vi* expirer; **~r** *n* moment *m* de repos *or* de répit; **breathing** *n* respiration *f*.

breathless ['brɛθlɪs] *a* essoufflé(e), haletant(e); oppressé(e).

breath-taking ['brɛθteɪkɪŋ] *a* stupéfiant(e), à vous couper le souffle.

breed [bri:d] *vb* (*pt, pp* **bred** [brɛd]) *vt* élever, faire l'élevage de // *vi* se reproduire // *n* race *f*, variété *f*; **~ing** *n* reproduction *f*; élevage *m*; (*upbringing*) éducation *f*.

breeze [bri:z] *n* brise *f*.

breezy ['bri:zɪ] *a* frais(fraîche); aéré(e); désinvolte, jovial(e).

brevity ['brɛvɪtɪ] *n* brièveté *f*.

brew [bru:] *vt* (*tea*) faire infuser; (*beer*) brasser; (*plot*) tramer, préparer // *vi* (*tea*) infuser; (*beer*) fermenter; (*fig*) se préparer, couver; **~er** *n* brasseur *m*; **~ery** *n* brasserie *f* (*fabrique*).

bribe [braɪb] *n* pot-de-vin *m* // *vt* acheter; soudoyer; **~ry** *n* corruption *f*.

brick [brɪk] *n* brique *f*; **~layer** *n* maçon *m*; **~works** *n* briqueterie *f*.

bridal ['braɪdl] *a* nuptial(e).

bride [braɪd] *n* mariée *f*, épouse *f*; **~groom** *n* marié *m*, époux *m*; **~smaid** *n* demoiselle *f* d'honneur.

bridge [brɪdʒ] *n* pont *m*; (*NAUT*) passerelle *f* (de commandement); (*of nose*) arête *f*; (*CARDS, DENTISTRY*) bridge *m* // *vt* (*river*) construire un pont sur; (*gap*) combler.

bridle ['braɪdl] *n* bride *f* // *vt* refréner, mettre la bride à; (*horse*) brider; **~ path** *n* piste *or* allée cavalière.

brief [bri:f] *a* bref(brève) // *n* (*LAW*) dossier *m*, cause *f* // *vt* donner des instructions à; **~s** *npl* slip *m*; **~case** *n* serviette *f*; porte-documents *m inv*; **~ing** *n* instructions *fpl*; **~ly** *ad* brièvement.

bright [braɪt] *a* brillant(e); (*room,*

weather) clair(e); (*person*) intelligent(e), doué(e); (*colour*) vif(vive); **~en** (*also:* **~en up**) *vt* (*room*) éclaircir; égayer // *vi* s'éclaircir; (*person*) retrouver un peu de sa gaieté.

brilliance ['brɪljəns] *n* éclat *m*.

brilliant ['brɪljənt] *a* brillant(e).

brim [brɪm] *n* bord *m*.

brine [braɪn] *n* eau salée; (*CULIN*) saumure *f*.

bring [brɪŋ], *pt, pp* **brought** *vt* (*thing*) apporter; (*person*) amener; **to ~ about** *vt* provoquer, entraîner; **to ~ back** *vt* rapporter; ramener; **to ~ down** *vt* abaisser; faire s'effondrer; **to ~ forward** *vt* avancer; **to ~ off** *vt* (*task, plan*) réussir, mener à bien; **to ~ out** *vt* (*meaning*) faire ressortir, mettre en relief; **to ~ round** *or* **to** *vt* (*unconscious person*) ranimer; **to ~ up** *vt* élever; (*question*) soulever; (*food: vomit*) vomir, rendre.

brink [brɪŋk] *n* bord *m*.

brisk [brɪsk] *a* vif(vive).

bristle ['brɪsl] *n* poil *m* // *vi* se hérisser.

Britain ['brɪtən] *n* (*also:* **Great ~**) Grande-Bretagne *f*.

British ['brɪtɪʃ] *a* britannique; **the ~** *npl* les Britanniques *mpl*; **the ~ Isles** *npl* les Iles *fpl* Britanniques; **B~ Rail (B.R.)** *n* compagnie ferroviaire britannique, ≈ S.N.C.F. *f*.

Briton ['brɪtən] *n* Britannique *m/f*.

Brittany ['brɪtənɪ] *n* Bretagne *f*.

brittle ['brɪtl] *a* cassant(e), fragile.

broach [brəutʃ] *vt* (*subject*) aborder.

broad [brɔ:d] *a* large; (*distinction*) général(e); (*accent*) prononcé(e); in **~ daylight** en plein jour; **~cast** *n* émission *f* // *vb* (*pt, pp* **broadcast**) *vt* radiodiffuser; téléviser // *vi* émettre; **~en** *vt* élargir // *vi* s'élargir; **~ly** *ad* en gros, généralement; **~-minded** *a* large d'esprit.

broccoli ['brɔkəlɪ] *n* brocoli *m*.

brochure ['brəuʃjuə*] *n* prospectus *m*, dépliant *m*.

broil [brɔɪl] *vt* griller.

broke [brəuk] *pt of* **break** // *a* (*col*) fauché(e).

broken ['brəukn] *pp of* **break** // *a:* **~ leg etc** jambe *etc* cassée; **in ~ English** dans un anglais approximatif *or* hésitant; **~-hearted** *a* (ayant) le cœur brisé.

broker ['brəukə*] *n* courtier *m*.

brolly ['brɔlɪ] *n* (*Brit col*) pépin *m*, parapluie *m*.

bronchitis [brɔŋ'kaɪtɪs] *n* bronchite *f*.

bronze [brɔnz] *n* bronze *m*.

brooch [brəutʃ] *n* broche *f*.

brood [bru:d] *n* couvée *f* // *vi* (*hen, storm*) couver; (*person*) méditer (sombrement), ruminer.

brook [bruk] *n* ruisseau *m*.

broom [brum] *n* balai *m*; **~stick** *n*

manche m à balai.

Bros. abbr = **Brothers**.

broth [brɔθ] n bouillon m de viande et de légumes.

brothel ['brɔθl] n maison close, bordel m.

brother ['brʌðə*] n frère m; ~-**in-law** n beau-frère m.

brought [brɔːt] pt, pp of **bring**.

brow [brau] n front m; (rare, gen: eye~) sourcil m; (of hill) sommet m.

brown [braun] a brun(e), marron inv // n (colour) brun m // vt brunir; (CULIN) faire dorer, faire roussir; ~ **bread** n pain m bis.

brownie ['brauni] n jeannette f, éclaireuse (cadette).

brown paper n papier m d'emballage.

brown sugar n cassonade f.

browse [brauz] vi (among books) bouquiner, feuilleter les livres.

bruise [bruːz] n bleu m, ecchymose f, contusion f // vt contusionner, meurtrir.

brunette [bruː'nɛt] n (femme) brune.

brunt [brʌnt] n: the ~ of (attack, criticism etc) le plus gros de.

brush [brʌʃ] n brosse f; (quarrel) accrochage m, prise f de bec // vt brosser; (also: ~ past, ~ against) effleurer, frôler; to ~ **aside** vt écarter, balayer; to ~ **up** vt (knowledge) rafraîchir, réviser; ~**wood** n broussailles fpl, taillis m.

Brussels ['brʌslz] n Bruxelles; ~ **sprout** n chou m de Bruxelles.

brutal ['bruːtl] a brutal(e).

brute [bruːt] n brute f // a: by ~ **force** par la force.

B.Sc. abbr see **bachelor**.

bubble ['bʌbl] n bulle f // vi bouillonner, faire des bulles; (sparkle, fig) pétiller; ~ **bath** n bain moussant.

buck [bʌk] n mâle m (d'un lapin, lièvre, daim etc); (US col) dollar m // vi ruer, lancer une ruade; to pass the ~ (to sb) se décharger de la responsabilité (sur qn); to ~ **up** vi (cheer up) reprendre du poil de la bête, se remonter.

bucket ['bʌkɪt] n seau m.

buckle ['bʌkl] n boucle f // vt boucler, attacher; (warp) tordre, gauchir; (: wheel) voiler.

bud [bʌd] n bourgeon m; (of flower) bouton m // vi bourgeonner; (flower) éclore.

Buddhism ['budɪzəm] n bouddhisme m.

budding ['bʌdɪŋ] a (poet etc) en herbe; (passion etc) naissant(e).

buddy ['bʌdɪ] n (US) copain m.

budge [bʌdʒ] vt faire bouger // vi bouger.

budgerigar ['bʌdʒərɪgaː*] n perruche f.

budget ['bʌdʒɪt] n budget m // vi: to ~ **for** sth inscrire qch au budget.

budgie ['bʌdʒɪ] n = **budgerigar**.

buff [bʌf] a (couleur f) chamois m // n (enthusiast) mordu(e).

buffalo, pl ~ or ~**es** ['bʌfələu] n buffle m; (US) bison m.

buffer ['bʌfə*] n tampon m; (COMPUT) mémoire f tampon.

buffet n ['bufeɪ] (food, Brit: bar) buffet m // vt ['bʌfɪt] gifler, frapper; secouer, ébranler; ~ **car** n (Brit RAIL) voiture-buffet f.

bug [bʌg] n (insect) punaise f; (: gen) insecte m, bestiole f; (fig: germ) virus m, microbe m; (: spy device) dispositif m d'écoute (électronique), micro clandestin // vt garnir de dispositifs d'écoute.

bugle ['bjuːgl] n clairon m.

build [bɪld] n (of person) carrure f, charpente f // vt (pt, pp **built**) construire, bâtir; to ~ **up** vt accumuler, amasser; accroître; ~**er** n entrepreneur m; ~**ing** n construction f; bâtiment m, construction; (habitation, offices) immeuble m; ~**ing society** n (Brit) société f de crédit immobilier.

built [bɪlt] pt, pp of **build**; ~-**in** a (cupboard) encastré(e); (device) incorporé(e); intégré(e); ~-**up area** n agglomération (urbaine); zone urbanisée.

bulb [bʌlb] n (BOT) bulbe m, oignon m; (ELEC) ampoule f.

bulge [bʌldʒ] n renflement m, gonflement m // vi faire saillie; présenter un renflement; to be bulging with être plein(e) à craquer de.

bulk [bʌlk] n masse f, volume m; in ~ (COMM) en vrac; the ~ of la plus grande or grosse partie de; ~**y** a volumineux(euse), encombrant(e).

bull [bul] n taureau m; ~**dog** n bouledogue m.

bulldozer ['buldəuzə*] n bulldozer m.

bullet ['bulɪt] n balle f (de fusil etc).

bulletin ['bulɪtɪn] n bulletin m, communiqué m.

bulletproof ['bulɪtpruːf] a (car) blindé(e); (vest etc) pare-balles inv.

bullfight ['bulfaɪt] n corrida f, course f de taureaux; ~**er** n torero m; ~**ing** n tauromachie f.

bullion ['buljən] n or m or argent m en lingots.

bullock ['bulək] n bœuf m.

bullring ['bulrɪŋ] n arènes fpl.

bull's-eye ['bulzaɪ] n centre m (de la cible).

bully ['bulɪ] n brute f, tyran m // vt tyranniser, rudoyer; (frighten) intimider.

bum [bʌm] n (col: backside) derrière m; (tramp) vagabond/e, traîne-savates m/f inv.

bumblebee ['bʌmblbiː] n bourdon m.

bump [bʌmp] n (blow) coup m, choc m;

(*jolt*) cahot *m*; (*on road etc, on head*) bosse *f* // *vt* heurter, cogner; **to ~ into** *vt fus* rentrer dans, tamponner; **~er** *n* pare-chocs *m inv* // *a*: **~er crop/harvest** récolte/moisson exceptionnelle.

bumptious ['bʌmpʃəs] *a* suffisant(e), prétentieux(euse).

bumpy ['bʌmpi] *a* cahoteux(euse).

bun [bʌn] *n* petit pain au lait; (*of hair*) chignon *m*.

bunch [bʌntʃ] *n* (*of flowers*) bouquet *m*; (*of keys*) trousseau *m*; (*of bananas*) régime *m*; (*of people*) groupe *m*; **~ of grapes** grappe *f* de raisin.

bundle ['bʌndl] *n* paquet *m* // *vt* (*also: ~ up*) faire un paquet de; (*put*): **to ~ sth/sb into** fourrer or enfourner qch/qn dans.

bungalow ['bʌŋgələu] *n* bungalow *m*.

bungle ['bʌŋgl] *vt* bâcler, gâcher.

bunion ['bʌnjən] *n* oignon *m* (*au pied*).

bunk [bʌŋk] *n* couchette *f*; **~ beds** *npl* lits superposés.

bunker ['bʌŋkə*] *n* (*coal store*) soute *f* à charbon; (*MIL, GOLF*) bunker *m*.

bunny ['bʌni] *n* (*also: ~ rabbit*) Jeannot *m* lapin.

bunting ['bʌntiŋ] *n* pavoisement *m*, drapeaux *mpl*.

buoy [bɔi] *n* bouée *f*; **to ~ up** *vt* faire flotter; (*fig*) soutenir, épauler; **~ant** *a* (*carefree*) gai(e), plein(e) d'entrain.

burden ['bə:dn] *n* fardeau *m*, charge *f* // *vt* charger; (*oppress*) accabler, surcharger.

bureau, *pl* **~x** [bjuə'rəu, -z] *n* (*Brit: writing desk*) bureau *m*, secrétaire *m*; (*US: chest of drawers*) commode *f*; (*office*) bureau, office *m*.

bureaucracy [bjuə'rɔkrəsi] *n* bureaucratie *f*.

burglar ['bə:glə*] *n* cambrioleur *m*; **~ alarm** *n* sonnerie *f* d'alarme; **~y** *n* cambriolage *m*.

Burgundy ['bə:gəndi] *n* Bourgogne *f*.

burial ['beriəl] *n* enterrement *m*.

burly ['bə:li] *a* de forte carrure, costaud(e).

Burma ['bə:mə] *n* Birmanie *f*.

burn [bə:n] *vt, vi* (*pt, pp* burned or burnt) brûler // *n* brûlure *f*; **to ~ down** *vt* incendier, détruire par le feu; **~er** *n* brûleur *m*.

burnt [bə:nt] *pt, pp* of **burn**.

burrow ['bʌrəu] *n* terrier *m* // *vt* creuser.

bursar ['bə:sə*] *n* économe *m/f*; (*Brit: student*) boursier/ère; **~y** *n* (*Brit*) bourse *f* (d'études).

burst [bə:st] *vb* (*pt, pp* burst) *vt* crever; faire éclater // *vi* éclater; (*tyre*) crever // *n* explosion *f*; (*also: ~ pipe*) rupture *f*; fuite *f*; **to ~ into flames** s'enflammer soudainement; **to ~ out laughing** éclater de rire; **to ~ into tears** fondre en

larmes; **to ~ing with** être plein (à craquer) de; regorger de; **to ~ into** *vt fus* (*room etc*) faire irruption dans; **to ~ open** *vi* s'ouvrir violemment or soudainement.

bury ['beri] *vt* enterrer.

bus, ~es [bʌs, 'bʌsiz] *n* autobus *m*.

bush [buʃ] *n* buisson *m*; (*scrub land*) brousse *f*; **to beat about the ~** tourner autour du pot.

bushy ['buʃi] *a* broussailleux(euse), touffu(e).

busily ['bizili] *ad* activement.

business ['biznis] *n* (*matter, firm*) affaire *f*; (*trading*) affaires *fpl*; (*job, duty*) travail *m*; **to be away on ~** être en déplacement d'affaires; **it's none of my ~** cela ne me regarde pas, ce ne sont pas mes affaires; **he means ~** il ne plaisante pas, il est sérieux; **~like** *a* sérieux(euse); efficace; **~man/woman** *n* homme/femme d'affaires; **~ trip** *n* voyage *m* d'affaires.

busker ['bʌskə*] *n* (*Brit*) musicien ambulant.

bus-stop ['bʌsstɔp] *n* arrêt *m* d'autobus.

bust [bʌst] *n* buste *m* // *a* (*col: broken*) fichu(e), fini(e); **to go ~** faire faillite.

bustle ['bʌsl] *n* remue-ménage *m*, affairement *m* // *vi* s'affairer, se démener.

busy ['bizi] *a* occupé(e); (*shop, street*) très fréquenté(e) // *vt*: **to ~ o.s.** s'occuper; **~body** *n* mouche *f* du coche, âme *f* charitable; **~ signal** *n* (*US TEL*) tonalité *f* occupé *inv*.

but [bʌt] ♦ *cj* mais; I'd love to come, **~** I'm busy j'aimerais venir mais je suis occupé ♦ *prep* (*apart from, except*) sauf, excepté; we've had nothing **~** trouble nous n'avons eu que des ennuis; no-one **~** him can do it lui seul peut le faire; **~** for you/your help sans toi/ton aide; anything **~** that tout sauf or excepté ça, tout mais pas ça

♦ *ad* (*just, only*) ne ... que; she's **~** a child elle n'est qu'une enfant; had I **~** known si seulement j'avais su; all **~** finished pratiquement terminé.

butcher ['butʃə*] *n* boucher *m* // *vt* massacrer; (*cattle etc for meat*) tuer.

butler ['bʌtlə*] *n* maître *m* d'hôtel.

butt [bʌt] *n* (*cask*) gros tonneau; (*thick end*) (gros) bout; (*of gun*) crosse *f*; (*of cigarette*) mégot *m*; (*Brit fig: target*) cible *f* // *vt* donner un coup de tête à; **to ~ in** *vi* (*interrupt*) s'immiscer dans la conversation.

butter ['bʌtə*] *n* beurre *m* // *vt* beurrer; **~cup** *n* bouton *m* d'or.

butterfly ['bʌtəflai] *n* papillon *m*; (*SWIMMING: also: ~ stroke*) brasse *f* papillon *inv*.

buttocks ['bʌtəks] *npl* fesses *fpl*.

button ['bʌtn] *n* bouton *m* // *vt* (*also: ~*

up) boutonner // vi se boutonner.

buttress ['bʌtrɪs] n contrefort m.

buxom ['bʌksəm] a aux formes avantageuses or épanouies.

buy [baɪ] vb (pt, pp **bought**) vt acheter; **to ~ sb sth/sth from sb** acheter qch à qn; **to ~ sb a drink** offrir un verre or à boire à qn; **~er** n acheteur/euse.

buzz [bʌz] n bourdonnement m; (col: phone call) coup m de fil // vi bourdonner.

buzzer ['bʌzə*] n timbre m électrique.

buzz word n (col) mot m à la mode.

by [baɪ] ♦ prep **1** (referring to cause, agent) par, de; **killed ~ lightning** tué par la foudre; **surrounded ~ a fence** entouré d'une barrière; **a painting ~ Picasso** un tableau de Picasso

2 (referring to method, manner, means): **~ bus/car** en autobus/voiture; **~ train** par le or en train; **to pay ~ cheque** payer par chèque; **~ saving hard, he ...** à force d'économiser, il ...

3 (via, through) par; **we came ~ Dover** nous sommes venus par Douvres

4 (close to, past) à côté de; **the house ~ the school** la maison à côté de l'école; **a holiday ~ the sea** des vacances au bord de la mer; **she sat ~ his bed** elle était assise à son chevet; **she went ~ me** elle est passée à côté de moi; **I go ~ the post office every day** je passe devant la poste tous les jours

5 (with time: not later than) avant; (: during): **~ daylight** à la lumière du jour; **by night** la nuit, de nuit; **~ 4 o'clock** avant 4 heures; **~ this time tomorrow** d'ici demain à la même heure; **~ the time I got here it was too late** lorsque je suis arrivé c'était déjà trop tard

6 (amount) à; **~ the kilo/metre** au kilo/au mètre; **paid ~ the hour** payé à l'heure

7 (MATH, measure): **to divide/multiply ~ 3** diviser/multiplier par 3; **a room 3 metres ~ 4** une pièce de 3 mètres sur 4; **it's broader ~ a metre** c'est plus large d'un mètre; **one ~ one** un à un; **little ~ little** petit à petit, peu à peu

8 (according to) d'après, selon; **it's 3 o'clock ~ my watch** il est 3 heures d'après ma montre; **it's all right ~ me** me je n'ai rien contre

9: **(all) ~ oneself** etc tout(e) seul(e)

10: **~ the way** au fait, à propos

♦ ad **1** see **go, pass** etc

2: **~ and ~** un peu plus tard, bientôt; **~ and large** dans l'ensemble.

bye(-bye) ['baɪ('baɪ)] excl au revoir!, salut!

by(e)-law ['baɪlɔ:] n arrêté municipal.

by-election ['baɪɪlɛkʃən] n (Brit) élection (législative) partielle.

bygone ['baɪɡɔn] a passé(e) // n: **let ~s**

be **~s** passons l'éponge, oublions le passé.

bypass ['baɪpɑ:s] n (route f de) contournement m; (MÉD) pontage m // vt éviter.

by-product ['baɪprɔdʌkt] n sous-produit m, dérivé m; (fig) conséquence f secondaire, retombée f.

bystander ['baɪstændə*] n spectateur/trice, badaud/e.

byte [baɪt] n (COMPUT) octet m.

byway ['baɪweɪ] n chemin m (écarté).

byword ['baɪwə:d] n: **to be a ~ for** être synonyme de (fig).

by-your-leave ['baɪjɔ:'li:v] n: **without so much as a ~** sans même demander la permission.

C

C [si:] n (MUS) do m.

C.A. abbr of **chartered accountant**.

cab [kæb] n taxi m; (of train, truck) cabine f; (horse-drawn) fiacre m.

cabaret ['kæbəreɪ] n attractions fpl, spectacle m de cabaret.

cabbage ['kæbɪdʒ] n chou m.

cabin ['kæbɪn] n cabane f, hutte f; (on ship) cabine f.

cabinet ['kæbɪnɪt] n (POL) cabinet m; (furniture) petit meuble à tiroirs et rayons; (also: display ~) vitrine f, petite armoire vitrée; **~-maker** n ébéniste m.

cable ['keɪbl] n câble m // vt câbler, télégraphier; **~-car** n téléphérique m; **~ television** n télévision f par câble.

cache [kæʃ] n cachette f.

cackle ['kækl] vi caqueter.

cactus, pl **cacti** ['kæktəs, -taɪ] n cactus m.

cadet [kə'dɛt] n (MIL) élève m officier.

cadge [kædʒ] vt se faire donner.

café ['kæfeɪ] n ≈ café(-restaurant) m (sans alcool).

cage [keɪdʒ] n cage f.

cagey ['keɪdʒɪ] a (col) réticent(e); méfiant(e).

cagoule [kə'ɡu:l] n K-way m ®.

Cairo ['kaɪərəu] n le Caire.

cajole [kə'dʒəul] vt couvrir de flatteries or de gentillesses.

cake [keɪk] n gâteau m; **~ of soap** savonnette f; **~d** a: **~d with** raidi(e) par, couvert(e) d'une croûte de.

calculate ['kælkjuleɪt] vt calculer; **calculation** [-'leɪʃən] n calcul m; **calculator** n machine f à calculer, calculatrice f.

calendar ['kæləndə*] n calendrier m; **~ year** n année civile.

calf [kɑ:f], pl **calves** n (of cow) veau m; (of other animals) petit m; (also: ~skin) veau m, vachette f; (ANAT) mollet m.

calibre, (US) **caliber** ['kælɪbə*] n calibre m.

call [kɔ:l] vt (gen, also TEL) appeler // vi appeler; (visit: also: ~ **in**, ~ **round**): to ~ **(for)** passer (prendre) // n (shout) appel m, cri m; (visit) visite f; (also: **telephone ~**) coup m de téléphone; communication f; **she's ~ed Suzanne** elle s'appelle Suzanne; **to be on ~** être de permanence; **to ~ back** vi (return) repasser; (TEL) rappeler; **to ~ for** vt fus demander; **to ~ off** vt annuler; **to ~ on** vt fus (visit) rendre visite à, passer voir; (request): **to ~ on sb to do** inviter qn à faire; **to ~ out** vi pousser un cri or des cris; **to ~ up** vt (MIL) appeler, mobiliser; **~box** n (Brit) cabine f téléphonique; **~er** n personne f qui appelle; visiteur m; **~ girl** n call-girl f; **~-in** n (US: phone-in) programme m à ligne ouverte; **~ing** n vocation f; (trade, occupation) état m; **~ing card** n (US) carte f de visite.

callous ['kæləs] a dur(e), insensible.

calm [kɑ:m] a calme // n calme m // vt calmer, apaiser; **to ~ down** vi se calmer, s'apaiser // vt calmer, apaiser.

Calor gas ['kælə*-] n ® butane m, butagaz m ®.

calorie ['kælərı] n calorie f.

calves [kɑ:vz] npl of **calf.**

camber ['kæmbə*] n (of road) bombement m.

Cambodia [kæm'bəudjə] n Cambodge m.

came [keɪm] pt of **come.**

camel ['kæməl] n chameau m.

cameo ['kæmɪəu] n camée m.

camera ['kæmərə] n appareil-photo m; (also: cine-~, movie ~) caméra f; in ~ à huis clos, en privé; **~man** n caméraman m.

camouflage ['kæməflɑ:ʒ] n camouflage m // vt camoufler.

camp [kæmp] n camp m // vi camper.

campaign [kæm'peɪn] n (MIL, POL etc) campagne f // vi (also fig) faire campagne.

campbed ['kæmp'bɛd] n (Brit) lit m de camp.

camper ['kæmpə*] n campeur/euse.

camping ['kæmpɪŋ] n camping m; **to go ~** faire du camping.

campsite ['kæmpsaɪt] n campement m.

campus ['kæmpəs] n campus m.

can [kæn] auxiliary vb see next headword // n (of milk, oil, water) bidon m; (tin) boîte f de conserve // vt mettre en conserve.

can [kæn] ♦ n, vt see previous headword ♦ auxiliary vb (negative **cannot, can't**; conditional and pt **could**) **1** (be able to) pouvoir; **you ~ do it if you try** vous pouvez le faire si vous essayez; **I ~'t hear you** je ne t'entends pas

2 (know how to) savoir; **I ~ swim/play**

tennis/drive je sais nager/jouer au tennis/conduire; **~ you speak French?** parlez-vous français?

3 (may) pouvoir; **~ I use your phone?** puis-je me servir de votre téléphone?

4 (expressing disbelief, puzzlement etc): **it ~'t be true!** ce n'est pas possible!; **what CAN he want?** qu'est-ce qu'il peut bien vouloir?

5 (expressing possibility, suggestion etc): **he could be in the library** il est peut-être dans la bibliothèque; **she could have been delayed** il se peut qu'elle ait été retardée.

Canada ['kænədə] n Canada m.

Canadian [kə'neɪdɪən] a canadien(ne) // n Canadien/ne.

canal [kə'næl] n canal m.

canary [kə'nɛərɪ] n canari m, serin m.

cancel ['kænsəl] vt annuler; (train) supprimer; (party, appointment) décommander; (cross out) barrer, rayer; (stamp) oblitérer; **~lation** [-'leɪʃən] n annulation f; suppression f; oblitération f; (TOURISM) réservation annulée.

cancer ['kænsə*] n cancer m; **C~** (sign) le Cancer.

candid ['kændɪd] a (très) franc(franche), sincère.

candidate ['kændɪdeɪt] n candidat/e.

candle ['kændl] n bougie f; (of tallow) chandelle f; (in church) cierge m; **by ~light** à la lumière d'une bougie; (dinner) aux chandelles; **~stick** n (also: ~ holder) bougeoir m; (bigger, ornate) chandelier m.

candour, (US) **candor** ['kændə*] n (grande) franchise or sincérité.

candy ['kændɪ] n sucre candi; (US) bonbon m; **~-floss** n (Brit) barbe f à papa.

cane [keɪn] n canne f // vt (Brit SCOL) administrer des coups de bâton à.

canister ['kænɪstə*] n boîte f.

cannabis ['kænəbɪs] n (drug) cannabis m; (also: ~ plant) chanvre indien.

canned ['kænd] a (food) en boîte, en conserve.

cannon, pl ~ or **~s** ['kænən] n (gun) canon m.

cannot ['kænɔt] = **can not.**

canny ['kænɪ] a madré(e), finaud(e).

canoe [kə'nu:] n pirogue f; (SPORT) canoë m.

canon ['kænən] n (clergyman) chanoine m; (standard) canon m.

can opener [-'əupnə*] n ouvre-boîte m.

canopy ['kænəpɪ] n baldaquin m; dais m.

can't [kænt] = **can not.**

cantankerous [kæn'tæŋkərəs] a querelleur(euse), acariâtre.

canteen [kæn'ti:n] n cantine f; (Brit: of cutlery) ménagère f.

canter ['kæntə*] *n* petit galop.
canvas ['kænvəs] *n* (gen) toile *f*.
canvassing ['kænvəsɪŋ] *n* (POL) prospection électorale, démarchage électoral; (COMM) démarchage, prospection.
canyon ['kænjən] *n* cañon *m*, gorge (profonde).
cap [kæp] *n* casquette *f*; (of pen) capuchon *m*; (of bottle) capsule *f* // *vt* capsuler; (outdo) surpasser.
capability [keɪpə'bɪlɪtɪ] *n* aptitude *f*, capacité *f*.
capable ['keɪpəbl] *a* capable.
capacity [kə'pæsɪtɪ] *n* capacité *f*, contenance *f*; aptitude *f*.
cape [keɪp] *n* (garment) cape *f*; (GEO) cap *m*.
capital ['kæpɪtl] *n* (also: ~ city) capitale *f*; (money) capital *m*; (also: ~ letter) majuscule *f*; ~ **gains tax** *n* impôt *m* sur les plus-values; ~**ism** *n* capitalisme *m*; ~**ist** *a*, *n* capitaliste (m/f); ~**ize**: to ~ize on *vt fus* profiter de; ~ **punishment** *n* peine capitale.
Capricorn ['kæprɪkɔ:n] *n* le Capricorne.
capsize [kæp'saɪz] *vt* faire chavirer // *vi* chavirer.
capsule ['kæpsju:l] *n* capsule *f*.
captain ['kæptɪn] *n* capitaine *m*.
caption ['kæpʃən] *n* légende *f*.
captive ['kæptɪv] *a*, *n* captif(ive).
capture ['kæptʃə*] *vt* capturer, prendre; (attention) capter // *n* capture *f*; (data ~) saisie *f* de données.
car [ka:*] *n* voiture *f*, auto *f*.
carafe [kə'ræf] *n* carafe *f*.
caramel ['kærəməl] *n* caramel *m*.
caravan ['kærəvæn] *n* caravane *f*; ~ **site** *n* (Brit) camping *m* pour caravanes.
carbohydrates [ka:bəu'haɪdreɪts] *npl* (foods) aliments *mpl* riches en hydrate de carbone.
carbon ['ka:bən] *n* carbone *m*; ~ **paper** *n* papier *m* carbone.
carburettor, (US) **carburetor** [ka:bju-'retə*] *n* carburateur *m*.
card [ka:d] *n* carte *f*; ~**board** *n* carton *m*; ~ **game** *n* jeu *m* de cartes.
cardiac ['ka:dɪæk] *a* cardiaque.
cardigan ['ka:dɪgən] *n* cardigan *m*.
cardinal ['ka:dɪnl] *a* cardinal(e) // *n* cardinal *m*.
card index ['ka:dɪndɛks] *n* fichier *m* (alphabétique).
care [kɛə*] *n* soin *m*, attention *f*; (worry) souci *m* // *vi*: to ~ **about** se soucier de, s'intéresser à; ~ **of** (c/o) chez, aux bons soins de; **in sb's** ~ à la garde de qn, confié à qn; **to take** ~ (to do) faire attention (à faire); **to take** ~ **of** *vt* s'occuper de, prendre soin de; **to** ~ **for** *vt fus* s'occuper de; (like) aimer; **I don't** ~ ça m'est bien égal, peu

m'importe.
career [kə'rɪə*] *n* carrière *f* // *vi* (also: ~ along) aller à toute allure.
carefree ['kɛəfri:] *a* sans souci, insouciant(e).
careful ['kɛəful] *a* soigneux(euse); (cautious) prudent(e); (be) ~! (fais) attention!; ~**ly** *ad* avec soin, soigneusement; prudemment.
careless ['kɛəlɪs] *a* négligent(e); (heedless) insouciant(e).
caress [kə'rɛs] *n* caresse *f* // *vt* caresser.
caretaker ['kɛəteɪkə*] *n* gardien/ne, concierge *m/f*.
car-ferry ['ka:fɛrɪ] *n* (on sea) ferry(-boat) *m*; (on river) bac *m*.
cargo, *pl* ~**es** ['ka:gəu] *n* cargaison *f*, chargement *m*.
car hire *n* location *f* de voiture.
Caribbean [kærɪ'bi:ən] *a*: the ~ (Sea) la mer des Antilles *or* Caraïbes.
caring ['kɛərɪŋ] *a* (person) bienveillant(e); (society, organization) humanitaire.
carnal ['ka:nl] *a* charnel(le).
carnation [ka:'neɪʃən] *n* œillet *m*.
carnival ['ka:nɪvəl] *n* (public celebration) carnaval *m*; (US: funfair) fête foraine.
carol ['kærəl] *n*: (Christmas) ~ chant *m* de Noël.
carp [ka:p] *n* (fish) carpe *f*; **to** ~ **at** *vt fus* critiquer.
car park ['ka:pa:k] *n* (Brit) parking *m*, parc *m* de stationnement.
carpenter ['ka:pɪntə*] *n* charpentier *m*.
carpentry ['ka:pɪntrɪ] *n* charpenterie *f*, métier *m* de charpentier; (woodwork: at school etc) menuiserie *f*.
carpet ['ka:pɪt] *n* tapis *m* // *vt* recouvrir (d'un tapis); ~ **slippers** *npl* pantoufles *fpl*; ~ **sweeper** *n* balai *m* mécanique.
carriage ['kærɪdʒ] *n* voiture *f*; (of goods) transport *m*; (: cost) port *m*; (of typewriter) chariot *m*; (bearing) maintien *m*, port *m*; ~ **return** *n* (on typewriter etc) retour *m* de chariot; ~**way** *n* (Brit: part of road) chaussée *f*.
carrier ['kærɪə*] *n* transporteur *m*, camionneur *m*; (MED) porteur/euse; (NAUT) porte-avions *m inv*; ~ **bag** *n* (Brit) sac *m* en papier *or* en plastique.
carrot ['kærət] *n* carotte *f*.
carry ['kærɪ] *vt* (subj: person) porter; (: vehicle) transporter; (a motion, bill) voter, adopter; (involve: responsibilities etc) comporter, impliquer // *vi* (sound) porter; **to be** *or* **get carried away** (fig) s'emballer, s'enthousiasmer; **to** ~ **on** *vi*: to ~ **on with sth/doing** continuer qch/à faire // *vt* entretenir, poursuivre; **to** ~ **out** *vt* (orders) exécuter; (investigation) effectuer; ~**cot** *n* porte-bébé *m*; ~**-on** *n* (col: fuss) histoires *fpl*.
cart [ka:t] *n* charrette *f* // *vt* transporter.

carton ['ka:tən] n (box) carton m; (of yogurt) pot m (en carton); (of cigarettes) cartouche f.

cartoon [ka:'tu:n] n (PRESS) dessin m (humoristique); (satirical) caricature f; (comic strip) bande dessinée; (CINEMA) dessin animé.

cartridge ['ka:trɪdʒ] n (for gun, pen) cartouche f; (for camera) chargeur m; (music tape) cassette f.

carve [ka:v] vt (meat) découper; (wood, stone) tailler, sculpter; **to ~ up** vt découper; (fig: country) morceler; **carving** n (in wood etc) sculpture f; **carving knife** n couteau m à découper.

car wash n station f de lavage (de voitures).

case [keɪs] n cas m; (LAW) affaire f, procès m; (box) caisse f, boîte f, étui m; (Brit: also: suit~) valise f; he hasn't put forward his ~ very well ses arguments ne sont guère convaincants; **in ~ of** en cas de; **in ~** he au cas où il; **just in ~** à tout hasard.

cash [kæʃ] n argent m; (COMM) argent liquide, numéraire m; liquidités fpl; (COMM: in payment) argent comptant, espèces fpl // vt encaisser; **to pay (in) ~** payer (en argent) comptant; **~ on delivery** (C.O.D.) (COMM) payable ou paiement à la livraison; **~book** n livre m de caisse; **~ card** n carte f de retrait; **~ desk** n (Brit) caisse f; **~ dispenser** n guichet m automatique de banque.

cashew [kæ'ʃu:] n (also: ~ nut) noix f de cajou.

cashier [kæ'ʃɪə*] n caissier/ère.

cashmere ['kæʃmɪə*] n cachemire m.

cash register n caisse enregistreuse.

casing ['keɪsɪŋ] n revêtement (protecteur), enveloppe (protectrice).

casino [kə'si:nəu] n casino m.

cask [ka:sk] n tonneau m.

casket ['ka:skɪt] n coffret m; (US: coffin) cercueil m.

casserole ['kæsərəul] n cocotte f; (food) ragoût m (en cocotte).

cassette [kæ'set] n cassette f, musicassette f; **~ player** n lecteur m de cassettes; **~ recorder** n magnétophone m à cassettes.

cast [ka:st] vb (pt, pp cast) vt (throw) jeter; (shed) perdre; se dépouiller de; (metal) couler, fondre; (THEATRE): **to ~** sb as Hamlet attribuer à qn le rôle d'Hamlet // n (THEATRE) distribution f; (mould) moule m; (also: plaster ~) plâtre m; **to ~ one's vote** voter, exprimer son suffrage; **to ~ off** vi (NAUT) larguer les amarres.

castaway ['ka:stəwəɪ] n naufragé/e.

caster sugar ['ka:stə*-] n (Brit) sucre m semoule.

casting ['ka:stɪŋ] a: **~ vote** (Brit) voix

prépondérante (pour départager).

cast iron n fonte f.

castle ['ka:sl] n château-fort m; (manor) château m.

castor ['ka:stə*] n (wheel) roulette f; **~ oil** n huile f de ricin.

castrate [kæs'treɪt] vt châtrer.

casual ['kæʒjul] a (by chance) de hasard, fait(e) au hasard, fortuit(e); (irregular: work etc) temporaire; (unconcerned) désinvolte; **~ wear** n vêtements mpl sport inv; **~ly** ad avec désinvolture, négligemment; fortuitement.

casualty ['kæʒjultɪ] n accidenté/e, blessé/e; (dead) victime f, mort/e.

cat [kæt] n chat m.

catalogue, (US) catalog ['kætələg] n catalogue m // vt cataloguer.

catalyst ['kætəlɪst] n catalyseur m.

catapult ['kætəpʌlt] n lance-pierres m inv, fronde m; (HISTORY) catapulte f.

catarrh [kə'ta:*] n rhume m chronique, catarrhe f.

catastrophe [kə'tæstrəfɪ] n catastrophe f.

catch [kætʃ] vb (pt, pp caught) vt (ball, train, thief, cold) attraper; (person: by surprise) prendre, surprendre; (understand) saisir; (get entangled) accrocher // vi (fire) prendre // n (fish etc caught) prise f; (thief etc caught) capture f; (trick) attrape f; (TECH) loquet m; cliquet m; **to ~ sb's attention** or **eye** attirer l'attention de qn; **to ~ fire** prendre feu; **to ~ sight of** apercevoir; **to ~ on** vi saisir; (grow popular) prendre; **to ~ up** vi se rattraper, combler son retard // vt (also: ~ up with) rattraper.

catching ['kætʃɪŋ] a (MED) contagieux(euse).

catchment area ['kætʃmənt-] n (Brit SCOL) aire f de recrutement; (GEO) bassin m hydrographique.

catch phrase n slogan m; expression toute faite.

catchy ['kætʃɪ] a (tune) facile à retenir.

category ['kætɪɡərɪ] n catégorie f.

cater ['keɪtə*] vi (provide food): **to ~ (for)** préparer des repas (pour), se charger de la restauration (pour); **to ~ for** vt fus (Brit: needs) satisfaire, pourvoir à; (: readers, consumers) s'adresser à, pourvoir aux besoins de; **~er** n traiteur m; fournisseur m; **~ing** n restauration f; approvisionnement m, ravitaillement m.

caterpillar ['kætəpɪlə*] n chenille f; **~ track** n chenille f.

cathedral [kə'θi:drəl] n cathédrale f.

catholic ['kæθəlɪk] a éclectique; universel(le); libéral(e); **C~** a, n (REL) catholique (m/f).

cat's-eye [kæts'aɪ] n (Brit AUT) (clou m à) catadioptre m.

cattle ['kætl] *npl* bétail *m*, bestiaux *mpl*.
catty ['kætɪ] *a* méchant(e).
caucus ['kɔ:kəs] *n* (POL: *group*) comité local d'un parti politique; (: US) comité électoral (pour désigner des candidats).
caught [kɔ:t] *pt, pp of* **catch.**
cauliflower ['kɔlɪflauə*] *n* chou-fleur *m*.
cause [kɔ:z] *n* cause *f* // *vt* causer.
caution ['kɔ:ʃən] *n* prudence *f*; (*warning*) avertissement *m* // *vt* avertir, donner un avertissement à.
cautious ['kɔ:ʃəs] *a* prudent(e).
cavalry ['kævəlrɪ] *n* cavalerie *f*.
cave [keɪv] *n* caverne *f*, grotte *f*; **to ~ in** *vi* (*roof etc*) s'effondrer; **~man** *n* homme *m* des cavernes.
caviar(e) ['kævɪɑ:*] *n* caviar *m*.
cavort [kə'vɔ:t] *vi* cabrioler, faire des cabrioles.
CB *n abbr* (= *Citizens' Band (Radio)*) CB *f*.
CBI *n abbr* (= *Confederation of British Industries*) groupement du patronat.
cc *abbr* = *carbon copy, cubic centimetres.*
cease [si:s] *vt, vi* cesser; **~fire** *n* cessez-le-feu *m*; **~less** *a* incessant(e), continuel(le).
cedar ['si:də*] *n* cèdre *m*.
ceiling ['si:lɪŋ] *n* plafond *m*.
celebrate ['sɛlɪbreɪt] *vt, vi* célébrer; **~d** *a* célèbre; **celebration** [-'breɪʃən] *n* célébration *f*.
celery ['sɛlərɪ] *n* céleri *m* (en branches).
cell [sɛl] *n* (*gen*) cellule *f*; (ELEC) élément *m* (*de pile*).
cellar ['sɛlə*] *n* cave *f*.
'cello ['tʃɛləu] *n* violoncelle *m*.
Celt [kɛlt, sɛlt] *n* Celte *m/f*.
Celtic ['kɛltɪk, 'sɛltɪk] *a* celte.
cement [sə'mɛnt] *n* ciment *m* // *vt* cimenter; **~ mixer** *n* bétonnière *f*.
cemetery ['sɛmɪtrɪ] *n* cimetière *m*.
censor ['sɛnsə*] *n* censeur *m* // *vt* censurer; **~ship** *n* censure *f*.
censure ['sɛnʃə*] *vt* blâmer, critiquer.
census ['sɛnsəs] *n* recensement *m*.
cent [sɛnt] *n* (US: *coin*) cent *m* (= 1:100 *du dollar*); *see also* **per.**
centenary [sɛn'ti:nərɪ] *n* centenaire *m*.
center ['sɛntə*] *n* (US) = **centre.**
centi... ['sɛntɪ] *prefix*: **~grade** *a* centigrade; **~metre**, (US) **~meter** *n* centimètre *m*.
centipede ['sɛntɪpi:d] *n* mille-pattes *m inv*.
central ['sɛntrəl] *a* central(e); **C~ America** *n* Amérique centrale; **~ heating** *n* chauffage central.
centre ['sɛntə*] *n* centre *m* // *vt* centrer; (PHOT) cadrer; **~-forward** *n* (SPORT) avant-centre *m*; **~-half** *n* (SPORT) demi-centre *m*.
century ['sɛntjurɪ] *n* siècle *m*; 20th ~

XXe siècle.
ceramic [sɪ'ræmɪk] *a* céramique.
cereal ['si:rɪəl] *n* céréale *f*.
ceremony ['sɛrɪmənɪ] *n* cérémonie *f*; **to stand on ~** faire des façons.
certain ['sə:tən] *a* certain(e); **to make ~ of** s'assurer de; **for ~** certainement, sûrement; **~ly** *ad* certainement; **~ty** *n* certitude *f*.
certificate [sə'tɪfɪkɪt] *n* certificat *m*.
certified ['sə:tɪfaɪd]: **~ mail** *n* (US): by **~ mail** en recommandé, avec avis de réception; **~ public accountant** *n* (US) expert-comptable *m*.
cervical ['sə:vɪkl] *a*: **~ cancer** cancer *m* du col de l'utérus; **~ smear** frottis vaginal.
cervix ['sə:vɪks] *n* col *m* de l'utérus.
cesspit ['sɛspɪt] *n* fosse *f* d'aisance.
cf. *abbr* (= *compare*) cf., voir.
ch. *abbr* (= *chapter*) chap.
chafe [tʃeɪf] *vt* irriter, frotter contre.
chaffinch ['tʃæfɪntʃ] *n* pinson *m*.
chain [tʃeɪn] *n* (*gen*) chaîne *f* // *vt* (*also:* **~ up**) enchaîner, attacher (avec une chaîne); **~ reaction** *n* réaction *f* en chaîne; **to ~ smoke** *vi* fumer cigarette sur cigarette; **~ store** *n* magasin *m* à succursales multiples.
chair [tʃɛə*] *n* chaise *f*; (*armchair*) fauteuil *m*; (*of university*) chaire *f* // *vt* (*meeting*) présider; **~lift** *n* télésiège *m*; **~man** *n* président *m*.
chalice ['tʃælɪs] *n* calice *m*.
chalk [tʃɔ:k] *n* craie *f*.
challenge ['tʃælɪndʒ] *n* défi *m* // *vt* défier; (*statement, right*) mettre en question, contester; **to ~ sb to do** mettre qn au défi de faire; **challenging** *a* de défi, provocateur(trice).
chamber ['tʃeɪmbə*] *n* chambre *f*; **~ of commerce** chambre de commerce; **~maid** *n* femme *f* de chambre; **~ music** *n* musique *f* de chambre.
champagne [ʃæm'peɪn] *n* champagne *m*.
champion ['tʃæmpɪən] *n* champion/ne; **~ship** *n* championnat *m*.
chance [tʃɑ:ns] *n* hasard *m*; (*opportunity*) occasion *f*, possibilité *f*; (*hope, likelihood*) chance *f* // *vt*: **to ~ it** risquer (le coup), essayer // *a* fortuit(e), de hasard; **to take a ~** prendre un risque; **by ~** par hasard.
chancellor ['tʃɑ:nsələ*] *n* chancelier *m*; **C~ of the Exchequer** *n* (*Brit*) chancelier de l'Échiquier.
chandelier [ʃændə'lɪə*] *n* lustre *m*.
change [tʃeɪndʒ] *vt* (*alter, replace*, COMM: *money*) changer; (*switch, substitute: gear, hands, trains, clothes, one's name etc*) changer de; (*transform*): **to ~ sb into** changer *or* transformer qn en // *vi* (*gen*) changer; (*change clothes*) se changer; (*be transformed*): **to ~ into** se

changer *or* transformer en // *n* changement *m*; (*money*) monnaie *f*; **to ~ one's mind** changer d'avis; **a ~ of clothes** des vêtements de rechange; **for a ~** pour changer; **~able** *a* (*weather*) variable; **~ machine** *n* distributeur *m* de monnaie; **~over** *n* (*to new system*) changement *m*, passage *m*.

changing ['tʃeɪndʒɪŋ] *a* changeant(e); **~ room** *n* (*Brit: in shop*) salon *m* d'essayage; (: *SPORT*) vestiaire *m*.

channel ['tʃænl] *n* (*TV*) chaîne *f*; (*waveband, groove, fig: medium*) canal *m*; (*of river, sea*) chenal *m* // *vt* canaliser; **through the usual ~s** en suivant la filière habituelle; **the (English) C~** la Manche; **the C~ Islands** les îles de la Manche, les îles anglo-normandes.

chant [tʃɑːnt] *n* chant *m*; mélopée *f*; psalmodie *f* // *vt* chanter; scander; psalmodier.

chaos ['keɪɔs] *n* chaos *m*.

chap [tʃæp] *n* (*Brit col: man*) type *m*.

chapel ['tʃæpəl] *n* chapelle *f*.

chaplain ['tʃæplɪn] *n* aumônier *m*.

chapped ['tʃæpt] *a* (*skin, lips*) gercé(e).

chapter ['tʃæptə*] *n* chapitre *m*.

char [tʃɑː*] *vt* (*burn*) carboniser // *n* (*Brit*) = **charlady**.

character ['kærɪktə*] *n* caractère *m*; (*in novel, film*) personnage *m*; (*eccentric*) numéro *m*, phénomène *m*; **~istic** [-'rɪstɪk] *a*, *n* caractéristique (*f*).

charcoal ['tʃɑːkəul] *n* charbon *m* de bois.

charge [tʃɑːdʒ] *n* accusation *f*; (*LAW*) inculpation *f*; (*cost*) prix (demandé); (*of gun, battery, MIL: attack*) charge *f* // *vt* (*LAW*): **to ~ sb** (**with**) inculper qn (de); (*gun, battery, MIL: enemy*) charger; (*customer, sum*) faire payer // *vi* (*gen with: up, along etc*) foncer; **~s** *npl*: **bank ~s** frais *mpl* de banque; **is there a ~?** doit-on payer?; **to reverse the ~s** (*TEL*) téléphoner en PCV; **to take ~ of** se charger de; **to be in ~ of** être responsable de, s'occuper de; **to ~ an expense (up) to sb** mettre une dépense sur le compte de qn; **~ card** *n* carte *f* de client (*émise par un grand magasin*).

charity ['tʃærɪtɪ] *n* charité *f*; institution *f* charitable *or* de bienfaisance, œuvre *f* (de charité).

charlady ['tʃɑːleɪdɪ] *n* (*Brit*) femme *f* de ménage.

charm [tʃɑːm] *n* charme *m* // *vt* charmer, enchanter; **~ing** *a* charmant(e).

chart [tʃɑːt] *n* tableau *m*, diagramme *m*; graphique *m*; (*map*) carte marine // *vt* dresser *or* établir la carte de.

charter ['tʃɑːtə*] *vt* (*plane*) affréter // *n* (*document*) charte *f*; **~ed accountant** *n* (*Brit*) expert-comptable *m*; **~ flight** *n* charter *m*.

chase [tʃeɪs] *vt* poursuivre, pourchasser // *n* poursuite *f*, chasse *f*.

chasm ['kæzəm] *n* gouffre *m*, abîme *m*.

chat [tʃæt] *vi* (*also:* **have a ~**) bavarder, causer // *n* conversation *f*; **~ show** *n* (*Brit*) entretien télévisé.

chatter ['tʃætə*] *vi* (*person*) bavarder // *n* bavardage *m*; **my teeth are ~ing** je claque des dents; **~box** *n* moulin *m* à paroles.

chatty ['tʃætɪ] *a* (*style*) familier(ère); (*person*) enclin(e) à bavarder.

chauffeur ['ʃəufə*] *n* chauffeur *m* (de maître).

chauvinist ['ʃəuvɪnɪst] *n* (*male ~*) phallocrate *m*; (*nationalist*) chauvin/e.

cheap [tʃiːp] *a* bon marché *inv*, pas cher(chère); (*joke*) facile, d'un goût douteux; (*poor quality*) à bon marché, de qualité médiocre // *ad* à bon marché, pour pas cher; **~en** *vt* rabaisser, déprécier; **~er** *a* à moins cher(chère); **~ly** *ad* à bon marché, à bon compte.

cheat [tʃiːt] *vi* tricher // *vt* tromper, duper; (*rob*) escroquer // *n* tricheur/euse; escroc *m*; (*trick*) duperie *f*, tromperie *f*.

check [tʃɛk] *vt* vérifier; (*passport, ticket*) contrôler; (*halt*) enrayer; (*restrain*) maîtriser // *n* vérification *f*; contrôle *m*; (*curb*) frein *m*; (*bill*) addition *f*; (*pattern: gen pl*) carreaux *mpl*; (*US*) = **cheque** // *a* (*also:* **~ed:** *pattern, cloth*) à carreaux; **to ~ in** *vi* (*in hotel*) remplir sa fiche (d'hôtel); (*at airport*) se présenter à l'enregistrement // *vt* (*luggage*) (faire) enregistrer; **to ~ out** *vi* (*in hotel*) régler sa note // *vt* (*luggage*) retirer; **to ~ up** *vi*: **to ~ up (on sth)** vérifier (qch); **to ~ up on sb** se renseigner sur le compte de qn; **~ered** *a* (*US*) = **chequered**; **~ers** *n* (*US*) jeu *m* de dames; **~-in (desk)** *n* enregistrement *m*; **~ing account** *n* (*US: current account*) compte courant; **~mate** *n* échec et mat *m*; **~out** *n* caisse *f*; **~point** *n* contrôle *m*; **~room** *n* (*US: left-luggage office*) consigne *f*; **~up** *n* (*MED*) examen médical, check-up *m*.

cheek [tʃiːk] *n* joue *f*; (*impudence*) toupet *m*, culot *m*; **~bone** *n* pommette *f*; **~y** *a* effronté(e), culotté(e).

cheep [tʃiːp] *vi* piauler.

cheer [tʃɪə*] *vt* acclamer, applaudir; (*gladden*) réjouir, réconforter // *vi* applaudir // *n* (*gen pl*) acclamations *fpl*, applaudissements *mpl*; bravos *mpl*; hourras *mpl*; **~s!** (à votre) santé!; **to ~ up** *vi* se dérider, reprendre courage // *vt* remonter le moral à *or* de, dérider, égayer; **~ful** *a* gai(e), joyeux(euse).

cheerio ['tʃɪərɪ'əu] *excl* (*Brit*) salut!, au revoir!

cheese [tʃiːz] *n* fromage *m*; **~board** *n* plateau *m* à fromages.

cheetah ['tʃiːtə] n guépard m.
chef [ʃef] n chef (cuisinier).
chemical ['kemɪkəl] a chimique // n produit m chimique.
chemist ['kemɪst] n (Brit: pharmacist) pharmacien/ne; (scientist) chimiste m/f; ~**ry** n chimie f; ~'**s** (shop) n (Brit) pharmacie f.
cheque [tʃek] n (Brit) chèque m; ~**book** n chéquier m, carnet m de chèques; ~ **card** n carte f (d'identité) bancaire.
chequered ['tʃekəd] a (fig) varié(e).
cherish ['tʃerɪʃ] vt chérir; (hope etc) entretenir.
cherry ['tʃerɪ] n cerise f.
chess [tʃes] n échecs mpl; ~**board** n échiquier m; ~**man** n pièce f (de jeu d'échecs).
chest [tʃest] n poitrine f; (box) coffre m, caisse f; ~ **of drawers** n commode f.
chestnut ['tʃesnʌt] n châtaigne f; (also: ~ **tree**) châtaignier m.
chew [tʃuː] vt mâcher; ~**ing gum** n chewing-gum m.
chic [ʃiːk] a chic inv, élégant(e).
chick [tʃɪk] n poussin m; (US col) pépée f.
chicken ['tʃɪkɪn] n poulet m; **to ~ out** vi (col) se dégonfler; ~**pox** n varicelle f.
chicory ['tʃɪkərɪ] n (for coffee) chicorée f; (salad) endive f.
chief [tʃiːf] n chef m // a principal(e); ~ **executive** n directeur général; ~**ly** ad principalement, surtout.
chiffon ['ʃɪfɔn] n mousseline f de soie.
chilblain ['tʃɪlbleɪn] n engelure f.
child, pl ~**ren** [tʃaɪld, 'tʃɪldrən] n enfant m/f; ~**birth** n accouchement m; ~**hood** n enfance f; ~**ish** a puéril(e), enfantin(e); ~**like** a innocent(e), pur(e); ~ **minder** n (Brit) garde f d'enfants.
Chile ['tʃɪlɪ] n Chili m.
chill [tʃɪl] n froid m; (MED) refroidissement m, coup m de froid // a froid(e), glacial(e) // vt faire frissonner; refroidir; (CULIN) mettre au frais, rafraîchir.
chil(l)i ['tʃɪlɪ] n piment m (rouge).
chilly ['tʃɪlɪ] a froid(e), glacé(e); (sensitive to cold) frileux(euse); **to feel ~** avoir froid.
chime [tʃaɪm] n carillon m // vi carillonner, sonner.
chimney ['tʃɪmnɪ] n cheminée f; ~ **sweep** n ramonneur m.
chimpanzee [tʃɪmpæn'ziː] n chimpanzé m.
chin [tʃɪn] n menton m.
China ['tʃaɪnə] n Chine f.
china ['tʃaɪnə] n porcelaine f; (vaisselle f en) porcelaine.
Chinese [tʃaɪ'niːz] a chinois(e) // n, pl

inv Chinois/e; (LING) chinois m.
chink [tʃɪŋk] n (opening) fente f, fissure f; (noise) tintement m.
chip [tʃɪp] n (gen pl: CULIN) frite f; (: US: also: **potato** ~) chip m; (of wood) copeau m; (of glass, stone) éclat m; (also: **micro**~) puce f // vt (cup, plate) ébrécher; **to ~ in** vi mettre son grain de sel.
chiropodist [kɪ'rɔpədɪst] n (Brit) pédicure m/f.
chirp [tʃəːp] vi pépier, gazouiller.
chisel ['tʃɪzl] n ciseau m.
chit [tʃɪt] n mot m, note f.
chitchat ['tʃɪttʃæt] n bavardage m.
chivalry ['ʃɪvəlrɪ] n chevalerie f; esprit m chevaleresque.
chives [tʃaɪvz] npl ciboulette f, civette f.
chock [tʃɔk] n cale f; ~**-a-block**, ~**-full** a plein(e) à craquer.
chocolate ['tʃɔklɪt] n chocolat m.
choice [tʃɔɪs] n choix m // a de choix.
choir ['kwaɪə*] n chœur m, chorale f; ~**boy** n jeune choriste m.
choke [tʃəuk] vi étouffer // vt étrangler; étouffer; (block) boucher, obstruer // n (AUT) starter m.
choose [tʃuːz], pt **chose**, pp **chosen** vt choisir; **to ~ to do** décider de faire, juger bon de faire.
choosy ['tʃuːzɪ] a: (**to be**) ~ (faire le) difficile.
chop [tʃɔp] vt (wood) couper (à la hache); (CULIN: also: ~ **up**) couper (fin), émincer, hacher (en morceaux) // n coup m (de hache, du tranchant de la main); (CULIN) côtelette f; ~**s** npl (jaws) mâchoires fpl; babines fpl.
chopper ['tʃɔpə*] n (helicopter) hélicoptère m, hélico m.
choppy ['tʃɔpɪ] a (sea) un peu agité(e).
chopsticks ['tʃɔpstɪks] npl baguettes fpl.
chord [kɔːd] n (MUS) accord m.
chore [tʃɔː*] n travail m de routine; **household** ~**s** travaux mpl du ménage.
chortle ['tʃɔːtl] vi glousser.
chorus ['kɔːrəs] n chœur m; (repeated part of song, also fig) refrain m.
chose [tʃəuz] pt of **choose**.
chosen ['tʃəuzn] pp of **choose**.
Christ [kraɪst] n Christ m.
christen ['krɪsn] vt baptiser.
Christian ['krɪstɪən] a, n chrétien(ne); ~**ity** [-'ænɪtɪ] n christianisme m; chrétienté f; ~ **name** n prénom m.
Christmas ['krɪsməs] n Noël m or f; **Merry ~!** joyeux Noël!; ~ **card** n carte f de Noël; ~ **Day** n le jour de Noël; ~ **Eve** n la veille de Noël; la nuit de Noël; ~ **tree** n arbre m de Noël.
chrome [krəum], **chromium** ['krəumɪəm] n chrome m.
chronic ['krɔnɪk] a chronique.
chronicle ['krɔnɪkl] n chronique f.
chronological [krɔnə'lɔdʒɪkəl] a

chronologique.

chrysanthemum [krɪ'sænθəməm] *n* chrysanthème *m*.

chubby ['tʃʌbɪ] *a* potelé(e), rondelet(te).

chuck [tʃʌk] *vt* lancer, jeter; **to ~ out** *vt* flanquer dehors *or* à la porte; **to ~ (up)** *vt* (*Brit*) lâcher, plaquer.

chuckle ['tʃʌkl] *vi* glousser.

chug [tʃʌg] *vi* faire teuf-teuf; souffler.

chum [tʃʌm] *n* copain/copine.

chunk [tʃʌŋk] *n* gros morceau; (*of bread*) quignon *m*.

church [tʃɜ:tʃ] *n* église *f*; **~yard** *n* cimetière *m*.

churlish ['tʃɜ:lɪʃ] *a* grossier(ère); hargneux(euse).

churn [tʃɜ:n] *n* (*for butter*) baratte *f*; (*for transport: also*: **milk ~**) (grand) bidon à lait; **to ~ out** *vt* débiter.

chute [ʃu:t] *n* glissoire *f*; (*also*: **rubbish ~**) vide-ordures *m inv*; (*Brit: children's slide*) toboggan *m*.

chutney ['tʃʌtnɪ] *n* condiment *m* à base de fruits.

CIA *n abbr* (*US*: = *Central Intelligence Agency*) CIA *f*.

CID *n abbr* (*Brit*: = *Criminal Investigation Department*) ≈ P.J. *f* (= *police judiciaire*).

cider ['saɪdə*] *n* cidre *m*.

cigar [sɪ'gɑ:*] *n* cigare *m*.

cigarette [sɪgə'rɛt] *n* cigarette *f*; **~ case** *n* étui *m* à cigarettes; **~ end** *n* mégot *m*.

cinder ['sɪndə*] *n* cendre *f*.

Cinderella [sɪndə'rɛlə] *n* Cendrillon *f*.

cine ['sɪnɪ]: **~-camera** *n* (*Brit*) caméra *f*; **~-film** *n* (*Brit*) film *m*.

cinema ['sɪnəmə] *n* cinéma *m*.

cinnamon ['sɪnəmən] *n* cannelle *f*.

cipher ['saɪfə*] *n* code secret; (*fig: faceless employee etc*) numéro *m*.

circle ['sə:kl] *n* cercle *m*; (*in cinema*) balcon *m* // *vi* faire *or* décrire des cercles // *vt* (*surround*) entourer, encercler; (*move round*) faire le tour de, tourner autour de.

circuit ['sə:kɪt] *n* circuit *m*; **~ous** [sə:'kjuɪtəs] *a* indirect(e), qui fait un détour.

circular ['sə:kjulə*] *a, n* circulaire (*f*).

circulate ['sə:kjuleɪt] *vi* circuler // *vt* faire circuler; **circulation** [-'leɪʃən] *n* circulation *f*; (*of newspaper*) tirage *m*.

circumflex ['sə:kəmflɛks] *n* (*also*: **~ accent**) accent *m* circonflexe.

circumstances ['sə:kəmstənsɪz] *npl* circonstances *fpl*; (*financial condition*) moyens *mpl*, situation financière.

circumvent [sə:kəm'vɛnt] *vt* tourner.

circus ['sə:kəs] *n* cirque *m*.

cistern ['sɪstən] *n* réservoir *m* (d'eau); (*in toilet*) réservoir de la chasse d'eau.

citizen ['sɪtɪzn] *n* (*POL*) citoyen/ne; (*resident*): **the ~s of this town** les

habitants de cette ville; **~ship** *n* citoyenneté *f*.

citrus fruit ['sɪtrəs-] *n* agrume *m*.

city ['sɪtɪ] *n* ville *f*, cité *f*; **the C~** la Cité de Londres (*centre des affaires*).

civic ['sɪvɪk] *a* civique; **~ centre** *n* (*Brit*) centre administratif (municipal).

civil ['sɪvɪl] *a* civil(e); poli(e), civil; **~ engineer** *n* ingénieur civil; **~ian** [sɪ'vɪlɪən] *a, n* civil(e).

civilization [sɪvɪlaɪ'zeɪʃən] *n* civilisation *f*.

civilized ['sɪvɪlaɪzd] *a* civilisé(e); (*fig*) où règnent les bonnes manières, empreint(e) d'une courtoisie de bon ton.

civil: **~ law** *n* code civil; (*study*) droit civil; **~ servant** *n* fonctionnaire *m/f*; **C~ Service** *n* fonction publique, administration *f*; **~ war** *n* guerre civile.

clad [klæd] *a*: **~ (in)** habillé(e) (de).

claim [kleɪm] *vt* revendiquer; demander, prétendre à; déclarer, prétendre // *vi* (*for insurance*) faire une déclaration de sinistre // *n* revendication *f*; demande *f*; prétention *f*, déclaration *f*; (*right*) droit *m*, titre *m*; (*insurance*) **~** demande *f* d'indemnisation, déclaration *f* de sinistre; **~ant** *n* (*ADMIN, LAW*) requérant/e.

clairvoyant [klɛə'vɔɪənt] *n* voyant/e, extra-lucide *m/f*.

clam [klæm] *n* palourde *f*.

clamber ['klæmbə*] *vi* grimper, se hisser.

clammy ['klæmɪ] *a* humide et froid(e) (au toucher), moite.

clamour, (*US*) **clamor** ['klæmə*] *vi*: **to ~ for** réclamer à grands cris.

clamp [klæmp] *n* étau *m* à main; agrafe *f*, crampon *m* // *vt* serrer; cramponner; **to ~ down on** *vt fus* sévir contre, prendre des mesures draconiennes à l'égard de.

clan [klæn] *n* clan *m*.

clang [klæŋ] *n* bruit *m or* fracas *m* métallique.

clap [klæp] *vi* applaudir; **~ping** *n* applaudissements *mpl*.

claret ['klærət] *n* (vin *m* de) bordeaux *m* (rouge).

clarinet [klærɪ'nɛt] *n* clarinette *f*.

clarity ['klærɪtɪ] *n* clarté *f*.

clash [klæʃ] *n* choc *m*; (*fig*) conflit *m* // *vi* se heurter; être *or* entrer en conflit.

clasp [klɑ:sp] *n* fermoir *m* // *vt* serrer, étreindre.

class [klɑ:s] *n* (*gen*) classe *f* // *vt* classer, classifier.

classic ['klæsɪk] *a* classique // *n* (*author, work*) classique *m*; **~al** *a* classique.

classified ['klæsɪfaɪd] *a* (*information*) secret(ète); **~ advertisements**, **~ ads** *npl* petites annonces.

classmate ['klɑ:smeɪt] *n* camarade *m/f* de classe.

classroom ['klɑ:srum] n (salle f de) classe f.

clatter ['klætə*] n cliquetis m // vi cliqueter.

clause [klɔ:z] n clause f; (LING) proposition f.

claw [klɔ:] n griffe f; (of bird of prey) serre f; (of lobster) pince f; **to ~ at** vt essayer de griffer or déchirer.

clay [kleɪ] n argile f.

clean [kli:n] a propre; (clear, smooth) net(te) // vt nettoyer; **to ~ out** vt nettoyer (à fond); **to ~ up** vt nettoyer; (fig) remettre de l'ordre dans; **~er** n (person) nettoyeur/euse, femme f de ménage; (also: **dry ~er**) teinturier/ière; (product) détachant m; **~ing** n nettoyage m; **~liness** ['klɛnlɪnɪs] n propreté f.

cleanse [klɛnz] vt nettoyer; purifier; **~r** n détergent m; (for face) démaquillant m; **cleansing department** n (Brit) service m de voirie.

clean-shaven ['kli:n'ʃeɪvn] a rasé(e) de près.

clear [klɪə*] a clair(e); (road, way) libre, dégagé(e) // vt dégager, déblayer, débarrasser; faire évacuer; (COMM: goods) liquider; (cheque) compenser; (LAW: suspect) innocenter; (obstacle) franchir or sauter sans heurter // vi (weather) s'éclaircir; (fog) se dissiper // ad: **~ of** à distance de, à l'écart de; **to ~ the table** débarrasser la table, desservir; **to ~ up** vi s'éclaircir, se dissiper // vt ranger, mettre en ordre; (mystery) éclaircir, résoudre; **~ance** n (removal) déblayage m; (free space) dégagement m; (permission) autorisation f; **~-cut** a précis(e), nettement défini(e); **~ing** n (in forest) clairière f; **~ing bank** n (Brit) banque f qui appartient à une chambre de compensation; **~ly** ad clairement; de toute évidence; **~way** n (Brit) route f à stationnement interdit.

cleaver ['kli:və*] n fendoir m, couperet m.

clef [klɛf] n (MUS) clé f.

cleft [klɛft] n (in rock) crevasse f, fissure f.

clench [klɛntʃ] vt serrer.

clergy ['klɔ:dʒɪ] n clergé m; **~man** n ecclésiastique m.

clerical ['klɛrɪkəl] a de bureau, d'employé de bureau; (REL) clérical(e), du clergé.

clerk [klɑ:k, (US) klɔ:rk] n employé/e de bureau; (US: salesman/woman) vendeur/euse.

clever ['klɛvə*] a (mentally) intelligent(e); (deft, crafty) habile, adroit(e); (device, arrangement) ingénieux(euse), astucieux(euse).

click [klɪk] vi faire un bruit sec or un dé-

clic // vt: **to ~ one's tongue** faire claquer sa langue; **to ~ one's heels** claquer des talons.

client ['klaɪənt] n client/e.

cliff [klɪf] n falaise f.

climate ['klaɪmɪt] n climat m.

climax ['klaɪmæks] n apogée m, point culminant; (sexual) orgasme m.

climb [klaɪm] vi grimper, monter // vt gravir, escalader, monter sur // n montée f, escalade f; **~-down** n reculade f, dérobade f; **~er** n (also: **rock ~er**) grimpeur/euse, varappeur/euse; **~ing** n (also: **rock ~ing**) escalade f, varappe f.

clinch [klɪntʃ] vt (deal) conclure, sceller.

cling [klɪŋ], pt, pp **clung** vi: **to ~ (to)** se cramponner (à), s'accrocher (à); (of clothes) coller (à).

clinic ['klɪnɪk] n centre médical.

clink [klɪŋk] vi tinter, cliqueter.

clip [klɪp] n (for hair) barrette f; (also: **paper ~**) trombone m; (holding hose etc) collier m or bague f (métallique) de serrage // vt (also: **~ together**: papers) attacher; (hair, nails) couper; (hedge) tailler; **~pers** npl tondeuse f; (also: **nail ~pers**) coupe-ongles m inv; **~ping** n (from newspaper) coupure f de journal.

cloak [kləuk] n grande cape // (fig) masquer, cacher; **~room** n (for coats etc) vestiaire m; (Brit: W.C.) toilettes fpl.

clock [klɔk] n (large) horloge f; (small) pendule f; **to ~ in** or **on** vi pointer (en arrivant); **to ~ off** or **out** vi pointer (en partant); **~wise** ad dans le sens des aiguilles d'une montre; **~work** n mouvement m (d'horlogerie); rouages mpl, mécanisme m // a mécanique.

clog [klɔg] n sabot m // vt boucher, encrasser // vi se boucher, s'encrasser.

cloister ['klɔɪstə*] n cloître m.

close a, ad and derivatives [kləus] a (near): **~ (to)** près (de), proche (de); (writing, texture) serré(e); (watch) étroit(e), strict(e); (examination) attentif(ive), minutieux(euse); (weather) lourd(e), étouffant(e) // ad près, à proximité; **~ to** prep près de; **~ by, ~ at hand** a, ad tout(e) près; **a ~ friend** un ami intime; **to have a ~ shave** (fig) l'échapper belle // vb and derivatives [kləuz] vt fermer // vi (shop etc) fermer; (lid, door etc) se fermer; (end) se terminer, se conclure // n (end) conclusion f; **to ~ down** vt, vi fermer (définitivement); **~d** a fermé(e); **~d shop** n organisation f qui n'admet que des travailleurs syndiqués; **~-knit** a (family, community) très uni(e); **~ly** ad (examine, watch) de près.

closet ['klɔzɪt] n (cupboard) placard m, réduit m.

close-up ['kləusʌp] n gros plan m.

closure ['kləuʒə*] n fermeture f.

clot [klɔt] *n* (*gen: blood* ~) caillot *m*; (*col: person*) ballot *m* // *vi* (*blood*) former des caillots; (: *external bleeding*) se coaguler.

cloth [klɔθ] *n* (*material*) tissu *m*, étoffe *f*; (*also: tea*~) torchon *m*; lavette *f*.

clothe [kləuð] *vt* habiller, vêtir; ~**s** *npl* vêtements *mpl*, habits *mpl*; ~**s brush** *n* brosse *f* à habits; ~**s line** *n* corde *f* (à linge); ~**s peg**, (*US*) ~**s pin** *n* pince *f* à linge.

clothing ['kləuðɪŋ] *n* =**clothes**.

cloud [klaud] *n* nuage *m*; ~**y** *a* nuageux(euse), couvert(e); (*liquid*) trouble.

clout [klaut] *vt* flanquer une taloche à.

clove [kləuv] *n* clou *m* de girofle; ~ **of garlic** gousse *f* d'ail.

clover ['kləuvə*] *n* trèfle *m*.

clown [klaun] *n* clown *m* // *vi* (*also:* ~ **about,** ~ **around**) faire le clown.

cloying ['klɔɪɪŋ] *a* (*taste, smell*) écœurant(e).

club [klʌb] *n* (*society*) club *m*; (*weapon*) massue *f*, matraque *f*; (*also: golf* ~) club // *vt* matraquer // *vi*: **to** ~ **together** s'associer; ~**s** *npl* (*CARDS*) trèfle *m*; ~ **car** *n* (*US RAIL*) wagon-restaurant *m*; ~**house** *n* pavillon *m*.

cluck [klʌk] *vi* glousser.

clue [klu:] *n* indice *m*; (*in crosswords*) définition *f*; **I haven't a** ~ je n'en ai pas la moindre idée.

clump [klʌmp] *n*: ~ **of trees** bouquet *m* d'arbres.

clumsy ['klʌmzɪ] *a* (*person*) gauche, maladroit(e); (*object*) malcommode, peu maniable.

clung [klʌŋ] *pt, pp* of **cling**.

cluster ['klʌstə*] *n* (petit) groupe // *vi* se rassembler.

clutch [klʌtʃ] *n* (*grip, grasp*) étreinte *f*, prise *f*; (*AUT*) embrayage *m* // *vt* agripper, serrer fort; **to** ~ **at** se cramponner à.

clutter ['klʌtə*] *vt* encombrer.

CND *abbr* = Campaign for Nuclear Disarmament.

Co. *abbr* of **county, company**.

c/o *abbr* (= *care of*) c/o, aux bons soins de.

coach [kəutʃ] *n* (*bus*) autocar *m*; (*horse-drawn*) diligence *f*; (*of train*) voiture *f*, wagon *m*; (*SPORT: trainer*) entraîneur/euse *f* // *vt* entraîner; ~ **trip** *n* excursion *f* en car.

coal [kəul] *n* charbon *m*; ~ **face** *n* front *m* de taille; ~**field** *n* bassin houiller.

coalition [kəuə'lɪʃən] *n* coalition *f*.

coalman, coal merchant ['kəulmən, 'kəulmɑ:tʃənt] *n* charbonnier *m*, marchand *m* de charbon.

coalmine ['kəulmaɪn] *n* mine *f* de charbon.

coarse [kɔ:s] *a* grossier(ère), rude.

coast [kəust] *n* côte *f* // *vi* (*with cycle etc*) descendre en roue libre; ~**al** *a* côtier(ère); ~**guard** *n* garde-côte *m*; ~**line** *n* côte *f*, littoral *m*.

coat [kəut] *n* manteau *m*; (*of animal*) pelage *m*, poil *m*; (*of paint*) couche *f* // *vt* couvrir, enduire; ~ **of arms** *n* blason *m*, armoiries *fpl*; ~ **hanger** *n* cintre *m*; ~**ing** *n* couche *f*, enduit *m*.

coax [kəuks] *vt* persuader par des cajoleries.

cob [kɔb] *n see* **corn**.

cobbler ['kɔblə*] *n* cordonnier *m*.

cobbles, cobblestones ['kɔblz, 'kɔblstəunz] *npl* pavés (ronds).

cobweb ['kɔbweb] *n* toile *f* d'araignée.

cocaine [kə'keɪn] *n* cocaïne *f*.

cock [kɔk] *n* (*rooster*) coq *m*; (*male bird*) mâle *m* // *vt* (*gun*) armer; ~**erel** *n* jeune coq *m*; ~**-eyed** *a* (*fig*) de travers; qui louche; qui ne tient pas debout (*fig*).

cockle ['kɔkl] *n* coque *f*.

cockney ['kɔknɪ] *n* cockney *m/f* (*habitant des quartiers populaires de l'East End de Londres*), ≈ faubourien/ne.

cockpit ['kɔkpɪt] *n* (*in aircraft*) poste *m* de pilotage, cockpit *m*.

cockroach ['kɔkrəutʃ] *n* cafard *m*.

cocktail ['kɔkteɪl] *n* cocktail *m*; ~ **cabinet** *n* (meuble-)bar *m*; ~ **party** *n* cocktail *m*.

cocoa ['kəukəu] *n* cacao *m*.

coconut ['kəukənʌt] *n* noix *f* de coco.

cod [kɔd] *n* morue (fraîche), cabillaud *m*.

C.O.D. *abbr* of **cash on delivery**.

code [kəud] *n* code *m*.

cod-liver oil *n* huile *f* de foie de morue.

coercion [kəu'ə:ʃən] *n* contrainte *f*.

coffee ['kɔfɪ] *n* café *m*; ~ **bar** *n* (*Brit*) café *m*; ~ **break** *n* pause-café *f*; ~**pot** *n* cafetière *f*; ~ **table** *n* (petite) table basse.

coffin ['kɔfɪn] *n* cercueil *m*.

cog [kɔg] *n* dent *f* (d'engrenage).

cogent ['kəudʒənt] *a* puissant(e), convaincant(e).

coil [kɔɪl] *n* rouleau *m*, bobine *f*; (*one loop*) anneau *m*, spire *f*; (*contraceptive*) stérilet *m* // *vt* enrouler.

coin [kɔɪn] *n* pièce *f* de monnaie // *vt* (*word*) inventer; ~**age** *n* monnaie *f*, système *m* monétaire; ~**-box** *n* (*Brit*) cabine *f* téléphonique.

coincide [kəuɪn'saɪd] *vi* coïncider; ~**nce** [kəu'ɪnsɪdəns] *n* coïncidence *f*.

coke [kəuk] *n* coke *m*.

colander ['kɔləndə*] *n* passoire *f* (à légumes).

cold [kəuld] *a* froid(e) // *n* froid *m*; (*MED*) rhume *m*; **it's** ~ il fait froid; **to be** ~ avoir froid; **to catch** ~ prendre *or* attraper froid; **to catch a** ~ attraper un rhume; **in** ~ **blood** de sang-froid; ~ **sore** *n* bouton *m* de fièvre.

coleslaw ['kəulslɔ:] n sorte de salade de chou cru.

colic ['kɔlɪk] n colique(s) f(pl).

collapse [kə'læps] vi s'effondrer, s'écrouler // n effondrement m, écroulement m.

collapsible [kə'læpsəbl] a pliant(e); télescopique.

collar ['kɔlə*] n (of coat, shirt) col m; ~bone n clavicule f.

collateral [kɔ'lætərl] n nantissement m.

colleague ['kɔli:g] n collègue m/f.

collect [kə'lɛkt] vt rassembler; ramasser; (as a hobby) collectionner; (Brit: call and pick up) (passer) prendre; (mail) faire la levée de, ramasser; (money owed) encaisser; (donations, subscriptions) recueillir // vi se rassembler; s'amasser; **to call** ~ (US TEL) téléphoner en PCV; ~**ion** [kə'lɛkʃən] n collection f; levée f; (for money) collecte f, quête f.

collector [kə'lɛktə*] n collectionneur m; (of taxes) percepteur m.

college ['kɔlɪdʒ] n collège m.

collide [kə'laɪd] vi: **to ~ (with)** entrer en collision (avec).

collie ['kɔlɪ] n (dog) colley m.

colliery ['kɔlɪərɪ] n mine f de charbon, houillère f.

collision [kə'lɪʒən] n collision f, heurt m.

colloquial [kə'ləukwɪəl] a familier(ère).

colon ['kəulən] n (sign) deux-points mpl; (MED) côlon m.

colonel ['kə:nl] n colonel m.

colonial [kə'ləunɪəl] a colonial(e).

colony ['kɔlənɪ] n colonie f.

colour, (US) **color** ['kʌlə*] n couleur f // vt colorer; peindre; (with crayons) colorier; (news) fausser, exagérer // vi (blush) rougir; ~s npl (of party, club) couleurs fpl; ~ **bar** n discrimination raciale (dans un établissement etc); ~**blind** a daltonien(ne); ~**ed** a coloré(e); (photo) en couleur // n: ~eds personnes fpl de couleur; ~ **film** n (for camera) pellicule f (en) couleur; ~**ful** a coloré(e), vif(vive); (personality) pittoresque, haut(e) en couleurs; ~**ing** n colorant m; (complexion) teint m; ~ **scheme** n combinaison f de(s) couleurs; ~ **television** n télévision f en couleur.

colt [kəult] n poulain m.

column ['kɔləm] n colonne f; ~**ist** ['kɔləmnɪst] n rédacteur/trice d'une rubrique.

coma ['kəumə] n coma m.

comb [kəum] n peigne m // vt (hair) peigner; (area) ratisser, passer au peigne fin.

combat ['kɔmbæt] n combat m // vt combattre, lutter contre.

combination [kɔmbɪ'neɪʃən] n (gen) combinaison f.

combine vb [kəm'baɪn] vt combiner; (one quality with another) joindre (à), allier (à) // vi s'associer; (CHEM) se combiner // n ['kɔmbaɪn] association f; (ECON) trust m; ~ **(harvester)** n moissonneuse-batteuse(-lieuse) f.

come [kʌm], pt came, pp come vi venir; arriver; **to ~ to** (decision etc) parvenir or arriver à; **to ~ undone/loose** se défaire/desserrer; **to ~ about** vi se produire, arriver; **to ~ across** vt fus rencontrer par hasard, tomber sur; **to ~ along** vi = **to come on**; **to ~ away** vi partir, s'en aller; se détacher; **to ~ back** vi revenir; **to ~ by** vt fus (acquire) obtenir, se procurer; **to ~ down** vi descendre; (prices) baisser; (buildings) s'écrouler; être démoli(e); **to ~ forward** vi s'avancer; se présenter, s'annoncer; **to ~ from** vt fus être originaire de; venir de; **to ~ in** vi entrer; **to ~ in for** vt fus (criticism etc) être l'objet de; **to ~ into** vt fus (money) hériter de; **to ~ off** vi (button) se détacher; (stain) s'enlever; (attempt) réussir; **to ~ on** vi (pupil, work, project) faire des progrès, avancer; (lights, electricity) s'allumer; (central heating) se mettre en marche; ~ **on!** viens!; allons!, allez!; **to ~ out** vi sortir; (book) paraître; (strike) cesser le travail, se mettre en grève; **to ~ round** vi (after faint, operation) revenir à soi, reprendre connaissance; **to ~ to** vi revenir à soi; **to ~ up** vi monter; **to ~ up against** vt fus (resistance, difficulties) rencontrer; **to ~ up with** vt fus: he came up with an idea il a eu une idée, il a proposé quelque chose; **to ~ upon** vt fus tomber sur; ~**back** n (THEATRE etc) rentrée f.

comedian [kə'mi:dɪən] n (in music hall etc) comique m; (THEATRE) comédien m.

comedown ['kʌmdaun] n déchéance f.

comedy ['kɔmɪdɪ] n comédie f.

comeuppance [kʌm'ʌpəns] n: **to get one's** ~ recevoir ce qu'on mérite.

comfort ['kʌmfət] n confort m, bien-être m; (solace) consolation f, réconfort m // vt consoler, réconforter; ~s npl aises fpl; ~**able** a confortable; ~**ably** ad (sit) confortablement; (live) à l'aise; ~ **station** n (US) toilettes fpl.

comic ['kɔmɪk] a (also: ~al) comique // n comique m; (magazine) illustré m; ~ **strip** n bande dessinée.

coming ['kʌmɪŋ] n arrivée f // a prochain(e), à venir; ~**(s) and going(s)** n(pl) va-et-vient m inv.

comma ['kɔmə] n virgule f.

command [kə'mɑ:nd] n ordre m, commandement m; (MIL: authority) commandement; (mastery) maîtrise f // vt (troops) commander; (be able to get) (pouvoir) disposer de, avoir à sa disposition; (*deserve*) avoir droit à; **~eer** [kɔmən'dɪə*] *vt* réquisitionner (par la force); **~er** *n* chef *m*; (*MIL*) commandant *m*.

commando [kə'mɑːndəu] *n* commando *m*; membre *m* d'un commando.

commemorate [kə'mɛməreɪt] *vt* commémorer.

commence [kə'mɛns] *vt*, *vi* commencer.

commend [kə'mɛnd] *vt* louer; recommander.

commensurate [kə'mɛnʃərɪt] *a*: ~ **with** en proportion de, proportionné(e) à.

comment ['kɔmɛnt] *n* commentaire *m* // *vi*: to ~ (on) faire des remarques (sur); **~ary** ['kɔməntəri] *n* commentaire *m*; (*SPORT*) reportage *m* (en direct); **~ator** ['kɔmənteɪtə*] *n* commentateur *m*; reporter *m*.

commerce ['kɔmə:s] *n* commerce *m*.

commercial [kə'mə:ʃəl] *a* commercial(e) // *n* (*TV*: *also*: ~ **break**) annonce *f* publicitaire, spot *m* (publicitaire).

commiserate [kə'mɪzəreɪt] *vi*: to ~ **with sb** témoigner de la sympathie pour qn.

commission [kə'mɪʃən] *n* (*committee, fee*) commission *f* // *vt* (*MIL*) nommer (à un commandement); (*work of art*) commander, charger un artiste de l'exécution de; **out of** ~ (*NAUT*) hors de service; **~aire** [kəmɪʃə'nɛə*] *n* (*Brit*: *at shop, cinema etc*) portier *m* (en uniforme); **~er** *n* membre *m* d'une commission; (*POLICE*) préfet *m* (de police).

commit [kə'mɪt] *vt* (*act*) commettre; (*to sb's care*) confier (à); **to ~ o.s. (to do)** s'engager (à faire); **to ~ suicide** se suicider; **~ment** *n* engagement *m*; (*obligation*) responsabilité(s) *f(pl)*.

committee [kə'mɪtɪ] *n* comité *m*.

commodity [kə'mɔdɪtɪ] *n* produit *m*, marchandise *f*, article *m*; (*food*) denrée *f*.

common ['kɔmən] *a* (*gen, also pej*) commun(e); (*usual*) courant(e) // *n* terrain communal; the C~s *npl* (*Brit*) la chambre des Communes; **in** ~ en commun; **~er** *n* roturier/ière; ~ **law** *n* droit coutumier; **~ly** *ad* communément, généralement; couramment; **C~ Market** *n* Marché commun; **~place** *a* banal(e), ordinaire; **~room** *n* salle commune; (*SCOL*) salle des professeurs; ~ **sense** *n* bon sens; the C~wealth *n* le Commonwealth.

commotion [kə'məuʃən] *n* désordre *m*, tumulte *m*.

communal ['kɔmjuːnl] *a* (*life*) communautaire; (*for common use*) commun(e).

commune *n* ['kɔmjuːn] (*group*) communauté *f* // *vi* [kə'mjuːn]: to ~ **with**

converser intimement avec; communier avec.

communicate [kə'mjuːnɪkeɪt] *vt*, *vi* communiquer.

communication [kəmjuːnɪ'keɪʃən] *n* communication *f*; ~ **cord** *n* (*Brit*) sonnette *f* d'alarme.

communion [kə'mjuːnɪən] *n* (*also*: Holy C~) communion *f*.

communism ['kɔmjunɪzəm] *n* communisme *m*; **communist** *a*, **n** communiste (*m/f*).

community [kə'mjuːnɪtɪ] *n* communauté *f*; ~ **centre** *n* foyer socio-éducatif, centre *m* de loisirs; ~ **chest** *n* (*US*) fonds commun.

commutation ticket [kɔmju'teɪʃən-] *n* (*US*) carte *f* d'abonnement.

commute [kə'mjuːt] *vi* faire le trajet journalier (de son domicile à un lieu de travail assez éloigné) // *vt* (*LAW*) commuer; **~r** *n* banlieusard/e (qui ... *see vi*).

compact *a* [kəm'pækt] compact(e) // *n* ['kɔmpækt] (*also*: **powder** ~) poudrier *m*; ~ **disk** *n* disque compact.

companion [kəm'pænɪən] *n* compagnon/compagne, camaraderie *f*.

company ['kʌmpəni] *n* (*also COMM, MIL, THEATRE*) compagnie *f*; **to keep sb** ~ tenir compagnie à qn; ~ **secretary** *n* (*COMM*) secrétaire général (*d'une société*).

comparative [kəm'pærətɪv] *a* comparatif(ive); (*relative*) relatif(ive); **~ly** *ad* (*relatively*) relativement.

compare [kəm'pɛə*] *vt*: to ~ **sth/sb with/to** comparer qch/qn avec *or* et/à // *vi*: to ~ (**with**) se comparer (à); être comparable (à); **comparison** [-'pærɪsn] *n* comparaison *f*.

compartment [kəm'pɑːtmənt] *n* (*also RAIL*) compartiment *m*.

compass ['kʌmpəs] *n* boussole *f*; **~es** *npl* compas *m*.

compassion [kəm'pæʃən] *n* compassion *f*, humanité *f*.

compatible [kəm'pætɪbl] *a* compatible.

compel [kəm'pɛl] *vt* contraindre, obliger; **~ling** *a* (*fig*: *argument*) irrésistible.

compendium [kəm'pɛndɪəm] *n* abrégé *m*.

compensate ['kɔmpənseɪt] *vt* indemniser, dédommager // *vi*: to ~ **for** compenser; **compensation** [-'seɪʃən] *n* compensation *f*; (*money*) dédommagement *m*, indemnité *f*.

compete [kəm'piːt] *vi* (*take part*) concourir; to ~ (**with**) rivaliser (avec), faire concurrence (à).

competence ['kɔmpɪtəns] *n* compétence *f*, aptitude *f*.

competent ['kɔmpɪtənt] *a* compétent(e), capable.

competition [kɒmpɪ'tɪʃən] *n* compétition *f*, concours *m*; (*ECON*) concurrence *f*.

competitive [kəm'petɪtɪv] *a* (*ECON*) concurrentiel(le); (*sport*) de compétition.

competitor [kəm'petɪtə*] *n* concurrent/e.

complacency [kəm'pleɪsnsɪ] *n* contentement *m* de soi, vaine complaisance.

complain [kəm'pleɪn] *vi*: **to ~ (about)** se plaindre (de); (*in shop etc*) réclamer (au sujet de); **~t** *n* plainte *f*; réclamation *f*; (*MED*) affection *f*.

complement ['kɒmplɪmənt] *n* complément *m*; (*especially of ship's crew etc*) effectif complet // ['kɒmplɪment] *vt* (*enhance*) compléter; **~ary** [kɒmplɪ-'mentərɪ] *a* complémentaire.

complete [kəm'pli:t] *a* complet(ète) // *vt* achever, parachever; (*a form*) remplir; **~ly** *ad* complètement; **completion** *n* achèvement *m*.

complex ['kɒmpleks] *a*, *n* complexe (*m*).

complexion [kəm'plekʃən] *n* (*of face*) teint *m*; (*of event etc*) aspect *m*, caractère *m*.

compliance [kəm'plaɪəns] *n* (*submission*) docilité *f*; (*agreement*): **~ with** le fait de se conformer à.

complicate ['kɒmplɪkeɪt] *vt* compliquer; **~d** *a* compliqué(e); **complication** [-'keɪʃən] *n* complication *f*.

compliment *n* ['kɒmplɪmənt] compliment *m* // *vt* ['kɒmplɪment] complimenter; **~s** *npl* compliments *mpl*, hommages *mpl*; vœux *mpl*; **to pay sb a ~** faire *or* adresser un compliment à qn; **~ary** [-'mentərɪ] *a* flatteur(euse); (*free*) à titre gracieux; **~ary ticket** *n* billet *m* de faveur.

comply [kəm'plaɪ] *vi*: **to ~ with** se soumettre à, se conformer à.

component [kəm'pəunənt] *n* composant *m*, élément *m*.

compose [kəm'pəuz] *vt* composer; **to ~ o.s.** se calmer, se maîtriser; prendre une contenance; **~d** *a* calme, posé(e); **~r** *n* (*MUS*) compositeur *m*.

composition [kɒmpə'zɪʃən] *n* composition *f*.

composure [kəm'pəuʒə*] *n* calme *m*, maîtrise *f* de soi.

compound ['kɒmpaund] *n* (*CHEM, LING*) composé *m*; (*enclosure*) enclos *m*, enceinte *f* // *a* composé(e); **~ fracture** *n* fracture compliquée.

comprehend [kɒmprɪ'hend] *vt* comprendre; **comprehension** [-'henʃən] *n* compréhension *f*.

comprehensive [kɒmprɪ'hensɪv] *a* (très) complet(ète); **~ policy** *n*

(*INSURANCE*) assurance *f* tous risques; **~ (school)** *n* (*Brit*) école secondaire non sélective avec libre circulation d'une section à l'autre, ≈ C.E.S. *m*.

compress *vt* [kəm'pres] comprimer // *n* ['kɒmpres] (*MED*) compresse *f*.

comprise [kəm'praɪz] *vt* (*also*: **be ~d of**) comprendre.

compromise ['kɒmprəmaɪz] *n* compromis *m* // *vt* compromettre // *vi* transiger, accepter un compromis.

compulsion [kəm'pʌlʃən] *n* contrainte *f*, force *f*.

compulsive [kəm'pʌlsɪv] *a* (*PSYCH*) compulsif(ive).

compulsory [kəm'pʌlsərɪ] *a* obligatoire.

computer [kəm'pju:tə*] *n* ordinateur *m*; (*mechanical*) calculatrice *f*; **~ize** *vt* traiter *or* automatiser par ordinateur; **~ programmer** *n* programmeur/euse; **~ programming** *n* programmation *f*; **~ science, computing** *n* informatique *f*.

comrade ['kɒmrɪd] *n* camarade *m/f*.

con [kɒn] *vt* duper; escroquer // *n* escroquerie *f*.

conceal [kən'si:l] *vt* cacher, dissimuler.

conceit [kən'si:t] *n* vanité *f*, suffisance *f*, prétention *f*; **~ed** *a* vaniteux(euse), suffisant(e).

conceive [kən'si:v] *vt*, *vi* concevoir.

concentrate ['kɒnsəntreɪt] *vi* se concentrer // *vt* concentrer.

concentration [kɒnsən'treɪʃən] *n* concentration *f*; **~ camp** *n* camp *m* de concentration.

concept ['kɒnsept] *n* concept *m*.

concern [kən'sə:n] *n* affaire *f*; (*COMM*) entreprise *f*, firme *f*; (*anxiety*) inquiétude *f*, souci *m* // *vt* concerner; **to be ~ed (about)** s'inquiéter (de), être inquiet (au sujet de); **~ing** *prep* en ce qui concerne, à propos de.

concert ['kɒnsət] *n* concert *m*; **~ed** [kən'sə:tɪd] *a* concerté(e); **~ hall** *n* salle *f* de concert.

concertina [kɒnsə'ti:nə] *n* concertina *m* // *vi* se télescoper, se caramboler.

concerto [kən'tʃə:təu] *n* concerto *m*.

conclude [kən'klu:d] *vt* conclure; **conclusion** [-'klu:ʒən] *n* conclusion *f*; **conclusive** [-'klu:sɪv] *a* concluant(e), définitif(ive).

concoct [kən'kɒkt] *vt* confectionner, composer; **~ion** [-'kɒkʃən] *n* mélange *m*.

concourse ['kɒŋkɔ:s] *n* (*hall*) hall *m*, salle *f* des pas perdus.

concrete ['kɒŋkri:t] *n* béton *m* // *a* concret(ète); en béton.

concur [kən'kə:*] *vi* être d'accord.

concurrently [kən'kʌrntlɪ] *ad* simultanément.

concussion [kən'kʌʃən] *n* (*MED*) commotion (cérébrale).

condemn [kən'dem] *vt* condamner.

condensation [kɔndɛn'seɪʃən] *n* condensation *f*.
condense [kən'dɛns] *vi* se condenser // *vt* condenser; **~d milk** *n* lait concentré (sucré).
condition [kən'dɪʃən] *n* condition *f* // *vt* déterminer, conditionner; **on ~ that** à condition que + *sub*, à condition de; **~al** *a* conditionnel(le); **~er** *n* (*for hair*) baume démêlant.
condolences [kən'dəʊlənsɪz] *npl* condoléances *fpl*.
condom ['kɔndəm] *n* préservatif *m*.
condominium [kɔndə'mɪnɪəm] *n* (*US: building*) immeuble *m* (en copropriété) // (*: rooms*) appartement *m* (dans un immeuble en copropriété).
condone [kən'dəʊn] *vt* fermer les yeux sur, approuver (tacitement).
conducive [kən'dju:sɪv] *a*: **~ to** favorable à, qui contribue à.
conduct *n* ['kɔndʌkt] conduite *f* // *vt* [kən'dʌkt] conduire; (*manage*) mener, diriger; (*MUS*) diriger; **to ~ o.s.** se conduire, se comporter; **~ed tour** *n* voyage organisé; visite guidée; **~or** *n* (*of orchestra*) chef *m* d'orchestre; (*on bus*) receveur *m*; (*US: on train*) chef de train; (*ELEC*) conducteur *m*; **~ress** *n* (*on bus*) receveuse *f*.
cone [kəʊn] *n* cône *m*; (*for ice-cream*) cornet *m*; (*BOT*) pomme *f* de pin, cône.
confectioner [kən'fɛkʃənə*] *n* (*of cakes*) pâtissier/ière; (*of sweets*) confiseur/euse; **~'s (shop)** *n* confiserie(-pâtisserie) *f*; **~y** *n* pâtisserie *f*; confiserie *f*.
confer [kən'fə:*] *vt*: **to ~ sth on** conférer qch à // *vi* conférer, s'entretenir.
conference ['kɔnfərns] *n* conférence *f*.
confess [kən'fɛs] *vt* confesser, avouer // *vi* se confesser; **~ion** [-'fɛʃən] *n* confession *f*.
confetti [kən'fɛtɪ] *n* confettis *mpl*.
confide [kən'faɪd] *vi*: **to ~ in** s'ouvrir à, se confier à.
confidence ['kɔnfɪdns] *n* confiance *f*; (*also*: self-~) assurance *f*, confiance en soi; (*secret*) confidence *f*; **in ~** (*speak, write*) en confidence, confidentiellement; **~ trick** *n* escroquerie *f*; **confident** *a* sûr(e), assuré(e); **confidential** [kɔnfɪ-'dɛnʃəl] *a* confidentiel(le).
confine [kən'faɪn] *vt* limiter, borner; (*shut up*) confiner, enfermer; **~s** ['kɔnfaɪnz] *npl* confins *mpl*, bornes *fpl*; **~d** *a* (*space*) restreint(e), réduit(e); **~ment** *n* emprisonnement *m*, détention *f*; (*MIL*) consigne *f* (au quartier); (*MED*) accouchement *m*.
confirm [kən'fə:m] *vt* (*report*, *REL*) confirmer; (*appointment*) ratifier; **~ation** [kɔnfə'meɪʃən] *n* confirmation *f*; **~ed** *a* invétéré(e), incorrigible.
confiscate ['kɔnfɪskeɪt] *vt* confisquer.

conflict *n* ['kɔnflɪkt] conflit *m*, lutte *f* // *vi* [kən'flɪkt] être *or* entrer en conflit; (*opinions*) s'opposer, se heurter; **~ing** *a* contradictoire.
conform [kən'fɔ:m] *vi*: **to ~ (to)** se conformer (à).
confound [kən'faʊnd] *vt* confondre.
confront [kən'frʌnt] *vt* confronter, mettre en présence; (*enemy, danger*) affronter, faire face à; **~ation** [kɔnfrən-'teɪʃən] *n* confrontation *f*.
confuse [kən'fju:z] *vt* embrouiller; (*one thing with another*) confondre; (*a person*) dérouté(e), désorienté(e); **confusing** *a* peu clair(e), déroutant(e); **confusion** [-'fju:ʒən] *n* confusion *f*.
congeal [kən'dʒi:l] *vi* (*blood*) se coaguler.
congenial [kən'dʒi:nɪəl] *a* sympathique, agréable.
congested [kən'dʒɛstɪd] *a* (*MED*) congestionné(e); (*fig*) surpeuplé(e); congestionné; bloqué(e).
congestion [kən'dʒɛstʃən] *n* congestion *f*; (*fig*) encombrement *m*.
congratulate [kən'grætjuleɪt] *vt*: **to ~ sb (on)** féliciter qn (de); **congratulations** [-'leɪʒnz] *npl* félicitations *fpl*.
congregate ['kɔngrɪgeɪt] *vi* se rassembler, se réunir.
congregation [kɔngrɪ'geɪʃən] *n* assemblée *f* (des fidèles).
congress ['kɔngrɛs] *n* congrès *m*; **~man** *n* (*US*) membre *m* du Congrès.
conjunction [kən'dʒʌŋkʃən] *n* conjonction *f*.
conjunctivitis [kəndʒʌŋktɪ'vaɪtɪs] *n* conjonctivite *f*.
conjure ['kʌndʒə*] *vt* faire apparaître (par la prestidigitation) // *vi* faire des tours de passe-passe; **to ~ up** *vt* (*ghost, spirit*) faire apparaître; (*memories*) évoquer; **~r** *n* prestidigitateur *m*, illusionniste *m/f*.
conk out [kɔŋk-] *vi* (*col*) tomber *or* rester en panne.
conman ['kɔnmæn] *n* escroc *m*.
connect [kə'nɛkt] *vt* joindre, relier; (*ELEC*) connecter; (*fig*) établir un rapport entre, faire un rapprochement entre // *vi* (*train*): **to ~ with** assurer la correspondance avec; **to be ~ed with** avoir un rapport avec; avoir des rapports avec, être en relation avec; (*related*) être allié(e) à, être parent/e de; **~ion** [-ʃən] *n* relation *f*, lien *m*; (*ELEC*) connexion *f*; (*TEL*) communication *f*; **in ~ion with** à propos de.
connive [kə'naɪv] *vi*: **to ~ at** se faire le complice de.
conquer ['kɔŋkə*] *vt* conquérir; (*feelings*) vaincre, surmonter.
conquest ['kɔŋkwɛst] *n* conquête *f*.
cons [kɔnz] *npl see* **convenience, pro.**
conscience ['kɔnʃəns] *n* conscience *f*.

conscientious [kɒnʃɪˈɛnʃəs] *a* consciencieux(euse); (*scruple, objection*) de conscience.

conscious [ˈkɒnʃəs] *a* conscient(e); **~ness** *n* conscience *f*; (MED) connaissance *f*.

conscript [ˈkɒnskrɪpt] *n* conscrit *m*.

consent [kənˈsɛnt] *n* consentement *m* // *vi*: to ~ (to) consentir (à).

consequence [ˈkɒnsɪkwəns] *n* suites *fpl*, conséquence *f*; importance *f*.

consequently [ˈkɒnsɪkwəntlɪ] *ad* par conséquent, donc.

conservation [kɒnsəˈveɪʃən] *n* préservation *f*, protection *f*.

conservative [kənˈsəːvətɪv] *a* conservateur(trice); (*cautious*) prudent(e); **C~** *a, n* (*Brit POL*) conservateur(trice).

conservatory [kənˈsəːvətrɪ] *n* (*greenhouse*) serre *f*.

conserve [kənˈsəːv] *vt* conserver, préserver; (*supplies, energy*) économiser // *n* confiture *f*, conserve *f* (de fruits).

consider [kənˈsɪdə*] *vt* considérer, réfléchir à; (*take into account*) penser à, prendre en considération; (*regard, judge*) considérer, estimer; **to ~ doing sth** envisager de faire qch.

considerable [kənˈsɪdərəbl] *a* considérable; **considerably** *ad* nettement.

considerate [kənˈsɪdərɪt] *a* prévenant(e), plein(e) d'égards.

consideration [kənsɪdəˈreɪʃən] *n* considération *f*; (*reward*) rétribution *f*, rémunération *f*.

considering [kənˈsɪdərɪŋ] *prep* étant donné.

consign [kənˈsaɪn] *vt* expédier, livrer; **~ment** *n* arrivage *m*, envoi *m*.

consist [kənˈsɪst] *vi*: to ~ of consister en, se composer de.

consistency [kənˈsɪstənsɪ] *n* consistance *f*; (*fig*) cohérence *f*.

consistent [kənˈsɪstənt] *a* logique, cohérent(e); ~ **with** compatible avec, en accord avec.

consolation [kɒnsəˈleɪʃən] *n* consolation *f*.

consonant [ˈkɒnsənənt] *n* consonne *f*.

conspicuous [kənˈspɪkjuəs] *a* voyant(e), qui attire la vue *or* l'attention.

conspiracy [kənˈspɪrəsɪ] *n* conspiration *f*, complot *m*.

constable [ˈkʌnstəbl] *n* (*Brit*) ≈ agent *m* de police, gendarme *m*; **chief ~** ≈ préfet *m* de police.

constabulary [kənˈstæbjulərɪ] *n* ≈ police *f*, gendarmerie *f*.

constant [ˈkɒnstənt] *a* constant(e); incessant(e); **~ly** *ad* constamment, sans cesse.

constipated [ˈkɒnstɪpeɪtɪd] *a* constipé(e).

constipation [kɒnstɪˈpeɪʃən] *n* constipation *f*.

constituency [kənˈstɪtjuənsɪ] *n* circonscription électorale.

constituent [kənˈstɪtjuənt] *n* électeur/trice; (*part*) élément constitutif, composant *m*.

constitution [kɒnstɪˈtjuːʃən] *n* constitution *f*; **~al** *a* constitutionnel(le).

constraint [kənˈstreɪnt] *n* contrainte *f*.

construct [kənˈstrʌkt] *vt* construire; **~ion** [-ʃən] *n* construction *f*; **~ive** *a* constructif(ive).

construe [kənˈstruː] *vt* analyser, expliquer.

consul [ˈkɒnsl] *n* consul *m*; **~ate** [ˈkɒnsjulɪt] *n* consulat *m*.

consult [kənˈsʌlt] *vt* consulter // *vi* consulter; se consulter; **~ant** *n* (MED) médecin consultant; (*other specialist*) consultant *m*, (expert-)conseil *m*; **~ing room** *n* (*Brit MED*) cabinet *m* de consultation.

consume [kənˈsjuːm] *vt* consommer; **~r** *n* consommateur/trice; **~r goods** *npl* biens *mpl* de consommation; **~r society** *n* société *f* de consommation.

consummate [ˈkɒnsʌmeɪt] *vt* consommer.

consumption [kənˈsʌmpʃən] *n* consommation *f*; (MED) consomption *f* (pulmonaire).

cont. *abbr* = continued.

contact [ˈkɒntækt] *n* contact *m*; (*person*) connaissance *f*, relation *f* // *vt* se mettre en contact *or* en rapport avec; ~ **lenses** *npl* verres *mpl* de contact.

contagious [kənˈteɪdʒəs] *a* contagieux(euse).

contain [kənˈteɪn] *vt* contenir; to ~ o.s. se contenir, se maîtriser; **~er** *n* récipient *m*; (*for shipping etc*) container *m*.

contaminate [kənˈtæmɪneɪt] *vt* contaminer.

cont'd *abbr* = continued.

contemplate [ˈkɒntəmpleɪt] *vt* contempler; (*consider*) envisager.

contemporary [kənˈtɛmpərərɪ] *a* contemporain(e); (*design, wallpaper*) moderne // *n* contemporain/e.

contempt [kənˈtɛmpt] *n* mépris *m*, dédain *m*; ~ **of court** (LAW) outrage *m* à l'autorité de la justice; **~uous** *a* dédaigneux(euse), méprisant(e).

contend [kənˈtɛnd] *vt*: to ~ that soutenir *or* prétendre que // *vi*: to ~ with rivaliser avec, lutter avec; **~er** *n* prétendant/e; adversaire *m/f*.

content [kənˈtɛnt] *a* content(e), satisfait(e) // *vt* contenter, satisfaire // *n* [ˈkɒntɛnt] contenu *m*; teneur *f*; **~s** *npl* contenu; (**table of**) **~s** table *f* des matières; **~ed** *a* content(e), satisfait(e).

contention [kənˈtɛnʃən] *n* dispute *f*,

contestation f; (argument) assertion f, affirmation f.

contest n ['kɔntest] combat m, lutte f; (competition) concours m // vt [kən'test] contester, discuter; (compete for) disputer; **~ant** [kən'testənt] n concurrent/e; (in fight) adversaire m/f.

context ['kɔntekst] n contexte m.

continent ['kɔntɪnənt] n continent m; the C~ (Brit) l'Europe continentale; **~al** [-'nentl] a continental(e) // n Européen/ne (continental(e)); **~al quilt** n (Brit) couette f.

contingency [kən'tɪndʒənsɪ] n éventualité f, événement imprévu; **~ plan** n plan m d'urgence.

continual [kən'tɪnjuəl] a continuel(le).

continuation [kəntɪnju'eɪʃən] n continuation f; (after interruption) reprise f; (of story) suite f.

continue [kən'tɪnju:] vi continuer // vt continuer; (start again) reprendre.

continuous [kən'tɪnjuəs] a continu(e), permanent(e); **~ stationery** n papier m en continu.

contort [kən'tɔ:t] vt tordre, crisper.

contour ['kɔntuə*] n contour m, profil m; (also: ~ line) courbe f de niveau.

contraband ['kɔntrəbænd] n contrebande f.

contraceptive [kɔntrə'septɪv] a contraceptif(ive), anticonceptionnel(le) // n contraceptif m.

contract n ['kɔntrækt] contrat m // vb [kən'trækt] vi (become smaller) se contracter, se resserrer; (COMM): to ~ to do sth s'engager (par contrat) à faire qch; **~ion** [-ʃən] n contraction f; **~or** n entrepreneur m.

contradict [kɔntrə'dɪkt] vt contredire; (be contrary to) démentir, être en contradiction avec.

contraption [kən'træpʃən] n (pej) machin m, truc m.

contrary ['kɔntrərɪ] a contraire, opposé(e); [kən'treərɪ] (perverse) contrariant(e), entêté(e) // n contraire m; on the ~ au contraire; unless you hear to the ~ sauf avis contraire.

contrast n ['kɔntrɑ:st] contraste m // vt [kən'trɑ:st] mettre en contraste, contraster.

contribute [kən'trɪbju:t] vi contribuer // vt: to ~ £10/an article to donner 10 livres/un article à; to ~ to (gen) contribuer à; (newspaper) collaborer à; **contribution** [kɔntrɪ'bju:ʃən] n contribution f; **contributor** n (to newspaper) collaborateur/trice.

contrive [kən'traɪv] vt combiner, inventer // vi: to ~ to do s'arranger pour faire, trouver le moyen de faire.

control [kən'trəul] vt maîtriser; (check) contrôler // n contrôle m, autorité f; maîtrise f; **~s** npl commandes fpl; every-thing is under ~ tout va bien, j'ai (or il a etc) la situation en main; to be in ~ of être maître de, maîtriser; être responsable de; the car went out of ~ j'ai (or il a etc) perdu le contrôle du véhicule; **~ panel** n tableau m de commande; **~ room** n salle f des commandes; (RADIO, TV) régie f; **~ tower** n (AVIAT) tour f de contrôle.

controversial [kɔntrə'və:ʃl] a discutable, controversé(e).

controversy ['kɔntrəvə:sɪ] n controverse f, polémique f.

convalesce [kɔnvə'les] vi relever de maladie, se remettre (d'une maladie).

convene [kən'vi:n] vt convoquer, assembler // vi se réunir, s'assembler.

convenience [kən'vi:nɪəns] n commodité f; at your ~ quand or comme cela vous convient; all modern ~s, all mod cons avec tout le confort moderne, tout confort.

convenient [kən'vi:nɪənt] a commode.

convent ['kɔnvənt] n couvent m.

convention [kən'venʃən] n convention f; **~al** a conventionnel(le).

conversant [kən'və:sənt] a: to be ~ with s'y connaître en; être au courant de.

conversation [kɔnvə'seɪʃən] n conversation f.

converse ['kɔnvə:s] n contraire m, inverse m // vi [kən'və:s] s'entretenir; **~ly** [-'və:slɪ] ad inversement, réciproquement.

convert vt [kən'və:t] (REL, COMM) convertir; (alter) transformer, aménager // n ['kɔnvə:t] converti/e; **~ible** a convertible // n (voiture f) décapotable f.

convey [kən'veɪ] vt transporter; (thanks) transmettre; (idea) communiquer; **~or belt** n convoyeur m, tapis roulant.

convict vt [kən'vɪkt] déclarer (or reconnaître) coupable // n ['kɔnvɪkt] forçat m, convict m; **~ion** [-ʃən] n condamnation f; (belief) conviction f.

convince [kən'vɪns] vt convaincre, persuader; **convincing** a persuasif(ive), convaincant(e).

convoluted [kɔnvə'lu:tɪd] a (argument) compliqué(e).

convulse [kən'vʌls] vt ébranler; to be **~d with laughter** se tordre de rire.

coo [ku:] vi roucouler.

cook [kuk] vt (faire) cuire // vi cuire; (person) faire la cuisine // n cuisinier/ière; **~book** n livre m de cuisine; **~er** n cuisinière f; **~ery** n cuisine f; **~ery book** n (Brit) = **~book**; **~ie** n (US) biscuit m, petit gâteau sec; **~ing** n cuisine f.

cool [ku:l] a frais(fraîche); (not afraid) calme; (unfriendly) froid(e); (impertinent) effronté(e) // vt, vi rafraîchir, refroidir.

coop [ku:p] n poulailler m // vt: **to ~ up** (fig) cloîtrer, enfermer.

cooperate [kəu'ɔpəreɪt] vi coopérer, collaborer; **cooperation** [-'reɪʃən] n coopération f, collaboration f.

cooperative [kəu'ɔpərətɪv] a coopératif(ive) // n coopérative f.

coordinate vt [kəu'ɔ:dɪneɪt] coordonner // n [kəu'ɔ:dɪnət] (MATH) coordonnée f; **~s** npl (clothes) ensemble m, coordonnés mpl.

cop [kɔp] n (col) flic m.

cope [kəup] vi se débrouiller; **to ~ with** faire face à; s'occuper de.

copper ['kɔpə*] n cuivre m; (col: policeman) flic m; **~s** npl petite monnaie.

coppice ['kɔpɪs] n, **copse** [kɔps] n taillis m.

copy ['kɔpɪ] n copie f; (book etc) exemplaire m // vt copier; **~right** n droit m d'auteur, copyright m.

coral ['kɔrəl] n corail m.

cord [kɔ:d] n corde f; (fabric) velours côtelé; whipcord m; corde f.

cordial ['kɔ:dɪəl] a cordial(e), chaleureux(euse) // n sirop m; cordial m.

cordon ['kɔ:dn] n cordon m; **to ~ off** vt boucler (par cordon de police).

corduroy ['kɔ:dərɔɪ] n velours côtelé.

core [kɔ:*] n (of fruit) trognon m, cœur m; (TECH) noyau m // vt enlever le trognon or le cœur de.

cork [kɔ:k] n liège m; (of bottle) bouchon m; **~screw** n tire-bouchon m.

corn [kɔ:n] n (Brit: wheat) blé m; (US: maize) maïs m; (on foot) cor m; **~ on the cob** (CULIN) épi m de maïs au naturel.

corned beef ['kɔ:nd-] n corned-beef m.

corner ['kɔ:nə*] n coin m; (AUT) tournant m, virage m // vt acculer, mettre au pied du mur; coincer; (COMM: market) accaparer // vi prendre un virage; **~stone** n pierre f angulaire.

cornet ['kɔ:nɪt] n (MUS) cornet m à pistons; (Brit: of ice-cream) cornet m (de glace).

cornflakes ['kɔ:nfleɪks] npl cornflakes mpl.

cornflour ['kɔ:nflauə*] n (Brit) farine f de maïs, maïzena f ®.

cornstarch ['kɔ:nstɑ:tʃ] n (US) = **cornflour**.

Cornwall ['kɔ:nwəl] n Cornouailles f.

corny ['kɔ:nɪ] a (col) rebattu(e), galvaudé(e).

coronary ['kɔrənərɪ] n: **~ (thrombosis)** infarctus m (du myocarde), thrombose f coronaire.

coronation [kɔrə'neɪʃən] n couronnement m.

coronet ['kɔrənɪt] n couronne f.

corporal ['kɔ:pərl] n caporal m, brigadier m // a: **~ punishment** châtiment corporel.

corporate ['kɔ:pərɪt] a en commun; constitué(e) (en corporation).

corporation [kɔ:pə'reɪʃən] n (of town) municipalité f, conseil municipal; (COMM) société f.

corps [kɔ:*], pl **corps** [kɔ:z] n corps m.

corpse [kɔ:ps] n cadavre m.

correct [kə'rɛkt] a (accurate) correct(e), exact(e); (proper) correct, convenable // vt corriger; **~ion** [-ʃən] n correction f.

correspond [kɔrɪs'pɔnd] vi correspondre; **~ence** n correspondance f; **~ence course** n cours m par correspondance; **~ent** n correspondant/e.

corridor ['kɔrɪdɔ:*] n couloir m, corridor m.

corrode [kə'rəud] vt corroder, ronger // vi se corroder.

corrugated ['kɔrəgeɪtɪd] a plissé(e); cannelé(e); ondulé(e); **~ iron** n tôle ondulée.

corrupt [kə'rʌpt] a corrompu(e) // vt corrompre; **~ion** [-ʃən] n corruption f.

Corsica ['kɔ:sɪkə] n Corse f.

cortège [kɔ:'teɪʒ] n cortège m (gén funèbre).

cosh [kɔʃ] n (Brit) matraque f.

cosmetic [kɔz'mɛtɪk] n produit m de beauté, cosmétique m.

cosset ['kɔsɪt] vt choyer, dorloter.

cost [kɔst] n coût m // vb (pt, pp cost) vi coûter // vt établir or calculer le prix de revient de; **~s** npl (LAW) dépens mpl; it **~s £5/too much** cela coûte cinq livres/ trop cher; **at all ~s** coûte que coûte, à tout prix.

co-star ['kəustɑ:*] n partenaire m/f.

cost-effective [kɔstɪ'fɛktɪv] a rentable.

costly ['kɔstlɪ] a coûteux(euse).

cost-of-living [kɔstəv'lɪvɪŋ] a: **~ allowance** indemnité f de vie chère; **~ index** indexe m du coût de la vie.

cost price n (Brit) prix coûtant or de revient.

costume ['kɔstju:m] n costume m; (lady's suit) tailleur m; (Brit: also: swimming ~) maillot m (de bain); **~ jewellery** n bijoux mpl de fantaisie.

cosy, (US) **cozy** ['kəuzɪ] a douillet(te).

cot [kɔt] n (Brit: child's) lit m d'enfant, petit lit; (US: campbed) lit de camp.

cottage ['kɔtɪdʒ] n petite maison (à la campagne), cottage m; **~ cheese** n fromage blanc (maigre); **~ industry** n industrie familiale or artisanale; **~ pie** n ≈ hachis m Parmentier.

cotton ['kɔtn] n coton m; **to ~ on to** vt fus (col) piger; **~ candy** n (US) barbe f à papa; **~ wool** n (Brit) ouate f, coton m hydrophile.

couch [kautʃ] n canapé m; divan m // vt formuler, exprimer.

couchette [ku:'ʃɛt] n couchette f.

cough [kɔf] *vi* tousser // *n* toux *f*; ~ **drop** *n* pastille *f* pour or contre la toux.

could [kud] *pt of* **can**; **~n't** = **could not.**

council ['kaunsl] *n* conseil *m*; **city or town** ~ conseil municipal; ~ **estate** *n* (*Brit*) (quartier *m* or zone *f* de) logements loués à/par la municipalité; ~ **house** *n* (*Brit*) maison *f* (à loyer modéré) louée par la municipalité; **~lor** *n* conseiller/ère.

counsel ['kaunsl] *n* avocat/e; consultation *f*, délibération *f*; **~lor** *n* conseiller/ère.

count [kaunt] *vt, vi* compter // *n* compte *m*; (*nobleman*) comte *m*; **to ~ on** *vt fus* compter sur; **~down** *n* compte *m* à rebours.

countenance ['kauntinəns] *n* expression *f* // *vt* approuver.

counter ['kauntə*] *n* comptoir *m*; (*in post office, bank*) guichet *m*; (*in game*) jeton *m* // *vt* aller à l'encontre de, opposer; (*blow*) parer // *ad*: ~ **to** à l'encontre de; contrairement à; **~act** *vt* neutraliser, contrebalancer; **~espionage** *n* contre-espionnage *m*.

counterfeit ['kauntəfit] *n* faux *m*, contrefaçon *f* // *vt* contrefaire // *a* faux(fausse).

counterfoil ['kauntəfɔil] *n* talon *m*, souche *f*.

countermand [kauntə'ma:nd] *vt* annuler.

counterpart ['kauntəpa:t] *n* (*of document etc*) double *m*; (*of person*) homologue *m/f*.

countess ['kauntis] *n* comtesse *f*.

countless ['kauntlis] *a* innombrable.

country ['kʌntri] *n* pays *m*; (*native land*) patrie *f*; (*as opposed to town*) campagne *f*; (*region*) région *f*, pays; ~ **dancing** *n* (*Brit*) danse *f* folklorique; ~ **house** *n* manoir *m*, (petit) château; **~man** *n* (*national*) compatriote *m*; (*rural*) habitant *m* de la campagne, campagnard *m*; **~side** *n* campagne *f*.

county ['kaunti] *n* comté *m*.

coup [ku:, -z] *n* beau coup; (*also*: ~ **d'état**) coup d'État.

couple ['kʌpl] *n* couple *m* // *vt* (*carriages*) atteler; (*TECH*) coupler; (*ideas, names*) associer; **a ~ of** deux.

coupon ['ku:pɔn] *n* coupon *m*, bon-prime *m*, bon-réclame *m*; (*COMM*) coupon.

courage ['kʌridʒ] *n* courage *m*.

courgette [kuə'ʒɛt] *n* (*Brit*) courgette *f*.

courier ['kuriə*] *n* messager *m*, courrier *m*; (*for tourists*) accompagnateur/trice.

course [kɔ:s] *n* cours *m*; (*of ship*) route *f*; (*for golf*) terrain *m*; (*part of meal*) plat *m*; **first ~** entrée *f*; **of ~** *ad* bien sûr; ~ **of action** parti *m*, ligne *f* de conduite; ~ **of lectures** série *f* de

conférences; ~ **of treatment** (*MED*) traitement *m*.

court [kɔ:t] *n* cour *f*; (*LAW*) cour, tribunal *m*; (*TENNIS*) court *m* // *vt* (*woman*) courtiser, faire la cour à; **to take to** ~ actionner or poursuivre en justice.

courteous ['kə:tiəs] *a* courtois(e), poli(e).

courtesy ['kə:təsi] *n* courtoisie *f*, politesse *f*; **by** ~ **of** avec l'aimable autorisation de.

court-house ['kɔ:thaus] *n* (*US*) palais *m* de justice.

courtier ['kɔ:tiə*] *n* courtisan *m*, dame *f* de cour.

court-martial, *pl* **courts-martial** ['kɔ:t'ma:ʃəl] *n* cour martiale, conseil *m* de guerre.

courtroom ['kɔ:trum] *n* salle *f* de tribunal.

courtyard ['kɔ:tja:d] *n* cour *f*.

cousin ['kʌzn] *n* cousin/e; **first** ~ cousin/e germain(e).

cove [kəuv] *n* petite baie, anse *f*.

covenant ['kʌvənənt] *n* contrat *m*, engagement *m*.

cover ['kʌvə*] *vt* couvrir // *n* (*for bed, of book, COMM*) couverture *f*; (*of pan*) couvercle *m*; (*over furniture*) housse *f*; (*shelter*) abri *m*; **to take** ~ (*shelter*) se mettre à l'abri; **under** ~ à l'abri; **under** ~ **of darkness** à la faveur de la nuit; **under separate** ~ (*COMM*) sous pli séparé; **to** ~ **up for sb** couvrir qn; **~age** *n* reportage *m*; (*INSURANCE*) couverture *f*; ~ **charge** *n* couvert *m* (supplément à payer); **~ing** *n* couverture *f*, enveloppe *f*; **~ing letter,** (*US*) ~ **letter** *n* lettre explicative; ~ **note** *n* (*INSURANCE*) police *f* provisoire.

covert ['kʌvət] *a* (*threat*) voilé(e), caché(e); (*attack*) indirect(e); (*glance*) furtif(ive).

cover-up ['kʌvərʌp] *n* tentative *f* pour étouffer une affaire.

covet ['kʌvit] *vt* convoiter.

cow [kau] *n* vache *f* // *cpd* femelle // *vt* effrayer, intimider.

coward ['kauəd] *n* lâche *m/f*; **~ice** [-is] *n* lâcheté *f*; **~ly** *a* lâche.

cowboy ['kaubɔi] *n* cow-boy *m*.

cower ['kauə*] *vi* se recroqueviller; trembler.

coxswain ['kɔksn] *n* (*abbr*: **cox**) barreur *m*; (*of ship*) patron *m*.

coy [kɔi] *a* faussement effarouché(e) or timide.

cozy ['kəuzi] *a* (*US*) = **cosy.**

CPA *n abbr* (*US*) *of* **certified public accountant.**

crab [kræb] *n* crabe *m*; ~ **apple** *n* pomme *f* sauvage.

crack [kræk] *n* fente *f*, fissure *f*; fêlure *f*; lézarde *f*; (*noise*) craquement *m*, coup (sec); (*joke*) plaisanterie *f*; (*col: attempt*): **to have a ~ at** essayer // *vt* fendre, fissurer; fêler; lézarder; (*whip*) faire claquer; (*nut*) casser // *a* (*athlete*) de première classe, d'élite; **to ~ down on** *vt fus* mettre un frein à; **to ~ up** *vi* être au bout de son rouleau, flancher; **~er** *n* pétard *m*; biscuit (salé), craquelin *m*.

crackle ['krækl] *vi* crépiter, grésiller.

cradle ['kreidl] *n* berceau *m*.

craft [krɑ:ft] *n* métier (artisanal); (*cunning*) ruse *f*, astuce *f*; (*boat*) embarcation *f*, barque *f*; **~sman** *n* artisan *m*, ouvrier (qualifié); **~smanship** *n* métier *m*, habileté *f*; **~y** *a* rusé(e), malin(igne), astucieux(euse).

crag [kræg] *n* rocher escarpé.

cram [kræm] *vt* (*fill*): **to ~ sth with** bourrer qch de; (*put*): **to ~ sth into** fourrer qch dans // *vi* (*for exams*) bachoter.

cramp [kræmp] *n* crampe *f* // *vt* gêner, entraver; **~ed** *a* à l'étroit, très serré(e).

cranberry ['krænbərı] *n* canneberge *f*.

crane [kreın] *n* grue *f*.

crank [kræŋk] *n* manivelle *f*; (*person*) excentrique *m/f*; **~shaft** *n* vilebrequin *m*.

cranny ['krænı] *n see* **nook**.

crash [kræʃ] *n* fracas *m*; (*of car, plane*) collision *f* // *vt* (*plane*) écraser // *vi* (*plane*) s'écraser; (*two cars*) se percuter, s'emboutir; (*fig*) s'effondrer; **to ~ into** se jeter *or* se fracasser contre; **~ course** *n* cours intensif; **~ helmet** *n* casque (protecteur); **~ landing** *n* atterrissage forcé *or* en catastrophe.

crate [kreit] *n* cageot *m*.

cravat(e) [krə'væt] *n* foulard (noué autour du cou).

crave [kreiv] *vt*, *vi*: **to ~ (for)** avoir une envie irrésistible de.

crawl [krɔ:l] *vi* ramper; (*vehicle*) avancer au pas // *n* (*SWIMMING*) crawl *m*.

crayfish ['kreifiʃ] *n* (*pl inv*) (*freshwater*) écrevisse *f*; (*saltwater*) langoustine *f*.

crayon ['kreiən] *n* crayon *m* (de couleur).

craze [kreiz] *n* engouement *m*.

crazy ['kreizı] *a* fou(folle); **~ paving** *n* dallage irrégulier (en pierres plates).

creak [kri:k] *vi* grincer; craquer.

cream [kri:m] *n* crème *f* // *a* (*colour*) crème *inv*; **~ cake** *n* (petit) gâteau à la crème; **~ cheese** *n* fromage *m* à la crème, fromage blanc; **~y** *a* crémeux(euse).

crease [kri:s] *n* pli *m* // *vt* froisser, chiffonner // *vi* se froisser, se chiffonner.

create [kri:'eit] *vt* créer; **creation** [-ʃən] *n* création *f*; **creative** *a* créateur(trice).

creature ['kri:tʃə•] *n* créature *f*.

crèche, creche [krɛʃ] *n* garderie *f*, crèche *f*.

credence ['kri:dns] *n*: **to lend** *or* **give ~** to ajouter foi à.

credentials [krı'dɛnʃlz] *npl* (*papers*) références *fpl*.

credit ['krɛdıt] *n* crédit *m* // *vt* (*COMM*) créditer; (*believe: also*: **give ~ to**) ajouter foi à, croire; **~s** *npl* (*CINEMA*) générique *m*; **to ~ sb with** (*fig*) prêter *or* attribuer à qn; **to be in ~** (*person, bank account*) être créditeur(trice); **~ card** *n* carte *f* de crédit; **~or** *n* créancier/ière.

creed [kri:d] *n* croyance *f*; credo *m*, principes *mpl*.

creek [kri:k] *n* crique *f*, anse *f*; (*US*) ruisseau *m*, petit cours d'eau.

creep [kri:p], *pt*, *pp* **crept** *vi* ramper; (*fig*) se faufiler, se glisser; (*plant*) grimper; **~er** *n* plante grimpante; **~y** *a* (*frightening*) qui fait frissonner, donne la chair de poule.

cremate [krı'meit] *vt* incinérer.

crematorium, *pl* **crematoria** [krɛmə-'tɔ:rıəm, -'tɔ:rıə] *n* four *m* crématoire.

crêpe [kreip] *n* crêpe *m*; **~ bandage** *n* (*Brit*) bande *f* Velpeau ®.

crept [krɛpt] *pt*, *pp of* **creep**.

crescent ['krɛsnt] *n* croissant *m*; rue *f* (en arc de cercle).

cress [krɛs] *n* cresson *m*.

crest [krɛst] *n* crête *f*; **~fallen** *a* déconfit(e), découragé(e).

crevice ['krɛvıs] *n* fissure *f*, lézarde *f*, fente *f*.

crew [kru:] *n* équipage *m*; **to have a ~-cut** avoir les cheveux en brosse; **~-neck** *n* col ras.

crib [krıb] *n* lit *m* d'enfant // *vt* (*col*) copier.

crick [krık] *n* crampe *f*.

cricket ['krıkıt] *n* (*insect*) grillon *m*, cri-cri *m inv*; (*game*) cricket *m*.

crime [kraım] *n* crime *m*; **criminal** ['krımınl] *a*, *n* criminel(le).

crimson ['krımzn] *a* cramoisi(e).

cringe [krındʒ] *vi* avoir un mouvement de recul; (*fig*) s'humilier, ramper.

crinkle ['krıŋkl] *vt* froisser, chiffonner.

cripple ['krıpl] *n* boiteux/euse, infirme *m/f* // *vt* estropier, paralyser.

crisis, *pl* **crises** ['kraısıs, -si:z] *n* crise *f*.

crisp [krısp] *a* croquant(e); (*fig*) vif(vive); brusque; **~s** *npl* (*Brit*) (pommes) chips *fpl*.

criss-cross ['krıskrɔs] *a* entrecroisé(e).

criterion, *pl* **criteria** [kraı'tıərıən, -'tıərıə] *n* critère *m*.

critic ['krıtık] *n* critique *m/f*; **~al** *a* critique; **~ally** *ad* (*examine*) d'un œil critique; (*speak etc*) sévèrement; **~ally ill** gravement malade; **~ism** ['krıtısızm] *n* critique *f*; **~ize** ['krıtısaız] *vt* critiquer.

croak [krəuk] *vi* (*frog*) coasser; (*raven*) croasser.
crochet ['krəuʃeɪ] *n* travail *m* au crochet.
crockery ['krɔkərɪ] *n* vaisselle *f*.
crocodile ['krɔkədaɪl] *n* crocodile *m*.
crocus ['krəukəs] *n* crocus *m*.
croft [krɔft] *n* (*Brit*) petite ferme.
crony ['krəunɪ] *n* copain/copine.
crook [kruk] *n* escroc *m*; (*of shepherd*) houlette *f*; **~ed** ['krukɪd] *a* courbé(e), tordu(e); (*action*) malhonnête.
crop [krɔp] *n* (*produce*) culture *f*; (*amount produced*) récolte *f*; (*riding ~*) cravache *f*; **to ~ up** *vi* surgir, se présenter, survenir.
cross [krɔs] *n* croix *f*; (BIOL) croisement *m* // *vt* (*street etc*) traverser; (*arms, legs, BIOL*) croiser; (*cheque*) barrer // a en colère, fâché(e); **to ~ o.s.** se signer, faire le signe de (la) croix; **to ~ out** *vt* barrer, biffer; **to ~ over** *vi* traverser; **~bar** *n* barre transversale; **~country (race)** *n* cross-(country) *m*; **~-examine** *vt* (LAW) faire subir un examen contradictoire à; **~-eyed** *a* qui louche; **~fire** *n* feux croisés; **~ing** *n* croisement *m*, carrefour *m*; (*sea passage*) traversée *f*; (*also:* **pedestrian ~ing**) passage clouté; **~ing guard** *n* (US) contractuel/ *le qui fait traverser la rue aux enfants*; **~ purposes** *npl:* **to be at ~ purposes** ne pas parler de la même chose; **~-reference** *n* renvoi *m*, référence *f*; **~roads** *n* carrefour *m*; **~ section** *n* (BIOL) coupe transversale; (*in population*) échantillon *m*; **~walk** *n* (US) passage clouté; **~wind** *n* vent *m* de travers; **~wise** *ad* en travers; **~word** *n* mots croisés *mpl*.
crotch [krɔtʃ] *n* (*of garment*) entre-jambes *m inv*.
crotchety ['krɔtʃɪtɪ] *a* (*a person*) grognon(ne), grincheux(euse).
crouch [krautʃ] *vi* s'accroupir; se tapir; se ramasser.
crow [krəu] *n* (*bird*) corneille *f*; (*of cock*) chant *m* du coq, cocorico *m* // *vi* (*cock*) chanter; (*fig*) pavoiser, chanter victoire.
crowbar ['krəuba:*] *n* levier *m*.
crowd [kraud] *n* foule *f* // *vt* bourrer, remplir // *vi* affluer, s'attrouper, s'entasser; **~ed** *a* bondé(e), plein(e); **~ed with** plein de.
crown [kraun] *n* couronne *f*; (*of head*) sommet *m* de la tête, calotte crânienne; (*of hat*) fond *m*; (*of hill*) sommet *m* // *vt* couronner; **~ jewels** *npl* joyaux *mpl* de la Couronne; **~ prince** *n* prince héritier.
crow's feet *npl* pattes *fpl* d'oie (*fig*).
crucial ['kru:ʃl] *a* crucial(e), décisif(ive).
crucifixion [kru:sɪ'fɪkʃən] *n* crucifiement *m*, crucifixion *f*.

crude [kru:d] *a* (*materials*) brut(e); non raffiné(e); (*fig: basic*) rudimentaire, sommaire; (: *vulgar*) cru(e), grossier(ère); **~ (oil)** *n* (pétrole) brut *m*.
cruel ['kruəl] *a* cruel(le); **~ty** *n* cruauté *f*.
cruet ['kru:ɪt] *n* huilier *m*; vinaigrier *m*.
cruise [kru:z] *n* croisière *f* // *vi* (*ship*) croiser; (*car*) rouler; (*aircraft*) voler; (*taxi*) être en maraude; **~r** *n* croiseur *m*.
crumb [krʌm] *n* miette *f*.
crumble ['krʌmbl] *vt* émietter // *vi* s'émietter; (*plaster etc*) s'effriter; (*land, earth*) s'ébouler; (*building*) s'écrouler, crouler; (*fig*) s'effondrer; **crumbly** *a* friable.
crumpet ['krʌmpɪt] *n* petite crêpe (épaisse).
crumple ['krʌmpl] *vt* froisser, friper.
crunch [krʌntʃ] *vt* croquer; (*underfoot*) faire craquer, écraser; faire crisser // *n* (*fig*) instant *m* or moment *m* critique, moment de vérité; **~y** *a* croquant(e), croustillant(e).
crusade [kru:'seɪd] *n* croisade *f*.
crush [krʌʃ] *n* foule *f*, cohue *f* // *vt* écraser; (*crumple*) froisser.
crust [krʌst] *n* croûte *f*.
crutch [krʌtʃ] *n* béquille *f*.
crux [krʌks] *n* point crucial.
cry [kraɪ] *vi* pleurer; (*shout: also:* **~ out**) crier // *n* cri *m*; **to ~ off** *vi* se dédire; se décommander.
cryptic ['krɪptɪk] *a* énigmatique.
crystal ['krɪstl] *n* cristal *m*; **~-clear** *a* clair(e) comme de l'eau de roche.
cub [kʌb] *n* petit *m* (*d'un animal*); (*also:* **~ scout**) louveteau *m*.
Cuba ['kju:bə] *n* Cuba *m*.
cubbyhole ['kʌbɪhəul] *n* cagibi *m*.
cube [kju:b] *n* cube *m* // *vt* (MATH) élever au cube; **cubic** *a* cubique; **cubic metre** *etc* mètre *m etc* cube; **cubic capacity** *n* cylindrée *f*.
cubicle ['kju:bɪkl] *n* box *m*, cabine *f*.
cuckoo ['kuku:] *n* coucou *m*; **~ clock** *n* (pendule *f* à) coucou *m*.
cucumber ['kju:kʌmbə*] *n* concombre *m*.
cuddle ['kʌdl] *vt* câliner, caresser // *vi* se blottir l'un contre l'autre.
cue [kju:] *n* (*snooker ~*) queue *f* de billard; (THEATRE etc) signal *m*.
cuff [kʌf] *n* (*Brit: of shirt, coat etc*) poignet *m*, manchette *f*; (*US: of trousers*) revers *m*; **off the ~** *ad* de chic, à l'improviste; **~link** *n* bouton *m* de manchette.
cul-de-sac ['kʌldəsæk] *n* cul-de-sac *m*, impasse *f*.
cull [kʌl] *vt* sélectionner.
culminate ['kʌlmɪneɪt] *vi:* **to ~ in** finir or se terminer par; (*end in*) mener à; **culmination** [-'neɪʃən] *n* point culmi-

nant.

culottes [kju:'lɔts] *npl* jupe-culotte *f*.

culpable ['kʌlpəbl] *a* coupable.

culprit ['kʌlprɪt] *n* coupable *m/f*.

cult [kʌlt] *n* culte *m*.

cultivate ['kʌltɪveɪt] *vt* (*also fig*) cultiver; **cultivation** [-'veɪʃən] *n* culture *f*.

cultural ['kʌltʃərəl] *a* culturel(le).

culture ['kʌltʃə*] *n* (*also fig*) culture *f*; **~d** *a* cultivé(e) (*fig*).

cumbersome ['kʌmbəsəm] *a* encombrant(e), embarrassant(e).

cunning ['kʌnɪŋ] *n* ruse *f*, astuce *f* // *a* rusé(e), malin(igne).

cup [kʌp] *n* tasse *f*; (*prize, event*) coupe *f*; (*of bra*) bonnet *m*.

cupboard ['kʌbəd] *n* placard *m*.

cup-tie ['kʌptaɪ] *n* (*Brit*) match *m* de coupe.

curate ['kjuərɪt] *n* vicaire *m*.

curator [kjuə'reɪtə*] *n* conservateur *m* (*d'un musée etc*).

curb [kə:b] *vt* refréner, mettre un frein à // *n* frein *m* (*fig*); (*US*) = **kerb**.

curdle ['kə:dl] *vi* (se) cailler.

cure [kjuə*] *vt* guérir; (*CULIN*) saler; fumer; sécher // *n* remède *m*.

curfew ['kə:fju:] *n* couvre-feu *m*.

curio ['kjuərɪəu] *n* bibelot *m*, curiosité *f*.

curiosity [kjuərɪ'ɔsɪtɪ] *n* curiosité *f*.

curious ['kjuərɪəs] *a* curieux(euse).

curl [kə:l] *n* boucle *f* (de cheveux) // *vt*, *vi* boucler; (*tightly*) friser; **to ~ up** *vi* s'enrouler; se pelotonner; **~er** *n* bigoudi *m*, rouleau *m*.

curly ['kə:lɪ] *a* bouclé(e); frisé(e).

currant ['kʌrnt] *n* raisin *m* de Corinthe, raisin sec.

currency ['kʌrnsɪ] *n* monnaie *f*; **to gain ~** (*fig*) s'accréditer.

current ['kʌrnt] *n* courant *m* // *a* courant(e); **~ account** *n* (*Brit*) compte courant; **~ affairs** *npl* (questions *fpl* d')actualité *f*; **~ly** *ad* actuellement.

curriculum, *pl* **~s** *or* **curricula** [kə'rɪkjuləm, -lə] *n* programme *m* d'études; **~ vitae (CV)** *n* curriculum vitae (C.V.) *m*.

curry ['kʌrɪ] *n* curry *m* // *vt*: **to ~ favour with** chercher à gagner la faveur *or* à s'attirer les bonnes grâces de.

curse [kə:s] *vi* jurer, blasphémer // *vt* maudire // *n* malédiction *f*; fléau *m*.

cursor ['kə:sə*] *n* (*COMPUT*) curseur *m*.

cursory ['kə:sərɪ] *a* superficiel(le), hâtif(ive).

curt [kə:t] *a* brusque, sec(sèche).

curtail [kə:'teɪl] *vt* (*visit etc*) écourter; (*expenses etc*) réduire.

curtain ['kə:tn] *n* rideau *m*.

curts(e)y ['kə:tsɪ] *n* révérence *f* // *vi* faire une révérence.

curve [kə:v] *n* courbe *f*; (*in the road*) tournant *m*, virage *m* // *vi* se courber; (*road*) faire une courbe.

cushion ['kuʃən] *n* coussin *m* // *vt* (*shock*) amortir.

custard ['kʌstəd] *n* (*for pouring*) crème anglaise.

custodian [kʌs'təudɪən] *n* gardien/ne; (*of collection etc*) conservateur/trice.

custody ['kʌstədɪ] *n* (*of child*) garde *f*; (*for offenders*) détention préventive.

custom ['kʌstəm] *n* coutume *f*, usage *m*; (*LAW*) droit coutumier, coutume; (*COMM*) clientèle *f*; **~ary** *a* habituel(le).

customer ['kʌstəmə*] *n* client/e.

customized ['kʌstəmaɪzd] *a* (*car etc*) construit(e) sur commande.

custom-made ['kʌstəm'meɪd] *a* (*clothes*) fait(e) sur mesure; (*other goods*) hors série, fait(e) sur commande.

customs ['kʌstəmz] *npl* douane *f*; **~ officer** *n* douanier *m*.

cut [kʌt] *vb* (*pt, pp* **cut**) *vt* couper; (*meat*) découper; (*shape, make*) tailler; couper; creuser; graver; (*reduce*) réduire // *vi* couper; (*intersect*) se couper // *n* (*gen*) coupure *f*; (*of clothes*) coupe *f*; (*of jewel*) taille *f*; (*in salary etc*) réduction *f*; (*of meat*) morceau *m*; **to ~ a tooth** percer une dent; **to ~ down** *vt fus* (*tree etc*) couper, abattre; (*reduce: also:* **~ down on**) réduire; **to ~ off** *vt* couper; (*fig*) isoler; **to ~ out** *vt* ôter; découper; tailler; **to ~ up** *vt* (*paper, meat*) découper; **~back** *n* réduction *f*.

cute [kju:t] *a* mignon(ne), adorable; (*clever*) rusé(e), astucieux(euse).

cuticle ['kju:tɪkl] *n* (*on nail*): **~ remover** *n* repousse-peaux *m inv*.

cutlery ['kʌtlərɪ] *n* couverts *mpl*.

cutlet ['kʌtlɪt] *n* côtelette *f*.

cut-: ~out *n* coupe-circuit *m inv*; (*cardboard* **~**) découpage *m*; **~-price,** (*US*) **~-rate** *a* au rabais, à prix réduit; **~ throat** *n* assassin *m* // *a* acharné(e).

cutting ['kʌtɪŋ] *a* tranchant(e), coupant(e); (*fig*) cinglant(e), mordant(e) // *n* (*Brit: from newspaper*) coupure *f* (de journal).

CV *n abbr of* **curriculum vitae**.

cwt *abbr of* **hundredweight(s)**.

cyanide ['saɪənaɪd] *n* cyanure *m*.

cycle ['saɪkl] *n* cycle *m* // *vi* faire de la bicyclette.

cycling ['saɪklɪŋ] *n* cyclisme *m*.

cyclist ['saɪklɪst] *n* cycliste *m/f*.

cygnet ['sɪgnɪt] *n* jeune cygne *m*.

cylinder ['sɪlɪndə*] *n* cylindre *m*; **~-head gasket** *n* joint *m* de culasse.

cymbals ['sɪmblz] *npl* cymbales *fpl*.

cynic ['sɪnɪk] *n* cynique *m/f*; **~al** *a* cynique; **~ism** ['sɪnɪsɪzəm] *n* cynisme *m*.

Cypriot ['sɪprɪət] *a* cypriote, chypriote // *n* Cypriote *m/f*, Chypriote *m/f*.

Cyprus ['saɪprəs] *n* Chypre *f*.

cyst [sɪst] n kyste m.
cystitis [sɪs'taɪtɪs] n cystite f.
czar [zɑ:*] n tsar m.
Czech [tʃɛk] a tchèque // n Tchèque m/f; (LING) tchèque m.
Czechoslovakia [tʃɛkəslə'vækɪə] n Tchécoslovaquie f; **~n** a tchécoslovaque // n Tchécoslovaque m/f.

D

D [di:] n (MUS) ré m.
dab [dæb] vt (eyes, wound) tamponner; (paint, cream) appliquer (par petites touches or rapidement).
dabble ['dæbl] vi: to ~ in faire or se mêler or s'occuper un peu de.
dad, daddy [dæd, 'dædɪ] n papa m.
daffodil ['dæfədɪl] n jonquille f.
daft [dɑ:ft] a idiot(e), stupide.
dagger ['dægə*] n poignard m.
daily ['deɪlɪ] a quotidien(ne), journalier(ère) // n quotidien m // ad tous les jours.
dainty ['deɪntɪ] a délicat(e), mignon(ne).
dairy ['dɛərɪ] n (shop) crémerie f, laiterie f; (on farm) laiterie f // a laitier(ère); ~ **produce** n produits laitiers.
dais ['deɪɪs] n estrade f.
daisy ['deɪzɪ] n pâquerette f; ~ **wheel** n (on printer) marguerite f.
dale [deɪl] n vallon m.
dam [dæm] n barrage m // vt endiguer.
damage ['dæmɪdʒ] n dégâts mpl, dommages mpl; (fig) tort m // vt endommager, abîmer; (fig) faire du tort à; ~s npl (LAW) dommages-intérêts mpl.
damn [dæm] vt condamner; (curse) maudire // n (col): I don't give a ~ je m'en fous // a (col: also: ~ed): this ~ ... ce sacré or foutu ...; ~ (it)! zut!
damp [dæmp] a humide // n humidité f // vt (also: ~en: cloth, rag) humecter; (enthusiasm etc) refroidir.
damson ['dæmzən] n prune f de Damas.
dance [dɑ:ns] n danse f; (ball) bal m // vi danser; ~ **hall** n salle f de bal, dancing m; ~ **r** n danseur/euse.
dancing ['dɑ:nsɪŋ] n danse f.
dandelion ['dændɪlaɪən] n pissenlit m.
dandruff ['dændrəf] n pellicules fpl.
Dane [deɪn] n Danois/e.
danger ['deɪndʒə*] n danger m; there is a ~ **of fire** il y a (un) risque d'incendie; in ~ en danger; he was in ~ **of falling** il risquait de tomber; ~**ous** a dangereux(euse).
dangle ['dæŋgl] vt balancer; (fig) faire miroiter // vi pendre, se balancer.
Danish ['deɪnɪʃ] a danois(e) // n (LING) danois m.
dapper ['dæpə*] a pimpant(e).
dare [dɛə*] vt: to ~ **sb to do** défier qn or mettre qn au défi de faire // vi: to ~ (to) **do sth** oser faire qch; I ~ **say** (I suppose) il est probable (que); ~**devil** n casse-cou m inv; **daring** a hardi(e), audacieux(euse) // n audace f, hardiesse f.
dark [dɑ:k] a (night, room) obscur(e), sombre; (colour, complexion) foncé(e), sombre; (fig) sombre // n: in the ~ dans le noir; in the ~ **about** (fig) ignorant tout de; **after** ~ après la tombée de la nuit; ~**en** vt obscurcir, assombrir // vi s'obscurcir, s'assombrir; ~ **glasses** npl lunettes noires; ~**ness** n obscurité f; ~ **room** n chambre noire.
darling ['dɑ:lɪŋ] a, n chéri(e).
darn [dɑ:n] vt repriser.
dart [dɑ:t] n fléchette f // vi: to ~ **towards** se précipiter or s'élancer vers; to ~ **away/along** partir/passer comme une flèche; ~**s** n jeu m de fléchettes; ~**board** n cible f (de jeu de fléchettes).
dash [dæʃ] n (sign) tiret m; (small quantity) goutte f, larme f // vt (missile) jeter or lancer violemment; (hopes) anéantir // vi: to ~ **towards** se précipiter or se ruer vers; to ~ **away** or **off** vi partir à toute allure.
dashboard ['dæʃbɔ:d] n (AUT) tableau m de bord.
dashing ['dæʃɪŋ] a fringant(e).
data ['deɪtə] npl données fpl; ~**base** n base f de données; ~ **processing** n traitement m (électronique) de l'information.
date [deɪt] n date f; rendez-vous m; (fruit) datte f // vt dater; ~ **of birth** date de naissance; to ~ ad à ce jour; out of ~ périmé(e); up to ~ à la page; mis(e) à jour; moderne; ~**d** a démodé(e).
daub [dɔ:b] vt barbouiller.
daughter ['dɔ:tə*] n fille f; ~**-in-law** n belle-fille f, bru f.
daunting ['dɔ:ntɪŋ] a intimidant(e), décourageant(e).
dawdle ['dɔ:dl] vi traîner, lambiner.
dawn [dɔ:n] n aube f, aurore f // vi (day) se lever, poindre; (fig) naître, se faire jour; it ~**ed on him that** ... il lui vint à l'esprit que ...
day [deɪ] n jour m; (as duration) journée f; (period of time, age) époque f, temps m; the ~ **before** la veille, le jour précédent; the ~ **after, the following** ~ le lendemain, le jour suivant; the ~ **after tomorrow** après-demain; the ~ **before yesterday** avant-hier; by ~ de jour; ~**break** n point m du jour; ~**dream** vi rêver (tout éveillé); ~**light** n (lumière f du) jour m; ~ **return** n (Brit) billet m d'aller-retour (valable pour la journée); ~**time** n jour m, journée f; ~**-to-~** a journalier(ère).
daze [deɪz] vt (subj: drug) hébéter; (: blow) étourdir // n: in a ~ hébété(e);

étourdi(e).

dazzle ['dæzl] *vt* éblouir, aveugler.

DC *abbr* (= *direct current*) courant continu.

deacon ['di:kən] *n* diacre *m*.

dead [dɛd] *a* mort(e); (*numb*) engourdi(e), insensible // *ad* absolument, complètement; **he was shot** ~ il a été tué d'un coup de revolver; ~ **on time** à l'heure pile; ~ **tired** éreinté(e), complètement fourbu(e); **to stop** ~ s'arrêter pile *or* net; **the** ~ les morts; **~en** *vt* (*blow, sound*) amortir; (*make numb*) endormir, rendre insensible; ~ **end** *n* impasse *f*; ~ **heat** *n* (*SPORT*): **to finish in a** ~ **heat** terminer ex-aequo; **~line** *n* date *f or* heure *f* limite; **~lock** *n* impasse *f* (*fig*); ~ **loss** *n*: **to be a** ~ **loss** (*col: person*) n'être bon(bonne) à rien; (*thing*) ne rien valoir; **~ly** *a* mortel(le); (*weapon*) meurtrier(ère); **~pan** *a* impassible.

deaf [dɛf] *a* sourd(e); **~en** *vt* rendre sourd; (*fig*) assourdir; **~ness** *n* surdité *f*; **~-mute** *n* sourd/e-muet/te.

deal [di:l] *n* affaire *f*, marché *m* // *vt* (*pt, pp* **dealt** [dɛlt]) (*blow*) porter; (*cards*) donner, distribuer; **a great** ~ (**of**) beaucoup (de); **to** ~ **in** *vt fus* faire le commerce de; **to** ~ **with** *vt fus* (*COMM*) traiter avec; (*handle*) s'occuper *or* se charger de; (*be about: book etc*) traiter de; **~er** *n* marchand *m*; **~ings** *npl* (*COMM*) transactions *fpl*; (*relations*) relations *fpl*, rapports *mpl*.

dean [di:n] *n* (*REL, Brit SCOL*) doyen *m*; (*US SCOL*) conseiller/ère (principal(e)) d'éducation.

dear [dɪə*] *a* cher(chère); (*expensive*) cher, coûteux(euse) // *n*: **my** ~ mon cher/ma chère; ~ **me!** mon Dieu!; **D~ Sir/Madam** (*in letter*) Monsieur/Madame; **~ly** *ad* (*love*) tendrement; (*pay*) cher.

death [dɛθ] *n* mort *f*; (*ADMIN*) décès *m*; ~ **certificate** *n* acte *m* de décès; ~ **duties** *npl* (*Brit*) droits *mpl* de succession; **~ly** *a* de mort; ~ **penalty** *n* peine *f* de mort; ~ **rate** *n* (taux *m* de) mortalité *f*.

debar [dɪ'ba:*] *vt*: **to** ~ **sb from doing** interdire à qn de faire.

debase [dɪ'beɪs] *vt* (*currency*) déprécier, dévaloriser; (*person*) abaisser, avilir.

debate [dɪ'beɪt] *n* discussion *f*, débat *m* // *vt* discuter, débattre.

debit ['dɛbɪt] *n* débit *m* // *vt*: **to** ~ **a sum to sb** *or* **to sb's account** porter une somme au débit de qn, débiter qn d'une somme.

debt [dɛt] *n* dette *f*; **to be in** ~ avoir des dettes, être endetté(e); **~or** *n* débiteur/trice.

debunk [dɪ'bʌŋk] *vt* (*theory, claim*)

montrer le ridicule de.

decade ['dɛkeɪd] *n* décennie *f*, décade *f*.

decadence ['dɛkədəns] *n* décadence *f*.

decaffeinated [dɪ'kæfɪneɪtɪd] *a* décaféiné(e).

decanter [dɪ'kæntə*] *n* carafe *f*.

decay [dɪ'keɪ] *n* décomposition *f*, pourrissement *m*; (*fig*) déclin *m*, délabrement *m*; (*also:* **tooth** ~) carie *f* (dentaire) // *vi* (*rot*) se décomposer, pourrir; (*fig*) se délabrer; décliner; se détériorer.

deceased [dɪ'si:st] *n* défunt/e.

deceit [dɪ'si:t] *n* tromperie *f*, supercherie *f*; **~ful** *a* trompeur(euse).

deceive [dɪ'si:v] *vt* tromper.

December [dɪ'sɛmbə*] *n* décembre *m*.

decent ['di:sənt] *a* décent(e), convenable; **they were very** ~ **about it** ils se sont montrés très chics.

deception [dɪ'sɛpʃən] *n* tromperie *f*.

deceptive [dɪ'sɛptɪv] *a* trompeur(euse).

decide [dɪ'saɪd] *vt* (*person*) décider; (*question, argument*) trancher, régler // *vi* se décider, décider; **to** ~ **to do/that** décider de faire/que; **to** ~ **on** décider, se décider pour; **~d** *a* (*resolute*) résolu(e), décidé(e); (*clear, definite*) net(te), marqué(e); **~dly** [-dɪdlɪ] *ad* résolument; incontestablement, nettement.

deciduous [dɪ'sɪdjuəs] *a* à feuilles caduques.

decimal ['dɛsɪməl] *a* décimal(e) // *n* décimale *f*; ~ **point** *n* ≈ virgule *f*.

decipher [dɪ'saɪfə*] *vt* déchiffrer.

decision [dɪ'sɪʒən] *n* décision *f*.

decisive [dɪ'saɪsɪv] *a* décisif(ive).

deck [dɛk] *n* (*NAUT*) pont *m*; (*of bus*): **top** ~ impériale *f*; (*of cards*) jeu *m*; **~chair** *n* chaise longue.

declaration [dɛklə'reɪʃən] *n* déclaration *f*.

declare [dɪ'klɛə*] *vt* déclarer.

decline [dɪ'klaɪn] *n* (*decay*) déclin *m*; (*lessening*) baisse *f* // *vt* refuser, décliner // *vi* décliner; être en baisse, baisser.

decorate ['dɛkəreɪt] *vt* (*adorn, give a medal to*) décorer; (*paint and paper*) peindre et tapisser; **decoration** [-'reɪʃən] *n* (*medal etc, adornment*) décoration *f*; **decorator** *n* peintre *m* en bâtiment.

decoy ['di:kɔɪ] *n* piège *m*.

decrease *n* ['di:kri:s] diminution *f* // *vt*, *vi* [di:'kri:s] diminuer.

decree [dɪ'kri:] *n* (*POL, REL*) décret *m*; (*LAW*) arrêt *m*, jugement *m*; ~ **nisi** *n* jugement *m* provisoire de divorce.

dedicate ['dɛdɪkeɪt] *vt* consacrer; (*book etc*) dédier.

dedication [dɛdɪ'keɪʃən] *n* (*devotion*) dévouement *m*.

deduce [dɪ'dju:s] *vt* déduire, conclure.

deduct [dɪ'dʌkt] *vt*: **to** ~ **sth (from)**

déduire qch (de), retrancher qch (de); *(from wage etc)* prélever qch (sur), retenir qch (sur); **~ion** [dɪ'dʌkʃən] *n (deducting, deducing)* déduction *f; (from wage etc)* prélèvement *m*, retenue *f*.
deed [di:d] *n* action *f*, acte *m; (LAW)* acte notarié, contrat *m*.
deep [di:p] *a (water, sigh, sorrow, thoughts)* profond(e); *(voice)* grave; **4 metres ~** de 4 mètres de profondeur *// ad*: **spectators stood 20 ~** il y avait 20 rangs de spectateurs; **~en** *vt (hole)* approfondir *// vi* s'approfondir; *(darkness)* s'épaissir; **~-freeze** *n* congélateur *m // vt* surgeler; **~-fry** *vt* faire frire (en friteuse); **~ly** *ad (breathe)* profondément; *(interested, moved)* vivement; *(grateful)* profondément, infiniment; **~-sea diving** *n* plongée sous-marine.
deer [dɪə*] *n (pl inv)*: **the ~** les cervidés *mpl (ZOOL)*; **(red) ~** cerf *m;* **(fallow) ~** daim *m;* **(roe) ~** chevreuil *m.*
deface [dɪ'feɪs] *vt* dégrader; barbouiller; rendre illisible.
default [dɪ'fɔ:lt] *vi (LAW)* faire défaut; *(gen)* manquer à ses engagements *// n (COMPUT: also: ~ value)* valeur *f* par défaut; **by ~** *(LAW)* par défaut, par contumace; *(SPORT)* par forfait.
defeat [dɪ'fi:t] *n* défaite *f // vt (team, opponents)* battre; *(fig: plans, efforts)* faire échouer.
defect *n* ['di:fɛkt] défaut *m // vi* [dɪ'fɛkt]: **to ~ to the enemy** passer à l'ennemi; **~ive** [dɪ'fɛktɪv] *a* défectueux(euse).
defence [dɪ'fɛns] *n* défense *f;* **in ~ of** pour défendre; **~less** *a* sans défense.
defend [dɪ'fɛnd] *vt* défendre; **~ant** *n* défendeur/deresse; *(in criminal case)* accusé/e, prévenu/e; **~er** *n* défenseur *m.*
defense [dɪ'fɛns] *n (US) =* **defence**.
defer [dɪ'fə:*] *vt (postpone)* différer, ajourner *// vi*: **to ~ to** déférer à, s'en remettre à.
defiance [dɪ'faɪəns] *n* défi *m;* **in ~ of** au mépris de.
defiant [dɪ'faɪənt] *a* provocant(e), de défi; *(person)* rebelle, intraitable.
deficiency [dɪ'fɪʃənsɪ] *n* insuffisance *f,* déficience *f;* carence *f.*
deficit ['defɪsɪt] *n* déficit *m.*
defile *vb* [dɪ'faɪl] *vt* souiller *// vi* défiler *// n* ['di:faɪl] défilé *m.*
define [dɪ'faɪn] *vt* définir.
definite ['defɪnɪt] *a (fixed)* défini(e), (bien) déterminé(e); *(clear, obvious)* net(te), manifeste; **he was ~ about it** il a été catégorique; il était sûr de son fait; **~ly** *ad* sans aucun doute.
definition [defɪ'nɪʃən] *n* définition *f.*
deflate [di:'fleɪt] *vt* dégonfler.
deflect [dɪ'flɛkt] *vt* détourner, faire dévier.
deformed [dɪ'fɔ:md] *a* difforme.

defraud [dɪ'frɔ:d] *vt* frauder; **to ~ sb of sth** escroquer qch à qn.
defrost [di:'frɒst] *vt (fridge)* dégivrer; **~er** *n (US: demister)* dispositif *m* antibuée *inv.*
deft [dɛft] *a* adroit(e), preste.
defunct [dɪ'fʌŋkt] *a* défunt(e).
defuse [di:'fju:z] *vt* désamorcer.
defy [dɪ'faɪ] *vt* défier; *(efforts etc)* résister à.
degenerate *vi* [dɪ'dʒɛnəreɪt] dégénérer *// a* [dɪ'dʒɛnərɪt] dégénéré(e).
degree [dɪ'gri:] *n* degré *m;* grade *m (universitaire);* **a (first) ~ in maths** une licence en maths; **by ~s** *(gradually)* par degrés; **to some ~** jusqu'à un certain point, dans une certaine mesure.
dehydrated [di:haɪ'dreɪtɪd] *a* déshydraté(e); *(milk, eggs)* en poudre.
de-ice [di:'aɪs] *vt (windscreen)* dégivrer.
deign [deɪn] *vi*: **to ~ to do** daigner faire.
deity ['di:ɪtɪ] *n* divinité *f;* dieu *m,* déesse *f.*
dejected [dɪ'dʒɛktɪd] *a* abattu(e), déprimé(e).
delay [dɪ'leɪ] *vt* retarder *// vi* s'attarder *// n* délai *m,* retard *m.*
delectable [dɪ'lɛktəbl] *a* délicieux(euse).
delegate *n* ['dɛlɪgɪt] délégué/e *// vt* ['dɛlɪgeɪt] déléguer.
delete [dɪ'li:t] *vt* rayer, supprimer.
deliberate *a* [dɪ'lɪbərɪt] *(intentional)* délibéré(e); *(slow)* mesuré(e) *// vi* [dɪ'lɪbəreɪt] délibérer, réfléchir; **~ly** *ad (on purpose)* exprès, délibérément.
delicacy ['dɛlɪkəsɪ] *n* délicatesse *f; (food)* mets fin *or* délicat, friandise *f.*
delicate ['dɛlɪkɪt] *a* délicat(e).
delicatessen [dɛlɪkə'tɛsn] *n* épicerie fine.
delicious [dɪ'lɪʃəs] *a* délicieux(euse).
delight [dɪ'laɪt] *n* (grande) joie, grand plaisir *// vt* enchanter; **~ed** *a*: **~ed (at or with/to do)** ravi(e) (de/de faire); **~ful** *a* adorable; merveilleux(euse); délicieux(euse).
delinquent [dɪ'lɪŋkwənt] *a, n* délinquant(e).
delirious [dɪ'lɪrɪəs] *a*: **to be ~** délirer.
deliver [dɪ'lɪvə*] *vt (mail)* distribuer; *(goods)* livrer; *(message)* remettre; *(speech)* prononcer; *(warning, ultimatum)* lancer; *(free)* délivrer; *(MED)* accoucher; **~y** *n* distribution *f;* livraison *f; (of speaker)* élocution *f; (MED)* accouchement *m.*
delude [dɪ'lu:d] *vt* tromper, leurrer.
delusion [dɪ'lu:ʒən] *n* illusion *f.*
delve [dɛlv] *vi*: **to ~ into** fouiller dans.
demand [dɪ'mɑ:nd] *vt* réclamer, exiger *// n* exigence *f; (claim)* revendication *f; (ECON)* demande *f;* **in ~** demandé(e), recherché(e); **on ~** sur demande; **~ing** *a (boss)* exigeant(e); *(work)* astrei-

gnant(e).

demean [dɪ'miːn] *vt*: **to ~ o.s.** s'abaisser.

demeanour, (*US*) **demeanor** [dɪ'miːnə•] *n* comportement *m*; maintien *m*.

demented [dɪ'mentɪd] *a* dément(e), fou(folle).

demise [dɪ'maɪz] *n* décès *m*.

demister [diː'mɪstə•] *n* (*AUT*) dispositif *m* anti-buée *inv*.

demo ['deməu] *n abbr* (col: = *demonstration*) manif *f*.

democracy [dɪ'mɔkrəsɪ] *n* démocratie *f*.

democrat ['deməkræt] *n* démocrate *m/f*; **~ic** [demə'krætɪk] *a* démocratique.

demolish [dɪ'mɔlɪʃ] *vt* démolir.

demonstrate ['demənstreɪt] *vt* démontrer, prouver // *vi*: **to ~ (for/against)** manifester (en faveur de/contre); **demonstration** [-'streɪʃən] *n* démonstration *f*, manifestation *f*; **demonstrator** *n* (*POL*) manifestant/e.

demote [dɪ'məut] *vt* rétrograder.

demure [dɪ'mjuə•] *a* sage, réservé(e); d'une modestie affectée.

den [den] *n* tanière *f*, antre *m*.

denatured alcohol [diː'neɪtʃəd-] *n* (*US*) alcool *m* à brûler.

denial [dɪ'naɪəl] *n* démenti *m*; dénégation *f*.

denim ['denɪm] *n* coton émerisé; **~s** *npl* (blue-)jeans *mpl*.

Denmark ['denmɑːk] *n* Danemark *m*.

denomination [dɪnɔmɪ'neɪʃən] *n* (*money*) valeur *f*; (*REL*) confession *f*; culte *m*.

denounce [dɪ'nauns] *vt* dénoncer.

dense [dens] *a* dense; (*stupid*) obtus(e), dur(e) *or* lent(e) à la comprenette.

density ['densɪtɪ] *n* densité *f*.

dent [dent] *n* bosse *f* // *vt* (*also*: **make a ~ in**) cabosser.

dental ['dentl] *a* dentaire; **~ surgeon** *n* (chirurgien/ne) dentiste.

dentist ['dentɪst] *n* dentiste *m/f*; **~ry** *n* art *m* dentaire.

denture(s) ['dentʃə(z)] *n(pl)* dentier *m*.

deny [dɪ'naɪ] *vt* nier; (*refuse*) refuser.

deodorant [diː'əudərənt] *n* désodorisant *m*, déodorant *m*.

depart [dɪ'pɑːt] *vi* partir; **to ~ from** (*fig: differ from*) s'écarter de.

department [dɪ'pɑːtmənt] *n* (*COMM*) rayon *m*; (*SCOL*) section *f*; (*POL*) ministère *m*, département *m*; **~ store** *n* grand magasin.

departure [dɪ'pɑːtʃə•] *n* départ *m*; (*fig*): **~ from** écart *m* par rapport à; **a new ~** une nouvelle voie; **~ lounge** *n* (*at airport*) salle *f* de départ.

depend [dɪ'pend] *vi*: **to ~ on** dépendre de; (*rely on*) compter sur; **it ~s** cela dépend; **~ing on the result ...** selon le résultat ...; **~able** *a* sûr(e), digne de confiance; **~ant** *n* personne *f* à charge;

~ent *a*: **to be ~ent (on)** dépendre (de) // *n* = **~ant**.

depict [dɪ'pɪkt] *vt* (*in picture*) représenter; (*in words*) (dé)peindre, décrire.

depleted [dɪ'pliːtɪd] *a* (considérablement) réduit(e) *or* diminué(e).

deploy [dɪ'plɔɪ] *vt* déployer.

deport [dɪ'pɔːt] *vt* déporter; expulser.

deportment [dɪ'pɔːtmənt] *n* maintien *m*, tenue *f*.

deposit [dɪ'pɔzɪt] *n* (*CHEM*, *COMM*, *GEO*) dépôt *m*; (*of ore, oil*) gisement *m*; (*part payment*) arrhes *fpl*, acompte *m*; (*on bottle etc*) consigne *f*; (*for hired goods etc*) cautionnement *m*, garantie *f* // *vt* déposer; mettre *or* laisser en dépôt; fournir *or* donner en acompte; laisser en garantie; **~ account** *n* compte *m* de dépôt.

depot ['depəu] *n* dépôt *m*.

depress [dɪ'pres] *vt* déprimer; (*press down*) appuyer sur, abaisser; **~ed** *a* (*person*) déprimé(e), abattu(e); (*area*) en déclin, touché(e) par le sous-emploi; **~ing** *a* déprimant(e); **~ion** [dɪ'preʃən] *n* dépression *f*.

deprivation [deprɪ'veɪʃən] *n* privation *f*; (*loss*) perte *f*.

deprive [dɪ'praɪv] *vt*: **to ~ sb of** priver qn de; enlever à qn; **~d** *a* déshérité(e).

depth [depθ] *n* profondeur *f*; **in the ~s of** au fond de; au cœur de; au plus profond de.

deputize ['depjutaɪz] *vi*: **to ~ for** assurer l'intérim de.

deputy ['depjutɪ] *a*: **~ head** directeur adjoint, sous-directeur *m* // *n* (*replacement*) suppléant/e, intérimaire *m/f*; (*second in command*) adjoint/e.

derail [dɪ'reɪl] *vt*: **to be ~ed** dérailler.

derby ['dɑːbɪ] *n* (*US: bowler hat*) (chapeau *m*) melon *m*.

derelict ['derɪlɪkt] *a* abandonné(e), à l'abandon.

deride [dɪ'raɪd] *vt* railler.

derisory [dɪ'raɪsərɪ] *a* (*sum*) dérisoire; (*smile, person*) moqueur(euse).

derive [dɪ'raɪv] *vt*: **to ~ sth from** tirer qch de; trouver qch dans // *vi*: **to ~ from** provenir de, dériver de.

derogatory [dɪ'rɔgətərɪ] *a* désobligeant(e); péjoratif(ive).

derv [dəːv] *n* (*Brit*) gas-oil *m*.

descend [dɪ'send] *vt*, *vi* descendre; **to ~ from** descendre de, être issu de.

descent [dɪ'sent] *n* descente *f*; (*origin*) origine *f*.

describe [dɪs'kraɪb] *vt* décrire; **description** [-'krɪpʃən] *n* description *f*; (*sort*) sorte *f*, espèce *f*.

desecrate ['desɪkreɪt] *vt* profaner.

desert *n* ['dezət] désert *m* // *vb* [dɪ'zəːt] *vt* déserter, abandonner // *vi* (*MIL*) déserter; **~er** *n* déserteur *m*; **~ island** *n* île déserte; **~s** *npl*: **to get one's just ~s**

n'avoir que ce qu'on mérite.
deserve [dɪ'zəːv] vt mériter; **deserving** a (person) méritant(e); (action, cause) méritoire.

design [dɪ'zaɪn] n (sketch) plan m, dessin m; (layout, shape) conception f, ligne f; (pattern) dessin m, motif(s) m(pl); (COMM) esthétique industrielle; (intention) dessein m // vt dessiner; concevoir; **to have ~s on** avoir des visées sur.

designer [dɪ'zaɪnə*] n (ART, TECH) dessinateur/trice; (fashion) modéliste m/f.

desire [dɪ'zaɪə*] n désir m // vt désirer, vouloir.

desk [dɛsk] n (in office) bureau m; (for pupil) pupitre m; (Brit: in shop, restaurant) caisse f; (in hotel, at airport) réception f.

desolate ['dɛsəlɪt] a désolé(e).

despair [dɪs'pɛə*] n désespoir m // vi: to ~ of désespérer de.

despatch [dɪs'pætʃ] n, vt = **dispatch**.

desperate ['dɛspərɪt] a désespéré(e); (fugitive) prêt(e) à tout; **~ly** ad désespérément; (very) terriblement, extrêmement.

desperation [dɛspə'reɪʃən] n désespoir m; **in ~** à bout de nerf; en désespoir de cause.

despicable [dɪs'pɪkəbl] a méprisable.

despise [dɪs'paɪz] vt mépriser, dédaigner.

despite [dɪs'paɪt] prep malgré, en dépit de.

despondent [dɪs'pɔndənt] a découragé(e), abattu(e).

dessert [dɪ'zəːt] n dessert m; **~spoon** n cuiller f à dessert.

destination [dɛstɪ'neɪʃən] n destination f.

destiny ['dɛstɪnɪ] n destinée f, destin m.

destitute ['dɛstɪtjuːt] a indigent(e).

destroy [dɪs'trɔɪ] vt détruire; **~er** n (NAUT) contre-torpilleur m.

destruction [dɪs'trʌkʃən] n destruction f.

detach [dɪ'tætʃ] vt détacher; **~ed** a (attitude) détaché(e); **~ed house** n pavillon m, maison(nette) (individuelle); **~ment** n (MIL) détachement m; (fig) détachement, indifférence f.

detail ['diːteɪl] n détail m // vt raconter en détail, énumérer; **in ~** en détail; **~ed** a détaillé(e).

detain [dɪ'teɪn] vt retenir; (in captivity) détenir; (in hospital) hospitaliser.

detect [dɪ'tɛkt] vt déceler, percevoir; (MED, POLICE) dépister; (MIL, RADAR, TECH) détecter; **~ion** [dɪ'tɛkʃən] n découverte f; dépistage m; détection f; **~ive** n agent m de la sûreté, policier m; private **~ive** détective privé; **~ive story** n roman policier.

detention [dɪ'tɛnʃən] n détention f; (SCOL) retenue f, consigne f.

deter [dɪ'təː*] vt dissuader.

detergent [dɪ'təːdʒənt] n détersif m, détergent m.

deteriorate [dɪ'tɪərɪəreɪt] vi se détériorer, se dégrader.

determine [dɪ'təːmɪn] vt déterminer; **to ~ to do** résoudre de faire, se déterminer à faire; **~d** a (person) déterminé(e).

deterrent [dɪ'tɛrənt] n effet m de dissuasion; force f de dissuasion.

detour ['diːtuə*] n détour m; (US AUT: diversion) déviation f.

detract [dɪ'trækt] vt: to ~ from (quality, pleasure) diminuer; (reputation) porter atteinte à.

detriment ['dɛtrɪmənt] n: to the ~ of au détriment de, au préjudice de; **~al** [dɛtrɪ'mɛntl] a: **~al to** préjudiciable or nuisible à.

devaluation [dɪvælju'eɪʃən] n dévaluation f.

devastating ['dɛvəsteɪtɪŋ] a dévastateur(trice).

develop [dɪ'vɛləp] vt (gen) développer; (habit) contracter; (resources) mettre en valeur, exploiter // vi se développer; (situation, disease: evolve) évoluer; (facts, symptoms: appear) se manifester, se produire; **~ing country** pays m en voie de développement; **~ment** n développement m; (of affair, case) rebondissement m, fait(s) nouveau(x).

device [dɪ'vaɪs] n (apparatus) engin m, dispositif m.

devil ['dɛvl] n diable m; démon m.

devious ['diːvɪəs] a (means) détourné(e); (person) sournois(e), dissimulé(e).

devise [dɪ'vaɪz] vt imaginer, concevoir.

devoid [dɪ'vɔɪd] a: ~ of dépourvu(e) de, dénué(e) de.

devolution [diːvə'luːʃən] n (POL) décentralisation f.

devote [dɪ'vəut] vt: to ~ sth to consacrer qch à; **~d** a dévoué(e); **to be ~d to** (book etc) être consacré(e) à; **~e** [dɛvəu'tiː] n (REL) adepte m/f; (MUS, SPORT) fervent/e.

devotion [dɪ'vəuʃən] n dévouement m, attachement m; (REL) dévotion f, piété f.

devour [dɪ'vauə*] vt dévorer.

devout [dɪ'vaut] a pieux(euse), dévot(e).

dew [djuː] n rosée f.

DHSS n abbr (Brit: = Department of Health and Social Security) ≈ ministère de la Santé et de la Sécurité Sociale.

diabetes [daɪə'biːtiːz] n diabète m; **diabetic** [-'bɛtɪk] a, n diabétique (m/f).

diabolical [daɪə'bɔlɪkl] a (col: weather) atroce; (: behaviour) infernal(e).

diagnosis, pl **diagnoses** [daɪəg'nəusɪs, -siːz] n diagnostic m.

diagonal [daɪˈægənl] *a* diagonal(e) // *n* diagonale *f*.

diagram [ˈdaɪəgræm] *n* diagramme *m*, schéma *m*; graphique *m*.

dial [ˈdaɪəl] *n* cadran *m* // *vt* (*number*) faire, composer.

dialect [ˈdaɪəlekt] *n* dialecte *m*.

dialling: ~ **code**, (*US*) **dial code** *n* indicatif *m* (téléphonique); ~ **tone**, (*US*) **dial tone** *n* tonalité *f*.

dialogue [ˈdaɪəlɔg] *n* dialogue *m*.

diameter [daɪˈæmɪtə*] *n* diamètre *m*.

diamond [ˈdaɪəmənd] *n* diamant *m*; (*shape*) losange *m*; ~**s** *npl* (*CARDS*) carreau *m*.

diaper [ˈdaɪəpə*] *n* (*US*) couche *f*.

diaphragm [ˈdaɪəfræm] *n* diaphragme *m*.

diarrhoea, (*US*) **diarrhea** [daɪəˈriːə] *n* diarrhée *f*.

diary [ˈdaɪərɪ] *n* (*daily account*) journal *m*; (*book*) agenda *m*.

dice [daɪs] *n* (*pl inv*) dé *m* // *vt* (*CULIN*) couper en dés or en cubes.

dictate *vt* [dɪkˈteɪt] dicter // *n* [ˈdɪkteɪt] injonction *f*.

dictation [dɪkˈteɪʃən] *n* dictée *f*.

dictator [dɪkˈteɪtə*] *n* dictateur *m*; ~**ship** *n* dictature *f*.

dictionary [ˈdɪkʃənrɪ] *n* dictionnaire *m*.

did [dɪd] *pt of* **do**.

didn't = **did not**.

die [daɪ] *vi* mourir; **to be dying for sth** avoir une envie folle de qch; **to be dying to do sth** mourir d'envie de faire qch; **to ~ away** *vi* s'éteindre; **to ~ down** *vi* se calmer, s'apaiser; **to ~ out** *vi* disparaître, s'éteindre.

diehard [ˈdaɪhɑːd] *n* réactionnaire *m/f*, jusqu'au-boutiste *m/f*.

Diesel [ˈdiːzəl]: ~ **engine** *n* moteur *m* diesel; ~ (**oil**) *n* carburant *m* diesel.

diet [ˈdaɪət] *n* alimentation *f*; (*restricted food*) régime *m* // *vi* (*also*: **be on a ~**) suivre un régime.

differ [ˈdɪfə*] *vi*: **to ~ from sth** être différent de; **différer** de; **to ~ from sb over sth** ne pas être d'accord avec qn au sujet de qch; ~**ence** *n* différence *f*; (*quarrel*) différend *m*, désaccord *m*; ~**ent** *a* différent(e); ~**entiate** [-ˈrenʃɪeɪt] *vi* se différencier; **to ~entiate between** faire une différence entre.

difficult [ˈdɪfɪkəlt] *a* difficile; ~**y** *n* difficulté *f*.

diffident [ˈdɪfɪdənt] *a* qui manque de confiance or d'assurance.

dig [dɪg] *vt* (*pt, pp* **dug**) (*hole*) creuser; (*garden*) bêcher // *n* (*prod*) coup *m* de coude; (*fig*) coup de griffe or de patte; **to ~ in** *vi* (*MIL: also*: ~ **o.s. in**) se retrancher; (*col: eat*) attaquer (un repas *etc*); **to ~ into** (*snow, soil*) creuser; **to ~ one's nails into** enfoncer ses ongles dans; **to ~ up** *vt* déterrer.

digest *vt* [daɪˈdʒest] digérer // *n* [ˈdaɪdʒest] sommaire *m*, résumé *m*; ~**ion** [dɪˈdʒestʃən] *n* digestion *f*.

digit [ˈdɪdʒɪt] *n* chiffre *m* (*de 0 à 9*); (*finger*) doigt *m*; ~**al** *a* digital(e); à affichage numérique or digital.

dignified [ˈdɪgnɪfaɪd] *a* digne.

dignity [ˈdɪgnɪtɪ] *n* dignité *f*.

digress [daɪˈgres] *vi*: **to ~ from** s'écarter de, s'éloigner de.

digs [dɪgz] *npl* (*Brit col*) piaule *f*, chambre meublée.

dilapidated [dɪˈlæpɪdeɪtɪd] *a* délabré(e).

dilemma [daɪˈlemə] *n* dilemme *m*.

diligent [ˈdɪlɪdʒənt] *a* appliqué(e), assidu(e).

dilute [daɪˈluːt] *vt* diluer.

dim [dɪm] *a* (*light, eyesight*) faible; (*memory, outline*) vague, indécis(e); (*stupid*) borné(e), obtus(e) // *vt* (*light*) réduire, baisser.

dime [daɪm] *n* (*US*) = 10 cents.

dimension [daɪˈmenʃən] *n* dimension *f*.

diminish [dɪˈmɪnɪʃ] *vt*, *vi* diminuer.

diminutive [dɪˈmɪnjutɪv] *a* minuscule, tout(e) petit(e).

dimmers [ˈdɪməz] *npl* (*US AUT*) phares *mpl* code *inv*; feux *mpl* de position.

dimple [ˈdɪmpl] *n* fossette *f*.

din [dɪn] *n* vacarme *m*.

dine [daɪn] *vi* dîner; ~**r** *n* (*person*) dîneur/euse; (*RAIL*) = **dining car**.

dinghy [ˈdɪŋgɪ] *n* youyou *m*; (*also*: **rubber ~**) canot *m* pneumatique; (*also*: **sailing ~**) voilier *m*, dériveur *m*.

dingy [ˈdɪndʒɪ] *a* miteux(euse), minable.

dining [ˈdaɪnɪŋ] *cpd*: ~ **car** *n* (*Brit*) wagon-restaurant *m*; ~ **room** *n* salle *f* à manger.

dinner [ˈdɪnə*] *n* dîner *m*; (*public*) banquet *m*; ~**'s ready!** à table!; ~ **jacket** *n* smoking *m*; ~ **party** *n* dîner *m*; ~ **time** *n* heure *f* du dîner.

dint [dɪnt] *n*: **by ~ of (doing)** à force de (faire).

dip [dɪp] *n* déclivité *f*; (*in sea*) baignade *f*, bain *m* // *vt* tremper, plonger; (*Brit AUT: lights*) mettre en code, baisser // *vi* plonger.

diploma [dɪˈpləumə] *n* diplôme *m*.

diplomacy [dɪˈpləuməsɪ] *n* diplomatie *f*.

diplomat [ˈdɪpləmæt] *n* diplomate *m*; ~**ic** [dɪpləˈmætɪk] *a* diplomatique.

dipstick [ˈdɪpstɪk] *n* (*AUT*) jauge *f* de niveau d'huile.

dire [daɪə*] *a* terrible, extrême, affreux(euse).

direct [daɪˈrekt] *a* direct(e) // *vt* diriger, orienter; **can you ~ me to ...?** pouvez-vous m'indiquer le chemin de ...?

direction [dɪˈrekʃən] *n* direction *f*; **sense of ~** sens *m* de l'orientation; ~**s** *npl* (*advice*) indications *fpl*; ~**s for use** mode *m* d'emploi.

directly [dɪˈrektlɪ] *ad* (*in straight line*)

directement, tout droit; (*at once*) tout de suite, immédiatement.

director [dɪˈrektə*] *n* directeur *m*; administrateur *m*; (*THEATRE*) metteur *m* en scène; (*CINEMA, TV*) réalisateur/trice.

directory [dɪˈrektərɪ] *n* annuaire *m*.

dirt [də:t] *n* saleté *f*; crasse *f*; ~-**cheap** *a* (ne) coûtant presque rien; ~**y** *a* sale // *vt* salir; ~**y trick** coup tordu.

disability [dɪsəˈbɪlɪtɪ] *n* invalidité *f*, infirmité *f*.

disabled [dɪsˈeɪbld] *a* infirme, invalide; (*maimed*) mutilé(e); (*through illness, old age*) impotent(e).

disadvantage [dɪsədˈvɑːntɪdʒ] *n* désavantage *m*, inconvénient *m*.

disagree [dɪsəˈgriː] *vi* (*differ*) ne pas concorder; (*be against, think otherwise*): to ~ (**with**) ne pas être d'accord (avec); ~**able** a désagréable; ~**ment** *n* désaccord *m*, différend *m*.

disappear [dɪsəˈpɪə*] *vi* disparaître; ~**ance** *n* disparition *f*.

disappoint [dɪsəˈpɔɪnt] *vt* décevoir; ~**ed** *a* déçu(e); ~**ing** a décevant(e); ~**ment** *n* déception *f*.

disapproval [dɪsəˈpruːvəl] *n* désapprobation *f*.

disapprove [dɪsəˈpruːv] *vi*: to ~ **of** désapprouver.

disarm [dɪsˈɑːm] *vt* désarmer; ~**ament** *n* désarmement *m*.

disarray [dɪsəˈreɪ] *n*: in ~ (*army, organization*) en déroute; (*hair, clothes*) en désordre.

disaster [dɪˈzɑːstə*] *n* catastrophe *f*, désastre *m*.

disband [dɪsˈbænd] *vt* démobiliser; disperser // *vi* se séparer; se disperser.

disbelief [dɪsbəˈliːf] *n* incrédulité *f*.

disc [dɪsk] *n* disque *m*; (*COMPUT*) = **disk**.

discard [dɪsˈkɑːd] *vt* (*old things*) se défaire de; (*fig*) écarter, renoncer à.

discern [dɪˈsə:n] *vt* discerner, distinguer; ~**ing** *a* judicieux(euse), perspicace.

discharge *vt* [dɪsˈtʃɑːdʒ] (*duties*) s'acquitter de; (*waste etc*) déverser; décharger; (*ELEC, MED*) émettre; (*patient*) renvoyer (chez lui); (*employee, soldier*) congédier, licencier; (*defendant*) relaxer, élargir // *n* [ˈdɪstʃɑːdʒ] (*ELEC, MED*) émission *f*; (*dismissal*) renvoi *m*; licenciement *m*; élargissement *m*.

discipline [ˈdɪsɪplɪn] *n* discipline *f*.

disc jockey *n* disque-jockey *m*.

disclaim [dɪsˈkleɪm] *vt* désavouer, dénier.

disclose [dɪsˈkləuz] *vt* révéler, divulguer; **disclosure** [-ˈkləuʒə*] *n* révélation *f*, divulgation *f*.

disco [ˈdɪskəu] *n abbr of* **discothèque**.

discomfort [dɪsˈkʌmfət] *n* malaise *m*,

gêne *f*; (*lack of comfort*) manque *m* de confort.

disconcert [dɪskənˈsə:t] *vt* déconcerter.

disconnect [dɪskəˈnekt] *vt* détacher; (*ELEC, RADIO*) débrancher; (*gas, water*) couper.

disconsolate [dɪsˈkɔnsəlɪt] *a* inconsolable.

discontent [dɪskənˈtent] *n* mécontentement *m*; ~**ed** a mécontent(e).

discontinue [dɪskənˈtɪnjuː] *vt* cesser, interrompre.

discord [ˈdɪskɔːd] *n* discorde *f*, dissension *f*; (*MUS*) dissonance *f*.

discothèque [ˈdɪskəutek] *n* discothèque *f*.

discount *n* [ˈdɪskaunt] remise *f*, rabais *m* // *vt* [dɪsˈkaunt] ne pas tenir compte de.

discourage [dɪsˈkʌrɪdʒ] *vt* décourager.

discover [dɪsˈkʌvə*] *vt* découvrir; ~**y** *n* découverte *f*.

discredit [dɪsˈkredɪt] *vt* mettre en doute; discréditer.

discreet [dɪˈskriːt] *a* discret(ète).

discrepancy [dɪˈskrepənsɪ] *n* divergence *f*, contradiction *f*.

discriminate [dɪˈskrɪmɪneɪt] *vi*: to ~ **between** établir une distinction entre, faire la différence entre; to ~ **against** pratiquer une discrimination contre; **discriminating** *a* qui a du discernement; **discrimination** [-ˈneɪʃən] *n* discrimination *f*; (*judgment*) discernement *m*.

discuss [dɪsˈkʌs] *vt* discuter de; (*debate*) discuter; ~**ion** [dɪsˈkʌʃən] *n* discussion *f*.

disdain [dɪsˈdeɪn] *n* dédain *m*.

disease [dɪˈziːz] *n* maladie *f*.

disembark [dɪsɪmˈbɑːk] *vt*, *vi* débarquer.

disengage [dɪsɪnˈgeɪdʒ] *vt* dégager; (*TECH*) déclencher; to ~ **the clutch** (*AUT*) débrayer.

disfigure [dɪsˈfɪgə*] *vt* défigurer.

disgrace [dɪsˈgreɪs] *n* honte *f*; (*disfavour*) disgrâce *f* // *vt* déshonorer, couvrir de honte; ~**ful** *a* scandaleux(euse), honteux(euse).

disgruntled [dɪsˈgrʌntld] *a* mécontent(e).

disguise [dɪsˈgaɪz] *n* déguisement *m* // *vt* déguiser; in ~ déguisé(e).

disgust [dɪsˈgʌst] *n* dégoût *m*, aversion *f* // *vt* dégoûter, écœurer; ~**ing** *a* dégoûtant(e); révoltant(e).

dish [dɪʃ] *n* plat *m*; to do *or* wash the ~es faire la vaisselle; **to** ~ **up** *vt* servir; ~**cloth** *n* (*for drying*) torchon *m*; (*for washing*) lavette *f*.

dishearten [dɪsˈhɑːtn] *vt* décourager.

dishevelled [dɪˈʃevəld] *a* ébouriffé(e); décoiffé(e); débraillé(e).

dishonest [dɪsˈɔnɪst] *a* malhonnête.

dishonour, (US) dishonor [dɪsˈɔnə*] *n*

déshonneur m; ~**able** a déshonorant(e).
dish towel n (US) torchon m.
dishwasher ['dɪʃwɔʃə*] n lave-vaisselle m; (person) plongeur/euse.
disillusion [dɪsɪ'luːʒən] vt désabuser, désenchanter.
disincentive [dɪsɪn'sɛntɪv] n: to be a ~ être démotivant(e); to be a ~ to sb démotiver qn.
disinfect [dɪsɪn'fɛkt] vt désinfecter; ~**ant** n désinfectant m.
disintegrate [dɪs'ɪntɪgreɪt] vi se désintégrer.
disinterested [dɪs'ɪntrəstɪd] a désintéressé(e).
disjointed [dɪs'dʒɔɪntɪd] a décousu(e), incohérent(e).
disk [dɪsk] n (COMPUT) disquette f; single-/double-sided ~ disquette une face/double face; ~ **drive** n lecteur m de disque or disquette, drive m; ~**ette** n (US) = **disk**.
dislike [dɪs'laɪk] n aversion f, antipathie f // vt ne pas aimer.
dislocate ['dɪsləkeɪt] vt disloquer; déboiter; désorganiser.
dislodge [dɪs'lɔdʒ] vt déplacer, faire bouger; (enemy) déloger.
disloyal [dɪs'lɔɪəl] a déloyal(e).
dismal ['dɪzml] a lugubre, maussade.
dismantle [dɪs'mæntl] vt démonter; (fort, warship) démanteler.
dismay [dɪs'meɪ] n consternation f.
dismiss [dɪs'mɪs] vt congédier, renvoyer; (idea) écarter; (LAW) rejeter // vi (MIL) rompre les rangs; ~**al** n renvoi m.
dismount [dɪs'maʊnt] vi mettre pied à terre.
disobedience [dɪsə'biːdɪəns] n désobéissance f.
disobedient [dɪsə'biːdɪənt] a désobéissant(e).
disobey [dɪsə'beɪ] vt désobéir à.
disorder [dɪs'ɔːdə*] n désordre m; (rioting) désordres mpl; (MED) troubles mpl; ~**ly** a en désordre; désordonné(e).
disorientated [dɪs'ɔːrɪenteɪtɪd] a désorienté(e).
disown [dɪs'əʊn] vt renier.
disparaging [dɪs'pærɪdʒɪŋ] a désobligeant(e).
dispassionate [dɪs'pæʃənət] a calme, froid(e); impartial(e), objectif(ive).
dispatch [dɪs'pætʃ] vt expédier, envoyer // n envoi m, expédition f; (MIL, PRESS) dépêche f.
dispel [dɪs'pɛl] vt dissiper, chasser.
dispensary [dɪs'pɛnsərɪ] n pharmacie f; (in chemist's) officine f.
dispense [dɪs'pɛns] vt distribuer, administrer; to ~ **with** vt fus se passer de; ~**r** n (container) distributeur m; **dispensing chemist** n (Brit) pharmacie f.

disperse [dɪs'pəːs] vt disperser; (knowledge) disséminer // vi se disperser.
dispirited [dɪs'pɪrɪtɪd] a découragé(e), déprimé(e).
displace [dɪs'pleɪs] vt déplacer.
display [dɪs'pleɪ] n étalage m; déploiement m; affichage m; (screen) écran m de visualisation, visuel m; (of feeling) manifestation f; (pej) ostentation f // vt montrer; (goods) mettre à l'étalage, exposer; (results, departure times) afficher; (pej) faire étalage de.
displease [dɪs'pliːz] vt mécontenter, contrarier; ~**d with** mécontent(e) de; **displeasure** [-'plɛʒə*] n mécontentement m.
disposable [dɪs'pəʊzəbl] a (pack etc) jetable; (income) disponible; ~ **nappy** n couche f à jeter, couche-culotte f.
disposal [dɪs'pəʊzl] n (availability, arrangement) disposition f; (of property) disposition f, cession f; (of rubbish) évacuation f, destruction f; at one's ~ à sa disposition.
dispose [dɪs'pəʊz] vt disposer; to ~ **of** vt (time, money) disposer de; (unwanted goods) se débarrasser de, se défaire de; (problem) expédier; ~**d** a: ~**d to do** disposé(e) à faire; **disposition** [-'zɪʃən] n disposition f; (temperament) naturel m.
disprove [dɪs'pruːv] vt réfuter.
dispute [dɪs'pjuːt] n discussion f; (also: industrial ~) conflit m // vt contester; (matter) discuter; (victory) disputer.
disqualify [dɪs'kwɔlɪfaɪ] vt (SPORT) disqualifier; to ~ **sb for sth/from doing** rendre qn inapte à qch/à faire; signifier à qn l'interdiction de faire; to ~ **sb (from driving)** retirer à qn son permis (de conduire).
disquiet [dɪs'kwaɪət] n inquiétude f, trouble m.
disregard [dɪsrɪ'gaːd] vt ne pas tenir compte de.
disrepair [dɪsrɪ'pɛə*] n mauvais état; to fall into ~ (building) tomber en ruine.
disreputable [dɪs'rɛpjutəbl] a (person) de mauvaise réputation; (behaviour) déshonorant(e).
disrupt [dɪs'rʌpt] vt (plans) déranger; (conversation) interrompre.
dissatisfaction [dɪssætɪs'fækʃən] n mécontentement m, insatisfaction f.
dissatisfied [dɪs'sætɪsfaɪd] vt disséquer.
dissect [dɪ'sɛkt] vt disséquer.
dissent [dɪ'sɛnt] n dissentiment m, différence f d'opinion.
dissertation [dɪsə'teɪʃən] n mémoire m.
disservice [dɪs'səːvɪs] n: to do sb a ~ rendre un mauvais service à qn; desservir qn.
dissimilar [dɪ'sɪmɪlə*] a: ~ (to) dissemblable (à), différent(e) (de).

dissipate ['dɪsɪpeɪt] *vt* dissiper; (*energy, efforts*) disperser.

dissolute ['dɪsəluːt] *a* débauché(e), dissolu(e).

dissolve [dɪ'zɔlv] *vt* dissoudre // *vi* se dissoudre, fondre; (*fig*) disparaître.

distance ['dɪstns] *n* distance *f*; **in the ~** au loin.

distant ['dɪstnt] *a* lointain(e), éloigné(e); (*manner*) distant(e), froid(e).

distaste [dɪs'teɪst] *n* dégoût *m*; **~ful** *a* déplaisant(e), désagréable.

distended [dɪs'tɛndɪd] *a* (*stomach*) dilaté(e).

distil [dɪs'tɪl] *vt* distiller; **~lery** *n* distillerie *f*.

distinct [dɪs'tɪŋkt] *a* distinct(e); (*preference, progress*) marqué(e); **as ~ from** par opposition à; **~ion** [dɪs'tɪŋkʃən] *n* distinction *f*; (*in exam*) mention *f* très bien; **~ive** *a* distinctif(ive).

distinguish [dɪs'tɪŋgwɪʃ] *vt* distinguer; différencier; **~ed** *a* (*eminent*) distingué(e); **~ing** *a* (*feature*) distinctif(ive), caractéristique.

distort [dɪs'tɔːt] *vt* déformer.

distract [dɪs'trækt] *vt* distraire, déranger; **~ed** *a* éperdu(e), égaré(e); **~ion** [dɪs'trækʃən] *n* distraction *f*; égarement *m*.

distraught [dɪs'trɔːt] *a* éperdu(e).

distress [dɪs'trɛs] *n* détresse *f*; (*pain*) douleur *f* // *vt* affliger; **~ing** *a* douloureux(euse), pénible.

distribute [dɪs'trɪbjuːt] *vt* distribuer; **distribution** [-'bjuːʃən] *n* distribution *f*; **distributor** *n* distributeur *m*.

district ['dɪstrɪkt] *n* (*of country*) région *f*; (*of town*) quartier *m*; (*ADMIN*) district *m*; **~ attorney** *n* (*US*) ≈ procureur *m* de la République; **~ nurse** *n* (*Brit*) infirmière visiteuse.

distrust [dɪs'trʌst] *n* méfiance *f*, doute *m* // *vt* se méfier de.

disturb [dɪs'təːb] *vt* troubler; (*inconvenience*) déranger; **~ance** *n* dérangement *m*; (*political etc*) troubles *mpl*; (*by drunks etc*) tapage *m*; **~ed** *a* (*worried, upset*) agité(e), troublé(e); **to be emotionally ~ed** avoir des problèmes affectifs; **~ing** *a* troublant(e), inquiétant(e).

disuse [dɪs'juːs] *n*: **to fall into ~** tomber en désuétude.

disused [dɪs'juːzd] *a* désaffecté(e).

ditch [dɪtʃ] *n* fossé *m* // *vt* (*col*) abandonner.

dither ['dɪðə*] *vi* hésiter.

ditto ['dɪtəu] *ad* idem.

dive [daɪv] *n* plongeon *m*; (*of submarine*) plongée *f*; (*AVIAT*) piqué *m*; (*pej*) bouge *m* // *vi* plonger; **~r** *n* plongeur *m*.

diversion [daɪ'vəːʃən] *n* (*Brit AUT*) déviation *f*; (*distraction, MIL*) diversion *f*.

divert [daɪ'vəːt] *vt* (*traffic*) dévier; (*river*) détourner; (*amuse*) divertir.

divide [dɪ'vaɪd] *vt* diviser; (*separate*) séparer // *vi* se diviser; **~d highway** *n* (*US*) route *f* à quatre voies.

dividend ['dɪvɪdɛnd] *n* dividende *m*.

divine [dɪ'vaɪn] *a* divin(e).

diving ['daɪvɪŋ] *n* plongée (sous-marine); **~ board** *n* plongeoir *m*.

divinity [dɪ'vɪnɪtɪ] *n* divinité *f*; théologie *f*.

division [dɪ'vɪʒən] *n* division *f*; séparation *f*.

divorce [dɪ'vɔːs] *n* divorce *m* // *vt* divorcer d'avec; **~d** *a* divorcé(e); **~e** [-'siː] *n* divorcé/e.

D.I.Y. *n abbr* (*Brit*) of **do-it-yourself**.

dizzy ['dɪzɪ] *a* (*height*) vertigineux(euse); **to make sb ~** donner le vertige à qn; **to feel ~** avoir la tête qui tourne.

DJ *n abbr of* **disc jockey**.

do [duː] ♦ *n* (*col: party etc*) soirée *f*, fête *f*
♦ *vb* (*pt* **did**, *pp* **done**) **1** (*in negative constructions*) non traduit; I **don't understand** je ne comprends pas
2 (*to form questions*) non traduit; **didn't you know?** vous ne le saviez pas?; **why didn't you come?** pourquoi n'êtes-vous pas venu?
3 (*for emphasis, in polite expressions*): **she does seem rather late** je trouve qu'elle est bien en retard; **~ sit down/help yourself** asseyez-vous/servez-vous je vous en prie
4 (*used to avoid repeating vb*): **she swims better than I ~** elle nage mieux que moi; **~ you agree? - yes, I ~/no, I don't** vous êtes d'accord? - oui/non; **she lives in Glasgow - so ~ I** elle habite Glasgow - moi aussi; **who broke it? - I did** qui l'a cassé? - c'est moi
5 (*in question tags*): **he laughed, didn't he?** il a ri, n'est-ce pas?; **I don't know him, ~ I?** je ne le connais pas, je crois
♦ *vt* (*gen: carry out, perform etc*) faire; **what are you doing tonight?** qu'est-ce que vous faites ce soir?; **to ~ the cooking/washing-up** faire la cuisine/la vaisselle; **to ~ one's teeth/hair/nails** se brosser les dents/se coiffer/se faire les ongles; **the car was ~ing 100** la voiture faisait du 100 (à l'heure)
♦ *vi* **1** (*act, behave*) faire; **~ as I ~** faites comme moi
2 (*get on, fare*) marcher; **the firm is ~ing well** l'entreprise marche bien; **how ~ you ~?** comment allez-vous?; (*on being introduced*) enchanté(e)!
3 (*suit*) aller; **will it ~?** est-ce que ça ira?
4 (*be sufficient*) suffire, aller; **will £10 ~?** est-ce que 10 livres suffiront?; **that'll**

~ ça suffit, ça ira; **that'll ~!** (*in annoyance*) ça va *or* suffit comme ça!; **to make ~ (with)** se contenter (de)
to do away with *vt fus* supprimer
to do up *vt* (*laces, dress*) attacher; (*buttons*) boutonner; (*zip*) fermer; (*renovate: room*) refaire; (*: house*) remettre à neuf
to do with *vt fus* (*need*): **I could ~ with a drink/some help** quelque chose à boire/un peu d'aide ne serait pas de refus; (*be connected*): **that has nothing to ~ with you** cela ne vous concerne pas; **I won't have anything to ~ with it** je ne veux pas m'en mêler
to do without *vi* s'en passer ♦ *vt fus* se passer de.
dock [dɔk] *n* dock *m*; (*LAW*) banc *m* des accusés // *vi* se mettre à quai; **~er** *n* docker *m*; **~yard** *n* chantier *m* de construction navale.
doctor ['dɔktə*] *n* médecin *m*, docteur *m*; (*Ph.D. etc*) docteur // *vt* (*fig*) falsifier; (*drink*) frelater; **D~ of Philosophy (Ph.D.)** *n* doctorat *m*; titulaire *m/f* d'un doctorat.
doctrine ['dɔktrɪn] *n* doctrine *f*.
document ['dɔkjumənt] *n* document *m*; **~ary** [-'mentərɪ] *a, n* documentaire (*m*).
dodge [dɔdʒ] *n* truc *m*; combine *f* // *vt* esquiver, éviter.
doe [dəu] *n* (*deer*) biche *f*; (*rabbit*) lapine *f*.
does [dʌz] *vb see* do; **doesn't** = **does not**.
dog [dɔg] *n* chien/ne // *vt* suivre de près; poursuivre, harceler; **~ collar** *n* collier *m* de chien; (*fig*) faux-col *m* d'ecclésiastique; **~-eared** *a* corné(e).
dogged ['dɔgɪd] *a* obstiné(e), opiniâtre.
dogsbody ['dɔgzbɔdɪ] *n* bonne *f* à tout faire, tâcheron *m*.
doings ['duːɪŋz] *npl* activités *fpl*.
do-it-yourself [duːɪtjɔː'self] *n* bricolage *m*.
doldrums ['dɔldrəmz] *npl*: **to be in the ~** avoir le cafard; être dans le marasme.
dole [dəul] *n* (*Brit: payment*) allocation *f* de chômage; **on the ~** au chômage; **to ~ out** *vt* donner au compte-goutte.
doleful ['dəulful] *a* triste, lugubre.
doll [dɔl] *n* poupée *f*; **to ~ o.s. up** se faire beau(belle).
dollar ['dɔlə*] *n* dollar *m*.
dolphin ['dɔlfɪn] *n* dauphin *m*.
domestic [də'mestɪk] *a* (*duty, happiness*) familial(e); (*policy, affairs, flights*) intérieur(e); (*animal*) domestique.
dominant ['dɔmɪnənt] *a* dominant(e).
dominate ['dɔmɪneɪt] *vt* dominer; **domineering** [-'nɪərɪŋ] *a* dominateur(trice), autoritaire.

dominion [də'mɪnɪən] *n* domination *f*; territoire *m*; dominion *m*.
domino, ~es ['dɔmɪnəu] *n* domino *m*; **~es** *n* (*game*) dominos *mpl*.
don [dɔn] *n* (*Brit*) professeur *m* d'université.
donate [də'neɪt] *vt* faire don de, donner.
done [dʌn] *pp of* do.
donkey ['dɔŋkɪ] *n* âne *m*.
donor ['dəunə*] *n* (*of blood etc*) donneur/euse; (*to charity*) donateur/trice.
don't [dəunt] *vb* = **do not**.
doodle ['duːdl] *vi* griffonner, gribouiller.
doom [duːm] *n* destin *m*; ruine *f* // *vt*: **to be ~ed (to failure)** être voué(e) à l'échec; **~sday** *n* le Jugement dernier.
door [dɔː*] *n* porte *f*; **~bell** *n* sonnette *f*; **~man** *n* (*in hotel*) portier *m*; (*in block of flats*) concierge *m*; **~mat** *n* paillasson *m*; **~step** *n* pas *m* de (la) porte, seuil *m*; **~way** *n* (embrasure *f* de) porte *f*.
dope [dəup] *n* (*col*) drogue *f* // *vt* (*horse etc*) doper.
dopey ['dəupɪ] *a* (*col*) à moitié endormi(e).
dormant ['dɔːmənt] *a* assoupi(e), en veilleuse; (*rule, law*) inappliqué(e).
dormitory ['dɔːmɪtrɪ] *n* dortoir *m*.
dose [dəus] *n* dose *f*; (*bout*) attaque *f*.
doss house ['dɔs-] *n* (*Brit*) asile *m* de nuit.
dot [dɔt] *n* point *m* // *vt*: **~ted with** parsemé(e) de; **on the ~** à l'heure tapante.
dote [dəut]: **to ~ on** *vt fus* être fou(folle) de.
dot-matrix printer [dɔt'meɪtrɪks-] *n* imprimante matricielle.
dotted line ['dɔtɪd-] *n* ligne pointillée.
double ['dʌbl] *n* double // *ad* (*fold*) en deux; (*twice*): **to cost ~ (sth)** coûter le double (de qch) *or* deux fois plus (que qch) // *n* double *m*; (*CINEMA*) doublure *f* // *vt* doubler; (*fold*) plier en deux // *vi* doubler; **on the ~**, (*Brit*) **at the ~** au pas de course; **~s** *n* (*TENNIS*) double *m*; **~ bass** *n* contrebasse *f*; **~ bed** *n* grand lit; **~-breasted** *a* croisé(e); **~cross** *vt* doubler, trahir; **~decker** *n* autobus *m* à impériale; **~ glazing** *n* (*Brit*) double vitrage *m*; **~ room** *n* chambre *f* pour deux personnes; **doubly** *ad* doublement, deux fois plus.
doubt [daut] *n* doute *m* // *vt* douter de; **to ~ that** douter que; **~ful** *a* douteux(euse); (*person*) incertain(e); **~less** *ad* sans doute, sûrement.
dough [dəu] *n* pâte *f*; **~nut** *n* beignet *m*.
douse [dauz] *vt* (*drench*) tremper, inonder; (*extinguish*) éteindre.
dove [dʌv] *n* colombe *f*.
Dover ['dəuvə*] *n* Douvres *m*.

dovetail ['dʌvteɪl] vi (fig) concorder.
dowdy ['daʊdɪ] a démodé(e); mal fagoté(e).
down [daʊn] n (fluff) duvet m // ad en bas // prep en bas de // vt (col: drink) vider; ~ **with X!** à bas X!; ~**-and-out** n clochard/e f; ~**at-heel** a éculé(e); (fig) miteux(euse); ~**cast** a démoralisé(e); ~**fall** n chute f; ruine f; ~**hearted** a découragé(e); ~**hill** ad: **to go** ~**hill** descendre; ~ **payment** n acompte m; ~**pour** n pluie torrentielle, déluge m; ~**right** a franc(franche); (refusal) catégorique; ~**stairs** ad au rez-de-chaussée; à l'étage inférieur; ~**stream** ad en aval; ~**to-earth** a terre à terre inv; ~**town** ad en ville; ~ **under** ad en Australie (or Nouvelle Zélande); ~**ward** ['daʊnwəd] a, ad, ~**wards** ['daʊnwədz] ad vers le bas.
dowry ['daʊrɪ] n dot f.
doz. abbr of **dozen**.
doze [daʊz] vi sommeiller; **to** ~ **off** vi s'assoupir.
dozen ['dʌzn] n douzaine f; **a** ~ **books** une douzaine de livres; ~**s of** des centaines or des milliers de.
Dr. abbr of **doctor, drive** (n).
drab [dræb] a terne, morne.
draft [drɑːft] n brouillon m; (COMM) traite f; (US MIL) contingent m; (: call-up) conscription f // vt faire le brouillon de; see also **draught**.
draftsman n (US) = **draughtsman**.
drag [dræg] vt traîner; (river) draguer // vi traîner // n (col) raseur/euse; corvée f; (women's clothing): **in** ~ (en) travesti; **to** ~ **on** vi s'éterniser.
dragon ['drægn] n dragon m.
dragonfly ['drægənflaɪ] n libellule f.
drain [dreɪn] n égout m; (on resources) saignée f // vt (land, marshes) drainer, assécher; (vegetables) égoutter; (reservoir etc) vider // vi (water) s'écouler; ~**age** n système m d'égouts; ~**ing board**, (US) ~**board** n égouttoir m; ~**pipe** n tuyau m d'écoulement.
dram [dræm] n petit verre.
drama ['drɑːmə] n (art) théâtre m, art m dramatique; (play) pièce f; (event) drame m; ~**tic** [drə'mætɪk] a dramatique; spectaculaire; ~**tist** ['dræmətɪst] n auteur m dramatique; ~**tize** vt (events) dramatiser; (adapt: for TV/cinema) adapter pour la télévision/pour l'écran.
drank [dræŋk] pt of **drink**.
drape [dreɪp] vt draper; ~**s** npl (US) rideaux mpl; ~**r** n (Brit) marchand/e de nouveautés.
drastic ['dræstɪk] a sévère; énergique.
draught, (US) **draft** [drɑːft] n courant m d'air; (NAUT) tirant m d'eau; ~**s** n (Brit) (jeu m de) dames fpl; **on** ~ (beer) à la pression; ~**board** n (Brit)

damier m.
draughtsman, (US) **draftsman** ['drɑːftsmən] n dessinateur/trice (industriel(le)).
draw [drɔː] vb (pt drew, pp drawn) vt tirer; (attract) attirer; (picture) dessiner; (line, circle) tracer; (money) retirer // vi (SPORT) faire match nul // n match nul; tirage m au sort; loterie f; **to** ~ **near** vi s'approcher; approcher; **to** ~ **out** vi (lengthen) s'allonger // vt (money) retirer; **to** ~ **up** vi (stop) s'arrêter // vt (document) établir, dresser; ~**back** n inconvénient m, désavantage m; ~**bridge** n pont-levis m.
drawer [drɔː*] n tiroir m; ['drɔːə*] (of cheque) tireur m.
drawing ['drɔːɪŋ] n dessin m; ~ **board** n planche f à dessin; ~ **pin** n (Brit) punaise f; ~ **room** n salon m.
drawl [drɔːl] n accent traînant.
drawn [drɔːn] pp of **draw**.
dread [drɛd] n épouvante f, effroi m // vt redouter, appréhender; ~**ful** a épouvantable, affreux(euse).
dream [driːm] n rêve m // vt, vi (pt, pp **dreamed** or **dreamt** [drɛmt]) rêver; ~**y** a rêveur(euse).
dreary ['drɪərɪ] a triste; monotone.
dredge [drɛdʒ] vt draguer.
dregs [drɛgz] npl lie f.
drench [drɛntʃ] vt tremper.
dress [drɛs] n robe f; (clothing) habillement m, tenue f // vi s'habiller // vt habiller; (wound) panser; (food) préparer; **to get** ~**ed** s'habiller; **to** ~ **up** vi s'habiller; (in fancy dress) se déguiser; ~ **circle** n (Brit) premier balcon; ~**er** n (THEATRE) habilleur/euse; (furniture) vaisselier m; ~**ing** n (MED) pansement m; (CULIN) sauce f, assaisonnement m; ~**ing gown** n (Brit) robe f de chambre; ~**ing room** n (THEATRE) loge f; (SPORT) vestiaire m; ~**ing table** n coiffeuse f; ~**maker** n couturière f; ~ **rehearsal** n (répétition) générale f; ~**y** a (col: clothes) (qui fait) habillé(e).
drew [druː] pt of **draw**.
dribble ['drɪbl] vi tomber goutte à goutte; (baby) baver // vt (ball) dribbler.
dried [draɪd] a (fruit, beans) sec(sèche); (eggs, milk) en poudre.
drier ['draɪə*] n = **dryer**.
drift [drɪft] n (of current etc) force f; direction f; (of sand etc) amoncellement m; (of snow) rafale f; coulée f; (: on ground) congère f; (general meaning) sens général // vi (boat) aller à la dérive, dériver; (sand, snow) s'amonceler, s'entasser; ~**wood** n bois m flotté.
drill [drɪl] n perceuse f; (bit) foret m; (of dentist) roulette f, fraise f; (MIL)

exercice *m* // *vt* percer // *vi* (for oil) faire un *or* des forage(s).

drink |drɪŋk| *n* boisson *f* // *vt*, *vi* (*pt* **drank**, *pp* **drunk**) boire; **to have a ~** boire quelque chose, boire un verre; prendre l'apéritif; **a ~ of water** un verre d'eau; **~er** *n* buveur/euse; **~ing water** *n* eau *f* potable.

drip |drɪp| *n* bruit *m* d'égouttement; goutte *f*; (*MED*) goutte-à-goutte *m inv*; perfusion *f* // *vi* tomber goutte à goutte; (*washing*) s'égoutter; (*wall*) suinter; **~dry** *a* (*shirt*) sans repassage; **~ping** *n* graisse *f* de rôti.

drive |draɪv| *n* promenade *f or* trajet *m* en voiture; (*also:* **~way**) allée *f*; (*energy*) dynamisme *m*, énergie *f*; (*PSYCH*) besoin *m*; pulsion *f*; (*push*) effort (concerté); campagne *f*; (*SPORT*) drive *m*; (*TECH*) entraînement *m*; traction *f*; transmission *f*; (*also:* **disk ~**) lecteur *m* de disquette // *vb* (*pt* **drove**, *pp* **driven**) *vt* conduire; (*nail*) enfoncer; (*push*) chasser, pousser; (*TECH: motor*) actionner; entraîner // *vi* (*AUT: at controls*) conduire; (*: travel*) aller en voiture; **left-/right-hand ~** conduite *f* à gauche/droite; **to ~ sb mad** rendre qn fou(folle).

drivel |'drɪvl| *n* (*col*) idioties *fpl*.

driven |'drɪvn| *pp of* **drive**.

driver |'draɪvə*| *n* conducteur/trice; (*of taxi, bus*) chauffeur *m*; **~'s license** *n* (*US*) permis *m* de conduire.

driveway |'draɪvweɪ| *n* allée *f*.

driving |'draɪvɪŋ| *n* conduite *f*; **~ in-structor** *n* moniteur *m* d'auto-école; **~ lesson** *n* leçon *f* de conduite; **~ licence** *n* (*Brit*) permis *m* de conduire; **~ mirror** *n* rétroviseur *m*; **~ school** *n* auto-école *f*; **~ test** *n* examen *m* du permis de conduire.

drizzle |'drɪzl| *n* bruine *f*, crachin *m*.

droll |drəʊl| *a* drôle.

drone |drəʊn| *n* bourdonnement *m*.

drool |dru:l| *vi* baver.

droop |dru:p| *vi* s'affaisser; tomber.

drop |drɔp| *n* goutte *f*; (*fall*) baisse *f*; (*also:* **parachute ~**) saut *m*; (*of cliff*) dénivellation *f*; à-pic *m* // *vt* laisser tomber; (*voice, eyes, price*) baisser; (*set down from car*) déposer // *vi* tomber; **~s** *npl* (*MED*) gouttes; **to ~ off** *vi* (*sleep*) s'assoupir // *vt* (*passenger*) déposer; **to ~ out** *vi* (*withdraw*) se retirer; (*student etc*) abandonner, décrocher; **~-out** *n* marginal/e; (*from studies*) drop-out *m/f*; **~pings** *npl* crottes *fpl*.

drought |draut| *n* sécheresse *f*.

drove |drəʊv| *pt of* **drive**.

drown |draun| *vt* noyer // *vi* se noyer.

drowsy |'drauzɪ| *a* somnolent(e).

drudgery |'drʌdʒərɪ| *n* corvée *f*.

drug |drʌg| *n* médicament *m*; (*narcotic*) drogue *f* // *vt* droguer **~ addict** *n* toxicomane *m/f*; **~gist** *n* (*US*) pharmacien/ne-droguiste; **~store** *n* (*US*) pharmacie-droguerie *f*, drugstore *m*.

drum |drʌm| *n* tambour *m*; (*for oil, petrol*) bidon *m* // *vi* tambouriner; **~s** *npl* batterie *f*; **~mer** *n* (joueur *m* de) tambour *m*.

drunk |drʌŋk| *pp of* **drink** // *a* ivre, soûl(e) // *n* (*also:* **~ard**) soûlard/e; homme/femme soûl(e); **~en** *a* ivre, soûl(e); ivrogne, d'ivrogne.

dry |draɪ| *a* sec(sèche); (*day*) sans pluie // *vt* sécher; (*clothes*) faire sécher // *vi* sécher; **to ~ up** *vi* se tarir; **~cleaner's** *n* teinturerie *f*; **~er** *n* séchoir *m*; (*US: spin-dryer*) essoreuse *f*; **~ goods store** *n* (*US*) magasin *m* de nouveautés; **~ness** *n* sécheresse *f*; **~ rot** *n* pourriture sèche (*du bois*).

dual |'djuəl| *a* double; **~ carriageway** *n* (*Brit*) route *f* à quatre voies *or* à chaussées séparées.

dubbed |dʌbd| *a* (*CINEMA*) doublé(e); (*nicknamed*) surnommé(e).

dubious |'dju:bɪəs| *a* hésitant(e), incertain(e); (*reputation, company*) douteux(euse).

duchess |'dʌtʃɪs| *n* duchesse *f*.

duck |dʌk| *n* canard *m* // *vi* se baisser vivement, baisser subitement la tête; **~ling** *n* caneton *m*.

duct |dʌkt| *n* conduite *f*, canalisation *f*; (*ANAT*) conduit *m*.

dud |dʌd| *n* (*shell*) obus non éclaté; (*object, tool*): **it's a ~** c'est de la camelote, ça ne marche pas // *a* (*Brit: cheque*) sans provision; (*: note, coin*) faux(fausse).

due |dju:| *a* dû(due); (*expected*) attendu(e); (*fitting*) qui convient // *n* dû *m* // *ad*: **~ north** droit vers le nord; **~s** *npl* (*for club, union*) cotisation *f*; (*in harbour*) droits *mpl* (de port); **in ~ course** en temps utile *or* voulu; finalement; **~ to** dû(due) à; causé(e) par; **he's ~ to finish tomorrow** normalement il doit finir demain.

duet |dju:'ɛt| *n* duo *m*.

duffel |dʌfl| *a*: **~ bag** sac *m* marin; **~ coat** duffel-coat *m*.

dug |dʌg| *pt, pp of* **dig**.

duke |dju:k| *n* duc *m*.

dull |dʌl| *a* ennuyeux(euse); terne; (*sound, pain*) sourd(e); (*weather, day*) gris(e), maussade; (*blade*) émoussé(e) // *vt* (*pain, grief*) atténuer; (*mind, senses*) engourdir.

duly |'dju:lɪ| *ad* (*on time*) en temps voulu; (*as expected*) comme il se doit.

dumb |dʌm| *a* muet(te); (*stupid*) bête; **dumbfounded** |dʌm'faundɪd| *a* sidéré(e).

dummy ['dʌmɪ] n (tailor's model) mannequin m; (SPORT) feinte f; (Brit: for baby) tétine f // a faux(fausse), factice.

dump [dʌmp] n tas m d'ordures; (place) décharge (publique); (MIL) dépôt m // vt (put down) déposer; déverser; (get rid of) se débarrasser de; ~ing n (ECON) dumping m; (of rubbish): 'no ~ing' 'décharge interdite'.

dumpling ['dʌmplɪŋ] n boulette f (de pâte).

dumpy ['dʌmpɪ] a courtaud(e), boulot(te).

dunce [dʌns] n âne m, cancre m.

dung [dʌŋ] n fumier m.

dungarees [dʌŋgə'ri:z] npl bleu(s) m(pl); salopette f.

dungeon ['dʌndʒən] n cachot m.

Dunkirk [dʌn'kə:k] n Dunkerque.

duplex ['du:pleks] n (US) maison jumelée; (: apartment) duplex m.

duplicate n ['dju:plɪkət] double m, copie exacte // vt ['dju:plɪkeɪt] faire un double de; (on machine) polycopier.

durable ['djuərəbl] a durable; (clothes, metal) résistant(e), solide.

duration [djuə'reɪʃən] n durée f.

duress [djuə'rɛs] n: under ~ sous la contrainte.

during ['djuərɪŋ] prep pendant, au cours de.

dusk [dʌsk] n crépuscule m.

dust [dʌst] n poussière f // vt (furniture) essuyer, épousseter; (cake etc): to ~ with saupoudrer de; ~bin n (Brit) poubelle f; ~er n chiffon m; ~ jacket n jacquette f; ~man n (Brit) boueux m, éboueur m; ~y a poussiéreux(euse).

Dutch [dʌtʃ] a hollandais(e), néerlandais(e) // n (LING) hollandais m; the ~ npl les Hollandais; to go ~ partager les frais; ~man/woman n Hollandais/e.

dutiful ['dju:tɪful] a (child) respectueux(euse).

duty ['dju:tɪ] n devoir m; (tax) droit m, taxe f; duties npl fonctions fpl; on ~ de service; (at night etc) de garde; off ~ libre, pas de service or de garde; ~-free a exempté(e) de douane, hors-taxe.

duvet ['du:veɪ] n (Brit) couette f.

dwarf [dwɔ:f] n nain/e // vt écraser.

dwell, pt, pp **dwelt** [dwel, dwelt] vi demeurer; to ~ on vt fus s'étendre sur; ~ing n habitation f, demeure f.

dwindle ['dwɪndl] vi diminuer, décroître.

dye [daɪ] n teinture f // vt teindre.

dying ['daɪɪŋ] a mourant(e), agonisant(e).

dyke [daɪk] n (Brit) digue f.

dynamic [daɪ'næmɪk] a dynamique.

dynamite ['daɪnəmaɪt] n dynamite f.

dynamo ['daɪnəməu] n dynamo f.

dyslexia [dɪs'lɛksɪə] n dyslexie f.

E

E [i:] n (MUS) mi m.

each [i:tʃ] a chaque // pronoun chacun(e); ~ one chacun(e); they hate ~ other ils se détestent (mutuellement); you are jealous of ~ other vous êtes jaloux l'un de l'autre; they have 2 books ~ ils ont 2 livres chacun.

eager ['i:gə*] a impatient(e); avide; ardent(e), passionné(e); to be ~ for désirer vivement, être avide de.

eagle ['i:gl] n aigle m.

ear [ɪə*] n oreille f; (of corn) épi m; ~ache n douleurs fpl aux oreilles; ~drum n tympan m.

earl [ə:l] n comte m.

earlier ['ə:lɪə*] a (date etc) plus rapproché(e); (edition etc) plus ancien(ne), antérieur(e) // ad plus tôt.

early ['ə:lɪ] ad tôt, de bonne heure; (ahead of time) en avance // a précoce; anticipé(e); qui se manifeste (or se fait) tôt or de bonne heure; to have an ~ night se coucher tôt or de bonne heure; in the ~ or ~ in the spring/19th century au début or commencement du printemps/19ème siècle; ~ retirement n retraite anticipée.

earmark ['ɪəma:k] vt: to ~ sth for réserver or destiner qch à.

earn [ə:n] vt gagner; (COMM: yield) rapporter.

earnest ['ə:nɪst] a sérieux(euse); in ~ ad sérieusement, pour de bon.

earnings ['ə:nɪŋz] npl salaire m; gains mpl.

earphones ['ɪəfəunz] npl écouteurs mpl.

earring ['ɪərɪŋ] n boucle f d'oreille.

earshot ['ɪəʃɔt] n: out of/within ~ hors de portée/à portée de la voix.

earth [ə:θ] n (gen; also ELEC: Brit) terre f; (of fox etc) terrier m // vt (Brit: ELEC) relier à la terre; ~enware n poterie f; faïence f; ~quake n tremblement m de terre, séisme m; ~y a (fig) terre à terre inv; truculent(e).

ease [i:z] n facilité f, aisance f // vt (soothe) calmer; (loosen) relâcher, détendre; (help pass): to ~ sth in/out faire pénétrer/sortir qch délicatement or avec douceur; faciliter la pénétration/la sortie de qch; at ~ à l'aise; (MIL) au repos; to ~ off or up vi diminuer; ralentir; se détendre.

easel ['i:zl] n chevalet m.

east [i:st] n est m // a d'est // ad à l'est, vers l'est; the E~ l'Orient m.

Easter ['i:stə*] n Pâques fpl; ~ egg n œuf m de Pâques.

easterly ['i:stəlɪ] a d'est.

eastern ['i:stən] a de l'est, oriental(e).

East Germany n Allemagne f de l'Est.

eastward(s) ['i:stwəd(z)] ad vers l'est, à l'est.

easy ['i:zɪ] a facile; (manner) aisé(e) // ad: **to take it** or **things** ~ ne pas se fatiguer; ne pas (trop) s'en faire; ~ **chair** n fauteuil m; ~**-going** a accommodant(e), facile à vivre.

eat, pt ate, pp eaten [i:t, eɪt, 'i:tn] vt, vi manger; **to ~ into, to ~ away at** vt fus ronger, attaquer.

eaves [i:vz] npl avant-toit m.

eavesdrop ['i:vzdrɔp] vi: **to ~ (on** a conversation) écouter (une conversation) de façon indiscrète.

ebb [ɛb] n reflux m // vi refluer; (fig: also: ~ **away**) décliner.

ebony ['ɛbənɪ] n ébène f.

eccentric [ɪk'sɛntrɪk] a, n excentrique (m/f).

echo, ~**es** ['ɛkəu] n écho m // vt répéter; faire chorus avec // vi résonner; faire écho.

eclipse [ɪ'klɪps] n éclipse f.

ecology [ɪ'kɔlədʒɪ] n écologie f.

economic [i:kə'nɔmɪk] a économique; (business etc) rentable; ~**al** a économique; (person) économe; ~**s** n économie f politique.

economize [ɪ'kɔnəmaɪz] vi économiser, faire des économies.

economy [ɪ'kɔnəmɪ] n économie f.

ecstasy ['ɛkstəsɪ] n extase f.

eczema ['ɛksɪmə] n eczéma m.

edge [ɛdʒ] n bord m; (of knife etc) tranchant m, fil m // vt border; **on ~** (fig) = edgy; **to ~ away from** s'éloigner furtivement de; ~**ways** ad latéralement; **he couldn't get a word in ~ways** il ne pouvait pas placer un mot.

edgy ['ɛdʒɪ] a crispé(e), tendu(e).

edible ['ɛdɪbl] a comestible; (meal) mangeable.

edict ['i:dɪkt] n décret m.

Edinburgh ['ɛdɪnbərə] n Édimbourg.

edit ['ɛdɪt] vt éditer; ~**ion** [ɪ'dɪʃən] n édition f; ~**or** n (in newspaper) rédacteur/trice; rédacteur/trice en chef; (of sb's work) éditeur/trice; ~**orial** [-'tɔ:rɪəl] a de la rédaction, éditorial(e) // n éditorial m.

educate ['ɛdjukeɪt] vt instruire; éduquer.

education [ɛdju'keɪʃən] n éducation f; (schooling) enseignement m, instruction f; ~**al** a pédagogique; scolaire; instructif(ive).

EEC n abbr (= European Economic Community) C.E.E. f (= Communauté économique européenne).

eel [i:l] n anguille f.

eerie ['ɪərɪ] a inquiétant(e), spectral(e), surnaturel(le).

effect [ɪ'fɛkt] n effet m // vt effectuer; ~**s** npl (THEATRE) effets mpl; **to take** ~

(law) entrer en vigueur, prendre effet; (drug) agir, faire son effet; **in ~** en fait; ~**ive** a efficace; ~**ively** ad efficacement; (in reality) effectivement; ~**iveness** n efficacité f.

effeminate [ɪ'fɛmɪnɪt] a efféminé(e).

efficiency [ɪ'fɪʃənsɪ] n efficacité f; rendement m.

efficient [ɪ'fɪʃənt] a efficace.

effort ['ɛfət] n effort m.

effusive [ɪ'fju:sɪv] a expansif(ive); chaleureux(euse).

e.g. ad abbr (= exempli gratia) par exemple, p. ex.

egg [ɛg] n œuf m; **to ~ on** vt pousser; ~**cup** n coquetier m; ~**plant** n (esp US) aubergine f; ~**shell** n coquille f d'œuf.

ego ['i:gəu] n moi m.

egotism ['ɛgəutɪzəm] n égotisme m.

egotist ['ɛgəutɪst] n égocentrique m/f.

Egypt ['i:dʒɪpt] n Égypte f; ~**ian** [ɪ'dʒɪpʃən] a égyptien(ne) // n Égyptien/ne.

eiderdown ['aɪdədaun] n édredon m.

eight [eɪt] num huit; ~**een** num dix-huit; **eighth** a, n huitième (m); ~**y** num quatre-vingt(s).

Eire ['ɛərə] n République f d'Irlande.

either ['aɪðə*] a l'un ou l'autre; (both, each) chaque; **on ~ side** de chaque côté // pronoun: ~ **(of them)** l'un ou l'autre; **I don't like ~** je n'aime ni l'un ni l'autre // ad non plus; **no, I don't ~** moi non plus // cj: ~ **good or bad** ou bon ou mauvais, soit bon soit mauvais.

eject [ɪ'dʒɛkt] vt expulser; éjecter.

eke [i:k]: **to ~ out** vt faire durer; augmenter.

elaborate a [ɪ'læbərɪt] compliqué(e), recherché(e), minutieux(euse) // vb [ɪ'læbəreɪt] vt élaborer // vi entrer dans les détails.

elapse [ɪ'læps] vi s'écouler, passer.

elastic [ɪ'læstɪk] a, n élastique (m); ~ **band** n (Brit) élastique m.

elated [ɪ'leɪtɪd] a transporté(e) de joie.

elbow ['ɛlbəu] n coude m.

elder ['ɛldə*] a aîné(e) // n (tree) sureau m; **one's ~s** ses aînés; ~**ly** a âgé(e) // npl: **the ~ly** les personnes âgées.

eldest ['ɛldɪst] a, n: **the ~** (child) l'aîné(e) (des enfants).

elect [ɪ'lɛkt] vt élire; **to ~ to do** choisir de faire // a: **the president ~** le président désigné; ~**ion** [ɪ'lɛkʃən] n élection f; ~**ioneering** [ɪlɛkʃə'nɪərɪŋ] n propagande électorale, manœuvres électorales; ~**or** n électeur/trice; ~**orate** n électorat m.

electric [ɪ'lɛktrɪk] a électrique; ~**al** a électrique; ~ **blanket** n couverture chauffante; ~ **fire** n radiateur m électrique.

electrician [ɪlɛk'trɪʃən] n électricien m.

electricity [ɪlek'trɪsɪtɪ] n électricité f.
electrify [ɪ'lektrɪfaɪ] vt (RAIL) électrifier; (audience) électriser.
electronic [ɪlek'trɒnɪk] a électronique; ~s n électronique f.
elegant ['elɪgənt] a élégant(e).
element ['elɪmənt] n (gen) élément m; (of heater, kettle etc) résistance f; ~ary [-'mentərɪ] a élémentaire; (school, education) primaire.
elephant ['elɪfənt] n éléphant m.
elevate ['elɪveɪt] vt élever.
elevator ['elɪveɪtə*] n élévateur m, monte-charge m inv; (US: lift) ascenseur m.
eleven [ɪ'levn] num onze; ~ses npl (Brit) ≈ pause-café f; ~th a onzième.
elicit [ɪ'lɪsɪt] vt: to ~ (from) obtenir (de), arracher (à).
eligible ['elɪdʒəbl] a éligible; (for membership) admissible.
elm [elm] n orme m.
elongated ['i:lɒŋgeɪtɪd] a étiré(e), allongé(e).
elope [ɪ'ləup] vi (lovers) s'enfuir (ensemble).
eloquent ['eləkwənt] a éloquent(e).
else [els] ad d'autre; something ~ quelque chose d'autre, autre chose; somewhere ~ ailleurs, autre part; everywhere ~ partout ailleurs; nobody ~ personne d'autre; where ~? à quel autre endroit?; little ~ pas grand-chose d'autre; ~where ad ailleurs, autre part.
elude [ɪ'lu:d] vt échapper à; (question) éluder.
elusive [ɪ'lu:sɪv] a insaisissable.
emaciated [ɪ'meɪsɪeɪtɪd] a émacié(e), décharné(e).
emancipate [ɪ'mænsɪpeɪt] vt émanciper.
embankment [ɪm'bæŋkmənt] n (of road, railway) remblai m, talus m; (riverside) berge f, quai m; (dyke) digue f.
embark [ɪm'bɑ:k] vi: to ~ (on) (s')embarquer (à bord de or sur) // vt embarquer; to ~ on (fig) se lancer or s'embarquer dans; ~ation [embɑ:'keɪʃən] n embarquement m.
embarrass [ɪm'bærəs] vt embarrasser, gêner; ~ed a gêné(e); ~ing a gênant(e), embarrassant(e); ~ment n embarras m, gêne f.
embassy ['embəsɪ] n ambassade f.
embed [ɪm'bed] vt enfoncer; sceller.
embers ['embəz] npl braise f.
embezzle [ɪm'bezl] vt détourner.
embitter [ɪm'bɪtə*] vt aigrir; envenimer.
embody [ɪm'bɒdɪ] vt (features) réunir, comprendre; (ideas) formuler, exprimer.
embossed [ɪm'bɒst] a repoussé(e); gaufré(e).

embrace [ɪm'breɪs] vt embrasser, étreindre; (include) embrasser, couvrir // vi s'étreindre, s'embrasser // n étreinte f.
embroider [ɪm'brɔɪdə*] vt broder; (fig: story) enjoliver; ~y n broderie f.
emerald ['emərəld] n émeraude f.
emerge [ɪ'mɜ:dʒ] vi apparaître, surgir.
emergence [ɪ'mɜ:dʒəns] n apparition f.
emergency [ɪ'mɜ:dʒənsɪ] n urgence f; in an ~ en cas d'urgence; ~ cord n (US) sonnette f d'alarme; ~ exit n sortie f de secours; ~ landing n atterrissage forcé; the ~ services npl (fire, police, ambulance) les services mpl d'urgence.
emery board ['emərɪ-] n lime f à ongles (en carton émerisé).
emigrate ['emɪgreɪt] vi émigrer.
eminent ['emɪnənt] a éminent(e).
emit [ɪ'mɪt] vt émettre.
emotion [ɪ'məuʃən] n émotion f; ~al a (person) émotif(ive), très sensible; (scene) émouvant(e); (tone, speech) qui fait appel aux sentiments.
emperor ['empərə*] n empereur m.
emphasis, pl -ases ['emfəsɪs, -si:z] n accent m; force f, insistance f.
emphasize ['emfəsaɪz] vt (syllable, word, point) appuyer or insister sur; (feature) souligner, accentuer.
emphatic [em'fætɪk] a (strong) énergique, vigoureux(euse); (unambiguous, clear) catégorique; ~ally ad avec vigueur or énergie; catégoriquement.
empire ['empaɪə*] n empire m.
employ [ɪm'plɔɪ] vt employer; ~ee [-'i:] n employé/e; ~er n employeur/euse; ~ment n emploi m; ~ment agency n agence f or bureau m de placement.
empower [ɪm'pauə*] vt: to ~ sb to do autoriser or habiliter qn à faire.
empress ['emprɪs] n impératrice f.
empty ['emptɪ] a vide; (threat, promise) en l'air, vain(e) // vt vider // vi se vider; (liquid) s'écouler // n (bottle) bouteille f vide; ~-handed a les mains vides.
emulate ['emjuleɪt] vt rivaliser avec, imiter.
emulsion [ɪ'mʌlʃən] n émulsion f; ~ (paint) n peinture f mate.
enable [ɪ'neɪbl] vt: to ~ sb to do permettre à qn de faire.
enact [ɪn'ækt] vt (law) promulguer; (play) jouer, représenter.
enamel [ɪ'næməl] n émail m.
encased [ɪn'keɪst] a: ~ in enfermé(e) dans, recouvert(e) de.
enchant [ɪn'tʃɑ:nt] vt enchanter; ~ing a ravissant(e), enchanteur(eresse).
encl. abbr (= enclosed) annexe(s).
enclose [ɪn'kləuz] vt (land) clôturer; (letter etc): to ~ (with) joindre (à); please find ~d veuillez trouver ci-joint.
enclosure [ɪn'kləuʒə*] n enceinte f;

(COMM) annexe *f.*

encompass [ɪn'kʌmpəs] *vt* encercler, entourer; *(include)* contenir, inclure.

encore [ɔŋ'kɔ:*] *excl, n* bis *(m).*

encounter [ɪn'kauntə*] *n* rencontre *f //* *vt* rencontrer.

encourage [ɪn'kʌrɪdʒ] *vt* encourager; **~ment** *n* encouragement *m.*

encroach [ɪn'krəutʃ] *vi*: to ~ (up)on empiéter *vi.*

encyclop(a)edia [ɛnsaɪkləu'pi:dɪə] *n* encyclopédie *f.*

end [ɛnd] *n (gen, also: aim)* fin *f; (of table, street etc)* bout *m,* extrémité *f //* *vt* terminer; *(also:* bring to an ~, put an ~ to) mettre fin à *// vi* se terminer, finir; in the ~ finalement; on ~ *(object)* debout, dressé(e); to stand on ~ *(hair)* se dresser sur la tête; for 5 hours on ~ durant 5 heures d'affilée *or* de suite; to ~ up *vi*: to ~ up in finir *or* se terminer par; *(place)* finir *or* aboutir à.

endanger [ɪn'deɪndʒə*] *vt* mettre en danger.

endearing [ɪn'dɪərɪŋ] *a* attachant(e).

endeavour, *(US)* **endeavor** [ɪn'devə*] *n* tentative *f,* effort *m // vi*: to ~ to do tenter *or* s'efforcer de faire.

ending ['ɛndɪŋ] *n* dénouement *m,* conclusion *f; (LING)* terminaison *f.*

endive ['ɛndaɪv] *n* chicorée *f.*

endless ['ɛndlɪs] *a* sans fin, interminable; *(patience, resources)* inépuisable, sans limites.

endorse [ɪn'dɔ:s] *vt (cheque)* endosser; *(approve)* appuyer, approuver, sanctionner; **~ment** *n (on driving licence)* contravention portée au permis de conduire.

endow [ɪn'dau] *vt (provide with money)* faire une donation à, doter; *(equip)*: to ~ with gratifier de, doter de.

endure [ɪn'djuə*] *vt* supporter, endurer *// vi* durer.

enemy ['ɛnəmɪ] *a, n* ennemi(e).

energetic [ɛnə'dʒɛtɪk] *a* énergique; actif(ive); qui fait se dépenser (physiquement).

energy ['ɛnədʒɪ] *n* énergie *f.*

enforce [ɪn'fɔ:s] *vt (LAW)* appliquer, faire respecter; **~d** *a* forcé(e).

engage [ɪn'geɪdʒ] *vt* engager; *(MIL)* engager le combat avec *// vi (TECH)* s'enclencher, s'engrener; to ~ in se lancer dans; **~d** *a (Brit: busy, in use)* occupé(e); *(betrothed)* fiancé(e); to get **~d** se fiancer; **~d tone** *n (Brit TEL)* tonalité *f* occupé *or* pas libre; **~ment** *n* obligation *f,* engagement *m;* rendez-vous *m inv; (to marry)* fiançailles *fpl; (MIL)* combat *m;* **~ment ring** *n* bague *f* de fiançailles.

engaging [ɪn'geɪdʒɪŋ] *a* engageant(e), attirant(e).

engender [ɪn'dʒɛndə*] *vt* produire, causer.

engine ['ɛndʒɪn] *n (AUT)* moteur *m; (RAIL)* locomotive *f;* ~ **driver** *n* mécanicien *m.*

engineer [ɛndʒɪ'nɪə*] *n* ingénieur *m; (US RAIL)* mécanicien *m;* **~ing** *n* engineering *m,* ingénierie *f; (of bridges, ships)* génie *m; (of machine)* mécanique *f.*

England ['ɪŋglənd] *n* Angleterre *f.*

English ['ɪŋglɪʃ] *a* anglais(e) *// n (LING)* anglais *m;* the ~ *npl* les Anglais; the ~ **Channel** *n* la Manche; **~man/woman** *n* Anglais/e.

engraving [ɪn'greɪvɪŋ] *n* gravure *f.*

engrossed [ɪn'grəust] *a*: ~ in absorbé(e) par, plongé(e) dans.

engulf [ɪn'gʌlf] *vt* engloutir.

enhance [ɪn'hɑ:ns] *vt* rehausser, mettre en valeur.

enjoy [ɪn'dʒɔɪ] *vt* aimer, prendre plaisir à; *(have: health, fortune)* jouir de; *(: success)* connaître; to ~ o.s. s'amuser; **~able** *a* agréable; **~ment** *n* plaisir *m.*

enlarge [ɪn'lɑ:dʒ] *vt* accroître; *(PHOT)* agrandir *// vi*: to ~ on *(subject)* s'étendre sur.

enlighten [ɪn'laɪtn] *vt* éclairer; **~ed** *a* éclairé(e); **~ment** *n*: the E~ment *(HISTORY)* ≈ le Siècle des lumières.

enlist [ɪn'lɪst] *vt* recruter; *(support)* s'assurer *// vi* s'engager.

enmity ['ɛnmɪtɪ] *n* inimitié *f.*

enormous [ɪ'nɔ:məs] *a* énorme.

enough [ɪ'nʌf] *a, n*: ~ **time/books** assez *or* suffisamment de temps/livres; have you got ~? (en) avez-vous assez? *// ad*: big ~ assez *or* suffisamment grand; he has not worked ~ il n'a pas assez *or* suffisamment travaillé; **~!** assez!, ça suffit!; that's ~, thanks cela suffit *or* c'est assez, merci; I've had ~ of him j'en ai assez de lui; ... which, funnily ~ ... qui, chose curieuse.

enquire [ɪn'kwaɪə*] *vt, vi =* **inquire**.

enrage [ɪn'reɪdʒ] *vt* mettre en fureur *or* en rage, rendre furieux(euse).

enrol [ɪn'rəul] *vt* inscrire *// vi* s'inscrire; **~ment** *n* inscription *f.*

ensign *(NAUT)* ['ɛnsən] enseigne *f,* pavillon *m; (MIL)* ['ɛnsaɪn] porte-étendard *m.*

ensue [ɪn'sju:] *vi* s'ensuivre, résulter.

ensure [ɪn'ʃuə*] *vt* assurer; garantir; to ~ that s'assurer que.

entail [ɪn'teɪl] *vt* entraîner, nécessiter.

entangle [ɪn'tæŋgl] *vt* emmêler, embrouiller.

enter ['ɛntə*] *vt (room)* entrer dans, pénétrer dans; *(club, army)* entrer à; *(competition)* s'inscrire à *or* pour; *(sb for a competition)* (faire) inscrire; *(write down)* inscrire, noter; *(COMPUT)* entrer, introduire *// vi* entrer; to ~ for *vt fus* s'inscrire à, se présenter pour *or* à; to ~ into *vt fus (explanation)* se lancer dans; (*debate*) prendre part à; (*agreement*) conclure; **to ~ (up)on** *vt fus* commencer.

enterprise ['entəpraɪz] *n* entreprise *f*; (*esprit m d'*)initiative *f*; **free ~** libre entreprise; **private ~** entreprise privée.

enterprising ['entəpraɪzɪŋ] *a* entreprenant(e), dynamique.

entertain [entə'teɪn] *vt* amuser, distraire; (*invite*) recevoir (à dîner); (*idea, plan*) envisager; **~er** *n* artiste *m/f* de variétés; **~ing** *a* amusant(e), distrayant(e); **~ment** *n* (*amusement*) distraction *f*, divertissement *m*, amusement *m*; (*show*) spectacle *m*.

enthralled [ɪn'θrɔːld] *a* captivé(e).

enthusiasm [ɪn'θuːzɪæzəm] *n* enthousiasme *m*.

enthusiast [ɪn'θuːzɪæst] *n* enthousiaste *m/f*; **~ic** [-'æstɪk] *a* enthousiaste; **to be ~ic about** être enthousiasmé(e) par.

entice [ɪn'taɪs] *vt* attirer, séduire.

entire [ɪn'taɪə*] *a* (tout) entier(ère); **~ly** *ad* entièrement, complètement; **~ty** [ɪn'taɪərətɪ] *n*: **in its ~ty** dans sa totalité.

entitle [ɪn'taɪtl] *vt* (*allow*): **to ~ sb to do** donner (le) droit à qn de faire; **to ~ sb to sth** donner droit à qch à qn; **~d** *a* (*book*) intitulé(e); **to be ~d to do** avoir le droit de *or* être habilité à faire.

entrance *n* ['entrns] entrée *f* // *vt* [ɪn'trɑːns] enchanter, ravir; **to gain ~ to** (*university etc*) être admis à; **~ examination** *n* examen *m* d'entrée; **~ fee** *n* droit d'inscription; (*to museum etc*) prix *m* d'entrée; **~ ramp** *n* (*US AUT*) bretelle *f* d'accès.

entrant ['entrnt] *n* participant/e; concurrent/e.

entreat [en'triːt] *vt* supplier.

entrenched [en'trentʃt] *a* retranché(e).

entrepreneur [ɔntrəprə'nə:*] *n* entrepreneur *m*.

entrust [ɪn'trʌst] *vt*: **to ~ sth to** confier qch à.

entry ['entrɪ] *n* entrée *f*; (*in register*) inscription *f*; **no ~** défense d'entrer, entrée interdite; (*AUT*) sens interdit; **~ form** *n* feuille *f* d'inscription; **~ phone** *n* interphone *m* (*à l'entrée d'un immeuble*).

envelop [ɪn'veləp] *vt* envelopper.

envelope ['envələup] *n* enveloppe *f*.

envious ['envɪəs] *a* envieux(euse).

environment [ɪn'vaɪərnmənt] *n* milieu *m*; environnement *m*; **~al** [-'mentl] *a* écologique; du milieu.

envisage [ɪn'vɪzɪdʒ] *vt* envisager; prévoir.

envoy ['envɔɪ] *n* envoyé/e.

envy ['envɪ] *n* envie *f* // *vt* envier; **to ~ sb sth** envier qch à qn.

epic ['epɪk] *n* épopée *f* // *a* épique.

epidemic [epɪ'demɪk] *n* épidémie *f*.

epilepsy ['epɪlepsɪ] *n* épilepsie *f*.

episode ['epɪsəud] *n* épisode *m*.

epistle [ɪ'pɪsl] *n* épître *f*.

epitome [ɪ'pɪtəmɪ] *n* résumé *m*; quintessence *f*, type *m*; **epitomize** *vt* résumer; illustrer, incarner.

equable ['ekwəbl] *a* égal(e); de tempérament égal.

equal ['iːkwl] *a* égal(e) // *n* égal/e // *vt* égaler; **~ to** (*task*) à la hauteur de; **~ity** [iː'kwɔlɪtɪ] *n* égalité *f*; **~ize** *vt*, *vi* égaliser; **~izer** *n* but égalisateur; **~ly** *ad* également; (*just as*) tout aussi.

equanimity [ekwə'nɪmɪtɪ] *n* égalité *f* d'humeur.

equate [ɪ'kweɪt] *vt*: **to ~ sth with** comparer qch à; assimiler qch à; **equation** [ɪ'kweɪʃən] *n* (*MATH*) équation *f*.

equator [ɪ'kweɪtə*] *n* équateur *m*.

equilibrium [iːkwɪ'lɪbrɪəm] *n* équilibre *m*.

equip [ɪ'kwɪp] *vt* équiper; **to be well ~ped** (*office etc*) être bien équipé(e); **he is well ~ped for the job** il a les compétences *or* les qualités requises pour ce travail; **~ment** *n* équipement *m*; (*electrical etc*) appareillage *m*, installation *f*.

equities ['ekwɪtɪz] *npl* (*Brit COMM*) actions cotées en Bourse.

equivalent [ɪ'kwɪvəlnt] *a*: **~ (to)** équivalent(e) (à) // *n* équivalent *m*.

equivocal [ɪ'kwɪvəkl] *a* équivoque; (*open to suspicion*) douteux(euse).

era ['ɪərə] *n* ère *f*, époque *f*.

eradicate [ɪ'rædɪkeɪt] *vt* éliminer.

erase [ɪ'reɪz] *vt* effacer; **~r** *n* gomme *f*.

erect [ɪ'rekt] *a* droit(e) // *vt* construire; (*monument*) ériger; élever; (*tent etc*) dresser; **~ion** [ɪ'rekʃən] *n* érection *f*.

ermine ['əːmɪn] *n* hermine *f*.

erode [ɪ'rəud] *vt* éroder; (*metal*) ronger.

erotic [ɪ'rɔtɪk] *a* érotique.

err [əː*] *vi* se tromper; (*REL*) pécher.

errand ['ernd] *n* course *f*, commission *f*.

erratic [ɪ'rætɪk] *a* irrégulier(ère); inconstant(e).

error ['erə*] *n* erreur *f*.

erupt [ɪ'rʌpt] *vi* entrer en éruption; (*fig*) éclater; **~ion** [ɪ'rʌpʃən] *n* éruption *f*.

escalate ['eskəleɪt] *vi* s'intensifier.

escalator ['eskəleɪtə*] *n* escalier roulant.

escapade [eskə'peɪd] *n* fredaine *f*; équipée *f*.

escape [ɪ'skeɪp] *n* évasion *f*; fuite *f*; (*of gas etc*) échappement *m*; fuite // *vi* s'échapper, fuir; (*from jail*) s'évader; (*fig*) s'en tirer; (*leak*) s'échapper; fuir // *vt* échapper à; **to ~ from** (*person*) échapper à; (*place*) s'échapper de; (*fig*) fuir; **escapism** *n* évasion *f* (*fig*).

escort *n* ['eskɔːt] escorte *f* // *vt* [ɪ'skɔːt] escorter.

Eskimo ['eskɪməu] *n* Esquimau/de.

especially [ɪ'speʃlɪ] *ad* particulièrement; surtout; exprès.

espionage ['espɪənɑːʒ] *n* espionnage *m*.

Esquire [ɪ'skwaɪə*] *n* (*abbr* Esq.): J. Brown, ~ Monsieur J. Brown.

essay ['eseɪ] *n* (*SCOL*) dissertation *f*; (*LITERATURE*) essai *m*.

essence ['esns] *n* essence *f*.

essential [ɪ'senʃl] *a* essentiel(le); (*basic*) fondamental(e) // *n*: ~s éléments essentiels; ~**ly** *ad* essentiellement.

establish [ɪ'stæblɪʃ] *vt* établir; (*business*) fonder, créer; (*one's power etc*) asseoir, affermir; ~**ment** *n* établissement *m*; création *f*; **the E~ment** les pouvoirs établis; l'ordre établi; les milieux dirigeants.

estate [ɪ'steɪt] *n* domaine *m*, propriété *f*; biens *mpl*, succession *f*; ~ **agent** *n* agent immobilier; ~ **car** *n* (*Brit*) break *m*.

esteem [ɪ'stiːm] *n* estime *f* // *vt* estimer; apprécier.

esthetic [ɪs'θetɪk] *a* (*US*) = **aesthetic**.

estimate *n* ['estɪmət] estimation *f*; (*COMM*) devis *m* // *vt* ['estɪmeɪt] estimer; **estimation** [-'meɪʃən] *n* opinion *f*; estime *f*.

estranged [ɪ'streɪndʒd] *a* séparé(e); dont on s'est séparé(e).

etc *abbr* (= et cetera) etc.

etching ['etʃɪŋ] *n* eau-forte *f*.

eternal [ɪ'təːnl] *a* éternel(le).

eternity [ɪ'təːnɪtɪ] *n* éternité *f*.

ethical ['eθɪkl] *a* moral(e).

ethics ['eθɪks] *n* éthique *f* // *npl* moralité *f*.

Ethiopia [iːθɪ'əupɪə] *n* Éthiopie *f*.

ethnic ['eθnɪk] *a* ethnique.

ethos ['iːθɔs] *n* génie *m*.

etiquette ['etɪket] *n* convenances *fpl*, étiquette *f*.

Eurocheque ['juərəutʃek] *n* eurochèque *m*.

Europe ['juərəp] *n* Europe *f*; ~**an** [-'piːən] *a* européen(ne) // *n* Européen/ne.

evacuate [ɪ'vækjueɪt] *vt* évacuer.

evade [ɪ'veɪd] *vt* échapper à; (*question etc*) éluder; (*duties*) se dérober à.

evaporate [ɪ'væpəreɪt] *vi* s'évaporer // *vt* faire évaporer; ~**d milk** *n* lait condensé non sucré.

evasion [ɪ'veɪʒən] *n* dérobade *f*; faux-fuyant *m*.

eve [iːv] *n*: on the ~ of à la veille de.

even ['iːvn] *a* régulier(ère), égal(e); (*number*) pair(e) // *ad* même; ~ **if** même si + *indic*; ~ **though** quand (bien) même + *cond*, alors même que + *cond*; ~ **more** encore plus; ~ **so** quand même; **not** ~ pas même; **to get** ~ **with sb** prendre sa revanche sur qn; **to** ~ **out** *vi* s'égaliser.

evening ['iːvnɪŋ] *n* soir *m*; (*as duration, event*) soirée *f*; **in the** ~ le soir; ~ **class** *n* cours *m* du soir; ~ **dress** *n* (*man's*) habit *m* de soirée, smoking *m*; (*woman's*) robe *f* de soirée.

event [ɪ'vent] *n* événement *m*; (*SPORT*) épreuve *f*; **in the** ~ **of** en cas de; ~**ful** *a* mouvementé(e).

eventual [ɪ'ventʃuəl] *a* final(e); ~**ity** [-'ælɪtɪ] *n* possibilité *f*, éventualité *f*; ~**ly** *ad* finalement.

ever ['evə*] *ad* jamais; (*at all times*) toujours; **the best** ~ le meilleur qu'on ait jamais vu; **have you** ~ **seen it?** l'as-tu déjà vu?, as-tu eu l'occasion *or* t'est-il arrivé de le voir?; ~ **since** *ad* depuis // *cj* depuis que; ~**green** *n* arbre *m* à feuilles persistantes; ~**lasting** *a* éternel(le).

every ['evrɪ] *a* chaque; ~ **day** tous les jours, chaque jour; ~ **other/third day** tous les deux/trois jours; ~ **other car** une voiture sur deux; ~ **now and then** de temps en temps; ~**body** *pronoun* tout le monde, tous *pl*; ~**day** *a* quotidien(ne); de tous les jours; ~**one** = ~**body**; ~**thing** *pronoun* tout; ~**where** *ad* partout.

evict [ɪ'vɪkt] *vt* expulser.

evidence ['evɪdns] *n* (*proof*) preuve(s) *f(pl)*; (*of witness*) témoignage *m*; (*sign*): **to show** ~ **of** donner des signes de; **to give** ~ témoigner, déposer.

evident ['evɪdnt] *a* évident(e); ~**ly** *ad* de toute évidence.

evil ['iːvl] *a* mauvais(e) // *n* mal *m*.

evoke [ɪ'vəuk] *vt* évoquer.

evolution [iːvə'luːʃən] *n* évolution *f*.

evolve [ɪ'vɔlv] *vt* élaborer // *vi* évoluer, se transformer.

ewe [juː] *n* brebis *f*.

ex- [eks] *prefix* ex-.

exact [ɪg'zækt] *a* exact(e) // *vt*: **to** ~ **sth (from)** extorquer qch (à); exiger qch (de); ~**ing** *a* exigeant(e); (*work*) fatigant(e); ~**ly** *ad* exactement.

exaggerate [ɪg'zædʒəreɪt] *vt*, *vi* exagérer; **exaggeration** [-'reɪʃən] *n* exagération *f*.

exalted [ɪg'zɔːltɪd] *a* élevé(e); (*person*) haut placé(e); (*elated*) exalté(e).

exam [ɪg'zæm] *n abbr* (*SCOL*) of **examination**.

examination [ɪgzæmɪ'neɪʃən] *n* (*SCOL, MED*) examen *m*.

examine [ɪg'zæmɪn] *vt* (*gen*) examiner; (*SCOL, LAW: person*) interroger; (*at customs: luggage*) inspecter; ~**r** *n* examinateur/trice.

example [ɪg'zɑːmpl] *n* exemple *m*; **for** ~ par exemple.

exasperate [ɪg'zɑːspəreɪt] *vt* exaspérer; **exasperation** [ɪgzɑːspə'reɪʃən] *n* exaspération *f*, irritation *f*.

excavate ['ekskəveɪt] *vt* excaver; (*object*) mettre au jour.

exceed [ɪk'siːd] vt dépasser; (one's powers) outrepasser; **~ingly** ad excessivement.

excellent ['eksələnt] a excellent(e).

except [ɪk'sept] prep (also: ~ for, ~ing) sauf, excepté, à l'exception de // vt excepter; ~ if/when sauf si/quand; ~ that excepté que, si ce n'est que; **~ion** [ɪk'sepʃən] n exception f; to take ~ion to s'offusquer de; **~ional** [ɪk'sepʃənl] a exceptionnel(le).

excerpt ['eksɔːpt] n extrait m.

excess [ɪk'ses] n excès m; ~ **baggage** n excédent m de bagages; ~ **fare** n supplément m; **~ive** a excessif(ive).

exchange [ɪks'tʃeɪndʒ] n échange m; (also: telephone ~) central m // vt: to ~ (for) échanger (contre); ~ **rate** n taux m des changes.

Exchequer [ɪks'tʃekə*] n: the ~ (Brit) l'Echiquier m, ≈ le ministère des Finances.

excise ['eksaɪz] n taxe f.

excite [ɪk'saɪt] vt exciter; to get ~d s'exciter; **~ment** n excitation f; **exciting** a passionnant(e).

exclaim [ɪk'skleɪm] vi s'exclamer; **exclamation** [eksklə'meɪʃən] n exclamation f; **exclamation mark** n point m d'exclamation.

exclude [ɪk'skluːd] vt exclure.

exclusive [ɪk'skluːsɪv] a exclusif(ive); (club, district) sélect(e); (item of news) en exclusivité; ~ **of VAT** TVA non comprise.

excruciating [ɪk'skruːʃɪeɪtɪŋ] a atroce, déchirant(e).

excursion [ɪk'skɔːʃən] n excursion f.

excuse n [ɪk'skjuːs] excuse f // vt [ɪk'skjuːz] excuser; to ~ **sb from** (activity) dispenser qn de; ~ **me**! excusez-moi!, pardon!; now if you will ~ me, ... maintenant, si vous (le) permettez ....

ex-directory ['eksdɪ'rektərɪ] a (Brit) sur la liste rouge.

execute ['eksɪkjuːt] vt exécuter.

execution [eksɪ'kjuːʃən] n exécution f; **~er** n bourreau m.

executive [ɪg'zekjutɪv] n (COMM) cadre m; (POL) exécutif m // a exécutif(ive).

exemplify [ɪg'zemplɪfaɪ] vt illustrer.

exempt [ɪg'zempt] a: ~ **from** exempté(e) or dispensé(e) de // vt: to ~ **sb from** exempter or dispenser qn de.

exercise ['eksəsaɪz] n exercice m // vt exercer; (patience etc) faire preuve de; (dog) promener // vi prendre de l'exercice; ~ **book** n cahier m.

exert [ɪg'zɔːt] vt exercer, employer; to ~ **o.s.** se dépenser; **~ion** [-ʃən] n effort m.

exhaust [ɪg'zɔːst] n (also: ~ **fumes**) gaz mpl d'échappement; (also: ~ **pipe**) tuyau m d'échappement // vt épuiser; **~ed** a épuisé(e); **~ion** [ɪg'zɔːstʃən] n épuisement m; **nervous ~ion** fatigue nerveuse; surmenage mental; **~ive** a très complet(ète).

exhibit [ɪg'zɪbɪt] n (ART) pièce f or objet m exposé(e); (LAW) pièce à conviction // vt exposer; (courage, skill) faire preuve de; **~ion** [eksɪ'bɪʃən] n exposition f.

exhilarating [ɪg'zɪləreɪtɪŋ] a grisant(e); stimulant(e).

exile ['eksaɪl] n exil m; (person) exilé/e // vt exiler.

exist [ɪg'zɪst] vi exister; **~ence** n existence f; to be in **~ence** exister; **~ing** a actuel(le).

exit ['eksɪt] n sortie f // vi (COMPUT, THEATRE) sortir; ~ **ramp** n (US AUT) bretelle f d'accès.

exodus ['eksədəs] n exode m.

exonerate [ɪg'zɔnəreɪt] vt: to ~ **from** disculper de.

exotic [ɪg'zɔtɪk] a exotique.

expand [ɪk'spænd] vt agrandir; accroître, étendre // vi (trade etc) se développer; s'accroître; s'étendre; (gas, metal) se dilater.

expanse [ɪk'spæns] n étendue f.

expansion [ɪk'spænʃən] n développement m, accroissement m; dilatation f.

expect [ɪk'spekt] vt (anticipate) s'attendre à, s'attendre à ce que + sub; (count on) compter sur, escompter; (hope for) espérer; (require) demander, exiger; (suppose) supposer; (await, also baby) attendre // vi: to be ~ing être enceinte; to ~ **sb to do** s'attendre à ce que qn fasse; attendre de qn qu'il fasse; **~ancy** n (anticipation) attente f; **life ~ancy** espérance f de vie; **~ant mother** n future maman; **~ation** [ekspek'teɪʃən] n attente f, prévisions fpl; espérance(s) f(pl).

expedience, expediency [ɪk'spiːdɪəns, ɪk'spiːdɪənsɪ] n: for the sake of ~ parce que c'est plus commode.

expedient [ɪk'spiːdɪənt] a indiqué(e), opportun(e); commode // n expédient m.

expedition [ekspə'dɪʃən] n expédition f.

expel [ɪk'spel] vt chasser, expulser; (SCOL) renvoyer, exclure.

expend [ɪk'spend] vt consacrer; (use up) dépenser; **~able** a remplaçable; **~iture** [ɪk'spendɪtʃə*] n dépense f; dépenses fpl.

expense [ɪk'spens] n dépense f; frais mpl; (high cost) coût m; ~**s** npl (COMM) frais mpl; at the ~ **of** aux dépens de; ~ **account** n (note f de) frais mpl.

expensive [ɪk'spensɪv] a cher(chère); coûteux(euse); to be ~ coûter cher.

experience [ɪk'spɪərɪəns] n expérience f // vt connaître; éprouver; **~d** a expérimenté(e).

experiment [ɪk'sperɪmənt] n expérience f // vi faire une expérience; to ~ **with**

expérimenter.

expert ['ɛkspɜ:t] *a* expert(e) // *n* expert *m*; **~ise** [-'ti:z] *n* (grande) compétence.

expire [ɪk'spaɪə*] *vi* expirer; **expiry** *n* expiration *f*.

explain [ɪk'spleɪn] *vt* expliquer; **explanation** [ɛksplə'neɪʃən] *n* explication *f*; **explanatory** [ɪk'splænətrɪ] *a* explicatif(ive).

explicit [ɪk'splɪsɪt] *a* explicite; (*definite*) formel(le).

explode [ɪk'spləud] *vi* exploser // *vt* faire exploser.

exploit *n* ['ɛksplɔɪt] exploit *m* // *vt* [ɪk'splɔɪt] exploiter; **~ation** [-'teɪʃən] *n* exploitation *f*.

exploratory [ɪk'splɔrətrɪ] *a* (*fig: talks*) préliminaire.

explore [ɪk'splɔ:*] *vt* explorer; (*possibilities*) étudier, examiner; **~r** *n* explorateur/trice.

explosion [ɪk'spləuʒən] *n* explosion *f*.

explosive [ɪk'spləusɪv] *a* explosif(ive) // *n* explosif *m*.

exponent [ɪk'spəunənt] *n* (*of school of thought etc*) interprète *m*, représentant *m*.

export *vt* [ɛk'spɔ:t] exporter // *n* ['ɛkspɔ:t] exportation *f* // *cpd* d'exportation; **~er** *n* exportateur *m*.

expose [ɪk'spəuz] *vt* exposer; (*unmask*) démasquer, dévoiler; **~d** *a* (*position*) exposé(e).

exposure [ɪk'spəuʒə*] *n* exposition *f*; (*PHOT*) (temps *m* de) pose *f*; (: *shot*) pose; **suffering from ~** (*MED*) souffrant des effets du froid et de l'épuisement; **~ meter** *n* posemètre *m*.

expound [ɪk'spaund] *vt* exposer.

express [ɪk'sprɛs] *a* (*definite*) formel(le), exprès(esse); (*Brit: letter etc*) exprès *inv* // *n* (*train*) rapide *m* // *ad* (*send*) exprès // *vt* exprimer; **~ion** [ɪk'sprɛʃən] *n* expression *f*; **~ly** *ad* expressément, formellement; **~way** *n* (*US: urban motorway*) voie *f* express (à plusieurs files).

exquisite [ɛk'skwɪzɪt] *a* exquis(e).

extend [ɪk'stɛnd] *vt* (*visit, street*) prolonger; (*building*) agrandir; (*offer*) présenter, offrir // *vi* (*land*) s'étendre.

extension [ɪk'stɛnʃən] *n* prolongation *f*; agrandissement *m*; (*building*) annexe *f*; (*to wire, table*) rallonge *f*; (*telephone: in offices*) poste *m*; (: *in private house*) téléphone *m* supplémentaire.

extensive [ɪk'stɛnsɪv] *a* étendu(e), vaste; (*damage, alterations*) considérable; (*inquiries*) approfondi(e); (*use*) largement répandu(e); **he's travelled ~ly** il a beaucoup voyagé.

extent [ɪk'stɛnt] *n* étendue *f*; **to some ~** dans une certaine mesure; **to what ~?** dans quelle mesure?, jusqu'à quel point?; **to the ~ of ...** au point de ....

extenuating [ɪk'stɛnjueɪtɪŋ] *a*: **~ circumstances** circonstances atténuantes.

exterior [ɛk'stɪərɪə*] *a* extérieur(e), du dehors // *n* extérieur *m*; dehors *m*.

external [ɛk'stə:nl] *a* externe.

extinct [ɪk'stɪŋkt] *a* éteint(e).

extinguish [ɪk'stɪŋgwɪʃ] *vt* éteindre; **~er** *n* extincteur *m*.

extort [ɪk'stɔ:t] *vt*: **to ~ sth (from)** extorquer qch (à); **~ionate** [ɪk'stɔ:ʃnət] *a* exorbitant(e).

extra ['ɛkstrə] *a* supplémentaire, de plus // *ad* (*in addition*) en plus // *n* supplément *m*; (*THEATRE*) figurant/e.

extra... ['ɛkstrə] *prefix* extra....

extract *vt* [ɪk'strækt] extraire; (*tooth*) arracher; (*money, promise*) soutirer // *n* ['ɛkstrækt] extrait *m*.

extracurricular ['ɛkstrəkə'rɪkjulə*] *a* parascolaire.

extradite ['ɛkstrədaɪt] *vt* extrader.

extramarital [ɛkstrə'mærɪtl] *a* extra-conjugal(e).

extramural [ɛkstrə'mjuərl] *a* hors-faculté *inv*.

extraordinary [ɪk'strɔ:dnrɪ] *a* extraordinaire.

extravagance [ɪk'strævəgəns] *n* prodigalités *fpl*; (*thing bought*) folie *f*, dépense excessive ou exagérée.

extravagant [ɪk'strævəgənt] *a* extravagant(e); (*in spending*) prodigue, dépensier(ère); dispendieux(euse).

extreme [ɪk'stri:m] *a, n* extrême (*m*); **~ly** *ad* extrêmement.

extricate ['ɛkstrɪkeɪt] *vt*: **to ~ sth (from)** dégager qch (de).

extrovert ['ɛkstrəvə:t] *n* extraverti/e.

eye [aɪ] *n* œil *m* (*pl* yeux); (*of needle*) trou *m*, chas *m* // *vt* examiner; **to keep an ~ on** surveiller; **~ball** *n* globe *m* oculaire; **~bath** *n* œillère *f* (*pour bains d'œil*); **~brow** *n* sourcil *m*; **~brow pencil** *n* crayon *m* à sourcils; **~drops** *npl* gouttes *fpl* pour les yeux; **~lash** *n* cil *m*; **~lid** *n* paupière *f*; **~liner** *n* eye-liner *m*; **~-opener** *n* révélation *f*; **~shadow** *n* ombre *f* à paupières; **~sight** *n* vue *f*; **~sore** *n* horreur *f*, chose *f* qui dépare ou enlaidit; **~ witness** *n* témoin *m* oculaire.

F

F [ɛf] *n* (*MUS*) fa *m*.

fable ['feɪbl] *n* fable *f*.

fabric ['fæbrɪk] *n* tissu *m*.

fabrication [fæbrɪ'keɪʃən] *n* invention(s) *f(pl)*, fabulation *f*; fait *m* (*or preuve f*) forgé(e) de toutes pièces.

fabulous ['fæbjuləs] *a* fabuleux(euse); (*col: super*) formidable.

face [feɪs] *n* visage *m*, figure *f*; expression *f*; (*of clock*) cadran *m*; (*of*

building) façade *f*; (*side, surface*) face *f*
// il va faire face à; ~ **down** (*person*) à plat
ventre; (*card*) face en dessous; **to make**
or pull a ~ faire une grimace; **in the** ~
of (*difficulties etc*) face à, devant; **on the**
~ **of it** à première vue; ~ **to** ~ face à
face; **to** ~ **up to** *vt fus* faire face à, affronter; ~ **cloth** *n* (*Brit*) gant *m* de
toilette; ~ **cream** *n* crème *f* pour le
visage; ~ **lift** *n* lifting *m*; (*of building*
etc) ravalement *m*, retapage *m*.
face value *n* (*of coin*) valeur nominale;
to take sth at ~ (*fig*) prendre qch pour
argent comptant.
facilities [fə'sɪlɪtɪz] *npl* installations *fpl*,
équipement *m*; **credit** ~ facilités *fpl* de
paiement.
facing ['feɪsɪŋ] *prep* face à, en face de //
n (*of wall etc*) revêtement *m*; (*SEWING*)
revers *m*.
facsimile [fæk'sɪmɪlɪ] *n* (*document*)
télécopie *f*; (*machine*) télécopieur *m*.
fact [fækt] *n* fait *m*; **in** ~ en fait.
factor ['fæktə*] *n* facteur *m*.
factory ['fæktərɪ] *n* usine *f*, fabrique *f*.
factual ['fæktjuəl] *a* basé(e) sur les faits.
faculty ['fækəltɪ] *n* faculté *f*; (*US: teach-*
ing staff) corps enseignant.
fad [fæd] *n* manie *f*; engouement *m*.
fade [feɪd] *vi* se décolorer, passer; (*light,*
sound, hope) s'affaiblir, disparaître;
(*flower*) se faner.
fag [fæg] *n* (*col: cigarette*) sèche *f*.
fail [feɪl] *vt* (*exam*) échouer à;
(*candidate*) recaler; (*subj: courage,*
memory) faire défaut à // *vi* échouer;
(*supplies*) manquer; (*eyesight, health,*
light) baisser, s'affaiblir; **to** ~ **to do sth**
(*neglect*) négliger de faire qch; (*be un-*
able) ne pas arriver *or* parvenir à faire
qch; **without** ~ à coup sûr; sans faute;
~**ing** *n* défaut *m* // *prep* faute de; ~**ure**
['feɪljə*] *n* échec *m*; (*person*) raté/e;
(*mechanical etc*) défaillance *f*.
faint [feɪnt] *a* faible; (*recollection*)
vague; (*mark*) à peine visible // *n*
évanouissement *m* // *vi* s'évanouir; **to**
feel ~ défaillir.
fair [fɛə*] *a* équitable, juste,
impartial(e); (*hair*) blond(e); (*skin,*
complexion) pâle, blanc(blanche);
(*weather*) beau(belle); (*good enough*)
assez bon(ne); (*sizeable*) considérable //
ad (*play*) franc-jeu // *n* foire *f*; (*Brit:*
funfair) fête (foraine); ~**ly** *ad* équita-
blement; (*quite*) assez; ~**ness** *n* justice
f, équité *f*, impartialité *f*.
fairy ['fɛərɪ] *n* fée *f*; ~ **tale** *n* conte *m*
de fées.
faith [feɪθ] *n* foi *f*; (*trust*) confiance *f*;
(*sect*) culte *m*, religion *f*; ~**ful** *a* fidèle;
~**fully** *ad* fidèlement.
fake [feɪk] *n* (*painting etc*) faux *m*;
(*photo*) trucage *m*; (*person*) imposteur
m // *a* faux(fausse); simulé(e) // *vt*

simuler; (*photo*) truquer; (*story*) fabriquer.
falcon ['fɔːlkən] *n* faucon *m*.
fall [fɔːl] *n* chute *f*; (*US: autumn*)
automne *m* // *vi* (*pt* fell, *pp* fallen)
tomber; ~**s** *npl* (*waterfall*) chute *f* d'eau,
cascade *f*; **to** ~ **flat** *vi* (*on one's face*)
tomber de tout son long, s'étaler; (*joke*)
tomber à plat; (*plan*) échouer; **to** ~
back *vi* reculer, se retirer; **to** ~ **back**
on *vt fus* se rabattre sur; **to** ~ **behind**
vi prendre du retard; **to** ~ **down** *vi*
(*person*) tomber; (*building, hopes*)
s'effondrer, s'écrouler; **to** ~ **for** *vt fus*
(*trick*) se laisser prendre à; (*person*)
tomber amoureux de; **to** ~ **in** *vi* s'effondrer; (*MIL*) se mettre en rangs; **to** ~
off *vi* tomber; (*diminish*) baisser,
diminuer; **to** ~ **out** *vi* (*friends etc*) se
brouiller; **to** ~ **through** *vi* (*plan,*
project) tomber à l'eau.
fallacy ['fæləsɪ] *n* erreur *f*, illusion *f*.
fallen ['fɔːlən] *pp of* **fall**.
fallout ['fɔːlaut] *n* retombées
(radioactives); ~ **shelter** *n* abri *m*
anti-atomique.
fallow ['fæləu] *a* en jachère; en friche.
false [fɔːls] *a* faux(fausse); **under** ~ **pre-**
tences sous un faux prétexte; ~ **teeth**
npl (*Brit*) fausses dents.
falter ['fɔːltə*] *vi* chanceler, vaciller.
fame [feɪm] *n* renommée *f*, renom *m*.
familiar [fə'mɪlɪə*] *a* familier(ère); **to**
be ~ **with** (*subject*) connaître; ~**ity**
[fəmɪlɪ'ærɪtɪ] *n* familiarité *f*.
family ['fæmɪlɪ] *n* famille *f*.
famine ['fæmɪn] *n* famine *f*.
famished ['fæmɪʃt] *a* affamé(e).
famous ['feɪməs] *a* célèbre; ~**ly** *ad* (*get*
on) fameusement, à merveille.
fan [fæn] *n* (*folding*) éventail *m*; (*ELEC*)
ventilateur *m*; (*person*) fan *m*,
admirateur/trice; supporter *m/f* // *vt*
éventer; (*fire, quarrel*) attiser; **to** ~
out *vi* se déployer (en éventail).
fanatic [fə'nætɪk] *n* fanatique *m/f*.
fan belt *n* courroie *f* de ventilateur.
fanciful ['fænsɪful] *a* fantaisiste.
fancy ['fænsɪ] *n* fantaisie *f*, envie *f*;
imagination *f* // *a* (de) fantaisie *inv* // *vt*
(*feel like, want*) avoir envie de;
(*imagine*) imaginer; **to take a** ~ **to** se
prendre d'affection pour; s'enticher de;
~ **dress** *n* déguisement *m*, travesti *m*;
~**-dress ball** *n* bal masqué *or* costumé.
fang [fæŋ] *n* croc *m*; (*of snake*) crochet
m.
fantastic [fæn'tæstɪk] *a* fantastique.
fantasy ['fæntəsɪ] *n* imagination *f*,
fantaisie *f*; chimère *f*.
far [fɑː*] *a*: **the** ~ **side/end** l'autre côté/
bout // *ad* loin; ~ **away** au loin, dans le
lointain; ~ **better** beaucoup mieux; ~
from loin de; **by** ~ de loin, de beaucoup;
go as ~ **as the farm** allez jusqu'à la

ferme; **as ~ as I know** pour autant que je sache; **~away** a lointain(e).

farce [fɑːs] n farce f.

farcical ['fɑːsɪkəl] a grotesque.

fare [fɛə*] n (on trains, buses) prix m du billet; (in taxi) prix de la course; (food) table f, chère f; **half ~** demi-tarif; **full ~** plein tarif.

Far East n: **the ~** l'Extrême-Orient m.

farewell [fɛə'wɛl] excl, a adieu (m).

farm [fɑːm] n ferme f // vt cultiver; **~er** n fermier/ère; cultivateur/trice; **~hand** n ouvrier/ère agricole; **~house** n (maison f de) ferme f; **~ing** n agriculture f; **~ worker** n = **~hand**; **~yard** n cour f de ferme.

far-reaching ['fɑː'riːtʃɪŋ] a d'une grande portée.

fart [fɑːt] (col!) n pet m // vi péter.

farther ['fɑːðə*] ad plus loin // a plus éloigné(e), plus lointain(e).

farthest ['fɑːðɪst] superlative of **far**.

fascinate ['fæsɪneɪt] vt fasciner; **fascinating** a fascinant(e).

fascism ['fæʃɪzəm] n fascisme m.

fashion ['fæʃən] n mode f; (manner) façon f, manière f // vt façonner; **in ~** à la mode; **out of ~** démodé(e); **~able** a à la mode; **~ show** n défilé m de mannequins or de mode.

fast [fɑːst] a rapide; (clock): **to be ~** avancer; (dye, colour) grand or bon teint inv // ad vite, rapidement; (stuck, held) solidement // n jeûne m // vi jeûner; **~ asleep** profondément endormi.

fasten ['fɑːsn] vt attacher, fixer; (coat) attacher, fermer // vi se fermer, s'attacher; **~er**, **~ing** n fermeture f, attache f.

fast food n fast food m, restauration f rapide.

fastidious [fæs'tɪdɪəs] a exigeant(e), difficile.

fat [fæt] a gros(se) // n graisse f; (on meat) gras m.

fatal ['feɪtl] a mortel(le); fatal(e); désastreux(euse); **~ity** [fə'tælɪtɪ] n (road death etc) victime f, décès m.

fate [feɪt] n destin m; (of person) sort m; **~ful** a fatidique.

father ['fɑːðə*] n père m; **~-in-law** n beau-père m; **~ly** a paternel(le).

fathom ['fæðəm] n brasse f (= 1828 mm) // vt (mystery) sonder, pénétrer.

fatigue [fə'tiːg] n fatigue f; (MIL) corvée f.

fatten ['fætn] vt, vi engraisser.

fatty ['fætɪ] a (food) gras(se) // n (col) gros/grosse.

fatuous ['fætjuəs] a stupide.

faucet ['fɔːsɪt] n (US) robinet m.

fault [fɔːlt] n faute f; (defect) défaut m; (GEO) faille f // vt trouver des défauts à, prendre en défaut; **it's my ~** c'est de ma faute; **to find ~ with** trouver à redire or

à critiquer à; **at ~** fautif(ive), coupable; **to a ~** à l'excès; **~less** a sans fautes; impeccable; irréprochable; **~y** a défectueux(euse).

fauna ['fɔːnə] n faune f.

faux pas ['fəu'pɑː] n impair m, bévue f, gaffe f.

favour, (US) **favor** ['feɪvə*] n faveur f; (help) service m // vt (proposition) être en faveur de; (pupil etc) favoriser; (team, horse) donner gagnant; **to do sb a ~** rendre un service à qn; **to find ~ with** trouver grâce aux yeux de; **in ~ of** en faveur de; **~able** a favorable; (price) avantageux(euse); **~ite** [-rɪt] a, n favori(te).

fawn [fɔːn] n faon m // a (also: **~-coloured**) fauve // vi: **to ~ (up)on** flatter servilement.

fax [fæks] n (document) télécopie f; (machine) télécopieur m.

FBI n abbr (US: = Federal Bureau of Investigation) F.B.I. m.

fear [fɪə*] n crainte f, peur f // vt craindre; **for ~ of** de peur que + sub or de + infinitive; **~ful** a craintif(ive); (sight, noise) affreux(euse), épouvantable.

feasible ['fiːzəbl] a faisable, réalisable.

feast [fiːst] n festin m, banquet m; (REL: also: **~ day**) fête f // vi festoyer.

feat [fiːt] n exploit m, prouesse f.

feather ['fɛðə*] n plume f.

feature ['fiːtʃə*] n caractéristique f; (article) chronique f, rubrique f // vt (subj: film) avoir pour vedette(s) // vi figurer (en bonne place); **~s** npl (of face) traits mpl; **~ film** n film principal.

February ['fɛbruərɪ] n février m.

fed [fɛd] pt, pp of **feed**.

federal ['fɛdərəl] a fédéral(e).

fed-up [fɛd'ʌp] a: **to be ~** en avoir marre or plein le dos.

fee [fiː] n rémunération f; (of doctor, lawyer) honoraires mpl; (of school, college etc) frais mpl de scolarité; (for examination) droits mpl.

feeble ['fiːbl] a faible.

feed [fiːd] n (of baby) tétée f; (of animal) fourrage m; pâture f; (on printer) mécanisme m d'alimentation // vt (pt, pp fed) nourrir; (Brit: baby) allaiter; donner le biberon à; (horse etc) donner à manger à; (machine) alimenter; (data, information): **to ~ into** fournir à; **to ~ on** vt fus se nourrir de; **~back** n feed-back m; **~ing bottle** n (Brit) biberon m.

feel [fiːl] n sensation f // vt (pt, pp felt) toucher; tâter, palper; (cold, pain) sentir; (grief, anger) ressentir, éprouver; (think, believe): **to ~ (that)** trouver que; **to ~ hungry/cold** avoir faim/froid; **to ~ lonely/better** se sentir seul/mieux; **I don't ~ well** je ne me sens pas bien; **to ~ like** (*want*) avoir envie de; **to ~ about** or **around** *vi* fouiller, tâtonner; **~er** *n* (*of insect*) antenne *f*; **to put out ~ers** or a **~er** tâter le terrain; **~ing** *n* sensation *f*, sentiment *m*.

feet [fi:t] *npl of* **foot**.

feign [feɪn] *vt* feindre, simuler.

fell [fɛl] *pt of* **fall** // *vt* (*tree*) abattre.

fellow ['fɛləu] *n* type *m*; compagnon *m*; (*of learned society*) membre *m* // *cpd*: **~ countryman** *n* compatriote *m*; **~ men** *npl* semblables *mpl*; **~ship** *n* association *f*; amitié *f*, camaraderie *f*; *sorte de bourse universitaire.*

felony ['fɛlənɪ] *n* crime *m*, forfait *m*.

felt [fɛlt] *pt, pp of* **feel** // *n* feutre *m*; **~tip pen** *n* stylo-feutre *m*.

female ['fi:meɪl] *n* (*ZOOL*) femelle *f*; (*pej: woman*) bonne femme // *a* (*BIOL, ELEC*) femelle; (*sex, character*) féminin(e); (*vote etc*) des femmes.

feminine ['fɛmɪnɪn] *a* féminin(e).

feminist ['fɛmɪnɪst] *n* féministe *m/f*.

fence [fɛns] *n* barrière *f*; (*col: person*) receleur/euse // *vt* (*also:* **~ in**) clôturer // *vi* faire de l'escrime; **fencing** *n* escrime *m*.

fend [fɛnd] *vi*: **to ~ for o.s.** se débrouiller (tout seul); **to ~ off** *vt* (*attack etc*) parer.

fender ['fɛndə*] *n* garde-feu *m inv*; (*US*) garde-boue *m inv*; pare-chocs *m inv*.

ferment *vi* [fə'mɛnt] fermenter // *n* ['fə:mɛnt] agitation *f*, effervescence *f*.

fern [fə:n] *n* fougère *f*.

ferocious [fə'rəuʃəs] *a* féroce.

ferret ['fɛrɪt] *n* furet *m*.

ferry ['fɛrɪ] *n* (*small*) bac *m*; (*large: also:* **~boat**) ferry(-boat) *m* // *vt* transporter.

fertile ['fə:taɪl] *a* fertile; (*BIOL*) fécond(e); **fertilizer** ['fə:tɪlaɪzə*] *n* engrais *m*.

fester ['fɛstə*] *vi* suppurer.

festival ['fɛstɪvəl] *n* (*REL*) fête *f*; (*ART, MUS*) festival *m*.

festive ['fɛstɪv] *a* de fête; **the ~ season** (*Brit: Christmas*) la période des fêtes.

festivities [fɛs'tɪvɪtɪz] *npl* réjouissances *fpl*.

festoon [fɛ'stu:n] *vt*: **to ~ with** orner de.

fetch [fɛtʃ] *vt* aller chercher; (*sell for*) se vendre.

fetching ['fɛtʃɪŋ] *a* charmant(e).

fête [feɪt] *n* fête *f*, kermesse *f*.

feud [fju:d] *n* dispute *f*, dissension *f*.

feudal ['fju:dl] *a* féodal(e).

fever ['fi:və*] *n* fièvre *f*; **~ish** *a* fiévreux(euse), fébrile.

few [fju:] *a* peu de; **they were ~** ils étaient peu (nombreux); **a ~** *a* quelques // *pronoun* quelques-uns; **~er** *a* moins de; moins (nombreux).

fiancé [fɪ'ã:ŋseɪ] *n* fiancé *m*; **~e** *n*

fiancée *f*.

fib [fɪb] *n* bobard *m*.

fibre, (*US*) **fiber** ['faɪbə*] *n* fibre *f*; **~-glass** *n* fibre de verre.

fickle ['fɪkl] *a* inconstant(e), volage, capricieux(euse).

fiction ['fɪkʃən] *n* romans *mpl*, littérature *f* romanesque; fiction *f*; **~al** *a* fictif(ive).

fictitious [fɪk'tɪʃəs] *a* fictif(ive), imaginaire.

fiddle ['fɪdl] *n* (*MUS*) violon *m*; (*cheating*) combine *f*; escroquerie *f* // *vt* (*Brit: accounts*) falsifier, maquiller; **to ~ with** *vt fus* tripoter.

fidget ['fɪdʒɪt] *vi* se trémousser, remuer.

field [fi:ld] *n* champ *m*; (*fig*) domaine *m*, champ; (*SPORT: ground*) terrain *m*; **~ marshal** *n* maréchal *m*; **~work** *n* travaux *mpl* pratiques (sur le terrain).

fiend [fi:nd] *n* démon *m*.

fierce [fɪəs] *a* (*look*) féroce, sauvage; (*wind, attack*) (très) violent(e); (*fighting, enemy*) acharné(e).

fiery ['faɪərɪ] *a* ardent(e), brûlant(e), fougueux(euse).

fifteen [fɪf'ti:n] *num* quinze.

fifth [fɪfθ] *a, n* cinquième (*m*).

fifty ['fɪftɪ] *num* cinquante; **~-~** *a*: **a ~~ chance** *etc* une chance *etc* sur deux // *ad* moitié-moitié.

fig [fɪg] *n* figue *f*.

fight [faɪt] *n* bagarre *f*; (*MIL*) combat *m*; (*against cancer etc*) lutte *f* // *vb* (*pt, pp* **fought**) *vt* se battre contre; (*cancer, alcoholism*) combattre, lutter contre // *vi* se battre; **~er** *n* lutteur *m* (*fig*); (*plane*) chasseur *m*; **~ing** *n* combats *mpl*.

figment ['fɪgmənt] *n*: **a ~ of the imagination** une invention.

figurative ['fɪgjurətɪv] *a* figuré(e).

figure ['fɪgə*] *n* (*DRAWING, GEOM*) figure *f*; (*number, cipher*) chiffre *m*; (*body, outline*) silhouette *f*, ligne *f*, formes *fpl* // *vt* (*US: appear*) figurer // *vi* (*US: make sense*) s'expliquer; **to ~ out** *vt* arriver à comprendre; calculer; **~head** *n* (*NAUT*) figure *f* de proue; (*pej*) prête-nom *m*; **~ of speech** *n* figure *f* de rhétorique.

file [faɪl] *n* (*tool*) lime *f*; (*dossier*) dossier *m*; (*folder*) dossier, chemise *f*; (*with hinges*) classeur *m*; (*COMPUT*) fichier *m*; (*row*) file *f* // *vt* (*nails, wood*) limer; (*papers*) classer; (*LAW: claim*) faire enregistrer; déposer // *vi*: **to ~ in/out** entrer/sortir l'un derrière l'autre; **to ~ past** défiler devant.

filing ['faɪlɪŋ] *n* (travaux *mpl* de) classement *m*; **~ cabinet** *n* classeur *m* (*meuble*).

fill [fɪl] *vt* remplir // *n*: **to eat one's ~** manger à sa faim; **to ~ in** *vt* (*hole*) boucher; (*form*) remplir; **to ~ up** *vt* remplir; ~ **it up, please** (*AUT*) le plein, s'il vous plaît.

fillet ['fılıt] *n* filet *m*; ~ **steak** *n* filet *m* de bœuf, tournedos *m*.

filling ['fılıŋ] *n* (*CULIN*) garniture *f*, farce *f*; (*for tooth*) plombage *m*; ~ **station** *n* station *f* d'essence.

film [fılm] *n* film *m*; (*PHOT*) pellicule *f*, film // *vt* (*scene*) filmer; ~ **star** *n* vedette *f* de cinéma; ~**strip** *n* (film *m* pour) projection *f* fixe.

filter ['fıltə*] *n* filtre *m* // *vt* filtrer; ~**lane** *n* (*Brit AUT*) voie *f* de sortie; ~**tipped** *a* à bout filtre.

filth [fılθ] *n* saleté *f*; ~**y** *a* sale, dégoûtant(e); (*language*) ordurier(ère).

fin [fın] *n* (*of fish*) nageoire *f*.

final ['faınl] *a* final(e), dernier(ère); définitif(ive) // *n* (*SPORT*) finale *f*; ~**s** *npl* (*SCOL*) examens *mpl* de dernière année; ~**e** [fı'nɑ:lı] *n* finale *m*; ~**ize** *vt* mettre au point; ~**ly** *ad* (*lastly*) en dernier lieu; (*eventually*) enfin, finalement.

finance [faı'næns] *n* finance *f*; ~**s** *npl* finances *fpl* // *vt* financer.

financial [faı'nænʃəl] *a* financier(ère).

find [faınd] *vt* (*pt, pp* **found**) trouver; (*lost object*) retrouver // *n* trouvaille *f*, découverte *f*; **to ~ sb guilty** (*LAW*) déclarer qn coupable; **to ~ out** *vt* se renseigner sur; (*truth, secret*) découvrir; (*person*) démasquer; **to ~ out about** se renseigner sur; (*by chance*) apprendre; ~**ings** *npl* (*LAW*) conclusions *fpl*, verdict *m*; (*of report*) constatations *fpl*.

fine [faın] *a* beau(belle); excellent(e); (*thin, subtle*) fin(e) // *ad* (*well*) très bien; (*small*) fin, finement // *n* (*LAW*) amende *f*; contravention *f* // *vt* (*LAW*) condamner à une amende; donner une contravention à; **to be ~** (*weather*) faire beau; ~ **arts** *npl* beaux-arts *mpl*.

finery ['faınərı] *n* parure *f*.

finger ['fıŋgə*] *n* doigt *m* // *vt* palper, toucher; (*MUS*) doigter; ~**nail** *n* auriculaire *m*/ index *m*; ~**nail** *n* ongle *m* (de la main); ~**print** *n* empreinte digitale; ~**tip** *n* bout *m* du doigt.

finicky ['fınıkı] *a* tatillon(ne), méticuleux(euse); minutieux(euse).

finish ['fınıʃ] *n* fin *f*; (*SPORT*) arrivée *f*; (*polish etc*) finition *f* // *vt* finir, terminer // *vi* finir, se terminer; (*session*) s'achever; **to ~ doing sth** finir de faire qch; **to ~ third** arriver *or* terminer troisième; **to ~ off** *vt* finir, terminer; (*kill*) achever; **to ~ up** *vi, vt* finir; ~**ing line** *n* ligne *f* d'arrivée; ~**ing school** *n* institution privée (*pour jeunes filles*).

finite ['faınaıt] *a* fini(e); (*verb*) conjugué(e).

Finland ['fınlənd] *n* Finlande *f*.

Finn [fın] *n* Finnois/e; Finlandais/e;

~**ish** *a* finnois(e); finlandais(e) // *n* (*LING*) finnois *m*.

fir [fə:*] *n* sapin *m*.

fire ['faıə*] *n* feu *m*; incendie *m* // *vt* (*discharge*): **to ~ a gun** tirer un coup de feu; (*fig*) enflammer, animer; (*dismiss*) mettre à la porte, renvoyer // *vi* tirer, faire feu; **on ~** en feu; ~ **alarm** *n* avertisseur *m* d'incendie; ~**arm** *n* arme *f* à feu; ~ **brigade**, (*US*) ~ **department** *n* (régiment *m* de sapeurs-)pompiers *mpl*; ~ **engine** *n* pompe à incendie; ~ **escape** *n* escalier *m* de secours; ~ **extinguisher** *n* extincteur *m*; ~**man** *n* pompier *m*; ~**place** *n* cheminée *f*; ~**side** *n* foyer *m*, coin *m* du feu; ~ **station** *n* caserne *f* de pompiers; ~**wood** *n* bois *m* de chauffage; ~**work** *n* feu *m* d'artifice; ~**works** *npl* (*display*) feu(x) d'artifice.

firing ['faıərıŋ] *n* (*MIL*) feu *m*, tir *m*; ~ **squad** *n* peloton *m* d'exécution.

firm [fə:m] *a* ferme // *n* compagnie *f*, firme *f*; ~**ly** *ad* fermement.

first [fə:st] *a* premier(ère) // *ad* (*before others*) le premier, la première; (*before other things*) en premier, d'abord; (*when listing reasons etc*) en premier lieu, premièrement // *n* (*person: in race*) premier/ère; (*SCOL*) mention *f* très bien; (*AUT*) première *f*; **at ~** au commencement, au début; ~ **of all** tout d'abord, pour commencer; ~ **aid** *n* premiers secours *or* soins *mpl*; ~**aid kit** *n* trousse *f* à pharmacie; ~**class** *a* de première classe; ~**hand** *a* de première main; ~ **lady** *n* (*US*) femme *f* du président; ~**ly** *ad* premièrement, en premier lieu; ~ **name** *n* prénom *m*; ~**rate** *a* excellent(e).

fish [fıʃ] *n* (*pl inv*) poisson *m*; poissons *mpl* // *vt, vi* pêcher; **to go ~ing** aller à la pêche; ~**erman** *n* pêcheur *m*; ~ **farm** *n* établissement *m* piscicole; ~ **fingers** *npl* (*Brit*) bâtonnets de poisson (congelés); ~**ing boat** *n* barque *f* de pêche; ~**ing line** *n* ligne *f* (de pêche); ~**ing rod** *n* canne *f* à pêche; ~**monger** *n* marchand *m* de poisson; ~**monger's (shop)** *n* poissonnerie *f*; ~ **sticks** *npl* (*US*) = ~ **fingers**; ~**y** *a* (*fig*) suspect(e), louche.

fist [fıst] *n* poing *m*.

fit [fıt] *a* (*MED, SPORT*) en (bonne) forme; (*proper*) convenable; approprié(e) // *vt* (*subj: clothes*) aller à; (*adjust*) ajuster; (*put in, attach*) installer, poser; adapter; (*equip*) équiper, garnir, munir // *vi* (*clothes*) aller; (*parts*) s'adapter; (*in space, gap*) entrer, s'adapter // *n* (*MED*) accès *m*, crise *f*; (*of coughing*) quinte *f*; ~ **to** en état de; ~ **for** digne de; apte à; **a ~ of anger** un accès de colère; **this dress is a tight/good ~** cette robe est un peu juste/

(me) va très bien; **by ~s and starts** par à-coups; **to ~ in** vi s'accorder; s'adapter; **to ~ out** (Brit: also: **~ up**) vt équiper; **~ful** a intermittent(e); **~ment** n meuble encastré, élément m; **~ness** n (MED) forme f physique; (of remark) à-propos m, justesse f; **~ted carpet** n moquette f; **~ted kitchen** n cuisine équipée; **~ter** n monteur m; (DRESSMAKING) essayeur/euse; **~ting** a approprié(e) // n (of dress) essayage m; (of piece of equipment) pose f, installation f; **~ting room** n cabine f d'essayage; **~tings** npl installations fpl.

five [faɪv] num cinq; **~r** n (col: Brit) billet m de cinq livres; (: US) billet de cinq dollars.

fix [fɪks] vt fixer; arranger; (mend) réparer // n: **to be in a ~** être dans le pétrin; **to ~ up** vt (meeting) arranger; **to ~ sb up with sth** faire avoir qch à qn; **~ation** [-'eɪʃən] n (PSYCH) fixation f; (fig) obsession f; **~ed** [fɪkst] a (prices etc) fixe; **~ture** ['fɪkstʃə*] n installation f (fixe); (SPORT) rencontre f (au programme).

fizz [fɪz] vi pétiller.

fizzle ['fɪzl] vi pétiller; **to ~ out** vi rater.

fizzy ['fɪzɪ] a pétillant(e); gazeux(euse).

flabbergasted ['flæbəgɑːstɪd] a sidéré(e), ahuri(e).

flabby ['flæbɪ] a mou(molle).

flag [flæg] n drapeau m; (also: ~stone) dalle f // vi faiblir; fléchir; **to ~ down** vt héler, faire signe de s'arrêter à.

flagpole ['flægpəul] n mât m.

flair [flɛə*] n flair m.

flak [flæk] n (MIL) tir antiaérien; (col: criticism) critiques fpl.

flake [fleɪk] n (of rust, paint) écaille f; (of snow, soap powder) flocon m // vi (also: ~ off) s'écailler.

flamboyant [flæm'bɔɪənt] a flamboyant(e), éclatant(e); (person) haut(e) en couleur.

flame [fleɪm] n flamme f.

flamingo [flə'mɪŋgəu] n flamant m (rose).

flammable ['flæməbl] a inflammable.

flan [flæn] n (Brit) tarte f.

flank [flæŋk] n flanc m // vt flanquer.

flannel ['flænl] n (Brit: also: face ~) gant m de toilette; (fabric) flanelle f; **~s** npl pantalon m de flanelle.

flap [flæp] n (of pocket, envelope) rabat m // vt (wings) battre (de) // vi (sail, flag) claquer; (col: also: **be in a ~**) paniquer.

flare [flɛə*] n fusée éclairante; (in skirt etc) évasement m; **to ~ up** vi s'embraser; (fig: person) se mettre en colère, s'emporter; (: revolt) éclater.

flash [flæʃ] n éclair m; (also: news ~) flash m (d'information); (PHOT) flash //

vt (switch on) allumer (brièvement); (send: message) câbler // vi briller; jeter des éclairs; (light on ambulance etc) clignoter; **in a ~** en un clin d'œil; **to ~ one's headlights** faire un appel de phares; **he ~ed by or past** il passa (devant nous) comme un éclair; **~bulb** n ampoule f de flash; **~cube** n cube-flash m; **~light** n lampe f de poche.

flashy ['flæʃɪ] a (pej) tape-à-l'œil inv, tapageur(euse).

flask [flɑːsk] n flacon m, bouteille f; (also: **vacuum ~**) bouteille f thermos ®.

flat [flæt] a plat(e); (tyre) dégonflé(e), à plat; (denial) catégorique; (MUS) bémolisé(e); (: voice) faux(fausse) // n (Brit: apartment) appartement m; (AUT) crevaison f; (MUS) bémol m; **to work ~ out** travailler d'arrache-pied; **~ly** ad catégoriquement; **~ten** vt (also: **~ten out**) aplatir.

flatter ['flætə*] vt flatter; **~ing** a flatteur(euse); **~y** n flatterie f.

flaunt [flɔːnt] vt faire étalage de.

flavour, (US) **flavor** ['fleɪvə*] n goût m, saveur f; (of ice cream etc) parfum m // vt parfumer; **vanilla-~ed** à l'arôme de vanille, vanillé(e); **~ing** n arôme m (synthétique).

flaw [flɔː] n défaut m.

flax [flæks] n lin m; **~en** a blond(e).

flea [fliː] n puce f.

fleck [flɛk] n tacheture f; moucheture f.

flee, pt, pp **fled** [fliː, flɛd] vt fuir, s'enfuir de // vi fuir, s'enfuir.

fleece [fliːs] n toison f // vt (col) voler, filouter.

fleet [fliːt] n flotte f; (of lorries etc) parc m, convoi m.

fleeting ['fliːtɪŋ] a fugace, fugitif(ive); (visit) très bref(brève).

Flemish ['flɛmɪʃ] a flamand(e).

flesh [flɛʃ] n chair f; **~ wound** n blessure superficielle.

flew [fluː] pt of **fly**.

flex [flɛks] n fil m or câble m électrique (souple) // vt fléchir; (muscles) tendre; **~ible** a flexible.

flick [flɪk] n petite tape; chiquenaude f; sursaut m; **to ~ through** vt fus feuilleter.

flicker ['flɪkə*] vi vaciller.

flier ['flaɪə*] n aviateur m.

flight [flaɪt] n vol m; (escape) fuite f; (also: **~ of steps**) escalier m; **~ attendant** n (US) steward m, hôtesse f de l'air; **~ deck** n (AVIAT) poste m de pilotage; (NAUT) pont d'envol.

flimsy ['flɪmzɪ] a (partition, fabric) peu solide, mince; (excuse) pauvre, mince.

flinch [flɪntʃ] vi tressaillir; **to ~ from** se dérober à, reculer devant.

fling [flɪŋ], pt, pp **flung** vt jeter, lancer.

flint [flɪnt] n silex m; (in lighter) pierre f (à briquet).

flip [flɪp] *n* chiquenaude *f*.

flippant ['flɪpənt] *a* désinvolte, irré-
vérencieux(euse).

flipper ['flɪpə*] *n* (*of seal etc*) nageoire
f; (*for swimming*) palme *f*.

flirt [fləːt] *vi* flirter // *n* flirteuse *f*.

flit [flɪt] *vi* voleter.

float [fləut] *n* flotteur *m*; (*in procession*)
char *m*; (*money*) réserve *f* // *vi* flotter //
vt faire flotter; (*loan, business*) lancer.

flock [flɔk] *n* troupeau *m*; (*of people*)
foule *f*.

flog [flɔg] *vt* fouetter.

flood [flʌd] *n* inondation *f*; (*of words,
tears etc*) flot *m*, torrent *m* // *vt* inonder;
~**ing** *n* inondation *f*; ~**light** *n*
projecteur *m* // *vt* éclairer aux
projecteurs, illuminer.

floor [flɔː] *n* sol *m*; (*storey*) étage *m*;
(*fig: at meeting*): **the** ~ l'assemblée *f*,
les membres *mpl* de l'assemblée // *vt*
terrasser; **on the** ~ par terre; **ground** ~,
(*US*) **first** ~ rez-de-chaussée *m*; **first** ~,
(*US*) **second** ~ premier étage; ~**board**
n planche *f* (*du plancher*); ~ **show** *n*
spectacle *m* de variétés.

flop [flɔp] *n* fiasco *m*.

floppy ['flɔpɪ] *a* lâche, flottant(e); ~
(**disk**) *n* (*COMPUT*) disquette *f*.

flora ['flɔːrə] *n* flore *f*.

florid ['flɔrɪd] *a* (*complexion*) fleuri(e);
(*style*) plein(e) de fioritures.

florist ['flɔrɪst] *n* fleuriste *m/f*.

flounce [flauns] *n* volant *m*.

flounder ['flaundə*] *vi* patauger // *n*
(*ZOOL*) flet *m*.

flour ['flauə*] *n* farine *f*.

flourish ['flʌrɪʃ] *vi* prospérer // *n*
fioriture *f*; (*of trumpets*) fanfare *f*.

flout [flaut] *vt* se moquer de, faire fi de.

flow [fləu] *n* flot *m*; courant *m*;
circulation *f*; (*tide*) flux *m* // *vi* couler;
(*traffic*) s'écouler; (*robes, hair*) flotter;
~ **chart** *n* organigramme *m*.

flower ['flauə*] *n* fleur *f* // *vi* fleurir; ~
bed *n* plate-bande *f*; ~**pot** *n* pot *m* (à
fleurs); ~**y** *a* fleuri(e).

flown [fləun] *pp* of **fly**.

flu [fluː] *n* grippe *f*.

fluctuate ['flʌktjueɪt] *vi* varier, fluctuer.

fluency ['fluːənsɪ] *n* facilité *f*.

fluent ['fluːənt] *a* (*speech*) coulant(e),
aisé(e); **he speaks** ~ **French** il parle le
français couramment.

fluff [flʌf] *n* duvet *m*; peluche *f*; ~**y** *a*
duveteux(euse); pelucheux(euse).

fluid ['fluːɪd] *a*, *n* fluide (*m*).

fluke [fluːk] *n* (*col: luck*) coup *m* de
veine.

flung [flʌŋ] *pt*, *pp* of **fling**.

fluoride ['fluərɑɪd] *n* fluor *m*.

flurry ['flʌrɪ] *n* (*of snow*) rafale *f*,
bourrasque *f*; ~ **of activity/excitement**
affairement *m*/excitation *f* soudain(e).

flush [flʌʃ] *n* rougeur *f*; excitation *f*;

(*fig: of youth, beauty etc*) éclat *m* // *vt*
nettoyer à grande eau // *vi* rougir // *a*: ~
with au ras de, de niveau avec; **to** ~ **the
toilet** tirer la chasse (d'eau); **to** ~ **out**
vt débusquer; ~**ed** *a* (tout(e)) rouge.

flustered ['flʌstəd] *a* énervé(e).

flute [fluːt] *n* flûte *f*.

flutter ['flʌtə*] *n* agitation *f*; (*of wings*)
battement *m* // *vi* battre des ailes,
voleter.

flux [flʌks] *n*: **in a state of** ~ fluctuant
sans cesse.

fly [flaɪ] *n* (*insect*) mouche *f*; (*on
trousers: also: flies*) braguette *f* // *vb* (*pt
flew, pp flown*) *vt* piloter; (*passengers,
cargo*) transporter (par avion);
(*distances*) parcourir // *vi* voler;
(*passengers*) aller en avion; (*escape*)
s'enfuir, fuir; (*flag*) se déployer; **to** ~
away *or* **off** *vi* (*bird, insect*) s'envoler;
~**ing** *n* (*activity*) aviation *f* // *a*: ~**ing
visit** visite *f* éclair *inv*; **with** ~**ing colours**
haut la main; ~**ing saucer** *n* soucoupe
volante; ~**ing start** *n*: **to get off to a**
~**ing start** faire un excellent départ;
~**over** *n* (*Brit: bridge*) saut-de-mouton
m; ~**sheet** *n* (*for tent*) double toit *m*.

foal [fəul] *n* poulain *m*.

foam [fəum] *n* écume *f*; (*on beer*)
mousse *f*; (*also: plastic* ~) mousse
cellulaire *or* de plastique // *vi* écumer;
(*soapy water*) mousser; ~ **rubber** *n*
caoutchouc *m* mousse.

fob [fɔb] *vt*: **to** ~ **sb off with** refiler à qn;
se débarrasser de qn avec.

focus ['fəukəs] *n* (*pl*: ~**es**) foyer *m*; (*of
interest*) centre *m* // *vt* (*field glasses etc*)
mettre au point // *vi*: **to** ~ (**on**) (*with
camera*) régler la mise au point (sur);
(*person*) fixer son regard (sur); **in** ~ au
point; **out of** ~ pas au point.

fodder ['fɔdə*] *n* fourrage *m*.

foe [fəu] *n* ennemi *m*.

fog [fɔg] *n* brouillard *m*; ~**gy** *a*: **it's**
~**gy** il y a du brouillard; ~**lamp** *n*
(*AUT*) phare *m* anti-brouillard.

foil [fɔɪl] *vt* déjouer, contrecarrer // *n*
feuille *f* de métal; (*kitchen* ~) papier *m*
d'alu(minium); (*FENCING*) fleuret *m*.

fold [fəuld] *n* (*bend, crease*) pli *m*;
(*AGR*) parc *m* à moutons; (*fig*) bercail
m // *vt* plier; **to** ~ **up** *vi* (*business*)
fermer boutique // *vt* (*map etc*) plier, replier; ~**er** *n* (*for papers*) chemise *f*;
classeur *m*; (*brochure*) dépliant *m*;
~**ing** *a* (*chair, bed*) pliant(e).

foliage ['fəulɪɪdʒ] *n* feuillage *m*.

folk [fəuk] *npl* gens *mpl* // *a* folklorique;
~**s** *npl* famille *f*, parents *mpl*; ~**lore**
['fəuklɔː*] *n* folklore *m*; ~ **song** *n*
chanson *f* folklorique.

follow ['fɔləu] *vt* suivre // *vi* suivre;
(*result*) s'ensuivre; **he** ~**ed suit** il fit de
même; **to** ~ **up** *vt* (*victory*) tirer parti
de; (*letter, offer*) donner suite à; (*case*)

suivre; **~er** n disciple m/f, partisan/e;
~ing a suivant(e) // n partisans mpl,
disciples mpl.

folly ['fɔlɪ] n inconscience f; sottise f.

fond [fɔnd] a (memory, look) tendre,
affectueux(euse); **to be ~ of** aimer
beaucoup.

fondle ['fɔndl] vt caresser.

food [fu:d] n nourriture f; **~ mixer** n
mixeur m; **~ poisoning** n intoxication f
alimentaire; **~ processor** n robot m de
cuisine; **~stuffs** npl denrées fpl
alimentaires.

fool [fu:l] n idiot/e; (HISTORY: of king)
bouffon m, fou m; (CULIN) purée f de
fruits à la crème // vt berner, duper // vi
(also: **~ around**) faire l'idiot or
l'imbécile; **~hardy** a téméraire, im-
prudent(e); **~ish** a idiot(e), stupide; im-
prudent(e); écervelé(e); **~proof** a
(plan etc) infaillible.

foot [fut] n (pl: feet) pied m; (measure)
pied (= 304 mm; 12 inches); (of animal)
patte f // vt (bill) casquer, payer; **on ~** à
pied; **~age** n (CINEMA: length) ≈ métrage m; (: material) séquences fpl;
~ball n ballon m (de football); (sport:
Brit) football m; (: US) football
américain; **~baller** (Brit) = **~ball
player**; **~ball ground** n terrain m de
football; **~ball player** n joueur m de
football; **~brake** n frein m à pied;
~bridge n passerelle f; **~hills** npl
contreforts mpl; **~hold** n prise f (de
pied); **~ing** n (fig) position f; **to lose
one's ~ing** perdre pied; **~lights** npl
rampe f; **~man** n laquais m; **~note** n
note f (en bas de page); **~path** n
sentier m; (in street) trottoir m; **~print**
n trace f (de pied); **~step** n pas m;
~wear n chaussure(s) f(pl).

for [fɔ:*] ♦ prep 1 (indicating destination, intention, purpose) pour; the train
~ London le train pour or (à destination)
de Londres; he went **~ the paper** il est
allé chercher le journal; **it's time ~
lunch** c'est l'heure du déjeuner; **what's it
~?** ça sert à quoi?; **what ~?** (why)
pourquoi?

2 (on behalf of, representing) pour; the
MP **~ Hove** le député de Hove; **to work
~ sb/sth** travailler pour qn/qch; **G ~**
George G comme Georges

3 (because of) pour; **~ this reason** pour
cette raison; **~ fear of being criticized**
de peur d'être critiqué

4 (with regard to) pour; **it's cold ~** July
il fait froid pour juillet; **a gift ~ languages** un don pour les langues

5 (in exchange for): **I sold it ~** £5 je l'ai
vendu 5 livres; **to pay 50 pence ~ a ticket** payer 50 pence un billet

6 (in favour of) pour; **are you ~ or
against us?** êtes-vous pour ou contre
nous?

7 (referring to distance) pendant, sur;
there are roadworks ~ 5 km il y a des
travaux sur or pendant 5 km; **we walked
~ miles** nous avons marché pendant des
kilomètres

8 (referring to time) pendant; depuis;
pour; **he was away ~ 2 years** il a été
absent pendant 2 ans; **she will be away
~ a month** elle sera absente (pendant)
un mois; **I have known her ~ years** je la
connais depuis des années; **can you do it
~ tomorrow?** est-ce que tu peux le faire
pour demain?

9 (with infinitive clauses): **it is not ~
me to decide** ce n'est pas à moi de
décider; **it would be best ~ you to leave**
le mieux serait que vous partiez; **there is
still time ~ you to do it** vous avez encore
le temps de le faire; **~ this to be possible ...** pour que cela soit possible ...

10 (in spite of): **~ all his work/efforts**
malgré tout son travail/tous ses efforts;
**~ all his complaints, he's very fond of
her** il a beau se plaindre, il l'aime
beaucoup

♦ cj (since, as: rather formal) car.

forage ['fɔrɪdʒ] n fourrage m.

foray ['fɔreɪ] n incursion f.

forbid [fə'bɪd], pt **forbad(e)**, pp **forbidden**
[fə'bɪd, -'bæd, -'bɪdn] vt défendre,
interdire; **to ~ sb to do** défendre or
interdire à qn de faire; **~den** a dé-
fendu(e); **~ding** a d'aspect or d'allure
sévère or sombre.

force [fɔ:s] n force f // vt forcer; the **F~s**
npl (Brit) l'armée f; **in ~** en force; **to
come into ~** entrer en vigueur; **~-feed**
vt nourrir de force; **~ful** a énergique,
volontaire.

forcibly ['fɔ:səblɪ] ad par la force, de
force; (vigorously) énergiquement.

ford [fɔ:d] n gué m.

fore [fɔ:*] n: **to the ~** en évidence.

forearm ['fɔ:rɑ:m] n avant-bras m inv.

foreboding [fɔ:'bəudɪŋ] n pressentiment
m (néfaste).

forecast ['fɔ:kɑ:st] n prévision f // vt
(irg: like cast) prévoir.

forecourt ['fɔ:kɔ:t] n (of garage) devant
m.

forefathers ['fɔ:fɑ:ðəz] npl ancêtres
mpl.

forefinger ['fɔ:fɪŋgə*] n index m.

forefront ['fɔ:frʌnt] n: **in the ~ of** au
premier rang or plan de.

forego vt = **forgo**.

foregone ['fɔ:gɔn] a: **it's a ~ conclusion**
c'est à prévoir, c'est couru d'avance.

foreground ['fɔ:graund] n premier plan.

forehead ['fɔrɪd] n front m.

foreign ['fɔrɪn] a étranger(ère); (trade)
extérieur(e); **~er** n étranger/ère; **~
secretary** n (Brit) ministre m des
Affaires étrangères; **F~ Office** n (Brit)
ministère m des Affaires étrangères.

foreleg ['fɔːlɛg] n patte f de devant; jambe antérieure.

foreman ['fɔːmən] n contremaître m.

foremost ['fɔːməust] a le(la) plus en vue; premier(ère) // ad: **first and ~** avant tout, tout d'abord.

forensic [fə'rɛnsɪk] a: ~ **medicine** médecine légale.

forerunner ['fɔːrʌnə*] n précurseur m.

foresee [fɔː'siː], pt **foresaw**, pp **foreseen** [fɔː'siː, -'sɔː, -'siːn] vt prévoir; ~**able** a prévisible.

foreshadow [fɔː'ʃædəu] vt présager, annoncer, laisser prévoir.

foresight ['fɔːsaɪt] n prévoyance f.

forest ['fɔrɪst] n forêt f.

forestall [fɔː'stɔːl] vt devancer.

forestry ['fɔrɪstrɪ] n sylviculture f.

foretaste ['fɔːteɪst] n avant-goût m.

foretell, pt, pp **foretold** [fɔː'tɛl, -'təuld] vt prédire.

forever [fə'rɛvə*] ad pour toujours; (fig) continuellement.

foreword ['fɔːwəːd] n avant-propos m inv.

forfeit ['fɔːfɪt] n prix m, rançon f // vt perdre; (one's life, health) payer de.

forgave [fə'geɪv] pt of **forgive**.

forge [fɔːdʒ] n forge f // vt (signature) contrefaire; (wrought iron) forger; **to ~ documents** fabriquer de faux papiers; **to ~ money** (Brit) fabriquer de la fausse monnaie; **to ~ ahead** vi pousser de l'avant, prendre de l'avance; ~**r** n faussaire m; ~**ry** n faux m, contrefaçon f.

forget [fə'gɛt], pt **forgot**, pp **forgotten** vt, vi oublier; ~**ful** a distrait(e), étourdi(e); ~**ful of** oublieux(euse) de; ~**-me-not** n myosotis m.

forgive [fə'gɪv], pt **forgave**, pp **forgiven** vt pardonner; **to ~ sb for sth** pardonner qch à qn; ~**ness** n pardon m.

forgo [fɔː'gəu], pt **forwent**, pp **forgone** vt renoncer à.

forgot [fə'gɔt] pt of **forget**.

forgotten [fə'gɔtn] pp of **forget**.

fork [fɔːk] n (for eating) fourchette f; (for gardening) fourche f; (of roads) bifurcation f; (of railways) embranchement m // vi (road) bifurquer; **to ~ out** (col: pay) vt allonger, se fendre de // vi casquer; ~**-lift truck** n chariot élévateur.

forlorn [fə'lɔːn] a (person) abandonné(e); (place) désert(e); (attempt, hope) désespéré(e).

form [fɔːm] n forme f; (SCOL) classe f; (questionnaire) formulaire m // vt former; **in top ~** en pleine forme.

formal ['fɔːməl] a (offer, receipt) en bonne et due forme; (person) cérémonieux(euse); (dinner) officiel(le); (ART, PHILOSOPHY) formel(le); ~**ly** ad officiellement, formellement; cérémo-

nieusement.

format ['fɔːmæt] n format m // vt (COMPUT) formater.

formation [fɔː'meɪʃən] n formation f.

formative ['fɔːmətɪv] a: ~ **years** années fpl d'apprentissage (fig) or de formation.

former ['fɔːmə*] a ancien(ne) (before n), précédent(e); **the ~ ... the latter** le premier ... le second, celui-là ... celui-ci; ~**ly** ad autrefois.

formidable ['fɔːmɪdəbl] a redoutable.

formula ['fɔːmjulə] n formule f.

forsake [fə'seɪk], pt **forsook**, pp **forsaken** [fə'seɪk, -'suk, -'seɪkən] vt abandonner.

fort [fɔːt] n fort m.

forte ['fɔːtɪ] n (point) fort m.

forth [fɔːθ] ad en avant; **to go back and ~** aller et venir; **and so ~** et ainsi de suite; ~**coming** a qui va paraître or avoir lieu prochainement; (character) ouvert(e), communicatif(ive); ~**right** a franc(franche), direct(e); ~**with** ad sur le champ.

fortify ['fɔːtɪfaɪ] vt fortifier; **fortified wine** n vin liquoreux or de liqueur.

fortnight ['fɔːtnaɪt] n quinzaine f, quinze jours mpl; ~**ly** a bimensuel(le) // ad tous les quinze jours.

fortunate ['fɔːtʃənɪt] a: **it is ~ that** c'est une chance que; ~**ly** ad heureusement.

fortune ['fɔːtʃən] n chance f; (wealth) fortune f; ~**teller** n diseuse f de bonne aventure.

forty ['fɔːtɪ] num quarante.

forward ['fɔːwəd] a (ahead of schedule) en avance; (movement, position) en avant, vers l'avant; (not shy) ouvert(e); direct(e); effronté(e) // n (SPORT) avant m // vt (letter) faire suivre; (parcel, goods) expédier; (fig) promouvoir, contribuer au développement or à l'avancement de; **to move ~** avancer; ~**(s)** ad en avant.

forwent [fɔː'wɛnt] pt of **forgo**.

fossil ['fɔsl] a, n fossile (m).

foster ['fɔstə*] vt encourager, favoriser; ~ **child** n enfant adopté; ~ **mother** n mère adoptive; mère nourricière.

fought [fɔːt] pt, pp of **fight**.

foul [faul] a (weather, smell, food) infect(e); (language) ordurier(ère); (deed) infâme // n (FOOTBALL) faute f // vt salir, encrasser; (football player) commettre une faute sur.

found [faund] pt, pp of **find** // vt (establish) fonder; ~**ation** [-'deɪʃən] n (act) fondation f; (base) fondement m; (also: ~**ation cream**) fond m de teint; ~**ations** npl (of building) fondations fpl.

founder ['faundə*] n fondateur m // vi couler, sombrer.

foundry ['faundrɪ] n fonderie f.

fount [faunt] n source f.

fountain ['fauntɪn] n fontaine f; ~ **pen** n stylo m (à encre).

four [fɔ:*] num quatre; **on all ~s** à quatre pattes; **~-poster** n (also: **~-poster
bed**) lit m à baldaquin; **~some**
['fɔ:səm] n partie f à quatre; sortie f à
quatre; **~teen** num quatorze; **~th** num
quatrième.
fowl [faul] n volaille f.
fox [fɔks] n renard m // vt mystifier.
foyer ['fɔɪeɪ] n vestibule m; (THEATRE)
foyer m.
fraction ['frækʃən] n fraction f.
fracture ['fræktʃə*] n fracture f.
fragile ['frædʒaɪl] a fragile.
fragment ['frægmənt] n fragment m.
fragrant ['freɪgrənt] a parfumé(e),
odorant(e).
frail [freɪl] a fragile, délicat(e).
frame [freɪm] n charpente f; (of picture)
cadre m; (of door, window) encadrement
m, chambranle m; (of spectacles: also:
~s) monture f // vt encadrer; **~ of mind**
n disposition f d'esprit; **~work** n
structure f.
France [frɑ:ns] n France f.
franchise ['fræntʃaɪz] n (POL) droit m
de vote; (COMM) franchise f.
frank [fræŋk] a franc(franche) // vt
(letter) affranchir; **~ly** ad franchement.
frantic ['fræntɪk] a frénétique.
fraternity [frə'tɜ:nɪtɪ] n (club) communauté f, confrérie f; (spirit) fraternité f.
fraud [frɔ:d] n supercherie f, fraude f,
tromperie f; imposteur m.
fraught [frɔ:t] a: **~ with** chargé(e) de,
plein(e) de.
fray [freɪ] n bagarre f // vi s'effilocher;
tempers were **~ed** les gens com-
mençaient à s'énerver.
freak [fri:k] n (also cpd) phénomène m,
créature ou événement exceptionnel par
sa rareté, son caractère d'anomalie.
freckle ['frɛkl] n tache f de rousseur.
free [fri:] a libre; (gratis) gratuit(e);
(liberal) généreux(euse), large // vt
(prisoner etc) libérer; (jammed object
or person) dégager; **~ (of charge), for ~**
ad gratuitement; **~dom** ['fri:dəm] n
liberté f; **~-for-all** n mêlée générale; **~
gift** n prime f; **~hold** n propriété
foncière libre; **~ kick** n coup franc;
~lance a indépendant(e); **~ly** ad librement; (liberally) libéralement;
~mason n franc-maçon m; **~post** n
franchise postale; **~-range** a (hen,
eggs) de ferme; **~ trade** n libre-
échange m; **~way** n (US) autoroute f;
~wheel vi descendre en roue libre; **~
will** n libre arbitre m; **of one's own ~**
will de son plein gré.
freeze [fri:z] vb (pt froze, pp frozen) vi
geler // vt geler; (food) congeler;
(prices, salaries) bloquer, geler // n gel
m; blocage m; **~-dried** a lyophilisé(e);
~r n congélateur m.
freezing ['fri:zɪŋ] a: **~ cold** a glacial(e);

~ point n point m de congélation; **3 degrees below ~** 3 degrés au-dessous de
zéro.
freight [freɪt] n (goods) fret m,
cargaison f; (money charged) fret, prix
m du transport; **~ train** n (US) train m
de marchandises.
French [frɛntʃ] a français(e) // n (LING)
français m; **the ~** npl les Français; **~
bean** n haricot vert; **~ fried potatoes**,
(US) **~ fries** npl (pommes de terre fpl)
frites fpl; **~man** n Français m; **~ window** n porte-fenêtre f; **~woman** n
Française f.
frenzy ['frɛnzɪ] n frénésie f.
frequent a ['fri:kwənt] fréquent(e) // vt
[frɪ'kwɛnt] fréquenter; **~ly** ad fréquemment.
fresh [frɛʃ] a frais(fraîche); (new)
nouveau(nouvelle); (cheeky) fami-
lier(ère), culotté(e); **~en** vi (wind, air)
fraîchir; **to ~en up** vi faire un brin de
toilette; **~er** n (Brit SCOL: col) bizuth
m, étudiant/e de 1ère année; **~ly** ad
nouvellement, récemment; **~man** n
(US) = **~er**; **~ness** n fraîcheur f;
~water a (fish) d'eau douce.
fret [frɛt] vi s'agiter, se tracasser.
friar ['fraɪə*] n moine m, frère m.
friction ['frɪkʃən] n friction f.
Friday ['fraɪdɪ] n vendredi m.
fridge [frɪdʒ] n (Brit) frigo m, frigidaire
m ®.
fried [fraɪd] pt, pp of fry // a frit(e); **~
egg** œuf m sur le plat.
friend [frɛnd] n ami/e; **~ly** a amical(e);
gentil(le); **~ship** n amitié f.
frieze [fri:z] n frise f, bordure f.
fright [fraɪt] n peur f, effroi m; **to take ~**
prendre peur, s'effrayer; **~en** vt effrayer, faire peur à; **~ened (of)** avoir
peur de (de); **~ening** a
effrayant(e); **~ful** a affreux(euse).
frigid ['frɪdʒɪd] a (woman) frigide.
frill [frɪl] n (of dress) volant m; (of shirt)
jabot m.
fringe [frɪndʒ] n frange f; (edge: of forest etc) bordure f; (fig): **on the ~** en
marge; **~ benefits** npl avantages
sociaux or en nature.
frisk [frɪsk] vt fouiller.
frisky ['frɪskɪ] a vif(vive), sémillant(e).
fritter ['frɪtə*] n beignet m; **to ~ away**
vt gaspiller.
frivolous ['frɪvələs] a frivole.
frizzy ['frɪzɪ] a crépu(e).
fro [frəu] see to.
frock [frɔk] n robe f.
frog [frɔg] n grenouille f; **~man** n
homme-grenouille m.
frolic ['frɔlɪk] vi folâtrer, batifoler.
from [frɔm] prep **1** (indicating starting
place, origin loc) de; **where do you come
~?, where are you ~?** d'où venez-vous?;
~ London to Paris de Londres à Paris; **a**

letter ~ my sister une lettre de ma sœur; to drink ~ the bottle boire à (même) la bouteille
2 (*indicating time*) (à partir) de; ~ one o'clock to or until or till two de une heure à deux heures; ~ January (on) à partir de janvier
3 (*indicating distance*) de; the hotel is one kilometre ~ the beach l'hôtel est à un kilomètre de la plage
4 (*indicating price, number etc*) de; the interest rate was increased ~ 9% to 10% le taux d'intérêt a augmenté de 9 à 10%
5 (*indicating difference*) de; he can't tell red ~ green il ne peut pas distinguer le rouge du vert
6 (*because of, on the basis of*): ~ what he says d'après ce qu'il dit; weak ~ hunger affaibli par la faim.

front [frʌnt] *n* (*of house, dress*) devant *m*; (*of coach, train*) avant *m*; (*of book*) couverture *f*; (*promenade: also*: sea ~) bord *m* de mer; (MIL, POL, METEOROLOGY) front *m*; (*fig: appearances*) contenance *f*, façade *f* // *a* de devant; premier(ère); in ~ (of) devant; ~ door *n* porte *f* d'entrée; (*of car*) portière *f* avant; ~ier [ˈfrʌntɪə*] *n* frontière *f*; ~ page *n* première page; ~ room *n* (*Brit*) pièce *f* de devant, salon *m*; ~ wheel drive *n* traction *f* avant.

frost [frɔst] *n* gel *m*, gelée *f*; (*also*: hoar~) givre *m*; ~bite *n* gelures *fpl*; ~ed *a* (*glass*) dépoli(e); ~y *a* (*window*) couvert(e) de givre; (*welcome*) glacial(e).

froth [ˈfrɔθ] *n* mousse *f*; écume *f*.

frown [fraun] *vi* froncer les sourcils.

froze [frəuz] *pt of* **freeze**; ~n *pp of* **freeze** // *a* (*food*) congelé(e).

fruit [fruːt] *n* (*pl inv*) fruit *m*; ~erer *n* fruitier *m*, marchand/e de fruits; ~erer's (shop) *n* fruiterie *f*; ~ful *a* fructueux(euse); (*plant, soil*) fécond(e); ~ion [fruːˈɪʃən] *n*: to come to ~ion se réaliser; ~ juice *n* jus *m* de fruit; ~ machine *n* (*Brit*) machine *f* à sous; ~ salad *n* salade *f* de fruits.

frustrate [frʌsˈtreɪt] *vt* frustrer; (*plot, plans*) faire échouer; ~d *a* frustré(e).

fry [fraɪ], *pt, pp* **fried** *vt* (faire) frire; the small ~ le menu fretin; ~ing pan *n* poêle *f* (à frire).

ft. *abbr of* **foot, feet**.

fuddy-duddy [ˈfʌdɪdʌdɪ] *n* (*pej*) vieux schnock.

fudge [fʌdʒ] *n* (CULIN) sorte de confiserie à base de sucre, de beurre et de lait.

fuel [fjuəl] *n* (*for heating*) combustible *m*; (*for propelling*) carburant *m*; ~ tank *n* cuve *f* à mazout, citerne *f*; (*in vehicle*) réservoir *m* de or à carburant.

fugitive [ˈfjuːdʒɪtɪv] *n* fugitif/ive.

fulfil [fulˈfɪl] *vt* (*function*) remplir; (*order*) exécuter; (*wish, desire*) satisfaire, réaliser; ~ment *n* (*of wishes*) réalisation *f*.

full [ful] *a* plein(e); (*details, information*) complet(ète); (*skirt*) ample, large // *ad*: to know ~ well that savoir fort bien que; I'm ~ (up) j'ai bien mangé; ~ employment *n* plein emploi; a ~ two hours deux bonnes heures; at ~ speed à toute vitesse; in ~ (*reproduce, quote*) intégralement; (*write name etc*) en toutes lettres; to pay in ~ tout payer; ~ moon *n* pleine lune; ~-scale *a* (*attack, war*) complet(ète), total(e); (*model*) grandeur nature *inv*; ~ stop *n* point *m*; ~-time *a, ad* (*work*) à plein temps // *n* (SPORT) fin *f* du match; ~y *ad* entièrement, complètement; ~y-fledged *a* (*teacher, barrister*) diplômé(e); (*citizen, member*) à part entière.

fulsome [ˈfulsəm] *a* (*pej*: *praise, gratitude*) excessif(ive).

fumble [ˈfʌmbl] *vi* fouiller, tâtonner; to ~ with *vt fus* tripoter.

fume [fjuːm] *vi* rager; ~s *npl* vapeurs *fpl*, émanations *fpl*, gaz *mpl*.

fun [fʌn] *n* amusement *m*, divertissement *m*; to have ~ s'amuser; for ~ pour rire; to make ~ of *vt fus* se moquer de.

function [ˈfʌŋkʃən] *n* fonction *f*; cérémonie *f*, soirée officielle // *vi* fonctionner; ~al *a* fonctionnel(le).

fund [fʌnd] *n* caisse *f*, fonds *m*; (*source, store*) source *f*, mine *f*; ~s *npl* fonds *mpl*.

fundamental [fʌndəˈmentl] *a* fondamental(e).

funeral [ˈfjuːnərəl] *n* enterrement *m*, obsèques *fpl* (*more formal occasion*); ~ parlour *n* dépôt *m* mortuaire; ~ service *n* service *m* funèbre.

fun fair *n* (*Brit*) fête (foraine).

fungus, *pl* **fungi** [ˈfʌŋgəs, -gaɪ] *n* champignon *m*; (*mould*) moisissure *f*.

funnel [ˈfʌnl] *n* entonnoir *m*; (*of ship*) cheminée *f*.

funny [ˈfʌnɪ] *a* amusant(e), drôle; (*strange*) curieux(euse), bizarre.

fur [fəː*] *n* fourrure *f*; (*Brit: in kettle etc*) (dépôt *m* de) tartre *m*; ~ coat *n* manteau *m* de fourrure.

furious [ˈfjuərɪəs] *a* furieux(euse); (*effort*) acharné(e).

furlong [ˈfəːlɔŋ] *n* = 201.17 *m* (*terme d'hippisme*).

furlough [ˈfəːləu] *n* permission *f*, congé *m*.

furnace [ˈfəːnɪs] *n* fourneau *m*.

furnish [ˈfəːnɪʃ] *vt* meubler; (*supply*) fournir; ~ings *npl* mobilier *m*, articles *mpl* d'ameublement.

furniture [ˈfəːnɪtʃə*] *n* meubles *mpl*, mobilier *m*; piece of ~ meuble *m*.

furrow [ˈfʌrəu] *n* sillon *m*.

furry [ˈfəːrɪ] *a* (*animal*) à fourrure; (*toy*) en peluche.

further ['fə:ðə*] a supplémentaire, autre; nouveau(nouvelle); plus loin // ad plus loin; (more) davantage; (moreover) de plus // vt faire avancer or progresser, promouvoir; ~ **education** n enseignement m post-scolaire (recyclage, formation professionnelle); ~**more** [fə:ðə'mɔ:*] ad de plus, en outre.
furthest ['fə:ðıst] superlative of **far**.
fury ['fjuərı] n fureur f.
fuse [fju:z] n fusible m; (for bomb etc) amorce f, détonateur m // vt, vi (metal) fondre; (fig) fusionner; **the lights have ~d** (Brit) les plombs ont sauté; ~ **box** n boîte f à fusibles.
fuss [fʌs] n chichis mpl, façons fpl, embarras mpl; (complaining) histoire(s) f(pl); **to make a ~** faire des façons etc; ~**y** a (person) tatillon(ne), difficile; chichiteux(euse) (dress, style) tarabiscoté(e).
future ['fju:tʃə*] a futur(e) // n avenir m; (LING) futur m; **in (the) ~** à l'avenir.
fuze [fju:z] (US) = **fuse**.
fuzzy ['fʌzı] a (PHOT) flou(e); (hair) crépu(e).

G

G [dʒi:] n (MUS) sol m.
gabble ['gæbl] vi bredouiller; jacasser.
gable ['geıbl] n pignon m.
gadget ['gædʒıt] n gadget m.
Gaelic ['geılık] a, n (LING) gaélique (m).
gag [gæg] n bâillon m; (joke) gag m // vt bâillonner.
gaiety ['geıtı] n gaieté f.
gaily ['geılı] ad gaiement.
gain [geın] n gain m, profit m // vt gagner // vi (watch) avancer; **to ~ in/by** gagner en/à; **to ~ 3lbs (in weight)** prendre 3 livres.
gait [geıt] n démarche f.
gal. abbr of **gallon**.
gale [geıl] n rafale f de vent; coup m de vent.
gallant ['gælənt] a vaillant(e), brave; (towards ladies) empressé(e), galant(e).
gall bladder ['gɔ:lblædə*] n vésicule f biliaire.
gallery ['gælərı] n galerie f; (also: **art ~**) musée m; (: private) galerie.
galley ['gælı] n (ship's kitchen) cambuse f; (ship) galère f.
Gallic ['gælık] a gaulois(e), français(e); (charm) latin(e).
gallon ['gæln] n gallon m (= 8 pints; Brit = 4.543 l; US = 3.785 l).
gallop ['gæləp] n galop m // vi galoper.
gallows ['gæləuz] n potence f.
gallstone ['gɔ:lstəun] n calcul m (biliaire).

galore [gə'lɔ:*] ad en abondance, à gogo (col).
galvanize ['gælvənaız] vt galvaniser; (fig): **to ~ sb into action** galvaniser qn.
gambit ['gæmbıt] n (fig): (opening) ~ manœuvre f stratégique.
gamble ['gæmbl] n pari m, risque calculé // vi, vt jouer // vi (on fig) miser sur; ~**r** n joueur m; **gambling** n jeu m.
game [geım] n jeu m; (event) match m; (HUNTING) gibier m // a brave; (ready): **to be ~ (for sth/to do)** être prêt(e) (à qch/à faire); **a ~ of football/tennis** une partie de football/tennis; **big ~** n gros gibier; ~**keeper** n garde-chasse m.
gammon ['gæmən] n (bacon) quartier m de lard fumé; (ham) jambon fumé.
gamut ['gæmət] n gamme f.
gang [gæŋ] n bande f, groupe m // vi: **to ~ up on sb** se liguer contre qn.
gangster ['gæŋstə*] n gangster m.
gangway ['gæŋweı] n passerelle f; (Brit: of bus) couloir central.
gaol [dʒeıl] n, vt (Brit) = **jail**.
gap [gæp] n trou m; (in time) intervalle m; (fig) lacune f; vide m.
gape [geıp] vi être or rester bouche bée; **gaping** a (hole) béant(e).
garage ['gærɑ:ʒ] n garage m.
garbage ['gɑ:bıdʒ] n ordures fpl, détritus mpl; ~ **can** n (US) poubelle f, boîte f à ordures.
garbled ['gɑ:bld] a déformé(e); faussé(e).
garden ['gɑ:dn] n jardin m; ~**er** n jardinier m; ~**ing** n jardinage m.
gargle ['gɑ:gl] vi se gargariser.
gargoyle ['gɑ:gɔıl] n gargouille f.
garish ['gɛərıʃ] a criard(e), voyant(e).
garland ['gɑ:lənd] n guirlande f; couronne f.
garlic ['gɑ:lık] n ail m.
garment ['gɑ:mənt] n vêtement m.
garrison ['gærısn] n garnison f.
garrulous ['gærjuləs] a volubile, loquace.
garter ['gɑ:tə*] n jarretière f; (US) jarretelle f.
gas [gæs] n gaz m; (US: gasoline) essence f // vt asphyxier; (MIL) gazer; ~ **cooker** n (Brit) cuisinière f à gaz; ~ **cylinder** n bouteille f de gaz; ~ **fire** n radiateur m à gaz.
gash [gæʃ] n entaille f; (on face) balafre f.
gasket ['gæskıt] n (AUT) joint m de culasse.
gas mask n masque m à gaz.
gas meter n compteur m à gaz.
gasoline ['gæsəli:n] n (US) essence f.
gasp [gɑ:sp] vi haleter; (fig) avoir le souffle coupé; **to ~ out** vt (say) dire dans un souffle or d'une voix entrecoupée.

gas ring n brûleur m.

gassy ['gæsɪ] a gazeux(euse).

gas tap n bouton m (de cuisinière à gaz); (on pipe) robinet m à gaz.

gate [geɪt] n (of garden) portail m; (of farm) barrière f; (of building) porte f; (of lock) vanne f; ~**crash** vt (Brit) s'introduire sans invitation dans; ~**way** n porte f.

gather ['gæðə*] vt (flowers, fruit) cueillir; (pick up) ramasser; (assemble) rassembler, réunir; recueillir; (understand) comprendre // vi (assemble) se rassembler; to ~ **speed** prendre de la vitesse; ~**ing** n rassemblement m.

gaudy ['gɔːdɪ] a voyant(e).

gauge [geɪdʒ] n (standard measure) calibre m; (RAIL) écartement m; (instrument) jauge f // vt jauger.

Gaul [gɔːl] n (country) Gaule f; (person) Gaulois/e.

gaunt [gɔːnt] a décharné(e); (grim, desolate) désolé(e).

gauntlet ['gɔːntlɪt] n (fig): to run the ~ through an angry crowd se frayer un passage à travers une foule hostile; to throw down the ~ jeter le gant.

gauze [gɔːz] n gaze f.

gave [geɪv] pt of **give**.

gay [geɪ] a (person) gai(e), réjoui(e); (colour) gai, vif(vive); (col) homosexuel(le).

gaze [geɪz] n regard m fixe // vi: to ~ at fixer du regard.

gazetteer [gæzə'tɪə*] n dictionnaire m géographique.

GB abbr of **Great Britain**.

GCE n abbr (Brit) = General Certificate of Education.

GCSE n abbr (Brit) = General Certificate of Secondary Education.

gear [gɪə*] n matériel m, équipement m; attirail m; (TECH) engrenage m; (AUT) vitesse f // (fig: adapt): to ~ sth to adapter qch à; top or (US) high/low/bottom ~ quatrième (or cinquième)/deuxième/première vitesse; in ~ en prise; ~ **box** n boîte f de vitesse; ~ **lever**, (US) ~ **shift** n levier m de vitesse.

geese [giːs] npl of **goose**.

gel [dʒel] n gelée f; (CHEM) colloïde m.

gelignite ['dʒelɪgnaɪt] n plastic m.

gem [dʒem] n pierre précieuse.

Gemini ['dʒemɪnaɪ] n les Gémeaux mpl.

gender ['dʒendə*] n genre m.

general ['dʒenərl] n général m // a général(e); in ~ en général; ~ **delivery** n (US) poste restante; ~ **election** n élection(s) législative(s); ~**ize** vi généraliser; ~**ly** ad généralement; ~ **practitioner (G.P.)** n généraliste m/f.

generate ['dʒenəreɪt] vt engendrer; (electricity) produire.

generation [dʒenə'reɪʃən] n génération f.

generator ['dʒenəreɪtə*] n générateur m.

generosity [dʒenə'rɔsɪtɪ] n générosité f.

generous ['dʒenərəs] a généreux(euse); (copious) copieux(euse).

genetic [dʒɪ'netɪk] a génétique.

Geneva [dʒɪ'niːvə] n Genève.

genial ['dʒiːnɪəl] a cordial(e), chaleureux(euse); (climate) clément(e).

genitals ['dʒenɪtlz] npl organes génitaux.

genius ['dʒiːnɪəs] n génie m.

gent [dʒent] n abbr of **gentleman**.

genteel [dʒen'tiːl] a de bon ton, distingué(e).

gentle ['dʒentl] a doux(douce).

gentleman ['dʒentlmən] n monsieur m; (well-bred man) gentleman m.

gently ['dʒentlɪ] ad doucement.

gentry ['dʒentrɪ] n petite noblesse.

gents [dʒents] n W.C. mpl (pour hommes).

genuine ['dʒenjuɪn] a véritable, authentique; sincère.

geography [dʒɪ'ɔgrəfɪ] n géographie f.

geology [dʒɪ'ɔlədʒɪ] n géologie f.

geometric(al) [dʒɪə'metrɪk(l)] a géométrique.

geometry [dʒɪ'ɔmətrɪ] n géométrie f.

geranium [dʒɪ'reɪnjəm] n géranium m.

geriatric [dʒerɪ'ætrɪk] a gériatrique.

germ [dʒəːm] n (MED) microbe m; (BIO, fig) germe m.

German ['dʒəːmən] a allemand(e) // n Allemand/e; (LING) allemand m; ~ **measles** n rubéole f.

Germany ['dʒəːmənɪ] n Allemagne f.

gesture ['dʒestʃə*] n geste m.

get [get], pt, pp **got**, pp **gotten** (US) vi **1** (become, be) devenir; to ~ old/tired devenir vieux/fatigué, vieillir/se fatiguer; to ~ **drunk** s'enivrer; to ~ **killed** se faire tuer; when do I ~ **paid?** quand est-ce que je serai payé?; it's ~ting late il se fait tard

2 (go): to ~ to/from aller à/de; to ~ **home** rentrer chez soi; how did you ~ here? comment es-tu arrivé ici?

3 (begin) commencer or se mettre à; I'm ~ting to like him je commence à l'apprécier; let's ~ **going** or **started** allons-y

4 (modal auxiliary vb): you've got to do it il faut que vous le fassiez; I've got to tell the police je dois le dire à la police
♦ vt
1: to ~ sth done (do) faire qch; (have done) faire faire qch; to ~ one's hair cut se faire couper les cheveux; to ~ sb to do sth faire faire qch à qn; to ~ sb drunk enivrer qn

2 (obtain: money, permission, results) obtenir, avoir; (find: job, flat) trouver; (fetch: person, doctor, object) aller cher-

cher; **to ~ sth for sb** procurer qch à qn; **~ me Mr Jones, please** (*on phone*) passez-moi Mr Jones, s'il vous plaît; **can I ~ you a drink?** est-ce que je peux vous servir à boire?
3 (*receive: present, letter*) recevoir, avoir; (*acquire: reputation*) avoir; (*: prize*) obtenir; **what did you ~ for your birthday?** qu'est-ce que tu as eu pour ton anniversaire?
4 (*catch*) prendre, saisir, attraper; (*hit: target etc*) atteindre; **to ~ sb by the arm/throat** prendre *or* saisir *or* attraper qn par le bras/à la gorge; **~ him!** arrête-le!
5 (*take, move*) faire parvenir; **do you think we'll ~ it through the door?** on arrivera à le faire passer par la porte?; **I'll ~ you there somehow** je me débrouillerai pour t'y emmener
6 (*catch, take: plane, bus etc*) prendre
7 (*understand*) comprendre, saisir; (*hear*) entendre; **I've got it!** j'ai compris!, je saisis!; **I didn't ~ your name** je n'ai pas entendu votre nom
8 (*have, possess*): **to have got** avoir; **how many have you got?** vous en avez combien?
to get about *vi* se déplacer; (*news*) se répandre
to get along *vi* (*agree*) s'entendre; (*depart*) s'en aller; (*manage*) = **to get by**
to get at *vt fus* (*attack*) s'en prendre à; (*reach*) attraper, atteindre
to get away *vi* partir, s'en aller; (*escape*) s'échapper
to get away with *vt fus* en être quitte pour; se faire passer *or* pardonner
to get back *vi* (*return*) rentrer ♦ *vt* récupérer, recouvrer
to get by *vi* (*pass*) passer; (*manage*) se débrouiller
to get down *vi, vt fus* descendre ♦ *vt* descendre; (*depress*) déprimer
to get down to *vt fus* (*work*) se mettre à (faire)
to get in *vi* rentrer; (*train*) arriver
to get into *vt fus* entrer dans; (*car, train etc*) monter dans; (*clothes*) mettre, enfiler, endosser; **to ~ into bed/a rage** se mettre au lit/en colère
to get off *vi* (*from train etc*) descendre; (*depart: person, car*) s'en aller; (*escape*) s'en tirer ♦ *vt* (*remove: clothes, stain*) enlever ♦ *vt fus* (*train, bus*) descendre de
to get on *vi* (*at exam etc*) se débrouiller; (*agree*): **to ~ on (with)** s'entendre (avec) ♦ *vt fus* monter dans; (*horse*) monter sur
to get out *vi* sortir; (*of vehicle*) descendre ♦ *vt* sortir
to get out of *vt fus* sortir de; (*duty etc*) échapper à, se soustraire à

to get over *vt fus* (*illness*) se remettre de
to get round *vt fus* contourner; (*fig: person*) entortiller
to get through *vi* (*TEL*) avoir la communication; **to ~ through to sb** atteindre qn
to get together *vi* se réunir ♦ *vt* assembler
to get up *vi* (*rise*) se lever ♦ *vt fus* monter
to get up to *vt fus* (*reach*) arriver à; (*prank etc*) faire.
getaway [gɛtəweɪ] *n* fuite *f*.
get-up ['gɛtʌp] *n* (*col*) accoutrement *m*.
geyser ['giːzə*] *n* chauffe-eau *m inv*; (*GEO*) geyser *m*.
Ghana ['gɑːnə] *n* Ghana *m*.
ghastly ['gɑːstlɪ] *a* atroce, horrible; (*pale*) livide, blême.
gherkin ['gəːkɪn] *n* cornichon *m*.
ghost [gəʊst] *n* fantôme *m*, revenant *m*.
giant ['dʒaɪənt] *n* géant(e) // *a* géant(e), énorme.
gibberish ['dʒɪbərɪʃ] *n* charabia *m*.
gibe [dʒaɪb] *n* sarcasme *m*.
giblets ['dʒɪblɪts] *npl* abats *mpl*.
Gibraltar [dʒɪ'brɔːltə*] *n* Gibraltar *m*.
giddy ['gɪdɪ] *a* (*dizzy*): **to be ~** avoir le vertige; (*height*) vertigineux(euse).
gift [gɪft] *n* cadeau *m*, présent *m*; (*donation, ability*) don *m*; **~ed** *a* doué(e); **~ token** *or* **voucher** *n* chèque-cadeau *m*.
gigantic [dʒaɪ'gæntɪk] *a* gigantesque.
giggle ['gɪgl] *vi* pouffer, ricaner sottement.
gill [dʒɪl] *n* (*measure*) = *0.25 pints* (*Brit* = *0.148 l*, *US* = *0.118 l*).
gills [gɪlz] *npl* (*of fish*) ouïes *fpl*, branchies *fpl*.
gilt [gɪlt] *n* dorure *f* // *a* doré(e); **~-edged** *a* (*COMM*) de premier ordre.
gimmick ['gɪmɪk] *n* truc *m*.
gin [dʒɪn] *n* (*liquor*) gin *m*.
ginger ['dʒɪndʒə*] *n* gingembre *m*; **~ ale**, **~ beer** *n* boisson gazeuse au gingembre; **~bread** *n* pain *m* d'épices.
gingerly ['dʒɪndʒəlɪ] *ad* avec précaution.
gipsy ['dʒɪpsɪ] *n* gitan/e, bohémien/ne.
giraffe [dʒɪ'rɑːf] *n* girafe *f*.
girder ['gəːdə*] *n* poutrelle *f*.
girdle ['gəːdl] *n* (*corset*) gaine *f*.
girl [gəːl] *n* fille *f*, fillette *f*; (*young unmarried woman*) jeune fille; (*daughter*) fille; **an English ~** une jeune Anglaise; **~friend** *n* (*of girl*) amie *f*; (*of boy*) petite amie.
giro ['dʒaɪrəʊ] *n* (*bank ~*) virement *m* bancaire; (*post office ~*) mandat *m*.
girth [gəːθ] *n* circonférence *f*; (*of horse*) sangle *f*.
gist [dʒɪst] *n* essentiel *m*.
give [gɪv] *vb* (*pt* **gave**, *pp* **given**) *vt*

donner // vi (break) céder; (stretch: fabric) se prêter; **to ~ sb stn, ~ sth to sb** donner qch à qn; **to ~ a cry/sigh** pousser un cri/un soupir; **to ~ away** vt donner; (give free) faire cadeau de; (betray) donner, trahir; (disclose) révéler; (bride) conduire à l'autel; **to ~ back** vt rendre; **to ~ in** vi céder // vt donner; **to ~ off** vt dégager; **to ~ out** vt distribuer; annoncer; **to ~ up** vi renoncer // vt renoncer à; **to ~ up smoking** arrêter de fumer; **to ~ o.s. up** se rendre; **to ~ way** vi céder; (Brit AUT) céder la priorité.

glacier ['glæsɪə*] n glacier m.

glad [glæd] a content(e).

gladly ['glædlɪ] ad volontiers.

glamorous ['glæmərəs] a séduisant(e).

glamour ['glæmə*] n éclat m, prestige m.

glance [glɑːns] n coup m d'œil // vi: **to ~** at jeter un coup d'œil à; **to ~ off** vt fus (bullet) ricocher sur; **glancing** a (blow) oblique.

gland [glænd] n glande f.

glare [glɛə*] n lumière éblouissante // vi briller d'un éclat aveuglant; **to ~** at lancer un or des regard(s) furieux à; **glaring** a (mistake) criant(e), qui saute aux yeux.

glass [glɑːs] n verre m; (also: looking ~) miroir m; **~es** npl lunettes fpl; **~ware** n verrerie f; **~y** a (eyes) vitreux(euse).

glaze [gleɪz] vt (door) vitrer; (pottery) vernir // n vernis m.

glazier ['gleɪzɪə*] n vitrier m.

gleam [gliːm] n lueur f // vi luire, briller; **~ing** a luisant(e).

glean [gliːn] vt (information) recueillir.

glee [gliː] n joie f.

glen [glɛn] n vallée f.

glib [glɪb] a qui a du bagou; facile.

glide [glaɪd] vi glisser; (AVIAT, birds) planer; **~r** n (AVIAT) planeur m; **gliding** n (AVIAT) vol m à voile.

glimmer ['glɪmə*] n lueur f.

glimpse [glɪmps] n vision passagère, aperçu m // vt entrevoir, apercevoir.

glint [glɪnt] vi étinceler.

glisten ['glɪsn] vi briller, luire.

glitter ['glɪtə*] vi scintiller, briller // n scintillement m.

gloat [gləʊt] vi: **to ~ (over)** jubiler (à propos de).

global ['gləʊbl] a mondial(e).

globe [gləʊb] n globe m.

gloom [gluːm] n obscurité f; (sadness) tristesse f, mélancolie f; **~y** a sombre, triste, mélancolique.

glorious ['glɔːrɪəs] a glorieux(euse); splendide.

glory ['glɔːrɪ] n gloire f; splendeur f // vi: **to ~** in se glorifier de.

gloss [glɒs] n (shine) brillant m, vernis

glossary ['glɒsərɪ] n glossaire m.

glossy ['glɒsɪ] a brillant(e), luisant(e).

glove [glʌv] n gant m; **~ compartment** n (AUT) boîte f à gants, vide-poches m inv.

glow [gləʊ] vi rougeoyer; (face) rayonner // n rougeoiement m.

glower ['glaʊə*] vi: **to ~ (at)** lancer des regards mauvais (à).

glue [gluː] n colle f // vt coller.

glum [glʌm] a maussade, morose.

glut [glʌt] n surabondance f.

glutton ['glʌtn] n glouton/ne; a **~ for work** un bourreau de travail.

gnarled [nɑːld] a noueux(euse).

gnat [næt] n moucheron m.

gnaw [nɔː] vt ronger.

go [gəʊ] vb (pt went, pp gone) vi aller; (depart) partir, s'en aller; (work) marcher; (be sold): **to ~ for £10** se vendre 10 livres; (fit, suit): **to ~ with** aller avec; (become): **to ~ pale/mouldy** pâlir/moisir; (break etc) céder // n (pl: ~es): **to have a ~ (at)** essayer (de faire); **to be on the ~** être en mouvement; **whose ~ is it?** à qui est-ce de jouer?; **he's going to do it** va faire, il est sur le point de faire; **to ~ for a walk** aller se promener; **to ~ dancing** aller danser; **how did it ~?** comment est-ce que ça s'est passé?; **to ~ round the back/by the shop** passer par derrière/devant le magasin; **to ~ about** vi (rumour) se répandre // vt fus: **how do I ~ about this?** comment dois-je m'y prendre (pour faire ceci)?; **to ~ ahead** vi (make progress) avancer; (get going) y aller; **to ~ along** vi aller, avancer // vt fus longer, parcourir; **to ~ away** vi partir, s'en aller; **to ~ back** vi rentrer; revenir; (go again) retourner; **to ~ back on** vt fus (promise) revenir sur; **to ~ by** vi (years, time) passer, s'écouler // vt fus s'en tenir à; en croire; **to ~ down** vi descendre; (ship) couler; (sun) se coucher // vt fus descendre; **to ~ for** vt fus (fetch) aller chercher; (like) aimer; (attack) s'en prendre à; attaquer; **to ~ in** vi entrer; **to ~ in for** vt fus (competition) se présenter à; (like) aimer; **to ~ into** vt fus entrer dans; (investigate) étudier, examiner; (embark on) se lancer dans; **to ~ off** vi partir, s'en aller; (food) se gâter; (explode) sauter; (event) se dérouler // vt fus ne plus aimer; **the gun went off** le coup est parti; **to ~ on** vi continuer; (happen) se passer; **to ~ on doing** continuer à faire; **to ~ out** vi sortir; (fire, light) s'éteindre; **to ~ over** vt fus (check) revoir, vérifier; **to ~ through** vt fus (town etc) traverser; **to ~ up** vi monter; (price) augmenter // vt fus gravir; **to ~ without** vt fus se passer de.

goad [gəud] vt aiguillonner.

go-ahead ['gəuəhɛd] a dynamique, entreprenant(e) // n feu vert.

goal [gəul] n but m; **~keeper** n gardien m de but; **~post** n poteau m de but.

goat [gəut] n chèvre f.

gobble ['gɔbl] vt (also: ~ **down**, ~ **up**) engloutir.

god [gɔd] n dieu m; **G~** n Dieu m; **~child** n filleul/e; **~daughter** n filleule f; **~dess** n déesse f; **~father** n parrain m; **~forsaken** a maudit(e); **~mother** n marraine f; **~send** n aubaine f; **~son** n filleul m.

goggles ['gɔglz] npl lunettes fpl (protectrices) (de motocycliste etc).

going ['gəuŋ] n (conditions) état m du terrain // a: **the ~ rate** le tarif (en vigueur).

gold [gəuld] n or m // a en or; **~en** a (made of gold) en or; (gold in colour) doré(e); **~fish** n poisson m rouge; **~plated** a plaqué(e) or inv; **~smith** n orfèvre m.

golf [gɔlf] n golf m; **~ ball** n balle f de golf; (on typewriter) boule m; **~ club** n club m de golf; (stick) club m, crosse f de golf; **~ course** n terrain m de golf; **~er** n joueur/euse de golf.

gone [gɔn] pp of go // a parti(e).

good [gud] a bon(ne); (kind) gentil(le); (child) sage // n bien m; **~s** npl marchandise f, articles mpl; **~!** bon!, très bien!; **to be ~ at** être bon en; **to be ~ for** être bon à; **it's ~ for you** c'est bon pour vous; **would you be ~ enough to ...?** auriez-vous la bonté or l'amabilité de ...?; **a ~ deal (of)** beaucoup (de); **a ~ many** beaucoup (de); **to make ~** vi (succeed) faire son chemin, réussir // vt (deficit) combler; (losses) compenser; **it's no ~ complaining** cela ne sert à rien de se plaindre; **for ~** pour de bon, une fois pour toutes; **~ morning/afternoon!** bonjour!; **~ evening!** bonsoir!; **~ night!** bonsoir!; (on going to bed) bonne nuit!; **~bye** excl au revoir!; **G~ Friday** n Vendredi saint; **~-looking** a bien inv; **~natured** a qui a un bon naturel; (discussion) enjoué(e); **~ness** n (of person) bonté f; **for ~ness sake!** je vous en prie!; **~ness gracious!** mon Dieu!; **~s train** n (Brit) train m de marchandises; **~will** n bonne volonté; (COMM) réputation f (auprès de la clientèle).

goose [gu:s], pl **geese** n oie f.

gooseberry ['guzbərɪ] n groseille f à maquereau; **to play ~** tenir la chandelle.

gooseflesh ['gu:sflɛʃ] n, **goose pimples** npl chair f de poule.

gore [gɔ:*] vt encorner // n sang m.

gorge [gɔ:dʒ] n gorge f // vt: **to ~ o.s. (on)** se gorger (de).

gorgeous ['gɔ:dʒəs] a splendide, superbe.

gorilla [gə'rɪlə] n gorille m.

gorse [gɔ:s] n ajoncs mpl.

gory ['gɔ:rɪ] a sanglant(e).

go-slow ['gəu'sləu] n (Brit) grève perlée.

gospel ['gɔspl] n évangile m.

gossip ['gɔsɪp] n bavardages mpl; commérage m, cancans mpl; (person) commère f // vi bavarder; (maliciously) cancaner, faire des commérages.

got [gɔt] pt, pp of get; **~ten** (US) pp of get.

gout [gaut] n goutte f.

govern ['gʌvn] vt gouverner.

governess ['gʌvənɪs] n gouvernante f.

government ['gʌvnmənt] n gouvernement m; (Brit: ministers) ministère m.

governor ['gʌvənə*] n (of state, bank) gouverneur m; (of school, hospital) administrateur m.

gown [gaun] n robe f; (of teacher; Brit: of judge) toge f.

G.P. n abbr of **general practitioner**.

grab [græb] vt saisir, empoigner; (property, power) se saisir de.

grace [greɪs] n grâce f // vt honorer; **5 days' ~** répit m de 5 jours; **to say ~** dire le bénédicité; (after meal) dire les grâces; **~ful** a gracieux(euse), élégant(e); **gracious** ['greɪʃəs] a bienveillant(e); de bonne grâce; miséricordieux(euse).

grade [greɪd] n (COMM) qualité f; calibre m; catégorie f; (in hierarchy) grade m, échelon m; (US SCOL) note f; classe f // vt classer; calibrer; graduer; **~ crossing** n (US) passage m à niveau; **~ school** n (US) école f primaire.

gradient ['greɪdɪənt] n inclinaison f, pente f.

gradual ['grædjuəl] a graduel(le), progressif(ive); **~ly** ad peu à peu, graduellement.

graduate n ['grædjuɪt] diplômé/e d'université // vi ['grædjueɪt] obtenir un diplôme d'université; **graduation** [-'eɪʃən] n cérémonie f de remise des diplômes.

graffiti [grə'fi:tɪ] npl graffiti mpl.

graft [grɑ:ft] n (AGR, MED) greffe f; (bribery) corruption f // vt greffer; **hard ~** n (col) boulot acharné.

grain [greɪn] n grain m.

gram [græm] n gramme m.

grammar ['græmə*] n grammaire f; **~ school** n (Brit) ≈ lycée m.

grammatical [grə'mætɪkl] a grammatical(e).

gramme [græm] n = **gram**.

grand [grænd] a magnifique, splendide; noble; **~children** npl petits-enfants mpl; **~dad** n grand-papa m; **~daughter** n petite-fille f; **~father** n grand-père m;

~**ma** n grand-maman f; ~**mother** n grand-mère f; ~**pa** n = ~**dad**; ~**parents** npl grand-père m et grand-mère f; ~ **piano** n piano m à queue; ~**son** n petit-fils m; ~**stand** n (SPORT) tribune f.

granite ['grænɪt] n granit m.

granny ['grænɪ] n grand-maman f.

grant [grɑːnt] vt accorder; (a request) accéder à; (admit) concéder // n (SCOL) bourse f; (ADMIN) subside m, subvention f; to take sth for ~ed considérer qch comme acquis.

granulated ['grænjuleɪtɪd] a: ~ **sugar** n sucre m en poudre.

grape [greɪp] n raisin m.

grapefruit ['greɪpfruːt] n pamplemousse m.

graph [grɑːf] n graphique m, courbe f; ~**ic** a graphique; (vivid) vivant(e); ~**ics** n arts mpl graphiques // npl graphisme m.

grapple ['græpl] vi: to ~ **with** être aux prises avec.

grasp [grɑːsp] vt saisir // n (grip) prise f; (fig) emprise f, pouvoir m; compréhension f, connaissance f; ~**ing** a avide.

grass [grɑːs] n herbe f; ~**hopper** n sauterelle f; ~-**roots** a de base; ~ **snake** n couleuvre f.

grate [greɪt] n grille f de cheminée // vi grincer // vt (CULIN) râper.

grateful ['greɪtful] a reconnaissant(e).

grater ['greɪtə•] n râpe f.

gratify ['grætɪfaɪ] vt faire plaisir à; (whim) satisfaire.

grating ['greɪtɪŋ] n (iron bars) grille f // a (noise) grinçant(e).

gratitude ['grætɪtjuːd] n gratitude f.

gratuity [grə'tjuːɪtɪ] n pourboire m.

grave [greɪv] n tombe f // a grave, sérieux(euse).

gravel ['grævl] n gravier m.

gravestone ['greɪvstəun] n pierre tombale.

graveyard ['greɪvjɑːd] n cimetière m.

gravity ['grævɪtɪ] n (PHYSICS) gravité f; pesanteur f; (seriousness) gravité.

gravy ['greɪvɪ] n jus m (de viande); sauce f.

gray [greɪ] a = **grey**.

graze [greɪz] vi paître, brouter // vt (touch lightly) frôler, effleurer; (scrape) écorcher // n écorchure f.

grease [griːs] n (fat) graisse f; (lubricant) lubrifiant m // vt graisser; lubrifier; ~**proof paper** n (Brit) papier sulfurisé; **greasy** a gras(se), graisseux(euse).

great [greɪt] a grand(e); (col) formidable; G~ **Britain** n Grande-Bretagne f; ~-**grandfather** n arrière-grand-père m; ~-**grandmother** n arrière-grand-mère f; ~**ly** ad très, grandement; (with verbs) beaucoup; ~**ness** n grandeur f.

Greece [griːs] n Grèce f.

greed [griːd] n (also: ~**iness**) avidité f; (for food) gourmandise f; ~**y** a avide; gourmand(e).

Greek [griːk] a grec(grecque) // n Grec/Grecque; (LING) grec m.

green [griːn] a vert(e); (inexperienced) (bien) jeune, naïf(ïve) // n vert m; (stretch of grass) pelouse f; (also: village ~) ≈ place f du village; ~s npl légumes verts; ~ **belt** n (round town) ceinture verte; ~ **card** n (AUT) carte verte; ~**ery** n verdure f; ~**gage** n reine-claude f; ~**grocer** n (Brit) marchand m de fruits et légumes; ~**house** n serre f.

Greenland ['griːnlənd] n Groenland m.

greet [griːt] vt accueillir; ~**ing** n salutation f; ~**ing(s) card** n carte f de vœux.

grenade [grə'neɪd] n grenade f.

grew [gruː] pt of **grow**.

grey [greɪ] a gris(e); (dismal) sombre; ~**hound** n lévrier m.

grid [grɪd] n grille f; (ELEC) réseau m.

grief [griːf] n chagrin m, douleur f.

grievance ['griːvəns] n doléance f, grief m.

grieve [griːv] vi avoir du chagrin; se désoler // vt faire de la peine à, affliger; to ~ **for** sb (dead person) pleurer qn.

grievous ['griːvəs] a: ~ **bodily harm** (LAW) coups mpl et blessures fpl.

grill [grɪl] n (on cooker) gril m // vt (Brit) griller; (question) cuisiner.

grille [grɪl] n grillage m; (AUT) calandre f.

grim [grɪm] a sinistre, lugubre.

grimace [grɪ'meɪs] n grimace f // vi grimacer, faire une grimace.

grimy ['graɪmɪ] a crasseux(euse).

grin [grɪn] n large sourire m // vi sourire.

grind [graɪnd] vt (pt, pp ground) écraser; (coffee, pepper etc) moudre; (US: meat) hacher; (make sharp) aiguiser // n (work) corvée f; to ~ **one's teeth** grincer des dents.

grip [grɪp] n étreinte f, poigne f; prise f; (holdall) sac m de voyage // vt saisir, empoigner; étreindre; to come to ~s **with** en venir aux prises avec.

gripping ['grɪpɪŋ] a prenant(e), palpitant(e).

grisly ['grɪzlɪ] a sinistre, macabre.

gristle ['grɪsl] n cartilage m (de poulet etc).

grit [grɪt] n gravillon m; (courage) cran m // vt (road) sabler; to ~ **one's teeth** serrer les dents.

groan [grəun] n gémissement m; grognement m // vi gémir; grogner.

grocer ['grəusə•] n épicier m; ~**ies** npl provisions fpl.

groin [grɔɪn] n aine f.

groom [gruːm] n palefrenier m; (also:

bride~) marié m // vt (horse) panser; (fig): to ~ sb for former qn pour.

groove [gru:v] n sillon m, rainure f.

grope [grəup] vi tâtonner; to ~ for vt fus chercher à tâtons.

gross [grəus] a grossier(ère); (COMM) brut(e); **~ly** ad (greatly) très, grandement.

grotto ['grɔtəu] n grotte f.

ground [graund] pt, pp of grind // n sol m, terre f; (land) terrain m, terres fpl; (SPORT) terrain; (US: also: ~ wire) terre; (reason: gen pl) raison f // vt (plane) empêcher de décoller, retenir au sol; (US: ELEC) équiper d'une prise de terre // vi (ship) s'échouer; **~s** npl (of coffee etc) marc m; (gardens etc) parc m, domaine m; **on the ~, to the ~** par terre; **to gain/lose ~** gagner/perdre du terrain; **~ cloth** n (US) = **~sheet**; **~ing** n (in education) connaissances fpl de base; **~less** a sans fondement; **~sheet** n (Brit) tapis m de sol; **~ staff** n équipage m au sol; **~ swell** n lame f or vague f de fond; **~work** n préparation f.

group [gru:p] n groupe m // vt (also: ~ together) grouper // vi (also: ~ together) se grouper.

grouse [graus] n (pl inv) (bird) grouse f // vi (complain) rouspéter, râler.

grove [grəuv] n bosquet m.

grovel ['grɔvl] vi ramper.

grow [grəu], pt grew, pp grown vi (plant) pousser, croître; (person) grandir; (increase) augmenter, se développer; (become): to ~ rich/weak s'enrichir/s'affaiblir // vt cultiver, faire pousser; to ~ up vi grandir; **~er** n producteur m; **~ing** a (fear, amount) croissant(e), grandissant(e).

growl [graul] vi grogner.

grown [grəun] pp of grow // a adulte; **~-up** n adulte m/f, grande personne.

growth [grəuθ] n croissance f, développement m; (what has grown) pousse f, poussée f; (MED) grosseur f, tumeur f.

grub [grʌb] n larve f; (col: food) bouffe f.

grubby ['grʌbɪ] a crasseux(euse).

grudge [grʌdʒ] n rancune f // vt: to ~ sb sth donner qch à qn à contre-cœur; reprocher qch à qn; to bear sb a ~ (for) garder rancune or en vouloir à qn (de).

gruelling ['gruəlɪŋ] a exténuant(e).

gruesome ['gru:səm] a horrible.

gruff [grʌf] a bourru(e).

grumble ['grʌmbl] vi rouspéter, ronchonner.

grumpy ['grʌmpɪ] a grincheux(euse).

grunt [grʌnt] vi grogner.

G-string ['dʒi:strɪŋ] n (garment) cache-sexe m inv.

guarantee [gærən'ti:] n garantie f // vt garantir.

guard [gɑ:d] n garde f; (one man) garde m; (Brit RAIL) chef m de train // vt garder, surveiller; **~ed** a (fig) prudent(e); **~ian** n gardien/ne; (of minor) tuteur/trice; **~'s van** n (Brit RAIL) fourgon m.

guerrilla [gə'rɪlə] n guérillero m; ~ warfare n guérilla f.

guess [gɛs] vi deviner // vt deviner; (US) croire, penser // n supposition f, hypothèse f; **~work** n hypothèse f.

guest [gɛst] n invité/e; (in hotel) client/e; **~-house** n pension f; ~ room n chambre f d'amis.

guffaw [gʌ'fɔ:] vi pouffer de rire.

guidance ['gaɪdəns] n conseils mpl.

guide [gaɪd] n (person, book etc) guide m; (also: **girl ~**) guide f // vt guider; **~book** n guide m; ~ dog n chien m d'aveugle; **~lines** npl (fig) instructions générales, conseils mpl.

guild [gɪld] n corporation f; cercle m, association f.

guile [gaɪl] n astuce f.

guillotine ['gɪləti:n] n guillotine f.

guilt [gɪlt] n culpabilité f; **~y** a coupable.

guinea pig ['gɪnɪpɪg] n cobaye m.

guise [gaɪz] n aspect m, apparence f.

guitar [gɪ'tɑ:*] n guitare f.

gulf [gʌlf] n golfe m; (abyss) gouffre m.

gull [gʌl] n mouette f.

gullet ['gʌlɪt] n gosier m.

gullible ['gʌlɪbl] a crédule.

gully ['gʌlɪ] n ravin m; ravine f; couloir m.

gulp [gʌlp] vi avaler sa salive; (from emotion) avoir la gorge serrée // vt (also: ~ down) avaler.

gum [gʌm] n (ANAT) gencive f; (glue) colle f; (sweet) boule f de gomme; (also: **chewing~**) chewing-gum m // vt coller; **~boots** npl (Brit) bottes fpl en caoutchouc.

gun [gʌn] n (small) revolver m, pistolet m; (rifle) fusil m, carabine f; (cannon) canon m; **~boat** n canonnière f; **~fire** n fusillade f; **~man** n bandit armé; **~ner** n artilleur m; **~point** n: at **~point** sous la menace du pistolet (or fusil); **~powder** n poudre f à canon; **~shot** n coup m de feu; **~smith** n armurier m.

gurgle ['gə:gl] vi gargouiller.

guru ['guru:] n gourou m.

gush [gʌʃ] vi jaillir; (fig) se répandre en effusions.

gusset ['gʌsɪt] n gousset m, soufflet m.

gust [gʌst] n (of wind) rafale f; (of smoke) bouffée f.

gusto ['gʌstəu] n enthousiasme m.

gut [gʌt] n intestin m, boyau m; (MUS etc) boyau; **~s** npl (courage) cran m.

gutter ['gʌtə*] n (of roof) gouttière f;

(*in street*) caniveau *m*.

guy [gaɪ] *n* (*also*: **~rope**) corde *f*; (*col: man*) type *m*; (*figure*) effigie de Guy Fawkes.

guzzle ['gʌzl] *vi* s'empiffrer // *vt* avaler gloutonnement.

gym [dʒɪm] *n* (*also*: **gymnasium**) gymnase *m*; (*also*: **gymnastics**) gym *f*; **~ shoes** *npl* chaussures *fpl* de gym(nastique); **~ slip** *n* (*Brit*) tunique *f* (d'écolière).

gymnast ['dʒɪmnæst] *n* gymnaste *m/f*; **~ics** [-'næstɪks] *n*, *npl* gymnastique *f*.

gynaecologist, (*US*) **gynecologist** [gaɪnɪ'kɔlədʒɪst] *n* gynécologue *m/f*.

gypsy ['dʒɪpsɪ] *n* = **gipsy**.

gyrate [dʒaɪ'reɪt] *vi* tournoyer.

H

haberdashery ['hæbə'dæʃərɪ] *n* (*Brit*) mercerie *f*.

habit ['hæbɪt] *n* habitude *f*; (*costume*) habit *m*, tenue *f*.

habitual [hə'bɪtjuəl] *a* habituel(le); (*drinker, liar*) invétéré(e).

hack [hæk] *vt* hacher, tailler // *n* (*cut*) entaille *f*; (*blow*) coup *m*; (*pej: writer*) nègre *m*.

hackneyed ['hæknɪd] *a* usé(e), rebattu(e).

had [hæd] *pt, pp of* **have**.

haddock, *pl* **~** *or* **~s** ['hædək] *n* églefin *m*; **smoked ~** haddock *m*.

hadn't ['hædnt] = **had not**.

haemorrhage, (*US*) **hemorrhage** ['hemərɪdʒ] *n* hémorragie *f*.

haggle ['hægl] *vi* marchander.

Hague [heɪg] *n*: **The ~** La Haye.

hail [heɪl] *n* grêle *f* // *vt* (*call*) héler; (*greet*) acclamer // *vi* grêler; **~stone** *n* grêlon *m*.

hair [hɛə*] *n* cheveux *mpl*; (*single hair: on head*) cheveu *m*; (: *on body*) poil *m*; **to do one's ~** se coiffer; **~brush** *n* brosse *f* à cheveux; **~cut** *n* coupe *f* (de cheveux); **~do** ['hɛədu:] *n* coiffure *f*; **~dresser** *n* coiffeur/euse; **~-dryer** *n* sèche-cheveux *m*; **~grip** *n* pince *f* à cheveux; **~pin** *n* épingle *f* à cheveux; **~pin bend,** (*US*) **~pin curve** *n* virage *m* en épingle à cheveux; **~raising** *a* à (vous) faire dresser les cheveux sur la tête; **~ remover** *n* dépilateur *m*; **~ spray** *n* laque *f* (pour les cheveux); **~style** *n* coiffure *f*; **~y** *a* poilu(e); chevelu(e); (*fig*) effrayant(e).

hake [heɪk] *n* colin *m*, merlu *m*.

half [hɑ:f] *n* (*pl* **halves**) moitié *f* // *a* demi(e) // *ad* à moitié, à demi; **~-an-hour** une demi-heure; **~ a dozen** une demi-douzaine; **~ a pound** une demi-livre, ≈ 250 g; **two and a ~** deux et demi; **a week and a ~** une semaine et demie; **~ (of it)** la moitié de; **~ (of)** la moitié de; **to cut sth in ~** couper qch en deux; **~ asleep** à moitié endormi(e); **~-back** *n* (*SPORT*) demi *m*; **~-breed,** **~-caste** *n* métis/se; **~-hearted** *a* tiède, sans enthousiasme; **~-hour** *n* demi-heure *f*; **~-mast: at ~-mast** (*flag*) en berne, à mi-mât; **~penny** ['heɪpnɪ] *n* (*Brit*) demi-penny *m*; **(at) ~-price** à moitié prix; **~ term** *n* (*Brit SCOL*) congé *m* de demi-trimestre; **~-time** *n* mi-temps *f*; **~way** *ad* à mi-chemin.

halibut ['hælɪbət] *n* (*pl inv*) flétan *m*.

hall [hɔ:l] *n* salle *f*; (*entrance way*) hall *m*, entrée *f*; (*corridor*) couloir *m*; (*mansion*) château *m*, manoir *m*; **~ of residence** *n* (*Brit*) pavillon *m* or résidence *f* universitaire.

hallmark ['hɔ:lmɑ:k] *n* poinçon *m*; (*fig*) marque *f*.

hallo [hə'ləu] *excl* = **hello**.

Hallowe'en [hæləu'i:n] *n* veille *f* de la Toussaint.

hallucination [həlu:sɪ'neɪʃən] *n* hallucination *f*.

hallway ['hɔ:lweɪ] *n* vestibule *m*; couloir *m*.

halo ['heɪləu] *n* (*of saint etc*) auréole *f*; (*of sun*) halo *m*.

halt [hɔ:lt] *n* halte *f*, arrêt *m* // *vt* faire arrêter // *vi* faire halte, s'arrêter.

halve [hɑ:v] *vt* (*apple etc*) partager *or* diviser en deux; (*expense*) réduire de moitié.

halves [hɑ:vz] *npl of* **half**.

ham [hæm] *n* jambon *m*.

hamburger ['hæmbə:gə*] *n* hamburger *m*.

hamlet ['hæmlɪt] *n* hameau *m*.

hammer ['hæmə*] *n* marteau *m* // *vt* (*fig*) éreinter, démolir // *vi* (*on door*) frapper à coups redoublés.

hammock ['hæmək] *n* hamac *m*.

hamper ['hæmpə*] *vt* gêner // *n* panier *m* (d'osier).

hamster ['hæmstə*] *n* hamster *m*.

hand [hænd] *n* main *f*; (*of clock*) aiguille *f*; (*handwriting*) écriture *f*; (*at cards*) jeu *m*; (*worker*) ouvrier/ère // *vt* passer, donner; **to give sb a ~** donner un coup de main à qn; **at ~** à portée de la main; **in ~** en main; (*work*) en cours; **to be on ~** (*person*) être disponible; (*emergency services*) se tenir prêt(e) (à intervenir); **to ~** (*information etc*) sous la main, à portée de la main; **on the one ~ ..., on the other ~** d'une part ..., d'autre part; **to ~ in** *vt* remettre; **to ~ out** *vt* distribuer; **to ~ over** *vt* transmettre; céder; **~bag** *n* sac *m* à main; **~book** *n* manuel *m*; **~brake** *n* frein *m* à main; **~cuffs** *npl* menottes *fpl*; **~ful** *n* poignée *f*.

handicap ['hændɪkæp] *n* handicap *m* // *vt* handicaper; **mentally/physically ~ped**

a handicapé(e) mentalement/physiquement.

handicraft ['hændɪkrɑ:ft] *n* travail *m* d'artisanat, technique artisanale.

handiwork ['hændɪwɔ:k] *n* ouvrage *m*; (*pej*) œuvre *f*.

handkerchief ['hæŋkətʃɪf] *n* mouchoir *m*.

handle ['hændl] *n* (*of door etc*) poignée *f*; (*of cup etc*) anse *f*; (*of knife etc*) manche *m*; (*of saucepan*) queue *f*; (*for winding*) manivelle *f* // *vt* toucher, manier; (*deal with*) s'occuper de; (*treat: people*) prendre; '~ with care' 'fragile'; to fly off the ~ s'énerver; ~**bar(s)** *n(pl)* guidon *m*.

hand-: ~**luggage** *n* bagages *mpl* à main; ~**made** *a* fait(e) à la main; ~**out** *n* documentation *f*, prospectus *m*; ~**rail** *n* rampe *f*, main courante; ~**shake** *n* poignée *f* de main.

handsome ['hænsəm] *a* beau(belle); généreux(euse); considérable.

handwriting ['hændraɪtɪŋ] *n* écriture *f*.

handy ['hændɪ] *a* (*person*) adroit(e); (*close at hand*) sous la main; (*convenient*) pratique; **handyman** *n* bricoleur *m*; (*servant*) homme *m* à tout faire.

hang [hæŋ], *pt*, *pp* **hung** *vt* accrocher; (*criminal*: *pt*, *pp* **hanged**) pendre // *vi* pendre; (*hair, drapery*) tomber; **to get the ~ of (doing) sth** (*col*) attraper le coup pour faire qch; **to ~ about** *vi* flâner, traîner; **to ~ on** *vi* (*wait*) attendre; **to ~ up** *vi* (*TEL*) raccrocher // *vt* accrocher, suspendre.

hangar ['hæŋə*] *n* hangar *m*.

hanger ['hæŋə*] *n* cintre *m*, portemanteau *m*.

hanger-on [hæŋər'ɔn] *n* parasite *m*.

hang-gliding ['hæŋglaɪdɪŋ] *n* vol *m* libre *or* sur aile delta.

hangover ['hæŋəʊvə*] *n* (*after drinking*) gueule *f* de bois.

hang-up ['hæŋʌp] *n* complexe *m*.

hanker ['hæŋkə*] *vi*: **to ~ after** avoir envie de.

hankie, hanky ['hæŋkɪ] *n abbr of* **handkerchief**.

haphazard [hæp'hæzəd] *a* fait(e) au hasard, fait(e) au petit bonheur.

happen ['hæpən] *vi* arriver; se passer, se produire; **as it ~s** justement; ~**ing** *n* événement *m*.

happily ['hæpɪlɪ] *ad* heureusement.

happiness ['hæpɪnɪs] *n* bonheur *m*.

happy ['hæpɪ] *a* heureux(euse); ~ **with** (*arrangements etc*) satisfait(e) de; ~ **birthday!** bon anniversaire!; ~**go-lucky** *a* insouciant(e).

harass ['hærəs] *vt* accabler, tourmenter; ~**ment** *n* tracasseries *fpl*.

harbour, (*US*) **harbor** ['hɑ:bə*] *n* port *m* // *vt* héberger, abriter.

hard [hɑ:d] *a* dur(e) // *ad* (*work*) dur; (*think, try*) sérieusement; **to look ~ at** regarder fixement; regarder de près; **no ~ feelings!** sans rancune!; **to be ~ of hearing** être dur(e) d'oreille; **to be ~ done by** être traité(e) injustement; ~**back** *n* livre relié; ~ **cash** *n* espèces *fpl*; ~ **disk** *n* (*COMPUT*) disque dur; ~**en** *vt* durcir; (*fig*) endurcir // *vi* durcir; ~**-headed** *a* réaliste; décidé(e); ~ **labour** *n* travaux forcés.

hardly ['hɑ:dlɪ] *ad* (*scarcely*) à peine; **it's ~ the case** ce n'est guère le cas; **that can ~ be true** cela ne peut tout de même pas être vrai; ~ **anywhere/ever** presque nulle part/jamais.

hardship ['hɑ:dʃɪp] *n* épreuves *fpl*; privations *fpl*.

hard-up [hɑ:d'ʌp] *a* (*col*) fauché(e).

hardware ['hɑ:dwɛə*] *n* quincaillerie *f*; (*COMPUT*) matériel *m*; ~ **shop** *n* quincaillerie *f*.

hard-wearing [hɑ:d'wɛərɪŋ] *a* solide.

hard-working [hɑ:d'wɜ:kɪŋ] *a* travailleur(euse).

hardy ['hɑ:dɪ] *a* robuste; (*plant*) résistant(e) au gel.

hare [hɛə*] *n* lièvre *m*; ~**-brained** *a* farfelu(e); écervelé(e).

harm [hɑ:m] *n* mal *m*; (*wrong*) tort *m* // *vt* (*person*) faire du mal ou du tort à; (*thing*) endommager; **out of ~'s way** à l'abri du danger, en lieu sûr; ~**ful** *a* nuisible; ~**less** *a* inoffensif(ive); sans méchanceté.

harmony ['hɑ:mənɪ] *n* harmonie *f*.

harness ['hɑ:nɪs] *n* harnais *m* // *vt* (*horse*) harnacher; (*resources*) exploiter.

harp [hɑ:p] *n* harpe *f* // *vi*: **to ~ on about** parler tout le temps de.

harrowing ['hærəʊɪŋ] *a* déchirant(e).

harsh [hɑ:ʃ] *a* (*hard*) dur(e); (*severe*) sévère; (*unpleasant*: *sound*) discordant(e); (: *colour*) criard(e); cru(e); (: *wine*) âpre.

harvest ['hɑ:vɪst] *n* (*of corn*) moisson *f*; (*of fruit*) récolte *f*; (*of grapes*) vendange *f* // *vi*, *vt* moissonner; récolter; vendanger.

has [hæz] *vb see* **have**.

hash [hæʃ] *n* (*CULIN*) hachis *m*; (*fig*: *mess*) gâchis *m*.

hasn't ['hæznt] = **has not**.

hassle ['hæsl] *n* chamaillerie *f*.

haste [heɪst] *n* hâte *f*; précipitation *f*; ~**n** ['heɪsn] *vt* hâter, accélérer // *vi* se hâter, s'empresser; **hastily** *ad* à la hâte; précipitamment; **hasty** *a* hâtif(ive); précipité(e).

hat [hæt] *n* chapeau *m*.

hatch [hætʃ] *n* (*NAUT*: *also*: ~**way**) écoutille *f*; (*also*: **service** ~) passe-plats *m inv* // *vi* éclore // *vt* faire éclore; (*plot*) tramer.

hatchback ['hætʃbæk] n (AUT) modèle m arrière.

hatchet ['hætʃɪt] n hachette f.

hate [heɪt] vt haïr, détester // n haine f; ~**ful** a odieux(euse), détestable.

hatred ['heɪtrɪd] n haine f.

hat trick n (SPORT, also fig) triplé m (3 buts réussis au cours du même match etc).

haughty ['hɔːtɪ] a hautain(e), arrogant(e).

haul [hɔːl] vt traîner, tirer // n (of fish) prise f; (of stolen goods etc) butin m; ~**age** n transport routier; ~**ier**, (US) ~**er** n transporteur (routier), camionneur m.

haunch [hɔːntʃ] n hanche f.

haunt [hɔːnt] vt (subj: ghost, fear) hanter; (: person) fréquenter // n repaire m.

have [hæv], pt, pp **had** ♦ auxiliary vb 1 (gen) avoir; être; **to ~ arrived/gone** être arrivé(e)/allé(e); **to ~ eaten/slept** avoir mangé/dormi; **he has been promoted** il a été promu

2 (in tag questions): **you've done it, ~n't you?** vous l'avez fait, n'est-ce pas?

3 (in short answers and questions): **no I ~n't!/yes we ~!** mais non!/mais si!; **so I ~!** ah oui!, oui c'est vrai!; **I've been there before, ~ you?** j'y suis déjà allé, et vous?

♦ modal auxiliary vb (be obliged): **to ~ (got) to do sth** devoir faire qch; être obligé(e) de faire qch; **she has (got) to do it** elle doit le faire, il faut qu'elle le fasse; **you ~n't to tell her** vous ne devez pas le lui dire

♦ vt 1 (possess, obtain) avoir; **he has (got) blue eyes/dark hair** il a les yeux bleus/les cheveux bruns; **may I ~ your address?** puis-je avoir votre adresse?

2 (+ noun: take, hold etc): **to ~ breakfast/a bath/a shower** prendre le petit déjeuner/un bain/une douche; **to ~ dinner/lunch** dîner/déjeuner; **to ~ a swim** nager; **to ~ a meeting** se réunir; **to ~ a party** organiser une fête

3: **to ~ sth done** faire faire qch; **to ~ one's hair cut** se faire couper les cheveux; **to ~ sb do sth** faire faire qch à qn

4 (experience, suffer) avoir; **to ~ a cold/flu** avoir un rhume/la grippe; **to ~ an operation** se faire opérer

5 (col: dupe) avoir; **he's been had** il s'est fait avoir or roulé

to have out vt: **to ~ it out with sb** (settle a problem etc) s'expliquer (franchement) avec qn.

haven ['heɪvn] n port m; (fig) havre m.

haven't ['hævnt] = **have not**.

haversack ['hævəsæk] n sac m à dos.

havoc ['hævək] n ravages mpl.

hawk [hɔːk] n faucon m.

hay [heɪ] n foin m; ~ **fever** n rhume m des foins; ~**stack** n meule f de foin.

haywire ['heɪwaɪə*] a (col): **to go ~** perdre la tête; mal tourner.

hazard ['hæzəd] n hasard m, chance f; danger m, risque m // vt risquer, hasarder; ~ **warning lights** npl (AUT) feux mpl de détresse.

haze [heɪz] n brume f.

hazelnut ['heɪzlnʌt] n noisette f.

hazy ['heɪzɪ] a brumeux(euse); (idea) vague; (photograph) flou(e).

he [hiː] pronoun il; **it is ~ who ...** c'est lui qui ...

head [hɛd] n tête f; (leader) chef m // vt (list) être en tête de; (group) être à la tête de; ~**s or tails** pile ou face; ~ **first** la tête la première; ~ **over heels in love** follement or éperdument amoureux(euse); **to ~ the ball** faire une tête; **to ~ for** vt fus se diriger vers; ~**ache** n mal m de tête; ~**dress** n coiffure f; ~**ing** n titre m; rubrique f; ~**lamp** n (Brit) = ~**light**; ~**land** n promontoire m, cap m; ~**light** n phare m; ~**line** n titre m; ~**long** ad (fall) la tête la première; (rush) tête baissée; ~**master** n directeur m, proviseur m; ~**mistress** n directrice f; ~ **office** n bureau central; ~**-on** a (collision) de plein fouet; ~**phones** npl casque m (à écouteurs); ~**quarters (HQ)** npl bureau or siège central; (MIL) quartier général; ~**-rest** n appui-tête m; ~**room** n (in car) hauteur f de plafond; (under bridge) hauteur limite; dégagement m; ~**scarf** n foulard m; ~**strong** a têtu(e), entêté(e); ~ **waiter** n maître m d'hôtel; ~**way** n: **to make ~way** avancer, faire des progrès; ~**wind** n vent m contraire; ~**y** a capiteux(euse); enivrant(e).

heal [hiːl] vt, vi guérir.

health [hɛlθ] n santé f; ~ **food shop** n magasin m diététique; **the H~ Service** n (Brit) ≈ la Sécurité Sociale; ~**y** a (person) en bonne santé; (climate, food, attitude etc) sain(e).

heap [hiːp] n tas m, monceau m // vt entasser, amonceler.

hear [hɪə*], pt, pp **heard** [hə:d] vt entendre; (news) apprendre; (lecture) assister à, écouter // vi entendre; **to ~ about** avoir des nouvelles de; entendre parler de; **to ~ from sb** recevoir des nouvelles de qn; ~**ing** n (sense) ouïe f; (of witnesses) audition f; (of a case) audience f; ~**ing aid** n appareil m acoustique; ~**say**: **by ~say** ad par ouï-dire m.

hearse [hə:s] n corbillard m.

heart [ha:t] n cœur m; ~**s** npl (CARDS) cœur; **at ~** au fond; **by ~** (learn, know) par cœur; ~ **attack** n crise f cardiaque; ~**beat** n battement m de cœur; ~**broken** a: **to be ~broken** avoir

beaucoup de chagrin; **~burn** n brûlures
fpl d'estomac; **~ failure** n arrêt m du
cœur; **~felt** a sincère.

hearth [hɑ:θ] n foyer m, cheminée f.

heartily ['hɑ:tɪlɪ] ad chaleureusement;
(laugh) de bon cœur; (eat) de bon
appétit; **to agree ~** être entièrement
d'accord.

hearty ['hɑ:tɪ] a chaleureux(euse);
robuste; vigoureux(euse).

heat [hi:t] n chaleur f; (fig) ardeur f; feu
m; (SPORT: also: **qualifying ~**)
éliminatoire f // vt chauffer; **to ~ up** vi
(liquids) chauffer; (room) se réchauffer
// vt réchauffer; **~ed** a chauffé(e); (fig)
passionné(e), échauffé(e), excité(e);
~er n appareil m de chauffage;
radiateur m.

heath [hi:θ] n (Brit) lande f.

heathen ['hi:ðn] a, n païen(ne).

heather ['hɛðə*] n bruyère f.

heating ['hi:tɪŋ] n chauffage m.

heatstroke ['hi:tstrəuk] n coup m de
chaleur.

heatwave ['hi:tweɪv] n vague f de
chaleur.

heave [hi:v] vt soulever (avec effort) //
vi se soulever; (retch) avoir des haut-le-
cœur // n (push) poussée f.

heaven ['hɛvn] n ciel m, paradis m; **~ly**
a céleste, divin(e).

heavily ['hɛvɪlɪ] ad lourdement; (drink,
smoke) beaucoup; (sleep, sigh)
profondément.

heavy ['hɛvɪ] a lourd(e); (work, sea,
rain, eater) gros(se); (drinker, smoker)
grand(e); **~ goods vehicle (HGV)** n
poids lourd (PL); **~weight** n (SPORT)
poids lourd.

Hebrew ['hi:bru:] a hébraïque // n
(LING) hébreu m.

Hebrides ['hɛbrɪdi:z] npl: **the ~** les Hé-
brides fpl.

heckle ['hɛkl] vt interpeller (un
orateur).

hectic ['hɛktɪk] a agité(e), trépidant(e).

he'd [hi:d] = **he would, he had**.

hedge [hɛdʒ] n haie f // vi se défiler; **to
~ one's bets** (fig) se couvrir.

hedgehog ['hɛdʒhɔg] n hérisson m.

heed [hi:d] vt (also: **take ~ of**) tenir
compte de, prendre garde à; **~less** a
insouciant(e).

heel [hi:l] n talon m // vt (shoe)
retalonner.

hefty ['hɛftɪ] a (person) costaud(e);
(parcel) lourd(e); (piece, price)
gros(se).

heifer ['hɛfə*] n génisse f.

height [haɪt] n (of person) taille f,
grandeur f; (of object) hauteur f; (of
plane, mountain) altitude f; (high
ground) hauteur, éminence f; (fig: of
glory) sommet m; (: of stupidity)
comble m; **~en** vt hausser, surélever;

(fig) augmenter.

heir [ɛə*] n héritier m; **~ess** n héritière
f; **~loom** n meuble m (or bijou m or tableau m) de famille.

held [hɛld] pt, pp of **hold**.

helicopter ['hɛlɪkɔptə*] n hélicoptère
m.

hell [hɛl] n enfer m; **~!** (col) merde!

he'll [hi:l] = **he will, he shall**.

hellish ['hɛlɪʃ] a infernal(e).

hello [hə'ləu] excl bonjour!; salut! (to sb
one addresses as 'tu'); (surprise) tiens!

helm [hɛlm] n (NAUT) barre f.

helmet ['hɛlmɪt] n casque m.

help [hɛlp] n aide f; (charwoman)
femme f de ménage; (assistant etc)
employée // vt aider; **~!** au secours!; **~
yourself** (to bread) servez-vous (de
pain); **he can't ~ it** il n'y peut rien; **~er**
n aide m/f, assistant/e; **~ful** a serviable,
obligeant(e); (useful) utile; **~ing** n
portion f; **~less** a impuissant(e); faible.

hem [hɛm] n ourlet m // vt ourler; **to ~
in** vt cerner.

he-man ['hi:mæn] n macho m.

hemorrhage ['hɛmɔrɪdʒ] n (US) =
haemorrhage.

hen [hɛn] n poule f.

hence [hɛns] ad (therefore) d'où, de là;
2 years ~ d'ici 2 ans; **~forth** ad
dorénavant.

henchman ['hɛntʃmən] n (pej) acolyte
m, séide m.

henpecked ['hɛnpɛkt] a dominé par sa
femme.

her [hə:*] pronoun (direct) la, l' + vowel or h mute; (indirect) lui; (stressed,
after prep) elle; see note at **she** // a
son(sa), ses pl; see also **me, my**.

herald ['hɛrəld] n héraut m // vt
annoncer.

herb [hə:b] n herbe f.

herd [hə:d] n troupeau m.

here [hɪə*] ad ici // excl tiens!, tenez!;
~! présent!; **~ is, ~ are** voici; **~'s my
sister** voici ma sœur; **~ he/she is** le/la
voici; **~ she comes** la voici qui vient;
~after ad après, plus tard; ci-après // n:
the ~after l'au-delà m; **~by** ad (in
letter) par la présente.

hereditary [hɪ'rɛdɪtrɪ] a héréditaire.

heresy ['hɛrəsɪ] n hérésie f.

hermit ['hə:mɪt] n ermite m.

hernia ['hə:nɪə] n hernie f.

hero, pl ~es ['hɪərəu] n héros m.

heroin ['hɛrəuɪn] n héroïne f.

heroine ['hɛrəuɪn] n héroïne f.

heron ['hɛrən] n héron m.

herring ['hɛrɪŋ] n hareng m.

hers [hə:z] pronoun le(la) sien(ne), les
siens(siennes); see also **mine**.

herself [hə:'sɛlf] pronoun (reflexive) se;
(emphatic) elle-même; (after prep) elle;
see also **oneself**.

he's [hi:z] = **he is, he has**.

hesitant ['hezɪtənt] a hésitant(e), indécis(e).

hesitate ['hezɪteɪt] vi: to ~ (about/to do) hésiter (sur/à faire); **hesitation** ['-teɪʃən] n hésitation f.

heyday ['heɪdeɪ] n: the ~ of l'âge m d'or de, les beaux jours de.

HGV n abbr of **heavy goods vehicle**.

hi [haɪ] excl salut!

hiatus [haɪ'eɪtəs] n trou m, lacune f; (LING) hiatus m.

hibernate ['haɪbəneɪt] vi hiberner.

hiccough, hiccup ['hɪkʌp] vi hoqueter // n hoquet m.

hide [haɪd] n (skin) peau f // vb (pt hid, pp hidden [hɪd, 'hɪdn]) vt: to ~ sth (from sb) cacher qch (à qn) // vi: to ~ (from sb) se cacher (de qn); ~-and-seek n cache-cache m; ~away n cachette f.

hideous ['hɪdɪəs] a hideux(euse) atroce.

hiding ['haɪdɪŋ] n (beating) correction f, volée f de coups; to be in ~ (concealed) se tenir caché(e).

hierarchy ['haɪərɑːkɪ] n hiérarchie f.

hi-fi ['haɪfaɪ] n hi-fi f inv // a hi-fi inv.

high [haɪ] a haut(e); (speed, respect, number) grand(e); (price) élevé(e); (wind) fort(e), violent(e); (voice) aigu(aiguë) // ad haut, en haut; 20 m ~ haut(e) de 20 m; ~boy n (US: tallboy) commode (haute); ~brow a, n intellectuel(le); ~chair n chaise haute (pour enfant); ~er education n études supérieures; ~-handed a autoritaire; très cavalier(ère); ~jack = hijack; ~ jump n (SPORT) saut m en hauteur; the H~lands npl les Highlands mpl; ~light n (fig: of event) point culminant // vt faire ressortir, souligner; ~ly ad très, fort, hautement; ~ly strung a nerveux(euse), toujours tendu(e); ~ness n hauteur f; Her H~ness son Altesse f; ~-pitched a aigu(aiguë); ~-rise block n tour f (d'habitation); ~ school n lycée m; (US) établissement m d'enseignement supérieur; ~ season n (Brit) haute saison; ~ street n (Brit) grand-rue f.

highway ['haɪweɪ] n grand'route f, route nationale; H~ Code n (Brit) code m de la route.

hijack ['haɪdʒæk] vt détourner (par la force); ~er n pirate m de l'air.

hike [haɪk] vi aller à pied // n excursion f à pied, randonnée f; (in prices) hausse f, augmentation f; ~r n promeneur/euse, excursionniste m/f.

hilarious [hɪ'lɛərɪəs] a (behaviour, event) désopilant(e).

hill [hɪl] n colline f; (fairly high) montagne f; (on road) côte f; ~side n (flanc m de) coteau m; ~y a vallonné(e); montagneux(euse).

hilt [hɪlt] n (of sword) garde f; to the ~ (fig: support) à fond.

him [hɪm] pronoun (direct) le, l' + vowel or h mute; (stressed, indirect, after prep) lui; see also me; ~self pronoun (reflexive) se; (emphatic) lui-même; (after prep) lui; see also oneself.

hind [haɪnd] a de derrière // n biche f.

hinder ['hɪndə*] vt gêner; (delay) retarder; (prevent): to ~ sb from doing empêcher qn de faire; **hindrance** ['hɪndrəns] n gêne f, obstacle m.

hindsight ['haɪndsaɪt] n: with ~ avec du recul, rétrospectivement.

Hindu ['hɪnduː] n Hindou/e.

hinge [hɪndʒ] n charnière f // vi (fig): to ~ on dépendre de.

hint [hɪnt] n allusion f; (advice) conseil m // vt: to ~ that insinuer que // vi: to ~ at faire une allusion à.

hip [hɪp] n hanche f.

hippopotamus, pl ~es or **hippopotami** [hɪpə'pɔtəməs, -'pɔtəmaɪ] n hippopotame m.

hire ['haɪə*] vt (Brit: car, equipment) louer; (worker) embaucher, engager // n location f; for ~ à louer; (taxi) libre; ~ purchase (H.P.) n (Brit) achat m (or vente f) à tempérament or crédit.

his [hɪz] pronoun le(la) sien(ne), les siens(siennes) // a son(sa), ses pl; see also my, mine.

hiss [hɪs] vi siffler.

historic(al) [hɪ'stɔrɪk(l)] a historique.

history ['hɪstərɪ] n histoire f.

hit [hɪt] vt (pt, pp hit) frapper; (knock against) cogner; (reach: target) atteindre, toucher; (collide with: car) entrer en collision avec, heurter; (fig: affect) toucher; (find) tomber sur // n coup m; (success) coup réussi; succès m; (song) chanson f à succès, tube m; to ~ it off with sb bien s'entendre avec qn; ~-and-run driver n chauffard m.

hitch [hɪtʃ] vt (fasten) accrocher, attacher; (also: ~ up) remonter d'une saccade // n (difficulty) anicroche f, contretemps m; to ~ a lift faire du stop.

hitch-hike ['hɪtʃhaɪk] vi faire de l'auto-stop; ~r n auto-stoppeur/euse.

hi-tech ['haɪ'tek] a à la pointe de la technologie, technologiquement avancé(e) // n high-tech m.

hitherto [hɪðə'tuː] ad jusqu'ici.

hive [haɪv] n ruche f; to ~ off vt mettre à part, séparer.

H.M.S. abbr = His (Her) Majesty's Ship.

hoard [hɔːd] n (of food) provisions fpl, réserves fpl; (of money) trésor m // vt amasser.

hoarding ['hɔːdɪŋ] n (Brit: for posters) panneau m d'affichage or publicitaire.

hoarfrost ['hɔːfrɔst] n givre m.

hoarse [hɔːs] a enroué(e).

hoax [həuks] n canular m.

hob [hɔb] *n* plaque chauffante.

hobble ['hɔbl] *vi* boitiller.

hobby ['hɔbɪ] *n* passe-temps favori; ~**horse** *n* (*fig*) dada *m*.

hobo ['həubəu] *n* (*US*) vagabond *m*.

hockey ['hɔkɪ] *n* hockey *m*.

hoe [həu] *n* houe *f*, binette *f*.

hog [hɔg] *n* sanglier *m* // *vt* (*fig*) accaparer; **to go the whole** ~ aller jusqu'au bout.

hoist [hɔɪst] *n* palan *m* // *vt* hisser.

hold [həuld] *vb* (*pt, pp* **held**) *vt* tenir; (*contain*) contenir; (*keep back*) retenir; (*believe*) maintenir; considérer; (*possess*) avoir; détenir // *vi* (*withstand pressure*) tenir (bon); (*be valid*) valoir // *n* prise *f*; (*fig*) influence *f*; (*NAUT*) cale *f*; ~ **the line!** (*TEL*) ne quittez pas!; **to** ~ **one's own** (*fig*) (bien) se défendre; (*sick person*) se maintenir; **to catch** *or* **get** (**a**) ~ **of** saisir; **to get** ~ **of** (*fig*) trouver; **to** ~ **back** *vt* retenir; (*secret*) cacher; **to** ~ **down** *vt* (*person*) maintenir à terre; (*job*) occuper; **to** ~ **off** *vt* tenir à distance; **to** ~ **on** *vi* tenir bon; (*wait*) attendre; ~ **on!** (*TEL*) ne quittez pas!; **to** ~ **on to** *vt fus* se cramponner à; (*keep*) conserver, garder; **to** ~ **out** *vi* offrir // *vi* (*resist*) tenir bon; **to** ~ **up** *vt* (*raise*) lever; (*support*) soutenir; (*delay*) retarder; ~**all** *n* (*Brit*) fourretout *m inv*; ~**er** *n* (*of ticket, record*) détenteur/trice; (*of office, title etc*) titulaire *m/f*; ~**ing** *n* (*share*) intérêts *mpl*; (*farm*) ferme *f*; ~**up** *n* (*robbery*) hold-up *m*; (*delay*) retard *m*; (*Brit*: *in traffic*) embouteillage *m*.

hole [həul] *n* trou *m*.

holiday ['hɔlədɪ] *n* vacances *fpl*; (*day off*) jour *m* de congé; (*public*) jour férié; **on** ~ en congé; ~ **camp** *n* (*for children*) colonie *f* de vacances; (*also*: ~ **centre**) camp *m* de vacances; ~**-maker** *n* (*Brit*) vacancier/ère; ~ **resort** *n* centre *m* de villégiature *or* de vacances.

holiness ['həulɪnɪs] *n* sainteté *f*.

Holland ['hɔlənd] *n* Hollande *f*.

hollow ['hɔləu] *a* creux(euse); (*fig*) faux(fausse) // *n* creux *m*; (*in land*) dépression *f* (de terrain), cuvette *f* // *vt*: **to** ~ **out** creuser, évider.

holly ['hɔlɪ] *n* houx *m*.

holocaust ['hɔləkɔ:st] *n* holocauste *m*.

holster ['həulstə*] *n* étui *m* de revolver.

holy ['həulɪ] *a* saint(e); (*bread, water*) bénit(e); (*ground*) sacré(e); **H~ Ghost** *or* **Spirit** *n* Saint-Esprit *m*.

home [həum] *n* foyer *m*, maison *f*; (*country*) pays natal, patrie *f*; (*institution*) maison *f* de famille; (*ECON, POL*) national(e), intérieur(e) // *ad* chez soi, à la maison; au pays natal; (*right in: nail etc*) à fond; **at** ~ chez soi, à la maison; **to go** (*or* **come**) ~ rentrer (chez soi), rentrer à la maison (*or* au

pays); **make yourself at** ~ faites comme chez vous; ~ **address** *n* domicile permanent; ~ **computer** *n* ordinateur *m* domestique; ~**land** *n* patrie *f*; ~**less** *a* sans foyer; sans abri; ~**ly** *a* simple, sans prétention; accueillant(e); ~**-made** *a* fait(e) à la maison; **H~ Office** *n* (*Brit*) Ministère *m* de l'Intérieur; ~ **rule** *n* autonomie *f*; **H~ Secretary** *n* (*Brit*) ministre *m* de l'Intérieur; ~**sick** *a*: **to be** ~**sick** avoir le mal du pays; s'ennuyer de sa famille; ~ **town** *n* ville natale; ~**ward** ['həumwəd] *a* (*journey*) du retour; ~**work** *n* devoirs *mpl*.

homogeneous [hɔməu'dʒi:nɪəs] *a* homogène.

homosexual [hɔməu'sɛksjuəl] *a, n* homosexuel(le).

honest ['ɔnɪst] *a* honnête; (*sincere*) franc(franche); ~**ly** *ad* honnêtement; franchement; ~**y** *n* honnêteté *f*.

honey ['hʌnɪ] *n* miel *m*; ~**comb** *n* rayon *m* de miel; ~**moon** *n* lune *f* de miel; (*trip*) voyage *m* de noces; ~**suckle** *n* (*BOT*) chèvrefeuille *m*.

honk [hɔŋk] *vi* klaxonner.

honorary ['ɔnərərɪ] *a* honoraire; (*duty, title*) honorifique.

honour, (*US*) honor ['ɔnə*] *vt* honorer // *n* honneur *m*; ~**able** *a* honorable; ~**s degree** *n* (*SCOL*) licence *avec* mention.

hood [hud] *n* capuchon *m*; (*Brit AUT*) capote *f*; (*US AUT*) capot *m*.

hoodlum ['hu:dləm] *n* truand *m*.

hoodwink ['hudwɪŋk] *vt* tromper.

hoof [hu:f] , *pl* ~**s** *or* **hooves** *n* sabot *m*.

hook [huk] *n* crochet *m*; (*on dress*) agrafe *f*; (*for fishing*) hameçon *m* // *vt* accrocher; (*dress*) agrafer.

hooligan ['hu:lɪgən] *n* voyou *m*.

hoop [hu:p] *n* cerceau *m*.

hoot [hu:t] *vi* (*AUT*) klaxonner; (*siren*) mugir; ~**er** *n* (*Brit AUT*) klaxon *m*; (*NAUT*) sirène *f*.

hoover ® ['hu:və*] (*Brit*) *n* aspirateur *m* // *vt* passer l'aspirateur dans *or* sur.

hooves [hu:vz] *npl of* **hoof**.

hop [hɔp] *vi* sauter; (*on one foot*) sauter à cloche-pied.

hope [həup] *vt, vi* espérer // *n* espoir *m*; **I** ~ **so** je l'espère; **I** ~ **not** j'espère que non; ~**ful** *a* (*person*) plein(e) d'espoir; (*situation*) prometteur(euse), encourageant(e); ~**fully** *ad* avec espoir, avec optimisme; avec un peu de chance; ~**less** *a* désespéré(e); (*useless*) nul(le).

hops [hɔps] *npl* houblon *m*.

horizon [hə'raɪzn] *n* horizon *m*; ~**tal** [hɔrɪ'zɔntl] *a* horizontal(e).

horn [hɔ:n] *n* corne *f*; (*MUS: also*: **French** ~) cor *m*; (*AUT*) klaxon *m*.

hornet ['hɔ:nɪt] *n* frelon *m*.

horny ['hɔ:nɪ] *a* corné(e); (*hands*) calleux(euse); (*col*) en rut, excité(e).

horoscope ['hɔrəskəup] n horoscope m.

horrendous [həˈrendəs] a horrible, affreux(euse).

horrible [ˈhɔrɪbl] a horrible, affreux(euse).

horrid [ˈhɔrɪd] a méchant(e), désagréable.

horrify [ˈhɔrɪfaɪ] vt horrifier.

horror [ˈhɔrə*] n horreur f; ~ **film** n film m d'épouvante.

horse [hɔːs] n cheval m; ~**back: on** ~**back** à cheval; ~ **chestnut** n marron m (d'Inde); ~**man/woman** n cavalier/ière; ~**power (h.p.)** n puissance f (en chevaux); ~**racing** n courses fpl de chevaux; ~**radish** n raifort m; ~**shoe** n fer m à cheval.

hose [həuz] n (also: ~**pipe**) tuyau m; (also: **garden** ~) tuyau d'arrosage.

hosiery [ˈhəuzɪərɪ] n (in shop) (rayon m des) bas mpl.

hospitable [ˈhɔspɪtəbl] a hospitalier(ère).

hospital [ˈhɔspɪtl] n hôpital m; **in** ~ à l'hôpital.

hospitality [hɔspɪˈtælɪtɪ] n hospitalité f.

host [həust] n hôte m; (in hotel etc) patron m; (REL) hostie f; (large number): **a** ~ **of** une foule de.

hostage [ˈhɔstɪdʒ] n otage m.

hostel [ˈhɔstl] n foyer m; (also: **youth** ~) auberge f de jeunesse.

hostess [ˈhəustɪs] n hôtesse f.

hostile [ˈhɔstaɪl] a hostile.

hostility [hɔˈstɪlɪtɪ] n hostilité f.

hot [hɔt] a chaud(e); (as opposed to only warm) très chaud; (spicy) fort(e); (fig) acharné(e); brûlant(e); violent(e), passionné(e); **to be** ~ (person) avoir chaud; (object) être (très) chaud; (weather) faire chaud; ~**bed** n (fig) foyer m, pépinière f; ~ **dog** n hot-dog m.

hotel [həuˈtel] n hôtel m.

hot: ~**headed** a impétueux(euse); ~**house** n serre chaude; ~ **line** n (POL) téléphone m rouge, ligne directe; ~**ly** ad passionnément, violemment; ~**plate** n (on cooker) plaque chauffante; ~**water bottle** n bouillotte f.

hound [haund] vt poursuivre avec acharnement // n chien courant.

hour [ˈauə*] n heure f; ~**ly** a, ad toutes les heures; (rate) horaire; ~**ly paid** a payé(e) à l'heure.

house n [haus] (pl: ~**s** [ˈhauzɪz]) maison f; (POL) chambre f; (THEATRE) salle f; auditoire m // vt [hauz] (person) loger, héberger; **on the** ~ (fig) aux frais de la maison; ~**boat** n bateau m (aménagé en habitation); ~**breaking** n cambriolage m (avec effraction); ~**coat** n peignoir m; ~**hold** n famille f, maisonnée f; ménage m; ~**keeper** n

gouvernante f; ~**keeping** n (work) ménage m; ~**keeping (money)** argent m du ménage; ~**-warming party** n pendaison f de crémaillère; ~**wife** n ménagère f; femme f au foyer; ~**work** n (travaux mpl du) ménage m.

housing [ˈhauzɪŋ] n logement m; ~ **development**, (Brit) ~ **estate** n cité f; lotissement m.

hovel [ˈhɔvl] n taudis m.

hover [ˈhɔvə*] vi planer; ~**craft** n aéroglisseur m.

how [hau] ad comment; ~ **are you?** comment allez-vous?; ~ **do you do?** bonjour; enchanté(e); ~ **far is it to ...?** combien y a-t-il jusqu'à ...?; ~ **long have you been here?** depuis combien de temps êtes-vous là?; ~ **lovely!** que or comme c'est joli!; ~ **many/much?** combien?; ~ **many people/much milk** combien de gens/lait; ~ **old are you?** quel âge avez-vous?; ~**ever** ad de quelque façon or manière que + sub; (+ adjective) quelque or si ... que + sub; (in questions) comment // cj pourtant, cependant.

howl [haul] vi hurler.

h.p., H.P. abbr of **hire purchase, horsepower.**

HQ abbr of **headquarters.**

hub [hʌb] n (of wheel) moyeu m; (fig) centre m, foyer m.

hubbub [ˈhʌbʌb] n brouhaha m.

hub cap n enjoliveur m.

huddle [ˈhʌdl] vi: **to** ~ **together** se blottir les uns contre les autres.

hue [hjuː] n teinte f, nuance f; ~ **and cry** n tollé (général), clameur f.

huff [hʌf] n: **in a** ~ fâché(e).

hug [hʌg] vt serrer dans ses bras; (shore, kerb) serrer // n étreinte f.

huge [hjuːdʒ] a énorme, immense.

hulk [hʌlk] n (ship) vieux rafiot; (car, building) carcasse f; (person) mastodonte m, malabar m.

hull [hʌl] n (of ship, nuts) coque f.

hullo [həˈləu] excl = **hello.**

hum [hʌm] vt (tune) fredonner // vi fredonner; (insect) bourdonner; (plane, tool) vrombir.

human [ˈhjuːmən] a humain(e) // n être humain.

humane [hjuːˈmeɪn] a humain(e), humanitaire.

humanitarian [hjuːmænɪˈtɛərɪən] a humanitaire.

humanity [hjuːˈmænɪtɪ] n humanité f.

humble [ˈhʌmbl] a humble, modeste // vt humilier.

humbug [ˈhʌmbʌg] n fumisterie f.

humdrum [ˈhʌmdrʌm] a monotone, routinier(ère).

humid [ˈhjuːmɪd] a humide.

humiliate [hjuːˈmɪlɪeɪt] vt humilier; **humiliation** [-ˈeɪʃən] n humiliation f.

humility [hju:'mɪlɪtɪ] *n* humilité *f*.
humorous ['hju:mərəs] *a* humoristique; (*person*) plein(e) d'humour.
humour, (*US*) **humor** ['hju:mə*] *n* humour *m*; (*mood*) humeur *f* // *vt* (*person*) faire plaisir à; se prêter aux caprices de.
hump [hʌmp] *n* bosse *f*.
hunch [hʌntʃ] *n* bosse *f*; (*premonition*) intuition *f*; ~**back** *n* bossu/e; ~**ed** *a* arrondi(e), voûté(e).
hundred ['hʌndrəd] *num* cent; ~s of des centaines de; ~**weight** *n* (*Brit*) = 50.8 *kg*; 112 *lb*; (*US*) = 45.3 *kg*; 100 *lb*.
hung [hʌŋ] *pt, pp of* hang.
Hungary ['hʌŋgərɪ] *n* Hongrie *f*.
hunger ['hʌŋgə*] *n* faim *f* // *vi*: to ~ for avoir faim de, désirer ardemment.
hungry ['hʌŋgrɪ] *a* affamé(e); to be ~ avoir faim.
hunk [hʌŋk] *n* (*of bread etc*) gros morceau.
hunt [hʌnt] *vt* (*seek*) chercher; (*SPORT*) chasser // *vi* chasser // *n* chasse *f*; ~**er** *n* chasseur *m*; ~**ing** *n* chasse *f*.
hurdle ['hə:dl] *n* (*SPORT*) haie *f*; (*fig*) obstacle *m*.
hurl [hə:l] *vt* lancer (avec violence).
hurrah, hurray [hu'rɑ:, hu'reɪ] *n* hourra *m*.
hurricane ['hʌrɪkən] *n* ouragan *m*.
hurried ['hʌrɪd] *a* pressé(e), précipité(e) // (*work*) fait(e) à la hâte; ~**ly** *ad* précipitamment, à la hâte.
hurry ['hʌrɪ] *n* hâte *f*, précipitation *f* // *vb* (*also*: ~ up) *vi* se presser, se dépêcher // *vt* (*person*) faire presser, faire se dépêcher; (*work*) presser; to be in a ~ être pressé(e); to do sth in a ~ faire qch en vitesse; to ~ in/out entrer/sortir précipitamment.
hurt [hə:t] *vb* (*pt, pp* hurt) *vt* (*cause pain to*) faire mal à; (*injure, fig*) blesser // *vi* faire mal // *a* blessé(e); ~**ful** *a* (*remark*) blessant(e).
hurtle ['hə:tl] *vi*: to ~ past passer en trombe; to ~ down dégringoler.
husband ['hʌzbənd] *n* mari *m*.
hush [hʌʃ] *n* calme *m*, silence *m* // *vt* faire taire; ~! chut!
husk [hʌsk] *n* (*of wheat*) balle *f*; (*of rice, maize*) enveloppe *f*.
husky ['hʌskɪ] *a* rauque // *n* chien *m* esquimau *or* de traîneau.
hustle ['hʌsl] *vt* pousser, bousculer // *n* bousculade *f*; ~ **and bustle** *n* tourbillon *m* (d'activité).
hut [hʌt] *n* hutte *f*; (*shed*) cabane *f*.
hutch [hʌtʃ] *n* clapier *m*.
hyacinth ['haɪəsɪnθ] *n* jacinthe *f*.
hydrant ['haɪdrənt] *n* prise *f* d'eau; (*also*: fire ~) bouche *f* d'incendie.
hydraulic [haɪ'drɔ:lɪk] *a* hydraulique.
hydroelectric [haɪdrəʊɪ'lektrɪk] *a* hydro-électrique.

hydrofoil ['haɪdrəʊfɔɪl] *n* hydrofoil *m*.
hydrogen ['haɪdrədʒən] *n* hydrogène *m*.
hyena [har'i:nə] *n* hyène *f*.
hygiene ['haɪdʒi:n] *n* hygiène *f*.
hymn [hɪm] *n* hymne *m*; cantique *m*.
hype [haɪp] *n* (*col*) campagne *f* publicitaire.
hypermarket ['haɪpəmɑ:kɪt] *n* hypermarché *m*.
hyphen ['haɪfɪn] *n* trait *m* d'union.
hypnotize ['hɪpnətaɪz] *vt* hypnotiser.
hypocrisy [hɪ'pɔkrɪsɪ] *n* hypocrisie *f*.
hypocrite ['hɪpəkrɪt] *n* hypocrite *m/f*; **hypocritical** [-'krɪtɪkl] *a* hypocrite.
hypothesis, *pl* **hypotheses** [haɪ'pɔθɪsɪs, -siːz] *n* hypothèse *f*.
hysterical [hɪ'sterɪkl] *a* hystérique.
hysterics [hɪ'sterɪks] *npl* (*violente*) crise de nerfs; (*laughter*) crise de rire.

I

I [aɪ] *pronoun* je; (*before vowel*) j'; (*stressed*) moi.
ice [aɪs] *n* glace *f*; (*on road*) verglas *m* // *vt* (*cake*) glacer; (*drink*) faire rafraîchir // *vi* (*also*: ~ over) geler; (*also*: ~ up) se givrer; ~ **axe** *n* piolet *m*; ~**berg** *n* iceberg *m*; ~**box** *n* (*US*) réfrigérateur *m*; (*Brit*) compartiment *m* à glace; (*insulated box*) glacière *f*; ~ **cream** *n* glace *f*; ~ **cube** *n* glaçon *m*; ~ **hockey** *n* hockey *m* sur glace.
Iceland ['aɪslənd] *n* Islande *f*.
ice-: ~ lolly *n* (*Brit*) esquimau *m*; ~ **rink** *n* patinoire *f*; ~ **skating** *n* patinage *m* (sur glace).
icicle ['aɪsɪkl] *n* glaçon *m* (*naturel*).
icing ['aɪsɪŋ] *n* (*AVIAT etc*) givrage *m*; (*CULIN*) glaçage *m*; ~ **sugar** *n* (*Brit*) sucre *m* glace.
icy ['aɪsɪ] *a* glacé(e); (*road*) verglacé(e); (*weather, temperature*) glacial(e).
I'd [aɪd] = **I would, I had.**
idea [aɪ'dɪə] *n* idée *f*.
ideal [aɪ'dɪəl] *n* idéal *m* // *a* idéal(e).
identical [aɪ'dentɪkl] *a* identique.
identification [aɪdentɪfɪ'keɪʃən] *n* identification *f*; **means of** ~ pièce *f* d'identité.
identify [aɪ'dentɪfaɪ] *vt* identifier.
identikit picture [aɪ'dentɪkɪt-] *n* portrait-robot *m*.
identity [aɪ'dentɪtɪ] *n* identité *f*; ~ **card** *n* carte *f* d'identité.
idiom ['ɪdɪəm] *n* langue *f*, idiome *m*; (*phrase*) expression *f* idiomatique.
idiosyncrasy [ɪdɪəʊ'sɪŋkrəsɪ] *n* particularité *f*, caractéristique *f*.
idiot ['ɪdɪət] *n* idiot/e, imbécile *m/f*; ~**ic** [-'ɔtɪk] *a* idiot(e), bête, stupide.
idle ['aɪdl] *a* sans occupation, désœuvré(e); (*lazy*) oisif(ive), paresseux(euse); (*unemployed*) au chômage;

(question, pleasures) vain(e), futile // *vt*: **to ~ away the time** passer son temps à ne rien faire; **to lie ~** être arrêté, ne pas fonctionner.

idol ['aɪdl] *n* idole *f*; **~ize** *vt* idolâtrer, adorer.

i.e. *ad abbr* (= *id est*) c'est-à-dire.

if [ɪf] *cj* si; **~ so** si c'est le cas; **~ not** sinon; **~ only** si seulement.

ignite [ɪgˈnaɪt] *vt* mettre le feu à, enflammer // *vi* s'enflammer.

ignition [ɪgˈnɪʃən] *n* (AUT) allumage *m*; **to switch on/off the ~** mettre/couper le contact; **~ key** *n* (AUT) clé *f* de contact.

ignorant ['ɪgnərənt] *a* ignorant(e); **to be ~ of** *(subject)* ne rien connaître en; *(events)* ne pas être au courant de.

ignore [ɪgˈnɔ:ʳ] *vt* ne tenir aucun compte de, ne pas relever; *(person)* faire semblant de ne pas reconnaître, ignorer; *(fact)* méconnaître.

ill [ɪl] *a* (sick) malade; *(bad)* mauvais(e) // *n* mal *m* // *ad*: **to speak** *etc* **~ of** dire *etc* du mal de; **to take** *or* **be taken ~** tomber malade; **~-advised** *a (decision)* peu judicieux(euse); *(person)* malavisé(e); **~-at-ease** *a* mal à l'aise.

I'll [aɪl] **= I will, I shall.**

illegal [ɪˈli:gl] *a* illégal(e).

illegible [ɪˈlɛdʒɪbl] *a* illisible.

illegitimate [ɪlɪˈdʒɪtɪmət] *a* illégitime.

ill-fated [ɪlˈfeɪtɪd] *a* malheureux(euse); *(day)* néfaste.

ill feeling *n* ressentiment *m*, rancune *f*.

illiterate [ɪˈlɪtərət] *a* illettré(e); *(letter)* plein(e) de fautes.

illness ['ɪlnɪs] *n* maladie *f*.

ill-treat [ɪlˈtri:t] *vt* maltraiter.

illuminate [ɪˈlu:mɪneɪt] *vt* *(room, street)* éclairer; *(building)* illuminer; **illumination** [-ˈneɪʃən] *n* éclairage *m*; illumination *f*.

illusion [ɪˈlu:ʒən] *n* illusion *f*; **to be under the ~ that** s'imaginer *or* croire que.

illustrate ['ɪləstreɪt] *vt* illustrer; **illustration** [-ˈstreɪʃən] *n* illustration *f*.

ill will *n* malveillance *f*.

I'm [aɪm] **= I am.**

image ['ɪmɪdʒ] *n* image *f*; *(public face)* image de marque; **~ry** *n* images *fpl*.

imaginary [ɪˈmædʒɪnərɪ] *a* imaginaire.

imagination [ɪmædʒɪˈneɪʃən] *n* imagination *f*.

imaginative [ɪˈmædʒɪnətɪv] *a* imaginatif(ive); plein(e) d'imagination.

imagine [ɪˈmædʒɪn] *vt* s'imaginer; *(suppose)* imaginer, supposer.

imbalance [ɪmˈbæləns] *n* déséquilibre *m*.

imitate ['ɪmɪteɪt] *vt* imiter; **imitation** [-ˈteɪʃən] *n* imitation *f*.

immaculate [ɪˈmækjulət] *a* impeccable; *(REL)* immaculé(e).

immaterial [ɪməˈtɪərɪəl] *a* sans importance, insignifiant(e).

immature [ɪməˈtjuəʳ] *a* *(fruit)* qui n'est pas mûr(e); *(person)* qui manque de maturité.

immediate [ɪˈmi:dɪət] *a* immédiat(e); **~ly** *ad* *(at once)* immédiatement; **~ly next to** juste à côté de.

immense [ɪˈmɛns] *a* immense; énorme.

immerse [ɪˈmə:s] *vt* immerger, plonger.

immersion heater [ɪˈmə:ʃən-] *n* (Brit) chauffe-eau *m* électrique.

immigrant ['ɪmɪgrənt] *n* immigrant/e; immigré/e.

immigration [ɪmɪˈgreɪʃən] *n* immigration *f*.

imminent ['ɪmɪnənt] *a* imminent(e).

immoral [ɪˈmɔrl] *a* immoral(e).

immortal [ɪˈmɔ:tl] *a, n* immortel(le).

immune [ɪˈmju:n] *a*: **~ (to)** immunisé(e) (contre).

immunity [ɪˈmju:nɪtɪ] *n* immunité *f*.

imp [ɪmp] *n* lutin *m*; *(child)* petit diable.

impact ['ɪmpækt] *n* choc *m*, impact *m*; *(fig)* impact.

impair [ɪmˈpɛəʳ] *vt* détériorer, diminuer.

impart [ɪmˈpɑ:t] *vt* communiquer, transmettre; confier, donner.

impartial [ɪmˈpɑ:ʃl] *a* impartial(e).

impassable [ɪmˈpɑ:səbl] *a* infranchissable; *(road)* impraticable.

impassive [ɪmˈpæsɪv] *a* impassible.

impatience [ɪmˈpeɪʃəns] *n* impatience *f*.

impatient [ɪmˈpeɪʃənt] *a* impatient(e); **to get** *or* **grow ~** s'impatienter.

impeccable [ɪmˈpɛkəbl] *a* impeccable, parfait(e).

impede [ɪmˈpi:d] *vt* gêner.

impediment [ɪmˈpɛdɪmənt] *n* obstacle *m*; *(also:* **speech ~)** défaut *m* d'élocution.

impending [ɪmˈpɛndɪŋ] *a* imminent(e).

imperative [ɪmˈpɛrətɪv] *a* nécessaire; urgent(e), pressant(e); *(tone)* impérieux(euse) // *n* (LING) impératif *m*.

imperfect [ɪmˈpə:fɪkt] *a* imparfait(e); *(goods etc)* défectueux(euse).

imperial [ɪmˈpɪərɪəl] *a* impérial(e); *(measure)* légal(e).

impersonal [ɪmˈpə:sənl] *a* impersonnel(le).

impersonate [ɪmˈpə:səneɪt] *vt* se faire passer pour; *(THEATRE)* imiter.

impertinent [ɪmˈpə:tɪnənt] *a* impertinent(e), insolent(e).

impervious [ɪmˈpə:vɪəs] *a* imperméable; *(fig)*: **~ to** insensible à; inaccessible à.

impetuous [ɪmˈpɛtjuəs] *a* impétueux(euse), fougueux(euse).

impetus ['ɪmpətəs] *n* impulsion *f*; *(of runner)* élan *m*.

impinge [ɪmˈpɪndʒ]: **to ~ on** *vt fus* *(person)* affecter, toucher; *(rights)* empiéter sur.

implement *n* ['ɪmplɪmənt] outil *m*, instrument *m*; *(for cooking)* ustensile *m* //

vt ['ɪmplɪmɛnt] exécuter, mettre à effet.
implicit [ɪm'plɪsɪt] *a* implicite; (*complete*) absolu(e), sans réserve.
imply [ɪm'plaɪ] *vt* suggérer, laisser entendre; indiquer, supposer.
impolite [ɪmpə'laɪt] *a* impoli(e).
import *vt* [ɪm'pɔ:t] importer // *n* ['ɪmpɔ:t] (*COMM*) importation *f*; (*meaning*) portée *f*, signification *f*.
importance [ɪm'pɔ:tns] *n* importance *f*.
important [ɪm'pɔ:tnt] *a* important(e).
importer [ɪm'pɔ:tə*] *n* importateur/trice.
impose [ɪm'pəʊz] *vt* imposer // *vi*: to ~ on sb abuser de la gentillesse (*or* crédulité) de qn.
imposing [ɪm'pəʊzɪŋ] *a* imposant(e), impressionnant(e).
imposition [ɪmpə'zɪʃən] *n* (*of tax etc*) imposition *f*; to be an ~ on (*person*) abuser de la gentillesse *or* la bonté de.
impossible [ɪm'pɒsɪbl] *a* impossible.
impotent ['ɪmpətnt] *a* impuissant(e).
impound [ɪm'paʊnd] *vt* confisquer, saisir.
impoverished [ɪm'pɒvərɪʃt] *a* pauvre, appauvri(e).
impractical [ɪm'præktɪkl] *a* pas pratique; (*person*) qui manque d'esprit pratique.
impregnable [ɪm'prɛgnəbl] *a* (*fortress*) imprenable; (*fig*) inattaquable; irréfutable.
impress [ɪm'prɛs] *vt* impressionner, faire impression sur; (*mark*) imprimer, marquer; to ~ sth on sb faire bien comprendre qch à qn.
impression [ɪm'prɛʃən] *n* impression *f*; (*of stamp, seal*) empreinte *f*; to be under the ~ that avoir l'impression que.
impressive [ɪm'prɛsɪv] *a* impressionnant(e).
imprint ['ɪmprɪnt] *n* (*PUBLISHING*) notice *f*.
imprison [ɪm'prɪzn] *vt* emprisonner, mettre en prison.
improbable [ɪm'prɒbəbl] *a* improbable; (*excuse*) peu plausible.
improper [ɪm'prɒpə*] *a* incorrect(e); (*unsuitable*) déplacé(e), de mauvais goût; indécent(e).
improve [ɪm'pru:v] *vt* améliorer // *vi* s'améliorer; (*pupil etc*) faire des progrès; ~**ment** *n* amélioration *f*; progrès *m*.
improvise ['ɪmprəvaɪz] *vt*, *vi* improviser.
impudent ['ɪmpjudnt] *a* impudent(e).
impulse ['ɪmpʌls] *n* impulsion *f*; on ~ impulsivement, sur un coup de tête.
impulsive [ɪm'pʌlsɪv] *a* impulsif(ive).
in [ɪn] ♦ *prep* **1** (*indicating place, position*) dans; ~ the house/the fridge dans la maison/le frigo; ~ the garden dans le *or* au jardin; ~ town en ville; ~

the country à la campagne; ~ school à l'école; ~ here/there ici/là
2 (*with place names: of town, region, country*): ~ London à Londres; ~ England en Angleterre; ~ Japan au Japon; ~ the United States aux États-Unis
3 (*indicating time: during*): ~ spring au printemps; ~ summer en été; ~ May/1992 en mai/1992; ~ the afternoon (dans) l'après-midi; at 4 o'clock ~ the afternoon à 4 heures de l'après-midi
4 (*indicating time: in the space of*) en; (*: future*) dans; I did it ~ 3 hours/days je l'ai fait en 3 heures/jours; I'll see you ~ 2 weeks *or* ~ 2 weeks' time je te verrai dans 2 semaines
5 (*indicating manner etc*) à; ~ a loud/soft voice à voix haute/basse; ~ pencil au crayon; ~ French en français; the boy ~ the blue shirt le garçon à *or* avec la chemise bleue
6 (*indicating circumstances*): ~ the sun au soleil; ~ the shade à l'ombre; ~ the rain sous la pluie
7 (*indicating mood, state*): ~ tears en larmes; ~ anger sous le coup de la colère; ~ despair au désespoir; ~ good condition en bon état; to live ~ luxury vivre dans le luxe
8 (*with ratios, numbers*): 1 ~ 10 (households), 1 (household) ~ 10 1 (ménage) sur 10; 20 pence ~ the pound 20 pence par livre sterling; they lined up ~ twos ils se mirent en rangs (deux) par deux; ~ hundreds par centaines
9 (*referring to people, works*) chez; the disease is common ~ children c'est une maladie courante chez les enfants; ~ (the works of) Dickens chez Dickens, dans (l'œuvre de) Dickens
10 (*indicating profession etc*) dans; to be ~ teaching être dans l'enseignement
11 (*after superlative*) de; the best pupil ~ the class le meilleur élève de la classe
12 (*with present participle*): ~ saying this en disant ceci
♦ *ad*: to be ~ (*person: at home, work*) être là; (*train, ship, plane*) être arrivé(e); (*in fashion*) être à la mode; to ask sb ~ inviter qn à entrer; to run/limp *etc* ~ entrer en courant/boitant *etc*
♦ *n*: the ~s and outs (of) (*of proposal, situation etc*) les tenants et aboutissants (de).
in., ins *abbr of* **inch(es)**.
inability [ɪnə'bɪlɪtɪ] *n* incapacité *f*.
inaccurate [ɪn'ækjurət] *a* inexact(e); (*person*) qui manque de précision.
inadequate [ɪn'ædɪkwət] *a* insuffisant(e), inadéquat(e).
inadvertently [ɪnəd'vɜ:tntlɪ] *ad* par mégarde.
inane [ɪ'neɪn] *a* inepte, stupide.
inanimate [ɪn'ænɪmət] *a* inanimé(e).
inappropriate [ɪnə'prəʊprɪət] *a*

inopportun(e), mal à propos; *(word, expression)* impropre.

inarticulate [ɪnɑ:ˈtɪkjulət] *a (person)* qui s'exprime mal; *(speech)* indistinct(e).

inasmuch as [ɪnəzˈmʌtʃæz] *ad* dans la mesure où; *(seeing that)* attendu que.

inauguration [ɪnɔ:gjuˈreɪʃən] *n* inauguration *f*; *(of president, official)* investiture *f*.

in-between [ɪnbɪˈtwi:n] *a* entre les deux.

inborn [ɪnˈbɔ:n] *a (feeling)* inné(e); *(defect)* congénital(e).

inbred [ɪnˈbred] *a* inné(e), naturel(le); *(family)* consanguin(e).

Inc. *abbr of* **incorporated**.

incapable [ɪnˈkeɪpəbl] *a* incapable.

incapacitate [ɪnkəˈpæsɪteɪt] *vt*: **to ~ sb from doing** rendre qn incapable de faire.

incense *n* [ˈɪnsɛns] encens *m* ‖ *vt* [ɪnˈsɛns] *(anger)* mettre en colère.

incentive [ɪnˈsɛntɪv] *n* encouragement *m*, raison *f* de se donner de la peine.

incessant [ɪnˈsɛsnt] *a* incessant(e); **~ly** *ad* sans cesse, constamment.

inch [ɪntʃ] *n* pouce *m (= 25 mm; 12 in a foot)*; **within an ~ of** à deux doigts de; **he didn't give an ~** *(fig)* il n'a pas voulu céder d'un pouce *or* faire la plus petite concession; **to ~ forward** *vi* avancer petit à petit.

incidence [ˈɪnsɪdns] *n (of crime, disease)* fréquence *f*.

incident [ˈɪnsɪdnt] *n* incident *m*; *(in book)* péripétie *f*.

incidental [ɪnsɪˈdɛntl] *a* accessoire; *(unplanned)* accidentel(le); **~ to** qui accompagne; **~ly** [-ˈdɛntəlɪ] *ad (by the way)* à propos.

incipient [ɪnˈsɪpɪənt] *a* naissant(e).

inclination [ɪnklɪˈneɪʃən] *n* inclination *f*.

incline *n* [ˈɪnklaɪn] pente *f*, plan incliné ‖ *vb* [ɪnˈklaɪn] *vt* incliner ‖ *vi*: **to ~ to** avoir tendance à; **to be ~d to do** être enclin(e) à faire; avoir tendance à faire.

include [ɪnˈklu:d] *vt* inclure, comprendre; **including** *prep* y compris.

inclusive [ɪnˈklu:sɪv] *a* inclus(e), compris(e) ‖ *ad*: **~ of tax** *etc* taxes *etc* comprises.

income [ˈɪnkʌm] *n* revenu *m*; **~ tax** *n* impôt *m* sur le revenu.

incompetent [ɪnˈkɔmpɪtnt] *a* incompétent(e), incapable.

incomplete [ɪnkəmˈpli:t] *a* incomplet(ète).

incongruous [ɪnˈkɔŋgruəs] *a* peu approprié(e); *(remark, act)* incongru(e), déplacé(e).

inconsistency [ɪnkənˈsɪstənsɪ] *n (of actions etc)* inconséquence *f*; *(of work)* irrégularité *f*; *(of statement etc)* incohérence *f*.

inconsistent [ɪnkənˈsɪstnt] *a* incon-

séquent(e); irrégulier(ère); peu cohérent(e).

inconspicuous [ɪnkənˈspɪkjuəs] *a* qui passe inaperçu(e); *(colour, dress)* discret(ète).

inconvenience [ɪnkənˈvi:njəns] *n* inconvénient *m*; *(trouble)* dérangement *m* ‖ *vt* déranger.

inconvenient [ɪnkənˈvi:njənt] *a* malcommode; *(time, place)* mal choisi(e), qui ne convient pas.

incorporate [ɪnˈkɔ:pəreɪt] *vt* incorporer; *(contain)* contenir; **~d** *a*: **~d company** *(US: abbr* Inc.*)* ≈ société *f* anonyme (S.A.).

incorrect [ɪnkəˈrɛkt] *a* incorrect(e); *(opinion, statement)* inexact(e).

increase *n* [ˈɪnkri:s] augmentation *f* ‖ *vi, vt* [ɪnˈkri:s] augmenter.

increasing [ɪnˈkri:sɪŋ] *a (number)* croissant(e); **~ly** de plus en plus.

incredible [ɪnˈkredɪbl] *a* incroyable.

incredulous [ɪnˈkredjuləs] *a* incrédule.

increment [ˈɪnkrɪmənt] *n* augmentation *f*.

incubator [ˈɪnkjubeɪtə*] *n* incubateur *m*; *(for babies)* couveuse *f*.

incumbent [ɪnˈkʌmbənt] *n (REL)* titulaire *m/f* ‖ *a*: **it is ~ on him to ...** il lui incombe *or* appartient de ....

incur [ɪnˈkɔ:*] *vt (expenses)* encourir; *(anger, risk)* s'exposer à; *(debt)* contracter; *(loss)* subir.

indebted [ɪnˈdɛtɪd] *a*: **to be ~ to sb (for)** être redevable à qn (de).

indecent [ɪnˈdi:snt] *a* indécent(e), inconvenant(e); **~ assault** *n (Brit)* attentat *m* à la pudeur; **~ exposure** *n* outrage *m* (public) à la pudeur.

indecisive [ɪndɪˈsaɪsɪv] *a* indécis(e); *(discussion)* peu concluant(e).

indeed [ɪnˈdi:d] *ad* en effet; d'ailleurs; vraiment; **yes ~!** certainement!

indefinite [ɪnˈdɛfɪnɪt] *a* indéfini(e); *(answer)* vague; *(period, number)* indéterminé(e); **~ly** *ad (wait)* indéfiniment.

indemnity [ɪnˈdɛmnɪtɪ] *n (insurance)* assurance *f*, garantie *f*; *(compensation)* indemnité *f*.

independence [ɪndɪˈpɛndns] *n* indépendance *f*.

independent [ɪndɪˈpɛndnt] *a* indépendant(e); **to become ~** s'affranchir.

index [ˈɪndɛks] *n (pl: ~es: in book)* index *m*; *(: in library etc)* catalogue *m*; *(pl:* indices [ˈɪndɪsi:z] *) (ratio, sign)* indice *m*; **~ card** *n* fiche *f*; **~ finger** *n* index *m*; **~-linked,** *(US)* **~ed** *a* indexé(e) (sur le coût de la vie *etc*).

India [ˈɪndɪə] *n* Inde *f*; **~n** *a* indien(ne) ‖ *n* Indien/ne; **Red ~n** Indien/ne (d'Amérique).

indicate [ˈɪndɪkeɪt] *vt* indiquer; **indica-**

tion [-'keɪʃən] *n* indication *f*, signe *m*.
indicative [ɪn'dɪkətɪv] *a* indicatif(ive) // *n* (*LING*) indicatif *m*; ~ **of** symptomatique de.
indicator ['ɪndɪkeɪtə*] *n* (*sign*) indicateur *m*; (*AUT*) clignotant *m*.
indices ['ɪndɪsiːz] *npl of* **index**.
indictment [ɪn'daɪtmənt] *n* accusation *f*.
indifference [ɪn'dɪfrəns] *n* indifférence *f*.
indifferent [ɪn'dɪfrənt] *a* indifférent(e); (*poor*) médiocre, quelconque.
indigenous [ɪn'dɪdʒɪnəs] *a* indigène.
indigestion [ɪndɪ'dʒestʃən] *n* indigestion *f*, mauvaise digestion *f*.
indignant [ɪn'dɪgnənt] *a*: ~ **at** (*at or about sth/with sb*) indigné(e) (de qch/contre qn).
indignity [ɪn'dɪgnɪtɪ] *n* indignité *f*, affront *m*.
indirect [ɪndɪ'rekt] *a* indirect(e).
indiscreet [ɪndɪ'skriːt] *a* indiscret(ète); (*rash*) imprudent(e).
indiscriminate [ɪndɪ'skrɪmɪnət] *a* (*person*) qui manque de discernement; (*admiration*) aveugle; (*killings*) commis(e) au hasard.
indisputable [ɪndɪ'spjuːtəbl] *a* incontestable, indiscutable.
individual [ɪndɪ'vɪdjuəl] *n* individu *m* // *a* individuel(le); (*characteristic*) particulier(ère), original(e).
indoctrination [ɪndɔktrɪ'neɪʃən] *n* endoctrinement *m*.
Indonesia [ɪndə'niːzɪə] *n* Indonésie *f*.
indoor ['ɪndɔː*] *a* d'intérieur; (*plant*) d'appartement; (*swimming pool*) couvert(e); (*sport, games*) pratiqué(e) en salle; ~**s** [ɪn'dɔːz] *ad* à l'intérieur; (*at home*) à la maison.
induce [ɪn'djuːs] *vt* persuader; (*bring about*) provoquer; ~**ment** *n* incitation *f*; (*incentive*) but *m*; (*pej: bribe*) pot-de-vin *m*.
induction [ɪn'dʌkʃən] *n* (*MED: of birth*) accouchement provoqué; ~ **course** *n* (*Brit*) stage *m* de mise au courant.
indulge [ɪn'dʌldʒ] *vt* (*whim*) céder à, satisfaire; (*child*) gâter // *vi*: **to** ~ **in sth** s'offrir qch, se permettre qch; se livrer à qch; ~**nce** *n* fantaisie *f* (que l'on s'offre); (*leniency*) indulgence *f*; ~**nt** *a* indulgent(e).
industrial [ɪn'dʌstrɪəl] *a* industriel(le); (*injury*) du travail; (*dispute*) ouvrier(ère); ~ **action** *n* action revendicative; ~ **estate** *n* (*Brit*) zone industrielle; ~**ist** *n* industriel *m*; ~ **park** *n* (*US*) = ~ **estate**.
industrious [ɪn'dʌstrɪəs] *a* travailleur(euse).
industry ['ɪndəstrɪ] *n* industrie *f*; (*diligence*) zèle *m*, application *f*.
inebriated [ɪ'niːbrɪeɪtɪd] *a* ivre.
inedible [ɪn'edɪbl] *a* immangeable;

(*plant etc*) non comestible.
ineffective [ɪnɪ'fektɪv], **ineffectual** [ɪnɪ'fektʃuəl] *a* inefficace; (*person*) incompétent(e).
inefficiency [ɪnɪ'fɪʃənsɪ] *n* inefficacité *f*.
inefficient [ɪnɪ'fɪʃənt] *a* inefficace.
inequality [ɪnɪ'kwɔlɪtɪ] *n* inégalité *f*.
inescapable [ɪnɪ'skeɪpəbl] *a* inéluctable, inévitable.
inevitable [ɪn'evɪtəbl] *a* inévitable; **inevitably** *ad* inévitablement.
inexpensive [ɪnɪk'spensɪv] *a* bon marché *inv*.
inexperienced [ɪnɪks'pɪərɪənst] *a* inexpérimenté(e).
infallible [ɪn'fælɪbl] *a* infaillible.
infamous ['ɪnfəməs] *a* infâme, abominable.
infancy ['ɪnfənsɪ] *n* petite enfance, bas âge; (*fig*) enfance, débuts *mpl*.
infant ['ɪnfənt] *n* (*baby*) nourrisson *m*; (*young child*) petit(e) enfant; ~ **school** *n* (*Brit*) classes *fpl* préparatoires (*entre 5 et 7 ans*).
infatuated [ɪn'fætjueɪtɪd] *a*: ~ **with** entiché(e) de.
infatuation [ɪnfætju'eɪʃən] *n* toquade *f*; engouement *m*.
infect [ɪn'fekt] *vt* infecter, contaminer; ~**ion** [ɪn'fekʃən] *n* infection *f*; contagion *f*; ~**ious** [ɪn'fekʃəs] *a* infectieux(euse); (*also fig*) contagieux(euse).
infer [ɪn'fəː*] *vt* conclure, déduire.
inferior [ɪn'fɪərɪə*] *a* inférieur(e); (*goods*) de qualité inférieure // *n* inférieur/e; (*in rank*) subalterne *m/f*; ~**ity** [ɪnfɪərɪ'ɔrətɪ] *n* infériorité *f*; ~**ity complex** *n* complexe *m* d'infériorité.
inferno [ɪn'fəːnəu] *n* enfer *m*; brasier *m*.
infertile [ɪn'fəːtaɪl] *a* stérile.
in-fighting ['ɪnfaɪtɪŋ] *n* querelles *fpl* internes.
infinite ['ɪnfɪnɪt] *a* infini(e).
infinitive [ɪn'fɪnɪtɪv] *n* infinitif *m*.
infinity [ɪn'fɪnɪtɪ] *n* infinité *f*; (*also MATH*) infini *m*.
infirmary [ɪn'fəːmərɪ] *n* hôpital *m*; (*in school, factory*) infirmerie *f*.
infirmity [ɪn'fəːmɪtɪ] *n* infirmité *f*.
inflamed [ɪn'fleɪmd] *a* enflammé(e).
inflammable [ɪn'flæməbl] *a* (*Brit*) inflammable.
inflammation [ɪnflə'meɪʃən] *n* inflammation *f*.
inflatable [ɪn'fleɪtəbl] *a* gonflable.
inflate [ɪn'fleɪt] *vt* (*tyre, balloon*) gonfler; (*fig*) grossir; gonfler; faire monter; **inflation** [ɪn'fleɪʃən] *n* (*ECON*) inflation *f*; **inflationary** [ɪn'fleɪʃnərɪ] *a* inflationniste.
inflict [ɪn'flɪkt] *vt*: **to** ~ **on** infliger à.
influence ['ɪnfluəns] *n* influence *f* // *vt* influencer; **under the** ~ **of drink** en état d'ébriété.

influential [ɪnflu'ɛnʃl] a influent(e).
influenza [ɪnflu'enzə] n grippe f.
influx ['ɪnflʌks] n afflux m.
inform [ɪn'fɔ:m] vt: **to ~ sb (of)** informer or avertir qn (de) // vi: **to ~ on sb** dénoncer qn, informer contre qn; **to ~ sb about** renseigner qn sur, mettre qn au courant de.
informal [ɪn'fɔ:ml] a (person, manner) simple, sans façon; (visit, discussion) dénué(e) de formalités; (announcement, invitation) non officiel(le); **~ity** [-'mælɪtɪ] n simplicité f, absence f de cérémonie; caractère non officiel.
informant [ɪn'fɔ:mənt] n informateur/trice.
information [ɪnfə'meɪʃən] n information f; renseignements mpl; (knowledge) connaissances fpl; **a piece of ~** un renseignement; **~ office** n bureau m de renseignements.
informative [ɪn'fɔ:mətɪv] a instructif(ive).
informer [ɪn'fɔ:mə*] n dénonciateur/trice; (also: police ~) indicateur/trice.
infringe [ɪn'frɪndʒ] vt enfreindre // vi: **to ~ on** empiéter sur; **~ment** n: **~ment (of)** infraction f (à).
infuriating [ɪn'fjuərɪeɪtɪŋ] a exaspérant(e).
ingenious [ɪn'dʒi:njəs] a ingénieux(euse).
ingenuity [ɪndʒɪ'nju:ɪtɪ] n ingéniosité f.
ingenuous [ɪn'dʒenjuəs] a naïf(ïve), ingénu(e).
ingot ['ɪŋgət] n lingot m.
ingrained [ɪn'greɪnd] a enraciné(e).
ingratiate [ɪn'greɪʃɪeɪt] vt: **to ~ o.s. with** s'insinuer dans les bonnes grâces de, se faire bien voir de.
ingredient [ɪn'gri:dɪənt] n ingrédient m; élément m.
inhabit [ɪn'hæbɪt] vt habiter.
inhabitant [ɪn'hæbɪtənt] n habitant/e.
inhale [ɪn'heɪl] vt inhaler; (perfume) respirer // vi (in smoking) avaler la fumée.
inherent [ɪn'hɪərənt] a: **~ (in or to)** inhérent(e) (à).
inherit [ɪn'herɪt] vt hériter (de); **~ance** n héritage m.
inhibit [ɪn'hɪbɪt] vt (PSYCH) inhiber; **to ~ sb from doing** empêcher or retenir qn de faire; **~ion** [-'bɪʃən] n inhibition f.
inhuman [ɪn'hju:mən] a inhumain(e).
initial [ɪ'nɪʃl] a initial(e) // n initiale f // vt parafer; **~s** npl initiales fpl; (as signature) parafe m; **~ly** ad initialement, au début.
initiate [ɪ'nɪʃɪeɪt] vt (start) entreprendre; amorcer; lancer; (person) initier.
initiative [ɪ'nɪʃɪətɪv] n initiative f.
inject [ɪn'dʒekt] vt (liquid) injecter; (person) faire une piqûre à; **~ion** [ɪn'dʒekʃən] n injection f, piqûre f.

injure ['ɪndʒə*] vt blesser; (wrong) faire du tort à; (damage: reputation etc) compromettre; **~d** a blessé(e).
injury ['ɪndʒərɪ] n blessure f; (wrong) tort m; **~ time** n (SPORT) arrêts mpl de jeu.
injustice [ɪn'dʒʌstɪs] n injustice f.
ink [ɪŋk] n encre f.
inkling ['ɪŋklɪŋ] n soupçon m, vague idée f.
inlaid ['ɪnleɪd] a incrusté(e); (table etc) marqueté(e).
inland a ['ɪnlənd] intérieur(e) // ad [ɪn'lænd] à l'intérieur, dans les terres; **I~ Revenue** n (Brit) fisc m.
in-laws ['ɪnlɔ:z] npl beaux-parents mpl; belle famille.
inlet ['ɪnlet] n (GEO) crique f.
inmate ['ɪnmeɪt] n (in prison) détenu/e; (in asylum) interné/e.
inn [ɪn] n auberge f.
innate [ɪ'neɪt] a inné(e).
inner ['ɪnə*] a intérieur(e); **~ city** n centre m de zone urbaine; **~ tube** n (of tyre) chambre f à air.
innings ['ɪnɪŋz] n (CRICKET) tour m de batte.
innocence ['ɪnəsns] n innocence f.
innocent ['ɪnəsnt] a innocent(e).
innocuous [ɪ'nɔkjuəs] a inoffensif(ive).
innuendo, ~es [ɪnju'endəu] n insinuation f, allusion (malveillante).
innumerable [ɪ'nju:mrəbl] a innombrable.
inordinately [ɪ'nɔ:dɪnətlɪ] ad démesurément.
in-patient ['ɪnpeɪʃənt] n malade hospitalisé(e).
input ['ɪnput] n (ELEC) énergie f, puissance f; (of machine) consommation f; (of computer) information fournie.
inquest ['ɪnkwest] n enquête (criminelle).
inquire [ɪn'kwaɪə*] vi demander // vt demander, s'informer de; **to ~ about** s'informer de, se renseigner sur; **to ~ into** vt fus faire une enquête sur; **inquiry** n demande f de renseignements; (LAW) enquête f, investigation f; **inquiry office** n (Brit) bureau m de renseignements.
inquisitive [ɪn'kwɪzɪtɪv] a curieux(euse).
inroad ['ɪnrəud] n incursion f.
insane [ɪn'seɪn] a fou(folle); (MED) aliéné(e).
insanity [ɪn'sænɪtɪ] n folie f; (MED) aliénation (mentale).
inscription [ɪn'skrɪpʃən] n inscription f; dédicace f.
inscrutable [ɪn'skru:təbl] a impénétrable.
insect ['ɪnsekt] n insecte m; **~icide** [ɪn'sektɪsaɪd] n insecticide m.
insecure [ɪnsɪ'kjuə*] a peu solide; peu

sûr(e); (person) anxieux(euse).

insensible [in'sɛnsɪbl] a insensible; (unconscious) sans connaissance.

insensitive [in'sɛnsɪtɪv] a insensible.

insert vt [in'sə:t] insérer // n ['insə:t] insertion f; **~ion** [in'sə:ʃən] n insertion f.

in-service [in'sə:vɪs] a (training) continu(e), en cours d'emploi; (course) d'initiation; de perfectionnement; de recyclage.

inshore [in'ʃɔ:*] a côtier(ère) // ad près de la côte; vers la côte.

inside ['in'said] n intérieur m // a intérieur(e) // ad à l'intérieur, dedans // prep à l'intérieur de; (of time): ~ 10 minutes en moins de 10 minutes; ~s npl (col) intestins mpl; ~ **forward** n (SPORT) intérieur m; ~ **lane** n (AUT: in Britain) voie f de gauche; ~ **out** ad à l'envers; (know) à fond; **to turn ~ out** retourner.

insight ['insait] n perspicacité f; (glimpse, idea) aperçu m.

insignificant [insig'nifiknt] a insignifiant(e).

insincere [insin'siə*] a hypocrite.

insinuate [in'sinjueit] vt insinuer.

insist [in'sist] vi insister; **to ~ on doing** insister pour faire; **to ~ that** insister pour que; (claim) maintenir or soutenir que; **~ent** a insistant(e), pressant(e).

insole ['insəul] n semelle intérieure; (fixed part of shoe) première f.

insolent ['insələnt] a insolent(e).

insomnia [in'sɒmnɪə] n insomnie f.

inspect [in'spɛkt] vt inspecter; (ticket) contrôler; **~ion** [in'spɛkʃən] n inspection f; contrôle m; **~or** n inspecteur/trice; (Brit: on buses, trains) contrôleur/euse.

inspire [in'spaiə*] vt inspirer.

install [in'stɔ:l] vt installer; **~ation** [instə'leiʃən] n installation f.

instalment, (US) **installment** [in'stɔ:l-mənt] n acompte m, versement partiel; (of TV serial etc) épisode m; **in ~s** (pay) à tempérament; (receive) en plusieurs fois.

instance ['instəns] n exemple m; **for ~** par exemple; **in many ~s** dans bien des cas; **in the first ~** tout d'abord, en premier lieu.

instant ['instənt] n instant m // a immédiat(e); urgent(e); (coffee, food) instantané(e), en poudre; **~ly** ad immédiatement, tout de suite.

instead [in'stɛd] ad au lieu de cela; **~ of** au lieu de; **~ of sb** à la place de qn.

instep ['instɛp] n cou-de-pied m; (of shoe) cambrure f.

instil [in'stil] vt: **to ~ (into)** inculquer (à); (courage) insuffler (à).

instinct ['instiŋkt] n instinct m.

institute ['institju:t] n institut m // vt

instituer, établir; (inquiry) ouvrir; (proceedings) entamer.

institution [insti'tju:ʃən] n institution f; établissement m (scolaire); établissement (psychiatrique).

instruct [in'strʌkt] vt instruire, former; **to ~ sb in sth** enseigner qch à qn; **to ~ sb to do** charger qn or ordonner à qn de faire; **~ion** [in'strʌkʃən] n instruction f; **~ions** npl directives fpl; **~ions** (for use) mode m d'emploi; **~or** n professeur m; (for skiing, driving) moniteur m.

instrument ['instrəmənt] n instrument m; **~al** [-'mɛntl] a: **to be ~al in** contribuer à; **~ panel** n tableau m de bord.

insufficient [insə'fiʃənt] a insuffisant(e).

insular ['insjulə*] a insulaire; (outlook) étroit(e); (person) aux vues étroites.

insulate ['insjuleit] vt isoler; (against sound) insonoriser; **insulating tape** n ruban isolant; **insulation** [-'leiʃən] n isolation f; insonorisation f.

insulin ['insjulin] n insuline f.

insult n ['insʌlt] insulte f, affront m // vt [in'sʌlt] insulter, faire un affront à.

insuperable [in'sju:prəbl] a insurmontable.

insurance [in'ʃuərəns] n assurance f; **fire/life ~** assurance-incendie/-vie; **~ policy** n police f d'assurance.

insure [in'ʃuə*] vt assurer.

intact [in'tækt] a intact(e).

intake ['inteik] n (TECH) admission f; adduction f; (of food) consommation f; (Brit SCOL): **an ~ of 200 a year** 200 admissions fpl par an.

integral ['intigrəl] a intégral(e); (part) intégrant(e).

integrate ['intigreit] vt intégrer // vi s'intégrer.

integrity [in'tɛgriti] n intégrité f.

intellect ['intəlɛkt] n intelligence f; **~ual** [-'lɛktjuəl] a, n intellectuel(le).

intelligence [in'tɛlɪdʒəns] n intelligence f; (MIL etc) informations fpl, renseignements mpl.

intelligent [in'tɛlɪdʒənt] a intelligent(e).

intend [in'tɛnd] vt (gift etc): **to ~ sth for** destiner qch à; **to ~ to do** avoir l'intention de faire; **~ed** a (insult) intentionnel(le); (journey) projeté(e); (effect) voulu(e).

intense [in'tɛns] a intense; (person) véhément(e); **~ly** ad intensément; profondément.

intensive [in'tɛnsɪv] a intensif(ive); **~ care unit** n service m de réanimation.

intent [in'tɛnt] n intention f // a attentif(ive), absorbé(e); **to all ~s and purposes** en fait, pratiquement; **to be ~ on doing sth** être (bien) décidé à faire qch.

intention [ɪn'tɛnʃən] n intention f; ~al a intentionnel(le), délibéré(e).

intently [ɪn'tɛntlɪ] ad attentivement.

interact [ɪntər'ækt] vi avoir une action réciproque.

interchange n ['ɪntətʃeɪndʒ] (exchange) échange m; (on motorway) échangeur m // vt [ɪntə'tʃeɪndʒ] échanger; mettre à la place l'un(e) de l'autre; ~able a interchangeable.

intercom ['ɪntəkɔm] n interphone m.

intercourse ['ɪntəkɔ:s] n rapports mpl.

interest ['ɪntrɪst] n intérêt m; (COMM: stake, share) intérêts mpl // vt intéresser; ~ed a intéressé(e); to be ~ed in s'intéresser à; ~ing a intéressant(e); ~ rate n taux m d'intérêt.

interfere [ɪntə'fɪə*] vi: to ~ in (quarrel, other people's business) se mêler à; to ~ with (object) tripoter, toucher à; (plans) contrecarrer; (duty) être en conflit avec.

interference [ɪntə'fɪərəns] n (gen) intrusion f; (PHYSICS) interférence f; (RADIO, TV) parasites mpl.

interim ['ɪntərɪm] a provisoire; (post) intérimaire // n: in the ~ dans l'intérim.

interior [ɪn'tɪərɪə*] n intérieur m // a intérieur(e).

interlock [ɪntə'lɔk] vi s'enclencher.

interloper ['ɪntələupə*] n intrus/e.

interlude ['ɪntəlu:d] n intervalle m; (THEATRE) intermède m.

intermediate [ɪntə'mi:dɪət] a intermédiaire; (SCOL: course, level) moyen(ne).

intermission [ɪntə'mɪʃən] n pause f; (THEATRE, CINEMA) entracte m.

intern [ɪn'tə:n] vt interner // n ['ɪntə:n] (US) interne m/f.

internal [ɪn'tə:nl] a interne; (dispute, reform etc) intérieur(e); ~ly ad intérieurement; 'not to be taken ~ly' 'pour usage externe'; I~ Revenue Service (IRS) n (US) fisc m.

international [ɪntə'næʃənl] a international(e).

interplay ['ɪntəpleɪ] n effet m réciproque, jeu m.

interpret [ɪn'tə:prɪt] vt interpréter // vi servir d'interprète; ~er n interprète m/f.

interrelated [ɪntərɪ'leɪtɪd] a en corrélation, en rapport étroit.

interrogate [ɪn'tɛrəugeɪt] vt interroger; (suspect etc) soumettre à un interrogatoire; **interrogation** [-'geɪʃən] n interrogation f; interrogatoire m; **interrogative** [ɪntə'rɔgətɪv] a interrogateur(trice).

interrupt [ɪntə'rʌpt] vt interrompre; ~ion [-'rʌpʃən] n interruption f.

intersect [ɪntə'sɛkt] vi couper, croiser // vi (roads) se croiser, se couper; ~ion [-'sɛkʃən] n intersection f; (of roads) croisement m.

intersperse [ɪntə'spə:s] vt: to ~ with parsemer de.

intertwine [ɪntə'twaɪn] vt entrelacer // vi s'entrelacer.

interval ['ɪntəvl] n intervalle m; (Brit: SCOL) récréation f; (: THEATRE) entracte m; (: SPORT) mi-temps f; at ~s par intervalles.

intervene [ɪntə'vi:n] vi (time) s'écouler (entre-temps); (event) survenir; (person) intervenir; **intervention** [-'vɛnʃən] n intervention f.

interview ['ɪntəvju:] n (RADIO, TV etc) interview f; (for job) entrevue f // vt interviewer; avoir une entrevue avec; ~er n interviewer m.

intestine [ɪn'tɛstɪn] n intestin m.

intimacy ['ɪntɪməsɪ] n intimité f.

intimate ['ɪntɪmət] a intime; (knowledge) approfondi(e) // vt ['ɪntɪmeɪt] suggérer, laisser entendre; (announce) faire savoir.

into ['ɪntu:] prep dans; ~ pieces/French en morceaux/français.

intolerable [ɪn'tɔlərəbl] a intolérable.

intolerance [ɪn'tɔlərns] n intolérance f.

intolerant [ɪn'tɔlərnt] a: ~ of intolérant(e) de; (MED) intolérant à.

intoxicate [ɪn'tɔksɪkeɪt] vt enivrer; ~d a ivre; **intoxication** [-'keɪʃən] n ivresse f.

intractable [ɪn'træktəbl] a (child, temper) indocile, insoumis(e); (problem) insoluble.

intransitive [ɪn'trænsɪtɪv] a intransitif(ive).

intravenous [ɪntrə'vi:nəs] a intraveineux(euse).

in-tray ['ɪntreɪ] n courrier m 'arrivée'.

intricate ['ɪntrɪkət] a complexe, compliqué(e).

intrigue [ɪn'tri:g] n intrigue f // vt intriguer // vi intriguer, comploter; **intriguing** a fascinant(e).

intrinsic [ɪn'trɪnsɪk] a intrinsèque.

introduce [ɪntrə'dju:s] vt introduire; to ~ sb (to sb) présenter qn (à qn); to ~ sb to (pastime, technique) initier qn à; **introduction** [-'dʌkʃən] n introduction f; (of person) présentation f; **introductory** a préliminaire, d'introduction.

intrude [ɪn'tru:d] vi (person) être importun(e); to ~ on (conversation etc) s'immiscer dans; ~r n intrus/e.

intuition [ɪntju:'ɪʃən] n intuition f.

inundate ['ɪnʌndeɪt] vt: to ~ with inonder de.

invade [ɪn'veɪd] vt envahir.

invalid n ['ɪnvəlɪd] malade m/f; (with disability) invalide m/f // a [ɪn'vælɪd] (not valid) invalide, non valide.

invaluable [ɪn'væljuəbl] a inestimable, inappréciable.

invariably [ɪn'vɛərɪəblɪ] ad invariablement; toujours.

invasion [ɪn'veɪʒən] n invasion f.
invent [ɪn'vɛnt] vt inventer; **~ion**
[ɪn'vɛnʃən] n invention f; **~ive** a
inventif(ive); **~or** n inventeur/trice.
inventory ['ɪnvəntrɪ] n inventaire m.
invert [ɪn'vɜːt] vt intervertir; (cup,
object) retourner; **~ed commas** npl
(Brit) guillemets mpl.
invest [ɪn'vɛst] vt investir // vi faire un
investissement.
investigate [ɪn'vɛstɪgeɪt] vt étudier,
examiner; (crime) faire une enquête
sur; **investigation** [-'geɪʃən] n examen
m; (of crime) enquête f, investigation f.
investment [ɪn'vɛstmənt] n investissement m, placement m.
investor [ɪn'vɛstə*] n épargnant/e,
actionnaire m/f.
invidious [ɪn'vɪdɪəs] a injuste; (task)
déplaisant(e).
invigilate [ɪn'vɪdʒɪleɪt] vt surveiller // vi
(in exam) être de surveillance.
invigorating [ɪn'vɪgəreɪtɪŋ] a vivi-
fiant(e); stimulant(e).
invisible [ɪn'vɪzɪbl] a invisible; **~ ink** n
encre f sympathique.
invitation [ɪnvɪ'teɪʃən] n invitation f.
invite [ɪn'vaɪt] vt inviter; (opinions etc)
demander; (trouble) chercher; **inviting**
a engageant(e), attrayant(e); (gesture)
encourageant(e).
invoice ['ɪnvɔɪs] n facture f.
involuntary [ɪn'vɔləntrɪ] a involontaire.
involve [ɪn'vɔlv] vt (entail) entraîner,
nécessiter; (associate): **to ~ sb (in)** impliquer qn (dans), mêler qn (à); faire
participer qn (à); **~d** a complexe; **to
feel ~d** se sentir concerné(e); **~ment** n
mise f en jeu; implication f; **~ment (in)**
participation f (à); rôle m (dans).
inward ['ɪnwəd] a (movement) vers
l'intérieur; (thought, feeling) profond(e),
intime; **~(s)** ad vers l'intérieur.
I/O abbr (COMPUT: = input/output) E/S.
iodine ['aɪədiːn] n iode m.
iota [aɪ'əʊtə] n (fig) brin m, grain m.
IOU n abbr (= I owe you) reconnaissance
f de dette.
IQ n abbr (= intelligence quotient) Q.I. m
(= quotient intellectuel).
IRA n abbr (= Irish Republican Army)
IRA f.
Iran [ɪ'rɑːn] n Iran m.
Iraq [ɪ'rɑːk] n Irak m.
irate [aɪ'reɪt] a courroucé(e).
Ireland ['aɪələnd] n Irlande f.
iris, **~es** ['aɪrɪs, -ɪz] n iris m.
Irish ['aɪrɪʃ] a irlandais(e) // npl: **the ~**
les Irlandais; **~man** n Irlandais m; **~
Sea** n mer f d'Irlande; **~woman** n
Irlandaise f.
irksome ['ɜːksəm] a ennuyeux(euse).
iron ['aɪən] n fer m; (for clothes) fer m
à repasser // a de or en fer // vt
(clothes) repasser; **to ~ out** vt

(crease) faire disparaître au fer; (fig)
aplanir; faire disparaître. **the ~ curtain** n le rideau de fer.
ironic(al) [aɪ'rɔnɪk(l)] a ironique.
ironing ['aɪənɪŋ] n repassage m; **~
board** n planche f à repasser.
ironmonger ['aɪənmʌŋgə*] n (Brit)
quincailler m; **~'s (shop)** n quincaillerie f.
irony ['aɪrənɪ] n ironie f.
irrational [ɪ'ræʃənl] a irrationnel(le);
déraisonnable; qui manque de logique.
irregular [ɪ'regjulə*] a irrégulier(ère).
irrelevant [ɪ'rɛləvənt] a sans rapport,
hors de propos.
irresistible [ɪrɪ'zɪstɪbl] a irrésistible.
irrespective [ɪrɪ'spɛktɪv]: **~ of** prep
sans tenir compte de.
irresponsible [ɪrɪ'spɔnsɪbl] a (act)
irréfléchi(e); (person) qui n'a pas le
sens des responsabilités.
irrigate ['ɪrɪgeɪt] vt irriguer; **irrigation**
[-'geɪʃən] n irrigation f.
irritable ['ɪrɪtəbl] a irritable.
irritate ['ɪrɪteɪt] vt irriter; **irritating** a
irritant(e); **irritation** [-'teɪʃən] n irritation f.
IRS n abbr of **Internal Revenue
Service.**
is [ɪz] vb see **be.**
Islam ['ɪzlɑːm] n Islam m.
island ['aɪlənd] n île f; (also: traffic ~)
refuge m (pour piétons); **~er** n
habitant/e d'une île, insulaire m/f.
isle [aɪl] n île f.
isn't ['ɪznt] = **is not.**
isolate ['aɪsəleɪt] vt isoler; **~d** a
isolé(e).
Israel ['ɪzreɪl] n Israël m; **~i** [ɪz'reɪlɪ] a
israélien(ne) // n Israélien/ne.
issue ['ɪʃuː] n question f, problème m;
(outcome) résultat m, issue f; (of banknotes etc) émission f; (of newspaper etc)
numéro m; (offspring) descendance f //
vt (rations, equipment) distribuer;
(orders) donner; (book) faire paraître,
publier; (banknotes, cheques, stamps)
émettre, mettre en circulation; **at ~** en
jeu, en cause; **to take ~ with sb (over)**
exprimer son désaccord avec qn (sur).
it [ɪt] pronoun **1** (specific: subject)
il(elle); (: direct object) le(la), l'; (: indirect object) lui; **~'s on the table** c'est
or il (or elle) est sur la table; **about/
from/of ~** en; **I spoke to him about ~** je
lui en ai parlé; **what did you learn from
~?** qu'est-ce que vous en avez retiré?;
I'm proud of ~ j'en suis fier; **in/to ~** y;
put the book in ~ mettez-y le livre; **he
agreed to ~** il y a consenti; **did you go to
~?** (party, concert etc) est-ce que vous y
êtes allé(s)?
2 (impersonal) il; ce; **~'s raining** il
pleut; **~'s Friday tomorrow** demain c'est
vendredi or nous sommes vendredi; **~'s**

Italian [ɪ'tæljən] *a* italien(ne) // *n* Italien/ne; (*LING*) italien *m*.

italic [ɪ'tælɪk] *a* italique.

Italy ['ɪtəlɪ] *n* Italie *f*.

itch [ɪtʃ] *n* démangeaison *f* // *vi* (*person*) éprouver des démangeaisons; (*part of body*) démanger; **I'm ~ing to do** l'envie me démange de faire; **~y** *a* qui démange; **to be ~y** = **to** ~.

it'd ['ɪtd] = **it would, it had.**

item ['aɪtəm] *n* (*gen*) article *m*; (*on agenda*) question *f*, point *m*; (*in programme*) numéro *m*; (*also*: **news** ~) nouvelle *f*; **~ize** *vt* détailler, spécifier.

itinerary [aɪ'tɪnərərɪ] *n* itinéraire *m*.

it'll ['ɪtl] = **it will, it shall.**

its [ɪts] *a* son(sa), ses *pl*.

it's [ɪts] = **it is, it has.**

itself [ɪt'sɛlf] *pronoun* (*emphatic*) lui-même(elle-même); (*reflexive*) se.

ITV *n abbr* (*Brit*: = *Independent Television*) chaîne fonctionnant en concurrence avec la BBC.

I.U.D. *n abbr* (= *intra-uterine device*) DIU *m* (dispositif intra-utérin), stérilet *m*.

I've [aɪv] = **I have.**

ivory ['aɪvərɪ] *n* ivoire *m*.

ivy ['aɪvɪ] *n* lierre *m*.

J

jab [dʒæb] *vt*: **to ~ sth into** enfoncer *or* planter qch dans // *n* coup *m*; (*MED*: col) piqûre *f*.

jack [dʒæk] *n* (*AUT*) cric *m*; (*CARDS*) valet *m*; **to ~ up** *vt* soulever (au cric).

jackal ['dʒækl] *n* chacal *m*.

jackdaw ['dʒækdɔ:] *n* choucas *m*.

jacket ['dʒækɪt] *n* veste *f*, veston *m*.

jack-knife ['dʒæknaɪf] *vi*: **the lorry ~d** la remorque (du camion) s'est mise en travers.

jack plug *n* (*ELEC*) jack *m*.

jackpot ['dʒækpɔt] *n* gros lot.

jaded ['dʒeɪdɪd] *a* éreinté(e), fatigué(e).

jagged ['dʒægɪd] *a* dentelé(e).

jail [dʒeɪl] *n* prison *f* // *vt* emprisonner, mettre en prison; **~er** *n* geôlier/ière.

jam [dʒæm] *n* confiture *f*; (*of shoppers etc*) cohue *f*; (*also*: **traffic** ~) embouteillage *m* // *vt* (*passage etc*) encombrer, obstruer; (*mechanism, drawer etc*) bloquer, coincer; (*RADIO*) brouiller // *vi* (*mechanism, sliding part*) se coincer, se bloquer; (*gun*) s'enrayer; **to ~ sth into** entasser *or* comprimer qch dans; enfoncer qch dans.

jangle ['dʒæŋgl] *vi* cliqueter.

janitor ['dʒænɪtə*] *n* (*caretaker*) huissier *m*; concierge *m*.

January ['dʒænjuərɪ] *n* janvier *m*.

Japan [dʒə'pæn] *n* Japon *m*; **~ese** [dʒæpə'ni:z] *a* japonais(e) // *n* (*pl inv*) Japonais/e; (*LING*) japonais *m*.

jar [dʒɑ:*] *n* (*glass*) pot *m*, bocal *m* // *vi* (*sound*) produire un son grinçant *or* discordant; (*colours etc*) détonner, jurer.

jargon ['dʒɑ:gən] *n* jargon *m*.

jaundice ['dʒɔ:ndɪs] *n* jaunisse *f*; **~d** *a* (*fig*) envieux(euse), désapprobateur(trice).

jaunt [dʒɔ:nt] *n* balade *f*; **~y** *a* enjoué(e); désinvolte.

javelin ['dʒævlɪn] *n* javelot *m*.

jaw [dʒɔ:] *n* mâchoire *f*.

jay [dʒeɪ] *n* geai *m*.

jaywalker ['dʒeɪwɔ:kə*] *n* piéton indiscipliné.

jazz [dʒæz] *n* jazz *m*; **to ~ up** *vt* animer, égayer.

jealous ['dʒɛləs] *a* jaloux(euse); **~y** *n* jalousie *f*.

jeans [dʒi:nz] *npl* (blue-)jean *m*.

jeer [dʒɪə*] *vi*: **to ~ (at)** huer; se moquer cruellement (de), railler.

jelly ['dʒɛlɪ] *n* gelée *f*; **~fish** *n* méduse *f*.

jeopardy ['dʒɛpədɪ] *n*: **to be in ~** être en danger *or* péril.

jerk [dʒə:k] *n* secousse *f*; saccade *f*; sursaut *m*, spasme *m* // *vt* donner une secousse à // *vi* (*vehicles*) cahoter.

jerkin ['dʒə:kɪn] *n* blouson *m*.

jersey ['dʒə:zɪ] *n* tricot *m*.

jest [dʒɛst] *n* plaisanterie *f*.

jet [dʒɛt] *n* (*gas, liquid*) jet *m*; (*AVIAT*) avion *m* à réaction, jet *m*; **~-black** *a* (d'un noir) de jais; **~ engine** *n* moteur *m* à réaction; **~ lag** *n* décalage *m* horaire.

jettison ['dʒɛtɪsn] *vt* jeter par-dessus bord.

jetty ['dʒɛtɪ] *n* jetée *f*, digue *f*.

Jew [dʒu:] *n* Juif *m*.

jewel ['dʒu:əl] *n* bijou *m*, joyau *m*; **~ler** *n* bijoutier/ère, joaillier *m*; **~ler's (shop)** *n* bijouterie *f*, joaillerie *f*; **~lery** *n* bijoux *mpl*.

Jewess ['dʒu:ɪs] *n* Juive *f*.

Jewish ['dʒu:ɪʃ] *a* juif(juive).

jib [dʒɪb] *n* (*NAUT*) foc *m*.

jibe [dʒaɪb] *n* sarcasme *m*.

jiffy ['dʒɪfɪ] *n* (col): **in a ~** en un clin d'œil.

jig [dʒɪg] *n* gigue *m*.

jigsaw ['dʒɪgsɔ:] *n* (*also*: ~ **puzzle**) puzzle *m*.

jilt [dʒɪlt] *vt* laisser tomber, plaquer.

jingle ['dʒɪŋgl] *n* (*advert*) couplet *m* publicitaire // *vi* cliqueter, tinter.

jinx [dʒɪŋks] *n* (col) (mauvais) sort.

jitters ['dʒɪtəz] *npl* (col): **to get the ~** avoir la trouille *or* la frousse.

job [dʒɔb] *n* travail *m*; (*employment*) emploi *m*, poste *m*, place *f*; **it's a good ~ that** — c'est heureux *or* c'est une chance que —; **just the ~!** (c'est) juste *or* exactement ce qu'il faut!; ~ **centre** n (Brit) agence f pour l'emploi; ~**less** a sans travail, au chômage.

jockey ['dʒɔkɪ] n jockey m // vi: to ~ for position manœuvrer pour être bien placé.

jocular ['dʒɔkjulə*] a jovial(e), enjoué(e); facétieux(euse).

jog [dʒɔg] vt secouer // vi (SPORT) faire du footing; **to** ~ **along** vi cahoter; trotter; ~**ging** n footing m.

join [dʒɔɪn] vt unir, assembler; (become member of) s'inscrire à; (meet) rejoindre, retrouver; se joindre à // vi (roads, rivers) se rejoindre, se rencontrer // n raccord m; **to** ~ **in** vi se mettre de la partie // vt fus se mêler à; (thanks etc) s'associer à; **to** ~ **up** vi s'engager.

joiner ['dʒɔɪnə*] n menuisier m; ~**y** n menuiserie f.

joint [dʒɔɪnt] n (TECH) jointure f; joint m; (ANAT) articulation f, jointure; (Brit: CULIN) rôti m; (col: place) boîte f // a commun(e); ~ **account** n (with bank etc) compte joint; ~**ly** ad ensemble, en commun.

joist [dʒɔɪst] n solive f.

joke [dʒəuk] n plaisanterie f; (also: **practical** ~) farce f // vi plaisanter; **to play a** ~ **on** jouer un tour à, faire une farce à; ~**r** n plaisantin m, blagueur/euse; (CARDS) joker m.

jolly ['dʒɔlɪ] a gai(e), enjoué(e) // ad (col) rudement, drôlement.

jolt [dʒəult] n cahot m, secousse f // vt cahoter, secouer.

Jordan ['dʒɔːdən] n Jordanie f.

jostle ['dʒɔsl] vt bousculer, pousser.

jot [dʒɔt] n: **not one** ~ pas un brin; **to** ~ **down** vt inscrire rapidement, noter; ~**ter** n (Brit) cahier m (de brouillon); bloc-notes m.

journal ['dʒəːnl] n journal m; ~**ism** n journalisme m; ~**ist** n journaliste m/f.

journey ['dʒəːnɪ] n voyage m; (distance covered) trajet m // vi voyager.

joy [dʒɔɪ] n joie f; ~**ful**, ~**ous** a joyeux(euse); ~ **ride** n virée f (gén avec une voiture volée); ~**stick** n (AVIAT, COMPUT) manche m à balai.

J.P. n abbr see **justice**.

Jr, Jun., Junr abbr of **junior**.

jubilant ['dʒuːbɪlnt] a triomphant(e); réjoui(e).

judge [dʒʌdʒ] n juge m // vt juger; **judg(e)ment** n jugement m; (punishment) châtiment m.

judicial [dʒuː'dɪʃl] a judiciaire.

judiciary [dʒuː'dɪʃɪərɪ] n (pouvoir m) judiciaire m.

judo ['dʒuːdəu] n judo m.

jug [dʒʌg] n pot m, cruche f.

juggernaut ['dʒʌgənɔːt] n (Brit: huge truck) mastodonte m.

juggle ['dʒʌgl] vi jongler; ~**r** n jongleur m.

Jugoslav etc ['juːgəuslɑːv] = **Yugoslav** etc.

juice [dʒuːs] n jus m.

juicy ['dʒuːsɪ] a juteux(euse).

jukebox ['dʒuːkbɔks] n juke-box m.

July [dʒuː'laɪ] n juillet m.

jumble ['dʒʌmbl] n fouillis m // vt (also: ~ **up**) mélanger, brouiller; ~ **sale** n (Brit) vente f de charité.

jumbo ['dʒʌmbəu] a: ~ **jet** avion géant, gros porteur (à réaction).

jump [dʒʌmp] vi sauter, bondir; (start) sursauter; (increase) monter en flèche // vt sauter, franchir // n saut m, bond m; sursaut m.

jumper ['dʒʌmpə*] n (Brit: pullover) pull-over m; (US: dress) robe-chasuble f; ~ **cables** npl (US) = **jump leads**.

jump leads npl (Brit) câbles mpl de démarrage.

jumpy ['dʒʌmpɪ] a nerveux(euse), agité(e).

junction ['dʒʌŋkʃən] n (Brit: of roads) carrefour m; (of rails) embranchement m.

juncture ['dʒʌŋktʃə*] n: **at this** ~ à ce moment-là, sur ces entrefaites.

June [dʒuːn] n juin m.

jungle ['dʒʌŋgl] n jungle f.

junior ['dʒuːnɪə*] a, n: **he's** ~ **to me** (by 2 years), **he's my** ~ (by 2 years) il est mon cadet (de 2 ans), il est plus jeune que moi (de 2 ans); **he's** ~ **to me** (seniority) il est en dessous de moi (dans la hiérarchie), j'ai plus d'ancienneté que lui; ~ **school** n (Brit) école f primaire, cours moyen.

junk [dʒʌŋk] n (rubbish) bric-à-brac m inv; ~ **food** n snacks mpl (vite prêts); ~ **shop** n (boutique f de) brocanteur m.

juror ['dʒuərə*] n juré m.

jury ['dʒuərɪ] n jury m.

just [dʒʌst] a juste // ad: **he's** ~ **done it/ left** il vient de le faire/partir; ~ **as I expected** exactement or précisément comme je m'y attendais; ~ **right/two o'clock** exactement or juste ce qu'il faut/ deux heures; **she's** ~ **as clever as you** elle est tout aussi intelligente que vous; **it's** ~ **as well that ...** heureusement que ...; ~ **as he was leaving** au moment or à l'instant précis où il partait; ~ **before/ enough/here** juste avant/assez/là; **it's** ~ **me/a mistake** ce n'est que moi/(rien) qu'une erreur; ~ **missed/caught** manqué/ attrapé de justesse; ~ **listen to this!** écoutez un peu ça!

justice ['dʒʌstɪs] n justice f; **J~ of the Peace (J.P.)** n juge m de paix.

justify ['dʒʌstɪfaɪ] vt justifier.

jut [dʒʌt] vi (also: ~ **out**) dépasser, faire saillie.

juvenile ['dʒuːvənaɪl] a juvénile; (court, books) pour enfants // n adolescent/e.

K

K *abbr* (= *one thousand*) K; (= *kilobyte*) Ko.

kangaroo [kæŋgə'ru:] *n* kangourou *m*.

karate [kə'rɑ:tɪ] *n* karaté *m*.

kebab [kə'bæb] *n* kébab *m*.

keel [ki:l] *n* quille *f*; **on an even ~** (*fig*) à flot.

keen [ki:n] *a* (*interest, desire, competition*) vif(vive); (*eye, intelligence*) pénétrant(e); (*edge*) effilé(e); (*eager*) plein(e) d'enthousiasme; **to be ~ to do** *or* **on doing sth** désirer vivement faire qch, tenir beaucoup à faire qch; **to be ~ on sth/sb** aimer beaucoup qch/qn.

keep [ki:p] *vb* (*pt, pp* **kept**) *vt* (*retain, preserve*) garder; (*hold back*) retenir; (*a shop, the books, a diary, a promise*) tenir; (*feed: one's family etc*) entretenir, assurer la subsistance de; (*chickens, bees etc*) élever // *vi* (*food*) se conserver; (*remain: in a certain state or place*) rester // *n* (*of castle*) donjon *m*; (*food etc*): **enough for his ~** assez pour (assurer) sa subsistance; (*col*): **for ~s** pour de bon, pour toujours; **to ~ doing sth** continuer à faire qch; faire qch continuellement; **to ~ sb from doing/sth from happening** empêcher qn de faire *or* que qn (ne) fasse/que qch (n')arrive; **to ~ sb happy/a place tidy** faire que qn soit content/qu'un endroit reste propre; **to ~ sth to o.s.** garder qch pour soi, tenir qch secret; **to ~ sth (back) from sb** cacher qch à qn; **to ~ time** (*clock*) être à l'heure, ne pas retarder; **to ~ on** *vi* continuer; **to ~ on doing** continuer à faire; **to ~ out** *vt* empêcher d'entrer; **'~ out'** 'défense d'entrer'; **to ~ up** *vi* se maintenir // *vt* continuer, maintenir; **to ~ up with** se maintenir au niveau de; **~er** *n* gardien/ne; **~-fit** *n* gymnastique *f* de maintien; **~ing** *n* (*care*) garde *f*; **in ~ing with** à l'avenant de; en accord avec; **~sake** *n* souvenir *m*.

keg [kɛg] *n* barrique *f*, tonnelet *m*.

kennel ['kɛnl] *n* niche *f*; **~s** *npl* chenil *m*.

kept [kɛpt] *pt, pp* of **keep**.

kerb [kə:b] *n* (*Brit*) bordure *f* du trottoir.

kernel ['kə:nl] *n* amande *f*; (*fig*) noyau *m*.

kettle ['kɛtl] *n* bouilloire *f*.

kettle drums *npl* timbales *fpl*.

key [ki:] *n* (*gen, mus*) clé *f*; (*of piano, typewriter*) touche *f* // *vt* (*also:* **~ in**) introduire au clavier; **~board** *n* clavier *m*; **~ed up** *a* (*person*) surexcité(e); **~hole** *n* trou *m* de la serrure; **~note** *n* (*fig*) note dominante; **~ ring** *n* porte-clés *m*.

khaki ['kɑ:kɪ] *a, n* kaki (*m*).

kick [kɪk] *vt* donner un coup de pied à // *vi* (*horse*) ruer // *n* coup *m* de pied; (*of rifle*) recul *m*; (*thrill*): **he does it for ~s** il le fait parce que ça l'excite, il le fait pour le plaisir; **to ~ off** *vi* (*sport*) donner le coup d'envoi.

kid [kɪd] *n* (*col: child*) gamin/e, gosse *m/f*; (*animal, leather*) chevreau *m* // *vi* (*col*) plaisanter, blaguer.

kidnap ['kɪdnæp] *vt* enlever, kidnapper; **~per** *n* ravisseur/euse; **~ping** *n* enlèvement *m*.

kidney ['kɪdnɪ] *n* (*anat*) rein *m*; (*culin*) rognon *m*.

kill [kɪl] *vt* tuer; (*fig*) faire échouer; détruire; supprimer // *n* mise *f* à mort; **~er** *n* tueur/euse; meurtrier/ère; **~ing** *n* meurtre *m*; tuerie *f*, massacre *m*; **~joy** *n* rabat-joie *m/f*.

kiln [kɪln] *n* four *m*.

kilo ['ki:ləu] *n* kilo *m*; **~byte** *n* (*comput*) kilo-octet *m*; **~gram(me)** ['kɪləugræm] *n* kilogramme *m*; **~metre**, (*US*) **~meter** ['kɪləmi:tə*] *n* kilomètre *m*; **~watt** ['kɪləuwɔt] *n* kilowatt *m*.

kilt [kɪlt] *n* kilt *m*.

kin [kɪn] *n see* **next, kith**.

kind [kaɪnd] *a* gentil(le), aimable // *n* sorte *f*, espèce *f*; (*species*) genre *m*; **to be two of a ~** se ressembler; **in ~** (*comm*) en nature.

kindergarten ['kɪndəgɑ:tn] *n* jardin *m* d'enfants.

kind-hearted [kaɪnd'hɑ:tɪd] *a* bon(bonne).

kindle ['kɪndl] *vt* allumer, enflammer.

kindly ['kaɪndlɪ] *a* bienveillant(e), plein(e) de gentillesse // *ad* avec bonté; **will you ~ ...** auriez-vous la bonté *or* l'obligeance de ....

kindness ['kaɪndnɪs] *n* bonté *f*, gentillesse *f*.

kindred ['kɪndrɪd] *a* apparenté(e); **~ spirit** âme *f* sœur.

king [kɪŋ] *n* roi *m*; **~dom** *n* royaume *m*; **~fisher** *n* martin-pêcheur *m*; **~-size** *a* long format *inv*; format géant *inv*.

kinky ['kɪŋkɪ] *a* (*fig*) excentrique; aux goûts spéciaux.

kiosk ['ki:ɔsk] *n* kiosque *m*; (*Brit tel*) cabine *f* (téléphonique).

kipper ['kɪpə*] *n* hareng fumé et salé.

kiss [kɪs] *n* baiser *m* // *vt* embrasser; **to ~ (each other)** s'embrasser.

kit [kɪt] *n* équipement *m*, matériel *m*; (*set of tools etc*) trousse *f*; (*for assembly*) kit *m*.

kitchen ['kɪtʃɪn] *n* cuisine *f*; **~ sink** *n* évier *m*.

kite [kaɪt] *n* (*toy*) cerf-volant *m*.

kith [kɪθ] *n*: **~ and kin** parents et amis *mpl*.

kitten ['kɪtn] *n* petit chat, chaton *m*.

kitty ['kɪtɪ] *n* (*money*) cagnotte *f*.

knack [næk] *n*: **to have the ~ (of doing)**

avoir le coup (pour faire); **there's a ~** il
y a un coup à prendre *or* une combine.
knapsack ['næpsæk] *n* musette *f*.
knead [ni:d] *vt* pétrir.
knee [ni:] *n* genou *m*; **~cap** *n* rotule *f*.
kneel, *pt*, *pp* **knelt** [ni:l, nɛlt] *vi* (*also*:
~ down) s'agenouiller.
knell [nɛl] *n* glas *m*.
knew [nju:] *pt of* **know**.
knickers ['nɪkəz] *npl* (*Brit*) culotte *f* (de
femme).
knife [naɪf] *n* (*pl* **knives**) couteau *m* // *vt*
poignarder, frapper d'un coup de
couteau.
knight [naɪt] *n* chevalier *m*; (*CHESS*)
cavalier *m*; **~hood** *n* (*title*): **to get a**
~hood être fait chevalier.
knit [nɪt] *vt* tricoter; (*fig*): **to ~ together**
vt unir // *vi* (*broken bones*) se ressouder;
~ting *n* tricot *m*; **~ting needle** *n*
aiguille *f* à tricoter; **~wear** *n* tricots
mpl, lainages *mpl*.
knives [naɪvz] *npl of* **knife**.
knob [nɔb] *n* bouton *m*.
knock [nɔk] *vt* frapper; heurter; (*fig*:
col) dénigrer // *vi* (*at door etc*): **to ~ at/**
on frapper à/sur // *n* coup *m*; **to ~**
down *vt* renverser; **to ~ off** *vi* (*col*:
finish) s'arrêter (de travailler); **to ~**
out *vt* assommer; (*BOXING*) mettre
k.-o.; **to ~ over** *vt* (*person*) renverser;
(*object*) faire tomber; **~er** *n* (*on door*)
heurtoir *m*; **~-kneed** *a* aux genoux cagneux; **~out** *n* (*BOXING*) knock-out *m*,
K.-O. *m*.
knot [nɔt] *n* (*gen*) nœud *m* // *vt* nouer;
~ty *a* (*fig*) épineux(euse).
know [nəu] *vt* (*pt* **knew**, *pp* **known**)
savoir; (*person, place*) connaître; **to ~**
how to do savoir (comment) faire; **to ~**
how to swim savoir nager; **to ~ about/of**
sth être au courant de/connaître qch; **to**
~ about *or* **of sb** avoir entendu parler de
qn; **~-all** *n* je-sais-tout *m/f*; **~-how** *n*
savoir-faire *m*, technique *f*, compétence
f; **~ing** *a* (*look etc*) entendu(e); **~ingly**
ad sciemment; (*smile, look*) d'un air
entendu.
knowledge ['nɔlɪdʒ] *n* connaissance *f*;
(*learning*) connaissances, savoir *m*;
~able *a* bien informé(e).
known [nəun] *pp of* **know**.
knuckle ['nʌkl] *n* articulation *f* (des
phalanges), jointure *f*.
Koran [kɔ'rɑ:n] *n* Coran *m*.
Korea [kə'rɪə] *n* Corée *f*.
kosher ['kəuʃə*] *a* kascher *inv*.

L

lab [læb] *n abbr* (= *laboratory*) labo *m*.
label ['leɪbl] *n* étiquette *f*; (*brand: of*
record) marque *f* // *vt* étiqueter.
laboratory [lə'bɔrətərɪ] *n* laboratoire *m*.

labour, (*US*) **labor** ['leɪbə*] *n* (*task*)
travail *m*; (*also*: **~ force**) main-d'œuvre
f; (*MED*) travail, accouchement *m* // *vi*:
to ~ (at) travailler dur (à), peiner
(sur); **in ~** (*MED*) en travail; **L~, the**
L~ party (*Brit*) le parti travailliste, les
travaillistes *mpl*; **~ed** *a* lourd(e),
laborieux(euse); **~er** *n* manœuvre *m*;
(*on farm*) ouvrier *m* agricole.
lace [leɪs] *n* dentelle *f*; (*of shoe etc*) lacet
m // *vt* (*shoe*) lacer.
lack [læk] *n* manque *m* // *vt* manquer de;
through *or* **for ~ of** faute de, par
manque de; **to be ~ing** manquer, faire
défaut; **to be ~ing in** manquer de.
lackadaisical [lækə'deɪzɪkl] *a* non-
chalant(e), indolent(e).
lacquer ['lækə*] *n* laque *f*.
lad [læd] *n* garçon *m*, gars *m*.
ladder ['lædə*] *n* échelle *f*; (*Brit: in*
tights) maille filée *f* // *vt, vi* (*Brit: tights*)
filer.
laden ['leɪdn] *a*: **~ (with)** chargé(e)
(de).
ladle ['leɪdl] *n* louche *f*.
lady ['leɪdɪ] *n* dame *f*; dame (du
monde); **L~ Smith** lady Smith; **the la-**
dies' (room) les toilettes *fpl* des dames;
~bird, (*US*) **~bug** *n* coccinelle *f*; **~-**
in-waiting *n* dame *f* d'honneur; **~like** *a*
distingué(e); **~ship** *n*: **your ~ship**
Madame la comtesse (*or* la baronne
etc).
lag [læg] *vi* (*also*: **~ behind**) rester en
arrière, traîner // *vt* (*pipes*) calorifuger.
lager ['lɑ:gə*] *n* bière blonde.
lagoon [lə'gu:n] *n* lagune *f*.
laid [leɪd] *pt, pp of* **lay**; **~ back** *a* (*col*)
relaxe, décontracté(e).
lain [leɪn] *pp of* **lie**.
lair [lɛə*] *n* tanière *f*, gîte *m*.
laity ['leɪɪtɪ] *n* laïques *mpl*.
lake [leɪk] *n* lac *m*.
lamb [læm] *n* agneau *m*.
lame [leɪm] *a* boiteux(euse).
lament [lə'mɛnt] *vt* pleurer, se lamenter
sur.
laminated ['læmɪneɪtɪd] *a* laminé(e);
(*windscreen*) (en verre) feuilleté.
lamp [læmp] *n* lampe *f*.
lampoon [læm'pu:n] *n* pamphlet *m*.
lamp: ~post *n* (*Brit*) réverbère *m*;
~shade *n* abat-jour *m inv*.
lance [lɑ:ns] *n* lance *f* // *vt* (*MED*)
inciser; **~ corporal** *n* (*Brit*) (soldat *m*
de) première classe *m*.
land [lænd] *n* (*as opposed to sea*) terre *f*
(ferme); (*country*) pays *m*; (*soil*) terre;
terrain *m*; (*estate*) terre(s), domaine(s)
m(pl) // *vi* (*from ship*) débarquer;
(*AVIAT*) atterrir; (*fig: fall*) (re)tomber //
vt (*obtain*) décrocher; (*passengers,*
goods) débarquer; **to ~ up** *vi* atterrir,
(finir par) se retrouver; **~ing** *n*
débarquement *m*; atterrissage *m*; (*of*

staircase) palier m; **~ing stage** n (*Brit*) débarcadère m, embarcadère m; **~lady** n propriétaire f, logeuse f; **~lord** n propriétaire m, logeur m; (*of pub etc*) patron m; **~mark** n (point m de) repère m; to be a ~mark (*fig*) faire date or époque; **~owner** n propriétaire foncier or terrien.

landscape ['lænskeɪp] n paysage m.

landslide ['lændslaɪd] n (GEO) glissement m (de terrain); (*fig:* POL) raz-de-marée (électoral).

lane [leɪn] n (*in country*) chemin m; (*in town*) ruelle f; (AUT) voie f; file f; (*in race*) couloir m.

language ['læŋgwɪdʒ] n langue f; (*way one speaks*) langage m; **bad ~** grossièretés fpl, langage grossier; **~ laboratory** n laboratoire m de langues.

languid ['læŋgwɪd] a languissant(e), langoureux(euse).

lank [læŋk] a (*hair*) raide et terne.

lanky ['læŋkɪ] a grand(e) et maigre, efflanqué(e).

lantern ['læntn] n lanterne f.

lap [læp] n (*of track*) tour m (de piste); (*of body*): in or on one's ~ sur les genoux // vt (*also:* ~ up) laper // vi (*waves*) clapoter.

lapel [lə'pɛl] n revers m.

Lapland ['læplænd] n Laponie f.

lapse [læps] n défaillance f // vi (LAW) cesser d'être en vigueur; se périmer; to ~ into bad habits prendre de mauvaises habitudes; ~ of time laps m de temps, intervalle m.

larceny ['lɑːsənɪ] n vol m.

lard [lɑːd] n saindoux m.

larder ['lɑːdə*] n garde-manger m inv.

large [lɑːdʒ] a grand(e); (*person, animal*) gros(grosse); at ~ (*free*) en liberté; (*generally*) en général; pour la plupart; **~ly** ad en grande partie.

lark [lɑːk] n (*bird*) alouette f; (*joke*) blague f, farce f; to ~ about vi faire l'idiot, rigoler.

laryngitis [lærɪn'dʒaɪtɪs] n laryngite f.

laser ['leɪzə*] n laser m; ~ **printer** n imprimante f laser.

lash [læʃ] n coup m de fouet; (*also:* eyelash) cil m // vt fouetter; (*tie*) attacher; to ~ out vi: to ~ out (at or against sb/sth) attaquer violemment (qn/qch); to ~ out (on sth) (*col: spend*) se fendre (de qch).

lass [læs] n (jeune) fille f.

lasso [læ'suː] n lasso m.

last [lɑːst] a dernier(ère) // ad en dernier // vi durer; ~ **week** la semaine dernière; ~ **night** hier soir; la nuit dernière; at ~ enfin; ~ **but one** avant-dernier(ère); **~-ditch** a (*attempt*) ultime, désespéré(e); **~ing** a durable; **~ly** ad en dernier lieu, pour finir; **~-minute** a de dernière minute.

latch [lætʃ] n loquet m.

late [leɪt] a (*not on time*) en retard; (*far on in day etc*) dernier(ère); tardif(ive); (*recent*) récent(e), dernier; (*former*) ancien(ne); (*dead*) défunt(e) // ad tard; (*behind time, schedule*) en retard; of ~ dernièrement; in ~ May vers la fin (du mois) de mai, fin mai; the ~ Mr X feu M. X; **~comer** n retardataire m/f; **~ly** ad récemment.

later ['leɪtə*] a (*date etc*) ultérieur(e); (*version etc*) plus récent(e) // ad plus tard; ~ on plus tard.

lateral ['lætərl] a latéral(e).

latest ['leɪtɪst] a tout(e) dernier(ère); at the ~ au plus tard.

lathe [leɪð] n tour m.

lather ['lɑːðə*] n mousse f (de savon).

Latin ['lætɪn] n latin m // a latin(e); ~ **America** n Amérique latine; **~-American** a d'Amérique latine.

latitude ['lætɪtjuːd] n latitude f.

latter ['lætə*] a deuxième, dernier(ère) // n: the ~ ce dernier, celui-ci; **~ly** ad dernièrement, récemment.

lattice ['lætɪs] n treillis m; treillage m.

laudable ['lɔːdəbl] a louable.

laugh [lɑːf] n rire m // vi rire; to ~ at vt fus se moquer de; (*joke*) rire de; to ~ off vt écarter or rejeter par une plaisanterie or par une boutade; **~able** a risible, ridicule; **~ing stock** n: the ~ing stock of la risée de; **~ter** n rire m; rires mpl.

launch [lɔːntʃ] n lancement m; (*boat*) chaloupe f; (*also:* motor ~) vedette f // vt (*ship, rocket, plan*) lancer; **~(ing) pad** n rampe f de lancement.

launder ['lɔːndə*] vt blanchir.

launderette [lɔːn'drɛt], (US) **laundromat** ['lɔːndrəmæt] n laverie f (automatique).

laundry ['lɔːndrɪ] n blanchisserie f; (*clothes*) linge m.

laureate ['lɔːrɪət] a see **poet**.

laurel ['lɔrl] n laurier m.

lava ['lɑːvə] n lave f.

lavatory ['lævətərɪ] n toilettes fpl.

lavender ['lævəndə*] n lavande f.

lavish ['lævɪʃ] a copieux(euse); somptueux(euse); (*giving freely*): ~ with prodigue de // vt: to ~ sth on sb prodiguer qch à qn; (*money*) dépenser qch sans compter pour qn/qch.

law [lɔː] n loi f; (*science*) droit m; **~-abiding** a respectueux(euse) des lois; ~ **and order** n l'ordre public; ~ **court** n tribunal m, cour f de justice; **~ful** a légal(e); permis(e).

lawn [lɔːn] n pelouse f; **~mower** n tondeuse f à gazon; ~ **tennis** n tennis m.

law school n faculté f de droit.

lawsuit ['lɔːsuːt] n procès m.

lawyer ['lɔːjə*] n (*consultant, with*

company) juriste m; *(for sales, wills etc)* ≈ notaire m; *(partner, in court)* ≈ avocat m.

lax [læks] a relâché(e).

laxative ['læksətɪv] n laxatif m.

laxity ['læksɪtɪ] n relâchement m.

lay [leɪ] pt of **lie** // a laïque; profane // vt *(pt, pp laid)* poser, mettre; *(eggs)* pondre; *(trap)* tendre; *(plans)* élaborer; **to ~ the table** mettre la table; **to ~ aside** or **by** vt mettre de côté; **to ~ down** vt poser; **to ~ down the law** faire la loi; **to ~ off** vt *(workers)* licencier; **to ~ on** vt *(water, gas)* mettre, installer; *(provide)* fournir; *(paint)* étaler; **to ~ out** vt *(design)* dessiner, concevoir; *(display)* disposer; *(spend)* dépenser; **to ~ up** vt *(to store)* amasser; *(car)* remiser; *(ship)* désarmer; *(subj: illness)* forcer à s'aliter; **~about** n fainéant/e; **~-by** n *(Brit)* aire f de stationnement (sur le bas-côté).

layer ['leɪə*] n couche f.

layman ['leɪmən] n laïque m; profane m.

layout ['leɪaut] n disposition f, plan m, agencement m; *(PRESS)* mise f en page.

laze [leɪz] vi paresser.

lazy ['leɪzɪ] a paresseux(euse).

lb. abbr of **pound** *(weight)*.

lead [li:d] n *(front position)* tête f; *(distance, time ahead)* avance f; *(clue)* piste f; *(to battery)* raccord m; *(ELEC)* fil m; *(for dog)* laisse f; *(THEATRE)* rôle principal; [lɛd] *(metal)* plomb m; *(in pencil)* mine f // vb *(pt, pp led)* vt mener, conduire; *(induce)* amener; *(be leader of)* être à la tête de; *(SPORT)* être en tête de // vi mener, être en tête; **to ~ sb astray** détourner qn du droit chemin; **to ~ away** vt emmener; **to ~ back** vt: **to ~ back to** ramener à; **to ~ on** vt *(tease)* faire marcher; **to ~ on to** *(induce)* amener à; **to ~ to** vt fus mener à; conduire à; aboutir à; **to ~ up to** vt fus conduire à.

leaden ['lɛdn] a *(sky, sea)* de plomb; *(heavy: footsteps)* lourd(e).

leader ['li:də*] n chef m; dirigeant/e, leader m; *(in newspaper)* éditorial m; **~ship** n direction f; qualités fpl de chef.

leading ['li:dɪŋ] a de premier plan; principal(e); **~ man/lady** n *(THEATRE)* vedette (masculine)/(féminine); **~ light** n *(person)* vedette f, sommité f.

leaf [li:f], pl **leaves** n feuille f; *(of table)* rallonge f // vi: **to ~ through sth** feuilleter qch; **to turn over a new ~** changer de conduite or d'existence.

leaflet ['li:flɪt] n prospectus m, brochure f; *(POL, REL)* tract m.

league [li:g] n ligue f; *(FOOTBALL)* championnat m; *(measure)* lieue f; **to be in ~ with** avoir partie liée avec, être de mèche avec.

leak [li:k] n *(out, also fig)* fuite f; *(in)* infiltration f // vi *(pipe, liquid etc)* fuir; *(shoes)* prendre l'eau // vt *(liquid)* répandre; *(information)* divulguer; **to ~ out** vi fuir; être divulgué(e).

lean [li:n] a maigre // vb *(pt, pp leaned or leant* [lɛnt] *)* vt: **to ~ sth on sth** appuyer qch sur qch // vi *(slope)* pencher; *(rest)*: **to ~ against** s'appuyer contre; être appuyé(e) contre; **to ~ on** s'appuyer sur; **to ~ back/forward** vi se pencher en arrière/avant; **to ~ out** vi se pencher au dehors; **to ~ over** vi se pencher; **~-to** n appentis m.

leap [li:p] n bond m, saut m // vi *(pt, pp leaped or leapt* [lɛpt]*)* bondir, sauter; **~frog** n jeu m de saute-mouton; **~ year** n année f bissextile.

learn, pt, pp **learned** or **learnt** [lə:n, -t] vt, vi apprendre; **to ~ how to do sth** apprendre à faire qch; **~ed** ['lə:nɪd] a érudit(e), savant(e); **~er** n débutant/e; *(Brit: also: ~er driver)* (conducteur/trice) débutant(e); **~ing** n savoir m.

lease [li:s] n bail m // vt louer à bail.

leash [li:ʃ] n laisse f.

least [li:st] a: **the ~ + noun** le(la) plus petit(e), le(la) moindre; *(smallest amount of)* le moins de; **the ~ + adjective** le(la) moins; **the ~ money** le moins d'argent; **at ~** au moins; **not in the ~** pas le moins du monde.

leather ['lɛðə*] n cuir m.

leave [li:v] vb *(pt, pp left)* vt laisser; *(go away from)* quitter // vi partir, s'en aller // n *(time off)* congé m; *(MIL, also: consent)* permission f; **to be left** rester; **there's some milk left over** il reste du lait; **on ~** en permission; **to ~ behind** vt *(person, object)* laisser; **to ~ out** vt oublier, omettre; **~ of absence** n congé exceptionnel; *(MIL)* permission spéciale.

leaves [li:vz] npl of **leaf**.

Lebanon ['lɛbənən] n Liban m.

lecherous ['lɛtʃərəs] a lubrique.

lecture ['lɛktʃə*] n conférence f; *(SCOL)* cours (magistral) // vi donner des cours; enseigner // vt *(scold)* sermonner, réprimander; **to ~ on** faire un cours (or son cours) sur; **to give a ~ on** faire une conférence sur; faire or donner un cours sur.

lecturer ['lɛktʃərə*] n *(speaker)* conférencier/ère; *(Brit: at university)* professeur m (d'université), ≈ maître assistant, maître de conférences.

led [lɛd] pt, pp of **lead**.

ledge [lɛdʒ] n *(of window, on wall)* rebord m; *(of mountain)* saillie f, corniche f.

ledger ['lɛdʒə*] n registre m, grand livre.

lee [li:] n côté m sous le vent.

leech [li:tʃ] n sangsue f.

leek [li:k] n poireau m.

leer [lɪə*] vi: to ~ at sb regarder qn d'un air mauvais or concupiscent.

leeway ['li:weɪ] n (fig): to have some ~ avoir une certaine liberté d'action.

left [left] pt, pp of **leave** // a gauche // ad à gauche // n gauche f; on the ~, to the ~ à gauche; the L~ (POL) la gauche; ~-handed a gaucher(ère); ~-hand side n gauche f, côté m gauche; ~-luggage (office) n (Brit) consigne f; ~-overs npl restes mpl; ~-wing a (POL) de gauche.

leg [leg] n jambe f; (of animal) patte f; (of furniture) pied m; (CULIN: of chicken) cuisse f; lst/2nd ~ (SPORT) match m aller/retour; (of journey) 1ère/2ème étape.

legacy ['legəsɪ] n héritage m, legs m.

legal ['li:gl] a légal(e); ~ **holiday** n (US) jour férié; ~ **tender** n monnaie légale.

legend ['ledʒənd] n légende f.

legible ['ledʒəbl] a lisible.

legislation [ledʒɪs'leɪʃən] n législation f; **legislature** ['ledʒɪslətʃə*] n corps législatif.

legitimate [lɪ'dʒɪtɪmət] a légitime.

leg-room ['legru:m] n place f pour les jambes.

leisure ['leʒə*] n loisir m, temps m libre; loisirs mpl; at ~ (tout) à loisir; à tête reposée; ~ **centre** n centre m de loisirs; ~**ly** a tranquille; fait(e) sans se presser.

lemon ['lemən] n citron m; ~**ade** n [-'neɪd] limonade f; ~ **tea** n thé m au citron.

lend [lend], pt, pp lent vt: to ~ sth (to sb) prêter qch (à qn).

length [leŋθ] n longueur f; (section: of road, pipe etc) morceau m, bout m; at ~ (at last) enfin, à la fin; (lengthily) longuement; ~**en** vt allonger, prolonger // vi s'allonger; ~**ways** ad dans le sens de la longueur, en long; ~**y** a (très) long(longue).

lenient ['li:nɪənt] a indulgent(e), clément(e).

lens [lenz] n lentille f; (of spectacles) verre m; (of camera) objectif m.

Lent [lent] n Carême m.

lent [lent] pt, pp of **lend**.

lentil ['lentl] n lentille f.

Leo ['li:əu] n le Lion.

leotard ['li:ətɑ:d] n maillot m (de danseur etc).

leper ['lepə*] n lépreux/euse.

leprosy ['leprəsɪ] n lèpre f.

lesbian ['lezbɪən] n lesbienne f.

less [les] a moins de // pronoun, ad moins; ~ than that/you moins que cela/vous; ~ than half moins de la moitié; ~ than ever moins que jamais; ~ and ~ de moins en moins; the ~ he works ... moins il travaille ....

lessen ['lesn] vi diminuer, s'amoindrir, s'atténuer // vt diminuer, réduire, atténuer.

lesser ['lesə*] a moindre; to a ~ extent à un degré moindre.

lesson ['lesn] n leçon f.

lest [lest] cj de peur de + infinitive, de peur que + sub.

let, pt, pp let [let] vt laisser; (Brit: lease) louer; to ~ sb do sth laisser qn faire qch; to ~ sb know sth faire savoir qch à qn, prévenir qn de qch; he ~ me go il m'a laissé partir; ~'s go allons-y; ~ him come qu'il vienne; 'to ~' 'à louer'; to ~ down vt (lower) baisser; (dress) rallonger; (hair) défaire; (disappoint) décevoir; to ~ go vi lâcher prise // vt lâcher; to ~ in vt laisser entrer; (visitor etc) faire entrer; to ~ off vt laisser partir; (firework etc) faire partir; (smell etc) dégager; to ~ on vi (col) dire; to ~ out vt laisser sortir; (dress) élargir; (scream) laisser échapper; to ~ up vi diminuer, s'arrêter.

lethal ['li:θl] a mortel(le), fatal(e).

letter ['letə*] n lettre f; ~ **bomb** n lettre piégée; ~**box** n (Brit) boîte f aux or à lettres; ~**ing** n lettres fpl; caractères mpl.

lettuce ['letɪs] n laitue f, salade f.

leukaemia, (US) leukemia [lu:'ki:mɪə] n leucémie f.

level ['levl] a plat(e), plan(e), uni(e); horizontal(e) // n niveau m; (flat place) terrain plat; (also: spirit ~) niveau à bulle // vt niveler, aplanir; to be ~ with être au même niveau que; 'A' ~s npl (Brit) ≈ baccalauréat m; 'O' ~s npl (Brit) ≈ B.E.P.C; on the ~ à l'horizontale; (fig: honest) régulier(ère); to ~ off or out vi (prices etc) se stabiliser; ~ **crossing** n (Brit) passage m à niveau; ~-**headed** a équilibré(e).

lever ['li:və*] n levier m // vt: to ~ up/out soulever/extraire au moyen d'un levier; ~**age** n: ~**age** (on or with) prise f (sur).

levy ['levɪ] n taxe f, impôt m // vt prélever, imposer, percevoir.

lewd [lu:d] a obscène, lubrique.

liability [laɪə'bɪlətɪ] n responsabilité f; (handicap) handicap m; **liabilities** npl obligations fpl, engagements mpl; (on balance sheet) passif m.

liable ['laɪəbl] a (subject): ~ to sujet(te) à; passible de; (responsible): ~ (for) responsable (de); (likely): ~ to do susceptible de faire.

liaison [li:'eɪzɔn] n liaison f.

liar ['laɪə*] n menteur/euse.

libel ['laɪbl] n écrit m diffamatoire; diffamation f // vt diffamer.

liberal ['lɪbərl] a libéral(e); (generous): ~ with prodigue de, généreux(euse) avec.

liberty ['lɪbətɪ] *n* liberté *f*; **to be at ~ to do** être libre de faire.

Libra ['liːbrə] *n* la Balance.

librarian [laɪ'brɛərɪən] *n* bibliothécaire *m/f*.

library ['laɪbrərɪ] *n* bibliothèque *f*.

libretto [lɪ'brɛtəu] *n* livret *m*.

Libya ['lɪbɪə] *n* Libye *f*.

lice [laɪs] *npl of* **louse**.

licence, (*US*) **license** ['laɪsns] *n* autorisation *f*, permis *m*; (*COMM*) licence *f*; (*RADIO*, *TV*) redevance *f*; (*also*: **driving ~**, (*US*) **driver's ~**) permis *m* (de conduire); (*excessive freedom*) licence; **~ number** *n* numéro *m* d'immatriculation; **~ plate** *n* plaque *f* minéralogique.

license ['laɪsns] *n* (*US*) = **licence** // *vt* donner une licence à; **~d** *a* (*for alcohol*) patenté(e) pour la vente des spiritueux.

lick [lɪk] *vt* lécher.

licorice ['lɪkərɪs] *n* = **liquorice**.

lid [lɪd] *n* couvercle *m*.

lie [laɪ] *n* mensonge *m* // *vi* mentir; (*pt* **lay**, *pp* **lain**) (*rest*) être étendu(e) or allongé(e) or couché(e); (*in grave*) être enterré(e), reposer; (*of object*: *be situated*) se trouver, être; **to ~ low** (*fig*) se cacher; **to ~ about** *vi* traîner; **to have a ~-down** (*Brit*) s'allonger, se reposer; **to have a ~-in** (*Brit*) faire la grasse matinée.

lieutenant [lef'tɛnənt, (*US*) luː'tɛnənt] *n* lieutenant *m*.

life [laɪf], *pl* **lives** *n* vie *f*; **~ assurance** *n* (*Brit*) assurance-vie *f*; **~belt** *n* (*Brit*) bouée *f* de sauvetage; **~boat** *n* canot *m* or chaloupe *f* de sauvetage; **~guard** *n* surveillant *m* de baignade; **~ insurance** = **~ assurance**; **~ jacket** *n* gilet *m* or ceinture *f* de sauvetage; **~less** *a* sans vie, inanimé(e); (*dull*) qui manque de vie or de vigueur; **~like** *a* qui semble vrai(e) or vivant(e); ressemblant(e); **~long** *a* de toute une vie, de toujours; **~ preserver** *n* (*US*) gilet *m* or ceinture *f* de sauvetage; bouée *f* de sauvetage; **~-saver** *n* surveillant *m* de baignade; **~ sentence** *n* condamnation *f* à vie or à perpétuité; **~-sized** *a* grandeur nature *inv*; **~ span** *n* (durée *f* de) vie *f*; **~style** *n* style *m* or mode *m* de vie; **~ support system** *n* (*MED*) respirateur artificiel; **~time** *n*: **in his ~time** de son vivant; **once in a ~time** une fois dans la or dans une vie.

lift [lɪft] *vt* soulever, lever; (*steal*) prendre, voler // *vi* (*fog*) se lever // *n* (*Brit*: *elevator*) ascenseur *m*; **to give sb a ~** (*Brit*) emmener or prendre qn en voiture; **~-off** *n* décollage *m*.

light [laɪt] *n* lumière *f*; (*daylight*) lumière, jour *m*; (*lamp*) lampe *f*; (*AUT*: **traffic ~**, **rear ~**) feu *m*; (: *headlamp*) phare *m*; (*for cigarette etc*): **have you got a ~?** avez-vous du feu? // *vt* (*pt*, *pp* **lighted** *or* **lit**) (*candle*, *cigarette*, *fire*) allumer; (*room*) éclairer // *a* (*room*, *colour*) clair(e); (*not heavy*, *also fig*) léger(ère); **to come to ~** être dévoilé(e) or découvert(e); **to ~ up** *vi* s'allumer; (*face*) s'éclairer // *vt* (*illuminate*) éclairer, illuminer; **~ bulb** *n* ampoule *f*; **~en** *vi* s'éclairer // *vt* (*give light to*) éclairer; (*make lighter*) éclaircir; (*make less heavy*) alléger; **~er** *n* (*also*: **cigarette ~er**) briquet *m*; (: *in car*) allume-cigare *m inv*; (*boat*) péniche *f*; **~-headed** *a* étourdi(e), écervelé(e); **~-hearted** *a* gai(e), joyeux(euse), enjoué(e); **~house** *n* phare *m*; **~ing** *n* (*on road*) éclairage *m*; (*in theatre*) éclairages; **~ly** *ad* légèrement; **to get off ~ly** s'en tirer à bon compte; **~ness** *n* clarté *f*; (*in weight*) légèreté *f*.

lightning ['laɪtnɪŋ] *n* éclair *m*, foudre *f*; **~ conductor**, (*US*) **~ rod** *n* paratonnerre *m*.

light pen *n* crayon *m* optique.

lightweight ['laɪtweɪt] *a* (*suit*) léger(ère); (*boxer*) poids léger *inv* // *n* (*BOXING*) poids léger.

like [laɪk] *vt* aimer (bien) // *prep* comme // *a* semblable, pareil(le) // *n*: **the ~** un(e) pareil(le) or semblable; le(la) pareil(le); (*pej*) (d')autres du même genre or acabit; **his ~s and dislikes** ses goûts *mpl* or préférences *fpl*; **I would ~**, **I'd ~** je voudrais, j'aimerais; **would you ~ a coffee?** voulez-vous du café?; **to be/ look ~ sb/sth** ressembler à qn/qch; **that's just ~ him** c'est bien de lui, ça lui ressemble; **do it ~ this** fais-le comme ceci; **nothing ~ ...** rien de tel que ...; **~able** *a* sympathique, agréable.

likelihood ['laɪklɪhud] *n* probabilité *f*.

likely ['laɪklɪ] *a* probable; plausible; **he's ~ to leave** il va sûrement partir, il risque fort de partir; **not ~!** pas de danger!

likeness ['laɪknɪs] *n* ressemblance *f*.

likewise ['laɪkwaɪz] *ad* de même, pareillement.

liking ['laɪkɪŋ] *n* affection *f*, penchant *m*; goût *m*.

lilac ['laɪlək] *n* lilas *m* // *a* lilas *inv*.

lily ['lɪlɪ] *n* lis *m*; **~ of the valley** *n* muguet *m*.

limb [lɪm] *n* membre *m*.

limber ['lɪmbə*]: **to ~ up** *vi* se dégourdir, se mettre en train.

limbo ['lɪmbəu] *n*: **to be in ~** (*fig*) être tombé(e) dans l'oubli.

lime [laɪm] *n* (*tree*) tilleul *m*; (*fruit*) lime *f*; (*GEO*) chaux *f*.

limelight ['laɪmlaɪt] *n*: **in the ~** (*fig*) en vedette, au premier plan.

limerick ['lɪmərɪk] *n* poème *m* humoristique (de 5 vers).

limestone ['laɪmstəʊn] *n* pierre *f* à chaux; (GEO) calcaire *m*.

limit ['lɪmɪt] *n* limite *f* // *vt* limiter; ~**ed** *a* limité(e), restreint(e); **to be** ~**ed to** se limiter à, ne concerner que; ~**ed (liability) company (Ltd)** *n* (Brit) ≈ société *f* anonyme (S.A.).

limp [lɪmp] *n*: **to have a** ~ boiter // *vi* boiter // *a* mou(molle).

limpet ['lɪmpɪt] *n* patelle *f*.

line [laɪn] *n* (gen) ligne *f*; (rope) corde *f*; (wire) fil *m*; (of poem) vers *m*; (row, series) rangée *f*; file *f*, queue *f*; (COMM: series of goods) article(s) *m(pl)* // *vt* (clothes): **to** ~ **(with)** doubler (de); (box): **to** ~ **(with)** garnir *or* tapisser (de); (subj: trees, crowd) border; **in his** ~ **of business** dans sa partie, dans son rayon; **in** ~ **with** en accord avec; **to** ~ **up** *vi* s'aligner, se mettre en rang(s) // *vt* aligner.

lined [laɪnd] *a* (face) ridé(e), marqué(e); (paper) réglé(e).

linen ['lɪnɪn] *n* linge *m* (de corps *or* de maison); (cloth) lin *m*.

liner ['laɪnə*] *n* paquebot *m* de ligne.

linesman ['laɪnzmən] *n* (TENNIS) juge *m* de ligne; (FOOTBALL) juge de touche.

line-up ['laɪnʌp] *n* file *f*; (SPORT) (composition *f* de l') équipe *f*.

linger ['lɪŋgə*] *vi* s'attarder; traîner; (smell, tradition) persister.

lingo, ~**es** ['lɪŋgəʊ] *n* (pej) jargon *m*.

linguistics [lɪŋ'gwɪstɪks] *n* linguistique *f*.

lining ['laɪnɪŋ] *n* doublure *f*.

link [lɪŋk] *n* (of a chain) maillon *m*; (connection) lien *m*, rapport *m* // *vt* relier, lier, unir; ~**s** *npl* (GOLF) (terrain *m* de) golf *m*; **to** ~ **up** *vt* relier // *vi* se rejoindre; s'associer.

lino ['laɪnəʊ], **linoleum** [lɪ'nəʊlɪəm] *n* linoléum *m*.

lion ['laɪən] *n* lion *m*; ~**ess** *n* lionne *f*.

lip [lɪp] *n* lèvre *f*; (of cup etc) rebord *m*; ~**read** *vi* lire sur les lèvres; ~ **salve** *n* pommade *f* rosat *or* pour les lèvres; ~ **service** *n*: **to pay** ~ **service to sth** ne reconnaître le mérite de qch que pour la forme; ~**stick** *n* rouge *m* à lèvres.

liqueur [lɪ'kjʊə*] *n* liqueur *f*.

liquid ['lɪkwɪd] *n* liquide *m* // *a* liquide.

liquidize ['lɪkwɪdaɪz] *vt* (CULIN) passer au mixer; ~**r** *n* mixer *m*.

liquor ['lɪkə*] *n* spiritueux *m*, alcool *m*; ~ **store** *n* (US) magasin *m* de vins et spiritueux.

liquorice ['lɪkərɪs] *n* réglisse *f*.

lisp [lɪsp] *n* zézaiement *m*.

list [lɪst] *n* liste *f*; (of ship) inclinaison *f* // *vt* (write down) inscrire; faire la liste de; (enumerate) énumérer // *vi* (ship) gîter, donner de la bande.

listen ['lɪsn] *vi* écouter; **to** ~ **to** écouter; ~**er** *n* auditeur/trice.

listless ['lɪstlɪs] *a* indolent(e), apathique.

lit [lɪt] *pt, pp of* **light**.

liter ['liːtə*] *n* (US) = **litre**.

literacy ['lɪtərəsɪ] *n* degré *m* d'alphabétisation, fait *m* de savoir lire et écrire.

literal ['lɪtərl] *a* littéral(e).

literary ['lɪtərərɪ] *a* littéraire.

literate ['lɪtərət] *a* qui sait lire et écrire, instruit(e).

literature ['lɪtərɪtʃə*] *n* littérature *f*; (brochures etc) copie *f* publicitaire, prospectus *mpl*.

lithe [laɪð] *a* agile, souple.

litigation [lɪtɪ'geɪʃən] *n* litige *m*; contentieux *m*.

litre, (US) **liter** ['liːtə*] *n* litre *m*.

litter ['lɪtə*] *n* (rubbish) détritus *mpl*, ordures *fpl*; (young animals) portée *f*; ~ **bin** *n* (Brit) boîte *f* à ordures, poubelle *f*; ~**ed** *a*: ~**ed with** jonché(e) de, couvert(e) de.

little ['lɪtl] *a* (small) petit(e); (not much): **it's** ~ c'est peu; ~ **milk** peu de lait // *ad* peu; **a** ~ un peu (de); ~ **by** ~ petit à petit, peu à peu.

live *vi* [lɪv] vivre; (reside) vivre, habiter // *a* [laɪv] (animal) vivant(e), en vie; (wire) sous tension; (broadcast) (transmis(e)) en direct; **to** ~ **down** *vt* faire oublier (avec le temps); **to** ~ **on** *vt fus* (food) vivre de // *vi* survivre; **to** ~ **together** *vi* vivre ensemble, cohabiter; **to** ~ **up to** *vt fus* se montrer à la hauteur de.

livelihood ['laɪvlɪhʊd] *n* moyens *mpl* d'existence.

lively ['laɪvlɪ] *a* vif(vive), plein(e) d'entrain.

liven up ['laɪvn ʌp] *vt* animer.

liver ['lɪvə*] *n* foie *m*.

livery ['lɪvərɪ] *n* livrée *f*.

lives [laɪvz] *npl of* **life**.

livestock ['laɪvstɒk] *n* cheptel *m*, bétail *m*.

livid ['lɪvɪd] *a* livide, blafard(e); (furious) furieux(euse), furibond(e).

living ['lɪvɪŋ] *a* vivant(e), en vie // *n*: **to earn** *or* **make a** ~ gagner sa vie; ~ **conditions** *npl* conditions *fpl* de vie; ~ **room** *n* salle *f* de séjour; ~ **wage** *n* salaire *m* permettant de vivre (décemment).

lizard ['lɪzəd] *n* lézard *m*.

load [ləʊd] *n* (weight) poids *m*; (thing carried) chargement *m*, charge *f*; (ELEC, TECH) charge // *vt* (also: ~ **up**): **to** ~ **(with)** (lorry, ship) charger (de); (gun, camera) charger (avec); (COMPUT) charger; **a** ~ **of**, ~**s of** (fig) un *or* des tas de, des masses de; ~**ed** *a* (dice) pipé(e); (question) insidieux(euse); (col: rich) bourré(e) de fric; (: drunk) bourré(e); ~**ing bay** *n* aire *f* de chargement.

loaf [ləʊf], *pl* **loaves** *n* pain *m*, miche *f* //

vi (*also*: ~ **about**, ~ **around**) fainéanter, traîner.

loan [ləun] *n* prêt *m* // *vt* prêter; **on** ~ prêté(e), en prêt.

loath [ləuθ] *a*: **to be** ~ **to do** répugner à faire.

loathe [ləuð] *vt* détester, avoir en horreur.

loaves [ləuvz] *npl of* **loaf**.

lobby ['lɔbɪ] *n* hall *m*, entrée *f*; (*POL*) groupe *m* de pression, lobby *m* // *vt* faire pression sur.

lobster ['lɔbstə*] *n* homard *m*.

local ['ləukl] *a* local(e) // *n* (*pub*) pub *m* or café *m* du coin; **the** ~**s** *npl* les gens *mpl* du pays *or* du coin; ~ **call** *n* communication urbaine; ~ **government** *n* administration locale *or* municipale.

locality [ləu'kælɪtɪ] *n* région *f*, environs *mpl*; (*position*) lieu *m*.

locate [ləu'keɪt] *vt* (*find*) trouver, repérer; (*situate*) situer.

location [ləu'keɪʃən] *n* emplacement *m*; **on** ~ (*CINEMA*) en extérieur.

loch [lɔx] *n* lac *m*, loch *m*.

lock [lɔk] *n* (*of door, box*) serrure *f*; (*of canal*) écluse *f*; (*of hair*) mèche *f*, boucle *f* // *vt* (*with key*) fermer à clé; (*immobilize*) bloquer // *vi* (*door etc*) fermer à clé; (*wheels*) se bloquer.

locker ['lɔkə*] *n* casier *m*.

locket ['lɔkɪt] *n* médaillon *m*.

locksmith ['lɔksmɪθ] *n* serrurier *m*.

lock-up ['lɔkʌp] *n* box *m*.

locomotive [ləukə'məutɪv] *n* locomotive *f*.

locum ['ləukəm] *n* (*MED*) suppléant/e (de médecin).

lodge [lɔdʒ] *n* pavillon *m* (de gardien); (*FREEMASONRY*) loge *f* // *vi* (*person*): **to** ~ (**with**) être logé(e) (chez), être en pension (chez) // *vt* (*appeal etc*) présenter; déposer; **to** ~ **a complaint** porter plainte; ~**r** *n* locataire *m/f*; (*with room and meals*) pensionnaire *m/f*.

lodgings ['lɔdʒɪŋz] *npl* chambre *f*; meublé *m*.

loft [lɔft] *n* grenier *m*.

lofty ['lɔftɪ] *a* élevé(e); (*haughty*) hautain(e).

log [lɔg] *n* (*of wood*) bûche *f*; (*book*) = logbook.

logbook ['lɔgbuk] *n* (*NAUT*) livre *m* or journal *m* de bord; (*AVIAT*) carnet *m* de vol; (*of car*) ≈ carte grise.

loggerheads ['lɔgəhedz] *npl*: **at** ~ (**with**) à couteaux tirés (avec).

logic ['lɔdʒɪk] *n* logique *f*; ~**al** *a* logique.

loin [lɔɪn] *n* (*CULIN*) filet *m*, longe *f*.

loiter ['lɔɪtə*] *vi* s'attarder; **to** ~ (**about**) traîner, musarder; (*pej*) rôder.

loll [lɔl] *vi* (*also*: ~ **about**) se prélasser, fainéanter.

lollipop ['lɔlɪpɔp] *n* sucette *f*; ~ **man/**

lady *n* (*Brit*) contractuel/le qui fait traverser la rue aux enfants.

London ['lʌndən] *n* Londres *m*; ~**er** *n* Londonien/ne.

lone [ləun] *a* solitaire.

loneliness ['ləunlɪnɪs] *n* solitude *f*, isolement *m*.

lonely ['ləunlɪ] *a* seul(e); solitaire, isolé(e).

long [lɔŋ] *a* long(longue) // *ad* longtemps // *vi*: **to** ~ **for sth** avoir très envie de qch; attendre qch avec impatience; **to** ~ **to do** avoir très envie de faire; attendre avec impatience de faire; **in the** ~ **run** à la longue; finalement; **so** *or* **as** ~ **as** pourvu que; **don't be** ~ dépêchez-vous; **how** ~ **is this river/course?** quelle est la longueur de ce fleuve/la durée de ce cours?; **6 metres** ~ (long) de 6 mètres; **6 months** ~ qui dure 6 mois, de 6 mois; **all night** ~ toute la nuit; **he no** ~**er comes** il ne vient plus; ~ **before** longtemps avant; **before** ~ (+ *future*) avant peu, dans peu de temps; (+ *past*) peu de temps après; **at** ~ **last** enfin; ~**-distance** *a* (*race*) de fond; (*call*) interurbain(e); ~**hand** *n* écriture normale *or* courante; ~**ing** *n* désir *m*, envie *f*, nostalgie *f*.

longitude ['lɔŋgɪtjuːd] *n* longitude *f*.

long: ~ **jump** *n* saut *m* en longueur; ~**-playing** *a*: ~**-playing record** (L.P.) *n* (disque *m*) 33 tours *m inv*; ~**-range** *a* à longue portée; ~**-sighted** *a* presbyte; (*fig*) prévoyant(e); ~**-standing** *a* de longue date; ~**-suffering** *a* empreint(e) d'une patience résignée; extrêmement patient(e); ~**-term** *a* à long terme; ~ **wave** *n* grandes ondes; ~**-winded** *a* intarissable, interminable.

loo [luː] *n* (*Brit col*) w.-c. *mpl*, petit coin.

look [luk] *vi* regarder; (*seem*) sembler, paraître, avoir l'air; (*building etc*): **to** ~ **south/on to the sea** donner au sud/sur la mer // *n* regard *m*; (*appearance*) air *m*, allure *f*, aspect *m*; ~**s** *npl* mine *f*; physique *m*, beauté *f*; **to** ~ **after** *vt fus* s'occuper de, prendre soin de; garder, surveiller; **to** ~ **at** *vt fus* regarder; **to** ~ **back** *vi*: **to** ~ **back at se** retourner pour regarder; **to** ~ **back on** (*event etc*) évoquer, repenser à; **to** ~ **down on** *vt fus* (*fig*) regarder de haut, dédaigner; **to** ~ **for** *vt fus* chercher; **to** ~ **forward to** *vt fus* attendre avec impatience; **we** ~ **forward to hearing from you** dans l'attente de vous lire; **to** ~ **into** *vt* examiner, étudier; **to** ~ **on** *vi* regarder (en spectateur); **to** ~ **out** *vi* (*beware*): **to** ~ **out** (**for**) prendre garde (à), faire attention (à); **to** ~ **out for** *vt fus* être à la recherche de; guetter; **to** ~ **round** *vi* regarder derrière soi, se retourner; **to** ~ **to** *vt fus* veiller à; (*rely on*) compter sur; **to** ~ **up** *vi* lever les yeux; (*improve*) s'améliorer // *vt* (*word*) chercher;

(friend) passer voir; **to ~ up to** *vt fus* avoir du respect pour; **~-out** *n* poste *m* de guet; guetteur *m*; **to be on the ~-out (for)** guetter.

loom [lu:m] *n* métier *m* à tisser // *vi* surgir; *(fig)* menacer.

loony ['lu:nɪ] *n (col)* timbré/e, cinglé/e.

loop [lu:p] *n* boucle *f*; **~hole** *n* porte *f* de sortie *(fig)*; échappatoire *f*.

loose [lu:s] *a (knot, screw)* desserré(e); *(stone)* branlant(e); *(clothes)* vague, ample, lâche; *(animal)* en liberté, échappé(e); *(life)* dissolu(e); *(morals, discipline)* relâché(e); *(thinking)* peu rigoureux(euse), vague; *(translation)* approximatif(ive); **~ change** *n* petite monnaie; **~ chippings** *npl (on road)* gravillons *mpl*; **to be at a ~ end** *or (US)* **at ~ ends** ne pas trop savoir quoi faire; **~ly** *ad* sans serrer; approximativement; **~n** *vt* desserrer, relâcher, défaire.

loot [lu:t] *n* butin *m* // *vt* piller.

lop [lɔp]: **to ~ off** *vt* couper, trancher.

lop-sided ['lɔp'saɪdɪd] *a* de travers, asymétrique.

lord [lɔ:d] *n* seigneur *m*; **L~** Smith lord Smith; **the L~** le Seigneur; **the (House of) L~s** *(Brit)* la Chambre des Lords; **~ship** *n*: **your L~ship** Monsieur le comte *(or* le baron *or* le Juge).

lore [lɔ:*] *n* tradition(s) *f(pl)*.

lorry ['lɔrɪ] *n (Brit)* camion *m*; **~ driver** *n (Brit)* camionneur *m*, routier *m*.

lose [lu:z], *pt, pp* **lost** *vt* perdre; *(opportunity)* manquer, perdre; *(pursuers)* distancer, semer // *vi* perdre; **to ~ (time) (clock)** retarder; **to get lost** *vi* se perdre; **~r** *n* perdant/e.

loss [lɔs] *n* perte *f*; **to be at a ~** être perplexe *or* embarrassé(e).

lost [lɔst] *pt, pp of* **lose** // *a* perdu(e); **~ property**, *(US)* **~ and found** *n* objets trouvés.

lot [lɔt] *n (at auctions)* lot *m*; *(destiny)* sort *m*, destinée *f*; **the ~** le tout; tous *mpl*, toutes *fpl*; **a ~** beaucoup; **a ~ of** beaucoup de; **~s of** des tas de; **to draw ~s (for sth)** tirer (qch) au sort.

lotion ['ləuʃən] *n* lotion *f*.

lottery ['lɔtərɪ] *n* loterie *f*.

loud [laud] *a* bruyant(e), sonore, fort(e); *(gaudy)* voyant(e), tapageur(euse) // *ad (speak etc)* fort; **~hailer** *n (Brit)* porte-voix *m inv*; **~ly** *ad* fort, bruyamment; **~speaker** *n* haut-parleur *m*.

lounge [laundʒ] *n* salon *m* // *vi* se prélasser, paresser; **~ suit** *n (Brit)* complet *m*; 'tenue de ville'.

louse [laus], *pl* **lice** *n* pou *m*.

lousy ['lauzɪ] *a (fig)* infect(e), moche.

lout [laut] *n* rustre *m*, butor *m*.

louvre, *(US)* **louver** ['lu:və*] *a (door, window)* à claire-voie.

lovable ['lʌvəbl] *a* très sympathique; adorable.

love [lʌv] *n* amour *m* // *vt* aimer; aimer beaucoup; **to be in ~ with** être amoureux(euse) de; **to make ~** faire l'amour; **'15 ~'** *(TENNIS)* '15 à rien *or* zéro'; **~ affair** *n* liaison (amoureuse); **~ life** *n* vie sentimentale.

lovely ['lʌvlɪ] *a (très)* joli(e); ravissant(e), charmant(e); agréable.

lover ['lʌvə*] *n* amant *m*; *(amateur)*: **a ~ of** un(e) ami(e) de; un(e) amoureux(euse) de.

loving ['lʌvɪŋ] *a* affectueux(euse), tendre, aimant(e).

low [ləu] *a* bas(basse) // *ad* bas // *n (METEOROLOGY)* dépression *f* // *vi (cow)* mugir; **to feel ~** se sentir déprimé(e); **to turn (down)** *vt* baisser; **~-cut** *a (dress)* décolleté(e); **~er** *vt* abaisser, baisser; **~-fat** *a* maigre; **~lands** *npl (GEO)* plaines *fpl*; **~ly** *a* humble, modeste; **~-lying** *a* à faible altitude.

loyal ['lɔɪəl] *a* loyal(e), fidèle; **~ty** *n* loyauté *f*, fidélité *f*.

lozenge ['lɔzɪndʒ] *n (MED)* pastille *f*; *(GEOM)* losange *m*.

L.P. *n abbr of* **long-playing record**.

L-plates ['ɛlpleɪts] *npl (Brit)* plaques *fpl* d'apprenti conducteur.

Ltd *abbr see* **limited**.

lubricant ['lu:brɪkənt] *n* lubrifiant *m*.

lubricate ['lu:brɪkeɪt] *vt* lubrifier, graisser.

luck [lʌk] *n* chance *f*; **bad ~** malchance *f*, malheur *m*; **good ~!** bonne chance!; **~ily** *ad* heureusement, par bonheur; **~y** *a (person)* qui a de la chance; *(coincidence)* heureux(euse); *(number etc)* qui porte bonheur.

ludicrous ['lu:dɪkrəs] *a* ridicule, absurde.

lug [lʌg] *vt* traîner, tirer.

luggage ['lʌgɪdʒ] *n* bagages *mpl*; **~ rack** *n (in train)* porte-bagages *m inv*; *(on car)* galerie *f*.

lukewarm ['lu:kwɔ:m] *a* tiède.

lull [lʌl] *n* accalmie *f* // *vt (child)* bercer; *(person, fear)* apaiser, calmer.

lullaby ['lʌləbaɪ] *n* berceuse *f*.

lumbago [lʌm'beɪgəu] *n* lumbago *m*.

lumber ['lʌmbə*] *n* bric-à-brac *m inv*; **~jack** *n* bûcheron *m*.

luminous ['lu:mɪnəs] *a* lumineux(euse).

lump [lʌmp] *n* morceau *m*; *(in sauce)* grumeau *m*; *(swelling)* grosseur *f* // *vt (also: ~ together)* réunir, mettre en tas; **~ sum** *n* somme globale *or* forfaitaire.

lunacy ['lu:nəsɪ] *n* démence *f*, folie *f*.

lunar ['lu:nə*] *a* lunaire.

lunatic ['lu:nətɪk] *a*, *n* fou(folle), dément(e).

lunch [lʌntʃ] *n* déjeuner *m*.

luncheon ['lʌntʃən] *n* déjeuner *m*; **~ meat** *n* sorte de saucisson; **~ voucher**

n chèque-repas *m*.
lung [lʌŋ] *n* poumon *m*.
lunge [lʌndʒ] *vi* (*also:* ~ **forward**) faire un mouvement brusque en avant; **to ~ at** envoyer *or* assener un coup à.
lurch [ləːtʃ] *vi* vaciller, tituber // *n* écart *m* brusque, embardée *f*; **to leave sb in the ~** laisser qn se débrouiller *or* se dépêtrer tout(e) seul(e).
lure [luə*] *n* appât *m*, leurre *m* // *vt* attirer *or* persuader par la ruse.
lurid ['luərɪd] *a* affreux(euse), atroce.
lurk [ləːk] *vi* se tapir, se cacher.
luscious ['lʌʃəs] *a* succulent(e); appétissant(e).
lush [lʌʃ] *a* luxuriant(e).
lust [lʌst] *n* luxure *f*; lubricité *f*; désir *m*; (*fig*): ~ **for** soif *f* de; **to ~ after** *vt fus* convoiter, désirer.
lusty ['lʌstɪ] *a* vigoureux(euse), robuste.
Luxembourg ['lʌksəmbəːg] *n* Luxembourg *m*.
luxurious [lʌg'zjuərɪəs] *a* luxueux(euse).
luxury ['lʌkʃərɪ] *n* luxe *m* // *cpd* de luxe.
lying ['laɪɪŋ] *n* mensonge(s) *m(pl)*.
lyric ['lɪrɪk] *a* lyrique; ~**s** *npl* (*of song*) paroles *fpl*; ~**al** *a* lyrique.

M

m. *abbr of* **metre, mile, million.**
M.A. *abbr see* **master.**
mac [mæk] *n* (*Brit*) imper(méable) *m*.
mace [meɪs] *n* masse *f*; (*spice*) macis *m*.
machine [mə'ʃiːn] *n* machine *f* // *vt* (*dress etc*) coudre à la machine; ~ **gun** *n* mitrailleuse *f*; ~**ry** *n* machinerie *f*, machines *fpl*; (*fig*) mécanisme(s) *m(pl)*.
mackerel ['mækrl] *n* (*pl inv*) maquereau *m*.
mackintosh ['mækɪntɔʃ] *n* (*Brit*) imperméable *m*.
mad [mæd] *a* fou(folle); (*foolish*) insensé(e); (*angry*) furieux(euse).
madam ['mædəm] *n* madame *f*.
madden ['mædn] *vt* exaspérer.
made [meɪd] *pt, pp of* **make.**
Madeira [mə'dɪərə] *n* (*GEO*) Madère *f*; (*wine*) madère *m*.
made-to-measure ['meɪdtə'meʒə*] *a* (*Brit*) fait(e) sur mesure.
madly ['mædlɪ] *ad* follement.
madman ['mædmən] *n* fou *m*, aliéné *m*.
madness ['mædnɪs] *n* folie *f*.
magazine [mægə'ziːn] *n* (*PRESS*) magazine *m*, revue *f*; (*MIL: store*) dépôt *m*, arsenal *m*; (*of firearm*) magasin *m*.
maggot ['mægət] *n* ver *m*, asticot *m*.
magic ['mædʒɪk] *n* magie *f* // *a* magique; ~**al** *a* magique; ~**ian** [mə'dʒɪʃən] *n* magicien/ne.
magistrate ['mædʒɪstreɪt] *n* magistrat *m*; juge *m*.

magnet ['mægnɪt] *n* aimant *m*; ~**ic** [-'netɪk] *a* magnétique.
magnificent [mæg'nɪfɪsnt] *a* superbe, magnifique.
magnify ['mægnɪfaɪ] *vt* grossir; (*sound*) amplifier; ~**ing glass** *n* loupe *f*.
magnitude ['mægnɪtjuːd] *n* ampleur *f*.
magpie ['mægpaɪ] *n* pie *f*.
mahogany [mə'hɔgənɪ] *n* acajou *m*.
maid [meɪd] *n* bonne *f*; **old ~** (*pej*) vieille fille.
maiden ['meɪdn] *n* jeune fille *f* // *a* (*aunt etc*) non mariée; (*speech, voyage*) inaugural(e); ~ **name** *n* nom *m* de jeune fille.
mail [meɪl] *n* poste *f*; (*letters*) courrier *m* // *vt* envoyer (par la poste); ~**box** *n* (*US*) boîte *f* aux lettres; ~**ing list** *n* liste *f* d'adresses; ~**order** *n* vente *f or* achat *m* par correspondance.
maim [meɪm] *vt* mutiler.
main [meɪn] *a* principal(e) // *n* (*pipe*) conduite principale, canalisation *f*; **the ~s** (*ELEC*) le secteur; **in the ~** dans l'ensemble; ~**frame** *n* (*COMPUT*) (gros) ordinateur, unité centrale; ~**land** *n* continent *m*; ~**ly** *ad* principalement, surtout; ~ **road** *n* grand-route *f*; ~**stream** *n* courant principal; ~**stay** *n* (*fig*) pilier *m*.
maintain [meɪn'teɪn] *vt* entretenir; (*continue*) maintenir, préserver; (*affirm*) soutenir; **maintenance** ['meɪntənəns] *n* entretien *m*; (*alimony*) pension *f* alimentaire.
maize [meɪz] *n* maïs *m*.
majestic [mə'dʒestɪk] *a* majestueux(euse).
majesty ['mædʒɪstɪ] *n* majesté *f*.
major ['meɪdʒə*] *n* (*MIL*) commandant *m* // *a* important(e), principal(e); (*MUS*) majeur(e).
Majorca [mə'jɔːkə] *n* Majorque *f*.
majority [mə'dʒɔrɪtɪ] *n* majorité *f*.
make [meɪk] *vt* (*pt, pp* **made**) faire; (*manufacture*) faire, fabriquer; (*cause to be*): **to ~ sb sad** *etc* rendre qn triste *etc*; (*force*): **to ~ sb do sth** obliger qn à faire qch, faire faire qch à qn; (*equal*): **2 and 2 ~ 4** 2 et 2 font 4 // *n* fabrication *f*; (*brand*) marque *f*; **to ~ a fool of sb** (*ridicule*) ridiculiser qn; (*trick*) avoir *or* duper qn; **to ~ a profit** faire un *or* des bénéfice(s); **to ~ a loss** essuyer une perte; **to ~ it** (*arrive*) arriver; (*achieve sth*) parvenir à qch; **what time do you ~ it?** quelle heure avez-vous?; **to ~ do with** se contenter de; se débrouiller avec; **to ~ for** *vt fus* (*place*) se diriger vers; **to ~ out** *vt* (*write out*) écrire; (: *cheque*) faire; (*understand*) comprendre; (*see*) distinguer; **to ~ up** *vt* (*invent*) inventer, imaginer; (*parcel*) faire // *vi* se réconcilier; (*with cosmetics*) se maquiller, se farder; **to ~ up for** *vt fus*

compenser; racheter; **~-believe** n: a world of ~-believe un pays de chimères; it's just ~-believe c'est pour faire semblant; c'est de l'invention pure; **~r** n fabricant m; **~shift** a provisoire, improvisé(e); **~-up** n maquillage m; **~-up remover** n démaquillant m.

making ['meɪkɪŋ] n (fig): in the ~ en formation or gestation; to have the ~s of (actor, athlete etc) avoir l'étoffe de.

malaria [mə'leərɪə] n malaria f.

Malaya [mə'leɪə] n Malaisie f.

male [meɪl] n (BIOL, ELEC) mâle m // a (sex, attitude) masculin(e); mâle; (child etc) du sexe masculin.

malevolent [mə'levələnt] a malveillant(e).

malfunction [mæl'fʌŋkʃən] n fonctionnement défectueux.

malice ['mælɪs] n méchanceté f, malveillance f; **malicious** [mə'lɪʃəs] a méchant(e), malveillant(e); (LAW) avec intention criminelle.

malign [mə'laɪn] vt diffamer, calomnier.

malignant [mə'lɪgnənt] a (MED) malin(igne).

mall [mɔːl] n (also: **shopping ~**) centre commercial.

mallet ['mælɪt] n maillet m.

malpractice [mæl'præktɪs] n faute professionnelle; négligence f.

malt [mɔːlt] n malt m // cpd (whisky) pur malt.

Malta ['mɔːltə] n Malte f.

mammal ['mæml] n mammifère m.

mammoth ['mæməθ] n mammouth m // a géant(e), monstre.

man [mæn], pl **men** n homme m; (CHESS) pièce f; (DRAUGHTS) pion m // vt garnir d'hommes; servir, assurer le fonctionnement de; être de service à; **an old ~** un vieillard; **~ and wife** mari et femme.

manage ['mænɪdʒ] vi se débrouiller // vt (be in charge of) s'occuper de; gérer; to ~ to do se débrouiller pour faire; réussir à faire; **~able** a maniable; faisable; **~ment** n administration f, direction f; **~r** n directeur m; administrateur m; (of hotel etc) gérant m; (of artist) impresario m; **~ress** [-ə'rɛs] n directrice f; gérante f; **~rial** [-ə'dʒɪərɪəl] a directorial(e); **managing** a: **managing director** directeur général.

mandarin ['mændərɪn] n (also: ~ orange) mandarine f; (person) mandarin m.

mandatory ['mændətərɪ] a obligatoire; (powers etc) mandataire.

mane [meɪn] n crinière f.

maneuver etc [mə'nuːvə*] (US) = **manoeuvre** etc.

manfully ['mænfəlɪ] ad vaillamment.

mangle ['mæŋgl] vt déchiqueter; mutiler.

mango, ~es ['mæŋgəu] n mangue f.

mangy ['meɪndʒɪ] a galeux(euse).

manhandle ['mænhændl] vt malmener.

manhole ['mænhəul] n trou m d'homme.

manhood ['mænhud] n âge m d'homme; virilité f.

man-hour ['mæn'auə*] n heure f de main-d'œuvre.

mania ['meɪnɪə] n manie f; **~c** ['meɪnɪæk] n maniaque m/f.

manic ['mænɪk] a maniaque.

manicure ['mænɪkjuə*] n manucure f; **~ set** n trousse f à ongles.

manifest ['mænɪfest] vt manifester // a manifeste, évident(e).

manifesto [mænɪ'festəu] n manifeste m.

manipulate [mə'nɪpjuleɪt] vt manipuler.

mankind [mæn'kaɪnd] n humanité f, genre humain.

manly ['mænlɪ] a viril(e); courageux(euse).

man-made ['mæn'meɪd] a artificiel(le).

manner ['mænə*] n manière f, façon f; **~s** npl manières; **~ism** n particularité f de langage (or de comportement), tic m.

manoeuvre, (US) **maneuver** [mə'nuːvə*] vt, vi manœuvrer // n manœuvre f.

manor ['mænə*] n (also: ~ house) manoir m.

manpower ['mænpauə*] n main-d'œuvre f.

mansion ['mænʃən] n château m, manoir m.

manslaughter ['mænslɔːtə*] n homicide m involontaire.

mantelpiece ['mæntlpiːs] n cheminée f.

manual ['mænjuəl] a manuel(le) // n manuel m.

manufacture [mænju'fæktʃə*] vt fabriquer // n fabrication f; **~r** n fabricant m.

manure [mə'njuə*] n fumier m; (artificial) engrais m.

manuscript ['mænjuskrɪpt] n manuscrit m.

many ['menɪ] a beaucoup de, de nombreux(euses) // pronoun beaucoup, un grand nombre; **a great ~** un grand nombre (de); **~ a ...** bien des ..., plus d'un(e) ....

map [mæp] n carte f // vt dresser la carte de; **to ~ out** vt tracer.

maple ['meɪpl] n érable m.

mar [mɑː*] vt gâcher, gâter.

marathon ['mærəθən] n marathon m.

marble ['mɑːbl] n marbre m; (toy) bille f.

March [mɑːtʃ] n mars m.

march [mɑːtʃ] vi marcher au pas; défiler // n marche f; (demonstration) rallye m.

mare [meə*] n jument f.

margarine [mɑːdʒə'riːn] n margarine f.

margin ['mɑːdʒɪn] n marge f; **~al**

(seat) n (POL) siège disputé.
marigold ['mærɪgəʊld] n souci m.
marijuana [mærɪ'wa:nə] n marijuana f.
marine [mə'ri:n] a marin(e) // n fusilier marin; (US) marine m.
marital ['mærɪtl] a matrimonial(e); ~ **status** situation f de famille.
mark [ma:k] n marque f; (of skid etc) trace f; (Brit SCOL) note f; (SPORT) cible f; (currency) mark m // vt marquer; (stain) tacher; (Brit SCOL) noter; corriger; **to ~ time** marquer le pas; **to ~ out** vt désigner; **~er** n (sign) jalon m; (bookmark) signet m.
market ['ma:kɪt] n marché m // vt (COMM) commercialiser; ~ **garden** n (Brit) jardin maraîcher; **~ing** n marketing m; **~place** n place f du marché; (COMM) marché m; ~ **research** n étude f de marché; ~ **value** n valeur marchande; valeur du marché.
marksman ['ma:ksmən] n tireur m d'élite.
marmalade ['ma:məleɪd] n confiture f d'oranges.
maroon [mə'ru:n] vt (fig): **to be ~ed** (in or at) être bloqué(e) (à) // a bordeaux inv.
marquee [ma:'ki:] n chapiteau m.
marriage ['mærɪdʒ] n mariage m; ~ **bureau** n agence matrimoniale; ~ **certificate** n extrait m d'acte de mariage.
married ['mærɪd] a marié(e); (life, love) conjugal(e).
marrow ['mærəʊ] n moelle f; (vegetable) courge f.
marry ['mærɪ] vt épouser, se marier avec; (subj: father, priest etc) marier // vi (also: **get married**) se marier.
Mars [ma:z] n (planet) Mars f.
marsh [ma:ʃ] n marais m, marécage m.
marshal ['ma:ʃl] n maréchal m; (US: fire, police) ≈ capitaine m // vt rassembler.
martyr ['ma:tə*] n martyr/e // vt martyriser; **~dom** n martyre m.
marvel ['ma:vl] n merveille f // vi: **to ~ (at)** s'émerveiller (de); **~lous**, (US) **~ous** a merveilleux(euse).
Marxist ['ma:ksɪst] a, n marxiste (m/f).
marzipan ['ma:zɪpæn] n pâte f d'amandes.
mascara [mæs'ka:rə] n mascara m.
masculine ['mæskjulɪn] a masculin(e).
mashed [mæʃt] a: ~ **potatoes** purée f de pommes de terre.
mask [ma:sk] n masque m // vt masquer.
mason ['meɪsn] n (also: **stone~**) maçon m; (also: **free~**) franc-maçon m; **~ry** n maçonnerie f.
masquerade [mæskə'reɪd] n bal masqué; (fig) mascarade f // vi: **to ~ as** se faire passer pour.
mass [mæs] n multitude f, masse f; (PHYSICS) masse; (REL) messe f // vi se

masser; **the ~es** les masses.
massacre ['mæsəkə*] n massacre m.
massage ['mæsa:ʒ] n massage m // vt masser.
massive ['mæsɪv] a énorme, massif(ive).
mass media ['mæs'mi:dɪə] npl mass-media mpl.
mass-production ['mæsprə'dʌkʃən] n fabrication f en série.
mast [ma:st] n mât m.
master ['ma:stə*] n maître m; (in secondary school) professeur m; (title for boys): **M~ X** Monsieur X // vt maîtriser; (learn) apprendre à fond; (understand) posséder parfaitement or à fond; ~ **key** n passe-partout m inv; **~ly** a magistral(e); **~mind** n esprit supérieur // vt diriger, être le cerveau de; **M~ of Arts/Science (M.A./M.Sc.)** n ≈ titulaire m/f d'une maîtrise (en lettres/sciences); **~piece** n chef-d'œuvre m; **~y** n maîtrise f; connaissance parfaite.
mat [mæt] n petit tapis; (also: **door~**) paillasson m // a = **matt**.
match [mætʃ] n allumette f; (game) match m, partie f; (fig) égal/e; mariage m; parti m // vt assortir; (go well with) aller bien avec, s'assortir à; (equal) égaler, valoir // vi être assorti(e); **to be a good ~** être bien assorti(e); **~box** n boîte f d'allumettes; **~ing** a assorti(e).
mate [meɪt] n camarade m/f de travail; (col) copain/copine; (animal) partenaire m/f, mâle/femelle; (in merchant navy) second m // vi s'accoupler // vt accoupler.
material [mə'tɪərɪəl] n (substance) matière f, matériau m; (cloth) tissu m, étoffe f // a matériel(le); (important) essentiel(le); **~s** npl matériaux mpl.
maternal [mə'tə:nl] a maternel(le).
maternity [mə'tə:nɪtɪ] n maternité f; ~ **dress** n robe f de grossesse; ~ **hospital** n maternité f.
math [mæθ] n (US) = **maths**.
mathematical [mæθə'mætɪkl] a mathématique.
mathematics [mæθə'mætɪks] n mathématiques fpl.
maths, (US) **math** [mæθs, mæθ] n math(s) fpl.
matinée ['mætɪneɪ] n matinée f.
mating ['meɪtɪŋ] n accouplement m.
matriculation [mətrɪkju'leɪʃən] n inscription f.
matrimonial [mætrɪ'məʊnɪəl] a matrimonial(e), conjugal(e).
matrimony ['mætrɪmənɪ] n mariage m.
matron ['meɪtrən] n (in hospital) infirmière-chef f; (in school) infirmière; **~ly** a de matrone; imposant(e).
mat(t) [mæt] a mat(e).
matted ['mætɪd] a emmêlé(e).
matter ['mætə*] n question f; (PHYSICS)

matière f, substance f; (content) contenu m, fond m; (MED: pus) pus m // vi importer; it doesn't ~ cela n'a pas d'importance; (I don't mind) cela ne fait rien; what's the ~? qu'est-ce qu'il y a?, qu'est-ce qui ne va pas?; no ~ what quoiqu'il arrive; as a ~ of course tout naturellement; as a ~ of fact en fait; ~-of-fact a terre à terre, neutre.

mattress ['mætrɪs] n matelas m.

mature [mə'tjuə*] a mûr(e); (cheese) fait(e) // vi mûrir; se faire.

maul [mɔːl] vt lacérer.

mauve [məuv] a mauve.

maximum ['mæksɪməm] a maximum // n (pl maxima ['mæksɪmə]) maximum m.

May [meɪ] n mai m.

may [meɪ] vi (conditional: might) (indicating possibility): he ~ come il se peut qu'il vienne; (be allowed to): ~ I smoke? puis-je fumer?; (wishes): ~ God bless you! (que) Dieu vous bénisse!

maybe ['meɪbiː] ad peut-être; ~ he'll ... peut-être qu'il ....

May Day n le Premier mai.

mayhem ['meɪhɛm] n grabuge m.

mayonnaise [meɪə'neɪz] n mayonnaise f.

mayor [mɛə*] n maire m; ~ess n maire m; épouse f du maire.

maze [meɪz] n labyrinthe m, dédale m.

M.D. abbr = Doctor of Medicine.

me [miː] pronoun me, m' + vowel; (stressed, after prep) moi; he heard ~ il m'a entendu(e); give ~ a book donnez-moi un livre; after ~ après moi.

meadow ['mɛdəu] n prairie f, pré m.

meagre, (US) meager ['miːgə*] a maigre.

meal [miːl] n repas m; (flour) farine f; ~time n l'heure f du repas.

mean [miːn] a (with money) avare, radin(e); (unkind) mesquin(e), méchant(e); (average) moyen(ne) // vt (pt, pp meant) (signify) signifier, vouloir dire; (intend): to ~ to do avoir l'intention de faire // n moyenne f; ~s npl moyens mpl; by ~s of par l'intermédiaire de; au moyen de; by all ~s je vous en prie; to be meant for sb/sth être destiné(e) à qn/qch; do you ~ it? vous êtes sérieux?; what do you ~? que voulez-vous dire?

meander [mɪ'ændə*] vi faire des méandres; (fig) flâner.

meaning ['miːnɪŋ] n signification f, sens m; ~ful a significatif(ive); ~less a dénué(e) de sens.

meant [mɛnt] pt, pp of **mean**.

meantime ['miːntaɪm] ad, **meanwhile** ['miːnwaɪl] ad (also: in the ~) pendant ce temps.

measles ['miːzlz] n rougeole f.

measly ['miːzlɪ] a (col) minable.

measure ['mɛʒə*] vt, vi mesurer // n mesure f; (ruler) règle (graduée); ~ments npl mesures fpl; chest/hip ~ment tour m de poitrine/hanches.

meat [miːt] n viande f; ~ball n boulette f de viande; ~y a avec beaucoup de viande, plein(e) de viande; (fig) substantiel(le).

Mecca ['mɛkə] n la Mecque.

mechanic [mɪ'kænɪk] n mécanicien m; ~s n mécanique f // npl mécanisme m; ~al a mécanique.

mechanism ['mɛkənɪzəm] n mécanisme m.

medal ['mɛdl] n médaille f; ~lion [mɪ'dælɪən] n médaillon m.

meddle ['mɛdl] vi: to ~ in se mêler de, s'occuper de; to ~ with toucher à.

media ['miːdɪə] npl media mpl.

mediaeval [mɛdɪ'iːvl] a = **medieval**.

median ['miːdɪən] n (US: also: ~ strip) bande médiane.

mediate ['miːdɪeɪt] vi s'interposer; servir d'intermédiaire.

Medicaid ['mɛdɪkeɪd] n (US) assistance médicale aux indigents.

medical ['mɛdɪkl] a médical(e).

Medicare ['mɛdɪkɛə*] n (US) assistance médicale aux personnes âgées.

medicated ['mɛdɪkeɪtɪd] a traitant(e), médicamenteux(euse).

medicine ['mɛdsɪn] n médecine f; (drug) médicament m.

medieval [mɛdɪ'iːvl] a médiéval(e).

mediocre [miːdɪ'əukə*] a médiocre.

meditate ['mɛdɪteɪt] vi méditer.

Mediterranean [mɛdɪtə'reɪnɪən] a méditerranéen(ne); the ~ (Sea) la (mer) Méditerranée.

medium ['miːdɪəm] a moyen(ne) // n (pl media: means) moyen m; (pl mediums: person) médium m; the happy ~ le juste milieu; ~ wave n ondes moyennes.

medley ['mɛdlɪ] n mélange m.

meek [miːk] a doux(douce), humble.

meet [miːt], pt, pp met vt rencontrer; (by arrangement) retrouver, rejoindre; (for the first time) faire la connaissance de; (go and fetch): I'll ~ you at the station j'irai te chercher à la gare; (fig) faire face à; satisfaire à; se joindre à // vi se rencontrer; se retrouver; (in session) se réunir; (join: objects) se joindre; to ~ with vt fus rencontrer; ~ing n rencontre f; (session: of club etc) réunion f; (interview) entrevue f; she's at a ~ing (COMM) elle est en conférence.

megabyte ['mɛgəbaɪt] n (COMPUT) méga-octet m.

megaphone ['mɛgəfəun] n porte-voix m inv.

melancholy ['mɛlənkəlɪ] n mélancolie f // a mélancolique.

mellow ['mɛləu] a velouté(e);

doux(douce); (*colour*) riche et profond(e); (*fruit*) mûr(e) // *vi* (*person*) s'adoucir.

melody ['mɛlədɪ] *n* mélodie *f*.

melon ['mɛlən] *n* melon *m*.

melt [mɛlt] *vi* fondre; (*become soft*) s'amollir; (*fig*) s'attendrir // *vt* faire fondre; (*person*) attendrir; **to ~ away** *vi* fondre complètement; **to ~ down** *vt* fondre; **~down** *n* fusion *f* (du cœur d'un réacteur nucléaire); **~ing pot** *n* (*fig*) creuset *m*.

member ['mɛmbə*] *n* membre *m*; M~ **of Parliament (MP)** (*Brit*) député *m*; M~ **of the European Parliament (MEP)** (*Brit*) Eurodéputé *m*; **~ship** *n* adhésion *f*; statut *m* de membre; (*nombre m de*) membres *mpl*, adhérents *mpl*; **~ship card** *n* carte *f* de membre.

memento [mə'mɛntəu] *n* souvenir *m*.

memo ['mɛməu] *n* note *f* (de service).

memoirs ['mɛmwɑ:z] *npl* mémoires *mpl*.

memorandum, *pl* **memoranda** [mɛmə'rændəm, -də] *n* note *f* (de service); (*DIPLOMACY*) mémorandum *m*.

memorial [mɪ'mɔ:rɪəl] *n* mémorial *m* // *a* commémoratif(ive).

memorize ['mɛməraɪz] *vt* apprendre par cœur; retenir.

memory ['mɛmərɪ] *n* mémoire *f*; (*recollection*) souvenir *m*.

men [mɛn] *npl of* **man**.

menace ['mɛnəs] *n* menace *f* // *vt* menacer.

mend [mɛnd] *vt* réparer; (*darn*) raccommoder, repriser // *n* reprise *f*; **on the ~** en voie de guérison.

menial ['mi:nɪəl] *a* de domestique, inférieur(e); subalterne.

meningitis [mɛnɪn'dʒaɪtɪs] *n* méningite *f*.

menopause ['mɛnəupɔ:z] *n* ménopause *f*.

menstruation [mɛnstru'eɪʃən] *n* menstruation *f*.

mental ['mɛntl] *a* mental(e).

mentality [mɛn'tælɪtɪ] *n* mentalité *f*.

mention ['mɛnʃən] *n* mention *f* // *vt* mentionner, faire mention de; **don't ~ it!** je vous en prie, il n'y a pas de quoi!

menu ['mɛnju:] *n* (*set ~, COMPUT*) menu *m*; (*printed*) carte *f*.

MEP *n abbr of* **Member of the European Parliament**.

mercenary ['mə:sɪnərɪ] *a* mercantile // *n* mercenaire *m*.

merchandise ['mə:tʃəndaɪz] *n* marchandises *fpl*.

merchant ['mə:tʃənt] *n* négociant *m*, marchand *m*; **~ bank** *n* (*Brit*) banque *f* d'affaires; **~ navy,** (*US*) **~ marine** *n* marine marchande.

merciful ['mə:sɪful] *a* miséricor-

dieux(euse), clément(e).

merciless ['mə:sɪlɪs] *a* impitoyable, sans pitié.

mercury ['mə:kjurɪ] *n* mercure *m*.

mercy ['mə:sɪ] *n* pitié *f*, merci *f*; (*REL*) miséricorde *f*; **at the ~ of** à la merci de.

mere [mɪə*] *a* simple; **~ly** *ad* simplement, purement.

merge [mə:dʒ] *vt* unir // *vi* se fondre; (*COMM*) fusionner; **~r** *n* (*COMM*) fusion *f*.

meringue [mə'ræŋ] *n* meringue *f*.

merit ['mɛrɪt] *n* mérite *m*, valeur *f* // *vt* mériter.

mermaid ['mə:meɪd] *n* sirène *f*.

merry ['mɛrɪ] *a* gai(e); M~ **Christmas!** Joyeux Noël!; **~-go-round** *n* manège *m*.

mesh [mɛʃ] *n* maille *f*; filet *m*.

mesmerize ['mɛzməraɪz] *vt* hypnotiser; fasciner.

mess [mɛs] *n* désordre *m*, fouillis *m*, pagaille *f*; (*MIL*) mess *m*, cantine *f*; **to ~ about** *or* **around** *vi* (*col*) perdre son temps; **to ~ about** *or* **around with** *vt fus* (*col*) chambarder, tripoter; **to ~ up** *vt* salir; chambarder; gâcher.

message ['mɛsɪdʒ] *n* message *m*.

messenger ['mɛsɪndʒə*] *n* messager *m*.

Messrs [mɛsrz] *abbr* (*on letters*) MM.

messy ['mɛsɪ] *a* sale; en désordre.

met [mɛt] *pt, pp of* **meet**.

metal ['mɛtl] *n* métal *m*; **~lic** [-'tælɪk] *a* métallique.

mete [mi:t]: **to ~ out** *vt fus* infliger.

meteorology [mi:tɪə'rɔlədʒɪ] *n* météorologie *f*.

meter ['mi:tə*] *n* (*instrument*) compteur *m*; (*US: unit*) = **metre**.

method ['mɛθəd] *n* méthode *f*; **~ical** [mɪ'θɔdɪkl] *a* méthodique.

Methodist ['mɛθədɪst] *a, n* méthodiste (*m/f*).

methylated spirit ['mɛθɪleɪtɪd-] *n* (*Brit: also:* **meths**) alcool *m* à brûler.

metre, (*US*) **meter** ['mi:tə*] *n* mètre *m*.

metric ['mɛtrɪk] *a* métrique.

metropolitan [mɛtrə'pɔlɪtən] *a* métropolitain(e); **the M~ Police** *n* (*Brit*) la police londonienne.

mettle ['mɛtl] *n* courage *m*.

mew [mju:] *vi* (*cat*) miauler.

mews [mju:z] *n*: **~ cottage** (*Brit*) maisonnette aménagée dans une ancienne écurie ou remise.

Mexico ['mɛksɪkəu] *n* Mexique *m*.

miaow [mi:'au] *vi* miauler.

mice [maɪs] *npl of* **mouse**.

micro ['maɪkrəu] *n* (*also:* **~computer**) micro-ordinateur *m*.

microchip ['maɪkrəutʃɪp] *n* puce *f*.

microphone ['maɪkrəfəun] *n* microphone *m*.

microscope ['maɪkrəskəup] *n* microscope *m*.

microwave ['maɪkrəuweɪv] n (also: ~ oven) four m à micro-ondes.

mid [mɪd] a: ~ May la mi-mai; ~ afternoon le milieu de l'après-midi; in ~ air en plein ciel; **~day** n midi m.

middle ['mɪdl] n milieu m; (waist) ceinture f, taille f // a du milieu; in the ~ of the night au milieu de la nuit; **~aged** a d'un certain âge; **the M~ Ages** npl le moyen âge; **~class** a ≈ bourgeois(e); **the ~ class(es)** n(pl) ≈ les classes moyennes; **M~ East** n Proche-Orient m, Moyen-Orient m; **~man** n intermédiaire m; ~ **name** n deuxième nom m; **~weight** n (BOXING) poids moyen.

middling ['mɪdlɪŋ] a moyen(ne).

midge [mɪdʒ] n moucheron m.

midget ['mɪdʒɪt] n nain/e.

Midlands ['mɪdləndz] npl comtés du centre de l'Angleterre.

midnight ['mɪdnaɪt] n minuit m.

midriff ['mɪdrɪf] n estomac m, taille f.

midst [mɪdst] n: in the ~ of au milieu de.

midsummer [mɪd'sʌmə*] n milieu m de l'été.

midway [mɪd'weɪ] a, ad: ~ (between) à mi-chemin (entre).

midweek [mɪd'wiːk] n milieu m de la semaine.

midwife, pl **midwives** ['mɪdwaɪf, -vz] n sage-femme f; **~ry** [-wɪfərɪ] n obstétrique f.

might [maɪt] vb see **may** // n puissance f, force f; **~y** a puissant(e).

migraine ['miːgreɪn] n migraine f.

migrant ['maɪgrənt] a (bird) migrateur(trice); (person) migrant(e); nomade; (worker) saisonnier(ère).

migrate [maɪ'greɪt] vi émigrer.

mike [maɪk] n abbr (= microphone) micro m.

mild [maɪld] a doux(douce); (reproach) léger(ère); (illness) bénin(igne).

mildew ['mɪldjuː] n mildiou m.

mildly ['maɪldlɪ] ad doucement; légèrement; **to put it ~** c'est le moins qu'on puisse dire.

mile [maɪl] n mil(l)e m (= 1609 m); **~age** n distance f en milles, ≈ kilométrage m; **~stone** n borne f; (fig) jalon m.

militant ['mɪlɪtnt] a, n militant(e).

military ['mɪlɪtərɪ] a militaire.

milk [mɪlk] n lait m // vt (cow) traire; (fig) dépouiller, plumer; ~ **chocolate** n chocolat m au lait; **~man** n laitier m; ~ **shake** n milk-shake m; **~y** a lacté(e); (colour) laiteux(euse); **M~y Way** n Voie lactée.

mill [mɪl] n moulin m; (factory) usine f, fabrique f; (spinning ~) filature f; (flour ~) minoterie f // vt moudre, broyer // vi (also: ~ about) grouiller.

miller ['mɪlə*] n meunier m.

millet ['mɪlɪt] n millet m.

milli... ['mɪlɪ] prefix: **~gram(me)** n milligramme m; **~metre**, (US) **~meter** n millimètre m.

millinery ['mɪlɪnərɪ] n modes fpl.

million ['mɪljən] n million m; **~aire** n millionnaire m.

millstone ['mɪlstəun] n meule f.

milometer [maɪ'lɒmɪtə*] n ≈ compteur m kilométrique.

mime [maɪm] n mime m // vt, vi mimer.

mimic ['mɪmɪk] n imitateur/trice // vt imiter, contrefaire; **~ry** n imitation f.

min. abbr of **minute(s)**, **minimum**.

mince [mɪns] vt hacher // vi (in walking) marcher à petits pas maniérés // n (Brit CULIN) viande hachée, hachis m; **~meat** n hachis de fruits secs utilisés en pâtisserie; ~ **pie** n sorte de tarte aux fruits secs; **~r** n hachoir m.

mind [maɪnd] n esprit m // vt (attend to, look after) s'occuper de; (be careful) faire attention à; (object to): **I don't ~ the noise** je ne crains pas le bruit, le bruit ne me dérange pas; **I don't ~ cela** ne me dérange pas; **it is on my ~ cela** me préoccupe; **to my ~** à mon avis or sens; **to be out of one's ~** ne plus avoir toute sa raison; **to bear sth in ~** tenir compte de qch; **to make up one's ~** se décider; **to ~ you, — remarquez —**; je vous assure —; **never ~** ne vous en faites pas; '~ **the step**' 'attention à la marche'; **~er** n (child~er) gardienne f; (bodyguard) ange gardien (fig); **~ful** a: **~ful of** attentif(ive) à, soucieux(euse) de; **~less** a irréfléchi(e).

mine [maɪn] pronoun le(la) mien(ne), les miens(miennes) // a: **this book is ~** ce livre est à moi // n mine f // vt (coal) extraire; (ship, beach) miner.

miner ['maɪnə*] n mineur m.

mineral ['mɪnərəl] a minéral(e) // n minéral m; **~s** npl (Brit: soft drinks) boissons gazeuses (sucrées); ~ **water** n eau minérale.

minesweeper ['maɪnswiːpə*] n dragueur m de mines.

mingle ['mɪŋgl] vi: **to ~ with** se mêler à.

miniature ['mɪnətʃə*] a (en) miniature // n miniature f.

minibus ['mɪnɪbʌs] n minibus m.

minimum ['mɪnɪməm] a, n minimum (m).

mining ['maɪnɪŋ] n exploitation minière // a minier(ère); de mineurs.

miniskirt ['mɪnɪskəːt] n mini-jupe f.

minister ['mɪnɪstə*] n (Brit POL) ministre m; (REL) pasteur m // vi: **to ~ to sb** donner ses soins à qn; **to ~ to sb's needs** pourvoir aux besoins de qn; **~ial** [-'tɪərɪəl] a (Brit POL) ministériel(le).

ministry ['mɪnɪstrɪ] n (Brit POL) ministère m; (REL): **to go into the ~**

devenir pasteur.
mink [mɪŋk] n vison m.
minnow ['mɪnəu] n vairon m.
minor ['maɪnə*] a petit(e), de peu
d'importance; (MUS) mineur(e) // n
(LAW) mineur/e.
minority [maɪ'nɔrɪtɪ] n minorité f.
mint [mɪnt] n (plant) menthe f; (sweet)
bonbon m à la menthe // vt (coins) battre; the (Royal) M~, (US) the (US) M~
≈ l'hôtel m de la Monnaie; in ~ condition à l'état de neuf.
minus ['maɪnəs] n (also: ~ sign) signe
m moins // prep moins.
minute a [maɪ'nju:t] minuscule; (detail)
minutieux(euse) // n ['mɪnɪt] minute f;
(official record) procès-verbal m, compte
rendu; ~s npl procès-verbal.
miracle ['mɪrəkl] n miracle m.
mirage ['mɪrɑ:ʒ] n mirage m.
mire ['maɪə*] n bourbe f, boue f.
mirror ['mɪrə*] n miroir m, glace f // vt
refléter.
mirth [mə:θ] n gaieté f.
misadventure [mɪsəd'ventʃə*] n
mésaventure f; **death by ~** décès
accidentel.
misapprehension ['mɪsæprɪ'henʃən] n
malentendu m, méprise f.
misbehave [mɪsbɪ'heɪv] vi se conduire
mal.
miscarriage ['mɪskærɪdʒ] n (MED)
fausse couche; ~ **of justice** erreur f
judiciaire.
miscellaneous [mɪsɪ'leɪnɪəs] a (items)
divers(es); (selection) varié(e).
mischief ['mɪstʃɪf] n (naughtiness)
sottises fpl; (harm) mal m, dommage
m; (maliciousness) méchanceté f; **mischievous** a (naughty) coquin(e), espiègle; (harmful) méchant(e).
misconception ['mɪskən'sepʃən] n idée
fausse.
misconduct [mɪs'kɔndʌkt] n inconduite
f; **professional ~** faute professionnelle.
misconstrue [mɪskən'stru:] vt mal
interpréter.
misdeed [mɪs'di:d] n méfait m.
misdemeanour, (US) **misdemeanor**
[mɪsdɪ'mi:nə*] n écart m de conduite;
infraction f.
miser ['maɪzə*] n avare m/f.
miserable ['mɪzərəbl] a malheu-
reux(euse); (wretched) misérable.
miserly ['maɪzəlɪ] a avare.
misery ['mɪzərɪ] n (unhappiness)
tristesse f; (pain) souffrances fpl;
(wretchedness) misère f.
misfire [mɪs'faɪə*] vi rater; (car engine)
avoir des ratés.
misfit ['mɪsfɪt] n (person) inadapté/e.
misfortune [mɪs'fɔ:tʃən] n malchance f,
malheur m.
misgiving(s) [mɪs'gɪvɪŋ(z)] n(pl)
craintes fpl, soupçons mpl.

misguided [mɪs'gaɪdɪd] a malavisé(e).
mishandle [mɪs'hændl] vt (treat
roughly) malmener; (mismanage) mal
s'y prendre pour faire or résoudre etc.
mishap ['mɪshæp] n mésaventure f.
misinterpret [mɪsɪn'tə:prɪt] vt mal
interpréter.
misjudge [mɪs'dʒʌdʒ] vt méjuger, se
méprendre sur le compte de.
mislay [mɪs'leɪ] vt égarer.
mislead [mɪs'li:d] vt irg induire en
erreur; ~**ing** a trompeur(euse).
misnomer [mɪs'nəumə*] n terme or
qualificatif trompeur or peu approprié.
misplace [mɪs'pleɪs] vt égarer.
misprint ['mɪsprɪnt] n faute f d'impression.
Miss [mɪs] n Mademoiselle.
miss [mɪs] vt (fail to get) manquer,
rater; (regret the absence of): **I ~ him/it**
il/cela me manque // vi manquer // n
(shot) coup manqué; **to ~ out** vt (Brit)
oublier.
misshapen [mɪs'ʃeɪpən] a difforme.
missile ['mɪsaɪl] n (AVIAT) missile m;
(object thrown) projectile m.
missing ['mɪsɪŋ] a manquant(e); (after
escape, disaster: person) disparu(e); **to
go ~** disparaître.
mission ['mɪʃən] n mission f; ~**ary** n
missionnaire m/f.
misspent ['mɪs'spent] a: **his ~ youth** sa
folle jeunesse.
mist [mɪst] n brume f, brouillard m // vi
(also: ~ **over**, ~ **up**) devenir bru-
meux(euse); (Brit: windows) s'embuer.
mistake [mɪs'teɪk] n erreur f, faute f //
vt (irg like take) mal comprendre; se
méprendre sur; **to make a ~** se tromper,
faire une erreur; **by ~** par erreur, par
inadvertance; **to ~ for** prendre pour; ~**n**
a (idea etc) erroné(e); **to be ~n** faire
erreur, se tromper.
mister ['mɪstə*] n (col) Monsieur m; see
Mr.
mistletoe ['mɪsltəu] n gui m.
mistook [mɪs'tuk] pt of **mistake**.
mistress ['mɪstrɪs] n maîtresse f; (Brit:
in primary school) institutrice f; see
Mrs.
mistrust [mɪs'trʌst] vt se méfier de.
misty ['mɪstɪ] a brumeux(euse).
misunderstand [mɪsʌndə'stænd] vt, vi
irg mal comprendre; ~**ing** n méprise f,
malentendu m.
misuse n [mɪs'ju:s] mauvais emploi; (of
power) abus m // vt [mɪs'ju:z] mal employer; abuser de.
mitigate ['mɪtɪgeɪt] vt atténuer.
mitt(en) ['mɪt(n)] n mitaine f; moufle f.
mix [mɪks] vt mélanger // vi se mélanger
// n mélange m; dosage m; **to ~ up** vt
mélanger; (confuse) confondre; ~**ed** a
(assorted) assortis(ies); (school etc)
mixte; ~**ed grill** n assortiment m de

grillades; **~ed-up** a (confused) désorienté(e), embrouillé(e); **~er** n (for food) batteur m, mixeur m; (person): **he is a good ~er** il est très liant; **~ture** n assortiment m, mélange m; (MED) préparation f; **~-up** n confusion f.

moan [məun] n gémissement m // vi gémir; (col: complain): **to ~ (about)** se plaindre (de).

moat [məut] n fossé m, douves fpl.

mob [mɔb] n foule f; (disorderly) cohue f; (pej): **the ~** la populace // vt assaillir.

mobile ['məubail] a mobile // n mobile m; **~ home** n caravane f.

mock [mɔk] vt ridiculiser, se moquer de // a faux(fausse); **~ery** n moquerie f, raillerie f.

mod [mɔd] a see **convenience**.

mode [məud] n mode m.

model ['mɔdl] n modèle m; (person: for fashion) mannequin m; (: for artist) modèle // vt modeler // vi travailler comme mannequin // a (railway: toy) modèle réduit inv; (child, factory) modèle; **to ~ clothes** présenter des vêtements.

modem ['məudɛm] n modem m.

moderate a n, ['mɔdərət] a modéré(e) // n (POL) modéré/e // vb ['mɔdəreit] vi se modérer, se calmer // vt modérer.

modern ['mɔdən] a moderne; **~ize** vt moderniser.

modest ['mɔdist] a modeste; **~y** n modestie f.

modicum ['mɔdikəm] n: **a ~ of** un minimum de.

modify ['mɔdifai] vt modifier.

mogul ['məugl] n (fig) nabab m.

mohair ['məuhɛə*] n mohair m.

moist [mɔist] a humide, moite; **~en** ['mɔisn] vt humecter, mouiller légèrement; **~ure** ['mɔistʃə*] n humidité f; (on glass) buée f; **~urizer** ['mɔistʃəraizə*] n produit hydratant.

molar ['məulə*] n molaire f.

molasses [məu'læsiz] n mélasse f.

mold [məuld] n, vt (US) = **mould**.

mole [məul] n (animal) taupe f; (spot) grain m de beauté.

molest [məu'lest] vt tracasser; molester.

mollycoddle ['mɔlikɔdl] vt chouchouter, couver.

molt [məult] vi (US) = **moult**.

molten ['məultən] a fondu(e).

mom [mɔm] n (US) = **mum**.

moment ['məumənt] n moment m, instant m; importance f; **at the ~** à ce moment; **~ary** a momentané(e), passager(ère); **~ous** ['-'mentəs] a important(e), capital(e).

momentum [məu'mentəm] n élan m, vitesse acquise; **to gather ~** prendre de la vitesse.

mommy ['mɔmi] n (US) = **mummy**.

Monaco ['mɔnəkəu] n Monaco m.

monarch ['mɔnək] n monarque m; **~y** n monarchie f.

monastery ['mɔnəstəri] n monastère m.

Monday ['mʌndi] n lundi m.

monetary ['mʌnitəri] a monétaire.

money ['mʌni] n argent m; **to make ~** gagner de l'argent; faire des bénéfices; rapporter; **~lender** n prêteur/euse; **~ order** n mandat m; **~-spinner** n (col) mine f d'or (fig).

mongrel ['mʌŋgrəl] n (dog) bâtard m.

monitor ['mɔnitə*] n (SCOL) chef m de classe; (TV, COMPUT) moniteur m // vt contrôler.

monk [mʌŋk] n moine m.

monkey ['mʌŋki] n singe m; **~ nut** n (Brit) cacahuète f; **~ wrench** n clé f à molette.

mono... ['mɔnəu] prefix: **~chrome** a monochrome.

monopoly [mə'nɔpəli] n monopole m.

monotone ['mɔnətəun] n ton m (or voix f) monocorde.

monotonous [mə'nɔtənəs] a monotone.

monsoon [mɔn'su:n] n mousson f.

monster ['mɔnstə*] n monstre m.

monstrous ['mɔnstrəs] a (huge) gigantesque; (atrocious) monstrueux(euse), atroce.

month [mʌnθ] n mois m; **~ly** a mensuel(le) // ad mensuellement // n (magazine) mensuel m, publication mensuelle.

monument ['mɔnjumənt] n monument m.

moo [mu:] vi meugler, beugler.

mood [mu:d] n humeur f, disposition f; **to be in a good/bad ~** être de bonne/mauvaise humeur; **~y** a (variable) d'humeur changeante, lunatique; (sullen) morose, maussade.

moon [mu:n] n lune f; **~light** n clair m de lune; **~lighting** n travail m au noir; **~lit** a éclairé(e) par la lune; (night) de lune.

moor [muə*] n lande f // vt (ship) amarrer // vi mouiller.

moorland ['muələnd] n lande f.

moose [mu:s] n (pl inv) élan m.

mop [mɔp] n balai m à laver // vt éponger, essuyer; **to ~ up** vt éponger; **~ of hair** tignasse f.

mope [məup] vi avoir le cafard, se morfondre.

moped ['məuped] n cyclomoteur m.

moral ['mɔrl] a moral(e) // n morale f; **~s** npl moralité f.

morale [mɔ'rɑ:l] n moral m.

morality [mə'ræliti] n moralité f.

morass [mə'ræs] n marais m, marécage m.

more [mɔ:*] ♦ a 1 (greater in number etc) plus (de), davantage; **~ people/work (than)** plus de gens/de travail (que)

2 (*additional*) encore (de); do you want (some) ~ tea? voulez-vous encore du thé?; I have no *or* I don't have any ~ money je n'ai plus d'argent; it'll take a few ~ weeks ça prendra encore quelques semaines
♦ *pronoun* plus, davantage; ~ than 10 plus de 10; it cost ~ than we expected cela a coûté plus que prévu; I want ~ j'en veux plus *or* davantage; is there any ~? est-ce qu'il en reste?; there's no ~ il n'y en a plus; a little ~ un peu plus; many/much ~ beaucoup plus, bien davantage
♦ *ad*: ~ dangerous/easily (than) plus dangereux/facilement (que); ~ and ~ expensive de plus en plus cher; ~ or less plus ou moins; ~ than ever plus que jamais.
moreover [mɔː'rəʊvə*] *ad* de plus.
morning ['mɔːnɪŋ] *n* matin *m*; matinée *f*; in the ~ le matin; 7 o'clock in the ~ 7 heures du matin.
Morocco [mə'rɒkəʊ] *n* Maroc *m*.
moron ['mɔːrɒn] *n* idiot/e, minus *m/f*.
Morse [mɔːs] *n* (*also*: ~ code) morse *m*.
morsel ['mɔːsl] *n* bouchée *f*.
mortal ['mɔːtl] *a*, *n* mortel(le); ~ity [-'tælɪtɪ] *n* mortalité *f*.
mortar ['mɔːtə*] *n* mortier *m*.
mortgage ['mɔːgɪdʒ] *n* hypothèque *f*; (*loan*) prêt *m* (*or* crédit *m*) hypothécaire; ~ company *n* (*US*) société *f* de crédit immobilier.
mortuary ['mɔːtjʊərɪ] *n* morgue *f*.
mosaic [məʊ'zeɪɪk] *n* mosaïque *f*.
Moscow ['mɒskəʊ] *n* Moscou *m*.
Moslem ['mɒzləm] *a*, *n* = **Muslim**.
mosque [mɒsk] *n* mosquée *f*.
mosquito [mɒs'kiːtəʊ], ~es *n* moustique *m*.
moss [mɒs] *n* mousse *f*.
most [məʊst] *a* la plupart de; le plus de // *pronoun* la plupart // *ad* le plus; (*very*) très, extrêmement; the ~ (*also*: + *adjective*) le plus; ~ of la plus grande partie de; ~ of them la plupart d'entre eux; I saw (the) ~ j'en ai vu la plupart; c'est moi qui en ai vu le plus; at the (very) ~ au plus; to make the ~ of profiter au maximum de; ~ly *ad* surtout, principalement.
MOT *n abbr* (*Brit*: = *Ministry of Transport*): the ~ (*test*) la visite technique (annuelle) obligatoire des véhicules à moteur.
motel [məʊ'tɛl] *n* motel *m*.
moth [mɒθ] *n* papillon *m* de nuit; mite *f*; ~ball *n* boule *f* de naphtaline.
mother ['mʌðə*] *n* mère *f* // *vt* (*care for*) dorloter; ~hood *n* maternité *f*; ~-in-law *n* belle-mère *f*; ~ly *a* maternel(le); ~-of-pearl *n* nacre *f*; ~-to-be *n* future maman *f*; ~ tongue *n* langue maternelle.

motion ['məʊʃən] *n* mouvement *m*; (*gesture*) geste *m*; (*at meeting*) motion *f* // *vt*, *vi*: to ~ (to) sb to do faire signe à qn de faire; ~less *a* immobile, sans mouvement; ~ picture *n* film *m*.
motivated ['məʊtɪveɪtɪd] *a* motivé(e).
motive ['məʊtɪv] *n* motif *m*, mobile *m*.
motley ['mɒtlɪ] *a* hétéroclite; bigarré(e), bariolé(e).
motor ['məʊtə*] *n* moteur *m*; (*Brit col: vehicle*) auto *f* // *a* à moteur(trice); ~bike *n* moto *f*; ~boat *n* bateau *m* à moteur; ~car *n* (*Brit*) automobile *f*; ~cycle *n* vélomoteur *m*; ~cyclist *n* motocycliste *m/f*; ~ing *n* (*Brit*) tourisme *m* automobile; ~ist *n* automobiliste *m/f*; ~ racing *n* (*Brit*) course *f* automobile; ~way *n* (*Brit*) autoroute *f*.
mottled ['mɒtld] *a* tacheté(e), marbré(e).
motto, ~es ['mɒtəʊ] *n* devise *f*.
mould, (*US*) **mold** [məʊld] *n* moule *m*; (*mildew*) moisissure *f* // *vt* mouler, modeler; (*fig*) façonner; ~er *vi* (*decay*) moisir; ~y *a* moisi(e).
moult, (*US*) **molt** [məʊlt] *vi* muer.
mound [maʊnd] *n* monticule *m*, tertre *m*.
mount [maʊnt] *n* mont *m*, montagne *f*; (*horse*) monture *f*; (*for jewel etc*) monture // *vt* monter // *vi* (*also*: ~ up) s'élever, monter.
mountain ['maʊntɪn] *n* montagne *f* // *cpd* de (la) montagne; ~eer [-'nɪə*] *n* alpiniste *m/f*; ~eering [-'nɪərɪŋ] *n* alpinisme *m*; ~ous *a* montagneux(euse); ~side *n* flanc *m* or versant *m* de la montagne.
mourn [mɔːn] *vt* pleurer // *vi*: to ~ (for) se lamenter (sur); ~er *n* parent/e *or* ami/e du défunt; personne *f* en deuil; ~ful *a* triste, lugubre; ~ing *n* deuil *m* // *cpd* (*dress*) de deuil; in ~ing en deuil.
mouse [maʊs], *pl* **mice** *n* (*also* COMPUT) souris *f*; ~trap *n* souricière *f*.
mousse [muːs] *n* mousse *f*.
moustache [məs'tɑːʃ] *n* moustache(s) *f(pl)*.
mousy ['maʊsɪ] *a* (*person*) effacé(e); (*hair*) d'un châtain terne.
mouth [maʊθ], ~s [maʊð, -ðz] *n* bouche *f*; (*of dog, cat*) gueule *f*; (*of river*) embouchure *f*; (*of bottle*) goulot *m*; (*opening*) orifice *m*; ~ful *n* bouchée *f*; ~ organ *n* harmonica *m*; ~piece *n* (*of musical instrument*) embouchure *f*; (*spokesman*) porte-parole *m inv*; ~wash *n* bain *m* de bouche; ~-watering *a* qui met l'eau à la bouche.
movable ['muːvəbl] *a* mobile.
move [muːv] *n* (*movement*) mouvement *m*; (*in game*) coup *m*; (: *turn to play*) tour *m*; (*change of house*) déménagement *m* // *vt* déplacer, bouger; (*emotion-*

ally) émouvoir; (POL: resolution etc) proposer // vi (gen) bouger, remuer; (traffic) circuler; (also: ~ house) déménager; **to ~ towards** se diriger vers; **to ~ sb to do sth** pousser or inciter qn à faire qch; **to get a ~ on** se dépêcher, se remuer; **to ~ about** or **around** vi (fidget) remuer; (travel) voyager, se déplacer; **to ~ along** vi se pousser; **to ~ away** vi s'en aller, s'éloigner; **to ~ back** vi revenir, retourner; **to ~ forward** vi avancer // vt avancer; (people) faire avancer; **to ~ in** (to a house) emménager // vt (onlookers) faire circuler; **to ~ out** vi (of house) déménager; **to ~ over** vi se pousser, se déplacer; **to ~ up** vi avancer; (employee) avoir de l'avancement.

movement ['mu:vmənt] n mouvement m.

movie ['mu:vɪ] n film m; **the ~s** le cinéma; **~ camera** n caméra f.

moving ['mu:vɪŋ] a en mouvement; émouvant(e).

mow, pt **mowed**, pp **mowed** or **mown** [meu, -n] vt faucher; (lawn) tondre; **to ~ down** vt faucher; **~er** n (also: lawnmower) tondeuse f à gazon.

MP n abbr of **member of parliament**.

m.p.h. abbr = miles per hour (60 m.p.h. = 96 km/h).

Mr, Mr. ['mɪstə*] n: **~ Smith** Monsieur Smith, M. Smith.

Mrs, Mrs. ['mɪsɪz] n: **~ Smith** Madame Smith, Mme Smith.

Ms, Ms. [mɪz] n (= Miss or Mrs): **~ Smith** ≈ Madame Smith, Mme Smith.

M.Sc. abbr see **master**.

much [mʌtʃ] a beaucoup de // ad, n or pronoun beaucoup; **how ~ is it?** combien est-ce que ça coûte?; **too ~** trop (de); **as ~ as** autant de.

muck [mʌk] n (mud) boue f; (dirt) ordures fpl; **to ~ about** or **around** vi (col) faire l'imbécile; (waste time) traînasser; **to ~ up** vt (col: ruin) gâcher, esquinter.

mud [mʌd] n boue f.

muddle ['mʌdl] n pagaille f; désordre m, fouillis m // vt (also: ~ up) brouiller, embrouiller; **to be in a ~** (person) ne plus savoir où l'on en est; **to ~ through** vi se débrouiller.

muddy ['mʌdɪ] a boueux(euse).

mud: **~guard** n garde-boue m inv; **~-slinging** n médisance f, dénigrement m.

muff [mʌf] n manchon m // vt (chance) rater, louper.

muffin ['mʌfɪn] n petit pain rond et plat.

muffle ['mʌfl] vt (sound) assourdir, étouffer; (against cold) emmitoufler.

muffler ['mʌflə*] n (US AUT) silencieux m.

mug [mʌg] n (cup) grande tasse (sans

soucoupe), chope f; (: for beer) chope; (col: face) bouille f; (: fool) poire f // vt (assault) agresser; **~ging** n agression f.

muggy ['mʌgɪ] a lourd(e), moite.

mule [mju:l] n mule f.

mull [mʌl]: **to ~ over** vt réfléchir à.

mulled [mʌld] a: **~ wine** vin chaud.

multi-level ['mʌltɪlevl] a (US) = **multistorey**.

multiple ['mʌltɪpl] a, n multiple (m); **~ sclerosis** n sclérose f en plaques.

multiplication [mʌltɪplɪ'keɪʃən] n multiplication f.

multiply ['mʌltɪplaɪ] vt multiplier // vi se multiplier.

multistorey ['mʌltɪ'stɔ:rɪ] a (Brit: building) à étages; (: car park) à étages or niveaux multiples.

mum [mʌm] n (Brit) maman f // a: **to keep ~** ne pas souffler mot.

mumble ['mʌmbl] vt, vi marmotter, marmonner.

mummy ['mʌmɪ] n (Brit: mother) maman f; (embalmed) momie f.

mumps [mʌmps] n oreillons mpl.

munch [mʌntʃ] vt, vi mâcher.

mundane [mʌn'deɪn] a banal(e), terre à terre inv.

municipal [mju:'nɪsɪpl] a municipal(e).

mural ['mjuərl] n peinture murale.

murder ['mə:də*] n meurtre m, assassinat m // vt assassiner; **~er** n meurtrier m, assassin m; **~ous** a meurtrier(ère).

murky ['mə:kɪ] a sombre, ténébreux(euse).

murmur ['mə:mə*] n murmure m // vt, vi murmurer.

muscle ['mʌsl] n muscle m; **to ~ in** vi s'imposer, s'immiscer.

muscular ['mʌskjulə*] a musculaire; (person, arm) musclé(e).

muse [mju:z] vi méditer, songer.

museum [mju:'zɪəm] n musée m.

mushroom ['mʌʃrum] n champignon m.

music ['mju:zɪk] n musique f; **~al** a musical(e); (person) musicien(ne) // n (show) comédie musicale; **~al instrument** n instrument m de musique; **~ian** [-'zɪʃən] n musicien(ne).

Muslim ['mʌzlɪm] a, n musulman(e).

muslin ['mʌzlɪn] n mousseline f.

mussel ['mʌsl] n moule f.

must [mʌst] auxiliary vb (obligation): **I ~ do it** je dois le faire, il faut que je le fasse; (probability): **he ~ be there by now** il doit y être maintenant, il y est probablement maintenant; **I ~ have made a mistake** j'ai dû me tromper // n nécessité f, impératif m; **it's a ~** c'est indispensable.

mustard ['mʌstəd] n moutarde f.

muster ['mʌstə*] vt rassembler.

mustn't ['mʌsnt] = **must not**.

musty ['mʌstɪ] a qui sent le moisi or le

renfermé.

mute [mju:t] *a, n* muet(te).

muted ['mju:tɪd] *a* assourdi(e); voilé(e).

mutiny ['mju:tɪnɪ] *n* mutinerie *f*.

mutter ['mʌtə*] *vt, vi* marmonner, marmotter.

mutton ['mʌtn] *n* mouton *m*.

mutual ['mju:tʃuəl] *a* mutuel(le), réciproque.

muzzle ['mʌzl] *n* museau *m*; (*protective device*) muselière *f*; (*of gun*) gueule *f*.

my [maɪ] *a* mon(ma), mes *pl*; ~ **house/car/gloves** ma maison/mon auto/mes gants; **I've washed ~ hair/cut ~ finger** je me suis lavé les cheveux/coupé le doigt.

myself [maɪ'self] *pronoun* (*reflexive*) me; (*emphatic*) moi-même; (*after prep*) moi; *see also* **oneself**.

mysterious [mɪs'tɪərɪəs] *a* mystérieux(euse).

mystery ['mɪstərɪ] *n* mystère *m*.

mystify ['mɪstɪfaɪ] *vt* mystifier; (*puzzle*) ébahir.

myth [mɪθ] *n* mythe *m*; ~**ology** [mɪ'θɒlədʒɪ] *n* mythologie *f*.

N

n/a *abbr* = *not applicable*.

nab [næb] *vt* pincer, attraper.

nag [næg] *vt* (*person*) être toujours après, reprendre sans arrêt; ~**ging** *a* (*doubt, pain*) persistant(e).

nail [neɪl] *n* (*human*) ongle *m*; (*metal*) clou *m* // *vt* clouer; **to ~ sb down to a date/price** contraindre qn à accepter *or* donner une date/un prix; ~**brush** *n* brosse *f* à ongles; ~**file** *n* lime *f* à ongles; ~ **polish** *n* vernis *m* à ongles; ~ **polish remover** *n* dissolvant *m*; ~ **scissors** *npl* ciseaux *mpl* à ongles; ~ **varnish** *n* (*Brit*) = ~ **polish**.

naïve [naɪ'i:v] *a* naïf(ïve).

naked ['neɪkɪd] *a* nu(e).

name [neɪm] *n* nom *m*; réputation *f* // *vt* nommer; citer; (*price, date*) fixer, donner; **by ~** par son nom; ~**less** *a* sans nom; (*witness, contributor*) anonyme; ~**ly** *ad* à savoir; ~**sake** *n* homonyme *m*.

nanny ['nænɪ] *n* bonne *f* d'enfants.

nap [næp] *n* (*sleep*) (petit) somme *m*; **to be caught ~ping** être pris à l'improviste *or* en défaut.

nape [neɪp] *n*: ~ **of the neck** nuque *f*.

napkin ['næpkɪn] *n* serviette *f* (de table).

nappy ['næpɪ] *n* (*Brit*) couche *f* (*gen pl*); ~ **rash** *n*: **to have ~ rash** avoir les fesses rouges.

narcissus, *pl* **narcissi** [nɑ:'sɪsəs, -saɪ] *n* narcisse *m*.

narcotic [nɑ:'kɒtɪk] *n* (*drug*) stupéfiant *m*; (*MED*) narcotique *m* // *a* narcotique.

narrative ['nærətɪv] *n* récit *m* // *a* narratif(ive).

narrow ['nærəu] *a* étroit(e); (*fig*) restreint(e), limité(e) // *vi* devenir plus étroit, se rétrécir; **to have a ~ escape** l'échapper belle; **to ~ sth down to** réduire qch à; ~**ly** *ad*: **he ~ly missed injury/the tree** il a failli se blesser/rentrer dans l'arbre; ~**-minded** *a* à l'esprit étroit, borné(e).

nasty ['nɑ:stɪ] *a* (*person*) méchant(e); très désagréable; (*smell*) dégoûtant(e); (*wound, situation*) mauvais(e).

nation ['neɪʃən] *n* nation *f*.

national ['næʃənl] *a* national(e) // *n* (*abroad*) ressortissant(e); (*when home*) national/e; ~ **dress** *n* costume national; **N~ Health Service (NHS)** *n* (*Brit*) service national de santé, ≈ Sécurité Sociale; **N~ Insurance** *n* (*Brit*) ≈ Sécurité Sociale; ~**ism** *n* nationalisme *m*; ~**ity** [-'nælɪtɪ] *n* nationalité *f*; ~**ize** *vt* nationaliser; ~**ly** *ad* du point de vue national; dans le pays entier.

nation-wide ['neɪʃənwaɪd] *a* s'étendant à l'ensemble du pays; (*problem*) à l'échelle du pays entier // *ad* à travers *or* dans tout le pays.

native ['neɪtɪv] *n* habitant/e du pays, autochtone *m/f*; (*in colonies*) indigène *m/f* // *a* du pays, indigène; (*country*) natal(e); (*ability*) inné(e); **a ~ of Russia** une personne originaire de Russie; **a ~ speaker of French** une personne de langue maternelle française; ~ **language** *n* langue maternelle.

NATO ['neɪtəu] *n abbr* (= *North Atlantic Treaty Organization*) O.T.A.N. *f*.

natural ['nætʃrəl] *a* naturel(le); ~ **gas** *n* gaz naturel; ~**ize** *vt* naturaliser; (*plant*) acclimater; **to become ~ized** (*person*) se faire naturaliser; ~**ly** *ad* naturellement.

nature ['neɪtʃə*] *n* nature *f*; **by ~** par tempérament, de nature.

naught [nɔ:t] *n* = **nought**.

naughty ['nɔ:tɪ] *a* (*child*) vilain(e), pas sage; (*story, film*) polisson(ne).

nausea ['nɔ:sɪə] *n* nausée *f*; **nauseate** ['nɔ:sɪeɪt] *vt* écœurer, donner la nausée à.

naval ['neɪvl] *a* naval(e); ~ **officer** *n* officier *m* de marine.

nave [neɪv] *n* nef *f*.

navel ['neɪvl] *n* nombril *m*.

navigate ['nævɪgeɪt] *vt* diriger, piloter // *vi* naviguer; **navigation** [-'geɪʃən] *n* navigation *f*; **navigator** *n* navigateur *m*.

navvy ['nævɪ] *n* (*Brit*) terrassier *m*.

navy ['neɪvɪ] *n* marine *f*; ~**(-blue)** *a* bleu marine *inv*.

Nazi ['nɑːtsɪ] *n* Nazi/e.

NB *abbr* (= *nota bene*) NB.

near [nɪə*] *a* proche // *ad* près // *prep* (*also*: ~ **to**) près de // *vt* approcher de;

~by [nɪə'baɪ] a proche // ad tout près, à proximité; **~ly** ad presque; **I ~ly fell** j'ai failli tomber; **~ miss** n collision évitée de justesse; (when aiming) coup manqué de peu or de justesse; **~side** n (AUT: right-hand drive) côté m gauche; **~-sighted** a myope.

neat [ni:t] a (person, work) soigné(e); (room etc) bien tenu(e) or rangé(e); (solution, plan) habile; (spirits) pur(e); **~ly** ad avec soin or ordre; habilement.

necessarily ['nɛsɪsrɪlɪ] ad nécessairement.

necessary ['nɛsɪsrɪ] a nécessaire.

necessity [nɪ'sɛsɪtɪ] n nécessité f; chose nécessaire or essentielle.

neck [nɛk] n cou m; (of horse, garment) encolure f; (of bottle) goulot m // vi (col) se peloter; **~ and ~** à égalité.

necklace ['nɛklɪs] n collier m.

neckline ['nɛklaɪn] n encolure f.

necktie ['nɛktaɪ] n cravate f.

need [ni:d] n besoin m // vt avoir besoin de; **to ~ to do** devoir faire; avoir besoin de faire; **you don't ~ to go** vous n'avez pas besoin or vous n'êtes pas obligé de partir.

needle ['ni:dl] n aiguille f // vt asticoter, tourmenter.

needless ['ni:dlɪs] a inutile.

needlework ['ni:dlwə:k] n (activity) travaux mpl d'aiguille; (object) ouvrage m.

needn't [ni:dnt] = need not.

needy ['ni:dɪ] a nécessiteux(euse).

negative ['nɛgətɪv] n (PHOT, ELEC) négatif m; (LING) terme m de négation // a négatif(ive).

neglect [nɪ'glɛkt] vt négliger // n (of person, duty, garden) le fait de négliger; (state of ~) abandon m.

negligee ['nɛglɪʒeɪ] n déshabillé m.

negligence ['nɛglɪdʒəns] n négligence f.

negotiate [nɪ'gəʊʃɪeɪt] vi, vt négocier; **negotiation** [-'eɪʃən] n négociation f, pourparlers mpl.

Negro ['ni:grəʊ] a (gen) noir(e); (music, arts) nègre, noir // n (pl: ~es) Noir/e.

neigh [neɪ] vi hennir.

neighbour, (US) neighbor ['neɪbə*] n voisin/e; **~hood** n quartier m; voisinage m; **~ing** a voisin(e), avoisinant(e); **~ly** a obligeant(e); (relations) de bon voisinage.

neither ['naɪðə*] a, pronoun aucun(e) (des deux), ni l'un(e) ni l'autre // cj: **I didn't move and ~ did Claude** je n'ai pas bougé, (et) Claude non plus; ..., **~ did I refuse** ..., (et or mais) je n'ai pas non plus refusé // ad: **~ good nor bad** ni bon ni mauvais.

neon ['ni:ɔn] n néon m; **~ light** n lampe f au néon.

nephew ['nɛvju:] n neveu m.

nerve [nə:v] n nerf m; (fig) sang-froid m, courage m; aplomb m, toupet m; **to have a fit of ~s** avoir le trac; **~-racking** a angoissant(e).

nervous ['nə:vəs] a nerveux(euse); inquiet(ète), plein(e) d'appréhension; **~ breakdown** n dépression nerveuse.

nest [nɛst] n nid m // vi (se) nicher, faire son nid; **~ egg** n (fig) bas m de laine, magot m.

nestle ['nɛsl] vi se blottir.

net [nɛt] n filet m // a net(te) // vt (fish etc) prendre au filet; (profit) rapporter; **~ball** n netball m; **~ curtains** npl voilages mpl.

Netherlands ['nɛðələndz] npl: **the ~** les Pays-Bas mpl.

nett [nɛt] a = **net.**

netting ['nɛtɪŋ] n (for fence etc) treillis m, grillage m.

nettle ['nɛtl] n ortie f.

network ['nɛtwə:k] n réseau m.

neurotic [njuə'rɔtɪk] a, n névrosé(e).

neuter ['nju:tə*] a, n neutre (m) // vt (cat etc) châtrer, couper.

neutral ['nju:trəl] a neutre // n (AUT) point mort; **~ize** vt neutraliser.

never ['nɛvə*] ad (ne ...) jamais; **~ again** plus jamais; **~ in my life** jamais de ma vie; see also **mind**; **~-ending** a interminable; **~theless** [nɛvəðə'lɛs] ad néanmoins, malgré tout.

new [nju:] a à nouveau(nouvelle); (brand new) neuf(neuve); **~born** a nouveau-né(e); **~comer** ['nju:kʌmə*] n nouveau venu/nouvelle venue; **~-fangled** ['nju:-fæŋgld] a (pej) ultramoderne (et farfelu(e)); **~-found** a de fraîche date; (friend) nouveau(nouvelle); **~ly** ad nouvellement, récemment; **~ly-weds** npl jeunes mariés mpl.

news [nju:z] n nouvelle(s) f(pl); (RADIO, TV) informations fpl, actualités fpl; **a piece of ~** une nouvelle; **~ agency** n agence f de presse; **~agent** n (Brit) marchand m de journaux; **~caster** n présentateur/trice; **~dealer** n (US) = **~agent**; **~ flash** n flash m d'information; **~letter** n bulletin m; **~paper** n journal m; **~print** n papier m (de) journal; **~reader** n = **~caster**; **~reel** n actualités (filmées); **~ stand** n kiosque m à journaux.

newt [nju:t] n triton m.

New Year ['nju:'jɪə*] n Nouvel An; **~'s Day** n le jour de l'An; **~'s Eve** n la Saint-Sylvestre.

New Zealand [nju:'zi:lənd] n la Nouvelle-Zélande; **~er** n Néo-zélandais/e.

next [nɛkst] a (seat, room) voisin(e), d'à côté; (meeting, bus stop) suivant(e); prochain(e) // ad la fois suivante; la prochaine fois; (afterwards) ensuite; **the ~ day** le lendemain, le jour suivant or d'après; ~ **year** l'année prochaine; **when do we meet** ~? quand nous revoyons-nous?; ~ **door** ad à côté; **~-of-kin** n parent m le plus proche; ~ **to** prep à côté de; ~ **to nothing** presque rien.

NHS n abbr of **National Health Service**.

nib [nɪb] n (of pen) (bec m de) plume f.

nibble ['nɪbl] vt grignoter.

nice [naɪs] a (holiday, trip) agréable; (flat, picture) joli(e); (person) gentil(le); (distinction, point) subtil(e); **~-looking** a joli(e); **~ly** ad agréablement; joliment; gentiment; subtilement.

niceties ['naɪsɪtɪz] npl subtilités fpl.

nick [nɪk] n encoche f // vt (col) faucher, piquer; **in the ~ of time** juste à temps.

nickel ['nɪkl] n nickel m; (US) pièce f de 5 cents.

nickname ['nɪkneɪm] n surnom m // vt surnommer.

niece [ni:s] n nièce f.

Nigeria [naɪ'dʒɪərɪə] n Nigéria m or f.

nigger ['nɪgə*] n (col!: highly offensive) nègre m, négresse f.

niggling ['nɪglɪŋ] a tatillon(ne).

night [naɪt] n nuit f; (evening) soir m; **at** ~ la nuit; **by** ~ de nuit; **the ~ before last** avant-hier soir; **~cap** n boisson prise avant le coucher; ~ **club** n boîte f de nuit; **~dress** n chemise f de nuit; **~fall** n tombée f de la nuit; **~gown** n, **~ie** ['naɪtɪ] n chemise f de nuit.

nightingale ['naɪtɪŋgeɪl] n rossignol m.

night life n vie f nocturne.

nightly ['naɪtlɪ] a de chaque nuit or soir; (by night) nocturne // ad chaque nuit or soir; nuitamment.

nightmare ['naɪtmɛə*] n cauchemar m.

night: ~ **porter** n gardien m de nuit, concierge m de service la nuit; ~ **school** n cours mpl du soir; ~ **shift** n équipe f de nuit; **~-time** n nuit f.

nil [nɪl] n rien m; (Brit SPORT) zéro m.

Nile [naɪl] n: **the** ~ le Nil.

nimble ['nɪmbl] a agile.

nine [naɪn] num neuf; **~teen** num dix-neuf; **~ty** num quatre-vingt-dix.

ninth [naɪnθ] num neuvième.

nip [nɪp] vt pincer.

nipple ['nɪpl] n (ANAT) mamelon m, bout m du sein.

nitrogen ['naɪtrədʒən] n azote m.

no [nəʊ] ♦ ad (opposite of 'yes') non; **are you coming?** - ~ **(I'm not)** est-ce que vous venez? - non; **would you like some more?** - ~ **thank you** vous en voulez encore? - non merci

♦ a (not any) pas de, aucun(e) (used with 'ne'); **I have** ~ **money/books** je n'ai pas d'argent/de livres; ~ **student would have done it** aucun étudiant ne l'aurait fait; **'**~ **smoking'** 'défense de fumer'; **'**~ **dogs'** 'les chiens ne sont pas admis'

♦ n (pl ~es) non m.

nobility [nəʊ'bɪlɪtɪ] n noblesse f.

noble ['nəʊbl] a noble.

nobody ['nəʊbədɪ] pronoun personne (with negative).

nod [nɒd] vi faire un signe de (la) tête (affirmatif ou amical); (sleep) somnoler // vt: **to** ~ **one's head** faire un signe de (la) tête; (in agreement) faire signe que oui // n signe m de (la) tête; **to** ~ **off** vi s'assoupir.

noise [nɔɪz] n bruit m; **noisy** a bruyant(e).

nominal ['nɒmɪnl] a (rent, fee) symbolique; (value) nominal(e).

nominate ['nɒmɪneɪt] vt (propose) proposer; (elect) nommer.

nominee [nɒmɪ'ni:] n candidat agréé; personne nommée.

non... [nɒn] prefix non-; **~-alcoholic** a non-alcoolisé(e); **~-committal** ['nɒnkə'mɪtl] a évasif(ive).

nondescript ['nɒndɪskrɪpt] a quelconque, indéfinissable.

none [nʌn] pronoun aucun/e; ~ **of you** aucun d'entre vous, personne parmi vous; **I've** ~ **left** je n'en ai plus; **he's** ~ **the worse for it** il ne s'en porte pas plus mal.

nonentity [nɒ'nentɪtɪ] n personne insignifiante.

nonetheless [nʌnðə'les] ad néanmoins.

non: **~-existent** a inexistant(e); **~-fiction** n littérature f non-romanesque.

nonplussed [nɒn'plʌst] a perplexe.

nonsense ['nɒnsəns] n absurdités fpl, idioties fpl; ~! ne dites pas d'idioties!

non: **~-smoker** n non-fumeur m; **~-stick** a qui n'attache pas; **~-stop** a direct(e), sans arrêt (or escale) // ad sans arrêt.

noodles ['nu:dlz] npl nouilles fpl.

nook [nuk] n: ~**s and crannies** recoins mpl.

noon [nu:n] n midi m.

no one ['nəʊwʌn] pronoun = **nobody**.

noose [nu:s] n nœud coulant; (hangman's) corde f.

nor [nɔ:*] cj = **neither** // ad see **neither**.

norm [nɔ:m] n norme f.

normal ['nɔ:ml] a normal(e); **~ly** ad normalement.

Normandy ['nɔ:məndɪ] n Normandie f.

north [nɔ:θ] n nord m // a du nord, nord inv // ad au or vers le nord; **N~ America** n Amérique f du Nord; **~-east** n nord-est m; **~erly** ['nɔ:ðəlɪ] a du nord; **~ern** ['nɔ:ðən] a du nord, septentrional(e); **N~ern Ireland** n Irlande f du Nord; **N~ Pole** n pôle m Nord; **N~ Sea** n mer f du Nord; **~ward(s)** ['nɔ:θwəd(z)] ad vers le nord; **~-west** n nord-ouest m.

Norway ['nɔ:weɪ] n Norvège f.

Norwegian [nɔ:'wi:dʒən] a norvé-

gien(ne) // *n* Norvégien/ne; *(LING)*
norvégien *m*.

nose [nəuz] *n* nez *m*; *(fig)* flair *m* // *vi*:
to ~ about fouiner *or* fureter (partout);
~-**dive** *n* (descente *f* en) piqué *m*; ~**y** *a*
= **nosy**.

nostalgia [nɔsˈtældʒɪə] *n* nostalgie *f*.

nostril [ˈnɔstrɪl] *n* narine *f*; *(of horse)*
naseau *m*.

nosy [ˈnəuzɪ] *a* curieux(euse).

not [nɔt] *ad* (ne ...) pas; he is ~ *or* isn't
here il n'est pas ici; you must ~ *or* you
mustn't do that tu ne dois pas faire ça;
it's too late, isn't it *or* is it ~? c'est trop
tard, n'est-ce pas?; ~ yet/now pas
encore/maintenant; ~ at all pas du tout;
see also **all, only**.

notably [ˈnəutəblɪ] *ad* en particulier;
(markedly) spécialement.

notary [ˈnəutərɪ] *n* *(also:* ~ **public)**
notaire *m*.

notch [nɔtʃ] *n* encoche *f*.

note [nəut] *n* note *f*; *(letter)* mot *m*;
(banknote) billet *m* // *vt* *(also:* ~ **down)**
noter; *(notice)* constater; ~**book** *n*
carnet *m*; ~**d** [ˈnəutɪd] *a* réputé(e);
~**pad** *n* bloc-notes *m*; ~**paper** *n* papier
m à lettres.

nothing [ˈnʌθɪŋ] *n* rien *m*; he does ~ il
ne fait rien; ~ new de nouveau; for
~ *(free)* pour rien, gratuitement.

notice [ˈnəutɪs] *n* avis *m*; *(of leaving)*
congé *m* // *vt* remarquer, s'apercevoir
de; to take ~ of prêter attention à; to
bring sth to sb's ~ porter qch à la
connaissance de qn; at short ~ dans un
délai très court; until further ~ jusqu'à
nouvel ordre; to hand in one's ~ donner
sa démission, démissionner; ~**able** *a*
visible; ~ **board** *n* *(Brit)* panneau *m*
d'affichage.

notify [ˈnəutɪfaɪ] *vt*: to ~ sth to sb
notifier qch à qn; to ~ sb of sth avertir
qn de qch.

notion [ˈnəuʃən] *n* idée *f*; *(concept)*
notion *f*.

notorious [nəuˈtɔːrɪəs] *a* notoire *(souvent en mal)*.

notwithstanding [nɔtwɪθˈstændɪŋ] *ad*
néanmoins // *prep* en dépit de.

nought [nɔːt] *n* zéro *m*.

noun [naun] *n* nom *m*.

nourish [ˈnʌrɪʃ] *vt* nourrir; ~**ing** *a*
nourrissant(e); ~**ment** *n* nourriture *f*.

novel [ˈnɔvl] *n* roman *m* // *a*
nouveau(nouvelle), original(e); ~**ist** *n*
romancier *m*; ~**ty** *n* nouveauté *f*.

November [nəuˈvɛmbə*] *n* novembre *m*.

now [nau] *ad* maintenant // *cj*: ~ *(that)*
maintenant que; right ~ tout de suite;
by ~ à l'heure qu'il est; just ~: I saw
her just ~ je viens de la voir, je l'ai vue
à l'instant; I'll read it just ~ je vais le
lire à l'instant *or* dès maintenant; ~ and

then, ~ and again de temps en temps;
from ~ on dorénavant; ~**adays**
[ˈnauədeɪz] *ad* de nos jours.

nowhere [ˈnəuwɛə*] *ad* nulle part.

nozzle [ˈnɔzl] *n* *(of hose)* jet *m*, lance *f*.

nuclear [ˈnjuːklɪə*] *a* nucléaire.

nucleus, *pl* **nuclei** [ˈnjuːklɪəs, ˈnjuːklɪaɪ]
n noyau *m*.

nude [njuːd] *a* nu(e) // *n* *(ART)* nu *m*; in
the ~ (tout(e)) nu(e).

nudge [nʌdʒ] *vt* donner un (petit) coup
de coude à.

nudist [ˈnjuːdɪst] *n* nudiste *m/f*.

nuisance [ˈnjuːsns] *n*: it's a ~ c'est
(très) ennuyeux *or* gênant; he's a ~ il
est assommant *or* casse-pieds; what a
~! quelle barbe!

null [nʌl] *a*: ~ and void nul(le) et non
avenu(e).

numb [nʌm] *a* engourdi(e).

number [ˈnʌmbə*] *n* nombre *m*;
(numeral) chiffre *m*; *(of house, car,
telephone, newspaper)* numéro *m* // *vt*
numéroter; *(include)* compter; a ~ of un
certain nombre de; to be ~ed among
compter parmi; they were seven in ~ ils
étaient (au nombre de) sept; ~ **plate** *n*
(Brit AUT) plaque *f* minéralogique *or*
d'immatriculation.

numeral [ˈnjuːmərəl] *n* chiffre *m*.

numerate [ˈnjuːmərɪt] *a*: to be ~ avoir
des notions d'arithmétique.

numerical [njuːˈmerɪkl] *a* numérique.

numerous [ˈnjuːmərəs] *a* nombreux(euse).

nun [nʌn] *n* religieuse *f*, sœur *f*.

nurse [nəːs] *n* infirmière *f* // *vt* *(patient,
cold)* soigner; *(baby: Brit)* bercer (dans
ses bras); (: *US*) allaiter, nourrir.

nursery [ˈnəːsərɪ] *n* *(room)* nursery *f*;
(institution) pouponnière *f*; *(for plants)*
pépinière *f*; ~ **rhyme** *n* comptine *f*,
chansonnette *f* pour enfants; ~ **school**
n école maternelle *f*; ~ **slope** *n* *(Brit
SKI)* piste *f* pour débutants.

nursing [ˈnəːsɪŋ] *n* *(profession)*
profession *f* d'infirmière; ~ **home** *n*
clinique *f*; maison *f* de convalescence.

nurture [ˈnəːtʃə*] *vt* élever.

nut [nʌt] *n* *(of metal)* écrou *m*; *(fruit)*
noix *f*, noisette *f*, cacahuète *f* *(terme
générique en anglais)*; he's ~s *(col)* il
est dingue; ~**crackers** *npl* casse-noix *m
inv*, casse-noisette(s) *m*.

nutmeg [ˈnʌtmeg] *n* (noix *f*) muscade *f*.

nutritious [njuːˈtrɪʃəs] *a* nutritif(ive),
nourrissant(e).

nutshell [ˈnʌtʃel] *n* coquille *f* de noix; in
a ~ en un mot.

nylon [ˈnaɪlɔn] *n* nylon *m* // *a* de *or* en
nylon.

O

oak [əuk] *n* chêne *m* // *a* de *or* en (bois de) chêne.

O.A.P. *abbr of* **old-age pensioner**.

oar [ɔ:*] *n* aviron *m*, rame *f*.

oasis, *pl* **oases** [əu'eɪsɪs] *n* oasis *f*.

oath [əuθ] *n* serment *m*; (*swear word*) juron *m*.

oatmeal ['əutmi:l] *n* flocons *mpl* d'avoine.

oats [əuts] *n* avoine *f*.

obedience [ə'bi:dɪəns] *n* obéissance *f*.

obedient [ə'bi:dɪənt] *a* obéissant(e).

obey [ə'beɪ] *vt* obéir à; (*instructions*) se conformer à // *vi* obéir.

obituary [ə'bɪtjuərɪ] *n* nécrologie *f*.

object *n* ['ɔbdʒɪkt] objet *m*; (*purpose*) but *m*, objet; (*LING*) complément *m* d'objet // *vi* [əb'dʒɛkt]: **to ~ to** (*attitude*) désapprouver; (*proposal*) protester contre; **expense is no ~** l'argent n'est pas un problème; **I ~!** je proteste!; **he ~ed that ...** il a fait valoir *or* a objecté que ...; **~ion** [əb'dʒɛkʃən] *n* objection *f*; (*drawback*) inconvénient *m*; **~ionable** [əb'dʒɛkʃənəbl] *a* très désagréable; choquant(e); **~ive** *n* objectif *m* // *a* objectif(ive).

obligation [ɔblɪ'geɪʃən] *n* obligation *f*, devoir *m*; (*debt*) dette *f* (de reconnaissance); **without ~** sans engagement.

oblige [ə'blaɪdʒ] *vt* (*force*): **to ~ sb to do** obliger *or* forcer qn à faire; (*do a favour*) rendre service à, obliger; **to be ~d to sb for sth** être obligé(e) à qn de qch; **obliging** *a* obligeant(e), serviable.

oblique [ə'bli:k] *a* oblique; (*allusion*) indirect(e).

obliterate [ə'blɪtəreɪt] *vt* effacer.

oblivion [ə'blɪvɪən] *n* oubli *m*.

oblivious [ə'blɪvɪəs] *a*: **~ of** oublieux(euse) de.

oblong ['ɔblɔŋ] *a* oblong(ue) // *n* rectangle *m*.

obnoxious [əb'nɔkʃəs] *a* odieux (euse); (*smell*) nauséabond(e).

oboe ['əubəu] *n* hautbois *m*.

obscene [əb'si:n] *a* obscène.

obscure [əb'skjuə*] *a* obscur(e) // *vt* obscurcir; (*hide: sun*) cacher.

observant [əb'zə:vnt] *a* observateur(trice).

observation [ɔbzə'veɪʃən] *n* observation *f*; (*by police etc*) surveillance *f*.

observatory [əb'zə:vətrɪ] *n* observatoire *m*.

observe [əb'zə:v] *vt* observer; (*remark*) faire observer *or* remarquer; **~r** *n* observateur/trice.

obsess [əb'sɛs] *vt* obséder; **~ive** *a* obsédant(e).

obsolescence [ɔbsə'lɛsns] *n* vieillis-sement *m*.

obsolete ['ɔbsəli:t] *a* dépassé(e); dé-modé(e).

obstacle ['ɔbstəkl] *n* obstacle *m*.

obstinate ['ɔbstɪnɪt] *a* obstiné(e); (*pain, cold*) persistant(e).

obstruct [əb'strʌkt] *vt* (*block*) boucher, obstruer; (*halt*) arrêter; (*hinder*) en-traver.

obtain [əb'teɪn] *vt* obtenir // *vi* avoir cours; **~able** *a* qu'on peut obtenir.

obtrusive [əb'tru:sɪv] *a* (*person*) importun(e); (*smell*) pénétrant(e); (*building etc*) trop en évidence.

obvious ['ɔbvɪəs] *a* évident(e), manifeste; **~ly** *ad* manifestement; bien sûr.

occasion [ə'keɪʒən] *n* occasion *f*; (*event*) événement *m* // *vt* occasionner, causer; **~al** *a* pris(e) *or* fait(e) *etc* de temps en temps; occasionnel(le); **~ally** *ad* de temps en temps, quelquefois.

occupation [ɔkju'peɪʃən] *n* occupation *f*; (*job*) métier *m*, profession *f*; **~al hazard** *n* risque *m* du métier.

occupier ['ɔkjupaɪə*] *n* occupant/e.

occupy ['ɔkjupaɪ] *vt* occuper; **to ~ o.s. with** *or* **by doing** s'occuper à faire.

occur [ə'kə:*] *vi* se produire; (*difficulty, opportunity*) se présenter; (*phenomenon, error*) se rencontrer; **to ~ to sb** venir à l'esprit de qn; **~rence** *n* présence *f*, existence *f*; cas *m*, fait *m*.

ocean ['əuʃən] *n* océan *m*; **~-going** *a* de haute mer.

o'clock [ə'klɔk] *ad*: **it is 5 ~** il est 5 heures.

OCR *n abbr of* **optical character recognition/reader**.

October [ɔk'təubə*] *n* octobre *m*.

octopus ['ɔktəpəs] *n* pieuvre *f*.

odd [ɔd] *a* (*strange*) bizarre, cu-rieux(euse); (*number*) impair(e); (*left over*) qui reste, en plus; (*not of a set*) dépareillé(e); **60~** 60 et quelques; **at ~ times** de temps en temps; **the ~ one out** l'exception *f*; **~s and ends** *npl* de petites choses; **~ity** *n* bizarrerie *f*; (*person*) excentrique *m/f*; **~ jobs** *npl* petits travaux divers; **~ly** *ad* bizarrement, curieusement; **~ments** *npl* (*COMM*) fins *fpl* de série; **~s** *npl* (*in betting*) cote *f*; **it makes no ~s** cela n'a pas d'importance; **at ~s** en désaccord.

odometer [ɔ'dɔmɪtə*] *n* odomètre *m*.

odour, **(**US**) odor** ['əudə*] *n* odeur *f*.

of [ɔv, əv] *prep* **1** (*gen*) de; **a friend ~ ours** un de nos amis; **a boy ~ 10** un garçon de 10 ans; **that was kind ~ you** c'était gentil de votre part

2 (*expressing quantity, amount, dates etc*) de; **a kilo ~ flour** un kilo de farine; **how much ~ this do you need?** combien vous en faut-il?; **there were 3 ~ them** (*people*) ils étaient 3; (*objects*) il y en

avait 3; 3 ~ **us** went 3 d'entre nous sont allé(e)s; **the 5th** ~ **July** le 5 juillet
3 (*from, out of*) en, de; **a statue** ~ **marble** une statue de *or* en marbre; **made** ~ **wood** (fait) en bois.

off [ɔf] *a, ad* (*engine*) coupé(e); (*tap*) fermé(e); (*Brit: food: bad*) mauvais(e), avancé(e); (: *milk*) tourné(e); (*absent*) absent(e); (*cancelled*) annulé(e) // *prep* de; sur; **to be** ~ (*to leave*) partir, s'en aller; **to be** ~ **work** être absent pour cause de maladie; **a day** ~ un jour de congé; **to have an** ~ **day** n'être pas en forme; **he had his coat** ~ il avait enlevé son manteau; **10%** ~ (*COMM*) 10% de rabais; ~ **the coast** au large de la côte; **I'm** ~ **meat** je ne mange plus de viande; je n'aime plus la viande; **on the** ~ **chance** à tout hasard.

offal [ˈɔfl] *n* (*CULIN*) abats *mpl*.

offbeat [ˈɔfbiːt] *a* excentrique.

off-colour [ˈɔfˈkʌlə*] *a* (*Brit: ill*) malade, mal fichu(e).

offence, (*US*) **offense** [əˈfens] *n* (*crime*) délit *m*, infraction *f*; **to take** ~ **at** se vexer de, s'offenser de.

offend [əˈfend] *vt* (*person*) offenser, blesser; ~**er** *n* délinquant/e; (*against regulations*) contrevenant/e.

offensive [əˈfensɪv] *a* offensant(e), choquant(e); (*smell etc*) très déplaisant(e); (*weapon*) offensif(ive) // *n* (*MIL*) offensive *f*.

offer [ˈɔfə*] *n* offre *f*, proposition *f* // *vt* offrir, proposer; **'on** ~ **'** (*COMM*) 'en promotion'; ~**ing** *n* offrande *f*.

offhand [ɔfˈhænd] *a* désinvolte // *ad* spontanément.

office [ˈɔfɪs] *n* (*place*) bureau *m*; (*position*) charge *f*, fonction *f*; **doctor's** ~ (*US*) cabinet (médical); **to take** ~ entrer en fonctions; ~ **automation** *n* bureautique *f*; ~ **block**, (*US*) ~ **building** *n* immeuble *m* de bureaux; ~ **hours** *npl* heures *fpl* de bureau; (*US MED*) heures de consultation.

officer [ˈɔfɪsə*] *n* (*MIL etc*) officier *m*; (*of organization*) membre *m* du bureau directeur; (*also*: **police** ~) agent *m* (de police).

office worker *n* employé/e de bureau.

official [əˈfɪʃl] *a* (*authorized*) officiel(le) // *n* officiel *m*; (*civil servant*) fonctionnaire *m/f*; employé/e; ~**dom** *n* administration *f*, bureaucratie *f*.

officiate [əˈfɪʃɪeɪt] *vi* (*REL*) officier; **to** ~ **at a marriage** célébrer un mariage.

officious [əˈfɪʃəs] *a* trop empressé(e).

offing [ˈɔfɪŋ] *n*: **in the** ~ (*fig*) en perspective.

off: ~**-licence** *n* (*Brit: shop*) débit *m* de vins et de spiritueux; ~**-line** *a, ad* (*COMPUT*) (en mode) autonome; (: *switched off*) non connecté(e); ~**-peak** *a* aux heures creuses; ~**-putting** *a*

(*Brit*) rébarbatif(ive); rebutant(e), peu engageant(e). ~**-season** *a, ad* hors-saison (*inv*).

offset [ˈɔfsɛt] *vt irg* (*counteract*) contrebalancer, compenser.

offshoot [ˈɔfʃuːt] *n* (*fig*) ramification *f*, antenne *f*; (: *of discussion etc*) conséquence *f*.

offshore [ɔfˈʃɔː*] *a* (*breeze*) de terre; (*island*) proche du littoral; (*fishing*) côtier(ère).

offside [ˈɔfˈsaɪd] *a* (*SPORT*) hors jeu // *n* (*AUT*: with right-hand drive) côté droit.

offspring [ˈɔfsprɪŋ] *n* progéniture *f*.

off: ~**-stage** *ad* dans les coulisses; ~**-the-peg**, (*US*) ~**-the-rack** *ad* en prêt-à-porter; ~**-white** *a* blanc cassé *inv*.

often [ˈɔfn] *ad* souvent; **how** ~ **do you go?** vous y allez tous les combien?; **how** ~ **have you gone there?** vous y êtes allé combien de fois?

ogle [ˈəʊgl] *vt* lorgner.

oh [əʊ] *excl* ô!, oh!, ah!

oil [ɔɪl] *n* huile *f*; (*petroleum*) pétrole *m*; (*for central heating*) mazout *m* // *vt* (*machine*) graisser; ~**can** *n* burette *f* de graissage; (*for storing*) bidon *m* à huile; ~**field** *n* gisement *m* de pétrole; ~ **filter** *n* (*AUT*) filtre *m* à huile; ~**-fired** *a* au mazout; ~ **painting** *n* peinture *f* à l'huile; ~ **rig** *n* derrick *m*; (*at sea*) plate-forme pétrolière; ~**skins** *npl* ciré *m*; ~ **tanker** *n* pétrolier *m*; ~ **well** *n* puits *m* de pétrole; ~**y** *a* huileux(euse); (*food*) gras(se).

ointment [ˈɔɪntmənt] *n* onguent *m*.

O.K., okay [ˈəʊˈkeɪ] *excl* d'accord! // *vt* approuver, donner son accord à; **is it** ~?, **are you** ~? ça va?

old [əʊld] *a* vieux(vieille); (*person*) vieux, âgé(e); (*former*) ancien(ne), vieux; **how** ~ **are you?** quel âge avez-vous?; **he's 10 years** ~ il a 10 ans, il est âgé de 10 ans; ~**er brother/sister** frère/sœur aîné(e); ~ **age** *n* vieillesse *f*; ~ **age pensioner (O.A.P.)** *n* (*Brit*) retraité/e; ~**-fashioned** *a* démodé(e); (*person*) vieux jeu *inv*.

olive [ˈɔlɪv] *n* (*fruit*) olive *f*; (*tree*) olivier *m* // *a* (*also*: ~**-green**) (vert) olive *inv*; ~ **oil** *n* huile *f* d'olive.

Olympic [əʊˈlɪmpɪk] *a* olympique; **the** ~ **Games, the** ~**s** les Jeux *mpl* olympiques.

omelet(te) [ˈɔmlɪt] *n* omelette *f*.

omen [ˈəʊmən] *n* présage *m*.

ominous [ˈɔmɪnəs] *a* menaçant(e), inquiétant(e); (*event*) de mauvais augure.

omit [əʊˈmɪt] *vt* omettre.

on [ɔn] ♦ *prep* **1** (*indicating position*) sur; ~ **the table** sur la table; ~ **the wall** sur le *or* au mur; ~ **the left** à gauche
2 (*indicating means, method, condition etc*): ~ **foot** à pied; ~ **the train/plane** (*be*) dans le train/l'avion; (*go*) en train/

avion; ~ **the telephone/radio/television** au téléphone/à la radio/à la télévision; **to be ~ drugs** se droguer; ~ **holiday** en vacances
3 (*referring to time*): ~ **Friday** vendredi; ~ **Fridays** le vendredi; ~ **June 20th** le 20 juin; **a week ~ Friday** vendredi en huit; ~ **arrival** à l'arrivée; ~ **seeing this** en voyant cela
4 (*about, concerning*) sur, de; **a book ~ Balzac/physics** un livre sur Balzac/de physique
♦ *ad* **1** (*referring to dress, covering*): **to have one's coat ~** avoir (mis) son manteau; **to put one's coat ~** mettre son manteau; **what's she got ~?** qu'est-ce qu'elle porte?; **screw the lid ~ tightly** vissez bien le couvercle
2 (*further, continuously*): **to walk** *etc* ~ continuer à marcher *etc*; ~ **and off** de temps à autre
♦ *a* **1** (*in operation: machine*) en marche; (*: radio, TV, light*) allumé(e); (*: tap, gas*) ouvert(e); (*: brakes*) mis(e); **is the meeting still ~?** (*not cancelled*) est-ce que la réunion a bien lieu?; (*in progress*) la réunion dure-t-elle encore?; **when is this film ~?** quand passe ce film?
2 (*col*): **that's not ~!** (*not acceptable*) cela ne se fait pas!; (*not possible*) pas question!

once [wʌns] *ad* une fois; (*formerly*) autrefois // *cj* une fois que; ~ **he had left/it was done** une fois qu'il fut parti/que ce fut terminé; **at ~** tout de suite, immédiatement; (*simultaneously*) à la fois; ~ **more** encore une fois; ~ **and for all** une fois pour toutes; ~ **upon a time** il y avait une fois, il était une fois.
oncoming [ˈɔnkʌmɪŋ] *a* (*traffic*) venant en sens inverse.
one [wʌn] ♦ *num* un(e); ~ **hundred and fifty cent** cinquante; ~ **day** un jour
♦ *a* **1** (*sole*) seul(e), unique; **the ~ book which** l'unique *or* le seul livre qui; **the ~ man who** le seul (homme) qui
2 (*same*) même; **they came in the ~ car** ils sont venus dans la même voiture
♦ *pronoun* **1**: **this** ~ celui-ci/celle-ci; **that** ~ celui-là/celle-là; **I've already got ~/a red** ~ j'en ai déjà un(e)/un(e) rouge; ~ **by** ~ un(e) à *or* par un(e)
2: ~ **another** l'un(e) l'autre; **to look at** ~ **another** se regarder
3 (*impersonal*) on; ~ **never knows** on ne sait jamais; **to cut ~'s finger** se couper le doigt.
one: **~-armed bandit** *n* machine *f* à sous; **~-day excursion** *n* (*US*) billet *m* d'aller-retour (valable pour la journée); **~-man** *a* (*business*) dirigé(e) *etc* par un seul homme; **~-man band** *n* homme-orchestre *m*; **~-off** *n* (*Brit col*) exemplaire *m* unique.

oneself [wʌnˈsɛlf] *pronoun* (*reflexive*) se; (*after prep*) soi(-même); (*emphatic*) soi-même; **to hurt** ~ se faire mal; **to keep sth for** ~ garder qch pour soi; **to talk to** ~ se parler à soi-même.
one: **~-sided** *a* (*argument*) unilatéral(e); **~-to-~** *a* (*relationship*) univoque; **~-upmanship** [-'ʌpmənʃɪp] *n* l'art de faire mieux que les autres; **~-way** *a* (*street, traffic*) à sens unique.
ongoing [ˈɔngəʊɪŋ] *a* en cours; suivi(e).
onion [ˈʌnjən] *n* oignon *m*.
on-line [ˈɔnˈlaɪn] *a, ad* (*COMPUT*) en ligne; (*: switched on*) connecté(e).
onlooker [ˈɔnlʊkə*] *n* spectateur/trice.
only [ˈəʊnlɪ] *ad* seulement // *a* seul(e), unique // *cj* seulement, mais; **an ~ child** un enfant unique; **not ~ ... but also** non seulement ... mais aussi; **I took ~ one** je n'en ai pris qu'un, j'en ai seulement pris un.
onset [ˈɔnsɛt] *n* début *m*; (*of winter, old age*) approche *f*.
onshore [ˈɔnˈʃɔː*] *a* (*wind*) du large.
onslaught [ˈɔnslɔːt] *n* attaque *f*, assaut *m*.
onto [ˈɔntu] *prep* =**on to**.
onus [ˈəʊnəs] *n* responsabilité *f*.
onward(s) [ˈɔnwəd(z)] *ad* (*move*) en avant.
ooze [uːz] *vi* suinter.
opaque [əʊˈpeɪk] *a* opaque.
OPEC [ˈəʊpɛk] *n abbr* (= *Organization of petroleum exporting countries*) O.P.E.P. *f* (= *Organisation des pays exportateurs de pétrole*).
open [ˈəʊpn] *a* ouvert(e); (*car*) découvert(e); (*road, view*) dégagé(e); (*meeting*) public(ique); (*admiration*) manifeste; (*question*) non résolu(e); (*enemy*) déclaré(e) // *vt* ouvrir // *vi* (*flower, eyes, door, debate*) s'ouvrir; (*shop, bank, museum*) ouvrir; (*book etc: commence*) commencer, débuter; **in the ~** (*air*) en plein air; **to ~ on to** *vt fus* (*subj: room, door*) donner sur; **to ~ up** *vt* ouvrir; (*blocked road*) dégager // *vi* s'ouvrir; **~ing** *n* ouverture *f*; (*opportunity*) occasion *f*; débouché *m*; (*job*) poste vacant; **~ly** *ad* ouvertement; **~-minded** *a* à l'esprit ouvert; **~-plan** *a* sans cloisons.
opera [ˈɔpərə] *n* opéra *m*; ~ **house** *n* opéra *m*.
operate [ˈɔpəreɪt] *vt* (*machine*) faire marcher, faire fonctionner; (*system*) pratiquer // *vi* fonctionner; (*drug*) faire effet; **to ~ on sb (for)** (*MED*) opérer qn (de).
operatic [ɔpəˈrætɪk] *a* d'opéra.
operating [ˈɔpəreɪtɪŋ] *a*: ~ **table/theatre** table *f*/salle *f* d'opération.
operation [ɔpəˈreɪʃən] *n* opération *f*; (*of machine*) fonctionnement *m*; **to be in ~** (*machine*) être en service; (*system*) être

en vigueur; **to have an ~** (*MED*) se faire opérer.

operative ['ɔpərətɪv] *a* (*measure*) en vigueur.

operator ['ɔpəreɪtə*] *n* (*of machine*) opérateur/trice; (*TEL*) téléphoniste *m/f*.

opinion [ə'pɪnɪən] *n* opinion *f*, avis *m*; **in my ~** à mon avis; **~ated** *a* aux idées bien arrêtées; **~ poll** *n* sondage *m* (d'opinion).

opponent [ə'pəunənt] *n* adversaire *m/f*.

opportunist [ɔpə'tjuːnɪst] *n* opportuniste *m/f*.

opportunity [ɔpə'tjuːnɪtɪ] *n* occasion *f*; **to take the ~ of doing** profiter de l'occasion pour faire; **en profiter pour faire**.

oppose [ə'pəuz] *vt* s'opposer à; **~d to** *a* opposé(e) à; **as ~d to** par opposition à; **opposing** *a* (*side*) opposé(e).

opposite ['ɔpəzɪt] *a* opposé(e); (*house etc*) d'en face // *ad* en face // *prep* en face de // *n* opposé *m*, contraire *m*; (*of word*) contraire.

opposition [ɔpə'zɪʃən] *n* opposition *f*.

oppress [ə'prɛs] *vt* opprimer.

opt [ɔpt] *vi*: **to ~ for** opter pour; **to ~ to do** choisir de faire; **to ~ out of** choisir de ne pas participer à *or* de ne pas faire.

optical ['ɔptɪkl] *a* optique; (*instrument*) d'optique; **~ character recognition/reader (OCR)** *n* lecture *f*/lecteur *m* optique.

optician [ɔp'tɪʃən] *n* opticien/ne.

optimist ['ɔptɪmɪst] *n* optimiste *m/f*; **~ic** [-'mɪstɪk] *a* optimiste.

option ['ɔpʃən] *n* choix *m*, option *f*; (*SCOL*) matière *f* à option; (*COMM*) option; **~al** *a* facultatif(ive); (*COMM*) en option.

or [ɔː*] *cj* ou; (*with negative*): **he hasn't seen ~ heard anything** il n'a rien vu ni entendu; **~ else** sinon; ou bien.

oral ['ɔːrəl] *a* oral(e) // *n* oral *m*.

orange ['ɔrɪndʒ] *n* (*fruit*) orange *f* // *a* orange *inv*.

orator ['ɔrətə*] *n* orateur/trice.

orbit ['ɔːbɪt] *n* orbite *f*.

orchard ['ɔːtʃəd] *n* verger *m*.

orchestra ['ɔːkɪstrə] *n* orchestre *m*; (*US: seating*) (fauteuils *mpl* d')orchestre; **orchestral** [-'kɛstrəl] *a* orchestral(e); (*concert*) symphonique.

orchid ['ɔːkɪd] *n* orchidée *f*.

ordain [ɔː'deɪn] *vt* (*REL*) ordonner; (*decide*) décréter.

ordeal [ɔː'diːl] *n* épreuve *f*.

order ['ɔːdə*] *n* ordre *m*; (*COMM*) commande *f* // *vt* ordonner; (*COMM*) commander; **in ~** en ordre; (*of document*) en règle; **in (working) ~** en état de marche; **in ~ of size** par ordre de grandeur; **in ~ to do/that** pour faire/que + *sub*; **on ~** (*COMM*) en commande; **to ~ sb to do** ordonner à qn de faire; **~**

form *n* bon *m* de commande; **~ly** *n* (*MIL*) ordonnance *f* // *a* (*room*) en ordre; (*mind*) méthodique; (*person*) qui a de l'ordre.

ordinary ['ɔːdnrɪ] *a* ordinaire, normal(e); (*pej*) ordinaire, quelconque; **out of the ~** exceptionnel(le).

ordnance ['ɔːdnəns] *n* (*MIL*: *unit*) service *m* du matériel.

ore [ɔː*] *n* minerai *m*.

organ ['ɔːgən] *n* organe *m*; (*MUS*) orgue *m*, orgues *fpl*; **~ic** [ɔː'gænɪk] *a* organique.

organization [ɔːgənaɪ'zeɪʃən] *n* organisation *f*.

organize ['ɔːgənaɪz] *vt* organiser; **~r** *n* organisateur/trice.

orgasm ['ɔːgæzəm] *n* orgasme *m*.

orgy ['ɔːdʒɪ] *n* orgie *f*.

Orient ['ɔːrɪənt] *n*: **the ~** l'Orient *m*; **oriental** [-'ɛntl] *a* oriental(e).

origin ['ɔrɪdʒɪn] *n* origine *f*.

original [ə'rɪdʒɪnl] *a* original(e); (*earliest*) originel(le) // *n* original *m*; **~ly** *ad* (*at first*) à l'origine.

originate [ə'rɪdʒɪneɪt] *vi*: **to ~ from** être originaire de; (*suggestion*) provenir de; **to ~ in** prendre naissance dans; avoir son origine dans.

Orkneys ['ɔːknɪz] *npl*: **the ~** (*also*: **the Orkney Islands**) les Orcades *fpl*.

ornament ['ɔːnəmənt] *n* ornement *m*; (*trinket*) bibelot *m*; **~al** [-'mɛntl] *a* décoratif(ive); (*garden*) d'agrément.

ornate [ɔː'neɪt] *a* très orné(e).

orphan ['ɔːfn] *n* orphelin/e // *vt*: **to be ~ed** devenir orphelin; **~age** *n* orphelinat *m*.

orthopaedic, (*US*) **orthopedic** [ɔːθə'piːdɪk] *a* orthopédique.

ostensibly [ɔs'tɛnsɪblɪ] *ad* en apparence.

ostentatious [ɔstɛn'teɪʃəs] *a* prétentieux(euse); ostentatoire.

ostracize ['ɔstrəsaɪz] *vt* frapper d'ostracisme.

ostrich ['ɔstrɪtʃ] *n* autruche *f*.

other ['ʌðə*] *a* autre // *pronoun*: **the ~ (one)** l'autre; **~s** (*~ people*) d'autres; **~ than** autrement que; à part; **~wise** *ad*, *cj* autrement.

otter ['ɔtə*] *n* loutre *f*.

ouch [autʃ] *excl* aïe!

ought, *pt* ought [ɔːt] *auxiliary vb*: **I ~ to do it** je devrais le faire, il faudrait que je le fasse; **this ~ to have been corrected** cela aurait dû être corrigé; **he ~ to win** il devrait gagner.

ounce [auns] *n* once *f* (= 28.35*g*; 16 *in a pound*).

our ['auə*] *a* notre, nos *pl*; *see also* **my**; **~s** *pronoun* le(la) nôtre, les nôtres; *see also* **mine**; **~selves** *pronoun pl* (*reflexive, after preposition*) nous; (*emphatic*) nous-mêmes; *see also* **oneself**.

oust [aust] *vt* évincer.

out [aut] *ad* dehors; (*published, not at home etc*) sorti(e); (*light, fire*) éteint(e); ~ **here** ici; ~ **there** là-bas; he's ~ (*absent*) il est sorti; (*unconscious*) il est sans connaissance; to be ~ **in** one's calculations s'être trompé dans ses calculs; to **run/back** *etc* ~ sortir en courant/en reculant *etc*; ~ **loud** *ad* à haute voix; ~ **of** (*outside*) en dehors de; (*because of: anger etc*) par; (*from among*): ~ **of** 10 sur 10; (*without*): ~ **of** petrol sans essence, à court d'essence; ~ **of order** (*machine*) en panne; (*TEL: line*) en dérangement; ~**-and-**~ *a* (*liar, thief etc*) véritable.

outback ['autbæk] *n* campagne isolée; (*in Australia*) intérieur *m*.

outboard ['autbɔ:d] *n*: ~ (**motor**) (moteur *m*) hors-bord *m*.

outbreak ['autbreik] *n* accès *m*; début *m*; éruption *f*.

outburst ['autbə:st] *n* explosion *f*, accès *m*.

outcast ['autkɑ:st] *n* exilé/e; (*socially*) paria *m*.

outcome ['autkʌm] *n* issue *f*, résultat *m*.

outcrop ['autkrɔp] *n* (*of rock*) affleurement *m*.

outcry ['autkrai] *n* tollé (général).

outdated [aut'deitid] *a* démodé(e).

outdo [aut'du:] *vt irg* surpasser.

outdoor [aut'dɔ:*] *a* de *or* en plein air; ~**s** *ad* dehors; au grand air.

outer ['autə*] *a* extérieur(e); ~ **space** *n* espace *m* cosmique.

outfit ['autfit] *n* équipement *m*; (*clothes*) tenue *f*; '~**ter's** (*Brit*) 'confection pour hommes'.

outgoing ['autgəuiŋ] *a* (*character*) ouvert(e), extraverti(e); ~**s** *npl* (*Brit: expenses*) dépenses *fpl*.

outgrow [aut'grəu] *vt irg* (*clothes*) devenir trop grand(e) pour.

outhouse ['authaus] *n* appentis *m*, remise *f*.

outing ['autiŋ] *n* sortie *f*; excursion *f*.

outlandish [aut'lændiʃ] *a* étrange.

outlaw ['autlɔ:] *n* hors-la-loi *m inv*.

outlay ['autlei] *n* dépenses *fpl*; (*investment*) mise *f* de fonds.

outlet ['autlet] *n* (*for liquid etc*) issue *f*, sortie *f*; (*US: ELEC*) prise *f* de courant; (*for emotion*) exutoire *m*; (*for goods*) débouché *m*; (*also: retail* ~) point *m* de vente.

outline ['autlain] *n* (*shape*) contour *m*; (*summary*) esquisse *f*, grandes lignes.

outlive [aut'liv] *vt* survivre à.

outlook ['autluk] *n* perspective *f*.

outlying ['autlaiiŋ] *a* écarté(e).

outmoded [aut'məudid] *a* démodé(e); dépassé(e).

outnumber [aut'nʌmbə*] *vt* surpasser en nombre.

out-of-date ['autəv'deit] *a* (*passport*) périmé(e); (*theory etc*) dépassé(e); (*custom*) désuet(ète); (*clothes etc*) démodé(e).

out-of-the-way ['autəvðə'wei] *a* (*place*) loin de tout.

outpatient ['autpeiʃənt] *n* malade *m/f* en consultation externe.

outpost ['autpəust] *n* avant-poste *m*.

output ['autput] *n* rendement *m*, production *f*; (*COMPUT*) sortie *f*.

outrage ['autreidʒ] *n* atrocité *f*, acte *m* de violence; scandale *m* // *vt* outrager; ~**ous** [-'reidʒəs] *a* atroce; scandaleux(euse).

outright *ad* [aut'rait] complètement; catégoriquement; carrément; sur le coup // *a* ['autrait] complet(ète); catégorique.

outset ['autset] *n* début *m*.

outside [aut'said] *n* extérieur *m* // *a* ['autsaid] *ad* (au) dehors, à l'extérieur // *prep* hors de, à l'extérieur de; **at the** ~ (*fig*) au plus *or* maximum; ~ **lane** *n* (*AUT: in Britain*) voie *f* de droite; ~**-left/-right** *n* (*FOOTBALL*) ailier gauche/droit; ~ **line** *n* (*TEL*) ligne extérieure; ~**r** *n* (*in race etc*) outsider *m*; (*stranger*) étranger/ère.

outsize ['autsaiz] *a* énorme; (*clothes*) grande taille *inv*.

outskirts ['autskə:ts] *npl* faubourgs *mpl*.

outspoken [aut'spəukən] *a* très franc(franche).

outstanding [aut'stændiŋ] *a* remarquable, exceptionnel(le); (*unfinished*) en suspens; en souffrance; non réglé(e).

outstay [aut'stei] *vt*: **to** ~ **one's welcome** abuser de l'hospitalité de son hôte.

outstretched [aut'stretʃt] *a* (*hand*) tendu(e); (*body*) étendu(e).

outstrip [aut'strip] *vt* (*competitors, demand*) dépasser.

out-tray ['auttrei] *n* courrier *m* 'départ'.

outward ['autwəd] *a* (*sign, appearances*) extérieur(e); (*journey*) (d')aller; ~**ly** *ad* extérieurement; en apparence.

outweigh [aut'wei] *vt* l'emporter sur.

outwit [aut'wit] *vt* se montrer plus malin que.

oval ['əuvl] *a, n* ovale (*m*).

ovary ['əuvəri] *n* ovaire *m*.

oven ['ʌvn] *n* four *m*; ~**proof** *a* allant au four.

over ['əuvə*] *ad* (par-)dessus // *a* (*or ad*) (*finished*) fini(e), terminé(e); (*too much*) en plus // *prep* sur; par-dessus; (*above*) au-dessus de; (*on the other side of*) de l'autre côté de; (*more than*) plus de; (*during*) pendant; ~ **here** ici; ~ **there** là-bas; **all** ~ (*everywhere*) partout; (*finished*) fini(e); ~ **and** ~ (*again*) à plusieurs reprises; ~ **and above** en plus de; **to ask sb** ~ inviter qn (à passer).

overall *a n,* [ˈəuvərɔ:l] *a (length)* total(e); *(study)* d'ensemble // *n (Brit)* blouse *f* // *ad* [əuvərˈɔ:l] dans l'ensemble, en général; **~s** *npl* bleus *mpl* (de travail).

overawe [əuvərˈɔ:] *vt* impressionner.

overbalance [əuvəˈbæləns] *vi* basculer.

overbearing [əuvəˈbɛərɪŋ] *a* impérieux(euse), autoritaire.

overboard [ˈəuvəbɔ:d] *ad (NAUT)* par-dessus bord.

overbook [əuvəˈbuk] *vt* faire du surbooking.

overcast [ˈəuvəka:st] *a* couvert(e).

overcharge [əuvəˈtʃa:dʒ] *vt:* to ~ sb for sth faire payer qch trop cher à qn.

overcoat [ˈəuvəkəut] *n* pardessus *m.*

overcome [əuvəˈkʌm] *vt irg* triompher de; surmonter; ~ with grief accablé(e) de douleur.

overcrowded [əuvəˈkraudɪd] *a* bondé(e).

overdo [əuvəˈdu:] *vt irg* exagérer; *(overcook)* trop cuire.

overdose [ˈəuvədəus] *n* dose excessive.

overdraft [ˈəuvədra:ft] *n* découvert *m.*

overdrawn [əuvəˈdrɔ:n] *a (account)* à découvert.

overdue [əuvəˈdju:] *a* en retard; *(recognition)* tardif(ive).

overflow [əuvəˈfləu] *vi* déborder // *n* [ˈəuvəfləu] trop-plein *m; (also:* ~ pipe) tuyau *m* d'écoulement, trop-plein *m.*

overgrown [əuvəˈgrəun] *a (garden)* envahi(e) par la végétation.

overhaul *vt* [əuvəˈhɔ:l] réviser // *n* [ˈəuvəhɔ:l] révision *f.*

overhead *ad* [əuvəˈhed] au-dessus // *a, n* [ˈəuvəhed] *a* aérien(ne); *(lighting)* vertical(e) // *n (US)* = ~s; **~s** *npl* frais généraux.

overhear [əuvəˈhɪə*] *vt irg* entendre (par hasard).

overheat [əuvəˈhi:t] *vi (engine)* chauffer.

overjoyed [əuvəˈdʒɔɪd] *a* ravi(e), enchanté(e).

overkill [ˈəuvəkɪl] *n:* that would be ~ ce serait trop.

overlap [əuvəˈlæp] *vi* se chevaucher.

overleaf [əuvəˈli:f] *ad* au verso.

overload [əuvəˈləud] *vt* surcharger.

overlook [əuvəˈluk] *vt (have view of)* donner sur; *(miss)* oublier, négliger; *(forgive)* fermer les yeux sur.

overnight *ad* [əuvəˈnaɪt] *(happen)* durant la nuit; *(fig)* soudain // *a* [ˈəuvənaɪt] d'une *(or* de) nuit; soudain(e); he stayed there ~ il y a passé la nuit.

overpower [əuvəˈpauə*] *vt* vaincre; *(fig)* accabler; **~ing** *a* irrésistible; *(heat, stench)* suffocant(e).

overrate [əuvəˈreɪt] *vt* surestimer.

override [əuvəˈraɪd] *vt (irg: like ride)*

(order, objection) passer outre à; *(decision)* annuler; **overriding** *a* prépondérant(e).

overrule [əuvəˈru:l] *vt (decision)* annuler; *(claim)* rejeter.

overrun [əuvəˈrʌn] *vt (irg: like run)* *(country)* occuper; *(time limit)* dépasser.

overseas [əuvəˈsi:z] *ad* outre-mer; *(abroad)* à l'étranger // *a (trade)* extérieur(e); *(visitor)* étranger(ère).

overseer [ˈəuvəsɪə*] *n (in factory)* contremaître *m.*

overshadow [əuvəˈʃædəu] *vt (fig)* éclipser.

overshoot [əuvəˈʃu:t] *vt irg* dépasser.

oversight [ˈəuvəsaɪt] *n* omission *f,* oubli *m.*

oversleep [əuvəˈsli:p] *vi irg* se réveiller (trop) tard.

overstep [əuvəˈstep] *vt:* to ~ the mark dépasser la mesure.

overt [əuˈvə:t] *a* non dissimulé(e).

overtake [əuvəˈteɪk] *vt irg* dépasser; *(AUT)* dépasser, doubler.

overthrow [əuvəˈθrəu] *vt irg (government)* renverser.

overtime [ˈəuvətaɪm] *n* heures *fpl* supplémentaires.

overtone [ˈəuvətəun] *n (also:* ~s) note *f,* sous-entendus *mpl.*

overture [ˈəuvətʃuə*] *n (MUS, fig)* ouverture *f.*

overturn [əuvəˈtə:n] *vt* renverser // *vi* se retourner.

overweight [əuvəˈweɪt] *a (person)* trop gros(se); *(luggage)* trop lourd(e).

overwhelm [əuvəˈwelm] *vt* accabler; submerger; écraser; **~ing** *a (victory, defeat)* écrasant(e); *(desire)* irrésistible.

overwork [əuvəˈwə:k] *n* surmenage *m.*

overwrought [əuvəˈrɔ:t] *a* excédé(e).

owe [əu] *vt* devoir; to ~ sb sth, to ~ sth to sb devoir qch à qn.

owing to [ˈəuɪŋtu:] *prep* à cause de, en raison de.

owl [aul] *n* hibou *m.*

own [əun] *vt* posséder // *a* propre; a room of my ~ une chambre à moi, ma propre chambre; to get one's ~ back prendre sa revanche; on one's ~ tout(e) seul(e); to ~ up *vi* avouer; **~er** *n* propriétaire *m/f;* **~ership** *n* possession *f.*

ox, *pl* **oxen** [ɔks, ˈɔksn] *n* bœuf *m.*

oxtail [ˈɔksteɪl] *n:* ~ soup soupe *f* à la queue de bœuf.

oxygen [ˈɔksɪdʒən] *n* oxygène *m;* ~ mask *n* masque *m* à oxygène.

oyster [ˈɔɪstə*] *n* huître *f.*

oz. *abbr* of **ounce(s).**

P

p [pi:] *abbr of* **penny, pence.**

pa [pɑ:] *n* (*col*) papa *m*.

P.A. *n abbr of* **personal assistant, public address system.**

p.a. *abbr of* **per annum.**

pace [peɪs] *n* pas *m*; (*speed*) allure *f*; vitesse *f* // *vi*: **to ~ up and down** faire les cent pas; **to keep ~ with** aller à la même vitesse que; (*events*) se tenir au courant de; **~maker** *n* (*MED*) stimulateur *m* cardiaque.

pacific [pə'sɪfɪk] *a* pacifique // *n*: **the P~ (Ocean)** le Pacifique, l'océan *m* Pacifique.

pack [pæk] *n* paquet *m*; ballot *m*; (*of hounds*) meute *f*; (*of thieves etc*) bande *f*; (*of cards*) jeu *m* // *vt* (*goods*) empaqueter, emballer; (*in suitcase etc*) emballer; (*box*) remplir; (*cram*) entasser; (*press down*) tasser; damer; **to ~ (one's bags)** faire ses bagages; **to ~ off** *vt* (*person*) envoyer (promener), expédier.

package ['pækɪdʒ] *n* paquet *m*; ballot *m*; (*also*: **~ deal**) marché global; forfait *m*; **~ tour** *n* voyage organisé.

packed lunch *n* repas froid.

packet ['pækɪt] *n* paquet *m*.

packing ['pækɪŋ] *n* emballage *m*; **~ case** *n* caisse *f* (d'emballage).

pact [pækt] *n* pacte *m*; traité *m*.

pad [pæd] *n* bloc(-notes) *m*; (*for inking*) tampon *m* encreur; (*col*: *flat*) piaule *f* // *vt* rembourrer; **~ding** *n* rembourrage *m*.

paddle ['pædl] *n* (*oar*) pagaie *f*; (*US*: *for table tennis*) raquette *f* de ping-pong // *vi* barboter, faire trempette // *vt*: **to ~ a canoe** *etc* pagayer; **~ steamer** *n* bateau *m* à aubes; **paddling pool** *n* (*Brit*) petit bassin.

paddy ['pædɪ] *n*: **~ field** *n* rizière *f*.

padlock ['pædlɔk] *n* cadenas *m*.

paediatrics, (*US*) **pediatrics** [pi:dɪ'ætrɪks] *n* pédiatrie *f*.

pagan ['peɪgən] *a, n* païen(ne).

page [peɪdʒ] *n* (*of book*) page *f*; (*also*: **~ boy**) groom *m*, chasseur *m*; (*at wedding*) garçon *m* d'honneur // *vt* (*in hotel etc*) (faire) appeler.

pageant ['pædʒənt] *n* spectacle *m* historique; grande cérémonie; **~ry** *n* apparat *m*, pompe *f*.

paid [peɪd] *pt, pp of* **pay** // *a* (*work, official*) rémunéré(e); **to put ~ to** (*Brit*) mettre fin à, régler.

pail [peɪl] *n* seau *m*.

pain [peɪn] *n* douleur *f*; **to be in ~** souffrir, avoir mal; **to take ~s to do** se donner du mal pour faire; **~ed** *a* peiné(e), chagrin(e); **~ful** *a* douloureux(euse); difficile, pénible; **~fully** *ad* (*fig*: *very*) terriblement; **~killer** *n* calmant *m*; **~less** *a* indolore.

painstaking ['peɪnzteɪkɪŋ] *a* (*person*) soigneux(euse); (*work*) soigné(e).

paint [peɪnt] *n* peinture *f* // *vt* peindre; (*fig*) dépeindre; **to ~ the door blue** peindre la porte en bleu; **~brush** *n* pinceau *m*; **~er** *n* peintre *m*; **~ing** *n* peinture *f*; (*picture*) tableau *m*; **~work** *n* peintures *fpl*; (*of car*) peinture *f*.

pair [pɛə*] *n* (*of shoes, gloves etc*) paire *f*; (*of people*) couple *m*; duo *m*; paire; **~ of scissors** (paire de) ciseaux *mpl*; **~ of trousers** pantalon *m*.

pajamas [pɪ'dʒɑ:məz] *npl* (*US*) pyjama(s) *m(pl)*.

Pakistan [pɑ:kɪ'stɑ:n] *n* Pakistan *m*; **~i** *a* pakistanais(e) // *n* Pakistanais/e.

pal [pæl] *n* (*col*) copain/copine.

palace ['pæləs] *n* palais *m*.

palatable ['pælɪtəbl] *a* bon(bonne), agréable au goût.

palate ['pælɪt] *n* palais *m* (*ANAT*).

palatial [pə'leɪʃəl] *a* grandiose, magnifique.

palaver [pə'lɑ:və*] *n* palabres *fpl* or *mpl*; histoire(s) *f(pl)*.

pale [peɪl] *a* pâle; **to grow ~** pâlir // *n*: **beyond the ~** au ban de la société.

Palestine ['pælɪstaɪn] *n* Palestine *f*; **Palestinian** [-'tɪnɪən] *a* palestinien(ne) // *n* Palestinien/ne.

palette ['pælɪt] *n* palette *f*.

paling ['peɪlɪŋ] *n* (*stake*) palis *m*; (*fence*) palissade *f*.

pall [pɔ:l] *n* (*of smoke*) voile *m* // *vi*: **to ~ (on)** devenir lassant (pour).

pallet ['pælɪt] *n* (*for goods*) palette *f*.

pallid ['pælɪd] *a* blême.

pallor ['pælə*] *n* pâleur *f*.

palm [pɑ:m] *n* (*ANAT*) paume *f*; (*also*: **~ tree**) palmier *m*; (*leaf, symbol*) palme *f* // *vt*: **to ~ sth off on sb** (*col*) refiler qch à qn; **P~ Sunday** le dimanche des Rameaux.

palpable ['pælpəbl] *a* évident(e), manifeste.

paltry ['pɔ:ltrɪ] *a* dérisoire; piètre.

pamper ['pæmpə*] *vt* gâter, dorloter.

pamphlet ['pæmflət] *n* brochure *f*.

pan [pæn] *n* (*also*: **sauce~**) casserole *f*; (*also*: **frying ~**) poêle *f*; (*of lavatory*) cuvette *f* // *vi* (*CINEMA*) faire un panoramique.

pancake ['pænkeɪk] *n* crêpe *f*.

panda ['pændə] *n* panda *m*; **~ car** *n* (*Brit*) ≈ voiture *f* pie *inv*.

pandemonium [pændɪ'məunɪəm] *n* tohu-bohu *m*.

pander ['pændə*] *vi*: **to ~ to** flatter bassement; obéir servilement à.

pane [peɪn] *n* carreau *m* (de fenêtre).

panel ['pænl] *n* (*of wood, cloth etc*) panneau *m*; (*RADIO, TV*) panel *m*;

invités *mpl*, experts *mpl*; **~ling**, (*US*) **~ing** *n* boiseries *fpl*.

pang [pæŋ] *n*: **~s of remorse** pincements *mpl* de remords; **~s of hunger/ conscience** tiraillements *mpl* d'estomac/de la conscience.

panic ['pænɪk] *n* panique *f*, affolement *m* // *vi* s'affoler, paniquer; **~ky** *a* (*person*) qui panique *or* s'affole facilement; **~-stricken** *a* affolé(e).

pansy ['pænzɪ] *n* (*BOT*) pensée *f*; (*col*) tapette *f*, pédé *m*.

pant [pænt] *vi* haleter.

panther ['pænθə*] *n* panthère *f*.

panties ['pæntɪz] *npl* slip *m*, culotte *f*.

pantihose ['pæntɪhəuz] *n* (*US*) collant *m*.

pantomime ['pæntəmaɪm] *n* (*Brit*) spectacle *m* de Noël.

pantry ['pæntrɪ] *n* garde-manger *m inv*; (*room*) office *f or m*.

pants [pænts] *n* (*Brit*: *woman's*) culotte *f*, slip *m*; (: *man's*) slip *m*, caleçon *m*; (*US*: *trousers*) pantalon *m*.

paper ['peɪpə*] *n* papier *m*; (*also*: **wall~**) papier peint; (*also*: **news~**) journal *m*; (*study*, *article*) article *m*; (*exam*) épreuve écrite // *a* en *or* de papier // *vt* tapisser (de papier peint); **~s** *npl* (*also*: **identity ~s**) papiers (d'identité); **~back** *n* livre *m* de poche; livre broché *or* non relié; **~ clip** *n* trombone *m*; **~ hankie** *n* mouchoir *m* en papier; **~weight** *n* presse-papiers *m inv*; **~work** *n* paperasserie *f*.

par [pɑ:*] *n* pair *m*; (*GOLF*) normale *f* du parcours; **on a ~ with** à égalité avec, au même niveau que.

parable ['pærəbl] *n* parabole *f* (*REL*).

parachute ['pærəʃu:t] *n* parachute *m*.

parade [pə'reɪd] *n* défilé m; (*inspection*) revue *f*; (*street*) boulevard *m* // *vt* (*fig*) faire étalage de // *vi* défiler.

paradise ['pærədaɪs] *n* paradis *m*.

paradox ['pærədɔks] *n* paradoxe *m*; **~ically** [-'dɔksɪklɪ] *ad* paradoxalement.

paraffin ['pærəfɪn] *n* (*Brit*): **~ (oil)** pétrole (lampant).

paragraph ['pærəgrɑ:f] *n* paragraphe *m*.

parallel ['pærəlɛl] *a* parallèle; (*fig*) analogue // *n* (*line*) parallèle *f*; (*fig*, *GEO*) parallèle *m*.

paralysis [pə'rælɪsɪs] *n* paralysie *f*.

paralyze ['pærəlaɪz] *vt* paralyser.

paramount ['pærəmaunt] *a*: **of ~ importance** de la plus haute *or* grande importance.

paranoid ['pærənɔɪd] *a* (*PSYCH*) paranoïaque; (*neurotic*) paranoïde.

paraphernalia [pærəfə'neɪlɪə] *n* attirail *m*, affaires *fpl*.

parasol ['pærə'sɔl] *n* ombrelle *f*; parasol *m*.

paratrooper ['pærətru:pə*] *n* parachutiste *m* (*soldat*).

parcel ['pɑ:sl] *n* paquet *m*, colis *m* // *vt* (*also*: **~ up**) empaqueter.

parch [pɑ:tʃ] *vt* dessécher; **~ed** *a* (*person*) assoiffé(e).

parchment ['pɑ:tʃmənt] *n* parchemin *m*.

pardon ['pɑ:dn] *n* pardon *m*; grâce *f* // *vt* pardonner à; (*LAW*) gracier; **~ me!** excusez-moi!; **I beg your ~!** pardon!, je suis désolé!; (**I beg your**) **~?**, (*US*) **~ me?** pardon?

parent ['pɛərənt] *n* père *m or* mère *f*; **~s** *npl* parents *mpl*.

Paris ['pærɪs] *n* Paris.

parish ['pærɪʃ] *n* paroisse *f*; (*civil*) ≈ commune *f* // *a* paroissial(e).

Parisian [pə'rɪzɪən] *a* parisien(ne) // *n* Parisien/ne.

park [pɑ:k] *n* parc *m*, jardin public // *vt* garer // *vi* se garer.

parking ['pɑ:kɪŋ] *n* stationnement *m*; **'no ~'** 'stationnement interdit'; **~ lot** *n* (*US*) parking *m*, parc *m* de stationnement; **~ meter** *n* parcomètre *m*; **~ ticket** *n* P.V. *m*.

parlance ['pɑ:lns] *n* langage *m*.

parliament ['pɑ:ləmənt] *n* parlement *m*; **~ary** [-'mɛntrɪ] parlementaire.

parlour, (*US*) **parlor** ['pɑ:lə*] *n* salon *m*.

parochial [pə'rəukɪəl] *a* paroissial(e); (*pej*) à l'esprit de clocher.

parody ['pærədɪ] *n* parodie *f*.

parole [pə'rəul] *n*: **on ~** en liberté conditionnelle.

parrot ['pærət] *n* perroquet *m*.

parry ['pærɪ] *vt* esquiver, parer à.

parsley ['pɑ:slɪ] *n* persil *m*.

parsnip ['pɑ:snɪp] *n* panais *m*.

parson ['pɑ:sn] *n* ecclésiastique *m*; (*Church of England*) pasteur *m*.

part [pɑ:t] *n* partie *f*; (*of machine*) pièce *f*; (*THEATRE etc*) rôle *m*; (*MUS*) voix *f*; partie; (*US*: *in hair*) raie *f* // *a* partiel(le) // *ad* = **partly** // *vt* séparer // *vi* (*people*) se séparer; (*roads*) se diviser; **to take ~ in** participer à, prendre part à; **for my ~** en ce qui me concerne; **to take sth in good ~** prendre qch du bon côté; **to take sb's ~** prendre le parti de qn, prendre parti pour qn; **for the most ~** en grande partie; dans la plupart des cas; **to ~ with** *vt fus* se séparer de; se défaire de; **~ exchange** *n* (*Brit*): **in ~ exchange** en reprise.

partial ['pɑ:ʃl] *a* partiel(le); (*unjust*) partial(e); **to be ~ to** aimer, avoir un faible pour.

participate [pɑ:'tɪsɪpeɪt] *vi*: **to ~ (in)** participer (à), prendre part (à); **participation** [-'peɪʃən] *n* participation *f*.

participle ['pɑ:tɪsɪpl] *n* participe *m*.

particle ['pɑ:tɪkl] *n* particule *f*.

particular [pə'tɪkjulə*] *a* particulier(ère); spécial(e); (*detailed*) détaillé(e); (*fussy*) difficile; méticuleux(euse); **~s** *npl* détails *mpl*; (*information*) renseignements *mpl*; **in ~** ad surtout, en particulier; **~ly** ad particulièrement; en particulier.

parting ['pɑ:tɪŋ] *n* séparation *f*; (*Brit: in hair*) raie *f* // *a* d'adieu.

partisan [pɑ:tɪ'zæn] *n* partisan/e // *a* partisan(e); de parti.

partition [pɑ:'tɪʃən] *n* (*POL*) partition *f*, division *f*; (*wall*) cloison *f*.

partly ['pɑ:tlɪ] *ad* en partie, partiellement.

partner ['pɑ:tnə*] *n* (*COMM*) associé/e; (*SPORT*) partenaire *m/f*; (*at dance*) cavalier/ère; **~ship** *n* association *f*.

partridge ['pɑ:trɪdʒ] *n* perdrix *f*.

part-time ['pɑ:t'taɪm] *a, ad* à mi-temps, à temps partiel.

party ['pɑ:tɪ] *n* (*POL*) parti *m*; (*team*) équipe *f*; groupe *m*; (*LAW*) partie *f*; (*celebration*) réception *f*; soirée *f*; fête *f* // *a* (*POL*) de *or* du parti; de partis; **~ dress** *n* robe habillée; **~ line** *n* (*TEL*) ligne partagée.

pass [pɑ:s] *vt* (*time, object*) passer; (*place*) passer devant; (*car, friend*) croiser; (*exam*) être reçu(e) à, réussir; (*candidate*) admettre; (*overtake, surpass*) dépasser; (*approve*) approuver, accepter // *vi* passer; (*SCOL*) être reçu(e) *or* admis(e), réussir // *n* (*permit*) laissez-passer *m inv*; carte *f* d'accès *or* d'abonnement; (*in mountains*) col *m*; (*SPORT*) passe *f*; (*SCOL: also*: ~ **mark**): **to get a ~** être reçu(e) (sans mention); **to ~ sth through a ring** *etc* (faire) passer qch dans un anneau *etc*; **to make a ~ at sb** (*col*) faire des avances à qn; **to ~ away** *vi* mourir; **to ~ by** *vi* passer // *vt* négliger; **to ~ on** *vt* (*news, object*) transmettre; (*illness*) passer; **to ~ out** *vi* s'évanouir; **to ~ up** *vt* (*opportunity*) laisser passer; **~able** *a* (*road*) praticable; (*work*) acceptable.

passage ['pæsɪdʒ] *n* (*also*: ~**way**) couloir *m*; (*gen, in book*) passage *m*; (*by boat*) traversée *f*.

passbook ['pɑ:sbuk] *n* livret *m*.

passenger ['pæsɪndʒə*] *n* passager/ère.

passer-by [pɑ:sə'baɪ] *n* passant/e.

passing ['pɑ:sɪŋ] *a* (*fig*) passager(ère); **in ~** en passant; **~ place** *n* (*AUT*) aire *f* de croisement.

passion ['pæʃən] *n* passion *f*; amour *m*; **~ate** *a* passionné(e).

passive ['pæsɪv] *a* (*also* LING) passif(ive).

Passover ['pɑ:səuvə*] *n* Pâque (*juive*).

passport ['pɑ:spɔ:t] *n* passeport *m*; **~ control** *n* contrôle *m* des passeports.

password ['pɑ:swə:d] *n* mot *m* de passe.

past [pɑ:st] *prep* (*further than*) au delà de, plus loin que; après; (*later than*) après // *a* passé(e); (*president etc*) ancien(ne) // *n* passé *m*; **he's ~ forty** il a dépassé la quarantaine, il a plus de *or* passé quarante ans; **for the ~ few/3 days** depuis quelques/3 jours; ces derniers/3 derniers jours; **he ran ~ me** il m'a dépassé en courant; il a passé devant moi en courant.

pasta ['pæstə] *n* pâtes *fpl*.

paste [peɪst] *n* (*glue*) colle *f* (de pâte); (*jewellery*) strass *m*; (*CULIN*) pâté *m* (à tartiner); pâte *f* // *vt* coller.

pasteurized ['pæstəraɪzd] *a* pasteurisé(e).

pastille ['pæstl] *n* pastille *f*.

pastime ['pɑ:staɪm] *n* passe-temps *m inv*, distraction *f*.

pastor ['pɑ:stə*] *n* pasteur *m*.

pastry ['peɪstrɪ] *n* pâte *f*; (*cake*) pâtisserie *f*.

pasture ['pɑ:stʃə*] *n* pâturage *m*.

pasty *n* ['pæstɪ] petit pâté (en croûte) // *a* ['peɪstɪ] pâteux(euse); (*complexion*) terreux(euse).

pat [pæt] *vt* donner une petite tape à.

patch [pætʃ] *n* (*of material*) pièce *f*; (*spot*) tache *f*; (*of land*) parcelle *f* // *vt* (*clothes*) rapiécer; (*to go through*) **a bad ~** (passer par) une période difficile; **to ~ up** *vt* réparer; **~y** *a* inégal(e).

pâté ['pæteɪ] *n* pâté *m*, terrine *f*.

patent ['peɪtnt] *n* brevet *m* (d'invention) // *vt* faire breveter // *a* patent(e), manifeste; **~ leather** *n* cuir verni.

paternal [pə'tə:nl] *a* paternel(le).

path [pɑ:θ] *n* chemin *m*, sentier *m*; allée *f*; (*of planet*) course *f*; (*of missile*) trajectoire *f*.

pathetic [pə'θetɪk] *a* (*pitiful*) pitoyable; (*very bad*) lamentable, minable; (*moving*) pathétique.

pathological [pæθə'lɔdʒɪkl] *a* pathologique.

pathos ['peɪθɔs] *n* pathétique *m*.

patience ['peɪʃns] *n* patience *f*; (*Brit: CARDS*) réussite *f*.

patient ['peɪʃnt] *n* patient/e; malade *m/f* // *a* patient(e).

patriotic [pætrɪ'ɔtɪk] *a* patriotique; (*person*) patriote.

patrol [pə'trəul] *n* patrouille *f* // *vt* patrouiller dans; **~ car** *n* voiture *f* de police; **~man** *n* (*US*) agent *m* de police.

patron ['peɪtrən] *n* (*in shop*) client/e; (*of charity*) patron/ne; **~ of the arts** mécène *m*; **~ize** ['pætrənaɪz] *vt* être (un) client *or* un habitué de; (*fig*) traiter avec condescendance.

patter ['pætə*] *n* crépitement *m*, tapotement *m*; (*sales talk*) boniment *m*.

pattern ['pætən] *n* modèle *m*; (*SEWING*) patron *m*; (*design*) motif *m*; (*sample*) échantillon *m*.

paunch [pɔ:ntʃ] *n* gros ventre, bedaine

f.

pauper ['pɔːpə*] *n* indigent/e.

pause [pɔːz] *n* pause *f*, arrêt *m*; (MUS) silence *m* // *vi* faire une pause, s'arrêter.

pave [peɪv] *vt* paver, daller; **to ~ the way for** ouvrir la voie à.

pavement ['peɪvmənt] *n* (*Brit*) trottoir *m*.

pavilion [pə'vɪlɪən] *n* pavillon *m*; tente *f*.

paving ['peɪvɪŋ] *n* pavage *m*, dallage *m*; **~ stone** *n* pavé *m*.

paw [pɔː] *n* patte *f*.

pawn [pɔːn] *n* gage *m*; (CHESS, *also fig*) pion *m* // *vt* mettre en gage; **~broker** *n* prêteur *m* sur gages; **~shop** *n* mont-de-piété *m*.

pay [peɪ] *n* salaire *m*; paie *f* // *vb* (*pt, pp* **paid**) *vt* payer // *vi* payer; (*be profitable*) être rentable; **to ~ attention (to)** prêter attention (à); **to ~ back** *vt* rembourser; **to ~ for** *vt* payer; **to ~ in** *vt* verser; **to ~ off** *vt* régler, acquitter; rembourser // *vi* (*scheme, decision*) se révéler payant(e); **to ~ up** *vt* régler; **~able** *a*: **~able to sb** à l'ordre de qn; **~ee** *n* bénéficiaire *m/f*; **~ envelope** *n* (US) = **~ packet**; **~ment** *n* paiement *m*; règlement *m*; versement *m*; **advance ~ment** acompte *m*; paiement anticipé; **monthly ~ment** mensualité *f*; **~ packet** *n* (*Brit*) paie *f*; **~phone** *n* cabine *f* téléphonique, téléphone public; **~roll** *n* registre *m* du personnel; **~ slip** *n* bulletin *m* de paie.

PC *n abbr of* **personal computer**.

p.c. *abbr of* **per cent**.

pea [piː] *n* (petit) pois.

peace [piːs] *n* paix *f*; (*calm*) calme *m*, tranquillité *f*; **~able** *a* paisible; **~ful** *a* paisible, calme.

peach [piːtʃ] *n* pêche *f*.

peacock ['piːkɔk] *n* paon *m*.

peak [piːk] *n* (*mountain*) pic *m*, cime *f*; (*fig: highest level*) maximum *m*; (: *of career, fame*) apogée *m*; **~ hours** *npl* heures *fpl* d'affluence.

peal [piːl] *n* (*of bells*) carillon *m*; **~s of laughter** éclats *mpl* de rire.

peanut ['piːnʌt] *n* arachide *f*, cacahuète *f*.

pear [pɛə*] *n* poire *f*.

pearl [pɜːl] *n* perle *f*.

peasant ['pɛznt] *n* paysan/ne.

peat [piːt] *n* tourbe *f*.

pebble ['pɛbl] *n* galet *m*, caillou *m*.

peck [pɛk] *vt* (*also*: **~ at**) donner un coup de bec à; (*food*) picorer // *n* coup *m* de bec; (*kiss*) bécot *m*; **~ing order** *n* ordre *m* des préséances; **~ish** *a* (*Brit col*): **I feel ~ish** je mangerais bien quelque chose.

peculiar [pɪ'kjuːlɪə*] *a* étrange, bizarre, curieux(euse); particulier(ère); **~ to**

particulier à.

pedal ['pɛdl] *n* pédale *f* // *vi* pédaler.

pedantic [pɪ'dæntɪk] *a* pédant(e).

peddler ['pɛdlə*] *n* marchand ambulant.

pedestal ['pɛdəstl] *n* piédestal *m*.

pedestrian [pɪ'dɛstrɪən] *n* piéton *m*; **~ crossing** *n* (*Brit*) passage clouté.

pediatrics [piːdɪ'ætrɪks] *n* (US) = **paediatrics**.

pedigree ['pɛdɪgriː] *n* ascendance *f*; (*of animal*) pedigree *m* // *cpd* (*animal*) de race.

pedlar ['pɛdlə*] *n* = **peddler**.

pee [piː] *vi* (*col*) faire pipi, pisser.

peek [piːk] *vi* jeter un coup d'œil (furtif).

peel [piːl] *n* pelure *f*, épluchure *f*; (*of orange, lemon*) écorce *f* // *vt* peler, éplucher // *vi* (*paint etc*) s'écailler; (*wallpaper*) se décoller.

peep [piːp] *n* (*Brit: look*) coup d'œil furtif; (*sound*) pépiement *m* // *vi* (*Brit*) jeter un coup d'œil (furtif); **to ~ out** *vi* se montrer (furtivement); **~hole** *n* judas *m*.

peer [pɪə*] *vi*: **to ~ at** regarder attentivement, scruter // *n* (*noble*) pair *m*; (*equal*) pair, égal/e; **~age** *n* pairie *f*.

peeved [piːvd] *a* irrité(e), ennuyé(e).

peevish ['piːvɪʃ] *a* grincheux(euse), maussade.

peg [pɛg] *n* cheville *f*; (*for coat etc*) patère *f*; (*Brit: also*: **clothes ~**) pince *f* à linge // *vt* (*prices*) contrôler, stabiliser.

Peking [piː'kɪŋ] *n* Pékin.

pelican crossing ['pɛlɪkən-] *n* (*Brit AUT*) feu *m* à commande manuelle.

pellet ['pɛlɪt] *n* boulette *f*; (*of lead*) plomb *m*.

pelmet ['pɛlmɪt] *n* cantonnière *f*; lambrequin *m*.

pelt [pɛlt] *vt*: **to ~ sb (with)** bombarder qn (de) // *vi* (*rain*) tomber à seaux // *n* peau *f*.

pelvis ['pɛlvɪs] *n* bassin *m*.

pen [pɛn] *n* (*for writing*) stylo *m*; (*for sheep*) parc *m*.

penal ['piːnl] *a* pénal(e); **~ize** *vt* pénaliser; (*fig*) désavantager.

penalty ['pɛnltɪ] *n* pénalité *f*; sanction *f*; (*fine*) amende *f*; (SPORT) pénalisation *f*; **~ (kick)** *n* (FOOTBALL) penalty *m*.

penance ['pɛnəns] *n* pénitence *f*.

pence [pɛns] *npl of* **penny**.

pencil ['pɛnsl] *n* crayon *m*; **~ case** *n* trousse *f* (d'écolier); **~ sharpener** *n* taille-crayon(s) *m inv*.

pendant ['pɛndnt] *n* pendentif *m*.

pending ['pɛndɪŋ] *prep* en attendant // *a* en suspens.

pendulum ['pɛndjuləm] *n* pendule *m*; (*of clock*) balancier *m*.

penetrate ['pɛnɪtreɪt] *vt* pénétrer dans; pénétrer.

penfriend ['penfrend] *n* (*Brit*) correspondant/e.

penguin ['peŋgwın] *n* pingouin *m*.

penicillin [penı'sılın] *n* pénicilline *f*.

peninsula [pə'nınsjulə] *n* péninsule *f*.

penis ['pi:nıs] *n* pénis *m*, verge *f*.

penitent ['penıtnt] *a* repentant(e).

penitentiary [penı'tenʃərı] *n* (*US*) prison *f*.

penknife ['pennaıf] *n* canif *m*.

pen name *n* nom *m* de plume, pseudonyme *m*.

penniless ['penılıs] *a* sans le sou.

penny, *pl* **pennies** *or* (*Brit*) **pence** ['penı, 'penız, pens] *n* penny *m* (*pl* pennies); (*US*) = **cent**.

penpal ['penpæl] *n* correspondant/e.

pension ['penʃən] *n* retraite *f*; (*MIL*) pension *f*; **~er** *n* (*Brit*) retraité/e.

penthouse ['penthaus] *n* appartement *m* (de luxe) en attique.

pent-up ['pentʌp] *a* (*feelings*) refoulé(e).

people ['pi:pl] *npl* gens *mpl*; personnes *fpl*; (*citizens*) peuple *m* // *n* (*nation, race*) peuple *m* // *vt* peupler; **several ~ came** plusieurs personnes sont venues; **the room was full of ~** la salle était pleine de monde *or* de gens.

pep [pep] *n* (*col*) entrain *m*, dynamisme *m*; **to ~ up** *vt* remonter.

pepper ['pepə*] *n* poivre *m*; (*vegetable*) poivron *m* // *vt* poivrer; **~mint** *n* (*plant*) menthe poivrée; (*sweet*) pastille *f* de menthe.

peptalk ['peptɔ:k] *n* (*col*) (petit) discours d'encouragement.

per [pə:*] *prep* par; **~ hour** (*miles etc*) à l'heure; (*fee*) (de) l'heure; **~ kilo** *etc* le kilo *etc*; **~ day/person** par jour/personne; **~ annum** *ad* par an; **~ capita** *a, ad* par personne, par habitant.

perceive [pə'si:v] *vt* percevoir; (*notice*) remarquer, s'apercevoir de.

per cent [pə'sent] *ad* pour cent.

percentage [pə'sentıdʒ] *n* pourcentage *m*.

perception [pə'sepʃən] *n* perception *f*; sensibilité *f*; perspicacité *f*.

perceptive [pə'septıv] *a* pénétrant(e); perspicace.

perch [pə:tʃ] *n* (*fish*) perche *f*; (*for bird*) perchoir *m* // *vi* (se) percher.

percolator ['pə:kəleıtə*] *n* percolateur *m*; cafetière *f* électrique.

perennial [pə'renıəl] *a* perpétuel(le); (*BOT*) vivace // *n* plante *f* vivace.

perfect *a, n* ['pə:fıkt] parfait(e) // *n* (*also*: **~ tense**) parfait *m* // *vt* [pə'fekt] parfaire; mettre au point; **~ly** *ad* parfaitement.

perforate ['pə:fəreıt] *vt* perforer, percer; **perforation** [-'reıʃən] *n* perforation *f*; (*line of holes*) pointillé *m*.

perform [pə'fɔ:m] *vt* (*carry out*) exé-cuter, remplir; (*concert etc*) jouer, donner // *vi* jouer; **~ance** *n* repré-sentation *f*, spectacle *m*; (*of an artist*) interprétation *f*; (*of player etc*) prestation *f*; (*of car, engine*) perfor-mance *f*; **~er** *n* artiste *m/f*; **~ing** *a* (*animal*) savant(e).

perfume ['pə:fju:m] *n* parfum *m*.

perfunctory [pə'fʌŋktərı] *a* négli-gent(e), pour la forme.

perhaps [pə'hæps] *ad* peut-être.

peril ['perıl] *n* péril *m*.

perimeter [pə'rımıtə*] *n* périmètre *m*; **~ wall** *n* mur *m* d'enceinte.

period ['pıərıəd] *n* période *f*; (*HISTORY*) époque *f*; (*SCOL*) cours *m*; (*full stop*) point *m*; (*MED*) règles *fpl* // *a* (*costume, furniture*) d'époque; **~ic** [-'ɔdık] *a* périodique; **~ical** [-'ɔdıkl] *a* périodique // *n* périodique *m*.

peripheral [pə'rıfərəl] *a* périphérique // *n* (*COMPUT*) périphérique *m*.

perish ['perıʃ] *vi* périr, mourir; (*decay*) se détériorer; **~able** *a* périssable.

perjury ['pə:dʒərı] *n* (*LAW: in court*) faux témoignage; (*breach of oath*) parjure *m*.

perk [pə:k] *n* avantage *m*, à-côté *m*; **to ~ up** *vi* (*cheer up*) se ragaillardir; **~y** *a* (*cheerful*) guilleret(te), gai(e).

perm [pə:m] *n* (*for hair*) permanente *f*.

permanent ['pə:mənənt] *a* permanent(e).

permeate ['pə:mıeıt] *vi* s'infiltrer // *vt* s'infiltrer dans; pénétrer.

permissible [pə'mısıbl] *a* permis(e), acceptable.

permission [pə'mıʃən] *n* permission *f*, autorisation *f*.

permissive [pə'mısıv] *a* tolérant(e); **the ~ society** la société de tolérance.

permit *n* ['pə:mıt] permis *m* // *vt* [pə'mıt] permettre; **to ~ sb to do** autoriser qn à faire, permettre à qn de faire.

perpendicular [pə:pən'dıkjulə*] *a, n* perpendiculaire (*f*).

perplex [pə'pleks] *vt* rendre perplexe; (*complicate*) embrouiller.

persecute ['pə:sıkju:t] *vt* persécuter.

persevere [pə:sı'vıə*] *vi* persévérer.

Persian ['pə:ʃən] *a* persan(e) // *n* (*LING*) persan *m*; **the (~) Gulf** le golfe Persique.

persist [pə'sıst] *vi*: **to ~ (in doing)** persister (à faire), s'obstiner (à faire); **~ent** *a* persistant(e), tenace.

person ['pə:sn] *n* personne *f*; **in ~** en personne; **~able** *a* de belle prestance, au physique attrayant; **~al** *a* personnel(le); individuel(le); **~al assis-tant (P.A.)** *n* secrétaire privé/e; **~al computer (PC)** *n* ordinateur individuel; **~ality** [-'nælıtı] *n* personnalité *f*; **~ally** *ad* personnellement.

personnel [pə:sə'nɛl] *n* personnel *m*.

perspective [pə'spɛktɪv] *n* perspective *f*.

perspiration [pə:spɪ'reɪʃən] *n* transpiration *f*.

persuade [pə'sweɪd] *vt*: to ~ sb to do sth persuader qn de faire qch, amener *or* décider qn à faire qch.

pert [pə:t] *a* (*bold*) effronté(e), impertinent(e).

pertaining [pə:'teɪnɪŋ]: ~ to *prep* relatif(ive) à.

peruse [pə'ru:z] *vt* lire (attentivement).

pervade [pə'veɪd] *vt* se répandre dans, envahir.

perverse [pə'və:s] *a* pervers(e); (*stubborn*) entêté(e), contrariant(e).

pervert *n* ['pə:və:t] perverti/e // *vt* [pə'və:t] pervertir.

pessimist ['pɛsɪmɪst] *n* pessimiste *m/f*; ~**ic** [-'mɪstɪk] *a* pessimiste.

pest [pɛst] *n* animal *m* (*or* insecte *m*) nuisible; (*fig*) fléau *m*.

pester ['pɛstə*] *vt* importuner, harceler.

pet [pɛt] *n* animal familier; (*favourite*) chouchou *m* // *vt* choyer // *vi* (*col*) se peloter.

petal ['pɛtl] *n* pétale *m*.

peter ['pi:tə*]: to ~ out *vi* s'épuiser; s'affaiblir.

petite [pə'ti:t] *a* menu(e).

petition [pə'tɪʃən] *n* pétition *f*.

petrified ['pɛtrɪfaɪd] *a* (*fig*) mort(e) de peur.

petrol ['pɛtrəl] *n* (*Brit*) essence *f*; two-star ~ essence *f* ordinaire; four-star ~ super *m*; ~ **can** *n* bidon *m* à essence.

petroleum [pə'trəʊlɪəm] *n* pétrole *m*.

petrol: ~ **pump** *n* (*Brit*) pompe *f* à essence; ~ **station** *n* (*Brit*) station-service *f*; ~ **tank** *n* (*Brit*) réservoir *m* d'essence.

petticoat ['pɛtɪkəʊt] *n* jupon *m*.

petty ['pɛtɪ] *a* (*mean*) mesquin(e); (*unimportant*) insignifiant(e), sans importance; ~ **cash** *n* menue monnaie; ~ **officer** *n* second-maître *m*.

petulant ['pɛtjʊlənt] *a* irritable.

pew [pju:] *n* banc *m* (d'église).

pewter ['pju:tə*] *n* étain *m*.

phantom ['fæntəm] *n* fantôme *m*; (*vision*) fantasme *m*.

pharmacy ['fɑ:məsɪ] *n* pharmacie *f*.

phase [feɪz] *n* phase *f*, période *f* // *vt*: to ~ sth in/out introduire/supprimer qch progressivement.

Ph.D. *abbr* (= *Doctor of Philosophy*) *title* ≈ Docteur *m* en Droit *or* Lettres *etc* // *n* ≈ doctorat *m*; titulaire *m* d'un doctorat.

pheasant ['fɛznt] *n* faisan *m*.

phenomenon, *pl* **phenomena** [fə'nɔmɪnən, -nə] *n* phénomène *m*.

philosophical [fɪlə'sɔfɪkl] *a* philosophique.

philosophy [fɪ'lɔsəfɪ] *n* philosophie *f*.

phobia ['fəʊbjə] *n* phobie *f*.

phone [fəʊn] *n* téléphone *m* // *vt* téléphoner; to be on the ~ avoir le téléphone; (*be calling*) être au téléphone; to ~ **back** *vt, vi* rappeler; to ~ **up** *vt* téléphoner à // *vi* téléphoner; ~ **book** *n* annuaire *m*; ~ **box** *or* **booth** *n* cabine *f* téléphonique; ~ **call** *n* coup *m* de fil *or* de téléphone; ~-**in** *n* (*Brit RADIO, TV*) programme *m* à ligne ouverte.

phonetics [fə'nɛtɪks] *n* phonétique *f*.

phoney ['fəʊnɪ] *a* faux(fausse), factice.

phonograph ['fəʊnəgrɑ:f] *n* (*US*) électrophone *m*.

phony ['fəʊnɪ] *a* = **phoney**.

photo ['fəʊtəʊ] *n* photo *f*.

photo... ['fəʊtəʊ] *prefix*: ~**copier** *n* machine *f* à photocopier; ~**copy** *n* photocopie *f* // *vt* photocopier; ~**graph** *n* photographie *f* // *vt* photographier; ~**grapher** [fə'tɔgrəfə*] *n* photographe *m/f*; ~**graphy** [fə'tɔgrəfɪ] *n* photographie *f*.

phrase [freɪz] *n* expression *f*; (*LING*) locution *f* // *vt* exprimer; ~ **book** *n* recueil *m* d'expressions (pour touristes).

physical ['fɪzɪkl] *a* physique; ~ **education** *n* éducation *f* physique; ~**ly** *ad* physiquement.

physician [fɪ'zɪʃən] *n* médecin *m*.

physicist ['fɪzɪsɪst] *n* physicien/ne.

physics ['fɪzɪks] *n* physique *f*.

physiotherapy [fɪzɪəʊ'θɛrəpɪ] *n* kinésithérapie *f*.

physique [fɪ'zi:k] *n* physique *m*; constitution *f*.

pianist ['pi:ənɪst] *n* pianiste *m/f*.

piano [pɪ'ænəʊ] *n* piano *m*.

pick [pɪk] *n* (*tool: also:* ~-axe) pic *m*, pioche *f* // *vt* choisir; (*gather*) cueillir; take your ~ faites votre choix; the ~ of le(la) meilleur(e) de; to ~ **off** *vt* (*kill*) (viser soigneusement et) abattre; to ~ **on** *vt fus* (*person*) harceler; to ~ **out** *vt* choisir; (*distinguish*) distinguer; to ~ **up** *vi* (*improve*) remonter, s'améliorer // *vt* ramasser; (*telephone*) décrocher; (*collect*) passer prendre; (*AUT: give lift to*) prendre; (*learn*) apprendre; to ~ **up** speed prendre de la vitesse; to ~ o.s. up se relever.

picket ['pɪkɪt] *n* (*in strike*) gréviste *m/f* participant à un piquet de grève; piquet *m* de grève // *vt* mettre un piquet de grève devant.

pickle ['pɪkl] *n* (*also:* ~**s**: *as condiment*) pickles *mpl* // *vt* conserver dans du vinaigre *or* dans de la saumure.

pickpocket ['pɪkpɔkɪt] *n* pickpocket *m*.

pickup ['pɪkʌp] *n* (*Brit: on record player*) bras *m* pick-up; (*small truck*) pick-up *m inv*.

picnic ['pɪknɪk] *n* pique-nique *m*.

pictorial [pɪk'tɔ:rɪəl] *a* illustré(e).

picture ['pɪktʃə*] *n* image *f*; (*painting*)

peinture f, tableau m; (photograph) photo(graphie) f; (drawing) dessin m; (film) film m // vt se représenter; (describe) dépeindre, représenter; **the ~s** (Brit) le cinéma; **~ book** n livre m d'images.

picturesque [pɪktʃə'resk] a pittoresque.

pie [paɪ] n tourte f; (of meat) pâté m en croûte.

piece [piːs] n morceau m; (of land) parcelle f; (item): **a ~ of furniture/ advice** un meuble/conseil // vt: **to ~ together** rassembler; **to take to ~s** démonter; **~meal** ad par bouts; **~work** n travail m aux pièces.

pie chart n graphique m à secteurs, camembert m.

pier [pɪə*] n jetée f; (of bridge etc) pile f.

pierce [pɪəs] vt percer, transpercer.

pig [pɪg] n cochon m, porc m.

pigeon ['pɪdʒən] n pigeon m; **~hole** n casier m.

piggy bank ['pɪgɪbæŋk] n tirelire f.

pigheaded ['pɪg'hedɪd] a entêté(e), têtu(e).

pigskin ['pɪgskɪn] n (peau m de) porc m.

pigsty ['pɪgstaɪ] n porcherie f.

pigtail ['pɪgteɪl] n natte f, tresse f.

pike [paɪk] n (spear) pique f; (fish) brochet m.

pilchard ['pɪltʃəd] n pilchard m (sorte de sardine).

pile [paɪl] n (pillar, of books) pile f; (heap) tas m; (of carpet) épaisseur f // vb (also: ~ up) vt empiler, entasser // vi s'entasser; **to ~ into** (car) s'entasser dans.

piles [paɪlz] npl hémorroïdes fpl.

pileup ['paɪlʌp] n (AUT) télescopage m, collision f en série.

pilfering ['pɪlfərɪŋ] n chapardage m.

pilgrim ['pɪlgrɪm] n pèlerin m.

pill [pɪl] n pilule f; **the ~** la pilule.

pillage ['pɪlɪdʒ] vt piller.

pillar ['pɪlə*] n pilier m; **~ box** n (Brit) boîte f aux lettres.

pillion ['pɪljən] n (of motor cycle) siège m arrière.

pillow ['pɪləu] n oreiller m; **~case** n taie f d'oreiller.

pilot ['paɪlət] n pilote m // cpd (scheme etc) pilote, expérimental(e) // vt piloter; **~ light** n veilleuse f.

pimp [pɪmp] n souteneur m, maquereau m.

pimple ['pɪmpl] n bouton m.

pin [pɪn] n épingle f; (TECH) cheville f // vt épingler; **~s and needles** fourmis fpl; **to ~ sb down** (fig) obliger qn à répondre; **to ~ sth on sb** (fig) mettre qch sur le dos de qn.

pinafore ['pɪnəfɔ:*] n tablier m.

pinball ['pɪnbɔ:l] n (also: ~ machine)

flipper m.

pincers ['pɪnsəz] npl tenailles fpl.

pinch [pɪntʃ] n pincement m; (of salt etc) pincée f // vt pincer; (col: steal) piquer, chiper // vi (shoe) serrer; **at a ~** à la rigueur.

pincushion ['pɪnkuʃən] n pelote f à épingles.

pine [paɪn] n (also: ~ tree) pin m // vi: **to ~ for** aspirer à, désirer ardemment; **to ~ away** vi dépérir.

pineapple ['paɪnæpl] n ananas m.

ping [pɪŋ] n (noise) tintement m; **~-pong** n ® ping-pong m ®.

pink [pɪŋk] a rose // n (colour) rose m; (BOT) œillet m, mignardise f.

pinpoint ['pɪnpɔɪnt] vt indiquer (avec précision).

pint [paɪnt] n pinte f (Brit = 0.57 l; US = 0.47 l); (Brit col) ≈ demi m, ≈ pot m.

pioneer [paɪə'nɪə*] n explorateur/trice; (early settler, fig) pionnier m.

pious ['paɪəs] a pieux(euse).

pip [pɪp] n (seed) pépin m; (Brit: time signal on radio) top m.

pipe [paɪp] n tuyau m, conduite f; (for smoking) pipe f; (MUS) pipeau m // vt amener par tuyau; **~s** npl (also: bag~s) cornemuse f; **to ~ down** vi (col) se taire; **~ cleaner** n cure-pipe m; **~ dream** n chimère f, utopie f; **~line** n pipe-line m; **~r** n joueur/euse de pipeau (or de cornemuse).

piping ['paɪpɪŋ] ad: **~ hot** très chaud(e).

pique ['piːk] n dépit m.

pirate ['paɪərət] n pirate m.

Pisces ['paɪsi:z] n les Poissons mpl.

piss [pɪs] vi (col) pisser; **~ed** a (col: drunk) bourré(e).

pistol ['pɪstl] n pistolet m.

piston ['pɪstən] n piston m.

pit [pɪt] n trou m, fosse f; (also: **coal ~**) puits m de mine; (also: **orchestra ~**) fosse f d'orchestre // vt: **to ~ sb against sb** opposer qn à qn; **~s** npl (AUT) aire f de service.

pitch [pɪtʃ] n (throw) lancement m; (MUS) ton m; (of voice) hauteur f; (Brit SPORT) terrain m; (NAUT) tangage m; (tar) poix f // vt (throw) lancer // vi (fall) tomber; (NAUT) tanguer; **to ~ a tent** dresser une tente; **~ed battle** n bataille rangée.

pitcher ['pɪtʃə*] n cruche f.

pitchfork ['pɪtʃfɔ:k] n fourche f.

piteous ['pɪtɪəs] a pitoyable.

pitfall ['pɪtfɔ:l] n trappe f, piège m.

pith [pɪθ] n (of plant) moelle f; (of orange) intérieur m de l'écorce; (fig) essence f; vigueur f.

pithy ['pɪθɪ] a piquant(e); vigoureux(euse).

pitiful ['pɪtɪful] a (touching) pitoyable; (contemptible) lamentable.

pitiless ['pɪtɪlɪs] a impitoyable.

pittance ['pɪtns] n salaire m de misère.
pity ['pɪtɪ] n pitié f // vt plaindre; **what a ~!** quel dommage!
pivot ['pɪvət] n pivot m.
pizza ['piːtsə] n pizza f.
placard ['plækɑːd] n affiche f.
placate [plə'keɪt] vt apaiser, calmer.
place [pleɪs] n endroit m, lieu m; (proper position, rank, seat) place f; (house) maison f, logement m; (home): at/to his ~ chez lui // vt (object) placer, mettre; (identify) situer; reconnaître; to take ~ avoir lieu; se passer; to change ~s with sb changer de place avec qn; to ~ an order passer une commande; out of ~ (not suitable) déplacé(e), inopportun(e); in the first ~ d'abord, en premier.
plague [pleɪg] n fléau m; (MED) peste f // vt (fig) tourmenter.
plaice [pleɪs] n (pl inv) carrelet m.
plaid [plæd] n tissu écossais.
plain [pleɪn] a (clear) clair(e), évident(e); (simple) simple, ordinaire; (frank) franc(franche); (not handsome) quelconque, ordinaire; (cigarette) sans filtre; (without seasoning etc) nature inv; (in one colour) uni(e) // ad franchement, carrément // n plaine f. ~ **chocolate** n chocolat m à croquer; ~ **clothes**: in ~ clothes (police) en civil; ~**ly** ad clairement; (frankly) carrément, sans détours.
plaintiff ['pleɪntɪf] n plaignant/e.
plait [plæt] n tresse f, natte f.
plan [plæn] n plan m; (scheme) projet m// vt (think in advance) projeter; (prepare) organiser // vi faire des projets.
plane [pleɪn] n (AVIAT) avion m; (tree) platane m; (tool) rabot m; (ART, MATH etc) plan m // a plan(e), plat(e) // vt (with tool) raboter.
planet ['plænɪt] n planète f.
plank [plæŋk] n planche f.
planning ['plænɪŋ] n planification f; **family** ~ planning familial; ~ **permission** n permis m de construire.
plant [plɑːnt] n plante f; (machinery) matériel m; (factory) usine f // vt planter; (colony) établir; (bomb) déposer, poser.
plaster ['plɑːstə*] n plâtre m; (also: ~ of Paris) plâtre à mouler; (Brit: also: sticking ~) pansement adhésif // vt plâtrer; (cover): to ~ with couvrir de; in ~ (leg etc) dans le plâtre; ~**ed** a (col) soûl(e).
plastic ['plæstɪk] n plastique m // a (made of plastic) en plastique; (flexible) plastique, malléable; (art) plastique; ~ **bag** n sac m en plastique.
plasticine ['plæstɪsiːn] n ® pâte f à modeler.
plastic surgery n chirurgie f esthétique.
plate [pleɪt] n (dish) assiette f; (sheet of metal, PHOT) plaque f; (in book) gravure f.
plateau, ~s or **~x** ['plætəu, -z] n plateau m.
plate glass n verre m (de vitrine).
platform ['plætfɔːm] n (at meeting) tribune f; (Brit: of bus) plate-forme f; (stage) estrade f; (RAIL) quai m; ~ **ticket** n (Brit) billet m de quai.
platinum ['plætɪnəm] n platine m.
platoon [plə'tuːn] n peloton m.
platter ['plætə*] n plat m.
plausible ['plɔːzɪbl] a plausible; (person) convaincant(e).
play [pleɪ] n jeu m; (THEATRE) pièce f (de théâtre) // vt (game) jouer à; (team, opponent) jouer contre; (instrument) jouer de; (play, part, piece of music, note) jouer // vi jouer; to ~ safe ne prendre aucun risque; to ~ down vt minimiser; to ~ up vi (cause trouble) faire des siennes; ~**boy** n playboy m; ~**er** n joueur/euse; (THEATRE) acteur/trice; (MUS) musicien/ne; ~**ful** a enjoué(e); ~**ground** n cour f de récréation; ~**group** n garderie f; ~**ing card** n carte f à jouer; ~**ing field** n terrain m de sport; ~**mate** n camarade m/f, copain/copine; ~**-off** n (SPORT) belle f; ~**pen** n parc m (pour bébé); ~**school** n = ~**group**; ~**thing** n jouet m; ~**wright** n dramaturge m.
plc abbr (= public limited company) SARL f.
plea [pliː] n (request) appel m; (excuse) excuse f; (LAW) défense f.
plead [pliːd] vt plaider; (give as excuse) invoquer // vi (LAW) plaider; (beg): to ~ **with sb** implorer qn.
pleasant ['plɛznt] a agréable; ~**ries** npl (polite remarks) civilités fpl.
please [pliːz] vt plaire à // vi (think fit): do as you ~ faites comme il vous plaira; ~! s'il te (or vous) plaît!; ~ **yourself!** à ta (or votre) guise!; ~**d** a: ~**d (with)** content(e) (de); ~**d to meet you** enchanté (de faire votre connaissance); **pleasing** a plaisant(e), qui fait plaisir.
pleasure ['plɛʒə*] n plaisir m; 'it's a ~' 'je vous en prie'.
pleat [pliːt] n pli m.
pledge [plɛdʒ] n gage m; (promise) promesse f // vt engager; promettre.
plentiful ['plɛntɪful] a abondant(e), copieux(euse).
plenty ['plɛntɪ] n abondance f; ~ **of** beaucoup de; (bien) assez de.
pliable ['plaɪəbl] a flexible; (person) malléable.
pliers ['plaɪəz] npl pinces fpl.
plight [plaɪt] n situation f critique.
plimsolls ['plɪmsəlz] npl (Brit) (chaussures fpl de) tennis fpl.
plinth [plɪnθ] n socle m.
plod [plɔd] vi avancer péniblement; (fig)

peiner; **~der** n bûcheur/euse.

plonk [plɔŋk] (col) n (Brit: wine) pinard m, piquette f // vt: **to ~ sth down** poser brusquement qch.

plot [plɔt] n complot m, conspiration f; (of story, play) intrigue f; (of land) lot m de terrain, lopin m // vt (mark out) pointer; relever; (conspire) comploter // vi comploter; **~ter** n (instrument) table traçante, traceur m.

plough, (US) **plow** [plau] n charrue f // vt (earth) labourer; **to ~ back** vt (COMM) réinvestir; **to ~ through** vt fus (snow etc) avancer péniblement dans.

ploy [plɔɪ] n stratagème m.

pluck [plʌk] vt (fruit) cueillir; (musical instrument) pincer; (bird) plumer // n courage m, cran m; **to ~ up courage** prendre son courage à deux mains; **~y** a courageux(euse).

plug [plʌg] n bouchon m, bonde f; (ELEC) prise f de courant; (AUT: also: **spark(ing) ~**) bougie f // vt (hole) boucher; (col: advertise) faire du battage pour, matraquer; **to ~ in** vt (ELEC) brancher.

plum [plʌm] n (fruit) prune f // a: **~ job** (col) travail m en or.

plumb [plʌm] a vertical(e) // n plomb m // ad (exactly) en plein // vt sonder.

plumber ['plʌmə*] n plombier m.

plumbing ['plʌmɪŋ] n (trade) plomberie f; (piping) tuyauterie f.

plummet ['plʌmɪt] vi plonger, dégringoler.

plump [plʌmp] a rondelet(te), dodu(e), bien en chair // vt: **to ~ sth (down)** on laisser tomber qch lourdement sur; **to ~ for** vt fus (col: choose) se décider pour.

plunder ['plʌndə*] n pillage m // vt piller.

plunge [plʌndʒ] n plongeon m // vt plonger // vi (fall) tomber, dégringoler; **to take the ~** se jeter à l'eau; **~r** n piston m; (débouchoir m à) ventouse f.

pluperfect [plu:'pə:fɪkt] n plus-que-parfait m.

plural ['pluərl] a pluriel(le) // n pluriel m.

plus [plʌs] n (also: **~ sign**) signe m plus // prep plus; **ten/twenty ~** plus de dix/vingt.

plush [plʌʃ] a somptueux(euse).

ply [plaɪ] n (of wool) fil m; (of wood) feuille f, épaisseur f // vt (tool) manier; (a trade) exercer // vi (ship) faire la navette; **to ~ sb with drink** donner continuellement à boire à qn; **~wood** n contre-plaqué m.

P.M. abbr of **Prime Minister.**

p.m. ad abbr (= post meridiem) de l'après-midi.

pneumatic drill [nju:'mætɪk-] n marteau-piqueur m.

pneumonia [nju:'məunɪə] n pneumonie f.

poach [pəutʃ] vt (cook) pocher; (steal) pêcher (or chasser) sans permis // vi braconner; **~er** n braconnier m.

P.O. Box n abbr of **Post Office Box.**

pocket ['pɔkɪt] n poche f // vt empocher; **to be out of ~** (Brit) en être de sa poche; **~book** n (wallet) portefeuille m; (notebook) carnet m; **~ knife** n canif m; **~ money** n argent m de poche.

pod [pɔd] n cosse f.

podgy ['pɔdʒɪ] a rondelet(te).

podiatrist [pɔ'di:ətrɪst] n (US) pédicure m/f, podologue m/f.

poem ['pəuɪm] n poème m.

poet ['pəuɪt] n poète m; **~ic** [-'ɛtɪk] a poétique; **~ laureate** n poète lauréat (nommé et appointé par la Cour royale); **~ry** n poésie f.

poignant ['pɔɪnjənt] a poignant(e); (sharp) vif(vive).

point [pɔɪnt] n (tip) pointe f; (in time) moment m; (in space) endroit m; (GEOM, SCOL, SPORT, on scale) point m; (subject, matter) point, sujet m; (also: **decimal ~**): **2 ~ 3 (2.3)** 2 virgule 3 (2,3) // vt (show) indiquer; (wall, window) jointoyer; (gun etc): **to ~ sth at** braquer or diriger qch sur // vi montrer du doigt; **~s** npl (AUT) vis platinées; (RAIL) aiguillage m; **to be on the ~ of doing sth** être sur le point de faire qch; **to make a ~** faire une remarque; **to get the ~** comprendre, saisir; **to come to the ~** en venir au fait; **there's no ~ (in doing)** cela ne sert à rien (de faire); **to ~ out** vt faire remarquer, souligner; **to ~ to** vt fus montrer du doigt; (fig) signaler; **~-blank** ad (also: **at ~-blank range**) à bout portant; (fig) catégorique; **~ed** a (shape) pointu(e); (remark) plein(e) de sous-entendus; **~edly** ad d'une manière significative; **~er** n (stick) baguette f; (needle) aiguille f; (dog) chien m d'arrêt; **~less** a inutile, vain(e); **~ of view** n point m de vue.

poise [pɔɪz] n (balance) équilibre m; (of head, body) port m; (calmness) calme m // vt placer en équilibre.

poison ['pɔɪzn] n poison m // vt empoisonner; **~ing** n empoisonnement m; **~ous** a (snake) venimeux(euse); (substance etc) vénéneux(euse).

poke [pəuk] vt (fire) tisonner; (jab with finger, stick etc) piquer; pousser du doigt; (put:): **to ~ sth in(to)** fourrer or enfoncer qch dans; **to ~ about** vi fureter.

poker ['pəukə*] n tisonnier m; (CARDS) poker m; **~-faced** a au visage impassible.

poky ['pəukɪ] a exigu(ë).

Poland ['pəulənd] n Pologne f.

polar ['pəulə*] a polaire; **~ bear** n ours

blanc.

Pole [pəul] n Polonais/e.

pole [pəul] n (of wood) mât m, perche f; (ELEC) poteau m; (GEO) pôle m; ~ **bean** n (US) haricot m (à rames); ~ **vault** n saut m à la perche.

police [pə'li:s] npl police f // vt maintenir l'ordre dans; ~ **car** n voiture f de police; ~**man** n agent m de police, policier m; ~ **station** n commissariat m de police; ~**woman** n femme-agent f.

policy ['pɔlɪsɪ] n politique f; (also: insurance ~) police f (d'assurance).

polio ['pəulɪəu] n polio f.

Polish ['pəulɪʃ] a polonais(e) // n (LING) polonais m.

polish ['pɔlɪʃ] n (for shoes) cirage m; (for floor) cire f, encaustique f; (for nails) vernis m; (shine) éclat m, poli m; (fig: refinement) raffinement m // vt (put polish on shoes, wood) cirer; (make shiny) astiquer, faire briller; (fig: improve) perfectionner; **to ~ off** vt (work) expédier; (food) liquider; ~**ed** a (fig) raffiné(e).

polite [pə'laɪt] a poli(e); ~**ness** n politesse f.

politic ['pɔlɪtɪk] a diplomatique; ~**al** [pə'lɪtɪkl] a politique; ~**ally** ad politiquement; ~**ian** [-'tɪʃən] n homme m politique, politicien m; ~**s** npl politique f.

polka ['pɔlkə] n polka f; ~ **dot** n pois m.

poll [pəul] n scrutin m, vote m; (also: opinion ~) sondage m (d'opinion) // vt obtenir.

pollen ['pɔlən] n pollen m.

polling ['pəulɪŋ] (Brit): ~ **booth** n isoloir m; ~ **day** n jour m des élections; ~ **station** n bureau m de vote.

pollution [pə'lu:ʃən] n pollution f.

polo ['pəuləu] n polo m; ~-**neck** a à col roulé.

polytechnic [pɔlɪ'teknɪk] n (college) I.U.T. m, Institut m Universitaire de Technologie.

polythene ['pɔlɪθi:n] n polyéthylène m; ~ **bag** n sac m en plastique.

pomegranate ['pɔmɪgrænɪt] n grenade f.

pomp [pɔmp] n pompe f, faste f, apparat m.

pompous ['pɔmpəs] a pompeux(euse).

pond [pɔnd] n étang m; mare f.

ponder ['pɔndə*] vt considérer, peser; ~**ous** a pesant(e), lourd(e).

pong [pɔŋ] n (Brit col) puanteur f.

pony ['pəunɪ] n poney m; ~**tail** n queue f de cheval; ~ **trekking** n (Brit) randonnée f à cheval.

poodle ['pu:dl] n caniche m.

pool [pu:l] n (of rain) flaque f; (pond) mare f; (artificial) bassin m; (also:

swimming ~) piscine f; (sth shared) fonds commun m; (money at cards) cagnotte f; (billiards) poule f // vt mettre en commun; **typing** ~ n pool m dactylographique; (football) ~**s** npl ≈ loto sportif.

poor [puə*] a pauvre; (mediocre) médiocre, faible, mauvais(e) // npl: **the** ~ les pauvres mpl; ~**ly** ad pauvrement; médiocrement // a souffrant(e), malade.

pop [pɔp] n (noise) bruit sec; (MUS) musique f pop; (US col: father) papa m // vt (put) fourrer, mettre (rapidement) // vi éclater; (cork) sauter; **to ~ in** vi entrer en passant; **to ~ out** vi sortir; **to ~ up** vi apparaître, surgir; ~ **concert** n concert m pop.

pope [pəup] n pape m.

poplar ['pɔplə*] n peuplier m.

poppy ['pɔpɪ] n coquelicot m; pavot m.

popsicle ['pɔpsɪkl] n (US) esquimau m.

popular ['pɔpjulə*] a populaire; (fashionable) à la mode; ~**ize** vt populariser; (science) vulgariser.

population [pɔpju'leɪʃən] n population f.

porcelain ['pɔ:slɪn] n porcelaine f.

porch [pɔ:tʃ] n porche m.

porcupine ['pɔ:kjupaɪn] n porc-épic m.

pore [pɔ:*] n pore m // vi: **to ~ over** s'absorber dans, être plongé(e) dans.

pork [pɔ:k] n porc m.

pornography [pɔ:'nɔgrəfɪ] n pornographie f.

porpoise ['pɔ:pəs] n marsouin m.

porridge ['pɔrɪdʒ] n porridge m.

port [pɔ:t] n (harbour) port m; (opening in ship) sabord m; (NAUT: left side) bâbord m; (wine) porto m; ~ **of call** escale f.

portable ['pɔ:təbl] a portatif(ive).

portent ['pɔ:tent] n présage m.

porter ['pɔ:tə*] n (for luggage) porteur m; (doorkeeper) gardien/ne; portier m.

portfolio [pɔ:t'fəulɪəu] n portefeuille m; (of artist) portfolio m.

porthole ['pɔ:thəul] n hublot m.

portion ['pɔ:ʃən] n portion f, part f.

portly ['pɔ:tlɪ] a corpulent(e).

portrait ['pɔ:treɪt] n portrait m.

portray [pɔ:'treɪ] vt faire le portrait de; (in writing) dépeindre, représenter.

Portugal ['pɔ:tjugl] n Portugal m.

Portuguese [pɔ:tju'gi:z] a portugais(e) // n (pl inv) Portugais/e; (LING) portugais m.

pose [pəuz] n pose f; (pej) affectation f // vi poser; (pretend): **to ~ as** se poser en // vt poser, créer.

posh [pɔʃ] a (col) chic inv.

position [pə'zɪʃən] n position f; (job) situation f.

positive ['pɔzɪtɪv] a positif(ive); (certain) sûr(e), certain(e); (definite) formel(le), catégorique; indéniable, réel(le).

posse ['pɒsɪ] n (US) détachement m.
possess [pə'zes] vt posséder; **~ion** [pə'zeʃən] n possession f.
possibility [pɒsɪ'bɪlɪtɪ] n possibilité f; éventualité f.
possible ['pɒsɪbl] a possible; as big as ~ aussi gros que possible.
possibly ['pɒsɪblɪ] ad (perhaps) peut-être; if you ~ **can** si cela vous est possible; I cannot ~ **come** il m'est impossible de venir.
post [pəust] n poste f; (Brit: collection) levée f; (: letters, delivery) courrier m; (job, situation) poste m; (pole) poteau m // vt (Brit: send by post; MIL) poster; (Brit: appoint): **to ~ to** affecter à; (notice) afficher; **~age** n affranchissement m; **~al order** n mandat(-poste) m; **~box** n (Brit) boîte f aux lettres; **~card** n carte postale; **~code** n (Brit) code postal.
poster ['pəustə*] n affiche f.
poste restante [pəust'restã:nt] n poste restante.
postgraduate ['pəust'grædjuət] n ≈ étudiant/e de troisième cycle.
posthumous ['pɒstjuməs] a posthume.
postman ['pəustmən] n facteur m.
postmark ['pəustmɑ:k] n cachet m (de la poste).
postmaster ['pəustmɑ:stə*] n receveur m des postes.
post-mortem ['pəust'mɔ:təm] n autopsie f.
post office ['pəustɒfɪs] n (building) poste f; (organization): the Post Office les Postes; **Post Office Box (P.O. Box)** n boîte postale (B.P.).
postpone [pəs'pəun] vt remettre (à plus tard), reculer.
posture ['pɒstʃə*] n posture f, attitude f.
postwar [pəust'wɔ:*] a d'après-guerre.
posy ['pəuzɪ] n petit bouquet.
pot [pɒt] n (for cooking) marmite f; casserole f; (for plants, jam) pot m; (col: marijuana) herbe f // vt (plant) mettre en pot; **to go to ~** (col: work, performance) aller à vau-l'eau.
potato, **~es** [pə'teɪtəu] n pomme f de terre; ~ **peeler** n épluche-légumes m.
potent ['pəutnt] a puissant(e); (drink) fort(e), très alcoolisé(e).
potential [pə'tenʃl] a potentiel(le) // n potentiel m; **~ly** ad en puissance.
pothole ['pɒthəul] n (in road) nid m de poule; (Brit: underground) gouffre m, caverne f; **potholing** n (Brit): **to go potholing** faire de la spéléologie.
potluck [pɒt'lʌk] n: **to take ~** tenter sa chance.
potshot ['pɒtʃɒt] n: **to take ~s or a ~ at** canarder.
potted ['pɒtɪd] a (food) en conserve; (plant) en pot.
potter ['pɒtə*] n potier m // vi: **to ~**

around, ~ **about** bricoler; **~y** n poterie f.
potty ['pɒtɪ] a (col: mad) dingue // n (child's) pot m.
pouch [pautʃ] n (ZOOL) poche f; (for tobacco) blague f.
poultry ['pəultrɪ] n volaille f.
pounce [pauns] vi: **to ~ (on)** bondir (sur), fondre sur.
pound [paund] n livre f (weight = 453g, 16 ounces; money = 100 pence); (for dogs, cars) fourrière f // vt (beat) bourrer de coups, marteler; (crush) piler, pulvériser // vi (beat) battre violemment, taper.
pour [pɔ:*] vt verser // vi couler à flots; (rain) pleuvoir à verse; **to ~ away** or **off** vt vider; **to ~ in** vi (people) affluer, se précipiter; **to ~ out** vi (people) sortir en masse // vt vider; déverser; (serve: a drink) verser; **~ing** a: **~ing rain** pluie torrentielle.
pout [paut] vi faire la moue.
poverty ['pɒvətɪ] n pauvreté f, misère f; **~-stricken** a pauvre, déshérité(e).
powder ['paudə*] n poudre f // vt poudrer; **to ~ one's face** or **nose** se poudrer; ~ **compact** n poudrier m; **~ed milk** n lait m en poudre; ~ **puff** n houppette f; ~ **room** n toilettes fpl (pour dames).
power ['pauə*] n (strength) puissance f, force f; (ability, POL: of party, leader) pouvoir m; (MATH) puissance; (of speech, thought) faculté f; (ELEC) courant m // vt faire marcher; **to be in** ~ (POL etc) être au pouvoir; ~ **cut** n (Brit) coupure f de courant; ~ **failure** n panne f de courant; **~ful** a puissant(e); **~less** a impuissant(e); ~ **point** n (Brit) prise f de courant; ~ **station** n centrale f électrique.
p.p. abbr (= per procurationem): ~ **J.** Smith pour M. J. Smith.
PR n abbr of **public relations.**
practicable ['præktɪkəbl] a (scheme) réalisable.
practical ['præktɪkl] a pratique; **~ity** [-'kælɪtɪ] n (no pl) (of situation etc) aspect m pratique; ~ **joke** n farce f; **~ly** ad (almost) pratiquement.
practice ['præktɪs] n pratique f; (of profession) exercice m; (at football etc) entraînement m; (business) cabinet m; clientèle f // vt, vi (US) = **practise**; **in ~** (in reality) en pratique; **out of ~** rouillé(e).
practise, (US) **practice** ['præktɪs] vt (work at: piano, one's backhand etc) s'exercer à, travailler; (train for: skiing, running etc) s'entraîner à; (a sport, religion, method) pratiquer; (profession) exercer // vi s'exercer, travailler; (train) s'entraîner; **practising** a (Christian etc) pratiquant(e); (lawyer) en exercice.
practitioner [præk'tɪʃənə*] n praticien/

ne.

prairie ['prɛərɪ] n savane f; (US): the ~s la Prairie.

praise [preɪz] n éloge(s) m(pl), louange(s) f(pl) // vt louer, faire l'éloge de.

pram [præm] n (Brit) landau m, voiture f d'enfant.

prance [prɑ:ns] vi (horse) caracoler.

prank [præŋk] n farce f.

prawn [prɔ:n] n crevette f (rose).

pray [preɪ] vi prier.

prayer [prɛə*] n prière f.

preach [pri:tʃ] vt, vi prêcher.

precaution [prɪ'kɔ:ʃən] n précaution f.

precede [prɪ'si:d] vt, vi précéder.

precedence ['presɪdəns] n préséance f.

precedent ['presɪdənt] n précédent m.

precinct ['pri:sɪŋkt] n (round cathedral) pourtour m, enceinte f; ~s npl (neighbourhood) alentours mpl, environs mpl; **pedestrian** ~ (Brit) zone piétonnière.

precious ['preʃəs] a précieux(euse).

precipitate a [prɪ'sɪpɪtɪt] (hasty) précipité(e) // vt [prɪ'sɪpɪteɪt] précipiter.

precise [prɪ'saɪs] a précis(e); ~ly ad précisément.

preclude [prɪ'klu:d] vt exclure.

precocious [prɪ'kəuʃəs] a précoce.

precondition [pri:kən'dɪʃən] n condition f nécessaire.

predecessor ['pri:dɪsesə*] n prédécesseur m.

predicament [prɪ'dɪkəmənt] n situation f difficile.

predict [prɪ'dɪkt] vt prédire; ~able a prévisible.

predominantly [prɪ'dɔmɪnəntlɪ] ad en majeure partie; surtout.

preen [pri:n] vt: to ~ itself (bird) se lisser les plumes; to ~ o.s. s'admirer.

prefab ['pri:fæb] n bâtiment préfabriqué.

preface ['prefəs] n préface f.

prefect ['pri:fekt] n (Brit: in school) élève chargé(e) de certaines fonctions de discipline; (in France) préfet m.

prefer [prɪ'fə:*] vt préférer; ~ably ['prefrəblɪ] ad de préférence; ~ence ['prefrəns] n préférence f; ~ential [prefə'renʃəl] a préférentiel(le); ~ential treatment traitement m de faveur.

prefix ['pri:fɪks] n préfixe m.

pregnancy ['pregnənsɪ] n grossesse f.

pregnant ['pregnənt] a enceinte af.

prehistoric ['pri:hɪs'tɔrɪk] a préhistorique.

prejudice ['predʒudɪs] n préjugé m; (harm) tort m, préjudice m // vt porter préjudice à; ~d a (person) plein(e) de préjugés; (view) préconçu(e), partial(e).

premarital ['pri:'mærɪtl] a avant le mariage.

premature ['prematʃuə*] a prématuré(e).

premier ['premɪə*] a premier(ère),

capital(e), primordial(e) // n (POL) premier ministre.

première ['premɪɛə*] n première f.

premise ['premɪs] n prémisse f; ~s npl locaux mpl; on the ~s sur les lieux; sur place.

premium ['pri:mɪəm] n prime f; to be at a ~ faire prime; ~ **bond** n (Brit) bon m à lot, obligation f à prime.

premonition [premə'nɪʃən] n prémonition f.

preoccupied [pri:'ɔkjupaɪd] a préoccupé(e).

prep [prep] n (SCOL: study) étude f; ~ **school** n = **preparatory school**.

prepaid [pri:'peɪd] a payé(e) d'avance.

preparation [prepə'reɪʃən] n préparation f; ~s npl (for trip, war) préparatifs mpl.

preparatory [prɪ'pærətərɪ]: ~ **school** n école primaire privée.

prepare [prɪ'pɛə*] vt préparer // vi: to ~ for se préparer à; ~d to prêt(e) à.

preposition [prepə'zɪʃən] n préposition f.

preposterous [prɪ'pɔstərəs] a absurde.

prerequisite [pri:'rekwɪzɪt] n condition f préalable.

prescribe [prɪ'skraɪb] vt prescrire.

prescription [prɪ'skrɪpʃən] n prescription f; (MED) ordonnance f.

presence ['prezns] n présence f; ~ **of mind** présence d'esprit.

present ['preznt] a présent(e) // n cadeau m; (also: ~ tense) présent m // vt [prɪ'zent] présenter; (give): to ~ sb with sth offrir qch à qn; to give sb a ~ offrir un cadeau à qn; at ~ en ce moment; ~ation [-'teɪʃən] n présentation f; (gift) cadeau m, présent m; (ceremony) remise f du cadeau; ~-day a contemporain(e), actuel(le); ~er [-'zentə*] n (RADIO, TV) présentateur/trice; ~ly ad (soon) tout à l'heure, bientôt; (at present) en ce moment.

preservative [prɪ'zə:vətɪv] n agent m de conservation.

preserve [prɪ'zə:v] vt (keep safe) préserver, protéger; (maintain) conserver, garder; (food) mettre en conserve // n (for game, fish) réserve f; (often pl: jam) confiture f; (: fruit) fruits mpl en conserve.

president ['prezɪdənt] n président/e; ~ial [-'denʃl] a présidentiel(le).

press [pres] n (tool, machine, newspapers) presse f; (for wine) pressoir m; (crowd) cohue f, foule f // vt (push) appuyer sur; (squeeze) presser, serrer; (clothes: iron) repasser; (pursue) talonner; (insist): to ~ sth on sb presser qn d'accepter qch // vi appuyer, peser; se presser; we are ~ed for time le temps nous manque; to ~ for sth faire pression pour obtenir qch; to ~ on vi continuer;

~ **conference** n conférence f de presse; **~ing** a urgent(e), pressant(e) // n repassage m; ~ **stud** n (Brit) bouton-pression m; **~-up** n (Brit) traction f.
pressure ['preʃə*] n (stress) tension f; ~ **cooker** n cocotte-minute f; ~ **gauge** n manomètre m; ~ **group** n groupe m de pression.
prestige [pres'ti:ʒ] n prestige m.
presumably [pri'zju:məbli] ad vraisemblablement.
presume [pri'zju:m] vt présumer, supposer; to ~ to do (dare) se permettre de faire.
presumption [pri'zʌmpʃən] n supposition f, présomption f; (boldness) audace f.
pretence, (US) **pretense** [pri'tens] n (claim) prétention f; to make a ~ of doing faire semblant de faire.
pretend [pri'tend] vt (feign) feindre, simuler // vi (feign) faire semblant; (claim): to ~ to sth prétendre à qch; to ~ to do faire semblant de faire.
pretense [pri'tens] n (US) = pretence.
pretension [pri'tenʃən] n prétention f.
pretext ['pri:tekst] n prétexte m.
pretty ['priti] a joli(e) // ad assez.
prevail [pri'veil] vi (win) l'emporter, prévaloir; (be usual) avoir cours; (persuade): to ~ (up)on sb to do persuader qn de faire; **~ing** a dominant(e).
prevalent ['prevələnt] a répandu(e), courant(e); (fashion) en vogue.
prevent [pri'vent] vt: to ~ (from doing) empêcher (de faire); **~ive** a préventif(ive).
preview ['pri:vju:] n (of film) avant-première f; (fig) aperçu m.
previous ['pri:viəs] a précédent(e); antérieur(e); **~ly** ad précédemment, auparavant.
prewar [pri:'wɔ:*] a d'avant-guerre.
prey [prei] n proie f // vi: to ~ on s'attaquer à.
price [prais] n prix m // vt (goods) fixer le prix de; tarifer; **~less** a sans prix, inestimable; ~ **list** n liste f des prix, tarif m.
prick [prik] n piqûre f // vt piquer; to ~ up one's ears dresser or tendre l'oreille.
prickle ['prikl] n (of plant) épine f; (sensation) picotement m.
prickly ['prikli] a piquant(e), épineux(euse); (fig: person) irritable; ~ **heat** n fièvre f miliaire.
pride [praid] n orgueil m; fierté f // vt: to ~ o.s. on se flatter de; s'enorgueillir de.
priest [pri:st] n prêtre m; **~hood** n prêtrise f, sacerdoce m.
prig [prig] n poseur/euse, fat m.
prim [prim] a collet monté inv, guindé(e).

primarily ['praimərili] ad principalement, essentiellement.
primary ['praiməri] a primaire; (first in importance) premier(ère), primordial(e); ~ **school** n (Brit) école primaire f.
prime [praim] a primordial(e), fondamental(e); (excellent) excellent(e) // vt (gun, pump) amorcer; (fig) mettre au courant; in the ~ of life dans la fleur de l'âge; **P~ Minister (P.M.)** n Premier ministre m.
primer ['praimə*] n (book) manuel m élémentaire; (paint) apprêt m.
primeval [prai'mi:vl] a primitif(ive); (forest) vierge.
primitive ['primitiv] a primitif(ive).
primrose ['primrəuz] n primevère f.
primus (stove) ['praiməs(stəuv)] n ® (Brit) réchaud m de camping.
prince [prins] n prince m.
princess [prin'ses] n princesse f.
principal ['prinsipl] a principal(e) // n (headmaster) directeur m, principal m.
principle ['prinsipl] n principe m; in/on ~ en/par principe.
print [print] n (mark) empreinte f; (letters) caractères mpl; (fabric) imprimé m; (ART) gravure f, estampe f; (PHOT) épreuve f // vt imprimer; (publish) publier; (write in capitals) écrire en majuscules; out of ~ épuisé(e); **~ed matter** n imprimés mpl; **~er** n imprimeur m; (machine) imprimante f; **~ing** n impression f; **~-out** n listage m.
prior ['praiə*] a antérieur(e), précédent(e) // n prieur m; ~ **to doing** avant de faire.
priority [prai'ɔriti] n priorité f.
prise [praiz] vt: to ~ open forcer.
prison ['prizn] n prison f // cpd pénitentiaire; **~er** n prisonnier/ère.
pristine ['pristi:n] a virginal(e).
privacy ['privəsi] n intimité f, solitude f.
private ['praivit] a privé(e); personnel(le); (house, car, lesson) particulier(ère) // n soldat m de deuxième classe; '~' (on envelope) 'personnelle'; in ~ en privé; ~ **enterprise** n l'entreprise privée; ~ **eye** n détective privé; **~ly** ad en privé; (within oneself) intérieurement; ~ **property** n propriété privée; **privatize** vt privatiser.
privet ['privit] n troène m.
privilege ['privilidʒ] n privilège m.
privy ['privi] a: to be ~ to être au courant de; ~ **council** n conseil privé.
prize [praiz] n prix m // a (example, idiot) parfait(e); (bull, novel) primé(e) // vt priser, faire grand cas de; ~ **giving** n distribution f des prix; **~winner** n gagnant/e.
pro [prəu] n (SPORT) professionnel/le; the **~s and cons** le pour et le contre.

probability [prɔbə'bɪlɪtɪ] *n* probabilité *f*.
probable ['prɔbəbl] *a* probable; **probably** *ad* probablement.
probation [prə'beɪʃən] *n* (*in employment*) essai *m*; (*LAW*) liberté surveillée; **on ~** (*employee*) à l'essai; (*LAW*) en liberté surveillée.
probe [prəub] *n* (*MED, SPACE*) sonde *f*; (*enquiry*) enquête *f*, investigation *f* // *vt* sonder, explorer.
problem ['prɔbləm] *n* problème *m*.
procedure [prə'si:dʒə*] *n* (*ADMIN, LAW*) procédure *f*; (*method*) marche *f* à suivre, façon *f* de procéder.
proceed [prə'si:d] *vi* (*go forward*) avancer; (*go about it*) procéder; (*continue*): **to ~ (with)** continuer, poursuivre; **to ~ to** aller à; passer à; **to ~ to do** se mettre à faire; **~ings** *npl* mesures *fpl*; (*LAW*) poursuites *fpl*; (*meeting*) réunion *f*, séance *f*; (*records*) compte rendu; actes *mpl*; **~s** ['prəusi:dz] *npl* produit *m*, recette *f*.
process ['prəuses] *n* processus *m*; (*method*) procédé *m* // *vt* traiter; **~ing** *n* traitement *m*.
procession [prə'seʃən] *n* défilé *m*, cortège *m*; **funeral ~** cortège *m* funèbre; convoi *m* mortuaire.
proclaim [prə'kleɪm] *vt* déclarer, proclamer.
procrastinate [prəu'kræstɪneɪt] *vi* faire traîner les choses, vouloir tout remettre au lendemain.
prod [prɔd] *vt* pousser.
prodigal ['prɔdɪgl] *a* prodigue.
prodigy ['prɔdɪdʒɪ] *n* prodige *m*.
produce *n* ['prɔdju:s] (*AGR*) produits *mpl* // *vt* [prə'dju:s] produire; (*to show*) présenter; (*cause*) provoquer, causer; (*THEATRE*) monter, mettre en scène; **~r** *n* (*THEATRE*) metteur *m* en scène; (*AGR, CINEMA*) producteur *m*.
product ['prɔdʌkt] *n* produit *m*.
production [prə'dʌkʃən] *n* production *f*; (*THEATRE*) mise *f* en scène; **~ line** *n* chaîne *f* (de fabrication).
productivity [prɔdʌk'tɪvɪtɪ] *n* productivité *f*.
profane [prə'feɪn] *a* sacrilège; (*lay*) profane.
profession [prə'feʃən] *n* profession *f*; **~al** *n* (*SPORT*) professionnel/le // *a* professionnel(le); (*work*) de professionnel.
professor [prə'fesə*] *n* professeur *m* (*titulaire d'une chaire*).
proficiency [prə'fɪʃənsɪ] *n* compétence *f*, aptitude *f*.
profile ['prəufaɪl] *n* profil *m*.
profit ['prɔfɪt] *n* bénéfice *m*; profit *m* // *vi*: **to ~ (by** *or* **from)** profiter (de); **~able** *a* lucratif(ive), rentable.
profiteering [prɔfɪ'tɪərɪŋ] *n* (*pej*) mercantilisme *m*.

profound [prə'faund] *a* profond(e).
profusely [prə'fju:slɪ] *ad* abondamment; avec effusion.
progeny ['prɔdʒɪnɪ] *n* progéniture *f*; descendants *mpl*.
programme, (*US*) **program** ['prəugræm] *n* programme *m*; (*RADIO, TV*) émission *f* // *vt* programmer; **~r**, (*US*) **programer** *n* programmeur/euse.
progress *n* ['prəugres] progrès *m* // *vi* [prə'gres] progresser, avancer; **in ~** en cours; **to make ~** progresser, faire des progrès, être en progrès; **~ive** ['gresɪv] *a* progressif(ive); (*person*) progressiste.
prohibit [prə'hɪbɪt] *vt* interdire, défendre.
project *n* ['prɔdʒekt] (*plan*) projet *m*, plan *m*; (*venture*) opération *f*, entreprise *f*; (*gen, SCOL: research*) étude *f*, dossier *m* // *vb* [prə'dʒekt] *vt* projeter // *vi* (*stick out*) faire saillie, s'avancer.
projection [prə'dʒekʃən] *n* projection *f*; saillie *f*.
projector [prə'dʒektə*] *n* projecteur *m*.
prolong [prə'lɔŋ] *vt* prolonger.
prom [prɔm] *n* abbr of **promenade**; (*US: ball*) bal *m* d'étudiants.
promenade [prɔmə'nɑ:d] *n* (*by sea*) esplanade *f*, promenade *f*; **~ concert** *n* concert *m* (de musique classique).
prominent ['prɔmɪnənt] *a* (*standing out*) proéminent(e); (*important*) important(e).
promiscuous [prə'mɪskjuəs] *a* (*sexually*) de mœurs légères.
promise ['prɔmɪs] *n* promesse *f* // *vt*, *vi* promettre; **promising** *a* prometteur(euse).
promote [prə'məut] *vt* promouvoir; (*venture, event*) organiser, mettre sur pied; (*new product*) lancer; **~r** *n* (*of sporting event*) organisateur/trice; **promotion** [-'məuʃən] *n* promotion *f*.
prompt [prɔmpt] *a* rapide // *ad* (*punctually*) à l'heure // *n* (*COMPUT*) message *m* (de guidage) // *vt* inciter; provoquer; (*THEATRE*) souffler (son rôle *or* ses répliques) à; **~ly** *ad* rapidement, sans délai; ponctuellement.
prone [prəun] *a* (*lying*) couché(e) (face contre terre); **~ to** enclin(e) à.
prong [prɔŋ] *n* pointe *f*; (*of fork*) dent *f*.
pronoun ['prəunaun] *n* pronom *m*.
pronounce [prə'nauns] *vt* prononcer // *vi*: **to ~ (up)on** se prononcer sur.
pronunciation [prənʌnsɪ'eɪʃən] *n* prononciation *f*.
proof [pru:f] *n* preuve *f*; (*test, of book, PHOT*) épreuve *f*; (*of alcohol*) degré *m* // *a*: **~ against** à l'épreuve de.
prop [prɔp] *n* support *m*, étai *m* // *vt* (*also*: **~ up**) étayer, soutenir; (*lean*): **to ~ sth against** appuyer qch contre *or* à.
propaganda [prɔpə'gændə] *n* propagandade *f*.

propel [prə'pɛl] *vt* propulser, faire avancer; **~ler** *n* hélice *f*; **~ling pencil** *n* (*Brit*) porte-mine *m inv*.

propensity [prə'pɛnsɪtɪ] *n* propension *f*.

proper ['prɔpə*] *a* (*suited, right*) approprié(e), bon(bonne); (*seemly*) correct(e), convenable; (*authentic*) vrai(e), véritable; (*col: real*) *n* + fini(e), vrai(e); **~ly** *ad* correctement, convenablement; bel et bien; **he doesn't eat/study ~ly** il mange/étudie mal; **~ noun** *n* nom *m* propre.

property ['prɔpətɪ] *n* (*things owned*) biens *mpl*; propriété(s) *f(pl)*; (*land*) terres *fpl*, domaine *m*; (*CHEM etc: quality*) propriété *f*; **~ owner** *n* propriétaire *m*.

prophecy ['prɔfɪsɪ] *n* prophétie *f*.

prophesy ['prɔfɪsaɪ] *vt* prédire.

prophet ['prɔfɪt] *n* prophète *m*.

proportion [prə'pɔ:ʃən] *n* proportion *f*; (*share*) part *f*; partie *f*; **~al**, **~ate** *a* proportionnel(le).

proposal [prə'pəuzl] *n* proposition *f*, offre *f*; (*plan*) projet *m*; (*of marriage*) demande *f* en mariage.

propose [prə'pəuz] *vt* proposer, suggérer // *vi* faire sa demande en mariage; **to ~ to do** avoir l'intention de faire.

proposition [prɔpə'zɪʃən] *n* proposition *f*.

propriety [prə'praɪɪtɪ] *n* (*seemliness*) bienséance *f*, convenance *f*.

prose [prəuz] *n* prose *f*; (*SCOL: translation*) thème *m*.

prosecute ['prɔsɪkju:t] *vt* poursuivre; **prosecution** [-'kju:ʃən] *n* poursuites *fpl* judiciaires; (*accusing side*) accusation *f*; **prosecutor** *n* procureur *m*; (*also: public prosecutor*) ministère public.

prospect *n* ['prɔspɛkt] perspective *f*; (*hope*) espoir *m*, chances *fpl* // *vt, vi* [prə'spɛkt] prospecter; **~s** *npl* (*for work etc*) possibilités *fpl* d'avenir, débouchés *mpl*; **prospective** [-'spɛktɪv] *a* (*possible*) éventuel(le); (*future*) futur(e).

prospectus [prə'spɛktəs] *n* prospectus *m*.

prosperity [prɔ'spɛrɪtɪ] *n* prospérité *f*.

prostitute ['prɔstɪtju:t] *n* prostituée *f*.

protect [prə'tɛkt] *vt* protéger; **~ion** *n* protection *f*; **~ive** *a* protecteur(trice).

protein ['prəuti:n] *n* protéine *f*.

protest *n* ['prəutɛst] protestation *f* // *vb* [prə'tɛst] *vi* protester // *vt* protester de.

Protestant ['prɔtɪstənt] *a, n* protestant(e).

protester [prə'tɛstə*] *n* manifestant/e.

protracted [prə'træktɪd] *a* prolongé(e).

protrude [prə'tru:d] *vi* avancer, dépasser.

proud [praud] *a* fier(ère); (*pej*) orgueilleux(euse).

prove [pru:v] *vt* prouver, démontrer // *vi*: **to ~ correct** *etc* s'avérer juste *etc*; **to ~ o.s.** montrer ce dont on est capable.

proverb ['prɔvə:b] *n* proverbe *m*.

provide [prə'vaɪd] *vt* fournir; **to ~ sb with sth** fournir qch à qn; **to ~ for** *vt fus* (*person*) subvenir aux besoins de; (*emergency*) prévoir; **~d (that)** *cj* à condition que + *sub*.

providing [prə'vaɪdɪŋ] *cj* à condition que + *sub*.

province ['prɔvɪns] *n* province *f*; **provincial** [prə'vɪnʃəl] *a* provincial(e).

provision [prə'vɪʒən] *n* (*supply*) provision *f*; (*supplying*) fourniture *f*; approvisionnement *m*; (*stipulation*) disposition *f*; **~s** *npl* (*food*) provisions *fpl*; **~al** *a* provisoire.

proviso [prə'vaɪzəu] *n* condition *f*.

provocative [prə'vɔkətɪv] *a* provocateur(trice), provocant(e).

provoke [prə'vəuk] *vt* provoquer; inciter.

prow [prau] *n* proue *f*.

prowess ['prauɪs] *n* prouesse *f*.

prowl [praul] *vi* (*also: ~ about, ~ around*) rôder // *n*: **on the ~** à l'affût; **~er** *n* rôdeur/euse.

proxy ['prɔksɪ] *n* procuration *f*.

prudent ['pru:dnt] *a* prudent(e).

prudish ['pru:dɪʃ] *a* prude, pudibond(e).

prune [pru:n] *n* pruneau *m* // *vt* élaguer.

pry [praɪ] *vi*: **to ~ into** fourrer son nez dans.

PS *n abbr* (= *postscript*) p.s.

psalm [sɑ:m] *n* psaume *m*.

pseudo- ['sju:dəu] *prefix* pseudo-; **pseudonym** *n* pseudonyme *m*.

psyche ['saɪkɪ] *n* psychisme *m*.

psychiatric [saɪkɪ'ætrɪk] *a* psychiatrique.

psychiatrist [saɪ'kaɪətrɪst] *n* psychiatre *m/f*.

psychic ['saɪkɪk] *a* (*also: ~al*) (*méta*)psychique; (*person*) doué(e) de télépathie *or* d'un sixième sens.

psychoanalyst [saɪkəu'ænəlɪst] *n* psychanalyste *m/f*.

psychological [saɪkə'lɔdʒɪkl] *a* psychologique.

psychologist [saɪ'kɔlədʒɪst] *n* psychologue *m/f*.

psychology [saɪ'kɔlədʒɪ] *n* psychologie *f*.

P.T.O. *abbr* (= *please turn over*) T.S.V.P.

pub [pʌb] *n abbr* (= *public house*) pub *m*.

pubic ['pju:bɪk] *a* pubien(ne), du pubis.

public ['pʌblɪk] *a* public/ique // *n* public *m*; **in ~** en public; **~ address system (P.A.)** *n* (système *m* de) sonorisation *f*; hauts-parleurs *mpl*.

publican ['pʌblɪkən] *n* patron *m* de pub.

public: ~ company *n* société *f*

anonyme (*cotée en bourse*); ~ **convenience** n (*Brit*) toilettes *fpl*; ~ **holiday** n jour férié; ~ **house** n (*Brit*) pub m.

publicity [pʌb'lisiti] n publicité f.

publicize ['pʌblisaiz] vt faire connaître, rendre public(ique).

publicly ['pʌbliklı] ad publiquement.

public: ~ **opinion** n opinion publique; ~ **relations (PR)** n relations publiques; ~ **school** n (*Brit*) école privée; (*US*) école publique; ~-**spirited** a qui fait preuve de civisme; ~ **transport** n transports *mpl* en commun.

publish ['pʌblıʃ] vt publier; ~**er** n éditeur m; ~**ing** n (*industry*) édition f.

puck [pʌk] n (*ICE HOCKEY*) palet m.

pucker ['pʌkə*] vt plisser.

pudding ['pudıŋ] n (*Brit: sweet*) dessert m, entremets m; (*sausage*) boudin m; **black** ~ boudin (noir).

puddle ['pʌdl] n flaque f d'eau.

puff [pʌf] n (*of smoke*) bouffée f // vt: **to** ~ **one's pipe** tirer sur sa pipe // vi sortir par bouffées; (*pant*) haleter; **to** ~ **out smoke** envoyer des bouffées de fumée; ~**ed** a (*col: out of breath*) tout(e) essoufflé(e); ~ **pastry** n pâte feuilletée; ~**y** a bouffi(e), boursouflé(e).

pull [pul] n (*tug*): **to give sth a** ~ tirer sur qch; (*fig*) influence f // vt tirer; (*muscle*) se claquer // vi tirer; **to** ~ **to pieces** mettre en morceaux; **to** ~ **one's punches** ménager son adversaire; **to** ~ **one's weight** y mettre du sien; **to** ~ **o.s. together** se ressaisir; **to** ~ **sb's leg** faire marcher qn; **to** ~ **apart** vt séparer; (*break*) mettre en pièces, démantibuler; **to** ~ **down** vt baisser, abaisser; (*house*) démolir; (*tree*) abattre; **to** ~ **in** vi (*AUT*) se ranger; (*RAIL*) entrer en gare; **to** ~ **off** vt enlever, ôter; (*deal etc*) conclure; **to** ~ **out** vi démarrer, partir; (*withdraw*) se retirer; (*AUT: come out of line*) déboîter // vt sortir; arracher; (*withdraw*) retirer; **to** ~ **over** vi (*AUT*) se ranger; **to** ~ **through** vi s'en sortir; **to** ~ **up** vi (*stop*) s'arrêter // vt remonter; (*uproot*) déraciner, arracher; (*stop*) arrêter.

pulley ['pulı] n poulie f.

pullover ['puləuvə*] n pull-over m, tricot m.

pulp [pʌlp] n (*of fruit*) pulpe f; (*for paper*) pâte f à papier.

pulpit ['pulpit] n chaire f.

pulsate [pʌl'seit] vi battre, palpiter; (*music*) vibrer.

pulse [pʌls] n (*of blood*) pouls m; (*of heart*) battement m; (*of music, engine*) vibrations *fpl*.

pummel ['pʌml] vt rouer de coups.

pump [pʌmp] n pompe f; (*shoe*) escarpin m // vt pomper; (*fig: col*) faire parler; **to** ~ **up** vt gonfler.

pumpkin ['pʌmpkın] n potiron m, citrouille f.

pun [pʌn] n jeu m de mots, calembour m.

punch [pʌntʃ] n (*blow*) coup m de poing; (*fig: force*) vivacité f, mordant m; (*tool*) poinçon m; (*drink*) punch m // vt (*hit*): **to** ~ **sb/sth** donner un coup de poing à qn/sur qch; (*make a hole*) poinçonner, perforer; ~ **line** n (*of joke*) conclusion f; ~-**up** n (*Brit col*) bagarre f.

punctual ['pʌŋktjuəl] a ponctuel(le).

punctuation [pʌŋktju'eiʃən] n ponctuation f.

puncture ['pʌŋktʃə*] n crevaison f.

pundit ['pʌndıt] n individu m qui pontifie, pontife m.

pungent ['pʌndʒənt] a piquant(e); (*fig*) mordant(e), caustique.

punish ['pʌnıʃ] vt punir; ~**ment** n punition f, châtiment m.

punk [pʌŋk] n (*also:* ~ **rocker**) punk m/f; (*also:* ~ **rock**) le punk; (*US col*) hoodlum) voyou m.

punt [pʌnt] n (*boat*) bachot m.

punter ['pʌntə*] n (*Brit: gambler*) parieur/euse.

puny ['pju:nı] a chétif(ive).

pup [pʌp] n chiot m.

pupil ['pju:pl] n élève m/f.

puppet ['pʌpıt] n marionnette f, pantin m.

puppy ['pʌpı] n chiot m, petit chien.

purchase ['pə:tʃıs] n achat m // vt acheter; ~**r** n acheteur/euse.

pure [pjuə*] a pur(e).

purely ['pjuəlı] ad purement.

purge [pə:dʒ] n (*MED*) purge f; (*POL*) épuration f, purge // vt purger.

purl [pə:l] n maille f à l'envers.

purple ['pə:pl] a violet(te); cramoisi(e).

purport [pə:'pɔ:t] vi: **to** ~ **to be/do** prétendre être/faire.

purpose ['pə:pəs] n intention f, but m; **on** ~ exprès; ~**ful** a déterminé(e), résolu(e).

purr [pə:*] vi ronronner.

purse [pə:s] n porte-monnaie m *inv*, bourse f // vt serrer, pincer.

purser ['pə:sə*] n (*NAUT*) commissaire m du bord.

pursue [pə'sju:] vt poursuivre.

pursuit [pə'sju:t] n poursuite f; (*occupation*) occupation f, activité f.

purveyor [pə'veıə*] n fournisseur m.

push [puʃ] n poussée f; (*effort*) gros effort; (*drive*) énergie f // vt pousser; (*button*) appuyer sur; (*thrust*): **to** ~ **sth (into)** enfoncer qch (dans); (*fig*) mettre en avant, faire de la publicité pour // vi pousser; appuyer; **to** ~ **aside** vt écarter; **to** ~ **off** vi (*col*) filer, ficher le camp; **to** ~ **on** vi (*continue*) continuer; **to** ~ **through** vt (*measure*) faire voter;

to ~ **up** vt (total, prices) faire monter; **~chair** n (Brit) poussette f; **~er** n (drug ~er) revendeur/euse (de drogue), ravitailleur/euse (en drogue); **~over** n (col): it's a ~over c'est un jeu d'enfant; **~-up** n (US) traction f; **~y** a (pej) arriviste.

puss, pussy(-cat) [pus, 'pusɪ(kæt)] n minet m.

put, pt, pp put [put] vt mettre, poser, placer; (say) dire, exprimer; (a question) poser; (estimate) estimer; to ~ **about** vi (NAUT) virer de bord // vt (rumour) faire courir; to ~ **across** vt (ideas etc) communiquer; faire comprendre; to ~ **away** vt (store) ranger; to ~ **back** vt (replace) remettre, replacer; (postpone) remettre; (delay) retarder; to ~ **by** vt (money) mettre de côté, économiser; to ~ **down** vt (parcel etc) poser, déposer; (pay) verser; (in writing) mettre par écrit, inscrire; (suppress: revolt etc) réprimer, faire cesser; (attribute) attribuer; to ~ **forward** vt (ideas) avancer, proposer; (date) avancer; to ~ **in** vt (gas, electricity) installer; (application, complaint) soumettre; to ~ **off** vt (light etc) éteindre; (postpone) remettre à plus tard, ajourner; (discourage) dissuader; to ~ **on** vt (clothes, lipstick etc) mettre; (light etc) allumer; (play etc) monter; (food, meal) servir; (: cook) mettre à cuire or à chauffer; (airs, weight) prendre; (brake) mettre; to ~ **out** vt mettre dehors; (one's hand) tendre; (news, rumour) faire courir, répandre; (light etc) éteindre; (person: inconvenience) déranger, gêner; to ~ **up** vt (raise) lever, relever, remonter; (pin up) afficher; (hang) accrocher; (build) construire, ériger; (a tent) monter; (increase) augmenter; (accommodate) loger; to ~ **up with** vt fus supporter.

putt [pʌt] vt poter (la balle) // n coup roulé; **~ing green** n green m.

putty ['pʌtɪ] n mastic m.

puzzle ['pʌzl] n énigme f, mystère m; (jigsaw) puzzle m; (also: crossword ~) problème m de mots croisés // vt intriguer, rendre perplexe // vi se creuser la tête.

pyjamas [pɪ'dʒɑːməz] npl (Brit) pyjama m.

pyramid ['pɪrəmɪd] n pyramide f.
Pyrenees [pɪrɪ'niːz] npl: the ~ les Pyrénées fpl.

Q

quack [kwæk] n (of duck) coin-coin m inv; (pej: doctor) charlatan m.
quad [kwɔd] abbr of **quadrangle**,

quadruplet.
quadrangle ['kwɔdræŋgl] n (MATH) quadrilatère m; (courtyard: abbr: quad) cour f.
quadruple [kwɔ'drupl] vt, vi quadrupler.
quadruplet [kwɔ'druːplɪt] n quadruplé·e.
quagmire ['kwægmaɪə*] n bourbier m.
quail [kweɪl] n (ZOOL) caille f // vi (person) perdre courage.
quaint [kweɪnt] a bizarre; (old-fashioned) désuet(ète); au charme vieillot, pittoresque.
quake [kweɪk] vi trembler // n abbr of earthquake.
qualification [kwɔlɪfɪ'keɪʃən] n (degree etc) diplôme m; (ability) compétence f, qualification f; (limitation) réserve f, restriction f.
qualified ['kwɔlɪfaɪd] a diplômé(e); (able) compétent(e), qualifié(e); (limited) conditionnel(le).
qualify ['kwɔlɪfaɪ] vt qualifier; (limit: statement) apporter des réserves à // vi: to ~ (as) obtenir son diplôme (de); to ~ (for) remplir les conditions requises (pour); (SPORT) se qualifier (pour).
quality ['kwɔlɪtɪ] n qualité f.
qualm [kwɑːm] n doute m; scrupule m.
quandary ['kwɔndrɪ] n: in a ~ devant un dilemme, dans l'embarras.
quantity ['kwɔntɪtɪ] n quantité f; ~ **surveyor** n métreur m vérificateur.
quarantine ['kwɔrntiːn] n quarantaine f.
quarrel ['kwɔrl] n querelle f, dispute f // vi se disputer, se quereller; **~some** a querelleur(euse).
quarry ['kwɔrɪ] n (for stone) carrière f; (animal) proie f, gibier m // vt (marble etc) extraire.
quart [kwɔːt] n ≈ litre m.
quarter ['kwɔːtə*] n quart m; (of year) trimestre m; (district) quartier m // vt partager en quartiers or en quatre; (MIL) caserner, cantonner; **~s** npl logement m; (MIL) quartiers mpl, cantonnement m; a ~ **of an hour** un quart d'heure; ~ **final** n quart m de finale; **~ly** a trimestriel(le) // ad tous les trois mois; **~master** n (MIL) intendant m militaire de troisième classe; (NAUT) maître m de manœuvre.
quartet(te) [kwɔː'tɛt] n quatuor m; (jazz players) quartette m.
quartz [kwɔːts] n quartz m.
quash [kwɔʃ] vt (verdict) annuler.
quaver ['kweɪvə*] vi trembler.
quay [kiː] n (also: ~side) quai m.
queasy ['kwiːzɪ] a (stomach) délicat(e); to feel ~ avoir mal au cœur.
queen [kwiːn] n (gen) reine f; (CARDS etc) dame f; ~ **mother** n reine mère f.
queer [kwɪə*] a étrange, curieux(euse); (suspicious) louche // n (col) homosexuel

m.

quell [kwɛl] *vt* réprimer, étouffer.

quench [kwɛntʃ] *vt* (*flames*) éteindre; **to ~ one's thirst** se désaltérer.

querulous ['kwɛrʊləs] *a* (*person*) récriminateur(trice); (*voice*) plaintif(ive).

query ['kwɪərɪ] *n* question *f*; (*doubt*) doute *m*; (*question mark*) point *m* d'interrogation // *vt* mettre en question *or* en doute.

quest [kwɛst] *n* recherche *f*, quête *f*.

question ['kwɛstʃən] *n* question *f* // *vt* (*person*) interroger; (*plan, idea*) mettre en question *or* en doute; **it's a ~ of doing** il s'agit de faire; **beyond ~** sans aucun doute; **out of the ~** hors de question; **~able** *a* discutable; **~ mark** *n* point *m* d'interrogation.

questionnaire [kwɛstʃə'nɛə*] *n* questionnaire *m.*

queue [kjuː] (*Brit*) *n* queue *f*, file *f* // *vi* faire la queue.

quibble ['kwɪbl] *vi* ergoter, chicaner.

quick [kwɪk] *a* rapide; (*reply*) prompt(e), rapide; (*mind*) vif(vive) // *ad* vite, rapidement // *n*: **cut to the ~** (*fig*) touché(e) au vif; **be ~!** dépêche-toi!; **~en** *vt* accélérer, presser; (*rouse*) stimuler // *vi* s'accélérer, devenir plus rapide; **~ly** *ad* vite, rapidement; **~sand** *n* sables mouvants; **~-witted** *a* à l'esprit vif.

quid [kwɪd] *n* (*pl inv*) (*Brit col*) livre *f.*

quiet ['kwaɪət] *a* tranquille, calme; (*ceremony, colour*) discret(ète) // *n* tranquillité *f*, calme *m* // *vt, vi* (*US*) = **~en**; **keep ~!** tais-toi!; **~en** (*also*: **~en down**) *vi* se calmer, s'apaiser // *vt* calmer, apaiser; **~ly** *ad* tranquillement, calmement; discrètement.

quilt [kwɪlt] *n* édredon *m*; (*continental ~*) couette *f.*

quin [kwɪn] *n abbr of* **quintuplet**.

quintuplet [kwɪn'tjuːplɪt] *n* quintuplé/e.

quip [kwɪp] *n* remarque piquante *or* spirituelle, pointe *f.*

quirk [kwəːk] *n* bizarrerie *f.*

quit, *pt, pp* **quit** *or* **quitted** [kwɪt] *vt* quitter // *vi* (*give up*) abandonner, renoncer; (*resign*) démissionner.

quite [kwaɪt] *ad* (*rather*) assez, plutôt; (*entirely*) complètement, tout à fait; **I ~ understand** je comprends très bien; **~ a few of them** un assez grand nombre d'entre eux; **~ (so)!** exactement!

quits [kwɪts] *a*: **~ (with)** quitte (envers); **let's call it ~** restons-en là.

quiver ['kwɪvə*] *vi* trembler, frémir.

quiz [kwɪz] *n* (*game*) jeu-concours *m*; test *m* de connaissances // *vt* interroger; **~zical** *a* narquois(e).

quota ['kwəʊtə] *n* quota *m.*

quotation [kwəʊ'teɪʃən] *n* citation *f*; (*of shares etc*) cote *f*, cours *m*; (*estimate*) devis *m*; **~ marks** *npl* guillemets *mpl.*

quote [kwəʊt] *n* citation *f* // *vt* (*sentence*) citer; (*price*) donner, fixer; (*shares*) coter // *vi*: **to ~ from** citer.

R

rabbi ['ræbaɪ] *n* rabbin *m.*

rabbit ['ræbɪt] *n* lapin *m*; **~ hutch** *n* clapier *m.*

rabble ['ræbl] *n* (*pej*) populace *f.*

rabies ['reɪbiːz] *n* rage *f.*

RAC *n abbr* (*Brit*) = *Royal Automobile Club.*

race [reɪs] *n* race *f*; (*competition, rush*) course *f* // *vt* (*person*) faire la course avec; (*horse*) faire courir; (*engine*) emballer // *vi* courir; (*engine*) s'emballer; **~ car** *n* (*US*) = **racing car**; **~ car driver** *n* (*US*) = **racing driver**; **~course** *n* champ *m* de courses; **~horse** *n* cheval *m* de course; **~track** *n* piste *f.*

racial ['reɪʃl] *a* racial(e); **~ist** *a, n* raciste (*m/f*).

racing ['reɪsɪŋ] *n* courses *fpl*; **~ car** *n* (*Brit*) voiture *f* de course; **~ driver** *n* (*Brit*) pilote *m* de course.

racism ['reɪsɪzəm] *n* racisme *m*; **racist** *a, n* raciste (*m/f*).

rack [ræk] *n* (*also*: **luggage ~**) filet *m* à bagages; (*also*: **roof ~**) galerie *f* // *vt* tourmenter; **to ~ one's brains** se creuser la cervelle.

racket ['rækɪt] *n* (*for tennis*) raquette *f*; (*noise*) tapage *m*; vacarme *m*; (*swindle*) escroquerie *f*; (*organized crime*) racket *m.*

racquet ['rækɪt] *n* raquette *f.*

racy ['reɪsɪ] *a* plein(e) de verve; osé(e).

radar ['reɪdɑː*] *n* radar *m.*

radial ['reɪdɪəl] *a* (*also*: **~-ply**) à carcasse radiale.

radiant ['reɪdɪənt] *a* rayonnant(e).

radiate ['reɪdɪeɪt] *vt* (*heat*) émettre, dégager // *vi* (*lines*) rayonner.

radiation [reɪdɪ'eɪʃən] *n* rayonnement *m*; (*radioactive*) radiation *f.*

radiator ['reɪdɪeɪtə*] *n* radiateur *m.*

radical ['rædɪkl] *a* radical(e).

radii ['reɪdɪaɪ] *npl of* **radius**.

radio ['reɪdɪəʊ] *n* radio *f*; **on the ~** à la radio.

radioactive [reɪdɪəʊ'æktɪv] *a* radioactif(ive).

radio station *n* station *f* de radio.

radish ['rædɪʃ] *n* radis *m.*

radius ['reɪdɪəs], *pl* **radii** *n* rayon *m.*

RAF *n abbr of* **Royal Air Force**.

raffle ['ræfl] *n* tombola *f.*

raft [rɑːft] *n* (*craft*; *also*: **life ~**) radeau *m.*

rafter ['rɑːftə*] *n* chevron *m.*

rag [ræg] *n* chiffon *m*; (*pej: newspaper*) feuille *f*, torchon *m*; (*for charity*) attractions organisées par les étudiants au profit d'œuvres de charité // *vt* (*Brit*) chahuter, mettre en boîte; **~s** *npl* haillons *mpl*; **~-and-bone man** *n* (*Brit*) = **~man**; **~ doll** *n* poupée *f* de chiffon.

rage [reɪdʒ] *n* (*fury*) rage *f*, fureur *f* // *vi* (*person*) être fou(folle) de rage; (*storm*) faire rage, être déchaîné(e); it's all the ~ cela fait fureur.

ragged ['rægɪd] *a* (*edge*) inégal(e), qui accroche; (*cuff*) effiloché(e); (*appearance*) déguenillé(e).

ragman ['rægmæn] *n* chiffonnier *m*.

raid [reɪd] *n* (*MIL*) raid *m*; (*criminal*) hold-up *m* inv; (*by police*) descente *f*, rafle *f* // *vt* faire un raid sur *or* un hold-up dans *or* une descente dans.

rail [reɪl] *n* (*on stair*) rampe *f*; (*on bridge, balcony*) balustrade *f*; (*of ship*) bastingage *m*; (*for train*) rail *m*; **~s** *npl* rails *mpl*, voie ferrée; **by ~** par chemin de fer; **~ing(s)** *n(pl)* grille *f*; **~way**, (*US*) **~road** *n* chemin *m* de fer; **~way line** *f* ligne *f* de chemin de fer; **~wayman** *n* cheminot *m*; **~way station** *n* gare *f*.

rain [reɪn] *n* pluie *f* // *vi* pleuvoir; in the ~ sous la pluie; it's **~ing** il pleut; **~bow** *n* arc-en-ciel *m*; **~coat** *n* imperméable *m*; **~drop** *n* goutte *f* de pluie; **~fall** *n* chute *f* de pluie; (*measurement*) hauteur *f* des précipitations; **~y** *a* pluvieux(euse).

raise [reɪz] *n* augmentation *f* // *vt* (*lift*) lever; hausser; (*build*) ériger; (*increase*) augmenter; (*a protest, doubt*) provoquer, causer; (*a question*) soulever; (*cattle, family*) élever; (*crop*) faire pousser; (*army, funds*) rassembler; (*loan*) obtenir; to ~ one's voice élever la voix.

raisin ['reɪzn] *n* raisin sec.

rake [reɪk] *n* (*tool*) râteau *m*; (*person*) débauché *m* // *vt* (*garden*) ratisser; (*with machine gun*) balayer.

rally ['rælɪ] *n* (*POL etc*) meeting *m*, rassemblement *m*; (*AUT*) rallye *m*; (*TENNIS*) échange *m* // *vt* rassembler, rallier // *vi* se rallier; (*sick person*) aller mieux; (*Stock Exchange*) reprendre; to ~ round *vt fus* se rallier à; venir en aide à.

RAM [ræm] *n abbr* (= *random access memory*) mémoire vive.

ram [ræm] *n* bélier *m* // *vt* enfoncer; (*soil*) tasser; (*crash into*) emboutir; percuter; éperonner.

ramble ['ræmbl] *n* randonnée *f* // *vi* (*pej: also: ~ on*) discourir, pérorer; **~r** *n* promeneur/euse, randonneur/euse; (*BOT*) rosier grimpant; **rambling** *a* (*speech*) décousu(e); (*BOT*) grimpant(e).

ramp [ræmp] *n* (*incline*) rampe *f*; dénivellation *f*; (*in garage*) pont *m*; on

~, off ~ (*US AUT*) bretelle *f* d'accès.

rampage [ræm'peɪdʒ] *n*: to be on the ~ se déchaîner.

rampant ['ræmpənt] *a* (*disease etc*) qui sévit.

ramshackle ['ræmʃækl] *a* (*house*) délabré(e); (*car etc*) déglingué(e).

ran [ræn] *pt of* **run**.

ranch [rɑːntʃ] *n* ranch *m*; **~er** *n* propriétaire *m* de ranch; cowboy *m*.

rancid ['rænsɪd] *a* rance.

rancour, (*US*) **rancor** ['ræŋkə*] *n* rancune *f*.

random ['rændəm] *a* fait(e) or établi(e) au hasard; (*COMPUT, MATH*) aléatoire // *n*: at ~ au hasard.

randy ['rændɪ] *a* (*Brit col*) excité(e); lubrique.

rang [ræŋ] *pt of* **ring**.

range [reɪndʒ] *n* (*of mountains*) chaîne *f*; (*of missile, voice*) portée *f*; (*of products*) choix *m*, gamme *f*; (*MIL: also: shooting ~*) champ *m* de tir; (*indoor*) stand *m* de tir; (*also: kitchen ~*) fourneau *m* (de cuisine) // *vt* (*place*) mettre en rang, placer; (*roam*) parcourir // *vi*: to ~ over couvrir; to ~ from ... to aller de ... à.

ranger ['reɪndʒə*] *n* garde forestier.

rank [ræŋk] *n* rang *m*; (*MIL*) grade *m*; (*Brit: also: taxi ~*) station *f* de taxis // *vi*: to ~ among compter or se classer parmi // *a* (qui sent) fort(e); extrême; the ~s (*MIL*) la troupe; the ~ and file (*fig*) la masse, la base.

rankle ['ræŋkl] *vi* (*insult*) rester sur le cœur.

ransack ['rænsæk] *vt* fouiller (à fond); (*plunder*) piller.

ransom ['rænsəm] *n* rançon *f*; to hold sb to ~ (*fig*) exercer un chantage sur qn.

rant [rænt] *vi* fulminer.

rap [ræp] *vt* frapper sur *or* à; taper sur.

rape [reɪp] *n* viol *m*; (*BOT*) colza *m* // *vt* violer; **~(seed) oil** *n* huile *f* de colza.

rapid ['ræpɪd] *a* rapide; **~s** *npl* (*GEO*) rapides *mpl*; **~ly** *ad* rapidement.

rapist ['reɪpɪst] *n* auteur *m* d'un viol.

rapport [ræ'pɔː*] *n* entente *f*.

rapture ['ræptʃə*] *n* extase *f*, ravissement *m*.

rare [reə*] *a* rare; (*CULIN: steak*) saignant(e).

rarely ['reəlɪ] *ad* rarement.

raring ['reərɪŋ] *a*: to be ~ to go (*col*) être très impatient(e) de commencer.

rascal ['rɑːskl] *n* vaurien *m*.

rash [ræʃ] *a* imprudent(e), irréfléchi(e) // *n* (*MED*) rougeur *f*, éruption *f*.

rasher ['ræʃə*] *n* fine tranche (de lard).

raspberry ['rɑːzbərɪ] *n* framboise *f*.

rasping ['rɑːspɪŋ] *a*: ~ noise grincement *m*.

rat [ræt] *n* rat *m*.

rate [reɪt] *n* (*ratio*) taux *m*, pourcentage

m; (speed) vitesse f, rythme m; (price) tarif m // vt classer; évaluer; to ~ sb/ sth as considérer qn/qch comme; ~s npl (Brit) impôts locaux; (fees) tarifs mpl; ~able value n (Brit) valeur locative imposable; ~payer n (Brit) contribuable m/f (payant les impôts locaux).

rather ['rɑːðə*] ad plutôt; it's ~ expensive c'est assez cher; (too much) c'est un peu cher; there's ~ a lot il y en a beaucoup; I would or I'd ~ go j'aimerais mieux or je préférerais partir.

rating ['reɪtɪŋ] n classement m; cote f; (NAUT: category) classe f; (: Brit : sailor) matelot m.

ratio ['reɪʃɪəu] n proportion f.

ration ['ræʃən] n (gen pl) ration(s) f(pl).

rational ['ræʃənl] a raisonnable, sensé(e); (solution, reasoning) logique; (MED) lucide; ~e [-'nɑːl] n raisonnement m; justification f; ~ize vt rationaliser; (conduct) essayer d'expliquer or de motiver.

rat race n foire f d'empoigne.

rattle ['rætl] n cliquetis m; (louder) bruit m de ferraille; (object: of baby) hochet m; (: of sports fan) crécelle f // vi cliqueter; faire un bruit de ferraille or du bruit // vt agiter (bruyamment); ~snake n serpent m à sonnettes.

raucous ['rɔːkəs] a rauque.

rave [reɪv] vi (in anger) s'emporter; (with enthusiasm) s'extasier; (MED) délirer.

raven ['reɪvən] n corbeau m.

ravenous ['rævənəs] a affamé(e).

ravine [rə'viːn] n ravin m.

raving ['reɪvɪŋ] a: ~ lunatic n fou furieux/folle furieuse.

ravishing ['rævɪʃɪŋ] a enchanteur(eresse).

raw [rɔː] a (uncooked) cru(e); (not processed) brut(e); (sore) à vif, irrité(e); (inexperienced) inexpérimenté(e); ~ deal n (col) sale coup m; ~ material n matière première.

ray [reɪ] n rayon m; ~ of hope n lueur f d'espoir.

raze [reɪz] vt raser, détruire.

razor ['reɪzə*] n rasoir m; ~ blade n lame f de rasoir.

Rd abbr of **road**.

re [riː] prep concernant.

reach [riːtʃ] n portée f, atteinte f; (of river etc) étendue f // vt atteindre; parvenir à // vi s'étendre; out of/within ~ hors de/à portée; to ~ out vi: to ~ out for allonger le bras pour prendre.

react [riː'ækt] vi réagir; ~ion [-'ækʃən] n réaction f.

reactor [riː'æktə*] n réacteur m.

read, pt, pp **read** [riːd, red] vi lire // vt lire; (understand) comprendre, interpréter; (study) étudier; (subj: instrument etc) indiquer, marquer; to ~ out

vt lire à haute voix; ~able a facile or agréable à lire; ~er n lecteur/trice; (book) livre m de lecture; (Brit: at university) maître m de conférences; ~ership n (of paper etc) (nombre m de) lecteurs mpl.

readily ['redɪlɪ] ad volontiers, avec empressement; (easily) facilement.

readiness ['redɪnɪs] n empressement m; in ~ (prepared) prêt(e).

reading ['riːdɪŋ] n lecture f; (understanding) interprétation f; (on instrument) indications fpl.

ready ['redɪ] a prêt(e); (willing) prêt, disposé(e); (quick) prompt(e); (available) disponible // ad: ~-cooked tout(e) cuit(e) (d'avance) // n: at the ~ (MIL) prêt à faire feu; (fig) tout(e) prêt(e) etc; to get ~ vi se préparer // vt préparer; ~-made a tout(e) fait(e); ~ money n (argent m) liquide m; ~ reckoner n barème m; ~-to-wear a en prêt-à-porter.

real [rɪəl] a réel(le); véritable; in ~ terms dans la réalité; ~ estate n biens fonciers or immobiliers; ~istic [-'lɪstɪk] a réaliste.

reality [riː'ælɪtɪ] n réalité f.

realization [rɪəlaɪ'zeɪʃən] n prise f de conscience; réalisation f.

realize ['rɪəlaɪz] vt (understand) se rendre compte de; (a project, COMM: asset) réaliser.

really ['rɪəlɪ] ad vraiment; ~? c'est vrai?

realm [relm] n royaume m.

realtor ['rɪəltə*] n (US) agent immobilier.

reap [riːp] vt moissonner; (fig) récolter.

reappear [riːə'pɪə*] vi réapparaître, reparaître.

rear [rɪə*] a de derrière, arrière inv; (AUT: wheel etc) arrière // n arrière m, derrière m // vt (cattle, family) élever // vi (also: ~ up: animal) se cabrer.

rear-view ['rɪəvjuː]: ~ mirror n (AUT) rétroviseur m.

reason ['riːzn] n raison f // vi: to ~ with sb raisonner qn, faire entendre raison à qn; to have ~ to think avoir lieu de penser; it stands to ~ that il va sans dire que; ~able a raisonnable; (not bad) acceptable; ~ably ad raisonnablement; ~ing n raisonnement m.

reassurance [riːə'ʃuərəns] n réconfort m; assurance f, garantie f.

reassure [riːə'ʃuə*] vt rassurer; to ~ sb of donner à qn l'assurance répétée de.

rebate ['riːbeɪt] n (on product) rabais m; (on tax etc) dégrèvement m; (repayment) remboursement m.

rebel n ['rebl] rebelle m/f // vi [rɪ'bel] se rebeller, se révolter; ~lious a rebelle.

rebound vi [rɪ'baund] (ball) rebondir // n ['riːbaund] rebond m.

rebuff [rɪ'bʌf] n rebuffade f.

rebuke [rɪ'bjuːk] vt réprimander.

rebut [rɪ'bʌt] vt réfuter.

recall [rɪ'kɔːl] vt rappeler; (remember) se rappeler, se souvenir de // n rappel m.

recant [rɪ'kænt] vi se rétracter; (REL) abjurer.

recap ['riːkæp] vt, vi récapituler.

recapitulate [riːkə'pɪtjuleɪt] vt, vi = recap.

rec'd abbr = received.

recede [rɪ'siːd] vi s'éloigner; reculer; redescendre; **receding** a (forehead, chin) fuyant(e); **receding hairline** front dégarni.

receipt [rɪ'siːt] n (document) reçu m; (for parcel etc) accusé m de réception; (act of receiving) réception f; ~s npl (COMM) recettes fpl.

receive [rɪ'siːv] vt recevoir.

receiver [rɪ'siːvə*] n (TEL) récepteur m, combiné m; (of stolen goods) receleur m; (LAW) administrateur m judiciaire.

recent ['riːsnt] a récent(e); ~ly ad récemment.

receptacle [rɪ'septɪkl] n récipient m.

reception [rɪ'sepʃən] n réception f; (welcome) accueil m, réception; ~ desk n réception f; ~ist n réceptionniste m/f.

recess [rɪ'ses] n (in room) renfoncement m; (for bed) alcôve f; (secret place) recoin m; (POL etc: holiday) vacances fpl; ~ion [-'seʃən] n récession f.

recipe ['resɪpɪ] n recette f.

recipient [rɪ'sɪpɪənt] n bénéficiaire m/f; (of letter) destinataire m/f.

recital [rɪ'saɪtl] n récital m.

recite [rɪ'saɪt] vt (poem) réciter.

reckless ['reklǝs] a (driver etc) imprudent(e).

reckon ['rekən] vt (count) calculer, compter; (consider) considérer, estimer; (think) : I ~ that ... je pense que ...; to ~ on vt fus compter sur, s'attendre à; ~ing n compte m, calcul m; estimation f.

reclaim [rɪ'kleɪm] vt (land) amender; (: from sea) assécher; (: from forest) défricher; (demand back) réclamer (le remboursement or la restitution de).

recline [rɪ'klaɪn] vi être allongé(e) or étendu(e); **reclining** a (seat) à dossier réglable.

recluse [rɪ'kluːs] n reclus/e, ermite m.

recognition [rekəg'nɪʃən] n reconnaissance f; **to gain** ~ être reconnu(e); **transformed beyond** ~ méconnaissable.

recognize ['rekəgnaɪz] vt: **to** ~ **(by/as)** reconnaître (à/comme étant).

recoil [rɪ'kɔɪl] vi (person): **to** ~ **(from)** reculer (devant) // n (of gun) recul m.

recollect [rekə'lekt] vt se rappeler, se souvenir de; ~**ion** [-'lekʃən] n souvenir m.

recommend [rekə'mend] vt recommander.

reconcile ['rekənsaɪl] vt (two people) réconcilier; (two facts) concilier, accorder; **to** ~ **o.s. to** se résigner à.

recondition [riːkən'dɪʃən] vt remettre à neuf; réviser entièrement.

reconnoitre, (US) **reconnoiter** [rekə'nɔɪtə*] (MIL) vt reconnaître // vi faire une reconnaissance.

reconstruct [riːkən'strʌkt] vt (building) reconstruire; (crime) reconstituer.

record n ['rekɔːd] rapport m, récit m; (of meeting etc) procès-verbal m; (register) registre m; (file) dossier m; (also: police ~) casier m judiciaire; (MUS: disc) disque m; (SPORT) record m // vt [rɪ'kɔːd] (set down) noter; (relate) rapporter; (MUS: song etc) enregistrer; **in** ~ **time** dans un temps record inv; **to keep a** ~ **of** noter; **off the** ~ a officieux(euse) // ad officieusement; ~ **card** n (in file) fiche f; ~**ed delivery** (Brit POST): ~**ed delivery letter** etc lettre etc recommandée; ~**er** n (LAW) avocat nommé à la fonction de juge; (MUS) flûte f à bec; ~ **holder** n (SPORT) détenteur/trice du record; ~**ing** n (MUS) enregistrement m; ~ **player** n électrophone m.

recount [rɪ'kaunt] vt raconter.

re-count n ['riːkaunt] (POL: of votes) pointage m // vt [riː'kaunt] recompter.

recoup [rɪ'kuːp] vt: **to** ~ **one's losses** récupérer ce qu'on a perdu, se refaire.

recourse [rɪ'kɔːs] n recours m; expédient m.

recover [rɪ'kʌvə*] vt récupérer // vi (from illness) se rétablir; (from shock) se remettre; (country) se redresser.

recovery [rɪ'kʌvərɪ] n récupération f; rétablissement m; redressement m.

recreation [rekrɪ'eɪʃən] n récréation f, détente f; ~**al** a pour la détente, récréatif(ive).

recruit [rɪ'kruːt] n recrue f // vt recruter.

rectangle ['rektæŋgl] n rectangle m; **rectangular** [-'tæŋgjulə*] a rectangulaire.

rectify ['rektɪfaɪ] vt (error) rectifier, corriger; (omission) réparer.

rector ['rektə*] n (REL) pasteur m; **rectory** n presbytère m.

recuperate [rɪ'kjuːpəreɪt] vi récupérer; (from illness) se rétablir.

recur [rɪ'kə:*] vi se reproduire; (idea, opportunity) se retrouver; (symptoms) réapparaître; ~**rent** a périodique, fréquent(e).

red [red] n rouge m; (POL: pej) rouge m/f // a rouge; **in the** ~ (account) à découvert; (business) en déficit; ~ **carpet treatment** n réception f en grande pompe; **R**~ **Cross** n Croix-Rouge f; ~ **currant** n groseille f (rouge); ~**den** vt, *vi* rougir; **~dish** *a* rougeâtre; (*hair*) plutôt roux(rousse).

redeem [rɪ'di:m] *vt* (*debt*) rembourser; (*sth in pawn*) dégager; (*fig, also REL*) racheter; **~ing** *a* (*feature*) qui sauve, qui rachète (le reste).

redeploy [ri:dɪ'plɔɪ] *vt* (*resources*) réorganiser.

red-haired [red'hɛəd] *a* roux(rousse).

red-handed [red'hændɪd] *a:* **to be caught ~** être pris(e) en flagrant délit *or* la main dans le sac.

redhead ['redhed] *n* roux/rousse.

red herring *n* (*fig*) diversion *f*, fausse piste.

red-hot [red'hɔt] *a* chauffé(e) au rouge, brûlant(e).

redirect [ri:daɪ'rɛkt] *vt* (*mail*) faire suivre.

red light *n*: **to go through a ~** (*AUT*) brûler un feu rouge; **red-light district** *n* quartier réservé.

redo [ri:'du:] *vt irg* refaire.

redolent ['redələnt] *a:* **~ of** qui sent; (*fig*) qui évoque.

redress [rɪ'drɛs] *n* réparation *f* // *vt* redresser.

Red Sea *n* la mer Rouge.

redskin ['redskɪn] *n* Peau-Rouge *m/f*.

red tape *n* (*fig*) paperasserie (administrative).

reduce [rɪ'dju:s] *vt* réduire; (*lower*) abaisser; **'~ speed now'** (*AUT*) 'ralentir'; **reduction** [rɪ'dʌkʃən] *n* réduction *f*; (*of price*) baisse *f*; (*discount*) rabais *m*; réduction.

redundancy [rɪ'dʌndənsɪ] *n* licenciement *m*, mise *f* au chômage.

redundant [rɪ'dʌndnt] *a* (*worker*) mis(e) au chômage, licencié(e); (*detail, object*) superflu(e); **to be made ~** être licencié(e), être mis(e) au chômage.

reed [ri:d] *n* (*BOT*) roseau *m*.

reef [ri:f] *n* (*at sea*) récif *m*, écueil *m*.

reek [ri:k] *vi*: **to ~ (of)** puer, empester.

reel [ri:l] *n* bobine *f*; (*TECH*) dévidoir *m*; (*FISHING*) moulinet *m*; (*CINEMA*) bande *f* // *vt* (*TECH*) bobiner; (*also:* **~ up**) enrouler // *vi* (*sway*) chanceler.

ref [rɛf] *n abbr* (*col: = referee*) arbitre *m*.

refectory [rɪ'fɛktərɪ] *n* réfectoire *m*.

refer [rɪ'fə:*] *vt*: **to ~ sth to** (*dispute, decision*) soumettre qch à; **to ~ sb to** (*inquirer: for information*) adresser *or* envoyer qn à; (*reader: to text*) renvoyer qn à; **to ~ to** *vt fus* (*allude to*) parler de, faire allusion à; (*apply to*) s'appliquer à; (*consult*) se reporter à.

referee [rɛfə'ri:] *n* arbitre *m*; (*Brit: for job application*) répondant/e.

reference ['rɛfrəns] *n* référence *f*, renvoi *m*; (*mention*) allusion *f*, mention *f*; (*for job application: letter*) références; lettre *f* de recommandation; (*: person*)

répondant/e; **with ~ to** en ce qui concerne; (*COMM: in letter*) me référant à; **~ book** *n* ouvrage *m* de référence.

refill *vt* [ri:'fɪl] remplir à nouveau; (*pen, lighter etc*) recharger // *n* ['ri:fɪl] (*for pen etc*) recharge *f*.

refine [rɪ'faɪn] *vt* (*sugar, oil*) raffiner; (*taste*) affiner; **~d** *a* (*person, taste*) raffiné(e).

reflect [rɪ'flɛkt] *vt* (*light, image*) réfléchir, refléter; (*fig*) refléter // *vi* (*think*) réfléchir, méditer; **to ~ on** *vt fus* (*discredit*) porter atteinte à, faire tort à; **~ion** [-'flɛkʃən] *n* réflexion *f*; (*image*) reflet *m*; (*criticism*): **~ion on** critique *f* de; atteinte *f* à; **on ~ion** réflexion faite.

reflex ['ri:flɛks] *a, n* réflexe (*m*); **~ive** [rɪ'flɛksɪv] *a* (*LING*) réfléchi(e).

reform [rɪ'fɔ:m] *n* réforme *f* // *vt* réformer; **the R~ation** [rɛfə'meɪʃən] *n* la Réforme; **~atory** *n* (*US*) ≈ centre *m* d'éducation surveillée.

refrain [rɪ'freɪn] *vi*: **to ~ from doing** s'abstenir de faire // *n* refrain *m*.

refresh [rɪ'frɛʃ] *vt* rafraîchir; (*subj: food*) redonner des forces à; (*: sleep*) reposer; **~er course** *n* (*Brit*) cours *m* de recyclage; **~ing** *a* (*drink*) rafraîchissant(e); (*sleep*) réparateur(trice); **~ments** *npl* rafraîchissements *mpl*.

refrigerator [rɪ'frɪdʒəreɪtə*] *n* réfrigérateur *m*, frigidaire *m*.

refuel [ri:'fjuəl] *vi* se ravitailler en carburant.

refuge ['rɛfju:dʒ] *n* refuge *m*; **to take ~ in** se réfugier dans.

refugee [rɛfju'dʒi:] *n* réfugié/e.

refund *n* ['ri:fʌnd] remboursement *m* // *vt* [rɪ'fʌnd] rembourser.

refurbish [ri:'fə:bɪʃ] *vt* remettre à neuf.

refusal [rɪ'fju:zəl] *n* refus *m*; **to have first ~ on** avoir droit de préemption sur.

refuse *n* ['rɛfju:s] ordures *fpl*, détritus *mpl* // *vt, vi* [rɪ'fju:z] refuser; **~ collection** *n* ramassage *m* d'ordures.

regain [rɪ'geɪn] *vt* regagner; retrouver.

regal ['ri:gl] *a* royal(e); **~ia** [rɪ'geɪlɪə] *n* insignes *mpl* de la royauté.

regard [rɪ'gɑ:d] *n* respect *m*, estime *f*, considération *f* // *vt* considérer; **to give one's ~s to** faire ses amitiés à; **'with kindest ~s'** 'bien amicalement'; **~ing, as ~s, with ~ to** *prep* en ce qui concerne; **~less** *ad* quand même; **~less of** sans se soucier de.

régime [reɪ'ʒi:m] *n* régime *m*.

regiment ['rɛdʒɪmənt] *n* régiment *m* // *vt* ['rɛdʒɪment] imposer une discipline trop stricte à; **~al** [-'mɛntl] *a* d'un *or* du régiment.

region ['ri:dʒən] *n* région *f*; **in the ~ of** (*fig*) aux alentours de; **~al** *a* régional(e).

register ['rɛdʒɪstə*] *n* registre *m*; (*also:* **electoral ~**) liste électorale // *vt* enregistrer, inscrire; *(birth)* déclarer; *(vehicle)* immatriculer; *(luggage)* enregistrer; *(letter)* envoyer en recommandé; *(subj: instrument)* marquer // *vi* se faire inscrire; *(at hotel)* signer le registre; *(make impression)* être (bien) compris(e); **~ed** *a (design)* déposé(e); *(Brit: letter)* recommandé(e); **~ed trademark** *n* marque déposée.

registrar ['rɛdʒɪstra:*] *n* officier *m* de l'état civil; secrétaire (général).

registration [rɛdʒɪs'treɪʃən] *n (act)* enregistrement *m*; inscription *f*; *(AUT: also:* ~ **number)** numéro *m* d'immatriculation.

registry ['rɛdʒɪstrɪ] *n* bureau *m* de l'enregistrement; ~ **office** *n (Brit)* bureau *m* de l'état civil; **to get married in a** ~ **office** ≈ se marier à la mairie.

regret [rɪ'grɛt] *n* regret *m* // *vt* regretter; **~fully** *ad* à or avec regret.

regular ['rɛgjulə*] *a* régulier(ère); *(usual)* habituel(le), normal(e); *(soldier)* de métier; *(COMM: size)* ordinaire // *n (client etc)* habitué/e; **~ly** *ad* régulièrement.

regulate ['rɛgjuleɪt] *vt* régler; **regulation** [-'leɪʃən] *n (rule)* règlement *m*; *(adjustment)* réglage *m*.

rehabilitation ['ri:həbɪlɪ'teɪʃən] *n (of offender)* réhabilitation *f*; *(of disabled)* rééducation *f*, réadaptation *f*.

rehearsal [rɪ'hə:səl] *n* répétition *f*.

rehearse [rɪ'hə:s] *vt* répéter.

reign [reɪn] *n* règne *m* // *vi* régner.

reimburse [ri:ɪm'bə:s] *vt* rembourser.

rein [reɪn] *n (for horse)* rêne *f*.

reindeer ['reɪndɪə*] *n (pl inv)* renne *m*.

reinforce [ri:ɪn'fɔ:s] *vt* renforcer; **~d concrete** *n* béton armé; **~ments** *npl (MIL)* renfort(s) *m(pl)*.

reinstate [ri:ɪn'steɪt] *vt* rétablir, réintégrer.

reject *n* ['ri:dʒɛkt] *(COMM)* article *m* de rebut // *vt* [rɪ'dʒɛkt] refuser; *(COMM: goods)* mettre au rebut; *(idea)* rejeter; **~ion** [rɪ'dʒɛkʃən] *n* rejet *m*, refus *m*.

rejoice [rɪ'dʒɔɪs] *vi:* **to** ~ **(at** *or* **over)** se réjouir (de).

rejuvenate [rɪ'dʒu:vəneɪt] *vt* rajeunir.

relapse [rɪ'læps] *n (MED)* rechute *f*.

relate [rɪ'leɪt] *vt (tell)* raconter; *(connect)* établir un rapport entre // *vi:* **to** ~ **to** se rapporter à; **~d** *a* apparenté(e); **relating to** *prep* concernant.

relation [rɪ'leɪʃən] *n (person)* parent/e; *(link)* rapport *m*, lien *m*; **~ship** *n* rapport *m*, lien *m*; *(personal ties)* relations *fpl*, rapports; *(also:* **family ~ship)** lien de parenté; *(affair)* liaison *f*.

relative ['rɛlətɪv] *n* parent/e // *a* relatif(ive); *(respective)* respectif(ive); **all her** ~**s** toute sa famille.

relax [rɪ'læks] *vi* se relâcher; *(person:*

unwind) se détendre // *vt* relâcher; *(mind, person)* détendre; **~ation** [ri:læk'seɪʃən] *n* relâchement *m*; détente *f*; *(entertainment)* distraction *f*; **~ed** *a* relâché(e); détendu(e); **~ing** *a* délassant(e).

relay ['ri:leɪ] *n (SPORT)* course *f* de relais // *vt (message)* retransmettre, relayer.

release [rɪ'li:s] *n (from prison, obligation)* libération *f*; *(of gas etc)* émission *f*; *(of film etc)* sortie *f*; *(record)* disque *m*; *(device)* déclencheur *m* // *vt (prisoner)* libérer; *(book, film)* sortir; *(report, news)* rendre public, publier; *(gas etc)* émettre, dégager; *(free: from wreckage etc)* dégager; *(TECH: catch, spring etc)* déclencher; *(let go)* relâcher; lâcher; desserrer.

relegate ['rɛləgeɪt] *vt* reléguer; *(SPORT):* **to be** ~**d** descendre dans une division inférieure.

relent [rɪ'lɛnt] *vi* se laisser fléchir; **~less** *a* implacable.

relevant ['rɛləvənt] *a* approprié(e); *(fact)* significatif(ive); *(information)* utile, pertinent(e); ~ **to** ayant rapport à, approprié à.

reliable [rɪ'laɪəbl] *a (person, firm)* sérieux(euse), fiable; *(method, machine)* fiable; **reliably** *ad:* **to be reliably informed** savoir de source sûre.

reliance [rɪ'laɪəns] *n:* ~ **(on)** confiance *f* (en); besoin *m* (de), dépendance *f* (de).

relic ['rɛlɪk] *n (REL)* relique *f*; *(of the past)* vestige *m*.

relief [rɪ'li:f] *n (from pain, anxiety)* soulagement *m*; *(help, supplies)* secours *m(pl)*; *(of guard)* relève *f*; *(ART, GEO)* relief *m*.

relieve [rɪ'li:v] *vt (pain, patient)* soulager; *(bring help)* secourir; *(take over from: gen)* relayer; *(: guard)* relever; **to** ~ **sb of sth** débarrasser qn de qch; **to** ~ **o.s.** se soulager, faire ses besoins.

religion [rɪ'lɪdʒən] *n* religion *f*; **religious** *a* religieux(euse); *(book)* de piété.

relinquish [rɪ'lɪŋkwɪʃ] *vt* abandonner; *(plan, habit)* renoncer à.

relish ['rɛlɪʃ] *n (CULIN)* condiment *m*; *(enjoyment)* délectation *f* // *vt (food etc)* savourer; **to** ~ **doing** se délecter à faire.

relocate [ri:ləu'keɪt] *vt* installer ailleurs // *vi* déménager, s'installer ailleurs.

reluctance [rɪ'lʌktəns] *n* répugnance *f*.

reluctant [rɪ'lʌktənt] *a* peu disposé(e), qui hésite; **~ly** *ad* à contrecœur, sans enthousiasme.

rely [rɪ'laɪ]: **to** ~ **on** *vt fus* compter sur; *(be dependent)* dépendre de.

remain [rɪ'meɪn] *vi* rester; **~der** *n* reste *m*; *(COMM)* fin *f* de série; **~ing** *a* qui reste; **~s** *npl* restes *mpl*.

remand [rɪ'mɑ:nd] *n:* **on** ~ en détention

# remark 154 report

préventive // vt: **to ~ in custody** écrouer; renvoyer en détention provisoire; **~ home** n (Brit) maison f d'arrêt.

remark [rɪ'mɑːk] n remarque f, observation f // vt (faire) remarquer; dire; (notice) remarquer; **~able** a remarquable.

remedial [rɪ'miːdɪəl] a (tuition, classes) de rattrapage.

remedy ['rɛmədɪ] n: **~ (for)** remède m (contre or à) // vt remédier à.

remember [rɪ'mɛmbə*] vt se rappeler, se souvenir de; **remembrance** n souvenir m; mémoire f.

remind [rɪ'maɪnd] vt: **to ~ sb of sth** rappeler qch à qn; **to ~ sb to do** faire penser à qn à faire, rappeler à qn qu'il doit faire; **~er** n rappel m; (note etc) pense-bête m.

reminisce [rɛmɪ'nɪs] vi: **to ~ (about)** évoquer ses souvenirs (de).

reminiscent [rɛmɪ'nɪsnt] a: **~ of** qui rappelle, qui fait penser à.

remiss [rɪ'mɪs] a négligent(e).

remission [rɪ'mɪʃən] n rémission f; (of debt, sentence) remise f; (of fee) exemption f.

remit [rɪ'mɪt] vt (send: money) envoyer; **~tance** n envoi m, paiement m.

remnant ['rɛmnənt] n reste m, restant m; **~s** npl (COMM) coupons mpl; fins fpl de série.

remorse [rɪ'mɔːs] n remords m; **~ful** a plein(e) de remords; **~less** a (fig) impitoyable.

remote [rɪ'məut] a éloigné(e), lointain(e); (person) distant(e); **~ control** n télécommande f; **~ly** ad au loin; (slightly) très vaguement.

remould ['riːməuld] n (Brit: tyre) pneu rechapé.

removable [rɪ'muːvəbl] a (detachable) amovible.

removal [rɪ'muːvəl] n (taking away) enlèvement m; suppression f; (Brit: from house) déménagement m; (from office: dismissal) renvoi m; (MED) ablation f; **~ van** n (Brit) camion m de déménagement.

remove [rɪ'muːv] vt enlever, retirer; (employee) renvoyer; (stain) faire partir; (doubt, abuse) supprimer; **~rs** npl (Brit: company) entreprise f de déménagement.

render ['rɛndə*] vt rendre; **~ing** n (MUS etc) interprétation f.

rendez-vous ['rɒndɪvuː] n rendez-vous m inv // vi opérer une jonction, se rejoindre.

renew [rɪ'njuː] vt renouveler; (negotiations) reprendre; (acquaintance) renouer; **~al** n renouvellement m; reprise f.

renounce [rɪ'nauns] vt renoncer à; (disown) renier.

renovate ['rɛnəveɪt] vt rénover; (art work) restaurer.

renown [rɪ'naun] n renommée f; **~ed** a renommé(e).

rent [rɛnt] n loyer m // vt louer; **~al** n (for television, car) (prix m de) location f.

rep [rɛp] n abbr (COMM: = representative) représentant m (de commerce); (THEATRE: = repertory) théâtre m de répertoire.

repair [rɪ'pɛə*] n réparation f // vt réparer; **in good/bad ~** en bon/mauvais état; **~ kit** n trousse f de réparations.

repartee [rɛpɑː'tiː] n repartie f.

repatriate [riː'pætrɪeɪt] vt rapatrier.

repay [riː'peɪ] vt irg (money, creditor) rembourser; (sb's efforts) récompenser; **~ment** n remboursement m; récompense f.

repeal [rɪ'piːl] n (of law) abrogation f; (of sentence) annulation f // vt abroger; annuler.

repeat [rɪ'piːt] n (RADIO, TV) reprise f // vt répéter; (pattern) reproduire; (promise, attack, also COMM: order) renouveler; (SCOL: a class) redoubler // vi répéter; **~edly** ad souvent, à plusieurs reprises.

repel [rɪ'pɛl] vt (lit, fig) repousser; **~lent** a repoussant(e) // n: **insect ~lent** insectifuge m.

repent [rɪ'pɛnt] vi: **to ~ (of)** se repentir (de); **~ance** n repentir m.

repertory ['rɛpətərɪ] n (also: **~ theatre**) théâtre m de répertoire.

repetition [rɛpɪ'tɪʃən] n répétition f.

repetitive [rɪ'pɛtɪtɪv] a (movement, work) répétitif(ive); (speech) plein(e) de redites.

replace [rɪ'pleɪs] vt (put back) remettre, replacer; (take the place of) remplacer; **~ment** n replacement m; remplacement m; (person) remplaçant/e.

replay ['riːpleɪ] n (of match) match rejoué; (of tape, film) répétition f.

replenish [rɪ'plɛnɪʃ] vt (glass) remplir (de nouveau); (stock etc) réapprovisionner.

replete [rɪ'pliːt] a rempli(e); (well-fed) rassasié(e).

replica ['rɛplɪkə] n réplique f, copie exacte.

reply [rɪ'plaɪ] n réponse f // vi répondre; **~ coupon** n coupon-réponse m.

report [rɪ'pɔːt] n rapport m; (PRESS etc) reportage m; (Brit: also: **school ~**) bulletin m (scolaire); (of gun) détonation f // vt rapporter, faire un compte rendu de; (PRESS etc) faire un reportage sur; (bring to notice: occurrence) signaler; (: person) dénoncer // vi (make a report) faire un rapport (or un reportage); (present o.s.): **to ~ (to sb)** se présenter (chez qn); ~ **card** n (US, Scottish) bulletin m scolaire; **~edly** ad: she is ~edly living in ... elle habitera ...; he ~edly told them to ... il leur aurait ordonné de ...; **~er** n reporter m.

repose [rɪ'pəuz] n: in ~ en or au repos.

represent [reprɪ'zent] vt représenter; **~ation** [-'teɪʃən] n représentation f; **~ations** npl (protest) démarche f; **~ative** a représentant/e; (US POL) député m // a représentatif(ive), caractéristique.

repress [rɪ'pres] vt réprimer; **~ion** [-'preʃən] n répression f.

reprieve [rɪ'priːv] n (LAW) grâce f; (fig) sursis m, délai m.

reprisal [rɪ'praɪzl] n représailles fpl.

reproach [rɪ'prəutʃ] n: to ~ sb with sth reprocher qch à qn; **~ful** a de reproche.

reproduce [riːprə'djuːs] vt reproduire // vi se reproduire; **reproduction** [-'dʌkʃən] n reproduction f.

reproof [rɪ'pruːf] n reproche m.

reptile ['reptaɪl] n reptile m.

republic [rɪ'pʌblɪk] n république f; **~an** a, n républicain(e).

repulsive [rɪ'pʌlsɪv] a repoussant(e), répulsif(ive).

reputable ['repjutəbl] a de bonne réputation; (occupation) honorable.

reputation [repju'teɪʃən] n réputation f.

repute [rɪ'pjuːt] n (bonne) réputation; **~d** a réputé(e); **~dly** ad d'après ce qu'on dit.

request [rɪ'kwest] n demande f; (formal) requête f // vt: to ~ (of or from sb) demander (à qn); ~ **stop** n (Brit: for bus) arrêt m facultatif.

require [rɪ'kwaɪə*] vt (need: subj: person) avoir besoin de; (: thing, situation) demander; (want) vouloir; exiger; (order) obliger; **~ment** n exigence f; besoin m; condition requise.

requisite ['rekwɪzɪt] n chose f nécessaire // a requis(e), nécessaire.

requisition [rekwɪ'zɪʃən] n: ~ (for) demande f (de) // vt (MIL) réquisitionner.

rescue ['reskjuː] n sauvetage m; (help) secours mpl // vt sauver; ~ **party** n équipe f de sauvetage; **~r** n sauveteur m.

research [rɪ'səːtʃ] n recherche(s) f(pl) // vt faire des recherches sur.

resemblance [rɪ'zembləns] n ressemblance f.

resemble [rɪ'zembl] vt ressembler à.

resent [rɪ'zent] vt éprouver du ressentiment de, être contrarié(e) par; **~ful** a irrité(e), plein(e) de ressentiment; **~ment** n ressentiment m.

reservation [rezə'veɪʃən] n (booking) réservation f; (doubt) réserve f; (protected area) réserve; (Brit: on road: also: central ~) bande f médiane; to

make a ~ (in a hotel/a restaurant/on a plane) réserver une chambre/une table/une place.

reserve [rɪ'zəːv] n réserve f; (SPORT) remplaçant/e // vt (seats etc) réserver, retenir; **~s** npl (MIL) réservistes mpl; in ~ en réserve; **~d** a réservé(e).

reshuffle [riː'ʃʌfl] n: Cabinet ~ (POL) remaniement ministériel.

residence ['rezɪdəns] n résidence f; ~ **permit** n (Brit) permis m de séjour.

resident ['rezɪdənt] n résident/e // a résidant(e); (area) résidentiel(le).

residue ['rezɪdjuː] n reste m; (CHEM, PHYSICS) résidu m.

resign [rɪ'zaɪn] vt (one's post) se démettre de // vi démissionner; to ~ o.s. to (endure) se résigner à; **~ation** [rezɪg'neɪʃən] n démission f; résignation f; **~ed** a résigné(e).

resilience [rɪ'zɪlɪəns] n (of material) élasticité f; (of person) ressort m.

resilient [rɪ'zɪlɪənt] a (person) qui réagit, qui a du ressort.

resist [rɪ'zɪst] vt résister à; **~ance** n résistance f.

resolution [rezə'luːʃən] n résolution f.

resolve [rɪ'zɔlv] n résolution f // vi (decide): to ~ to do résoudre or décider de faire // vt (problem) résoudre.

resort [rɪ'zɔːt] n (town) station f; (recourse) recours m // vi: to ~ to avoir recours à; in the last ~ en dernier ressort.

resounding [rɪ'zaundɪŋ] a retentissant(e).

resource [rɪ'sɔːs] n ressource f; **~s** npl ressources.

respect [rɪs'pekt] n respect m // vt respecter; **~s** npl respects, hommages mpl; with ~ to en ce qui concerne; in this ~ sous ce rapport, à cet égard; **~able** a respectable; **~ful** a respectueux(euse).

respite ['respaɪt] n répit m.

resplendent [rɪs'plendənt] a resplendissant(e).

respond [rɪs'pɔnd] vi répondre; (to treatment) réagir.

response [rɪs'pɔns] n réponse f; (to treatment) réaction f.

responsibility [rɪspɔnsɪ'bɪlɪtɪ] n responsabilité f.

responsible [rɪs'pɔnsɪbl] a (liable): ~ (for) responsable (de); (person) digne de confiance; (job) qui comporte des responsabilités; **responsibly** ad avec sérieux.

responsive [rɪs'pɔnsɪv] a qui n'est pas réservé(e) or indifférent(e).

rest [rest] n repos m; (stop) arrêt m, pause f; (MUS) silence m; (support) support m, appui m; (remainder) reste m, restant m // vi se reposer; (be *supported*): **to ~ on** appuyer *or* reposer sur; (*remain*) rester // *vt* (*lean*): to ~ sth on/against appuyer qch sur/contre; **the ~ of them** les autres; **it ~s with him to** c'est à lui de.

restaurant ['rɛstərɔŋ] *n* restaurant *m*; ~ **car** *n* (*Brit*) wagon-restaurant *m*.

restful ['rɛstful] *a* reposant(e).

restitution [rɛstɪ'tjuːʃən] *n* (*act*) restitution *f*; (*reparation*) réparation *f*.

restive ['rɛstɪv] *a* agité(e), impatient(e); (*horse*) rétif(ive).

restless ['rɛstlɪs] *a* agité(e).

restoration [rɛstə'reɪʃən] *n* restauration *f*; restitution *f*.

restore [rɪ'stɔː*] *vt* (*building*) restaurer; (*sth stolen*) restituer; (*peace, health*) rétablir.

restrain [rɪs'treɪn] *vt* (*feeling*) contenir; (*person*): **to ~ (from doing)** retenir (de faire); ~**ed** *a* (*style*) sobre; (*manner*) mesuré(e); ~**t** *n* (*restriction*) contrainte *f*; (*moderation*) retenue *f*.

restrict [rɪs'trɪkt] *vt* restreindre, limiter; ~**ion** [-kʃən] *n* restriction *f*, limitation *f*.

rest room *n* (*US*) toilettes *fpl*.

result [rɪ'zʌlt] *n* résultat *m* // *vi*: **to ~ in** aboutir à, se terminer par; **as a ~ of** à la suite de.

resume [rɪ'zjuːm] *vt*, *vi* (*work, journey*) reprendre.

résumé ['reɪzjumeɪ] *n* résumé *m*; (*US*) curriculum vitae *m*.

resumption [rɪ'zʌmpʃən] *n* reprise *f*.

resurgence [rɪ'sɜːdʒəns] *n* réapparition *f*.

resurrection [rɛzə'rɛkʃən] *n* résurrection *f*.

resuscitate [rɪ'sʌsɪteɪt] *vt* (*MED*) réanimer.

retail [rɪ'teɪl] *n* (*vente f au*) détail *m* // *cpd* de *or* au détail // *vt* vendre au détail; ~**er** *n* détaillant/e; ~ **price** *n* prix *m* de détail.

retain [rɪ'teɪn] *vt* (*keep*) garder, conserver; (*employ*) engager; ~**er** *n* (*servant*) serviteur *m*; (*fee*) acompte *m*, provision *f*.

retaliate [rɪ'tælɪeɪt] *vi*: **to ~ (against)** se venger (de); **retaliation** [-'eɪʃən] *n* représailles *fpl*, vengeance *f*.

retarded [rɪ'tɑːdɪd] *a* retardé(e).

retch [rɛtʃ] *vi* avoir des haut-le-cœur.

retentive [rɪ'tɛntɪv] *a*: ~ **memory** excellente mémoire.

retina ['rɛtɪnə] *n* rétine *f*.

retinue ['rɛtɪnjuː] *n* suite *f*, cortège *m*.

retire [rɪ'taɪə*] *vi* (*give up work*) prendre sa retraite; (*withdraw*) se retirer, partir; (*go to bed*) (aller) se coucher; ~**d** *a* (*person*) retraité(e); ~**ment** *n* retraite *f*; **retiring** *a* (*person*) réservé(e).

retort [rɪ'tɔːt] *vi* riposter.

retrace [riː'treɪs] *vt* reconstituer; **to ~ one's steps** revenir sur ses pas.

retract [rɪ'trækt] *vt* (*statement, claws*) rétracter; (*undercarriage, aerial*) rentrer, escamoter // *vi* se rétracter; rentrer.

retrain [riː'treɪn] *vt* (*worker*) recycler.

retread ['riːtrɛd] *n* (*tyre*) pneu rechapé.

retreat [rɪ'triːt] *n* retraite *f* // *vi* battre en retraite; (*flood*) reculer.

retribution [rɛtrɪ'bjuːʃən] *n* châtiment *m*.

retrieval [rɪ'triːvəl] *n* (*see vb*) récupération *f*; réparation *f*; recherche *f* et extraction *f*.

retrieve [rɪ'triːv] *vt* (*sth lost*) récupérer; (*situation, honour*) sauver; (*error, loss*) réparer; (*COMPUT*) rechercher; ~**r** *n* chien *m* d'arrêt.

retrospect ['rɛtrəspɛkt] *n*: **in ~** rétrospectivement, après coup; ~**ive** [-'spɛktɪv] *a* (*law*) rétroactif(ive).

return [rɪ'tɜːn] *n* (*going or coming back*) retour *m*; (*of sth stolen etc*) restitution *f*; (*recompense*) récompense *f*; (*FINANCE: from land, shares*) rapport *m*; (*report*) relevé *m*, rapport *m* // *cpd* (*journey*) de retour; (*Brit: ticket*) aller et retour; (*match*) retour // *vi* (*person etc: come back*) revenir; (: *go back*) retourner // *vt* rendre; (*bring back*) rapporter; (*send back*) renvoyer; (*put back*) remettre; (*POL: candidate*) élire; ~**s** *npl* (*COMM*) recettes *fpl*; bénéfices *mpl*; **in ~ (for)** en échange (de); **by ~ (of post)** par retour (du courrier); **many happy ~s (of the day)!** bon anniversaire!

reunion [riː'juːnɪən] *n* réunion *f*.

reunite [riː.juː'naɪt] *vt* réunir.

rev [rɛv] *n abbr* (= *revolution: AUT*) tour *m* // *vb* (*also:* ~ **up**) *vt* emballer // *vi* s'emballer.

revamp ['riː'væmp] *vt* (*house*) retaper; (*firm*) réorganiser.

reveal [rɪ'viːl] *vt* (*make known*) révéler; (*display*) laisser voir; ~**ing** *a* révélateur(trice); (*dress*) au décolleté généreux *or* suggestif.

revel ['rɛvl] *vi*: **to ~ in sth/in doing** se délecter de qch/à faire.

revelry ['rɛvlrɪ] *n* festivités *fpl*.

revenge [rɪ'vɛndʒ] *n* vengeance *f*; (*in game etc*) revanche *f* // *vt* venger; **to take ~** se venger.

revenue ['rɛvənjuː] *n* revenu *m*.

reverberate [rɪ'vɜːbəreɪt] *vi* (*sound*) retentir, se répercuter; (*light*) se réverbérer.

reverence ['rɛvərəns] *n* vénération *f*, révérence *f*.

Reverend ['rɛvərənd] *a* (*in titles*): **the ~ John Smith** (*Anglican*) le révérend John Smith; (*Catholic*) l'abbé (John) Smith; (*Protestant*) le pasteur (John) Smith.

reversal [rɪ'vɜːsl] *n* (*of opinion*) revirement *m*.

reverse [rɪ'vəːs] n contraire m, opposé m; (back) dos m, envers m; (AUT: also: ~ **gear**) marche f arrière // a (order, direction) opposé(e), inverse // vt (turn) renverser, retourner; (change) renverser, changer complètement; (LAW: judgment) réformer // vi (Brit AUT) faire marche arrière; ~**d charge call** n (Brit TEL) communication f en PCV; **reversing lights** npl (Brit AUT) feux mpl de marche arrière or de recul.

revert [rɪ'vəːt] vi: to ~ to revenir à, retourner à.

review [rɪ'vjuː] n revue f; (of book, film) critique f // vt passer en revue; faire la critique de; ~**er** n critique m.

revile [rɪ'vaɪl] vt injurier.

revise [rɪ'vaɪz] vt (manuscript) revoir, corriger; (opinion) réviser, modifier; (study: subject, notes) réviser; **revision** [rɪ'vɪʒən] n révision f.

revival [rɪ'vaɪvəl] n reprise f; rétablissement m; (of faith) renouveau m.

revive [rɪ'vaɪv] vt (person) ranimer; (custom) rétablir; (hope, courage) redonner; (play, fashion) reprendre // vi (person) reprendre connaissance; (hope) renaître; (activity) reprendre.

revolt [rɪ'vəult] n révolte f // vi se révolter, se rebeller // vt révolter, dégoûter; ~**ing** a dégoûtant(e).

revolution [revə'luːʃən] n révolution f; (of wheel etc) tour m, révolution; ~**ary** a, n révolutionnaire (m/f).

revolve [rɪ'vɒlv] vi tourner.

revolver [rɪ'vɒlvə*] n revolver m.

revolving [rɪ'vɒlvɪŋ] a (chair) pivotant(e); (light) tournant(e); ~ **door** n (porte f à) tambour m.

revulsion [rɪ'vʌlʃən] n dégoût m, répugnance f.

reward [rɪ'wɔːd] n récompense f // vt: to ~ (**for**) récompenser (de); ~**ing** a (fig) qui (en) vaut la peine, gratifiant(e).

rewire [riː'waɪə*] vt (house) refaire l'installation électrique de.

reword [riː'wəːd] vt formuler or exprimer différemment.

rheumatism ['ruːmətɪzəm] n rhumatisme m.

Rhine [raɪn] n: the ~ le Rhin.

rhinoceros [raɪ'nɒsərəs] n rhinocéros m.

Rhone [rəun] n: the ~ le Rhône.

rhubarb ['ruːbɑːb] n rhubarbe f.

rhyme [raɪm] n rime f; (verse) vers mpl.

rhythm ['rɪðm] n rythme m.

rib [rɪb] n (ANAT) côte f // vt (mock) taquiner.

ribald ['rɪbəld] a paillard(e).

ribbon ['rɪbən] n ruban m; **in** ~**s** (torn) en lambeaux.

rice [raɪs] n riz m.

rich [rɪtʃ] a riche; (gift, clothes) somptueux(euse); **the** ~ npl les riches mpl; ~**es** npl richesses fpl; ~**ly** ad richement; (deserved, earned) largement, grandement; ~**ness** n richesse f.

rickets ['rɪkɪts] n rachitisme m.

rickety ['rɪkɪtɪ] a branlant(e).

rickshaw ['rɪkʃɔː] n pousse(-pousse) m inv.

rid, pt, pp **rid** [rɪd] vt: to ~ **sb of** débarrasser qn de; **to get** ~ **of** se débarrasser de.

ridden ['rɪdn] pp of **ride**.

riddle ['rɪdl] n (puzzle) énigme f // vt: **to be** ~**d with** être criblé(e) de.

ride [raɪd] n promenade f, tour m; (distance covered) trajet m // vb (pt **rode**, pp **ridden** [rəud, 'rɪdn]) vi (as sport) monter (à cheval), faire du cheval; (go somewhere: on horse, bicycle) aller (à cheval or bicyclette etc); (journey: on bicycle, motor-cycle, bus) rouler // vt (a certain horse) monter; (distance) parcourir, faire; to ~ **a horse/bicycle/ camel** monter à cheval/à bicyclette/à dos de chameau; **to ~ at anchor** (NAUT) être à l'ancre; **to take sb for a ~** (fig) faire marcher qn; rouler qn; ~**r** n cavalier/ ère; (in race) jockey m; (on bicycle) cycliste m/f; (on motorcycle) motocycliste m/f; (in document) annexe f, clause additionnelle.

ridge [rɪdʒ] n (of hill) faîte m; (of roof, mountain) arête f; (on object) strie f.

ridicule ['rɪdɪkjuːl] n ridicule m; dérision f.

ridiculous [rɪ'dɪkjuləs] a ridicule.

riding ['raɪdɪŋ] n équitation f; ~ **school** n manège m, école f d'équitation.

rife [raɪf] a répandu(e); ~ **with** abondant(e) en.

riffraff ['rɪfræf] n racaille f.

rifle ['raɪfl] n fusil m (à canon rayé) // vt vider, dévaliser; ~ **range** n champ m de tir; (indoor) stand m de tir.

rift [rɪft] n fente f, fissure f; (fig: disagreement) désaccord m.

rig [rɪg] n (also: oil ~: on land) derrick m; (: at sea) plate-forme pétrolière f // vt (election etc) truquer; **to ~ out** vt (Brit) habiller; (: pej) fringuer, attifer; **to ~ up** vt arranger, faire avec des moyens de fortune; ~**ging** n (NAUT) gréement m.

right [raɪt] a (true) juste, exact(e); (correctly chosen: answer, road etc) bon(bonne); (suitable) approprié(e), convenable; (just) juste, équitable; (morally good) bien inv; (not left) droit(e) // n (title, claim) droit m; (not left) droite f // ad (answer) correctement; (not on the left) à droite // vt redresser // excl bon!; **to be ~** (person) avoir raison; (answer) être juste or correct(e); **by** ~**s** en toute justice; **on the** ~ à droite; **to be in the** ~ avoir raison; ~ **now** en ce moment même; tout de suite; ~ **against the wall** tout contre le mur; ~ **ahead** tout droit; droit devant; ~ **in the middle** en plein milieu; ~ **away** immédiatement; ~ **angle** *n* angle droit; ~**eous** ['raɪtʃəs] *a* droit(e), vertueux(euse) (*anger*) justifié(e); ~**ful** *a* (*heir*) légitime; ~**handed** *a* (*person*) droitier(ère); ~**hand man** *n* bras droit (*fig*); ~**hand side** *n* côté droit; ~**ly** *ad* bien, correctement; (*with reason*) à juste titre; ~ **of way** *n* droit *m* de passage; (*AUT*) priorité *f*; ~**wing** *a* (*POL*) de droite.

rigid ['rɪdʒɪd] *a* rigide; (*principle*) strict(e).

rigmarole ['rɪgmərəul] *n* galimatias *m*, comédie *f*.

rigorous ['rɪgərəs] *a* rigoureux(euse).

rile [raɪl] *vt* agacer.

rim [rɪm] *n* bord *m*; (*of spectacles*) monture *f*; (*of wheel*) jante *f*.

rind [raɪnd] *n* (*of bacon*) couenne *f*; (*of lemon etc*) écorce *f*.

ring [rɪŋ] *n* anneau *m*; (*on finger*) bague *f*; (*also*: **wedding** ~) alliance *f*; (*for napkin, of people, objects*) cercle *m*; (*of spies*) réseau *m*; (*of smoke etc*) rond; (*arena*) piste *f*, arène *f*; (*for boxing*) ring *m*; (*sound of bell*) sonnerie *f*; (*telephone call*) coup *m* de téléphone // *vb* (*pt* **rang**, *pp* **rung**) *vi* (*person, bell*) sonner; (*also*: ~ **out**: *voice, words*) retentir; (*TEL*) téléphoner // *vt* (*Brit TEL*: *also*: ~ **up**) téléphoner à; **to** ~ **the bell** sonner; **to** ~ **back** *vt*, *vi* (*TEL*) rappeler; **to** ~ **off** *vi* (*Brit TEL*) raccrocher; ~**ing** *n* tintement *m*; sonnerie *f*; (*in ears*) bourdonnement *m*; ~**ing tone** *n* (*Brit TEL*) sonnerie *f*; ~**leader** *n* (*of gang*) chef *m*, meneur *m*.

ringlets ['rɪŋlɪts] *npl* anglaises *fpl*.

ring road *n* (*Brit*) route *f* de ceinture.

rink [rɪŋk] *n* (*also*: **ice** ~) patinoire *f*.

rinse [rɪns] *vt* rincer.

riot ['raɪət] *n* émeute *f*, bagarres *fpl* // *vi* faire une émeute, manifester avec violence; **to run** ~ se déchaîner; ~**ous** *a* tapageur(euse); tordant(e).

rip [rɪp] *n* déchirure *f* // *vt* déchirer // *vi* se déchirer; ~**cord** *n* poignée *f* d'ouverture.

ripe [raɪp] *a* (*fruit*) mûr(e); (*cheese*) fait(e); ~**n** *vt* mûrir // *vi* mûrir; se faire.

rip-off ['rɪpɔf] *n* (*col*): **it's a** ~! c'est du vol manifeste!

ripple ['rɪpl] *n* ride *f*, ondulation *f*; égrènement *m*, cascade *f* // *vi* se rider, onduler // *vt* rider, faire onduler.

rise [raɪz] *n* (*slope*) côte *f*, pente *f*; (*hill*) élévation *f*; (*increase: in wages: Brit*) augmentation *f*; (: *in prices, temperature*) hausse *f*; augmentation; (*fig: to power etc*) essor *m*, ascension *f* // *vi* (*pt*

rose, *pp* risen ['rəuz, rɪzn]) s'élever, monter; (*prices*) augmenter, monter; (*waters, river*) monter; (*sun, wind, person: from chair, bed*) se lever; (*also*: ~ up: *rebel*) se révolter; se rebeller; **to give** ~ **to** donner lieu à; **to** ~ **to the occasion** se montrer à la hauteur; **rising** *a* (*increasing: number, prices*) en hausse; (*tide*) montant(e); (*sun, moon*) levant(e) // *n* (*uprising*) soulèvement *m*, insurrection *f*.

risk [rɪsk] *n* risque *m*; danger *m* // *vt* risquer; **at** ~ en danger; **at one's own** ~ à ses risques et périls; ~**y** *a* risqué(e).

rissole ['rɪsəul] *n* croquette *f*.

rite [raɪt] *n* rite *m*; **last** ~s derniers sacrements.

ritual ['rɪtjuəl] *a* rituel(le) // *n* rituel *m*.

rival ['raɪvl] *n* rival/e; (*in business*) concurrent/e // *a* rival(e); qui fait concurrence // *vt* être en concurrence avec; **to** ~ **sb/sth in** rivaliser avec qn/qch de; ~**ry** *n* rivalité *f*, concurrence *f*.

river ['rɪvə*] *n* rivière *f*; (*major, also fig*) fleuve *m* // *cpd* (*port, traffic*) fluvial(e); **up/down** ~ en amont/aval; ~**bank** *n* rive *f*, berge *f*.

rivet ['rɪvɪt] *n* rivet *m* // *vt* riveter; (*fig*) river, fixer.

Riviera [rɪvɪ'ɛərə] *n*: **the** (French) ~ la Côte d'Azur; **the Italian** ~ la Riviera (italienne).

road [rəud] *n* route *f*; (*small*) chemin *m*; (*in town*) rue *f*; (*fig*) chemin, voie *f*; **major/minor** ~ route principale *or* à priorité/voie secondaire; ~**block** *n* barrage routier; ~**hog** *n* chauffard *m*; ~ **map** *n* carte routière; ~ **safety** *n* sécurité routière; ~**side** *n* bord *m* de la route, bas-côté *m*; ~**sign** *n* panneau *m* de signalisation; ~**way** *n* chaussée *f*; ~**works** *npl* travaux *mpl* (de réfection des routes); ~**worthy** *a* en bon état de marche.

roam [rəum] *vi* errer, vagabonder // *vt* parcourir, errer par.

roar [rɔ:*] *n* rugissement *m*; (*of crowd*) hurlements *mpl*; (*of vehicle, thunder, storm*) grondement *m* // *vi* rugir; hurler; gronder; **to** ~ **with laughter** éclater de rire; **to do a** ~**ing trade** faire des affaires d'or.

roast [rəust] *n* rôti *m* // *vt* (*meat*) (faire) rôtir; ~ **beef** *n* rôti *m* de bœuf, rosbif *m*.

rob [rɔb] *vt* (*person*) voler; (*bank*) dévaliser; **to** ~ **sb of sth** voler *or* dérober qch à qn; (*fig: deprive*) priver qn de qch; ~**ber** *n* bandit *m*, voleur *m*; ~**bery** *n* vol *m*.

robe [rəub] *n* (*for ceremony etc*) robe *f*; (*also*: **bath** ~) peignoir *m*; (*US*) couverture *f* // *vt* revêtir (d'une robe).

robin ['rɔbɪn] *n* rouge-gorge *m*.

robot ['rəubɔt] *n* robot *m*.

robust [rəu'bʌst] *a* robuste; (*material, appetite*) solide.

rock [rɔk] *n* (*substance*) roche *f*, roc *m*; (*boulder*) rocher *m*; roche; (*Brit: sweet*) ≈ sucre *m* d'orge // *vt* (*swing gently: cradle*) balancer; (*: child*) bercer; (*shake*) ébranler, secouer // *vi* (se) balancer; être ébranlé(e) or secoué(e); **on the ~s** (*drink*) avec des glaçons; (*ship*) sur les écueils; (*marriage etc*) en train de craquer; **~ and roll** *n* rock (and roll) *m*, rock'n'roll *m*; **~-bottom** *n* (*fig*) niveau le plus bas // *a* (*fig: prices*) sacrifié(e); **~ery** *n* (jardin *m* de) rocaille *f*.

rocket ['rɔkɪt] *n* fusée *f*; (*MIL*) fusée, roquette *f*.

rocking ['rɔkɪŋ]: **~ chair** *n* fauteuil *m* à bascule; **~ horse** *n* cheval *m* à bascule.

rocky ['rɔkɪ] *a* (*hill*) rocheux(euse); (*path*) rocailleux(euse); (*unsteady: table*) branlant(e).

rod [rɔd] *n* (*metallic*) tringle *f*; (*TECH*) tige *f*; (*wooden*) baguette *f*; (*also: fishing ~*) canne *f* à pêche.

rode [rəud] *pt of* **ride**.

rodent ['rəudnt] *n* rongeur *m*.

rodeo ['rəudɪəu] *n* rodéo *m*.

roe [rəu] *n* (*species: also: ~ deer*) chevreuil *m*; (*of fish, also: hard ~*) œufs *mpl* de poisson; **soft ~** laitance *f*.

rogue [rəug] *n* coquin/e.

role [rəul] *n* rôle *m*.

roll [rəul] *n* rouleau *m*; (*of banknotes*) liasse *f*; (*also: bread ~*) petit pain; (*register*) liste *f*; (*sound: of drums etc*) roulement *m*; (*movement: of ship*) roulis *m* // *vt* rouler; (*also: ~ up: string*) enrouler; (*also: ~ out: pastry*) étendre au rouleau // *vi* rouler; (*wheel*) tourner; **to ~ about** *or* **around** *vi* rouler ça et là; (*person*) se rouler par terre; **to ~ by** *vi* (*time*) s'écouler, passer; **to ~ in** *vi* (*mail, cash*) affluer; **to ~ over** *vi* se retourner; **to ~ up** *vi* (*col: arrive*) arriver, s'amener // *vt* (*carpet*) rouler; **~ call** *n* appel *m*; **~er** *n* rouleau *m*; (*wheel*) roulette *f*; **~er coaster** *n* montagnes *fpl* russes; **~er skates** *npl* patins *mpl* à roulettes.

rolling ['rəulɪŋ] *a* (*landscape*) ondulé(e)(euse); **~ pin** *n* rouleau *m* à pâtisserie; **~ stock** *n* (*RAIL*) matériel roulant.

ROM [rɔm] *n abbr* (= *read only memory*) mémoire morte.

Roman ['rəumən] *a* romain(e) // *n* Romain/e; **~ Catholic** *a*, *n* catholique (*m/f*).

romance [rə'mæns] *n* histoire *f* (*or* film *m or* aventure *f*) romanesque; (*charm*) poésie *f*; (*love affair*) idylle *f*.

Romania [rəu'meɪnɪə] *n* = **Rumania**.

Roman numeral *n* chiffre romain.

romantic [rə'mæntɪk] *a* romantique; sentimental(e).

Rome [rəum] *n* Rome.

romp [rɔmp] *n* jeux bruyants // *vi* (*also: ~ about*) s'ébattre, jouer bruyamment.

rompers ['rɔmpəz] *npl* barboteuse *f*.

roof, *pl* **~s** [ruːf] *n* toit *m*; (*of tunnel, cave*) plafond *m* // *vt* couvrir (d'un toit); **the ~ of the mouth** la voûte du palais; **~ing** *n* toiture *f*; **~ rack** *n* (*AUT*) galerie *f*.

rook [ruk] *n* (*bird*) freux *m*; (*CHESS*) tour *f*.

room [ruːm] *n* (*in house*) pièce *f*; (*also: bed~*) chambre *f* (à coucher); (*in school etc*) salle *f*; (*space*) place *f*; **~s** *npl* (*lodging*) meublé *m*; **'~s to let'**, (*US*) **'~s for rent'** 'chambres à louer'; **~ing house** *n* (*US*) maison *f or* immeuble *m* de rapport; **~mate** *n* camarade *m/f* de chambre; **~ service** *n* service *m* des chambres (*dans un hôtel*); **~y** *a* spacieux(euse); (*garment*) ample.

roost [ruːst] *n* juchoir *m* // *vi* se jucher.

rooster ['ruːstə*] *n* coq *m*.

root [ruːt] *n* (*BOT, MATH*) racine *f*; (*fig: of problem*) origine *f*, fond *m* // *vi* (*plant*) s'enraciner; **to ~ about** *vi* (*fig*) fouiller; **to ~ for** *vt fus* applaudir; **to ~ out** *vt* extirper.

rope [rəup] *n* corde *f*; (*NAUT*) cordage *m* // *vt* (*box*) corder; (*climbers*) encorder; **to ~ sb in** (*fig*) embringuer qn; **to know the ~s** (*fig*) être au courant, connaître les ficelles.

rosary ['rəuzərɪ] *n* chapelet *m*.

rose [rəuz] *pt of* **rise** // *n* rose *f*; (*also: ~bush*) rosier *m*; (*on watering can*) pomme *f* // *a* rose.

rosé ['rəuzeɪ] *n* rosé *m*.

rose: **~bud** *n* bouton *m* de rose; **~bush** *n* rosier *m*.

rosemary ['rəuzmərɪ] *n* romarin *m*.

roster ['rɔstə*] *n*: **duty ~** tableau *m* de service.

rostrum ['rɔstrəm] *n* tribune *f* (*pour un orateur etc*).

rosy ['rəuzɪ] *a* rose; **a ~ future** un bel avenir.

rot [rɔt] *n* (*decay*) pourriture *f*; (*fig: pej*) idioties *fpl*, balivernes *fpl* // *vt*, *vi* pourrir.

rota ['rəutə] *n* liste *f*, tableau *m* de service; **on a ~ basis** par roulement.

rotary ['rəutərɪ] *a* rotatif(ive).

rotate [rəu'teɪt] *vt* (*revolve*) faire tourner; (*change round: crops*) alterner; (*: jobs*) faire à tour de rôle // *vi* (*revolve*) tourner; **rotating** *a* (*movement*) tournant(e).

rote [rəut] *n*: **by ~** machinalement, par cœur.

rotten ['rɔtn] *a* (*decayed*) pourri(e); (*dishonest*) corrompu(e); (*col: bad*) mauvais(e), moche; **to feel ~** (*ill*) être mal fichu(e).

rough [rʌf] a (cloth, skin) rêche, rugueux(euse); (terrain) accidenté(e); (path) rocailleux(euse); (voice) rauque, rude; (person, manner: coarse) rude, fruste; (: violent) brutal(e); (district, weather) mauvais(e); (plan) ébauché(e); (guess) approximatif(ive) // n (GOLF) rough m; to ~ it vivre à la dure; **to sleep** ~ (Brit) coucher à la dure; **~age** n fibres fpl diététiques; **~-and-ready** a rudimentaire; **~cast** n crépi m; ~ **copy**, ~ **draft** n brouillon m; **~ly** ad (handle) rudement, brutalement; (make) grossièrement; (approximately) à peu près, en gros.

roulette [ru:'let] n roulette f.

Roumania [ru:'meɪnɪə] n = **Rumania**.

round [raund] a rond(e) // n rond m, cercle m; (Brit: of toast) tranche f; (duty: of policeman, milkman etc) tournée f; (: of doctor) visites fpl; (game: of cards, in competition) partie f; (BOXING) round m; (of talks) série f // vt (corner) tourner; (bend) prendre; (cape) doubler // prep autour de // ad: all ~ tout autour; **the long way** ~ (par) le chemin le plus long; **all the year** ~ toute l'année; **it's just** ~ **the corner** c'est juste après le coin; (fig) c'est tout près; ~ **the clock** ad 24 heures sur 24; **to go** ~ faire le tour or un détour; **to go** ~ **to sb's (house)** aller chez qn; **go** ~ **the back** passez par derrière; **to go** ~ **a house** visiter une maison, faire le tour d'une maison; **enough to go** ~ assez pour tout le monde; **to go** ~ **the** ~**s** (disease, story) circuler; ~ **of ammunition** n cartouche f; ~ **of applause** n ban m, applaudissements mpl; ~ **of drinks** n tournée f; ~ **of sandwiches** n sandwich m; **to** ~ **off** vt (speech etc) terminer; **to** ~ **up** vt rassembler; (criminals) effectuer une rafle de; (prices) arrondir (au chiffre supérieur); **~about** n (Brit AUT) rond-point m (à sens giratoire); (: at fair) manège m (de chevaux de bois) // a (route, means) détourné(e); **~ers** npl (game) ≈ balle f au camp; **~ly** ad (fig) tout net, carrément; **~-shouldered** a au dos rond; ~ **trip** n (voyage m) aller et retour m; **~up** n rassemblement m; (of criminals) rafle f.

rouse [rauz] vt (wake up) réveiller; (stir up) susciter; provoquer; éveiller; **rousing** a (welcome) enthousiaste.

rout [raut] n (MIL) déroute f.

route [ru:t] n itinéraire m; (of bus) parcours m; (of trade, shipping) route f; ~ **map** n (Brit: for journey) croquis m d'itinéraire.

routine [ru:'ti:n] a (work) ordinaire, courant(e); (procedure) d'usage // n (pej) routine f; (THEATRE) numéro m; **daily** ~ occupations journalières.

roving ['rəuvɪŋ] a (life) vagabond(e).

row [rəu] n (line) rangée f; (of people, seats, KNITTING) rang m; (behind one another: of cars, people) file f; [rau] (noise) vacarme m; (dispute) dispute f, querelle f; (scolding) réprimande f, savon m // vi (in boat) ramer; (as sport) faire de l'aviron; [rau] se disputer, se quereller // vt (boat) faire aller à la rame or à l'aviron; **in a** ~ (fig) d'affilée; **~boat** n (US) canot m (à rames).

rowdy ['raudɪ] a chahuteur(euse); bagarreur(euse) // n voyou m.

rowing ['rəuɪŋ] n canotage m; (as sport) aviron m; ~ **boat** n (Brit) canot m (à rames).

royal ['rɔɪəl] a royal(e); **R~ Air Force (RAF)** n armée de l'air britannique.

royalty ['rɔɪəltɪ] n (royal persons) (membres mpl de la) famille royale; (payment: to author) droits mpl d'auteur; (: to inventor) royalties fpl.

r.p.m. abbr (AUT: = revs per minute) tr/mn (= tours/minute).

R.S.V.P. abbr (= répondez s'il vous plaît) R.S.V.P.

Rt Hon. abbr (Brit: = Right Honourable) titre donné aux députés de la Chambre des communes.

rub [rʌb] n (with cloth) coup m de chiffon or de torchon; (on person) friction f // vt frotter; frictionner; **to** ~ **sb up** or (US) ~ **sb the wrong way** prendre qn à rebrousse-poil; **to** ~ **off** vi partir; **to** ~ **off on** vt fus déteindre sur; **to** ~ **out** vt effacer.

rubber ['rʌbə*] n caoutchouc m; (Brit: eraser) gomme f (à effacer); ~ **band** n élastique m; ~ **plant** n caoutchouc m (plante verte).

rubbish ['rʌbɪʃ] n (from household) ordures fpl; (fig: pej) choses fpl sans valeur; camelote f; bêtises fpl, idioties fpl; ~ **bin** n (Brit) boîte f à ordures, poubelle f; ~ **dump** n (in town) décharge publique, dépotoir m.

rubble ['rʌbl] n décombres mpl; (smaller) gravats mpl.

ruby ['ru:bɪ] n rubis m.

rucksack ['rʌksæk] n sac m à dos.

ructions ['rʌkʃənz] npl grabuge m.

rudder ['rʌdə*] n gouvernail m.

ruddy ['rʌdɪ] a (face) coloré(e); (col: damned) sacré(e), fichu(e).

rude [ru:d] a (impolite: person) impoli(e); (: word, manners) grossier(ère); (shocking) indécent(e), inconvenant(e).

rueful ['ru:ful] a triste.

ruffian ['rʌfɪən] n brute f, voyou m.

ruffle ['rʌfl] vt (hair) ébouriffer; (clothes) chiffonner; (water) agiter; (fig: person) émouvoir, faire perdre son flegme à.

rug [rʌg] n petit tapis m; (Brit: for knees) couverture f.

rugby ['rʌgbɪ] n (also: ~ **football**) rugby

m.

rugged ['rʌgɪd] *a (landscape)* accidenté(e); *(features, kindness, character)* rude; *(determination)* farouche.

rugger ['rʌgə*] *n (Brit col)* rugby *m.*

ruin ['ruːɪn] *n* ruine *f // vt* ruiner; *(spoil: clothes)* abîmer; **~s** *npl* ruine(s).

rule [ruːl] *n* règle *f*; *(regulation)* règlement *m*; *(government)* autorité *f*, gouvernement *m // vt (country)* gouverner; *(person)* dominer; *(decide)* décider *// vi* commander; décider; *(LAW)* statuer; **as a ~** normalement, en règle générale; **to ~ out** *vt* exclure; **~d** *a (paper)* réglé(e); **~r** *n (sovereign)* souverain/e; *(leader)* chef *m* (d'État); *(for measuring)* règle *f*; **ruling** *a (party)* au pouvoir; *(class)* dirigeant(e) *// n (LAW)* décision *f.*

rum [rʌm] *n* rhum *m // a (col)* bizarre.

Rumania [ruːˈmeɪnɪə] *n* Roumanie *f.*

rumble ['rʌmbl] *vi* gronder; *(stomach, pipe)* gargouiller.

rummage ['rʌmɪdʒ] *vi* fouiller.

rumour, *(US)* **rumor** ['ruːmə*] *n* rumeur *f*, bruit *m* (qui court) *// vt*: it is ~ed that le bruit court que.

rump [rʌmp] *n (of animal)* croupe *f*; **~ steak** *n* rumsteck *m.*

rumpus ['rʌmpəs] *n (col)* tapage *m*, chahut *m*; *(quarrel)* prise *f* de bec.

run [rʌn] *n (pas m de) course *f*; *(outing)* tour *m* or promenade *f* (en voiture); parcours *m*, trajet *m*; *(series)* suite *f*, série *f*; *(THEATRE)* série de représentations; *(SKI)* piste *f*; *(in tights, stockings)* maille filée, échelle *f // vb (pt ran, pp run) vt (operate: business)* diriger; *(: competition, course)* organiser; *(: hotel, house)* tenir; *(COMPUT)* exécuter; *(force through: rope, pipe)*: to ~ sth through faire passer qch à travers; *(to pass: hand, finger)*: to ~ sth over promener or passer qch sur; *(water, bath)* faire couler *// vi* courir; *(pass: road etc)* passer; *(work: machine, factory)* marcher; *(bus, train: operate)* être en service; *(: travel)* circuler; *(continue: play)* se jouer; *(: contract)* être valide; *(slide: drawer etc)* glisser; *(flow: river, bath)* couler; *(colours, washing)* déteindre; *(in election)* être candidat, se présenter; **there was a ~ on** *(meat, tickets)* les gens se sont rués sur; **in the long ~** à longue échéance; à la longue; en fin de compte; **on the ~** en fuite; **I'll ~ you to the station** je vais vous emmener or conduire à la gare; **to ~ a risk** courir un risque; **to ~ about** or **around** *vi (children)* courir çà et là; **to ~ across** *vt fus (find)* trouver par hasard; **to ~ away** *vi* s'enfuir; **to ~ down** *vt (production)* réduire progressivement; *(factory)* réduire progressivement la production de; *(AUT)*

renverser; *(criticize)* critiquer, dénigrer; **to be ~ down** *(person: tired)* être fatigué(e) or à plat; **to ~ in** *vt (Brit: car)* roder; **to ~ into** *vt fus (meet: person)* rencontrer par hasard; *(: trouble)* se heurter à; *(collide with)* heurter; **to ~ off** *vi* s'enfuir *// vt (water)* laisser s'écouler; **to ~ out** *vi (person)* sortir en courant; *(liquid)* couler; *(lease)* expirer; *(money)* être épuisé(e); **to ~ out of** *vt fus* se trouver à court de; **to ~ over** *vt (AUT)* écraser *// vt fus (revise)* revoir, reprendre; **to ~ through** *vt fus (instructions)* reprendre, revoir; **to ~ up** *vt (debt)* laisser accumuler; **to ~ up against** *(difficulties)* se heurter à; **~away** *a (horse)* emballé(e); *(truck)* fou(folle); *(inflation)* galopant(e).

rung [rʌŋ] *pp of* ring *// n (of ladder)* barreau *m.*

runner ['rʌnə*] *n (in race: person)* coureur/euse; *(: horse)* partant *m*; *(on sledge)* patin *m*; *(for drawer etc)* coulisseau *m*; *(carpet: in hall etc)* chemin *m*; **~ bean** *n (Brit)* haricot *m* (à rames); **~-up** *n* second/e.

running ['rʌnɪŋ] *n* course *f*; direction *f*; organisation *f*; marche *f*, fonctionnement *m // a (water)* courant(e); *(costs)* de gestion; *(commentary)* suivi(e); **to be in/out of the ~ for sth** être/ne pas être sur les rangs pour qch; **6 days ~** 6 jours de suite.

runny ['rʌnɪ] *a* qui coule.

run-of-the-mill ['rʌnəvðə'mɪl] *a* ordinaire, banal(e).

runt [rʌnt] *n (also pej)* avorton *m.*

run-up ['rʌnʌp] *n*: **~ to sth** *(election etc)* période *f* précédant qch.

runway ['rʌnweɪ] *n (AVIAT)* piste *f* (d'envol or d'atterrissage).

rupee [ruːˈpiː] *n* roupie *f.*

rupture ['rʌptʃə*] *n (MED)* hernie *f.*

rural ['ruərl] *a* rural(e).

rush [rʌʃ] *n* course précipitée; *(of crowd)* ruée *f*, bousculade *f*; *(hurry)* hâte *f*, bousculade; *(current)* flot *m*; *(BOT)* jonc *m // vt* transporter or envoyer d'urgence; *(attack: town etc)* prendre d'assaut *// vi* se précipiter; **~ hour** *n* heures *fpl* de pointe or d'affluence.

rusk [rʌsk] *n* biscotte *f.*

Russia ['rʌʃə] *n* Russie *f*; **~n** *a* russe *// n* Russe *m/f*; *(LING)* russe *m.*

rust [rʌst] *n* rouille *f // vi* rouiller.

rustic ['rʌstɪk] *a* rustique.

rustle ['rʌsl] *vi* bruire, produire un bruissement *// vt (paper)* froisser; *(US: cattle)* voler.

rustproof ['rʌstpruːf] *a* inoxydable.

rusty ['rʌstɪ] *a* rouillé(e).

rut [rʌt] *n* ornière *f*; *(ZOOL)* rut *m*; **to be in a ~** suivre l'ornière, s'encroûter.

ruthless ['ru:θlɪs] a sans pitié, impitoyable.

rye [raɪ] n seigle m.

S

Sabbath ['sæbəθ] n (Jewish) sabbat m; (Christian) dimanche m.

sabotage ['sæbətɑːʒ] n sabotage m // vt saboter.

saccharin(e) ['sækərɪn] n saccharine f.

sachet ['sæʃeɪ] n sachet m.

sack [sæk] n (bag) sac m // vt (dismiss) renvoyer, mettre à la porte; (plunder) piller, mettre à sac; **to get the ~** être renvoyé(e) or mis(e) à la porte; **~ing** n toile f à sac; renvoi m.

sacrament ['sækrəmənt] n sacrement m.

sacred ['seɪkrɪd] a sacré(e).

sacrifice ['sækrɪfaɪs] n sacrifice m // vt sacrifier.

sad [sæd] a (unhappy) triste; (deplorable) triste, fâcheux(euse).

saddle ['sædl] n selle f // vt (horse) seller; **to be ~d with sth** (col) avoir qch sur les bras; **~bag** n sacoche f.

sadistic [sə'dɪstɪk] a sadique.

sadness ['sædnɪs] n tristesse f.

s.a.e. n abbr = stamped addressed envelope.

safe [seɪf] a (out of danger) hors de danger, en sécurité; (not dangerous) sans danger; (cautious) prudent(e); (sure: bet etc) assuré(e) // n coffre-fort m; **~ from** à l'abri de; **~ and sound** sain(e) et sauf(sauve); **(just) to be on the ~ side** pour plus de sûreté, par précaution; **~-conduct** n sauf-conduit m; **~-deposit** n (vault) dépôt m de coffres-forts; (box) coffre-fort m; **~guard** n sauvegarde f, protection f // vt sauvegarder, protéger; **~keeping** n bonne garde; **~ly** ad sans danger, sans risque; (without mishap) sans accident.

safety ['seɪftɪ] n sécurité f; **~ belt** n ceinture f de sécurité; **~ pin** n épingle f de sûreté or de nourrice; **~ valve** n soupape f de sûreté.

sag [sæg] vi s'affaisser, fléchir; pendre.

sage [seɪdʒ] n (herb) sauge f; (man) sage m.

Sagittarius [sædʒɪ'tɛərɪəs] n le Sagittaire.

Sahara [sə'hɑːrə] n: the ~ (Desert) le (désert du) Sahara.

said [sɛd] pt, pp of say.

sail [seɪl] n (on boat) voile f; (trip): **to go for a ~** faire un tour en bateau // vt (boat) manœuvrer, piloter // vi (travel: ship) avancer, naviguer; (: passenger) aller or se rendre (en bateau); (set off) partir, prendre la mer; (SPORT) faire de la voile; **they ~ed into Le Havre** ils sont

entrés dans le port du Havre; **to ~ through** vi, vt fus (fig) réussir haut la main; **~boat** n (US) bateau m à voiles, voilier m; **~ing** n (SPORT) voile f; **to go ~ing** faire de la voile; **~ing ship** n grand voilier; **~or** n marin m, matelot m.

saint [seɪnt] n saint/e.

sake [seɪk] n: **for the ~ of** pour (l'amour de), dans l'intérêt de; par égard pour.

salad ['sæləd] n salade f; **~ bowl** n saladier m; **~ cream** n (Brit) (sorte f de) mayonnaise f; **~ dressing** n vinaigrette f.

salary ['sælərɪ] n salaire m, traitement m.

sale [seɪl] n vente f; (at reduced prices) soldes mpl; **'for ~'** 'à vendre'; **on ~** en vente; **on ~ or return** vendu(e) avec faculté de retour; **~room** n salle f des ventes; **~s assistant, (US) ~s clerk** n vendeur/euse; **~sman** n vendeur m; (representative) représentant m de commerce; **~swoman** n vendeuse f.

salient ['seɪlɪənt] a saillant(e).

sallow ['sæləʊ] a cireux(euse).

salmon ['sæmən] n (pl inv) saumon m.

saloon [sə'luːn] n (US) bar m; (Brit AUT) berline f; (ship's lounge) salon m.

salt [sɔlt] n sel m // vt saler // cpd de sel; (CULIN) salé(e); **to ~ away** n (col: money) mettre de côté; **~ cellar** n salière f; **~-water** a (d'eau) de mer; **~y** a salé(e).

salute [sə'luːt] n salut m // vt saluer.

salvage ['sælvɪdʒ] n (saving) sauvetage m; (things saved) biens sauvés or récupérés // vt sauver, récupérer.

salvation [sæl'veɪʃən] n salut m; **S~ Army** n Armée f du Salut.

same [seɪm] a même // pronoun: **the ~** le(la) même, les mêmes; **the ~ book as** le même livre que; **at the ~ time** en même temps; **all or just the ~** tout de même, quand même; **to do the ~** faire de même, en faire autant; **to do the ~ as sb** faire comme qn; **the ~ to you!** et à vous de même!; (after insult) toi-même!

sample ['sɑːmpl] n échantillon m; (MED) prélèvement m // vt (food, wine) goûter.

sanctimonious [sæŋktɪ'məʊnɪəs] a moralisateur(trice).

sanction ['sæŋkʃən] n sanction f.

sanctity ['sæŋktɪtɪ] n sainteté f, caractère sacré.

sanctuary ['sæŋktjuərɪ] n (holy place) sanctuaire m; (refuge) asile m; (for wild life) réserve f.

sand [sænd] n sable m // vt sabler.

sandal ['sændl] n sandale f.

sandbox ['sændbɒks] n (US) = sandpit.

sandcastle ['sændkɑːsl] n château m de sable.

sandpaper ['sændpeɪpə*] n papier m de verre.

sandpit ['sændpɪt] n (for children) tas m de sable.

sandstone ['sændstəʊn] n grès m.

sandwich ['sændwɪtʃ] n sandwich m // vt (also: ~ **in**) intercaler; cheese/ham ~ sandwich au fromage/jambon; ~ **board** n panneau publicitaire (porté par un homme-sandwich); ~ **course** n (Brit) cours m de formation professionnelle.

sandy ['sændɪ] a sablonneux(euse); couvert(e) de sable; (colour) sable inv, blond roux inv.

sane [seɪn] a (person) sain(e) d'esprit; (outlook) sensé(e), sain(e).

sang [sæŋ] pt of sing.

sanitary ['sænɪtərɪ] a (system, arrangements) sanitaire; (clean) hygiénique; ~ **towel**, (US) ~ **napkin** n serviette f hygiénique.

sanitation [sænɪ'teɪʃən] n (in house) installations fpl sanitaires; (in town) système m sanitaire; ~ **department** n (US) service m de voirie.

sanity ['sænɪtɪ] n santé mentale; (common sense) bon sens.

sank [sæŋk] pt of sink.

Santa Claus [sæntə'klɔːz] n le Père Noël.

sap [sæp] n (of plants) sève f // vt (strength) saper, miner.

sapling ['sæplɪŋ] n jeune arbre m.

sapphire ['sæfaɪə*] n saphir m.

sarcasm ['sɑːkæzm] n sarcasme m, raillerie f.

sardine [sɑː'diːn] n sardine f.

Sardinia [sɑː'dɪnɪə] n Sardaigne f.

sash [sæʃ] n écharpe f.

sat [sæt] pt, pp of sit.

satchel ['sætʃl] n cartable m.

sated ['seɪtɪd] a repu(e); blasé(e).

satellite ['sætəlaɪt] a, n satellite (m).

satin ['sætɪn] n satin m // a en or de satin, satiné(e).

satire ['sætaɪə*] n satire f.

satisfaction [sætɪs'fækʃən] n satisfaction f.

satisfactory [sætɪs'fæktərɪ] a satisfaisant(e).

satisfy ['sætɪsfaɪ] vt satisfaire, contenter; (convince) convaincre, persuader; ~**ing** a satisfaisant(e).

Saturday ['sætədɪ] n samedi m.

sauce [sɔːs] n sauce f; ~**pan** n casserole f.

saucer ['sɔːsə*] n soucoupe f.

saucy ['sɔːsɪ] a impertinent(e).

Saudi ['saʊdɪ]: ~ **Arabia** n Arabie Saoudite; ~ **(Arabian)** a saoudien(ne) // n Saoudien/ne.

sauna ['sɔːnə] n sauna m.

saunter ['sɔːntə*] vi: to ~ to aller en flânant or se balader jusqu'à.

sausage ['sɔsɪdʒ] n saucisse f; ~ **roll** n

friand m.

savage ['sævɪdʒ] a (cruel, fierce) brutal(e), féroce; (primitive) primitif(ive), sauvage // n sauvage m/f // vt attaquer férocement.

save [seɪv] vt (person, belongings) sauver; (money) mettre de côté, économiser; (time) (faire) gagner; (food) garder; (COMPUT) sauvegarder; (avoid: trouble) éviter // vi (also: ~ **up**) mettre de l'argent de côté // n (SPORT) arrêt m (du ballon) // prep sauf, à l'exception de.

saving ['seɪvɪŋ] n économie f // a: **the** ~ **grace** of ce qui rachète; ~**s** npl économies fpl; ~**s bank** n caisse f d'épargne.

saviour, (US) **savior** ['seɪvjə*] n sauveur m.

savour, (US) **savor** ['seɪvə*] vt savourer; ~**y** a savoureux(euse); (dish: not sweet) salé(e).

saw [sɔː] pt of see // n (tool) scie f // vt (pt sawed, pp sawed or sawn [sɔːn]) scier; ~**dust** n sciure f; ~**mill** n scierie f; ~**n-off shotgun** n carabine f à canon scié.

saxophone ['sæksəfəʊn] n saxophone m.

say [seɪ] n: to have one's ~ dire ce qu'on a à dire; to have a or some ~ in sth avoir son mot à dire dans qch // vt (pt, pp said) dire; could you ~ that again? pourriez-vous répéter ceci?; that goes without ~ing cela va sans dire, cela va de soi; ~**ing** n dicton m, proverbe m.

scab [skæb] n croûte f; (pej) jaune m.

scaffold ['skæfəʊld] n échafaud m; ~**ing** n échafaudage m.

scald [skɔːld] n brûlure f // vt ébouillanter.

scale [skeɪl] n (of fish) écaille f; (MUS) gamme f; (of ruler, thermometer etc) graduation f, échelle (graduée); (of salaries, fees etc) barème m; (of map, also size, extent) échelle // vt (mountain) escalader; ~**s** npl balance f; (larger) bascule f; **on a large** ~ sur une grande échelle, en grand; ~ **of charges** tableau m des tarifs; (ECON) barème m des redevances; **to** ~ **down** vt réduire; ~ **model** n modèle m à l'échelle.

scallop ['skɔləp] n coquille f Saint-Jacques.

scalp [skælp] n cuir chevelu // vt scalper.

scamper ['skæmpə*] vi: to ~ **away**, ~ **off** détaler.

scampi ['skæmpɪ] npl langoustines (frites), scampi mpl.

scan [skæn] vt scruter, examiner; (glance at quickly) parcourir; (TV, RADAR) balayer.

scandal ['skændl] n scandale m; (gossip) ragots mpl.

Scandinavia [skændɪ'neɪvɪə] *n* Scandinavie *f*; **~n** *a* scandinave // *n* Scandinave *m/f*.

scant [skænt] *a* insuffisant(e); **~y** *a* peu abondant(e), insuffisant(e), maigre.

scapegoat ['skeɪpgəut] *n* bouc *m* émissaire.

scar [ska:] *n* cicatrice *f*.

scarce [skɛəs] *a* rare, peu abondant(e); **~ly** *ad* à peine, presque pas; **scarcity** *n* rareté *f*, manque *m*, pénurie *f*.

scare [skɛə*] *n* peur *f*, panique *f* // *vt* effrayer, faire peur à; **to ~ sb stiff** faire une peur bleue à qn; **bomb ~** alerte *f* à la bombe; **~crow** *n* épouvantail *m*; **~d** *a*: **to be ~d** avoir peur.

scarf, pl scarves [ska:f, ska:vz] *n* (*long*) écharpe *f*; (*square*) foulard *m*.

scarlet ['ska:lɪt] *a* écarlate.

scathing ['skeɪðɪŋ] *a* cinglant(e), acerbe.

scatter ['skætə*] *vt* éparpiller, répandre; (*crowd*) disperser // *vi* se disperser; **~brained** *a* écervelé(e), étourdi(e).

scavenger ['skævəndʒə*] *n* éboueur *m*.

scene [si:n] *n* (THEATRE, *fig etc*) scène *f*; (*of crime, accident*) lieu(x) *m(pl)*, endroit *m*; (*sight, view*) spectacle *m*, vue *f*; **~ry** *n* (THEATRE) décor(s) *m(pl)*; (*landscape*) paysage *m*; **scenic** *a* scénique; offrant de beaux paysages *or* panoramas.

scent [sɛnt] *n* parfum *m*, odeur *f*; (*fig: track*) piste *f*; (*sense of smell*) odorat *m*.

sceptical ['skɛptɪkəl] *a* sceptique.

schedule ['ʃedju:l, (US) 'skedju:l] *n* programme *m*, plan *m*; (*of trains*) horaire *m*; (*of prices etc*) barème *m*, tarif *m* // *vt* prévoir; **on ~** à l'heure (prévue); **à la date prévue; to be ahead of/behind ~** avoir de l'avance/du retard; **~d flight** *n* vol régulier.

scheme [ski:m] *n* plan *m*, projet *m*; (*method*) procédé *m*; (*dishonest plan, plot*) complot *m*, combine *f*; (*arrangement*) arrangement *m*, classification *f*; (*pension ~ etc*) régime *m* // *vt, vi* comploter, manigancer; **scheming** *a* rusé(e), intrigant(e) // *n* manigances *fpl*, intrigues *fpl*.

scholar ['skɔlə*] *n* érudit/e; **~ly** *a* érudit(e), savant(e); **~ship** *n* érudition *f*; (*grant*) bourse *f* (d'études).

school [sku:l] *n* (*gen*) école *f*; (*in university*) faculté *f*; (*secondary school*) collège *m*, lycée *m* // *cpd* scolaire // *vt* (*animal*) dresser; **~book** *n* livre *m* scolaire *or* de classe; **~boy** *n* écolier *m*; collégien *m*, lycéen *m*; **~children** *npl* écoliers *mpl*, collégiens *mpl*, lycéens *mpl*; **~days** *npl* années *fpl* de scolarité; **~girl** *n* écolière *f*; collégienne *f*, lycéenne *f*; **~ing** *n* instruction *f*, études *fpl*; **~master** *n* (*primary*) instituteur *m*; (*secondary*) professeur *m*;

~mistress *n* institutrice *f*; professeur *m*; **~teacher** *n* instituteur/trice; professeur *m*.

sciatica [saɪ'ætɪkə] *n* sciatique *f*.

science ['saɪəns] *n* science *f*; **~ fiction** *n* science-fiction *f*; **scientific** [-'tɪfɪk] *a* scientifique; (*eminent*) savant *m*; **scientist** *n* scientifique *m/f*;

scissors ['sɪzəz] *npl* ciseaux *mpl*.

scoff [skɔf] *vt* (Brit col: *eat*) avaler, bouffer // *vi*: **to ~ (at)** (*mock*) se moquer (de).

scold [skəuld] *vt* gronder, attraper.

scone [skɔn] *n* sorte de petit pain rond au lait.

scoop [sku:p] *n* pelle *f* (à main); (*for ice cream*) boule *f* à glace; (PRESS) reportage exclusif *or* à sensation; **to ~ out** *vt* évider, creuser; **to ~ up** *vt* ramasser.

scooter ['sku:tə*] *n* (*motor cycle*) scooter *m*; (*toy*) trottinette *f*.

scope [skəup] *n* (*capacity: of plan, undertaking*) portée *f*, envergure *f*; (: *of person*) compétence *f*, capacités *fpl*; (*opportunity*) possibilités *fpl*; **within the ~ of** dans les limites de.

scorch [skɔ:tʃ] *vt* (*clothes*) brûler (légèrement), roussir; (*earth, grass*) dessécher, brûler.

score [skɔ:*] *n* score *m*, décompte *m* des points; (MUS) partition *f*; (*twenty*) vingt // *vt* (*goal, point*) marquer; (*success*) remporter // *vi* marquer des points; (FOOTBALL) marquer un but; (*keep score*) compter les points; **on that ~** sur ce chapitre, à cet égard; **to ~ 6 out of 10** obtenir 6 sur 10; **to ~ out** *vt* rayer, barrer, biffer; **~board** *n* tableau *m*.

scorn [skɔ:n] *n* mépris *m*, dédain *m*.

Scorpio ['skɔ:pɪəu] *n* le Scorpion.

Scot [skɔt] *n* Écossais/e.

scotch [skɔtʃ] *vt* faire échouer; enrayer; étouffer; **S~** *n* whisky *m*, scotch *m*.

scot-free ['skɔt'fri:] *ad*: **to get off ~** (*unpunished*) s'en tirer sans être puni.

Scotland ['skɔtlənd] *n* Écosse *f*.

Scots [skɔts] *a* écossais(e); **~man/ woman** *n* Écossais/e.

Scottish ['skɔtɪʃ] *a* écossais(e).

scoundrel ['skaundrl] *n* vaurien *m*.

scour ['skauə*] *vt* (*clean*) récurer; frotter; décaper; (*search*) battre, parcourir.

scourge [skə:dʒ] *n* fléau *m*.

scout [skaut] *n* (MIL) éclaireur *m*; (*also*: **boy ~**) scout *m*; **to ~ around** *vi* explorer, chercher.

scowl [skaul] *vi* se renfrogner, avoir l'air maussade; **to ~ at** regarder de travers.

scrabble ['skræbl] *vi* (*claw*): **to ~ (at)** gratter; (*also*: **~ around**: *search*) chercher à tâtons // *n* ® Scrabble *m* ®.

scraggy ['skrægɪ] *a* décharné(e).

scram [skræm] *vi (col)* ficher le camp.

scramble ['skræmbl] *n* bousculade *f*, ruée *f* // *vi* avancer tant bien que mal (à quatre pattes *or* en grimpant); **to ~ out** sortir *or* descendre à toute vitesse; **to ~ for** se bousculer *or* se disputer pour (avoir); **~d eggs** *npl* œufs brouillés.

scrap [skræp] *n* bout *m*, morceau *m*; *(fight)* bagarre *f*; *(also: ~ iron)* ferraille *f* // *vt* jeter, mettre au rebut; *(fig)* abandonner, laisser tomber // *vi (fight)* se bagarrer; **~s** *npl (waste)* déchets *mpl*; **~book** *n* album *m*; **~ dealer** *n* marchand *m* de ferraille.

scrape [skreıp] *vt, vi* gratter, racler // *n*: **to get into a ~** s'attirer des ennuis; **to ~ through** réussir de justesse; **~r** *n* grattoir *m*, racloir *m*.

scrap: **~ heap** *n (fig)*: **on the ~ heap** au rancart *or* rebut; **~ merchant** *n (Brit)* marchand *m* de ferraille; **~ paper** *n* papier *m* brouillon.

scratch [skrætʃ] *n* égratignure *f*, rayure *f*; éraflure *f*; *(from claw)* coup *m* de griffe // *a*: **~ team** équipe de fortune *or* improvisée // *vt (record)* rayer; *(paint etc)* érafler; *(with claw, nail)* griffer // *vi* (se) gratter; **to start from ~** partir de zéro; **to be up to ~** être à la hauteur.

scrawl [skrɔ:l] *vi* gribouiller.

scrawny ['skrɔ:nı] *a* décharné(e).

scream [skri:m] *n* cri perçant, hurlement *m* // *vi* crier, hurler.

scree [skri:] *n* éboulis *m*.

screech [skri:tʃ] *vi* hurler; *(tyres, brakes)* crisser, grincer.

screen [skri:n] *n* écran *m*, paravent *m*; *(CINEMA, TV)* écran; *(fig)* rideau *m* // *vt* masquer, cacher; *(from the wind etc)* abriter, protéger; *(film)* projeter; *(candidates etc)* filtrer; **~ing** *n (MED)* test *m (or tests)* de dépistage; **~play** *n* scénario *m*.

screw [skru:] *n* vis *f*; *(propeller)* hélice *f* // *vt* visser; **to ~ up** *vt (paper etc)* froisser; *(col: ruin)* bousiller; **~driver** *n* tournevis *m*.

scribble ['skrıbl] *vt* gribouiller, griffonner.

script [skrıpt] *n (CINEMA etc)* scénario *m*, texte *m*; *(in exam)* copie *f*.

Scripture ['skrıptʃə*] *n* Ecriture Sainte.

scroll [skrəul] *n* rouleau *m*.

scrounge [skraundʒ] *vt (col)*: **to ~ sth (off *or* from sb)** se faire payer qch (par qn), emprunter qch (à qn) // *vi*: **to ~ on sb** vivre aux crochets de qn.

scrub [skrʌb] *n (clean)* nettoyage *m* (à la brosse); *(land)* broussailles *fpl* // *vt (floor)* nettoyer à la brosse; *(pan)* récurer; *(washing)* frotter; *(reject)* annuler.

scruff [skrʌf] *n*: **by the ~ of the neck** par la peau du cou.

scruffy ['skrʌfı] *a* débraillé(e).

scrum(mage) ['skrʌm(ıdʒ)] *n (RUGBY)* mêlée *f*.

scruple ['skru:pl] *n* scrupule *m*.

scrutiny ['skru:tını] *n* examen minutieux.

scuff [skʌf] *vt* érafler.

scuffle ['skʌfl] *n* échauffourée *f*, rixe *f*.

scullery ['skʌlərı] *n* arrière-cuisine *f*.

sculptor ['skʌlptə*] *n* sculpteur *m*.

sculpture ['skʌlptʃə*] *n* sculpture *f*.

scum [skʌm] *n* écume *f*, mousse *f*; *(pej: people)* rebut *m*, lie *f*.

scupper ['skʌpə*] *vt* saborder.

scurrilous ['skʌrıləs] *a* haineux(euse), virulent(e); calomnieux(euse).

scurry ['skʌrı] *vi* filer à toute allure; **to ~ off** détaler, se sauver.

scuttle ['skʌtl] *n (NAUT)* écoutille *f*; *(also: coal ~)* seau *m* (à charbon) // *vt (ship)* saborder // *vi (scamper)*: **to ~ away, ~ off** détaler.

scythe [saıð] *n* faux *f*.

SDP *n abbr (Brit)* = *Social Democratic Party.*

sea [si:] *n* mer *f* // *cpd* marin(e), de (la) mer, maritime; **by ~** *(travel)* par mer, en bateau; **on the ~** *(boat)* en mer; *(town)* au bord de la mer; **to be all at ~** *(fig)* nager complètement; **out to ~** au large; **(out) at ~** en mer; **~board** *n* côte *f*; **~food** *n* fruits *mpl* de mer; **~ front** *n* bord *m* de mer; **~gull** *n* mouette *f*.

seal [si:l] *n (animal)* phoque *m*; *(stamp)* sceau *m*, cachet *m*; *(impression)* cachet, estampille *f* // *vt* sceller; *(envelope)* coller; *(: with seal)* cacheter; **to ~ off** *vt (close)* condamner; *(forbid entry to)* interdire l'accès de.

sea level *n* niveau *m* de la mer.

seam [si:m] *n* couture *f*; *(of coal)* veine *f*, filon *m*.

seaman ['si:mən] *n* marin *m*.

seamy ['si:mı] *a* louche, mal famé(e).

seance ['seıɔns] *n* séance *f* de spiritisme.

seaplane ['si:pleın] *n* hydravion *m*.

search [sə:tʃ] *n (for person, thing)* recherche(s) *f(pl)*; *(of drawer, pockets)* fouille *f*; *(LAW: at sb's home)* perquisition *f* // *vt* fouiller; *(examine)* examiner minutieusement; scruter // *vi*: **to ~ for** chercher; **to ~ through** *vt fus* fouiller; **in ~ of** à la recherche de; **~ing** *a* pénétrant(e); minutieux(euse); **~light** *n* projecteur *m*; **~ party** *n* expédition *f* de secours; **~ warrant** *n* mandat *m* de perquisition.

seashore ['si:ʃɔ:*] *n* rivage *m*, plage *f*, bord *m* de (la) mer.

seasick ['si:sık] *a* qui a le mal de mer.

seaside ['si:saıd] *n* bord *m* de la mer; **~ resort** *n* station *f* balnéaire.

season ['si:zn] *n* saison *f* // *vt* assaisonner, relever; **~al** *a* saisonnier(ère); **~ed** *a (fig)* expérimenté(e);

~ **ticket** n carte f d'abonnement.
seat [si:t] n siège m; (in bus, train: place) place f; (PARLIAMENT) siège; (buttocks) postérieur m; (of trousers) fond m // vt faire asseoir, placer; (have room for) avoir des places assises pour, pouvoir accueillir; ~ **belt** n ceinture f de sécurité.
sea water n eau f de mer.
seaweed ['si:wi:d] n algues fpl.
seaworthy ['si:wə:ði] a en état de naviguer.
sec. abbr of **second(s)**.
secluded [si'klu:did] a retiré(e), à l'écart.
seclusion [si'klu:ʒən] n solitude f.
second ['sɛkənd] num deuxième, second(e) // ad (in race etc) en seconde position // n (unit of time) seconde f; (in series, position) deuxième m/f, second/e; (AUT: also: ~ gear) seconde f; (COMM: imperfect) article m de second choix // vt (motion) appuyer; ~**ary** a secondaire; ~**ary school** n collège m, lycée m; ~**-class** a de deuxième classe // ad (RAIL) en seconde; ~**hand** a d'occasion; de seconde main; ~ **hand** n (on clock) trotteuse f; ~**ly** ad deuxièmement; ~**ment** [si'kɔndmənt] n (Brit) détachement m; ~**-rate** a de deuxième ordre, de qualité inférieure; ~ **thoughts** npl doutes mpl; on ~ **thoughts** or (US) **thought** à la réflexion.
secrecy ['si:krəsı] n secret m.
secret ['si:krıt] a secret(ète) // n secret m; **in** ~ ad en secret, secrètement, en cachette.
secretary ['sɛkrətərı] n secrétaire m/f; (COMM) secrétaire général; **S~ of State (for)** (Brit POL) ministre m (de).
secretive ['si:krətıv] a réservé(e); (pej) cachottier(ère), dissimulé(e).
sectarian [sɛk'tɛərıən] a sectaire.
section ['sɛkʃən] n coupe f, section f; (department) section; (COMM) rayon m; (of document) section, article m, paragraphe m.
sector ['sɛktə*] n secteur m.
secular ['sɛkjulə*] a profane; laïque; séculier(ère).
secure [si'kjuə*] a (free from anxiety) sans inquiétude, sécurisé(e); (firmly fixed) solide, bien attaché(e) (or fermé(e) etc); (in safe place) en lieu sûr, en sûreté // vt (fix) fixer, attacher; (get) obtenir, se procurer.
security [si'kjuərıtı] n sécurité f, mesures fpl de sécurité; (for loan) caution f, garantie f.
sedan [sı'dæn] n (US AUT) berline f.
sedate [sı'deıt] a calme; posé(e) // vt donner des sédatifs à.
sedative ['sɛdıtıv] n calmant m, sédatif m.
seduce [sı'dju:s] vt (gen) séduire; se-

duction [-'dʌkʃən] n séduction f; **seductive** [-'dʌktıv] a séduisant(e), séducteur(trice).
see [si:] vb (pt saw, pp seen) vt (gen) voir; (accompany): **to ~ sb to the door** reconduire or raccompagner qn jusqu'à la porte // vi voir // n évêché m; **to ~ that** (ensure) veiller à ce que + sub, faire en sorte que + sub, s'assurer que; ~ **you soon!** à bientôt!; **to ~ about** vt fus s'occuper de; **to ~ off** vt accompagner (à la gare or à l'aéroport etc); **to ~ through** vt mener à bonne fin // vt fus voir clair dans; **to ~ to** vt fus s'occuper de, se charger de.
seed [si:d] n graine f; (fig) germe m; (TENNIS) tête f de série; **to go to ~** monter en graine; (fig) se laisser aller; ~**ling** n jeune plant m, semis m; ~**y** a (shabby) minable, miteux(euse).
seeing ['si:ıŋ] cj: ~ (that) vu que, étant donné que.
seek [si:k], pt, pp **sought** vt chercher, rechercher.
seem [si:m] vi sembler, paraître; **there ~s to be ...** il semble qu'il y a ...; **on dirait qu'il y a ...**; ~**ingly** ad apparemment.
seen [si:n] pp of **see**.
seep [si:p] vi suinter, filtrer.
seesaw ['si:sɔ:] n (jeu m de) bascule f.
seethe [si:ð] vi être en effervescence; **to ~ with anger** bouillir de colère.
see-through ['si:θru:] a transparent(e).
segregate ['sɛgrıgeıt] vt séparer, isoler.
seize [si:z] vt (grasp) saisir, attraper; (take possession of) s'emparer de; (LAW) saisir; **to ~ (up)on** vt fus saisir, sauter sur; **to ~ up** vi (TECH) se gripper.
seizure ['si:ʒə*] n (MED) crise f, attaque f; (LAW) saisie f.
seldom ['sɛldəm] ad rarement.
select [sı'lɛkt] a choisi(e), d'élite; select inv // vt sélectionner, choisir; ~**ion** [-'lɛkʃən] n sélection f, choix m.
self [sɛlf] n (pl selves): **the ~** le moi inv // prefix auto-; ~**-catering** a (Brit) avec cuisine, où l'on peut faire sa cuisine; ~**-centred**, (US) ~**-centered** a égocentrique; ~**-coloured**, (US) ~**-colored** a uni(e); ~**-confidence** n confiance f en soi; ~**-conscious** a timide, qui manque d'assurance; ~**-contained** a (Brit: flat) avec entrée particulière, indépendant(e); ~**-control** n maîtrise f de soi; ~**-defence**, (US) ~**-defense** n légitime défense f; ~**-discipline** n discipline personnelle; ~**-employed** a qui travaille à son compte; ~**-evident** a évident(e), qui va de soi; ~**-governing** a autonome; ~**-indulgent** a qui ne se refuse rien; ~**-interest** n intérêt personnel; ~**ish** a égoïste; ~**ishness** n égoïsme m; ~**less** a désintéressé(e);

~-**pity** n apitoiement m sur soi-même; ~-**possessed** a assuré(e); ~-**preservation** n instinct m de conservation; ~-**respect** n respect m de soi, amour-propre m; ~-**righteous** a satisfait(e) de soi, pharisaïque; ~-**sacrifice** n abnégation f; ~-**satisfied** a content(e) de soi, suffisant(e); ~-**service** a, n libre-service (m), self-service (m); ~-**sufficient** a indépendant(e); ~-**taught** a autodidacte.

sell [sɛl], pt, pp **sold** vt vendre // vi se vendre; **to** ~ **at** or **for** 10 F se vendre 10 F; **to** ~ **off** vt liquider; **to** ~ **out** vi: **to** ~ **out** (**to sb/sth**) (COMM) vendre son fonds or son affaire (à qn/qch); vendre tout son stock de; **the tickets are all sold out** il ne reste plus de billets; ~-**by date** n date f limite de vente; ~-**er** n vendeur/euse, marchand/e; ~**ing price** n prix m de vente.

sellotape ['sɛləuteɪp] n ® (Brit) papier collant, scotch m ®.

sellout ['sɛlaut] n trahison f, capitulation f; (of tickets): **it was a** ~ tous les billets ont été vendus.

selves [sɛlvz] npl of **self**.

semblance ['sɛmbləns] n semblant m.

semen ['siːmən] n sperme m.

semester [sɪ'mɛstə*] n (US) semestre m.

semi ['sɛmɪ] prefix semi-, demi-; à demi, à moitié; ~**circle** n demi-cercle m; ~**colon** n point-virgule m; ~**detached (house)** n (Brit) maison jumelée or jumelle; ~**final** n demi-finale f.

seminar ['sɛmɪnɑː*] n séminaire m.

seminary ['sɛmɪnərɪ] n (REL: for priests) séminaire m.

semiskilled ['sɛmɪ'skɪld] a: ~ **worker** n ouvrier/ère spécialisé(e).

senate ['sɛnɪt] n sénat m; **senator** n sénateur m.

send [sɛnd], pt, pp **sent** vt envoyer; **to** ~ **away** vt (letter, goods) envoyer, expédier; **to** ~ **away for** vt fus commander par correspondance, se faire envoyer; **to** ~ **back** vt renvoyer; **to** ~ **for** vt fus envoyer chercher; faire venir; **to** ~ **off** vt (goods) envoyer, expédier; (Brit SPORT: player) expulser or renvoyer du terrain; **to** ~ **out** vt (invitation) envoyer (par la poste); **to** ~ **up** vt (person, price) faire monter; (Brit: parody) mettre en boîte, parodier; ~**er** n expéditeur/trice; ~-**off** n: **a good** ~-**off** des adieux chaleureux.

senior ['siːnɪə*] a (older) aîné(e), plus âgé(e); (of higher rank) supérieur(e) // n aîné/e; (in service) personne f qui a plus d'ancienneté; ~ **citizen** n personne âgée; ~**ity** [-'ɔrɪtɪ] n priorité f d'âge, ancienneté f.

sensation [sɛn'seɪʃən] n sensation f; ~**al** a qui fait sensation; (marvellous) sensationnel(le).

sense [sɛns] n sens m; (feeling) sentiment m; (meaning) signification f; (wisdom) bon sens // vt sentir, pressentir; **it makes** ~ c'est logique; ~**s** npl raison f; ~**less** a insensé(e), stupide; (unconscious) sans connaissance.

sensibility [sɛnsɪ'bɪlɪtɪ] n sensibilité f; **sensibilities** npl susceptibilité f.

sensible ['sɛnsɪbl] a sensé(e), raisonnable; sage; pratique.

sensitive ['sɛnsɪtɪv] a sensible.

sensual ['sɛnsjuəl] a sensuel(le).

sensuous ['sɛnsjuəs] a voluptueux(euse), sensuel(le).

sent [sɛnt] pt, pp of **send**.

sentence ['sɛntns] n (LING) phrase f; (LAW: judgment) condamnation f, sentence f; (: punishment) peine f // vt: **to** ~ **sb to death/to 5 years** condamner qn à mort/à 5 ans.

sentiment ['sɛntɪmənt] n sentiment m; (opinion) opinion f, avis m; ~**al** [-'mɛntl] a sentimental(e).

sentry ['sɛntrɪ] n sentinelle f, factionnaire m.

separate a ['sɛprɪt] séparé(e), indépendant(e), différent(e) // vb ['sɛpəreɪt] vt séparer // vi se séparer; ~**s** npl (clothes) coordonnés mpl; ~**ly** ad séparément; **separation** [-'reɪʃən] n séparation f.

September [sɛp'tɛmbə*] n septembre m.

septic ['sɛptɪk] a septique; (wound) infecté(e); ~ **tank** n fosse f septique.

sequel ['siːkwl] n conséquence f; séquelles fpl; (of story) suite f.

sequence ['siːkwəns] n ordre m, suite f.

sequin ['siːkwɪn] n paillette f.

serene [sɪ'riːn] a serein(e), calme, paisible.

sergeant ['sɑːdʒənt] n sergent m; (POLICE) brigadier m.

serial ['sɪərɪəl] n feuilleton m; ~ **number** n numéro m de série.

series ['sɪərɪs] n (pl inv) série f; (PUBLISHING) collection f.

serious ['sɪərɪəs] a sérieux(euse), réfléchi(e); grave; ~**ly** ad sérieusement, gravement.

sermon ['sɜːmən] n sermon m.

serrated [sɪ'reɪtɪd] a en dents de scie.

servant ['sɜːvənt] n domestique m/f; (fig) serviteur/servante.

serve [sɜːv] vt (employer etc) servir, être au service de; (purpose) servir à; (customer, food, meal) servir; (apprenticeship) faire, accomplir; (prison term) faire; purger // vi (also TENNIS) servir; (be useful): **to** ~ **as/for/ to do** servir de/à/à faire // n (TENNIS) service m; **it** ~**s him right** c'est bien fait pour lui; **to** ~ **out**, ~ **up** vt (food) servir.

service ['sə:vɪs] n (gen) service m; (AUT: maintenance) révision f // vt (car, washing machine) réviser; **the S~s** les forces armées; **to be of ~ to sb** rendre service à qn; **dinner ~** service m de table; **~able** a pratique, commode; **~ charge** n (Brit) service m; **~man** n militaire m; **~ station** n station-service f.

serviette [sə:vɪ'ɛt] n (Brit) serviette f (de table).

session ['sɛʃən] n (sitting) séance f; (SCOL) année f scolaire (or universitaire).

set [sɛt] n série f, assortiment m; (of tools etc) jeu m; (RADIO, TV) poste m; (TENNIS) set m; (group of people) cercle m, milieu m; (CINEMA) plateau m; (THEATRE: stage) scène f; (: scenery) décor m; (MATH) ensemble m; (HAIR-DRESSING) mise f en plis // a (fixed) fixe, déterminé(e); (ready) prêt(e) // vb (pt, pp set) vt (place) mettre, poser, placer; (fix, establish) fixer; (: record) établir; (adjust) régler; (decide: rules etc) fixer, choisir; (TYP) composer // vi (sun) se coucher; (jam, jelly, concrete) prendre; **to be ~ on doing** être résolu à faire; **~ (to music)** mettre en musique; **to ~ on fire** mettre le feu à; **to ~ free** libérer; **to ~ sth going** déclencher qch; **to ~ sail** partir, prendre la mer; **to ~ about** vt fus (task) entreprendre, se mettre à; **to ~ aside** vt mettre de côté; **to ~ back** vt (in time): **to ~ back (by)** retarder (de); **to ~ off** vi se mettre en route, partir // vt (bomb) faire exploser; (cause to start) déclencher; (show up well) mettre en valeur, faire valoir; **to ~ out** vi: **to ~ out to do** entreprendre de faire; avoir pour but or intention de faire // vt (arrange) disposer; (state) présenter, exposer; **to ~ up** vt (organization) fonder, constituer; **~back** n (hitch) revers m, contretemps m; **~ menu** n menu m.

settee [sɛ'ti:] n canapé m.

setting ['sɛtɪŋ] n cadre m; (of jewel) monture f.

settle ['sɛtl] vt (argument, matter) régler; (problem) résoudre; (MED: calm) calmer // vi (bird, dust etc) se poser; (sediment) se déposer; (also: ~ down) s'installer, se fixer; se calmer; se ranger; **to ~ for sth** accepter qch, se contenter de qch; **to ~ in** vi s'installer; **to ~ on sth** opter or se décider pour qch; **to ~ up with sb** régler (ce que l'on doit à) qn; **~ment** n (payment) règlement m; (agreement) accord m; (colony) colonie f; (village etc) établissement m; hameau m; **~r** n colon m.

setup ['sɛtʌp] n (arrangement) manière f dont les choses sont organisées; (situation) situation f, allure f des choses.

seven ['sɛvn] num sept; **~teen** num dix-sept; **~th** num septième; **~ty** num soixante-dix.

sever ['sɛvə*] vt couper, trancher; (relations) rompre.

several ['sɛvərl] a, pronoun plusieurs m/ fpl; **~ of us** plusieurs d'entre nous.

severance ['sɛvərəns] n (of relations) rupture f; **~ pay** n indemnité f de licenciement.

severe [sɪ'vɪə*] a sévère, strict(e); (serious) grave, sérieux(euse); (hard) rigoureux(euse), dur(e); (plain) sévère, austère; **severity** [sɪ'vɛrɪtɪ] n sévérité f; gravité f; rigueur f.

sew [səu], pt **sewed**, pp **sewn** vt, vi coudre; **to ~ up** vt (re)coudre.

sewage ['su:ɪdʒ] n vidange(s) f(pl).

sewer ['su:ə*] n égout m.

sewing ['səuɪŋ] n couture f; **~ machine** n machine f à coudre.

sewn [səun] pp of **sew**.

sex [sɛks] n sexe m; **to have ~ with** avoir des rapports (sexuels) avec; **~ist** a, n sexiste (m/f).

sexual ['sɛksjuəl] a sexuel(le).

sexy ['sɛksɪ] a sexy inv.

shabby ['ʃæbɪ] a miteux(euse); (behaviour) mesquin(e), méprisable.

shack [ʃæk] n cabane f, hutte f.

shackles ['ʃæklz] npl chaînes fpl, entraves fpl.

shade [ʃeɪd] n ombre f; (for lamp) abat-jour m inv; (of colour) nuance f, ton m; (small quantity): **a ~ of** un soupçon de // vt abriter du soleil, ombrager; **in the ~** à l'ombre; **a ~ smaller** un tout petit peu plus petit.

shadow ['ʃædəu] n ombre f // vt (follow) filer; **~ cabinet** n (Brit POL) cabinet parallèle formé par le parti qui n'est pas au pouvoir; **~y** a ombragé(e); (dim) vague, indistinct(e).

shady ['ʃeɪdɪ] a ombragé(e); (fig: dishonest) louche, véreux(euse).

shaft [ʃɑ:ft] n (of arrow, spear) hampe f; (AUT, TECH) arbre m; (of mine) puits m; (of lift) cage f; (of light) rayon m, trait m.

shaggy ['ʃægɪ] a hirsute; en broussaille.

shake [ʃeɪk] vb (pt **shook**, pp **shaken** [ʃuk, 'ʃeɪkn]) vt secouer; (bottle, cocktail) agiter; (house, confidence) ébranler // vi trembler // n secousse f; **to ~ one's head** (in refusal) dire or faire non de la tête; (in dismay) secouer la tête; **to ~ hands with sb** serrer la main à qn; **to ~ off** vt secouer; (fig) se débarrasser de; **to ~ up** vt secouer; **shaky** a (hand, voice) tremblant(e); (building) branlant(e), peu solide.

shall [ʃæl] auxiliary vb: **I ~ go** j'irai; **~ I open the door?** j'ouvre la porte?; **I'll get the coffee, ~ I?** je vais chercher le café, d'accord?

shallow ['ʃæləu] *a* peu profond(e); *(fig)* superficiel(le).

sham [ʃæm] *n* frime *f*; *(jewellery, furniture)* imitation *f*.

shambles ['ʃæmblz] *n* confusion *f*, pagaïe *f*, fouillis *m*.

shame [ʃeɪm] *n* honte *f* // *vt* faire honte à; **it is a ~ (that/to do)** c'est dommage (que + *sub*/de faire); **what a ~!** quel dommage!; **~faced** *a* honteux(euse), penaud(e), **~ful** *a* honteux(euse), scandaleux(euse); **~less** *a* éhonté(e), effronté(e); *(immodest)* impudique.

shampoo [ʃæm'pu:] *n* shampooing *m* // *vt* faire un shampooing à; **~ and set** *n* shampooing *m* et mise *f* en plis.

shamrock ['ʃæmrɔk] *n* trèfle *m* *(emblème national de l'Irlande).*

shandy ['ʃændɪ] *n* bière panachée.

shan't [ʃɑ:nt] = **shall not.**

shanty town ['ʃæntɪ-] *n* bidonville *m*.

shape [ʃeɪp] *n* forme *f* // *vt* façonner, modeler; *(statement)* formuler; *(sb's ideas)* former; *(sb's life)* déterminer // *vi* *(also:* ~ **up**: *events)* prendre tournure; (*: person)* faire des progrès, s'en sortir; **to take ~** prendre forme *or* tournure; **-shaped** *suffix*: **heart-shaped** en forme de cœur; **~less** *a* informe, sans forme; **~ly** *a* bien proportionné(e), beau(belle).

share [ʃɛə*] *n* *(thing received, contribution)* part *f*; *(COMM)* action *f* // *vt* partager; *(have in common)* avoir en commun; **to ~ out** *(among or between)* partager (entre); **~holder** *n* actionnaire *m/f*.

shark [ʃɑ:k] *n* requin *m*.

sharp [ʃɑ:p] *a* *(razor, knife)* tranchant(e), bien aiguisé(e); *(point)* aigu(guë); *(nose, chin)* pointu(e); *(outline)* net(te); *(cold, pain)* vif(vive); *(MUS)* dièse; *(voice)* coupant(e); *(person: quick-witted)* vif(vive), éveillé(e); (*: unscrupulous)* malhonnête // *n* *(MUS)* dièse *m* // *ad:* **at 2 o'clock** ~ à 2 heures pile *or* tapantes; **~en** *vt* aiguiser; *(pencil)* tailler; *(fig)* aviver; **~ener** *n* *(also:* **pencil ~ener)** taille-crayon(s) *m inv*; **~eyed** *a* à qui rien n'échappe; **~ly** *ad* *(turn, stop)* brusquement; *(stand out)* nettement; *(criticize, retort)* sèchement, vertement.

shatter ['ʃætə*] *vt* briser; *(fig: upset)* bouleverser; (*: ruin)* briser, ruiner *// vi* voler en éclats, se briser.

shave [ʃeɪv] *vt* raser // *vi* se raser // *n:* **to have a ~** se raser; **~r** *n* *(also:* **electric ~r)** rasoir *m* électrique.

shaving ['ʃeɪvɪŋ] *n* *(action)* rasage *m*; **~s** *npl* *(of wood etc)* copeaux *mpl*; **~ brush** *n* blaireau *m*; **~ cream** *n* crème *f* à raser.

shawl [ʃɔ:l] *n* châle *m*.

she [ʃi:] *pronoun* elle; **~-cat** *n* chatte *f*;

~-elephant *n* éléphant *m* femelle; *NB: for ships, countries follow the gender of your translation.*

sheaf [ʃi:f], *pl* **sheaves** *n* gerbe *f*.

shear [ʃɪə*] *vt* *(pt* **~ed**, *pp* **~ed** *or* **shorn)** *(sheep)* tondre; **to ~ off** *vi* *(branch)* partir, se détacher; **~s** *npl* *(for hedge)* cisaille(s) *f(pl)*.

sheath [ʃi:θ] *n* gaine *f*, fourreau *m*, étui *m*; *(contraceptive)* préservatif *m*.

sheaves [ʃi:vz] *npl of* **sheaf.**

shed [ʃɛd] *n* remise *f*, resserre *f* // *vt* *(pt, pp* **shed)** *(leaves, fur etc)* perdre; *(tears)* verser, répandre.

she'd [ʃi:d] = **she had, she would.**

sheen [ʃi:n] *n* lustre *m*.

sheep [ʃi:p] *n* *(pl inv)* mouton *m*; **~dog** *n* chien *m* de berger; **~ish** *a* penaud(e), timide; **~skin** *n* peau *f* de mouton.

sheer [ʃɪə*] *a* *(utter)* pur(e), pur et simple; *(steep)* à pic, abrupt(e); *(almost transparent)* extrêmement fin(e) // *ad* à pic, abruptement.

sheet [ʃi:t] *n* *(on bed)* drap *m*; *(of paper)* feuille *f*; *(of glass, metal)* feuille, plaque *f*.

sheik(h) [ʃeɪk] *n* cheik *m*.

shelf [ʃelf], *pl* **shelves** *n* étagère *f*, rayon *m*.

shell [ʃel] *n* *(on beach)* coquillage *m*; *(of egg, nut etc)* coquille *f*; *(explosive)* obus *m*; *(of building)* carcasse *f* // *vt* *(crab, prawn etc)* décortiquer; *(peas)* écosser; *(MIL)* bombarder (d'obus).

she'll [ʃi:l] = **she will, she shall.**

shellfish ['ʃelfɪʃ] *n* *(pl inv)* *(crab etc)* crustacé *m*; *(scallop etc)* coquillage *m*; *(pl: as food)* crustacés *m*; coquillages.

shelter ['ʃeltə*] *n* abri *m*, refuge *m* // *vt* abriter, protéger; *(give lodging to)* donner asile à // *vi* s'abriter, se mettre à l'abri.

shelve [ʃelv] *vt* *(fig)* mettre en suspens *or* en sommeil; **~s** *npl of* **shelf.**

shepherd ['ʃepəd] *n* berger *m* // *vt* *(guide)* guider, escorter; **~'s pie** *n* ≈ hachis *m* Parmentier.

sheriff ['ʃerɪf] *n* shérif *m*.

sherry ['ʃerɪ] *n* xérès *m*, sherry *m*.

she's [ʃi:z] = **she is, she has.**

Shetland ['ʃetlənd] *n* *(also:* **the ~s, the ~ Isles)** les îles *fpl* Shetland.

shield [ʃi:ld] *n* bouclier *m* // *vt:* **to ~ (from)** protéger (de *or* contre).

shift [ʃɪft] *n* *(change)* changement *m*; *(of workers)* équipe *f*, poste *m* // *vt* déplacer, changer de place; *(remove)* enlever // *vi* changer de place, bouger; **~less** *a* *(person)* fainéant(e); **~ work** *n* travail *m* en équipe *or* par relais *or* par roulement; **~y** *a* sournois(e); *(eyes)* fuyant(e).

shilling ['ʃɪlɪŋ] *n* *(Brit)* shilling *m* *(= 12 old pence; 20 in a pound).*

shilly-shally ['ʃɪlɪʃælɪ] *vi* tergiverser,

atermoyer.

shimmer ['ʃɪmə*] vi miroiter, chatoyer.
shin [ʃɪn] n tibia m.
shine [ʃaɪn] n éclat m, brillant m // vb (pt, pp **shone**) vi briller // vt faire briller or reluire; (torch): **to ~ on** braquer sur.
shingle ['ʃɪŋgl] n (on beach) galets mpl; (on roof) bardeau m; **~s** n (MED) zona m.
shiny ['ʃaɪnɪ] a brillant(e).
ship [ʃɪp] n bateau m; (large) navire m // vt transporter (par mer); (send) expédier (par mer); (load) charger, embarquer; **~building** n construction navale; **~ment** n cargaison f; **~ping** n (ships) navires mpl; (traffic) navigation f; **~shape** a en ordre impeccable; **~wreck** n épave f; (event) naufrage m // vt: **to be ~wrecked** faire naufrage; **~yard** n chantier naval.
shire ['ʃaɪə*] n (Brit) comté m.
shirk [ʃə:k] vt esquiver, se dérober à.
shirt [ʃə:t] n (man's) chemise f; **in ~ sleeves** en bras de chemise.
shit [ʃɪt] excl (col!) merde! (!).
shiver ['ʃɪvə*] vi frissonner.
shoal [ʃəʊl] n (of fish) banc m.
shock [ʃɔk] n (impact) choc m, heurt m; (ELEC) secousse f; (emotional) choc, secousse; (MED) commotion f, choc // vt choquer, scandaliser; bouleverser; **~ absorber** n amortisseur m; **~ing** a choquant(e), scandaleux(euse); épouvantable; révoltant(e).
shod [ʃɔd] pt, pp of **shoe**.
shoddy ['ʃɔdɪ] a de mauvaise qualité, mal fait(e).
shoe [ʃu:] n chaussure f, soulier m; (also: horse~) fer m à cheval // vt (pt, pp **shod**) (horse) ferrer; **~horn** n chausse-pied m; **~lace** n lacet m (de soulier); **~ polish** n cirage m; **~shop** n magasin de chaussures; **~string** n (fig): **on a ~string** avec un budget dérisoire.
shone [ʃɔn] pt, pp of **shine**.
shoo [ʃu:] excl (allez,) ouste!
shook [ʃʊk] pt of **shake**.
shoot [ʃu:t] n (on branch, seedling) pousse f // vb (pt, pp **shot**) vt (game) chasser; tirer; abattre; (person) blesser (or tuer) d'un coup de fusil (or de revolver); (execute) fusiller; (film) tourner // vi (with gun, bow): **to ~ (at)** tirer (sur); (FOOTBALL) shooter, tirer; **to ~ down** vt (plane) abattre; **to ~ in/out** vi entrer/sortir comme une flèche; **to ~ up** vi (fig) monter en flèche; **~ing** n (shots) coups mpl de feu, fusillade f; (HUNTING) chasse f; **~ing star** n étoile filante.
shop [ʃɔp] n magasin m; (workshop) atelier m // vi (also: go ~ping) faire ses courses or ses achats; **~ assistant** n

(Brit) vendeur/euse; **~ floor** n (Brit: fig) ouvriers mpl; **~keeper** n marchand/e, commerçant/e; **~lifting** n vol m à l'étalage; **~per** n personne f qui fait ses courses, acheteur/euse; **~ping** n (goods) achats mpl, provisions fpl; **~ping bag** n sac m (à provisions); **~ping centre**, (US) **~ping center** n centre commercial; **~-soiled** a défraîchi(e), qui a fait la vitrine; **~ steward** n (Brit INDUSTRY) délégué/e syndical(e); **~ window** n vitrine f.
shore [ʃɔ:*] n (of sea, lake) rivage m, rive f // vt: **to ~ (up)** étayer.
shorn [ʃɔ:n] pp of **shear**.
short [ʃɔ:t] a (not long) court(e); (soon finished) court, bref(brève); (person, step) petit(e); (curt) brusque, sec(sèche); (insufficient) insuffisant(e) // n (also: ~ film) court métrage; (a pair of) **~s** un short; **to be ~ of sth** être à court de or manquer de qch; **in ~** bref; en bref; **~ of doing** à moins de faire; **everything ~ of** tout sauf; **it is ~ for** c'est l'abréviation or le diminutif de; **to cut ~** (speech, visit) abréger, écourter; (person) couper la parole à; **to fall ~ of** ne pas être à la hauteur de; **to stop ~** s'arrêter net; **to stop ~ of** ne pas aller jusqu'à; **~age** n manque m, pénurie f; **~bread** n ≈sablé m; **~change** vt ne pas rendre assez à; **~circuit** n court-circuit m; **~coming** n défaut m; **~(crust) pastry** n (Brit) pâte brisée; **~cut** n raccourci m; **~en** vt raccourcir; (text, visit) abréger; **~fall** n déficit m; **~hand** n (Brit) sténo(graphie) f; **~hand typist** n (Brit) sténodactylo m/f; **~ list** n (Brit: for job) liste f des candidats sélectionnés; **~ly** ad bientôt, sous peu; **~sighted** a (Brit) myope; (fig) qui manque de clairvoyance; **~staffed** a à court de personnel; **~ story** n nouvelle f; **~tempered** a qui s'emporte facilement; **~term** a (effect) à court terme; **~wave** n (RADIO) ondes courtes.
shot [ʃɔt] pt, pp of **shoot** // n coup m (de feu); (person) tireur m; (try) coup, essai m; (injection) piqûre f; (PHOT) photo f; **like a ~** comme une flèche; (very readily) sans hésiter; **~gun** n fusil m de chasse.
should [ʃʊd] auxiliary vb: **I ~ go now** je devrais partir maintenant; **he ~ be there now** il devrait être arrivé maintenant; **I ~ go if I were you** si j'étais vous j'irais; **I ~ like to** j'aimerais bien, volontiers.
shoulder ['ʃəʊldə*] n épaule f; (Brit: of road): **hard ~** accotement m // vt (fig) endosser, se charger de; **~ bag** n sac m à bandoulière; **~ blade** n omoplate f; **~ strap** n bretelle f.
shouldn't ['ʃʊdnt] = **should not**.
shout [ʃaʊt] n cri m // vt crier // vi crier,

pousser des cris; **to ~ down** *vt* huer; **~ing** *n* cris *mpl*.

shove [ʃʌv] *vt* pousser; (*col: put*): **to ~ sth in** fourrer *or* ficher qch dans; **to ~ off** *vi* (*NAUT*) pousser au large; (*fig: col*) ficher le camp.

shovel ['ʃʌvl] *n* pelle *f*.

show [ʃəu] *n* (*of emotion*) manifestation *f*, démonstration *f*; (*semblance*) semblant *m*, apparence *f*; (*exhibition*) exposition *f*, salon *m*; (*THEATRE*) spectacle *m*, représentation *f*; (*CINEMA*) séance *f* // *vb* (*pt* ~**ed**, *pp* **shown**) *vt* montrer; (*courage etc*) faire preuve de, manifester; (*exhibit*) exposer // *vi* se voir, être visible; **on ~** (*exhibits etc*) exposé(e); **to ~ in** *vt* (*person*) faire entrer; **to ~ off** *vi* (*pej*) crâner // *vt* (*display*) faire valoir; (*pej*) faire étalage de; **to ~ out** *vt* (*person*) reconduire (jusqu'à la porte); **to ~ up** *vi* (*stand out*) ressortir; (*col: turn up*) se montrer // *vt* démontrer; (*unmask*) démasquer, dénoncer; **~ business** *n* le monde du spectacle; **~down** *n* épreuve *f* de force.

shower ['ʃauə*] *n* (*rain*) averse *f*; (*of stones etc*) pluie *f*, grêle *f*; (*also: ~bath*) douche *f* // *vi* prendre une douche, se doucher // *vt*: **to ~ sb with** (*gifts etc*) combler qn de; (*abuse etc*) accabler qn de; (*missiles*) bombarder qn de; **~proof** *a* imperméable.

showing ['ʃəuiŋ] *n* (*of film*) projection *f*.

show jumping *n* concours *m* hippique.

shown [ʃəun] *pp* of **show**.

show-off ['ʃəuɔf] *n* (*col: person*) crâneur/euse, m'as-tu-vu/e.

showroom ['ʃəurum] *n* magasin *m* or salle *f* d'exposition.

shrank [ʃræŋk] *pt* of **shrink**.

shrapnel ['ʃræpnl] *n* éclats *mpl* d'obus.

shred [ʃred] *n* (*gen pl*) lambeau *m*, petit morceau // *vt* mettre en lambeaux, déchirer; (*CULIN*) râper; couper en lanières; **~der** *n* (*for vegetables*) râpeur *m*; (*for documents*) destructeur *m* de documents.

shrewd [ʃru:d] *a* astucieux(euse), perspicace.

shriek [ʃri:k] *vt, vi* hurler, crier.

shrill [ʃril] *a* perçant(e), aigu(guë), strident(e).

shrimp [ʃrimp] *n* crevette grise.

shrine [ʃrain] *n* châsse *f*; (*place*) lieu *m* de pèlerinage.

shrink [ʃriŋk], *pt* **shrank**, *pp* **shrunk** *vi* rétrécir; (*fig*) se réduire; se contracter // *vt* (*wool*) (faire) rétrécir // *n* (*col: pej*) psychanalyste *m/f*; **to ~ from (doing) sth** reculer devant (la pensée de faire) qch; **~age** *n* rétrécissement *m*; **~wrap** *vt* emballer sous film plastique.

shrivel ['ʃrivl] (*also: ~ up*) *vt* ratatiner, flétrir // *vi* se ratatiner, se flétrir.

shroud [ʃraud] *n* linceul *m* // *vt*: **~ed in mystery** enveloppé(e) de mystère.

Shrove Tuesday ['ʃrəuv-] *n* (le) Mardi gras.

shrub [ʃrʌb] *n* arbuste *m*; **~bery** *n* massif *m* d'arbustes.

shrug [ʃrʌg] *vt, vi*: **to ~ (one's shoulders)** hausser les épaules; **to ~ off** *vt* faire fi de.

shrunk [ʃrʌŋk] *pp* of **shrink**.

shudder ['ʃʌdə*] *vi* frissonner, frémir.

shuffle ['ʃʌfl] *vt* (*cards*) battre; **to ~ (one's feet)** traîner les pieds.

shun [ʃʌn] *vt* éviter, fuir.

shunt [ʃʌnt] *vt* (*RAIL: direct*) aiguiller; (*: divert*) détourner.

shut, *pt, pp* **shut** [ʃʌt] *vt* fermer // *vi* (se) fermer; **to ~ down** *vt, vi* fermer définitivement; **to ~ off** *vt* couper, arrêter; **to ~ up** *vi* (*col: keep quiet*) se taire // *vt* (*close*) fermer; (*silence*) faire taire; **~ter** *n* volet *m*; (*PHOT*) obturateur *m*.

shuttle ['ʃʌtl] *n* navette *f*; (*also: ~ service*) (service *m* de) navette *f*.

shuttlecock ['ʃʌtlkɔk] *n* volant *m* (*de badminton*).

shy [ʃai] *a* timide.

siblings ['sibliŋz] *npl* enfants *mpl* d'un même couple.

Sicily ['sisili] *n* Sicile *f*.

sick [sik] *a* (*ill*) malade; (*vomiting*): **to be ~** vomir; (*humour*) noir(e), macabre; **to feel ~** avoir envie de vomir, avoir mal au cœur; **to be ~ of** (*fig*) en avoir assez de; **~ bay** *n* infirmerie *f*; **~en** *vt* écœurer // *vi*: **to be ~ening for sth** (*cold etc*) couver qch.

sickle ['sikl] *n* faucille *f*.

sick: ~ leave *n* congé *m* de maladie; **~ly** *a* maladif(ive), souffreteux(euse); (*causing nausea*) écœurant(e); **~ness** *n* maladie *f*; (*vomiting*) vomissement(s) *m(pl)*; **~ pay** *n* indemnité *f* de maladie.

side [said] *n* côté *m*; (*of lake, road*) bord *m* // *cpd* (*door, entrance*) latéral(e) // *vi*: **to ~ with sb** prendre le parti de qn, se ranger du côté de qn; **by the ~ of** au bord de; **~ by ~** côte à côte; **to take ~s (with)** prendre parti (pour); **~board** *n* buffet *m*; **~boards** (*Brit*), **~burns** *npl* (*whiskers*) pattes *fpl*; **~ effect** *n* (*MED*) effet *m* secondaire; **~light** *n* (*AUT*) veilleuse *f*; **~line** *n* (*SPORT*) (ligne *f* de) touche *f*; (*fig*) activité *f* secondaire; **~long** *a* oblique, de coin; **~saddle** *ad* en amazone; **~ show** *n* attraction *f*; **~step** *vt* (*fig*) éluder; éviter; **~ street** *n* rue transversale; **~track** *vt* (*fig*) faire dévier de son sujet; **~walk** *n* (*US*) trottoir *m*; **~ways** *ad* de côté.

siding ['saidiŋ] *n* (*RAIL*) voie *f* de garage.

sidle ['saidl] *vi*: **to ~ up (to)** s'approcher furtivement (de).

siege [si:dʒ] *n* siège *m*.

sieve [sɪv] *n* tamis *m*, passoire *f*.

sift [sɪft] *vt* passer au tamis *or* au crible; *(fig)* passer au crible.

sigh [saɪ] *n* soupir *m* // *vi* soupirer, pousser un soupir.

sight [saɪt] *n* *(faculty)* vue *f*; *(spectacle)* spectacle *m*; *(on gun)* mire *f* // *vt* apercevoir; **in ~** visible; *(fig)* en vue; **out of ~** hors de vue; **~seeing** *n* tourisme *m*; **to go ~seeing** faire du tourisme.

sign [saɪn] *n* *(gen)* signe *m*; *(with hand etc)* signe, geste *m*; *(notice)* panneau *m*, écriteau *m* // *vt* signer; **to ~ on** *vi* *(MIL)* s'engager; *(as unemployed)* s'inscrire au chômage // *vt* *(MIL)* engager; *(employee)* embaucher; **to ~ over** *vt*: **to ~ sth over to sb** céder qch par écrit à qn; **to ~ up** *vt* *(MIL)* engager // *vi* s'engager.

signal ['sɪgnl] *n* signal *m* // *vi* *(AUT)* mettre son clignotant // *vt* *(person)* faire signe à; *(message)* communiquer par signaux; **~-man** *n* *(RAIL)* aiguilleur *m*.

signature ['sɪgnətʃə*] *n* signature *f*; **~ tune** *n* indicatif musical.

signet ring ['sɪgnət-] *n* chevalière *f*.

significance [sɪg'nɪfɪkəns] *n* signification *f*; importance *f*.

significant [sɪg'nɪfɪkənt] *a* significatif(ive); *(important)* important(e), considérable.

signpost ['saɪnpəust] *n* poteau indicateur.

silence ['saɪlns] *n* silence *m* // *vt* faire taire, réduire au silence; **~r** *n* *(on gun, Brit AUT)* silencieux *m*.

silent ['saɪlnt] *a* silencieux(euse); *(film)* muet(te); **to remain ~** garder le silence, ne rien dire; **~ partner** *n* *(COMM)* bailleur *m* de fonds, commanditaire *m*.

silhouette [sɪlu:'et] *n* silhouette *f*.

silicon chip ['sɪlɪkən-] *n* puce *f* électronique.

silk [sɪlk] *n* soie *f* // *cpd* de or en soie; **~y** *a* soyeux(euse).

silly ['sɪlɪ] *a* stupide, sot(te), bête.

silt [sɪlt] *n* vase *f*; limon *m*.

silver ['sɪlvə*] *n* argent *m*; *(money)* monnaie *f* (en pièces d'argent); *(also:* **~ware**) argenterie *f* // *cpd* d'argent, en argent; **~ paper** *n* *(Brit)* papier *m* d'argent *or* d'étain; **~-plated** *a* plaqué(e) argent; **~smith** *n* orfèvre *m/f*; **~y** *a* argenté(e).

similar ['sɪmɪlə*] *a*: **~ (to)** semblable (à); **~ly** *ad* de la même façon, de même.

simile ['sɪmɪlɪ] *n* comparaison *f*.

simmer ['sɪmə*] *vi* cuire à feu doux, mijoter.

simpering ['sɪmpərɪŋ] *a* minaudier(ère), nunuche.

simple ['sɪmpl] *a* simple; **simplicity** [-'plɪsɪtɪ] *n* simplicité *f*.

simultaneous [sɪməl'teɪnɪəs] *a* simultané(e).

sin [sɪn] *n* péché *m* // *vi* pécher.

since [sɪns] *ad, prep* depuis // *cj* *(time)* depuis que; *(because)* puisque, étant donné que, comme; **~ then** depuis ce moment-là.

sincere [sɪn'sɪə*] *a* sincère; **sincerity** [-'serɪtɪ] *n* sincérité *f*.

sinew ['sɪnju:] *n* tendon *m*; **~s** *npl* muscles *mpl*.

sinful ['sɪnful] *a* coupable.

sing [sɪŋ], *pt* **sang**, *pp* **sung** *vt*, *vi* chanter.

singe [sɪndʒ] *vt* brûler légèrement; *(clothes)* roussir.

singer ['sɪŋə*] *n* chanteur/euse.

singing ['sɪŋɪŋ] *n* chant *m*.

single ['sɪŋgl] *a* seul(e), unique; *(unmarried)* célibataire; *(not double)* simple // *n* *(Brit: also:* **~ ticket**) aller *m* (simple); *(record)* 45 tours *m*; **~s** *npl* *(TENNIS)* simple *m*; **to ~ out** *vt* choisir; distinguer; **~ bed** *n* lit *m* à une place *or* d'une personne; **~-breasted** *a* droit(e); **~ file** *n*: **in ~ file** en file indienne; **~-handed** *ad* tout(e) seul(e), sans (aucune) aide; **~-minded** *a* résolu(e), tenace; **~ room** *n* chambre *f* à un lit *or* pour une personne.

singlet ['sɪŋglɪt] *n* tricot *m* de corps.

singly ['sɪŋglɪ] *ad* séparément.

singular ['sɪŋgjulə*] *a* singulier(ère), étrange; *(LING)* (au) singulier, du singulier // *n* *(LING)* singulier *m*.

sinister ['sɪnɪstə*] *a* sinistre.

sink [sɪŋk] *n* évier *m* // *vb* *(pt* **sank**, *pp* **sunk**) *vt* *(ship)* (faire) couler, faire sombrer; *(foundations)* creuser; *(piles etc)*: **to ~ sth into** enfoncer qch dans // *vi* couler, sombrer; *(ground etc)* s'affaisser; **to ~ in** *vi* s'enfoncer, pénétrer.

sinner ['sɪnə*] *n* pécheur/eresse.

sinus ['saɪnəs] *n* *(ANAT)* sinus *m inv*.

sip [sɪp] *vt* boire à petites gorgées.

siphon ['saɪfən] *n* siphon *m*; **to ~ off** *vt* siphonner.

sir [sə*] *n* monsieur *m*; **S~ John Smith** sir John Smith; **yes ~** oui Monsieur.

siren ['saɪərn] *n* sirène *f*.

sirloin ['sə:lɔɪn] *n* aloyau *m*.

sissy ['sɪsɪ] *n* *(col: coward)* poule mouillée.

sister ['sɪstə*] *n* sœur *f*; *(nun)* religieuse *f*, (bonne) sœur; *(Brit: nurse)* infirmière *f* en chef; **~-in-law** *n* belle-sœur *f*.

sit [sɪt], *pt, pp* **sat** *vi* s'asseoir; *(assembly)* être en séance, siéger; *(for painter)* poser // *vt* *(exam)* passer, se présenter à; **to ~ down** *vi* s'asseoir; **to ~ in on** *vt fus* assister à; **to ~ up** *vi* s'asseoir; *(not go to bed)* rester debout, ne pas se coucher.

sitcom ['sɪtkɔm] *n abbr* (= *situation*

comedy) comédie f de situation.
site [saɪt] *n* emplacement *m*, site *m*; (*also*: **building ~**) chantier *m*.
sit-in ['sɪtɪn] *n* (*demonstration*) sit-in *m inv*, occupation *f* de locaux.
sitting ['sɪtɪŋ] *n* (*of assembly etc*) séance *f*; (*in canteen*) service *m*; **~ room** *n* salon *m*.
situated ['sɪtjueɪtɪd] *a* situé(e).
situation [sɪtju'eɪʃən] *n* situation *f*; '**~s vacant/wanted**' (*Brit*) 'offres/demandes d'emploi'.
six [sɪks] *num* six; **~teen** *num* seize; **~th** *a* sixième; **~ty** *num* soixante.
size [saɪz] *n* taille *f*; dimensions *fpl*; (*of clothing*) taille; (*of shoes*) pointure *f*; (*glue*) colle *f*; **to ~ up** *vt* juger, jauger; **~able** *a* assez grand(e) *or* gros(se); assez important(e).
sizzle ['sɪzl] *vi* grésiller.
skate [skeɪt] *n* patin *m*; (*fish: pl inv*) raie *f* // *vi* patiner; **~board** *n* skateboard *m*, planche *f* à roulettes; **~r** *n* patineur/euse; **skating** *n* patinage *m*; **skating rink** *n* patinoire *f*.
skeleton ['skelɪtn] *n* squelette *m*; (*outline*) schéma *m*; **~ key** *n* passepartout *m*; **~ staff** *n* effectifs réduits.
skeptical ['skeptɪkl] *a* (*US*) = **sceptical**.
sketch [sketʃ] *n* (*drawing*) croquis *m*, esquisse *f*; (*THEATRE*) sketch *m*, saynète *f* // *vt* esquisser, faire un croquis *or* une esquisse de; **~ book** *n* carnet *m* à dessin; **~y** *a* incomplet(ète), fragmentaire.
skewer ['skjuːə*] *n* brochette *f*.
ski [skiː] *n* ski *m* // *vi* skier, faire du ski; **~ boot** *n* chaussure *f* de ski.
skid [skɪd] *vi* déraper.
skier ['skiːə*] *n* skieur/euse.
skiing ['skiːɪŋ] *n* ski *m*.
ski jump *n* saut *m* à skis.
skilful ['skɪlful] *a* habile, adroit(e).
ski lift *n* remonte-pente *m inv*.
skill [skɪl] *n* habileté *f*, adresse *f*, talent *m*; **~ed** *a* habile, adroit(e); (*worker*) qualifié(e).
skim [skɪm] *vt* (*milk*) écrémer; (*soup*) écumer; (*glide over*) raser, effleurer // *vi*: **to ~ through** (*fig*) parcourir; **~med milk** *n* lait écrémé.
skimp [skɪmp] *vt* (*work*) bâcler, faire à la va-vite; (*cloth etc*) lésiner sur; **~y** *a* étriqué(e); maigre.
skin [skɪn] *n* peau *f* // *vt* (*fruit etc*) éplucher; (*animal*) écorcher; **~-deep** *a* superficiel(le); **~ diving** *n* plongée sous-marine; **~ny** *a* maigre, maigrichon(ne); **~tight** *a* (*dress etc*) collant(e), ajusté(e).
skip [skɪp] *n* petit bond *or* saut; (*container*) benne *f* // *vi* gambader, sautiller; (*with rope*) sauter à la corde // *vt* (*pass over*) sauter.
ski: **~ pants** *npl* fuseau *m* (de ski); **~**

pole *n* bâton *m* de ski.
skipper ['skɪpə*] *n* (*NAUT*, *SPORT*) capitaine *m*.
skipping rope ['skɪpɪŋ-] *n* (*Brit*) corde *f* à sauter.
skirmish ['skɜːmɪʃ] *n* escarmouche *f*, accrochage *m*.
skirt [skɜːt] *n* jupe *f* // *vt* longer, contourner.
ski suit *n* combinaison *f* (de ski).
skit [skɪt] *n* sketch *m* satirique.
skittle ['skɪtl] *n* quille *f*; **~s** *n* (*game*) (jeu *m* de) quilles *fpl*.
skive [skaɪv] *vi* (*Brit col*) tirer au flanc.
skulk [skʌlk] *vi* rôder furtivement.
skull [skʌl] *n* crâne *m*.
skunk [skʌŋk] *n* mouffette *f*.
sky [skaɪ] *n* ciel *m*; **~light** *n* lucarne *f*; **~scraper** *n* gratte-ciel *m inv*.
slab [slæb] *n* plaque *f*; dalle *f*.
slack [slæk] *a* (*loose*) lâche, desserré(e); (*slow*) stagnant(e); (*careless*) négligent(e), peu sérieux(euse) *or* consciencieux(euse) // *n* (*in rope etc*) mou *m*; **~s** *npl* pantalon *m*; **~en** (*also*: **~en off**) *vi* ralentir, diminuer // *vt* relâcher.
slag [slæg] *n* scories *fpl*; **~ heap** *n* crassier *m*.
slain [sleɪn] *pp of* **slay**.
slam [slæm] *vt* (*door*) (faire) claquer; (*throw*) jeter violemment, flanquer; (*criticize*) éreinter, démolir // *vi* claquer.
slander ['slɑːndə*] *n* calomnie *f*; diffamation *f*.
slang [slæŋ] *n* argot *m*.
slant [slɑːnt] *n* inclinaison *f*; (*fig*) angle *m*, point *m* de vue; **~ed** *a* tendancieux(euse); **~ing** *a* en pente, incliné(e); couché(e).
slap [slæp] *n* claque *f*, gifle *f*; tape *f* // *vt* donner une claque *or* une gifle *or* une tape à // *ad* (*directly*) tout droit, en plein; **~dash** *a* fait(e) sans soin *or* à la va-vite; (*person*) insouciant(e), négligent(e); **~stick** *n* (*comedy*) grosse farce, style *m* tarte à la crème; **~-up** *a*: **a ~-up meal** (*Brit*) un repas extra *or* fameux.
slash [slæʃ] *vt* entailler, taillader; (*fig: prices*) casser.
slat [slæt] *n* latte *f*, lame *f*.
slate [sleɪt] *n* ardoise *f* // *vt* (*fig: criticize*) éreinter, démolir.
slaughter ['slɔːtə*] *n* carnage *m*, massacre *m* // *vt* (*animal*) abattre; (*people*) massacrer.
slave [sleɪv] *n* esclave *m/f* // *vi* (*also*: **~ away**) trimer, travailler comme un forçat; **~ry** *n* esclavage *m*.
slay [sleɪ], *pt* **slew**, *pp* **slain** *vt* (*formal*) tuer.
sleazy ['sliːzɪ] *a* miteux(euse), minable.
sledge [sledʒ] *n* luge *f*; **~hammer** *n* marteau *m* de forgeron.
sleek [sliːk] *a* (*hair, fur*) brillant(e),

luisant(e); (*car, boat*) aux lignes pures or élégantes.

sleep [sli:p] *n* sommeil *m* // *vi* (*pt, pp* slept [slɛpt]) dormir; (*spend night*) dormir, coucher; **to go to ~** s'endormir; **to ~ in** *vi* (*lie late*) faire la grasse matinée; (*oversleep*) se réveiller trop tard; **~er** *n* (*person*) dormeur/euse; (*Brit RAIL: on track*) traverse *f*; (: *train*) train *m* de voitures-lits; **~ing bag** *n* sac *m* de couchage; **~ing car** *n* wagon-lits *m*, voiture-lits *f*; **~ing pill** *n* somnifère *m*; **~less** *a*: **a ~less night** une nuit blanche; **~walker** *n* somnambule *m/f*; **~y** *a* qui a envie de dormir; (*fig*) endormi(e).

sleet [sli:t] *n* neige fondue.

sleeve [sli:v] *n* manche *f*.

sleigh [sleɪ] *n* traîneau *m*.

sleight [slaɪt] *n*: **~ of hand** tour *m* de passe-passe.

slender ['slɛndə*] *a* svelte, mince; faible, ténu(e).

slept [slɛpt] *pt, pp* of **sleep**.

slew [slu:] *vi* virer, pivoter // *pt* of **slay**.

slice [slaɪs] *n* tranche *f*; (*round*) rondelle *f* // *vt* couper en tranches (or en rondelles).

slick [slɪk] *a* brillant(e) en apparence; mielleux(euse) // *n* (*also*: **oil ~**) nappe *f* de pétrole, marée noire.

slide [slaɪd] *n* (*in playground*) toboggan *m*; (*PHOT*) diapositive *f*; (*Brit: also*: **hair ~**) barrette *f*; (*in prices*) chute *f*, baisse *f* // *vb* (*pt, pp* slid [slɪd]) *vt* (*faire*) glisser // *vi* glisser; **~ rule** *n* règle *f* à calcul; **sliding** *a* (*door*) coulissant(e); **sliding scale** *n* échelle *f* mobile.

slight [slaɪt] *a* (*slim*) mince, menu(e); (*frail*) frêle; (*trivial*) faible, insignifiant(e); (*small*) petit(e), léger(ère) (*before n*) // *n* offense *f*, affront *m* // *vt* (*offend*) blesser, offenser; **not in the ~est** pas le moins du monde, pas du tout; **~ly** *ad* légèrement, un peu.

slim [slɪm] *a* mince // *vi* maigrir, suivre un régime amaigrissant.

slime [slaɪm] *n* vase *f*; substance visqueuse.

slimming ['slɪmɪŋ] *n* amaigrissement *m*.

sling [slɪŋ] *n* (*MED*) écharpe *f* // *vt* (*pt, pp* slung) lancer, jeter.

slip [slɪp] *n* faux pas *m*; (*mistake*) erreur *f*, étourderie *f*; bévue *f*; (*underskirt*) combinaison *f*; (*of paper*) petite feuille, fiche *f* // *vt* (*slide*) glisser // *vi* (*slide*) glisser; (*move smoothly*): **to ~ into/out of** se glisser or se faufiler dans/hors de; (*decline*) baisser; **to ~ sth on/off** enfiler/enlever qch; **to give sb the ~** fausser compagnie à qn; **a ~ of the tongue** un lapsus; **to ~ away** *vi* s'esquiver; **~ped disc** *n* déplacement *m* de vertèbres.

slipper ['slɪpə*] *n* pantoufle *f*.

slippery ['slɪpərɪ] *a* glissant(e); insaisissable.

slip road *n* (*Brit: to motorway*) bretelle *f* d'accès.

slipshod ['slɪpʃɔd] *a* négligé(e), peu soigné(e).

slip-up ['slɪpʌp] *n* bévue *f*.

slipway ['slɪpweɪ] *n* cale *f* (de construction or de lancement).

slit [slɪt] *n* fente *f*; (*cut*) incision *f*; (*tear*) déchirure *f* // *vt* (*pt, pp* slit) fendre; couper; inciser; déchirer.

slither ['slɪðə*] *vi* glisser, déraper.

sliver ['slɪvə*] *n* (*of glass, wood*) éclat *m*; (*of cheese etc*) petit morceau, fine tranche.

slob [slɔb] *n* (*col*) rustaud/e.

slog [slɔg] (*Brit*) *n* gros effort; tâche fastidieuse // *vi* travailler très dur.

slogan ['sləugən] *n* slogan *m*.

slop [slɔp] *vi* (*also*: **~ over**) se renverser; déborder // *vt* répandre; renverser.

slope [sləup] *n* pente *f*, côte *f*; (*side of mountain*) versant *m*; (*slant*) inclinaison *f* // *vi*: **to ~ down** être or descendre en pente; **to ~ up** monter.

sloppy ['slɔpɪ] *a* (*work*) peu soigné(e), bâclé(e); (*appearance*) négligé(e), débraillé(e); (*film etc*) sentimental(e).

slot [slɔt] *n* fente *f* // *vt*: **to ~ sth into** encastrer or insérer qch dans // *vi*: **to ~ into** s'encastrer or s'insérer dans; **~ machine** *n* (*Brit: vending machine*) distributeur *m*, machine *f* à sous; (*for gambling*) appareil *m* or machine *f* à sous.

sloth [sləuθ] *n* (*laziness*) paresse *f*.

slouch [slautʃ] *vi* avoir le dos rond, être voûté(e); **to ~ about** *vi* (*laze*) traîner à ne rien faire.

slovenly ['slʌvənlɪ] *a* sale, débraillé(e).

slow [sləu] *a* lent(e); (*watch*): **to be ~** retarder // *ad* lentement // *vt, vi* (*also*: **~ down, ~ up**) ralentir; ' **~** ' (*road sign*) 'ralentir'; **~ly** *ad* lentement; **~ motion** *n*: **in ~ motion** au ralenti.

sludge [slʌdʒ] *n* boue *f*.

slug [slʌg] *n* limace *f*; (*bullet*) balle *f*; **~gish** *a* mou(molle), lent(e).

sluice [slu:s] *n* vanne *f*; écluse *f*.

slum [slʌm] *n* taudis *m*.

slumber ['slʌmbə*] *n* sommeil *m*.

slump [slʌmp] *n* baisse soudaine, effondrement *m*; crise *f* // *vi* s'effondrer, s'affaisser.

slung [slʌŋ] *pt, pp* of **sling**.

slur [slə:*] *n* bredouillement *m*; (*smear*): **~ (on)** atteinte *f* (à); insinuation *f* (contre) // *vt* mal articuler.

slush [slʌʃ] *n* neige fondue; **~ fund** *n* caisse noire, fonds secrets.

slut [slʌt] *n* souillon *f*.

sly [slaɪ] *a* rusé(e); sournois(e).

smack [smæk] *n* (*slap*) tape *f*; (*on face*)

gifle f // vt donner une tape à; gifler; (child) donner la fessée à // vi: **to ~ of** avoir des relents de, sentir.

small [smɔːl] a petit(e); **~ ads** npl (Brit) petites annonces; **~ change** n petite or menue monnaie; **~holder** n (Brit) petit cultivateur; **~ hours** npl: **in the ~ hours** au petit matin; **~pox** n variole f; **~ talk** n menus propos.

smart [smɑːt] a élégant(e), chic inv; (clever) intelligent(e), astucieux(euse), futé(e); (quick) rapide, vif(vive), prompt(e) // vi faire mal, brûler; **to ~en up** vi devenir plus élégant(e), se faire beau(belle) // vt rendre plus élégant(e).

smash [smæʃ] n (also: **~-up**) collision f, accident m // vt casser, briser, fracasser; (opponent) écraser; (hopes) ruiner, détruire; (SPORT: record) pulvériser // vi se briser, se fracasser; s'écraser; **~ing** a (col) formidable.

smattering ['smætərɪŋ] n: **a ~ of** quelques notions de.

smear [smɪə*] n tache f, salissure f; trace f; (MED) frottis m // vt enduire; (fig) porter atteinte à.

smell [smɛl] n odeur f; (sense) odorat m // vb (pt, pp smelt or smelled [smɛlt, smɛld]) vt sentir // vi (food etc): **to ~ (of)** sentir; (pej) sentir mauvais; **it ~s good/~s of garlic** ça sent bon/sent l'ail; **~y** a qui sent mauvais, malodorant(e).

smile [smaɪl] n sourire m // vi sourire.

smirk [smɜːk] n petit sourire suffisant or affecté.

smith [smɪθ] n maréchal-ferrant m; forgeron m; **~y** ['smɪðɪ] n forge f.

smock [smɔk] n blouse f, sarrau m.

smog [smɔg] n brouillard mêlé de fumée.

smoke [sməʊk] n fumée f // vt, vi fumer; **~d** a (bacon, glass) fumé(e); **~r** n (person) fumeur/euse; (RAIL) wagon m fumeurs; **~ screen** n rideau m or écran m de fumée; (fig) paravent m; **smoking** n: **'no smoking'** (sign) 'défense de fumer'; **smoky** a enfumé(e).

smolder ['sməʊldə*] vi (US) = **smoulder**.

smooth [smuːð] a lisse; (sauce) onctueux(euse); (flavour, whisky) moelleux(euse); (movement) régulier(ère), sans à-coups or heurts; (person) doucereux(euse), mielleux(euse) // vt lisser, défroisser; (also: **~ out**: creases, difficulties) faire disparaître.

smother ['smʌðə*] vt étouffer.

smoulder, (US) **smolder** ['sməʊldə*] vi couver.

smudge [smʌdʒ] n tache f, bavure f // vt salir, maculer.

smug [smʌg] a suffisant(e), content(e) de soi.

smuggle ['smʌgl] vt passer en contrebande or en fraude; **~r** n contrebandier/ère; **smuggling** n contrebande f.

smutty ['smʌtɪ] a (fig) grossier(ère), obscène.

snack [snæk] n casse-croûte m inv; **~ bar** n snack(-bar) m.

snag [snæg] n inconvénient m, difficulté f.

snail [sneɪl] n escargot m.

snake [sneɪk] n serpent m.

snap [snæp] n (sound) claquement m, bruit sec; (photograph) photo f, instantané m; (game) sorte de jeu de bataille // a subit(e); fait(e) sans réfléchir // vt faire claquer; (break) casser net; (photograph) prendre un instantané de // vi se casser net or avec un bruit sec; **to ~ open/shut** s'ouvrir/se refermer brusquement; **to ~ at** vt fus (subj: dog) essayer de mordre; **to ~ off** vt (break) casser net; **to ~ up** vt sauter sur, saisir; **~py** a prompt(e); (slogan) qui a du punch; **~shot** n photo f, instantané m.

snare [snɛə*] n piège m.

snarl [snɑːl] vi gronder.

snatch [snætʃ] n (fig) vol m; (small amount): **~es of** des fragments mpl or bribes fpl de // vt saisir (d'un geste vif); (steal) voler.

sneak [sniːk] vi: **to ~ in/out** entrer/sortir furtivement or à la dérobée; **~ers** npl chaussures fpl de tennis or basket; **~y** a sournois(e).

sneer [snɪə*] vi ricaner, sourire d'un air sarcastique.

sneeze [sniːz] vi éternuer.

sniff [snɪf] vi renifler // vt renifler, flairer.

snigger ['snɪgə*] vi ricaner; pouffer de rire.

snip [snɪp] n petit bout; (bargain) (bonne) occasion or affaire f // vt couper.

sniper ['snaɪpə*] n (marksman) tireur embusqué.

snippet ['snɪpɪt] n bribes fpl.

snivelling ['snɪvlɪŋ] a (whimpering) larmoyant(e), pleurnicheur(euse).

snob [snɔb] n snob m/f; **~bish** a snob inv.

snooker ['snuːkə*] n sorte de jeu de billard.

snoop ['snuːp] vi: **to ~ on sb** espionner qn; **to ~ about somewhere** fourrer son nez quelque part.

snooty ['snuːtɪ] a snob inv, prétentieux(euse).

snooze [snuːz] n petit somme // vi faire un petit somme.

snore [snɔː*] vi ronfler; **snoring** n ronflement(s) m(pl).

snorkel ['snɔːkl] n (of swimmer) tuba m.

snort [snɔːt] vi grogner; (horse) renâcler.

snotty ['snɔtɪ] *a* morveux(euse).

snout [snaut] *n* museau *m*.

snow [snəu] *n* neige *f* // *vi* neiger; ~**ball** *n* boule *f* de neige; ~**bound** *a* enneigé(e), bloqué(e) par la neige; ~**drift** *n* congère *f*; ~**drop** *n* perce-neige *m*; ~**fall** *n* chute *f* de neige; ~**flake** *n* flocon *m* de neige; ~**man** *n* bonhomme *m* de neige; ~**plough**, (US) ~**plow** *n* chasse-neige *m inv*; ~**shoe** *n* raquette *f* (*pour la neige*); ~**storm** *n* tempête *f* de neige.

snub [snʌb] *vt* repousser, snober // *n* rebuffade *f*; ~-**nosed** *a* au nez retroussé.

snuff [snʌf] *n* tabac *m* à priser.

snug [snʌg] *a* douillet(te), confortable.

snuggle ['snʌgl] *vi*: **to** ~ **up to sb** se serrer *or* se blottir contre qn.

so [səu] ♦ *ad* **1** (*thus, likewise*) ainsi; if ~ si oui; ~ **do/have I** moi aussi; it's 5 **o'clock** - ~ **it is!** il est 5 heures - en effet! *or* c'est vrai!; **I hope/think** ~ je l'espère/le crois; ~ **far** jusqu'ici, jusqu'à maintenant; (*in past*) jusque-là
2 (*in comparisons etc: to such a degree*) si, tellement; ~ **big (that)** si *or* tellement grand (que); **she's not** ~ **clever as her brother** elle n'est pas aussi intelligente que son frère
3: ~ **much** *a, ad* tant (de); **I've got** ~ **much work** j'ai tant de travail; **I love you** ~ **much** je vous aime tant; ~ **many** tant (de)
4 (*phrases*): **10 or** ~ à peu près *or* environ 10; ~ **long!** (*col: goodbye*) au revoir!, à un de ces jours!
♦ *cj* **1** (*expressing purpose*): ~ **as to do** pour *or* afin de faire; ~ **(that)** pour que *or* afin que + *sub*
2 (*expressing result*) donc, par conséquent; ~ **that** si bien que, de (telle) sorte que.

soak [səuk] *vt* faire tremper // *vi* tremper; **to** ~ **in** *vi* être absorbé(e); **to** ~ **up** *vt* absorber.

so-and-so ['səuənsəu] *n* (*somebody*) un tel(une telle).

soap [səup] *n* savon *m*; ~**flakes** *npl* paillettes *fpl* de savon; ~ **opera** *n* feuilleton télévisé; ~ **powder** *n* lessive *f*; ~**y** *a* savonneux(euse).

soar [sɔ:*] *vi* monter (en flèche), s'élancer.

sob [sɔb] *n* sanglot *m* // *vi* sangloter.

sober ['səubə*] *a* qui n'est pas (*or* plus) ivre; (*sedate*) sérieux(euse), sensé(e); (*moderate*) mesuré(e); (*colour, style*) sobre, discret(ète); **to** ~ **up** *vt* dégriser // *vi* se dégriser.

so-called ['səu'kɔ:ld] *a* soi-disant *inv*.

soccer ['sɔkə*] *n* football *m*.

social ['səuʃl] *a* social(e) // *n* (petite) fête; ~ **club** *n* amicale *f*, foyer *m*;

~**ism** *n* socialisme *m*; ~**ist** *a, n* socialiste (*m/f*); ~**ize** *vi*: **to** ~**ize (with)** lier connaissance (avec); parler (avec); ~ **security** *n* aide sociale; ~ **work** *n* assistance sociale; ~ **worker** *n* assistant/e social(e).

society [sə'saɪətɪ] *n* société *f*; (*club*) société, association *f*; (*also*: **high** ~) (haute) société, grand monde.

sociology [səusɪ'ɔlədʒɪ] *n* sociologie *f*.

sock [sɔk] *n* chaussette *f* // *vt* (*col: hit*) flanquer un coup à.

socket ['sɔkɪt] *n* cavité *f*; (*ELEC: also:* **wall** ~) prise *f* de courant; (*: for light bulb*) douille *f*.

sod [sɔd] *n* (*of earth*) motte *f*; (*Brit col!*) con *m* (!); salaud *m* (!).

soda ['səudə] *n* (*CHEM*) soude *f*; (*also:* ~ **water**) eau *f* de Seltz; (*US: also:* ~ **pop**) soda *m*.

sodden ['sɔdn] *a* trempé(e); détrempé(e).

sofa ['səufə] *n* sofa *m*, canapé *m*.

soft [sɔft] *a* (*not rough*) doux(douce); (*not hard*) doux; mou(molle); (*not loud*) doux, léger(ère); (*kind*) doux, gentil(le); (*weak*) indulgent(e); (*stupid*) stupide, débile; ~ **drink** *n* boisson non alcoolisée; ~**en** ['sɔfn] *vt* (r)amollir; adoucir; atténuer // *vi* se ramollir; s'adoucir; s'atténuer; ~**ly** *ad* doucement; gentiment; ~**ness** *n* douceur *f*.

software ['sɔftwɛə*] *n* (*COMPUT*) logiciel *m*, software *m*.

soggy ['sɔgɪ] *a* trempé(e); détrempé(e).

soil [sɔɪl] *n* (*earth*) sol *m*, terre *f* // *vt* salir; (*fig*) souiller.

solace ['sɔlɪs] *n* consolation *f*.

solar ['səulə*] *a* solaire.

sold [səuld] *pt, pp* of **sell**; ~ **out** *a* (*COMM*) épuisé(e).

solder ['səuldə*] *vt* souder (*au fil à souder*) // *n* soudure *f*.

soldier ['səuldʒə*] *n* soldat *m*, militaire *m*.

sole [səul] *n* (*of foot*) plante *f*; (*of shoe*) semelle *f*; (*fish: pl inv*) sole *f* // *a* seul(e), unique.

solemn ['sɔləm] *a* solennel(le); sérieux(euse), grave.

sole trader *n* (*COMM*) chef *m* d'entreprise individuelle.

solicit [sə'lɪsɪt] *vt* (*request*) solliciter // *vi* (*prostitute*) racoler.

solicitor [sə'lɪsɪtə*] *n* (*Brit: for wills etc*) ≈ notaire *m*; (*: in court*) ≈ avocat *m*.

solid ['sɔlɪd] *a* (*not hollow*) plein(e), compact(e), massif(ive); (*strong, sound, reliable, not liquid*) solide; (*meal*) consistant(e), substantiel(le) // *n* solide *m*.

solidarity [sɔlɪ'dærɪtɪ] *n* solidarité *f*.

solitary ['sɔlɪtərɪ] *a* solitaire; ~ **con-**

finement n (LAW) isolement m.
solo ['səuləu] n solo m; **~ist** n soliste m/f.
soluble ['sɔljubl] a soluble.
solution [sə'lu:ʃən] n solution f.
solve [sɔlv] vt résoudre.
solvent ['sɔlvənt] a (COMM) solvable // n (CHEM) (dis)solvant m.
some [sʌm] ♦ a 1 (a certain amount or number of): ~ tea/water/ice cream du thé/de l'eau/de la glace; ~ children/apples des enfants/pommes
2 (certain: in contrasts): ~ people say that ... il y a des gens qui disent que ...; ~ films were excellent, but most were mediocre certains films étaient excellents, mais la plupart étaient médiocres
3 (unspecified): ~ woman was asking for you il y avait une dame qui vous demandait; he was asking for ~ book (or other) il demandait un livre quelconque; ~ day un de ces jours; ~ day next week un jour la semaine prochaine
♦ pronoun 1 (a certain number) quelques-un(e)s, certain(e)s; I've got ~ (books etc) j'en ai (quelques-uns); ~ (of them) have been sold certains ont été vendus
2 (a certain amount) un peu; I've got ~ (money, milk) j'en ai un peu
♦ ad: ~ 10 people quelque 10 personnes, 10 personnes environ.
somebody ['sʌmbədɪ] pronoun = someone.
somehow ['sʌmhau] ad d'une façon ou d'une autre; (for some reason) pour une raison ou une autre.
someone ['sʌmwʌn] pronoun quelqu'un.
someplace ['sʌmpleɪs] ad (US) = somewhere.
somersault ['sʌməsɔ:lt] n culbute f, saut périlleux // vi faire la culbute or un saut périlleux; (car) faire un tonneau.
something ['sʌmθɪŋ] pronoun quelque chose m; ~ interesting quelque chose d'intéressant.
sometime ['sʌmtaɪm] ad (in future) un de ces jours, un jour ou l'autre; (in past): ~ last month au cours du mois dernier.
sometimes ['sʌmtaɪmz] ad quelquefois, parfois.
somewhat ['sʌmwɔt] ad quelque peu, un peu.
somewhere ['sʌmwɛə*] ad quelque part.
son [sʌn] n fils m.
song [sɔŋ] n chanson f.
sonic ['sɔnɪk] a (boom) supersonique.
son-in-law ['sʌnɪnlɔ:] n gendre m, beau-fils m.
sonny ['sʌnɪ] n (col) fiston m.
soon [su:n] ad bientôt; (early) tôt; ~

afterwards peu après; see also as; **~er** ad (time) plus tôt; (preference): I would **~er** do j'aimerais autant or je préférerais faire; **~er or later** tôt ou tard.
soot [sut] n suie f.
soothe [su:ð] vt calmer, apaiser.
sophisticated [sə'fɪstɪkeɪtɪd] a raffiné(e); sophistiqué(e); hautement perfectionné(e), très complexe.
sophomore ['sɔfəmɔ:*] n (US) étudiant/e de seconde année.
sopping ['sɔpɪŋ] a (also: ~ wet) tout(e) trempé(e).
soppy ['sɔpɪ] a (pej) sentimental(e).
soprano [sə'prɑ:nəu] n (voice) soprano m; (singer) soprano m/f.
sorcerer ['sɔ:sərə*] n sorcier m.
sore [sɔ:*] a (painful) douloureux(euse), sensible; (offended) contrarié(e), vexé(e) // n plaie f; **~ly** ad (tempted) fortement.
sorrow ['sɔrəu] n peine f, chagrin m.
sorry ['sɔrɪ] a désolé(e); (condition, excuse) triste, déplorable; ~! pardon!, excusez-moi!; to feel ~ for sb plaindre qn.
sort [sɔ:t] n genre m, espèce f, sorte f // vt (also: ~ out: papers) trier; classer; ranger; (: letters etc) trier; (: problems) résoudre, régler; **~ing office** n bureau m de tri.
SOS n abbr (= save our souls) S.O.S. m.
so-so ['səusəu] ad comme ci comme ça.
sought [sɔ:t] pt, pp of **seek**.
soul [səul] n âme f; **~-destroying** a démoralisant(e); **~ful** a plein(e) de sentiment.
sound [saund] a (healthy) en bonne santé, sain(e); (safe, not damaged) solide, en bon état; (reliable, not superficial) sérieux(euse), solide; (sensible) sensé(e) // ad: ~ asleep dormant d'un profond sommeil // n (noise) son m; bruit m; (GEO) détroit m, bras m de mer // vt (alarm) sonner; (also: ~ out: opinions) sonder // vi sonner, retentir; (fig: seem) sembler (être); to ~ like ressembler à; ~ barrier n mur m du son; ~ effects npl bruitage m; **~ly** ad (sleep) profondément; (beat) complètement, à plate couture; **~proof** a insonorisé(e); **~track** n (of film) bande f sonore.
soup [su:p] n soupe f, potage m; in the ~ (fig) dans le pétrin; ~ plate n assiette creuse or à soupe; **~spoon** n cuiller f à soupe.
sour ['sauə*] a aigre; it's ~ grapes (fig) c'est du dépit.
source [sɔ:s] n source f.
south [sauθ] n sud m // a sud inv, du sud // ad au sud, vers le sud; **S~ Africa** n Afrique f du Sud; **S~ African** a sud-africain(e) // n Sud-Africain/e; **S~**

America n Amérique f du Sud; **S~ American** a sud-américain/e // n Sud-Américain/e; **~-east** n sud-est m; **~erly** ['sʌðəlɪ] a du sud; au sud; **~ern** ['sʌðən] a (du) sud; méridional(e); exposé(e) au sud; **S~ Pole** n Pôle m Sud; **~ward(s)** ad vers le sud; **~-west** n sud-ouest m.

souvenir [suːvə'nɪə*] n souvenir m (objet).

sovereign ['sɔvrɪn] a, n souverain(e).

soviet ['səuvɪət] a soviétique; **the S~ Union** l'Union f soviétique.

sow n [sau] truie f // vt [səu] (pt ~ed, pp sown [səun]) semer.

soya ['sɔɪə], (US) **soy** [sɔɪ] n: **~ bean** n graine f de soja; **~ sauce** n sauce f de soja.

spa [spaː] n (town) station thermale; (US: also: **health ~**) établissement m de cure de rajeunissement etc.

space [speɪs] n (gen) espace m; (room) place f; espace; (length of time) laps m de temps // cpd spatial(e) // vt (also: **~ out**) espacer; **~craft** n engin spatial; **~man/woman** n astronaute m/f, cosmonaute m/f; **~ship** n = **~craft**; **spacing** n espacement m.

spade [speɪd] n (tool) bêche f, pelle f; (child's) pelle; **~s** npl (CARDS) pique m.

Spain [speɪn] n Espagne f.

span [spæn] pt de **spin** // n (of bird, plane) envergure f; (of arch) portée f; (in time) espace m de temps, durée f // vt enjamber, franchir; (fig) couvrir, embrasser.

Spaniard ['spænjəd] n Espagnol/e.

spaniel ['spænjəl] n épagneul m.

Spanish ['spænɪʃ] a espagnol(e), d'Espagne // n (LING) espagnol m; **the ~** npl les Espagnols mpl.

spank [spæŋk] vt donner une fessée à.

spanner ['spænə*] n (Brit) clé f (de mécanicien).

spar [spaː*] n espar m // vi (BOXING) s'entraîner.

spare [spɛə*] a de réserve, de rechange; (surplus) de or en trop, de reste // n (part) pièce f de rechange, pièce détachée // vt (do without) se passer de; (afford to give) donner, accorder, passer; (refrain from hurting) épargner; (refrain from using) ménager; **to ~** (surplus) en surplus, de trop; **~ part** n pièce f de rechange, pièce détachée; **~ time** n moments mpl de loisir; **~ wheel** n (AUT) roue f de secours.

sparing ['spɛərɪŋ] a: **to be ~ with** ménager; **~ly** ad avec modération.

spark [spaːk] n étincelle f; **~(ing) plug** n bougie f.

sparkle ['spaːkl] n scintillement m, étincellement m, éclat m // vi étinceler, scintiller; (bubble) pétiller; **sparkling** a étincelant(e), scintillant(e); (wine) mousseux(euse), pétillant(e).

sparrow ['spærəu] n moineau m.

sparse [spaːs] a clairsemé(e).

spartan ['spaːtən] a (fig) spartiate.

spasm ['spæzəm] n (MED) spasme m; (fig) accès m; **~odic** [-'mɔdɪk] a (fig) intermittent(e).

spastic ['spæstɪk] n handicapé/e moteur.

spat [spæt] pt, pp of **spit**.

spate [speɪt] n (fig): **~ of** avalanche f or torrent m de; **in ~** (river) en crue.

spatter ['spætə*] vt éclabousser // vi gicler.

spawn [spɔːn] vi frayer // n frai m.

speak [spiːk], pt **spoke**, pp **spoken** vt (language) parler; (truth) dire // vi parler; (make a speech) prendre la parole; **to ~ to sb/of or about sth** parler à qn/de qch; **~ up!** parle plus fort!; **~er** n (in public) orateur m; (also: **loud~er**) haut-parleur m; (POL): **the S~er** est le président de la chambre des Communes (Brit) or des Représentants (US).

spear [spɪə*] n lance f; **~head** vt (attack etc) mener.

spec [spɛk] n (col): **on ~** à tout hasard.

special ['spɛʃl] a spécial(e); **~ist** n spécialiste m/f; **~ity** [spɛʃɪ'ælɪtɪ] n spécialité f; **~ize** vi: **to ~ize (in)** se spécialiser (dans); **~ly** ad spécialement, particulièrement.

species ['spiːʃiːz] n espèce f.

specific [spə'sɪfɪk] a précis(e); particulier(ère), (BOT, CHEM etc) spécifique; **~ally** ad expressément, explicitement.

specimen ['spɛsɪmən] n spécimen m, échantillon m; (MED) prélèvement m.

speck [spɛk] n petite tache, petit point; (particle) grain m.

speckled ['spɛkld] a tacheté(e), moucheté(e).

specs [spɛks] npl (col) lunettes fpl.

spectacle ['spɛktəkl] n spectacle m; **~s** npl lunettes fpl; **spectacular** [-'tækjulə*] a spectaculaire // n (CINEMA etc) superproduction f.

spectator [spɛk'teɪtə*] n spectateur/trice.

spectrum, pl spectra ['spɛktrəm, -rə] n spectre m; (fig) gamme f.

speculation [spɛkju'leɪʃən] n spéculation f; conjectures fpl.

speech [spiːtʃ] n (faculty) parole f; (talk) discours m, allocution f; (manner of speaking) façon f de parler, langage m; (enunciation) élocution f; **~less** a muet(te).

speed [spiːd] n vitesse f; (promptness) rapidité f; **at full or top ~** à toute vitesse or allure; **to ~ up** vi aller plus vite, accélérer // vt accélérer; **~boat** n vedette f, hors-bord m inv; **~ily** ad rapidement, promptement; **~ing** n (AUT) excès m de vitesse; **~ limit** n limitation f de vitesse, vitesse maximale permise; **~ometer** [spɪ'dɒmɪtə*] n compteur m (de vitesse); **~way** (SPORT) piste f de vitesse pour motos; (also: **~way racing**) épreuve(s) f(pl) de vitesse de motos; **~y** a rapide, prompt(e).

spell [spɛl] n (also: **magic ~**) sortilège m, charme m; (period of time) (courte) période // vt (pt, pp spelt (Brit) or **~ed** [spɛlt, spɛld]) (in writing) écrire, orthographier; (aloud) épeler; (fig) signifier; **to cast a ~ on sb** jeter un sort à qn; **he can't ~** il fait des fautes d'orthographe; **~bound** a envoûté(e), subjugué(e); **~ing** n orthographe f.

spend, pt, pp spent [spɛnd, spɛnt] vt (money) dépenser; (time, life) passer; consacrer; **~thrift** n dépensier/ère.

sperm [spə:m] n spermatozoïde m; (semen) sperme m.

spew [spju:] vt vomir.

sphere [sfɪə*] n sphère f.

spice [spaɪs] n épice f.

spick-and-span ['spɪkən'spæn] a impeccable.

spicy ['spaɪsɪ] a épicé(e), relevé(e); (fig) piquant(e).

spider ['spaɪdə*] n araignée f.

spike [spaɪk] n pointe f.

spill, pt, pp spilt or **~ed** [spɪl, -t, -d] vt renverser; répandre // vi se répandre; **to ~ over** vi déborder.

spin [spɪn] n (revolution of wheel) tour m; (AVIAT) (chute f en) vrille f; (trip in car) petit tour, balade f // vb (pt spun, span, pp spun) vt (wool etc) filer; (wheel) faire tourner // vi tourner, tournoyer; **to ~ out** vt faire durer.

spinach ['spɪnɪtʃ] n épinard m; (as food) épinards.

spinal ['spaɪnl] a vertébral(e), spinal(e); **~ cord** n moelle épinière.

spindly ['spɪndlɪ] a grêle, filiforme.

spin-dryer [spɪn'draɪə*] n (Brit) essoreuse f.

spine [spaɪn] n colonne vertébrale; (thorn) épine f, piquant m.

spinning ['spɪnɪŋ] n (of thread) filage m; (by machine) filature f; **~ top** n toupie f; **~ wheel** n rouet m.

spin-off ['spɪnɒf] n avantage inattendu; sous-produit m.

spinster ['spɪnstə*] n célibataire f; vieille fille.

spiral ['spaɪərl] n spirale f // a en spirale // vi (fig) monter en flèche; **~ staircase** n escalier m en colimaçon.

spire ['spaɪə*] n flèche f, aiguille f.

spirit ['spɪrɪt] n (soul) esprit m, âme f; (ghost) esprit, revenant m; (mood) esprit, état m d'esprit; (courage) courage m, énergie f; **~s** npl (drink) spiritueux mpl, alcool m; **in good ~s** de bonne humeur; **~ed** a vif(vive), fougueux(euse), plein(e) d'allant; **~ level** n niveau m à bulle.

spiritual ['spɪrɪtjuəl] a spirituel(le); religieux(euse).

spit [spɪt] n (for roasting) broche f // vi (pt, pp spat) cracher; (sound) crépiter.

spite [spaɪt] n rancune f, dépit m // vt contrarier, vexer; **in ~ of** en dépit de, malgré; **~ful** a malveillant(e), rancunier(ère).

spittle ['spɪtl] n salive f; bave f; crachat m.

splash [splæʃ] n éclaboussement m; (of colour) tache f // excl (sound) plouf // vt éclabousser // vi (also: **~ about**) barboter, patauger.

spleen [spli:n] n (ANAT) rate f.

splendid ['splɛndɪd] a splendide, superbe, magnifique.

splint [splɪnt] n attelle f, éclisse f.

splinter ['splɪntə*] n (wood) écharde f; (metal) éclat m // vi se fragmenter.

split [splɪt] n fente f, déchirure f; (fig: POL) scission f // vb (pt, pp split) vt fendre, déchirer; (party) diviser; (work, profits) partager, répartir // vi (divide) se diviser; **to ~ up** vi (couple) se séparer, rompre; (meeting) se disperser.

splutter ['splʌtə*] vi bafouiller; postillonner.

spoil, pt, pp spoilt or **~ed** [spɔɪl, -t, -d] vt (damage) abîmer; (mar) gâcher; (child) gâter; **~s** npl butin m; **~sport** n trouble-fête m, rabat-joie m.

spoke [spəuk] pt of speak // n rayon m.

spoken ['spəukn] pp of speak.

spokesman ['spəuksmən], **spokes-woman** ['-wumən] n porte-parole m inv.

sponge [spʌndʒ] n éponge f // vt éponger // vi: **to ~ off** or **on** vivre aux crochets de; **~ bag** n (Brit) trousse f de toilette; **~ cake** n ≈ biscuit m de Savoie.

sponsor ['spɒnsə*] n (RADIO, TV) personne f (or organisme m) qui assure le patronage // vt patronner; parrainer; **~ship** n patronage m; parrainage m.

spontaneous [spɒn'teɪnɪəs] a spontané(e).

spooky ['spu:kɪ] a qui donne la chair de poule.

spool [spu:l] n bobine f.

spoon [spu:n] n cuiller f; **~-feed** vt nourrir à la cuiller; (fig) mâcher le travail à; **~ful** n cuillerée f.

sport [spɔːt] n sport m; (person) chic type/chic fille // vt arborer; **~ing** a sportif(ive); **to give sb a ~ing chance** donner sa chance à qn; **~ jacket** n (US) = **~s jacket**; **~s car** n voiture f de sport; **~s jacket** n veste f de sport; **~sman** n sportif m; **~smanship** n esprit sportif, sportivité f; **~swear** n vêtements mpl de sport; **~swoman** n sportive f; ~**y** a sportif(ive).

spot [spɔt] n tache f; (dot: on pattern) pois m; (pimple) bouton m; (place) endroit m, coin m; (small amount): **a** ~ **of** un peu de // vt (notice) apercevoir; repérer; **on the** ~ sur place, sur les lieux; ~ **check** n sondage m, vérification ponctuelle; ~**less** a immaculé(e); ~**light** n projecteur m; (AUT) phare m auxiliaire; ~**ted** a tacheté(e), moucheté(e); à pois; ~**ty** a (face) boutonneux(euse).

spouse [spauz] n époux/épouse.

spout [spaut] n (of jug) bec m; (of liquid) jet m // vi jaillir.

sprain [spreɪn] n entorse f, foulure f // vt: **to** ~ **one's ankle** se fouler or se tordre la cheville.

sprang [spræŋ] pt of **spring**.

sprawl [sprɔːl] vi s'étaler.

spray [spreɪ] n jet m (en fines gouttelettes); (container) vaporisateur m, bombe f; (of flowers) petit bouquet // vt vaporiser, pulvériser; (crops) traiter.

spread [spred] n propagation f; (distribution) répartition f; (CULIN) pâte f à tartiner // vb (pt, pp spread) vt étendre, étaler; répandre; propager // vi s'étendre; se répandre; se propager; ~-**eagled** ['spredɪːgld] a étendu(e) bras et jambes écartés; ~**sheet** n (COMPUT) tableur m.

spree [spriː] n: **to go on a** ~ faire la fête.

sprightly ['spraɪtlɪ] a alerte.

spring [sprɪŋ] n (leap) bond m, saut m; (coiled metal) ressort m; (season) printemps m; (of water) source f // vi (pt sprang, pp sprung) bondir, sauter; **to** ~ **from** provenir de; **to** ~ **up** vi (problem) se présenter, surgir; ~**board** n tremplin m; ~**clean** n (also: ~-cleaning) grand nettoyage de printemps; ~**time** n printemps m; ~**y** a élastique, souple.

sprinkle ['sprɪŋkl] vt (pour) répandre; verser; **to** ~ **water etc on**, ~ **with water etc** asperger d'eau etc; **to** ~ **sugar etc on**, ~ **with sugar etc** saupoudrer de sucre etc; ~**r** n (for lawn) arroseur m; (to put out fire) diffuseur m d'extincteur automatique d'incendie.

sprint [sprɪnt] n sprint m // vi sprinter.

sprout [spraut] vi germer, pousser; ~**s** npl (also: **Brussels** ~**s**) choux mpl de Bruxelles.

spruce [spruːs] n épicéa m // a net(te), pimpant(e).

sprung [sprʌŋ] pp of **spring**.

spry [spraɪ] a alerte, vif(vive).

spun [spʌn] pt, pp of **spin**.

spur [spəː*] n éperon m; (fig) aiguillon m // vt (also: ~ **on**) éperonner; aiguillonner; **on the** ~ **of the moment** sous l'impulsion du moment.

spurious ['spjuərɪəs] a faux(fausse).

spurn [spəːn] vt repousser avec mépris.

spurt [spəːt] vi jaillir, gicler.

spy [spaɪ] n espion/ne // vi: **to** ~ **on** espionner, épier // vt (see) apercevoir; ~**ing** n espionnage m.

sq. (MATH), **Sq.** (in address) abbr of **square**.

squabble ['skwɔbl] vi se chamailler.

squad [skwɔd] n (MIL, POLICE) escouade f, groupe m; (FOOTBALL) contingent m.

squadron ['skwɔdrn] n (MIL) escadron m; (AVIAT, NAUT) escadrille f.

squalid ['skwɔlɪd] a sordide, ignoble.

squall [skwɔːl] n rafale f, bourrasque f.

squalor ['skwɔlə*] n conditions fpl sordides.

squander ['skwɔndə*] vt gaspiller, dilapider.

square [skwɛə*] n carré m; (in town) place f; (instrument) équerre f // a carré(e); (honest) honnête, régulier(ère); (col: ideas, tastes) vieux jeu inv, qui retarde // vt (arrange) régler; arranger; (MATH) élever au carré // vi (agree) cadrer, s'accorder; **all** ~ quitte; à égalité; **a** ~ **meal** un repas convenable; **2 metres** ~ (de) 2 mètres sur 2; **1** ~ **metre** 1 mètre carré.

squash [skwɔʃ] n (Brit: drink): **lemon/orange** ~ citronnade f/orangeade f; (SPORT) squash m // vt écraser.

squat [skwɔt] a petit(e) et épais(se), ramassé(e) // vi s'accroupir; ~**ter** n squatter m.

squawk [skwɔːk] vi pousser un or des gloussement(s).

squeak [skwiːk] vi grincer, crier.

squeal [skwiːl] vi pousser un or des cri(s) aigu(s) or perçant(s).

squeamish ['skwiːmɪʃ] a facilement dégoûté(e); facilement scandalisé(e).

squeeze [skwiːz] n pression f; restrictions fpl de crédit // vt presser; (hand, arm) serrer; **to** ~ **out** vt exprimer; (fig) soutirer.

squelch [skweltʃ] vi faire un bruit de succion; patauger.

squib [skwɪb] n pétard m.

squid [skwɪd] n calmar m.

squiggle ['skwɪgl] n gribouillis m.

squint [skwɪnt] vi loucher // n: **he has a** ~ il louche, il souffre de strabisme; **to** ~ **at sth** regarder qch du coin de l'œil; (quickly) jeter un coup d'œil à qch.

squire ['skwaɪə*] n (Brit) propriétaire terrien.

squirm [skwəːm] vi se tortiller.

squirrel ['skwɪrəl] n écureuil m.

squirt [skwəːt] vi jaillir, gicler.

Sr abbr of **senior**.

St abbr of **saint**, **street**.

stab [stæb] n (with knife etc) coup m (de couteau etc); (col: try): **to have a** ~ **at (doing) sth** s'essayer à (faire) qch // vt poignarder.

stable ['steibl] n écurie f // a stable.

stack [stæk] n tas m, pile f // vt empiler, entasser.

stadium ['steidiəm] n stade m.

staff [staːf] n (work force) personnel m; (: Brit SCOL) professeurs mpl; (: servants) domestiques mpl; (MIL) état-major m; (stick) perche f, bâton m // vt pourvoir en personnel.

stag [stæg] n cerf m.

stage [steidʒ] n scène f; (profession): the ~ le théâtre; (point) étape f, stade m; (platform) estrade f // vt (play) monter, mettre en scène; (demonstration) organiser; (fig: perform: recovery etc) effectuer; in ~s par étapes, par degrés; ~coach n diligence f; ~door n entrée f des artistes; ~ manager n régisseur m.

stagger ['stægə*] vi chanceler, tituber // vt (person) stupéfier; bouleverser; (hours, holidays) étaler, échelonner.

stagnate [stæg'neit] vi stagner, croupir.

stag party n enterrement m de vie de garçon.

staid [steid] a posé(e), rassis(e).

stain [stein] n tache f; (colouring) colorant m // vt tacher; (wood) teindre; ~ed glass window n vitrail m; ~less a (steel) inoxydable; ~ remover n détachant m.

stair [steə*] n (step) marche f; ~s npl escalier m; on the ~s dans l'escalier; ~case, ~way n escalier m.

stake [steik] n pieu m, poteau m; (BETTING) enjeu m // vt risquer, jouer; to be at ~ être en jeu.

stale [steil] a (bread) rassis(e); (beer) éventé(e); (smell) de renfermé.

stalemate ['steilmeit] n pat m; (fig) impasse f.

stalk [stɔːk] n tige f // vt traquer // vi marcher avec raideur.

stall [stɔːl] n éventaire m, étal m; (in stable) stalle f // vt (AUT) caler // vi (AUT) caler; (fig) essayer de gagner du temps; ~s npl (Brit: in cinema, theatre) orchestre m.

stallion ['stæliən] n étalon m (cheval).

stalwart ['stɔːlwət] n partisan m fidèle.

stamina ['stæminə] n vigueur f, endurance f.

stammer ['stæmə*] n bégaiement m // vi bégayer.

stamp [stæmp] n timbre m; (mark, also fig) empreinte f; (on document) cachet m // vi (also: ~ one's foot) taper du pied // vt tamponner, estamper; (letter) timbrer; ~ album n album m de timbres(-poste); ~ collecting n philatélie f.

stampede [stæm'piːd] n ruée f.

stance [stæns] n position f.

stand [stænd] n (position) position f; (MIL) résistance f; (structure) guéridon m; support m; (COMM) étalage m, stand m; (SPORT) tribune f // vb (pt, pp stood) vi (be upright) se tenir (debout); (rise) se lever, se mettre debout; (be placed) se trouver // vt (place) mettre, poser; (tolerate, withstand) supporter; to make a ~ prendre position; to ~ for parliament (Brit) se présenter aux élections (comme candidat à la députation); to ~ by vi (be ready) se tenir prêt(e) // vt fus (opinion) s'en tenir à; to ~ down vi (withdraw) se retirer; to ~ for vt fus (signify) représenter, signifier; (tolerate) supporter, tolérer; to ~ in for vt fus remplacer; to ~ out vi (be prominent) ressortir; to ~ up vi (rise) se lever, se mettre debout; to ~ up for vt fus défendre; to ~ up to vt fus tenir tête à, résister à.

standard ['stændəd] n niveau voulu; (flag) étendard m // a (size etc) ordinaire, normal(e); courant(e); ~s npl (morals) morale f, principes mpl; ~ lamp n (Brit) lampadaire m; ~ of living n niveau m de vie.

stand-by ['stændbai] n remplaçant/e; to be on ~ se tenir prêt(e) (à intervenir); être de garde; ~ ticket n (AVIAT) billet m sans garantie.

stand-in ['stændin] n remplaçant/e; (CINEMA) doublure f.

standing ['stændiŋ] a debout inv // n réputation f, rang m, standing m; of many years' ~ qui dure or existe depuis longtemps; ~ order n (Brit: at bank) virement m automatique, prélèvement m bancaire; ~ orders npl (MIL) règlement m; ~ room n places fpl debout.

stand-offish [stænd'ɔfiʃ] a distant(e), froid(e).

standpoint ['stændpɔint] n point m de vue.

standstill ['stændstil] n: at a ~ à l'arrêt; (fig) au point mort; to come to a ~ s'immobiliser, s'arrêter.

stank [stæŋk] pt of **stink**.

staple ['steipl] n (for papers) agrafe f // a (food etc) de base, principal(e) // vt agrafer; ~r n agrafeuse f.

star [staː*] n étoile f; (celebrity) vedette f // vi: to ~ (in) être la vedette (de) // vt (CINEMA) avoir pour vedette.

starboard ['staːbəd] n tribord m.

starch [staːtʃ] n amidon m.

stardom ['staːdəm] n célébrité f.

stare [steə*] n regard m fixe // vi: to ~ at regarder fixement.

starfish ['staːfiʃ] n étoile f de mer.

stark [staːk] a (bleak) désolé(e), morne // ad: ~ naked complètement nu(e).

starling ['staːliŋ] n étourneau m.

starry ['staːri] a étoilé(e); ~-eyed a (innocent) ingénu(e).

start [staːt] n commencement m, début m; (of race) départ m; (sudden

movement) sursaut *m // vt* commencer *//
vi* partir, se mettre en route; *(jump)*
sursauter; to ~ **doing** *or* **to do sth** se
mettre à faire qch; **to ~ off** *vi*
commencer; *(leave)* partir; **to ~ up** *vi*
commencer; *(car)* démarrer *// vt* déclencher; *(car)* mettre en marche; ~**er** *n*
(AUT) démarreur *m*; *(SPORT)* starter *m*; *(: runner, horse)* partant *m*;
(Brit CULIN) entrée *f*; ~**ing point** *n*
point *m* de départ.

startle ['stɑːtl] *vt* faire sursauter; donner
un choc à.

starvation [stɑːˈveɪʃən] *n* faim *f*, famine
f.

starve [stɑːv] *vi* mourir de faim; être
affamé(e) *// vt* affamer.

state [steɪt] *n* état *m // vt* déclarer,
affirmer; formuler; the S~s les États-
Unis *mpl*; **to be in a ~** être dans tous ses
états; ~**ly** *a* majestueux(euse),
imposant(e); ~**ment** *n* déclaration *f*;
(LAW) déposition *f*; ~**sman** *n* homme *m*
d'État.

static ['stætɪk] *n* *(RADIO)* parasites *mpl*
// a statique.

station ['steɪʃən] *n* gare *f*; poste *m*
(militaire *or* de police *etc*); *(rank)*
condition *f*, rang *m // vt* placer, poster.

stationary ['steɪʃnərɪ] *a* à l'arrêt,
immobile.

stationer ['steɪʃənə*] *n* papetier/ère;
~**'s (shop)** *n* papeterie *f*; ~**y** *n* papier
m à lettres, petit matériel de bureau.

station master *n* *(RAIL)* chef *m* de
gare.

station wagon *n* *(US)* break *m*.

statistic [stəˈtɪstɪk] *n* statistique *f*; ~**s** *n*
(science) statistique *f*.

statue ['stætjuː] *n* statue *f*.

status ['steɪtəs] *n* position *f*, situation *f*;
prestige *m*; statut *m*; ~ **symbol** *n*
marque *f* de standing.

statute ['stætjuːt] *n* loi *f*; ~**s** *npl* *(of
club etc)* statuts *mpl*; **statutory** *a*
statutaire, prévu(e) par un article de loi.

staunch [stɔːntʃ] *a* sûr(e), loyal(e).

stave [steɪv] *n* *(MUS)* portée *f // vt*: **to ~
off** *(attack)* parer; *(threat)* conjurer.

stay [steɪ] *n* *(period of time)* séjour *m //
vi* rester; *(reside)* loger; *(spend some
time)* séjourner; **to ~ put** ne pas bouger;
to ~ with friends loger chez des amis; **to
~ the night** passer la nuit; **to ~ behind**
vi rester en arrière; **to ~ in** *vi* *(at
home)* rester à la maison; **to ~ on** *vi*
rester; **to ~ out** *vi* *(of house)* ne pas
rentrer; **to ~ up** *vi* *(at night)* ne pas se
coucher; ~**ing power** *n* endurance *f*.

stead [sted] *n*: **in sb's ~** à la place de
qn; **to stand sb in good ~** être très utile
or servir beaucoup à qn.

steadfast ['stedfɑːst] *a* ferme, résolu(e).

steadily ['stedɪlɪ] *ad* progressivement;
sans arrêt; *(walk)* d'un pas ferme.

steady ['stedɪ] *a* stable, solide, ferme;
(regular) constant(e), régulier(ère);
(person) calme, pondéré(e) *// vt*
stabiliser; assujettir; calmer; **to ~ o.s.**
reprendre son aplomb.

steak [steɪk] *n* *(meat)* bifteck *m*, steak
m; *(fish)* tranche *f*.

steal [stiːl], *pt* **stole,** *pp* **stolen** *vt, vi*
voler.

stealth [stelθ] *n*: **by ~** furtivement; ~**y**
a furtif(ive).

steam [stiːm] *n* vapeur *f // vt* passer à la
vapeur; *(CULIN)* cuire à la vapeur *// vi*
fumer; *(ship)*: **to ~ along** filer; ~ **engine** *n* locomotive *f* à vapeur; ~**er** *n*
(bateau *m* à) vapeur *m*; ~**roller** *n*
rouleau compresseur; ~**ship** *n* = ~**er**;
~**y** *a* embué(e), humide.

steel [stiːl] *n* acier *m // cpd* d'acier;
~**works** *n* aciérie *f*.

steep [stiːp] *a* raide, escarpé(e); *(price)*
très élevé(e), excessif(ive) *// vt* (faire)
tremper.

steeple ['stiːpl] *n* clocher *m*.

steer [stɪə*] *n* bœuf *m // vt* diriger,
gouverner; guider *// vi* tenir le
gouvernail; ~**ing** *n* *(AUT)* conduite *f*;
~**ing wheel** *n* volant *m*.

stem [stem] *n* *(of plant)* tige *f*; *(of leaf,
fruit)* queue *f*; *(of glass)* pied *m // vt*
contenir, endiguer, juguler; **to ~ from**
vt fus provenir de, découler de.

stench [stentʃ] *n* puanteur *f*.

stencil ['stensl] *n* stencil *m*; pochoir *m //
vt* polycopier.

stenographer [steˈnɔgrəfə*] *n* *(US)*
sténographe *m/f*.

step [step] *n* pas *m*; *(stair)* marche *f*;
(action) mesure *f*, disposition *f // vi*: **to
~ forward** faire un pas en avant,
avancer; ~**s** *npl* *(Brit)* = **stepladder**; **to
be in/out of ~ (with)** *(fig)* aller dans le
sens (de)/être déphasé(e) (par rapport
à); **to ~ down** *vi* *(fig)* se retirer, se
désister; **to ~ off** *vt fus* descendre de;
to ~ up *vt* augmenter; intensifier;
~**brother** *n* demi-frère *m*; ~**daughter**
n belle-fille *f*; ~**father** *n* beau-père *m*;
~**ladder** *n* escabeau *m*; ~**mother** *n*
belle-mère *f*; ~**ping stone** *n* pierre *f* de
gué; *(fig)* tremplin *m*; ~**sister** *n* demi-
sœur *f*; ~**son** *n* beau-fils *m*.

stereo ['stɛrɪəu] *n* *(system)* stéréo *f*;
(record player) chaîne *f* stéréo *// a* *(also:*
~**phonic)** stéréophonique.

sterile ['sterail] *a* stérile; **sterilize**
['sterilaiz] *vt* stériliser.

sterling ['stɜːlɪŋ] *a* *(silver)* de bon aloi,
fin(e); *(fig)* à toute épreuve, excellent(e)
// n *(ECON)* livres *fpl* sterling *inv*; **a
pound ~** une livre sterling.

stern [stɜːn] *a* sévère *// n* *(NAUT)* arrière
m, poupe *f*.

stew [stjuː] *n* ragoût *m // vt, vi* cuire à la
casserole.

steward ['stju:əd] *n* (AVIAT, NAUT, RAIL) steward *m*; (*in club etc*) intendant *m*; **~ess** *n* hôtesse *f*.

stick [stɪk] *n* bâton *m*; morceau *m* // *vb* (*pt, pp* **stuck**) *vt* (*glue*) coller; (*thrust*): **to ~ sth into** piquer *or* planter *or* enforcer *or* enfoncer qch dans; (*col: put*) mettre, fourrer; (*col: tolerate*) supporter // *vi* se planter; tenir; (*remain*) rester; **to ~ out, to ~ up** *vi* dépasser, sortir; **to ~ up for** *vt fus* défendre; **~er** *n* autocollant *m*; **~ing plaster** *n* sparadrap *m*, pansement adhésif.

stickler ['stɪklə*] *n*: **to be a ~ for** être pointilleux(euse) sur.

stick-up ['stɪkʌp] *n* braquage *m*, hold-up *m*.

sticky ['stɪkɪ] *a* poisseux(euse); (*label*) adhésif(ive).

stiff [stɪf] *a* raide, rigide; dur(e); (*difficult*) difficile, ardu(e); (*cold*) froid(e), distant(e); (*strong, high*) fort(e), élevé(e); **~en** *vt* raidir, renforcer // *vi* se raidir; se durcir; **~ neck** *n* torticolis *m*.

stifle ['staɪfl] *vt* étouffer, réprimer.

stigma, *pl* (BOT, MED, REL) **~ta**, (*fig*) **~s** ['stɪgmə, stɪg'mɑ:tə] *n* stigmate *m*.

stile [staɪl] *n* échalier *m*.

stiletto [stɪ'letəu] *n* (Brit: also: **~ heel**) talon *m* aiguille.

still [stɪl] *a* immobile; calme, tranquille // *ad* (*up to this time*) encore, toujours; (*even*) encore; (*nonetheless*) quand même, tout de même; **~born** *a* mort-né(e); **~ life** *n* nature morte.

stilt [stɪlt] *n* échasse *f*; (*pile*) pilotis *m*.

stilted ['stɪltɪd] *a* guindé(e), emprunté(e).

stimulate ['stɪmjuleɪt] *vt* stimuler.

stimulus, *pl* **stimuli** ['stɪmjuləs, 'stɪmjulaɪ] *n* stimulant *m*; (BIOL, PSYCH) stimulus *m*.

sting [stɪŋ] *n* piqûre *f*; (*organ*) dard *m* // *vt, vi* (*pt, pp* **stung**) piquer.

stingy ['stɪndʒɪ] *a* avare, pingre.

stink [stɪŋk] *n* puanteur *f* // *vi* (*pt* **stank**, *pp* **stunk**) puer, empester; **~ing** *a* (*fig: col*) infect(e), vache; **a ~ing ...** un(e) foutu(e) ....

stint [stɪnt] *n* part *f* de travail // *vi*: **to ~ on** lésiner sur, être chiche de.

stir [stə:*] *n* agitation *f*, sensation *f* // *vt* remuer // *vi* remuer, bouger; **to ~ up** *vt* exciter.

stirrup ['stɪrəp] *n* étrier *m*.

stitch [stɪtʃ] *n* (SEWING) point *m*; (KNITTING) maille *f*; (MED) point de suture; (*pain*) point de côté // *vt* coudre, piquer; suturer.

stoat [stəut] *n* hermine *f* (*avec son pelage d'été*).

stock [stɔk] *n* réserve *f*, provision *f*; (COMM) stock *m*; (AGR) cheptel *m*, bétail *m*; (CULIN) bouillon *m*;

(FINANCE) valeurs *fpl*, titres *mpl* // *a* (*fig: reply etc*) courant(e); classique // *vt* (*have in stock*) avoir, vendre; **in/out of ~** en stock *or* en magasin/épuisé(e); **to take ~** (*fig*) faire le point; **~s and shares** valeurs (mobilières), titres; **to ~ up** *vi*: **to ~ up (with)** s'approvisionner (en).

stockbroker ['stɔkbrəukə*] *n* agent *m* de change.

stock cube *n* bouillon-cube *m*.

stock exchange *n* Bourse *f* (des valeurs).

stocking ['stɔkɪŋ] *n* bas *m*.

stock: **~ market** *n* Bourse *f*, marché financier; **~ phrase** *n* cliché *m*; **~pile** *n* stock *m*, réserve *f* // *vt* stocker, accumuler; **~taking** *n* (Brit COMM) inventaire *m*.

stocky ['stɔkɪ] *a* trapu(e), râblé(e).

stodgy ['stɔdʒɪ] *a* bourratif(ive), lourd(e).

stoke [stəuk] *vt* garnir, entretenir; chauffer.

stole [stəul] *pt of* **steal** // *n* étole *f*.

stolen ['stəuln] *pp of* **steal**.

stolid ['stɔlɪd] *a* impassible, flegmatique.

stomach ['stʌmək] *n* estomac *m*; (*abdomen*) ventre *m* // *vt* supporter, digérer; **~ ache** *n* mal *m* à l'estomac *or* au ventre.

stone [stəun] *n* pierre *f*; (*pebble*) caillou *m*, galet *m*; (*in fruit*) noyau *m*; (MED) calcul *m*; (Brit: weight) = 6.348 kg; 14 pounds // *cpd* de *or* en pierre // *vt* dénoyauter; **~-cold** *a* complètement froid(e); **~-deaf** *a* sourd(e) comme un pot; **~work** *n* maçonnerie *f*.

stood [stud] *pt, pp of* **stand**.

stool [stu:l] *n* tabouret *m*.

stoop [stu:p] *vi* (*also:* **have a ~**) être voûté(e); (*bend*) se baisser.

stop [stɔp] *n* arrêt *m*; halte *f*; (*in punctuation*) point *m* // *vt* arrêter; (*break off*) interrompre; (*also:* **put a ~ to**) mettre fin à // *vi* s'arrêter; (*rain, noise etc*) cesser, s'arrêter; **to ~ doing sth** cesser *or* arrêter de faire qch; **to ~ dead** *vi* s'arrêter net; **to ~ off** *vi* faire une courte halte; **to ~ up** *vt* (*hole*) boucher; **~gap** *n* (*person*) bouche-trou *m*; (*measure*) mesure *f* intérimaire; **~lights** *npl* (AUT) signaux *mpl* de stop, feux *mpl* arrière; **~over** *n* halte *f*; (AVIAT) escale *f*.

stoppage ['stɔpɪdʒ] *n* arrêt *m*; (*of pay*) retenue *f*; (*strike*) arrêt de travail.

stopper ['stɔpə*] *n* bouchon *m*.

stop press *n* nouvelles *fpl* de dernière heure.

stopwatch ['stɔpwɔtʃ] *n* chronomètre *m*.

storage ['stɔ:rɪdʒ] *n* emmagasinage *m*; (COMPUT) mise *f* en mémoire *or* réserve; **~ heater** *n* radiateur *m* électrique par accumulation.

store [stɔː*] n provision f, réserve f; (depot) entrepôt m; (Brit: large shop) grand magasin; (US) magasin m // vt emmagasiner; ~s npl provisions; **to ~ up** vt mettre en réserve, emmagasiner; **~room** n réserve f, magasin m.

storey, (US) **story** ['stɔːrɪ] n étage m.

stork [stɔːk] n cigogne f.

storm [stɔːm] n orage m, tempête f; ouragan m // vi (fig) fulminer // vt prendre d'assaut; **~y** a orageux(euse).

story ['stɔːrɪ] n histoire f; récit m; (US) = storey; **~book** n livre m d'histoires or de contes.

stout [staut] a solide; (brave) intrépide; (fat) gros(se), corpulent(e) // n bière brune.

stove [stəuv] n (for cooking) fourneau m; (: small) réchaud m; (for heating) poêle m.

stow [stəu] vt ranger; cacher; **~away** n passager/ère clandestin(e).

straddle ['strædl] vt enjamber, être à cheval sur.

straggle ['strægl] vi être (or marcher) en désordre; **~r** n traînard/e.

straight [streɪt] a droit(e); (frank) honnête, franc(franche) // ad (tout) droit; (drink) sec, sans eau; **to put** or **get** ~ mettre en ordre, mettre de l'ordre dans; ~ **away**, ~ **off** (at once) tout de suite; **~en** vt (also: ~en out) redresser; **~-faced** a impassible; **~forward** a simple; honnête, direct(e).

strain [streɪn] n (TECH) tension f; pression f; (physical) effort m; (mental) tension (nerveuse); (MED) entorse f; (streak, trace) tendance f; élément m // vt tendre fortement; mettre à l'épreuve; (filter) passer, filtrer // vi peiner, fournir un gros effort; **~s** npl (MUS) accords mpl, accents mpl; **~ed** a (laugh etc) forcé(e), contraint(e); (relations) tendu(e); **~er** n passoire f.

strait [streɪt] n (GEO) détroit m; **~jacket** n camisole f de force; **~-laced** a collet monté inv.

strand [strænd] n (of thread) fil m, brin m; **~ed** a en rade, en plan.

strange [streɪndʒ] a (not known) inconnu(e); (odd) étrange, bizarre; **~r** n inconnu/e; étranger/ère.

strangle ['stræŋgl] vt étrangler; **~hold** n (fig) emprise totale, mainmise f.

strap [stræp] n lanière f, courroie f, sangle f; (of slip, dress) bretelle f // vt attacher (avec une courroie etc).

strategic [strəˈtiːdʒɪk] a stratégique.

strategy ['strætɪdʒɪ] n stratégie f.

straw [strɔː] n paille f; **that's the last ~!** ça c'est le comble!

strawberry ['strɔːbərɪ] n fraise f.

stray [streɪ] a (animal) perdu(e), errant(e) // vi s'égarer; ~ **bullet** n balle

perdue.

streak [striːk] n raie f, bande f, filet m; (fig: of madness etc): **a ~ of** une or des tendance(s) à // vt zébrer, strier // vi: **to ~ past** passer à toute allure.

stream [striːm] n ruisseau m; courant m, flot m; (of people) défilé ininterrompu, flot // vt (SCOL) répartir par niveau // vi ruisseler; **to ~ in/out** entrer/sortir à flots.

streamer ['striːmə*] n serpentin m, banderole f.

streamlined ['striːmlaɪnd] a (AVIAT) fuselé(e), profilé(e); (AUT) aérodynamique; (fig) rationalisé(e).

street [striːt] n rue f // cpd de la rue; des rues; **~car** n (US) tramway m; ~ **lamp** n réverbère m; ~ **plan** n plan m des rues; **~wise** a (col) futé(e), réaliste.

strength [strɛŋθ] n force f; (of girder, knot etc) solidité f; **~en** vt fortifier; renforcer; consolider.

strenuous ['strɛnjuəs] a vigoureux(euse), énergique; (tiring) ardu(e), fatigant(e).

stress [strɛs] n (force, pressure) pression f; (mental strain) tension (nerveuse); (accent) accent m // vt insister sur, souligner.

stretch [strɛtʃ] n (of sand etc) étendue f // vi s'étirer; (extend): **to ~ to** or **as far as** s'étendre jusqu'à // vt tendre, étirer; (spread) étendre; (fig) pousser (au maximum); **to ~ out** vi s'étendre // vt (arm etc) allonger, tendre; (to spread) étendre.

stretcher ['strɛtʃə*] n brancard m, civière f.

strewn [struːn] a: ~ **with** jonché(e) de.

stricken ['strɪkən] a (person) très éprouvé(e); (city, industry etc) dévasté(e); ~ **with** (disease etc) frappé(e) or atteint(e) de.

strict [strɪkt] a strict(e).

stride [straɪd] n grand pas, enjambée f // vi (pt **strode**, pp **stridden** [strəud, 'strɪdn]) marcher à grands pas.

strife [straɪf] n conflit m, dissensions fpl.

strike [straɪk] n grève f; (of oil etc) découverte f; (attack) raid m // vb (pt, pp **struck**) vt frapper; (oil etc) trouver, découvrir // vi faire grève; (attack) attaquer; (clock) sonner; **on** ~ (workers) en grève; **to ~ a match** frotter une allumette; **to ~ down** vt (fig) terrasser; **to ~ out** vt rayer; **to ~ up** vt (MUS) se mettre à jouer; **to ~ up a friendship with** se lier d'amitié avec; **~r** n gréviste m/f; (SPORT) buteur m; **striking** a frappant(e), saisissant(e).

string [strɪŋ] n ficelle f, fil m; (row) rang m; chapelet m; file f; (MUS) corde f // vt (pt, pp **strung**): **to ~ out** échelonner; **to ~ together** enchaîner; the

~s *npl* (*MUS*) les instruments *mpl* à cordes; **to pull** ~s (*fig*) faire jouer le piston; ~ **bean** *n* haricot vert; ~(**ed**) **instrument** *n* (*MUS*) instrument *m* à cordes.

stringent ['strɪndʒənt] *a* rigoureux(euse); (*need*) impérieux(euse).

strip [strɪp] *n* bande *f* // *vt* déshabiller; dégarnir, dépouiller; (*also:* ~ **down**: *machine*) démonter // *vi* se déshabiller; ~ **cartoon** *n* bande dessinée.

stripe [straɪp] *n* raie *f*, rayure *f*; ~**d** *a* rayé(e), à rayures.

strip lighting *n* éclairage *m* au néon *or* fluorescent.

stripper ['strɪpə*] *n* strip-teaseuse *f*.

strive, *pt* **strove**, *pp* **striven** [straɪv, strəuv, 'strɪvn] *vi*: **to** ~ **to do** s'efforcer de faire.

strode [strəud] *pt of* **stride**.

stroke [strəuk] *n* coup *m*; (*MED*) attaque *f*; (*caress*) caresse *f* // *vt* caresser; **at a** ~ d'un (seul) coup.

stroll [strəul] *n* petite promenade // *vi* flâner, se promener nonchalamment; ~**er** *n* (*US*) poussette *f*.

strong [strɔŋ] *a* fort(e); vigoureux(euse); solide; vif(vive); **they are 50** ~ ils sont au nombre de 50; ~**box** *n* coffre-fort *m*; ~**hold** *n* bastion *m*; ~**ly** *ad* fortement, avec force; vigoureusement; solidement; ~**room** *n* chambre forte.

strove [strəuv] *pt of* **strive**.

struck [strʌk] *pt, pp of* **strike**.

structural ['strʌktʃərəl] *a* structural(e); (*CONSTR*) de construction; affectant les parties portantes.

structure ['strʌktʃə*] *n* structure *f*; (*building*) construction *f*; édifice *m*.

struggle ['strʌgl] *n* lutte *f* // *vi* lutter, se battre.

strum [strʌm] *vt* (*guitar*) gratter de.

strung [strʌŋ] *pt, pp of* **string**.

strut [strʌt] *n* étai *m*, support *m* // *vi* se pavaner.

stub [stʌb] *n* bout *m*; (*of ticket etc*) talon *m* // *vt*: **to** ~ **one's toe** se heurter le doigt de pied; **to** ~ **out** *vt* écraser.

stubble ['stʌbl] *n* chaume *m*; (*on chin*) barbe *f* de plusieurs jours.

stubborn ['stʌbən] *a* têtu(e), obstiné(e), opiniâtre.

stucco ['stʌkəu] *n* stuc *m*.

stuck [stʌk] *pt, pp of* **stick** // *a* (*jammed*) bloqué(e), coincé(e); ~-**up** *a* prétentieux(euse).

stud [stʌd] *n* clou *m* (à grosse tête); bouton *m* de col; (*of horses*) écurie *f*, haras *m*; (*also:* ~ **horse**) étalon *m* // *vt* (*fig*): ~**ded with** parsemé(e) *or* criblé(e) de.

student ['stju:dənt] *n* étudiant/e // *cpd* estudiantin(e); universitaire; d'étudiant; ~ **driver** *n* (*US*) (conducteur/trice)

débutant(e).

studio ['stju:dɪəu] *n* studio *m*, atelier *m*.

studious ['stju:dɪəs] *a* studieux(euse), appliqué(e); (*studied*) étudié(e); ~**ly** *ad* (*carefully*) soigneusement.

study ['stʌdɪ] *n* étude *f*; (*room*) bureau *m* // *vt* étudier; examiner // *vi* étudier, faire ses études.

stuff [stʌf] *n* chose(s) *f(pl)*, truc *m*; affaires *fpl*, trucs; (*substance*) substance *f* // *vt* rembourrer; (*CULIN*) farcir; ~**ing** *n* bourre *f*, rembourrage *m*; (*CULIN*) farce *f*; ~**y** *a* (*room*) mal ventilé(e) *or* aéré(e); (*ideas*) vieux jeu *inv*.

stumble ['stʌmbl] *vi* trébucher; **to** ~ **across** (*fig*) tomber sur; **stumbling block** *n* pierre *f* d'achoppement.

stump [stʌmp] *n* souche *f*; (*of limb*) moignon *m* // *vt*: **to be** ~**ed** sécher, ne pas savoir que répondre.

stun [stʌn] *vt* étourdir; abasourdir.

stung [stʌŋ] *pt, pp of* **sting**.

stunk [stʌŋk] *pp of* **stink**.

stunt [stʌnt] *n* tour *m* de force; truc *m* publicitaire; (*AVIAT*) acrobatie *f* // *vt* retarder, arrêter; ~**ed** *a* rabougri(e); ~**man** *n* cascadeur *m*.

stupendous [stju:'pɛndəs] *a* prodigieux(euse), fantastique.

stupid ['stju:pɪd] *a* stupide, bête; ~**ity** [-'pɪdɪtɪ] *n* stupidité *f*, bêtise *f*.

sturdy ['stə:dɪ] *a* robuste, vigoureux(euse); solide.

stutter ['stʌtə*] *vi* bégayer.

sty [staɪ] *n* (*of pigs*) porcherie *f*.

stye [staɪ] *n* (*MED*) orgelet *m*.

style [staɪl] *n* style *m*; (*distinction*) allure *f*, cachet *m*, style; **stylish** *a* élégant(e), chic *inv*; **stylist** *n* (*hair stylist*) coiffeur/euse.

stylus ['staɪləs] *n* (*of record player*) pointe *f* de lecture.

suave [swɑ:v] *a* doucereux(euse), onctueux(euse).

sub... [sʌb] *prefix* sub..., sous-; ~**conscious** *a* subconscient(e) // *n* subconscient *m*; ~**contract** *vt* sous-traiter.

subdue [səb'dju:] *vt* subjuguer, soumettre; ~**d** *a* contenu(e), atténué(e); (*light*) tamisé(e); (*person*) qui a perdu de son entrain.

subject *n* ['sʌbdʒɪkt] sujet *m*; (*SCOL*) matière *f* // *vt* [səb'dʒɛkt]: **to** ~ **to** soumettre à; exposer à; **to be** ~ **to** (*law*) être soumis(e) à; (*disease*) être sujet(te) à; ~**ive** [səb'dʒɛktɪv] *a* subjectif(ive); ~ **matter** *n* sujet *m*; contenu *m*.

subjunctive [səb'dʒʌŋktɪv] *n* subjonctif *m*.

sublet [sʌb'lɛt] *vt* sous-louer.

submachine gun ['sʌbmə'ʃi:n-] *n* fusil-mitrailleur *m*.

submarine [sʌbmə'ri:n] *n* sous-marin

m.

submerge [səb'mə:dʒ] *vt* submerger; immerger // *vi* plonger.

submission [səb'mɪʃən] *n* soumission *f.*

submissive [səb'mɪsɪv] *a* soumis(e).

submit [səb'mɪt] *vt* soumettre // *vi* se soumettre.

subnormal [sʌb'nɔ:məl] *a* au-dessous de la normale; (*backward*) arriéré(e).

subordinate [sə'bɔ:dɪnət] *a, n* subordonné(e).

subpoena [səb'pi:nə] *n* (LAW) citation *f*, assignation *f.*

subscribe [səb'skraɪb] *vi* cotiser; to ~ to (*opinion, fund*) souscrire à; (*newspaper*) s'abonner à; être abonné/e à; ~r *n* (*to periodical, telephone*) abonné/e.

subscription [səb'skrɪpʃən] *n* souscription *f*; abonnement *m.*

subsequent ['sʌbsɪkwənt] *a* ultérieur(e), suivant(e); consécutif(ive); ~ly *ad* par la suite.

subside [səb'saɪd] *vi* s'affaisser; (*flood*) baisser; (*wind*) tomber; ~nce [-'saɪdns] *n* affaissement *m.*

subsidiary [səb'sɪdɪərɪ] *a* subsidiaire, accessoire // *n* filiale *f.*

subsidize ['sʌbsɪdaɪz] *vt* subventionner.

subsidy ['sʌbsɪdɪ] *n* subvention *f.*

substance ['sʌbstəns] *n* substance *f*; (*fig*) essentiel *m.*

substantial [səb'stænʃl] *a* substantiel(le); (*fig*) important(e).

substantiate [səb'stænʃɪeɪt] *vt* étayer, fournir des preuves à l'appui de.

substitute ['sʌbstɪtju:t] *n* (*person*) remplaçant/e; (*thing*) succédané *m* // *vt*: to ~ sth/sb for substituer qch/qn à, remplacer par qch/qn.

subterranean [sʌbtə'reɪnɪən] *a* souterrain(e).

subtitle ['sʌbtaɪtl] *n* (CINEMA) sous-titre *m.*

subtle ['sʌtl] *a* subtil(e).

subtotal [sʌb'təʊtl] *n* total partiel.

subtract [səb'trækt] *vt* soustraire, retrancher; ~ion [-'trækʃən] *n* soustraction *f.*

suburb ['sʌbə:b] *n* faubourg *m*; the ~s la banlieue; ~an [sə'bə:bən] *a* de banlieue, suburbain(e); ~ia [sə'bə:bɪə] *n* la banlieue.

subway ['sʌbweɪ] *n* (US) métro *m*; (Brit) passage souterrain.

succeed [sək'si:d] *vi* réussir; avoir du succès // *vt* succéder à; to ~ in doing réussir à faire; ~ing *a* (*following*) suivant(e).

success [sək'sɛs] *n* succès *m*; réussite *f*; ~ful *a* (*venture*) couronné(e) de succès; to be ~ful (in doing) réussir (à faire); ~fully *ad* avec succès.

succession [sək'sɛʃən] *n* succession *f.*

successive [sək'sɛsɪv] *a* successif(ive);

consécutif(ive).

such [sʌtʃ] *a* tel(telle); (*of that kind*): ~ a book un livre de ce genre or pareil, un tel livre; ~ books des livres de ce genre or pareils, de tels livres; (*so much*): ~ courage un tel courage // *ad* si; ~ a long trip un si long voyage; ~ good books de si bons livres; ~ a lot of tellement or tant de; ~ as (*like*) tel(telle) que, comme; a noise ~ as to un bruit de nature à; as ~ *ad* en tant que tel(telle), à proprement parler; ~-and-~ *a* tel(telle) ou tel(telle).

suck [sʌk] *vt* sucer; (*breast, bottle*) téter; ~er *n* (BOT, ZOOL, TECH) ventouse *f*; (col) naïf/ive, poire *f.*

suction ['sʌkʃən] *n* succion *f.*

sudden ['sʌdn] *a* soudain(e), subit(e); all of a ~ soudain, tout à coup; ~ly *ad* brusquement, tout à coup, soudain.

suds [sʌdz] *npl* eau savonneuse.

sue [su:] *vt* poursuivre en justice, intenter un procès à.

suede [sweɪd] *n* daim *m*, cuir suédé // *cpd* de daim.

suet ['suɪt] *n* graisse *f* de rognon or de bœuf.

suffer ['sʌfə*] *vt* souffrir, subir; (*bear*) tolérer, supporter // *vi* souffrir; ~er *n* malade *m/f*; victime *m/f*; ~ing *n* souffrance(s) *f(pl).*

sufficient [sə'fɪʃənt] *a* suffisant(e); ~ money suffisamment d'argent; ~ly *ad* suffisamment, assez.

suffocate ['sʌfəkeɪt] *vi* suffoquer, étouffer.

suffused [sə'fju:zd] *a*: to be ~ with baigner dans, être imprégné(e) de.

sugar ['ʃʊgə*] *n* sucre *m* // *vt* sucrer; ~ beet *n* betterave sucrière; ~ cane *n* canne *f* à sucre; ~y *a* sucré(e).

suggest [sə'dʒɛst] *vt* suggérer, proposer; dénoter; ~ion [-'dʒɛstʃən] *n* suggestion *f.*

suicide ['suɪsaɪd] *n* suicide *m.*

suit [su:t] *n* (*man's*) costume *m*, complet *m*; (*woman's*) tailleur *m*, ensemble *m*; (CARDS) couleur *f* // *vt* aller à; convenir à; (*adapt*): to ~ sth to adapter or approprier qch à; ~able *a* qui convient; approprié(e); ~ably *ad* comme il se doit (or se devait *etc*), convenablement.

suitcase ['su:tkeɪs] *n* valise *f.*

suite [swi:t] *n* (*of rooms, also* MUS) suite *f*; (*furniture*): bedroom/dining room ~ (ensemble *m* de) chambre *f* à coucher/ salle *f* à manger.

suitor ['su:tə*] *n* soupirant *m*, prétendant *m.*

sulfur ['sʌlfə*] *n* (US) = **sulphur.**

sulk [sʌlk] *vi* bouder; ~y *a* boudeur(euse), maussade.

sullen ['sʌlən] *a* renfrogné(e), maussade; morne.

sulphur, (US) sulfur ['sʌlfə*] *n* soufre

m.

sultana [sʌl'tɑːnə] *n* (*fruit*) raisin (sec) de Smyrne.

sultry ['sʌltrɪ] *a* étouffant(e).

sum [sʌm] *n* somme *f*; (*SCOL etc*) calcul *m*; **to ~ up** *vt, vi* résumer.

summarize ['sʌməraɪz] *vt* résumer.

summary ['sʌmərɪ] *n* résumé *m* // *a* (*justice*) sommaire.

summer ['sʌmə*] *n* été *m* // *cpd* d'été, estival(e); **~house** *n* (*in garden*) pavillon *m*; **~time** *n* (*season*) été *m*; **~ time** *n* (*by clock*) heure *f* d'été.

summit ['sʌmɪt] *n* sommet *m*.

summon ['sʌmən] *vt* appeler, convoquer; **to ~ up** *vt* rassembler, faire appel à; **~s** *n* citation *f*, assignation *f*.

sump [sʌmp] *n* (*Brit AUT*) carter *m*.

sun [sʌn] *n* soleil *m*; **in the ~** au soleil; **~bathe** *vi* prendre un bain de soleil; **~burn** *n* coup de soleil; (*tan*) bronzage *m*.

Sunday ['sʌndɪ] *n* dimanche *m*; **~ school** *n* ≈ catéchisme *m*.

sundial ['sʌndaɪəl] *n* cadran *m* solaire.

sundown ['sʌndaun] *n* coucher *m* du soleil.

sundry ['sʌndrɪ] *a* divers(e), différent(e); **all and ~** tout le monde, n'importe qui; **sundries** *npl* articles divers.

sunflower ['sʌnflauə*] *n* tournesol *m*.

sung [sʌŋ] *pp of* sing.

sunglasses ['sʌnɡlɑːsɪz] *npl* lunettes *fpl* de soleil.

sunk [sʌŋk] *pp of* sink.

sun: **~light** *n* (lumière *f* du) soleil *m*; **~ny** *a* ensoleillé(e); (*fig*) épanoui(e), radieux(euse); **~rise** *n* lever *m* du soleil; **~ roof** *n* (*AUT*) toit ouvrant; **~set** *n* coucher *m* du soleil; **~shade** *n* (*over table*) parasol *m*; **~shine** *n* (lumière *f* du) soleil *m*; **~stroke** *n* insolation *f*, coup *m* de soleil; **~tan** *n* bronzage *m*; **~tan oil** *n* huile *f* solaire.

super ['suːpə*] *a* (*col*) formidable.

superannuation [suːpərænjuˈeɪʃən] *n* cotisations *fpl* pour la pension.

superb [suːˈpɜːb] *a* superbe, magnifique.

supercilious [suːpəˈsɪlɪəs] *a* hautain(e), dédaigneux(euse).

superficial [suːpəˈfɪʃəl] *a* superficiel(le).

superintendent [suːpərɪnˈtɛndənt] *n* directeur/trice; (*POLICE*) ≈ commissaire *m*.

superior [suˈpɪərɪə*] *a, n* supérieur(e); **~ity** [-ˈɔrɪtɪ] *n* supériorité *f*.

superlative [suˈpɜːlətɪv] *a* sans pareil(le), suprême // *n* (*LING*) superlatif *m*.

superman ['suːpəmæn] *n* surhomme *m*.

supermarket ['suːpəmɑːkɪt] *n* supermarché *m*.

supernatural [suːpəˈnætʃərəl] *a* surnaturel(le).

superpower ['suːpəpauə*] *n* (*POL*) superpuissance *f*.

supersede [suːpəˈsiːd] *vt* remplacer, supplanter.

superstitious [suːpəˈstɪʃəs] *a* superstitieux(euse).

supervise ['suːpəvaɪz] *vt* surveiller; diriger; **supervision** [-ˈvɪʒən] *n* surveillance *f*; contrôle *m*; **supervisor** *n* surveillant/e; (*in shop*) chef *m* de rayon.

supine ['suːpaɪn] *a* couché(e) *or* étendu(e) sur le dos.

supper ['sʌpə*] *n* dîner *m*; (*late*) souper *m*.

supple ['sʌpl] *a* souple.

supplement *n* ['sʌplɪmənt] supplément *m* // *vt* [sʌplɪˈmɛnt] ajouter à, compléter; **~ary** [-ˈmɛntərɪ] *a* supplémentaire.

supplier [səˈplaɪə*] *n* fournisseur *m*.

supply [səˈplaɪ] *vt* (*provide*) fournir; (*equip*): **to ~ (with)** approvisionner *or* ravitailler (en); fournir (en); alimenter (en) // *n* provision *f*, réserve *f*; (*supplying*) approvisionnement *m*; (*TECH*) alimentation *f* // *cpd* (*teacher etc*) suppléant(e); **supplies** *npl* (*food*) vivres *mpl*; (*MIL*) subsistances *fpl*.

support [səˈpɔːt] *n* (*moral, financial etc*) soutien *m*, appui *m*; (*TECH*) support *m*, soutien // *vt* soutenir, supporter; (*financially*) subvenir aux besoins de; (*uphold*) être pour, être partisan de, appuyer; **~er** *n* (*POL etc*) partisan/e; (*SPORT*) supporter *m*.

suppose [səˈpəuz] *vt, vi* supposer; imaginer; **to be ~d to do** être censé(e) faire; **~dly** [səˈpəuzɪdlɪ] *ad* soi-disant; **supposing** *cj* si, à supposer que + *sub*.

suppress [səˈprɛs] *vt* réprimer; supprimer; étouffer; refouler.

supreme [suˈpriːm] *a* suprême.

surcharge ['sɜːtʃɑːdʒ] *n* surcharge *f*; (*extra tax*) surtaxe *f*.

sure [ʃuə*] *a* (*gen*) sûr(e); (*definite, convinced*) sûr, certain(e); **~!** (*of course*) bien sûr!; **~ enough** effectivement; **to make ~ of sth** s'assurer de *or* vérifier qch; **to make ~ that** s'assurer *or* vérifier que; **~ly** *ad* sûrement; certainement.

surety ['ʃuərətɪ] *n* caution *f*.

surf [sɜːf] *n* ressac *m*.

surface ['sɜːfɪs] *n* surface *f* // *vt* (*road*) poser le revêtement de // *vi* remonter à la surface; faire surface; **~ mail** *n* courrier *m* par voie de terre (*or* maritime).

surfboard ['sɜːfbɔːd] *n* planche *f* de surf.

surfeit ['sɜːfɪt] *n*: **a ~ of** un excès de; une indigestion de.

surfing ['sɜːfɪŋ] *n* surf *m*.

surge [sɜːdʒ] *n* vague *f*, montée *f* // *vi*

déferler.

surgeon ['sə:dʒən] *n* chirurgien *m*.

surgery ['sə:dʒərɪ] *n* chirurgie *f*; (*Brit: room*) cabinet *m* (de consultation); **to undergo ~** être opéré(e); **~ hours** *npl* (*Brit*) heures *fpl* de consultation.

surgical ['sə:dʒɪkl] *a* chirurgical(e); **~ spirit** *n* (*Brit*) alcool *m* à 90°.

surly ['sə:lɪ] *a* revêche, maussade.

surname ['sə:neɪm] *n* nom *m* de famille.

surplus ['sə:pləs] *n* surplus *m*, excédent *m* // *a* en surplus, de trop.

surprise [sə'praɪz] *n* (*gen*) surprise *f*; (*astonishment*) étonnement *m* // *vt* surprendre; étonner; **surprising** *a* surprenant(e), étonnant(e); **surprisingly** *ad* (*easy, helpful*) étonnamment, étrangement.

surrender [sə'rɛndə*] *n* reddition *f*, capitulation *f* // *vi* se rendre, capituler.

surreptitious [sʌrəp'tɪʃəs] *a* subreptice, furtif(ive).

surrogate ['sʌrəgɪt] *n* substitut *m*; **~ mother** *n* mère porteuse *or* de substitution.

surround [sə'raund] *vt* entourer; (*MIL etc*) encercler; **~ing** *a* environnant(e); **~ings** *npl* environs *mpl*, alentours *mpl*.

surveillance [sə:'veɪləns] *n* surveillance *f*.

survey *n* ['sə:veɪ] enquête *f*, étude *f*; (*in housebuying etc*) inspection *f*, (*rapport m d'*)expertise *f*; (*of land*) levé *m* // *vt* [sə:'veɪ] passer en revue; enquêter sur; inspecter; **~or** *n* expert *m*; (*arpenteur m*) géomètre *m*.

survival [sə'vaɪvl] *n* survie *f*; (*relic*) vestige *m*.

survive [sə'vaɪv] *vi* survivre; (*custom etc*) subsister // *vt* survivre à; **survivor** *n* survivant/e.

susceptible [sə'sɛptəbl] *a*: **~ (to)** sensible (à); (*disease*) prédisposé(e) (à).

suspect *a n,* ['sʌspɛkt] suspect(e) *m* // *vt* [səs'pɛkt] soupçonner, suspecter.

suspend [səs'pɛnd] *vt* suspendre; **~ed sentence** *n* condamnation *f* avec sursis; **~er belt** *n* porte-jarretelles *m inv*; **~ers** *npl* (*Brit*) jarretelles *fpl*; (*US*) bretelles *fpl*.

suspense [səs'pɛns] *n* attente *f*; (*in film etc*) suspense *m*.

suspension [səs'pɛnʃən] *n* (*gen, AUT*) suspension *f*; (*of driving licence*) retrait *m* provisoire; **~ bridge** *n* pont suspendu.

suspicion [səs'pɪʃən] *n* soupçon(s) *m(pl)*.

suspicious [səs'pɪʃəs] *a* (*suspecting*) soupçonneux(euse), méfiant(e); (*causing suspicion*) suspect(e).

sustain [səs'teɪn] *vt* supporter; soutenir; corroborer; (*suffer*) subir; recevoir; **~ed** *a* (*effort*) soutenu(e), prolongé(e).

sustenance ['sʌstɪnəns] *n* nourriture *f*; moyens *mpl* de subsistance.

swab [swɔb] *n* (*MED*) tampon *m*; prélèvement *m*.

swagger ['swægə*] *vi* plastronner.

swallow ['swɔləu] *n* (*bird*) hirondelle *f* // *vt* avaler; (*fig*) gober; **to ~ up** *vt* engloutir.

swam [swæm] *pt of* **swim**.

swamp [swɔmp] *n* marais *m*, marécage *m* // *vt* submerger.

swan [swɔn] *n* cygne *m*.

swap [swɔp] *vt*: **to ~ (for)** échanger (contre), troquer (contre).

swarm [swɔ:m] *n* essaim *m* // *vi* fourmiller, grouiller.

swarthy ['swɔ:ðɪ] *a* basané(e), bistré(e).

swastika ['swɔstɪkə] *n* croix gammée.

swat [swɔt] *vt* écraser.

sway [sweɪ] *vi* se balancer, osciller; tanguer // *vt* (*influence*) influencer.

swear [swɛə*], *pt* **swore**, *pp* **sworn** *vi* jurer; **to ~ to sth** jurer de qch; **~word** *n* gros mot, juron *m*.

sweat [swɛt] *n* sueur *f*, transpiration *f* // *vi* suer.

sweater ['swɛtə*] *n* tricot *m*, pull *m*.

sweaty ['swɛtɪ] *a* en sueur, moite *or* mouillé(e) de sueur.

Swede [swi:d] *n* Suédois/e.

swede [swi:d] *n* (*Brit*) rutabaga *m*.

Sweden ['swi:dn] *n* Suède *f*.

Swedish ['swi:dɪʃ] *a* suédois(e) // (*LING*) suédois *m*.

sweep [swi:p] *n* coup *m* de balai; (*curve*) grande courbe; (*range*) champ *m*; (*also*: **chimney ~**) ramoneur *m* // *vb* (*pt, pp* **swept**) *vt* balayer // *vi* avancer majestueusement *or* rapidement; s'élancer; s'étendre; **to ~ away** *vt* balayer; entraîner; emporter; **to ~ past** *vi* passer majestueusement *or* rapidement; **to ~ up** *vt, vi* balayer; **~ing** *a* (*gesture*) large; circulaire; a **~ing statement** une généralisation hâtive.

sweet [swi:t] *n* (*Brit: pudding*) dessert *m*; (*candy*) bonbon *m* // *a* doux(douce); (*not savoury*) sucré(e); (*fresh*) frais(fraîche), pur(e); (*fig*) agréable, doux; gentil(le); mignon(ne); **~corn** *n* maïs doux; **~en** *vt* sucrer; adoucir; **~heart** *n* amoureux/euse; **~ness** *n* goût sucré; douceur *f*; **~ pea** *n* pois *m* de senteur.

swell [swɛl] *n* (*of sea*) houle *f* // *a* (*col: excellent*) chouette // *vb* (*pt* **~ed**, *pp* **swollen** *or* **~ed**) *vt* augmenter; grossir // *vi* grossir, augmenter; (*sound*) s'enfler; (*MED*) enfler; **~ing** *n* (*MED*) enflure *f*; grosseur *f*.

sweltering ['swɛltərɪŋ] *a* étouffant(e), oppressant(e).

swept [swɛpt] *pt, pp of* **sweep**.

swerve [swə:v] *vi* faire une embardée *or*

swift [swɪft] n (bird) martinet m // a
rapide, prompt(e).

swig [swɪg] n (col: drink) lampée f.

swill [swɪl] n pâtée f // vt (also: ~ out, ~
down) laver à grande eau.

swim [swɪm] n: to go for a ~ aller nager
or se baigner // vb (pt swam, pp swum)
vi nager; (SPORT) faire de la natation;
(head, room) tourner // vt traverser (à
la nage); faire (à la nage); ~**mer** n
nageur/euse; ~**ming** n nage f, natation
f; ~**ming cap** n bonnet m de bain;
~**ming costume** n (Brit) maillot m (de
bain); ~**ming pool** n piscine f; ~**suit**
n maillot m (de bain).

swindle [swɪndl] n escroquerie f.

swine [swaɪn] n (pl inv) pourceau m,
porc m; (col!) salaud m (!).

swing [swɪŋ] n balançoire f;
(movement) balancement m, oscillations
fpl; (MUS) swing m; rythme m // vb (pt,
pp swung) vt balancer, faire osciller
(also: ~ round) tourner, faire virer // vi
se balancer, osciller; (also: ~ round)
virer, tourner; to be in full ~ battre son
plein; ~ **door**, (US) ~**ing door** n porte
battante.

swingeing [swɪndʒɪŋ] a (Brit)
écrasant(e); considérable.

swipe [swaɪp] vt (hit) frapper à toute
volée; gifler; (col: steal) piquer.

swirl [swəːl] vi tourbillonner, tournoyer.

swish [swɪʃ] a (col: smart) rupin(e) // vi
siffler.

Swiss [swɪs] a suisse // n (pl inv) Suisse/
esse.

switch [swɪtʃ] n (for light, radio etc)
bouton m; (change) changement m,
revirement m // vt (change) changer;
intervertir; **to ~ off** vt éteindre;
(engine) arrêter; **to ~ on** vt allumer;
(engine, machine) mettre en marche;
~**board** n (TEL) standard m.

Switzerland [swɪtsələnd] n Suisse f.

swivel [swɪvl] vi (also: ~ round)
pivoter, tourner.

swollen [swəʊlən] pp of swell.

swoon [swuːn] vi se pâmer.

swoop [swuːp] n (also: ~ down) descendre en piqué, piquer.

swop [swɒp] vt = swap.

sword [sɔːd] n épée f; ~**fish** n espadon
m.

swore [swɔː*] pt of swear.

sworn [swɔːn] pp of swear.

swot [swɒt] vt, vi bûcher, potasser.

swum [swʌm] pp of swim.

swung [swʌŋ] pt, pp of swing.

syllable [sɪləbl] n syllabe f.

syllabus [sɪləbəs] n programme m.

symbol [sɪmbl] n symbole m.

symmetry [sɪmɪtrɪ] n symétrie f.

sympathetic [sɪmpə'θetɪk] a compa-
tissant(e); bienveillant(e), compré-

hensif(ive); ~ **towards** bien disposé(e)
envers.

sympathize [sɪmpəθaɪz] vi: to ~ with
sb plaindre qn; s'associer à la douleur
de qn; ~**r** n (POL) sympathisant/e.

sympathy [sɪmpəθɪ] n compassion f; in
~ with en accord avec; (strike) en or
par solidarité avec; with our deepest ~
en vous priant d'accepter nos sincères
condoléances.

symphony [sɪmfənɪ] n symphonie f.

symptom [sɪmptəm] n symptôme m;
indice m.

synagogue [sɪnəgɒg] n synagogue f.

syndicate [sɪndɪkɪt] n syndicat m,
coopérative f.

synonym [sɪnənɪm] n synonyme m.

syntax [sɪntæks] n syntaxe f.

synthetic [sɪn'θetɪk] a synthétique.

syphon [saɪfən] n, vb = siphon.

Syria [sɪrɪə] n Syrie f.

syringe [sɪ'rɪndʒ] n seringue f.

syrup [sɪrəp] n sirop m; (also: golden
~) mélasse raffinée.

system [sɪstəm] n système m; (order)
méthode f; (ANAT) organisme m; ~**atic**
[-'mætɪk] a systématique; méthodique;
~ **disk** n (COMPUT) disque m système;
~**s analyst** n analyste-programmeur
m/f.

T

ta [tɑː] excl (Brit col) merci!

tab [tæb] n (loop on coat etc) attache f;
(label) étiquette f; **to keep ~s on** (fig)
surveiller.

tabby [tæbɪ] n (also: ~ cat) chat/te ti-
gré(e).

table [teɪbl] n table f // vt (Brit: motion
etc) présenter; **to lay** or **set the ~** mettre le couvert or la table; ~ **of contents** n table f des matières; ~**cloth** n
nappe f; ~ **d'hôte** [tɑː:bl'dəʊt] a (meal)
à prix fixe; ~ **lamp** n lampe
décorative; ~**mat** n (for plate)
napperon m, set m; (for hot dish)
dessous-de-plat m inv; ~**spoon** n cuiller
f de service; (also: ~**spoonful:** as
measurement) cuillerée f à soupe.

tablet [tæblɪt] n (MED) comprimé m; (:
for sucking) pastille f; (for writing) bloc
m; (of stone) plaque f.

table: ~ **tennis** n ping-pong m, tennis
m de table; ~ **wine** n vin m de table.

tabulate [tæbjuleɪt] vt (data, figures)
mettre sous forme de table(s).

tacit [tæsɪt] a tacite.

tack [tæk] n (nail) petit clou; (stitch)
point m de bâti; (NAUT) bord m, bordée
f // vt clouer; bâtir // vi tirer un or des
bord(s).

tackle [tækl] n matériel m, équipement
m; (for lifting) appareil m de levage;

(RUGBY) plaquage m // vt (difficulty) s'attaquer à; (RUGBY) plaquer.

tacky ['tækɪ] a collant(e); pas sec(sèche).

tact [tækt] n tact m; **~ful** a plein(e) de tact.

tactical ['tæktɪkl] a tactique.

tactics ['tæktɪks] n, npl tactique f.

tactless ['tæktlɪs] a qui manque de tact.

tadpole ['tædpəʊl] n têtard m.

taffy ['tæfɪ] n (US) (bonbon m au) caramel m.

tag [tæg] n étiquette f; **to ~ along** vi suivre.

tail [teɪl] n queue f; (of shirt) pan m // vt (follow) suivre, filer; **to ~ away, ~ off** vi (in size, quality etc) baisser peu à peu; **~back** n (Brit AUT) bouchon m; **~ coat** n habit m; **~ end** n bout m, fin f; **~gate** n (AUT) hayon m arrière.

tailor ['teɪlə*] n tailleur m (artisan); **~ing** n (cut) coupe f; **~-made** a fait(e) sur mesure; (fig) conçu(e) spécialement.

tailwind ['teɪlwɪnd] n vent m arrière inv.

tainted ['teɪntɪd] a (food) gâté(e); (water, air) infecté(e); (fig) souillé(e).

take, pt took, pp taken [teɪk, tuk, 'teɪkn] vt prendre; (gain: prize) remporter; (require: effort, courage) demander; (tolerate) accepter, supporter; (hold: passengers etc) contenir; (accompany) emmener, accompagner; (bring, carry) apporter, emporter; (exam) passer, se présenter à; **to ~ sth from** (drawer etc) prendre qch dans; (person) prendre qch à; I ~ it that je suppose que; **to ~ for a walk** (child, dog) emmener promener; **to ~ after** vt fus ressembler à; **to ~ apart** vt démonter; **to ~ away** vt emporter; enlever; **to ~ back** vt (return) rendre, rapporter; (one's words) retirer; **to ~ down** vt (building) démolir; (letter etc) prendre, écrire; **to ~ in** vt (deceive) tromper, rouler; (understand) comprendre, saisir; (include) couvrir, inclure; (lodger) prendre; **to ~ off** vi (AVIAT) décoller // vt (remove) enlever; (imitate) imiter, pasticher; **to ~ on** vt (work) accepter, se charger de; (employee) prendre, embaucher; (opponent) accepter de se battre contre; **to ~ out** vt sortir; (remove) enlever; (licence) prendre, se procurer; **to ~ sth out of sth** enlever qch de; (drawer, pocket etc) prendre qch dans qch; **to ~ over** vt (business) reprendre // vi: **to ~ over from sb** prendre la relève de qn; **to ~ to** vt fus (person) se prendre d'amitié pour; (activity) prendre goût à; **to ~ up** vt (one's story, a dress) reprendre; (occupy: time, space) prendre, occuper; (engage in: hobby etc) se mettre à; **~away** a (food) à emporter; **~-home**

pay n salaire net; **~off** n (AVIAT) décollage m; **~out** a (US) = **~away**; **~over** n (COMM) rachat m.

takings ['teɪkɪŋz] npl (COMM) recette f.

talc [tælk] n (also: **~um powder**) talc m.

tale [teɪl] n (story) conte m, histoire f; (account) récit m; (pej) histoire f; **to tell ~s** (fig) rapporter.

talent ['tælnt] n talent m, don m; **~ed** a doué(e), plein(e) de talent.

talk [tɔːk] n propos mpl; (gossip) racontars mpl (pej); (conversation) discussion f; (interview) entretien m; (a speech) causerie f, exposé m // vi (chatter) bavarder; **~s** npl (POL etc) entretiens mpl; conférence f; **to ~ about** parler de; (converse) s'entretenir or parler de; **to ~ sb out of/into doing** persuader qn de ne pas faire/de faire; **to ~ shop** parler métier or affaires; **to ~ over** vt discuter (de); **~ative** a bavard(e); **~ show** n causerie (télévisée or radiodiffusée).

tall [tɔːl] a (person) grand(e); (building, tree) haut(e); **to be 6 feet ~** ≈ mesurer 1 mètre 80; **~boy** n (Brit) grande commode; **~ story** n histoire f invraisemblable.

tally ['tælɪ] n compte m // vi: **to ~ (with)** correspondre (à).

talon ['tælən] n griffe f; (eagle) serre f.

tame [teɪm] a apprivoisé(e); (fig: story, style) insipide.

tamper ['tæmpə*] vi: **to ~ with** toucher à (en cachette ou sans permission).

tampon ['tæmpən] n tampon m hygiénique or périodique.

tan [tæn] n (also: **sun~**) bronzage m // vt, vi bronzer, brunir // a (colour) brun roux inv.

tang [tæŋ] n odeur (or saveur) piquante.

tangent ['tændʒənt] n (MATH) tangente f; **to go off at a ~** (fig) changer complètement de direction.

tangerine [tændʒə'riːn] n mandarine f.

tangle ['tæŋgl] n enchevêtrement m // vt enchevêtrer.

tank [tæŋk] n réservoir m; (for processing) cuve f; (for fish) aquarium m; (MIL) char m d'assaut, tank m.

tanker ['tæŋkə*] n (ship) pétrolier m, tanker m; (truck) camion-citerne m.

tantalizing ['tæntəlaɪzɪŋ] a (smell) extrêmement appétissant(e); (offer) terriblement tentant(e).

tantamount ['tæntəmaunt] a: **~ to** qui équivaut à.

tantrum ['tæntrəm] n accès m de colère.

tap [tæp] n (on sink etc) robinet m; (gentle blow) petite tape // vt frapper or taper légèrement; (resources) exploiter, utiliser; (telephone) mettre sur écoute; **on ~** (fig: resources) disponible; **~-dancing** n claquettes fpl.

tape [teɪp] n ruban m; (also: **magnetic**

~) bande f (magnétique) // vt (record) enregistrer (sur bande); ~ **measure** n mètre m à ruban.

taper ['teɪpə*] n cierge m // vi s'effiler.

tape recorder n magnétophone m.

tapestry ['tæpɪstrɪ] n tapisserie f.

tar [ta:] n goudron m.

target ['ta:gɪt] n cible f; (fig: objective) objectif m.

tariff ['tærɪf] n (COMM) tarif m; (taxes) tarif douanier.

tarmac ['ta:mæk] n (Brit: on road) macadam m; (AVIAT) aire f d'envol.

tarnish ['ta:nɪʃ] vt ternir.

tarpaulin [ta:'pɔ:lɪn] n bâche goudronnée.

tarragon ['tærəgən] n estragon m.

tart [ta:t] n (CULIN) tarte f; (Brit col: pej: woman) poule f // a (flavour) âpre, aigrelet(te); **to ~ o.s. up** (col) se faire beau(belle); (: pej) s'attifer.

tartan ['ta:tn] n tartan m // a écossais(e).

tartar ['ta:tə*] n (on teeth) tartre m; ~ **sauce** n sauce f tartare.

task [ta:sk] n tâche f; **to take to ~** prendre à partie; ~ **force** n (MIL, POLICE) détachement spécial.

tassel ['tæsl] n gland m; pompon m.

taste [teɪst] n goût m; (fig: glimpse, idea) idée f, aperçu m // vt goûter // vi: **to ~ of** (fish etc) avoir le or un goût de; **it ~s like fish** ça a un or le goût de poisson, on dirait du poisson; **you can ~ the garlic (in it)** on sent bien l'ail; **can I have a ~ of this wine?** puis-je goûter un peu de ce vin?; **to have a ~ for sth** aimer qch, avoir un penchant pour qch; **in good/bad ~** de bon/mauvais goût; ~**ful** a de bon goût; ~**less** a (food) qui n'a aucun goût; (remark) de mauvais goût; **tasty** a savoureux(euse), délicieux(euse).

tatters ['tætəz] npl: **in ~** (also: tattered) en lambeaux.

tattoo [tə'tu:] n tatouage m; (spectacle) parade f militaire // vt tatouer.

taught [tɔ:t] pt, pp of teach.

taunt [tɔ:nt] n raillerie f // vt railler.

Taurus ['tɔ:rəs] n le Taureau.

taut [tɔ:t] a tendu(e).

tawdry ['tɔ:drɪ] a (d'un mauvais goût) criard.

tax [tæks] n (on goods etc) taxe f; (on income) impôts mpl, contributions fpl // vt taxer; imposer; (fig: strain: patience etc) mettre à l'épreuve; ~**able** a (income) imposable; ~**ation** [-'seɪʃən] n taxation f; impôts mpl, contributions fpl; ~ **avoidance** n évasion fiscale; ~ **collector** n percepteur m; ~ **disc** n (Brit AUT) vignette f (automobile); ~ **evasion** n fraude fiscale; ~**-free** a exempt(e) d'impôts.

taxi ['tæksɪ] n taxi m // vi (AVIAT) rouler

(lentement) au sol; ~ **driver** n chauffeur m de taxi; ~ **rank** (Brit), ~ **stand** n station f de taxis.

tax: ~ **payer** n contribuable m/f; ~ **relief** n dégrèvement or allègement fiscal; ~ **return** n déclaration f d'impôts or de revenus.

TB n abbr = tuberculosis.

tea [ti:] n thé m; (Brit: snack: for children) goûter m; **high ~** (Brit) collation combinant goûter et dîner; ~ **bag** n sachet m de thé; ~ **break** n (Brit) pause-thé f.

teach [ti:tʃ], pt, pp **taught** vt: **to ~ sb sth, ~ sth to sb** apprendre qch à qn; (in school etc) enseigner qch à qn // vi enseigner; ~**er** n (in secondary school) professeur m; (in primary school) instituteur/trice; ~**ing** n enseignement m.

tea cosy n couvre-théière m.

teacup ['ti:kʌp] n tasse f à thé.

teak [ti:k] n teck m.

team [ti:m] n équipe f; (of animals) attelage m; ~**work** n travail m d'équipe.

teapot ['ti:pɔt] n théière f.

tear n [tɛə*] déchirure f; [tɪə*] larme f // vb [tɛə*] (pt tore, pp torn) vt déchirer // vi se déchirer; **in ~s** en larmes; **to ~ along** vi (rush) aller à toute vitesse; **to ~ up** vt (sheet of paper etc) déchirer, mettre en morceaux or pièces; ~**ful** a larmoyant(e); ~ **gas** n gaz m lacrymogène.

tearoom ['ti:ru:m] n salon m de thé.

tease [ti:z] vt taquiner; (unkindly) tourmenter.

tea set n service m à thé.

teaspoon ['ti:spu:n] n petite cuiller f; (also: ~**ful**: as measurement) ≈ cuillerée f à café.

teat [ti:t] n tétine f.

teatime ['ti:taɪm] n l'heure f du thé.

tea towel n (Brit) torchon m (à vaisselle).

technical ['tɛknɪkl] a technique; ~**ity** [-'kælɪtɪ] n technicité f; (detail) détail m technique.

technician [tɛk'nɪʃən] n technicien/ne.

technique [tɛk'ni:k] n technique f.

technological [tɛknə'lɔdʒɪkl] a technologique.

technology [tɛk'nɔlədʒɪ] n technologie f.

teddy (bear) ['tɛdɪ(bɛə*)] n ours m (en peluche).

tedious ['ti:dɪəs] a fastidieux(euse).

tee [ti:] n (GOLF) tee m.

teem [ti:m] vi: **to ~ (with)** grouiller (de); **it is ~ing (with rain)** il pleut à torrents.

teenage ['ti:neɪdʒ] a (fashions etc) pour jeunes, pour adolescents; ~**r** n jeune m/f, adolescent/e.

teens [ti:nz] *npl*: **to be in one's ~** être adolescent(e).

tee-shirt ['ti:ʃə:t] *n* = **T-shirt**.

teeter ['ti:tə*] *vi* chanceler, vaciller.

teeth [ti:θ] *npl of* **tooth**.

teethe [ti:ð] *vi* percer ses dents.

teething ['ti:ðɪŋ]: **~ ring** *n* anneau *m* (*pour bébé qui perce ses dents*); **~ troubles** *npl* (*fig*) difficultés initiales.

teetotal ['ti:'təutl] *a* (*person*) qui ne boit jamais d'alcool.

telegram ['tɛlɪgræm] *n* télégramme *m*.

telegraph ['tɛlɪgrɑ:f] *n* télégraphe *m*.

telephone ['tɛlɪfəun] *n* téléphone *m* // *vt* (*person*) téléphoner à; (*message*) téléphoner; **~ booth**, (*Brit*) **~ box** *n* cabine *f* téléphonique; **~ call** *n* coup *m* de téléphone, appel *m* téléphonique, communication *f* téléphonique; **~ directory** *n* annuaire *m* (du téléphone); **~ number** *n* numéro *m* de téléphone; **~ operator** *n* téléphoniste *m/f*, standardiste *m/f*; **telephonist** [tə'lɛfənɪst] *n* (*Brit*) téléphoniste *m/f*.

telephoto ['tɛlɪ'fəutəu] *a*: **~ lens** *n* téléobjectif *m*.

telescope ['tɛlɪskəup] *n* télescope *m*.

televise ['tɛlɪvaɪz] *vt* téléviser.

television ['tɛlɪvɪʒən] *n* télévision *f*; **~ set** *n* poste *m* de télévision.

telex ['tɛlɛks] *n* télex *m*.

tell [tɛl], *pt*, *pp* **told** *vt* dire; (*relate: story*) raconter; (*distinguish*): **to ~ sth from** distinguer qch de // *vi* (*talk*): **to ~ (of)** parler (de); (*have effect*) se faire sentir, se voir; **to ~ sb to do** dire à qn de faire; **to ~ off** *vt* réprimander, gronder; **~er** *n* (*in bank*) caissier/ère; **~ing** *a* (*remark, detail*) révélateur(trice); **~tale** *a* (*sign*) éloquent(e), révélateur(trice).

telly ['tɛlɪ] *n abbr* (*Brit col*: = **television**) télé *f*.

temp [tɛmp] *n abbr* (= *temporary*) (secrétaire *f*) intérimaire *f*.

temper ['tɛmpə*] *n* (*nature*) caractère *m*; (*mood*) humeur *f*; (*fit of anger*) colère *f* // *vt* (*moderate*) tempérer, adoucir; **to be in a ~** être en colère; **to lose one's ~** se mettre en colère.

temperament ['tɛmprəmənt] *n* (*nature*) tempérament *m*; **~al** [-'mɛntl] *a* capricieux(euse).

temperate ['tɛmprət] *a* modéré(e); (*climate*) tempéré(e).

temperature ['tɛmprətʃə*] *n* température *f*; **to have** *or* **run a ~** avoir de la fièvre.

tempest ['tɛmpɪst] *n* tempête *f*.

template ['tɛmplɪt] *n* patron *m*.

temple ['tɛmpl] *n* (*building*) temple *m*; (*ANAT*) tempe *f*.

temporary ['tɛmpərərɪ] *a* temporaire, provisoire; (*job, worker*) temporaire; **~ secretary** *n* (secrétaire *f*) intérimaire *f*.

tempt [tɛmpt] *vt* tenter; **to ~ sb into doing** induire qn à faire; **~ation** [-'teɪʃən] *n* tentation *f*.

ten [tɛn] *num* dix.

tenable ['tɛnəbl] *a* défendable.

tenacity [tə'næsɪtɪ] *n* ténacité *f*.

tenancy ['tɛnənsɪ] *n* location *f*; état *m* de locataire.

tenant ['tɛnənt] *n* locataire *m/f*.

tend [tɛnd] *vt* s'occuper de // *vi*: **to ~ to do** avoir tendance à faire.

tendency ['tɛndənsɪ] *n* tendance *f*.

tender ['tɛndə*] *a* tendre; (*delicate*) délicat(e); (*sore*) sensible; (*affectionate*) tendre, doux(douce) // *n* (*COMM: offer*) soumission *f* // *vt* offrir.

tenement ['tɛnəmənt] *n* immeuble *m* (de rapport).

tenet ['tɛnət] *n* principe *m*.

tennis ['tɛnɪs] *n* tennis *m*; **~ ball** *n* balle *f* de tennis; **~ court** *n* (court *m* de) tennis; **~ player** *n* joueur/euse de tennis; **~ racket** *n* raquette *f* de tennis; **~ shoes** *npl* (chaussures *fpl* de) tennis *mpl*.

tenor ['tɛnə*] *n* (*MUS*) ténor *m*; (*of speech etc*) sens général.

tense [tɛns] *a* tendu(e) // *n* (*LING*) temps *m*.

tension ['tɛnʃən] *n* tension *f*.

tent [tɛnt] *n* tente *f*.

tentative ['tɛntətɪv] *a* timide, hésitant(e); (*conclusion*) provisoire.

tenterhooks ['tɛntəhuks] *npl*: **on ~** sur des charbons ardents.

tenth [tɛnθ] *num* dixième.

tent: ~ peg *n* piquet *m* de tente; **~ pole** *n* montant *m* de tente.

tenuous ['tɛnjuəs] *a* ténu(e).

tenure ['tɛnjuə*] *n* (*of property*) bail *m*; (*of job*) période *f* de jouissance; statut *m* de titulaire.

tepid ['tɛpɪd] *a* tiède.

term [tə:m] *n* (*limit*) terme *m*; (*word*) terme, mot *m*; (*SCOL*) trimestre *m*; (*LAW*) session *f* // *vt* appeler; **~s** *npl* (*conditions*) conditions *fpl*; (*COMM*) tarif *m*; **~ of imprisonment** peine *f* de prison; **in the short/long ~** à court/long terme; **to come to ~s with** (*problem*) faire face à.

terminal ['tə:mɪnl] *a* terminal(e); (*disease*) dans sa phase terminale // *n* (*ELEC*) borne *f*; (*for oil, ore etc, COMPUT*) terminal *m*; (*also:* **air ~**) aérogare *f*; (*Brit: also:* **coach ~**) gare routière.

terminate ['tə:mɪneɪt] *vt* mettre fin à // *vi*: **to ~ in** finir en *or* par.

terminus ['tə:mɪnəs, 'tə:mɪnaɪ] *n* terminus *m inv*.

terrace ['tɛrəs] *n* terrasse *f*; (*Brit: row of houses*) rangée *f* de maisons (*attenantes les unes aux autres*); **the ~s** (*Brit SPORT*) les gradins *mpl*; **~d** *a* (*garden*) en terrasses.

terracotta ['tɛrə'kɔtə] *n* terre cuite.
terrain [tɛ'reɪn] *n* terrain *m* (sol).
terrible ['tɛrɪbl] *a* terrible, atroce;
(*weather, work*) affreux(euse), épouvantable; **terribly** *ad* terriblement; (*very badly*) affreusement mal.
terrier ['tɛrɪə*] *n* terrier *m* (chien).
terrific [tə'rɪfɪk] *a* fantastique, incroyable, terrible; (*wonderful*) formidable, sensationnel(le).
terrify ['tɛrɪfaɪ] *vt* terrifier.
territory ['tɛrɪtərɪ] *n* territoire *m*.
terror ['tɛrə*] *n* terreur *f*; **~ism** *n* terrorisme *m*; **~ist** *n* terroriste *m/f*.
terse [tə:s] *a* (*style*) concis(e); (*reply*) laconique.
Terylene ['tɛrɪliːn] *n* ® tergal *m* ®.
test [tɛst] *n* (*trial, check*) essai *m*; (: *of goods in factory*) contrôle *m*; (*of courage etc*) épreuve *f*; (MED) examens *mpl*; (CHEM) analyses *fpl*; (*exam: of intelligence etc*) test *m* (d'aptitude); (: *in school*) interrogation *f* de contrôle; (*also: driving ~*) (examen du) permis *m* de conduire // *vt* essayer; contrôler; mettre à l'épreuve; examiner; analyser; tester; faire subir une interrogation (de contrôle) à.
testament ['tɛstəmənt] *n* testament *m*; **the Old/New T~** l'Ancien/le Nouveau Testament.
testicle ['tɛstɪkl] *n* testicule *m*.
testify ['tɛstɪfaɪ] *vi* (LAW) témoigner, déposer; **to ~ to sth** (LAW) attester qch; (*gen*) témoigner de qch.
testimony ['tɛstɪmənɪ] *n* (LAW) témoignage *m*, déposition *f*.
test: **~ match** *n* (CRICKET, RUGBY) match international; **~ pilot** *n* pilote *m* d'essai; **~ tube** *n* éprouvette *f*.
tetanus ['tɛtənəs] *n* tétanos *m*.
tether ['tɛðə*] *vt* attacher // *n*: **at the end of one's ~** à bout (de patience).
text [tɛkst] *n* texte *m*; **~book** *n* manuel *m*.
textile ['tɛkstaɪl] *n* textile *m*.
texture ['tɛkstʃə*] *n* texture *f*; (*of skin, paper etc*) grain *m*.
Thames [tɛmz] *n*: **the ~** la Tamise.
than [ðæn, ðən] *cj* que; (*with numerals*): **more ~ 10/once** plus de 10/d'une fois; **I have more/less ~ you** j'en ai plus/moins que toi; **she has more apples ~ pears** elle a plus de pommes que de poires.
thank [θæŋk] *vt* remercier, dire merci à; **~ you (very much)** merci (beaucoup); **~s** *npl* remerciements *mpl* // *excl* merci!; **~s to** *prep* grâce à; **~ful** *a*: **~ful (for)** reconnaissant(e) (de); **~less** *a* ingrat(e); **T~sgiving (Day)** *n* jour *m* d'action de grâce.
that [ðæt] ♦ *a* (*demonstrative*: *pl* those) ce, cet + *vowel or h mute*, *f* cette; **~ man/woman/book** cet homme/cette femme/ce livre; (*not 'this'*) cet homme-là/cette femme-là/ce livre-là; **~ one** celui-là(celle-là)
♦ *pronoun* 1 (*demonstrative*: *pl* those) ce; (*not 'this one'*) cela, ça; **who's ~?** qui est-ce?; **what's ~?** qu'est-ce que c'est?; **is ~ you?** c'est toi?; **I prefer this to ~** je préfère ceci à cela *or* ça; **~'s what he said** c'est *or* voilà ce qu'il a dit; **~ is (to say)** c'est-à-dire, à savoir
2 (*relative: subject*) qui; (: *object*) que; (: *indirect*) lequel(laquelle), *pl* lesquels(lesquelles); **the book ~ I read** le livre que j'ai lu; **the books ~ are in the library** les livres qui sont dans la bibliothèque; **all ~ I have** tout ce que j'ai; **the box ~ I put it in** la boîte dans laquelle je l'ai mis; **the people ~ I spoke to** les gens auxquels *or* à qui j'ai parlé
3 (*relative: of time*) où; **the day ~ he came** le jour où il est venu
♦ *cj* que; **he thought ~ I was ill** il pensait que j'étais malade
♦ *ad* (*demonstrative*): **I can't work ~ much** je ne peux pas travailler autant que cela; **I didn't know it was ~ bad** je ne savais pas que c'était si *or* aussi mauvais; **it's about ~ high** c'est à peu près de cette hauteur.
thatched [θætʃt] *a* (*roof*) de chaume; **~ cottage** chaumière *f*.
thaw [θɔː] *n* dégel *m* // *vi* (*ice*) fondre; (*food*) dégeler // *vt* (*food*) (faire) dégeler; **it's ~ing** (*weather*) il dégèle.
the [ðiː, ðə] *definite article* 1 (*gen*) le, *f* la, l' + *vowel or h mute*, *pl* les (NB: à + le(s) = au(x); de + le = du; de + les = des); **~ boy/girl/ink** le garçon/la fille/l'encre; **~ children** les enfants; **~ history of ~ world** l'histoire du monde; **give it to ~ postman** donne-le au facteur; **to play ~ piano/flute** jouer du piano/de la flûte; **~ rich and ~ poor** les riches et les pauvres
2 (*in titles*): **Elizabeth ~ First** Élisabeth première; **Peter ~ Great** Pierre le Grand
3 (*in comparisons*): **~ more he works, ~ more he earns** plus il travaille, plus il gagne de l'argent.
theatre, (*US*) **theater** ['θɪətə*] *n* théâtre *m*; **~-goer** *n* habitué(e) du théâtre.
theatrical [θɪ'ætrɪkl] *a* théâtral(e).
theft [θɛft] *n* vol *m* (larcin).
their [ðɛə*] *a* leur, *pl* leurs; **~s** *pronoun* le(la) leur, les leurs; *see also* my, mine.
them [ðɛm, ðəm] *pronoun* (*direct*) les; (*indirect*) leur; (*stressed, after prep*) eux(elles); *see also* me.
theme [θiːm] *n* thème *m*; **~ song** *n* chanson principale.
themselves [ðəm'sɛlvz] *pl pronoun* (*reflexive*) se; (*emphatic*) eux-mêmes(elles-mêmes); *see also* oneself.
then [ðɛn] *ad* (*at that time*) alors, à ce

moment-là; (*next*) puis, ensuite; (*and also*) et puis (*therefore*) alors, dans ce cas // *a*: **the ~ president** le président d'alors *or* de l'époque; **by ~** (*past*) à ce moment-là; (*future*) d'ici là; **from ~ on** dès lors.

theology [θɪ'ɔlədʒɪ] *n* théologie *f*.

theoretical [θɪə'rɛtɪkl] *a* théorique.

theory ['θɪərɪ] *n* théorie *f*.

therapy ['θɛrəpɪ] *n* thérapie *f*.

there ['ðɛə*] *ad* **1**: **~ is, ~ are** il y a; **~ are 3 of them** (*people, things*) il y en a 3; **~ has been an accident** il y a eu un accident

2 (*referring to place*) là, là-bas; **it's ~** c'est là (-bas); **in/on/up/down ~** là-dedans/là-dessus/là-haut/en bas; **he went ~ on Friday** il y est allé vendredi; **I want that book ~** je veux ce livre-là; **he is!** le voilà!

3: **~, ~** (*esp to child*) allons, allons!

thereabouts [ðɛərə'bauts] *ad* (*place*) par là, près de là; (*amount*) environ, à peu près.

thereafter [ðɛər'ɑ:ftə*] *ad* par la suite.

thereby [ðɛə'baɪ] *ad* ainsi.

therefore ['ðɛəfɔ:*] *ad* donc, par conséquent.

there's ['ðɛəz] = **there is, there has**.

thermal ['θə:ml] *a* thermique.

thermometer [θə'mɔmɪtə*] *n* thermomètre *m*.

Thermos ['θə:məs] *n* ® (*also*: **~ flask**) thermos *m or f inv* ®.

thermostat ['θə:məustæt] *n* thermostat *m*.

thesaurus [θɪ'sɔ:rəs] *n* dictionnaire *m* synonymique.

these [ðiːz] *pl pronoun* ceux-ci(celles-ci) // *pl a* ces; (*not 'those'*): **~ books** ces livres-ci.

thesis, *pl* **theses** ['θiːsɪs, 'θiːsiːz] *n* thèse *f*.

they [ðeɪ] *pl pronoun* ils(elles); (*stressed*) eux(elles); **~ say that ...** (*it is said that*) on dit que ...; **~'d** = **they had, they would; ~'ll** = **they shall, they will; ~'re** = **they are; ~'ve** = **they have**.

thick [θɪk] *a* épais(se); (*crowd*) dense; (*stupid*) bête, borné(e) // *n*: **in the ~ of** au beau milieu de, en plein cœur de; **it's 20 cm ~** ça a 20 cm d'épaisseur; **~en** *vi* s'épaissir // *vt* (*sauce etc*) épaissir; **~ness** *n* épaisseur *f*; **~set** *a* trapu(e), costaud(e); **~skinned** *a* (*fig*) peu sensible.

thief, *pl* **thieves** [θiːf, θiːvz] *n* voleur/euse.

thigh [θaɪ] *n* cuisse *f*.

thimble ['θɪmbl] *n* dé *m* (à coudre).

thin [θɪn] *a* mince; (*person*) maigre; (*soup*) peu épais(se); (*hair, crowd*) clairsemé(e); (*fog*) léger(ère) // *vt* (*hair*) éclaircir; **to ~** (**down**) (*sauce,*

paint) délayer.

thing [θɪŋ] *n* chose *f*; (*object*) objet *m*; (*contraption*) truc *m*; **~s** *npl* (*belongings*) affaires *fpl*; **the best ~ would be to** le mieux serait de; **how are ~s?** comment ça va?

think [θɪŋk] , *pt, pp* **thought** *vi* penser, réfléchir // *vt* penser, croire; (*imagine*) s'imaginer; **to ~ of** penser à; **what did you ~ of them?** qu'avez-vous pensé d'eux?; **I'll ~ about it** je vais y réfléchir; **to ~ of doing** avoir l'idée de faire; **I ~ so/not** je crois *or* pense que oui/non; **to ~ well of** avoir une haute opinion de; **to ~ over** *vt* bien réfléchir à; **to ~ up** *vt* inventer, trouver; **~ tank** *n* groupe *m* de réflexion.

third [θə:d] *num* troisième // *n* troisième *m/f*; (*fraction*) tiers *m*; (*Brit* SCOL: *degree*) ≈ licence *f* avec mention passable; **~ly** *ad* troisièmement; **~ party insurance** *n* (*Brit*) assurance *f* au tiers; **~-rate** *a* de qualité médiocre; **the T~ World** *n* le Tiers-Monde.

thirst [θə:st] *n* soif *f*; **~y** *a* (*person*) qui a soif, assoiffé(e).

thirteen ['θə:'tiːn] *num* treize.

thirty ['θə:tɪ] *num* trente.

this [ðɪs] ♦ *a* (*demonstrative: pl* these) ce, cet + *vowel or h mute, f* cette; **~ man/woman/book** cet homme/cette femme/ce livre; (*not 'that'*) cet homme-ci/cette femme-ci/ce livre-ci; **~ one** celui-ci(celle-ci)

♦ *pronoun* (*demonstrative: pl* these) ce; (*not 'that one'*) celui-ci(celle-ci), ceci; **who's ~?** qui est-ce?; **what's ~?** qu'est-ce que c'est?; **I prefer ~ to that** je préfère ceci à cela; **~ is what he said** voici ce qu'il a dit; **~ is Mr Brown** (*in introductions*) je vous présente Mr Brown; (*in photo*) c'est Mr Brown; (*on telephone*) ici Mr Brown

♦ *ad* (*demonstrative*): **it was about ~ big** c'était à peu près de cette grandeur *or* grand comme ça; **I didn't know it was ~ bad** je ne savais pas que c'était si *or* aussi mauvais.

thistle ['θɪsl] *n* chardon *m*.

thong [θɔŋ] *n* lanière *f*.

thorn [θɔ:n] *n* épine *f*.

thorough ['θʌrə] *a* (*search*) minutieux(euse); (*knowledge, research*) approfondi(e); (*work*) consciencieux(euse); (*cleaning*) à fond; **~bred** *n* (*horse*) pur-sang *m inv*; **~fare** *n* rue *f*; **'no ~fare'** 'passage interdit'; **~ly** *ad* minutieusement; en profondeur; à fond; **he ~ly agreed** il était tout à fait d'accord.

those [ðəuz] *pl pronoun* ceux-là(celles-là) // *pl a* ces; (*not 'these'*): **~ books** ces livres-là.

though [ðəu] *cj* bien que + *sub*, quoique

+ *sub* // *ad* pourtant.

thought [θɔ:t] *pt, pp of* **think** // *n* pensée *f*; (*opinion*) avis *m*; (*intention*) intention *f*; **~ful** *a* pensif(ive); réfléchi(e); (*considerate*) prévenant(e); **~less** *a* étourdi(e); qui manque de considération.

thousand ['θauzənd] *num* mille; **one ~** mille; **~s of** des milliers de; **~th** *num* millième.

thrash [θræʃ] *vt* rouer de coups; donner une correction à; (*defeat*) battre à plate couture; **to ~ about** *vi* se débattre; **to ~ out** *vt* débattre de.

thread [θrɛd] *n* fil *m*; (*of screw*) pas *m*, filetage *m* // *vt* (*needle*) enfiler; **~bare** *a* râpé(e), élimé(e).

threat [θrɛt] *n* menace *f*; **~en** *vi* (*storm*) menacer // *vt*: **to ~en sb with sth/to do** menacer qn de qch/de faire.

three [θri:] *num* trois; **~-dimensional** *a* à trois dimensions; (*film*) en relief; **~-piece suit** *n* complet *m* (avec gilet); **~-piece suite** *n* salon *m* comprenant un canapé et deux fauteuils assortis; **~-ply** *a* (*wood*) à trois épaisseurs; (*wool*) trois fils *inv*.

thresh [θrɛʃ] *vt* (*AGR*) battre.

threshold ['θrɛʃhəuld] *n* seuil *m*.

threw [θru:] *pt of* **throw**.

thrifty ['θrɪftɪ] *a* économe.

thrill [θrɪl] *n* frisson *m*, émotion *f* // *vi* tressaillir, frissonner // *vt* (*audience*) électriser; **to be ~ed** (*with gift etc*) être ravi; **~er** *n* film *m* (*or* roman *m* *or* pièce *f*) à suspense; **~ing** *a* saisissant(e), excitant(e).

thrive, *pt* **thrived, throve**, *pp* **thrived, thriven** [θraɪv, θrəuv, 'θrɪvn] *vi* pousser *or* se développer bien; (*business*) prospérer; **he ~s on it** cela lui réussit; **thriving** *a* vigoureux(euse); prospère.

throat [θrəut] *n* gorge *f*; **to have a sore ~** avoir mal à la gorge.

throb [θrɔb] *vi* (*heart*) palpiter; (*engine*) vibrer; (*with pcin*) lanciner; (*wound*) causer des élancements.

throes [θrəuz] *npl*: **in the ~ of** au beau milieu de; en proie à.

throne [θrəun] *n* trône *m*.

throng [θrɔŋ] *n* foule *f* // *vt* se presser dans.

throttle ['θrɔtl] *n* (*AUT*) accélérateur *m* // *vt* étrangler.

through [θru:] *prep* à travers; (*time*) pendant, durant; (*by means of*) par, par l'intermédiaire de; (*owing to*) à cause de // *a* (*ticket, train, passage*) direct(e) // *ad* à travers; **to put sb ~ to sb** (*TEL*) passer qn à qn; **to be ~** (*TEL*) avoir la communication; (*have finished*) avoir fini; **'no ~ way'** (*Brit*) 'impasse'; **~out** *prep* (*place*) partout dans; (*time*) durant tout(e) le(la) // *ad* partout.

throve [θrəuv] *pt of* **thrive**.

throw [θrəu] *n* jet *m*; (*SPORT*) lancer *m*

// *vt* (*pt* **threw**, *pp* **thrown** [θru:, θrəun]) lancer, jeter; (*SPORT*) lancer; (*rider*) désarçonner; (*fig*) décontenancer; (*pottery*) tourner; **to ~ a party** donner une réception; **to ~ away** *vt* jeter; **to ~ off** *vt* se débarrasser de; **to ~ out** *vt* jeter dehors; (*reject*) rejeter; **to ~ up** *vi* vomir; **~away** *a* à jeter; **~-in** *n* (*SPORT*) remise *f* en jeu.

thru [θru:] *prep, a, ad* (*US*) = **through**.

thrush [θrʌʃ] *n* grive *f*.

thrust [θrʌst] *n* (*TECH*) poussée *f* // *vt* (*pt, pp* **thrust**) pousser brusquement; (*push in*) enfoncer.

thud [θʌd] *n* bruit sourd.

thug [θʌg] *n* voyou *m*.

thumb [θʌm] *n* (*ANAT*) pouce *m* // *vt* (*book*) feuilleter; **to ~ a lift** faire de l'auto-stop, arrêter une voiture; **~tack** *n* (*US*) punaise *f* (*clou*).

thump [θʌmp] *n* grand coup; (*sound*) bruit sourd // *vt* cogner sur // *vi* cogner, frapper.

thunder ['θʌndə*] *n* tonnerre *m* // *vi* tonner; (*train etc*): **to ~ past** passer dans un grondement *or* un bruit de tonnerre; **~bolt** *n* foudre *f*; **~clap** *n* coup *m* de tonnerre; **~storm** *n* orage *m*; **~y** *a* orageux(euse).

Thursday ['θɜ:zdɪ] *n* jeudi *m*.

thus [ðʌs] *ad* ainsi.

thwart [θwɔ:t] *vt* contrecarrer.

thyme [taɪm] *n* thym *m*.

tiara [tɪ'ɑ:rə] *n* (*woman's*) diadème *m*.

tick [tɪk] *n* (*sound: of clock*) tic-tac *m*; (*mark*) coche *f*; (*ZOOL*) tique *f*; (*Brit col*): **in a ~** dans un instant // *vi* faire tic-tac // *vt* cocher; **to ~ off** *vt* cocher; (*person*) réprimander, attraper; **to ~ over** *vi* (*engine*) tourner au ralenti; (*fig*) aller *or* marcher doucettement.

ticket ['tɪkɪt] *n* billet *m*; (*for bus, tube*) ticket *m*; (*in shop: on goods*) étiquette *f*; (*: from cash register*) reçu *m*, ticket; (*for library*) carte *f*; **~ collector** *n* contrôleur/euse; **~ office** *n* guichet *m*, bureau *m* de vente des billets.

tickle ['tɪkl] *n* chatouillement *m* // *vt* chatouiller; (*fig*) plaire à; faire rire.

tidal ['taɪdl] *a* à marée; **~ wave** *n* raz-de-marée *m inv*.

tidbit ['tɪdbɪt] *n* (*US*) = **titbit**.

tiddlywinks ['tɪdlɪwɪŋks] *n* jeu *m* de puce.

tide [taɪd] *n* marée *f*; (*fig: of events*) cours *m* // *vt*: **to ~ sb over** dépanner qn; **high/low ~** marée haute/basse.

tidy ['taɪdɪ] *a* (*room*) bien rangé(e); (*dress, work*) net(nette), soigné(e); (*person*) ordonné(e), qui a le sens de l'ordre // *vt* (*also: ~ up*) ranger; **to ~ o.s. up** s'arranger.

tie [taɪ] *n* (*string etc*) cordon *m*; (*Brit: also: neck~*) cravate *f*; (*fig: link*) lien *m*; (*SPORT: draw*) égalité *f* de points;

match nul // vt (parcel) attacher; (ribbon) nouer // vi (SPORT) faire match nul; finir à égalité de points; **to ~ sth in a bow** faire un nœud à or avec qch; **to ~ a knot in sth** faire un nœud à qch; **to ~ down** vt attacher; (fig): **to ~ sb down to** contraindre qn à accepter; **to ~ up** vt (parcel) ficeler; (dog, boat) attacher; (arrangements) conclure; **to be ~d up** (busy) être pris or occupé.

tier [tɪə*] n gradin m; (of cake) étage m.

tiff [tɪf] n petite querelle.

tiger ['taɪgə*] n tigre m.

tight [taɪt] a (rope) tendu(e), raide; (clothes) étroit(e), très juste; (budget, programme, bend) serré(e); (control) strict(e), sévère; (col: drunk) ivre, rond(e) // ad (squeeze) très fort; (shut) à bloc, hermétiquement; **~s** npl (Brit) collant m; **~en** vt (rope) tendre; (screw) resserrer; (control) renforcer // vi se tendre, se resserrer; **~-fisted** a avare; **~ly** ad (grasp) bien, très fort; **~rope** n corde f raide.

tile [taɪl] n (on roof) tuile f; (on wall or floor) carreau m.

till [tɪl] n caisse (enregistreuse) // vt (land) cultiver // prep, cj = until.

tiller ['tɪlə*] n (NAUT) barre f (du gouvernail).

tilt [tɪlt] vt pencher, incliner // vi pencher, être incliné(e).

timber ['tɪmbə*] n (material) bois m de construction; (trees) arbres mpl.

time [taɪm] n temps m; (epoch: often pl) époque f, temps; (by clock) heure f; (moment) moment m; (occasion, also MATH) fois f; (MUS) mesure f // vt (race) chronométrer; (programme) minuter; (remark etc) choisir le moment de; **a long ~** un long moment, longtemps; **for the ~ being** pour le moment; **4 at a ~** 4 à la fois; **from ~ to ~** de temps en temps; **in ~** (soon enough) à temps; (after some time) avec le temps, à la longue; (MUS) en mesure; **in a week's ~** dans une semaine; **in no ~** en un rien de temps; **any ~** n'importe quand; **on ~** à l'heure; **5 ~s 5** 5 fois 5; **what ~ is it?** quelle heure est-il?; **to have a good ~** bien s'amuser; **~'s up!** c'est l'heure!; **~ bomb** n bombe f à retardement; **~ lag** n décalage m; (in travel) décalage horaire; **~less** a éternel(le); **~ly** a opportun(e); **~ off** n temps m libre; **~r** n (~ switch) minuteur m; (in kitchen) compte-minutes m inv; **~scale** n délais mpl; **~ switch** n (Brit) minuteur m; (for lighting) minuterie f; **~table** n (RAIL) (indicateur m) horaire m; (SCOL) emploi m du temps; **~ zone** n fuseau m horaire.

timid ['tɪmɪd] a timide; (easily scared) peureux(euse).

timing ['taɪmɪŋ] n minutage m; chronométrage m; **the ~ of his resignation** le moment choisi pour sa démission.

timpani ['tɪmpənɪ] npl timbales fpl.

tin [tɪn] n étain m; (also: ~ plate) fer-blanc m; (Brit: can) boîte f (de conserve); (for baking) moule m (à gâteau); **~foil** n papier m d'étain.

tinge [tɪndʒ] n nuance f // vt: **~d with** teinté(e) de.

tingle ['tɪŋgl] vi picoter.

tinker ['tɪŋkə*] n rétameur ambulant; (gipsy) romanichel m; **to ~ with** vt fus bricoler, rafistoler.

tinkle ['tɪŋkl] vi tinter.

tinned [tɪnd] a (Brit: food) en boîte, en conserve.

tin opener ['-əupnə*] n (Brit) ouvre-boîte(s) m.

tinsel ['tɪnsl] n guirlandes fpl de Noël (argentées).

tint [tɪnt] n teinte f; (for hair) shampooing colorant; **~ed** a (hair) teint(e); (spectacles, glass) teinté(e).

tiny ['taɪnɪ] a minuscule.

tip [tɪp] n (end) bout m; (protective: on umbrella etc) embout m; (gratuity) pourboire m; (for coal) terril m; (Brit: for rubbish) décharge f; (advice) tuyau m // vt (waiter) donner un pourboire à; (tilt) incliner; (overturn: also: ~ over) renverser; (empty: also: ~ out) déverser; **~-off** n (hint) tuyau m; **~ped** a (Brit: cigarette) (à bout) filtre inv.

tipsy ['tɪpsɪ] a un peu ivre, éméché(e).

tiptoe ['tɪptəu] n: **on ~** sur la pointe des pieds.

tiptop ['tɪp'tɔp] a: **in ~ condition** en excellent état.

tire ['taɪə*] n (US) = tyre // vt fatiguer // vi se fatiguer; **~d** a fatigué(e); **to be ~d of** en avoir assez de, être las(lasse) de; **~some** a ennuyeux(euse); **tiring** a fatigant(e).

tissue ['tɪʃuː] n tissu m; (paper handkerchief) mouchoir m en papier, kleenex m ®; **~ paper** n papier m de soie.

tit [tɪt] n (bird) mésange f; **to give ~ for tat** rendre coup pour coup.

titbit ['tɪtbɪt], (US) **tidbit** ['tɪdbɪt] n (food) friandise f; (news) potin m.

titivate ['tɪtɪveɪt] vt pomponner.

title ['taɪtl] n titre m; **~ deed** n (LAW) titre (constitutif) de propriété; **~ role** n rôle principal.

titter ['tɪtə*] vi rire (bêtement).

titular ['tɪtjulə*] a (in name only) nominal(e).

TM abbr of **trademark.**

to [tuː, tə] ♦ prep **1** (direction) à; **to go ~ France/Portugal/London/school** aller en France/au Portugal/à Londres/à l'école; **to go ~ Claude's/the doctor's** aller chez Claude/le docteur; **the road ~**

Edinburgh la route d'Édimbourg
2 (*as far as*) (jusqu')à; **to count ~ 10** compter jusqu'à 10; **from 40 ~ 50 people** de 40 à 50 personnes
3 (*with expressions of time*): **a quarter ~ 5** 5 heures moins le quart; **it's twenty ~ 3** il est 3 heures moins vingt
4 (*for, of*) de; **the key ~ the front door** la clé de la porte d'entrée; **a letter ~ his wife** une lettre (adressée) à sa femme
5 (*expressing indirect object*) à; **to give sth ~ sb** donner qch à qn; **to talk ~ sb** parler à qn
6 (*in relation to*) à; **3 goals ~ 2** 3 (buts) à 2; **30 miles ~ the gallon** ≈ 9,4 litres aux cent (km)
7 (*purpose, result*): **to come ~ sb's aid** venir au secours de qn, porter secours à qn; **to sentence sb ~ death** condamner qn à mort; **~ my surprise** à ma grande surprise
♦ **with vb 1** (*simple infinitive*): **~ go/eat** aller/manger
2 (*following another vb*): **to want/try/ start ~ do** vouloir/essayer de/ commencer à faire; *see also relevant verb*
3 (*with vb omitted*): **I don't want ~** je ne veux pas
4 (*purpose, result*) pour; **I did it ~ help you** je l'ai fait pour vous aider
5 (*equivalent to relative clause*): **I have things ~ do** j'ai des choses à faire; **the main thing is ~ try** l'important est d'essayer
6 (*after adjective etc*): **ready ~ go** prêt(e) à partir; **too old/young ~ ...** trop vieux/jeune pour ...; *see also relevant adjective etc*
♦ *ad*: **push/pull the door ~** tirez/poussez la porte.
toad [təud] *n* crapaud *m*; **~stool** *n* champignon (vénéneux).
toast [təust] *n* (*CULIN*) pain grillé, toast *m*; (*drink, speech*) toast *m* // *vt* (*CULIN*) faire griller; (*drink to*) porter un toast à; **a piece** *or* **slice of ~** un toast; **~er** *n* grille-pain *m inv*.
tobacco [tə'bækəu] *n* tabac *m*; **~nist** *n* marchand(e) de tabac; **~nist's (shop)** *n* (bureau *m* de) tabac *m*.
toboggan [tə'bɔgən] *n* toboggan *m*; (*child's*) luge *f*.
today [tə'deɪ] *ad, n* (*also fig*) aujourd'hui *m*.
toddler ['tɔdlə*] *n* enfant *m/f* qui commence à marcher, bambin *m*.
toddy ['tɔdɪ] *n* grog *m*.
to-do [tə'du:] *n* (*fuss*) histoire *f*, affaire *f*.
toe [təu] *n* doigt *m* de pied, orteil *m*; (*of shoe*) bout *m*; **to ~ the line** (*fig*) obéir, se conformer.
toffee ['tɔfɪ] *n* caramel *m*.
toga ['təugə] *n* toge *f*.

together [tə'gɛðə*] *ad* ensemble; (*at same time*) en même temps; **~ with** *prep* avec.
toil [tɔɪl] *n* dur travail, labeur *m*.
toilet ['tɔɪlət] *n* (*Brit: lavatory*) toilettes *fpl*, cabinets *mpl* // *cpd* (*bag, soap etc*) de toilette; **~ bowl** *n* cuvette *f* des w.-c.; **~ paper** *n* papier *m* hygiénique; **~ries** *npl* articles *mpl* de toilette; **~ roll** *n* rouleau *m* de papier hygiénique; **~ water** *n* eau *f* de toilette.
token ['təukən] *n* (*sign*) marque *f*, témoignage *m*; (*voucher*) bon *m*, coupon *m*; **book/record ~** *n* (*Brit*) chèque-livre/-disque *m*.
told [təuld] *pt, pp of* **tell**.
tolerable ['tɔlərəbl] *a* (*bearable*) tolérable; (*fairly good*) passable.
tolerant ['tɔlərnt] *a*: **~ (of)** tolérant(e) (à l'égard de).
tolerate ['tɔləreɪt] *vt* supporter; (*MED, TECH*) tolérer.
toll [təul] *n* (*tax, charge*) péage *m* // *vi* (*bell*) sonner; **the accident ~ on the roads** le nombre des victimes de la route.
tomato, ~es [tə'mɑ:təu] *n* tomate *f*.
tomb [tu:m] *n* tombe *f*.
tomboy ['tɔmbɔɪ] *n* garçon manqué.
tombstone ['tu:mstəun] *n* pierre tombale.
tomcat ['tɔmkæt] *n* matou *m*.
tomorrow [tə'mɔrəu] *ad, n* (*also fig*) demain (*m*); **the day after ~** après-demain; **a week ~** demain en huit; **~ morning** demain matin.
ton [tʌn] *n* tonne *f* (*Brit* = 1016 kg; *US* = 907 kg; *metric* = 1000 kg); (*NAUT: also*: **register ~**) tonneau *m* (= 2.83 *cu.m*); **~s of** (*col*) des tas de.
tone [təun] *n* ton *m*; (*of radio*) tonalité *f* // *vi* s'harmoniser; **to ~ down** *vt* (*colour, criticism*) adoucir; (*sound*) baisser; **to ~ up** *vt* (*muscles*) tonifier; **~-deaf** *a* qui n'a pas d'oreille.
tongs [tɔŋz] *npl* pinces *fpl*; (*for coal*) pincettes *fpl*; (*for hair*) fer *m* à friser.
tongue [tʌŋ] *n* langue *f*; **~ in cheek** *ad* ironiquement; **~-tied** *a* (*fig*) muet(te); **~-twister** *n* phrase *f* très difficile à prononcer.
tonic ['tɔnɪk] *n* (*MED*) tonique *m*; (*also*: **~ water**) tonic *m*.
tonight [tə'naɪt] *ad, n* cette nuit; (*this evening*) ce soir.
tonsil ['tɔnsl] *n* amygdale *f*; **~litis** [-'laɪtɪs] *n* amygdalite *f*.
too [tu:] *ad* (*excessively*) trop; (*also*) aussi; **~ much** *ad* trop // *a* trop de; **~ many** *a* trop de; **~ bad!** tant pis!
took [tuk] *pt of* **take**.
tool [tu:l] *n* outil *m* // *vt* travailler, ouvrager; **~ box** *n* boîte *f* à outils.
toot [tu:t] *vi* siffler; (*with car-horn*) klaxonner.

tooth [tu:θ], pl **teeth** n (ANAT TECH), dent f; **~ache** n mal m de dents; **~brush** n brosse f à dents; **~paste** n (pâte f) dentifrice m; **~pick** n cure-dent m.

top [tɔp] n (of mountain, head) sommet m; (of page, ladder) haut m; (of box, cupboard, table) dessus m; (lid: of box, jar) couvercle m; (: of bottle) bouchon m; (toy) toupie f // a du haut; (in rank) premier(ère); (best) meilleur(e) // vt (exceed) dépasser; (be first in) être en tête de; **on ~** of sur; (in addition to) en plus de; **from ~ to bottom** de fond en comble; **to ~ up**, (US) **to ~ off** vt remplir; **~ floor** n dernier étage; **~ hat** n haut-de-forme m; **~-heavy** a (object) trop lourd(e) du haut.

topic ['tɔpɪk] n sujet m, thème m; **~al** a d'actualité.

top: ~less a (bather etc) aux seins nus; **~-level** a (talks) à l'échelon le plus élevé.

topple ['tɔpl] vt renverser, faire tomber // vi basculer; tomber.

top-secret ['tɔp'si:krɪt] a ultra-secret(ète).

topsy-turvy ['tɔpsi'tə:vi] a, ad sens dessus-dessous.

torch [tɔ:tʃ] n torche f; (Brit: electric) lampe f de poche.

tore [tɔ:*] pt of **tear**.

torment n ['tɔ:mɛnt] tourment m // vt [tɔ:'mɛnt] tourmenter; (fig: annoy) agacer.

torn [tɔ:n] pp of **tear**.

tornado, **~es** [tɔ:'neɪdəu] n tornade f.

torpedo, **~es** [tɔ:'pi:dəu] n torpille f.

torrent ['tɔrnt] n torrent m.

tortoise ['tɔ:təs] n tortue f; **~shell** ['tɔ:təʃɛl] a en écaille.

torture ['tɔ:tʃə*] n torture f // vt torturer.

Tory ['tɔ:ri] (Brit POL) a tory (pl tories), conservateur(trice) // n tory m/f, conservateur/trice.

toss [tɔs] vt lancer, jeter; (pancake) faire sauter; (head) rejeter en arrière; **to ~ a coin** jouer à pile ou face; **to ~ up for sth** jouer qch à pile ou face; **to ~ and turn** (in bed) se tourner et se retourner.

tot [tɔt] n (Brit: drink) petit verre; (child) bambin m.

total ['təutl] a total(e) // n total m // vt (add up) faire le total de, totaliser; (amount to) s'élever à.

totally ['təutəli] ad totalement.

totter ['tɔtə*] vi chanceler.

touch [tʌtʃ] n contact m, toucher m; (sense, also skill: of pianist etc) toucher; (fig: note, also FOOTBALL) touche f // vt (gen) toucher; (tamper with) toucher à; **a ~ of** (fig) un petit peu de; une touche de; **in ~ with** en contact or rapport avec; **to get in ~ with** prendre contact

avec; **to lose ~** (friends) se perdre de vue; **to ~ on** vt fus (topic) effleurer, toucher; **to ~ up** vt (paint) retoucher; **~-and-go** a incertain(e); **~down** n atterrissage m; (on sea) amerrissage m; (US FOOTBALL) but m; **~ed** a touché(e); (col) cinglé(e); **~ing** a touchant(e), attendrissant(e); **~line** n (SPORT) (ligne f de) touche f; **~y** a (person) susceptible.

tough [tʌf] a dur(e); (resistant) résistant(e), solide; (meat) dur(e), coriace.

toupee ['tu:pei] n postiche m.

tour ['tuə*] n voyage m; (also: package ~) voyage organisé; (of town, museum) tour m, visite f; (by artist) tournée f // vt visiter; **~ing** n voyages mpl touristiques, tourisme m.

tourism ['tuərizm] n tourisme m.

tourist ['tuərist] n touriste m/f // ad (travel) en classe touriste // cpd touristique; **~ office** n syndicat m d'initiative.

tournament ['tuənəmənt] n tournoi m.

tousled ['tauzld] a (hair) ébouriffé(e).

tout [taut] vi: **to ~ for** essayer de raccrocher, racoler // n (also: ticket ~) revendeur m de billets.

tow [təu] vt remorquer; **'on ~'**, (US) **'in ~'** (AUT) 'véhicule en remorque'.

toward(s) [tə'wɔ:d(z)] prep vers; (of attitude) envers, à l'égard de; (of purpose) pour.

towel ['tauəl] n serviette f (de toilette); (also: tea ~) torchon m; **~ling** n (fabric) tissu-éponge m; **~ rail**, (US) **~ rack** n porte-serviettes m inv.

tower ['tauə*] n tour f; **~ block** n (Brit) tour f (d'habitation); **~ing** a très haut(e), imposant(e).

town [taun] n ville f; **to go to ~** aller en ville; (fig) y mettre le paquet; **~ centre** n centre m de la ville, centre-ville m; **~ clerk** n ≈ secrétaire m/f de mairie; **~ council** n conseil municipal; **~ hall** n ≈ mairie f; **~ plan** n plan m de ville; **~ planning** n urbanisme m.

towrope ['təurəup] n (câble m de) remorque f.

tow truck n (US) dépanneuse f.

toy [tɔi] n jouet m; **to ~ with** vt fus jouer avec; (idea) caresser.

trace [treis] n trace f // vt (draw) tracer, dessiner; (follow) suivre la trace de; (locate) retrouver; **tracing paper** n papier-calque m.

track [træk] n (mark) trace f; (path: gen) chemin m, piste f; (: of bullet etc) trajectoire f; (: of suspect, animal) piste; (RAIL) voie ferrée, rails mpl; (on tape, SPORT) (on record) plage f // vt suivre la trace or la piste de; **to keep ~ of** suivre; **to ~ down** vt (prey) trouver et capturer; (sth lost) finir par retrouver; **~suit** n survêtement m.

tract [trækt] n (GEO) étendue f, zone f; (pamphlet) tract m.

tractor ['træktə*] n tracteur m.

trade [treɪd] n commerce m; (skill, job) métier m // vi faire du commerce; **to ~ with/in** faire du commerce avec/le commerce de; **to ~ in** vt (old car etc) faire reprendre; **~ fair** n foire (-exposition) commerciale; **~-in price** n prix m à la reprise; **~mark** n marque f de fabrique; **~name** n marque déposée; **~r** n commerçant/e, négociant/e; **~sman** n (shopkeeper) commerçant; **~ union** n syndicat m; **~ unionist** n syndicaliste m/f; **trading** n affaires fpl, commerce m; **trading estate** n (Brit) zone industrielle.

tradition [trə'dɪʃən] n tradition f; **~al** a traditionnel(le).

traffic ['træfɪk] n trafic m; (cars) circulation f // vi: **to ~ in** (pej: liquor, drugs) faire le trafic de; **~ circle** n (US) rond-point m; **~ jam** n embouteillage m; **~ lights** npl feux mpl (de signalisation); **~ warden** n contractuel/le.

tragedy ['trædʒədɪ] n tragédie f.

tragic ['trædʒɪk] a tragique.

trail [treɪl] n (tracks) trace f, piste f; (path) chemin m, piste; (of smoke etc) traînée f // vt traîner, tirer; (follow) suivre // vi traîner; **to ~ behind** vi traîner, être à la traîne; **~er** n (AUT) remorque f; (US) caravane f; (CINEMA) bande-annonce f; **~er truck** n (US) (camion m) semi-remorque m.

train [treɪn] n train m; (in underground) rame f; (of dress) traîne f // vt (apprentice, doctor etc) former; (sportsman) entraîner; (dog) dresser; (memory) exercer; (point: gun etc): **to ~ sth on** braquer qch sur // vi recevoir sa formation; s'entraîner; **one's ~ of thought** le fil de sa pensée; **~ed a** qualifié(e), qui a reçu une formation; dressé(e); **~ee** [treɪ'niː] n stagiaire m/f; (in trade) apprenti/e; **~er** n (SPORT) entraîneur/euse; (of dogs etc) dresseur/euse; **~ing** n formation f; entraînement m; dressage m; **in ~ing** (SPORT) à l'entraînement; (fit) en forme; **~ing college** n école professionnelle; (for teachers) ≈ école normale; **~ing shoes** npl chaussures fpl de sport.

traipse [treɪps] vi (se) traîner, déambuler.

trait [treɪt] n trait m (de caractère).

traitor ['treɪtə*] n traître m.

tram [træm] n (Brit: also: **~car**) tram(way) m.

tramp [træmp] n (person) vagabond/e, clochard/e; (col: pej: woman): **to be a ~** être coureuse // vi marcher d'un pas lourd // vt (walk through: town, streets) parcourir à pied.

trample ['træmpl] vt: **to ~ (underfoot)** piétiner; (fig) bafouer.

trampoline ['træmpəliːn] n trampolino m.

tranquil ['træŋkwɪl] a tranquille; **~lizer** n (MED) tranquillisant m.

transact [træn'zækt] vt (business) traiter; **~ion** [-'zækʃən] n transaction f; **~ions** npl (minutes) actes mpl.

transatlantic ['trænzət'læntɪk] a transatlantique.

transfer n ['trænsfə*] (gen, also SPORT) transfert m; (POL: of power) passation f; (picture, design) décalcomanie f; (: stick-on) autocollant m // vt [træns'fə:*] transférer; passer; décalquer.

transform [træns'fɔ:m] vt transformer.

transfusion [træns'fju:ʒən] n transfusion f.

transient ['trænzɪənt] a transitoire, éphémère.

transistor [træn'zɪstə*] n (ELEC; also: **~ radio**) transistor m.

transit ['trænzɪt] n: **in ~** en transit.

transitive ['trænzɪtɪv] a (LING) transitif(ive).

translate [trænz'leɪt] vt traduire; **translation** [-'leɪʃən] n traduction f; (SCOL: as opposed to prose) version f; **translator** n traducteur/trice.

transmission [trænz'mɪʃən] n transmission f.

transmit [trænz'mɪt] vt transmettre; (RADIO, TV) émettre; **~ter** n émetteur m.

transparency [træns'pɛərnsɪ] n (Brit PHOT) diapositive f.

transparent [træns'pærnt] a transparent(e).

transpire [træn'spaɪə*] vi (turn out): **it ~d that ...** on a appris que ...; (happen) arriver.

transplant vt [træns'plɑ:nt] transplanter; (seedlings) repiquer // n ['trænsplɑ:nt] (MED) transplantation f.

transport n ['trænspɔ:t] transport m // vt [træns'pɔ:t] transporter; **~ation** [-'teɪʃən] n (moyen m de) transport m; (of prisoners) transportation f; **~ café** n (Brit) ≈ restaurant m de routiers.

trap [træp] n (snare, trick) piège m; (carriage) cabriolet m // vt prendre au piège; (immobilize) bloquer; (jam) coincer; **~ door** n trappe f.

trapeze [trə'pi:z] n trapèze m.

trappings ['træpɪŋz] npl ornements mpl; attributs mpl.

trash [træʃ] n (pej: goods) camelote f; (: nonsense) sottises fpl; **~ can** n (US) boîte f à ordures.

trauma ['trɔ:mə] n traumatisme m; **~tic** [-'mætɪk] a traumatisant(e).

travel ['trævl] n voyage(s) m(pl) // vi voyager; (move) aller, se déplacer // vt (distance) parcourir; **~ agency** n agence f de voyages; ~ **agent** n agent m de voyages; ~**ler**, (US) ~**er** n voyageur/euse; ~**ler's cheque** n chèque m de voyage; ~**ling**, (US) ~**ing** n voyage(s) m(pl) // cpd (bag, clock) de voyage; (expenses) de déplacement; ~ **sickness** n mal m de la route (or de mer or de l'air).

travesty ['trævəstɪ] n parodie f.

trawler ['trɔːlə*] n chalutier m.

tray [treɪ] n (for carrying) plateau m; (on desk) corbeille f.

treachery ['tretʃərɪ] n traîtrise f.

treacle ['triːkl] n mélasse f.

tread [trɛd] n pas m; (sound) bruit m de pas; (of tyre) chape f, bande f de roulement // vi (pt trod, pp trodden) marcher; **to ~ on** vt fus marcher sur.

treason ['triːzn] n trahison f.

treasure ['trɛʒə*] n trésor m // vt (value) tenir beaucoup à; (store) conserver précieusement.

treasurer ['trɛʒərə*] n trésorier/ère.

treasury ['trɛʒərɪ] n trésorerie f; **the T~**, (US) **the T~ Department** le ministère des Finances.

treat [triːt] n petit cadeau, petite surprise // vt traiter; **to ~ sb to sth** offrir qch à qn.

treatise ['triːtɪz] n traité m (ouvrage).

treatment ['triːtmənt] n traitement m.

treaty ['triːtɪ] n traité m.

treble ['trɛbl] a triple // vt, vi tripler; ~ **clef** n clé f de sol.

tree [triː] n arbre m.

trek [trɛk] n voyage m; randonnée f; (tiring walk) tirée f // vi (as holiday) faire de la randonnée.

tremble ['trɛmbl] vi trembler.

tremendous [trɪ'mɛndəs] a (enormous) énorme, fantastique; (excellent) formidable.

tremor ['trɛmə*] n tremblement m; (also: earth ~) secousse f sismique.

trench [trɛntʃ] n tranchée f.

trend [trɛnd] n (tendency) tendance f; (of events) cours m; (fashion) mode f; ~**y** a (idea) dans le vent; (clothes) dernier cri inv.

trepidation [trɛpɪ'deɪʃən] n vive agitation.

trespass ['trɛspəs] vi: **to ~ on** s'introduire sans permission dans; (fig) empiéter sur; **'no ~ing'** 'propriété privée', 'défense d'entrer'.

tress [trɛs] n boucle f de cheveux.

trestle ['trɛsl] n tréteau m; ~ **table** n table f à tréteaux.

trial ['traɪəl] n (LAW) procès m, jugement m; (test: of machine etc) essai m; (hardship) épreuve f; (worry) souci m; **by ~ and error** par tâtonnements.

triangle ['traɪæŋgl] n (MATH, MUS) triangle m.

tribe [traɪb] n tribu f.

tribunal [traɪ'bjuːnl] n tribunal m.

tributary ['trɪbjʊtərɪ] n (river) affluent m.

tribute ['trɪbjuːt] n tribut m, hommage m; **to pay ~ to** rendre hommage à.

trice [traɪs] n: **in a ~** en un clin d'œil.

trick [trɪk] n ruse f; (clever act) astuce f; (joke) tour m; (CARDS) levée f // vt attraper, rouler; **to play a ~ on sb** jouer un tour à qn; **that should do the ~** ça devrait faire l'affaire; ~**ery** n ruse f.

trickle ['trɪkl] n (of water etc) filet m // vi couler en un filet or goutte à goutte.

tricky ['trɪkɪ] a difficile, délicat(e).

tricycle ['traɪsɪkl] n tricycle m.

trifle ['traɪfl] n bagatelle f; (CULIN) ≈ diplomate m // ad: **a ~ long** un peu long; **trifling** a insignifiant(e).

trigger ['trɪgə*] n (of gun) gâchette f; **to ~ off** vt déclencher.

trim [trɪm] a net(te); (house, garden) bien tenu(e); (figure) svelte // n (haircut etc) légère coupe; (embellishment) finitions fpl; (on car) garnitures fpl // vt couper légèrement; (decorate): **to ~ (with)** décorer (de); (NAUT: a sail) gréer; ~**mings** npl décorations fpl; (extras: gen CULIN) garniture f.

trinket ['trɪŋkɪt] n bibelot m; (piece of jewellery) colifichet m.

trip [trɪp] n voyage m; (excursion) excursion f; (stumble) faux pas // vi (stumble) faire un faux pas, trébucher; (go lightly) marcher d'un pas léger; **on a ~** en voyage; **to ~ up** vi trébucher // vt faire un croc-en-jambe à.

tripe [traɪp] n (CULIN) tripes fpl; (pej: rubbish) idioties fpl.

triple ['trɪpl] a triple.

triplets ['trɪplɪts] npl triplés/ées.

tripod ['traɪpɔd] n trépied m.

trite [traɪt] a banal(e).

triumph ['traɪʌmf] n triomphe m // vi: **to ~ (over)** triompher (de).

trivia ['trɪvɪə] npl futilités fpl.

trivial ['trɪvɪəl] a insignifiant(e); (commonplace) banal(e).

trod [trɔd] pt of **tread**; ~**den** pp of **tread**.

trolley ['trɔlɪ] n chariot m.

trombone [trɔm'bəʊn] n trombone m.

troop [truːp] n bande f, groupe m; ~**s** npl (MIL) troupes fpl; (: men) hommes mpl, soldats mpl; **to ~ in/out** vi entrer/sortir en groupe; ~**er** n (MIL) soldat m de cavalerie; ~**ing the colour** n (ceremony) le salut au drapeau.

trophy ['trəʊfɪ] n trophée m.

tropic ['trɔpɪk] n tropique m; ~**al** a tropical(e).

trot [trɔt] n trot m // vi trotter; **on the ~** (Brit fig) d'affilée.

trouble ['trʌbl] n difficulté(s) f(pl), problème(s) m(pl); (worry) ennuis mpl, soucis mpl; (bother, effort) peine f;

(POL) conflits mpl, troubles mpl; (MED):
stomach etc ~ troubles gastriques // vt
déranger, gêner; (worry) inquiéter //
vi: to ~ to do prendre la peine de faire;
~s npl (POL etc) troubles mpl; to be in
~ avoir des ennuis; (ship, climber etc)
être en difficulté; it's no ~! je vous en
prie!; what's the ~? qu'est-ce qui ne va
pas?; ~d a (person) inquiet(ète);
(epoch, life) agité(e); ~maker n
élément perturbateur, fauteur m de troubles; ~shooter n (in conflict) concilia-
teur m; ~some a ennuyeux(euse),
gênant(e).

trough [trɔf] n (also: drinking ~)
abreuvoir m; (also: feeding ~) auge f;
(channel) chenal m.

trousers ['trauzəz] npl pantalon m;
short ~ culottes courtes.

trout [traut] n (pl inv) truite f.

trowel ['trauəl] n truelle f.

truant ['truənt] n: to play ~ (Brit) faire
l'école buissonnière.

truce [tru:s] n trêve f.

truck [trʌk] n camion m; (RAIL) wagon
m à plate-forme; (for luggage) chariot
m (à bagages); ~ driver n camionneur
m; ~ farm n (US) jardin maraîcher.

truculent ['trʌkjulənt] a agressif(ive).

trudge [trʌdʒ] vi marcher lourdement,
se traîner.

true [tru:] a vrai(e); (accurate)
exact(e); (genuine) vrai, véritable;
(faithful) fidèle.

truffle ['trʌfl] n truffe f.

truly ['tru:lı] ad vraiment, réellement;
(truthfully) sans mentir; (faithfully)
fidèlement.

trump [trʌmp] n atout m; ~ed-up a
inventé(e) (de toutes pièces).

trumpet ['trʌmpıt] n trompette f.

truncheon ['trʌntʃən] n bâton m
(d'agent de police); matraque f.

trundle ['trʌndl] vt, vi: to ~ along rouler
bruyamment.

trunk [trʌŋk] n (of tree, person) tronc
m; (of elephant) trompe f; (case) malle
f; (US AUT) coffre m; ~s npl (also:
swimming ~s) maillot m or slip m de
bain.

truss [trʌs] n (MED) bandage m
herniaire; to ~ (up) vt (CULIN) brider.

trust [trʌst] n confiance f; (LAW)
fidéicommis m; (COMM) trust m // vt
(rely on) avoir confiance en; (entrust):
to ~ sth to sb confier qch à qn; ~ed a
en qui l'on a confiance; ~ee [trʌs'ti:] n
(LAW) fidéicommissaire m/f; (of school
etc) administrateur/trice; ~ful, ~ing a
confiant(e); ~worthy a digne de
confiance.

truth, ~s [tru:θ, tru:ðz] n vérité f; ~ful
a (person) qui dit la vérité; (description) exact(e), vrai(e).

try [traı] n essai m, tentative f; (RUGBY)

essai // vt (LAW) juger; (test: sth new)
essayer, tester; (strain) éprouver // vi
essayer; to ~ to do essayer de faire;
(seek) chercher à faire; to ~ on vt
(clothes) essayer; to ~ out vt essayer,
mettre à l'essai; ~ing a pénible.

T-shirt ['ti:ʃə:t] n tee-shirt m.

T-square ['ti:skwɛə*] n équerre f en T.

tub [tʌb] n cuve f; baquet m; (bath) baignoire f.

tuba ['tju:bə] n tuba m.

tubby ['tʌbı] a rondelet(te).

tube [tju:b] n tube m; (Brit: underground) métro m; (for tyre) chambre f
à air.

tubing ['tju:bıŋ] n tubes mpl; a piece of
~ un tube.

TUC n abbr (Brit: = Trades Union
Congress) confédération f des syndicats
britanniques.

tuck [tʌk] n (SEWING) pli m, rempli m //
vt (put) mettre; to ~ away vt cacher,
ranger; to ~ in vt rentrer; (child)
border // vi (eat) manger de bon appétit;
attaquer le repas; to ~ up vt (child)
border; ~ shop n boutique f à
provisions (dans une école).

Tuesday ['tju:zdı] n mardi m.

tuft [tʌft] n touffe f.

tug [tʌg] n (ship) remorqueur m // vt
tirer (sur); ~-of-war n lutte f à la
corde.

tuition [tju:'ıʃən] n (Brit) leçons fpl; (:
private ~) cours particuliers; (US:
school fees) frais mpl de scolarité.

tulip ['tju:lıp] n tulipe f.

tumble ['tʌmbl] n (fall) chute f, culbute
f // vi tomber, dégringoler; (with
somersault) faire une or des culbute(s);
to ~ to sth (col) réaliser qch; ~down a
délabré(e); ~ dryer n (Brit) séchoir m
(à linge) à air chaud.

tumbler ['tʌmblə*] n verre (droit),
gobelet m.

tummy ['tʌmı] n (col) ventre m.

tumour ['tju:mə*], (US) **tumor**
['tu:mə*] n tumeur f.

tuna ['tju:nə] n (pl inv) (also: ~ fish)
thon m.

tune [tju:n] n (melody) air m // vt (MUS)
accorder; (RADIO, TV, AUT) régler, mettre au point; to be in/out of ~ (instrument) être accordé/désaccordé;
(singer) chanter juste/faux; to ~ in
(to) (RADIO, TV) se mettre à l'écoute
(de); to ~ up vi (musician) accorder
son instrument; ~ful a mélodieux(euse).

tunic ['tju:nık] n tunique f.

tuning ['tju:nıŋ] n réglage m; ~ fork n
diapason m.

Tunisia [tju:'nızıə] n Tunisie f.

tunnel ['tʌnl] n tunnel m; (in mine)
galerie f.

turbulence ['tə:bjuləns] n (AVIAT)
turbulence f.

tureen [tə'ri:n] n soupière f.

turf [tə:f] n gazon m; (clod) motte f (de gazon) // vt gazonner; **to ~ out** vt (col) jeter; jeter dehors.

turgid ['tə:dʒɪd] a (speech) pompeux(euse).

Turk [tə:k] n Turc/Turque.

Turkey ['tə:kɪ] n Turquie f.

turkey ['tə:kɪ] n dindon m, dinde f.

Turkish ['tə:kɪʃ] a turc(turque) // n (LING) turc m.

turmoil ['tə:mɔɪl] n trouble m, bouleversement m.

turn [tə:n] n tour m; (in road) tournant m; (tendency: of mind, events) tournure f; (performance) numéro m; (MED) crise f, attaque f // vt tourner; (collar, steak) retourner; (milk) faire tourner; (change): **to ~ sth into** changer qch en // vi tourner; (person: look back) se (re)tourner; (reverse direction) faire demi-tour; (change) changer; (become) devenir; **to ~ into** se changer en; **a good ~** un service; **it gave me quite a ~** ça m'a fait un coup; **'no left ~'** (AUT) 'défense de tourner à gauche'; **it's your ~** c'est (à) votre tour; **in ~** à son tour; **à tour de rôle**; **to take ~s** se relayer; **to take ~s at** faire à tour de rôle; **to ~ away** vi se détourner, tourner la tête; **to ~ back** vi revenir, faire demi-tour; **to ~ down** vt (refuse) rejeter, refuser; (reduce) baisser; (fold) rabattre; **to ~ in** vi (col: go to bed) aller se coucher // vt (fold) rentrer; **to ~ off** vi (from road) tourner // vt (light, radio etc) éteindre; (engine) arrêter; **to ~ on** vt (light, radio etc) allumer; (engine) mettre en marche; **to ~ out** vt (light, gas) éteindre // vi: **to ~ out to be ...** s'avérer ..., se révéler ...; **to ~ over** vi (person) se retourner // vt (object) retourner; (page) tourner; **to ~ round** vi faire demi-tour; (rotate) tourner; **to ~ up** vi (person) arriver, se pointer; (lost object) être retrouvé(e) // vt (collar) remonter; (increase: sound, volume etc) mettre plus fort; **~ing** n (in road) tournant m; **~ing point** n (fig) tournant m, moment décisif.

turnip ['tə:nɪp] n navet m.

turnout ['tə:naut] n (nombre m de personnes dans l')assistance f.

turnover ['tə:nəuvə*] n (COMM: amount of money) chiffre m d'affaires; (: of goods) roulement m; (CULIN) sorte de chausson.

turnpike ['tə:npaɪk] n (US) autoroute f à péage.

turnstile ['tə:nstaɪl] n tourniquet m (d'entrée).

turntable ['tə:nteɪbl] n (on record player) platine f.

turn-up ['tə:nʌp] n (Brit: on trousers) revers m.

turpentine ['tə:pəntaɪn] n (also: **turps**) (essence f de) térébenthine f.

turquoise ['tə:kwɔɪz] n (stone) turquoise f // a turquoise inv.

turret ['tʌrɪt] n tourelle f.

turtle ['tə:tl] n tortue marine; **~neck (sweater)** n pullover m à col montant.

tusk [tʌsk] n défense f.

tussle ['tʌsl] n bagarre f, mêlée f.

tutor ['tju:tə*] n (in college) directeur/trice d'études; (private teacher) précepteur/trice; **~ial** [-'tɔ:rɪəl] n (SCOL) (séance f de) travaux mpl pratiques.

tuxedo [tʌk'si:dəu] n (US) smoking m.

TV [ti:'vi:] n abbr (= television) télé f.

twang [twæŋ] n (of instrument) son vibrant; (of voice) ton nasillard.

tweed [twi:d] n tweed m.

tweezers ['twi:zəz] npl pince f à épiler.

twelfth [twelfθ] num douzième.

twelve [twelv] num douze; **at ~ (o'clock)** à midi; (midnight) à minuit.

twentieth ['twentɪθ] num vingtième.

twenty ['twentɪ] num vingt.

twice [twaɪs] ad deux fois; **~ as much** deux fois plus.

twiddle ['twɪdl] vt, vi: **to ~ (with) sth** tripoter qch; **to ~ one's thumbs** (fig) se tourner les pouces.

twig [twɪg] n brindille f // vt, vi (col) piger.

twilight ['twaɪlaɪt] n crépuscule m.

twin [twɪn] a, n jumeau(elle) // vt jumeler; **~(-bedded) room** n chambre f à deux lits.

twine [twaɪn] n ficelle f // vi (plant) s'enrouler.

twinge [twɪndʒ] n (of pain) élancement m; (of conscience) remords m.

twinkle ['twɪŋkl] vi scintiller; (eyes) pétiller.

twirl [twə:l] vt faire tournoyer // vi tournoyer.

twist [twɪst] n torsion f, tour m; (in wire, flex) tortillon m; (in story) coup m de théâtre // vt tordre; (weave) entortiller; (roll around) enrouler; (fig) déformer // vi s'entortiller; s'enrouler; (road) serpenter.

twit [twɪt] n (col) crétin/e.

twitch [twɪtʃ] vi se convulser; avoir un tic.

two [tu:] num deux; **to put ~ and ~ together** (fig) faire le rapport; **~-door** a (AUT) à deux portes; **~-faced** a (pej: person) faux(fausse); **~fold** ad: **to increase ~fold** doubler; **~-piece (suit)** n (costume m) deux-pièces m inv; **~-piece (swimsuit)** n (maillot m de bain) deux-pièces m inv; **~-seater** n (plane) (avion m) biplace m; (car) voiture f à deux places; **~some** n (people) couple m; **~-way** a (traffic) dans les deux sens.

tycoon [taɪˈkuːn] *n*: (*business*) ~ gros homme d'affaires.

type [taɪp] *n* (*category*) genre *m*, espèce *f*; (*model*) modèle *m*; (*example*) type *m*; (*TYP*) type, caractère *m* // *vt* (*letter etc*) taper (à la machine); **~-cast** *a* (*actor*) condamné(e) à toujours jouer le même rôle; **~face** *n* (*TYP*) police *f* (de caractères); **~script** *n* texte dactylographié; **~writer** *n* machine *f* à écrire; **~written** *a* dactylographié(e).

typhoid ['taɪfɔɪd] *n* typhoïde *f*.

typical ['tɪpɪkl] *a* typique, caractéristique.

typing ['taɪpɪŋ] *n* dactylo(graphie) *f*.

typist ['taɪpɪst] *n* dactylo *m/f*.

tyrant ['taɪərnt] *n* tyran *m*.

tyre, (*US*) **tire** ['taɪə*] *n* pneu *m*; ~ **pressure** *n* pression *f* (de gonflage).

U

U-bend ['juːˈbɛnd] *n* (*AUT*, *in pipe*) coude *m*.

udder ['ʌdə*] *n* pis *m*, mamelle *f*.

UFO ['juːfəu] *n abbr* (= *unidentified flying object*) ovni *m*.

Uganda [juːˈgændə] *n* Ouganda *m*.

ugh [əːh] *excl* pouah!

ugly ['ʌglɪ] *a* laid(e), vilain(e); (*fig*) répugnant(e).

UK *n abbr see* **united**.

ulcer ['ʌlsə*] *n* ulcère *m*; (*also*: **mouth** ~) aphte *f*.

Ulster ['ʌlstə*] *n* Ulster *m*.

ulterior [ʌlˈtɪərɪə*] *a* ultérieur(e); ~ **motive** *n* arrière-pensée *f*.

ultimate ['ʌltɪmət] *a* ultime, final(e); (*authority*) suprême; **~ly** *ad* en fin de compte; finalement; par la suite.

ultrasound ['ʌltrəsaund] *n* (*MED*) ultrason *m*.

umbilical cord [ʌmbɪˈlaɪkl-] *n* cordon ombilical.

umbrella [ʌmˈbrɛlə] *n* parapluie *m*.

umpire ['ʌmpaɪə*] *n* arbitre *m*.

umpteen [ʌmpˈtiːn] *a* je ne sais combien de; **for the ~th time** pour la nième fois.

UN, UNO *n abbr of* **United Nations (Organization)**.

unable [ʌnˈeɪbl] *a*: **to be ~ to** ne (pas) pouvoir, être dans l'impossibilité de; être incapable de.

unaccompanied [ʌnəˈkʌmpənɪd] *a* (*child, lady*) non accompagné(e).

unaccountably [ʌnəˈkauntəblɪ] *ad* inexplicablement.

unaccustomed [ʌnəˈkʌstəmd] *a* inaccoutumé(e), inhabituel(le); **to be ~ to sth** ne pas avoir l'habitude de qch.

unanimous [juːˈnænɪməs] *a* unanime; **~ly** *ad* à l'unanimité.

unarmed [ʌnˈɑːmd] *a* (*without a*

weapon) non armé(e); (*combat*) sans armes.

unassuming [ʌnəˈsjuːmɪŋ] *a* modeste, sans prétentions.

unattached [ʌnəˈtætʃt] *a* libre, sans attaches.

unattended [ʌnəˈtɛndɪd] *a* (*car, child, luggage*) sans surveillance.

unauthorized [ʌnˈɔːθəraɪzd] *a* non autorisé(e), sans autorisation.

unavoidable [ʌnəˈvɔɪdəbl] *a* inévitable.

unaware [ʌnəˈwɛə*] *a*: **to be ~ of** ignorer, ne pas savoir, être inconscient(e) de; **~s** *ad* à l'improviste, au dépourvu.

unbalanced [ʌnˈbælənst] *a* déséquilibré(e).

unbearable [ʌnˈbɛərəbl] *a* insupportable.

unbeknown(st) [ʌnbɪˈnəun(st)] *ad*: ~ **to** à l'insu de.

unbelievable [ʌnbɪˈliːvəbl] *a* incroyable.

unbend [ʌnˈbɛnd] *vb* (*irg*) *vi* se détendre // *vt* (*wire*) redresser, détordre.

unbias(s)ed [ʌnˈbaɪəst] *a* impartial(e).

unborn [ʌnˈbɔːn] *a* à naître.

unbreakable [ʌnˈbreɪkəbl] *a* incassable.

unbroken [ʌnˈbrəukən] *a* intact(e); continu(e).

unbutton [ʌnˈbʌtn] *vt* déboutonner.

uncalled-for [ʌnˈkɔːldfɔː*] *a* déplacé(e), injustifié(e).

uncanny [ʌnˈkænɪ] *a* étrange, troublant(e).

unceasing [ʌnˈsiːsɪŋ] *a* incessant(e), continu(e).

unceremonious [ʌnsɛrɪˈməunɪəs] *a* (*abrupt, rude*) brusque.

uncertain [ʌnˈsəːtn] *a* incertain(e); mal assuré(e); **~ty** *n* incertitude *f*, doutes *mpl*.

unchecked [ʌnˈtʃɛkt] *a* non réprimé(e).

uncivilized [ʌnˈsɪvɪlaɪzd] *a* (*gen*) non civilisé(e); (*fig: behaviour etc*) barbare.

uncle ['ʌŋkl] *n* oncle *m*.

uncomfortable [ʌnˈkʌmfətəbl] *a* inconfortable; (*uneasy*) mal à l'aise, gêné(e); désagréable.

uncommon [ʌnˈkɔmən] *a* rare, singulier(ère), peu commun(e).

uncompromising [ʌnˈkɔmprəmaɪzɪŋ] *a* intransigeant(e), inflexible.

unconcerned [ʌnkənˈsəːnd] *a*: **to be ~ (about)** ne pas s'inquiéter de.

unconditional [ʌnkənˈdɪʃənl] *a* sans conditions.

unconscious [ʌnˈkɔnʃəs] *a* sans connaissance, évanoui(e); (*unaware*) inconscient(e) // *n*: **the ~** l'inconscient *m*; **~ly** *ad* inconsciemment, sans s'en rendre compte.

uncontrollable [ʌnkənˈtrəuləbl] *a* irrépressible; indiscipliné(e).

unconventional [ʌnkənˈvɛnʃənl] *a*

non conventionnel(le).

uncouth [ʌn'ku:θ] *a* grossier(ère), fruste.

uncover [ʌn'kʌvə*] *vt* découvrir.

undecided [ʌndɪ'saɪdɪd] *a* indécis(e), irrésolu(e).

under ['ʌndə*] *prep* sous; (*less than*) (de) moins de; au-dessous de; (*according to*) selon, en vertu de // *ad* au-dessous; en dessous; **from ~ sth** de dessous *or* de sous qch; **~ there** là-dessous; **~ repair** en (cours de) réparation.

under... ['ʌndə*] *prefix* sous-; **~-age** *a* qui n'a pas l'âge réglementaire; **~carriage** *n* (*Brit AVIAT*) train *m* d'atterrissage; **~charge** *vt* ne pas faire payer assez à; **~coat** *n* (*paint*) couche *f* de fond; **~cover** *a* secret(ète), clandestin(e); **~current** *n* courant sous-jacent; **~cut** *vt irg* vendre moins cher que; **~developed** *a* sous-développé(e); **~dog** *n* opprimé *m*; **~done** *a* (*CULIN*) saignant(e); (*pej*) pas assez cuit(e); **~estimate** *vt* sous-estimer, mésestimer; **~fed** *a* sous-alimenté(e); **~foot** *ad* sous les pieds; **~go** *vt irg* subir; (*treatment*) suivre; **~graduate** *n* étudiant/e (qui prépare la licence); **~ground** *n* (*Brit*: *railway*) métro *m*; (*POL*) clandestinité *f* // *a* souterrain(e); (*fig*) clandestin(e); **~growth** *n* broussailles *fpl*, sous-bois *m*; **~hand(ed)** *a* (*fig*) sournois(e), en dessous; **~lie** *vt irg* être à la base de; **~line** *vt* souligner; **~ling** ['ʌndəlɪŋ] *n* (*pej*) sous-fifre *m*, subalterne *m*; **~mine** *vt* saper, miner; **~neath** [ʌndə'ni:θ] *ad* (en) dessous // *prep* sous, au-dessous de; **~paid** *a* sous-payé(e); **~pants** *npl* caleçon *m*, slip *m*; **~pass** *n* (*Brit*) passage souterrain; (: *on motorway*) passage inférieur; **~privileged** *a* défavorisé(e), économiquement faible; **~rate** *vt* sous-estimer, mésestimer; **~shirt** *n* (*US*) tricot *m* de corps; **~shorts** *npl* (*US*) caleçon *m*, slip *m*; **~side** *n* dessous *m*; **~skirt** *n* (*Brit*) jupon *m*.

understand [ʌndə'stænd] *vb* (*irg: like stand*) *vt, vi* comprendre; **I ~ that ...** je me suis laissé dire que ...; je crois comprendre que ...; **~able** *a* compréhensible; **~ing** *a* compréhensif(ive) // *n* compréhension *f*; (*agreement*) accord *m*.

understatement ['ʌndəsteɪtmənt] *n*: **that's an ~** c'est (bien) peu dire, le terme est faible.

understood [ʌndə'stud] *pt, pp of* **understand** // *a* entendu(e); (*implied*) sous-entendu(e).

understudy ['ʌndəstʌdɪ] *n* doublure *f*.

undertake [ʌndə'teɪk] *vt irg* entreprendre; se charger de; **to ~ to do sth** s'engager à faire qch.

undertaker ['ʌndəteɪkə*] *n* entrepreneur *m* des pompes funèbres, croque-mort *m*.

undertaking ['ʌndəteɪkɪŋ] *n* entreprise *f*; (*promise*) promesse *f*.

undertone ['ʌndətəun] *n*: **in an ~** à mi-voix.

underwater [ʌndə'wɔ:tə*] *ad* sous l'eau // *a* sous-marin(e).

underwear ['ʌndəwεə*] *n* sous-vêtements *mpl*; (*women's only*) dessous *mpl*.

underworld ['ʌndəwə:ld] *n* (*of crime*) milieu *m*, pègre *f*.

underwriter ['ʌndəraɪtə*] *n* (*INSURANCE*) souscripteur *m*.

undies ['ʌndɪz] *npl* (*col*) dessous *mpl*, lingerie *f*.

undo [ʌn'du:] *vt irg* défaire; **~ing** *n* ruine *f*, perte *f*.

undoubted [ʌn'dautɪd] *a* indubitable, certain(e); **~ly** *ad* sans aucun doute.

undress [ʌn'drɛs] *vi* se déshabiller.

undue [ʌn'dju:] *a* indu(e), excessif(ive).

undulating ['ʌndjuleɪtɪŋ] *a* ondoyant(e), onduleux(euse).

unduly [ʌn'dju:lɪ] *ad* trop, excessivement.

unearth [ʌn'ə:θ] *vt* déterrer; (*fig*) dénicher.

unearthly [ʌn'ə:θlɪ] *a* surnaturel(le); (*hour*) indu(e), impossible.

uneasy [ʌn'i:zɪ] *a* mal à l'aise, gêné(e); (*worried*) inquiet(ète).

unemployed [ʌnɪm'plɔɪd] *a* sans travail, au chômage // *n*: **the ~** les chômeurs *mpl*.

unemployment [ʌnɪm'plɔɪmənt] *n* chômage *m*.

unending [ʌn'ɛndɪŋ] *a* interminable.

unerring [ʌn'ə:rɪŋ] *a* infaillible, sûr(e).

uneven [ʌn'i:vn] *a* inégal(e); irrégulier(ère).

unexpected [ʌnɪk'spɛktɪd] *a* inattendu(e), imprévu(e); **~ly** *ad* à l'improviste.

unfailing [ʌn'feɪlɪŋ] *a* inépuisable; infaillible.

unfair [ʌn'fɛə*] *a*: **~ (to)** injuste (envers).

unfaithful [ʌn'feɪθful] *a* infidèle.

unfamiliar [ʌnfə'mɪlɪə*] *a* étrange, inconnu(e).

unfashionable [ʌn'fæʃnəbl] *a* (*clothes*) démodé(e); (*district*) déshérité(e), pas à la mode.

unfasten [ʌn'fɑ:sn] *vt* défaire; détacher.

unfavourable, (*US*) **unfavorable** [ʌn'feɪvərəbl] *a* défavorable.

unfeeling [ʌn'fi:lɪŋ] *a* insensible, dur(e).

unfit [ʌn'fɪt] *a* en mauvaise santé; pas en forme; (*incompetent*): **~ (for)** impropre (à); (*work, service*) inapte (à).

unfold [ʌn'fəuld] *vt* déplier; (*fig*) ré-

véler, exposer // *vi* se dérouler.
unforeseen [ˈʌnfɔːˈsiːn] *a* imprévu(e).
unforgettable [ʌnfəˈgetəbl] *a* inoubliable.
unfortunate [ʌnˈfɔːtʃnət] *a* malheureux(euse); (*event, remark*) malencontreux(euse); **~ly** *ad* malheureusement.
unfounded [ʌnˈfaundɪd] *a* sans fondement.
unfriendly [ʌnˈfrendlɪ] *a* froid(e), inamical(e).
ungainly [ʌnˈgeɪnlɪ] *a* gauche, dégingandé(e).
ungodly [ʌnˈgɔdlɪ] *a*: **at an ~ hour** à une heure indue.
ungrateful [ʌnˈgreɪtful] *a* ingrat(e).
unhappiness [ʌnˈhæpɪnɪs] *n* tristesse *f*, peine *f*.
unhappy [ʌnˈhæpɪ] *a* triste, malheureux(euse); **~ with** (*arrangements etc*) mécontent(e) de, peu satisfait(e) de.
unharmed [ʌnˈhɑːmd] *a* indemne, sain(e) et sauf(sauve).
unhealthy [ʌnˈhelθɪ] *a* (*gen*) malsain(e); (*person*) maladif(ive).
unheard-of [ʌnˈhɜːdɔv] *a* inouï(e), sans précédent.
uniform [ˈjuːnɪfɔːm] *n* uniforme *m* // *a* uniforme.
uninhabited [ʌnɪnˈhæbɪtɪd] *a* inhabité(e).
union [ˈjuːnjən] *n* union *f*; (*also:* **trade ~**) syndicat *m* // *cpd* du syndicat, syndical(e); **U~ Jack** *n* drapeau du Royaume-Uni.
unique [juːˈniːk] *a* unique.
unit [ˈjuːnɪt] *n* unité *f*; (*section: of furniture etc*) élément *m*, bloc *m*; (*team, squad*) groupe *m*, service *m*.
unite [juːˈnaɪt] *vt* unir // *vi* s'unir; **~d** uni(e), unifié(e); (*efforts*) conjugué(e); **U~d Kingdom (UK)** *n* Royaume-Uni *m*; **U~d Nations (Organization) (UN, UNO)** *n* (Organisation *f* des) Nations Unies (O.N.U.); **U~d States (of America) (US, USA)** *n* États-Unis *mpl*.
unit trust *n* (*Brit*) société *f* d'investissement; ≈ SICAV *f*.
unity [ˈjuːnɪtɪ] *n* unité *f*.
universal [juːnɪˈvɜːsl] *a* universel(le).
universe [ˈjuːnɪvɜːs] *n* univers *m*.
university [juːnɪˈvɜːsɪtɪ] *n* université *f*.
unjust [ʌnˈdʒʌst] *a* injuste.
unkempt [ʌnˈkempt] *a* mal tenu(e), débraillé(e); mal peigné(e).
unkind [ʌnˈkaɪnd] *a* peu gentil(le), méchant(e).
unknown [ʌnˈnəun] *a* inconnu(e).
unlawful [ʌnˈlɔːful] *a* illégal(e).
unleash [ʌnˈliːʃ] *vt* détacher; (*fig*) déchaîner, déclencher.
unless [ʌnˈles] *cj*: **~ he leaves** à moins qu'il (ne) parte; **~ we leave** à moins de

partir, à moins que nous (ne) partions; **~ otherwise stated** sauf indication contraire.
unlike [ʌnˈlaɪk] *a* dissemblable, différent(e) // *prep* à la différence de, contrairement à.
unlikely [ʌnˈlaɪklɪ] *a* improbable; invraisemblable.
unlisted [ʌnˈlɪstɪd] *a* (*US TEL*) sur la liste rouge.
unload [ʌnˈləud] *vt* décharger.
unlock [ʌnˈlɔk] *vt* ouvrir.
unlucky [ʌnˈlʌkɪ] *a* malchanceux(euse); (*object, number*) qui porte malheur; **to be ~** ne pas avoir de chance.
unmarried [ʌnˈmærɪd] *a* célibataire.
unmistakable [ʌnmɪsˈteɪkəbl] *a* indubitable; qu'on ne peut pas ne pas reconnaître.
unmitigated [ʌnˈmɪtɪgeɪtɪd] *a* non mitigé(e), absolu(e), pur(e).
unnatural [ʌnˈnætʃrəl] *a* non naturel(le); contre nature.
unnecessary [ʌnˈnesəsərɪ] *a* inutile, superflu(e).
unnoticed [ʌnˈnəutɪst] *a*: **(to go) ~** (passer) inaperçu(e).
UNO [ˈjuːnəu] *n abbr of* **United Nations Organization**.
unobtainable [ʌnəbˈteɪnəbl] *a* (*TEL*) impossible à obtenir.
unobtrusive [ʌnəbˈtruːsɪv] *a* discret(ète).
unofficial [ʌnəˈfɪʃl] *a* non officiel(le); (*strike*) ≈ non sanctionné(e) par la centrale.
unpack [ʌnˈpæk] *vi* défaire sa valise.
unpalatable [ʌnˈpælətəbl] *a* (*truth*) désagréable (à entendre).
unparalleled [ʌnˈpærəleld] *a* incomparable, sans égal.
unpleasant [ʌnˈpleznt] *a* déplaisant(e), désagréable.
unplug [ʌnˈplʌg] *vt* débrancher.
unpopular [ʌnˈpɔpjulə*] *a* impopulaire.
unprecedented [ʌnˈpresɪdəntɪd] *a* sans précédent.
unpredictable [ʌnprɪˈdɪktəbl] *a* imprévisible.
unprofessional [ʌnprəˈfeʃənl] *a* (*conduct*) contraire à la déontologie.
unqualified [ʌnˈkwɔlɪfaɪd] *a* (*teacher*) non diplômé(e), sans titres; (*success*) sans réserve, total(e).
unquestionably [ʌnˈkwestʃənəblɪ] *ad* incontestablement.
unravel [ʌnˈrævl] *vt* démêler.
unreal [ʌnˈrɪəl] *a* irréel(le).
unrealistic [ʌnrɪəˈlɪstɪk] *a* irréaliste; peu réaliste.
unreasonable [ʌnˈriːznəbl] *a* qui n'est pas raisonnable.
unrelated [ʌnrɪˈleɪtɪd] *a* sans rapport; sans lien de parenté.
unreliable [ʌnrɪˈlaɪəbl] *a* sur qui (or

quoi) on ne peut pas compter, peu fiable.
unremitting [ʌnrɪ'mɪtɪŋ] *a* inlassable, infatigable, acharné(e).

unreservedly [ʌnrɪ'zɜːvɪdlɪ] *ad* sans réserve.

unrest [ʌn'rɛst] *n* agitation *f*, troubles *mpl*.

unroll [ʌn'rəul] *vt* dérouler.

unruly [ʌn'ruːlɪ] *a* indiscipliné(e).

unsafe [ʌn'seɪf] *a* dangereux(euse), hasardeux(euse).

unsaid [ʌn'sɛd] *a*: to leave sth ~ passer qch sous silence.

unsatisfactory ['ʌnsætɪs'fæktərɪ] *a* qui laisse à désirer.

unsavoury, (US) **unsavory** [ʌn'seɪvərɪ] *a* (*fig*) peu recommandable, répugnant(e).

unscathed [ʌn'skeɪðd] *a* indemne.

unscrew [ʌn'skruː] *vt* dévisser.

unscrupulous [ʌn'skruːpjuləs] *a* sans scrupules.

unsettled [ʌn'sɛtld] *a* perturbé(e); instable; incertain(e).

unshaven [ʌn'ʃeɪvn] *a* non *or* mal rasé(e).

unsightly [ʌn'saɪtlɪ] *a* disgracieux(euse), laid(e).

unskilled [ʌn'skɪld] *a*: ~ **worker** manœuvre *m*.

unspeakable [ʌn'spiːkəbl] *a* indicible; (*awful*) innommable.

unstable [ʌn'steɪbl] *a* instable.

unsteady [ʌn'stɛdɪ] *a* mal assuré(e), chancelant(e), instable.

unstuck [ʌn'stʌk] *a*: to come ~ se décoller; (*fig*) faire fiasco.

unsuccessful [ʌnsək'sɛsful] *a* (*attempt*) infructueux(euse); (*writer, proposal*) qui n'a pas de succès; (*marriage*) malheureux(euse), qui ne réussit pas; to be ~ (*in attempting sth*) ne pas réussir; ne pas avoir de succès; (*application*) ne pas être retenu(e).

unsuitable [ʌn'suːtəbl] *a* qui ne convient pas, peu approprié(e); inopportun(e).

unsure [ʌn'ʃuə*] *a* pas sûr(e); to be ~ of o.s. manquer de confiance en soi.

unsympathetic [ʌnsɪmpə'θɛtɪk] *a* (*person*) antipathique; (*attitude*) hostile.

untapped [ʌn'tæpt] *a* (*resources*) inexploité(e).

unthinkable [ʌn'θɪŋkəbl] *a* impensable, inconcevable.

untidy [ʌn'taɪdɪ] *a* (*room*) en désordre; (*appearance*) désordonné(e), débraillé(e); (*person*) sans ordre, désordonné; débraillé; (*work*) peu soigné(e).

untie [ʌn'taɪ] *vt* (*knot, parcel*) défaire; (*prisoner, dog*) détacher.

until [ən'tɪl] *prep* jusqu'à; (*after negative*) avant // *cj* jusqu'à ce que + *sub*, en attendant que + *sub*; (*in past,*

after negative) avant que + *sub*; ~ **now** jusqu'à présent, jusqu'ici; ~ **then** jusque-là.

untimely [ʌn'taɪmlɪ] *a* inopportun(e); (*death*) prématuré(e).

untold [ʌn'təuld] *a* incalculable; indescriptible.

untoward [ʌntə'wɔːd] *a* fâcheux(euse), malencontreux(euse).

untranslatable [ʌntrænz'leɪtəbl] *a* intraduisible.

unused [ʌn'juːzd] *a* neuf(neuve).

unusual [ʌn'juːʒuəl] *a* insolite, exceptionnel(le), rare.

unveil [ʌn'veɪl] *vt* dévoiler.

unwavering [ʌn'weɪvərɪŋ] *a* inébranlable.

unwelcome [ʌn'wɛlkəm] *a* importun(e); de trop.

unwell [ʌn'wɛl] *a* indisposé(e), souffrant(e); to feel ~ ne pas se sentir bien.

unwieldy [ʌn'wiːldɪ] *a* difficile à manier.

unwilling [ʌn'wɪlɪŋ] *a*: to be ~ to do ne pas vouloir faire; ~**ly** *ad* à contrecœur, contre son gré.

unwind [ʌn'waɪnd] *vb* (*irg*) *vt* dérouler // *vi* (*relax*) se détendre.

unwise [ʌn'waɪz] *a* déraisonnable.

unwitting [ʌn'wɪtɪŋ] *a* involontaire.

unworkable [ʌn'wəːkəbl] *a* (*plan*) inexploitable.

unworthy [ʌn'wəːðɪ] *a* indigne.

unwrap [ʌn'ræp] *vt* défaire; ouvrir.

unwritten [ʌn'rɪtn] *a* (*agreement*) tacite.

up [ʌp] ♦ *prep*: he went ~ the stairs/the hill il a monté l'escalier/la colline; the cat was ~ a tree le chat était dans un arbre; they live further ~ the street ils habitent plus haut dans la rue
♦ *ad* **1** (*upwards, higher*): ~ **in the sky/ the mountains** (là-haut) dans le ciel/les montagnes; put it a bit higher ~ mettez-le un peu plus haut; ~ **there** là-haut; ~ **above** au-dessus
2: to be ~ (*out of bed*) être levé(e); (*prices etc*) avoir augmenté *or* monté
3: ~ **to** (*as far as*) jusqu'à; ~ **to now** jusqu'à présent
4: to be ~ **to** (*depending on*): it's ~ **to you** c'est à vous de décider; (*equal to*): he's not ~ **to** it (*job, task etc*) il n'en est pas capable; (*col: be doing*): what is he ~ **to**? qu'est-ce qu'il peut bien faire?
♦ *n*: ~**s and downs** hauts et bas *mpl*.

up-and-coming [ʌpənd'kʌmɪŋ] *a* plein(e) d'avenir *or* de promesses.

upbringing ['ʌpbrɪŋɪŋ] *n* éducation *f*.

update [ʌp'deɪt] *vt* mettre à jour.

upheaval [ʌp'hiːvl] *n* bouleversement *m*; branle-bas *m*; crise *f*.

uphill [ʌp'hɪl] *a* qui monte; (*fig: task*) difficile, pénible // *ad*: to go ~ monter.

uphold [ʌp'həuld] *vt irg* maintenir;

soutenir.

upholstery [ʌp'həulstəri] n rembourrage m; (of car) garniture f.

upkeep ['ʌpki:p] n entretien m.

upon [ə'pɒn] prep sur.

upper ['ʌpə*] a supérieur(e); du dessus // n (of shoe) empeigne f; ~-**class** a ≈ bourgeois(e); ~ **hand** n: to have the ~ hand avoir le dessus; ~**most** a le(la) plus haut(e).

upright ['ʌprait] a droit(e); vertical(e); (fig) droit, honnête // n montant m.

uprising ['ʌpraiziŋ] n soulèvement m, insurrection f.

uproar ['ʌprɔ:*] n tumulte m, vacarme m.

uproot [ʌp'ru:t] vt déraciner.

upset n ['ʌpsɛt] dérangement m // vt [ʌp'sɛt] (irg: like set) (glass etc) renverser; (plan) déranger; (person: offend) contrarier; (: grieve) faire de la peine à; bouleverser // a [ʌp'sɛt] contrarié(e); peiné(e); (stomach) détraqué(e), dérangé(e).

upshot ['ʌpʃɔt] n résultat m.

upside-down ['ʌpsaid'daun] ad à l'envers.

upstairs [ʌp'stɛəz] ad en haut // a (room) du dessus, d'en haut.

upstart ['ʌpstɑ:t] n parvenu/e.

upstream [ʌp'stri:m] ad en amont.

uptake ['ʌpteik] n: he is quick/slow on the ~ il comprend vite/est lent à comprendre.

uptight [ʌp'tait] a (col) très tendu(e), crispé(e).

up-to-date ['ʌptə'deit] a moderne; très récent(e).

upturn ['ʌptə:n] n (in luck) retournement m; (COMM: in market) hausse f.

upward ['ʌpwəd] a ascendant(e); vers le haut; ~(s) ad vers le haut.

urban ['ə:bən] a urbain(e).

urbane [ə:'bein] a urbain(e), courtois(e).

urchin ['ə:tʃin] n gosse m, garnement m.

urge [ə:dʒ] n besoin m; envie f; forte envie, désir m // vt: to ~ sb to do sth exhorter qn à faire, pousser qn à faire; recommander vivement à qn de faire.

urgency ['ə:dʒənsi] n urgence f; (of tone) insistance f.

urgent ['ə:dʒənt] a urgent(e).

urine ['juərin] n urine f.

urn [ə:n] n urne f; (also: tea ~) fontaine f à thé.

US, USA n abbr of **United States (of America)**.

us [ʌs] pronoun nous; see also me.

use n [ju:s] emploi m, utilisation f; usage m // vt [ju:z] se servir de, utiliser, employer; she ~d to do it elle le faisait (autrefois), elle avait coutume de le faire; in ~ en usage; out of ~ hors d'usage; to be of ~ servir, être utile; it's no ~ ça ne sert à rien; to be ~d to avoir l'habitude de, être habitué(e) à; to ~ up vt finir, épuiser; consommer; ~d a (car) d'occasion; ~ful a utile; ~fulness n utilité f; ~less a inutile; ~r n utilisateur/trice, usager m; ~r-friendly a (computer) convivial(e), facile d'emploi.

usher ['ʌʃə*] n placeur m; ~ette [-'rɛt] n (in cinema) ouvreuse f.

USSR n: the ~ l'URSS f.

usual ['ju:ʒuəl] a habituel(le); as ~ comme d'habitude; ~ly ad d'habitude, d'ordinaire.

utensil [ju:'tɛnsl] n ustensile m; kitchen ~s batterie f de cuisine.

uterus ['ju:tərəs] n utérus m.

utility [ju:'tiliti] n utilité f; (also: public ~) service public; ~ **room** n buanderie f.

utmost ['ʌtməust] a extrême, le(la) plus grand(e) // n: to do one's ~ faire tout son possible.

utter ['ʌtə*] a total(e), complet(ète) // vt prononcer, proférer; émettre; ~**ance** n paroles fpl; ~**ly** ad complètement, totalement.

U-turn ['ju:'tə:n] n demi-tour m.

V

v. abbr of **verse, versus, volt**; (= vide) voir.

vacancy ['veikənsi] n (Brit: job) poste vacant; (room) chambre f disponible.

vacant ['veikənt] a (post) vacant(e); (seat etc) libre, disponible; (expression) distrait(e); ~ **lot** n (US) terrain inoccupé; (for sale) terrain à vendre.

vacate [və'keit] vt quitter.

vacation [və'keiʃən] n vacances fpl.

vaccinate ['væksineit] vt vacciner.

vacuum ['vækjum] n vide m; ~ **bottle** n (US) = ~ **flask**; ~ **cleaner** n aspirateur m; ~ **flask** n (Brit) bouteille f thermos ®; ~-**packed** a emballé(e) sous vide.

vagina [və'dʒainə] n vagin m.

vagrant ['veigrnt] n vagabond/e, mendiant/e.

vague [veig] a vague, imprécis(e); (blurred: photo, memory) flou(e); ~**ly** ad vaguement.

vain [vein] a (useless) vain(e); (conceited) vaniteux(euse); in ~ en vain.

valentine ['væləntain] n (also: ~ card) carte f de la Saint-Valentin.

valiant ['væliənt] a vaillant(e).

valid ['vælid] a valide, valable; (excuse) valable.

valley ['væli] n vallée f.

valour, (US) valor ['vælə*] n courage m.

valuable ['væljuəbl] *a (jewel)* de grande valeur; *(time)* précieux(euse); **~s** *npl* objets *mpl* de valeur.

valuation [vælju'eɪʃən] *n* évaluation *f*, expertise *f*.

value ['vælju:] *n* valeur *f // vt (fix price)* évaluer, expertiser; *(cherish)* tenir à; **~ added tax (VAT)** *n (Brit)* taxe *f* à la valeur ajoutée (T.V.A.); **~d** *a (appreciated)* estimé(e).

valve [vælv] *n (in machine)* soupape *f*; *(on tyre)* valve *f*; *(in radio)* lampe *f*.

van [væn] *n (AUT)* camionnette *f*; *(Brit RAIL)* fourgon *m*.

vandal ['vændl] *n* vandale *m/f*; **~ism** *n* vandalisme *m*; **~ize** *vt* saccager.

vanilla [və'nɪlə] *n* vanille *f*.

vanish ['vænɪʃ] *vi* disparaître.

vanity ['vænɪtɪ] *n* vanité *f*; **~ case** *n* sac *m* de toilette.

vantage ['va:ntɪdʒ] *n*: **~ point** bonne position.

vapour, (US) vapor ['veɪpə*] *n* vapeur *f*; *(on window)* buée *f*.

variable ['vɛərɪəbl] *a* variable; *(mood)* changeant(e).

variance ['vɛərɪəns] *n*: **to be at ~ (with)** être en désaccord (avec); *(facts)* être en contradiction (avec).

varicose ['værɪkəus] *a*: **~ veins** varices *fpl*.

varied ['vɛərɪd] *a* varié(e), divers(e).

variety [və'raɪətɪ] *n* variété *f*; *(quantity)* nombre *m*, quantité *f*; **~ show** *n* (spectacle *m* de) variétés *fpl*.

various ['vɛərɪəs] *a* divers(e), différent(e); *(several)* divers, plusieurs.

varnish ['va:nɪʃ] *n* vernis *m // vt* vernir.

vary ['vɛərɪ] *vt, vi* varier, changer.

vase [va:z] *n* vase *m*.

vaseline ['væsɪli:n] *n* ® vaseline *f*.

vast [va:st] *a* vaste, immense; *(amount, success)* énorme; **~ly** *ad* infiniment, extrêmement.

VAT [væt] *n abbr of* **value added tax**.

vat [væt] *n* cuve *f*.

vault [vɔ:lt] *n (of roof)* voûte *f*; *(tomb)* caveau *m*; *(in bank)* salle *f* des coffres; chambre forte; *(jump)* saut *m // vt (also: ~ over)* sauter (d'un bond).

vaunted ['vɔ:ntɪd] *a*: **much-~** tant célébré(e).

VCR *n abbr of* **video cassette recorder**.

VD *n abbr of* **venereal disease**.

VDU *n abbr of* **visual display unit**.

veal [vi:l] *n* veau *m*.

veer [vɪə*] *vi* tourner; virer.

vegetable ['vedʒtəbl] *n* légume *m // a* végétal(e).

vegetarian [vedʒɪ'tɛərɪən] *a, n* végétarien(ne).

vehement ['vi:ɪmənt] *a* violent(e), impétueux(euse); *(impassioned)* ardent(e).

vehicle ['vi:ɪkl] *n* véhicule *m*.

veil [veɪl] *n* voile *m // vt* voiler.

vein [veɪn] *n* veine *f*; *(on leaf)* nervure *f*; *(fig: mood)* esprit *m*.

velvet ['velvɪt] *n* velours *m*.

vending machine ['vendɪŋ-] *n* distributeur *m* automatique.

veneer [və'nɪə*] *n* placage *m* de bois; *(fig)* vernis *m*.

venereal [vɪ'nɪərɪəl] *a*: **~ disease (VD)** *n* maladie vénérienne.

Venetian [vɪ'ni:ʃən] *a*: **~ blind** store vénitien.

vengeance ['vendʒəns] *n* vengeance *f*; **with a ~** *(fig)* vraiment, pour de bon.

venison ['venɪsn] *n* venaison *f*.

venom ['venəm] *n* venin *m*.

vent [vent] *n* conduit *m* d'aération; *(in dress, jacket)* fente *f // vt (fig: one's feelings)* donner libre cours à.

ventilate ['ventɪleɪt] *vt (room)* ventiler, aérer; **ventilator** *n* ventilateur *m*.

ventriloquist [ven'trɪləkwɪst] *n* ventriloque *m/f*.

venture ['ventʃə*] *n* entreprise *f // vt* risquer, hasarder *// vi* s'aventurer, se risquer.

venue ['venju:] *n* lieu *m* de rendez-vous *or* rencontre.

verb [və:b] *n* verbe *m*; **~al** *a* verbal(e); *(translation)* littéral(e).

verbatim [və:'beɪtɪm] *a, ad* mot pour mot.

verdict ['və:dɪkt] *n* verdict *m*.

verge [və:dʒ] *n (Brit)* bord *m*; **on the ~ of doing** sur le point de faire; **to ~ on** *vt fus* approcher de.

vermin ['və:mɪn] *npl* animaux *mpl* nuisibles; *(insects)* vermine *f*.

vermouth ['və:məθ] *n* vermouth *m*.

versatile ['və:sətaɪl] *a* polyvalent(e).

verse [və:s] *n* vers *mpl*; *(stanza)* strophe *f*; *(in bible)* verset *m*.

version ['və:ʃən] *n* version *f*.

versus ['və:səs] *prep* contre.

vertical ['və:tɪkl] *a* vertical(e) *// n* verticale *f*; **~ly** *ad* verticalement.

vertigo ['və:tɪgəu] *n* vertige *m*.

verve [və:v] *n* brio *m*; enthousiasme *m*.

very ['verɪ] *ad* très *// a*: **the ~ book which** le livre même que; **at the ~ end** tout à la fin; **the ~ last** le tout dernier; **at the ~ least** au moins; **~ much** beaucoup.

vessel ['vesl] *n (ANAT, NAUT)* vaisseau *m*; *(container)* récipient *m*.

vest [vest] *n (Brit)* tricot *m* de corps; *(US: waistcoat)* gilet *m*; **~ed interests** *npl (COMM)* droits acquis.

vestry ['vestrɪ] *n* sacristie *f*.

vet [vet] *n abbr (= veterinary surgeon)* vétérinaire *m/f // vt* examiner minutieusement; *(text)* revoir.

veteran ['vetərn] *n* vétéran *m*; *(also: war ~)* ancien combattant.

veterinary ['vetrɪnərɪ] *a* vétérinaire; **~**

surgeon, *(US)* **veterinarian** [vɛtrə-'nɛərɪən] *n* vétérinaire *m/f*.

veto ['viːtəu] *n* (*pl* ~es) veto *m* // *vt* opposer son veto à.

vex [vɛks] *vt* fâcher, contrarier; ~**ed** *a* (*question*) controversé(e).

VHF *abbr* (= *very high frequency*) VHF *f*.

via ['vaɪə] *prep* par, via.

viable ['vaɪəbl] *a* viable.

vibrate [vaɪˈbreɪt] *vi*: to ~ (**with**) vibrer (de); (*resound*) retentir (de).

vicar ['vɪkəʳ] *n* pasteur *m* (*de l'Église anglicane*); ~**age** *n* presbytère *m*.

vicarious [vɪˈkɛərɪəs] *a* indirect(e).

vice [vaɪs] *n* (*evil*) vice *m*; (*TECH*) étau *m*.

vice- [vaɪs] *prefix* vice-.

vice squad *n* ≈ brigade mondaine.

vice versa ['vaɪsɪ'vəːsə] *ad* vice versa.

vicinity [vɪˈsɪnɪtɪ] *n* environs *mpl*, alentours *mpl*.

vicious ['vɪʃəs] *a* (*remark*) cruel(le), méchant(e); (*blow*) brutal(e); ~ **circle** *n* cercle vicieux.

victim ['vɪktɪm] *n* victime *f*.

victor ['vɪktəʳ] *n* vainqueur *m*.

Victorian [vɪkˈtɔːrɪən] *a* victorien(ne).

victory ['vɪktərɪ] *n* victoire *f*.

video ['vɪdɪəu] *cpd* vidéo *inv* // *n* (~ *film*) vidéo *f*; (*also*: ~ **cassette**) vidéocassette *f*; (*also*: ~ **cassette recorder**) magnétoscope *m*; ~ **tape** *n* bande *f* vidéo *inv*; (*cassette*) vidéocassette *f*.

vie [vaɪ] *vi*: to ~ **with** rivaliser avec.

Vienna [vɪˈenə] *n* Vienne *f*.

Vietnam [vjɛt'næm] *n* Viet-Nam *m*, Vietnam *m*; ~**ese** [-nəˈmiːz] *a* vietnamien(ne) // *n* (*pl inv*) Vietnamien/ne.

view [vjuː] *n* vue *f*; (*opinion*) avis *m*, vue // *vt* (*situation*) considérer; (*house*) visiter; **on** ~ (*in museum etc*) exposé(e); **in full** ~ **of** sous les yeux de; (*building etc*) devant; **in** ~ **of the fact that** étant donné que; ~**er** *n* (*viewfinder*) viseur *m*; (*small projector*) visionneuse *f*; (*TV*) téléspectateur/trice; ~**finder** *n* viseur *m*; ~**point** *n* point *m* de vue.

vigil ['vɪdʒɪl] *n* veille *f*.

vigorous ['vɪgərəs] *a* vigoureux(euse).

vile [vaɪl] *a* (*action*) vil(e); (*smell*) abominable; (*temper*) massacrant(e).

villa ['vɪlə] *n* villa *f*.

village ['vɪlɪdʒ] *n* village *m*; ~**r** *n* villageois/e.

villain ['vɪlən] *n* (*scoundrel*) scélérat *m*; (*criminal*) bandit *m*; (*in novel etc*) traître *m*.

vindicate ['vɪndɪkeɪt] *vt* défendre avec succès; justifier.

vindictive [vɪnˈdɪktɪv] *a* vindicatif(ive), rancunier(ère).

vine [vaɪn] *n* vigne *f*; (*climbing plant*) plante grimpante.

vinegar ['vɪnɪgəʳ] *n* vinaigre *m*.

vineyard ['vɪnjɑːd] *n* vignoble *m*.

vintage ['vɪntɪdʒ] *n* (*year*) année *f*, millésime *m*; ~ **wine** *n* vin *m* de grand cru.

violate ['vaɪəleɪt] *vt* violer.

violence ['vaɪələns] *n* violence *f*; (*POL etc*) incidents violents.

violent ['vaɪələnt] *a* violent(e).

violet ['vaɪələt] *a* (*colour*) violet(te) // *n* (*plant*) violette *f*.

violin [vaɪəˈlɪn] *n* violon *m*; ~**ist** *n* violoniste *m/f*.

VIP *n abbr* (= *very important person*) V.I.P. *m*.

virgin ['vəːdʒɪn] *n* vierge *f* // *a* vierge.

Virgo ['vəːgəu] *n* la Vierge.

virile ['vɪraɪl] *a* viril(e).

virtually ['vəːtjuəlɪ] *ad* (*almost*) pratiquement.

virtue ['vəːtjuː] *n* vertu *f*; (*advantage*) mérite *m*, avantage *m*; **by** ~ **of** par le fait de.

virtuous ['vəːtjuəs] *a* vertueux(euse).

virus ['vaɪərəs] *n* virus *m*.

visa ['viːzə] *n* visa *m*.

visibility [vɪzɪˈbɪlɪtɪ] *n* visibilité *f*.

visible ['vɪzəbl] *a* visible.

vision ['vɪʒən] *n* (*sight*) vue *f*, vision *f*; (*foresight*, *in dream*) vision.

visit ['vɪzɪt] *n* visite *f*; (*stay*) séjour *m* // *vt* (*person*) rendre visite à; (*place*) visiter; ~**ing hours** *npl* (*in hospital etc*) heures *fpl* de visite; ~**or** *n* visiteur/ euse; (*in hotel*) client/e; ~**ors' book** *n* livre *m* d'or; (*in hotel*) registre *m*.

visor ['vaɪzəʳ] *n* visière *f*.

vista ['vɪstə] *n* vue *f*, perspective *f*.

visual ['vɪzjuəl] *a* visuel(le); ~ **aid** *n* support visuel (pour l'enseignement); ~ **display unit (VDU)** *n* console *f* de visualisation, visuel *m*.

visualize ['vɪzjuəlaɪz] *vt* se représenter; (*foresee*) prévoir.

vital ['vaɪtl] *a* vital(e); ~**ly** *ad* extrêmement; ~ **statistics** *npl* (*fig*) mensurations *fpl*.

vitamin ['vɪtəmɪn] *n* vitamine *f*.

vivacious [vɪˈveɪʃəs] *a* animé(e), qui a de la vivacité.

vivid ['vɪvɪd] *a* (*account*) frappant(e); (*light*, *imagination*) vif(vive); ~**ly** *ad* (*describe*) d'une manière vivante; (*remember*) de façon précise.

V-neck ['viːnɛk] *n* décolleté *m* en V.

vocabulary [vəuˈkæbjulərɪ] *n* vocabulaire *m*.

vocal ['vəukl] *a* vocal(e); (*articulate*) qui sait s'exprimer; ~ **chords** *npl* cordes vocales.

vocation [vəuˈkeɪʃən] *n* vocation *f*; ~**al** *a* professionnel(le).

vociferous [vəˈsɪfərəs] *a* bruyant(e).

vodka ['vɔdkə] n vodka f.

vogue [vəug] n mode f; (popularity) vogue f.

voice [vɔɪs] n voix f; (opinion) avis m // vt (opinion) exprimer, formuler.

void [vɔɪd] n vide m // a nul(le); ~ of vide de, dépourvu(e) de.

volatile ['vɔlətaɪl] a volatil(e); (fig) versatile.

volcano, ~es [vɔl'keɪnəu] n volcan m.

volition [və'lɪʃən] n: of one's own ~ de son propre gré.

volley ['vɔlɪ] n (of gunfire) salve f; (of stones etc) pluie f, volée f; (TENNIS etc) volée f; ~ball n volley(-ball) m.

volt [vəult] n volt m; ~age n tension f, voltage m.

volume ['vɔljuːm] n volume m.

voluntarily ['vɔləntrɪlɪ] ad volontairement; bénévolement.

voluntary ['vɔləntərɪ] a volontaire; (unpaid) bénévole.

volunteer [vɔlən'tɪə*] n volontaire m/f // vi (MIL) s'engager comme volontaire; to ~ to do se proposer pour faire.

vomit ['vɔmɪt] vt, vi vomir.

vote [vəut] n vote m, suffrage m; (cast) voix f, vote; (franchise) droit m de vote // vt (chairman) élire // vi voter; ~ of censure motion f de censure; ~ of thanks discours m de remerciement; ~r n électeur/trice; **voting** n scrutin m.

vouch [vautʃ]: to ~ for vt fus se porter garant de.

voucher ['vautʃə*] n (for meal, petrol) bon m; (receipt) reçu m.

vow [vau] n vœu m, serment m // vi jurer.

vowel ['vauəl] n voyelle f.

voyage ['vɔɪɪdʒ] n voyage m par mer, traversée f.

vulgar ['vʌlgə*] a vulgaire.

vulnerable ['vʌlnərəbl] a vulnérable.

vulture ['vʌltʃə*] n vautour m.

W

wad [wɔd] n (of cotton wool, paper) tampon m; (of banknotes etc) liasse f.

waddle ['wɔdl] vi se dandiner.

wade [weɪd] vi: to ~ through marcher dans, patauger dans // vt passer à gué.

wafer ['weɪfə*] n (CULIN) gaufrette f.

waffle ['wɔfl] n (CULIN) gaufre f; (col) rabâchage m; remplissage m.

waft [wɔft] vt porter // vi flotter.

wag [wæg] vt agiter, remuer // vi remuer.

wage [weɪdʒ] n (also: ~s) salaire m, paye f // vt: to ~ war faire la guerre; ~ packet n (enveloppe f de) paye f.

wager ['weɪdʒə*] n pari m.

waggle ['wægl] vt, vi remuer.

wag(g)on ['wægən] n (horse-drawn) chariot m; (Brit RAIL) wagon m (de marchandises).

wail [weɪl] vi gémir; (siren) hurler.

waist [weɪst] n taille f, ceinture f; ~coat n (Brit) gilet m; ~line n (tour m de) taille f.

wait [weɪt] n attente f // vi attendre; to lie in ~ for guetter; to ~ for attendre; I can't ~ to (fig) je meurs d'envie de; to ~ behind vi rester (à attendre); to ~ on vt fus servir; ~er n garçon m (de café), serveur m; ~ing n: 'no ~ing' (Brit AUT) 'stationnement interdit'; ~ing list n liste f d'attente; ~ing room n salle f d'attente; ~ress n serveuse f.

waive [weɪv] vt renoncer à, abandonner.

wake [weɪk] vb (pt woke, ~d, pp woken, ~d) vt (also: ~ up) réveiller // vi (also: ~ up) se réveiller // n (for dead person) veillée f mortuaire; (NAUT) sillage m; ~n vt, vi = wake.

Wales [weɪlz] n pays m de Galles.

walk [wɔːk] n promenade f; (short) petit tour; (gait) démarche f; (path) chemin m; (in park etc) allée f // vi marcher; (for pleasure, exercise) se promener // vt (distance) faire à pied; (dog) promener; 10 minutes' ~ from à 10 minutes de marche de; from all ~s of life de toutes conditions sociales; to ~ out on vt fus (col) quitter, plaquer; ~er n (person) marcheur/euse; ~ie-talkie ['wɔːkɪ'tɔːkɪ] n talkie-walkie m; ~ing n marche f à pied; ~ing stick n canne f; ~out n (of workers) grève-surprise f; ~over n (col) victoire f ou examen etc facile; ~way n promenade f.

wall [wɔːl] n mur m; (of tunnel, cave) paroi f; ~ed a (city) fortifié(e).

wallet ['wɔlɪt] n portefeuille m.

wallflower ['wɔːlflauə*] n giroflée f; to be a ~ (fig) faire tapisserie.

wallop ['wɔləp] vt (col) taper sur.

wallow ['wɔləu] vi se vautrer.

wallpaper ['wɔːlpeɪpə*] n papier peint.

wally ['wɔlɪ] n (col) imbécile m/f.

walnut ['wɔːlnʌt] n noix f; (tree) noyer m.

walrus, pl ~ or ~es ['wɔːlrəs] n morse m.

waltz [wɔːlts] n valse f // vi valser.

wan [wɔn] a pâle; triste.

wand [wɔnd] n (also: magic ~) baguette f (magique).

wander ['wɔndə*] vi (person) errer, aller sans but; (thoughts) vagabonder; (river) serpenter // vt errer dans.

wane [weɪn] vi (moon) décroître; (reputation) décliner.

wangle ['wæŋgl] vt (Brit col) se débrouiller pour avoir; carotter.

want [wɔnt] vt vouloir; (need) avoir besoin de; (lack) manquer de // n: for ~ of par manque de, faute de; ~s npl (*needs*) besoins *mpl*; **to ~ to do** vouloir faire; **to ~ sb to do** vouloir que qn fasse; **~ing** *a*: **to be found ~ing** ne pas être à la hauteur.

wanton ['wɔntn] *a* capricieux(euse); dévergondé(e).

war [wɔː*] *n* guerre *f*; **to make ~ (on)** faire la guerre (à).

ward [wɔːd] *n* (*in hospital*) salle *f*; (*POL*) section électorale; (*LAW*: *child*) pupille *m/f*; **to ~ off** *vt* parer, éviter.

warden ['wɔːdn] *n* (*Brit*: *of institution*) directeur/trice; (*of park, game reserve*) gardien/ne; (*Brit*: *also*: **traffic ~**) contractuel/le.

warder ['wɔːdə*] *n* (*Brit*) gardien *m* de prison.

wardrobe ['wɔːdrəʊb] *n* (*cupboard*) armoire *f*; (*clothes*) garde-robe *f*; (*THEATRE*) costumes *mpl*.

warehouse ['wɛəhaʊs] *n* entrepôt *m*.

wares [wɛəz] *npl* marchandises *fpl*.

warfare ['wɔːfɛə*] *n* guerre *f*.

warhead ['wɔːhɛd] *n* (*MIL*) ogive *f*.

warily ['wɛərɪlɪ] *ad* avec prudence.

warm [wɔːm] *a* chaud(e); (*thanks, welcome, applause*) chaleureux(euse); **it's ~** il fait chaud; **I'm ~** j'ai chaud; **to ~ up** *vi* (*person, room*) se réchauffer; (*water*) chauffer; (*athlete, discussion*) s'échauffer // *vt* réchauffer; chauffer; (*engine*) faire chauffer; **~-hearted** *a* affectueux(euse); **~ly** *ad* chaudement; vivement; chaleureusement; **~th** *n* chaleur *f*.

warn [wɔːn] *vt* avertir, prévenir; **~ing** *n* avertissement *m*; (*notice*) avis *m*; **~ing light** *n* avertisseur lumineux; **~ing triangle** *n* (*AUT*) triangle *m* de présignalisation.

warp [wɔːp] *vi* travailler, se voiler // *vt* voiler; (*fig*) pervertir.

warrant ['wɔrnt] *n* (*guarantee*) garantie *f*; (*LAW*: *to arrest*) mandat *m* d'arrêt; (: *to search*) mandat de perquisition.

warranty ['wɔrəntɪ] *n* garantie *f*.

warren ['wɔrən] *n* (*of rabbits*) terriers *mpl*, garenne *f*.

warrior ['wɔrɪə*] *n* guerrier/ère.

Warsaw ['wɔːsɔː] *n* Varsovie.

warship ['wɔːʃɪp] *n* navire *m* de guerre.

wart [wɔːt] *n* verrue *f*.

wartime ['wɔːtaɪm] *n*: **in ~** en temps de guerre.

wary ['wɛərɪ] *a* prudent(e).

was [wɔz] *pt of* **be**.

wash [wɔʃ] *vt* laver // *vi* se laver // *n* (*paint*) badigeon *m*; (*washing programme*) lavage *m*; (*of ship*) sillage *m*; **to have a ~** se laver, faire sa toilette; **to ~ away** *vt* (*stain*) enlever au lavage; (*subj: river etc*) emporter; **to ~ off** *vi* partir au lavage; **to ~ up** *vi* (*Brit*) faire la vaisselle; (*US*) se débarbouiller; **~able** *a* lavable; **~basin**, (*US*) **~bowl**

n lavabo *m*; **~cloth** *n* (*US*) gant *m* de toilette; **~er** *n* (*TECH*) rondelle *f*, joint *m*; **~ing** *n* (*linen etc*) lessive *f*; **~ing machine** *n* machine *f* à laver; **~ing powder** *n* (*Brit*) lessive *f* (en poudre); **~ing-up** *n* vaisselle *f*; **~ing-up liquid** *n* produit *m* pour la vaisselle; **~-out** *n* (*col*) désastre *m*; **~room** *n* toilettes *fpl*.

wasn't ['wɔznt] = **was not**.

wasp [wɔsp] *n* guêpe *f*.

wastage ['weɪstɪdʒ] *n* gaspillage *m*; (*in manufacturing, transport etc*) déchet *m*; **natural ~** départs naturels.

waste [weɪst] *n* gaspillage *m*; (*of time*) perte *f*; (*rubbish*) déchets *mpl*; (*also*: **household ~**) ordures *fpl* // *a* (*material*) de rebut; (*land*) inculte // *vt* gaspiller; (*time, opportunity*) perdre; **~s** *npl* étendue *f* désertique; **to ~** (*destroy*) dévaster; **to ~ away** *vi* dépérir; **~ disposal unit** *n* (*Brit*) broyeur *m* d'ordures; **~ful** *a* gaspilleur(euse); (*process*) peu économique; **~ ground** *n* (*Brit*) terrain *m* vague; **~paper basket** *n* corbeille *f* à papier; **~ pipe** (tuyau *m* de) vidange *f*.

watch [wɔtʃ] *n* montre *f*; (*act of watching*) surveillance *f*; guet *m*; (*guard*: *MIL*) sentinelle *f*; (: *NAUT*) homme *m* de quart; (*NAUT*: *spell of duty*) quart *m* // *vt* (*look at*) observer; (: *match, programme*) regarder; (*spy on, guard*) surveiller; (*be careful of*) faire attention à // *vi* regarder; (*keep guard*) monter la garde; **to ~ out** *vi* faire attention; **~dog** *n* chien *m* de garde; **~ful** *a* attentif(ive), vigilant(e); **~maker** *n* horloger/ère; **~man** *n* gardien *m*; (*also*: **night ~man**) veilleur *m* de nuit; **~strap** *n* bracelet *m* de montre.

water ['wɔːtə*] *n* eau *f* // *vt* (*plant*) arroser // *vi* (*eyes*) larmoyer; **in British ~s** dans les eaux territoriales Britanniques; **to ~ down** *vt* (*milk*) couper d'eau; (*fig: story*) édulcorer; **~colour** *n* aquarelle *f*; **~colours** *npl* couleurs *fpl* pour aquarelle; **~cress** *n* cresson *m* (de fontaine); **~fall** *n* chute *f* d'eau; **~ heater** *n* chauffe-eau *m*; **~ ice** *n* sorbet *m*; **~ing can** *n* arrosoir *m*; **~ lily** *n* nénuphar *m*; **~logged** *a* détrempé(e), imbibé(e) d'eau; **~line** *n* (*NAUT*) ligne *f* de flottaison; **~ main** *n* canalisation *f* d'eau; **~mark** *n* (*on paper*) filigrane *m*; **~melon** *n* pastèque *f*; **~proof** *a* imperméable; **~shed** *n* (*GEO*) ligne *f* de partage des eaux; (*fig*) moment *m* critique, point décisif; **~skiing** *n* ski *m* nautique; **~tight** *a* étanche; **~way** *n* cours *m* d'eau navigable; **~works** *npl* station *f* hydraulique; **~y** *a* (*colour*) délavé(e); (*coffee*) trop faible.

watt [wɔt] *n* watt *m*.

wave [weɪv] *n* vague *f*; (*of hand*) geste *m*, signe *m*; (*RADIO*) onde *f*; (*in hair*) ondulation f // vi faire signe de la main; (flag) flotter au vent // vt (handkerchief) agiter; (stick) brandir; **~length** n longueur f d'ondes.

waver ['weɪvə*] vi vaciller; (voice) trembler; (person) hésiter.

wavy ['weɪvɪ] a ondulé(e); onduleux(euse).

wax [wæks] n cire f; (for skis) fart m // vt cirer; (car) lustrer // vi (moon) croître; **~works** npl personnages mpl de cire; musée m de cire.

way [weɪ] n chemin m, voie f; (path, access) passage m; (distance) distance f; (direction) chemin m, direction f; (manner) façon f, manière f; (habit) habitude f, façon f; (condition) état m; **which ~?** — **this** — par où or de quel côté? — par ici; **on the ~** (en route) en route; **to be on one's ~** être en route; **to be in the ~** bloquer le passage; (fig) gêner; **to go out of one's ~ to do** (fig) se donner du mal pour faire; **to lose one's ~** perdre son chemin; **in a ~** d'un côté; **in some ~s** à certains égards; d'un côté; **by the ~ ...** à propos ...; **'~ in'** (Brit) 'entrée'; **'~ out'** (Brit) 'sortie'.

waylay [weɪ'leɪ] vt irg attaquer; (fig): **I got waylaid** quelqu'un m'a accroché.

wayward ['weɪwəd] a capricieux(euse), entêté(e).

W.C. ['dʌblju:'si:] n (Brit) w.-c. mpl, waters mpl.

we [wi:] pl pronoun nous.

weak [wi:k] a faible; (health) fragile; (beam etc) peu solide; **~en** vi faiblir // vt affaiblir; **~ling** n gringalet m; faible m/f; **~ness** n faiblesse f; (fault) point m faible.

wealth [welθ] n (money, resources) richesse(s) f(pl); (of details) profusion f; **~y** a riche.

wean [wi:n] vt sevrer.

weapon ['wepən] n arme f.

wear [weə*] n (use) usage m; (deterioration through use) usure f; (clothing): **sports/baby~** vêtements mpl de sport/pour bébés // vb (pt **wore**, pp **worn**) vt (clothes) porter; mettre; (damage: through use) user // vi (last) faire de l'usage; (rub etc through) s'user; **evening ~** tenue f de soirée; **to ~ away** vt user, ronger // vi s'user, être rongé(e); **to ~ down** vt user; (strength) épuiser; **to ~ off** vi disparaître; **to ~ on** vi se poursuivre; passer; **to ~ out** vt user; (person, strength) épuiser; **~ and tear** n usure f.

weary ['wɪərɪ] a (tired) épuisé(e); (dispirited) las(lasse); abattu(e).

weasel ['wi:zl] n (ZOOL) belette f.

weather ['weðə*] n temps m // vt (wood) faire mûrir; (tempest, crisis) essuyer, être pris(e) dans; survivre à, tenir le coup durant; **under the ~** (fig:

ill) mal fichu(e); **~-beaten** a (person) hâlé(e); (building) dégradé(e) par les intempéries; **~cock** n girouette f; **~ forecast** n prévisions fpl météorologiques, météo f; **~ vane** n = **~cock**.

weave [wi:v], pt **wove**, pp **woven** [wi:v, wəuv, 'wəuvn] vt (cloth) tisser; (basket) tresser; **~r** n tisserand/e.

web [web] n (of spider) toile f; (on foot) palmure f; (fabric, also fig) tissu m.

wed [wed], pt, pp **wedded** vt épouser // vi se marier.

we'd [wi:d] = **we had, we would**.

wedding ['wedɪŋ] n mariage m; **silver/golden ~ anniversary** noces fpl d'argent/d'or; **~ day** n jour m du mariage; **~ dress** n robe f de mariage; **~ ring** n alliance f.

wedge [wedʒ] n (of wood etc) coin m; (under door etc) cale f; (of cake) part f // vt (fix) caler; (push) enfoncer, coincer.

wedlock ['wedlɔk] n (union f du) mariage m.

Wednesday ['wednzdɪ] n mercredi m.

wee [wi:] a (Scottish) petit(e); tout(e) petit(e).

weed [wi:d] n mauvaise herbe f // vt désherber; **~killer** n désherbant m; **~y** a (man) gringalet.

week [wi:k] n semaine f; **a ~ today/on Friday** aujourd'hui/vendredi en huit; **~day** n jour m de semaine; (COMM) jour ouvrable; **~end** n week-end m; **~ly** ad une fois par semaine, chaque semaine // a, n hebdomadaire (m).

weep [wi:p], pt, pp **wept** vi (person) pleurer; **~ing willow** n saule pleureur.

weigh [weɪ] vt, vi peser; **to ~ down** vt (branch) faire plier; (fig: with worry) accabler; **to ~ up** vt examiner.

weight [weɪt] n poids m; **to lose/put on ~** maigrir/grossir; **~ing** n (allowance) indemnité f, allocation f; **~ lifter** n haltérophile m; **~y** a lourd(e).

weir [wɪə*] n barrage m.

weird [wɪəd] a bizarre; (eerie) surnaturel(le).

welcome ['welkəm] a bienvenu(e) // n accueil m // vt accueillir; (also: **bid ~**) souhaiter la bienvenue à; (be glad of) se réjouir de; **to be ~** être le(la) bienvenu(e); **thank you — you're ~!** merci — de rien or il n'y a pas de quoi.

weld [weld] n soudure f // vt souder.

welfare ['welfeə*] n bien-être m; **~ state** n État-providence m.

well [wel] n puits m // ad bien // a: **to be ~** aller bien // excl eh bien!; bon!; enfin!; **as ~** aussi, également; **as ~ as** aussi bien que or de; en plus de; **~ done!** bravo!; **get ~ soon** remets-toi vite!; **to do ~** in sth bien réussir en or dans qch; **to ~ up** vi monter.

we'll [wi:l] = **we will, we shall.**

well: **~-behaved** *a* sage obéissant(e);
~-being *n* bien-être *m*; **~-built** *a*
(*person*) bien bâti(e); **~-dressed** *a* bien
habillé(e), bien vêtu(e); **~-heeled** *a*
(*col: wealthy*) fortuné(e), riche.

wellingtons ['wɛlɪŋtənz] *npl* (*also:*
wellington boots) bottes *fpl* de caoutchouc.

well: **~-known** *a* (*person*) bien
connu(e); **~-mannered** *a* bien éle-
vé(e); **~-meaning** *a* bien intention-
né(e); **~-off** *a* aisé(e), assez riche; **~-
read** *a* cultivé(e); **~-to-do** *a* aisé(e),
assez riche; **~-wisher** *n*: scores of **~-
wishers** had gathered de nombreux amis
et admirateurs s'étaient rassemblés.

Welsh [wɛlʃ] *a* gallois(e) // *n* (*LING*)
gallois *m*; the **~** *npl* les Gallois *mpl*;
~man/woman *n* Gallois/e; **~ rarebit**
n croûte *f* au fromage.

went [wɛnt] *pt of* **go.**

wept [wɛpt] *pt, pp of* **weep.**

were [wɜ:*] *pt of* **be.**

we're [wɪə*] = **we are.**

weren't [wɜ:nt] = **were not.**

west [wɛst] *n* ouest *m* // *a* ouest *inv*, de
or à l'ouest // *ad* à *or* vers l'ouest; **the
W~** *n* l'Occident *m*, l'Ouest; **the W~
Country** (*Brit*) le sud-ouest de l'Angleterre; **~erly** *a* (*wind*) d'ouest; **~ern**
a occidental(e), de *or* à l'ouest // *n*
(*CINEMA*) western *m*; **W~ Germany** *n*
Allemagne *f* de l'Ouest; **W~ Indian** *a*
antillais(e) // *n* Antillais/e; **W~ Indies**
npl Antilles *fpl*; **~ward(s)** *ad* vers
l'ouest.

wet [wɛt] *a* mouillé(e); (*damp*) humide;
(*soaked*) trempé(e); (*rainy*) pluvieux
(euse); **to get ~** se mouiller; '**~ paint**'
'attention peinture fraîche'; **~ blanket**
n (*fig*) rabat-joie *m inv*; **~ suit** *n*
combinaison *f* de plongée.

we've [wi:v] = **we have.**

whack [wæk] *vt* donner un grand coup à.

whale [weɪl] *n* (*ZOOL*) baleine *f*.

wharf, *pl* **wharves** [wɔ:f, wɔ:vz] *n* quai
m.

what [wɔt] *a* quel(le), *pl*
quels(quelles); **~ size is he?** quelle taille
fait-il?; **~ colour is it?** de quelle couleur
est-ce?; **~ books do you need?** quels livres vous faut-il?; **~ a mess!** quel désordre!

♦ *pronoun* **1** (*interrogative*) que, *prep* +
quoi; **~ are you doing?** que faites-vous?,
qu'est-ce que vous faites?; **~ is happening?** qu'est-ce qui se passe?, que se
passe-t-il?; **~ are you talking about?** de
quoi parlez-vous?; **~ is it called?**
comment est-ce que ça s'appelle?; **~
about me?** et moi?; **~ about doing ...?**
et si on faisait ...?

2 (*relative: subject*) ce qui; (: *direct
object*) ce que; (: *indirect object*) ce +

prep + quoi, ce dont; **I saw ~ you did/
was on the table** j'ai vu ce que vous avez
fait/ce qui était sur la table; **tell me ~
you remember** dites-moi ce dont vous
vous souvenez

♦ *excl* (*disbelieving*) quoi!, comment!

whatever [wɔt'ɛvə*] *a*: **~ book** quel que
soit le livre que (*or* qui) + *sub*;
n'importe quel livre // *pronoun*: **do ~ is
necessary** faites (tout) ce qui est
nécessaire; **~ happens** quoi qu'il arrive;
no reason ~ *or* whatsoever pas la moindre raison; **nothing ~** rien du tout.

wheat [wi:t] *n* blé *m*, froment *m*.

wheedle ['wi:dl] *vt*: **to ~ sb into doing
sth** cajoler *or* enjôler qn pour qu'il fasse
qch; **to ~ sth out of sb** obtenir qch de qn
par des cajoleries.

wheel [wi:l] *n* roue *f*; (*AUT: also:* steering **~**) volant *m*; (*NAUT*) gouvernail *m* //
vt pousser, rouler // *vi* (*also:* **~ round**)
tourner; **~barrow** *n* brouette *f*; **~chair**
n fauteuil roulant; **~ clamp** *n* (*AUT*)
sabot *m* (de Denver).

wheeze [wi:z] *vi* respirer bruyamment.

when [wɛn] ♦ *ad* quand; **~ did it happen?** c'est arrivé quand?

♦ *cj* **1** (*at, during, after the time that*)
quand, lorsque; **she was reading ~ I
came in** elle lisait quand *or* lorsque je
suis entré

2 (*on, at which*): **on the day ~ I met
him** le jour où je l'ai rencontré

3 (*whereas*) alors que; **you said I was
wrong ~ in fact I was right** vous avez dit
que j'avais tort alors qu'en fait j'avais
raison.

whenever [wɛn'ɛvə*] *ad* quand donc //
cj quand; (*every time that*) chaque fois
que; **you may leave ~ you like** vous
pouvez partir quand vous voudrez.

where [wɛə*] *ad, cj* où; **this is ~** c'est là
que; **~abouts** *ad* où donc // *n*: sb's
~abouts l'endroit où se trouve qn; **~as**
cj alors que; **~by** *pronoun* par lequel
(*or* laquelle etc); **~upon** *cj* sur quoi, et
sur ce; **wherever** [-'ɛvə*] *ad* où donc //
cj où que + *sub*; **~withal** *n* moyens
mpl.

whet [wɛt] *vt* aiguiser.

whether ['wɛðə*] *cj* si; **I don't know ~
to accept or not** je ne sais pas si je dois
accepter ou non; **it's doubtful ~** il est
peu probable que; **~ you go or not** que
vous y alliez ou non.

which [wɪtʃ] ♦ *a* **1** (*interrogative: direct, indirect*) quel(le), *pl* quels(quelles); **~ picture do you want?** quel
tableau voulez-vous?; **~ one?** lequel(laquelle)?

2: in ~ case auquel cas

♦ *pronoun* **1** (*interrogative*) lequel(laquelle), *pl* lesquels(lesquelles); **I don't
mind ~** peu importe lequel; **~ (of these)
are yours?** lesquels sont à vous?; **here**

are the books — tell me ~ you want voici les livres — dites-moi lesquels or ceux que vous voulez

2 (*relative: subject*) qui; (: *object*) que, prep + lequel(laquelle) (NB: *à* + *lequel* = auquel; *de* + *lequel* = duquel); **the apple ~ you ate**/~ **is on the table** la pomme que vous avez mangée/qui est sur la table; **the chair on ~ you are sitting** la chaise sur laquelle vous êtes assis; **the book of ~ you spoke** le livre dont vous avez parlé; **he said he knew, ~ is true/I feared** il a dit qu'il le savait, ce qui est vrai/ce que je craignais; **after ~** après quoi.

whichever |wɪtʃˈɛvə*| a: **take ~ book you prefer** prenez le livre que vous préférez, peu importe lequel; **~ way you** de quelque façon que vous + sub.

whiff |wɪf| n bouffée f.

while |waɪl| n moment m // cj pendant que; (*as long as*) tant que; (*whereas*) alors que; bien que + sub; **for a ~** pendant quelque temps; **to ~ away** vt (*time*) (faire) passer.

whim |wɪm| n caprice m.

whimper |ˈwɪmpə*| vi geindre.

whimsical |ˈwɪmzɪkl| a (*person*) capricieux(euse); (*look*) étrange.

whine |waɪn| vi gémir, geindre; pleurnicher.

whip |wɪp| n fouet m; (*for riding*) cravache f; (*POL: person*) chef m de file (*assurant la discipline dans son groupe parlementaire*) // vt fouetter; (*snatch*) enlever (or sortir) brusquement; **~ped cream** n crème fouettée; **~-round** n (*Brit*) collecte f.

whirl |wəːl| vt faire tourbillonner; faire tournoyer // vi tourbillonner; **~pool** n tourbillon m; **~wind** n tornade f.

whirr |wəː*| vi bruire; ronronner; vrombir.

whisk |wɪsk| n (*CULIN*) fouet m // vt fouetter, battre; **to ~ sb away** or **off** emmener qn rapidement.

whisker |ˈwɪskə*| n: **~s** (*of animal*) moustaches fpl; (*of man*) favoris mpl.

whisky, (*Irish, US*) **whiskey** |ˈwɪskɪ| n whisky m.

whisper |ˈwɪspə*| vt, vi chuchoter.

whistle |ˈwɪsl| n (*sound*) sifflement m; (*object*) sifflet m // vi siffler.

white |waɪt| a blanc(blanche); (*with fear*) blême // n blanc m; (*person*) blanc/blanche; **~ coffee** n (*Brit*) café m au lait, (*café*) crème m; **~-collar worker** n employé-de bureau; **~ elephant** n (*fig*) objet dispendieux et superflu; **~ lie** n pieux mensonge; **~ paper** n (*POL*) livre blanc; **~wash** vt blanchir à la chaux; (*fig*) blanchir.

whiting |ˈwaɪtɪŋ| n (*pl inv*) (*fish*) merlan m.

Whitsun |ˈwɪtsn| n la Pentecôte.

whittle |ˈwɪtl| vt: **to ~ away,** **~ down** (*costs*) réduire, rogner.

whizz |wɪz| vi aller (or passer) à toute vitesse; **~ kid** n (*col*) petit prodige.

who |huː| pronoun qui.

whodunit |huːˈdʌnɪt| n (*col*) roman policier.

whoever |huːˈɛvə*| pronoun: **~ finds it** celui(celle) qui le trouve, (qui que ce soit), quiconque le trouve; **ask ~ you like** demandez à qui vous voulez; **~ he marries** qui que ce soit or quelle que soit la personne qu'il épouse; **~ told you that?** qui a bien pu vous dire ça?

whole |həul| a (*complete*) entier(ère), tout(e); (*not broken*) intact(e), complet(ète) // n (*total*) totalité f; (*sth not broken*) tout m; **the ~ of the town** la ville tout entière; **on the ~, as a ~** dans l'ensemble; **~-hearted** a sans réserve(s), sincère; **~meal** a (*bread, flour*) complet(ète); **~sale** n (*vente f* en) gros m // a de gros; (*destruction*) systématique; **~saler** n grossiste m/f; **~some** a sain(e); (*advice*) salutaire; **~wheat** a = **~meal**; **wholly** ad entièrement, tout à fait.

whom |huːm| pronoun **1** (*interrogative*) qui; **~ did you see?** qui avez-vous vu?; **to ~ did you give it?** à qui l'avez-vous donné?

2 (*relative*) que, prep + qui (*check syntax of French verb used*): **the man ~ I saw**/**to ~ I spoke** l'homme que j'ai vu/à qui j'ai parlé.

whooping cough |ˈhuːpɪŋkɔf| n coqueluche f.

whore |hɔː*| n (*col; pej*) putain f.

whose |huːz| ♦ a **1** (*possessive: interrogative*): **~ book is this?** à qui est ce livre?; **~ pencil have you taken?** à qui est le crayon que vous avez pris?, c'est le crayon de qui que vous avez pris?; **~ daughter are you?** de qui êtes-vous la fille?

2 (*possessive: relative*): **the man ~ son you rescued** l'homme dont or de qui vous avez sauvé le fils; **the girl ~ sister you were speaking to** la fille à la sœur de qui or de laquelle vous parliez; **the woman ~ car was stolen** la femme dont la voiture a été volée

♦ pronoun à qui; **~ is this?** à qui est ceci?; **I know ~ it is** je sais à qui c'est.

why |waɪ| ad pourquoi // excl tiens!, voyons!; **the reason ~** la raison pour laquelle; **tell me ~** dites-moi pourquoi; **~ not?** pourquoi pas?; **~ever** ad pourquoi donc, mais pourquoi.

wick |wɪk| n mèche f (*de bougie*).

wicked |ˈwɪkɪd| a mauvais(e), méchant(e); inique; cruel(le); (*mischievous*) malicieux(euse).

wicker |ˈwɪkə*| n osier m; (*also:* **~work**) vannerie f.

wicket ['wıkıt] n (CRICKET) guichet m; espace compris entre les deux guichets.

wide [waıd] a large; (area, knowledge) vaste, très étendu(e); (choice) grand(e) // ad: **to open ~** ouvrir tout grand; **to shoot ~** tirer à côté; **~-angle lens** n objectif m grand-angulaire; **~-awake** a bien éveillé(e); **~ly** ad (differing) radicalement; (spaced) sur une grande étendue; (believed) généralement; **~n** vt élargir; **~ open** a grand(e) ouvert(e); **~spread** a (belief etc) très répandu(e).

widow ['wıdəu] n veuve f; **~er** n veuf m.

width [wıdθ] n largeur f.

wield [wi:ld] vt (sword) manier; (power) exercer.

wife, **wives** [waıf, waıvz] n femme (mariée), épouse f.

wig [wıg] n perruque f.

wiggle ['wıgl] vt agiter, remuer.

wild [waıld] a sauvage; (sea) déchaîné(e); (idea, life) fou(folle); extravagant(e); **~s** npl régions fpl sauvages; **~erness** ['wıldənıs] n désert m, région f sauvage; **~-goose chase** n (fig) fausse piste; **~life** n faune f (et flore f) sauvage(s); **~ly** ad (applaud) frénétiquement; (hit, guess) au hasard; (happy) follement.

wilful ['wılful] a (person) obstiné(e); (action) délibéré(e); (crime) prémédité(e).

will [wıl] ♦ auxiliary vb 1 (forming future tense): **I ~ finish it tomorrow** je le finirai demain; **I ~ have finished it by tomorrow** je l'aurai fini d'ici demain; **~ you do it?** — yes **I ~/no I won't** le ferez-vous? — oui/non
2 (in conjectures, predictions): **he ~ or he'll be there by now** il doit être arrivé à l'heure qu'il est; **that ~ be the postman** ça doit être le facteur
3 (in commands, requests, offers): **~ you be quiet!** voulez-vous bien vous taire!; **~ you help me?** est-ce que vous pouvez m'aider?; **~ you have a cup of tea?** voulez-vous une tasse de thé?; **I won't put up with it!** je ne le tolérerai pas!
♦ vt (pt, pp **~ed**): **to ~ sb to do** souhaiter ardemment que qn fasse; **he ~ed himself to go on** par un suprême effort de volonté, il continua
♦ n volonté f; testament m.

willing ['wılıŋ] a de bonne volonté, serviable; **he's ~ to do it** il est disposé à le faire, il veut bien le faire; **~ly** ad volontiers; **~ness** a bonne volonté.

willow ['wıləu] n saule m.

will power n volonté f.

willy-nilly [wılı'nılı] ad bon gré mal gré.

wilt [wılt] vi dépérir.

wily ['waılı] a rusé(e).

win [wın] n (in sports etc) victoire f // vb (pt, pp **won** [wʌn]) vt (battle, money) gagner; (prize) remporter; (popularity) acquérir // vi gagner; **to ~ over**, (Brit) **~ round** vt gagner, se concilier.

wince [wıns] vi tressaillir.

winch [wıntʃ] n treuil m.

wind n [wınd] (also MED) vent m // vb [waınd] (pt, pp **wound** [waund]) vt enrouler; (wrap) envelopper; (clock, toy) remonter; (take breath away: [wınd]) couper le souffle à // vi (road, river) serpenter; **to ~ up** vt (clock) remonter; (debate) terminer, clôturer; **~fall** n coup m de chance; **~ing** a (road) sinueux(euse); (staircase) tournant(e); **~ instrument** n (MUS) instrument m à vent; **~mill** n moulin m à vent.

window ['wındəu] n fenêtre f; (in car, train, also: **~pane**) vitre f; (in shop etc) vitrine f; **~ box** n jardinière f; **~ cleaner** n (person) laveur/euse de vitres; **~ ledge** n rebord m de la fenêtre; **~ pane** n vitre f, carreau m; **~sill** n (inside) appui m de la fenêtre; (outside) rebord m de la fenêtre.

windpipe ['wındpaıp] n gosier m.

windscreen, (US) **windshield** ['wındskri:n, 'wındʃi:ld] n pare-brise m inv; **~ washer** n lave-glace m inv; **~ wiper** n essuie-glace m inv.

windswept ['wındswεpt] a balayé(e) par le vent.

windy ['wındı] a venté(e), venteux(euse); **it's ~** il y a du vent.

wine [waın] n vin m; **~ cellar** n cave f à vins; **~ glass** n verre m à vin; **~ list** n carte f des vins; **~ tasting** n dégustation f (de vins); **~ waiter** n sommelier m.

wing [wıŋ] n aile f; **~s** npl (THEATRE) coulisses fpl; **~er** n (SPORT) ailier m.

wink [wıŋk] n clin m d'œil // vi faire un clin d'œil; (blink) cligner des yeux.

winner ['wınə*] n gagnant/e.

winning ['wınıŋ] a (team) gagnant(e); (goal) décisif(ive); **~s** npl gains mpl; **~ post** n poteau m d'arrivée.

winter ['wıntə*] n hiver m // vi hiverner; **~ sports** npl sports mpl d'hiver.

wintry ['wıntrı] a hivernal(e).

wipe [waıp] n coup m de torchon (or de chiffon or d'éponge) // vt essuyer; **to ~ off** vt essuyer; **to ~ out** vt (debt) régler; (memory) oublier; (destroy) anéantir; **to ~ up** vt essuyer.

wire ['waıə*] n fil m (de fer); (ELEC) fil électrique; (TEL) télégramme m // vt (house) faire l'installation électrique de; (also: **~ up**) brancher.

wireless ['waıəlıs] n (Brit) télégraphie f sans fil; (set) T.S.F. f.

wiring ['waıərıŋ] n installation f électrique.

wiry ['waɪərɪ] *a* noueux(euse), nerveux(euse).

wisdom ['wɪzdəm] *n* sagesse *f*; (*of action*) prudence *f*; ~ **tooth** *n* dent *f* de sagesse.

wise [waɪz] *a* sage, prudent(e), judicieux(euse).

...wise [waɪz] *suffix*: time~ en ce qui concerne le temps, question temps.

wish [wɪʃ] *n* (*desire*) désir *m*; (*specific desire*) souhait *m*, vœu *m* // *vt* souhaiter, désirer, vouloir; best ~**es** (*on birthday etc*) meilleurs vœux; **with best** ~**es** (*in letter*) bien amicalement; **to** ~ **sb goodbye** dire au revoir à qn; **he** ~**ed me well** il me souhaitait de réussir; **to** ~ **to do/sb to do** désirer *or* vouloir faire/que qn fasse; **to** ~ **for** souhaiter; **it's** ~**ful thinking** c'est prendre ses désirs pour des réalités.

wishy-washy [wɪʃɪ'wɔʃɪ] *a* (*col*: *colour*) délavé(e); (: *ideas, argument*) faiblard(e).

wisp [wɪsp] *n* fine mèche (*de cheveux*); (*of smoke*) mince volute *f*.

wistful ['wɪstful] *a* mélancolique.

wit [wɪt] *n* (*gen pl*) intelligence *f*, esprit *m*; présence *f* d'esprit; (*wittiness*) esprit; (*person*) homme/femme d'esprit.

witch [wɪtʃ] *n* sorcière *f*.

with [wɪð, wɪθ] *prep* **1** (*in the company of*) avec; (*at the home of*) chez; **we stayed** ~ **friends** nous avons logé chez des amis; **I'll be** ~ **you in a minute** je suis à vous dans un instant
2 (*descriptive*): **a room** ~ **a view** une chambre avec vue; **the man** ~ **the grey hat/blue eyes** l'homme au chapeau gris/ aux yeux bleus
3 (*indicating manner, means, cause*): ~ **tears in her eyes** les larmes aux yeux; **to walk** ~ **a stick** marcher avec une canne; **red** ~ **anger** rouge de colère; **to shake** ~ **fear** trembler de peur; **to fill sth** ~ **water** remplir qch d'eau
4: **I'm** ~ **you** (*I understand*) je vous suis; **to be** ~ **it** (*col*: *up-to-date*) être dans le vent.

withdraw [wɪθ'drɔː] *vb* (*irg*) *vt* retirer // *vi* se retirer; (*go back on promise*) se rétracter; ~**al** *n* retrait *m*; (*MED*) état *m* de manque; ~**n** *a* (*person*) renfermé(e).

wither ['wɪðə*] *vi* se faner.

withhold [wɪθ'həuld] *vt* irg (*money*) retenir; (*decision*) remettre; (*permission*): **to** ~ (**from**) refuser (à); (*information*): **to** ~ (**from**) cacher (à).

within [wɪð'ɪn] *prep* à l'intérieur de // *ad* à l'intérieur; ~ **sight of** en vue de; ~ **a mile of** à moins d'un mille de; ~ **the week** avant la fin de la semaine.

without [wɪð'aut] *prep* sans.

withstand [wɪθ'stænd] *vt irg* résister à.

witness ['wɪtnɪs] *n* (*person*) témoin *m*; (*evidence*) témoignage *m* // *vt* (*event*) être témoin de; (*document*) attester l'authenticité de; ~ **box**, (*US*) ~ **stand** *n* barre *f* des témoins.

witticism ['wɪtɪsɪzm] *n* mot *m* d'esprit.

witty ['wɪtɪ] *a* spirituel(le), plein(e) d'esprit.

wives [waɪvz] *npl of* **wife**.

wizard ['wɪzəd] *n* magicien *m*.

wk *abbr of* **week**.

wobble ['wɔbl] *vi* trembler; (*chair*) branler.

woe [wəu] *n* malheur *m*.

woke [wəuk] *pt of* **wake**; ~**n** *pp of* **wake**.

wolf, *pl* **wolves** [wulf, wulvz] *n* loup *m*.

woman, *pl* **women** ['wumən, 'wɪmɪn] *n* femme *f*; ~ **doctor** *f* médecin *m*; **women's lib** *n* (*col*) MLF *m*.

womb [wuːm] *n* (*ANAT*) utérus *m*.

women ['wɪmɪn] *npl of* **woman**.

won [wʌn] *pt, pp of* **win**.

wonder ['wʌndə*] *n* merveille *f*, miracle *m*; (*feeling*) émerveillement *m* // *vi*: **to** ~ **whether** se demander si; **to** ~ **at** s'étonner de; s'émerveiller de; **to** ~ **about** songer à; **it's no** ~ **that** il n'est pas étonnant que + *sub*; ~**ful** *a* merveilleux(euse).

won't [wəunt] = **will not**.

woo [wuː] *vt* (*woman*) faire la cour à.

wood [wud] *n* (*timber, forest*) bois *m*; ~ **carving** *n* sculpture *f* en or sur bois; ~**ed** *a* boisé(e); ~**en** *a* en bois; (*fig*) raide; inexpressif(ive); ~**pecker** *n* pic *m* (*oiseau*); ~**wind** *n* (*MUS*) bois *m*; **the** ~**wind** (*MUS*) les bois; ~**work** *n* menuiserie *f*; ~**worm** *n* ver *m* du bois.

wool [wul] *n* laine *f*; **to pull the** ~ **over sb's eyes** (*fig*) en faire accroire à qn; ~**len**, (*US*) ~**en** *a* de laine; (*industry*) lainier(ère); ~**lens** *npl* lainages *mpl*; ~**ly**, (*US*) ~**y** *a* laineux(euse); (*fig*: *ideas*) confus(e).

word [wɜːd] *n* mot *m*; (*spoken*) mot, parole *f*; (*promise*) parole; (*news*) nouvelles *fpl* // *vt* rédiger, formuler; **in other** ~**s** en d'autres termes; **to break/ keep one's** ~ manquer à/tenir sa parole; ~**ing** *n* termes *mpl*, langage *m*; libellé *m*; ~ **processing** *n* traitement *m* de texte; ~ **processor** *n* machine *f* de traitement de texte.

wore [wɔː*] *pt of* **wear**.

work [wɜːk] *n* travail *m*; (*ART*, *LITERATURE*) œuvre *f* // *vi* travailler; (*mechanism*) marcher, fonctionner; (*plan etc*) marcher; (*medicine*) agir // *vt* (*clay, wood etc*) travailler; (*mine etc*) exploiter; (*machine*) faire marcher *or* fonctionner; **to be out of** ~ être au chômage; ~**s** *n* (*Brit*: *factory*) usine *f* // *npl* (*of clock, machine*) mécanisme *m*; **to** ~ **loose** *vi* se défaire, se desserrer; **to**

~ **on** vt fus travailler à; (principle) se baser sur; **to** ~ vi (plans etc) marcher // vt (problem) résoudre; (plan) élaborer; it ~s out at £100 ça fait 100 livres; **to get** ~**ed up** se mettre dans tous ses états; ~**able** a (solution) réalisable; ~**aholic** n bourreau m de travail; ~**er** n travailleur/euse, ouvrier/ère; ~**force** n main-d'œuvre f; ~**ing class** n classe ouvrière; ~**ing-class** a ouvrier(ère); ~**ing man** n travailleur m; ~**ing order** n: **in** ~**ing order** en état de marche; ~**man** n ouvrier m; ~**manship** n métier m, habileté f; facture f; ~**sheet** n feuille f de programmation; ~**shop** n atelier m; ~ **station** n poste m de travail; ~**-to-rule** n (Brit) grève f du zèle.

world [wə:ld] n monde m // cpd (champion) du monde; (power, war) mondial(e); **to think the** ~ **of sb** (fig) ne jurer que par qn; ~**ly** a de ce monde; ~**-wide** a universel(le).

worm [wə:m] n ver m.

worn [wɔ:n] pp of **wear** // a usé(e); ~-**out** a (object) complètement usé(e); (person) épuisé(e).

worried ['wʌrɪd] a inquiet(ète).

worry ['wʌrɪ] n souci m // vt inquiéter // vi s'inquiéter, se faire du souci.

worse [wə:s] a pire, plus mauvais(e) // ad plus mal // n pire m; **a change for the** ~ une détérioration; ~**n** vt, vi empirer; ~ **off** a moins à l'aise financièrement; (fig): **you'll be** ~ **off this way** ça ira moins bien de cette façon.

worship ['wə:ʃɪp] n culte m // vt (God) rendre un culte à; (person) adorer; **Your W**~ (Brit: to mayor) Monsieur le Maire; (: to judge) Monsieur le Juge.

worst [wə:st] a le(la) pire, le(la) plus mauvais(e) // ad le plus mal // n pire m; **at** ~ au pis aller.

worsted ['wustɪd] n: (wool) ~ laine peignée.

worth [wə:θ] n valeur f // a: **to be** ~ valoir; **it's** ~ **it** cela en vaut la peine; **it is** ~ **one's while (to do)** on gagne (à faire); ~**less** a qui ne vaut rien; ~**while** a (activity) qui en vaut la peine; (cause) louable.

worthy [wə:ðɪ] a (person) digne; (motive) louable; ~ **of** digne de.

would [wud] auxiliary vb **1** (conditional tense): **if you asked him he** ~ **do it** si vous le lui demandiez, il le ferait; **if you had asked him he** ~ **have done it** si vous le lui aviez demandé, il l'aurait fait

2 (in offers, invitations, requests): ~ **you like a biscuit?** voulez-vous or voudriez-vous un biscuit?; ~ **you close the door please?** voulez-vous fermer la porte, s'il vous plaît

3 (in indirect speech): **I said I** ~ **do it** j'ai dit que je le ferais

4 (emphatic): **it WOULD have to snow today!** naturellement il neige or il fallait qu'il neige aujourd'hui!

5 (insistence): **she** ~**n't do it** elle n'a pas voulu or elle a refusé de le faire

6 (conjecture): **it** ~ **have been midnight** il devait être minuit

7 (indicating habit): **he** ~ **go there on Mondays** il y allait le lundi.

would-be ['wudbi:] a (pej) soi-disant.

wouldn't ['wudnt] = **would not**.

wound vb [waund] pt, pp of **wind** // n, vt [wu:nd] n blessure f // vt blesser.

wove [wəuv] pt of **weave**; ~**n** pp of **weave**.

wrangle ['ræŋgl] n dispute f.

wrap [ræp] n (stole) écharpe f; (cape) pèlerine f // vt (also: ~ **up**) envelopper; ~**per** n (Brit: of book) couverture f; ~**ping paper** n papier m d'emballage; (for gift) papier cadeau.

wrath [rɔθ] n courroux m.

wreak [ri:k] vt: **to** ~ **havoc on** avoir un effet désastreux sur; **to** ~ **vengeance (on)** se venger (de).

wreath, ~**s** [ri:θ, ri:ðz] n couronne f.

wreck [rɛk] n (sea disaster) naufrage m; (ship) épave f; (pej: person) loque humaine // vt démolir; (ship) provoquer le naufrage de; (fig) briser, ruiner; ~**age** n débris mpl; (of building) décombres mpl; (of ship) épave f.

wren [rɛn] n (ZOOL) roitelet m.

wrench [rɛntʃ] n (TECH) clé f (à écrous); (tug) violent mouvement de torsion; (fig) arrachement m // vt tirer violemment sur, tordre; **to** ~ **sth from** arracher qch violemment à or de.

wrestle ['rɛsl] vi: **to** ~ **(with sb)** lutter (avec qn); **to** ~ **with** (fig) se débattre avec, lutter contre; ~**r** n lutteur/euse; **wrestling** n lutte f; (also: **all-in wrestling**) catch m.

wretched ['rɛtʃɪd] a misérable; (col) maudit(e).

wriggle ['rɪgl] vi se tortiller.

wring [rɪŋ], pt, pp **wrung** vt tordre; (wet clothes) essorer; (fig): **to** ~ **sth out of** arracher qch à.

wrinkle ['rɪŋkl] n (on skin) ride f; (on paper etc) pli m // vt rider, plisser // vi se plisser.

wrist [rɪst] n poignet m; ~**watch** n montre-bracelet f.

writ [rɪt] n acte m judiciaire.

write [raɪt], pt **wrote**, pp **written** vt, vi écrire; **to** ~ **down** vt noter; (put in writing) mettre par écrit; **to** ~ **off** vt (debt) passer aux profits et pertes; (depreciate) amortir; **to** ~ **out** vt écrire; (copy) recopier; **to** ~ **up** vt rédiger; ~**-off** n perte totale; ~**r** n auteur m, écrivain m.

writhe [raɪð] vi se tordre.

writing ['raɪtɪŋ] n écriture f; (of

author) œuvres *fpl*; **in ~** par écrit; **~ paper** *n* papier *m* à lettres.
written ['rɪtn] *pp* of **write**.
wrong [rɔŋ] *a* faux(fausse); (*incorrectly chosen: number, road etc*) mauvais(e); (*not suitable*) qui ne convient pas; (*wicked*) mal; (*unfair*) injuste // *ad* faux // *n* tort *m* // *vt* faire du tort à, léser; **you are ~ to do it** tu as tort de le faire; **you are ~ about that, you've got it** tu te trompes; **to be in the ~** avoir tort; **what's ~?** qu'est-ce qui ne va pas?; **to go ~** (*person*) se tromper; (*plan*) mal tourner; (*machine*) tomber en panne; **~ful** *a* injustifié(e); **~ly** *ad* à tort.
wrote [rəut] *pt* of **write**.
wrought [rɔːt] *a*: **~ iron** fer forgé.
wrung [rʌŋ] *pt, pp* of **wring**.
wry [raɪ] *a* désabusé(e).
wt. *abbr* of **weight**.

X Y Z

Xmas ['eksməs] *n abbr* of **Christmas**.
X-ray [eks'reɪ] *n* rayon *m* X; (*photograph*) radio(graphie) *f*.
xylophone ['zaɪləfəun] *n* xylophone *m*.
yacht [jɔt] *n* yacht *m*; voilier *m*; **~ing** *n* yachting *m*, navigation *f* de plaisance.
Yank [jæŋk], **Yankee** ['jæŋkɪ] *n* (*pej*) Amerloque *m/f*.
yap [jæp] *vi* (*dog*) japper.
yard [jɑːd] *n* (*of house etc*) cour *f*; (*measure*) yard *m* (= *914 mm; 3 feet*); **~stick** *n* (*fig*) mesure *f*, critère *m*.
yarn [jɑːn] *n* fil *m*; (*tale*) longue histoire.
yawn [jɔːn] *n* bâillement *m* // *vi* bâiller; **~ing** *a* (*gap*) béant(e).
yd. *abbr* of **yard(s)**.
yeah [jɛə] *ad* (*col*) ouais.
year [jɪə*] *n* an *m*, année *f*; **to be 8 ~s old** avoir 8 ans; **an eight-~-old child** un enfant de huit ans; **~ly** *a* annuel(le) // *ad* annuellement.
yearn [jəːn] *vi*: **to ~ for sth** aspirer à qch, languir après qch; **to ~ to do** aspirer à faire; **~ing** *n* désir ardent, envie *f*.
yeast [jiːst] *n* levure *f*.
yell [jɛl] *vi* hurler.
yellow ['jɛləu] *a, n* jaune (*m*).
yelp [jɛlp] *vi* japper; glapir.
yeoman ['jəumən] *n*: **Y~ of the Guard** hallebardier *m* de la garde royale.
yes [jɛs] *ad* oui; (*answering negative question*) si // *n* oui *m*; **to say/answer ~** dire/répondre oui.
yesterday ['jɛstədɪ] *ad, n* hier (*m*); **~ morning/evening** hier matin/soir; **all day ~** toute la journée d'hier.
yet [jɛt] *ad* encore; déjà // *cj* pourtant, néanmoins; **it is not finished ~** ce n'est pas encore fini *or* toujours pas fini; **the best ~** le meilleur jusqu'ici *or* jusque-là;

as ~ jusqu'ici, encore.
yew [juː] *n* if *m*.
yield [jiːld] *n* production *f*, rendement *m*; rapport *m* // *vt* produire, rendre, rapporter; (*surrender*) céder // *vi* céder; (*US AUT*) céder la priorité.
YMCA *n abbr* (= *Young Men's Christian Association*) YMCA *m*.
yoga ['jəugə] *n* yoga *m*.
yog(h)ourt, yog(h)urt ['jəugət] *n* yaourt *m*.
yoke [jəuk] *n* joug *m*.
yolk [jəuk] *n* jaune *m* (d'œuf).
yonder ['jɔndə*] *ad* là(-bas).
you [juː] *pronoun* **1** (*subject*) tu; (*polite form*) vous; (*pl*) vous; **~ French enjoy your food** vous autres Français, vous aimez bien manger; **~ and I will go** toi et moi *or* vous et moi, nous irons
2 (*object: direct, indirect*) te, t' + *vowel*; vous; **I know ~** je te *or* vous connais; **I gave it to ~** je te l'ai donné, je vous l'ai donné
3 (*stressed*) toi; vous; **I told you to do it** c'est à toi *or* vous que j'ai dit de le faire
4 (*after prep, in comparisons*) toi; vous; **it's for ~** c'est pour toi *or* vous; **she's younger than ~** elle est plus jeune que toi *or* vous
5 (*impersonal: one*) on; **fresh air does ~ good** l'air frais fait du bien; **~ never know** on ne sait jamais.
you'd [juːd] = **you had, you would**.
you'll [juːl] = **you will, you shall**.
young [jʌŋ] *a* jeune // *npl* (*of animal*) petits *mpl*; (*people*): **the ~** les jeunes, la jeunesse; **~er** *a* (*brother etc*) cadet(te); **~ster** *n* jeune *m* (garçon *m*); (*child*) enfant *m/f*.
your [jɔː*] *a* ton(ta), tes *pl*; (*polite form, pl*) votre, vos *pl*; *see also* **my**.
you're [juə*] = **you are**.
yours [jɔːz] *pronoun* le(la) tien(ne), les tiens(tiennes); (*polite form, pl*) le(la) vôtre, les vôtres; **yours sincerely/faithfully** je vous prie d'agréer l'expression de mes sentiments les meilleurs/mes sentiments respectueux *or* dévoués; *see also* **mine**.
yourself [jɔː'sɛlf] *pronoun* (*reflexive*) te; (*: polite form*) vous; (*after prep*) toi; vous; (*emphatic*) toi-même; vous-même; **yourselves** *pl pronoun* vous; (*emphatic*) vous-mêmes; *see also* **oneself**.
youth [juːθ] *n* jeunesse *f*; (*young man*) (*pl ~s* [juːðz]) jeune homme *m*; **~ club** *n* centre *m* de jeunes; **~ful** *a* jeune; de jeunesse; juvénile; **~ hostel** *n* auberge *f* de jeunesse.
you've [juːv] = **you have**.
YTS *n abbr* (*Brit*: = *Youth Training Scheme*) ≈ TUC *m*.
Yugoslav ['juːgəuslɑːv] *a* yougoslave // *n* Yougoslave *m/f*.

Yugoslavia ['juːgəu'slɑːvɪə] *n* Yougoslavie *f*.
yuppie ['jʌpɪ] *n* yuppie *m/f*.
YWCA *n abbr* (= *Young Women's Christian Association*) YWCA *m*.
zany ['zeɪnɪ] *a* farfelu(e), loufoque.
zap [zæp] *vt* (*COMPUT*) effacer.
zeal [ziːl] *n* zèle *m*, ferveur *f*; empressement *m*.
zebra ['ziːbrə] *n* zèbre *m*; ~ **crossing** *n* (*Brit*) passage *m* pour piétons.
zero ['zɪərəu] *n* zéro *m*.
zest [zest] *n* entrain *m*, élan *m*; zeste *m*.
zigzag ['zɪgzæg] *n* zigzag *m*.
Zimbabwe [zɪm'bɑːbwɪ] *n* Zimbabwe

m.
zinc [zɪŋk] *n* zinc *m*.
zip [zɪp] *n* (*also*: ~ **fastener**, (*US*) ~**per**) fermeture *f* éclair ® // *vt* (*also*: ~ **up**) fermer avec une fermeture éclair ®; ~ **code** *n* (*US*) code postal.
zodiac ['zəudɪæk] *n* zodiaque *m*.
zone [zəun] *n* zone *f*; (*subdivision of town*) secteur *m*.
zoo [zuː] *n* zoo *m*.
zoology [zuː'ɔlədʒɪ] *n* zoologie *f*.
zoom [zuːm] *vi*: to ~ **past** passer en trombe; ~ **lens** *n* zoom *m*.
zucchini [tsuː'kiːnɪ] *n(pl)* (*US*) courgette(s) *f(pl)*.

FRENCH VERB FORMS

1 Participe présent *2* Participe passé *3* Présent *4* Imparfait *5* Futur *6* Conditionnel *7* Subjonctif présent

acquérir *1* acquérant *2* acquis *3* acquiers, acquérons, acquièrent *4* acquérais *5* acquerrai *7* acquière

ALLER *1* allant *2* allé *3* vais, vas, va, allons, allez, vont *4* allais *5* irai *6* irais *7* aille

asseoir *1* asseyant *2* assis *3* assieds, asseyons, asseyez, asseyent *4* asseyais *5* assiérai *7* asseye

atteindre *1* atteignant *2* atteint *3* atteins, atteignons *4* atteignais *7* atteigne

AVOIR *1* ayant *2* eu *3* ai, as, a, avons, avez, ont *4* avais *5* aurai *6* aurais *7* aie, aies, ait, ayons, ayez, aient

battre *1* battant *2* battu *3* bats, bat, battons *4* battais *7* batte

boire *1* buvant *2* bu *3* bois, buvons, boivent *4* buvais *7* boive

bouillir *1* bouillant *2* bouilli *3* bous, bouillons *4* bouillais *7* bouille

conclure *1* concluant *2* conclu *3* conclus, concluons *4* concluais *7* conclue

conduire *1* conduisant *2* conduit *3* conduis, conduisons *4* conduisais *7* conduise

connaître *1* connaissant *2* connu *3* connais, connaît, connaissons *4* connaissais *7* connaisse

coudre *1* cousant *2* cousu *3* couds, cousons, cousez, cousent *4* cousais *7* couse

courir *1* courant *2* couru *3* cours, courons *4* courais *5* courrai *7* coure

couvrir *1* couvrant *2* couvert *3* couvre, couvrons *4* couvrais *7* couvre

craindre *1* craignant *2* craint *3* crains, craignons *4* craignais *7* craigne

croire *1* croyant *2* cru *3* crois, croyons, croient *4* croyais *7* croie

croître *1* croissant *2* crû *3* crois, croissons *4* croissais *7* croisse

cueillir *1* cueillant *2* cueilli *3* cueille, cueillons *4* cueillais *5* cueillerai *7* cueille

devoir *1* devant *2* dû, due, dus, dues *3* dois, devons, doivent *4* devais *5* devrai *7* doive

dire *1* disant *2* dit *3* dis, disons, dites, disent *4* disais *7* dise

dormir *1* dormant *2* dormi *3* dors, dormons *4* dormais *7* dorme

écrire *1* écrivant *2* écrit *3* écris, écrivons *4* écrivais *7* écrive

ÊTRE *1* étant *2* été *3* suis, es, est, sommes, êtes, sont *4* étais *5* serai *6* serais *7* sois, sois, soit, soyons, soyez, soient

FAIRE *1* faisant *2* fait *3* fais, fais, fait, faisons, faites, font *4* faisais *5* ferai *6* ferais *7* fasse

falloir *2* fallu *3* faut *4* fallait *5* faudra *7* faille

FINIR *1* finissant *2* fini *3* finis, finis, finit, finissons, finissez, finissent *4* finissais *5* finirai *6* finirais *7* finisse

fuir *1* fuyant *2* fui *3* fuis, fuyons, fuient *4* fuyais *7* fuie

joindre *1* joignant *2* joint *3* joins, joignons *4* joignais *7* joigne

lire *1* lisant *2* lu *3* lis, lisons *4* lisais *7* lise

luire *1* luisant *2* lui *3* luis, luisons *4* luisais *7* luise

maudire *1* maudissant *2* maudit *3* maudis, maudissons *4* maudissait *7* maudisse

mentir *1* mentant *2* menti *3* mens, mentons *4* mentais *7* mente

mettre *1* mettant *2* mis *3* mets, mettons *4* mettais *7* mette

mourir *1* mourant *2* mort *3* meurs, mourons, meurent *4* mourais *5* mourrai *7* meure

naître *1* naissant *2* né *3* nais, naît, naissons *4* naissais *7* naisse

offrir *1* offrant *2* offert *3* offre, offrons *4* offrais *7* offre

PARLER *1* parlant *2* parlé *3* parle, parles, parle, parlons, parlez, parlent *4* parlais, parlais, parlait, parlions, parliez, parlaient *5* parlerai, parleras, parlera, parlerons, parlerez, parleront *6* parlerais, parlerais, parlerait, parlerions, parleriez, parleraient *7* parle, parles, parle, parlions, parliez, parlent *impératif* parle! parlez!

partir *1* partant *2* parti *3* pars, partons *4* partais *7* parte

plaire *1* plaisant *2* plu *3* plais, plaît, plaisons *4* plaisais *7* plaise

pleuvoir *1* pleuvant *2* plu *3* pleut, pleuvent *4* pleuvait *5* pleuvra *7* pleuve

pourvoir *1* pourvoyant *2* pourvu *3* pourvois, pourvoyons, pourvoient *4* pourvoyais *7* pourvoie

pouvoir *1* pouvant *2* pu *3* peux, peut, pouvons, peuvent *4* pouvais *5* pourrai *7* puisse

prendre *1* prenant *2* pris *3* prends, prenons, prennent *4* prenais *7* prenne

prévoir *like voir* *5* prévoirai

RECEVOIR *1* recevant *2* reçu *3* reçois, reçois, reçoit, recevons, recevez, reçoivent *4* recevais *5* recevrai *6* recevrais *7* reçoive

RENDRE *1* rendant *2* rendu *3* rends, rends, rend, rendons, rendez, rendent *4* rendais *5* rendrai *6* rendrais *7* rende

résoudre *1* résolvant *2* résolu *3* résous, résout, résolvons *4* résolvais *7* résolve

rire *1* riant *2* ri *3* ris, rions *4* riais *7* rie

savoir *1* sachant *2* su *3* sais, savons, savent *4* savais *5* saurai *7* sache *impératif* sache, sachons, sachez

servir *1* servant *2* servi *3* sers, servons *4* servais *7* serve

sortir *1* sortant *2* sorti *3* sors, sortons *4* sortais *7* sorte

souffrir *1* souffrant *2* souffert *3* souffre, souffrons *4* souffrais *7* souffre

suffire *1* suffisant *2* suffi *3* suffis, suffisons *4* suffisais *7* suffise

suivre *1* suivant *2* suivi *3* suis, suivons *4* suivais *7* suive

taire *1* taisant *2* tu *3* tais, taisons *4* taisais *7* taise

tenir *1* tenant *2* tenu *3* tiens, tenons, tiennent *4*

tenais 5 tiendrai 7 tienne
vaincre 1 vainquant 2 vaincu 3 vaincs, vainc, vainquons 4 vainquais 7 vainque
valoir 1 valant 2 valu 3 vaux, vaut, valons 4 valais 5 vaudrai 7 vaille
venir 1 venant 2 venu 3 viens, venons, viennent 4 venais 5 viendrai 7 vienne

vivre 1 vivant 2 vécu 3 vis, vivons 4 vivais 7 vive
voir 1 voyant 2 vu 3 vois, voyons, voient 4 voyais 5 verrai 7 voie
vouloir 1 voulant 2 voulu 3 veux, veut, voulons, veulent 4 voulais 5 voudrai 7 veuille *impératif* veuillez

LE VERBE ANGLAIS

present	pt	pp	present	pt	pp
arise	arose	arisen	**dwell**	dwelt	dwelt
awake	awoke	awaked	**eat**	ate	eaten
be (am, is, are; being)	was, were	been	**fall**	fell	fallen
			feed	fed	fed
			feel	felt	felt
bear	bore	born(e)	**fight**	fought	fought
beat	beat	beaten	**find**	found	found
become	became	become	**flee**	fled	fled
begin	began	begun	**fling**	flung	flung
behold	beheld	beheld	**fly (flies)**	flew	flown
bend	bent	bent	**forbid**	forbade	forbidden
beseech	besought	besought	**forecast**	forecast	forecast
beset	beset	beset	**forego**	forewent	foregone
bet	bet, betted	bet, betted	**foresee**	foresaw	foreseen
bid	bid, bade	bid, bidden	**foretell**	foretold	foretold
bind	bound	bound	**forget**	forgot	forgotten
bite	bit	bitten	**forgive**	forgave	forgiven
bleed	bled	bled	**forsake**	forsook	forsaken
blow	blew	blown	**freeze**	froze	frozen
break	broke	broken	**get**	got	got, (*US*) gotten
breed	bred	bred			
bring	brought	brought	**give**	gave	given
build	built	built	**go (goes)**	went	gone
burn	burnt, burned	burnt, burned	**grind**	ground	ground
			grow	grew	grown
burst	burst	burst	**hang**	hung, hanged	hung, hanged
buy	bought	bought			
can	could	(been able)	**have (has; having)**	had	had
cast	cast	cast			
catch	caught	caught	**hear**	heard	heard
choose	chose	chosen	**hide**	hid	hidden
cling	clung	clung	**hit**	hit	hit
come	came	come	**hold**	held	held
cost	cost	cost	**hurt**	hurt	hurt
creep	crept	crept	**keep**	kept	kept
cut	cut	cut	**kneel**	knelt, kneeled	knelt, kneeled
deal	dealt	dealt			
dig	dug	dug	**know**	knew	known
do (3rd person; he/she/it/does)	did	done	**lay**	laid	laid
			lead	led	led
			lean	leant, leaned	leant, leaned
draw	drew	drawn	**leap**	leapt, leaped	leapt, leaped
dream	dreamed, dreamt	dreamed, dreamt	**learn**	learnt, learned	learnt, learned
drink	drank	drunk			
drive	drove	driven	**leave**	left	left

221

present	pt	pp	present	pt	pp
lend	lent	lent	speak	spoke	spoken
let	let	let	speed	sped,	sped,
lie	lay	lain		speeded	speeded
(lying)			spell	spelt,	spelt,
light	lit,	lit,		spelled	spelled
	lighted	lighted	spend	spent	spent
lose	lost	lost	spill	spilt,	spilt,
make	made	made		spilled	spilled
may	might	—	spin	spun	spun
mean	meant	meant	spit	spat	spat
meet	met	met	split	split	split
mistake	mistook	mistaken	spoil	spoiled,	spoiled,
mow	mowed	mown,		spoilt	spoilt
		mowed	spread	spread	spread
must	(had to)	(had to)	spring	sprang	sprung
pay	paid	paid	stand	stood	stood
put	put	put	steal	stole	stolen
quit	quit,	quit,	stick	stuck	stuck
	quitted	quitted	sting	stung	stung
read	read	read	stink	stank	stunk
rid	rid	rid	stride	strode	stridden
ride	rode	ridden	strike	struck	struck,
ring	rang	rung			stricken
rise	rose	risen	strive	strove	striven
run	ran	run	swear	swore	sworn
saw	sawed	sawn	sweep	swept	swept
say	said	said	swell	swelled	swollen,
see	saw	seen			swelled
seek	sought	sought	swim	swam	swum
sell	sold	sold	swing	swung	swung
send	sent	sent	take	took	taken
set	set	set	teach	taught	taught
shake	shook	shaken	tear	tore	torn
shall	should	—	tell	told	told
shear	sheared	shorn,	think	thought	thought
		sheared	throw	threw	thrown
shed	shed	shed	thrust	thrust	thrust
shine	shone	shone	tread	trod	trodden
shoot	shot	shot	wake	woke,	woken,
show	showed	shown		waked	waked
shrink	shrank	shrunk	waylay	waylaid	waylaid
shut	shut	shut	wear	wore	worn
sing	sang	sung	weave	wove,	woven,
sink	sank	sunk		weaved	weaved
sit	sat	sat	wed	wedded,	wedded,
slay	slew	slain		wed	wed
sleep	slept	slept	weep	wept	wept
slide	slid	slid	win	won	won
sling	slung	slung	wind	wound	wound
slit	slit	slit	withdraw	withdrew	withdrawn
smell	smelt,	smelt,	withhold	withheld	withheld
	smelled	smelled	withstand	withstood	withstood
sow	sowed	sown,	wring	wrung	wrung
		sowed	write	wrote	written